Scholastic's

The Magic School Bus™

Science Explorations

B

SCHOLASTIC INC.

Senior Vice President, Director of Education: Dr. Ernest Fleishman
Editor in Chief: Catherine Vanderhoof
Managing Editor: Sandy Kelley
Written by Richard Chevat
Science Consultant: Pauline Lang
Vice President, Director, Editorial Design and Production: Will Kefauver
Project Art Director: Joan Michael
Art Director: Kathy Massaro
Cover illustration and interior illustrations: John Speirs
Assistant Production Director: Bryan Samolinski

Based on the award-winning Magic School Bus books by Joanna Cole, illustrated by Bruce Degen.
Based on the Magic School Bus animated television series produced by Scholastic Productions Inc.

Printed in the U.S.A.
ISBN 0-590-48768-X
5 6 7 8 9 10 14 99 98 97 96 95

Table of Contents

Hi, I'm Phoebe. Welcome to Ms. Frizzle's class. I'm new here too. Let me tell you, things were a lot different at my old school.

THE ANT

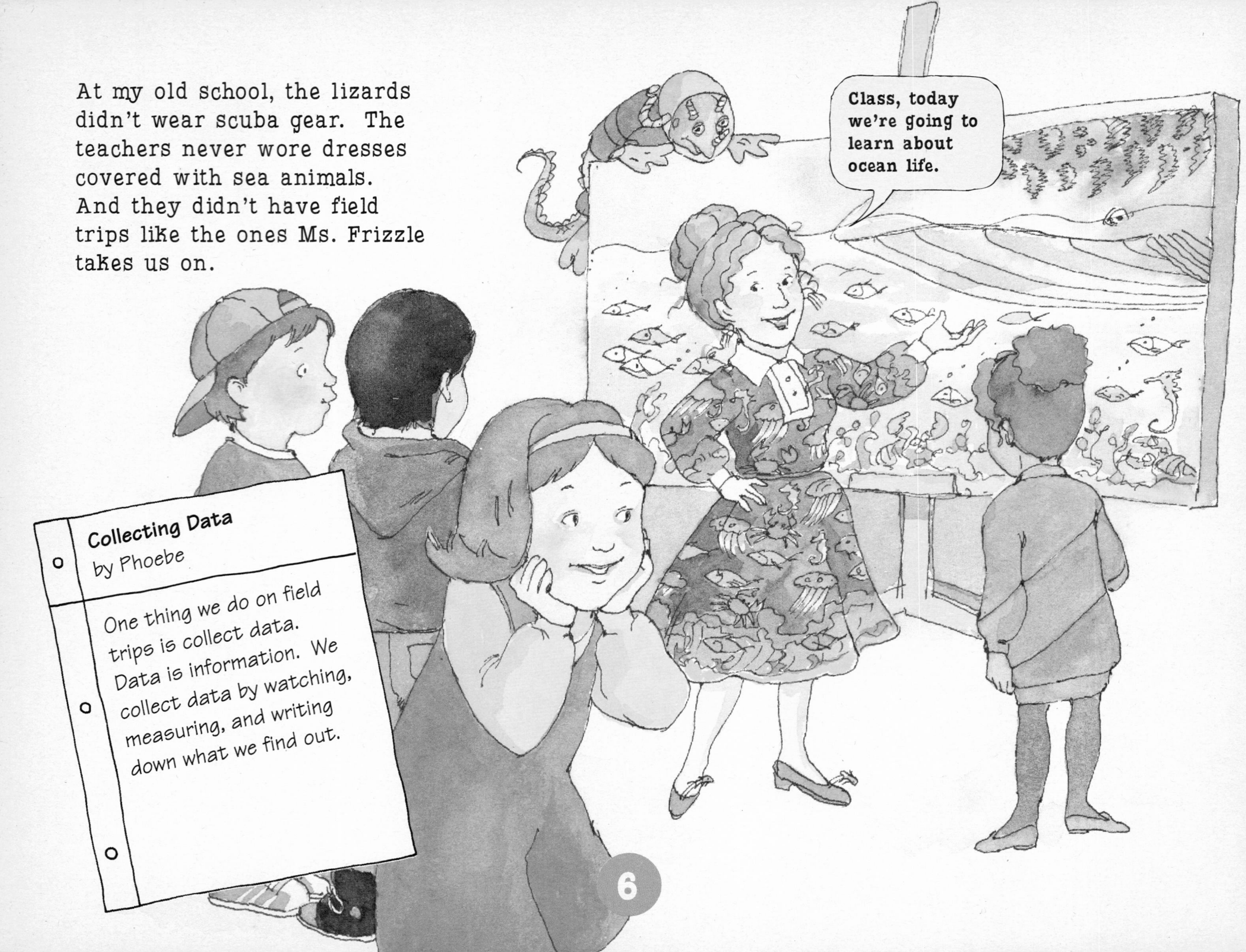
At my old school, the lizards didn't wear scuba gear. The teachers never wore dresses covered with sea animals. And they didn't have field trips like the ones Ms. Frizzle takes us on.
Class, today we're going to learn about ocean life.
Collecting Data
by Phoebe
One thing we do on field trips is collect data. Data is information. We collect data by watching, measuring, and writing down what we find out.

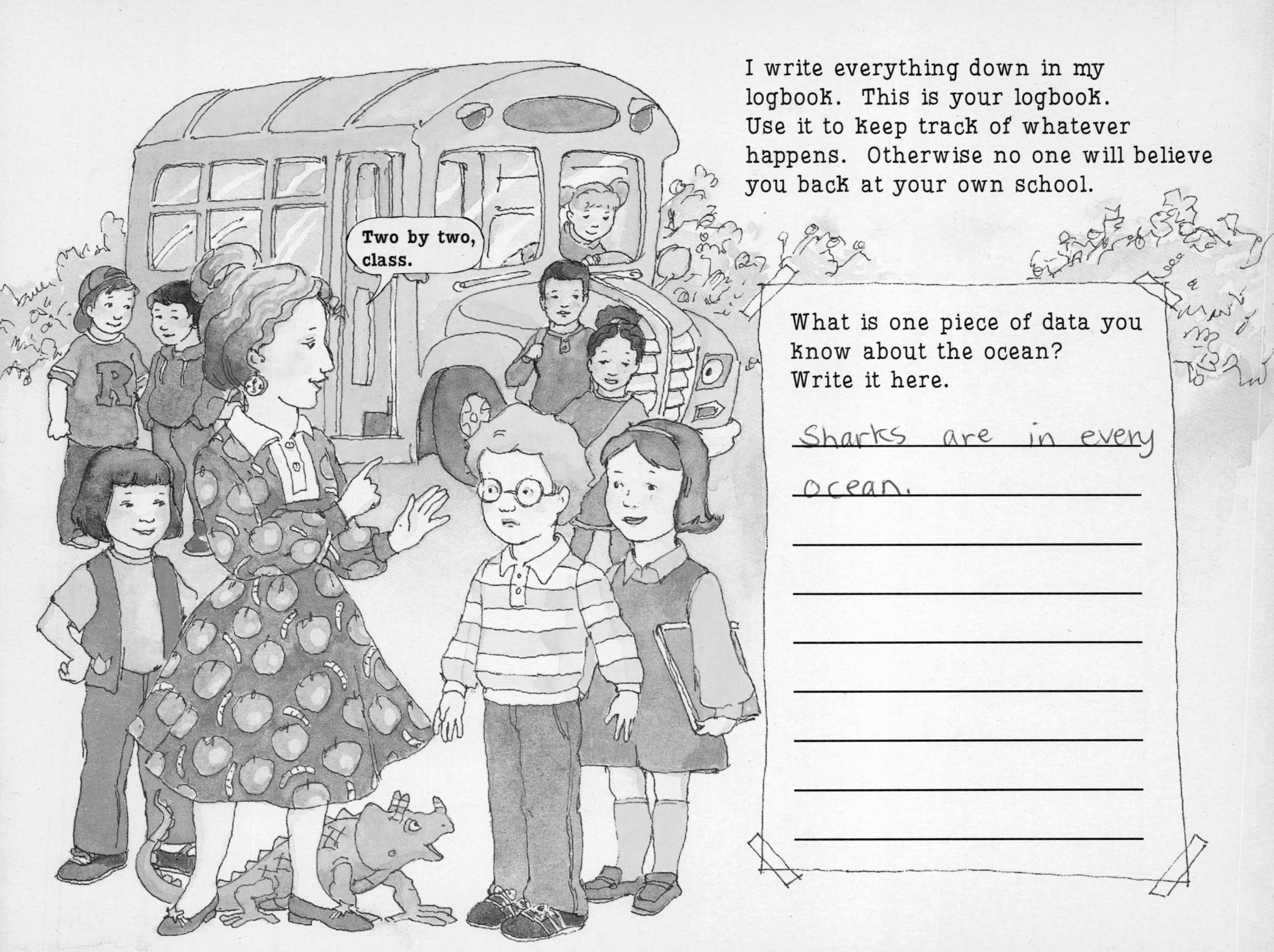
Two by two, class.
I write everything down in my logbook. This is your logbook. Use it to keep track of whatever happens. Otherwise no one will believe you back at your own school.
What is one piece of data you know about the ocean? Write it here.
Sharks are in every ocean.

Outta Space

How Far Are the Planets?
by Ralphie

Earth is about 93 million miles (150 million kilometers) from the Sun. But if Earth was only one foot (3 decimeters) from the Sun, this is about how far the other planets would be from the Sun:

Mercury - 5 inches (13cm)
Venus - 9 inches (23 cm)
Earth - 1 foot (30 cm)
Mars - 1 foot, 6 inches (46 cm)
Jupiter - 5 feet, 2 inches ($1\frac{1}{2}$ meters)
Saturn - 9 feet, 6 inches (almost 3 meters)
Uranus - 19 feet (almost 6 meters)
Neptune - 30 feet ($9\frac{1}{3}$ meters)
Pluto - 39 feet (12 meters)

The solar system is made up of the Sun and all the planets and other things that circle around it.

The planets are very far apart — millions of miles. To help you understand how big the solar system is, think about this. If you were in a plane flying from Earth to the Sun, the trip would take you almost 18 years.

The solar system is so big, it's hard to imagine.
It's hard to imagine how we are going to get home.

Make a floor map of the solar system.

Use a measuring tape and paper.

1. Cut 9 small slips of paper. Write the name of a different planet on each one.

2. Write "SUN" on a piece of paper. Tape it to a wall, near the floor.

3. Measure one foot (3 decimeters) from the wall. Put the paper that says Earth there.

4. Measure the distances for the other planets. Use the chart on page 8. Put the paper for each planet in the right spot.

Can you fit the whole solar system in your classroom? _____yes _____ no

There are two groups of planets in the solar system. Can you guess from your map which planets go in each group? Write the names of the planets in their correct group.

Inner Planets	Outer Planets

Spinning Tops

How Long Is an Orbit?
by Dorothy Ann

The Earth takes about 365 days to orbit the Sun. That's why a year is 365 days long. It takes the Moon about 28 days to go around the Earth.

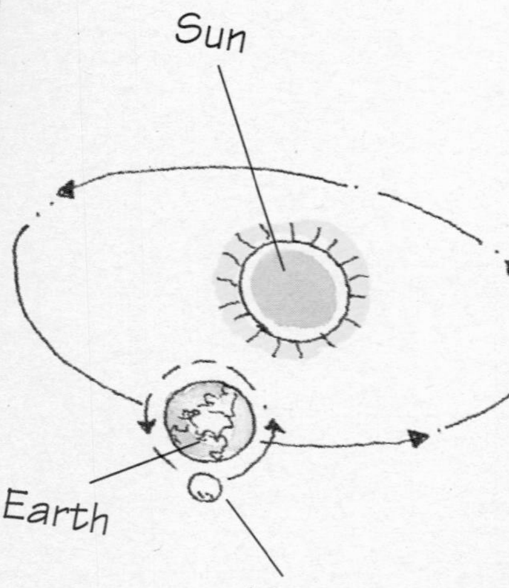

The moons and planets in the solar system move in curved paths called orbits. Earth orbits the Sun. The Moon orbits Earth.

Act out the orbits of the Earth, Sun, and Moon.

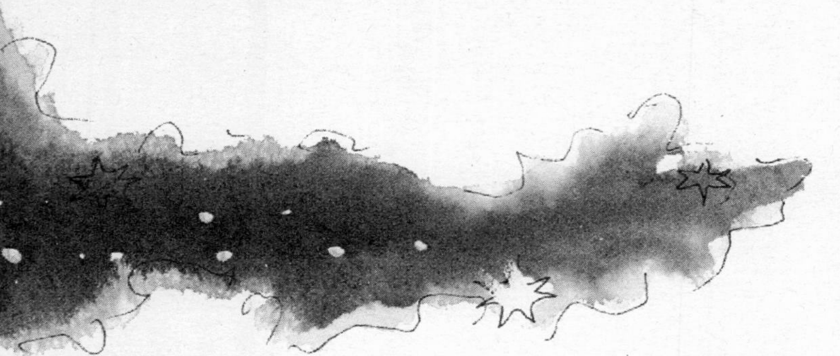

The man in the moon must get awfully dizzy.

Get two friends. One of you will be the Sun, one the Earth, and one the Moon.

1. Let the Sun stand still.

2. Earth should move slowly around the Sun in a circle, like this:

3. While Earth moves, the Moon should circle around Earth. The real Moon circles Earth $13\frac{1}{2}$ times during one trip around the Sun. Can your "Moon" do that?

4. After you've done that for a while, add something new. Earth and Moon should spin around as they move. The Sun should spin too.

5. Now add one more thing. Have the Sun move in a straight line, while Earth and the Moon keep moving in their circles. Can you do everything at the same time?

Earth spins around once every day. How many times would it spin in one trip around the Sun?

____

Picture a Planet

Why did Saturn go to a jewelry store?
To buy a new ring!
Saturn

The Rings of Saturn
by Tim

Saturn has many rings. The rings are made of billions of chunks of ice, rocks, and dust.

Every planet is different. They are different sizes and different colors. Some are solid. Some are clouds of gas. Some have no moons, and some have many.

Scientists have learned a lot about other planets by looking at them through telescopes.

Draw pictures of these three planets, using the information in each box. Look in books if you need help.

Earth

- About 8,000 miles (12,880 kilometers) across
- One moon
- Mainly covered with water
- Looks like a blue marble with white swirls

Mars

- Smaller than Earth
- Two moons
- Red with dark areas and white ice caps at north and south poles

Jupiter

- More than 10 times larger than Earth
- Covered with dark and light striped clouds
- Large red spot
- 16 moons
- A very thin ring

What's for Lunch?

Some animals eat plants. Some animals eat other animals. And some animals eat both plants and other animals.
What's that?
A salad.
Good, I want to watch an animal eating a plant.
Plant Food
by Wanda
Food starts with green plants. These plants can make their own food with energy from the sun. Some animals eat the plants. Other animals eat animals that have eaten plants.

Which of these animals eat only plants? Which eat only other animals? Which eat both? Fill in the chart. Look in books if you need help.

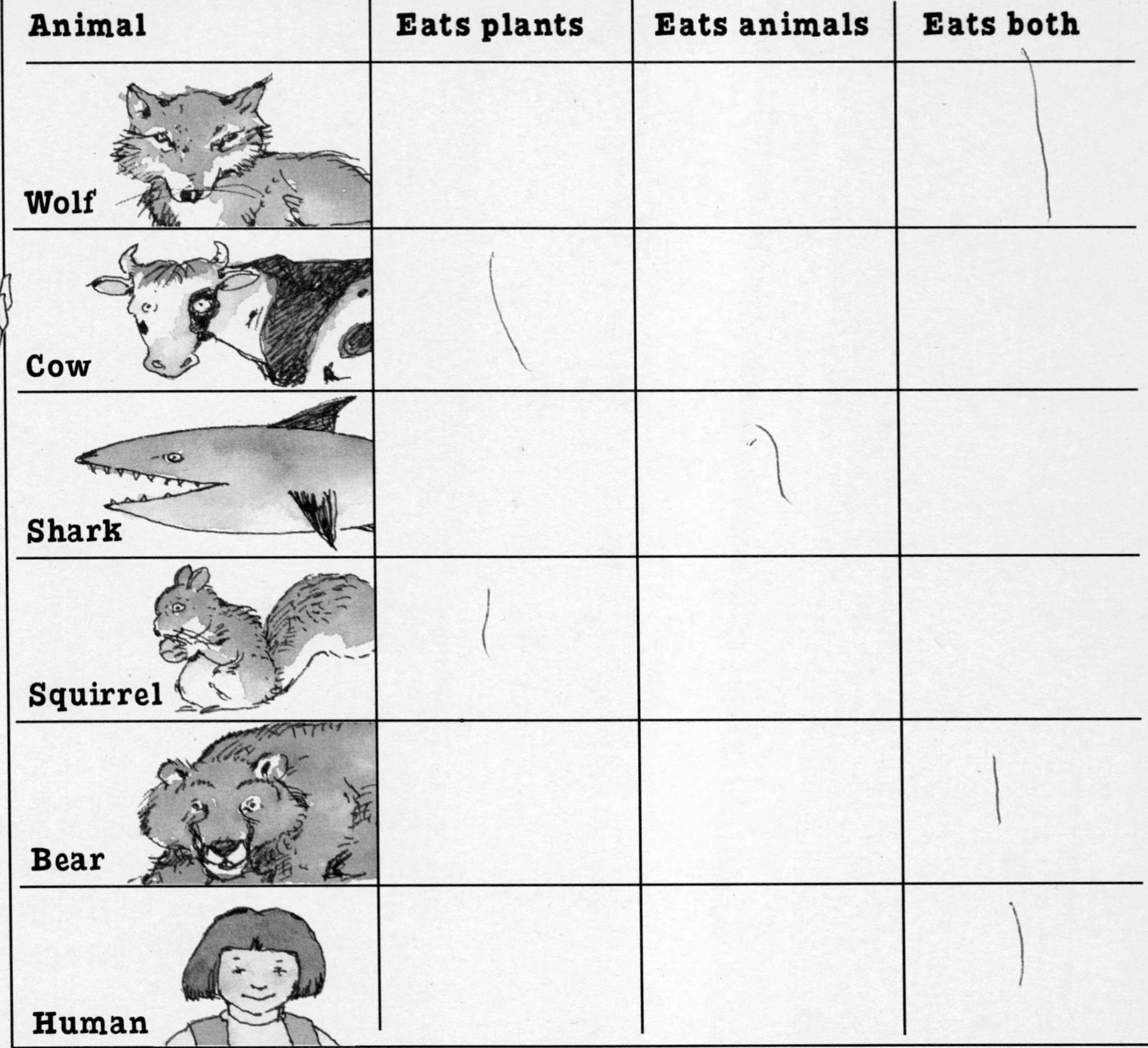

Animal	Eats plants	Eats animals	Eats both
Wolf			
Cow			
Shark			
Squirrel			
Bear			
Human			

Plant Food

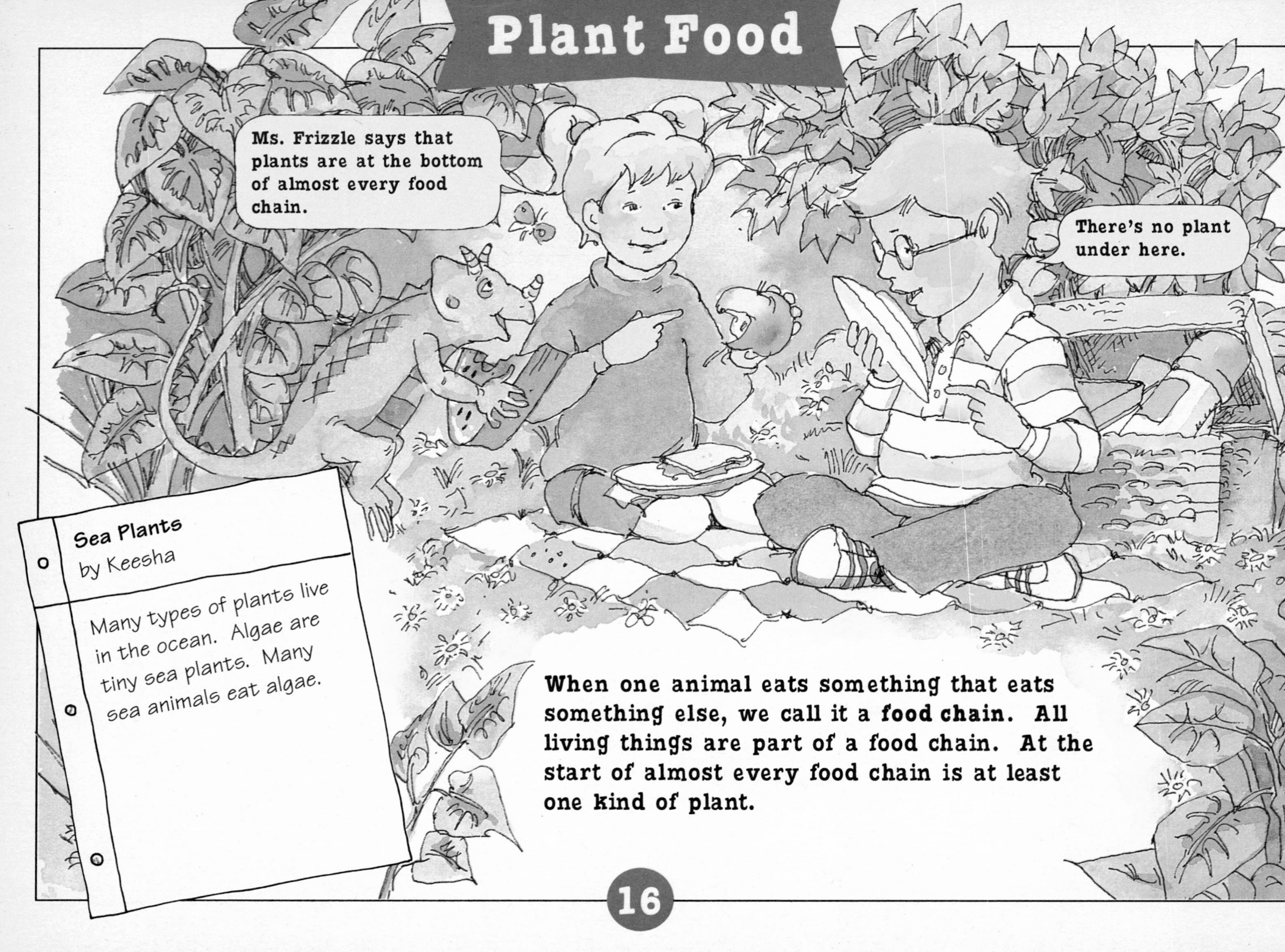

Ms. Frizzle says that plants are at the bottom of almost every food chain.
There's no plant under here.
Sea Plants
by Keesha
Many types of plants live in the ocean. Algae are tiny sea plants. Many sea animals eat algae.

When one animal eats something that eats something else, we call it a **food chain**. All living things are part of a food chain. At the start of almost every food chain is at least one kind of plant.

The food chains on this page have a beginning and an end.

Can you fill in the middle? You can draw any type of animal you want. You can draw more than one animal. Remember, each animal has to eat the animal or plant that comes before it.

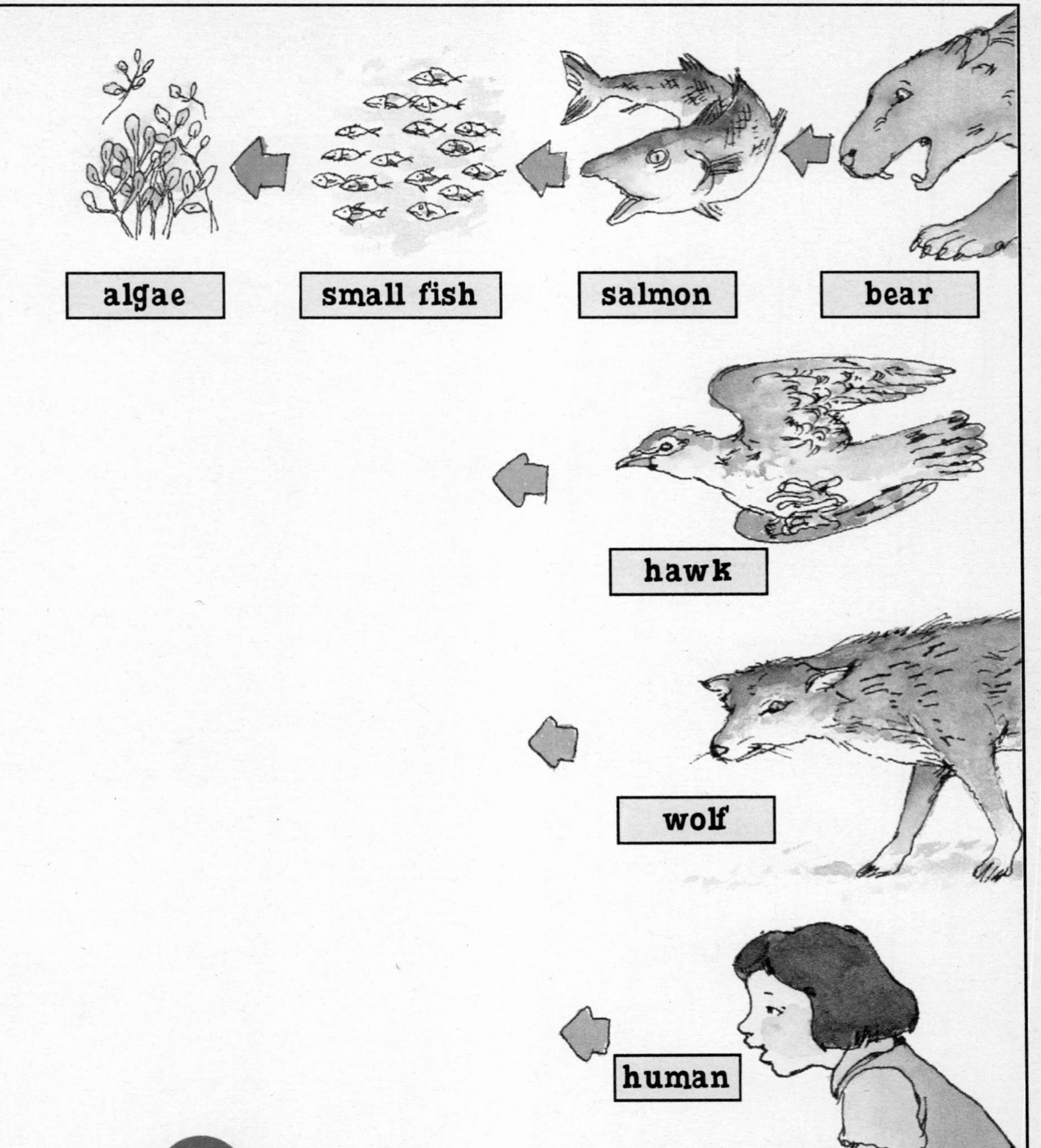

Rub a Dub

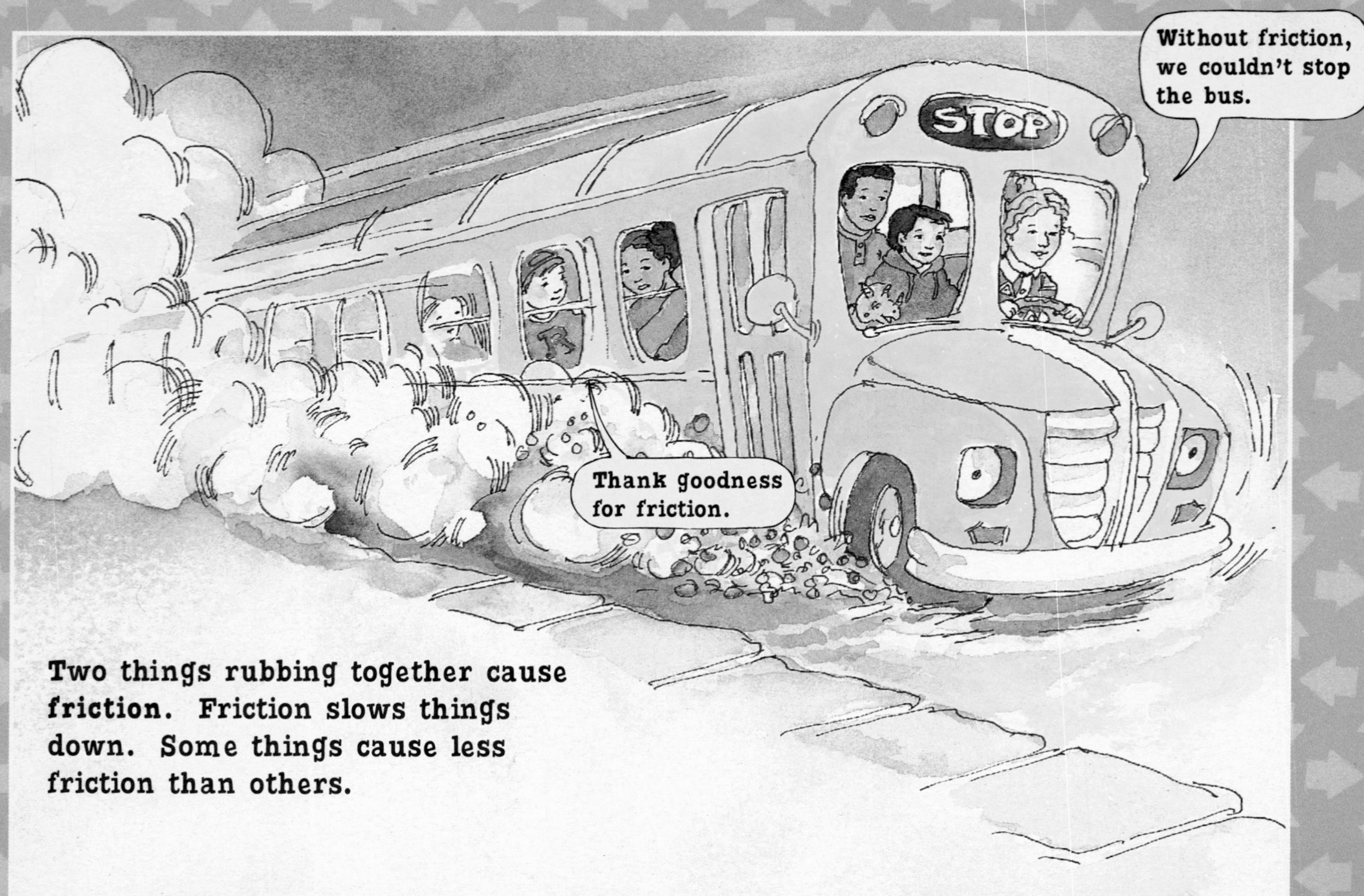

Two things rubbing together cause friction. Friction slows things down. Some things cause less friction than others.

Friction Races

Friction makes things hard to move.

Which shapes cause less friction? Find out by using different shapes and comparing them. You'll need some wooden or plastic blocks and a straw.

1. Pick out 2 or 3 blocks to use. One should be round, like a ball or a tube. The other blocks can be shaped like a square or a triangle, or anything else.

2. Mark off a racecourse on the floor with a piece of tape for the beginning and one for the end.

3. Put one block at the Start line. Use the straw to blow the block to the Finish line. Be sure to blow each block along the course the same way. Have a friend time you with a watch or by counting.

4. Write the results in the chart.

Shape of Block	Time

What happened? Did one shape move faster than the others? Which one?

____

____

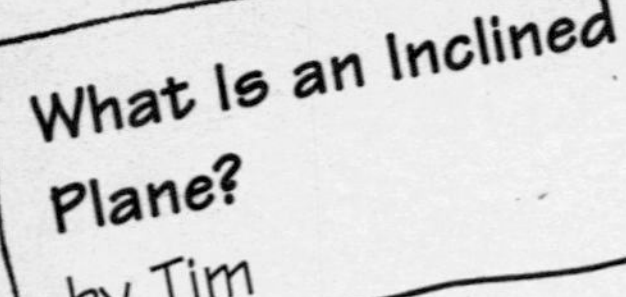

Anything that slants can be an inclined plane. A ramp is an inclined plane. People loading or unloading a truck often use a ramp to help them move things. A slide is also an inclined plane.

Class, an inclined plane makes it easier to move something up or down.

This slide makes it easier to get off the bus.

And more fun, too!

Machines make it easier for you to move things. One kind of machine is an inclined plane. It can help you move a heavy object to a higher or lower place.

Test how a ramp can help you move a marble.

You will need:

a marble

a ramp (a paper-towel tube makes a good ramp)

10 books, each about $\frac{1}{2}$ inch ($1\frac{1}{2}$ centimeters) thick

a yardstick or meterstick

1. Find a place with a smooth floor. Lean the ramp on one book.

2. Hold the marble at the top of the ramp. Let it roll.

3. Measure how far the marble rolls. Start measuring at the bottom of the ramp. In the chart, record how far it goes.

4. Make a guess. What will happen if you raise the ramp?________________________

5. Raise the ramp to 4 books. Then to 7 books. Then to 10 books. Do steps 2 and 3 each time. Which height made the marble roll farthest?________________________

Number of Books	My Guess	How Far?

Mix Masters

Class, what happens when you mix sand and water at the beach?
You get a suntan.
This bag is a mixture of red, green, and brown candy.
No, it isn't. I ate all the red ones.

Part of chemistry is mixing things together. Sometimes when we mix two things together, we can take them apart easily. Sometimes when we mix them together, they change into something new.

Make a mixture out of sand and water.

You'll need:

2 clear jars
a measuring cup
water
sand
pencil or stick
a coffee filter

1. Measure 2 cups ($\frac{1}{2}$ liter) of water into a jar.

2. Measure a half cup (125 ml) of sand. Pour the sand into the water.

3. What happens to the sand?

____

4. Stir the water and sand mixture with a pencil or a stick. Can you see the sand?

____

5. Now hold the coffee filter over the second jar. Slowly pour the mixture into the filter so the water goes into the empty jar.

6. Look in the coffee filter. What do you see?

____

Measure it in the measuring cup. What is in the filter?

____

7. Look in the second jar. What do you see?

____

Measure it in the measuring cup. What is in the second jar?

____

Do the Dough

When we put things together, they sometimes change into something new. Then it is very hard to take them apart again.

Sometimes when we mix things together, they change.

Being mixed into this class would change anybody.

Make modeling clay by mixing ingredients and changing them into something new. Work with a friend. You will need:

4 cups (1 liter) flour
1 cup (250 ml) salt
$1\frac{1}{2}$ cups (375 ml) warm water
2 mixing bowls
large spoon

Before you start, look at the flour, salt, and water. Touch them. Write down what you see.

What is the flour like?

____

What is the salt like?

____

What is the water like?

____

What do you think will happen when you mix everything together?

____

____

1. Mix the salt and the warm water together. Stir for 30 seconds.

2. Put the flour in the other bowl. Mix the salt and water mixture into the flour.

3. Shape the mix into a ball and squeeze it with your hands for at least five minutes. That's called "kneading the dough."

4. You can mold the dough into any shape. If it doesn't stick together, it may need a few more drops of water. Also try kneading it more.

Your dough will dry in the air, or you can ask an adult to bake it in an oven at 300 degrees for about an hour. You can paint the dough when it is dry. Or if you want colored dough, add food coloring to the water before you start.

How is the dough different from the flour, salt, and water?

____

____

What happens when you let the dough dry?

____

____

Could you take the flour, water, and salt apart again?

____

____

Weather Report

What are we doing up here?
Ms. Frizzle wanted to show us a drizzle.
F
C

Weather is happening all the time. Whatever is going on in the air around us is the **weather**.

What's the Temperature?

by Keesha

A thermometer measures temperature. That tells us how hot or cold the air is.

a thermometer

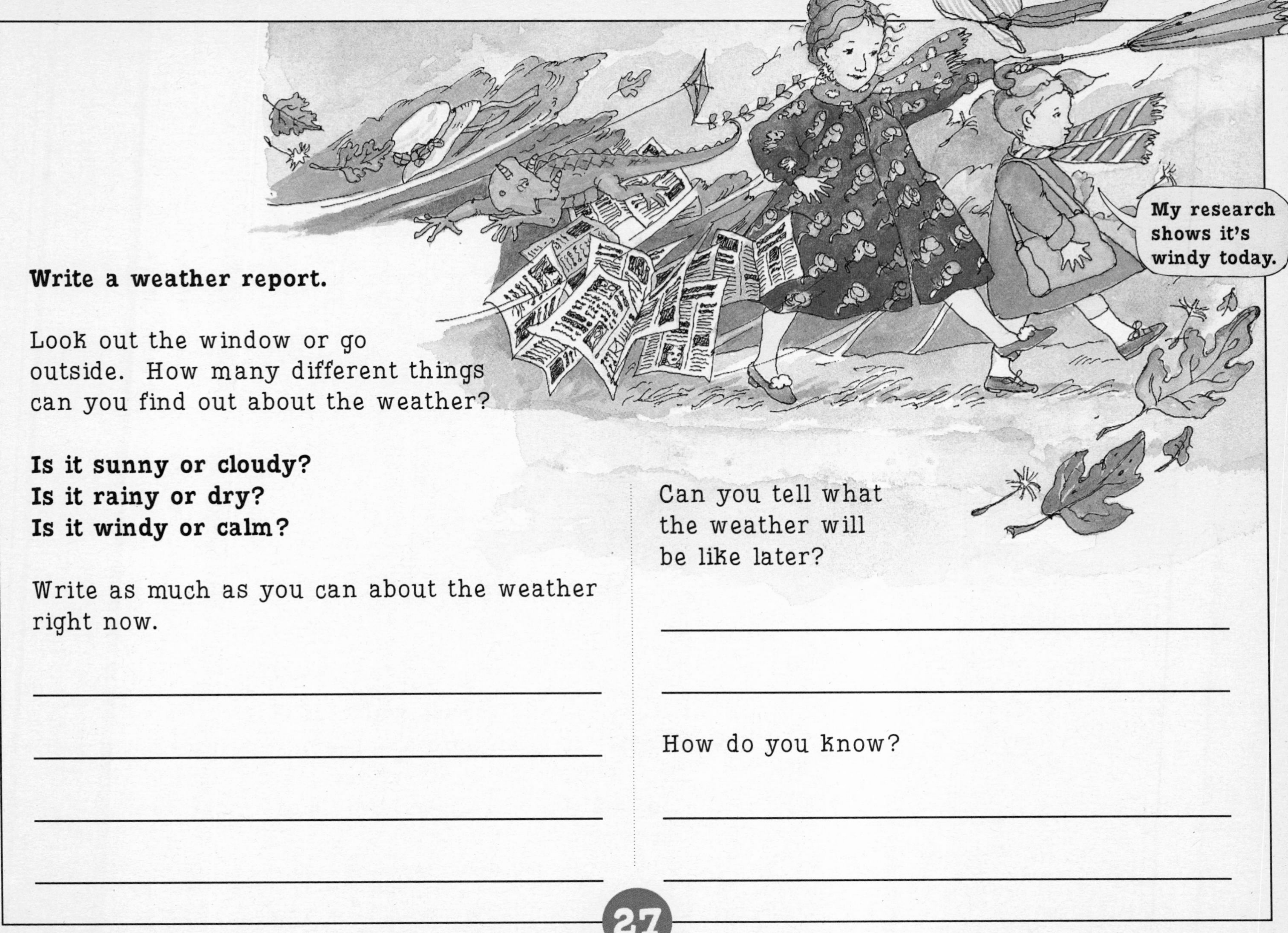
My research shows it's windy today.

Write a weather report.

Look out the window or go outside. How many different things can you find out about the weather?

Is it sunny or cloudy?
Is it rainy or dry?
Is it windy or calm?

Write as much as you can about the weather right now.

____

____

____

____

Can you tell what the weather will be like later?

____

____

How do you know?

____

____

Where Does the Water Go?

Types of Clouds
by Arnold
There are different types of clouds. Cirrus clouds are thin and wispy. Cumulus clouds are thick and fleecy. Cumulo-nimbus clouds are thick, dark-gray thunderclouds.
cirrus clouds
cumulus clouds
cumulo-nimbus clouds
Did you hear the weather report?
Yes. It said cloudy with a chance of buses.

Heat from the sun makes water on Earth evaporate. It turns into a gas and floats into the sky. In the sky it turns back into tiny drops of water. The drops hang close together and form clouds.

How does water form clouds?

Get a clean, clear bottle or jar. Put in a little bit of hot water.

Put some ice cubes in a plastic bag. Put them over the top of the jar. What happens?

____

How is what happens in the jar like a cloud?

____

Draw a picture of what happens in the jar.

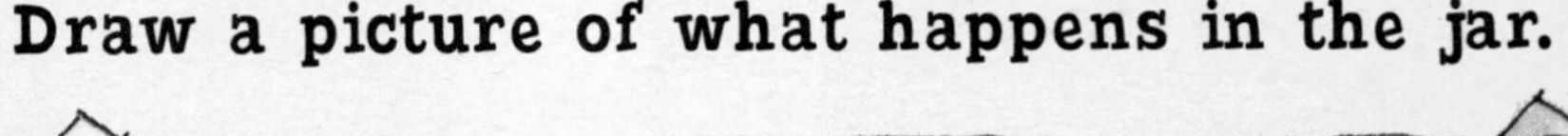

Please Be Seeded

Inside a Seed
by Carlos
Inside a seed there is already a tiny baby plant, ready to grow. There is also food for the plant and tough skin or a shell to protect it.
baby plant
food
outer shell
Keesha, what did the flower say to her guests?
I don't know, Ralphie.
Please be seeded! Get it? Seated? Seeded?
Seeds are one way that plants make new plants. Each plant has its own kind of seed. Inside the seed is everything the baby plant needs to grow, except water and light.

Take two beans. Beans are seeds.

Look at your seeds. Use a magnifying glass if you have one. Can you see different parts of the seed? Draw what you see.

My seed

2/5/97 19:45 - Lucas predicts that only the wet one will have sprouts ("I know that!")
We put four beans in each one: 1 kidney, 1 pinto, 1 red, 1 black.

1. Wet a paper towel, and fold it over. Stuff it in a plastic bag. Then place a seed in the bag, with the towel all around it. Label that bag with the number **1**.

2. Take another paper towel, and without making it wet, fold it and place it in a plastic bag. Put a seed in that towel. Label that bag with the number **2**.

3. Place both bags side by side on a shelf where they will get some light, but not direct sun. What do you think will happen?

____

4. Check the seeds every day. Make sure that the towel in Bag 1 is always damp.

Draw what happens.

Did something different happen in each bag? Why do you think this happened?

____

____

Flower Power

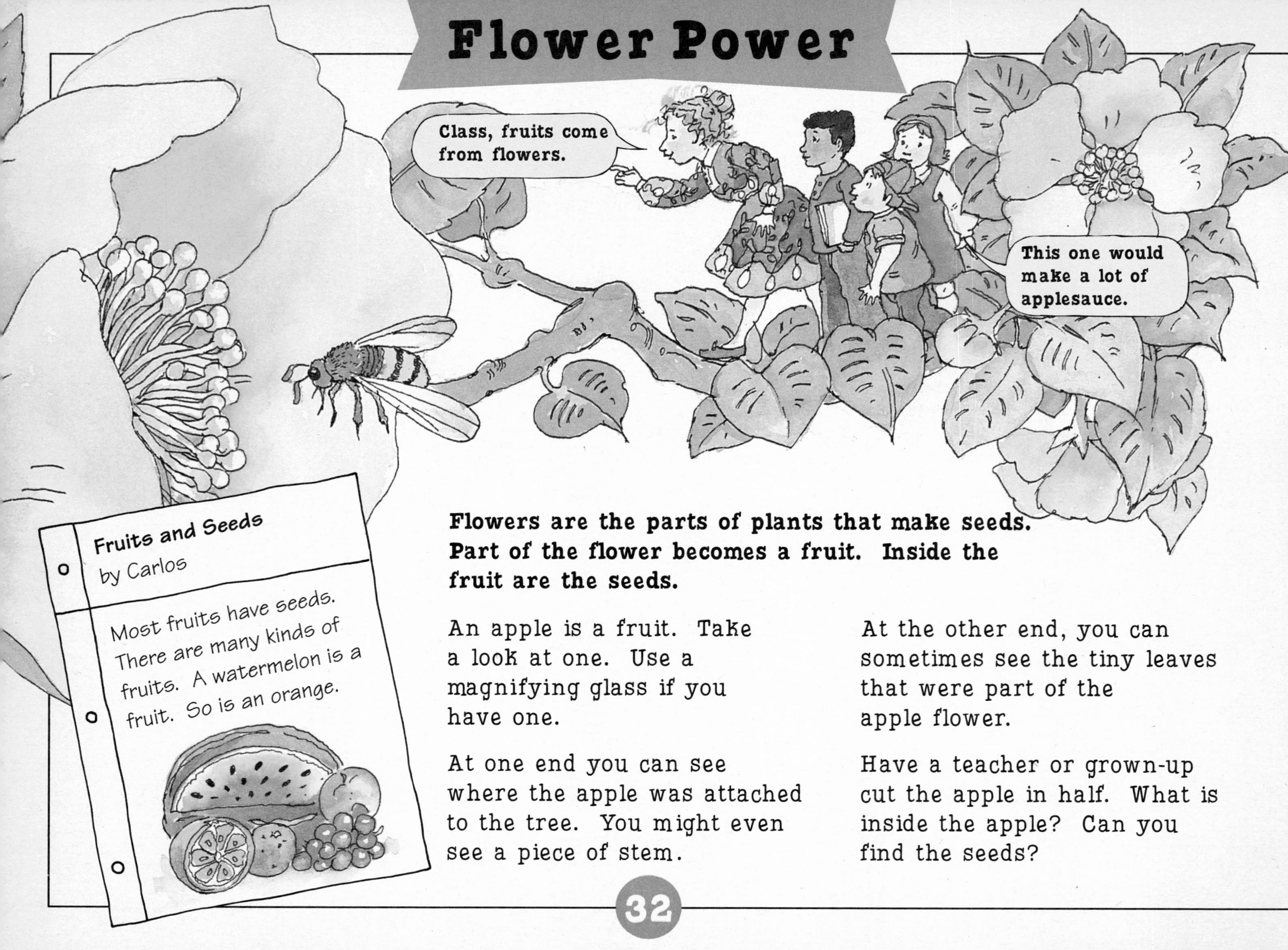

Class, fruits come from flowers.
This one would make a lot of applesauce.
Fruits and Seeds
by Carlos
Most fruits have seeds. There are many kinds of fruits. A watermelon is a fruit. So is an orange.

Flowers are the parts of plants that make seeds. Part of the flower becomes a fruit. Inside the fruit are the seeds.

An apple is a fruit. Take a look at one. Use a magnifying glass if you have one.

At one end you can see where the apple was attached to the tree. You might even see a piece of stem.

At the other end, you can sometimes see the tiny leaves that were part of the apple flower.

Have a teacher or grown-up cut the apple in half. What is inside the apple? Can you find the seeds?

My research shows that apples grow from the flowers on apple trees.

The apple is one fruit, but there are many other kinds of fruits. How can you tell if something is a fruit or not? Is a banana a fruit? Is a potato? Look for other examples of fruits at home or at the grocery store.

Try to answer these questions about the foods you look at:

1. Does it have seeds?
2. Did it grow from a flower?
3. Can you find where the fruit was attached to the stem?

Bring in a list of the fruits you found and a list of the plant foods you found that weren't fruits.

Fruits	Not Fruits

Ant Antics

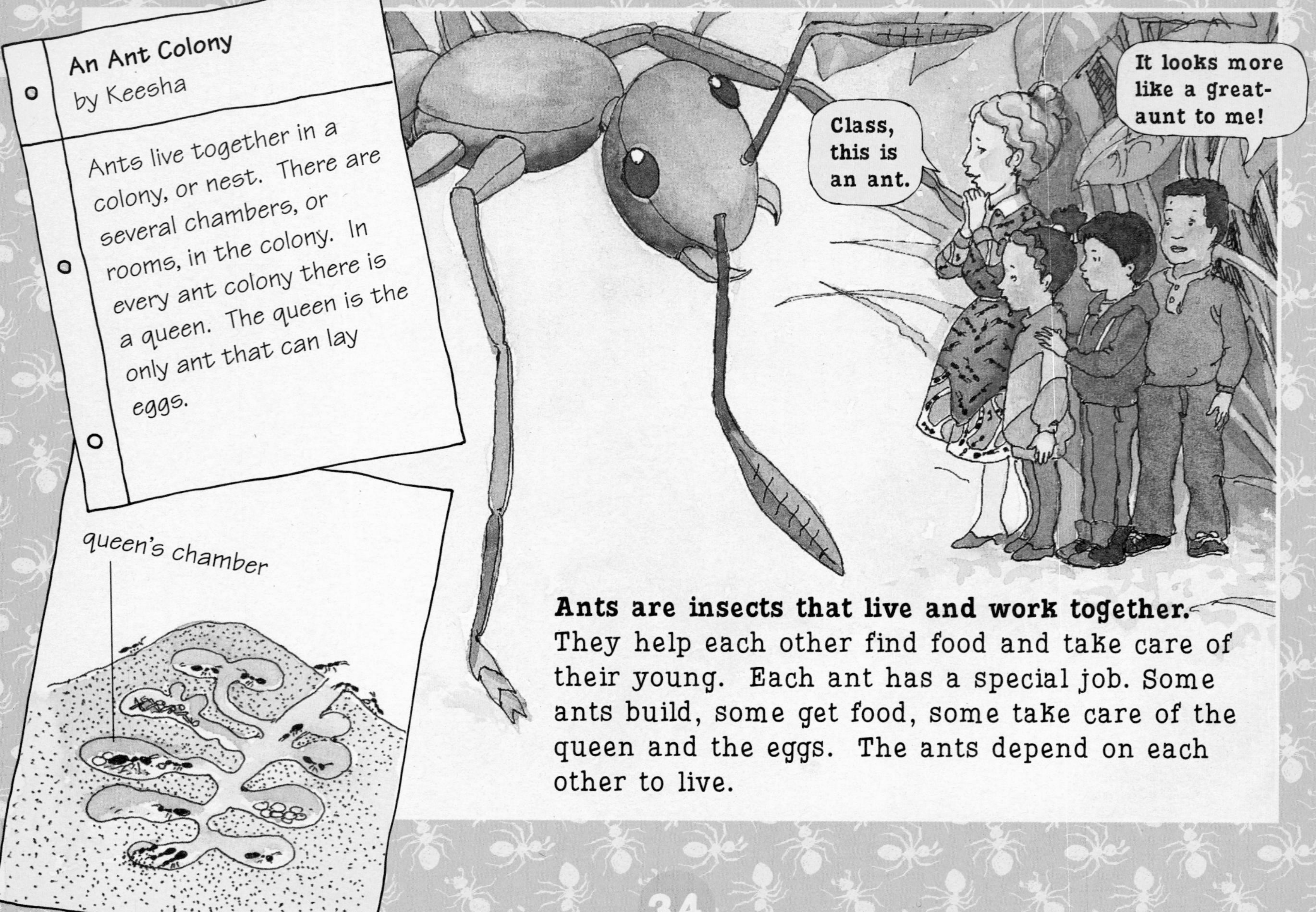

An Ant Colony
by Keesha
Ants live together in a colony, or nest. There are several chambers, or rooms, in the colony. In every ant colony there is a queen. The queen is the only ant that can lay eggs.
queen's chamber
Class, this is an ant.
It looks more like a great-aunt to me!

Ants are insects that live and work together. They help each other find food and take care of their young. Each ant has a special job. Some ants build, some get food, some take care of the queen and the eggs. The ants depend on each other to live.

People live together in homes and towns and cities. Like ants, people have different jobs and depend on each other. How are ants and people alike? How are they different? List some ways in each column.

In some ways, people are like ants.
But not in every way, thank goodness!

Ants are like people because:	Ants are not like people because:

Now Smell This

Ants can't talk, but they can tell each other where food is.
Hey, do you know where lunch is?
Do I look like an ant?
This is very touching.
Ant Senses
by Wanda
Ants have eyes, but they mainly use smell and touch. They use their antennae to touch things, including other ants.

Ants can't talk, but they can send messages to each other.

When an ant finds food, it goes back to the nest, leaving a trail of smells. Then it uses its antennae to tap other ants and "tell" them it found food. The other ants follow the smell trail back to the food.

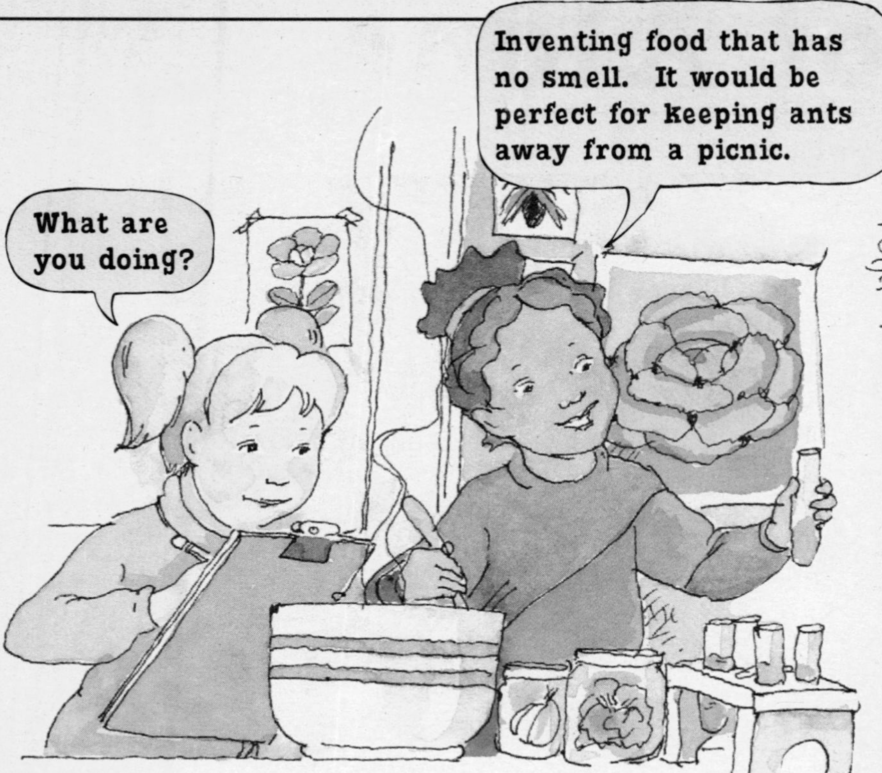

Ants have to communicate without talking.

How good are you at communicating without talking?

Play this game and see what kind of "ant-ics" you come up with.

You need four people to play. Divide into two teams.

Find the Food

1. One person from each team leaves the room.

2. The other two people take a block or a book or any other small object and together hide it somewhere in the room. That is the "food."

3. Call the other two players into the room. Each of the players who hid the food tries to tell his or her teammate where it is. None of the players can point. And none of the players can use words or sounds of any kind.

4. The first player who finds the "food" wins for that team.

5. Switch players. The players who were the "hiders" go outside while the players who were the "finders" hide the "food" in a different place.

Home — Not Alone

The Biggest Dam
by Tim
The biggest beaver dam ever discovered was 4,000 feet (1,200 meters) long. It was built by beavers near Berlin, Germany.
The door to a beaver lodge is underwater.
Why couldn't they have front steps like everyone else?

A Beaver Lodge

Beavers build their own homes, and they make the ponds they live in. Beavers make ponds by damming up rivers. Then they build a home, called a **lodge**, in the middle of the pond.

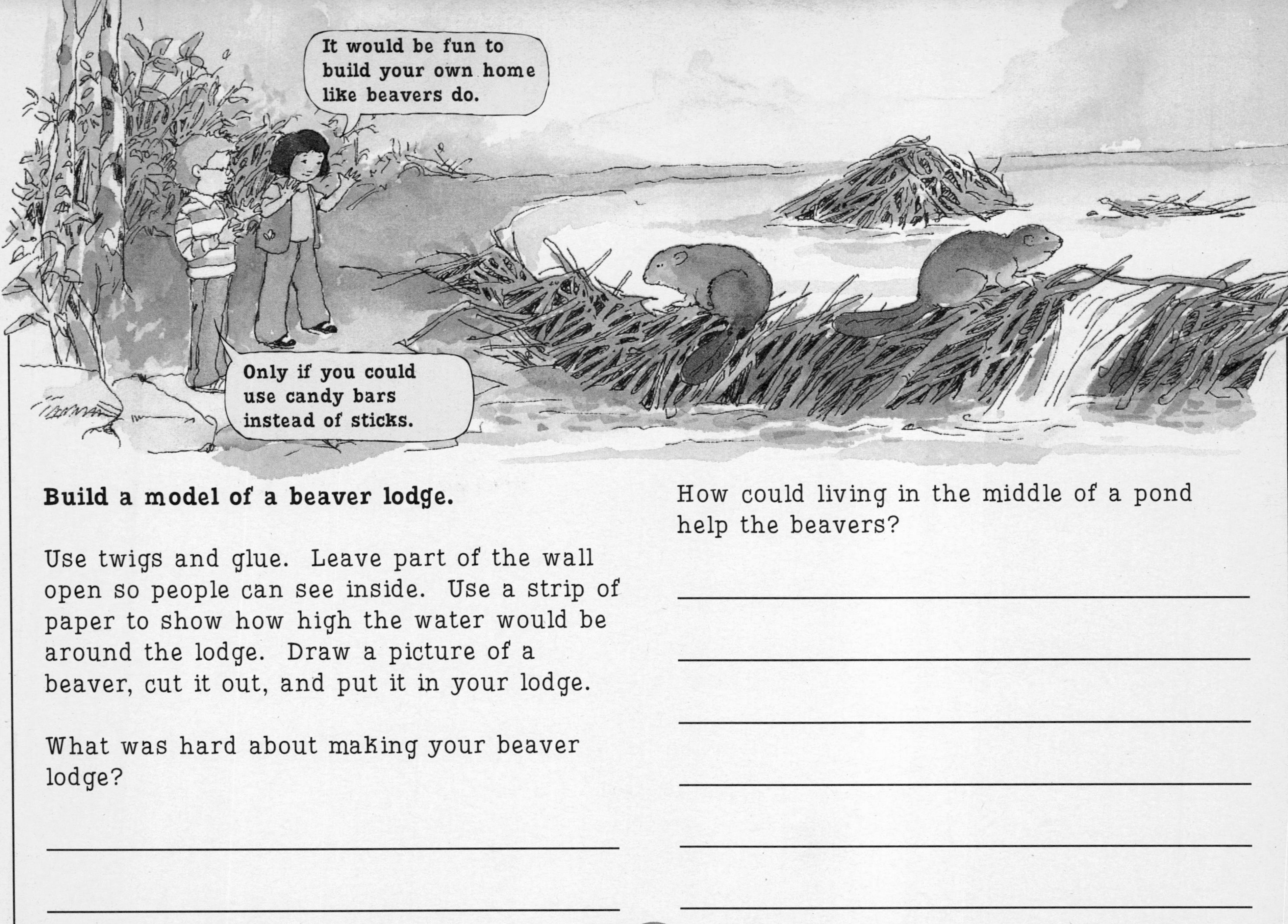

Build a model of a beaver lodge.

Use twigs and glue. Leave part of the wall open so people can see inside. Use a strip of paper to show how high the water would be around the lodge. Draw a picture of a beaver, cut it out, and put it in your lodge.

What was hard about making your beaver lodge?

____

____

How could living in the middle of a pond help the beavers?

____

____

____

____

____

____

Home Is Where the Habitat Is

According to my research, an animal's neighborhood is called a habitat.
I call this neighborhood wet.
Human Habitats
by Phoebe
Human beings live in many different types of habitats. People often change their habitats. They cut down trees or plant crops or dam rivers. All of these things change a habitat.

The neighborhood an animal lives in is called a habitat.

There are many different types of animal habitats. Some birds live in forests. Others live in meadows.

Many different animals can live in the same neighborhood. Animals in the same habitat might eat the same food or live in the same places. Or one kind of animal might eat another.

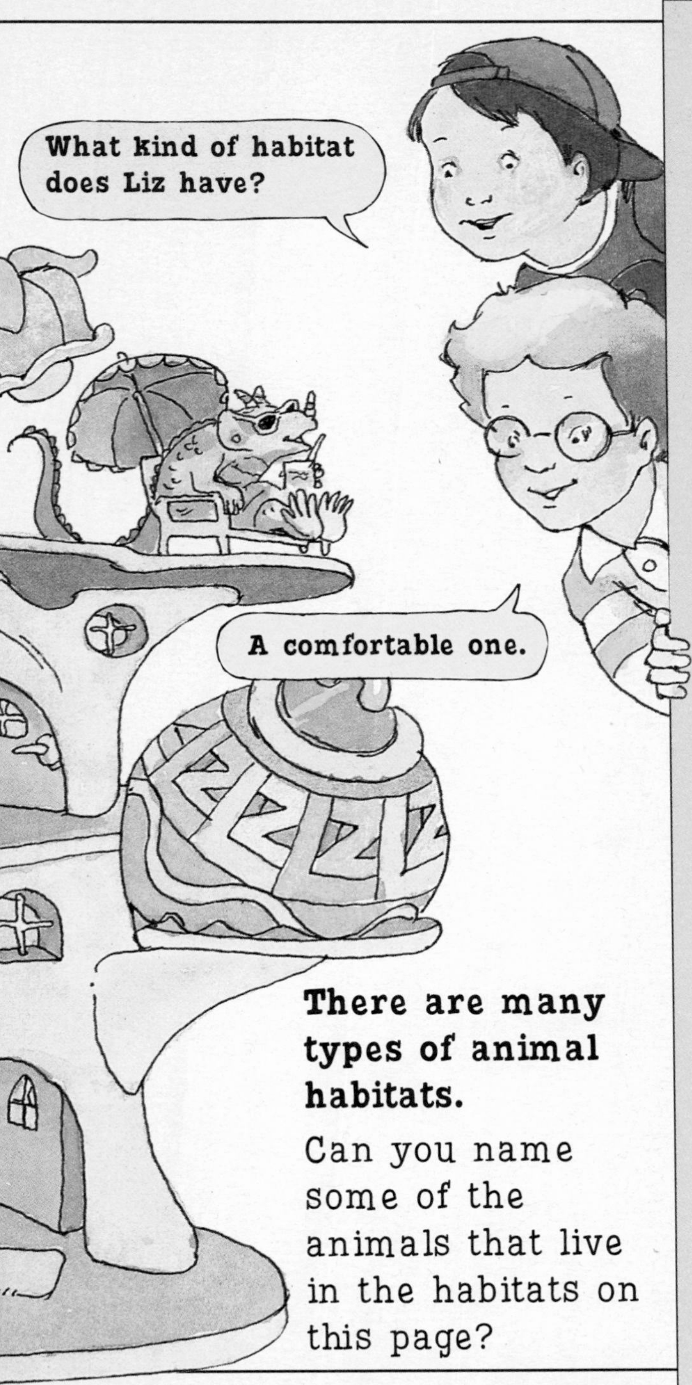

What kind of habitat does Liz have?
A comfortable one.

There are many types of animal habitats.

Can you name some of the animals that live in the habitats on this page?

Zounds!

Sounds are made when something shakes, or **vibrates.** Things that are different sizes make different sounds. A big drum makes a booming sound. A little drum makes a higher, lighter sound.

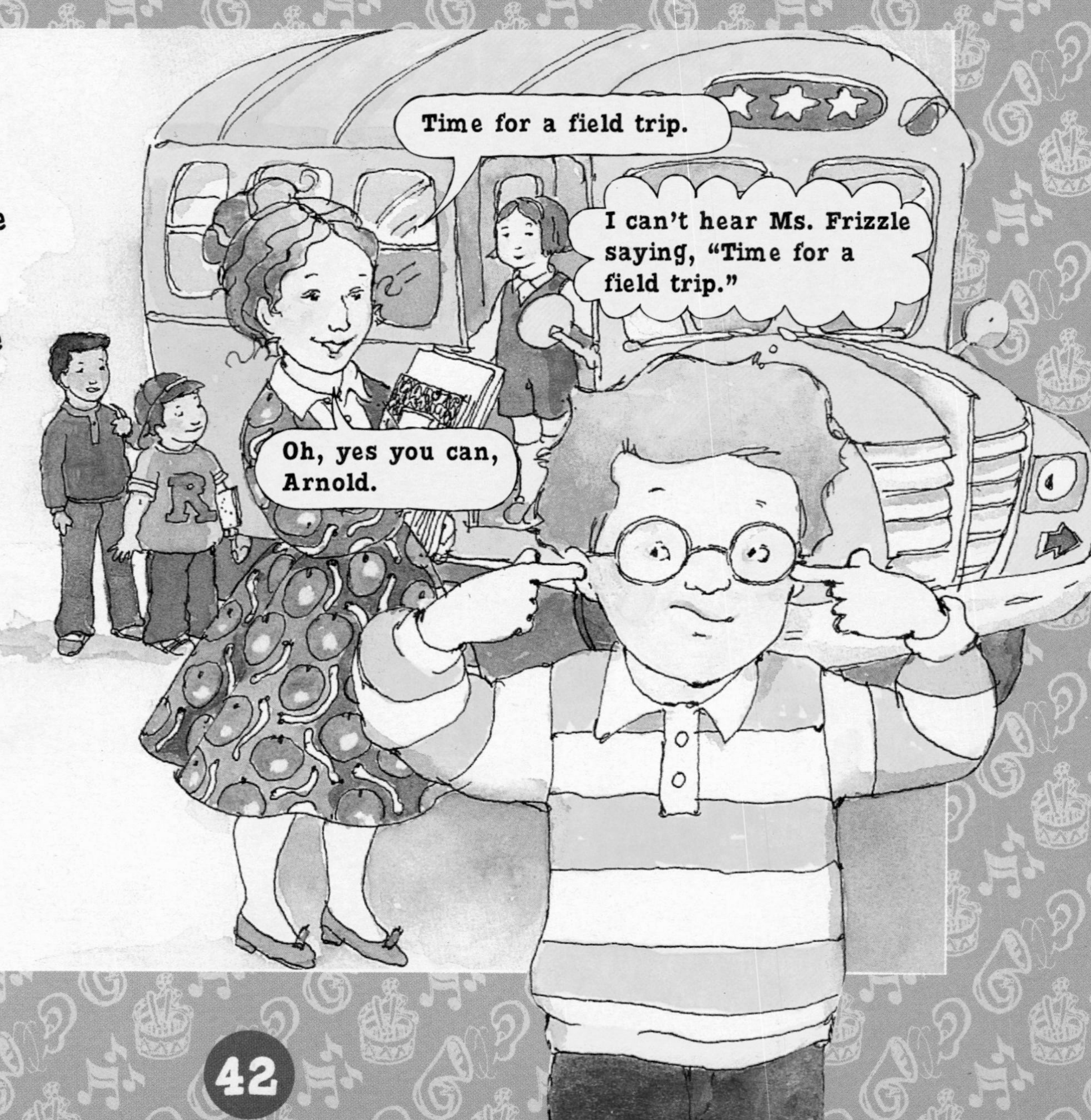

Time for a field trip.
I can't hear Ms. Frizzle saying, "Time for a field trip."
Oh, yes you can, Arnold.

Making Music
by Phoebe

Instruments all make sound by vibrating. When you hit a drum, the drum head vibrates. When you strum a guitar, the strings vibrate.

You can't see a sound. But you can see how something vibrating causes sound.

Make a musical instrument out of rubber bands.

1. Use the top from a shoebox or some other cardboard box. You can decorate your box top with colored paper and glue.

2. Stretch rubber bands of different sizes across the box top the long way.

3. Pluck on the rubber bands.

Ralphie, what are you doing?

Carlos asked me to shake hands.

Can you see the rubber bands vibrate?

Yes______ No______

Do they make sounds?

Yes______ No______

Do different types of rubber bands make different sounds?

Yes______ No______

Can you write a rule that tells how the size of the rubber band changes the sound it makes? Try it!

____

____

____

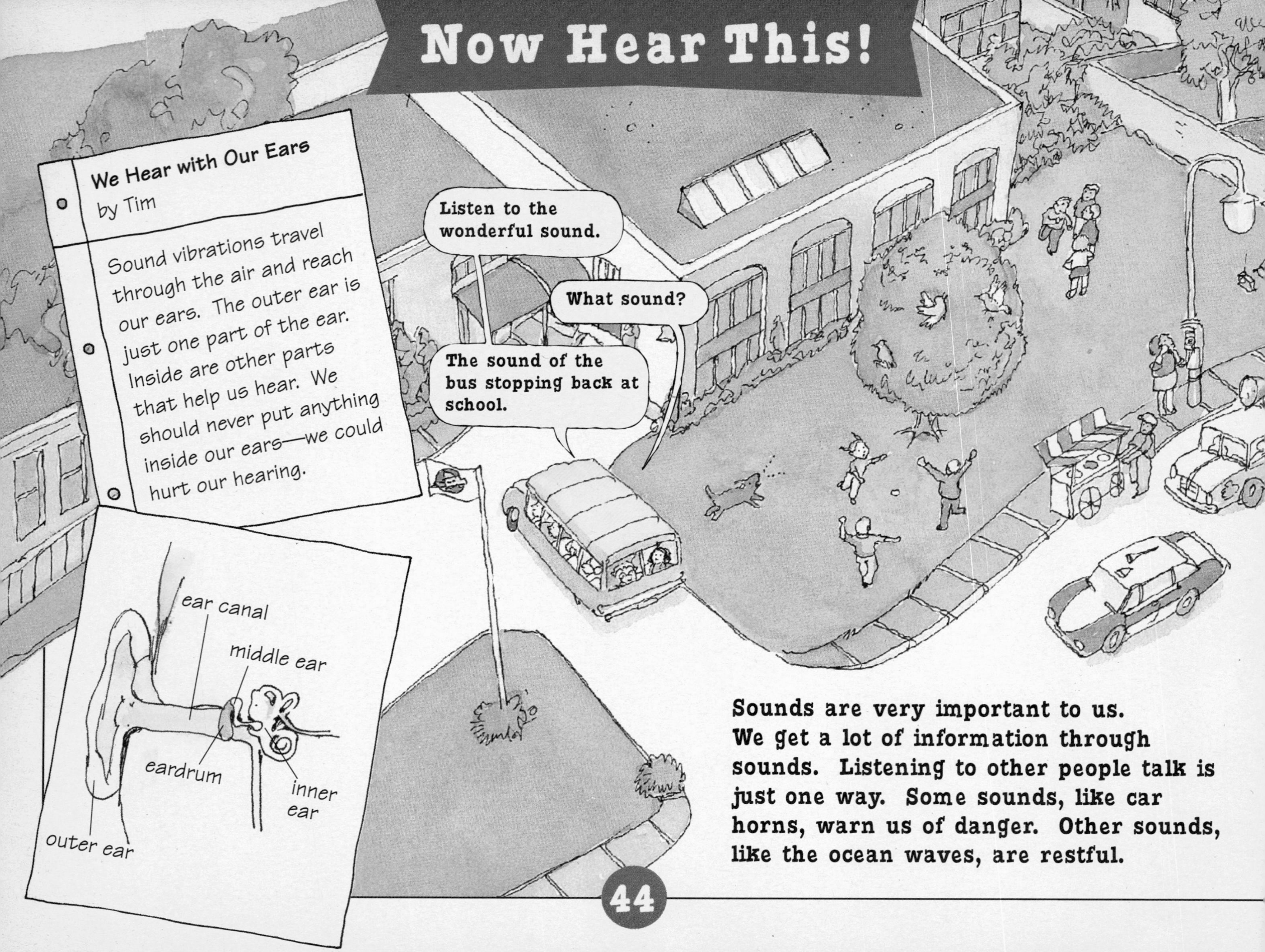
Now Hear This!
We Hear with Our Ears
by Tim
Sound vibrations travel through the air and reach our ears. The outer ear is just one part of the ear. Inside are other parts that help us hear. We should never put anything inside our ears—we could hurt our hearing.
ear canal
middle ear
eardrum
inner ear
outer ear
Listen to the wonderful sound.
What sound?
The sound of the bus stopping back at school.
Sounds are very important to us. We get a lot of information through sounds. Listening to other people talk is just one way. Some sounds, like car horns, warn us of danger. Other sounds, like the ocean waves, are restful.

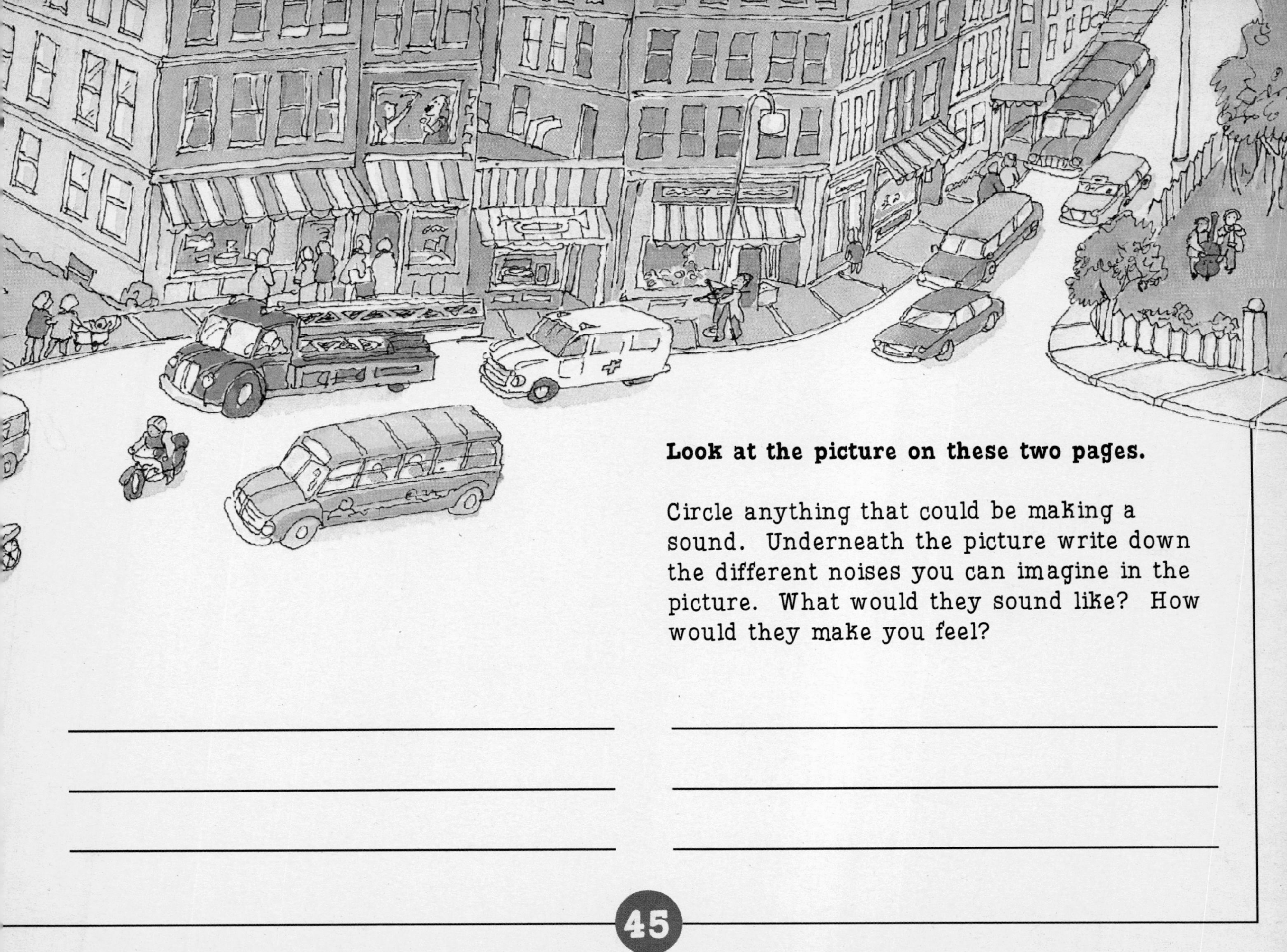

Look at the picture on these two pages.

Circle anything that could be making a sound. Underneath the picture write down the different noises you can imagine in the picture. What would they sound like? How would they make you feel?

The Line Is Busy

You don't have to
come any closer.
I can hear you fine.

Sound in the Water
by Dorothy Ann

Sound can travel far underwater. Low sounds made by humpback whales can travel for thousands of miles.

Sound usually reaches our ears by traveling through air. But sound can also travel through water or the ground. It can move through anything that can vibrate.

Sound can travel through water, wood, even string.

Make a cup telephone to see how this is true. You'll need:

2 paper or plastic-foam cups
a 10-foot (3-meter) piece of string

1. Make a small hole at the bottom of each of the two cups.

2. Put one end of the string through the hole in one cup. Knot the string to keep it in the cup.

3. Do the same with the other end of the string and the other cup. Stretch the string tight between the two cups.

4. Take turns talking and listening.

Hello. Ralphie isn't in right now. Please leave a message after the beep.

What happened when you used your "telephone"?

____

____

How did the sound travel from one cup to the other?

____

Try different kinds of string. Did one kind work better?

____

Something to Chew On

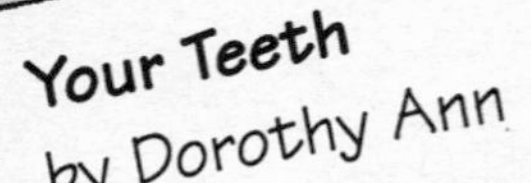

Your Teeth
by Dorothy Ann

You have a few different types of teeth in your mouth. Different teeth do different jobs. Incisors are pointy and sharp for biting. Molars are flat for grinding and mashing.

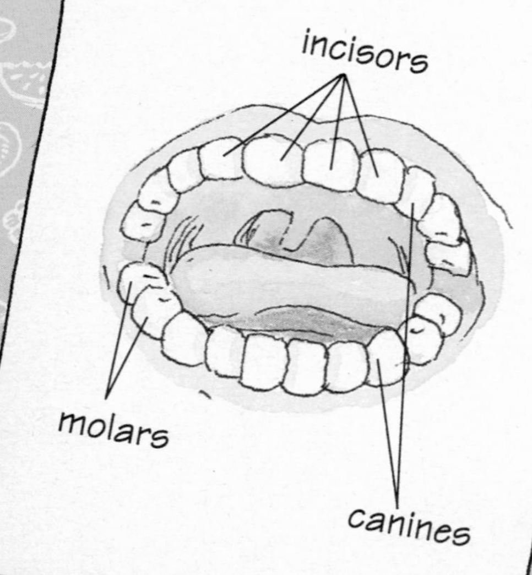

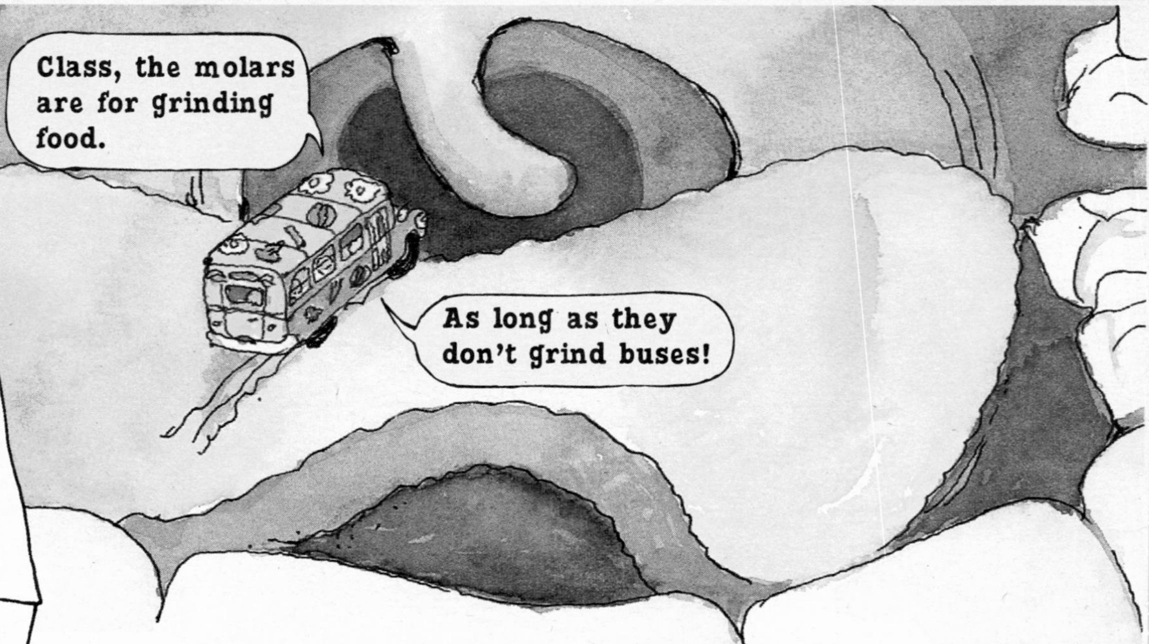

Class, the molars are for grinding food.
As long as they don't grind buses!

Your body uses food for energy. It also turns food into new bones, skin, and muscles. Before your body can use food, it has to be digested.

When you chew your food, you grind it up into little pieces. The watery liquid in your mouth, called **saliva**, helps make the food soft. This gets the food ready for its trip inside your body.

Animals eat different kinds of food. They also have different kinds of teeth. What kinds of teeth do you think these animals have? What kinds of foods do they eat? Do they have to mash lots of plants? Or do they have to cut lots of meat? Draw in their teeth, and explain why they have that kind. Look in books if you need help.

Wolf

____

____

Hippo

____

____

Shark

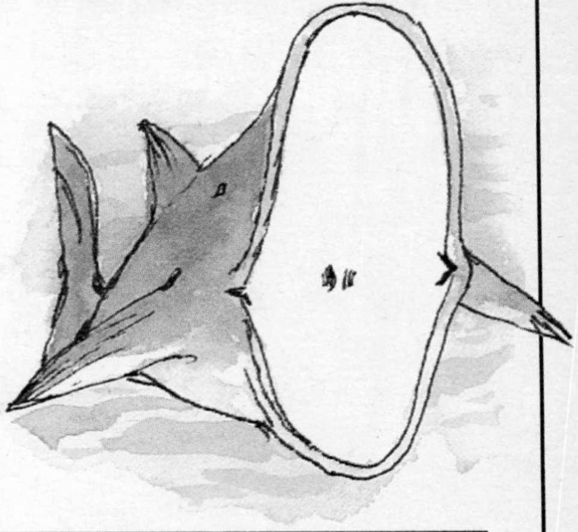

____

____

Horse

____

____

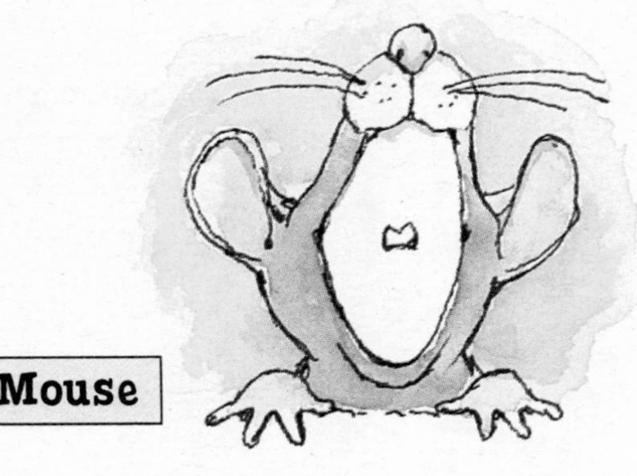

Mouse

____

____

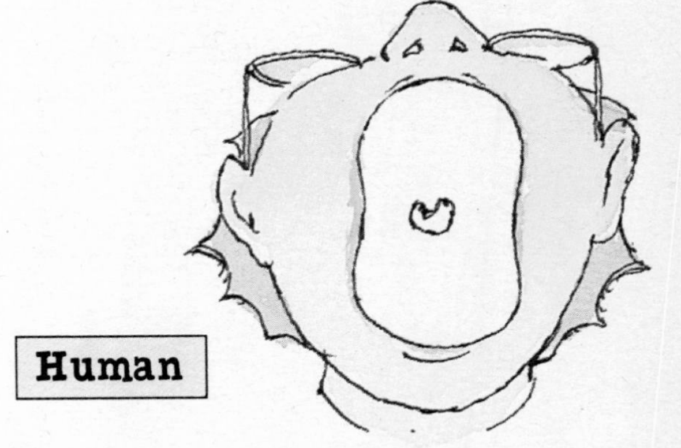

Human

____

____

It Takes Guts

When you eat, you chew your food and swallow it. Then it travels through your body through a long tube. The food is digested. It is broken into smaller parts so your body can use it.

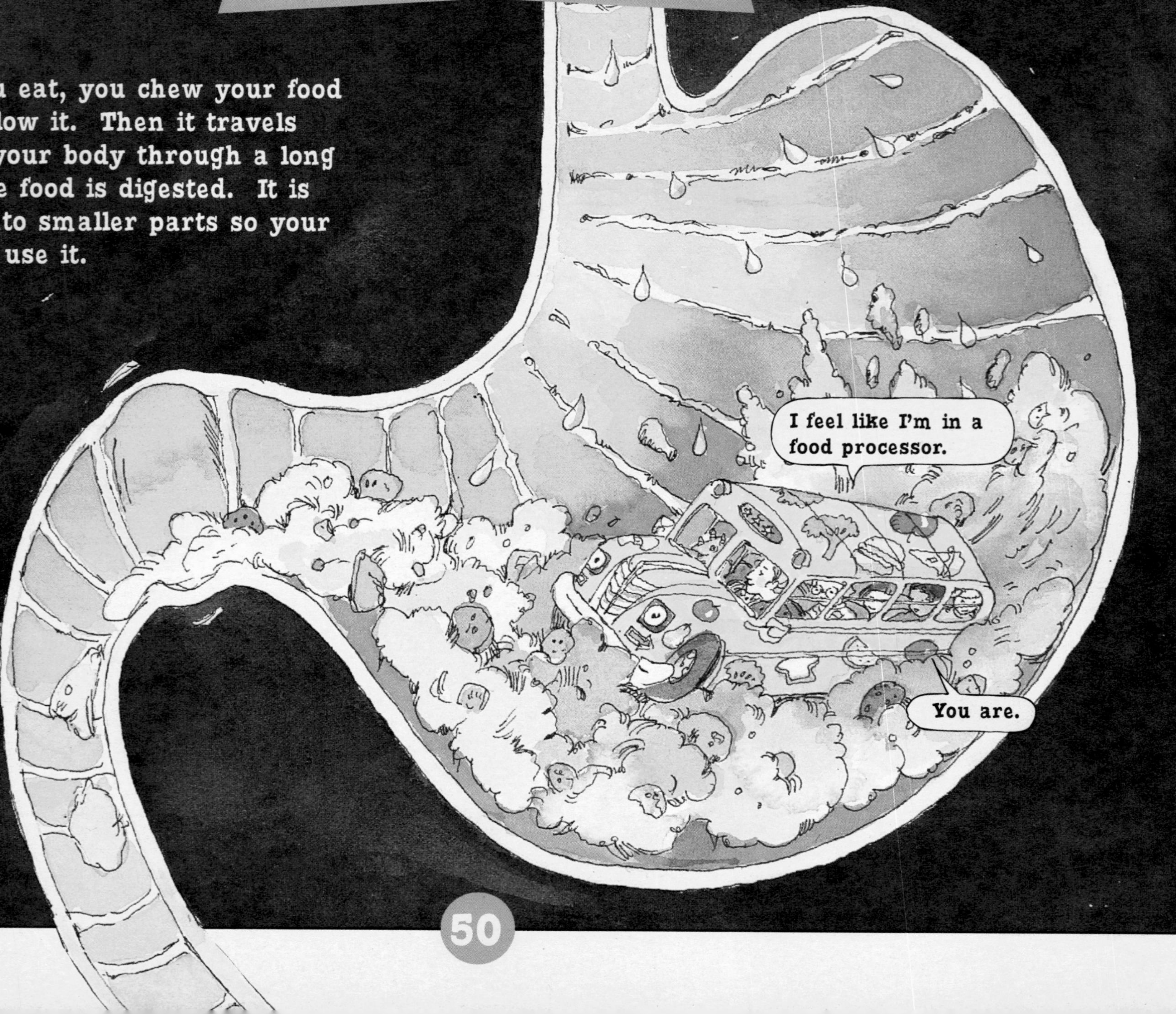

I feel like I'm in a food processor.
You are.

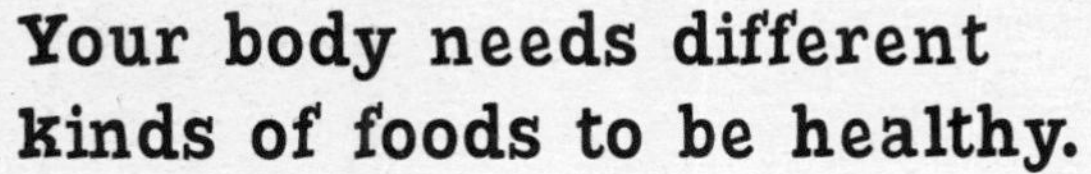

Your body needs different kinds of foods to be healthy.

The food pyramid tells you how much of each type of food you should eat every day. List the foods you ate yesterday next to each group below.

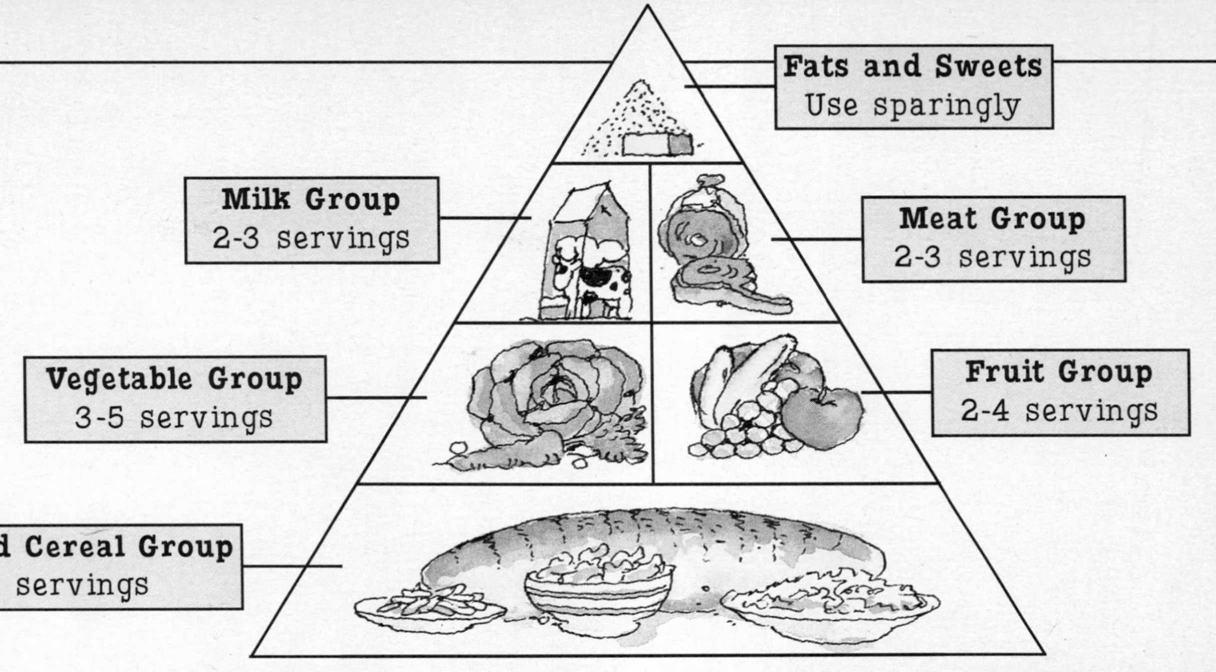

Kind of Food	What I Ate Yesterday
Bread, cereal, rice, pasta	
Fruits	
Vegetables	
Milk, yogurt, cheese	
Meat, chicken, fish, eggs, beans	
Sweets and fats	

What Rot!

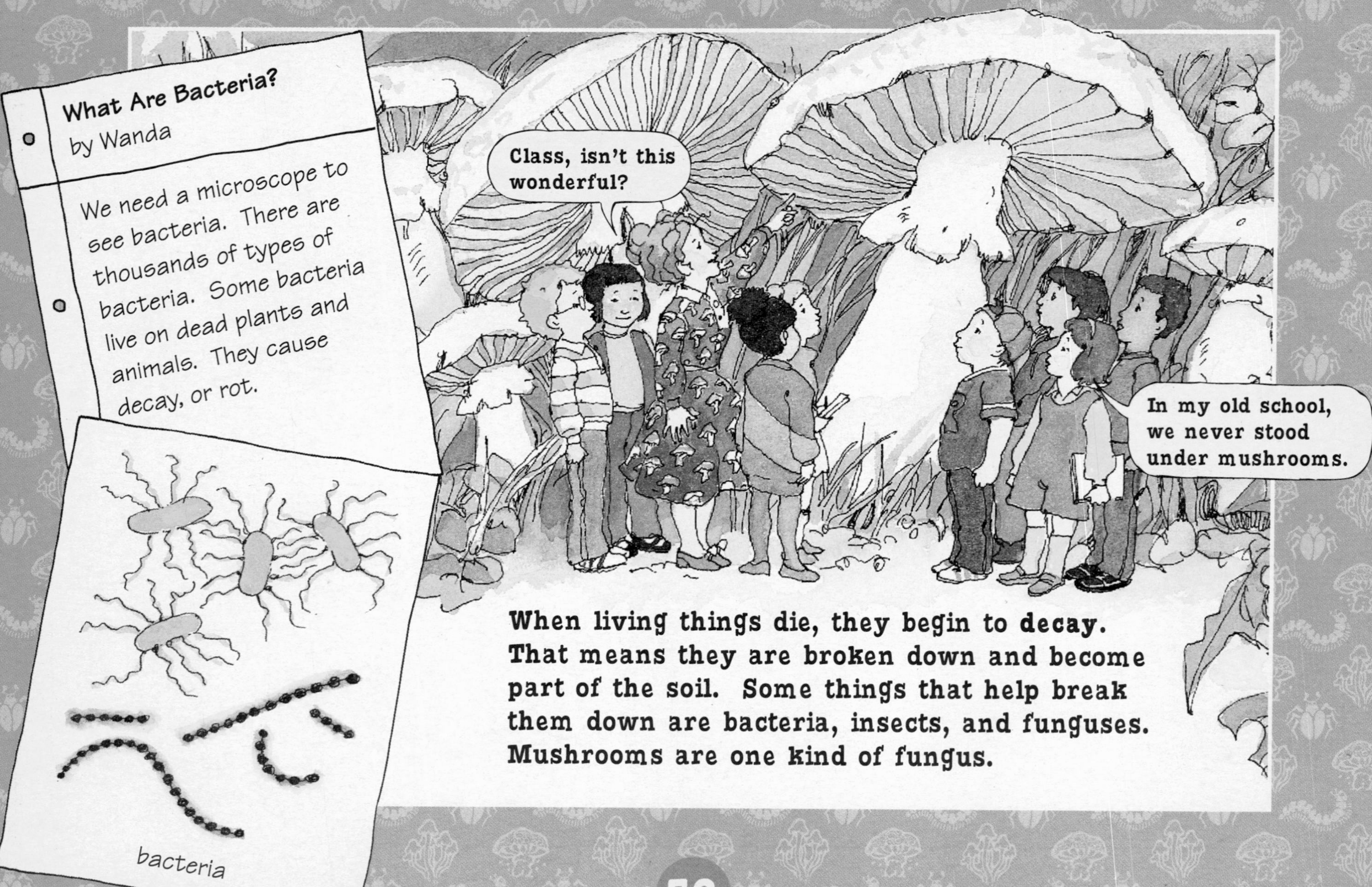

What Are Bacteria?
by Wanda
We need a microscope to see bacteria. There are thousands of types of bacteria. Some bacteria live on dead plants and animals. They cause decay, or rot.
bacteria
Class, isn't this wonderful?
In my old school, we never stood under mushrooms.

When living things die, they begin to **decay**. That means they are broken down and become part of the soil. Some things that help break them down are bacteria, insects, and funguses. Mushrooms are one kind of fungus.

What happens when something rots?

Make a rot museum. Get some small glass or plastic jars with lids. Put different foods in each jar: a piece of fruit, a vegetable, a piece of bread or cheese. You can also use grass clippings or other plants.

Check on the jars every day and record what you see.
How do the foods change? Do they rot in different ways? Do you see anything growing in the jars?

Rot Record

Jar	Day	What Happened

Home in the Log

Where Does the Log Go?
by Arnold
When a tree grows, it stores lots of nutrients, or food. When it dies, it begins to rot. As it rots, the nutrients go back into the soil. New trees use them to grow.
Home, home, in the log!

A dead, rotting log is home to hundreds of plants and animals. Bacteria, insects, small animals, and other creatures can live there. Some creatures eat the dead wood. Some animals eat other animals. Over time, the log rots away until it disappears.

How many of these things can you find in the rotting log?

Circle the animals and plants you find in the picture below.

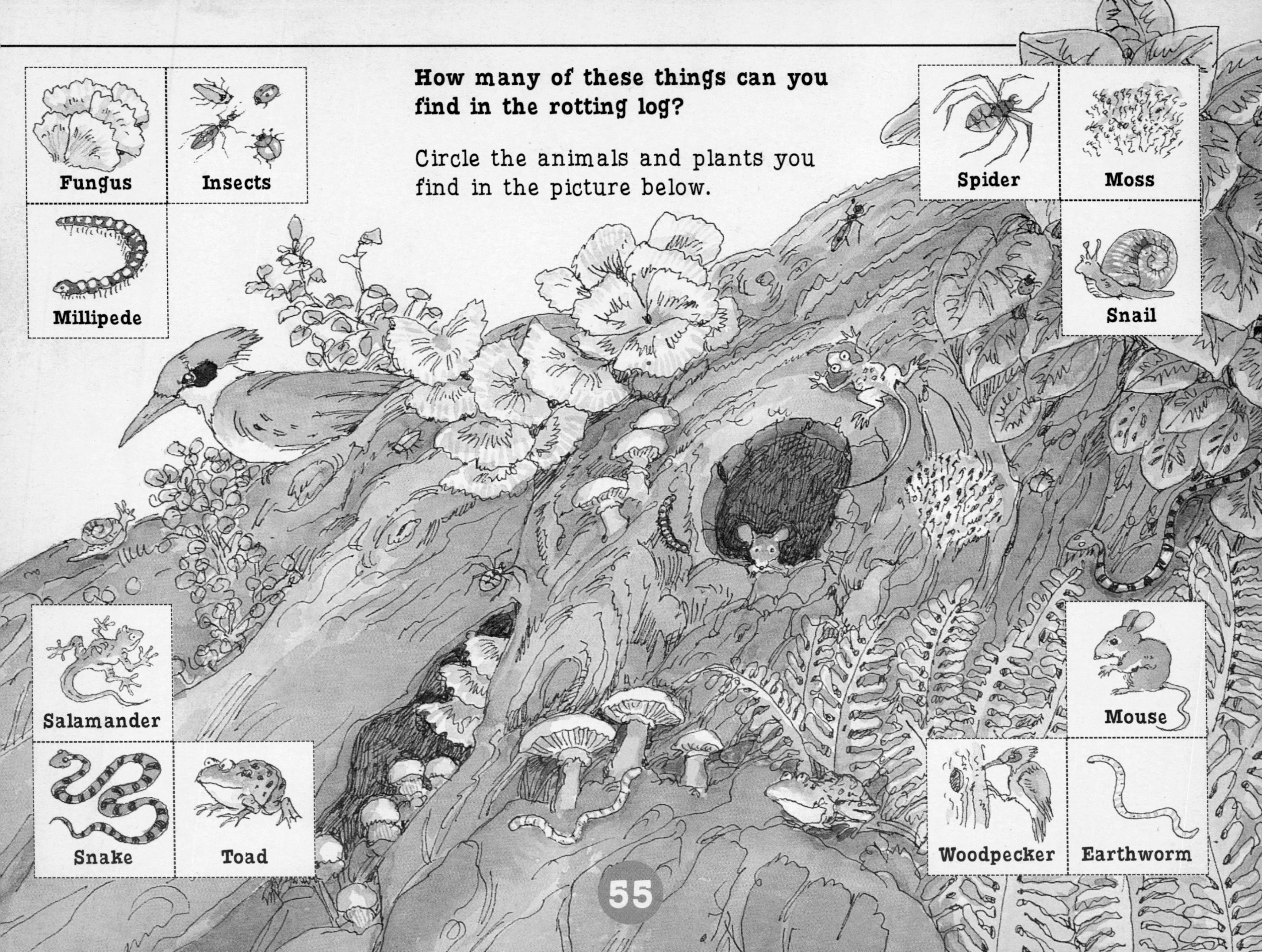

That's Sick!

Sometimes germs make you sick. A germ is a tiny living thing that gets into your body. You can only get sick from someone else if you catch his or her germs.

Ralphie, what's wrong?

I told Ms. Frizzle I had a cold and couldn't go on the field trip. She said I was the field trip!

Why Do You Get Shots?
by Carlos

Some germs are called viruses. A shot puts a very weak form of a virus in your body. Your body learns how to fight the virus this way. Then it can stop other viruses of the same type.

My research shows that six kids in the class have had the chicken pox, eight have had colds, and one gets bus sick a lot.

When you're sick, your body is fighting germs that have gotten inside you. You can help your body by resting, staying warm, and drinking plenty of liquids.

What do you do when you have a cold? Write some of the things here:

____

____

Pretend you're a doctor. Mr. Smith is one of your patients. He has a cold. Write a letter to Mr. Smith telling him what he should do to get better.

Dear Mr. Smith,

____

____

____

____

____

____

____

____

____

____

____

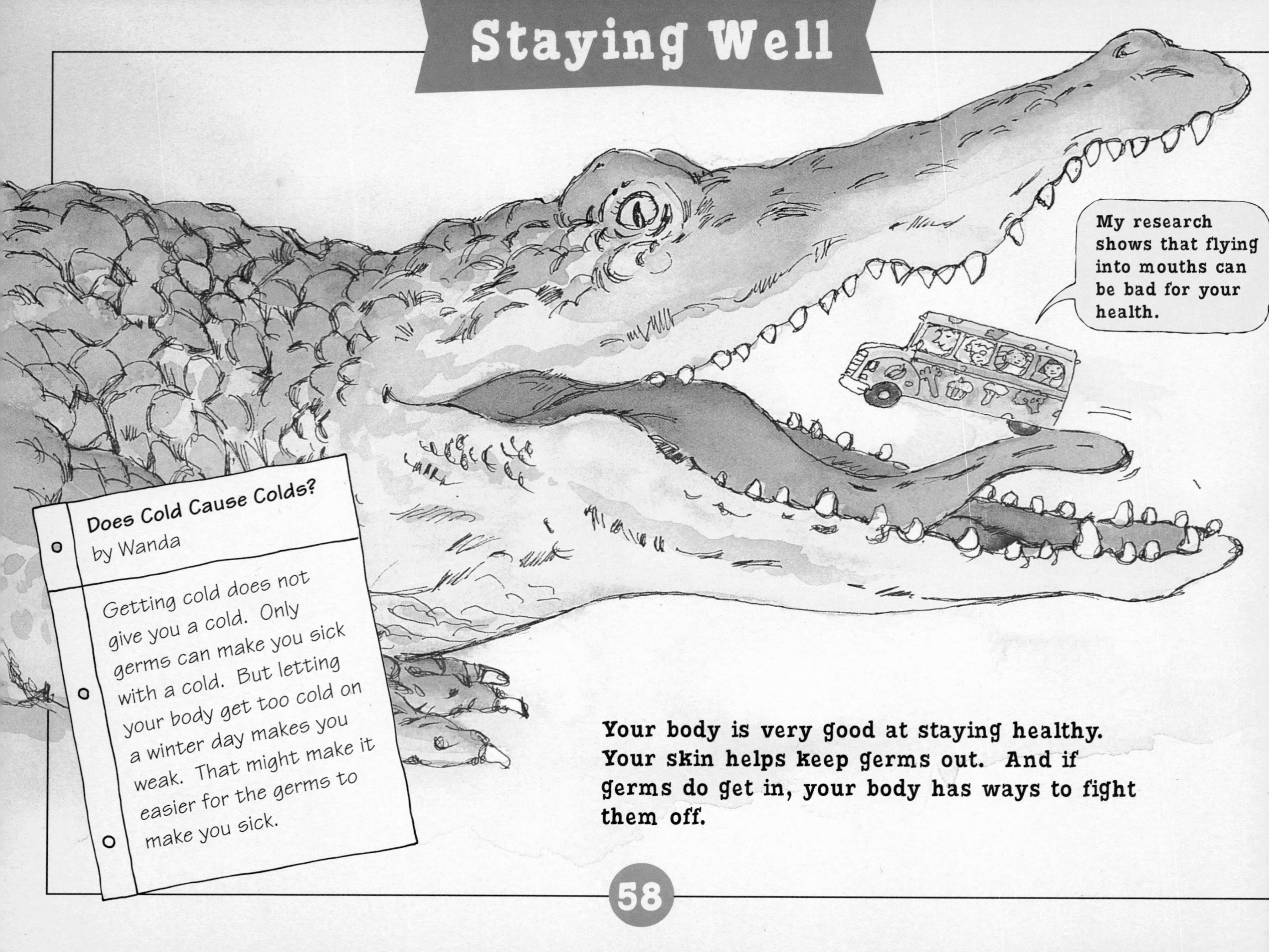

My research shows that flying into mouths can be bad for your health.
Does Cold Cause Colds?
by Wanda
Getting cold does not give you a cold. Only germs can make you sick with a cold. But letting your body get too cold on a winter day makes you weak. That might make it easier for the germs to make you sick.

Your body is very good at staying healthy. Your skin helps keep germs out. And if germs do get in, your body has ways to fight them off.

Here are some of the things we can do to stay healthy:

- We can eat healthy foods.
- We can get plenty of rest.
- We can go to the doctor for checkups.
- We can dress warmly when it's cold outside.
- We can wash our hands before we eat.
- We can be careful not to put things in our mouth that might have germs.

Draw a poster on this page. Tell people some of the things they can do to help their bodies stay healthy.

It's cool to stay warm.

Dry Up!

Is a Desert Hot or Cold?

by Tim

A desert can be hot or cold. Some deserts are in very hot places, like the Sahara in Africa. Other deserts are in cold places, like the South Pole.

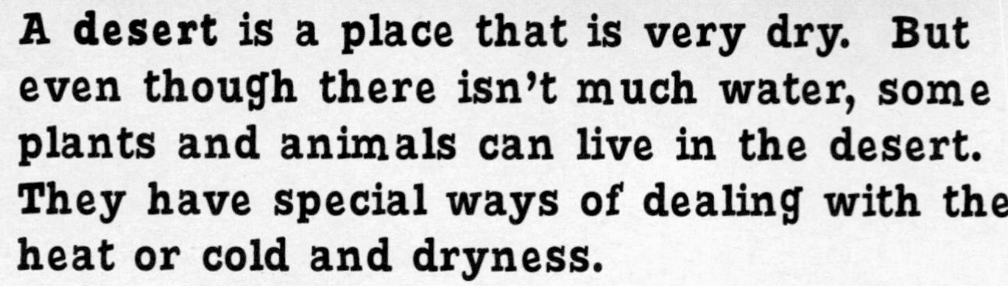

A desert is a place that is very dry. But even though there isn't much water, some plants and animals can live in the desert. They have special ways of dealing with the heat or cold and dryness.

To survive in the hot desert, a **cactus** has a thick, waxy skin to keep water in. It has spines to keep animals from eating it. It does not have leaves, because leaves would lose too much water.

The **creosote bush** has very small leaves. They are coated with a thick sap to keep water in. If it gets too dry, the plant goes to "sleep" until the rains come.

Design your own desert plant.

Draw a picture, and then write about each part of your plant. Explain how the plant can live in the desert. How does it store water? How does it collect water?

My Desert Plant

Built for the Hot Desert

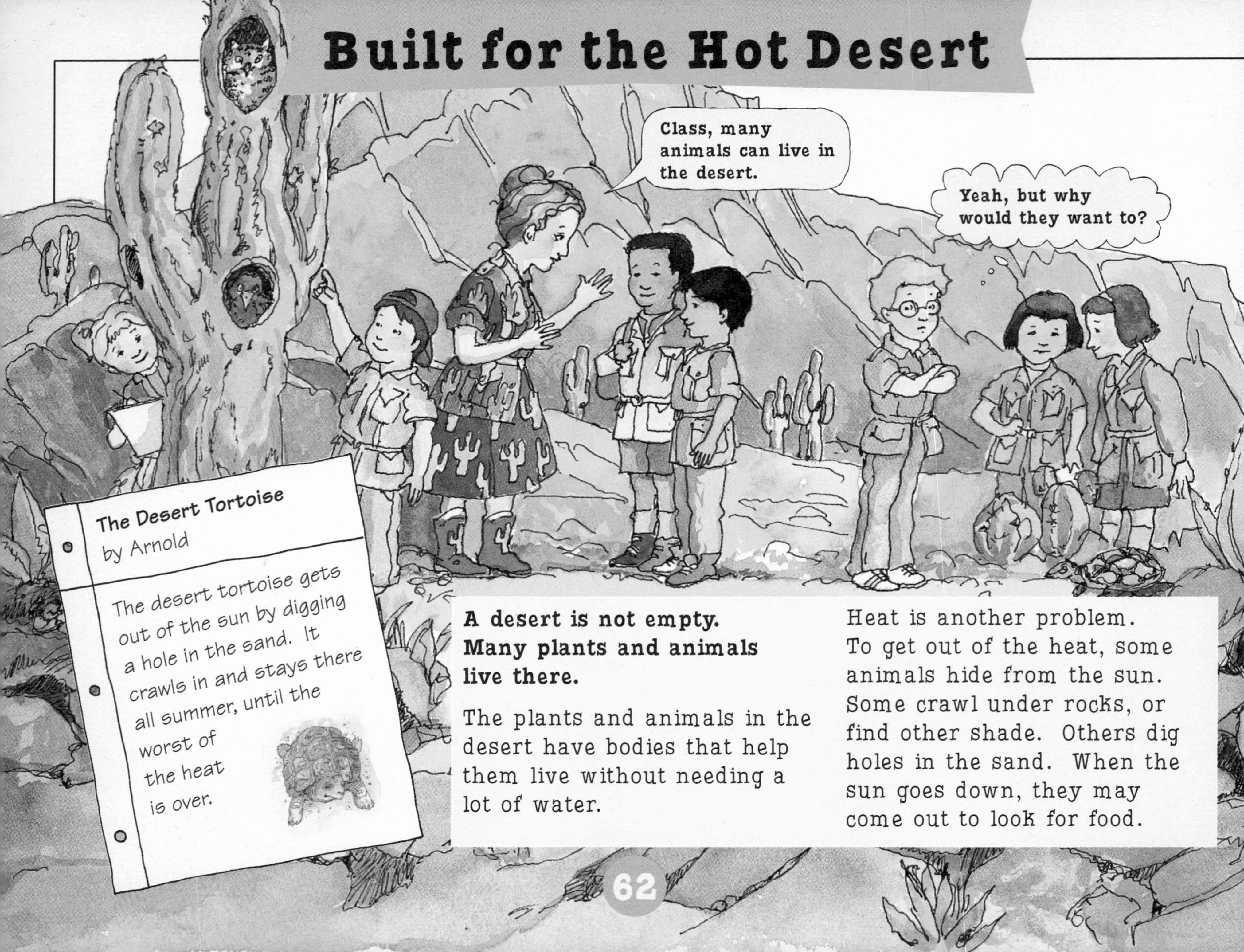

Class, many animals can live in the desert.
Yeah, but why would they want to?

The Desert Tortoise
by Arnold

The desert tortoise gets out of the sun by digging a hole in the sand. It crawls in and stays there all summer, until the worst of the heat is over.

A desert is not empty. Many plants and animals live there.

The plants and animals in the desert have bodies that help them live without needing a lot of water.

Heat is another problem. To get out of the heat, some animals hide from the sun. Some crawl under rocks, or find other shade. Others dig holes in the sand. When the sun goes down, they may come out to look for food.

Which is cooler—staying in the shade or hiding under the sand? You can find out.

1. On a hot, sunny day fill a deep box with sand, and place it outside in the morning. Put it where it will be in the sun all day. Then go back in the afternoon.

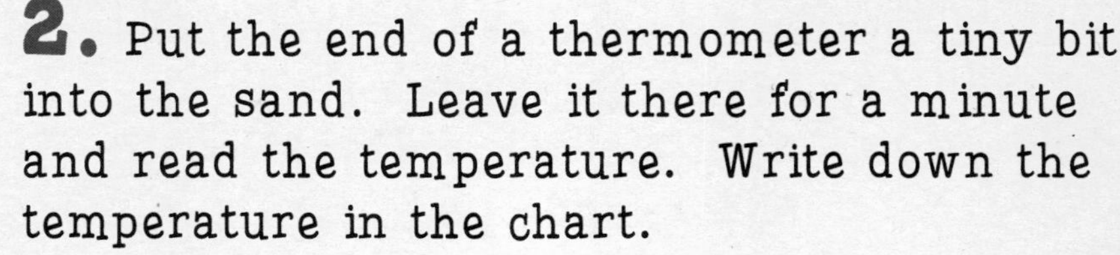

2. Put the end of a thermometer a tiny bit into the sand. Leave it there for a minute and read the temperature. Write down the temperature in the chart.

3. Push another thermometer deep into the sand. Leave it there a minute, then read the temperature. Write it down.

4. Now find a shady spot under a tree or next to a building. Put a thermometer on the ground and wait a minute. Read the temperature. Write it down.

Temperature at top of sand: ________________

Temperature under sand: ________________

Temperature in shade: ________________

Which place was coolest? ________________

Most of the things you read in this book are true. But some things are made up just for fun. Next to each sentence, write T for true or M for made up.

___ **1.** You could fly in a plane from Earth to the Sun.

___ **2.** Many types of plants live in the ocean.

___ **3.** Without friction, you could not stop a bus.

___ **4.** School buses sometimes fall out of rain clouds.

___ **5.** Inside a seed is a tiny plant.

___ **6.** Ants use smells to send messages.

___ **7.** Some teachers can hear what you are thinking.

___ **8.** Over time, rot makes dead things disappear.

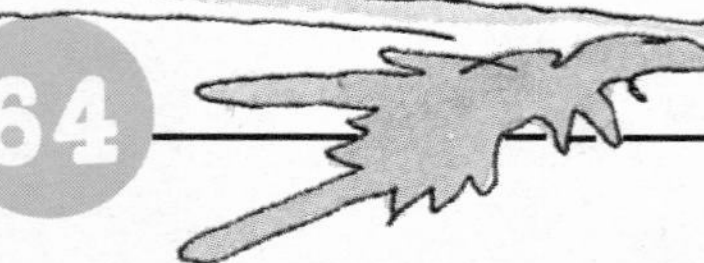

Mr. Frederick Mil
479 Carleton Ave.
Glen Ellyn, IL 60137
July
2009

MW01025396

NEW TESTAMENT
TEXT & TRANSLATION
COMMENTARY

NEW TESTAMENT TEXT AND TRANSLATION COMMENTARY

Commentary on the variant readings of the ancient New Testament manuscripts and how they relate to the major English translations

PHILIP W. COMFORT

Visit Tyndale's exciting Web site at www.tyndale.com

New Testament Text and Translation Commentary

Library of Congress Cataloging-in-Publication Data

New Testament text and translation commentary : commentary on the variant readings of the ancient New Testament manuscripts and how they relate to the major English translations / Philip W. Comfort.
p. cm.
Includes bibliographical references and index.
ISBN-13: 978-1-4143-1034-3 (hc : alk. paper)
ISBN-10: 1-4143-1034-X (hc : alk. paper)
1. Bible. N.T.—Manuscripts, Greek. 2. Bible. N.T.—Criticism, Textual. 3. Bible. N.T.—Translating. I. Title.
BS1904.5.C66 2008
225.4'86—dc22 2008031065

Printed in the United States of America

14 13 12 11 10 09 08
7 6 5 4 3 2 1

CONTENTS

PREFACE

The purpose of this work is to provide scholars, pastors, students, and serious Bible readers with a commentary on the variant readings in the New Testament that have significance for Bible interpretation and Bible translation—and to do so in a format that is communicative and informative to English readers as well as those who know Greek.

Many readers of the New Testament are perplexed by, or at least curious about, the number of differences that exist between modern English versions and the King James Version. Furthermore, readers of the New Testament regularly encounter notes in the margins of their English Bibles that mention variant readings present in the underlying Greek manuscripts. Each of the modern English versions usually has at least 500 such notes for the New Testament; some (such as the New King James Version and the New Jerusalem Bible) have as many as 1,000. Yet explanations rarely accompany these notes, so most readers have no idea why certain readings were preferred over others or why it was important to mention the variant at all. In total, there are about 3,000 textual variants noted in the array of contemporary English versions—variants that impact interpretation and exposition. Commentators, preachers, and students need to be aware of these variants and understand them for enriched interpretation, homiletics, and study of the New Testament text. However, when one of my New Testament students at Wheaton College a number of years ago asked me, "Where is there a book that explains these textual variants?" I had to tell him, "There isn't one, really—unless you know Greek." Since then, I have felt the need to provide such a book for English readers as well as for those who know Greek and are seeking information on how textual criticism might affect translation and exegesis. This volume is my attempt to provide such a tool.

This volume has been a long time in the making—well over fifteen years—so I am glad to see it finally come into print. My son, John Comfort, spent countless hours studying the English versions in this book, making many significant contributions. I owe him many thanks for his labor. I also want to acknowledge the editorial skills of David Barrett, Patrick LaCosse, and Matthew Wolf, each of whom made this book better. I offer my thanks to Mark Taylor and Mark Norton for believing in this book, and to Bruce Metzger for always encouraging me in the task of textual criticism. I dedicate this volume to the members of the Bible Translation Committee who produced the New Living Translation. As a member of this committee, I had the happy task of serving as the New Testament textual critic. I hope this volume will help many other translators, as well as scholars, pastors, teachers, and students, make wise choices about the New Testament text and its translation.

INTRODUCTION

In this introduction, I briefly explain the practice of New Testament textual criticism (section 1) as well as the histories and textual tendencies of the major printed editions of the Greek New Testament (section 2) and the standard English versions (section 3). In addition, I have provided a list of sigla and abbreviations (section 4), an explanation of how to use this commentary (section 5), and a glossary of technical terms (section 6).

After the introduction follows the commentary—from Matthew to Revelation—covering every textual variation noted in the major English translations. The notes explain every major textual difference between the following versions of the New Testament: King James Version (KJV), New King James Version (NKJV), Revised Standard Version (RSV), New Revised Standard Version (NRSV), English Standard Version (ESV), New American Standard Bible (NASB), New International Version (NIV), Today's New International Version (TNIV), New English Bible (NEB), Revised English Bible (REB), New Jerusalem Bible (NJB), New American Bible (NAB), New Living Translation (NLT, revised), Holman Christian Standard Bible (HCSB), and the NET Bible: New English Translation (NET). Within each note, each textual variant is marked as to whether that reading is found in the Nestle-Aland/United Bible Society Greek New Testament edition (noted as NU), the Westcott-Hort Greek New Testament edition (noted as WH), or the Textus Receptus (noted as TR). Frequently, the notes explain textual differences between modern versions on the one hand and the Textus Receptus and KJV (and NKJV) on the other. Many of these variations are noted in the margins of modern versions in deference to the KJV tradition. The notes in this volume also explain significant differences among the modern versions.

In addition to the notes that focus on textual variations among the English versions, there is another kind of note that is intended to help English readers and Greek students understand other significant textual differences which (1) have influenced English versions in minor matters, (2) reflect a completely different textual tradition (this often occurs in the D-text in Acts), or (3) present an interesting interpretation. These notes provide English translations and explanations of many of the variants listed in the critical apparatus of the Nestle-Aland text.

1. The Practice of New Testament Textual Criticism[1]

Because the New Testament is an ancient document—published before the time of the printing press—it exists in many handwritten manuscripts. And since there is not complete agreement

[1] Much of the material in this section first appeared in chapter 6 (pp. 289-297) of my book *Encountering the Manuscripts* (Nashville, Tenn.: Broadman & Holman, 2005). It is used and adapted here with permission.

of wording among these manuscripts, textual critics must sort through their variant readings to reconstruct the original wording of the Greek New Testament. This process is called textual criticism. As defined by the *Oxford Classical Dictionary*, textual criticism is "the technique and art of restoring a text to its original state, as far as possible, in the editing of Greek and Latin authors" (1970, 1048).

The discipline of textual criticism is necessary for all ancient works, such as Homer's *Iliad*, Virgil's *Aeneid*, and the Greek New Testament. In order to accomplish this task, textual critics need manuscripts—the more the better and (usually) the earlier the better. Textual critics working with nonbiblical literature are often frustrated by the fact that so few manuscripts for the work in question exist or the fact that there is a large gap of time (several centuries) between the original composition and the extant copies. By contrast, New Testament textual critics have many early and reliable manuscripts. The time gap between the autographs and the earliest extant copies is quite close—no more than 100 years for most of the books of the New Testament. Thus, we are in a good position to recover most of the original wording of the Greek New Testament. Such optimism was held by the well-known textual critics of the nineteenth century—most notably, Samuel Tregelles, B. F. Westcott, and F. J. A. Hort, who, although acknowledging that we may never recover all of the original text of the New Testament books with absolute certainty, believed that the careful work of textual criticism could bring us extremely close. In the twentieth century, two eminent textual critics, Bruce Metzger and Kurt Aland, affirmed this same purpose, and were instrumental in the production of the two critical editions of the Greek New Testament that are widely used today.

Tregelles, Hort, Metzger, and Aland, as well as Constantine von Tischendorf, the nineteenth-century scholar who famously discovered Codex Sinaiticus, all provided histories of the transmission of the New Testament text and methodologies for recovering the original wording. Their views of textual criticism were derived from their actual experience of working with manuscripts and doing textual criticism in preparing critical editions of the Greek New Testament. Successive generations of scholars, working with ever-increasing quantities of manuscripts (especially earlier ones) and refining their methodologies, have continued with the task of recovering the original wording of the Greek New Testament.

By contrast, a certain number of textual critics in recent years have abandoned the notion that the original wording of the Greek New Testament can ever be recovered. Let us take, for example, Bart Ehrman (author of *The Orthodox Corruption of Scripture*) and David Parker (author of *The Living Text of the Gospels*). Having analyzed their positions, J. K. Elliott writes, "Both [men] emphasise the living and therefore changing text of the New Testament and the needlessness and inappropriateness of trying to establish one immutable original text. The changeable text in all its variety is what we textual critics should be displaying" (1999, 17). Elliott then speaks for himself on the matter: "Despite my own published work in trying to prove the originality of the text in selected areas of textual variation, . . . I agree that the task of trying to establish the original words of the original authors with 100% certainty is impossible. More dominant in text critics' thinking now is the need to plot the changes in the history of the text" (1999, 18).

Not one textual critic could or would ever say that any of the critical editions of the Greek New Testament replicates the original wording with 100 percent accuracy. But an accurate reconstruction has to be the goal of those who practice textual criticism as classically defined. To veer from this is to stray from the essential task of textual criticism. It is an illuminating exercise "to plot the changes in the history of the text," but this assumes a known starting point. And what can that starting point be if not the original text? In analyzing Ehrman's book, *The Orthodox Corruption of Scripture*, Silva notes this same paradox: "Although this book is appealed to in support of blurring the notion of an original text, there is hardly a page in that book that does not in fact mention such a text or assume its accessibility . . . Ehrman's book is unimaginable unless he can identify an initial form of the text that can be differentiated from a later alteration" (2002, 149). In short, one cannot speak about the text being corrupted if there is not an original text to be corrupted.

I am not against reconstructing the history of the text. In fact, I devoted many years to studying all the early Greek New Testament manuscripts (those dated before A.D. 300) and compiling a fresh edition of them in *The Text of the Earliest New Testament Greek Manuscripts* (coedited with David Barrett). This work provides a representative sampling of New Testament books that were actually read by Christians in the earliest centuries of the church. But whatever historical insights we may gain by studying the varying manuscript traditions as texts unto themselves, this is no reason to abandon the goal of producing the best critical edition possible, one that most likely replicates the original wording. Thus, I echo Silva's comments entirely, when he says: "I would like to affirm—not only with Hort, but with practically all students of ancient documents—that the recovery of the original text (i.e., the text in its initial form, prior to the alterations produced in the copying process) remains the primary task of textual criticism" (2002, 149).

For my own part, my work with the significant textual variants leads me to conclude, with some degree of certainty, that for any given passage of scripture, the original text usually stands somewhere either in the critical edition produced by Westcott and Hort or that produced by Nestle, Aland, et al. Many of the papyri discoveries in the twentieth century affirm readings in Westcott and Hort, but these readings were not always accepted by Aland and the UBS committee. On the other hand, several of the readings in the early papyri show that the text of Westcott and Hort needed to be revised, and this was done in the Nestle-Aland/UBS edition. And there are still other readings (relatively few in number) which, in my estimation, are likely original but were not adopted by either edition. Finally, I must admit that there are several instances where one or more variant readings have equal qualifications to claim the right as being "the original wording." Many textual critics would say the same—though probably about different textual-variant units than the ones I consider. But there is, by no means, a large number of such textual variants. And these few recalcitrant cases should not cause us to abandon the task of recovering the original wording of the Greek New Testament. New insights have come and will keep coming, in the form of actual documents, new methodologies, and new understandings. These will help us continue the valid and necessary task of seeking to reconstruct the original with a high degree of accuracy.

Theories and Methodologies of Textual Criticism

THE NATURE OF TEXTUAL CORRUPTION

Textual critics deal with two different kinds of corruptions of the original: transcriptional errors and deliberate changes. Transcriptional errors are the most common type found in the manuscripts of the Greek New Testament. These accidental changes caused by faulty copying are broken down into the following categories:

Dittography: An error involving the repetition of a word, letter, or phrase, caused by the eye skipping backward in the copying process. For example, if the original text of Matt 22:32 read:

ουκ εστιν θεος νεκρων

"He is not God of the dead"

a scribe committing dittography could produce the following:

ουκ εστιν θεος θεος νεκρων

"God is not God of the dead"

Haplography (or Scribal Leap): An error involving the omission of a word, letter, or phrase, caused by the eye skipping that portion in the copying process. Because the scribe moved forward in his copying, this error is sometimes called "a scribal leap." If the original were:

ουκ εστιν θεος θεος νεκρων

"God is not God of the dead"

a scribe committing haplography could produce:

ουκ εστιν θεος νεκρων

"He is not God of the dead"

Homoeoarchton (or Homoioarchton): An omission in which the eye of the copyist slips accidentally from one word to a similar word having a similar beginning. If the original text of Eph 1:15 read:

την αγαπην την εις παντας τους αγιους

"love which you have for all the saints"

a scribe whose eye slipped from the first to the third word would write:

την εις παντας τους αγιους

"which you have for all the saints"

Homoeoteleuton (or Homoioteleuton): An omission in which the eye of the copyist slips accidentally from one word to a similar word having a similar ending. If the original text of Matt 27:11 had:

επηρωτησεν αυτον ο ηγεμων λεγων

"the governor asked him, saying"

a scribe confounded by the similar endings of the last two words might write:

επηρωτησεν αυτον λεγων

"he asked him, saying"

Transposition: An error in which two letters or two (or more) words are accidentally reversed. If the original text of Heb 12:15 read:

τις ριζα πικριας ανω φυουσα ενοχλη

"some root of bitterness, springing up, might cause trouble"

a scribe might accidentally transpose two letters in the middle of the last word:

τις ριζα πικριας ανω φυουσα εν χολη

"some root of bitterness, springing up with gall"

Textual critics also deal with *purposeful* scribal alteration. The two most common types of deliberate changes are conflated readings and interpolations. A conflation is the scribal technique of resolving a discrepancy between two or more variant readings by including all of them. For example, in John 1:34, some manuscripts read "Son of God" and other manuscripts read "chosen of God." A few manuscripts conflate the two readings and say, "chosen Son of God" (see note on John 1:34). This phenomenon is more prevalent in later manuscripts because the scribe was confronted with greater variation among the extant witnesses. Interpolations are scribal additions to the manuscript that attempt to clarify the meaning of the text. For example, in 1 Corinthians 3:3, the best textual evidence supports the reading "jealousy and strife" in a list of vices. Certain scribes couldn't resist adding another vice found in a similar list in Galatians 5:20; so they added "divisions" to the list. These kinds of interpolations account for a host of variants.

METHODS OF TEXTUAL CRITICISM

Textual critics have developed theories and methodologies for deciding which reading is most likely original. These theories and methodologies generally fall into two categories: (1) those that pertain to external evidence (with a focus on the classification of manuscripts or studies of the documents themselves) and (2) those that pertain to internal evidence (with a focus on discerning the most likely reading from which all others deviated).

External Evidence

Various New Testament textual critics have posited canons for determining the original wording primarily on the basis of external or documentary evidence—the character and reliability of the documents themselves. This endeavor began in the early 1700s, when scholars became dissatisfied with perceived inaccuracies in the Textus Receptus. In 1707, John Mill of Oxford produced an edition of the Textus Receptus with an extensive critical apparatus. His thorough prolegomena detailed several principles for textual criticism which took into account the genealogical relationship that exists between manuscripts copied from the same exemplar. Though he did not change the Textus Receptus, he laid the foundations for modern textual criticism. In the 1730s, Bengel became the first person to categorize manuscripts according to their age and location and to formulate the significant principle that textual witnesses must be weighed and not merely counted—that is, the testimony of a few witnesses may be accepted over against that of a larger number, if the few witnesses are deemed more reliable.

The earliest critical editions of the Greek New Testament represent attempts to produce a critical text largely on the basis of external evidence. Perhaps the most important methodological development from this period came when Westcott and Hort concluded that Codex Vaticanus and Codex Sinaiticus (along with a few other early manuscripts) presented a text that most closely replicated the original writing. Based on this theory, they developed a genealogical tree that linked extant witnesses (such as Vaticanus and Sinaiticus) to the original autographs. According to their theory, Vaticanus was almost perfectly transmitted from the original. It was a "Neutral Text"—i.e., a text void of corruption. Their theory was revolutionary, and their edition was responsible for overthrowing the Textus Receptus. Westcott and Hort's postulate of a "Neutral Text" was rejected, however, by many textual critics who became skeptical of recovering the original text through genealogical means. It was judged by several scholars that Westcott and Hort had begged the question, subjectively selecting Codex Vaticanus as the pure text and then using that selection to declare the other manuscripts impure. Thus, Westcott and Hort's theory was no longer heartily endorsed.

Internal Evidence

Left without a solid methodology for making external judgments, textual critics turned more and more to internal evidence. They began to endorse the canon that the reading that is most likely original is the one that best explains the variants. This canon is a development of Bengel's maxim (1855, xiii), *proclivi scriptioni praestat ardua* ("the harder reading is to be preferred"), which he formulated in response to his own question as to which variant reading is likely to have been the source from which the others arose. In practice, applying this central canon of internal criticism involves testing a given reading against several criteria, which various scholars have posited and implemented over the past three hundred years of New Testament textual criticism. Having made a thorough historical survey of the development of canons for internal criticism, Eldon Epp (1976, 243) summarized all the criteria as follows:

1. A variant's status as the shorter or shortest reading.
2. A variant's status as the harder or hardest reading.
3. A variant's fitness to account for the origin, development, or presence of all other readings.

4. A variant's conformity to the author's style and vocabulary.
5. A variant's conformity to the author's theology or ideology.
6. A variant's conformity to Koine (rather than Attic) Greek.
7. A variant's conformity to Semitic forms of expression.
8. A variant's lack of conformity to parallel passages or to contextual information.
9. A variant's lack of conformity to Old Testament passages.
10. A variant's lack of conformity to liturgical forms and usages.
11. A variant's lack of conformity to extrinsic doctrinal views.

The preference for the shorter reading was the primary canon of Griesbach, as espoused in his prolegomena to *Novum Testamentum Graece* (1796). This guideline has usually been observed by textual critics ever since. But the work of Royse in recent years has called it into question. Studying the habits of the scribes of $\mathfrak{P}^{45}$, $\mathfrak{P}^{46}$, $\mathfrak{P}^{47}$, $\mathfrak{P}^{66}$, $\mathfrak{P}^{72}$, and $\mathfrak{P}^{75}$, Royse came to the conclusion that each of these scribes was more inclined to omit words than add words (1981, 2-3).

Some scholars have therefore drawn the conclusion that the longer reading is to be preferred over the shorter (for example, see Head 1990, 247). But Griesbach's principle is still valid if we remember that he "qualified it carefully by excepting certain variants, such as those that could be explained by homoeoteleuton" (Silva 1992b, 23). The kind of omissions noted by Royse often are of nonessential terms or are the result of scribal inadvertence. Thus, the principle still stands with respect to judging between truly shorter readings and readings with longer verbiage. In most instances, the longer verbiage is the result of scribal gap-filling[2] and expansion. Thus, while it cannot be said that the longer reading is always suspect, any reading which looks like an attempt to fill in textual gaps is suspect as a scribal addition.

The evaluation of internal evidence by these criteria is not immune to problems of subjectivity. Quite often, two textual critics, using the same list of principles to examine the same variant unit, will not agree. For example, with respect to #4, one critic might argue that one variant was produced by a copyist attempting to emulate the author's style; the other will claim the same variant has to be original because it accords with the author's style. And with respect to #5, one critic might argue that one variant was produced by an orthodox scribe attempting to rid the text of a reading that could be used to promote heterodoxy; another will claim that the same variant has to be original because it is orthodox and accords with Christian doctrine (thus a heterodoxical scribe must have changed it). Thus, internal arguments—in and of themselves—often lead to opposite decisions about textual variants, because each textual critic has his or her own subjective biases.

Reasoned Eclecticism

Thus it is the case that neither external evidence nor internal evidence can be given absolute sway in all circumstances. Textual critics must always operate with one eye on the external evidence and one eye on the internal evidence. This method has been called "reasoned eclecticism." According to Holmes (1989, 55), "Reasoned eclecticism applies a combination of internal and external considerations, evaluating the character of the variants in light of the manuscripts evidence and vice versa in order to obtain a balanced view of the matter and as a check upon purely subjective tendencies." Holmes further expands on this method in an article entitled "The Case for Reasoned Eclecticism" (2002, 77-100), wherein he makes a solid case for this method as being the most viable for the actual practice of New Testament textual criticism. First, he urges that the critic must

---

[2] Scribes at times felt information was missing from the text (especially in narratives), which called for some kind of completion. Gaps were often automatically filled mentally in the reading process. However, scribes made additions to the text, so as to make the text more lucid for their readers. Such insertions, whether one word or one sentence, account for the ever-expanding text of the New Testament throughout the course of its transmission. Such gap-filling is nowhere more evident than in the interpolations that occur in the D-text of Acts. For more on this phenomenon, see appendix A.

know and use the documents, citing the famous dictum of Hort, "Knowledge of documents should precede final judgment upon readings" (1882, 31). But he then explains that this can take us only so far—in two respects. First, he argues that "documentary evidence can take us back to the earliest recoverable (or surviving) stage of the textual tradition, but it cannot us take us any further. That is, on the basis of external evidence alone we cannot determine whether the earliest recoverable stage of the textual transmission is the autograph or a copy of it" (2002, 83). Second, the extant documentary evidence often presents a situation where one cannot clearly determine which reading has the best documentary support. In the end, then, Holmes concurs with Zuntz, who said that documentary evidence can "throw a very considerable weight into the scales of probability [but] will not by itself suffice to determine [a] choice between competing readings" (1953, 283).

Those who practice textual criticism know this all too well. The situation then becomes one of emphasis. Does one give more weight to documentary evidence or to internal consideration? Scholars such as Tregelles, Hort, and Colwell (see comments below) place more emphasis on the documents. I tend to follow their lead. Other scholars, such as Kilpatrick, Boismard, and Elliott, place more emphasis on internal criticism, such that they advocate "thorough-going eclecticism" (see a good article on this by Elliott 2002, 101-124). Other scholars practice reasoned eclecticism, as explained by Holmes. Among those are Aland and Metzger, though each has his own emphasis.[3]

Refining the Documentary Approach

All textual critics—including those working with the classics—implement both external and internal criticism in selecting the reading which is most likely original. And all textual critics must do this on a variant-unit by variant-unit basis. Some give priority of place to internal over external evidence; others do the opposite. The editors of NU demonstrate that they tried to do both; this can be seen in Metzger's discussions in *A Textual Commentary on the Greek New Testament*. However, it is my observation that the resultant eclectic text exhibits too much dependence on internal evidence, emphasizing the "local" aspect of the "local-genealogical" method, to use Aland's language. This means that the decision making, on a variant-unit by variant-unit basis, produced a text with an uneven documentary presentation. Furthermore, the committee setting, with members voting on each significant textual variant, cannot help but produce a text with uneven documentation. All eclectic texts reconstruct a text that no ancient Christian actually read, even though they approach a close replication of the original writings. However, the NU edition's eclecticism extends even to following different manuscripts within the same sentence.[4]

In my view, an eclectic approach that gives greater weight to external (documentary) evidence is best. Such an approach labors to select a premier group of manuscripts as the primary witnesses for certain books and/or sections of the New Testament, not for the entire New Testament, since each book of the New Testament was, in its earliest form, a separate publication.[5] Once the best manuscripts for each book or group of books in the New Testament are established, these manuscripts need to be pruned of obvious errors and singular variants. Then these should be the manuscripts used for determining the most likely original wording. The burden of proof on textual critics is to demonstrate that the best manuscripts, when challenged by the testimony of other witnesses, do *not* contain the original wording. The part of this process that corresponds to Aland's "localness" (internal evidence) is that the text must be determined on a variant-unit basis. However, my view of the "genealogical" (external evidence) aspect is that it must be preestablished

---

[3] Aland calls his method "local-genealogical." For more detailed interaction with the methods of Aland and Metzger, see appendices B and C.

[4] For specific examples of this, see appendix B. I expand on my preference for favoring documentary evidence in appendix D.

[5] Hort overreached in embracing Codex Vaticanus as the preeminent text for the entire New Testament, when we now know that there are superior witnesses for certain sections of the New Testament. The same can be said for Tischendorf, who was too enthusiastic about his prize find, Codex Sinaiticus. However, for several books of the New Testament, we can hardly do better than start with Codex Vaticanus and/or Codex Sinaiticus—if only for the simple reason that they often contain more extant text than the earlier papyri and that they usually provide witness to an early text.

for an entire book and not re-created verse by verse, which results in a very uneven documentary presentation. Of course, internal criticism will have to come into play when documentary evidence is evenly divided, or when some feature of the text strongly calls for it. And, on occasion, it must be admitted that two (or more) readings are equally good candidates for being deemed the original wording.

THE MOST RELIABLE WITNESSES

In what follows I list what I have concluded to be the most reliable witnesses for each major section or book of the New Testament. In my application of the eclectic approach throughout this commentary, I give preference to these witnesses unless internal evidence strongly favors a different reading. In the main, I see the proto-Alexandrian manuscripts as being the best witnesses to the original text. Some may call this a subjective predetermination. But I honestly say that this favoritism has come from studying thousands of textual variants, as well as studying scribal tendencies, and usually coming to the conclusion that the proto-Alexandrian manuscripts have preserved the most primitive, if not the original, wording. Of course, these manuscripts are not perfect. $\mathfrak{P}^{75}$, one of the most pristine manuscripts, has flaws. Nonetheless, its fidelity and acuity far outweigh its imperfections. In my book, *The Quest for the Original Text of the New Testament,* I described various groupings of the papyrus manuscripts exhibiting textual affinities on a book-by-book basis. These groupings covered the early papyri from $\mathfrak{P}^{1}$ to $\mathfrak{P}^{92}$.[6] The selections I list below largely follow Metzger's identification of witnesses, but I modify and expand Metzger's list of proto-Alexandrian manuscripts in two ways: (1) I add more manuscripts, especially the more recently published papyri; (2) I specify the proto-Alexandrian manuscripts by New Testament book or section. Thus, the proto-Alexandrian manuscripts are as follows:

Gospels: $\mathfrak{P}^{1}$ $\mathfrak{P}^{4+64+67}$ $\mathfrak{P}^{5}$ $\mathfrak{P}^{28}$ $\mathfrak{P}^{35}$ $\mathfrak{P}^{39}$ $\mathfrak{P}^{66c}$ $\mathfrak{P}^{71}$ $\mathfrak{P}^{75}$ $\mathfrak{P}^{77}$ $\mathfrak{P}^{90}$ $\mathfrak{P}^{95}$ $\mathfrak{P}^{101}$ $\mathfrak{P}^{103}$ $\mathfrak{P}^{104}$ $\mathfrak{P}^{106}$ $\mathfrak{P}^{107}$ $\mathfrak{P}^{108}$ $\mathfrak{P}^{119}$ $\mathfrak{P}^{120}$
Acts: $\mathfrak{P}^{45}$ $\mathfrak{P}^{53}$ $\mathfrak{P}^{91}$ 0189
Paul's Epistles: $\mathfrak{P}^{13}$ (Hebrews) $\mathfrak{P}^{15+16}$ $\mathfrak{P}^{30}$ $\mathfrak{P}^{40}$ $\mathfrak{P}^{46}$ $\mathfrak{P}^{65}$ $\mathfrak{P}^{92}$ 0220
General Epistles: $\mathfrak{P}^{20}$ $\mathfrak{P}^{23}$ $\mathfrak{P}^{72}$ (in part) $\mathfrak{P}^{81}$ $\mathfrak{P}^{100}$
Revelation: $\mathfrak{P}^{18}$ $\mathfrak{P}^{24}$ $\mathfrak{P}^{47}$ $\mathfrak{P}^{98}$ $\mathfrak{P}^{115}$

The Gospels

PREMIER WITNESSES

Primary Manuscripts (with substantial extant text): $\mathfrak{P}^{4+64+67}$ $\mathfrak{P}^{75}$ $\mathfrak{P}^{66c}$ B א (but not in John 1–8)
Primary Manuscripts Dated After 400: C (in part) L W (in Luke 1–8, John) Z Δ Ξ Ψ (in Mark) 33 (in part)
Secondary Manuscripts (with smaller portions of text): $\mathfrak{P}^{1}$ $\mathfrak{P}^{7}$ $\mathfrak{P}^{28}$ $\mathfrak{P}^{35}$ $\mathfrak{P}^{39}$ $\mathfrak{P}^{71}$ $\mathfrak{P}^{77}$ $\mathfrak{P}^{101}$ $\mathfrak{P}^{106}$ $\mathfrak{P}^{108}$ $\mathfrak{P}^{111}$

Unquestionably, $\mathfrak{P}^{75}$ (containing Luke and John) and B constitute the best witnesses for the Gospels. We can add several other manuscripts to the $\mathfrak{P}^{75}$/B group. One of the primary additions is $\mathfrak{P}^{4+64+67}$ (as one codex). Other members of the group are $\mathfrak{P}^{1}$, $\mathfrak{P}^{28}$, $\mathfrak{P}^{35}$, $\mathfrak{P}^{39}$, $\mathfrak{P}^{71}$, $\mathfrak{P}^{77}$, $\mathfrak{P}^{101}$, $\mathfrak{P}^{106}$, $\mathfrak{P}^{108}$, and $\mathfrak{P}^{111}$.

---

[6] In some significant articles written during the past few years, Eldon Epp has also explored grouping manuscripts into what he calls "textual clusters" (1989). He sees the papyri as belonging to one of four clusters, which he calls the "A" group—later Alexandrian papyri; the "B" group—early papyri that have affinities with Vaticanus (B); the "C" group—the papyri that are linked with what used to be called "Caesarean," and the "D" group—those papyri that have associations with Bezae (D). My groupings are not as broad-based, because I think groups need to be established for books or sections of the New Testament (such as the Gospels and Paul's Epistles), rather than for the entire New Testament. Nonetheless, there is a great deal of overlap between my groupings and Epp's. With the appearance of more published papyri ($\mathfrak{P}^{100}$ to $\mathfrak{P}^{115}$ in 1998–1999), we can expand the population of each broad group and then establish tighter textual communities—that is, manuscripts showing a high degree of textual agreement. Admittedly, this is somewhat of a tenuous procedure because of the fragmentary condition of several of the papyri. Nonetheless, it is a fruitful exercise to compare the smaller manuscripts with the larger papyri in an effort to establish textual relationships.

I think $\mathfrak{P}^{66c}$ ($\mathfrak{P}^{66}$ corrected) also belongs in this group, though it is a bit more removed. A later yet extremely significant member of this group is Codex Vaticanus (B), as well as Sinaiticus (א), though it is not as prominent. (Sinaiticus cannot be included in John 1–8, where it is inclined to expand the text—showing "Western" tendencies—as demonstrated by Fee. See Epp and Fee 1993, 221-243.) With the addition of $\mathfrak{P}^{4+64+67}$ to this group, as well as $\mathfrak{P}^{66c}$, it is apparent that manuscripts with this kind of text existed before $\mathfrak{P}^{75}$—as early as 150–175 (the time period for $\mathfrak{P}^{4+64+67}$ and $\mathfrak{P}^{66}$), and it is also known that this text was maintained throughout the third and fourth centuries. Thus, we have evidence of a relatively pure form of the gospel text from the mid-second century to the mid-fourth century.

The leading manuscripts of this group, $\mathfrak{P}^{4+64+67}$ and $\mathfrak{P}^{75}$, have overlapping text in Luke and therefore can be compared in this gospel. In a paper given in November of 1998 at the Society of Biblical Literature annual meeting, William Warren demonstrated that there is 93 percent agreement between $\mathfrak{P}^{4}$ and $\mathfrak{P}^{75}$ in Luke (as well as 93 percent between $\mathfrak{P}^{4}$ and B). In my own comparative study of $\mathfrak{P}^{4}$ and $\mathfrak{P}^{75}$, I observed that both $\mathfrak{P}^{4}$ and $\mathfrak{P}^{75}$ are identical in forty complete verses, with only five significant exceptions (Luke 3:22, 36; 5:39; 6:11, 14). The proportion of concurrence in these two manuscripts is amazing. Out of approximately 400 words, they differ in less than 10. This is 97.5 percent agreement. Unfortunately, $\mathfrak{P}^{64+67}$ (containing portions of Matthew) cannot be compared with $\mathfrak{P}^{75}$, because there is no overlapping text. However, we can compare $\mathfrak{P}^{64+67}$ with B and א, the natural extensions of a $\mathfrak{P}^{75}$-type of text. My studies show that $\mathfrak{P}^{64+67}$ agrees with B in 10 out of 13 variant-units, and with א in 12 out of 13.

OTHER MEMBERS OF THIS GOSPEL GROUP

Certain early papyri can be compared with $\mathfrak{P}^{75}$ and $\mathfrak{P}^{4+64+67}$ because they have overlapping text. However, other early papyri can be compared only with B and א. This comparison shows that several papyri also belong to this group. These manuscripts are $\mathfrak{P}^{1}$, $\mathfrak{P}^{7}$, $\mathfrak{P}^{28}$, $\mathfrak{P}^{35}$, $\mathfrak{P}^{39}$, $\mathfrak{P}^{71}$, $\mathfrak{P}^{77}$, $\mathfrak{P}^{101}$, $\mathfrak{P}^{106}$, $\mathfrak{P}^{108}$, $\mathfrak{P}^{111}$. The data are as follows:

$\mathfrak{P}^{1}$ concurs with B in 11 out of 12 variant-units.

$\mathfrak{P}^{7}$ (dated third/fourth century? by Aland) concurs completely with $\mathfrak{P}^{4}$ and $\mathfrak{P}^{75}$ in Luke 4:1-2, even with respect to making πνευματι a nomen sacrum in 4:2.

$\mathfrak{P}^{28}$ shows more agreement with $\mathfrak{P}^{75}$ than any other single manuscript—in 7 out of 10 variant-units.

$\mathfrak{P}^{35}$ concurs with B in 6 out of 6 variant-units.

$\mathfrak{P}^{39}$ agrees with $\mathfrak{P}^{75}$ (in its corrected form) verbatim—with the exception of two transposed words and one δε found in $\mathfrak{P}^{75}$—thus, making $\mathfrak{P}^{39}$ agree with $\mathfrak{P}^{75}$ in 6 out of 7 variant-units and with B in all 7 units.

$\mathfrak{P}^{71}$ agrees with B in 5 out of 5 variants.

$\mathfrak{P}^{77}$ concurs with א in 6 out of 6 variants, and with B in 4 out of 6. $\mathfrak{P}^{103}$, probably belonging to the same codex as $\mathfrak{P}^{77}$, shows the same tendencies.

$\mathfrak{P}^{101}$ concurs with א in 8 out of 10 variants, and with B in 7 out of 10.

$\mathfrak{P}^{106}$ shares twelve verses (John 1:29-35, 40-46) and about 100 words with $\mathfrak{P}^{75}$. Out of 10 variant-units, $\mathfrak{P}^{106}$ concurs with $\mathfrak{P}^{75}$ 8 out of 10 times. $\mathfrak{P}^{106}$ shows strong alignment with other manuscripts in this group: with B 9 times out of 10; with א 8 times out of 10, and with $\mathfrak{P}^{66}$ 8 times out of 10.

$\mathfrak{P}^{108}$ agrees with א in 7 out of 7 variant-units.

$\mathfrak{P}^{111}$ concurs with the text of $\mathfrak{P}^{75}$ completely, except in one variant in 17:22 (του versus οτε). Even though the mutual text is small (Luke 17:11-13, 22-23), the two manuscripts concur in 8 out of 9 variant-units.

$\mathfrak{P}^{66c}$ also belongs in this group. Fee's studies (1965, 1968b) on $\mathfrak{P}^{66c}$ and $\mathfrak{P}^{75}$ in John 1–9 show that $\mathfrak{P}^{66c}$ demonstrates more agreement with $\mathfrak{P}^{75}$ than does $\mathfrak{P}^{66*}$. This means that $\mathfrak{P}^{66}$ was often corrected in the direction of $\mathfrak{P}^{75}$ in John 1–9. In John 10–21 the percentage of

> agreement between $\mathfrak{P}^{66c}$ and $\mathfrak{P}^{75}$ (for its extant portion, 10:1–15:8) and B (for 15:9–21:22) goes up significantly. Of the 450 corrections in $\mathfrak{P}^{66}$, about 50 are of nonsense readings. Of the remaining 400, 284 make the text of $\mathfrak{P}^{66}$ normative (i.e., in agreement with a text supported by all witnesses). Of the remaining 116 corrections, 88 brought the text into conformity with $\mathfrak{P}^{75}$ (in John 1:1–13:10; 14:8–15:10) or with B (in the remaining sections of John). This means that 75 percent (88 of 116) of the substantive changes conformed $\mathfrak{P}^{66}$ to a $\mathfrak{P}^{75}$/B-type text.

With respect to the premier group of gospel witnesses, it should be observed that many of these manuscripts seem to be the work of professionals because they display what is known as the professional book hand: $\mathfrak{P}^{4+64+67}$, $\mathfrak{P}^{39}$, $\mathfrak{P}^{66c}$, $\mathfrak{P}^{75}$, and $\mathfrak{P}^{77}$ (see Comfort 2005, 20). Among all the copyists, professionals would be the ones most likely to produce the best copies. Second, this group has representation from the second century to the early fourth—from manuscripts like $\mathfrak{P}^{4+64+67}$, $\mathfrak{P}^{66c}$, and $\mathfrak{P}^{77}$ (of the second century), to $\mathfrak{P}^{75}$ (ca. 175–200), to $\mathfrak{P}^{28}$, $\mathfrak{P}^{39}$, $\mathfrak{P}^{106}$, and $\mathfrak{P}^{111}$ (of the third century), and on to B and ℵ of the fourth century. The manuscripts in this group serve as the primary manuscripts for reconstructing the original text of the Gospels. For Matthew, it appears that most of the early papyri support the readings of ℵ over against B, when the two differ. In Luke and John, it is the other way around.

One final note is due concerning the Gospel of Mark. Ironically, the earliest gospel has not been preserved in very many early manuscripts. And to add to the irony (and mystery), Mark is traditionally said to have taken his gospel with him to Egypt (Eusebius, *Hist. eccl.* 2.16)—and yet there are hardly any early extant copies of Mark among the many discoveries of manuscripts in Egypt. The earliest copy of Mark is preserved in $\mathfrak{P}^{45}$, but it is not a very faithful copy. In the book of Mark especially, the scribe of $\mathfrak{P}^{45}$ exerted many personal liberties in making a text that replicated more the *thought* of his exemplar than the actual words. As is well known, $\mathfrak{P}^{45}$ has marked affinities with the fifth-century manuscript, W. The more "normal" text of Mark is preserved in one early fourth-century manuscript, $\mathfrak{P}^{88}$, and two later fourth-century manuscripts, ℵ and B. Until there are more discoveries of early copies of Mark, it is difficult to reconstruct the early history of the text.

A few witnesses have been identified as "Caesarean" in the Gospel of Mark. These manuscripts probably came from Origen's text, a text that he took with him from Alexandria to Caesarea and that bears a mixture of so-called "Western" and Alexandrian readings. These witnesses are Codex Koridethi (Θ) 28 565 700 f^{1} f^{13}, the Armenian and Georgian versions, $\mathfrak{P}^{45}$ and W (in 1:1–5:30).

Acts

THE ALEXANDRIAN TEXT

Primary Manuscripts (with substantial extant text): $\mathfrak{P}^{45}$ B ℵ
Primary Manuscripts Dated After 400: $\mathfrak{P}^{74}$ A C (in part) Ψ 33 81 104 326 1739
Secondary Manuscripts (with smaller portions of text): $\mathfrak{P}^{8}$ $\mathfrak{P}^{41}$ $\mathfrak{P}^{50}$ $\mathfrak{P}^{53}$ $\mathfrak{P}^{91}$ 0189

THE WESTERN TEXT AND D-TEXT

Primary Manuscripts: D it^{d}
Secondary Manuscripts: $\mathfrak{P}^{29(?)}$ $\mathfrak{P}^{38}$ $\mathfrak{P}^{48}$ $\mathfrak{P}^{112}$; also it^{h} syr^{hmg} syr^{h**} Cyprian Augustine

The book of Acts existed in two distinct forms in the early church—the Alexandrian and the Western. The Alexandrian text is found in manuscripts such as $\mathfrak{P}^{45}$ $\mathfrak{P}^{74}$ ℵ A B C Ψ 0189 33. The Western text is found in a few third-century papyri ($\mathfrak{P}^{29}$ $\mathfrak{P}^{38}$ $\mathfrak{P}^{48}$), a fifth-century papyrus ($\mathfrak{P}^{112}$), the uncial 0171 (ca. 300), and Codex Bezae (D, fifth century). The Western text is also attested to by the African Old Latin manuscripts (including it^{h}), marginal readings in the Harclean Syriac translation (noted as syr^{hmg} or syr^{h**}), and the writings of Cyprian and Augustine. The Western text, which is nearly one-tenth longer than the Alexandrian, is more colorful and filled with added circumstantial details. The Western text must be referred to loosely because it is a conglomerate of variant readings which are (1) generally non-Alexandrian, (2) found in early Western witnesses, (3) found in D, and (4) even found in witnesses that are not normally considered "Western"—i.e., Marcion, Tatian, and Irenaeus.

The leading witness of the Western text is Codex Bezae (D) of the fifth century. But this form of the Western text was not created by the scribe who produced Codex Bezae, even though he himself may have added his own enhancements. The creation of the text as later found in D could have happened prior to the third century. Aland and Aland state, "When and how the Greek exemplar of D originated is unknown ($\mathfrak{P}^{29}$, $\mathfrak{P}^{38}$, $\mathfrak{P}^{48}$, and 0171 of the third and fourth centuries show earlier or related forms), but the additions, omissions, and alterations of the text (especially in Luke and Acts) betray the touch of a significant theologian. . . . When D supports the early tradition the manuscript has a genuine significance, but it (as well as its precursors and followers) should be examined most carefully when it opposes the early tradition" (1987, 108). Metzger considered the early Western text to be the work of a reviser "who was obviously a meticulous and well-informed scholar, [who] eliminated seams and gaps and added historical, biographical, and geographical details. Apparently the reviser did his work at an early date, before the text of Acts had come to be generally regarded as a sacred text that must be preserved inviolate" (Introduction to Acts, TCGNT).

Theories abound as to which form of the text is the original one—or even if Luke wrote both (see Metzger's excellent survey in TCGNT). The major scholarly consensus is that the Alexandrian text is primary and the Western secondary. J. H. Ropes (1926, ccxxii) considered the Western text to be "a paraphrastic rewriting of the original," the "work of a single editor trying to improve the work on a large scale." R. P. C. Hanson (1965, 215-224) characterized this reviser as an interpolator who made large insertions into an Alexandrian type text. Hanson hypothesized "that these interpolations were made in Rome between A.D. 120 and 150, at a time when the book of Acts was not yet regarded as sacrosanct and inspired."

More often than not, the editors of the NU text considered the Alexandrian text, as the shorter text, to have preserved the original wording. My view is that in nearly every instance where the D-text stands alone (against other witnesses—especially the Alexandrian), it is a case of the Western scribe functioning as a reviser who enhanced the text with redactional fillers. This person (whom I often refer to as the "reviser" or "D-reviser" in the commentary notes) must have been a knowledgeable researcher, who had a penchant for adding historical, biographical, and geographical details (as noted by Metzger). More than anything, he was intent on filling in gaps in the narrative by adding circumstantial details. Furthermore, he shaped the text to favor the Gentiles over the Jews, to promote Paul's apostolic mission, and to heighten the activity of the Holy Spirit in the work of the apostles.

Paul's Epistles and Hebrews

Primary Manuscripts (with substantial extant text): $\mathfrak{P}^{13}$ (for Hebrews) $\mathfrak{P}^{46}$ א B
Primary Manuscripts Dated After 400: A C I H^{p} 33 81 104 326 1739
Secondary Manuscripts (with smaller portions of text): $\mathfrak{P}^{13}$ $\mathfrak{P}^{15+16}$ $\mathfrak{P}^{27}$ $\mathfrak{P}^{30}$ $\mathfrak{P}^{40}$ $\mathfrak{P}^{49+65}$ $\mathfrak{P}^{92}$

It is not as easy to determine the primary manuscripts for Paul's Epistles as it is for the Gospels. $\mathfrak{P}^{46}$ has to be considered as a primary manuscript because of its early date (second century) and coverage of text (Romans—2 Thessalonians, including Hebrews), although its textual testimony is not as pure as that found in $\mathfrak{P}^{75}$ for the Gospels.

The three most comprehensive and significant studies of the textual character of $\mathfrak{P}^{46}$ were done by Kenyon, Sanders, and Zuntz. Both Kenyon and Sanders affirm the Alexandrian textual character of $\mathfrak{P}^{46}$, noting especially its affinities with B. According to Kenyon's tabulation (1936, xv-xvi), $\mathfrak{P}^{46}$ and B have the following percentages of agreement: Romans (66%), 1 Corinthians (75%), 2 Corinthians (77%), Galatians (73%), Ephesians (83%), Philippians (73%), Colossians (78%), and

Hebrews (79%). $\mathfrak{P}^{46}$ also has an affinity with א (but the percentages of agreement are about 5% lower for each book than for B). Note the extremely high agreement in Ephesians and Hebrews, and lower agreement in Romans—this is because B is noted for its "Western" tendencies in Romans. $\mathfrak{P}^{46}$ also shows great affinity with other witnesses. Zuntz (1953, 265) affirmed an early eastern group of manuscripts for the Pauline corpus: $\mathfrak{P}^{46}$ B 1739 Coptic Sahidic, Coptic Bohairic, Clement, and Origen. The relationship between $\mathfrak{P}^{46}$ and 1739 is noteworthy because 1739 is a tenth-century manuscript that was copied from a fourth-century manuscript of excellent quality. According to a colophon, the scribe of 1739 for the Pauline Epistles followed a manuscript which came from the library of Pamphilus in Caesarea and which contained an Origenian text (Zuntz 1953, 71-78; Metzger 1992, 65). The three manuscripts, $\mathfrak{P}^{46}$ B and 1739, form a clear textual line: from $\mathfrak{P}^{46}$ (early second century) to B (early fourth century) to 1739 (tenth century).

The most thorough study on the text of $\mathfrak{P}^{46}$ was done by Günther Zuntz (1953, 83), who wrote:

> Within the wider affinities of the "Alexandrian" tradition, the Vaticanus is now seen to stand out as a member of a group with $\mathfrak{P}^{46}$ and the pre-ancestor of 1739. The early date of the text-form which this group preserves is fixed by its oldest member and its high quality is borne out by many striking instances. B is in fact a witness for a text, not of C. A.D. 360, but of C. A.D. 200.

Although he was quick to point out the many scribal blunders found in $\mathfrak{P}^{46}$, Zuntz was just as eager to demonstrate that $\mathfrak{P}^{46}$ is a representative of "a text of the superior, early-Alexandrian type" (1953, 247). This quotation from Zuntz encapsulates his impression of $\mathfrak{P}^{46}$'s text:

> The excellent quality of the text represented by our oldest manuscript, $\mathfrak{P}^{46}$, stands out again. As so often before, we must here again be careful to distinguish between the very poor work of the scribe who penned it and the basic text which he so poorly rendered. $\mathfrak{P}^{46}$ abounds with scribal blunders, omissions, and also additions. In some of them the scribe anticipated the errors of later copyists; in some others he shares an older error; but the vast majority are his own uncontested property. Once they have been discarded, there remains a text of outstanding (though not absolute) purity. (1953, 212-213)

Thus, Zuntz made it clear that $\mathfrak{P}^{46}$ B and 1739 are primary manuscripts for Paul's Major Epistles and Hebrews (which was considered part of the Pauline corpus by the early church). The other primary manuscripts are א, A, and C (where extant). A textual comparison of these manuscripts with the secondary manuscripts listed above yields the following results:

$\mathfrak{P}^{13}$ agrees with $\mathfrak{P}^{46}$ in 40 out of 50 variants (80%), and it agrees with B in 13 out of 18 variants (B lacks much of Hebrews). No other textual affinities are clearly manifest, even with א and 1739.

$\mathfrak{P}^{15+16}$ shows the greatest affinity with B (34 out of 43 variants = 79%); and א (32 out of 43 = 74%). It demonstrates only 55% agreement with $\mathfrak{P}^{46}$. By way of comparison, $\mathfrak{P}^{15+16}$ shows significant divergence from D (agreeing only 15 out of 33 variants) and F G (11 out of 33).

$\mathfrak{P}^{27}$ demonstrates the greatest affinity with B and א (both 10 out of 11 variants), as well as with A (9 out of 11 variants), and C (8 out of 11 variants). $\mathfrak{P}^{27}$'s agreement with $\mathfrak{P}^{46}$ is less: 7 out of 11. For comparison purposes, $\mathfrak{P}^{27}$ demonstrates significant divergence from D (agreeing only 5 out of 11 variants) and from F G (6 out of 11 variants).

$\mathfrak{P}^{30}$ displays the highest agreement with א (11 out of 13 variants) and then with B (9 out of 13 variants). Its text cannot be compared to $\mathfrak{P}^{46+65}$ because there is no overlap among these manuscripts. For comparison purposes, $\mathfrak{P}^{30}$ demonstrates significant divergence from D (agreeing only 5 out of 13 variants).

$\mathfrak{P}^{40}$ exhibits the highest agreement with א (13 out of 15 variants) and then with A and B (both 12 out of 13 variants). Its text does not overlap with $\mathfrak{P}^{46}$. By way of comparison, $\mathfrak{P}^{40}$ demonstrates significant divergence from D (agreeing only 6 out of 13 variants) and from F G (3 out of 13 variants).

$\mathfrak{P}^{49+65}$ demonstrates the greatest affinity with B and ℵ (both 14 out of 16 variants), as well as with A (12 out of 16 variants). It shows less agreement with $\mathfrak{P}^{46}$ (8 out of 14 variants). For comparison purposes, $\mathfrak{P}^{49+65}$ demonstrates significant divergence from D (agreeing only 7 out of 16 variants) and from F G (5 out of 16 variants).

$\mathfrak{P}^{92}$ exhibits the greatest affinity with ℵ (6 out of 7 variants) and B (5 out of 7). For comparison purposes, $\mathfrak{P}^{92}$ exhibits divergence from D F G (agreeing only 3 out of 7 variants for each manuscript).

The data clearly show that ℵ and B had their precursors—namely, papyri from the third century—$\mathfrak{P}^{15+16}$, $\mathfrak{P}^{27}$, $\mathfrak{P}^{30}$, $\mathfrak{P}^{40}$, $\mathfrak{P}^{49+65}$, $\mathfrak{P}^{92}$. Significantly, none of these papyri exhibit a marked affinity with $\mathfrak{P}^{46}$ in the Pauline Epistles. Only $\mathfrak{P}^{13}$, in Hebrews, has this textual closeness with $\mathfrak{P}^{46}$ (with 80% agreement). Thus, we must be wary of $\mathfrak{P}^{46}$'s independence, while also recognizing its witness to the original text. It should also be noted that the early papyri agree slightly more with ℵ than with B. This probably affirms the impression that B tends to expand the text (its "Western" tendencies) in Paul's Epistles, while ℵ is more pure. The situation seems to be that any combination of the papyri with ℵ or B must be seriously considered as providing solid testimony for the original text—and even more so when the papyri agree with both ℵ and B. Disregarding the places where B aligns with the "Western" manuscripts D F G, its testimony with ℵ and the above noted papyri often represents the original text. Another strong witness is the manuscript 1739. Lightfoot (1893, 380) was convinced that where ℵ B and 1739 concur in supporting a Pauline reading, the original text is invariably reflected. Add to this the testimony of $\mathfrak{P}^{46}$ and the other papyri, and the certainty becomes greater.

Paul's Pastoral Epistles

Primary Manuscripts (with substantial extant text): ℵ (B lacks Pastorals) I 1739
Secondary Manuscripts (with smaller portions of text): $\mathfrak{P}^{32}$

The Pastoral Epistles have a different history than the other Pauline Epistles because they were private letters to individuals, which would not have been circulated among the churches in its early years. Gradually, the Pastoral Epistles gained recognition and acceptance into the Pauline canon. (The Epistle to Philemon, although also a personal letter, gained immediate recognition because of its connection with Colossians.) There is only one early copy of one Pastoral Epistle, $\mathfrak{P}^{32}$, displaying part of Titus (ch 2). This manuscript, dated around 175, was probably the work of a professional scribe. Although $\mathfrak{P}^{32}$ cannot be compared with B because Vaticanus lacks the Pastoral Epistles, it shows affinity with ℵ (and slightly less affinity with F G). Overall, the best witness for the Pastoral Epistles is ℵ.

The General Epistles

Primary Manuscripts (with substantial extant text): $\mathfrak{P}^{72}$ (for 1 Peter) ℵ B
Primary Manuscripts Dated After 400: $\mathfrak{P}^{74}$ A C 33 81 104 326 1739
Secondary Manuscripts (with smaller portions of text): $\mathfrak{P}^{20}$ $\mathfrak{P}^{23}$ $\mathfrak{P}^{81}$ $\mathfrak{P}^{100}$ 0232

The General Epistles (also known as the Catholic Epistles) have had a textual and canonical history distinct from the Four Gospels and Paul's Epistles. From as early as the second century, the Four Gospels were collected together into one volume, as were Paul's Epistles (minus the Pastorals). But this was not so for the other New Testament books. In fact, only a few other books were widely read in the churches—namely, 1 Peter and 1 John. The other General Epistles had a difficult time making it into the New Testament canon: James, because of its apparent opposition to Pauline soteriology; 2 Peter, because of its dissimilarity to 1 Peter; 2 John, 3 John, and Jude, because of their obscurity. Interestingly, the book of Acts was often attached to the General Epistles, as is shown by the ordering in Codex Vaticanus (where the General Epistles follow Acts). Given their preference for Codex Vaticanus, Westcott and Hort's text follows this order. The seventh-century papyrus, $\mathfrak{P}^{74}$, has only Acts and the General Epistles in one codex. It is a good witness for both.

As canonical lists were made, indicating which books belonged in the New Testament, the Catholic Epistles were most often disputed. The Muratorian Canon, a list expressing the views of Roman church leaders in about A.D. 180, included only 1 and 2 John and Jude among General Epistles. Origen stated that 1 Peter and 1 John were the only undisputed writings of the seven, but he accepted all of them as canonical. All seven appeared in Codex Claromontanus (Egypt, sixth century), Codex Sinaiticus, Codex Vaticanus (both fourth century), Athanasius's Thirty-Ninth Festal Letter (A.D. 367), Jerome's writings (about A.D. 394), Codex Alexandrinus (fifth century), and Augustine's writings (fourth to fifth centuries). The textual situation for each book or section must be discussed separately.

JAMES

James has been preserved in three third-century manuscripts, exhibiting the following affinities:

$\mathfrak{P}^{20}$ bears resemblance to ℵ (in 10 out of 14 variants) and B (also in 10 out of 14 variants).
$\mathfrak{P}^{23}$ shows affinities with ℵ A C (in 7 of 8 variants).
$\mathfrak{P}^{100}$ agrees predominantly with B (in 22 out of 27 variants) and then with ℵ and C (both 18 of 27 variants).

The entire text of James is best preserved in the fourth-century manuscript, Codex Vaticanus (B) and the fifth-century manuscripts, Codex Alexandrinus (A) and Codex Ephraemi Rescriptus (C).

1 PETER

Peter's first epistle, accepted from the beginning as authentic and apostolic, was well preserved in its early textual transmission. This textual fidelity is manifest in one late third-century manuscript, $\mathfrak{P}^{72}$ (Papyrus Bodmer VII-VIII), and another fourth-century manuscript, $\mathfrak{P}^{81}$. Excluding singular variants, $\mathfrak{P}^{72}$ displays a text that resembles B and yet is closer to the original than B, while $\mathfrak{P}^{81}$ has more affinity with ℵ than with B. $\mathfrak{P}^{74}$, of the seventh century, also has a fairly good text for 1 Peter.

2 PETER AND JUDE

The original text of 2 Peter and Jude was not as well preserved in the early period of textual transmission, because these books were not readily acknowledged as apostolic, canonical texts by all the sectors of the early church. The manuscript evidence for these books is quite diverse, marked by independence. This is evident in the two papyri, $\mathfrak{P}^{72}$ (especially for Jude) and $\mathfrak{P}^{78}$. All in all, Codex Alexandrinus (A) is usually the best witness for these epistles. $\mathfrak{P}^{74}$, B, and C are also good witnesses.

JOHN'S EPISTLES

The best manuscript for John's Epistles is B, followed by ℵ. Codex A tends to be expansive and erratic in these epistles. Several Western witnesses, especially in the Vulgate manuscripts, have extended interpolations (see notes on 2:17; 4:3; 5:6b, 7b-8a, 9, 10, 20). First John has one early, third-century witness, $\mathfrak{P}^{9}$, but it is fragmentary, and its textual character is unreliable. Second John also has a third-century witness, 0232; its testimony *is* reliable.

Revelation

Primary Manuscripts (with substantial extant text): $\mathfrak{P}^{47}$ $\mathfrak{P}^{115}$ ℵ A C
Primary Later Manuscripts: 2053 2062 2344
Secondary Manuscripts (with smaller portions of text): $\mathfrak{P}^{18}$ $\mathfrak{P}^{24}$ $\mathfrak{P}^{85}$ $\mathfrak{P}^{98}$

According to Joseph Schmid (1955–1956; a magnum opus on the text of Revelation), the best text is preserved in A and C, supported by a few select minuscules (2053 2062 2344). This text seems to have been antedated by three third-century manuscripts, $\mathfrak{P}^{18}$ (which has agreement with C in 10 out of 11 variants), $\mathfrak{P}^{24}$ (though the extant text is too small to be certain), and $\mathfrak{P}^{115}$. Concerning $\mathfrak{P}^{115}$, the textual affinities are as follows:

> $\mathfrak{P}^{115}$ agrees with $\mathfrak{P}^{47}$ in 52 out of 131 variants (40% agreement).
> $\mathfrak{P}^{115}$ agrees with א in 81 out of 165 variants (49% agreement).
> $\mathfrak{P}^{115}$ agrees with A in 109 out of 165 variants (66% agreement).
> $\mathfrak{P}^{115}$ agrees with C in 94 out of 137 variants (68% agreement).
> Thus, $\mathfrak{P}^{115}$ belongs in the A C group, though marginally.

Schmid thinks the second-best text is that found in א and $\mathfrak{P}^{47}$. (This group would also have to include $\mathfrak{P}^{85}$, which accords almost completely with $\mathfrak{P}^{47}$.) But this seems too simplistic of a hierarchy. Often, when A and C stand against א and $\mathfrak{P}^{47}$, one is hard-pressed to say which combination is superior. It is true that א displays several omissions and some interpolations in Revelation, but Codex A is full of accidental omissions, especially in the first half of the book (as the commentary notes reveal). The scribe of A seems to have been very fatigued or inattentive when copying the first half of Revelation. Thus, we should be hesitant to accept the general maxim that A has the best text of Revelation. Perhaps, it is better to say A *and* C together preserve one of the purest forms of the original text, but not necessarily any more pristine than that found in the combined testimony of א and $\mathfrak{P}^{47}$. This must be decided on a case-by-case basis.

Two other important sources for the Apocalypse are a mass of manuscripts that follow Andreas of Caesarea's commentary on Revelation (marked as Maj^{A}) and a common group of other Byzantine (or Koine) manuscripts (marked as Maj^{K}). The siglum Maj indicates the agreement of Maj^{A} and Maj^{K}. The manuscript 046 usually agrees with Maj^{K}, and the manuscript P concurs with Maj^{A}.

Finally, it should be noted that Erasmus's edition of Revelation (which eventually became the Textus Receptus) was largely based on one twelfth-century manuscript (1), which lacked the last six verses. Furthermore, in other parts of this manuscript, the Greek commentary became mingled in with the text. For many of these corrupted parts, as well as for the missing final verses, Erasmus used the Latin Vulgate to re-create the Greek text. As one might expect, this procedure produced a Greek edition with readings that have never been found in any Greek manuscript but are still perpetuated in the Textus Receptus (Metzger 1992, 99-100). A good and thorough description of all the witnesses to the book of Revelation is provided by Aune (1997, cxxxvi-cxlviii).

2. Significant Editions of the Greek New Testament

This commentary interacts with four editions of the Greek New Testament: (1) the Textus Receptus, (2) Westcott and Hort's *The New Testament in the Original Greek*, (3) the United Bible Societies' *Greek New Testament* (third and fourth editions), and (4) the Nestle-Aland *Novum Testamentum Graece* (twenty-sixth and twenty-seventh editions).

The Textus Receptus (TR)

The Textus Receptus (abbreviated TR in the commentary) has its roots in the early fourth century, when Lucian of Antioch produced a major recension of the New Testament (see Jerome's introduction to his Latin translation of the Gospels, PL 29:527c). This text is sometimes called "Syrian," because of its association with Antioch in Syria. Lucian's work was a definite recension (i.e., a purposely created edition), in contrast to the Alexandrian text-type (see appendix D). The Alexandrian scribes did some minimal editing, such as we would call copy editing. By contrast, the Syrian text is the result of a much larger endeavor; it is characterized by smoothness of language, which is achieved by the removal of obscurities and awkward grammatical constructions, and by the conflation of variant readings.

Lucian's text was produced prior to the Diocletian persecution (ca. 303), during which many copies of the New Testament were confiscated and destroyed. Not long after this period of devastation, Constantine came to power and recognized Christianity as a legal religion. There was, of course, a great need for copies of the New Testament to be made and distributed to churches throughout the Mediterranean world. It was at this time that Lucian's text began to be propagated by bishops going out from Antioch to churches throughout the East. Lucian's text soon became standard in the Eastern Church. For century after century—from the sixth to the fourteenth—the great majority of Greek New Testament manuscripts were produced in Byzantium, the capital of the Eastern Empire. All of these copies bore the same kind of text, one directly descended from Lucian's Syrian recension. When the first Greek New Testament was printed (ca. 1525), it was based on a Greek text that Erasmus had compiled using a few late Byzantine manuscripts (notably, minuscules 1 and 2 of the twelfth century). This text went through a few more revisions by Robert Stephanus and then by Theodore Beza. Beza's text was published by the Elzevir brothers in 1624, with a second edition in 1633. In this printing they announced that their edition contained "the text which is now received by all, in which we give nothing changed or corrupted." In this way, "textus receptus" (the "received text") became the name of this form of the Greek New Testament.

The edition of the Textus Receptus cited throughout this commentary is that of Stephanus (1550). The Elzevirs' text (1624) is virtually the same. Both can be called the Textus Receptus (TR).

In recent years, a few scholars have attempted to defend the validity of the Textus Receptus or what they would call the Majority Text. The Majority Text is nearly the same as the Textus Receptus, since TR was derived from manuscripts produced in Byzantium, where the majority of other Greek New Testaments were produced. The two terms are not completely synonymous, however, because TR did not attempt to reproduce the reading found in a statistical majority of witnesses. Thus, it does not consistently reflect the Majority Text throughout. Majority Text is more nearly synonymous with the Byzantine text-type because it was in Byzantium (and surrounding regions) that Lucian's recension was copied again and again in thousands of manuscripts.

Modern advocates of the superiority of the Majority Text over other text-types are Hodges and Farstad, who produced *The Greek New Testament according to the Majority Text*. Their arguments are more theological than textual. They reason that God would not have allowed a corrupt or inferior text to be found in the majority of manuscripts, while permitting a superior text to be hidden away in a few early manuscripts somewhere in the sands of Egypt. Further, they argue that the church's adoption of the Majority Text was a vindication of its correctness, while the obscurity of the Egyptian text was a sign of its rejection.

Most contemporary scholars contend that a minority of manuscripts—primarily the earliest ones—preserve the most authentic wording of the text. Those who defend the Majority Text (and its well-known incarnations, TR and KJV) would have to prove that these earlier manuscripts, usually having a slimmer text than what appears in later manuscripts, were purposefully trimmed at an early stage in the textual transmission. In other words, they would have to present good arguments as to why early scribes would have purposely excised the following passages: Matthew 5:44b; 6:13b; 16:2b-3; 17:21; 18:11; 20:16b, 22-23; 23:14; 27:35b; Mark 7:16; 9:44, 46; 11:26; 15:28; 16:8-20; Luke 4:4b; 9:54c-56; 11:2; 17:36; 22:43-44; 23:17, 34; John 5:3b-4; 7:53—8:11; Acts 8:37; 15:34; 24:6b-8a; 28:16b, 29; Romans 16:24; 1 John 5:6b-8a. Had these portions originally been in the text, there are no good explanations why they would have been eliminated. On the other hand, there are several good explanations why they were added, such as gospel harmonization, the insertion of oral traditions, and theological enhancements (see commentary on the above passages). It is true that some of the earliest scribes were prone to shorten their texts in the interest of readability, but these deletions usually involved only a few words. Thus, most scholars see TR as being the culmination of textual accretions.

Westcott and Hort, The New Testament in the Original Greek (WH)

Aided by the work of scholars such as Tregelles and Tischendorf, two British scholars, Brooke Westcott and Fenton Hort, worked together for twenty-eight years to produce an edition entitled *The New Testament in the Original Greek* (2 volumes, 1881–1882; abbreviated WH in the commentary). In this publication, they made known their theory (which was chiefly Hort's) that Codex Vaticanus and Codex Sinaiticus (along with a few other early manuscripts) represented a text that most closely replicated the original writing. This is the text, which they called the Neutral Text, that Westcott and Hort attempted to reproduce in their edition. Their work was historically significant in that it dethroned reliance on the Textus Receptus.

In my opinion, Westcott and Hort's edition is still to this day, even with so many more manuscript discoveries, a very close reproduction of the primitive text of the New Testament. Of course, like many others, I think they gave too much weight to Codex Vaticanus alone. This criticism aside, the Westcott and Hort text is extremely reliable. In my own studies of textual variants, in many instances where I would disagree with the wording in the NU edition in favor of a particular variant reading, I would later check with WH and realize that they had come to the same decision. This revealed to me that I was working on a similar methodological basis as they. Since the era of Westcott and Hort, hundreds of other manuscripts have been discovered, notably the early papyri. Were Westcott and Hort alive today, they would be pleased to see that several of these papyri affirm their view that Codex Vaticanus and Codex Sinaiticus are reliable witnesses of a very primitive form of the Greek New Testament. They would have undoubtedly altered some of their textual choices based on the evidence of the papyri. For example, the testimony of $\mathfrak{P}^{75}$ (with א and B) in several Lukan passages clearly indicates that Westcott and Hort were wrong to have excluded several passages in Luke 22–24 based on their theory of "Western noninterpolations."

The Nestle-Aland Novum Testamentum Graece (26th and 27th editions) and The United Bible Societies' Greek New Testament (3rd and 4th corrected editions) (NU)

In the commentary these two editions, which have the same text, are referred to jointly as NU; when it is necessary to refer to the volumes individually, the sigla NA^{26}, NA^{27}, UBS^{3}, and UBS^{4} are used.

The United Bible Societies prepared an edition of the *Greek New Testament* as a tool for their Bible translators, in which a full citation of witnesses was given in the critical apparatus for significant variants. After the United Bible Societies had published two editions of the *Greek New Testament*, they decided to unite with the work being done on the twenty-sixth edition of the Nestle-Aland text, a scholarly reference tool.

Thus, the United Bible Societies' third edition of the *Greek New Testament* and the Nestle-Aland twenty-sixth edition of *Novum Testament Graece* have the same text. Each, however, has different punctuation and a different critical apparatus. The United Bible Societies' text has a plenary listing of witnesses for select variation units; the Nestle-Aland text has a condensed listing of the manuscript evidence for almost all the variant-units. Both works have since gone into another edition (the fourth and twenty-seventh, respectively), manifesting a multitude of corrections to the critical apparatus but not to the wording of the text itself.

In *The Text of the New Testament*, Kurt and Barbara Aland argue that the Nestle-Aland text "comes closer to the original text of the New Testament than did Tischendorf or Westcott and Hort, not to mention von Soden" (1991, 32). And in several other passages they intimate that this text may very well be the original text. This is evident in Kurt Aland's defense (1979, 14) of NA^{26} as the new "standard text":

> The new "standard text" has passed the test of the early papyri and uncials. It corresponds, in fact, to the text of the early time. . . . At no place and at no time do we find readings here [in the

> earliest manuscripts] that require a change in the "standard text." If the investigation conducted here in all its brevity and compactness could be presented fully, the detailed apparatus accompanying each variant would convince the last doubter. A hundred years after Westcott-Hort, the goal of an edition of the New Testament "in the original Greek" seems to have been reached. . . . The desired goal appears now to have been attained, to offer the writings of the New Testament in the form of the text that comes nearest to that which, from the hand of their authors or redactors, they set out on their journey in the church of the first and second centuries.

Though the Alands should be commended for their work, it remains to be seen whether or not the Nestle-Aland text is the best replication of the original text. As noted before, I have my doubts (see appendix D, "The Importance of the Documentary Considerations"). Nonetheless, the Nestle-Aland Greek text is now truly recognized as the standard text, accepted by most of the academic community as representing the best attempt at reconstructing the original text of the Greek New Testament.

Since the scholarly community worldwide is most familiar with NU, this is the edition given first in each listing of textual variants. The NU reading is printed as it stands in the UBS^{4} edition, including accents. All the variants are unaccented, as in the critical apparatus of NA^{27}. This presentation should not be interpreted as implying, however, that this text is "inspired" or infallible—as many scholars will readily attest. The NU editors were able to take into consideration the newly discovered documents as they sought to produce a more accurate text. In many places they no doubt have achieved their goal to produce a more accurate text than did Westcott and Hort. However, their strong reliance on the eclectic method has produced an uneven documentary text (see appendixes B and D). In some, but not all, instances, the Nestle-Aland text presents an advance beyond Westcott and Hort.

Nonetheless, the reader will see that the NU and WH editions often agree on matters of major textual significance. Where the WH and NU diverge, however, NU far more frequently concurs with TR than does WH. Furthermore, where WH and NU differ, I am inclined quite frequently to agree with WH on the basis of documentary evidence.

3. Significant English Versions

Most variant readings are accompanied by a listing of the English versions that follow them. The translations consulted for this commentary are listed here in the order in which they are cited:

KJV	King James Version, 1611
NKJV	New King James Version, 1982
RSV	Revised Standard Version, 1946
NRSV	New Revised Standard Version, 1990
ESV	English Standard Version, 2001
NASB	New American Standard Bible, 1964, 1995
NIV	New International Version, 1978
TNIV	Today's New International Version, 2005
NEB	New English Bible, 1961
REB	Revised English Bible, 1989
NJB	New Jerusalem Bible, 1986
NAB	New American Bible, 1984 (revised NT)
NLT	New Living Translation (second edition), 2004
HCSB	Holman Christian Standard Bible, 2004
NET	The NET Bible (New English Translation), 1996

KJV and NKJV have the closest textual affinity of any two translations and appear together; they are followed by RSV, NRSV, ESV, and NASB—each revisions of the Authorized Version. (The ASV is cited only occasionally because it is not a translation in current use.) After the "standard" versions, various independent translations are listed: NIV and its revision, TNIV; NEB and its revision, REB. NJB and NAB are independent of one another but appear together because they are both Catholic versions. Finally, the three most recent independent translations are listed, NLT, HCSB, and NET.

King James Version (1611)—KJV

For the New Testament, the King James translators essentially used the Textus Receptus (see the discussion under "Textus Receptus" above).The King James translators did well with the resources that were available to them, but those resources were flawed, especially with respect to the New Testament text. Since the King James Version was published, earlier and better manuscripts have been discovered, thereby enabling better critical editions of the Greek New Testament and better English translations.

New King James Version (1982)—NKJV

NKJV is a revision of KJV which modernizes its language but does not depart from KJV's textual decisions. The New Testament of NKJV is thus based on the Textus Receptus, with several marginal notes on readings in the Majority Text (noted in NKJV as M-Text; see discussion under "Textus Receptus" above). NKJV also lists many textual differences between TR and the text of NA^{26}/UBS^{3} (noted as NU-Text or U-Text). The reader can thus note how many significant differences there are between the two texts.

American Standard Version (1901)—ASV

The ASV (essentially the same as the English Revised Version, 1881, with minor changes made for American readers) is the best English translation reflecting the Greek text produced by the end of nineteenth century through the labors of men like Tregelles, Tischendorf, Westcott, and Hort. These men were greatly influenced by Codex Sinaiticus and Codex Vaticanus, but not by the papyri, since only a few had been discovered and published by then. Thus, ASV reflects the influence of these two great uncial manuscripts and serves as a point of comparison with the subsequent twentieth-century versions. In this commentary, it is cited sparingly.

Revised Standard Version (1952)—RSV

The RSV is a revision of ASV. It was felt that ASV suffered from being too rigid; it needed reworking to make it more idiomatic. The demand for revision was strengthened by the discovery of several important biblical manuscripts in the 1930s and 1940s—namely, the Dead Sea Scrolls for the Old Testament and the Chester Beatty Papyri for the New Testament. The RSV New Testament was based on the seventeenth edition of the Nestle text (1941).

New Revised Standard Version (1990)—NRSV

The NRSV is an authorized revision of RSV. Of all the translations, it is the one that most closely follows the text of NA^{27}/UBS^{4}. No doubt, this is due to the fact that Bruce Metzger served on both the editorial committees—a leading member of the NA^{27}/UBS^{4} committee and the chairperson for the NRSV committee.

English Standard Version (2001)—ESV

A separate revision of RSV was undertaken by evangelical scholars in the late 1990s, resulting in the ESV. Like NRSV, its translators started with NA^{27}/UBS^{4} as the textual base for the New Testament.

In the end, its text lies somewhere between RSV and NRSV; the translators were less likely than the NRSV committee to change RSV readings in the direction of NA^{27}/UBS^4.

New American Standard Bible (1964, 1995)—NASB

The NASB is generally respected as a good study Bible that closely reflects the wording of the original languages, yet is not a fluid translation for Bible reading. Furthermore, this translation is clearly lacking in terms of textual fidelity: though it was originally supposed to follow the twenty-third edition of the Nestle text, it tends to follow the Textus Receptus. This commentary cites the 1964 edition, as this is the version that most readers have in hand. An updated version appeared in 1995, but this update has only a few textual changes in the translation, with a few more changes in the marginal notes.

New International Version (1978, 1983)—NIV

The NIV is an excellent translation in fairly contemporary English. The New Testament essentially follows the United Bible Societies' first edition of the *Greek New Testament* (1966). It diverges from NA^{27}/UBS^4 in about 350 significant places—many in agreement with TR. This book cites the 1983 edition, which introduced numerous revisions to the original NIV and is the edition most people own.

New English Bible (1961)—NEB

The NEB is worthwhile to analyze because it reflects a very eclectic Greek text. After the translation appeared, the Greek text followed by the translation committee was produced by R. V. G. Tasker. The committee's verse-by-verse decision making produced a text that is very uneven and yet very interesting. The translators adopted readings never before adopted by English translators.

Revised English Bible (1989)—REB

The REB is a revision of The New English Bible (NEB). The revisers of the New Testament used NA^{26}. This choice resulted in several textual changes from NEB, which had followed a very eclectic text. The translators of NEB had adopted readings never before put into print by English translators, but the scholars working on REB adjusted many of these readings back toward the norm. At the same time, they also made some significant textual changes, the most outstanding of which was their treatment of the story of the woman caught in adultery (John 7:53–8:11). Reflecting the overwhelming evidence of the Greek manuscripts, this story is not included in the main body of John's Gospel. Rather, it is printed as an appendix after the Gospel of John.

New Jerusalem Bible (1986)—NJB

The New Jerusalem Bible is a revision of the Jerusalem Bible, a translation widely accepted among Roman Catholics for liturgical purposes, for study, and for private reading. The new edition incorporated progress in scholarship over the two decades since the preparation of the first edition. NJB generally has been well received (in Catholic circles and beyond) as an excellent study text. NJB is worthy of analysis because it displays an eclectic text—especially in the book of Acts, where many "Western" readings were adopted.

The New American Bible (1970; 1984 revised NT)—NAB

The New American Bible is the first American Catholic Bible to be translated from the original languages (the Jerusalem Bible was originally a French translation). Although this translation was published in 1970, work had begun on this version several decades before. Only after Pope Pius's encyclical *Divino Afflante Spiritu* (1967), however, would a Catholic Bible based on Greek and Hebrew be accepted. Prior to Pius's encyclical, an American translation based on the Latin Vulgate, called the Confraternity Bible, was published. NAB's New Testament was revised (in 1984) based on NA[26]. The translation is fairly literal and has very few marginal notes. It does not follow the "Western" readings, unlike NJB.

New Living Translation (1996, 2004)—NLT

The NLT is a complete revision of The Living Bible. The Living Bible was a paraphrase of the American Standard Version, whose New Testament was based upon the Greek text of Westcott and Hort. When it came time to revise The Living Bible, it was deemed appropriate for a translation committee to base its work on the most recent critical editions of the Greek New Testament, the Nestle-Aland *Novum Testamentum Graece* (twenty-seventh edition) and the United Bible Societies' *Greek New Testament* (fourth corrected edition). The New Testament translators also made judicious evaluation of the manuscript evidence itself. As a result, their textual decisions often depart from the Nestle-Aland text. These departures sometimes affirmed the Westcott and Hort text and at other times affirmed a different manuscript tradition altogether. (Of all the translations, this is the one whose textual decisions I am most familiar with, since I was New Testament coordinator for the project.)

Holman Christian Standard Bible (2004)—HCSB

The Holman Christian Standard Bible was originally intended to be a fresh translation of the Majority Text; however, the textual basis was changed early on to the modern critical editions of the Hebrew Bible and Greek New Testament. In the New Testament, HCSB essentially follows NA[27]/UBS[4], although it frequently provides TR readings in the footnotes.

The NET Bible (New English Translation) (1996)—NET

The NET Bible is another recent independent translation, known for its extensive translators' notes. Rather than establishing any printed edition of the Greek New Testament as the basis for NET, textual consultants determined which readings to follow on a case-by-case basis. NET differs from NA[27]/UBS[4] in several hundred places. Its textual decisions are very transparent, since many of the translators' notes interact with the manuscript evidence.

On occasion, a few other versions are noted, usually because they display readings not found or noted in any of the other versions. These include the English Revised Version (ERV, 1881), *The New Testament: A New Translation* (MOFFATT, 1922), *The Complete Bible: An American Translation* (GOODSPEED, 1935), *The New Testament in the Language of the People* (WILLIAMS, 1956), The New Testament in Modern English (PHILLIPS, 1958), and Today's English Version (TEV, 1966).

I have done my best to cite each version with the appropriate textual variants. This was not always easy to do, because translators have the freedom to render a Greek text in a variety of ways, some of which may inadvertently follow a textual variant they were not aware of. Translators at times take liberties in the interest of producing a more readable text, much the same as ancient scribes. Often the modern translators hit upon the same solution as one of their ancient predecessors. In most cases, translations do not note which reading they are following. I have therefore matched the English version with what appears to be its corresponding textual variant. However, if a translation appears to be following one variant, but a marginal note shows that the translators intended to follow a different variant, I have taken them at their word. In these cases, I have listed that version in parentheses as following the intended reading. In this kind of detailed work there will inevitably be errors in citations of witnesses and versions. I welcome suggestions for emendations in future printings.

4. Abbreviations

Manuscripts and Ancient Versions

In order to represent the testimony of a great number of ancient witnesses in a compact format, textual critics have developed a body of symbols (called *sigla;* singular *siglum*). The following sigla are used in this commentary. A fuller listing can be found in the introduction and appendixes to UBS^{4} and NA^{27}.

PAPYRI

$\mathfrak{P}^{1}$ Matt 1; early 3rd c.
$\mathfrak{P}^{3}$ Luke 7, 10; 6th–7th c.
$\mathfrak{P}^{4}$ Luke 1–6; late 2nd c. (same codex as $\mathfrak{P}^{64+67}$)
$\mathfrak{P}^{5}$ John 1, 16, 20; early 3rd c.
$\mathfrak{P}^{10}$ Rom 1; 4th c.
$\mathfrak{P}^{13}$ Heb 2–5, 10–12; early 3rd c.
$\mathfrak{P}^{15+16}$ (probably part of same codex) 1 Cor 7–8; Phil 3–4; late 3rd c.
$\mathfrak{P}^{20}$ Jas 2–3; 3rd c.
$\mathfrak{P}^{22}$ John 15–16; mid 3rd c.
$\mathfrak{P}^{23}$ Jas 1; ca. 200
$\mathfrak{P}^{24}$ Rev 5–6; ca. 300
$\mathfrak{P}^{25}$ Matt 18–19; 4th c.
$\mathfrak{P}^{26}$ Rom 1; ca. 600
$\mathfrak{P}^{27}$ Rom 8–9; 3rd c.
$\mathfrak{P}^{30}$ 1 Thess 4–5; 2 Thess 1; early 3rd c.
$\mathfrak{P}^{32}$ Titus 1–2; late 2nd c.
$\mathfrak{P}^{34}$ 1 Cor 16; 2 Cor 5, 10–11; 7th c.
$\mathfrak{P}^{35}$ Matt 25; 4th c.
$\mathfrak{P}^{37}$ Matt 26; late 3rd c.
$\mathfrak{P}^{38}$ Acts 18–19; ca. 300
$\mathfrak{P}^{39}$ John 8; first half of 3rd c.
$\mathfrak{P}^{40}$ Rom 1–4, 6, 9; 3rd c.
$\mathfrak{P}^{45}$ Gospels and Acts; early 3rd c.
$\mathfrak{P}^{46}$ Paul's Major Epistles (less the Pastorals); late 2nd c.
$\mathfrak{P}^{47}$ Rev 9–17; 3rd c.
$\mathfrak{P}^{48}$ Acts 23; 3rd c.
$\mathfrak{P}^{49}$ Eph 4–5; 3rd c. (same codex as $\mathfrak{P}^{65}$)
$\mathfrak{P}^{50}$ Acts 8, 10; late 4th c.
$\mathfrak{P}^{51}$ Gal 1; ca. 400
$\mathfrak{P}^{52}$ John 18; ca. 125
$\mathfrak{P}^{53}$ Matt 26; Acts 9–10; mid 3rd c.
$\mathfrak{P}^{54}$ Jas 2–3; 5th c.
$\mathfrak{P}^{59}$ John 1–2, 11–12, 17–18; 7th c.
$\mathfrak{P}^{60}$ John 16–19; 7th c.
$\mathfrak{P}^{61}$ Rom 16; 1 Cor 1, 5–6; Phil 3; Col 1, 5; 1 Thess 1; Titus 3; Phlm; ca. 700
$\mathfrak{P}^{64+67}$ Matt 3, 5, 26; late 2nd c. (same codex as $\mathfrak{P}^{4}$)
$\mathfrak{P}^{65}$ 1 Thess 1–2; 3rd c. (same codex as $\mathfrak{P}^{49}$)

$\mathfrak{P}^{66}$ John; late 2nd c.
$\mathfrak{P}^{66c1}$ designates the corrections of the original scribe.
$\mathfrak{P}^{66c2}$ designates the corrections of a second scribe in the scriptorium.
$\mathfrak{P}^{66c3}$ designates the corrections of a third scribe who was also the paginator.
$\mathfrak{P}^{70}$ Matt 2–3, 11–12, 24; 3rd c.
$\mathfrak{P}^{72}$ 1–2 Peter, Jude; ca. 300
$\mathfrak{P}^{74}$ Acts, General Epistles; 7th c.
$\mathfrak{P}^{75}$ Luke and John; ca. 200
$\mathfrak{P}^{77}$ Matt 23; late 2nd c. (probably same codex as $\mathfrak{P}^{103}$)
$\mathfrak{P}^{84}$ Mark 2, 6; John 5, 17; 6th c.
$\mathfrak{P}^{85}$ Rev 9–10; ca. 400
$\mathfrak{P}^{87}$ Phlm; late 2nd c.
$\mathfrak{P}^{88}$ Mark 2; 4th c.
$\mathfrak{P}^{90}$ John 18–19; late 2nd c.
$\mathfrak{P}^{91}$ Acts 2–3; 3rd c.
$\mathfrak{P}^{92}$ Eph 1; 2 Thess 1; ca. 300
$\mathfrak{P}^{98}$ Rev 1:13–20; late 2nd c.
$\mathfrak{P}^{99}$ portions of Rom, 2 Cor, Gal, Eph; ca. 400
$\mathfrak{P}^{100}$ Jas 3–5; ca. 300
$\mathfrak{P}^{101}$ Matt 3–4; 3rd c.
$\mathfrak{P}^{103}$ Matt 13–14; late 2nd c. (probably same codex as $\mathfrak{P}^{77}$)
$\mathfrak{P}^{104}$ Matt 21; 2nd c.
$\mathfrak{P}^{106}$ John 1; 3rd c.
$\mathfrak{P}^{109}$ John 21; late 2nd c.
$\mathfrak{P}^{110}$ Matt 10; ca. 300
$\mathfrak{P}^{112}$ Acts 26; 5th c.
$\mathfrak{P}^{113}$ Rom 2; ca. 200
$\mathfrak{P}^{115}$ Rev 2–3, 5–6, 8–15; 3rd c.
$\mathfrak{P}^{119}$ John 1; mid 3rd c.
$\mathfrak{P}^{120}$ John 1; ca. 300
$\mathfrak{P}^{121}$ John 19; ca. 200
$\mathfrak{P}^{122}$ John 21; 4th c.

UNCIALS

These manuscripts are written in uncial script on parchment or vellum, as opposed to papyrus.

א (Sinaiticus) most of NT; 4th c.
$א^{1}$ designates the corrector who worked on the manuscript before it left the scriptorium.
$א^{2}$ designates a group of correctors working in Caesarea in the sixth or seventh century, who corrected the manuscript in general conformity to the Byzantine text.
A (Alexandrinus) most of NT; 5th c.
B (Vaticanus) most of NT; 4th c.
B^{1} designates a corrector who was nearly contemporary with the original scribe.
B^{2} designates a tenth- or eleventh-century corrector, who also retouched the writing and added accents and punctuation marks.
C (Ephraemi Rescriptus) most of NT with many lacunae; 5th c.
D (Bezae) Gospels, Acts; 5th c.
D (Claromontanus) Paul's Epistles; 6th c. (different ms than Bezae)
E (Laudianus 35) Acts; 6th c.

F	(Augensis) Paul's Epistles; 9th c.
G	(Boernerianus) Paul's Epistles; 9th c.
H	(Coislinianus) Paul's Epistles; 6th c.
I	(Freerianus or Washington) Paul's Epistles; 5th c.
K	(Cyprius) Gospels; 9th c.
K	(Mosquensis) Acts and Epistles; 9th c.
L	(Regius) Gospels; 8th c.
M	(Campianus) Gospels; 9th c.
N	(Petropolitanus Purpureus) Gospels; 6th c.
P	(Porphyrianus) Acts—Revelation; 9th c.
Q	(Guelferbytanus B) Luke, John; 5th c.
S	(Vaticanus 354) Gospels; 949
T	(Borgianus) Luke, John; 5th c.
U	(Nanianus) Gospels; 9th c.
W	(Washingtonianus or the Freer Gospels) Gospels; 5th c.
X	(Monacensis) Gospels; 10th c.
Z	(Dublinensis) Matthew; 6th c.
Γ	(036) Gospels; 10th c.
Δ	(037) Gospels; 9th c.
Θ	(038) Gospels; 9th c.
Ξ	(040) Luke; 6th c.
Π	(041) Gospels; 9th c.
Σ	(042) Matthew, Mark; 6th c.
Φ	(043) Matthew, Mark; 6th c.
Ψ	(044) Gospels, Acts, Paul's Epistles; 9th c.
048	Acts, Paul's Epistles, General Epistles; 5th c.
059	Mark 15; 4th–5th c.
067	Matt 14, 24–26; Mark 9, 14; 6th c.
083	(with 0112) Mark 13–16; John 1, 2–4; 6th–7th c.
087	Matt 1–2, 19, 21; Mark 12; John 18; 6th c.
099	Mark 16; 7th c.
0102	Matt 21–24; Luke 3–4, 21; 7th c.
0126	Mark 5–6; 8th c.
0130	Mark 1–2; Luke 1, 2; 9th c.
0131	Mark 7–9; 9th c.
0132	Mark 5; 9th c.
0167	Mark 4, 6; 7th c.
0171	Matt 10; Luke 22; ca. 300
0187	Mark 6; 6th c.
0189	Acts 5; ca. 200
0250	Gospels; 8th c.
0266	Luke 20; 6th c.
0274	Mark 6–10; 5th c.
0278	Paul's Epistles; 9th c.

MINUSCULES

These are written in lowercase cursive script, usually on vellum or parchment.

1	Gospels, Acts, Paul's Epistles; 12th c.
20	Gospels; 11th c.
22	Gospels; 12th c.

28	Gospels; 11th c.
33	All NT except Rev; 9th c.
81	Acts, Paul's Epistles 1044
137	Gospels; 11th c.
138	Gospels; 11th c.
209	All NT; 14th–15th c.
225	Gospels; 1192
274	Gospels; 10th c.
304	Gospels; 12th c.
435	Gospels; 12th–13th c.
565	Gospels; 9th c.
579	Gospels; 13th c.
700	Gospels; 11th c.
892	Gospels; 9th c.
954	Gospels; 15th c.
983	Gospels; 12th c.
1216	Gospels; 11th c.
1241	Gospels, Acts, Paul's Epistles; 12th c.
1424	(or Family 1424—a group of 29 manuscripts sharing nearly the same text) most of NT; 9th–10th c.
1582	Gospels; 949
1739	Acts, Paul's Epistles; 10th c.
2053	Rev; 13th c.
2344	Rev; 11th c.
f^1	(a family of manuscripts including 1, 118, 131, 209) Gospels; 12th–14th c.
f^{13}	(a family of manuscripts including 13, 69, 124, 174, 230, 346, 543, 788, 826, 828, 983, 1689, 1709—known as the Ferrar group) Gospels; 11th–15th c.
Maj	The Majority Text; that is, a group consisting of thousands of minuscules which display a similar text. In the commentary, a few minuscules from this group are occasionally cited on their own: 1110, 1215, 1217, and 1221.
Maj^A	This siglum only occurs in Revelation and indicates a large group of manuscripts which contain a commentary on Revelation by Andreas of Caesarea.
Maj^K	This siglum also occurs only in Revelation and indicates the large group of manuscripts which do not contain Andreas's commentary.

ANCIENT VERSIONS

Syriac (syr)

syr^c	(Syriac Curetonianus) Gospels; 5th c.
syr^h	(Syriac Harclean) All NT; 616
syr^{h**}	This siglum denotes a reading in syr^h that is set off by asterisks, indicating some question about its originality.
syr^{hmg}	This siglum denotes a reading from the margin of syr^h.
syr^p	(Peshitta) All NT except Revelation and shorter General Epistles; 4th–5th c.
syr^{pal}	(Palestinian Syriac) Gospels; 5th–6th c.
syr^s	(Syriac Sinaiticus) Gospels; 4th c.

Old Latin (it)

it^a	(Vercellenis) Gospels; 4th c.
it^{aur}	(Aureus) Gospels; 7th c.
it^b	(Veronensis) Gospels; 5th c.

it^{d}	(Cantabrigiensis—the Latin text of Bezae) Gospels, Acts, 3 John; 5th c.
it^{e}	(Palatinus) Gospels; 5th c.
it^{f}	(Brixianus) Gospels; 6th c.
it^{ff2}	(Corbeiensis II) Gospels; 5th c.
it^{g1}	(Sangermanensis) Matthew; 8th–9th c.
it^{gig}	(Gigas) Gospels; Acts; 13th c.
it^{h}	(Fleury palimpset) Matt 3–14, 18–28; Acts; Revelation; Peter's Epistles; 1 John; 5th c.
it^{i}	(Vindobonensis) Mark 2–15; Luke 10–23; 5th c.
it^{k}	(Bobbiensis) Matthew, Mark; ca. 400
it^{l}	(Rehdigeranus) Gospels; Acts 8–11, 15; James; 1 Peter; John's Epistles; 8th c.
it^{q}	(Monacensis) Gospels; 6th–7th c.
it^{r}	(Usserianus) Gospels, Paul's Epistles, Peter's Epistles, 1 John; 7th c.
it^{w}	(Wernigerodensis) Acts; 14th–15th c.; Peter's Epistles; 1 John; 6th c.

Vulgate

The following sigla represent the major editions of the Vulgate.

vg^{cl}	(Clementine) *Biblia Sacra Vulgatae Editionis Sixti Quinti Pont. Max. iussu recognita atque edita;* 1592
vgst	(Stuttgart) *Biblia sacra iuxta Vulgatam versionem;* 1969
vg^{ww}	(Wordsworth and White) *Novum Testamentum Domini nostri Iesu Christi latine secundum editionem Sancti Hieronymi;* 1889–1954
lat	Indicates a reading supported by the Vulgate and some of the Old Latin mss.

Coptic

The Coptic translations of the New Testament date from the 3rd century onward.

cop^{ach}	(Akhmimic) John; James; 4th c.
cop^{ach2}	(Subakhmimic) John; 4th c.
cop^{bo}	(Bohairic = north Egypt) All NT; 9th c.
cop^{fay}	(Fayyumic = central Egypt) John; 4th–5th c.
cop^{G67}	(a Middle Egyptian ms) Acts; 5th c.
cop^{mae}	(Middle Egyptian) Matthew; 4th–5th c.
cop^{sa}	(Sahidic = southern Egypt) All NT; 4th–5th c.

Armenian

arm — All NT; 12th c.

Ethiopic

eth — All NT; 14th c.

Georgian

geo — All NT; 11th c.

Slavonic

slav — All NT; 10th–12th c.

Other text-critical sigla

B^{vid}	A superscript *vid* (short for Latin *videtur,* "it seems so") indicates that the reading appears to be in the witness, but a lacuna or other damage to the ms makes it somewhat uncertain.
B^{*,c,1,2}	A superscript *c* or numbers designate corrections made in the manuscript. An asterisk designates the original, pre-corrected reading.
892^{mg}	A superscript *mg* indicates that the reading is found in the margin of the

manuscript. These readings could represent corrections or alternative readings suggested by the scribe.

892[txt]	A superscript *txt* indicates that the reading is found in the text, as opposed to the margin.
v.r.	A *variant reading* listed in a manuscript.
33[s]	A superscript *s* indicates that the reading is found in a supplement—a later addition to the manuscript.
2053[com]	A superscript *com* indicates that the reading appears in a commentary by the Church Fathers.
pc	This abbreviation of Latin *pauci* shows that the reading is found in a few manuscripts which depart from the reading in the Majority Text.

Ancient Authors

The following abbreviations are used for ancient works.

1 Apol.	Justin Martyr, *First Apology*
1 Clem.	*1 Clement*
Ann.	Tacitus, *Annals*
Ant.	Josephus, *Jewish Antiquities*
b. Ber.	Babylonian tractate *Berakot*
Bacch.	Euripides, *Bacchanals*
Cels.	Origen, *Against Celsus*
Claud.	Suetonius, *Claudius*
Comm. Jo.	Origen, *Commentary on John*
Comm. Matt.	Origen, *Commentary on Matthew*
Comm. Rom.	Origen, *Commentary on Romans*
Cons.	Augustine, *De consensus evangelistarum* (*Harmony of the Gospels*)
Dial.	Justin Martyr, *Dialogue with Trypho*
Dial.	Pseudo-Athanasius, *Dialogue with Zaccheus*
Did.	*Didache*
Epist.	Jerome, *Epistulae*
Fel.	Augustine, *Against Felix*
Geogr.	Ptolemy, *Geography*
Gos. Pet.	*Gospel of Peter*
Haer.	Irenaeus, *Against Heresies*
Hist. eccl.	Eusebius, *Ecclesiastical History*
J.W.	Josephus, *Jewish War*
Life	Josephus, *The Life*
LXX	Septuagint
Marc.	Tertullian, *Against Marcion*
Onom.	Eusebius, *Onomasticon*
Or. Bas.	Gregory of Nazianzus, *Oratio in laudem Basilii*
Pan.	Epiphanius, *Panarion* (*Refutation of all Heresies*)
Phaen.	Aratus, *Phaenomena*
Prom.	Aeschylus, *Prometheus Bound*
Pyth.	Pindar, *Pythian Odes*
Quaest. Mar.	Eusebius, *Quaestiones ad Marinum*
Tg. Ps.-J.	*Targum Pseudo-Jonathan*

Modern Works

The following abbreviations are used for modern reference works:

BDAG — Bauer, W., F. W. Danker, W. F. Arndt, and F. W. Gingrich. *Greek-English Lexicon of the New Testament and Other Early Christian Literature*. 3rd ed. Chicago: University of Chicago Press, 2000.

DJG — Green, J. B. and S. McKnight. *Dictionary of Jesus and the Gospels*. Downers Grove: InterVarsity Press, 1992.

ISBE — Bromiley, G. W. *International Standard Bible Encyclopedia*. 4 vols. Grand Rapids: Eerdmans, 1979–1988.

LSJ — Liddell, Henry G., Robert Scott, and Henry Jones. *A Greek-English Lexicon*. Revised ed. with supplement. Oxford: Clarendon, 1968.

MM — Moulton, J. H., and G. Milligan. *The Vocabulary of the Greek Testament*. Peabody, MA: Hendrickson, 1997.

NIDCC — Douglas, J. D. *New International Dictionary of the Christian Church*. Grand Rapids: Zondervan, 1974.

P.Oxy. — Egyptian Exploration Society, *The Oxyrhynchus Papyri*. 71 vols. London, 1898–2007.

PL — Patrologia latina. Edited by J.-P. Migne. 217 vols. Paris, 1844–1864.

Syntax — Turner, Nigel. *Syntax*. Vol. 3 of *A Grammar of New Testament Greek*. Edited by James Hope Moulton. Edinburgh: T&T Clark, 1978.

TCGNT — Metzger, Bruce. *A Textual Commentary on the Greek New Testament*. 2nd ed. New York: United Bible Societies, 1994.

Text of Earliest MSS — Comfort, Philip W., and David P. Barrett. *The Text of the Earliest New Testament Greek Manuscripts*. Carol Stream: Tyndale House Publishers, 2001.

5. How to Use the Commentary

The sigla TR, WH, and NU are used throughout to show which variant reading is found in a particular edition: NU = Nestle-Aland and United Bible Societies' Greek text; WH = Westcott and Hort; TR = Textus Receptus. For each variant-unit where there is significant textual variation (and influence on English versions), the NU reading is listed first (in Greek words fully accented, with an English translation), followed by manuscript support and English version selection. The NU reading is always cited first for the sake of consistency and because this is the standard text used worldwide. Its primary position does not necessarily mean that I think it always preserves the original text; in fact, I disagree in many instances—as do many other textual critics and translators. This is made clear in the notes. (appendix D provides a complete index to all such notes.)

Frequently, the NU reading is the same as WH; less frequently, the same as TR. If both WH and NU have the same reading, it is listed as WH NU. If all three have the same readings, it is listed TR WH NU. (Parentheses are used to indicate that the particular Greek edition supports a given reading but may have a slight difference in wording.) After the citation of the NU reading, there follows each variant reading in Greek (not accented, as in the critical apparatus of NA^{27}), with notation of which Greek edition (if any) follows that reading. Each variant reading is followed by manuscript support and English versions. Then the commentary follows.

Other variant units, which have not had noticeable impact on English versions, are not formulated in the same way. These are simply discussed in paragraph format. Notes on the Western text (otherwise known as the D-text) in the commentary on Acts have a special format, which is explained in the introduction to Acts.

My intention in this work is to analyze all textual variants that affect meaning, particularly those that have impacted major English translations. There are other significant textual variants that have not affected translations but are important to exegesis. As such, many of the variants listed in the textual apparatus of NA^{27} will be covered, but not all. The obvious exclusions are as follows:

1. Word transpositions where meaning is not affected.
2. Addition or deletion of articles, unless the variant clearly alters meaning.
3. Addition or deletion of conjunctions, unless the variant clearly alters meaning.
4. Conjectural readings (marked *cj* in the critical apparatus of NA^{27}).
5. Spelling variants of proper nouns, unless the spelling affects meaning or has etymological significance.
6. Stylistic variants (for example, ουχ versus ουκ).
7. Addition or deletion of possessive pronoun after articular nouns, where the article itself could indicate possession (for example, την σαρκαν versus την σαρκαν αυτου, when both mean "his flesh").
8. Variants which change two verbs joined by και into one verb plus a participle—or conversely, one verb plus a participle made into two verbs joined by και (see John 13:12).
9. Variants involving changes in tense for the same verb, which do not significantly alter the meaning of the text.
10. Variants involving true synonyms, especially for verbs such as φημι and λεγω.
11. Variants with support from only one witness (i.e., singular variants) will not be covered, unless that reading is early or extremely interesting. The same generally holds true for variants that have no support from any Greek witnesses—only from the ancient versions. However, some of these are discussed because of their historical value.

The reader will notice three other features in the notes: (1) I have used my own English translation of the Greek because it is often necessary to be very literal and/or to add material [in brackets] for clarity. (2) I have cited many but not all of the witnesses in support of various readings. I have included ancient versions and the church fathers only when it was clear that their testimony was significant. (3) I have added many technical "notes" after the textual evidence. These are important because they provide firsthand observations about certain readings in various manuscripts. Notes on readings in the early New Testament papyri will often refer readers to a more detailed analysis in a work entitled *The Text of the Earliest New Testament Greek Manuscripts* (Comfort and Barrett), abbreviated as *Text of Earliest MSS*.

Finally, I would be remiss if I did not mention how frequently I consulted *The Textual Commentary on the Greek New Testament* (abbreviated as TCGNT), written by Bruce Metzger. This work (in two editions: 1975 and 1994) is an excellent companion to the United Bible Societies' *Greek New Testament* (third edition and fourth edition) because it sets forth the reasons that led the committee (for whom Metzger was the spokesperson) to "adopt certain variant readings for inclusion in the text and to relegate certain other readings to the apparatus." Thus, Metzger's work provides a report of how the committee evaluated and resolved the problems concerning the 1,440 sets of variant readings supplied in the critical apparatus of the Bible Societies' edition.

6. Glossary

Akhmimic A dialect of Coptic once spoken in Akhmim (ancient Panopolis) in Upper Egypt.

anacoluthon A rhetorical device that can be loosely defined as a change of syntax within a sentence. More specifically, anacoluthons (or "anacoluthia") are created when a sentence abruptly changes from one structure to another.

anarthrous An adjective or noun which is not determined by an article.

arthrous An adjective or noun determined by an article.

Bohairic A dialect of Coptic once spoken around Memphis in the Nile Delta; currently a liturgical language for Coptic Christians.

codex/codices An ancient form of a book produced by sewing together sheets of papyrus or vellum (animal skins). The codex replaced the scroll in the early Christian community as the format in which to copy the Scriptures.

conflation The scribal technique of resolving a discrepancy between two or more readings by including all of them.

conjectural emendation The text-critical technique of making an educated guess as to what the original text might have been, without any direct manuscript evidence.

Coptic A language spoken in ancient Egypt.

critical edition An edition of an ancient text that is based on a collation of variant readings and that includes editorial decisions about which readings are most likely original.

D-text The text present in Codex Bezae (D) and related manuscripts.

diglot A manuscript which presents a text in two languages at once.

diorthotes A scribe in a scriptorium who proofread and corrected manuscripts.

diple A single chevron (>) mark made by a scribe in a manuscript; it indicated that the marked text needed to be checked for accuracy.

dittography The accidental, erroneous act of repeating a word, phrase or combination of letters by a scribe or copyist.

editio princeps The first published transcription of an ancient text.

exegesis Study of a text in order to understand its full meaning.

exemplar A manuscript that is being copied, or the parent manuscript against which another manuscript is corrected.

extant A manuscript or reading that exists and is known today.

external evidence Evidence for a given reading based on extant manuscripts.

folio A leaf (sheet of paper, parchment, or papyrus) in a codex.

gap-filling The addition of words to a text by a scribe who perceived a narrative gap (see appendix A).

gematria The interpretation of words and names based on the numerical values of their letters.

gloss A note made in the margins or between the lines of a book, in which the meaning of the text in its original language is explained, sometimes in another language. Sometimes they were included by later copyists as part of the biblical text itself.

hapax legomenon A word that occurs only one time in a corpus.

haplography The act of writing once what should be written twice (e.g., "endodontics" becomes "endontics").

harmonization The process of changing a text in one Bible passage to make it match the wording in another passage; this frequently occurs in the Gospels.

hendiadys Literally, "one through two", the use of two nouns to describe a single object, such as "sound and fury" for "furious sound"; it is a common Greek construction.

homoeoarchton Literally, "the same beginning"; it is often the cause of omissions in textual transmission, as the eye loses its place in the exemplar and picks up the same sequence of letters at another place.

homoeoteleuton Literally, "the same ending"; it is often the cause of omissions in textual transmission, as the eye loses its place in the exemplar and picks up the same sequence of letters at another place.

incipit The first few words of a manuscript, which were often used as a title (e.g., the Hebrew Bible uses "In the wilderness" as the title for the book of Numbers).

internal evidence Evidence for a given reading based on how that reading and other variants most likely developed.

interpolation An entry or passage in a text that was not written by the original author.

lacuna/lacunae Gaps in the text created by missing fragments in a manuscript.

lectionary A collection or arrangement of Scripture readings used in Christian liturgies.

local-genealogical method A method of textual criticism in which decisions are made on a case-by-case basis, taking into account all available external and internal evidence for the possible variant readings.

Majority Text Readings from the majority of manuscripts, representing the Byzantine text-type.

majuscules Capital letters used in manuscript copying.

manuscript A copy of the ancient text in the language in which it was written.

minuscules Manuscripts written in lowercase cursive script.

nomen sacrum/nomina sacra A "sacred name" that is typically distinguished in ancient manuscripts by contraction (abbreviation) and an overbar.

obelus/obeli A mark in Greek manuscripts which signifies that a correction needs to be made, or that a particular reading is spurious.

opisthograph A scroll with writing on both the front and back.

overbar A horizontal line written over a contraction (abbreviation) in an ancient manuscript.

palimpsest A vellum or parchment manuscript whose original writing was scraped off and replaced with a newer text; very often the older text is more valuable as an ancient witness.

papyrology The study of ancient papyrus manuscripts.

papyrus A writing surface prepared from strips of papyrus reed pounded together to make a flat surface.

parablepsis The skipping of a copyist's eye from one place in the text to another; it is the cause of many transcriptional errors.

parchment A writing surface prepared from animal skins that have had the hair removed and been rubbed smooth.

partitive genitive The use of the genitive case to indicate what the main noun is part of. For example, in the expression "firstborn of the dead," the phrase "the dead" is marked by "of" to show that the firstborn is part of the body of dead people.

proto-Alexandrian A New Testament manuscript which predates the Alexandrian manuscripts but appears to have been used in making those manuscripts.

quire A group of four sheets in a codex that are folded together.

recension The intentional creation of an authoritative edition of a text.

recto This does *not* indicate the right-hand page, as with modern publishing. Instead, it refers to the side of the papyrus sheet with the grains running horizontally, meant to be read first.

Sahidic The predominant dialect of Coptic in pre-Islamic Egypt.

scribes Men and women trained to make new copies of earlier manuscripts.

scriptio continua Text written continuously with no space between words, a practice exhibited in all early Greek manuscripts.

scriptoral practices The methods and practices of a particular scribe or group (school) of scribes.

scriptorium A room or building (usually attached to a library) set apart for scribes to do their work of copying.

Septuagint A translation of the Old Testament into Greek, made in the third century B.C. and widely used in the early church (abbreviated as LXX).

siglum/sigla A symbol which represents the testimony of an ancient witness or witnesses to a given reading.

singular reading A textual variant that occurs in only a single manuscript.

stemma A genealogical reconstruction of the manuscript tradition; a "family tree" of manuscripts.

stichoi Notations at the end of a manuscript section recording how many lines were copied; they were a means of determining how much the scribe should be paid.

text-type A family of manuscripts that share largely the same text. Usually described in geographic terms, e.g., the Byzantine text-type is typical of manuscripts copied in Byzantium.

textual critic A person who studies manuscripts and their transmission and makes decisions about which reading among the variants is most likely original.

textual transmission The process of manually transmitting a written text from copy to copy.

Textus Receptus The "received text," an edition of the Greek New Testament on which the King James Version was based.

transposition A scribal error in which two letters are accidentally reversed.

variant readings The different readings for a section of text as they appear various witnesses.

variant-unit A place of disagreement among the witnesses to a text, where the various readings must be compared and evaluated.

versions Translations of ancient texts into other languages.

verso This does *not* indicate the left-hand page, as with modern publishing. Instead, it refers to the side of the papyrus sheet with the grains running vertically, meant to be read second.

Vulgate The translation of the Hebrew and Greek Scriptures into common Latin by Jerome (ca. 400).

Gospel according to MATTHEW

Inscription (Title)

WH NU	κατα μαθθαιον "According to Matthew" א B (NIV TNIV NLT NET)
variant 1	ευαγγελιον κατα μαθθαιον "Gospel according to Matthew" Paris Papyrus D W f[13] 33 Maj NKJV RSV NRSV ESV NASB NEB REB NJB NAB HCSB
variant 2/(TR)	αγιον ευαγγελιον κατα μαθθαιον "Holy Gospel according to Matthew" M f[1] (KJV)
variant 3	untitled 𝔓[1] none

In its original composition, the first verse of Matthew's gospel functioned as the title or incipit. Therefore, variant 3 accurately reflects the absence of a separate title in the original text. 𝔓[1] displays the very first page of Matthew's gospel with the upper margin almost completely intact (on the verso). The only writing that shows is the letter α, the mark for page 1; there is no title. On the recto, a later scribe (in an entirely different hand) may have added a titular descriptor for the Gospel (only three incomplete words are extant).

Variant 1 represents the first stage in giving inscriptions to the Gospels. Each gospel was titled separately because each gospel often was a book by itself (see comments on the title to John). Such titles were often expanded, as in TR. The WH NU reading reflects the second stage in titling the Gospels, a stage when all four gospels were placed together in one codex and were titled under one head: The Gospel—According to Matthew, According to Mark, According to Luke, According to John. This titling was mostly influenced by Codex Vaticanus, which has κατα μαθθαιον, κατα μαρκον, κατα λουκαν, κατα ιωαννην written for both the inscription and subscription in each gospel. Codex Sinaiticus has the same titling for the inscription, but in the subscription for Mark, Luke, and John, the word ευαγγελιον ("Gospel") comes first (see comments on Matthew's subscription). This reflects the fact that each gospel was titled separately in the earlier history of textual transmission.

Matthew 1:3

The two earliest extant manuscripts (𝔓[1] B) read Ζαρε ("Zare") instead of Ζαρα ("Zara"), found in all other manuscripts.

Matthew 1:6

In later manuscripts (C L W Maj) ο βασιλευς ("the king") is added to the second mention of "David." According to the earliest manuscripts (𝔓[1] ℵ B), τον βασιλεα ("the king") appears only in the first mention of David in this verse.

Matthew 1:7-8

WH NU — Ἀσάφ. [8] Ἀσάφ
"Asaph. [8] Asaph"
𝔓[1] ℵ B C (D) f[1,13] it cop
NKJVmg RSVmg NRSV ESV NJBmg NAB NLT HCSB NETmg

variant/TR — Ασα. [8] Ασα
"Asa. [8] Asa"
L W 33 Maj
KJV NKJV RSV NRSVmg ESVmg NASB NIV TNIV NEB REB NJB HCSBmg NET

A small fragment of 𝔓[1], which showed the second occurrence of the name "Asaph," was lost shortly after the manuscript's discovery. Fortunately, the original photograph of the manuscript shows this portion. The reading that appears in the variant is the orthographically "correct" spelling because Abijah was the father of Asa, according to 1 Chr 3:10-11. However, the documentary evidence strongly supports the "incorrect" spelling. Apparently, Matthew wrote Ασαφ, following a spelling he copied from a genealogical record other than that found in most copies of the Septuagint (which read Ασα). Later, scribes changed it to "Asa," probably because they did not want readers to think this king was the psalmist "Asaph" (see Pss 50, 73–83).

Matthew 1:10

WH NU — Ἀμώς. Ἀμώς
"Amos. Amos"
ℵ B C (D) f[1]
NKJVmg RSV NRSV ESV NJBmg NAB NLT HCSB NETmg

variant/TR — Αμων. Αμων
"Amon. Amon"
L W f[13] Maj
KJV NKJV RSVmg NRSVmg ESVmg NASB NIV TNIV NEB REB NJB NET

The same kind of spelling variant occurred in this verse as in Matt 1:7-8. The "correct" spelling is Αμων ("Amon"), king of Judah, according to 1 Chr 3:14. However, several Greek witnesses of 2 Kgs 21:18-25 and 2 Chr 33:20-25 read Αμως ("Amos"), an incorrect spelling. Because of superior external testimony, we have to assume that the original text of Matthew also read Αμος ("Amos").

Matthew 1:11

Several late manuscripts (M Θ f[1] 33 syr[h], the last of which uses markings to indicate the insertion is not original) add another person to the genealogy—namely, Joakim (Ιωακιμ)—in between Josiah and Jeconiah. This was an attempt to harmonize Matthew's account to 1 Chr 3:15-16. But Matthew's record is not an attempt to reproduce an entire father-to-son lineage; certain individuals were omitted, Joakim being one of them.

Matthew 1:16

TR WH NU	Ἰωσὴφ τὸν ἄνδρα Μαρίας, ἐξ ἧς ἐγεννήθη Ἰησοῦς ὁ λεγόμενος Χριστός "Joseph the husband of Mary, of whom was born Jesus who is called Christ" 𝔓[1] א B C L W (f[1]) 33 syr[p,h] Maj all
variant 1	Ιωσηφ τον ω μηνστευθεισα παρθενος Μαριαμ εγγενησεν Ιησουν τον λεγομενον Χριστον "Joseph, to whom was betrothed Mary, a virgin, who gave birth to Jesus who is called Christ" Θ f[13] it NEBmg NJBmg
variant 2	"Joseph, to whom was betrothed the virgin Mary who [feminine] bore Jesus the Christ" syr[c] none
variant 3	"Joseph, to whom Mary a virgin was betrothed, was the father of Jesus who is called Christ" syr[s] NEBmg NJBmg (see also MOFFATT)

Variant 2 is a paraphrase of variant 1, and both represent attempts by later scribes to emphasize Mary's virginity and thereby affirm the virgin birth. Variant 3, however, presents a completely different reading. The NJBmg says that the Sinaitic Syriac (syr[s]) reading must have arisen as a result of a misunderstanding of the first variant. But that is not correct, because in 1:25 syr[s] has the textual change, "she [Mary] bore to him [Joseph] a son," instead of "she bore a son." This shows an intentional change. Therefore, the reading of syr[s] in 1:18 makes Jesus the son of Joseph, not the son of Mary. This is not a bald denial of the virgin birth, although it could look that way at first glance; rather, it appears to be an attempt to make Joseph the legal father of Jesus, not his biological father (Brown 1977, 62-64).

Although various scholars have attempted to show that other historical documents concur with the third variant, Metzger (TCGNT) has sufficiently countered such attempts. This reading has no documentary support from any Greek witnesses and contradicts the intent of the passage, which is to show that Jesus' birth is directly connected with Mary, not Joseph. Therefore, the TR WH NU reading, supported by the early papyrus 𝔓[1] and other important witnesses (א B C W), is to be accepted as original.

Matthew 1:18

TR WH NU	τοῦ δὲ Ἰησοῦ Χριστοῦ ἡ γένεσις "the birth of [the] Jesus Christ" 𝔓1 א C (L) Z (f1,13 33) KJV NKJV RSV NRSV ESV NASB NIV TNIV REB NJB NAB NLT HCSB NET
variant 1	"the birth of the Christ" it syrc,s RSVmg ESVmg NEB
variant 2	του δε Χριστου Ιησου η γενεσις "the birth of the Christ Jesus" B none
variant 3	του δε Ιησου η γενεσις "the birth of [the] Jesus" W none

The Greek expression of the TR WH NU reading is difficult because it literally means "the birth of the Jesus Christ." The definite article before the title "Jesus Christ" does not appear in any other place in the NT except in inferior manuscripts in Acts 8:37; 1 John 4:3; and Rev 12:17 (Westcott and Hort 1882, 7). This would give copyists cause to make the changes as noted above.

Variant 1 is a natural translation modification, variant 2 reflects Pauline usage, and variant 3 is a simplification. Since the best evidence supports the TR WH NU reading, we should take it as is and attempt to understand the function of the article as being referential. In other words, the author is saying, "the birth of the Jesus just mentioned [1:16], the one who is the Messiah, was as follows."

Several manuscripts (L f13 Maj) read γεννησις instead of γενεσις (in 𝔓1 א B C W Z). Both words can be translated "birth," but the variant γεννησις is an attempt to link Jesus' birth with the verb used throughout the preceding genealogy, γενναω.

Matthew 1:22

One scribe (D) and several ancient translators (it syrs copsa) added "Isaiah" before "the prophet" so as to specify the prophet that Matthew was quoting.

Matthew 1:23

Instead of the reading, και καλεσουσιν το ονομα αυτου Εμμανουηλ ("and they will call his name Emmanuel"), supported by א B 071, some other witnesses read και καλεσεις το ονομα αυτου Εμμανουηλ ("and you will call his name Emmanuel")—so D copbo Origen Eusebius. The variant reflects scribal conformity of this verse to 1:21 or Isa 7:14 (LXX). In the Matthew passage, "you" refers to Joseph; in the Isaiah passage, "you" refers to Ahaz. The writer of this gospel adapted the OT quotation to a broader scope of participation—all who recognize Jesus as the Messiah will call him "Emmanuel," God with us.

Matthew 1:25

WH NU ἔτεκεν υἱόν
"she gave birth to a son"
ℵ B Z[vid] 071[vid] f[1,13] 33
NKJVmg RSV NRSV ESV NASB NIV TNIV NEB REB NJB NAB NLT HCSB NET

variant/TR ετεκεν τον υιον αυτης τον πρωτοτοκον
"she gave birth to her firstborn son"
C D L W 087 Maj
KJV NKJV NRSVmg HCSBmg

Since the word "firstborn" could imply that other offspring followed, it could be argued that "firstborn" was dropped from the original by scribes who wanted to support the view of Mary's perpetual virginity. However, if this were the case, we would expect to see, in the same manuscripts, the same deletion in Luke 2:7 (the parallel passage), but we do not. Thus, it is far more likely that the variant reading in 1:25 reflects scribal conformity to Luke 2:7, which has "firstborn" in every manuscript except W. TR (followed by KJV and NKJV) reflects this harmonization.

Matthew 2:5

One thirteenth-century Greek manuscript (4) and a few ancient versions (syr[h] cop[bo]) add "Micah" before "the prophet." Although this is correct (the quotation comes from Mic 5:2), Matthew chose not to identify the specific prophet. One scribe (it[a]) mistakenly attributed the quote to Isaiah, the most popular prophet to be quoted in the NT.

Matthew 2:18

WH NU κλαυθμὸς καὶ ὀδυρμὸς πολύς
"weeping and great mourning"
ℵ B Z 0250 f[1]
RSV NRSV ESV NASB NIV TNIV NEB REB NJB NAB NLT HCSB NET

variant/TR θρηνος και κλαυθμος και οδυρμος πολυς
"lamentation and weeping and great mourning"
C D L W 0233 f[13] 33 Maj
KJV NKJV HCSBmg NETmg

Because Matthew's rendition of Jer 31:15 (38:15 in the LXX) differs significantly from the Septuagint, various scribes wanted to conform Matthew's rendition to the Septuagint. One way to do this was to add θρηνος και ("weeping and"). Such alterations were common in the fourth century (and thereafter), when scribes tended to produce a standardized text by harmonizing OT quotations in the NT with the Greek OT.

Matthew 3:3

One ancient version (syr[s]) omits the first and third clauses of the Isa 40:3 citation, leaving only, "Prepare the way of [the] Lord." Another ancient Old Latin version (it[k]) omits the third clause.

Matthew 3:7

TR NU — ἐρχομένους ἐπὶ τὸ βάπτισμα αὐτοῦ
"they were coming to his baptism"
א[1] C D L W 0233 f[1,13] 33 Maj it syr cop[bo]
KJV NKJV (NIV) TNIV NAB HCSB NET

variant/WH — ερχομενους επι το βαπτισμα
"they were coming to the baptism"
א* B cop[sa] Origen
RSV NRSV ESV NASB NEB REB NJB NLT

The variant has the earliest support and likely represents Matthew's original thought—that the religious leaders were coming to observe the baptism John was doing. (It is possible but not likely that this reading means they were coming to be baptized, for that would be more naturally expressed by ερχομενους εις το βαπτισμα.) The TR NU reading probably reflects a late addition, intended to distinguish John's baptism from Christian baptism. Most modern versions follow the variant, while the modern NU text uncharacteristically supports the KJV and NKJV.

Matthew 3:11a

𝔓[101] has the reading ο δε ερχομενος ισχυροτερος μου εστιν ("the coming one is greater than I") as opposed to ο δε οπισω μου ερχομενος ισχυροτερος μου εστιν ("the one coming after me is greater than I"). 𝔓[101] is the only Greek manuscript that supports this reading. It is also found in two Old Latin manuscripts (it[a,d]) and some Coptic manuscripts.

Matthew 3:11b

TR WH NU — βαπτίσει ἐν πνεύματι ἁγίῳ καὶ πυρί
"he will baptize in the Holy Spirit and fire"
א B C L W
all

variant — βαπτισει εν πνευματι αγιω
"he will baptize in the Holy Spirit"
Maj
NKJVmg

The omission might be a scribal attempt to simplify a difficult statement (how would Jesus baptize *in fire*?). The expression is probably a hendiadys (one thought expressed by two words); in other words, the baptism in the Holy Spirit is a fire baptism, a baptism that brings purification (see Zech 13:9; Mal 3:2).

Matthew 3:15-16

In between these verses, two Old Latin manuscripts (it[a,g1]) add, "and when he was baptized a great light shone from the water so that all who were gathered were frightened." F. F. Bruce (1989, 127-128) notes that this addition is present in Tatian's Diatessaron. A similar statement, according to Epiphanius (*Pan.* 30.13.7-8), appears in the *Gospel of the Ebionites:* "And immediately a great light shone round about that place." These additions, though colorful, likely do not go back to Matthew's original text. In fact, none of the gospels speaks of the presence of light at Jesus' baptism.

Matthew 3:16

TR NU	ἠνεῴχθησαν [αὐτῷ] οἱ οὐρανοι "the heavens were opened to him" א[1] C D[s] L W 0233 f[1,13] Maj KJV NKJV RSVmg NRSV ESV NJBmg NAB NLTmg HCSB NETmg
variant/WH	ηνεωχθησαν οι ουρανοι "the heavens were opened" א* B syr[c,s] cop[sa] Irenaeus—according to P.Oxy. 405[vid] RSV ESVmg NASB NIV TNIV NEB REB NJB NLT HCSBmg NET

The earliest extant manuscript that preserves Matthew's record of Jesus' baptism is P.Oxy. 405, which preserves a portion of Irenaeus's *Against Heresies* 3.9, in which Matt 3:16-17 is quoted. According to Grenfell and Hunt (1903, 10-11), this manuscript should be dated in the late second century. If so, this manuscript represents an early copy of Irenaeus's original work, which was produced around A.D. 150–175. The account of Jesus' baptism, as recorded in Matt 3:16-17, is repeated in the course of Irenaeus's argument. Matthew's text is designated with a diple (>) at the beginning of each line of the quotation. In standard scriptorial practice, a diple indicated that the wording needed fixing or, at least, checking. A careful transcriptional reconstruction reveals that this manuscript most likely concurs with א* and B. This early manuscript support affirms the WH reading as well as the decision of most modern English translators to go with the shorter text.

The TR NU reading portrays the opening of the heavens as a private experience. However, since the manuscript support for the omission of αυτω ("to him") is strong, it is likely that a later scribe added αυτω in an attempt to harmonize this part of the verse to 16b, which states that Jesus (not the crowd gathered there) saw the Spirit of God descending upon him. It is also possible that scribes harmonized Matthew to Mark, who portrays the baptism as Jesus' private experience (Jesus sees the heavens opened and hears the heavenly voice). But the whole tenor of Matthew's account implies a public unveiling. Indeed, the last statement of the pericope is God's public proclamation: "This is my beloved Son, in whom I am well pleased," as opposed to the private affirmation, "You are my beloved Son, in whom I am well pleased" (an inferior reading, see note on 3:17).

Matthew 3:17

TR WH NU unanimously agree that the voice out of heaven says ουτος εστιν ο υιος μου ο αγαπητος, εν ω ευδοκησα ("This is my beloved Son in whom I am well pleased"). This reading, which is followed by all English versions, has excellent manuscript support: 𝔓[101] א B C Irenaeus (according to P.Oxy. 405[vid]) Maj. A Western reading begins the quote by saying συ ει ο υιος μου ("you are my beloved Son in whom I am well pleased")—so D it[a] syr[c,s]. This variant is an attempt (1) to conform Matthew's account to Mark and Luke, which both have God the Father speaking directly to his Son (see Mark 1:11; Luke 3:22), and (2) to make the scene at Jesus' baptism a personal epiphany for Jesus. The scribe of D (followed by other Western witnesses) seems to have had an adoptionist view of Jesus' baptism—that is, the baptism was the time that Jesus was filled with God's Spirit and thereby was made God's Son (see note on Luke 3:22, where D's adoptionist tendencies are most apparent).

But the point of Matthew's account is to emphasize the Father's open affirmation of his love for his Son and his commissioning him to begin his ministry. No one else on earth shared this relationship and commission. By this announcement, reminiscent of Ps 2:7 and Isa 42:1, God was publicly declaring Jesus to be both the Messiah and Suffering Servant (Morris 1992, 67-68). This heavenly, divine proclamation came not for Jesus' sake but for the sake of the bystanders, including John the Baptist (see John 1:32-34). Elsewhere in the Gospels, the heavenly voice proclaims the Father's love and selection of his Son for the sake of those standing by (see, for example, the transfiguration account, Matt 17:5; Mark 9:7; Luke 9:35). In John 12:28-30, Jesus explicitly states that the Father spoke from heaven for the sake of the people, not for his sake. The people (who had come from all around Judea, 3:5) needed to hear the Father's love and commissioning of Jesus because Jesus was about to begin his public ministry. In light of Matthew's perspective on this, we can see why 3:16 was also not originally written as a private experience (see note on 3:16).

Matthew 4:4

According to TR WH NU, supported by ℵ B C, Jesus tells Satan, "man does not live by bread alone but by every word proceeding through the mouth of God." A few witnesses, chiefly Western (D it[a,b]), shorten the quotation by dropping the expression εκπορευομενω δια στοματος ("proceeding through [the] mouth"), resulting in this wording: "man does not live by bread alone but by every word of God." A scribe must have thought it too strange to have every word proceeding *through* the mouth of God and deleted that part to make it easier to understand. Morris (1992, 74) provides a good explanation of the original's difficult wording: "'Through' is unusual in such a connection; it perhaps hints that what has been spoken is more than a casual utterance. It does not originate on the lips, so to speak, but comes from the inner being."

Matthew 4:10

TR WH NU	ὕπαγε, σατανᾶ
"Go away, Satan."
ℵ B C*vid W Δ 0233 f[1,13]
all

variant	υπαγε οπισω μου, σατανα
"Get behind me, Satan."
C[2] D L Z 33 Maj
NKJVmg

The variant reading is a harmonization to Matt 16:23, where Jesus told Peter (who had tried to dissuade Jesus from going to the cross), "Get behind me, Satan (= adversary)."

Matthew 4:12

Many manuscripts (C[2] L W Θ f[1,13] Maj) add ο Ιησους ("Jesus") to the beginning of this verse. The addition is a reintroduced, inserted subject (from 4:10). This shows the influence of oral reading on the written text. The same addition occurs in most English versions (see, for example, NRSV NIV NLT) for the same reason: Matthew 4:12 begins a new section, so the subject, "Jesus," is inserted into the translation.

Matthew 4:17

TR WH NU	μετανοεῖτε· ἤγγικεν γὰρ ἡ βασιλεία τῶν οὐρανῶν "Repent, for the kingdom of heaven is near." ℵ B C D L W f[1,13] 33 cop all
variant	"the kingdom of heaven is near" it[k] syr[c,s] NEBmg

Tasker (1964, 411), speaking for the NEB translators, considered the possibility that the words μετανοειτε ("repent") and γαρ ("for") "were a later assimilation of the text to 3.2, particularly as Matthew never elsewhere associates the call to repentance with Jesus." However, since the words are present in all Greek witnesses, the NEB translators included them in the text. And, indeed, they should be included, for it is very likely that the translators of it[k] and syr[c,s] omitted the words to avoid having Jesus repeating John the Baptist's message verbatim (see 3:2) because it might look like Jesus was John's follower.

Matthew 4:24

A few significant witnesses (B C* f[13] Eusebius) do not include the fourth και ("and") in this sentence; therefore, it is bracketed in NA[27]: συνεχομενους [και] δαιμονιζομενους. With the inclusion of the και (found in ℵ C[2] D W f[1] Maj), the verse reads, "They brought to him all the sick, those having various diseases and torments, those being demon-possessed, and epileptics and paralytics." With the exclusion of the και, the verse reads, "They brought to him all the sick, those having various diseases and tormented demoniacs and epileptics and paralytics." The variant reading, adopted by WH and likely original, indicates that the ones suffering from torments were those who were demon-possessed. These are not two different kinds of people. Not one English translation reflects this, not even in a note.

Matthew 5:4-5

In almost all the Greek manuscripts Matt 5:4 comes before Matt 5:5, but the order is reversed in D 33 it[b,f,q] syr[c] cop[bo] Clement Origen and the Eusebian canons. Some textual critics consider the original order to have been 5:5, 4 (so Tischendorf), or that 5:4 was a gloss on 5:3 (see NJBmg). However, the reversed order, which occurred as early as the second century (viz., the witness of Clement and Origen), was probably an attempt to join the "the meek" of v. 5 with "the poor" of v. 3. But the better-attested order preserves the rhetorical pattern of the beatitudes. According to Green (1975, 76), it presents four pairs of virtues dovetailed in the order A B A' B' C D C' D', as follows:

A poor in spirit/theirs is the kingdom

B mourning/will be comforted

A' meek/will inherit the earth

B' hungering for righteousness/will be filled

C merciful/will receive mercy

D pure in heart/will see God

C' peacemakers/will be called sons of God

D' persecuted for righteousness/theirs is the kingdom

Matthew 5:11

WH NU εἴπωσιν πᾶν πονηρὸν καθ' ὑμῶν [ψευδόμενοι]
"they speak all kinds of evil against you falsely"
א B
RSV NRSV ESV NASB NIV TNIV NEB REB NJB NAB NLT HCSB NET

variant 1/TR ειπωσιν παν πονηρον ρημα καθ υμων ψευδομενοι
"they speak every evil word [or, thing] against you falsely"
C W Θ 0196 $f^{1,13}$ Maj
KJV (NKJV)

variant 2 ειπωσιν παν πονηρον καθ υμων
"they speak all kinds of evil against you"
D it syr^{s}
NRSVmg NLTmg NETmg

The first variant, adding ρημα, is a natural completion of a perceived gap—i.e., it fills out the expression "they speak every evil ______ against you." The KJV translators, following TR, understood ρημα to mean "thing" (instead of "word") and therefore rendered it, "they speak all manner of evil against you." The second variant, which omits ψευδομενοι ("falsely"), represents a terser, more difficult reading. Because a more difficult reading is likely to be original, it could be argued that the word "falsely" was added to make the sense clearer. On the other hand, it could be argued that the word was dropped because the sense is too restrictive: blessing should come for being spoken against—period. Since these internal arguments neutralize each other, the balance goes to the external testimony, which strongly favors the inclusion of "falsely," for it is present in many ancient and diverse witnesses.

Matthew 5:19

Some important manuscripts (א* D W) omit the last clause of this verse: ος δ αν ποιηση και διδαξη, ουτος μεγας κληθησεται εν τη βασιλεια των ουρανων ("but whoever does [them] and teaches [them], this one will be called great in the kingdom of heaven"). The omission is most likely due to homoeoteleuton (the previous sentence ends with the same last six words). The scribe of D continued the omission to the end of 5:20, which ends with the same last three words.

Matthew 5:22

WH NU πᾶς ὁ ὀργιζόμενος τῷ ἀδελφῷ αὐτοῦ
"everyone being angry with his brother"
$\mathfrak{P}^{64+67}$ א* B 1424^{mg} Origen MSS[according to Apollinaris, Augustine, Jerome]
NKJVmg RSV NRSV ESV NASB NIV TNIV NEB REB NJB NAB NLT HCSB NET

variant/TR πας ο οργιζομενους τω αδελφω αυτου εικη
"everyone being angry with his brother without cause"
$א^{2}$ D L W Θ 0233 $f^{1,13}$ 33 Maj Diatessaron it syr cop MSS[according to Origen, Apollinaris, Jerome]
KJV NKJV RSVmg NRSVmg ESVmg NASBmg NIVmg TNIVmg NEBmg NLTmg NETmg

UBS[3] cites $\mathfrak{P}^{67vid}$, but there is no need to affix the "vid" (indicating probable but uncertain inclusion) to this papyrus—for it clearly does not have the additional word εικη. This was adjusted to 𝔓[67] in the third corrected edition and then to 𝔓[64] in the fourth edition. Actually, the manuscript should be cited as 𝔓[64+67] because the two portions belong to the same codex, as does 𝔓[4] (see *Text of Earliest MSS,* 71). The addition of the qualifier ϵικη ("without cause") must have occurred somewhat early in the transmission of the NT text, perhaps in the early third century, inasmuch as its presence is noted in various manuscripts by Origen, Apollonaris, Jerome, and Augustine. A marginal note in 1424 (ninth century) indicates that the qualifier was not in certain Greek manuscripts or in the *Gospel of the Nazarenes* (second century). Clearly, this addition was an attempt to soften Jesus' bold assertion and to thereby justify anger if it is for a good reason. But this insertion must be rejected on internal grounds (had it originally been in the text, why would it have been deleted?) and on documentary grounds. The second-century manuscript, 𝔓[64+67], does not include this word, nor do ℵ* B and Origen. Nonetheless, the longer reading was accepted into TR and popularized by KJV—"whosoever is angry with his brother without a cause shall be in danger of the judgment." Modern versions, while rejecting it, note it out of respect for its long-standing history in texts and translations.

Matthew 5:25

WH NU
καὶ ὁ κριτὴς τῷ ὑπηρέτῃ
"and the judge to the officer"
𝔓[64+67] ℵ B 0275 f[1,13] it[k]
RSV NRSV ESV NASB NEB REB NJB NLT HCSB

variant/TR
και ο κριτης σϵ παραδω τω υπηρϵτη
"and the judge hand you over to the officer"
(D) L W Θ 0233 33 Maj syr[c,s] cop
KJV NKJV NIV TNIV NAB HCSBmg NET

NA[27] lists 𝔓[64] as supporting the NU text; but because 𝔓[64] and 𝔓[67] are portions of the same manuscript, it should be listed as 𝔓[64+67] (see *Text of Earliest MSS,* 71). The difference between the two readings is that the variant repeats σϵ παραδω ("hand you over") from the previous clause: "lest your opponent hand you over [σϵ παραδω] to the judge, and the judge hand you over [σϵ παραδω] to the officer." This repetition could have been original and then later excised in Alexandrian manuscripts for the sake of refinement, but it is more likely (and in keeping with the habit of copyists) that certain scribes repeated the phrase.

Matthew 5:27

WH NU
ἐρρέθη· οὐ μοιχεύσεις.
"it was said, 'Do not commit adultery.'"
𝔓[64+67] ℵ B
NKJVmg RSV NRSV ESV NASB NIV TNIV NEB REB NJB NAB NLT HCSB NET

variant/TR
ϵρρϵθη τοις αρχαιοις· ου μοιχϵυσϵις
"it was said to those of old, 'Do not commit adultery.'"
L Δ Θ 0233 f[13] 33
KJV NKJV

The addition of the expression, "to those of old," reflects scribal conformity to the immediate context—to Matt 5:33 (not Matt 21:33 as noted in NA[27]).

Matthew 5:28

TR WH NU πᾶς ὁ βλέπων γυναῖκα πρὸς τὸ ἐπιθυμῆσαι αὐτήν
"everyone looking at a woman with a view to desiring her"
(ℵ[1] αυτης) B D L W Θ 0233 f[13] 33 Maj
KJV NKJV ESV NASB HCSB NET

variant πας ο βλεπωη γυναικα προς επιθυμησαι
"everyone looking at a woman with desire"
𝔓[64+67] ℵ* Tertullian Clement
RSV NRSV NIV TNIV NEB REB NJB NAB NLT

It is difficult to decide which reading is original because both readings have early testimony and make good sense. The correction in ℵ[1] represents a grammatical refinement—from Koine to classical usage. This factor, plus the fact that the variant has such early testimony (notably from the second-century manuscript 𝔓[64+67]), slightly favors the shorter reading. Hence, most modern versions follow the variant.

Matthew 5:30

This verse is omitted in D syr[s] and one cop[bo] manuscript. Since this verse and the previous have the same ending in syr[s], it is likely that the verse was dropped accidentally due to homoeoteleuton. (This could also explain the omission in D.) But this verse is essential to complete Jesus' thought about lust: It begins with the eyes (5:29) and leads to the hand (5:30), which is the member of the body that can carry out the desire of the eye.

Matthew 5:32

TR WH NU all read και ος εαν απολελυμενην γαμηση, μοιχαται ("and whatever man marries a divorced woman commits adultery"), based on the testimony of ℵ L W Θ 0250 f[1,13] Maj. All English versions follow this reading. This strong statement is characteristic of Jesus' tenor in the Sermon on the Mount. Without qualification, Jesus says that marriage to a divorced woman is adultery. The D-text (D it[a,b,k] and, according to Origen, some other manuscripts unknown to us today) omit this clause. Why? It is possible that the D-editor/scribe did not agree with this statement and simply expunged it (it is also deleted in the D-text at 19:9, a parallel passage). Or it is possible that he perceived it to be superfluous inasmuch as the previous clause implies the same—since whoever divorces his wife makes her an adulteress, it goes without saying that whoever marries a divorced woman also commits adultery. Codex Vaticanus (B), however, puts the onus on the woman alone: και ο απολελυμενην γαμησας, μοιχαται ("and the divorced woman who marries commits adultery"). Textual variation occurs in Matt 19:9 with respect to the same expression (see comments there).

Matthew 5:44

WH NU προσεύχεσθε ὑπὲρ τῶν διωκόντων ὑμᾶς
"pray for those persecuting you"
ℵ B f[1] it[k] syr[c,s] cop[sa] Origen
NKJVmg RSV NRSV ESV NASB NIV TNIV NEB REB NJB NAB NLT HCSB NET

variant/TR ευλογειτε τους καταρωμενους υμας, καλως

ποιειτε τοις μισουσιν υμας προσευχεσθε υπερ των επηρεαζοντων υμας και διωκοντων υμας
"bless those who curse you, do good to those who hate you, pray for those who despitefully use you and persecute you"
D L W Θ f[13] 33 Maj
KJV NKJV NIVmg NEBmg NJBmg NLTmg HCSBmg NETmg

The textual evidence favors the shorter reading on three counts: (1) the Greek manuscripts are one century earlier (fourth century) for the shorter reading than those for the longer (fifth century and beyond); (2) the citations of the church fathers for the shorter reading come from earlier fathers; (3) the additional words in the longer reading must have been borrowed from Luke's account of the Sermon on the Mount (Luke 6:27-28), for had they originally been in Matthew's gospel, there is no good explanation for how they were dropped.

Jesus did say that we should bless those who curse us and do good to those who hate us, but these were not his words as recorded by Matthew. These were the words recorded by Luke. Apparently, Jesus gave several similar sermons using similar and dissimilar language at will; therefore, the "Sermon on the Mount" in Matthew is not a verbatim copy of Luke's "Sermon on the Plain." Various scribes, however, thought it their duty to make one gospel harmonize with the other in passages that they perceived were covering the same event. TR incorporates most of these harmonizations, which were then translated into KJV and NKJV. Most modern versions do not include the harmonization here.

Matthew 5:47a

Many manuscripts (L W Θ 33 Maj—but not TR) substitute the noun φιλους ("friends") for αδελφους ("brothers"). The change was suggested by the verb ασπασησθε ("greet"), which was commonly used to describe a daily exchange among friends.

Matthew 5:47b

WH NU οὐχὶ καὶ οἱ ἐθνικοὶ τὸ αὐτο ποιοῦσιν
"Don't the Gentiles do the same?"
א B D Z
KJV NKJVmg RSV NRSV ESV NASB NIV NEB REB NLT HCSB NET

variant/TR ουχι και οι τελωναι το αυτο ποιουσιν
"Don't the tax collectors do the same?"
L W Θ Maj
NKJV NJB HCSBmg

The word τελωναι ("tax collectors") is a carryover from the previous verse. If we trust the documentary evidence, the variant cannot be original. The entire verse is lacking in some witnesses (it[k] syr[s]), probably due to homoeoteleuton—both 5:46 and 5:47 end with the same last three words.

Matthew 6:1

WH NU τὴν δικαιοσύνην ὑμῶν
"your righteousness"
א*,2 B D 0250 f[1]
(RSV NRSV) ESV NASB NIV TNIV NEB REB NJB NAB NLT HCSB NET

variant 1/TR — την ελεημοσυνην υμων
"your alms[giving]"
L W Z Θ f[13] 33 Maj
KJV NKJV NJBmg HCSBmg

variant 2 — την δοσις υμων
"your gift [giving]"
א[1] syr[c] cop[bo]
none

According to WH NU, the full rendering is: "don't practice your righteousness before people." The first variant was probably a harmonization to 6:2 or an early gloss on δικαιοσυνη ("righteousness"), since "righteousness" in Hebrew was often rendered as ελεημοσυνην ("alms") in the Septuagint. The second variant is also an attempt to explain just what it means "to do righteousness before people" by indicating that it was a matter of giving gifts (presumably to the temple) in the sight of others. Jesus began with a general condemnation of ostentatious displays of religion and then followed with examples. He did not begin with almsgiving first. Most modern English versions try to reflect this.

Matthew 6:4, 6

WH NU — ὁ πατήρ σου ὁ βλέπων ἐν τῷ κρυπτῷ ἀποδώσει σοι
"your Father who sees in secret will reward you"
א B D Z f[1,13] 33 it[k] syr[c] cop Origen
RSV NRSV ESV NASB NIV TNIV NEB REB NJB NAB NLT HCSB NET

variant/TR — ο πατηρ σου ο βλεπων εν τω κρυπτω αποδωσει σοι εν τω φανερω
"your Father who sees in secret will reward you openly"
L W Θ Maj it syr
KJV NKJV NRSVmg NEBmg HCSBmg NETmg

The addition εν τω φανερω ("in the open" = "openly") was probably created to give symmetrical, antithetical balance to the expression εν τω κρυπτω ("in secret" = "secretly"). Had it originally been in the text, there is no good way to explain its omission in so many early and diverse witnesses. This addition, which helps for oral reading, skews the passage's disparagement of any kind of ostentatiousness. All true acts of righteousness should be done for God (not people) to see; and the reward should come in like manner—from God to the believer, not for others to see.

Matthew 6:8

In this verse, the divine title is πατηρ ("Father") according to early and diverse testimony: א* D L W Z 0170[vid]. This is the wording adopted by NA[27] and all English versions. However, WH adopted the reading θεος ο πατηρ ("God the Father") based on א[1] B cop[sa] Origen (noted in ASVmg). Usually, a reading supported by א and B in Matthew is considered to be original, but the weight of other authorities is against it in this case (especially since the testimony of א* stands against א[1]). This reading, which used to be part of the Nestle text, was relegated to the apparatus in NA[27]/UBS[4] for internal reasons: (1) Matthew never uses the expression elsewhere; (2) it was adapted from Pauline usage (TCGNT). Another variant, ο πατηρ υμων ο ουρανοις ("your heavenly Father"), found in 047 892[c] syr[h], came from scribal harmonization to Matt 6:9.

Matthew 6:11

The expression τον αρτον ημων τον επιουσιον, usually translated "our daily bread," gave ancient translators and commentators difficulty because the word επιουσιον occurs only here and in Luke 11:3 in the NT and because it does not appear in other Hellenistic literature (Metzger 1958, 52-54). Origen thought the word was "coined by the evangelist" (BDAG 376). The meaning of the word is sought from its derivation: (1) επι and ουσια, translated as "necessary for existence" (so Origen, Chrysostom, and Jerome); (2) επι την ουσα, translated as "for this day"; or (3) η επιουσα, rendered as "for the following day." The word, found in all NT Greek manuscripts (the earliest being the amulet P.Antinoopolis 2.54 of the third century), either speaks of what is necessary for existence or of what meets our day-by-day need. Most modern translators opt for a translation that addresses the daily need. Some ancient translators did the same, while others focused on the issue of sustaining existence: (1) *cottidianum* ("daily") in Old Latin; (2) *supersubstantialem* ("that which substantiates") in vg; (3) "necessary" in syr$^{h,(p)}$; (4) "of tomorrow" in cop^{sa}; (5) *crastinum* ("of tomorrow") in cop$^{mae(?)}$ cop^{bo}; (6) *mahar* ("tomorrow") in *Gospel of the Hebrews*.

The word could also have eschatological significance, if it is derived from επειναι, "for the future." In his *Commentary on Matthew* (6:11) Jerome wrote, "In the Gospel according to Hebrews, for 'substantial bread' I found 'mahar,' which means 'belonging to tomorrow'; so the sense is: our bread of the morrow, that is, of the future, give us this day." This means that "the disciples are to pray for tomorrow's bread today, since tomorrow would be the day of the Messiah (cf. Exod 16:22ff.) on which work would not be possible" (Albright and Mann 1971, 76). This interpretation coincides nicely with the emphasis in the first part of the prayer on the coming of the kingdom. However, the other translations mentioned above are also based on solid exegesis because the Lord's Prayer does address our need to depend on God for our everyday existence.

Matthew 6:13

WH NU	omit doxology at end of prayer (see various forms below) ℵ B D Z 0170 f^{1} NKJVmg RSV NRSV ESV NIV TNIV NEB REB NJB NAB NLT HCSBmg NET
variant 1	add αμην ("amen") 17 vg^{cl} none
variant 2	add "because yours is the power forever." it^{k} syr^{p} none
variant 3	add "because yours is the power and the glory forever. Amen." cop^{sa,fay} (*Didache* omits αμην) none
variant 4	add "because yours is the kingdom and the glory forever. Amen." syr^{c} none

variant 5/TR add οτι σου εστιν η βασιλεια και η δυναμις και η δοξα εις τους αιωνας. αμην.
"because yours is the kingdom and the power and the glory forever. Amen."
L W Δ Θ 0233 f[13] 33 Maj syr
KJV NKJV RSVmg NRSVmg ESVmg NASB NIVmg TNIVmg NEBmg NJBmg NLTmg HCSB NETmg

variant 6 add οτι σου εστιν η βασιλεια του πατρος και του υιου και του αγιου πνευματος εις τους αιωνας. αμην.
"because yours is the kingdom of the Father and the Son and the Holy Spirit forever. Amen."
157 (1253)
none

There are other minor variations than those listed above (see NA[27] and UBS[4]), but these represent the six basic variations of the doxology that were added to the Lord's Prayer. The testimony of the earliest extant witnesses reveals that the prayer concluded with a petition for deliverance from evil. The variety among the variants speaks against the genuineness of any of the additions. What is presented above shows the continual expansion of the addition—from the simple "amen" in variant 1 to the elaborate Trinitarian doxology in variant 6. In the first stage of additions, it appears that scribes used "power" and/or "glory" (probably adapted from verses such as 1 Chr 29:11; Ps 62:3 LXX; Dan 2:37; 1 Pet 4:11; Jude 25). This is the reading in the *Didache*, and this same ending (in transposed order—glory and power) appears at the end of the late-third century Christian prayer (see P.Oxy. 407). In the next stage, "kingdom" and "amen" were added.

The longer form probably came from the *Didache* (also known as "The Teaching of the Twelve"), which was written in Syria or Palestine during the early second century. The *Didache* was compiled from various sources that give details about the traditions of well-established church communities. This is probably why Westcott and Hort (1882, 9) could say that the "doxology originated in liturgical use in Syria, and was thence adopted into the Greek and Syriac Syrian texts of the N.T." As such, a longer form of the Lord's Prayer may have been in use as early as the end of the first century. This was elongated still further by the addition of "kingdom" to the wording found in the *Didache:* "power and glory." This particular form—"kingdom, power, and glory"— became popular by its inclusion in TR and KJV.

Tregelles and Tischendorf were the first textual critics to omit the ending. The first English translators to exclude the ending to the Lord's Prayer were those who produced the English Revised Version (1884) and the American Standard Version (1901). Most twentieth-century translators have done the same. The NASB, which tends to be quite conservative, is an exception. But the ending has become so ingrained in Christian tradition that it has not dropped from use in private prayers or in public worship—with the exception of the Roman Catholic churches. When reciting the Lord's Prayer, most Christians do not stop after saying "but deliver us from evil." Most go on to say, "For yours is the kingdom, and the power, and the glory, forever. Amen."

Why do people feel compelled to end with this assertive doxology? Probably for the same reason that motivated some early scribes to add it. This profound prayer invites a glorious, uplifting conclusion—especially in oral reading.

Matthew 6:15

NU ἐὰν δὲ μὴ ἀφῆτε τοῖς ἀνθρώποις
"but if you do not forgive people"
ℵ D f[1] 892*
NRSV NASB NEB REB NJB NAB NLT HCSB NET

variant/TR WH εαν δε μη αφητε τοις ανθρωποις τα παραπτωματα αυτων
"but if you do not forgive people their trespasses"
B L W Θ 0233 f^{13} 33 Maj
KJV NKJV RSV ESV NIV TNIV HCSBmg

The textual evidence is evenly divided here, as well as the internal evidence. On one hand, it could be argued that "their trespasses" was carried over from 6:14; on the other hand, it could be argued that it was dropped by scribes who considered it redundant (note that the expression appears again in 6:15b). The textual decisions of the English versions display the ambiguity.

Matthew 6:18

WH NU ὁ πατήρ σου ὁ βλέπων ἐν τῷ κρυφαίῳ ἀποδώσει σοι
"your Father who sees in secret will reward you"
א B (D^c)
NKJVmg RSV NRSV ESV NASB NIV TNIV NEB REB NJB NLT HCSB NET

variant/TR ο πατηρ σου ο βελπων εν τω κρυπτω αποδωσει σοι εν τω φανερω
"your Father who sees in secret will reward you openly"
L W Θ 0233 0250 f^{13} 33 Maj
KJV NKJV NRSVmg HCSBmg

The synonymous expression εν τω κρυπτω ("in secret"), borrowed from 6:4, was substituted in later manuscripts for εν τω κρυφαιω. At the end of the verse, some late manuscripts add εν τω φανερω ("in the open" = "openly"), borrowed from inferior manuscripts in 6:4 (see note there) and 6:6. This expansion was incorporated in TR and carried over to KJV and NKJV.

Matthew 6:25

TR WH NU τί φάγητε [ἢ τί πίητε]
"what you eat or what you drink"
B W f^{13} 33 it cop^{bo}
KJV NKJV RSV NRSV ESV NASB NIV TNIV NEB REB NAB NLT HCSB NET

variant 1 τι φαγητε και τι πιητε
"what you eat and what you drink"
L Θ 0233 Maj $syr^{h,p}$
none

variant 2 τι φαγητε
"what you eat"
א f^1 $it^{a,b,k}$ syr^c cop^{sa}
NRSVmg NJB

The reading which TR WH NU follow could be an assimilation to 6:31; so also the first variant. Often a variant in two forms shows the work of scribal addition. The sense and poetic balance of the passage (τι φαγητε . . . τι ενδυσησθε = "what you eat . . . what you are clothed with") are all the better without η τι πιητε ("or what you drink") as in the second variant, which was followed by NJB.

Matthew 6:28

(TR) WH NU καταμάθετε τὰ κρίνα τοῦ ἀγροῦ πῶς αὐξάνουσιν· οὐ κοπιῶσιν οὐδὲ νήθουσιν
"consider how the lilies of the field grow, they neither labor nor spin"
ℵ[1] (B 33 κοπιουσιν) Θ f[1] (L W 0233 0281 f[13] Maj)
all

variant καταμαθετε τα κρινα του αργου πως ου ξαινουσιν ουδε νηθουσιν ουδε κοπιωσιν
"consider how the lilies of the field do not card nor spin nor labor"
ℵ* (P.Oxy. 655 ου ξανει ουδε νηθει = "they do not card or spin")
NEBmg

A translation of P.Oxy. 655 I a, b is as follows: "[Take no thought] from morning until evening or from evening until morning, either for your food, what you will eat, or for your clothes, what you will put on. You are far better than the lilies which do not card or spin . . . . Having one garment, what do you [lack]? . . . Who could add to your span of life?"

T. C. Skeat (1938, 211-214) was given a clue to understanding a correction in ℵ after he examined P.Oxy. 655 (a late second-century noncanonical gospel, which was later identified as the *Gospel of Thomas*) and determined that the reading was ξανει ("card"), not αυξανει ("grow"), as originally transcribed by Grenfell and Hunt. This led Skeat to reexamine this verse in Codex Sinaiticus (ℵ) under ultraviolet light and determine the reading (listed as the variant) underneath the corrected reading (listed above as text). The presence of ξαινω in ℵ and P.Oxy. 655 is significant; it could very well reflect the original text—how easy it would be for ου ξαινουσιν ("they do not card") to become αυξανουσιν ("they grow") in the copying process—especially since there was no space between letters. If the second variant reflects the original, the statement indicates that there are three things lilies do not do: they do not card (i.e., comb wool), spin, or labor (with no mention of growth per se). This pattern mirrors the triple verbal description about the birds: "they neither sow nor reap nor gather into barns" (6:26). (See note on Luke 12:27 concerning a similar variant.)

Matthew 6:33

TR NU τὴν βασιλείαν [τοῦ θεοῦ] καὶ τὴν δικαιοσύνην αὐτοῦ
"the kingdom of God and his righteousness"
L W Θ 0233 f[1,13] 33 Maj syr
KJV NKJV NRSV ESV NEB REB NAB NLT HCSB

variant 1/WH την βασιλειαν και την δικαιοσυνην αυτου
"the kingdom and his righteousness"
ℵ (it[k]) cop[sa,bo] Eusebius
RSV NRSVmg NASB NIV TNIV NJB NLTmg HCSBmg NET

variant 2 την δικαιοσυνην και την βασιλειαν αυτου
"the righteousness and his kingdom"
B
none

variant 3	την βασιλειαν των ουρανων και την δικαιοσυνην αυτου "the kingdom of the heavens and his righteousness" Clement none
variant 4	την βασιλειαν του θεου "the kingdom of God" 245 none

Normally, the testimony of later manuscripts such as L W Θ 0233 $f^{1,13}$ 33 Maj should not be given more weight than the testimony of Alexandrian manuscripts such as ℵ and B, neither of which include a modifying phrase after "kingdom." Metzger's argument (see TCGNT) that Matthew almost always used a modifier after "kingdom" is a strong one. But it could be for this very reason that later scribes added "of God" or "of the heavens." If either of these expressions were originally in the text, why would the scribes of ℵ and B delete them? Since this cannot be adequately explained, the first or second variant more likely reflects the original text. These readings emphasize the need for people to seek the kind of righteousness Jesus described in the Sermon on the Mount as a prerequisite for entering the kingdom.

Matthew 7:2

Instead of the simple μετρηθησεται ("it will be measured") found in the earliest manuscripts, a few later manuscripts (Θ 0233 f^{13}) have the compound αντιμετρηθησεται ("it will be measured in return"), most likely borrowed from Luke 6:38.

Matthew 7:13

TR NU	πλατεῖα ἡ πύλη καὶ εὐρύχωρος ἡ ὁδὸς ἡ ἀπάγουσα εἰς τὴν ἀπώλειαν "wide is the gate and broad is the road leading to destruction" ℵ[2] B C L W Δ Θ $f^{1,13}$ 33 all
variant/WH	πλατεια και ευρυχωρος η οδος η απαγουσα εις την απολειαν "wide and broad is the road leading to destruction" ℵ* it[a,k] Clement Hippolytus Cyprian RSVmg NRSVmg ESVmg NEBmg NJBmg

The words η πυλη ("the gate") may have been added by scribes to complete the parallelism with 7:14, or the words may have been deleted so as to make the adjectives "wide and broad" describe only "the road." The omission also occurs in 7:14 in most of the same witnesses (it[a,k] Clement Hippolytus Cyprian). Thus, the changes seem purposeful, not accidental. The TR NU reading focuses on the gate that opens the way to the road going to destruction; the variant reading focuses only on the road leading to destruction. Both readings equally convey the image Jesus used to contrast the narrow way of righteous living to the broad way of unrighteous living. Nonetheless, the TR NU reading is more consistent with the following verse, which characterizes both the gate and the road.

Matthew 7:14

The TR WH NU reading has τι στενη η πυλη ("how narrow [is] the gate"), based on א[2] (B[2]) C L W Θ f[1,13] Maj. A variant reads οτι στενη η πυλη ("because narrow [is] the gate"), found in א* 700[c] (B* οτι δε). Though it is difficult to be dogmatic about which reading is original (there is only a one-letter difference: τι/οτι), it seems that the TR WH NU reading originated from a scribe or scribes who could not understand how οτι could immediately follow 7:13 and still make good sense. Thus, the explanatory οτι ("because") was changed to an interjection τι ("how"). But the οτι of 7:14 is the second of two explanatory statements emphasizing the necessity of entering the narrow gate. The first explanatory statement (introduced with οτι) provides the contrast by speaking of the broad way that leads to destruction; the second provides a description of the narrow way leading to life.

Matthew 7:22

In this verse, a few witnesses (syr[c] Justin Origen) display an addition borrowed from a parallel passage (Luke 13:26): "did we not eat and drink in your name?" As the verse stands in all other manuscripts, the emphasis is on what people did in the name of Jesus and how they thought it gave them the right to enter the kingdom. The addition offers another plea: "weren't we your companions and friends, even those who ate and drank with you—how could you not let us into your kingdom?"

Matthew 7:27

The expression επνευσαν οι ανεμοι και ("the winds blew and") was accidentally omitted in two manuscripts (א* 33) due to homoeoteleuton (the previous clause ends with the same last six letters: ποταμοι και). All other manuscripts include these words.

Matthew 7:29

WH NU — οἱ γραμματεῖς αὐτῶν
"their scribes"
א B
RSV NRSV ESV NASB NIV TNIV NEB REB NJB NAB NLT HCSB NET

variant 1/TR — οι γραμματεις
"the scribes"
L 565 700 Maj
KJV NKJV

variant 2 — οι γραμμαεις αυτων και οι Φαρισαοι
"their scribes and the Pharisees"
C* W 33 syr
NJBmg

In context, Matthew was comparing Jesus' manner of teaching (with authority) with that of the scribes or their (the peoples') scribes (who apparently lacked authority). Both the WH NU reading and second variant have the expression "their scribes" (as opposed to "the scribes") backed by overwhelmingly solid manuscript authority. The first variant is perhaps an effort to categorize all scribes as "the scribes"—a distinct category of Jewish educators. The second variant is a natural scribal expansion inasmuch as the two groups, "scribes and Pharisees," often appear side by side in the Gospels.

Matthew 8:3, 7

Scribes (C² L W Θ Maj) inserted ο Ιησους ("Jesus") before λεγων ("saying") in order to get a specific subject into the verse, especially since the subject was unnamed at the beginning of the chapter. Many modern translators have done the same thing (see NIV NEB NJB). But according to the best manuscript evidence (א B C*), the subject is left unspecified until 8:4. The same scribes again inserted ο Ιησους ("Jesus") at the beginning of 8:7 for the same reason; most modern translations do the same.

Matthew 8:5, 8, 13

In a few witnesses (syr^s Clement Eusebius), the εκατονταρχος ("centurion"—leader of a hundred soldiers) in these three verses has become χιλιαρχος ("chiliarch"—leader of a thousand soldiers). It has been argued that "centurion" was borrowed from Luke and that "chiliarch" is therefore original (Allen 1912, 78). If this was the case, however, one would think that at least one Greek manuscript would have preserved the reading "chiliarch," but none of them do.

Matthew 8:9

NU reads εγω ανθρωπος ειμι υπο εξουιαν ("I also am a man under authority") based on the authority of C L W Θ f^{1,13} 33. Other witnesses (א B it Diatessaron) have an additional word at the end: τασσομενος ("placed"), which is included in WH in brackets. Usually a reading supported by א B is more likely to be original than one upheld by C L W Θ, but in this case most scholars suspect that the variant reveals scribal conformity to Luke 7:8.

Matthew 8:10

WH NU	παρ᾽ οὐδενὶ τοσαύτην πίστιν ἐν τῷ ᾽Ισραὴλ εὗρον "with no one in Israel I found such faith" B W (f¹ 0281) it^k cop^bo RSVmg NRSV ESV NASB NIV TNIV REB NJB NAB NLT HCSB NET
variant/TR	ουδε εν τω Ισραηλ τοσαυτην πιστιν ευρον "not even in Israel I found such faith" א C L Θ 0233 0250 f¹³ 33 Maj KJV NKJV RSV NRSVmg ESVmg NASBmg NEB

The WH NU reading and the variant are divided as to manuscript support. The variant reading may have been created by scribes attempting to conform this verse to Luke 7:9. This reading has been popularized by its inclusion in TR and its presence in KJV and NKJV. But a few modern versions (RSV NEB) follow it as well.

Matthew 8:13

At the end of the verse, some manuscripts (א*,2 C Θ f¹ 33) add και υποστρεψας ο εκατονταρχος εις τον οικον αυτου εν αυτη τη ωρα ευρεν τον παιδα υγιαινοντα ("and when the centurion returned to his house that very hour he found the child well"). This is clearly a case of a scribe borrowing from Luke 7:10 to fill a gap in this verse.

Matthew 8:15

WH NU — διηκόνει αὐτῷ
"she was serving him"
B C Θ 0233
NKJVmg RSV NRSV ESV NASB NIV TNIV NEB REB NJB NAB NLT HCSB

variant/TR — διηκονει αυτοις
"she was serving them"
ℵ[1] L Δ $f^{1,13}$ 33 $syr^{c,s}$ cop^{bo}
KJV NKJV NET

The variant (followed by KJV NKJV and, oddly enough, NET) is probably the result of a scribe conforming Matthew to parallel passages (Mark 1:31; Luke 4:39). WH NU preserve Matthew's original wording, which is christocentric. Since Christ did the healing, he is the one Peter's mother-in-law served.

Matthew 8:18

WH NU — ὄχλον
"a crowd"
B cop^{saMSS}
NASB NIV TNIV REB NJB NAB NLT HCSBmg

variant 1 — οχλους
"crowds"
ℵ* f^{1}
NEB HCSB

variant 2/TR — πολλους οχλους
"great crowds"
ℵ[2] C L Θ 0233 f^{13} 33 Maj
KJV NKJV RSV NRSV ESV NET

variant 3 — πολυν οχλον
"a great crowd"
W 1424 cop^{saMS}
none

The addition of πολλους ("many" = great) does not accord with Matthew's style; it is probably a scribal embellishment borrowed from Mark 4:36. Matthew wrote either οχλον (as in WH NU) or οχλους (as in the first variant); the plural accords with Matthean style. English translations are divided on this variant.

Matthew 8:21

TR NU — ἕτερος δὲ τῶν μαθητῶν [αὐτοῦ]
"another of his disciples"
C L W Θ 0250 $f^{1,13}$ Maj
KJV NKJV NRSV NIV TNIV NEB REB NAB NLT HCSB

variant/WH — ετερος δε των μαθητων
"another of the disciples"
ℵ B 33 it^{a} cop^{sa}
RSV ESV NASB NJB NET

The context of this textual variant is important. A certain disciple is making an excuse for not following Jesus immediately: "Lord, first let me go and bury my father." Thus, the omission of αυτου ("his") is significant. It may have been deleted so that readers would not think that one of Jesus' very own disciples (whether of the twelve or of the seventy-two) was excusing himself from following Jesus. In this case, the sense is that one of the people who had been following Jesus declined total commitment. Perhaps Matthew intended this meaning, and the variant reading reflects what he originally wrote. If so, the addition of αυτου ("his") can be explained as a rote scribal insertion—inasmuch as it was customary for this possessive pronoun to appear after "disciples" in Matthew.

Matthew 8:28

WH NU	τὴν χώραν τῶν Γαδαρηνῶν "the country of the Gadarenes" (Γαζαρηνων א*) B C Θ syr[h,p,s] NKJVmg RSV NRSV ESV NASB NIV TNIV NEB REB NJB NAB NLT HCSB NET
variant 1/TR	την χωραν των Γεργεσηνων "the country of the Gergesenes" א[2] L W f[1,13] Maj KJV NKJV RSVmg NRSVmg ESVmg NIVmg TNIVmg NJBmg NABmg NLTmg HCSBmg NETmg
variant 2	την χωραν των Γερασηνων "the country of the Gerasenes" 892[c] syr[hmg] cop[sa] RSVmg NRSVmg ESVmg NIVmg TNIVmg NJBmg NABmg NLTmg NETmg

In every instance in the Synoptic Gospels where the writer records Jesus' visit to the region on the eastern side of the Sea of Galilee (where he healed the demoniac), there is textual variation as to what this region is named. In this verse, Mark 5:1, and Luke 8:26 all three readings occur: "Gerasenes," "Gergesenes," and "Gadarenes." "The variations in the readings in the three synoptical gospels reflect the perplexities of the scribes" (Bruce 1979, 144).

Origen (*Comm. Jo.* 5.41.24) spoke of this confusion while commenting on John 1:28. Origen objected to Gadara (a reading he saw in a few manuscripts), which is about five miles southeast of the Sea of Galilee. He also rejected Gerasa, which is thirty miles southeast of the Sea of Galilee. Origen suggested the name Gergesa on the basis of some local tradition and because its name was supposed to mean "dwelling of those that have driven away." Fond of finding etymological significance in names, Origen said the name suited the place because there the citizens asked Jesus to leave their territory.

"Gadarenes" has the best testimony in Matthew, and adequately suits the context for the story. Josephus (*Life* 42.9) said that Gadara had territory and villages on the border of the lake; one of these villages must have been called "Gerasa," which is the name found in the best manuscripts in Mark 5:1 and Luke 8:26. The first variant, "Gergesenes," probably shows the influence Origen had on later traditions; and the second variant, "Gerasenes," is scribal harmonization to Mark 5:1 and Luke 8:26.

Matthew 8:29a

WH NU — υἱὲ τοῦ θεοῦ
"Son of God"
ℵ B C* L f^1 33
RSV NRSV ESV NASB NIV TNIV NEB REB NJB NAB NLT HCSB NET

variant/TR — Ιησους, υιε του θεου
"Jesus, Son of God"
C^3 W Θ 0242^{vid} f^{13} Maj
KJV NKJV HCSBmg

The addition of "Jesus" in the variant is likely a harmonization to Mark 1:24, a parallel verse. This reading has been popularized by its inclusion in TR and its presence in KJV and NKJV. Either way, it is significant to note that the demons recognized that Jesus was the Son of God.

Matthew 8:29b

TR WH NU have the expression βασανισαι ημας ("torture us") based on excellent testimony: $ℵ^1$ B C L. A few manuscripts (ℵ* W) substitute the verb απολεσαι ("to destroy"). The variant is the result of scribal conformity to Luke 4:34, a parallel verse. With either reading, the demons' question is the same: Has the eschaton (the end of the age) already come? These evil spirits feared that their punishment was imminent.

Matthew 8:31

WH NU — ἀπόστειλον ἡμᾶς εἰς τὴν ἀγέλην τῶν χοίρων
"send us into the herd of pigs"
ℵ B Θ 0242^{vid} f^1 33
NKJVmg RSV NRSV ESV NASB NIV TNIV NEB REB NJB NAB NLT HCSB NET

variant/TR — επιτρεψον ημιν απελθειν εις την αγελην των χοιρων
"allow us to be sent into the herd of pigs"
C L W f^{13} Maj
KJV NKJV

The variant is probably the result of scribal conformity to Luke 8:32, a parallel verse. It was included in TR and has been popularized by KJV and NKJV.

Matthew 9:1

A few manuscripts (C^3 $Θ^c$ f^{13}) insert the name of the subject, ο Ιησους ("Jesus"), because this begins a new section. Many English translators do the same.

Matthew 9:2, 5

WH NU have αφιενται σου αι αμαρτιαι ("your sins are forgiven") based on the fairly good testimony of ℵ B D. The variant changes the verb to αφεωνται ("have been forgiven"), as found in C L W Θ 0233 $f^{1,13}$ Maj. Scribes may have found the present tense bothersome because it usually has a durative function ("your sins are being forgiven"). Turner (*Syntax* 3.64), however, explains this as a punctiliar present: "sins receive forgiveness herewith." The variant reading was created to fix the perceived tense problem or to harmonize this text with Luke 5:20. Mark 2:5 has similar textual variation.

Matthew 9:8

WH NU	οἱ ὄχλοι ἐφοβήθησαν "the crowds were afraid" ℵ B D W 0281 f^1 33 it $syr^{p,s}$ cop NKJVmg RSV NRSV ESV NLT HCSB NET
variant 1/TR	οι οχλοι εθαυμασαν "the crowds marveled" C L Θ 0233 f^{13} Maj syr^h KJV NKJV NASB NIV TNIV NEB REB NJB NAB HCSBmg NETmg
variant 2	omit Irenaeus none

The WH NU reading has excellent manuscript evidence and recently gained additional support from 0281 (seventh century), a manuscript discovered (with other manuscripts) at St. Catherine's Monastery. Furthermore, the WH NU reading is more difficult than the others because the expected response to witnessing a miracle is awe and praise, not fear and praise ("they were afraid and glorified God"). Some commentators argue that εφοβηθησαν should be translated as "they were awestruck," but that is closer to the word Mark used: εξιστασθαι ("to astonish," Mark 2:12). Matthew and Luke both speak of the people being afraid (see Luke 5:26). People are afraid of the unknown, the new, and the supernatural. Jesus' transfiguration and resurrection were new, supernatural events—in both cases Matthew says that witnesses of these events "were afraid" (see 17:6; 28:9-10). In this case, the crowds were afraid because they saw something entirely new: a man forgiving the sins of another man and healing him to prove it. They sensed that Jesus was no mere mortal, no normal rabbi, but a supernatural human being endowed with authority from God.

Matthew 9:12

In typical fashion (see 4:12; 8:3, 7; 9:1), several scribes (C L W Θ 0233^c $f^{1,13}$ 33 Maj) inserted ο Ιησους ("Jesus") in the beginning of the sentence so as to get a specific subject into the verse. Many modern translations do the same thing (see NIV NEB NLT).

Matthew 9:13

WH NU	οὐ γὰρ ἦλθον καλέσαι δικαίους ἀλλὰ ἁμαρτωλούς "for I have not come to call [the] righteous but sinners" ℵ B D W Δ 0233 f^1 33 NKJVmg RSV NRSV ESV NASB NIV TNIV NEB REB NJB NAB NLT HCSB NET
variant/TR	ου γαρ ηλθον καλεσαι δικαιους αλλα αμαρτωλους εις μετανοιαν "for I have not come to call the righteous but sinners to repentance" C L Θ 0281 f^{13} Maj KJV NKJV HCSBmg

The expansion in the variant reading is the result of harmonization to Luke 5:32 or the result of oral/aural gap filling—inasmuch as the ear expects the infinitive "to call" to be followed by a prepositional phrase indicating to what one is called.

Matthew 9:14

TR NU οἱ Φαρισαῖοι νηστεύομεν [πολλά]
"the Pharisees fast often"
ℵ[2] C D L W Θ 0233 f[1,13] 33 Maj
KJV NKJV RSVmg NRSV NAB NLTmg HCSB NET

variant 1 οι Φαρισαιοι νηστευομεν πυκνα
"the Pharisees fast frequently"
ℵ[1]
none

variant 2/WH οι Φαρισαιοι νηστευομεν
"the Pharisees fast"
ℵ* B 0281
NKJVmg RSV NRSVmg ESV NASB NIV TNIV NEB REB NJB NLT

The word πολλα ("often") is a likely scribal addition (probably taken from Luke 5:33) intended to make a more effective contrast between the fasting of the Pharisees and John's disciples with the lack thereof on the part of Jesus' disciples. Indeed, many copyists would not want readers to think that Jesus condemned fasting completely. The corrector of ℵ (who was a contemporary with the scribe who produced the manuscript) may have been the first scribe to create the addition πολλα ("frequently"); the next corrector of ℵ (working in the sixth or seventh century) changed πολλα to πυκνα. Thus, the original text went from having no adverb to having different ones. Nearly all the modern versions, contra NU, follow the second variant (as in WH) in not including any adverb.

Matthew 9:15

The D-text has some interesting variants, which reveal the editorial liberty this scribe took with the text. Instead of νυμφωνος ("bride chamber"), found in most Greek manuscripts, D reads νυμφιου ("bridegroom")—either as the result of conformity to the second part of the verse or through a misunderstanding of the phrase "friends of the bridegroom" or "guests of the bridegroom" (literally "sons of the bride chamber"). Instead of the verb πενθειν ("to mourn"), D (also W it cop[bo]) reads νηστευειν ("to fast"), which is a harmonization to the previous verse and to the next clause of this verse. While Jesus, the bridegroom, was with his friends, they should not mourn but celebrate; when he left, then they would fast. At the end of the verse, D (also it syr[hmg]) adds εν εκειναις ταις ημεραις ("in those days")—an editorial expansion.

Matthew 9:18

Some of the textual variants in this verse can be explained by the fact that ancient manuscripts were written with no spaces between words. In this case, the text was written αρχωνειςελθων, which could be interpreted as αρχων εις ελθων ("one ruler coming") or αρχων εισελθων ("a ruler coming to"). Thus, either reading could be original (see O'Callaghan 1981, 104-106). The ambiguity caused by the εις is eliminated in ℵ and B (followed by WH), which read αρχων προσελθων.

Matthew 9:26

TR WH NU all read εξηλθεν η φημη αυτη ("this report went out"), with the support of B W f^{13} Maj. This reading is followed by all English versions. There are two variants on this: (1) εξηλθεν η φημη αυτου ("his fame went out") in D cop^{sa}; (2) εξηλθεν η φημη αυτης ("the report of [about] her went out") in ℵ C* Θ f^{1} 33. The second variant, which has good documentary support, might be original because scribes did not think the girl should be given preeminent notice—rather what Jesus did (the miracle of raising the girl from the dead) should be prominent. Thus, the expression "the report about her" was probably changed to "this report" (which requires only a one-letter change—from αυτης to αυτη) or to "his fame" (probably borrowed from Luke 4:14).

Matthew 9:34

TR WH NU — include verse: οἱ δὲ Φαρισαῖοι ἔλεγον· ἐν τῷ ἄρχοντι τῶν δαιμονίων ἐκβάλλει τὰ δαιμόνια.
"But the Pharisees said, 'By the ruler of demons he casts out demons.'"
ℵ B C L W Θ $f^{1,13}$ 33
KJV NKJV RSV NRSV ESV NASB NIV TNIV NEBmg REBmg NJB NAB NLT HCSB NET

variant — omit verse
D $it^{a,d,k}$ syr^{s} Hilary
RSVmg NRSVmg NEB REB NJBmg NETmg

Several scholars affirm the omission of this verse, arguing that it is an assimilation to Matt 12:24 and its parallel in Luke 11:15 (Tasker 1964, 412). Other scholars argue that 10:25 presupposes this statement (Carson 1984, 234), for in 10:25 Jesus mentions that the Jewish leaders had already maligned him by associating him with Beelzebul. The cause for omission in the "Western" witnesses noted above cannot be ascribed to transcriptional error. Perhaps it was excised because the previous verse provides a more positive ending to the pericope. But when all is said about internal evidence, the verdict for its inclusion in the text is determined by its strong documentary attestation. It is included in all the English versions except the NEB and REB.

Matthew 10:3

TR WH NU — Θαδδαῖος
"Thaddaeus"
ℵ B f^{13} cop
NKJVmg RSV NRSV ESV NASB NIV TNIV REB NJB NAB NLT HCSB NET

variant 1 — Λεββαιος
"Lebbaeus"
D it^{k} MSS[according to Augustine]
RSVmg ESVmg NEB REBmg NLTmg NETmg

variant 2 — Λεββαιος ο επικληθεις Θαδδαιος
"Lebbaeus, the one called Thaddaeus"
(C) L W Θ f^{1} 33 Maj it^{f}
KJV NKJV RSVmg NRSVmg ESVmg NLTmg HCSBmg NETmg

variant 3 — Θαδδαιος ο επικληθεις Λεββαιος
"Thaddeaus, the one called Lebbaeus"
13
none

variant 4 — "Judas Zelotes"
it[a,b,g1,h,q]
none

variant 5 — "Judas the son of James" (after Simon the Cananean in 10:4)
syr[s]
none

A comparison of the listing of apostles in Matt 10:2-4, Mark 3:16-19, and Luke 6:13-16 indicates Thaddaeus must be the same person as Judas son of James or Judas brother of James (possibly the author of Jude):

1. & 2. Peter and Andrew

3. & 4. James and John, sons of Zebedee

5. & 6. Philip and Bartholomew

7. & 8. Thomas and Matthew

9. James (the son of Alphaeus) and

10a. Thaddaeus or Lebbaeus (in Matthew, Mark)

11a. Simon the Cananean (in Matthew, Mark)

10b. Simon the Zealot (in Luke, Acts)

11b. Judas the son of James (in Luke, Acts)

12. Judas Iscariot

In the lists of the twelve disciples in the Synoptic Gospels and Acts, the first four pairs are consistent; the last two are not. By comparing the list above, it seems likely that the last four disciples (9-12) were:

9. James the son of Alphaeus

10. Thaddaeus, also called Judas the son of James

11. Simon the Cananaean, also called Simon the Zealot

12. Judas Iscariot

The textual variations in this verse (as in Mark 2:18—see comments there) are the result of scribes attempting to harmonize the accounts. Either "Lebbaeus" or "Thaddaeus" is original (most likely the latter), based on the combined manuscript evidence of A B. The other readings are conflations or harmonizations to the other gospels.

Matthew 10:4a

WH NU — Σίμων ὁ Καναναῖος
"Simon the Cananean" (Simon the Zealot)
B C (D) L f^1 33
NKJVmg RSV NRSV ESV NASB NIV TNIV NEB REB NJB NAB NLT HCSB NET

variant/TR Σιμων ο Καναιτης
"Simon the Cananite"
א W Θ f^{13} Maj
KJV NKJV

The variant reading is not just an alternate spelling of the same name. The name Καναναιος ("Cananean") is the Aramaic form of "Zealot." The name Καναιτης describes a man from Cana. If the WH NU reading is correct, then it is possible that this disciple of Jesus was zealous for the law or was "a zealous nationalist prior to his call to follow Jesus. . . . Later, the term *zealot* was used to designate the religiously motivated Jewish revolutionaries who were active in guerilla-type warfare in the period leading up to A.D. 70 and the destruction of Jerusalem" (DJG 181).

Matthew 10:4b

The best manuscript evidence (א B L W etc.) supports the reading Ιουδας ο Ισκαριωτης ("Judas Iscariot"), which all English translations follow. However, some interesting variants appear in the textual tradition: Ιουδας ο Σκαριωτης ("Judas the Scarioth") in D and Old Latin; Ιουδας Ισκαριωθ ("Judas from Kerioth") in C; Ιουδας ο Σιμωνος Ισκαριωτου ("Judas Simon Iscariot") in Origen. Scholars have conjectured several meanings for Judas's surname. Among the possibilities suggested, three are legitimate: (1) "man of Kerioth," a city in Moab (Jer 48:24; Amos 2:2) or in southern Judah (Josh 15:25); (2) "the dyer," reflecting Judas's occupation; (3) σικαριος, a Greek word meaning "assassin" (see Acts 21:38). Of the three, the first meaning seems to be the most viable. According to some ancient manuscripts, Judas's father is said to be "of Kerioth" in John 6:71 (א* Θ f^{13}); 12:4 (D); 13:2 (D it^{e}); 14:22 (D). But in other manuscripts at John 6:71 and 13:26, Judas's father is given the same epithets as those listed above. In this verse, it is safest to side with the best manuscript evidence (i.e., that supporting WH NU). The first variant may reflect the Greek word σικαριος (Latin *sicarius*), the second shows conformity to Mark 3:19 and Luke 6:16, and the third is a harmonization to John 6:71.

Matthew 10:8

TR WH NU ἀσθενοῦντας θεραπεύετε, νεκροὺς ἐγείρετε
"heal the sick, raise the dead"
א B C* D 0281^{vid} $f^{1,13}$ 33 it syr^{s} cop^{bo}
all

variant ασθενουντας θεραπευετε
"heal the sick"
C^{3} L Θ Maj syr^{p} cop^{sa} Eusebius
NKJVmg

Most likely the words νεκρους εγειρετε ("raise the dead") were deleted by scribes who thought it impossible that Jesus would give disciples the power to raise the dead. In fact, there is no record of them having done so in the Gospels—unless the plural "we must do the works of him who sent us" in John 9:3-4 is meant to include the disciples (see note there).

Matthew 10:10

Instead of the TR WH NU reading, "the laborer is worthy of his food" (της τροφης αυτου), which is supported by all the early manuscripts, a few manuscripts (K 565 892 it syr[hmg]) read "the laborer is worthy of his wages" (του μισθου αυτου). The variant arose as an attempt to conform Matt 10:10 to 1 Tim 5:18. However, the point of the Matthean passage is that the disciples should receive food, not wages, from those who received their message.

Matthew 10:12

At the end of the verse (after the words, "As you enter the house, greet it"), several manuscripts (א*,2 D L W 0281[vid]) add, λεγοντες ειρηνη τω οικω τουτω ("saying, 'peace to this house'"). The addition, though found in a number of witnesses, was probably taken from Luke 10:5 by scribes who considered Matthew's wording to be too terse.

Matthew 10:19

In a few manuscripts (D L) the second clause of this verse, δοθησεται γαρ υμιν εν εκεινη ωρα τι λαλησητε ("for in that hour it will be given to you what to say"), has been omitted—probably due to homoeoteleuton (the previous clause also ends with τι λαλησητε).

Matthew 10:23

WH NU read Οταν δε διωκωσιν υμας εν τη πολει ταυτη, φευγετε εις την ετεραν ("when they persecute you in that city flee to a different one") based on the good testimony of א B W 33, and this is what is found in all English versions. Other manuscripts (C D L Θ 0171[vid] Maj—so TR) replace the last word, ετεραν, with αλλην ("another one"). Another variant reading is as follows: οταν δε διωκωσιν υμας εν τη πολει ταυτη, φευγετε εις την αλλην, εαν δε εν τη αλλη διωκωσιν υμας φευγετε εις την αλλην ("when they persecute you in that city flee to another; and if they persecute you in the other, flee to another"). This is found in D 0171[vid] (L) f[1,13] it syr[s].

It is possible that the last variant is original and the shorter reading resulted from homoeoteleuton—in some manuscripts both clauses end with the same word, αλλην. The longer reading also seems more compatible with the prediction that follows in the second half of the verse, wherein Jesus says that the disciples would not exhaust all the cities of Israel prior to his coming. However, the longer reading could be nothing more than a natural scribal expansion prompted by the term ετεραν ("a different one") (Westcott and Hort 1882, 12). Therefore, the shorter reading, which has good support and also suits the context, is to be preferred.

Neither reading negates the difficulty of the passage, which says that Jesus would return before the disciples had time to go through all the cities of Israel (in their flight from persecution). Carson (1984, 251) wrongly says that B and D omit "of Israel" (B and D omit only the article before "Israel"); otherwise, this omission would significantly alter the text by no longer delimiting the geographical location.

Matthew 10:25

TR NU Βεελζεβουλ
"Beelzebul"
𝔓[110] C (D L) W Θ f[1,13] 33 Maj
NKJVmg RSV NRSV ESV NASB NIVmg TNIV REB NJB NAB NLT HCSB NET

variant 1/WH Βεεζεβουλ
"Beezebul"
א B
NLTmg

variant 2 *Beelzebub*
it[c] syr[p,s]
KJV NKJV NIV NEB NLTmg

Most of the Greek manuscripts read "Beelzebul," which is likely the right form of this word. (This reading now has the support of the recently published papyrus 𝔓[110], dated ca. 300). The religious leaders may have invented this term by combining two Hebrew words: *ba'al* ("lord," see Hos 2:16 [18]), which stood for the local Canaanite fertility god; and *zebul* ("exalted dwelling," see 1 Kgs 8:13). The first variant is simply a spelling change that avoids the λζ combination, which is unusual in Greek. The second variant in the Old Latin and Syriac versions is an attempt to identify this one with the god of Ekron (see 2 Kgs 1:2-3, 6, 16), an idol worshiped by pagans. As all idolatry was regarded as devil worship (Lev 17:7; Deut 32:17; Ps 106:37; 1 Cor 10:20), there seems to have been something peculiarly satanic about the worship of this hateful god, which caused his name to become a synonym of Satan. Though we nowhere read that Jesus was actually called "Beelzebul," he was charged with being in league with Satan under that name (12:24, 26), and more than once was charged with "having a devil" or "demon" (Mark 3:30; John 7:20; 8:48). Here it is used to denote the most opprobrious language that could be applied by one to another.

Matthew 10:35-36

In most manuscripts it says that a "man" (ανθρωπον) will be against his father and mother. In D it syr[c,s] "man" was changed to "son" (υιον) to make the text conform completely to the wording in Mic 7:6.

Matthew 10:37

TR WH NU read και ο φιλων υιον η θυγατερα υπερ εμε ουκ εστιν μου αξιος ("and the one who loves his son or daughter more than me is not worthy of me") based on א B[mg] C L W etc., which is followed by all the English versions. Some manuscripts (𝔓[19] B[txt] D it[d]) omit this clause; 𝔓[19] also omits all of 10:38— perhaps due to homoeoteleuton (10:37a and 10:38 both end with αξιος). However, it is possible that the exemplar of 𝔓[19] did not include 10:37b and that homoeoteleuton accounts only for the omission of 10:38. The scribe of B originally wrote 10:37, lacking the clause noted above, and then added it in the lower margin. D presents an abbreviated rendition of this pericope (10:34-42), omitting 10:37b and 10:41b.

Are we to conclude, then, that scribal error alone accounts for the omission here, or was there some exegetical reason for deleting (or adding) this? As an argument for the longer reading, it could be said that 10:37b was deleted by scribes to achieve harmony with 10:35, which speaks only of the children's relationship to their parents.

Matthew 10:42

The Greek expression found in the best witnesses (𝔓19 ℵ B C W etc.), ποτηριον ψυχρου ("cup of cold"), lacks the substantive after the adjective "cold." Thus, the word υδατος ("water") is a natural addition included in D and found in many ancient versions (Old Latin, Syriac, Armenian, Ethiopic, and Georgian) and in English versions.

Matthew 11:2a

TR WH NU read Ιωαννης ακουσας εν τω δεσμωτηριω τα εργα του Χριστου ("in prison John heard about the works of the Christ"), based on the excellent authority of 𝔓19vid ℵ B C L W etc. The name Χριστου ("Christ") was changed to Ιησου ("Jesus") in D syr[c]. The variant reading came into existence because some scribe(s) thought it odd that John the Baptist would question whether Jesus was the Christ in the same context in which he is called "the Christ." Thus, "Christ" was changed to "Jesus." This sort of smoothing over difficult readings is typical in D.

Matthew 11:2b

WH NU πέμψας διὰ τῶν μαθητῶν αὐτοῦ
"he sent [a message] by way of his disciples"
ℵ B C* D W Z Δ Θ 0233 f[13] 33 cop[sa]
NKJVmg RSV NRSV ESV NASB NIV TNIV NEB REB NJB NAB NLT HCSB NET

variant/TR πεμψας δυο των μαθητων αυτου
"he sent two of his disciples"
C[3] L f[1] Maj cop[bo] Origen
KJV NKJV NRSVmg

Although it is possible that δια was confused for δυο (or vice versa), it is more likely that δυο is the result of a scribal attempt to harmonize this verse to Luke 7:18. The reading δια has excellent manuscript support.

Matthew 11:15

WH NU ὁ ἔχων ὦτα ἀκουέτω
"the one having ears let him hear"
B D 700 it[k] syr[s]
RSVmg NRSV ESV NIV TNIV NEB REB NJB NAB HCSB NET

variant/TR ο εχων ωτα ακουειν ακουετω
"the one having ears to hear let him hear"
ℵ C L W Z Θ f[1,13] 33 Maj syr[c,h,p] cop
KJV NKJV RSV NRSVmg NASB NLT HCSBmg

The variant reading is the result of scribes harmonizing this expression with that found in Mark (4:9, 23; 7:16) and Luke (8:8; 14:35). The resultant expanded text sounds better in oral reading than does the shorter text.

Matthew 11:19

WH NU ἐδικαιώθη ἡ σοφία ἀπὸ τῶν ἔργων αὐτῆς
"wisdom is justified by her works"
ℵ B* W syr[h,p] cop[bo] MSS[according to Jerome] (f[13] it[k] add παντων = "all [her works]")
NKJVmg RSV NRSV ESV NASB NIV TNIV NEB REB NJB NAB NLT HCSB NET

variant/TR εδικαιωθη η σοφια απο των τεκνων αυτης
"wisdom is justified by her children"
B[2] C D L Θ f[1] 33 Maj syr[c,s]
KJV NKJV RSVmg NRSVmg ESVmg NJBmg HCSBmg NETmg

The WH NU reading has superior manuscript support inasmuch as it is found in ℵ B* W, several early versions (notably it[k], syr, cop), and was known by Jerome to be the reading in some manuscripts (which had to be earlier than ca. 400). The variant has support from later manuscripts and is probably the result of a scribal attempt to conform this verse to Luke 7:35, a parallel passage. Wisdom, though momentarily jeered, is always proven correct by her future deeds. The emphasis in Luke is on Wisdom's future generations.

Matthew 12:4

WH NU τοὺς ἄρτους τῆς προθέσεως ἔφαγον
"they ate the bread of presentation"
ℵ B
NASB TNIV NJB NLT HCSB NET

variant/TR τους αρτους της προθεσεως εφαγεν
"he ate the bread of presentation"
𝔓[70] C D L W Θ f[1,13] 33 Maj
KJV NKJV RSV NRSV ESV NIV NEB REB NAB HCSBmg

The variant reading was rejected by the NU editors on the grounds that it represents conformity to the parallel passages in Mark 2:26 and Luke 6:4. But the variant has the earliest (𝔓[70]) and most diverse testimony. It is also the more difficult reading because the OT passage alluded to here (1 Sam 21:1-6) implies that David and his men—not just David— ate the bread, as does the previous verse, which speaks of "the ones with him" (i.e., David's companions). Thus, the WH NU reading could represent conformity to the immediate context or the OT passage.

Matthew 12:15

TR NU ἠκολούθησαν αὐτῷ [ὄχλοι] πολλοί
"many crowds followed him"
C D L W Θ (0233) 0281 f[1,13] 33 Maj
KJV NKJV NRSV TNIV NAB HCSB NET

variant/WH ηκολουθησαν αυτω πολλοι
"many followed him"
ℵ B
NKJVmg RSV NRSVmg ESV NASB NIV NEB REB NJB NLT HCSBmg NETmg

The variant is likely the original reading because of its presence in ℵ and B. This shorter reading cannot be discounted as Alexandrian trimming because the scribes of ℵ and B did not shorten the same expression (οχλοι πολλοι) in any of the other five occurrences in Matthew (see

4:25; 8:1; 13:2; 15:30; 19:2). The NU reading, therefore, would have to be the result of scribal conformity to Matthean style.

Matthew 12:21

This is the last verse of a four-verse (12:18-21) quotation of Isa 42:1-4. In 12:21, Matthew follows the Septuagint ("and in his name the Gentiles will hope"), which is distinctly different from the Masoretic Text ("and the islands will wait for his law"). However, Matthew left out the preposition επι before the dative τω ονοματι αυτω ("his name"), which was filled in by a few manuscripts (W 0233) to conform Matthew's quote to the Septuagint.

Matthew 12:22

WH NU — τὸν κωφὸν λαλεῖν καὶ βλέπειν
"the mute person [was able] to speak and to see"
ℵ B D
NKJVmg RSV NRSV ESV NASB (NIV) TNIV NAB NLT HCSB NET

variant 1 — τον κωφον και τυφλον λαλειν και βλεπειν
"the mute and blind person [was able] to speak and to see"
L W Δ Θ 0233 $f^{1,13}$
NEB REB NJB

variant 2/TR — τον τυφλον και κωφον λαλειν και βλεπειν
"the blind and mute person [was able] to speak and to see"
C 0281 33 Maj
KJV NKJV

According to the WH NU reading, Jesus healed a person who was demon-possessed, blind, and mute, with the result that "the mute person" (τον κωφον) spoke and saw. But because it sounds awkward that the mute person spoke and saw, scribes introduced the additions found in the two variants. The transposition of words in the variants reveals the secondary nature of both additions.

Matthew 12:24, 27

TR NU — βεελζεβουλ
"Beelzebul"
($\mathfrak{P}^{21}$ 12:24 only—missing in 12:27) C D L W 0233 0281 Θ $f^{1,13}$ 33 Maj
RSV NRSV ESV NASB NIVmg TNIV REB NJB NAB NLT HCSB NET

variant 1/WH — Βεεζεβουλ
"Beezebul"
ℵ B
NIVmg

variant 2 — *Beelzebub*
it^{c} $syr^{c,p}$
KJV NKJV NIV NEB NJBmg

See comments on 10:25.

Matthew 12:30

TR WH NU read ο μη συναγων μετ εμου σκορπιζει ("the one not gathering with me scatters"), based on B C D L W f[1,13] Maj. A variant reading adds με ("me") to the end of this statement, making it read, "the one not gathering with me scatters me." This is supported by א 33 syr[hmg] cop[bo] Origen Athanasius. To modern sensibilities, the variant reading sounds odd. Not one English version has adopted the variant reading or noted it. But this must not have sounded odd to some ancient scribes, exegetes, and translators, who retained the reading "scatters me." The metaphor speaks of gathering and scattering sheep. We do not think of scattering sheep as including the shepherd, but he is so identified with his flock that, inasmuch as Jesus is united to those who are his own, to scatter his sheep is to scatter or divide Jesus himself. Compare Acts 9:4, where Jesus says to Paul, "Why do you persecute *me?*" when, in fact, Paul was persecuting Christians. To hurt the believers is to hurt Jesus. Thus, the expression "scatters me" may be equivalent to "divides me," which is congruent with the thrust of this passage, in which Jesus argues that any kingdom divided against itself will not stand (12:25-29).

Uncomfortable with the expression "scatters me," several scribes may have shortened it to "scatters." Of course, the opposite could have happened: "me" could have been added to achieve balance with the previous clause "the one not with me is against me." Good sense can be made of either reading. The same textual variation occurs in Luke 11:23, with documentary support favoring the shorter reading (see comments there).

Matthew 12:47

TR NU	[εἶπεν δέ τις αὐτῷ· ἰδοὺ ἡ μήτηρ σου καὶ οἱ ἀδελφοί σου ἔξω ἑστήκασιν ζητοῦντες σοι λαλῆσαι.] "And someone said to him, 'Behold, your mother and brothers are outside wanting to speak with you.'" א[(1)] C (D) W Z Θ f[(1),13] (33) Maj syr[h,p] cop[bo] KJV NKJV RSVmg NRSV ESVmg NASB NIV TNIV NEB REB NJBmg NAB NLT HCSB NET
variant/WH	omit verse א* B L it[k] syr[c,s] cop[sa] RSV NRSVmg ESV NIVmg TNIVmg NJB NABmg NLTmg HCSBmg NETmg

The arguments in favor of the TR NU reading are twofold: (1) The verse was omitted due to homoeoteleuton (both 12:46 and 12:47 end with the same word (λαλησαι). (2) Jesus' response in 12:48 requires a response to someone's statement. If 12:47 were missing, Jesus would not be answering anyone. The arguments for the variant are twofold: (1) The array of witnesses supporting the omission is substantial, calling into question whether homoeoteleuton could have occurred in so many witnesses. (2) Scribes would have been prompted by the context to fill in the gap between 12:46 and 12:48, whereas Matthew may have expected readers to fill this gap in their own minds as they read. All things being equal, the variant, found in WH, has better support and is the reading which was most likely changed.

Matthew 13:4

Some late manuscripts (K Θ f[13]) and several ancient versions (it[b,h] syr[c,h] cop[sa,bo]) add του ουρανου ("of heaven") after τα πετεινα ("the birds"). This was a harmonization to Luke 8:5.

Matthew 13:9, 43

WH NU ὁ ἔχων ὦτα ἀκουέτω
"the one having ears let him hear"
ℵ* B (0242 for 13:43—missing in 13:9)
RSV NRSV ESV NASB NIV TNIV NEB REB NJB NAB HCSB NET

variant/TR ο εχων ωτα ακουειν ακουετω
"the one having ears to hear let him hear"
ℵ[2] C D W Z Θ $f^{1,13}$ 33 Maj
KJV NKJV RSVmg NRSVmg ESVmg NLT HCSBmg

The same variation occurred in Matt 11:15 (see comments there). The longer reading is probably the result of conformity to Mark 4:9; Luke 8:8. The sense of the saying is not affected either way, but the longer reading makes for better oral reading.

Matthew 13:14

D and a few Old Latin manuscripts fill out the quotation from Isa 6:9 by adding πορευθητι και ειπε τω λαω τουτω ("go to this people and say") prior to the reading of the original text.

Matthew 13:28

Following the text of B 1424 cop, WH omits δουλοι ("slaves"). This reflects WH's strong preference for B.

Matthew 13:35a

TR WH NU διὰ τοῦ προφήτου
"through the prophet"
ℵ[1] B C D L W 0233 0242 Maj it syr cop Eusebius
KJV NKJV RSV NRSV ESV NASB NIV TNIV NEBmg REB NJB NAB NLT HCSB NET

variant 1 δια Ησαιου του προφητου
"through Isaiah the prophet"
ℵ* Θ $f^{1,13}$ 33 Porphyry[according to Jerome] MSS[according to Eusebius and Jerome]
RSVmg NRSVmg NEB REBmg

variant 2 δια Ασαφ του προφητου
"through Asaph the prophet"
MSS[according to Jerome]
none

This textual problem hinges on the fact that Asaph, not Isaiah, was the prophet Matthew quoted. This problem was discussed as early as the third century. Eusebius said that some copyists must not have understood that "the prophet" meant by Matthew was Asaph, and therefore "added in the Gospel δια Ησαιου του προφητου ['through Isaiah the prophet'], but in the accurate copies it stands without the addition δια Ησαιου ['through Isaiah']." Thus, Eusebius was arguing for the shorter reading, declaring that it was in the accurate copies (see Tregelles 1857, 1:47). Jerome conjectured that Ασαφ was the original reading, for it was found in all the old manuscripts, but then was removed by ignorant men and replaced with Ησαιου. However, not one extant manuscript reads Ασαφ. What is interesting, though, is that Jerome was responding to Porphyry (a third-century critic of Christianity), who used this verse to show that Matthew was ignorant. Thus, we know that in the third century some manuscripts must have read "Isaiah."

Quite possibly, later scribes expunged "Isaiah" from the text in order to correct Matthew's mistake. This might have been what happened in א, where the corrector א[1] deleted "Isaiah." In other manuscripts Matthew was similarly corrected elsewhere (see comments on 27:9). It is for this reason that Hort (1882, 13) judged the reading with "Isaiah" to be original, which was then changed by deleting "Isaiah" or adding "Asaph." Only one English translation, the NEB, has placed "Isaiah" in the text (see Tasker 1964, 412 for his reasons), but this was changed in the REB, which now follows TR WH NU.

In defense of the shorter reading, it could be said that "Isaiah" was inserted because it was typical for Matthew to name "Isaiah" in prophetic quotations (3:3; 4:14; 8:17; 12:17) and, where he did not do so, for scribes to add his name (see 1:22; 2:5 and comments). This kind of insertion may have found its way into א* and been subsequently corrected in א[1].

Matthew 13:35b

TR NU	κεκρυμμένα ἀπὸ καταβολῆς [κόσμου] "things hidden from the world's foundation" א*,2 C D L W Θ 0233 f[13] Maj Clement all
variant/WH	κεκρυμμενα απο καταβολης "things hidden from the foundation" א[1] B f[1] it[e,k] Origen NRSVmg NLTmg

According to the longer reading, the prophet spoke "things that were hidden from *the world's* foundation." This is a quotation taken from Ps 78:2. The Hebrew text says that these things were hidden "from of old," which, in the context of the psalm, probably refers to the beginning of the nation of Israel. The Septuagint says that these things were hidden "from the beginning," which could convey "the beginning of creation." If Matthew was following the Hebrew text here, the shorter reading is more likely original: "these things were hidden from the foundation (of Israel)." If Matthew was following the Greek text, the longer reading is more appropriate. Since the internal evidence can be seen to support either reading, we must turn to the external evidence, which slightly favors the omission of κοσμου ("of the world").

Matthew 13:36

In usual fashion, the subject, ο Ιησους ("Jesus"), is inserted in later manuscripts: C L W Θ 0233 f[13] 33 Maj. Several modern English versions do the same because this is a new section.

According to the best documentary evidence—the three earliest manuscripts (א* B 0242[vid])—Matthew wrote the verb διασαφησον (which means "to thoroughly explain"). Later documents (א[2] D C L W) read φρασον (meaning simply "explain"), which was probably a harmonization to Matt 15:15.

Matthew 13:37

Instead of ο υιος του ανθρωπου ("the Son of Man"), supported by most manuscripts, one manuscript (28) reads ο υιος του θεου ("the Son of God"), and another witness (Epiphanius) reads ο θεος ("God").

Matthew 13:43

See comments on 13:9 above.

Matthew 13:44

B cop[bo] and Origen omit παντα ("everything"). WH follows this slim testimony.

Matthew 13:51

WH NU Συνήκατε ταῦτα πάντα;
"Have you understood all these things?"
ℵ B D Θ syr[s]
NKJVmg RSV NRSV ESV NASB NIV (TNIV) NEB REB NJB NAB NLT HCSB NET

variant/TR λεγει αυτοις ο Ιησους, Συνηκατε ταυτα παντα;
"Jesus says to them, 'Have you understood all these things?'"
C L W 0233 f[1,13] 33 Maj
KJV NKJV HCSBmg

The first addition in the variant is intended to help readers immediately understand that the speaker is Jesus, who has not been mentioned by name since 13:1.

Matthew 13:55

WH NU Ιωσηφ
"Joseph"
ℵ[2] B C Θ f[1] 33 syr
RSV NRSV ESV NASB NIV TNIV NEB REB NJB NAB NLT HCSB NET

variant 1/TR Ιωσης
"Joses"
𝔓[103] L W Δ 0106 f[13] it[k]
KJV NKJV NLTmg HCSBmg

variant 2 Ιωαννης
"John"
ℵ*[vid] D
NLTmg

Of the names of Jesus' four brothers mentioned here, the first, third, and fourth are textually certain—James, Simon, and Jude. The second is uncertain, as the above evidence shows. Of the three variants, Matthew could have written either "Joseph" or "Joses." Both readings have early and diverse support—𝔓[103] (ca. 200) providing the earliest witness to "Joses." According to Metzger, "Joses" is the Galilean pronunciation (*yose*) of the correct Hebrew *yosep* ("Joseph"). Nonetheless, "Joses" appears to be a harmonization to Mark 6:3. The other variant, "John," could have arisen due to the natural association of "James and John" found frequently in the Gospels (TCGNT). It is also possible that the variants were created by scribes who believed in Mary's perpetual virginity and therefore wanted to avoid having one of Joseph's sons called by his same name, for that could indicate that Joseph and Mary had sexual intercourse. Of course, those who espouse this view say that all of Jesus' "brothers and sisters" were his cousins or half-siblings. (See comments on Mark 3:32.)

Matthew 13:57

The WH NU reading, following B D Θ 0281 33 700, has ουκ προφητης ατιμος ει μη εν τη πατριδι, which is literally translated as "a prophet is not dishonored except in the father-country." The nonspecificity of τη πατριδι led various scribes (א Z f[13]) to add ιδια ("his own") or αυτου ("his"—as in L W f[1] Maj—so TR) or both (as in C). The first variant is a harmonization to John 4:44, the second variant is a harmonization to Mark 6:4, and the third variant is a conflation of the first two.

Matthew 14:2

Nearly all the Greek manuscripts read, ουτος εστιν Ιωαννης ο Βαπτιστης ("this is John the Baptist"). But D and several Old Latin manuscripts add "whom I beheaded."

Matthew 14:3a

The verse begins with the statement, "For Herod had arrested John, bound him, and put him in prison," following the testimony of א C D L W etc. A few manuscripts (B Θ f[13]) have the addition τοτε ("then") before the verb κρατητας ("had arrested") to help the reader understand that 14:3 chronologically occurs before 14:1-2. Such an addition is not needed because this is sufficiently conveyed by the aorist verbs with a pluperfect sense.

Matthew 14:3b

TR WH NU — Ἡρῳδιάδα τὴν γυναῖκα Φιλίππου τοῦ ἀδελφοῦ αὐτοῦ·
"Herodias, his brother Philip's wife"
א B C L W Δ Θ f[1,13] 33
all

variant — Ηρωδιαδα την γυναικα του αδελφου αυτου
"Herodias, his brother's wife"
D it[a,c,d,e] Augustine
RSVmg NRSVmg

According to Matthew, Herodias was originally married to a son of Herod the Great called Philip. This Philip is most likely the person Josephus simply calls "Herod, son of Herod the Great and Mariamne" (*Ant.* 18.5.4), whom scholars refer to as Herod Philip. Herodias later left Herod Philip to marry Herod Antipas, a move which violated the OT law (Lev 18:16) and prompted John the Baptist's critique. Herod Philip and Herodias had a daughter named Salome, who later married another son of Herod the Great named Philip (known as Philip the Tetrarch, mentioned in Luke 3:1). Perhaps to avoid confusion with Philip the Tetrarch, scribes dropped the name "Philip" from Matthew's text. This was done in D and it[a,c,d,e], and probably by Luke himself in Luke 3:19.

Matthew 14:12

WH NU — ἦραν τὸ πτῶμα
"they carried the corpse"
א B C D L Θ f[1,13] 33
NAB HCSB

variant/TR ηραν το σωμα
"they carried the body"
W 0106 Maj
KJV NKJV RSV NRSV ESV NASB NIV TNIV NEB REB NJB NLT HCSBmg NET

Quite possibly, πτωμα ("corpse") was borrowed from the parallel passage, Mark 6:29; but it is more likely that πτωμα was changed to σωμα, either by accident (a scribe mistaking one word for the other) or by intention—to soften the description of John's cadaver. Nearly all English translations do the same kind of softening; only the NAB and HCSB read "corpse."

Matthew 14:14

In typical fashion, several manuscripts (C L W 067 0106[vid] Maj) display the added, specific subject, ο Ιησους ("Jesus"), carried over from the previous verse.

Matthew 14:15

א B Z[vid] 33 read οι μαθηται ("the disciples"), to which was added αυτου ("his") in several manuscripts (C D L W Θ $f^{1,13}$ Maj—so TR). This is a typical scribal expansion in the Gospels. The original readers would have known that "the disciples" were Jesus' disciples. Therefore, the possessive pronoun "his" is an addition intended to help later readers.

Matthew 14:16

Since the specified subject ο Ιησους ("Jesus") is not present in several manuscripts (א* D Z[vid] it[e,k] syr[c,s,p] cop[sa,bo]), it is very likely that it was added by scribes, as was often done in the text of Matthew.

Matthew 14:21

A few witnesses (D Θ f^1 it) reverse the order of the phrase γυναικων και παιδιων ("women and children"). In Near Eastern culture, children often had higher social status than women, and this change might reflect that bias. We can be certain that the change was calculated, because the same witnesses have the same transposition in 15:38 (see comments there).

Matthew 14:24

WH NU τὸ δὲ πλοῖον ἤδη σταδίους πολλοὺς ἀπὸ τῆς γῆς
"the boat was many stadia away from the land"
B f^{13} cop[sa]
NKJVmg RSV (NRSV ESV NASB) NEBmg (NAB NLT) HCSB (NET)

variant 1 το δε πλοιον απεχειν της γης σταδιους ικανους
"the boat was considerable stadia away from the land"
Θ (700) syr[c,p]
NIV TNIV NEB REB NJB

variant 2/TR το δε πλοιον μεσον της θαλασσης ην
"the boat was in the middle of the sea"
א C L W 073 0106 f^1 33 Maj
KJV NKJV HCSBmg

variant 3 το δε πλοιον ην εις μεσον της θαλασσης
"the boat was [went] into the middle of the sea"
D 1424 it[e]
none

The second variant has the best manuscript support (the third is a variation of the second); however, its agreement with Mark 6:47 causes one to suspect it as a case of scribal harmonization. The first variant also appears to be the work of harmonization—in this case, to John 6:19. The difference is not insignificant. To be in the middle of the Sea of Galilee means to be about three or four miles from shore; to be many stadia from land could mean they were just a half mile from shore or four miles from shore. John tells us specifically that they were 25 to 30 stadia (one *stadion* was about 600 feet or 185 meters) away from shore, which is about four miles out. This puts the boat in the middle of the Sea of Galilee, which is about seven miles across. To be in the middle of the sea (which was about 200 feet deep at that point) during a violent storm was cause for great consternation, and it increases the drama of Jesus' rescue.

Matthew 14:27

The absence of ο Ιησους ("Jesus") in some witnesses (א* D 073) and its presence in two different places in various manuscripts (before αυτοις in א[1] B and after αυτοις in C L W Θ 0106 f[1,13] Maj) reveals that it is a scribal insertion, intended to specify the subject. The insertion spoils the suspense of the narrative, which intentionally does not name "Jesus" because the disciples are uncertain of who this apparition-like visitor is until he identifies himself by saying, εγω ειμι ("I am").

Matthew 14:29

WH NU Πέτρος περιεπάτησεν ἐπὶ τὰ ὕδατα καὶ ἦλθεν πρὸς τὸν Ἰησοῦν.
"Peter walked upon the waters and came to(ward) Jesus."
(א ελθειν ουν ηλθεν = "to come, then he came") B C*[vid] 700
RSV NRSV ESV NASB NIV TNIV NEB REB NJB NAB (NLT) HCSB NET

variant 1/TR Πετρος περιπατειν επι τα υδατα ελθειν προς τον Ιησουν
"Peter walked upon the waters to come to(ward) Jesus"
א[1] C[2] D L W Θ 073 0106 f[1,13] 33 Maj
KJV NKJV

The change in the variant reflects scribal interpretation. Since, as v. 30 implies, Peter did not walk on the water all the way to Jesus, a scribe wanted to clarify that it was only Peter's intention "to come" to Jesus, not that he actually made it to him. But the WH NU reading is itself ambiguous; it can mean that Peter "came to Jesus" or "came toward Jesus." Apparently, Peter made it most of the way, because when he started to sink, Jesus needed only to reach out his hand to catch him (Carson 1984, 346).

Matthew 14:30

TR NU τὸν ἄνεμον [ἰσχυρόν]
"the strong wind"
B[1] C D L (W adds σφορδα = "very") Θ 0106 f[1,13] Maj
KJV NKJV RSVmg NRSV ESVmg NEB REB NAB NLT HCSB NET

variant/WH τον ανεμον
"the wind"
ℵ B* 073 33 cop[sa,bo]
NKJVmg RSV NRSVmg ESV NASB NIV TNIV NJB HCSBmg

It is possible that ισχυρον was accidentally dropped due to homoeoteleuton—the two previous words both end with ον. But it is more likely that the adjective was added to intensify the description of the wind. Several modern versions, following the testimony of ℵ B* etc., exhibit the shorter reading.

Matthew 15:4

WH NU θεὸς εἶπεν
"God said"
ℵ[1] B D 073 f[1,13] syr[c,p,s]
RSV NRSV NASB NIV TNIV NEB REB NJB NAB NLT HCSB NET

variant/TR θεος ενετειλατο λεγων
"God commanded saying"
ℵ*[,2] C L W 0106 33 Maj syr[h]
KJV NKJV NRSVmg ESV HCSBmg

The WH NU reading cannot be dismissed as Alexandrian trimming because the witnesses are not all Alexandrian. The variant was created to conform the verb of 15:4 with εντολην ("commandment") in 15:3.

Matthew 15:5

This verse is difficult to interpret because it literally reads, "But you say, whoever says to his father and mother, 'it is a gift,' whatever from me you might have benefited from." Something has to be added to the end of the statement for it to make sense. The scribe of ℵ* added ουδεν εστιν ("it is nothing"). This yields the sense, "because I have given it as a gift to God, what you might have benefited from me is now nothing." In other words, the statement says that a child was allowed, by religious tradition, to forego taking care of his or her parents in lieu of making an offering to God (see comments on 15:6a). Most English translations expand the text to provide the reader with a meaning similar to this.

Matthew 15:6a

WH NU οὐ μὴ τιμήσει τὸν πατέρα αὐτοῦ
"by no means does he [have to] honor his father"
ℵ B D it[a,e] syr[c] cop[sa]
NKJVmg RSV NRSV ESV NASBmg NIV NAB NLT HCSB NET

variant 1/TR add η την μητερα αυτου ("or his mother")
C L W Θ 0106 f[1] Maj
KJV NKJV NASB NIVmg TNIV NEB REB NJB NLTmg HCSBmg

variant 2 add η την μητερα ("or the [his] mother")
073 f[13] 33
none

variant 3 add και την μητερα αυτου ("and his mother")
Φ 565 cop[bo]
none

The first part of 15:6 completes the statement begun in 15:5 (see comments there). The shorter reading has the best testimony, and all the variants are expansions attempting to achieve parallelism with 15:4-5, which mention both father and mother.

Matthew 15:6b

WH NU τὸν λόγον τοῦ θεοῦ
"the word of God"
א[1] B D Θ it syr cop
RSV NRSV ESV NASB NIV TNIV NJB NAB NLT HCSB NET

variant 1 τον νομον του θεου
"the law of God"
א*[,2] C 073 f[13] Ptolemy
RSVmg NRSVmg ESVmg NEB REB

variant 2/TR την εντολην του θεου
"the commandment of God"
L W 0106 f[1] 33 Maj
KJV NKJV NRSVmg

According to the WH NU reading, Jesus said, "You nullify the word of God by your tradition." The second variant can easily be dismissed because it has inferior documentary attestation and it is an expected addition inasmuch as the previous verses speak about "the commandment" of God. The true reading has to be one of the other two readings, both of which have fairly good support. Since the WH NU reading may be considered a harmonization to Mark 7:13, it is likely that Jesus was contrasting "the law of God," the Torah (variant 1), with the traditions of the Jews—the interpretations which were to guide Jewish practice of the law. This reading also has good documentary support, including א* (which was changed to λογον then back to νομον) and the early witness of Ptolemy (ca. A.D. 180).

Matthew 15:8

WH NU ὁ λαὸς οὗτος τοῖς χείλεσιν με τιμᾷ
"this people honors me with the [their] lips"
א B D L Θ 073 f[13] 33 syr[c,s] cop
RSV NRSV ESV NASB NIV TNIV NEB REB NJB NAB NLT HCSB NET

variant/TR εγγιζει μοι ο λαος ουτος τω στοματι αυτων και τοις χειλεσιν με τιμα
"this people draws near to me with their mouth and honors me with the [their] lips"
C W 0106 (f[1]) Maj
KJV NKJV HCSBmg

The expanded text is the result of scribal conformity of the OT quotation to Isa 29:13 (LXX). This kind of conformity was especially prevalent in the fourth century and thereafter because it was then that New Testaments were often bound together with Old Testaments in one Bible codex, thereby increasing the temptation for scribes to create harmony between OT quotes appearing in the NT and the OT text itself.

Matthew 15:14

The statement τυφλοι εισιν οδηγοι τυφλων ("they are blind guides of the blind") in NU is supported by א[1] C L W Z Θ f[1,13] 0106 33 Maj (with various orders). However, other manuscripts (א*,2 B D 0237) omit the last word τυφλων (so WH), resulting in "they are blind guides." This shorter reading, with good documentary support, is more likely original because scribes probably added τυφλων to achieve balance with the next statement in the second half of the verse: "and if the blind lead the blind."

Matthew 15:16

In typical fashion, several manuscripts (C L W Maj) add the specific subject, ο Ιησους ("Jesus"), to this verse because it is a new paragraph. Most modern translations do the same.

Matthew 15:18-19

The words εξερχεται κακεινα κοινοι τον ανθρωπον εκ γαρ της καρδιας ("[things] come out, and that defiles the man, for out of the heart") are omitted in א* W 33[vid] due to haplography—the eye of the scribe passing from the word καρδιας ("heart"), which appears just before the words so quoted, to the next appearance of καρδιας several words away.

Matthew 15:31

According to the NU text, following the testimony of C L W Δ 0233, the reading is βλεποντας κωφους λαλουντας ("they were seeing the mutes speaking"). A few other manuscripts (B Θ it[e]) read βλεποντας κωφους ακουοντας ("they were seeing the mutes hearing"). A few other manuscripts (N O Σ) read βλεποντας κωφους ακουοντας και λαλουντας ("they were seeing the mutes hearing and speaking"). Since the word κωφους describes one who is both deaf and mute, the result of a healing would bring both hearing and speaking. To onlookers, however, "speaking" is easily observable, "hearing" is not. Thus, the first variant is the more difficult reading. It also has the support of the earliest manuscript, B. For these reasons, the first variant is probably the original reading, which was then changed to "speaking" in manuscripts supporting the NU text. The second variant is a conflation of these two readings.

Matthew 15:38

Several witnesses (ℵ D Θ f^1 cop) reverse the order of γυναικων και παιδιων ("women and children"). The same change occurred in 14:21 (see comments there), involving several of the same witnesses.

Matthew 15:39

WH NU — Μαγαδάν
"Magadan"
ℵ* B D
NKJVmg RSV NRSV ESV NASB NIV TNIV NEB REB NJB NAB NLT HCSB NET

variant 1 — Μαγεδαν
"Magedan"
ℵ[2] it Eusebius
none

variant 2/TR — Μαγδαλα
"Magdala"
L Θ $f^{1,13}$ Maj
KJV NKJV NRSVmg HCSBmg

variant 3 — Μαγδαλαν
"Magdalan"
C N W 33
NRSVmg

The WH NU reading has a place-name ("Magadan") that is unknown. Arguing for the second variant ("Magdala"), some scholars have suggested that it would be easy for scribes to mistake ΜΑΓΔΑΛΑ ("Magdala") for ΜΑΓΑΔΑΝ ("Magadan") because in the uncial letters of ancient manuscripts the letters *delta, alpha,* and *lambda* look alike (Albright and Mann 1971, 189-190). But this does not account for the Greek letter *nu* at the end of ΜΑΓΑΔΑΝ ("Magadan"), which is distinctly different from *delta, alpha,* and *lambda.* Thus, most other scholars adopt the more difficult reading ("Magadan") because it has the best external support. (See comments on Mark 8:10.)

Matthew 16:2b-3a

TR WH NU — [ὀψίας γενομένης λέγετε· εὐδία, πυρράζει γὰρ ὁ οὐρανός·[3]καὶ πρωΐ· σήμερον χειμών, πυρράζει γὰρ στυγνάζων ὁ οὐρανός. τὸ μὲν πρόσωπον τοῦ οὐρανοῦ γινώσκετε διακρίνειν, τὰ δὲ σημεῖα τῶν καιρῶν οὐ δύνασθε;]
"When it is evening you say, 'It will be fair weather because the sky is red.' [3] And in the morning, 'It will be stormy today because the sky is red and overcast.' You can read the signs of the weather, but you can't read the signs of the time?"
C D L W Θ f^1 33 Maj $syr^{h,p}$ Eusebius (several late MSS add υποκριται ["hypocrites"] after ουρανος ["sky"])
KJV NKJV RSV NRSV ESV NASB NIV TNIV NEBmg NJB NAB NLT HCSB NET

variant omit verses
א B X Γ f^{13} syr[c,s] cop[sa] Origen MSS[according to Jerome]
RSVmg NRSVmg ESVmg NIVmg TNIVmg NEB REB NJBmg NLTmg HCSBmg

Had the additional words been original, there is no good reason to explain why the scribes of א B would have intentionally deleted them, and there is no way to explain the omission as a transcriptional accident. Thus, it is far more likely that this portion, bracketed in NU and double-bracketed in WH, was inserted later by a scribe who either borrowed the concept from Luke 12:54-56 (as a metaphor for "the signs of the times") or from an oral or other written tradition, thereby providing an actual example of what it meant for the ancients to interpret the appearance of the sky (see Westcott and Hort 1882, 13). Among the added words, there are several that are never used by Matthew or (in two instances) by any other writer in the NT: (1) ευδια (appears only here in the NT), (2) πυρραζει (appears only here in the NT and was used only by Byzantine writers; BDAG 899), (3) στυγναζω (appears only here and in Mark 10:22). This strongly suggests that a scribe added the words that appear in the TR WH NU reading (see Hirunuma 1981, 39-45).

But the question remains: Why was this addition made? A close look at the context supplies the answer. According to Matthew's account, the Jewish leaders came to Jesus twice, each time asking him to give them a sign to prove that he was truly the Messiah sent from God. In Matt 12:38, the leaders simply asked for a sign. In response, Jesus said that no sign would be given to them except the sign of Jonah, who depicted Christ's death, burial, and resurrection (12:39-40). Later, the Jewish leaders asked Jesus for a sign "from heaven" (Matt 16:1). Again, Jesus told them that no sign would be given them except the sign of Jonah (16:4)—according to the reading of the shorter version. But the query for "a sign from heaven" does not seem to be answered by Jesus pointing to Jonah. This created a disappointment for various readers—a gap in the text that called for some kind of filling. Therefore, a scribe decided to fill the gap and did so by borrowing from the thought of Luke 12:54-56 and some other unknown source (perhaps the scribe's own knowledge). He added words about signs in the "sky" as complementing a request about a sign from "heaven."

Luke 12:54-56 is an interesting passage, with a different setting than the Matthean account. In Luke 12 no one asks Jesus for a sign from heaven. Rather, Jesus is depicted as condemning that generation of Jews for not realizing what was happening in their lifetimes—the very Messiah, the Son of God, was among them, and they did not realize it. So he told them that they could discern the weather by watching for various signs in the sky and on the earth but they could not discern "the signs of the times." The sign in the sky was western clouds signaling the coming of rain; the sign on the earth was a south wind signaling the coming of heat. The longer reading in Matthew speaks only of signs in the sky: red sky in the evening signals good weather for the next day; red sky in the morning signals bad weather for that day. In this regard, Matt 16:2b-3a and Luke 12:54-55 are different, but Matt 16:3b and Luke 12:56 are nearly identical, with the exception that the Matthean account refers only to the signs of the sky.

Whoever filled the gap in Matthew must have done so by the middle of the fourth century, because we know that around 380 Jerome saw manuscripts with and without the extra words. In fact, Jerome indicated that the extra words were not present in most of the manuscripts known to him. Nonetheless, he included them in his Latin translation. Most English translations do exactly what Jerome did: they include the words, knowing there is some significant doubt about their authenticity. The only modern English versions to exclude the passage are the NEB and REB. All others retain the words and append a footnote about their absence in various manuscripts.

Matthew 16:4

WH NU τὸ σημεῖον Ἰωνᾶ
"the sign of Jonah"
ℵ B D L 700
NKJVmg RSV NRSV ESV NASB NIV TNIV NEB REB NJB NAB (NLT) HCSB NET

variant/TR το σημειον Ιωνα του προφητου
"the sign of Jonah the prophet"
C W Θ f[1,13] 33 Maj
KJV NKJV HCSBmg

The variant is a scribal addition intended to clarify for the reader that this "Jonah" was Jonah the prophet.

Matthew 16:8

WH NU ἄρτους οὐκ ἔχετε
"you have no bread"
ℵ B D Θ f[13] 700
NKJVmg RSV NRSV ESV NASB NIV TNIV REB NJB NAB NLT HCSB NET

variant/TR αρτους ουκ ελαβετε
"you brought no bread"
C L W f[1] 33 Maj
KJV NKJV NEB

Although one word could have easily been confused for the other (εχετε and ελαβετε have the same first letter and last three letters), it is likely that the variant is the result of a scribe conforming this verse stylistically to the context, where the verb λαμβανω is used three times (see 16:7, 9, 10).

Matthew 16:13

WH NU τίνα λέγουσιν οἱ ἄνθρωποι εἶναι τὸν υἱὸν τοῦ ἀνθρώπου;
"Who do people say the Son of Man is?"
ℵ B 0281 cop Origen
RSV NRSV ESV NASB NIV TNIV NEB REB NJB NAB NLT HCSB NET

variant/TR τινα με λεγουσιν οι ανθρωποι ειναι τον υιον του ανθρωπου
"Who do people say that I, the Son of Man, am?"
D L Θ f[1,13] 33 Maj (C W in transposed order) syr
KJV NKJV NEBmg HCSBmg

The variant is the result of a scribe making the text more suitable for public reading, for the insertion of με helps the reader immediately realize that Jesus was asking for self-identification as the "Son of Man."

Matthew 16:20

In typical fashion, some manuscripts (L W Θ f[1,13] 33 Maj) add αυτου ("his") after μαθηταις ("disciples") so as to distinguish Jesus' disciples from any others.

Matthew 16:20

WH NU — ὁ χριστός
"the Christ"
ℵ* B L Δ Θ $f^{1,13}$ it $syr^{c,p}$ cop^{sa} Origen
RSV NRSV ESV NASB NIV TNIV NEB REB NJB NAB NLT HCSB NET

variant/TR — Ιησους ο χριστος
"Jesus the Christ"
$ℵ^{2}$ C (D) W Maj syr^{h} cop^{bo}
KJV NKJV NRSVmg HCSBmg NETmg

Even though it could be posited that the variant is the more unusual of the two readings (Jesus warned them that "they should tell no one that he is Jesus the Christ"), the shorter reading has the best manuscript support. But the discrepancy is not easily solved, especially since the same kind of scribal change occurred in the next verse (see comments there).

Matthew 16:21

TR WH NU — ὁ Ἰησοῦς
"Jesus"
$ℵ^{2}$ C L W Θ $f^{1,13}$ Maj (B^{2} D omit the article)
KJV NKJV RSV NRSV ESV NIV TNIV NEB REB NJB NAB NLT HCSB NET

variant 1 — omit
$ℵ^{1}$ Irenaeus
none

variant 2 — Ιησους χριστος
"Jesus Christ"
ℵ* B* $cop^{sa,bo}$
NASB NLTmg

This is a difficult textual variant because the external and internal evidence conflict with each other. (It should be noted that ℵ displays all three variants. "Jesus Christ" was originally included, later deleted, and subsequently corrected to "Jesus.") Usually a reading supported by ℵ* B* is accepted as original, but the absence of "Christ" in so many other manuscripts has led scholars to think that the second variant is a scribal addition prompted by Jesus having just been called "the Christ" in 16:18. Allen (1912, 181) says, "it is the work of a scribe who wished to emphasize the fact that this was a turning point in Christ's ministry and teaching." But it could have been the work of Matthew himself who begins the book (1:1) with the same title, "Jesus Christ," repeats it in 1:18 (where there is also textual variation—see comments), and uses it again here—each at a critical point in the Gospel. The change from "Jesus Christ" to "Jesus" can be explained as a change from the more unusual to the usual, for in the Gospels the reader usually encounters the reading "Jesus" at the beginning of new episodes, not "Jesus Christ."

The eclectic approach to textual criticism (as applied to the NU text) allows for the testimony of ℵ and B to be accepted in 16:20 and then rejected in 16:21. But a documentary approach cautions against this. This approach looks to the external testimony first and then seeks to substantiate that testimony on internal grounds. If internal arguments are inadequate, then it is possible that the reading with inferior manuscript support could be original. In this case, it appears that in Matt 16:18, Peter calls Jesus "the Christ." Jesus then tells the disciples not to tell anyone he is "the Christ." In 16:21, which marks a major turning point in the ministry of Jesus as he faces his destiny of suffering and death in Jerusalem, Matthew says "Jesus Christ began to explain to his disciples that he had to go to Jerusalem and suffer many things."

Matthew 17:2

As a harmonization to Matt 28:3, D it^{MSS} syr^{c} cop^{boMSS} read λευκα ως το χιων ("white as the snow"), instead of λευκα ως το φως ("white as the light"), found in all other manuscripts.

Matthew 17:4

WH NU ποιήσω ὧδε τρεῖς σκηνάς
"I will make three tabernacles here"
ℵ B C* 700* it^{b}
NKJVmg RSV NRSV ESV NASB NIV TNIV NEB REB NJB NAB NLT HCSB NET

variant/TR ποιησωμεν ωδε τρεις σκηνας
"we will make three tabernacles here"
C^{3} D L W Θ 0281 f^{1,13} 33 Maj
KJV NKJV HCSBmg NETmg

According to superior manuscript support, Peter was speaking for himself when he said, "I will make three tents here." But in other manuscripts, he spoke for himself and his two companions, James and John. This is reflected in TR, followed by KJV and NKJV.

Matthew 17:9

WH NU regard the verb εγερθη ("has been raised") as original, following the slim testimony of B and D. This yields the translation, "Tell no one the vision until the Son of Man has been raised from the dead," which is followed by all English versions. A variant reading has the active voice verb, αναστη ("rises"), found in ℵ C L (W) Z Θ f^{1,13} 33 Maj. This produces the translation, "Tell no one the vision until the Son of Man rises from the dead."

The WH NU reading was accepted, not because of its external testimony, which is meager, but because the variant is suspect as having been harmonized to Mark 9:9 (see TCGNT). In most instances in the NT, Jesus is said to have been raised from the dead (passive voice) by the power of God, but there are a few instances that speak of him rising from the dead (active voice) by his own power (see 1 Thess 4:14; also John 10:18; Rom 14:9). Therefore, it is more likely that Matthew himself used Mark's word, αναστη ("rises"), and that the scribes of B and D changed it to the more ordinary, εγερθη ("has been raised").

Matthew 17:11a

The scribes of C Θ f^{13} Maj inserted the specific subject, Ιησους ("Jesus"), carried over from 17:9. This was a common scribal insertion.

Matthew 17:11b

WH NU 'Ηλίας μὲν ἔρχεται
"Elijah indeed is coming"
ℵ B D W Θ f^{1} 33
NKJVmg RSV NRSV ESV NASB NIV TNIV NEB REB NJB NAB HCSB NET

variant/TR Ηλιας μεν ερχεται πρωτον
"Elijah indeed is coming first"
C (L) Z f[13] Maj
KJV NKJV NLT HCSBmg

The additional word πρωτον ("first"), found in the variant, is a scribal carryover from the previous verse.

Matthew 17:12-13

The last clause of 17:12 and all of 17:13 are transposed in D and Old Latin manuscripts in order to place the statement about the disciples understanding that Jesus was speaking about John the Baptist next to Jesus' discussion about him. In these manuscripts it reads:

> "'But I tell you, Elijah has already come, and they did not recognize him; but they did to him whatever they pleased.' Then the disciples understood that he was speaking to them about John the Baptist. 'So also the Son of Man is about to suffer at their hands.'"

But the WH NU reading, having superior attestation (all Greek MSS except D), reads:

> "'But I tell you, Elijah has already come, and they did not recognize him; but they did to him whatever they pleased. So also the Son of Man is about to suffer at their hands.' Then the disciples understood that he was speaking to them about John the Baptist."

Matthew 17:15

TR NU κακῶς πάσχει
"he suffers terribly"
C D W f[1,13] 33 Maj
KJV NKJV RSV NRSV ESV NIV TNIV (NEB) REB NJB NLT HCSB NET

variant/WH κακως εχει
"he is ill"
א B L Z[vid] Θ
NASB

The variant reading has superior documentary support; however, it is suspected to be a scribal change because the expression κακως εχει ("he is ill") is a common idiom in the Greek NT. Furthermore, certain scribes may have considered πασχει ("he suffers") to be the result of a transcriptional error (the two words have the same last three letters) and therefore corrected it to the more usual εχει. Both readings, however, convey the same idea.

Matthew 17:17

Instead of the expression γενεα απιστος και διεστραμμενη ("faithless and depraved generation"), found in most manuscripts, a few witnesses (Z Φ) read γενεα πονηρα και διεστραμμενη ("evil and depraved generation"), harkening back to Matt 12:39 and 16:4.

Matthew 17:20

WH NU — διὰ τὴν ὀλιγοπιστίαν ὑμῶν
"because of your little faith"
ℵ B Θ 0281 f[1,13] 33 syr[c] cop
RSV NRSV ESV NASB NIV TNIV NEB REB NJB NAB NLT HCSB NET

variant/TR — δια την απιστιαν
"because of your unbelief"
C D L W Maj syr[h,p]
KJV NKJV HCSBmg

The word απιστιαν ("unbelief") is a scribal substitution, carried over from 17:17. But there is a difference between the faithless generation of Jews who rejected Jesus as the Messiah and the disciples who had faith but not enough, in this case, to cast out the demons. The word ολιγοπιστιαν ("little faith") is found only here in the NT; its cognate ολιγοπιστος was used almost exclusively by Matthew (6:30; 8:26; 14:31; 16:8; 17:20; cf. Luke 12:28), and Jesus often used the word to describe the disciples' lack of adequate faith, not their unbelief.

Matthew 17:21

WH NU — omit verse
ℵ* B Θ 0281 33 892* it[e] syr[c,s] cop[sa]
NKJVmg RSV NRSV ESV NASBmg NIV TNIV NEB REB NJB NAB NLT HCSBmg NET

variant/TR — add verse
τουτο δε το γενος ουκ εκπορευεται ει μη εν προσευχη και νηστεια.
"But this kind does not come out except by prayer and fasting."
ℵ[2] C D L W f[1,13] Maj (syr[h,p]) Origen
KJV NKJV RSVmg NRSVmg ESVmg NASB NIVmg NEBmg NABmg NLTmg HCSB NETmg

The external evidence against including this verse is substantial, including ℵ* B (the two earliest manuscripts), 0281 (a seventh-century manuscript discovered at St. Catherine's Monastery in the late twentieth century), and early witnesses of Old Latin, Coptic, and Syriac. If the verse was originally part of Matthew's gospel, there is no good reason to explain why it was dropped from so many early and diverse witnesses. Thus, it is far more likely that this added verse was assimilated from Mark 9:29 in its long form, which has the additional words "and fasting." In fact, the same manuscripts (ℵ[2] C D L W f[1,13] Maj) that have the long form in Mark 9:29 have the additional verse here. Thus, a scribe took the full verse of Mark 9:29 as presented in his manuscript and inserted it here; most other manuscripts maintained this insertion in the transmission of the text. (The short form in Mark 9:29 appears in ℵ* B.) The verse is included in KJV and NKJV and excluded in all other modern versions except NASB and HCSB which include the verse in brackets.

Matthew 17:22

WH NU — Συστρεφομένων δὲ αὐτῶν ἐν τῇ Γαλιλαίᾳ
"as they [the disciples] were gathering together in Galilee"
ℵ B 0281[vid] f[1]
NKJVmg RSV NRSV ESV NASB NIV TNIV NEB REB NJB NAB NLT HCSB NET

variant/TR Αναστρεφομενων δε αυτων εν τη Γαλιλαια
"as they [the disciples] were living in Galilee"
C (D) L W Θ f[13] 33 Maj
KJV NKJV RSVmg NRSVmg ESVmg HCSBmg

The WH NU reading has better manuscript support. The rare word συστρεφομενων, appearing only twice in the NT, was changed to the more common one, αναστερφομενων, in later manuscripts. The WH NU reading implies that many of Jesus' disciples (besides the Twelve) were gathering together in Galilee in preparation for the journey to Jerusalem for the Passover. This tells us that not all of Jesus' disciples accompanied him all the time in his Galilean ministry; rather, various disciples came to him on various occasions such as this one. Before going to Jerusalem, however, Jesus told them that he would be betrayed, crucified, then raised from the dead on the third day.

Matthew 17:23

Instead of the verb εγερθησεται ("he will be raised"), a few important witnesses (B 047 f[13]) read αναστησεται ("he will rise"). In connection with what was discussed in 17:9 (see above), the rarer form is αναστησεται.

Matthew 17:26

Several manuscripts (W f[13] Maj) supply the name ο Πετρος ("Peter") to give the reading a specific subject. This addition is found in TR, and followed by KJV and NKJV. Other versions (such as NRSV and NLT) supply the subject as well. At the end of this verse, one twelfth-century Greek manuscript (713) adds, "Simon said, 'Yes.' Jesus says, 'Then you also give, as being a foreigner to them.'" According to Metzger (TCGNT), the same kind of expansion occurs in the Arabic form of the Diatessaron and in Ephraem's commentary on the Diatessaron.

Matthew 18:2

As is typical for the transmission of the gospel texts, a specific subject, ο Ιησους ("Jesus"), was added in D W Θ 078[cvid] f[13] Maj.

Matthew 18:10

Borrowing from 18:6, the scribe of D and some ancient translators (it syr[c] cop[sa]) added των πιστευοντων εις εμε ("the ones believing in me") after των μικρων τουτων ("these little ones"), producing the full expression, "these little ones who believe in me."

Matthew 18:11

WH NU omit verse
ℵ B L* Θ* f[1,13] 33 it[e] syr[s] cop[sa] Origen
RSV NRSV ESV NASBmg NIV TNIV NEB REB NJB NAB NLT HCSBmg NET

variant1/TR add verse, as Ηλθεν γαρ ο υιος του ανθρωπου σωσαι το απολωλος
"For the Son of Man came to save the lost."
D L[c] W Θ[c] 078[vid] Maj syr[c,p]
KJV NKJV RSVmg NRSVmg ESVmg NASB NIVmg NEBmg REBmg NJBmg NABmg NLTmg HCSB NETmg

variant 2 add verse, as Ηλθεν γαρ ο υιος του ανθρωπου ζητησαι και σωσαι το απολωλος
"For the Son of Man came to seek and to save the lost."
L[mg] 892[c] it[c] syr[h]
none

The absence of this verse in several important and diverse witnesses attests to the fact that it was not part of the original text of Matthew. It was borrowed from Luke 19:10, a passage not at all parallel to this one. Most likely the addition first appeared in the shorter form (variant 1), and was later expanded to the longer form (variant 2), which concurs exactly with Luke 19:10. The manuscript L demonstrates all three phases: L* omits the verse; L[c] has the shorter form of the addition; and L[mg] has the longer form.

Very likely this verse was inserted in Matt 18 to provide some sort of bridge between verses 10 and 12. In other words, a scribe perceived there was a semantic gap that needed filling. Luke 19:10 was used to introduce the illustration of a shepherd seeking out its lost sheep (the longer form also speaks of "seeking out," which makes the connection even clearer). However, the text must be read without the bridge that 18:11 provides. Verse 12 follows verse 10 in the original in that it provides yet another reason for why the "little ones who believe in Jesus" should not be despised: The shepherd is concerned for each and every sheep in the flock. In a flock of 100 sheep, if even one leaves, he will seek it out and find it.

Matthew 18:14

Several manuscripts (B N Θ 078 0281 f[13] 33) read του πατρος μου ("my Father") instead of του πατρος υμων ("your Father"), found in ℵ D L W Δ f[1] (the NU reading). Though it is difficult to determine which one Matthew wrote (the two expressions are used with equal frequency), the reading "my Father" is probably the result of scribal harmonization to 18:10.

Matthew 18:15

TR NU ἐὰν δὲ ἁμαρτήσῃ [εἰς σὲ] ὁ ἀδελφός σου
"if your brother sins against you"
D L W Θ 078 f[13] 33 Maj it syr
KJV NKJV RSV NRSV ESV NASBmg NIV NEBmg REBmg NAB NLT HCSB NET

variant/WH εαν δε αμαρτηση ο αδελφος σου
"if your brother sins"
ℵ B 0281 f[1] cop[sa] Origen
NRSVmg NASB TNIV NEB REB NJB NLTmg HCSBmg NETmg

There is no adequate explanation, on transcriptional grounds, to explain why the words εις σε ("against you") would have been omitted from manuscripts such as ℵ B 0281. The TR NU reading almost certainly contains a scribal interpolation, influenced by 18:21, where Peter asks Jesus, "How often shall my brother sin against me and I forgive him?" The interpolation could also have been created to limit what kind of sin warranted reproof from one believer to another—i.e., only sin that directly offended a fellow believer. But in the early Christian community the believers were encouraged to warn and restore a fellow believer who was living a sinful life or about to fall away from the faith (see Gal 6:1; Heb 2:1; 1 John 5:16; Jude 22-23), whether or not that sin had caused offense between them. Indeed, the entire tenor of the Matthean passage (18:15-17) supports the view that the sin Jesus was speaking about was a sin that could cause the sinning believer to leave the Christian community, "the church." Note that Jesus says that the restored sinner is "regained," while the obstinate sinner is to be considered "a Gentile or tax collector" (i.e., an outcast from the Christian community). This was a serious sin that called for restoration—not just between individuals, but between the sinner and the church.

Matthew 18:20

D* it[g1] syr[s] read ουκ εισιν γαρ δυο η τρεις συνηγμενοι εις το εμον ονομα, παρ οις ουκ ειμι εν μεσω αυτων ("for there are not two or three gathered together in my name with whom I am not present"). Evidently, the scribe of D (and others) mistook the first word ου ("where") for ουκ ("not") and then made the subsequent changes (Westcott and Hort 1882, 15).

Matthew 18:26

WH NU — μακροθύμησον ἐπ' ἐμοί
"be patient with me"
B D Θ 700 syr[c,s]
NRSV ESV NASB NIV TNIV NEB REB NJB NAB NLT HCSB NET

variant/TR — Κυριε, μακροθυμησον επ εμε
"Lord, be patient with me"
א L W 058 0281 f[1,13] 33 Maj it cop
KJV NKJV RSV

Though the textual evidence is evenly divided, the variant reading seems more likely to have been changed to the WH NU reading than vice versa, because scribes may have thought that the vocative expression "Lord" should be attributed only to Jesus (which in this case it is not) and therefore deleted it.

Matthew 18:29

WH NU — πεσὼν οὖν ὁ σύνδουλος αὐτοῦ
"then his fellow servant falling down"
א B C* D L Θ 058 f[1] syr cop
NKJVmg RSV NRSV ESV NASB NIV TNIV NAB NLT HCSB NET

variant/TR — πεσων ουν ο συνδουλος αυτου εις τους ποδας αυτου
"then his fellow servant falling down at his feet"
C[2] W f[13] 33 Maj
KJV NKJV NEB REB NJB HCSBmg

Although it could be argued that the WH NU reading is the result of scribal conformity to 18:26, its documentary evidence is very strong. Therefore, the variant must be considered an insertion that adds color to the narrative.

Matthew 18:35

WH NU ἐὰν μὴ ἀφῆτε ἕκαστος τῷ ἀδελφῷ αὐτου ἀπὸ τῶν καρδιῶν ὑμῶν
"unless each one, from your hearts, forgives his brother"
א B D L Θ f[1] syr[c,s] cop
RSV NRSV ESV NASB NIV TNIV NEB REB NJB NAB NLT HCSB NET

variant/TR εαν μη αφητε εκαστος τω αδελφω αυτου απο των καρδιων υμων τα παραπτωματα αυτων
"unless each one, from your hearts, forgives his brother his trespasses"
C W f[13] 33 Maj
KJV NKJV HCSBmg

The variant reading is a scribal expansion taken from Matt 6:14-15. In this verse (which summarizes an entire section on forgiveness, beginning in 18:21), the emphasis is on forgiving the person who has sinned against another, no matter the offense.

Matthew 19:4

WH NU ὁ κτίσας
"the one who created [them]"
B Θ f[1] it[e] cop Origen
NKJVmg ESV NASB TNIV HCSB NET

variant/TR ο ποιησας
"the one who made [them]"
א C D (L) W Z f[13] Maj syr
KJV NKJV RSV NRSV NIV NEB REB NJB NAB NLT HCSBmg

Scholars generally argue that the variant is the result of scribal conformity to the following predicate, εποιησεν ("he made"), or to the Septuagintal passage quoted, Gen 1:27. Since the same kind of harmonization to the Septuagint occurred in the next verse in most of the same manuscripts (see note), it is safe to say that the WH NU reading is Matthean. The variant, however, hardly changes the meaning. Indeed, most English translators have felt more comfortable with "he made" than "he created"—and may have been following either text.

Matthew 19:5

The simple verb κολληθησεται ("join"), supported by B D W Θ 078, was changed to the compound προσκολληθησεται ("join together") in א C L Z f[1] 33, due to the influence of the Septuagint (Gen 1:27).

Matthew 19:7

The word αυτην ("her"), as found in B C W 078 087 f[13] Maj, but not in א D L Z Θ f[1], was probably supplied by scribes as the correct object of the infinitive απολυσαι ("to divorce"). It is bracketed in NU, but probably should be omitted.

Matthew 19:8

A few manuscripts (א Φ) add a specific subject, ο Ιησους ("Jesus"), who has not been named since 19:1. This is a typical addition in ancient gospel narratives and modern English translations (see NIV NLT).

Matthew 19:9

(TR) WH NU ὃς ἂν ἀπολύσῃ τὴν γυναῖκα αὐτοῦ μὴ ἐπὶ πορνείᾳ καὶ γαμήσῃ ἄλλην μοιχᾶται
"whoever divorces his wife, except for infidelity, and marries another, he commits adultery"
א C^3 D L (W) Z Θ 078 Maj
all

variant 1 ος αν απολυση την γυναικα αυτου ποιει αυτην μοιχευθηναι
"whoever divorces his wife makes her commit adultery"
C* N
RSVmg NRSVmg ESVmg

variant 2 ος αν απολυση την γυναικα παρεκτος λογου πορνειας ποιει αυτην μοιχευθηναι
"whoever divorces his wife, except for the matter of unchastity, makes her commit adultery"
B f^1 cop^{bo}
none

variant 3 ος αν απολυση την γυναικα παρεκτος λογου πορνειας και γαμηση αλλην μοιχαται
"whoever divorces his wife, except for the matter of unchastity, and marries another, he commits adultery"
D f^{13} 33 it cop^{sa}
none

It should be noted that $\mathfrak{P}^{25vid}$ supports either variant 1 or variant 2 because it shows the last word μοιχευθηναι. According to some manuscripts (א C^3 D L) the verse ends after μοιχαται or μοιχευθηναι. However, several manuscripts have an additional clause in two forms:

addition 1 και ο απολελυμενην γαμων μοιχαται
"and the one marrying a divorced woman commits adultery"
(B) C* W Z Θ 078 (Maj)—so TR
KJV NKJV RSVmg NRSVmg ESVmg NEBmg REBmg NLTmg HCSBmg

addition 2 ωσαυτως και ο γαμων απολελυμενην μοιχαται
"so that also the one marrying a divorced woman commits adultery"
$\mathfrak{P}^{25}$
none

The issue at stake in the first set of textual variations is whether (1) the man commits adultery by marrying another woman after divorcing his wife or (2) the divorced woman is put into a situation where she cannot but commit adultery if she marries another man. The other issue pertains to the clause, "except for unchastity," which may be original or may have been borrowed from 5:32, where the text is firm on this clause. The various changes in the manuscripts represent differing exegetical viewpoints among the scribes; in other words, the changes are not due to any kind of transcriptional error. Whatever the original reading, the man who divorces his wife is at fault because his remarriage is sin and so is the remarriage of his former wife. The only way for the man not to be held culpable is if the woman was unchaste, which is what nearly all the manuscripts say and which is affirmed by Jesus' words in 5:32.

The issue in the second set of variants is just as critical, for it directly addresses the issue of a man marrying a divorced woman. Not only are divorced women who remarry culpable, so are those who marry them. Of course, Matthew may not have written this here, but it is fairly certain that he did so in 5:32 (the parallel passage), for the clause is included in all Greek manuscripts except D (see note).

Matthew 19:10

𝔓71vid ℵ B Θ (so WH) read οι μαθηται ("the disciples") versus the reading in NU, οι μαθηται αυτου ("his disciples"), supported by 𝔓25 C D L W Z Maj. The shorter reading could likely be original because of earlier documentary support. Even though Metzger (see TCGNT on Mark 6:41) argues that later copyists tended to identify "his disciples" as "the disciples," the gospel writers themselves vacillated between the two.

Matthew 19:16

WH NU	Διδάσκαλε "Teacher" ℵ B D L f1 ita,e NKJVmg RSV NRSV ESV NASB NIV TNIV NEB REB NJB NAB NLT HCSB NET
variant/TR	Διδασκαλε αγαθε "Good teacher" C W Θ f13 33 Maj syr KJV NKJV NLTmg

The variant reading is the product of scribal harmonization to the other gospel parallels, Mark 10:17 and Luke 18:18 (see note on 19:17).

Matthew 19:17

WH NU	εἷς ἐστιν ὁ ἀγαθός "there is one who is good" ℵ B (D) L Θ (f1) ita,d copbo NKJVmg RSV NRSV ESV NASB NIV TNIV NEB REB NJB NAB NLT HCSB NET
variant 1/TR	ουδεις αγαθος ει μη εις ο θεος "there is no one good, except one—God" C (W) f13 33 Maj syrh,p copsa KJV NKJV HCSBmg
variant 2	"there is one who is good—God" it syrc none

The first variant is a natural translational expansion of the WH NU reading in that it supplies what is implicit—namely, that God is the only one who is good. The second variant has to follow the textual variant of the previous verse, which reads, "Good teacher." In fact, the same manuscripts support the same variants in 19:16 as in 19:17. But it is a manifest harmonization to Mark 10:18 and Luke 18:19. The WH NU reading allows for the interpretation that Jesus could be referring to himself when he says, "there is one who is good."

Matthew 19:20

(WH) NU πάντα ταῦτα ἐφύλαξα
"All these things I have kept."
ℵ* B L Θ f[1]
NKJVmg RSV NRSV ESV NASB NIV TNIV NEB REB NJB NAB NLT HCSB NET

variant/TR παντα ταυτα εφυλαξα εκ νεοτητος μου
"All these things I have kept from my youth."
ℵ[2] C (D) W f[13] 33 Maj it syr cop
KJV NKJV NRSVmg HCSBmg

In context, a young man had just asked Jesus what he could do to inherit eternal life. Jesus then told him that he had to keep the commandments. The young man said he had done so. The variant reading, providing the expansion, is a harmonization to Mark 10:20 and Luke 18:21. More manuscripts demonstrate harmonization here than in 19:16-17. It was a common phenomenon, especially in the fourth century and thereafter, for scribes to harmonize the Synoptic Gospels, thereby sacrificing the literary uniqueness of each work. The entire pericope of the rich young ruler is—in keeping with Matthean style—terser than in Mark and Luke.

Matthew 19:22

Based on the testimony of C D W Θ f[1,13] Maj, TR NU read ακουσας . . . τον λογον (having heard the word). This is slightly expanded in B it syr[c,s,p] (so WH) to ακουσας . . . τον λογον τουτον ("having heard this word"). Most English versions do the same. The original text is probably found in ℵ L Z 0281, which simply read ακουσας ("having heard"). This variant has just as good external testimony as the TR NU reading and is the reading that best explains the other two. Uncomfortable with a participial phrase lacking an object after ακουσας ("having heard"), scribes and ancient translators filled the gap with either "the word" or "this word." The editors of NU adopted a reading supported by a group of manuscripts (led by C D W) whose testimony was rejected six times in the six verses that make up this pericope, calling into question why its testimony should be accepted here.

Matthew 19:24

Jesus' statement, "It is easier for a camel to go through an eye of a needle than for a rich man to enter the kingdom of God," was subject to all kinds of textual variation. Among the many variants, there are two notable ones: (1) In some witnesses (59 geo arm), the Greek word for "camel" (καμηλον) has been changed to καμιλον, meaning "rope" or "ship's cable." This change, of course, tones down the extent of Jesus' hyperbole, but the saying about the camel was a well-known proverb to show absolute impossibility. The same proverb appears in the Qur'an (7.38), and a similar proverb is found in the Talmud (*b. Ber.* 55b). "It is a way of indicating something unusually difficult, well-nigh impossible" (Hill 1972, 284). (2) The other significant change is that some scribes (Z f[1] 33 syr[c,s]) changed "kingdom of God" (found in all other manuscripts), an expression that rarely occurs in Matthew, to "kingdom of the heavens," an expression that is patently Matthean.

Matthew 19:29a

WH NU — ἢ πατέρα ἢ μητέρα
"or father or mother"
B it[a]
NKJVmg RSV NRSV ESV NASB NIV TNIV NEB REB NJB NAB NLT HCSB NET

variant 1/TR — η πατερα η μητερα η γυναικα
"or father or mother or wife"
א C L W Θ f[13] 33
KJV NKJV NASBmg TNIVmg HCSBmg

variant 2 — η μητερα
"or mother"
D it[b,d]
none

variant 3 — η γοινες
"or parents"
f[1] (it[e])
none

According to the WH NU reading, the full rendering of this statement is: "everyone who has left home or brothers or sisters or father or mother or children or lands on account of my name." There are several differences among the manuscripts in the list of items and relatives that a disciple of Jesus must forsake in order to follow him. Among the three variants, two can easily be discounted: variant 2 as the result of homoeoteleuton (πατερα/μητερα), and variant 3 as an abbreviated translation of "father or mother" or a harmonization to Luke 18:29. But the first variant cannot be easily dismissed because it has good textual support and is the reading that scribes would be tempted to change, since it seems too demanding for Jesus to require that disciples leave their wives. It is true that the first variant could be the result of harmonization to Luke 18:29, but the same can be argued against the WH NU reading—that it is the result of harmonization to Mark 10:29.

Even if the WH NU reading is followed, an exegete cannot say that Jesus never spoke of a male disciple forsaking his wife to follow him, because this is made explicit in Luke 18:29 (where the word "wives" appears in all manuscripts). Jesus did not command this specifically, but his statement does imply that some men had left their wives to follow him. The exact circumstances that warranted a man leaving his wife and whether it was temporary or permanent are unclear.

Matthew 19:29b

Instead of the word εκατονταπλασιονα ("hundredfold"), supported by א C D W Θ f[1,13] 33 Maj, some witnesses (B L Origen) read πολλαπλασιονα ("manifold"). The former may be the result of harmonization to Mark 10:30; the latter, to Luke 18:30. Either way, the meaning is not significantly altered.

Matthew 20:7

At the end of this verse, several manuscripts (C* W f[13] 33 Maj) add και ο εαν η δικαιον λημψεσθε ("and you will receive whatever [amount] is right"). This is clearly a scribal addition carried over from 20:4.

Matthew 20:16

WH NU	omit second sentence of verse א B L Z 085 cop[sa] NKJVmg RSV NRSV ESV NASB NIV TNIV NEB REB NJB NAB NLT HCSB NET
variant/TR	add πολλοι γαρ εισιν κλητοι, ολιγοι δε εκλεκτοι "For many are called but few are chosen." C D W Θ f[1,13] 33 Maj it syr KJV NKJV NRSVmg HCSBmg

Although it could be argued that this sentence was accidentally dropped from the text due to homoeoteleuton (the first sentence ends with εσχατοι and the second with εκλεκτοι), it is far more likely that scribes added it from 22:14. But whereas the statement perfectly suits the conclusion to the parable of the wedding feast in Matt 22:1-14 (where several are invited but only a few attend), it is an odd addendum to the parable here. Exegetes who use the inferior text will have a difficult time explaining how the statement "many are called but few are chosen" has anything to do with a parable in which all were called and chosen to work in the vineyard. The point of this parable is captured by the shorter, superior text, "the last will be first and the first, last," because this cancels human endeavor to outdo others and exalts God's sovereignty to give grace as he pleases.

Matthew 20:17

The manuscripts B C W 085 33 Maj read τους δωδεκα μαθητας ("the twelve disciples"), whereas א D L Θ f[1,13] read τους δωδεκα ("the Twelve"). Either reading could be original because both have good support and because the gospel writers alternated between the nomenclature "the twelve disciples" and "the Twelve."

Matthew 20:22b-23a

WH NU	δύνασθε πιεῖν τὸ ποτήριον ὃ ἐγὼ μέλλω πίνειν; λέγουσιν αὐτῷ· δυνάμεθα. [23]λέγει αὐτοῖς, τὸ μὲν ποτήριον μου πίεσθε, "Are you able to drink the cup which I am about to drink?" [23]They say to him, "We are able." He says to them, "Indeed you will drink my cup." א B D L Z Θ 085 f[1,13] syr[c,s] cop[sa] NKJVmg RSV NRSV ESV NASB NIV TNIV NEB REB NJB NAB NLT HCSB NET
variant/TR	Δυνασθε πιειν το ποτηριον ο εγω μελλω πινειν η το βαπτισμα ο εγω βαπτιζομαι βαπτισθηναι; λεγουσιν αυτω, δυναμεαθα. [23]λεγει αυτοις, Το μεν ποτηριον μου πιεσθε και ο βαπτισμα ο εγω βαπτιζομαι βαπτισθησεσθε. "Are you able to drink the cup which I am about to drink or be baptized with the baptism that I will be baptized with?" They say to him, "We are able." [23]He says to them, Indeed you will drink my cup and be baptized with the baptism that I will be baptized with." C W 33 Maj syr[h] KJV NKJV NRSVmg HCSBmg NETmg

The variant reading is a scribal expansion borrowed verbatim from Mark 10:38-39. The manuscripts C and W are notorious for scribal harmonization of the Synoptic Gospels; the majority of manuscripts (Maj) followed suit. This reading was accepted into TR, and has been popularized by its presence in the KJV and NKJV.

Matthew 20:28

At the end of this verse some witnesses, namely D (Φ it syr[c]), have an addendum to Jesus' speech, translated as follows:

> "But as for you, from littleness you seek to grow great and from greatness you make yourselves small. When you are invited to a banquet do not take one of the places of honour, because someone more important than you may arrive and then the steward will have to say, "Move down lower," and you would be covered with confusion. Take the lowest place, and then if someone less important than you comes in, the steward will say to you, 'Move up higher,' and that will be to your advantage." (NJBmg)

The first sentence of this addition comes from an unknown source, perhaps an apocryphal gospel. The rest of the addition is borrowed from Luke 14:8-10. It is remarkable that this interpolation should have been put at the end of the Matthean pericope (20:20-28), as compared to the Lukan parallel (Luke 22:24-27), whose last verse is far more conducive to this addition than what is in Matthew.

Matthew 20:30a

TR NU	ἐλέησον ἡμᾶς, [κύριε] "Have mercy on us, Lord." 𝔓[45vid] C W f[1] 33 Maj syr[p] KJV NKJV RSVmg NRSV NAB NET
variant 1/WH	Κυριε, ελεησον ημας "Lord, have mercy on us." B L Z 085 0281 RSV ESV NASB NIV TNIV NJB NLT HCSB
variant 2	ελεησον ημας "Have mercy on us." ℵ D Θ f[13] it syr[c] ESVmg NEB REB

See next note.

Matthew 20:30b

TR WH NU	υἱὸς Δαυίδ "son of David" (nominative) B K W Z Γ Δ (none?)
variant 1	υιε Δαυιδ "son of David" (as a vocative) 𝔓[45vid] C D 085 0281 f[1] 33 all

variant 2 Ιησου, υιε Δαυιδ
"Jesus, son of David"
א L Θ f^{13}
none

It is necessary to break up the variants for 20:30a and 20:30b into two separate listings because the manuscripts are not consistent with respect to word order, the presence or absence of the titles "Lord" and "Son of David," as well as whether "son" is nominative (υιος) or vocative (υιε). All things considered, it seems that "Lord" appeared just after "have mercy" and that it was followed by the vocative "son of David." The addition of "Jesus" is the result of harmonization to Mark 10:47 and Luke 18:38 (parallel verses which have the word "Jesus"). The variant having only "Lord," though the shortest reading, has only slim Western support and is also suspect as having been harmonized to Matt 9:27 (a previous account of blind men being healed). This reading, however, was favored by the translators of NEB and REB.

Matthew 20:33

One Syriac manuscript (syr[c]) adds "and we could see you" to the final words of this verse, thereby creating the dramatic statement, "open our eyes and we could see you." This is a good example of narrative gap-filling. After this verse, one Old Latin manuscript (it[c]) adds: "Jesus said to them, 'Do you believe that I am able to do this?' They said to him, 'Yes, Lord.'" This interpolation, borrowed from Matt 9:28, repeats the idea that Jesus calls upon people to have faith in him before he heals them.

Matthew 21:4-5

According to most manuscripts, the prophet whom Matthew quotes is left unnamed. However, some scribes could not resist adding "Zechariah" (M[mg] it[a,c,h] and one Coptic Bohairic MS), while others added "Isaiah" (Ethiopic and Vulgate MSS and one Coptic Bohairic MS). Each scribal addition is correct but incomplete because the quotation comes from two messianic prophecies, Isa 62:11 and Zech 9:9. Matthew, however, must have been thinking of only one prophet (του προφητου), namely Zechariah, because most of the quotation comes from him (only the introductory words, "fear not, daughter of Zion," are from Isaiah).

Matthew 21:5-7

According to א B and other manuscripts, the text reads επιβεβηκως επι ονον και επι πωλον υιον υποζυγιου ("mounted on a donkey and on a colt, the foal of a donkey"). This is a difficult reading, for it seems to say that Jesus used two animals for his triumphal entry, when it is possible for him to ride on only one. The other gospel writers made it clear that there was only one animal. Some scholars have suggested that Matthew did not understand the parallelism of the Hebrew poetry in Zech 9:9—the second poetic line provides a further description of the first line; therefore, one animal (not two) is depicted. Perhaps Matthew did understand this and intended that και be understood to mean "even": "mounted on a donkey / even on a colt, the foal of a donkey." However, the fact that επι ("on") appears twice discounts this approach; the text still suggests that two animals are here depicted. To get around this problem, several scribes (C D W Θ f^{13} 33 Maj—so TR) omitted the second επι. Other scribes (א[1] L Z) tried to solve the problem by deleting υιον ("foal"). The textual changes continue in 21:7, where several manuscripts (D Θ Φ f^{13} 33) read the singular "it" (αυτον or αυτω) for "them" (αυτων). This change was an attempt to have the text say that the disciples put their garments only on the foal, not on both the donkey and the foal, which is to say that Jesus would ride only on the foal. We would have expected, however, that the scribes would have gone all the way and changed the expression και επεκαθισεν επανω αυτων ("and he sat on them") to και επεκαθισεν επανω αυτου ("and he sat on it"). But not one scribe touched the last word, probably because αυτων can be understood as referring to the garments, not the animals—that is, Jesus sat on the garments that were placed on the animal(s).

Matthew 21:9

At the end of this quote a few witnesses (Φ syr[c]) add, "and many came out to meet him, rejoicing and glorifying God for all the things they saw." This addition is a scribal adaptation taken from verses like Luke 19:37 and John 12:13.

Matthew 21:12

WH NU	τὸ ἱερόν "the temple" ℵ B L Θ 0281[vid] f[13] 33 NKJVmg RSVmg NRSV ESV NASB NIV TNIV NEB REB NJB NAB NLT HCSB NET
variant/TR	το ιερον του θεου "the temple of God" C D W f[1] Maj it syr KJV NKJV RSV NRSVmg ESVmg HCSBmg

It is possible that scribes added "of God" when they realized the close connection between this verse and Mal 3:1-4, which predicts that the Messiah would suddenly come to God's temple and purge it (Westcott and Hort 1882, 15). Or it is possible that other scribes deleted it because "of God" does not appear in the parallel passages (Mark 11:15; Luke 19:45). But on the basis of documentary support, it must be judged that the variant is a scribal expansion, which happens to give good effect in that the expression "God's temple" stands in strong contrast to the temple profaned with men's merchandizing. Nevertheless, the addition is not necessary, because the next verse (a quotation from Isa 56:7) brings out the contrast even more vigorously: "My house will be called a house of prayer, but you are making it a den of robbers."

Matthew 21:13

According to ℵ B L Θ 0281 cop[bo], the last part of the verse reads αυτον ποιειτε σπηλαιον ληστων ("you are making it a den of robbers"); these manuscripts contain the present tense ποιειτε, which emphasizes the ongoing profanation of the temple. Other witnesses (C D W f[13] Maj) have the aorist εποιησατε ("you made"), and others (f[1]) have the perfect πεποικατε ("you have made")—in conformity to Mark 11:17.

Matthew 21:28-31

One look at the critical apparatus of NA[27] or UBS[4] for these verses will discourage even the most diligent student from trying to decode, let alone resolve, the textual problems herein. Among the many variants, there are three basic renditions of the story. The first is followed by all the English versions, and the other two are noted in NLTmg. The three are as follows:

1. When the father asks his first son to go and work in the vineyard, he says no, but later

repents and goes. When the second son is asked, he says yes but does not go. When Jesus asks the Jewish leaders which of the two did the father's will, they say, "the first." This reading is supported by ℵ C* K W Δ it[c] syr[c,h,p], and is the NU text.

2. When the father asks his first son to go and work in the vineyard, he says yes but does not go. When the second son is asked, he says no, but later repents and goes. When Jesus asks the Jewish leaders which of the two did the father's will, they say, "the second." This reading is supported by B Θ f[13] 700 and other minuscules (so WH), among which there are several different synonyms used to describe the second son: ο υστερος ("the latter"), ο εσχατος ("the last"), ο δευτερος ("the second").

3. When the father asks his first son to go and work in the vineyard, he says no, but later repents and goes. When the second son is asked, he says yes but does not go. When Jesus asks the Jewish leaders which of the two did the father's will, they say, "the second." This reading is supported by D it syr[s] and other MSS[according to Jerome].

The first and second readings communicate the same moral truth: It is the son who says no, repents, then goes to work who is the one that does the Father's will.

The discrepancy is whether it is the first son or the second son who eventually becomes obedient. When Jesus spoke this parable, it is doubtful that he intended the first son to represent the Jews and the second son, the Gentiles. But this is a natural explication for this passage and one that Christian exegetes would employ. For this reason, it is not improbable that the first reading was transposed by scribes in order to yield this interpretation (as in the second reading). Yet it is possible that the second reading is original because it suits the context so well. According to the conclusion of the parable (21:31-32), it would seem that the father typifies John the Baptist; the first son symbolizes the Jewish leaders who appear to listen to John but do not really obey the message in getting ready for Jesus the Messiah; and the second son represents the tax collectors and prostitutes who do not appear to have listened to John but eventually do because they accept Jesus as the Messiah. But how do we account for the third reading? Is this just another aberration of D and its allied Western witnesses, or does it—as the most difficult reading of the three—represent the original text? Many scholars dismiss it as nonsensical; others (notably Jerome) perceive it as portraying the Jewish leaders' perverse thinking: Instead of giving Jesus the expected answer, "the first son," the Jewish leaders intentionally tried to spoil the point of Jesus' parable by giving the wrong answer. In response, Jesus reproves them by saying, "the tax collectors and prostitutes will enter the kingdom of heaven before you do." But was this Matthew's literary ingenuity or that of the scribe of Codex Bezae (D)? Most likely it is the latter, for this scribe (or his predecessor) is known for the liberties he took with the text in the interest of making it more interesting literature (see note on 21:32 and discussion in Aland and Aland 1987, 307-311).

Matthew 21:32

The WH NU reading is υμεις δε ιδοντες ουδε μετεμεληθητε υστερον του πιστευσαι αυτω ("but you, having seen [it], did not later repent to believe in him"), supported by B Θ 0102 f[1,13] (ℵ C L W Maj read ου instead of ουδε). But D it[c,e] syr[s] read υμεις δε ιδοντες μετεμεληθητε υστερον του πιστευσαι αυτω. Is this reading the result of an accidental omission of the negative particle (ου or ουδε), or is it an intentional change? There are two ways to translate the reading in D: (1) "but you, having seen [it], later repented to believe in him," or (2) "but you, having seen [it], later changed your minds about believing in him." (The "it" in both renderings refers to the message of John the Baptist and the influence it had on the common people, while "him" refers to John the Baptist.) The second rendering accords with the way D changed the story of the two sons in the preceding parable (see note above)—that is, the religious leaders are like the second son, who first says yes then changes his mind. Jesus, of course, does not agree that such a son does his father's will; quite the opposite, the second son (like the religious leaders) thinks he is doing the father's will when, in fact, he is not. Thus, Jesus reproves the Pharisees in 21:31, telling them, "the tax collectors and prostitutes will enter the kingdom of heaven before you do." Of course, this calls for a complex reading of the text—one that is looking for irony. The scribe of the D-text was capable of such irony and may have adjusted the text here to give this effect, unless D is just faulty here and we have misconstrued our reading of D.

Matthew 21:44

TR WH NU	[καὶ ὁ πεσὼν ἐπὶ τὸν λίθον τοῦτον συνθλασθήσεται· ἐφ' ὃν δ' ἂν πέσῃ λικμήσει αὐτόν.] "And the one falling on this stone will be broken to pieces; and it will crush anyone on whom it falls." א B C L W Z (Θ) 0102 f[1,13] Maj syr[c,h,p] cop KJV NKJV RSVmg NRSV ESV NASB NIV TNIV NEBmg REBmg NJBmg NAB NLT HCSB NET
variant	omit verse 𝔓[104] D 33 it syr[s] Origen Eusebius RSV NRSVmg ESVmg NIVmg TNIVmg NEB REB NJB NABmg NLTmg HCSBmg NETmg

This verse is included in WH NU but is bracketed to signal the editors' doubts about it being a part of Matthew's original composition. The inclusion of the verse has good documentary support, the kind that would usually affirm legitimacy for most textual variants. However, it is challenged by the testimony of 𝔓[104], one of the very earliest manuscripts (early second century; see the discussion in Comfort 2005, 160-163). Although 𝔓[104] is not cited in NA[27] or UBS[4], the reconstruction of its text can be done only with the exclusion of v. 44 (see *Text of Earliest MSS*, 644). The added testimony of D 33 it syr[s] Origen and Eusebius strongly suggests that the verse was borrowed from Luke 20:18. Had the verse originally been in Matthew, it is difficult to explain what would have prompted its deletion. These concerns should give more translators cause for relegating the verse to the margin.

The first quote, in Matt 21:42, is taken from Ps 118:22-23; it is quoted in all the gospels to underscore the reality that Jesus, though rejected by the Jews, would become the cornerstone of the church. The next verse affirms this truth when it says, "the kingdom of God will be taken away from you [the Jews] and given to a people who will produce its fruit." Then follows 21:44: "he who falls on this stone will be broken to pieces, but he on whom it falls will be crushed" (taken from Isa 8:14-15 and Dan 2:34-35, 44-45). This prophecy depicts Christ as both the stone over which the Jews stumbled and were broken (cf. Rom 9:30-33; 1 Cor 1:23) and the stone that will smash all kingdoms in the process of establishing God's kingdom.

Matthew 22:7

WH NU	ὁ δὲ βασιλεὺς ὠργίσθη "and the king was angry" א B L 085 f[1] syr[c,s] cop[sa] RSV NRSV ESV NASB NIV TNIV NEB REB NJB NAB NLT HCSB NET

variant 1/TR καὶ ακουσας ο βασιλευς εκεινος ωργισθη
"and having heard, that king was angry"
C (D) W 0102 Maj
KJV NKJV HCSBmg

variant 2 ο δε βασιλευς ακουσας ωργισθη
"but having heard, the king was angry"
Θ f^{13} syr^{p}
none

The variants present the work of scribes and ancient translators filling in a gap in the chain of narrative events: The king had to *hear* about what happened to his servants before he could act on it (by sending his soldiers to destroy those who had murdered his servants). Often, however, the gospel writers did not include every action in a narrative because they assumed readers could use their imagination to fill in the gaps.

Matthew 22:10

TR NU read ο γαμος (the wedding feast) in the expression, "the wedding feast was filled with guests." This reading is supported by B^{1} D W Θ 085 0161^{vid} $f^{1,13}$ 33 Maj. However, a variant reading ο νυμφων ("the wedding hall") has excellent documentation (ℵ B* L 0102—so WH) and may also be the superior reading on internal grounds, inasmuch as γαμος is more likely a reading created to bring the text into conformity with the immediate context (see 22:2-4, 8-9, 12, where γαμος appears three times), whereas νυμφων is unique.

Matthew 22:13

WH NU δήσαντες αὐτοῦ πόδας καὶ χεῖρας ἐκβάλετε αὐτὸν εἰς τὸ σκότος τὸ ἐξώτερον
"binding his hands and feet, throw him into outer darkness"
ℵ B L Θ 085 $f^{1,(13)}$ cop
NKJVmg RSV NRSV ESV NASB NIV TNIV NEB REB NJB NAB NLT HCSB NET

variant 1 αρατε αυτον ποδων και χειρων και βαλετε αυτον εις το σκοτος το εξωτερον
"take him, hands and feet, and throw him into outer darkness"
D it ($syr^{c,s}$)
none

variant 2/TR δησαντες αυτου ποδας και χειρας αρατε αυτον και εκβαλετε αυτον εις το σκοτος το εξωτερον
"binding his hands and feet, take him away, and throw him into outer darkness"
C W 0102 33 Maj
KJV NKJV HCSBmg

The first variant, represented by the D-text, excludes any mention of binding. The second variant, found in TR, has some minor gap-filling of action-sequencing: binding, taking away, and throwing him out. This was typical in later manuscripts.

Matthew 22:30

WH NU	ὡς ἄγγελοι ἐν τῷ οὐρανῷ εἰσιν "they are like angels in heaven" B D 700 NKJVmg RSV NRSV ESV NASB NIV TNIV NEB REB NJB NAB NLT HCSB NET
variant 1	ως οι αγγελοι εν τω ουρανω εισιν "they are like the angels in heaven" Θ f[1] none
variant 2/TR	ως αγγελοι θεου εν τω ουρανω εισιν "they are like angels of God in heaven" א L f[13] 33 (W Maj add οι before αγγελοι = the angels) KJV NKJV RSVmg NRSVmg HCSBmg NETmg

The WH NU reading is likely the one from which the others diverged. The anarthrous αγγελοι ("angels") emphasizes the nature of being, not the personal identity of the being. Resurrected believers will not be the same as the angels of God in personality or classification of "being" (humans will always be humans and angels will always be angels); resurrected believers will, like angels, share in the nature of being unmarried.

Matthew 22:32

WH NU	οὐκ ἔστιν [ὁ] θεὸς νεκρῶν ἀλλὰ ζώντων. "He is not the God of dead ones but of living ones." B L Δ f[1] 33 RSV NRSV ESV NASB NIV TNIV NEB NJB NAB NLT HCSB NET
variant 1	ουκ εστιν θεος νεκρων αλλα ζωντων "He is not [a] God of dead ones but of living ones." א D W none
variant 2/TR	ουκ εστιν ο θεος θεος νεκρων αλλα ζωντων "God is not the God of dead ones but of living ones." (Θ f[13]) 0102 Maj KJV NKJV REB HCSBmg

In defense of the second variant, it is possible that the second occurrence of θεος ("God") dropped out of the text due to haplography or was deleted as a perceived dittography, for in ancient texts the double nomina sacra $\overline{\text{ΘCΘC}}$ could cause either kind of mistake. But it appears that this text was read carefully by ancient scribes who wanted to make the sense absolutely clear; thus, some added the article (as in the WH NU reading), and others added the article before the first θεος and added a second θεος (as in the second variant). Thus, the first variant is most likely the original reading—and one that yields very good sense in that it emphasizes the kind of God he is. The God of Abraham, Isaac, and Jacob is not a God (anarthrous θεος) of dead people but of living people.

Matthew 22:37

According to the best manuscript evidence (א B L W), Jesus says the greatest commandment is "to love the Lord your God with all your heart and with all your soul and with all your mind." This is a verbatim quotation of Deut 6:5, with the exception of the last word, which is "might" instead of "mind." A few ancient translators (it[c] syr[c,s]), subsequently, changed "mind" to "might," thereby producing a version harmonized to the OT, as well as to Mark 12:30. Certain scribes (Θ 0107 f[13]) added "might" (ισχυι) to the list, probably influenced by Luke 10:27.

Matthew 23:4

TR NU φορτία βαρέα [καὶ δυσβάστακτα]
"heavy burdens and hard to bear"
B D[c] (D* reads αδυσβαστακτα—"not hard to bear") W Θ 0102 0107 f[13] 33 Maj
KJV NKJV RSV NRSV ESV NAB HCSB NET

variant 1/WH φορτια βαρεα
"heavy burdens"
L f[1] it syr cop[bo]
RSVmg NRSVmg ESVmg NASB NIV TNIV NEB REB NJB NLT HCSBmg

variant 2 φορτια δυσβαστακτα
"burdens hard to bear"
700 1010
none

variant 3 μεγαλα βαρεα
"great burdens"
א
none

It is quite possible that the words και δυσβαστακτα ("and hard to bear") were transported by scribes from Luke 11:46 or that they were accidentally deleted by other scribes due to oversight (the eye passing from και to και) or perceived redundancy. In any case, the words add color to Jesus' description of a load placed on one's shoulders that is so heavy it cannot be borne—such were the rules that the Jewish leaders put on the Jewish populace. In any event, NU aligns with TR in this case, and the versions are split.

Matthew 23:5

WH NU μεγαλύνουσιν τὰ κράσπεδα
"they enlarge the tassels"
א B D Θ f[1]
RSV NRSV ESV NJB NAB NLT HCSB NET

variant/TR μεγαλυνουσιν τα κρασπεδα των ιματιων αυτων
"they enlarge the tassels of their garments"
L W 0102 0107 f[13] 33 Maj
KJV NKJV NASB NIV TNIV NEB REB HCSBmg

The WH NU reading has the earliest documentation (א B), as well as support from other manuscripts. The expansion in the variant is the result of scribal embellishment, intended to help readers understand where the tassels were located. Many English translators did the same.

Matthew 23:7

WH NU καλεῖσθαι ὑπὸ τῶν ἀνθρώπων ῥαββί
"to be called by people, 'Rabbi'"
ℵ B L Δ Θ 0102 f[1] cop syr[p]
RSV NRSV ESV NASB NIV TNIV NEB REB NJB NAB NLT HCSB NET

variant/TR καλεισθαι υπο των ανθρωπων ραββι, ραββι
"to be called by people, 'Rabbi, Rabbi'"
D W 0107 f[13] Maj syr[c,h,s]
KJV NKJV

Most likely scribes expanded the text to give it more literary flair. The single title is historically accurate—a teacher was called by his title, "Rabbi," only once (see the instances where Jesus was called "Rabbi"—26:25, 49; Mark 9:5; 11:21; 14:45; John 1:49; 3:2). The double title became part of TR, and was popularized by KJV and NKJV.

Matthew 23:8

WH NU ὑμῶν ὁ διδάσκαλος
"your teacher"
ℵ[1] B 33 892*
NKJVmg RSV NRSV ESV NASB NIV TNIV NEB REB NJB NAB NLT HCSB NET

variant 1 υμων ο καθηγητης
"your instructor"
ℵ[*,2] D L (W) Θ 0107 f[1,13]
none

variant 2/TR υμων ο καθηγητης, ο χριστος
"your instructor, the Christ"
K Γ Δ 0102 892[c] Maj syr[c]
KJV NKJV HCSBmg

The variants in this verse were probably all taken from 23:10, where ο καθηγητης ("the instructor") appears as a synonym for ο διδασκαλος ("the teacher") and where Jesus names the one teacher as "the Christ." In Jesus' day rabbis were teachers of the law. In the NT, a teacher was usually called διδασκαλος. In 23:10, however, the word καθηγητης is used in all manuscripts—its only occurrence in the NT; it means "a guide, an instructor, a teacher." Thus, the two variants show assimilation to 23:10.

Matthew 23:14

WH NU omit verse
ℵ B D L Z Θ f[1] 33 it[a,e] syr[s] cop[sa]
NKJVmg RSV NRSV ESV NASBmg NIV TNIV NEB REB NJB NAB NLT HCSBmg NET

variant/TR add verse 14
Ουαι δε υμιν, γραμματεις και Φαρισαιοι υποκριται, οτι κατεσθιετε τας οικιας των χηρων και προφασει μακρα προσευχομενοι· δια τουτο λημψεσθε περισσοτερον κριμα.
"Woe to you, scribes and Pharisees, hypocrites, because you devour widows'

houses and for a pretense make long prayers; therefore, you will receive the greater judgment."
before verse 13: W 0102 0107 Maj it^{f} syr^{h,p}
RSVmg NRSVmg
after verse 13: f^{13} it syr^{c} (so TR)
KJV NKJV RSVmg NRSVmg ESVmg NASB NIVmg NEBmg REBmg NJBmg NABmg NLTmg HCSB NETmg

This verse, not present in the earliest manuscripts and several other witnesses, was taken from Mark 12:40 or Luke 20:47 and inserted in later manuscripts either before or after 23:13. This kind of gospel harmonization became especially prevalent after the fourth century. It is noteworthy that KJV and NKJV did not follow TR in placing the verse before verse 13, but after it. The verse is noted in modern versions out of deference for its place in English Bible history. Undoubtedly, the HCSB includes the verse out of deference to its KJV- and NKJV-friendly readership, but this does not help these readers understand that KJV is based on inferior manuscript support.

Matthew 23:19

WH NU τυφλοι
"blind men"
ℵ D L Z Θ f^{1} syr^{c,s}
RSV NRSV ESV NASB NIV TNIV NEB REB NJB NAB NLT HCSB NET

variant/TR μωροι και τυφλοι
"fools and blind men"
B C W 0102 f^{13} 33 Maj
KJV NKJV HCSBmg

The expanded reading of the variant is probably a carryover from 23:17. It is included in the TR and KJV tradition.

Matthew 23:21

TR WH NU καὶ ἐν τῷ κατοικοῦντι αὐτόν
"and the one dwelling in it"
ℵ B Θ f^{1,13} cop
all

variant και εν τω κατοικησαντι αυτον
"and the one having dwelt in it"
C D K L W Z Δ 0102
NKJVmg

The difference between a present participle, κατοικουντι (TR WH NU), and an aorist participle, κατοικησαντι (variant), may be significant in this verse because it could make a statement about God's continuing or past presence in the temple: "he swears by the temple and the one dwelling/having dwelt in it." Unless the aorist participle is inceptive ("the one having come to dwell"), the temporal quality of the aorist could mean that at the time Jesus said this he did not consider that God was still dwelling in the temple. Of course, the scribes who wrote the variant could have also thought that, from their temporal perspective, God no longer dwelt in the temple. This is especially suggested by 23:38, where Jesus pronounces the anathema: "your house is left to you desolate" (see note on 23:38).

Nonetheless, the present participle has the best authority and allows for the interpretation that, from Jesus' perspective at that time (i.e., before his entrance into Jerusalem and his subsequent rejection), God still dwelt in the temple. This would soon change, as is evidenced by Jesus' proclamation in 23:38 and the tearing of the veil in the temple when Jesus was crucified (27:51).

Matthew 23:25

Based on the testimony of ℵ B D, the last word of this verse is ακρασιας; it means "self-indulgence." It was changed in three ways: (1) αδικιας ("unrighteousness") in C K it[f] syr[p] Maj (see NKJVmg); (2) ακαθαρσιας ("impurity") in Σ syr[s] cop; (3) πλεονεξιας ("greed") in M. The variants are scribal alternatives to this unusual word, which appears only here and in 1 Cor 7:5 in the NT.

Matthew 23:26

NU	καθάρισον πρῶτον τὸ ἐντὸς τοῦ ποτηρίου, ἵνα γένηται καὶ τὸ ἐκτὸς αὐτοῦ καθαρόν "first cleanse the inside of the cup, that the outside of it may also become clean" D Θ f[1] it[a,e] syr[s] NRSV NEB REB NAB NLTmg HCSB NET
variant/TR WH	καθαρισον πρωτον το εντος του ποτηριου και της παροψιδος ινα γενηται και το εκτος αυτων καθαρον "first cleanse the inside of the cup and the dish, that the outside of them may also become clean" ℵ (B[2]) C L W 0102 0281 Maj KJV NKJV RSV NRSVmg ESV NASB NIV TNIV NJB NLT HCSBmg NETmg

A few manuscripts not listed above (B* f[13] 28) read the singular αυτου, even though they have the added expression και της παροψιδος ("and the dish") that requires the plural αυτων. This shows that the text was originally singular; the variant is an addition taken from the previous verse.

Matthew 23:35

According to most manuscripts, this verse reads, "all the righteous blood shed on earth may come upon you—from the blood of righteous Abel to the blood of Zechariah son of Barachiah, whom you murdered between the sanctuary and the altar." Most scholars think Jesus was summarizing the OT history of martyrdom. Genesis 4:8 records the murder of Abel, and 2 Chr 24:20-22 records the murder of a priest named Zechariah. Since the Hebrew OT canon began with Genesis and ended with 2 Chronicles, this was Jesus' way of saying "from the beginning to the end of Scripture."

The Zechariah who was murdered in 2 Chr 24:20-22, however, was not the son of Barachiah but the son of Jehoiada. For this reason some manuscripts (ℵ* 6 13) omitted υιου βαραχιου ("son of Barachiah") after "Zechariah" (see ESVmg), and the *Gospel of the Nazarenes* (according to Jerome's *Commentary on Matthew*) reads "son of Jehoiada." But all the other witnesses read "son of Barachiah"—the earliest witness being provided by the second-century manuscript 𝔓[77] (which shows [βαρα]χιου). Thus, it must be judged that this is what Matthew wrote.

Did Matthew confuse two names or was Matthew thinking of the prophet Zechariah, son of Barachiah (Zech 1:1)? The patronym supports the latter, and so does the context, which speaks of how Jerusalem rejected all the prophets (23:34, 37). Jesus' saying, therefore, refers to the martyrdoms of the first to the last prophet. (Abel was considered a prophet because his death had prophetic implications—see Heb 11:4.) Most scholars reject this view because there is no record of Zechariah the prophet having been murdered, and because Jesus' description of where the murder occurred seems to concur with what was described in 2 Chr 24:20-22. Thus, some scholars have conjectured that Zechariah was the grandson of one called Barachiah (Carson 1984, 486; Morris 1992, 589), or even that Barachiah was also called Jehoiada.

Matthew 23:38

TR NU ἀφίεται ὑμῖν ὁ οἶκος ὑμῶν ἔρημος
"your house is left to you desolate"
𝔓[77vid] א C D W Θ 0102 f[1,13] Maj syr[h,p] Clement Eusebius
KJV NKJV RSV NRSV ESV NASB NIV TNIV NEBmg REB NJB NAB NLT HCSB NET

variant/WH αφιεται υμιν ο οικος υμων
"your house is left to you"
B L syr[s] cop[sa]
RSVmg NRSVmg NEB REBmg NLTmg

The second-century manuscript, 𝔓[77] (P.Oxy. 2683 + P.Oxy. 4405), has some lacunae in this verse. It can most likely be reconstructed as αφιεται υμιν ο [οικος υμων ερημο]ς. As such, 𝔓[77] most likely supports the TR NU reading. (For more details, see *Text of Earliest MSS,* 611.) This second-century manuscript provides the earliest witness to the presence of ερημος ("desolate") in this verse. This witness, combined with that of several other manuscripts, was enough to prompt the NU editors to include the word in the text (a change from previous editions of NU). The only argument against this reading is that scribes could have added the word ερημος to make it conform to Jer 12:7 or 22:5, the OT passages behind this verse. But it is more likely that ερημος was dropped because scribes thought the word was superfluous following αφιεται ("is left") (TCGNT). In either case, Jesus was predicting God's abandonment of Jerusalem and the temple as the result of the Jews rejecting their Messiah. Ultimately, this abandonment and desolation would be realized in the destruction of Jerusalem and the temple in A.D. 70 (see note on Luke 13:35).

Matthew 24:6

With the support of א B D L Θ f[1] 33, WH NU read δει γαρ γενεσθαι, which is literally translated as "it is necessary to happen." Since the phrase begs some kind of filler as the subject of the infinitive γενεσθαι, various scribes obliged: (1) δει γαρ παντα γενεσθαι ("it is necessary for everything to happen") in C W 0102 f[13] Maj (so TR); (2) δει γαρ ταυτα γενεσθαι ("it is necessary for these things to happen") in 565 syr[s]; (3) δει γαρ παντα ταυτα γενεσθαι ("it is necessary for all these things to happen") in 1241 (it[f]). English translators do the same kind of supplying.

Matthew 24:7

WH NU	ἔσονται λιμοὶ καὶ σεισμοί "there will be famines and earthquakes" (א) B D it syr[s] cop NKJVmg RSV NRSV ESV NASB NIV TNIV NEB REB NJB NAB NLT HCSB NET
variant/TR	εσονται λιμοι και λοιμοι και σεισμοι "there will be famines and pestilences and earthquakes" C Θ 0102 f[1,13] Maj (L W 33 in transposed order) KJV NKJV NRSVmg HCSBmg NETmg

The manuscript evidence slightly favors the WH NU reading. It is possible that λοιμοι ("pestilences") was accidentally dropped from the text because it looks so similar to λιμοι ("famines"), but it is more likely that λοιμοι was added to make this verse harmonize with the parallel passage, Luke 21:11. The word transposition in L W 33 is further evidence of an addition.

Matthew 24:31

At the end of this verse a few witnesses (D 1093 it) add another statement, taken almost verbatim from Luke 21:28, αρχομενον δε τουτων γινεσθαι αναβλεψατε και επαρατε τας κεφαλας υμων, διοτι εγγιζει η απολυτρωσις υμων ("when you see these things beginning to occur, look up and lift up your heads because your redemption draws near"). The redemption that comes with Christ's parousia is a Lukan theme, not Matthean.

Matthew 24:36

WH NU	Περὶ δὲ τῆς ἡμέρας ἐκείνης καὶ ὥρας οὐδεὶς οἶδεν, οὐδὲ οἱ ἄγγελοι τῶν οὐρανῶν οὐδὲ ὁ υἱός, εἰ μὴ ὁ πατὴρ μόνος. "But concerning that day and hour no one knows, not even the angels of heaven, nor the Son, no one except the Father." א*,2 B D Θ f[13] it MSS[according to Jerome] RSV NRSV ESV NASB NIV TNIV NEB REB NJB NAB NLT HCSB NETmg
variant/TR	Περι δε της ημερας εκεινης και ωρας ουδεις οιδεν, ουδε οι αγγελοι των ουρανων, ει μη ο πατηρ μονος "But concerning that day and hour no one knows, not even the angels of heaven, no one except the Father." א[1] L W f[1] 33 Maj syr cop MSS[according to Jerome] KJV NKJV RSVmg NRSVmg ESVmg NIVmg TNIVmg NJBmg NLTmg HCSBmg NET

The same omission of "nor the Son" occurs in the parallel passage, Mark 13:32, but in very few manuscripts. The documentary support in favor of its inclusion is impressive in both gospels. Some have argued that the words were added in א*,2 B D etc. in order to harmonize Matthew with Mark (see note in NET), but it is far more likely that the words were omitted in א[1] L W f[1] Maj because scribes found it difficult to conceive of Jesus not knowing something his Father knew—specifically, the time of the second coming. How could Jesus not know the time of his return when he had just predicted all the events that would lead up to it? This is hard to answer. What can be said is that the Son, after his incarnation, took a position of dependence on his Father. The Son, who was one with the Father, acted and spoke in dependence on the Father. If the Father did not reveal something to him, it was not revealed. The timing of the second coming was the Father's prerogative (see Acts 1:7).

Matthew 24:42

WH NU οὐκ οἴδατε ποίᾳ ἡμέρᾳ ὁ κύριος ὑμῶν ἔρχεται
"you do not know which day your Lord comes"
א B D W Θ
NKJVmg RSV NRSV ESV NASB NIV TNIV NEB REB NJB NAB NLT HCSB NET

variant/TR ουκ οιδατε ποια ωρα ο κυριος υμων ερχεται
"you do not know which hour your Lord comes"
K L 0281 Maj syr[p,s]
KJV NKJV NRSVmg HCSBmg NETmg

The variant reading, poorly attested, is the result of harmonization to 24:44 (and perhaps Luke 12:40).

Matthew 24:48

WH NU χρονίζει μου ὁ κύριος
"my master is delaying"
א B 33 cop[sa,bo]
NKJVmg RSV NRSV ESV NASB (NIV TNIV NJB) NAB (NLT) HCSB NET

variant/TR χρονιζει μου ο κυριος ελθειν
"my master is delaying to come"
W f[(1),13] Maj syr (C D L Θ 067 0281 word transposition)
KJV NKJV (NEB REB)

Considering that the point of this parable (24:45-51) is to teach the believers about being ready for the Lord's parousia ("coming"), it was only natural for scribes to add a word that emphasized the Lord's coming.

Matthew 25:1

TR WH NU ἐξῆλθον εἰς ὑπάντησιν τοῦ νυμφίου
"they went out to meet the bridegroom"
א B (C) L W Z 0249 f[13] 33 Maj
all

variant εξηλθον εις υπαντησιν του νυμφιου και της νυμφης
"they went out to meet the bridegroom and the bride"
D Θ f[1] syr
RSVmg NRSVmg ESVmg

In a parable about Jesus coming as the bridegroom, many readers would expect that the one who is waiting for him is the bride. This expectation is heightened by the fact that the NT speaks of Christ and the church as bridegroom and bride (John 3:29; 2 Cor 11:2; Eph 5:25-32; Rev 21:2). But for the sake of emphasizing individual readiness for the day of his coming, Jesus used ten bridesmaids, not one bride, to illustrate the importance of being ready. According to custom, on the evening of the wedding the bridegroom would go to the bride's house and take her to his home for the wedding festivities. Along the way, a procession of family and friends would follow the bridegroom and the bride, lighting up the way with their torches. In this parable we see ten bridesmaids who evidently would accompany the bridegroom back to the bride's home; five sensible bridesmaids took enough oil to keep their torches burning, while the other five did not. There is no mention of the bride because this would distract from the lesson of the parable: a call to individual readiness. The scribes and ancient translators (mainly of a "Western" tradition) who added "and the bride" did so (1) to get every character in the scene (according to the historical custom) or (2) to reflect the NT theme of Christ, the bridegroom, coming for the church, his bride.

Matthew 25:6

At the end of the verse, several manuscripts (A C D L W etc.) add αυτου ("him") to provide an object for εξερχεσθε εις απαντησιν ("go out to meet"). But the addition is not needed, and the testimony of ℵ and B (contra NU) is sufficient to show that Matthew did not write it (so WH).

Matthew 25:9

WH NU μήποτε οὐ μὴ ἀρκέσῃ ἡμῖν καὶ ὑμῖν
"No, there will certainly not be enough for us and you."
B C D K W Δ f^1
NRSV ESV NEB REB NLT HCSB NET

variant/TR μηποτε ουκ αρκεση ημιν και υμιν
"No, there may not be enough for us and you."
ℵ A L Z (Θ) f^{13} 33
KJV NKJV RSV NASB NIV TNIV NJB NAB

The WH NU reading, which has good support, indicates that the sensible bridesmaids were absolutely certain that they did not have enough oil for themselves and the foolish bridesmaids. The variant reading, which has nearly as good support, indicates that the sensible bridesmaids were hesitant about giving the foolish bridesmaids any oil in case there would not be enough.

Matthew 25:13

WH NU οὐκ οἴδατε τὴν ἡμέραν οὐδὲ τὴν ὥραν
"you do not know the day nor the hour"
𝔓[35] ℵ A B C* D L W f^1 syr cop
NKJVmg RSV NRSV ESV NASB NIV TNIV NEB REB NJB NAB (NLT) HCSB NET

variant/TR ουκ οιδατε την ημεραν ουδε την ωραν εν η ο υιος του ανθρωπου ερχεται
"you do not know the day nor the hour in which the Son of Man comes"
C^3 f^{13} Maj
KJV NKJV NRSVmg HCSBmg NETmg

The manuscript evidence for the WH NU reading is impressive. The addition is a natural scribal expansion borrowed from 24:44. The proclamation without the addition is a potent conclusion to the pericope (25:1-13).

Matthew 25:15-16

The word ευθεως ("immediately") is best placed at the beginning of 25:16 (as in WH NU—followed by modern versions), not at the end of 25:15 (as in TR—followed by KJV and NKJV). It is Matthean style for the word ευθεως ("immediately") to appear at the beginning of clauses, not at the end.

Matthew 25:29-30

At the end of this verse a few manuscripts (C^3 H 892^{mg}) add ταυτα λεγων εφωνει· ο εχων ωτα ακουειν ακουετω ("these things saying, he cried out, 'He who has ears to hear let him hear'"). A few other manuscripts (Γ f^{13}) add the same expression at the end of 25:30. This scribal addition, borrowed from 11:15 and 13:9, makes a good refrain that is especially effective here for oral reading.

Matthew 25:31

WH NU — οἱ ἄγγελοι
"the angels"
א B D L Θ f^1 33 cop^{sa}
NKJVmg RSV NRSV ESV NASB NIV TNIV NEB REB NJB NAB NLT HCSB NET

variant/TR — οι αγιοι αγγελοι
"the holy angels"
A W f^{13} Maj it^f $syr^{h,p}$
KJV NKJV HCSBmg

The word αγιοι could have been originally in the text and then was dropped accidentally, since αγιοι and αγγελοι begin and end with the same letters. However, since the manuscript evidence favors the WH NU reading, it is more likely that the variant reflects scribal interpolation influenced by Mark 8:38 or Luke 9:26.

Matthew 25:41

TR WH NU state that the eternal fires "were prepared" (ητοιμασμενον) for the devil and his angels. This has excellent support ($\mathfrak{P}^{45}$ א A B L W Θ 067 0128 f^{13} 33 Maj syr cop), and is followed by all English versions. A few other witnesses (D f^1 it), primarily "Western," have the change: ο ητοιμασεν πατηρ μου ("which my Father prepared").

It is possible that the TR WH NU reading is the result of scribes making it a passive statement so as to avoid directly saying that God the Father prepared the eternal fires. But the variant reading could be the result of scribes trying to make this verse parallel with 25:34. In the end, the TR WH NU reading has to be accepted because it has superior documentary witness.

Matthew 26:3

WH NU — οἱ ἀρχιερεῖς καὶ οἱ πρεσβύτεροι
"the chief priests and the elders"
$\mathfrak{P}^{45}$ א A B D L Θ 0293 $f^{1,13}$ syr^s cop
NKJVmg RSV NRSV ESV NASB NIV TNIV NEB REB NJB NAB NLT HCSB NET

variant 1/TR	οι αρχιερεις και οι γραμματευς και οι πρεσβυτεροι "the chief priests and the scribes and the elders" Maj it syr^{h,p} KJV NKJV HCSBmg
variant 2	οι αρχιερεις και οι Φαρισαιοι "the chief priests and the Pharisees" W none

According to Matthew, two groups of people were responsible for plotting Jesus' death: the chief priests and the elders of the people, who were the leading members of the Jewish religion and Jewish society. These men are identified by Matthew as the prime movers behind Jesus' murder (26:14; 27:1; 28:12). Along with them, Matthew mentions in other passages "the scribes" (26:57; 27:41) and "the Pharisees" (27:62), each of which was added here by various scribes.

Matthew 26:7

The adjective βαρυτιμου, meaning "very expensive, very precious," appears only here in the NT, according to B W 0239. This was probably changed (in ℵ A D L etc.) to the more ordinary word, πολυτιμου ("costly"), influenced by the parallel account on the anointing in John 12:3.

Matthew 26:14

In a few manuscripts (D Θ^{cvid}) Judas is called Ιουδας Σκαριωτης ("Judas Scarioth"), as opposed to Ιουδας Ισκαριωτης ("Judas Iscariot"), found in all other manuscripts, including 𝔓$^{64+67}$, the earliest witness. (See comments on 10:4b.)

Matthew 26:20

TR NU	τῶν δώδεκα "the Twelve" 𝔓$^{64+67vid?}$ 𝔓^{37vid} 𝔓^{45vid} B D f^{1,13} KJV NKJV RSVmg NRSV ESV NIV TNIV NJB NAB NLTmg HCSB NET
variant/WH	των δωδεκα μαθητων "the twelve disciples" ℵ A L W Δ Θ 33 RSV NRSVmg ESVmg NASB NEB REB NLT NETmg

Even though both 𝔓^{37} and 𝔓^{45} are listed as "vid," it is certain that both did not include the word μαθητων because line spacing would not accommodate it. 𝔓^{37} has the typical abbreviation for "Twelve," as $\overline{\iota\beta}$; and 𝔓^{45} has it written out as [δω]δεκα. 𝔓$^{64+67}$ is less certain, but line lengths of the manuscript suggest that it reads $\overline{\iota\beta}$ (see *Text of Earliest MSS,* 69). The testimony of the papyri (with B and D) created a change in the NU text. Prior to NA^{26}, the NU text included the word μαθητων ("disciples"). But the early evidence shows that this must have been a later addition. Such an addition is not necessary in light of the fact that Jesus' closest followers were often designated by the gospel writers as simply "the Twelve."

Matthew 26:27

WH NU λαβὼν ποτήριον
"taking a cup"
ℵ B L W Z Δ Θ 0281 0298 f[1] 33 cop Origen
RSV NRSV ESV NASB NEB REB NJB NAB NLT HCSB

variant/TR λαβων το ποτηριον
"taking the cup"
𝔓[37vid] 𝔓[45] A C D f[13]
KJV NKJV NIV TNIV NET

Given that scribes would be more inclined to add a definite article before "cup" (especially since the cup here is the cup of the Lord's Supper) than to delete an article, it is quite likely that ℵ B L W etc. preserve the original wording. Most of the translations, accordingly, did not follow the second reading. Nevertheless, the testimony of 𝔓[37vid] and 𝔓[45] may have encouraged the translators of NIV TNIV and NET to add the definite article before "cup."

Matthew 26:28

WH NU τὸ αἷμα μου τῆς διαθήκης
"my blood of the covenant"
𝔓[37] 𝔓[45vid] ℵ B L Z Θ 0298[vid] 33
NKJVmg RSV NRSV ESV NASB NIV TNIV NEB REB NJB NAB NLT HCSB NET

variant/TR το αιμα μου της καινης διαθηκης
"my blood of the new covenant"
A C D W f[1,13] Maj syr cop
KJV NKJV RSVmg NRSVmg ESVmg NIVmg TNIVmg NJBmg NLTmg HCSBmg NETmg

The WH NU reading has excellent documentation—the four earliest Greek manuscripts attesting to the reading "covenant." (According to spacing, 𝔓[45] could not have contained the word καινης; see *Text of Earliest MSS,* 164.) Influenced by Luke 22:20, which contains the word "new" before "covenant," later scribes harmonized the Matthean account to Luke's (see note on Luke 22:20). Of course, Jesus was instituting a new covenant, even "the new covenant" God promised through Jeremiah (31:31-34). So, it is not wrong to call this the new covenant, but it is not what Matthew wrote.

Matthew 26:39

At the end of this verse, some late manuscripts (C[3mg] f[13] 69) and lectionaries (124 230 348 543 713 788 826 828 983) add the pericope from Luke 22:43-44 (in the manuscripts) and Luke 22:43-45a (in the lectionaries). The earliest witness to the inclusion of this pericope in Matt 26 is a marginal gloss written by the third corrector of C, who lived in Constantinople in the ninth century. The pericope fits as well in the garden scene in Matthew as it does in Luke (see comments on Luke 22:43-44), but it is a spurious addition in both books. Its placement in Matthew shows that it was very likely a piece of floating oral tradition. The same kind of multiple placement occurred with the pericope of the adulteress (see comments on John 7:53–8:11), also a piece of floating oral tradition.

Matthew 26:42

WH NU	εἰ οὐ δύναται τοῦτο παρελθεῖν "if this cannot pass" 𝔓^{37} ℵ B L NKJVmg RSV NRSV ESV NASB (NLT) HCSB
variant 1	ει ου δυναται τουτο το ποτηριον παρελθειν "if it is not possible to let this cup pass" Θ it syr^{p,s} none
variant 2	ει ου δυναται τουτο παρελθειν απ εμου "if it is not possible to let this pass from me" A C W 067 f^{13} none
variant 3/TR	ει ου δυναται τουτο το ποτηριον παρελθειν απ εμου "if it is not possible to let this cup pass from me" Maj KJV NKJV NIV TNIV NEB REB NJB NAB HCSBmg NET

The WH NU reading has the best manuscript support and is the shortest of all the readings—both signs that it is original. The three variants represent natural scribal expansions that help fill out the sense (many translators did the same by adding "cup"); the expansions became accretive, culminating in the majority of the manuscripts (and TR). The resultant text harmonizes with Mark 14:36.

Matthew 26:44

Several manuscripts (𝔓^{37} A D K f^{1} 565) omit εκ τριτου ("for the third [time]") from this verse. Since the omission cannot be blamed on harmonization or any apparent transcriptional error, it is possible that the shorter text is original. If so, it must be judged that εκ τριτου ("for the third [time]") was added to complement εκ δευτερου ("for the second [time]") in 26:42.

Matthew 26:49-50

The words Χαιρε, ραββι, και κατεφιλησεν αυτον. ο δε Ιησους ειπεν αυτω ("'Greetings, Rabbi,' and he kissed him. And Jesus said to him") are missing from 𝔓^{37} due to homoeoteleuton. The eye of the scribe passed from ειπεν αυτω (which is the reading in 𝔓^{37}) in 26:49 to the same words in 26:50, and he continued copying from there.

Matthew 26:59

WH NU	οἱ δὲ ἀρχιερεῖς "and the chief priests" ℵ B D L Θ f^{13} cop RSV NRSV ESV NASB NIV TNIV NEB REB NJB NAB NLT HCSB NET
variant/TR	οι δε αρχιερεις και οι πρεσβυτεροι "and the chief priests and the elders" A C W f^{1} 33 Maj KJV NKJV

The WH NU reading is strongly supported by early and diverse testimony. The addition is a carryover from 25:57, which found its way into TR, and from there into KJV and NKJV.

Matthew 26:60

Several manuscripts (A C D f[13] 33 Maj—so TR) add ψευδομαρτυρες ("false witnesses") at the end of the verse to provide a noun after δυο ("two").

Matthew 26:63

According to the best manuscript authority (א A B D), the text says ημιν ειπης ει συ ει ο χριστος ο υιος του θεου ("tell us if you are the Christ, the Son of God"). But certain scribes (C* N W Δ cop[sa,bo]), recalling the declaration Peter made in 16:16, could not resist adding του ζωντος—creating the reading, "the Christ, the Son of the living God." The same kind of change occurred in John 6:69 (see note).

Matthew 26:69

Instead of Ιησου του Γαλιλαιου ("Jesus of Galilee"), found in most manuscripts, a few witnesses (C syr[p]) read Ιησου του Ναζωραιου ("Jesus of Nazareth"), so as to conform this verse to 26:71 and to the title commonly used in the NT. In fact, this is the only place in the NT where the expression "Jesus of Galilee" appears; the Lord was better known as "Jesus of Nazareth" (which occurs about twenty times in the NT). Therefore, this is clearly a case where the unusual was changed to the usual.

Matthew 26:73

A few manuscripts (C* Σ syr[h**]) add Γαλιλαιος ει και ("you are a Galilean and") before η λαλια σου δηλον σε ποιε ("your speech makes it clear who you are") in order to make it explicit that the maidservant knew exactly what kind of accent Peter had—a Galilean accent.

Matthew 27:2

WH NU	Πιλάτῳ τῷ ἡγεμόνι "Pilate the governor" א B L 0281 33 syr[p,s] cop Origen NKJVmg RSV NRSV ESV NASB NIV TNIV NEB REB NJB NAB NLT HCSB NET
variant/TR	Ποντιω Πιλατω τω ηγεμονι "Pontius Pilate the governor" A C W Θ 0250 f[1,13] Maj KJV NKJV HCSBmg NETmg

According to the documentary evidence, his name was most likely written here simply as "Pilate," and was changed in other manuscripts to the dual name "Pontius Pilate" because the full name is used in all other NT occurrences (Luke 3:1; Acts 4:27; 1 Tim 6:13).

Matthew 27:4

TR NU	αἷμα ἀθῷον "innocent blood" א A B* C W Δ f[1,13] 33 Origen all
variant 1/WH	αιμα δικαιον "righteous blood" B[1] L Θ it NRSVmg
variant 2	αιμα του δικαιου "blood of the righteous one" syr[s] none

The expression "innocent blood" frequently appears in the Septuagint to describe the murder of a man who did not deserve to die (Prov 6:17; Lam 4:13; Joel 4:19; Jonah 1:14). It would seem perfectly natural for Judas to have this sentiment about Jesus and to express it in these terms; indeed, the manuscript evidence supports this. But Christians knew that Jesus was not just innocent; he was righteous. Indeed, in Peter's second gospel message he blames the Jews for murdering "the holy and righteous one" (Acts 3:14-15). Thus, some Christian scribes changed "innocent" to "righteous"—and a few (notably Tatian) took it a step further by writing "the blood of the righteous one."

Matthew 27:5

WH NU	ῥίψας τὰ ἀργύρια εἰς τὸν ναόν "throwing the silver coins into the temple" (א adds τριακοντα = "thirty") B L Θ f[13] 33 ESV NASB NIV TNIV NAB NLT HCSB NET
variant/TR	ριψας τα αργυρια εν τω ναω "throwing the silver coins in the temple" A C W f[1] Maj KJV NKJV RSV NRSV NEB REB NJB

The difference between the two prepositions (εις/εν) would usually be insignificant, but in this case the significance pertains to where Judas was when he threw the coins. Generally speaking, in Matthean usage and NT usage, ναος describes the inner sanctuary, not the temple proper or temple precinct (usually called ιερον). Thus, Judas could have violated the boundaries, crossing over from the outer court to the inner court, and thrown the coins into (εις) the holy place. Or he could have entered into the holy place and thrown the coins down while in (εν) there. Unless the WH NU reading is the result of Alexandrian refinement (see TCGNT), the manuscript support for it is superior to that for the variant.

Matthew 27:9

TR WH NU	Ἰερεμίου τοῦ προφήτου "Jeremiah the prophet" א A B C L W all

variant 1 Ζαχαριου του προφητου
"Zechariah the prophet"
22 syr[hmg]
NRSVmg NETmg

variant 2 Ιησαιου του προφητου
"Isaiah the prophet"
21 it[l]
NRSVmg NETmg

variant 3 του προφητου
"the prophet"
Φ 33 it[a,b] syr[p,s] cop[boMS] MSS[according to Augustine]
NETmg

The ascription of this prophecy to Jeremiah is difficult because the passage seems to come from Zech 11:12-13. (The passage in Matt 27:9b-10 reads, "And they took the thirty pieces of silver, the price of the one on whom the price had been set, on whom some of the people of Israel had set a price, and they gave them for the potter's field, as the Lord commanded me," NRSV.) Because of the difficulty of assigning this prophecy to Jeremiah, some scribes changed "Jeremiah" to "Zechariah" (variant 1), and others dropped the name before the prophet (variant 3). Still others changed the name to "Isaiah," probably because he is the most quoted prophet in the NT. But Matthew's ascription of the prophecy to Jeremiah is not wrong, because although the quotation comes mainly from Zech 11:12-13, it also comes from Jer 19:1-11; 32:6-9. Zechariah's words do not mention the purchase of a field, but Jeremiah's words do. In fact, it is Jeremiah who speaks of innocent blood (Jer 19:4) and of changing the name of a potter's field (Jer 19:6). And it is Jeremiah who purchased a potter's field (Jer 32:6-9). Thus, Jeremiah received the credit because he was the more prominent prophet (see Carson 1984, 562-563).

Matthew 27:11

The words ο ηγεμων ("the governor") are missing from W Θ, probably due to homoeoteleuton; the next word has the same ending: λεγων ("saying").

Matthew 27:16a

NU [Ἰησοῦν] Βαραββᾶν
"Jesus Barabbas"
S[mg] Θ f[1] 700* syr[s] MSS[according to Origen]
NKJVmg RSVmg NRSV TNIV NEB REB NJBmg NAB NLTmg HCSBmg NET

variant 1/TR WH Βαραββαν
"Barabbas"
ℵ A B D L W 0250 f[13] 33 700[c]
KJV NKJV RSV NRSVmg ESV NASB NIV TNIVmg NEBmg NJB NLT HCSB NETmg

See comments on 27:17.

Matthew 27:16b

At the end of this verse a few manuscripts (Φ syr[s]) add ος δια φονον και στασιν ην βεβλημενος εις φυλακην ("who, because of murder and insurrection, was put in prison"). This addition, perhaps adapted from Mark 15:7, provides the reader with background information about who Barabbas was and why he was in prison.

Matthew 27:17

NU [Ἰησοῦν τὸν] Βαραββᾶν
"Jesus Barabbas"
S^mg (Θ 700 omit τον) f[1] syr[s] MSS[according to Origen]
RSVmg NRSV TNIV NEB REB NJBmg NAB NLTmg HCSBmg NET

variant 1/TR WH Βαραββαν
"Barabbas"
א A D L W f[13] 565 700[c] (B 1010 MSS[according to Origen] add τον)
KJV NKJV RSV NRSVmg ESV NASB NIV TNIVmg NEBmg NJB NABmg NLT HCSB NETmg

The NU reading is supported only by some so-called "Caesarean" witnesses. Some scholars, however, think that Ιησους ("Jesus") was in the archetype of B because the article τον was left before Βαραββαν, implying that the name "Jesus" appeared before "Barabbas" in the scribe's exemplar. Several later manuscripts have glosses that indicate "Jesus" appeared in earlier manuscripts. A marginal note to Codex S (from the tenth century) says, "In many ancient copies which I have met with I found Barabbas himself likewise called 'Jesus.'" According to Metzger, about twenty minuscules contain a marginal note stating that in very ancient manuscripts Barabbas is called Jesus; in one of these the note is attributed to Origen. Since Origen himself calls attention to this in his *Commentary on Matthew* the reading must be of great antiquity (TCGNT). Another argument in favor of the reading "Jesus Barabbas" is that it is offset with the wording "Jesus, the one called Christ"—as if the second title serves to distinguish the two men called Jesus (see note in NET).

But if the reading "Jesus Barabbas" is ancient, why does it not appear in the most ancient manuscripts (namely, א A B D W)? Was it suppressed in most manuscripts, only to show up later, in ninth to twelfth century witnesses? Or was it added by some scribe early in the history of the transmission of the text because he considered "Barabbas" to not really be a name (it means "son of a father") or because he wanted to add some drama to Matthew's narrative? Perhaps the crowd outside Pilate's palace had been shouting, "give us Jesus, give us Jesus." To which Pilate responded, "Do you want Jesus the one called Barabbas or do you want Jesus the one called Christ?" Instead of asking for Jesus the Christ, they get Jesus the murderer. The irony is blatant: the murdering Jesus is set free, while the freeing Jesus is murdered.

In any case, the unusualness of the reading "Jesus Barabbas" made the NU editors consider it to be the one Matthew wrote, which was later changed because scribes could not conceive of anyone but the Messiah being called "Jesus." In fact, Origen (*Comm. Matt.* 121) said that in all of Scripture no one who was called Jesus was a sinner. Many ancients may have shared Origen's sentiment and excised it from the text. Some modern translators (NRSV TNIV NEB REB NAB NET), however, have ventured to put "Jesus Barabbas" side by side with "Jesus the Christ."

Matthew 27:24

WH NU ἀθῷος εἰμι ἀπὸ τοῦ αἵματος τούτου
"I am innocent of the blood of this man."
B D Θ it syr[s]
NKJVmg RSV NRSV ESV NASB NIV TNIV NEB REB NJB NAB NLT HCSB NET

variant/TR αθωος ειμι απο του αιματος του δικαιου τουτου
"I am innocent of the blood of this just man."
ℵ (A) L W f[1,13] Maj syr[h,p]
KJV NKJV RSVmg NRSVmg ESVmg NJBmg HCSBmg

The WH NU reading could be the result of homoeoteleuton—του δικαιου accidentally being omitted before τουτου. However, it is more likely that the variant reading is a scribal interpolation adapted from Pilate's wife's comment about Jesus being a just man (27:19; cf. Luke 23:14 and John 19:6). This bit of gap-filling is important for the narrative of Jesus' trial because it tells us that Pilate thought Jesus was innocent of the crimes charged against him and even more, that Jesus was a just man. But as WH NU read, it must be inferred that Pilate thought Jesus was innocent or he would not have washed his hands of Jesus' blood.

Matthew 27:28

According to early and diverse testimony (ℵ*,2 A L W Θ 0250 f[1,13] cop), the Roman soldiers stripped Jesus (εκδυσαντες αυτον), then put a scarlet robe on him. All translations follow this reading. A few other manuscripts (ℵ[1] B 1424) indicate that they clothed him (ενδυσαντες αυτον) with a scarlet robe. And yet other manuscripts (D it syr[s]) indicate that they clothed him and then put a scarlet robe on him. The first variant has excellent testimony and makes good sense. Since Jesus had just been stripped for the flogging he received (27:26), it would seem more likely that the soldiers clothed him than stripped him again. However, it is possible that this reading displays harmonization to Mark 15:17 or John 19:2, or it could be the work of narrative gap-filling.

Matthew 27:32

One manuscript (33) adds the interesting detail, borrowed from Mark 15:21, that Simon the Cyrenian was "coming in from the country" (ερχομενον απ αγρου) when he was conscripted by the Roman soldiers to carry Jesus' cross. The D-text (D it) adds εις απαντησιν αυτου ("when he met him").

Matthew 27:34

WH NU οἶνον μετὰ χολῆς μεμιγμένον
"wine mixed with gall"
ℵ B D K L f[1,13] 33
NKJVmg RSV NRSV ESV NASB NIV TNIV NEB REB NJB NAB (NLT) HCSB NET

variant/TR οξος μετα χολης μεμιγμενον
"sour wine mixed with gall"
A W 0250 0281 Maj
KJV NKJV HCSBmg

The WH NU reading has excellent documentary attestation. The variant reading is the result of scribal conformity to the other gospels (Mark 15:36; Luke 23:36; John 19:29) or to Ps 68:22 (LXX; 69:22 in English Bible).

Matthew 27:35

WH NU	διεμερίσαντο τὰ ἱμάτια αὐτοῦ βάλλοντες κλῆρον "they divided his garments [by] casting lots" א A B D L W 33 NKJVmg RSV NRSV ESV NASB NIV TNIV NEB REB NJB NAB NLT HCSB NET
variant/TR	διεμερισαντο τα ιματια αυτου βαλλοντες κληρον ινα πληρωθη το ρηθεν δια του προφητου, Διεμερισαντο τα ιματια μου εαυτοις και επι τον ιματισμον μου εβαλον κληρον "they divided his garments [by] casting lots, that it might be fulfilled what was spoken through the prophet, 'They parted my garments among them, and for my vesture they cast lots.'" Δ Θ 0250 f[1,13] 1424 it Eusebius KJV NKJV NRSVmg NIVmg NLTmg HCSBmg

Because of the excellent support for the shorter text, it must be judged that the long addition came from John 19:24, coupled with a typical Matthean introduction to a prophetic citation (see 4:14). It was natural for scribes, wanting to emulate Matthew's style, to make this addition, because Matthew had a penchant for showing how various events in Jesus' life and ministry fulfilled the OT Scriptures (in this case, Ps 22:18, from the most quoted chapter in the NT concerning the crucifixion). Some of the same scribes (Θ 0250 f[1,13]) also made this addition in Mark 15:27.

Matthew 27:38

In one Old Latin manuscript (it[c]) the two thieves crucified with Jesus are given names: *Zoatham* and *Camma*. The same scribe gave nearly the same names in Mark 15:27: *Zoathan* and *Chammata*. In Luke 23:32 the scribe of the minuscule manuscript 1 gave them the names *Joathas* and *Maggatras*. Such name giving was typical of scribes who thought there was a gap in the text if significant figures were left unnamed. Even the best of scribes, the copyist of 𝔓[75], could not resist; he gave the name Νευης ("Nineveh") to the rich antagonist of the beggar, who is named Lazarus. Later, Priscillian gave him the name *Finees* (see note on Luke 16:19).

Matthew 27:41

TR WH NU	οἱ ἀρχιερεῖς ἐμπαίζοντες μετὰ τῶν γραμματέων καὶ πρεσβυτέρων "the chief priests with the scribes and elders were mocking [Jesus]" (א) A B C L Θ f[1,13] 33 all
variant 1	οι αρχιερεις εμπαιζοντες μετα των γραμματεων και Φαρισαιων "the chief priests with the scribes and Pharisees were mocking [Jesus]" D W it syr[s] none

variant 2 οι αρχιερεις εμπαιζοντες μετα των γραμματεων και πρεσβυτερων και Φαρισαιων
"the chief priests with the scribes and the elders and Pharisees"
Maj it[f] syr[h,p]
NKJVmg HCSBmg

The variant readings present scribal attempts to include the Pharisees among those mocking Jesus because they were one of the religious groups who were responsible for Jesus' crucifixion (12:14; 27:62).

Matthew 27:42

WH NU βασιλεὺς 'Ισραήλ ἐστιν καταβάτω νῦν ἀπὸ τοῦ σταυροῦ καὶ πιστεύσομεν.
"He is Israel's king. Let him come down from the cross now and we will believe."
(א reads πιστευσωμεν) B D L 33 cop[sa]
NKJVmg RSV NRSV ESV NASB NIV TNIV NEB REB NJB NAB NLT HCSB NET

variant/TR ει βασιλευς Ισραηλ εστιν καταβατω νυν απο του σταυρου και πιστευσωμεν
"If he is Israel's king, let him come down now from the cross and we would believe."
(A reads πιστευομεν) W Θ f[1,13] Maj syr cop[bo]
KJV NKJV HCSBmg

If scribes did not understand that the reading of the text was to be taken sarcastically (something like, "Some king of Israel you are!"), then it would be natural for them to make the sentence conditional—both by adding ει ("if") at the beginning and by changing the future tense verb for "believe" to a subjunctive. Some of the manuscripts (א A) evidence a mixture of the two changes.

Matthew 27:46

TR NU ἠλι ἠλι
"Eli, Eli"
A D (L) W Θ f[1,13] Maj
KJV NKJV RSV NRSV ESV NASB TNIV NEB REB NJB NAB NLT HCSB NET

variant/WH ηλοι ηλοι
"Eloi, Eloi"
א B 33 cop
NIV TNIVmg NLTmg

The TR NU reading reflects the Hebrew word *eli* ("my God"), whereas the variant comes from the Aramaic word *elahi* ("my God"). Although it could be argued that the variant is the result of scribal conformity to Mark 15:34, it reflects the actual language Jesus spoke and has excellent manuscript support (albeit almost all Egyptian).

Furthermore, it would be easier for the bystanders to mistake the three-syllable Aramaic word for the three-syllable word "Elijah" than to confuse ηλι for "Elijah." Jesus was crying out to God, and in the words of Ps 22:1 was asking God why he had forsaken him. The crowds thought he was crying to Elijah, who, according to some Jewish traditions, would come to the rescue of those in distress (TDNT 2.930-931). The remaining words of Jesus' cry, *lema sabachthani,* are clearly Aramaic. The reason this expression appears with various spellings among the MSS is that Greek scribes found it difficult to transliterate the Aramaic.

Matthew 27:49

TR NU λοιποὶ ἔλεγον· ἄφες ἴδωμεν εἰ ἔρχεται Ἠλίας σώσων αὐτόν.
"Others said, 'Leave him alone, let us see if Elijah comes to save him.'"
A D W Θ $f^{1,13}$ Maj it syr cop[sa,bo]
all

variant/WH λοποι ελεγον· αφες ιδωμεν ει ερχεται Ηλιας σωσων αυτον. αλλος δε λαβων λογχην ενυξεν αυτου την πλευραν, και εξηλθεν υδωρ και αιμα.
"Others said, 'Leave him alone, let us see if Elijah comes to save him.' But another took his spear and pierced his side, and out came water and blood."
א B C L Γ
RSVmg NRSVmg NASBmg NLTmg

The general consensus among scholars about the variant is that it was interpolated from John 19:34 (see Metzger's assessment in TCGNT). However, the variant cannot be easily dismissed, for the following reasons: (1) The manuscript evidence for its inclusion is strong; indeed, the testimony of א B C has far more often refuted that of A D W than vice versa in the NU text—why not here? The scribes of B (especially) and א usually refrained from being gospel harmonists. (2) If it was taken from John 19:34, why was it not taken verbatim? As it is, the order of the last words in Matthew is "water and blood," whereas in John it is "blood and water," and there are four other words used in Matthew that do not appear in John (αλλος δε λαβων and εξηλθεν). (3) The reason scribes would want to delete it from the text is because the spearing (according to John) happened after Jesus' death, whereas here it occurs just before his death (see 27:50). Thus, the deletion was made in the interest of avoiding a discrepancy among the Gospels. Such harmonization was done full-scale in manuscripts like A D W. (4) Another reason for scribes to delete it is that it appears to present a jarring contradiction to what was just described: While many of the bystanders were waiting to see if Elijah would come and save Jesus, a Roman soldier (in complete opposition to this sentiment) lances Jesus with his spear. Therefore, the longer text should not be easily dismissed because, in fact, it is the harder reading and has excellent documentary support. At the least, it should be included in the text with single brackets (WH includes it with double brackets).

Matthew 27:56

Instead of Ιωσηφ ("Joseph"), found in א D* L W Θ, several witnesses (A B C D[c] $f^{1,13}$ 33 Maj) read Ιωση ("Joses"). Perhaps the variant was created by scribes who did not want a brother of Jesus being named after his father Joseph because it could imply that Joseph had more children by Mary after the birth of Jesus. (See note on 13:55 for the same textual variant concerning the name of one of Jesus' brothers.)

Matthew 27:64

WH NU — οἱ μαθηταὶ αὐτοῦ κλέψωσιν αὐτόν
"his disciples may steal it [Jesus' body]"
A B C* D K W Δ Θ $f^{1,13}$ 33
NKJVmg RSV NRSV ESV NASB NIV TNIV NEB REB NJB NAB NLT HCSB NET

variant/TR — οι μαθηται αυτου νυκτος κλεψωσιν αυτον
"his disciples may steal it [Jesus' body] at night"
C^3 L Γ syr^s
KJV NKJV

The WH NU reading has excellent manuscript support. The insertion of "at night" is an extra detail supplied by scribes to make this statement harmonize with 28:13.

Matthew 28:2

WH NU — ἀπεκύλισεν τὸν λίθον
"he [the angel] rolled away the stone"
א B D syr^s cop^{sa}
NKJVmg RSV NRSV ESV NASB NIV TNIV NEB REB NJB NAB NLT HCSB NET

variant 1/TR — απεκυλισεν τον λιθον απο της θυρας
"he [the angel] rolled away the stone from the entrance"
A C K W Δ syr^p
KJV NKJV

variant 2 — απεκυλισεν τον λιθον απο της θυρας του μνημειου
"he [the angel] rolled away the stone from the entrance of the tomb"
L Γ Θ $f^{1,13}$ 33
none

The WH NU reading has early and diverse documentary support. The variant readings are natural scribal expansions.

Matthew 28:6

WH NU — τὸν τόπον ὅπου ἔκειτο
"the place where he was lying"
א B Θ 33 it^e syr^s cop
RSV NRSV ESV NASB NIV TNIV NEB REB NJB NAB NLT HCSB NET

variant 1/TR — τον τοπον οπου εκειτο ο κυριος
"the place where the Lord was lying"
A C D L W 0148 $f^{1,13}$ Maj
KJV NKJV RSVmg NRSVmg ESVmg NETmg

variant 2 — τον τοπον οπου εκειτο ο Ιησους
"the place where Jesus was lying"
Φ
NETmg

variant 3 τον τοπον οπου εκειτο το σωμα του Ιησου
"the place where the body of Jesus was lying"
1424
NETmg

The WH NU reading has early and diverse textual support. All the variants are scribal expansions intended to help the readability of the text. The first variant is well-known because of its inclusion in TR and its presence in KJV and NKJV.

Matthew 28:7

A few witnesses (D 565 syr[s]) read ηγερθη ("he was raised"), instead of the fuller expression ηγερθη απο των νεκρων ("he was raised from the dead") found in all other manuscripts. Because of its sparse textual attestation, the short reading must be judged as stylistic trimming.

Matthew 28:9

WH NU καὶ ἰδοὺ Ἰησοῦς ὑπήντησεν αὐταῖς
"and behold Jesus met them"
ℵ B D W Θ f[13] 33 syr[p] cop
NKJVmg RSV NRSV ESV NASB NIV TNIV NEB REB NJB NAB NLT HCSB NET

variant/TR Ως δε επορευοντο απαγγειλαι τοις μαθηταις αυτου· και ιδου Ιησους υπηντησεν αυταις
"And as they went to tell his disciples—and behold, Jesus met them."
A C L 0148 f[1] Maj syr[h]
KJV NKJV HCSBmg

It is possible that the shorter text is the result of homoeoteleuton—the previous verse ends with exactly the same last four words: απαγγειλαι τοις μαθηταις αυτου ("to tell his disciples"). Or it could be that the shorter text is the result of scribes excising a redundant statement (see 28:8). However, the shorter text has the best documentary attestation. Furthermore, the longer text—an attempt at narrative gap-filling—is quite awkward inasmuch as the inserted clause does not conjoin well with the next clause beginning with και ("and"). The KJV translators, following TR, avoided this problem by simply not translating και.

Matthew 28:10

A few late witnesses (157 2211) read μαθηταις μου ("my disciples") instead of αδελφοις μου ("my brothers"), found in all other manuscripts. It is extremely significant that Jesus now calls his disciples his "brothers" because the resurrection created a new relationship by providing for the regeneration of those who believe in Jesus (see John 20:17; 1 Pet 1:3).

Matthew 28:17

Several manuscripts (A W Γ Θ 0148 f[1,13] Maj—so TR) add an object (either αυτον or αυτω) after προσεκυνησαν ("they worshiped") to complete the verb: "seeing Jesus, they worshiped him." Most English versions do the same. Without the object, the sense is that seeing Jesus caused them to worship—the worship could have been directed toward God the Father, Jesus, or both.

Matthew 28:20

WH NU	omit αμην ("amen") at end of verse א A* B D W f^1 33 cop^{sa} NKJVmg RSV NRSV ESV NASB NIV TNIV NEB REB NJB NAB NLT HCSB NET
Variant/TR	add αμην ("amen") at end of verse A^c Θ f^{13} Maj it syr KJV NKJV NRSVmg NETmg

Because the books of the NT were read aloud in church meetings, it became customary to end the reading with an "amen." Gradually, this spoken word was added to the printed page of many manuscripts. This addition took place in all four gospels and Acts. Some of the Epistles were originally concluded by the writer with "amen"; to those that were not, many scribes appended "amen." Thus, in one manuscript or another, every book of the NT ends with "amen." But only a few of these may have been written by the original writer (see the endings of Galatians, Jude, and 2 Peter).

Subscription

B concludes the book with κατα Μαθθαιον ("According to Matthew"). See note on "Inscription" (the first note in Matthew) for discussion.

Gospel according to MARK

Inscription (Title)

WH NU	Κατα Μαρκαν "According to Mark" א B (NIV TNIV NLT NET)
variant 1	Ευαγγελιον κατα Μαρκαν "Gospel according to Mark" A D L W Θ f[13] 33 Maj NKJV RSV NRSV ESV NASB NEB REB NJB NAB HCSB
variant 2/TR	Το Κατα Μαρκον Αγιον Ευαγγελιον "The Holy Gospel according to Mark" (or, "The Gospel according to Saint Mark") 209 579 KJV

All the titles given to the second gospel are scribal creations. In its original composition, the first verse of this gospel functioned as the title (see note on 1:1). Variant 1 (even though it is found in manuscripts later than א and B) probably represents the first stage in giving inscriptions to the Gospels. Each gospel was titled separately because each gospel often was a book by itself (see comments on the inscription to each of the gospels). The WH NU reading reflects the second stage in titling the gospels, a stage when all four gospels were placed together in one codex and were titled under one head: The Gospel—According to Matthew, According to Mark, According to Luke, According to John. This titling was mostly influenced by Codex Vaticanus, which has κατα μαθθαιον, κατα μαρκον, κατα λουκαν, κατα ιωαννην written for both the inscription and subscription in each respective gospel. Codex Sinaiticus has the same titling for the inscription, but in the subscription for Mark, Luke, and John ευαγγελιον ("Gospel") comes first (Matthew lacks a subscription in א). This reflects the fact that each gospel was titled separately in the earlier history of textual transmission.

Mark 1:1

TR NU	Ἀρχὴ τοῦ εὐαγγελίου Ἰησοῦ Χριστοῦ [υἱοῦ θεοῦ] "[The] beginning of the gospel of Jesus Christ, Son of God" א[1] B D L W it syr cop (A f[1,13] Maj add του before θεου) KJV NKJV RSV NRSV ESV NASB NIV TNIVmg NEB REB NJB NAB NLT HCSB NET

variant 1/WH Αρχη του ευαγγελιου Ιησου χριστου
"[The] beginning of the gospel of Jesus Christ"
א* Θ (28) cop^{saMS} Origen
RSVmg NRSVmg ESVmg NASBmg NIVmg TNIV NEBmg REBmg NJBmg NABmg NLTmg HCSBmg NETmg

variant 2 Αρχη του ευαγγελιου
"[The] beginning of the Gospel"
Irenaeus Epiphanius
none

This verse (without a verb) was either Mark's title for his gospel or an incipit introducing this gospel's theme: the gospel about (or proclaimed by) Jesus Christ, God's Son. When first written, the title may have been brief ("beginning of the Gospel") and then expanded by the additions, "Jesus Christ" and "Son of God." It was typical for scribes to expand titles to NT books (see, for example, the note on Rev 1:1). However, most scholars argue for the TR NU reading because of its excellent documentary attestation and because it suits Mark's literary plan. It is argued that "the Son of God" is essential to Mark's title because it introduces a major theme in Mark: Jesus' divine sonship. Hurtado (1989, 23) said, "the claim that Jesus is the Son of God appears at several points in Mark, indicating that Jesus' divine sonship is an important part of Mark's portrait (cf. 1:11; 3:11; 5:7; 9:7; 14:61-62; 15:39), and this causes most scholars to believe that the title was originally here in the opening of the book and that it was accidentally omitted in some manuscripts."

The usual explanation for a scribe accidentally dropping the title is that the title would have been written with the last four words in nomina sacra form as follows: ΕΥΑΓΓΕΛΙΟΥ$\overline{\text{ΙΥ}}\overline{\text{ΧΥ}}\overline{\text{ΥΥ}}\overline{\text{ΘΥ}}$ (see TCGNT). It is argued that the last four words look so much alike that the last four letters $\overline{\text{ΥΥ}}\overline{\text{ΘΥ}}$ (= "Son of God") could have been easily dropped. As a case in point, Codex Sinaiticus was emended by the first corrector (who added $\overline{\text{ΥΥ}}\overline{\text{ΘΥ}}$) before it left the scriptorium. However, it must be noted that υιος ("Son") was not among the earliest divine names to be written as a nomen sacrum. In fact, many of the earliest manuscripts did not do so (such as $\mathfrak{P}^{4+64+67}$), while a few did (such as $\mathfrak{P}^{1}$, $\mathfrak{P}^{40}$, $\mathfrak{P}^{101}$); most of the early scribes vacillated (such as $\mathfrak{P}^{45}$, $\mathfrak{P}^{46}$, $\mathfrak{P}^{66}$, $\mathfrak{P}^{75}$)—writing it both as a nomen sacrum and in full. Thus, if the omission of υιου θεου happened early in the history of textual transmission (which appears to be the case), it cannot necessarily be blamed on four nomina sacra strung together. As a case in point, Codex Vaticanus is written as ευαγγελιου $\overline{\text{ΙΥ}}$ $\overline{\text{ΧΥ}}$ υιου $\overline{\text{ΘΥ}}$. "Son" is not treated as a nomen sacrum. It is noteworthy that all the English versions except the TNIV (which departs from the NIV here) have kept the full title, "Jesus Christ, Son of God," and nearly every version has noted the shorter variant.

One final issue has to be addressed here: the punctuation at the end of the verse. According to NA^{27} and UBS^{4}, the verse ends with a full stop, making it a verbless title (so most modern translations). In other texts (such as TR, followed by KJV), the verse ends with a comma, thereby joining 1:1 to 1:2. The decision is exegetical; there is nothing in the ancient manuscripts to suggest one way of punctuation against the other. Several church fathers treated 1:2-3 as a parenthesis, thereby joining 1:1 to 1:4. Taking this logic a step further, Lachmann conjectured that 1:2-3 was not written by Mark but inserted later by a scribe. But not one manuscript attests to this. Therefore, 1:1 is a verbless title not intended to be attached grammatically to what follows, and 1:2-3 serves as an opening quotation for the Gospel, thematically connected with 1:4.

Mark 1:2a

WH NU γέγραπται ἐν τῷ Ἠσαΐᾳ τῷ προφήτῃ
"it has been written in Isaiah the prophet"
א B L Δ 33 565 cop
NKJVmg RSV NRSV ESV NASB NIV TNIV NEB REB NJB NAB NLT HCSB NET

variant/TR γεγραπται εν τοις προφηταις
"it has been written in the prophets"
A W f[13] Maj
KJV NKJV RSVmg NRSVmg ESVmg HCSBmg NETmg

Various scribes, aware that Mark was citing more than one prophet in the following verses (1:2-3), changed "Isaiah the prophet" to "the prophets" (so TR and KJV). In 1:2 Mark quoted first from Exod 23:20 (LXX) and then from Mal 3:1 (Hebrew text), and in 1:3 he quoted Isa 40:3 (LXX)—or perhaps Mark was using an early Jewish collection of texts relating to the Messiah (Cole 1961, 57). Whatever his source, Mark attributed the text to Isaiah only. It may be that he was more familiar with Isaiah, or that he thought Isaiah's name was the one which his readers most often associated with prophecies about the Messiah. The quote from Malachi speaks of a messenger who would prepare the way for the Messiah. Both quotes refer specifically to verses 4-8. All modern versions follow the superior reading.

Mark 1:2b

WH NU ὃς κατασκευάσει τὴν ὁδόν σου
"[he] who will prepare your way"
א B D K L P W Θ 700*
RSV NRSV ESV NASB NIV TNIV NEB REB NJB NAB NLT HCSB NET

variant/TR ος κατασκευασει την οδον σου εμπροσθεν σου
"[he] who will prepare your way before you"
A f[1,13] 33 Maj
KJV NKJV NRSVmg HCSBmg

The extended reading is the result of scribal harmonization to Matt 11:10. This harmonization found its way into TR, followed by KJV and NKJV.

Mark 1:3

According to most manuscripts, the text reads ευθειας ποιειτε τας τριβους αυτου ("make his paths straight"), but some Western witnesses (D it) conformed the quote to Isa 40:3 (LXX) by changing αυτου ("his") to του θεου ημων ("our God"). At the end of this verse, two witnesses (W it[c]) extend the Isaiah quotation by adding Isa 40:4-8. The scribes who did this may have been influenced by Luke 3:4-6, a citation of Isa 40:3-5.

Mark 1:4

NU ἐγένετο Ἰωάννης [ὁ] βαπτίζων ἐν τῇ ἐρήμῳ καὶ κηρύσσων
"John was the one baptizing in the wilderness and proclaiming"
א L Δ cop[bo]
none

variant 1/WH εγενετο Ιωαννης ο βαπτιζων εν τη ερημω κηρυσσων
"John the baptizing one [= John the Baptist] appeared in the wilderness proclaiming"
B 33
RSV NRSV ESV NASB NIV TNIV NEB REB NJB NAB (NLT) HCSB NET

variant 2/TR εγενετο Ιωαννης βαπτιζων εν τη ερημω και κηρυσσων
"John came baptizing in the wilderness and proclaiming"
A W f[1,13] Maj
KJV NKJV NRSVmg

variant 3 εγενετο Ιωαννης εν τη ερημω βαπτιζων και κηρυσσων
"John appeared in the wilderness, baptizing and proclaiming"
D Θ 28 700 it syr[p]
none

Of the four variants, the NU reading represents the most difficult reading in that it describes (in a participial phrase) John as "the one baptizing and proclaiming" (Guelich 1989, 16). Even though this is the more difficult construction, it accords with Markan style (see 6:14, 24). The first variant shows that the scribes understood "John the baptizing one" to be equivalent to a title, "John the Baptist." Interestingly, all the modern English versions followed this variant. The second and third variants are scribal attempts to circumvent the articular participial phrase.

Mark 1:8

NU reads, εγω εβαπτισμα υμας υδατι, αυτος δε βαπτισει υμας εν πνευματι αγιω ("I baptize you in [or, with] water, but he will baptize you in [or, with] the Holy Spirit"). According to א B Δ 33, the first clause does not have the preposition εν ("in") before υδατι ("water"), whereas A D L W f[1,13] Maj do have the preposition. According to B and L, the second clause does not have the preposition εν, whereas א A D W 33 f[1,13] Maj do have it. None of these changes really affect translation or interpretation of the verse because the dative without the preposition can be rendered as "with water" or "in water" and as "with Spirit" or "in spirit," and the preposition εν can be translated as "in" or "with." Therefore, depending on one's theological perspective on water baptism, this verse can be interpreted to say that John the Baptist baptized "with water" (for those who believe in sprinkling) or "in water" (for those who believe in immersion). The same is true for the Spirit-baptism: It can mean that the Spirit is the agent of baptism (for example, "we are baptized by the Spirit into one body"—1 Cor 12:13) or it can mean believers are immersed in the Holy Spirit. In the final analysis, a modern exegete can still read the text in any of the four ways just mentioned, no matter what the wording is.

Mark 1:10

WH NU τὸ πνεῦμα ὡς περιστερὰν καταβαῖνον εἰς αὐτόν
"the Spirit of God like a dove descending into [or, to] him"
B D f[13]
none

variant 1 το πνευμα ως περιστεραν καταβαινον επ αυτον
"the Spirit of God like a dove descending on him"
A L Θ f[1] Maj syr
all

variant 2/TR το πνευμα ως περιστεραν καταβαινον και μενον επ αυτον
"the Spirit of God like a dove descending and remaining on him"
א (W) 33 it
none

The two variants are the result of scribal conformity to the other gospels—the first variant to Matt 3:16 and Luke 3:22, the second to John 1:33. In these gospels (followed by the variant readings), the Spirit is said to descend upon Jesus after his baptism. But in the WH NU reading of Mark 1:10, the Spirit is said to enter into Jesus after his baptism. This is a significant difference because whereas "upon" suggests that Jesus was anointed and empowered with the Spirit, "into" suggests that Jesus was penetrated and inhabited by the Spirit. This reading could be readily used by adoptionists to prooftext the baptismal regeneration of Jesus. In fact, the Ebionites (who were basically adoptionist) held such a view about Jesus (ISBE 2.10). According to Epiphanius (*Pan.* 30.13.7-8), the *Gospel of the Ebionites* reads, "After the people were baptized, Jesus also came and was baptized by John. And as he came up from the water, the heavens were opened, and he saw the Holy Spirit descending in the form of a dove and *entering into him.*" In truth, if εις is the original reading here, it need not be seen as supporting a heterodox view of Christ. The term εις has a much broader semantic range than the common gloss "into" suggests. In Matt 27:30, for example, the term clearly means "on" or "upon."

Mark 1:14

WH NU τὸ εὐαγγέλιον τοῦ θεοῦ
"the gospel of God"
א B L Θ f[1,13] 33 Origen
NKJVmg RSV NRSV ESV NASB NIV TNIV NEB REB NJB NAB NLT HCSB NET

variant/TR το ευαγγελιον της βασιλειας του θεου
"the gospel of the kingdom of God"
A D W Maj
KJV NKJV HCSBmg NETmg

The expansion in the variant is the result of scribal harmonization, either to the immediate context (the next verse speaks of Jesus proclaiming the imminence of the kingdom) or to Matt 4:17. TR, followed by KJV and NKJV, typically incorporated such harmonizations.

Mark 1:24

According to excellent testimony (A B C D W), the demon-possessed man says to Jesus, οιδα σε τις ει, ο αγιος του θεου ("I know who you are: the Holy One of God"). By way of conformity to the immediate context, where we see the spirit speaking in the plural ("Have you come to destroy us?"), some witnesses (א L Δ) switch to the plural (οιδαμεν="we know").

Mark 1:27

WH NU τί ἐστιν τοῦτο διδαχὴ καινὴ κατ᾽ ἐξουσίαν· καὶ τοῖς πνεύμασι τοῖς ἀκαθάρτοις ἐπιτάσσει, καὶ ὑπακούουσιν αὐτῷ.
"What is this? A new teaching with authority. And he commands the unclean spirits and they obey him."
ℵ B L 33 (f[1]) 28* (565*)
NKJVmg NRSV ESV TNIV NLT HCSB NET

variant 1/TR τι εστιν τουτο; τις η διδαχη η καινη αυτη; οτι κατ εξουσιαν και τοις πνευμασι τοις ακαθαρτοις επιτασσει και υπακουουσιν αυτω.
"What is this? What new teaching is this? For with authority indeed he commands the unclean spirits and they obey him."
(A) C (f[13] 565[mg]) Maj
KJV NKJV NLT HCSBmg

variant 2 τις η διδαχη εκεινη η καινη αυτη η εξουσια οτι και τοις πνευμασι τοις ακαθαρτοις επιτασσει και υπακουουσιν αυτω;
"What is this new teaching with authority, because he commands even the unclean spirits and they obey him?"
D (W it syr[s])
NJB

variant 3 τι εστιν τουτο; διδαχη καινη αυτη, οτι κατ εξουσιαν και τοις πνευμασι τοις ακαθαρτοις επιτασσει.
"What is this? This is a new teaching, because with authority indeed he commands the unclean spirits and they obey him."
Θ (700)
RSV NRSVmg NASB NIV NEB REB NJBmg NAB

The difficulty posed by the WH NU reading is that the crowd asks a question out loud and then immediately provides its own affirmative answer. Faced with this awkwardness, several scribes adjusted the text to two questions (as in variant 1) or to one long question (in variant 2, which conforms to Luke 4:36). The third variant, also showing some scribal expansion, comes closest to preserving the same semantic form as WH NU, which is most likely the original reading.

Mark 1:29

TR WH NU ἐκ τῆς συναγωγῆς ἐξελθόντες ἦλθον εἰς τὴν οἰκίαν
"departing the synagogue they went into the house"
ℵ A C L 33 Maj
KJV NKJV NRSV ESVmg NASB NIV TNIV NEB REB NJBmg NLT HCSB NET

variant εκ της συναγωγης εξελθων ηλθεν εις την οικιαν
"departing the synagogue he went into the house"
B (D W Θ) f[1,13] 565 700
RSV NRSVmg ESV NJB NAB

The testimony is evenly divided between the reading with the plural participle and verb (as in TR WH NU) and the reading with the singular participle and verb (as in the variant). The former, however, is the more difficult reading because it has "they" (which we would assume meant Jesus and all the disciples, including James and John) went "with James and John." At this point in the narrative, Jesus had called only four disciples, all of whom are mentioned here: Peter, Andrew, James, and John. Thus, after saying that Jesus and the disciples went to Peter and Andrew's house, Mark added (almost as an afterthought) "with James and John" so as to include them all. The variant arose as an attempt to smooth out the awkwardness of the text or to conform it to Matt 8:14 and Luke 4:38.

Mark 1:32-34

In these verses there are several minor yet noteworthy variants:

1. In 1:32, TR NU have the expression οτε εδυ ο ηλιος ("when the sun set"), supported by ℵ A C L W Θ 33 f[1,13] Maj. This is classical Greek; Koine Greek would read οτε εδυσεν ο ηλιος ("when the sun set")—found in B D (so WH; see Guelich 1989, 63).

2. In 1:32, W and syr[s] omit και τους δαιμονιζομενους ("and the demon-possessed"); ℵ* omits this phrase, all of 1:33, and the first part of 1:34 up to the word νοσιος ("sickness"); all of this text was then added by a corrector. The omissions appear to be scribal accidents.

3. At the end of 1:34, D repeats (by dittography) the entire first part of 1:34 up to the word εξεβαλεν ("he cast out").

Mark 1:34

TR NU	ᾔδεισαν αὐτόν "they knew him" ℵ* A 0130 Maj all
variant 1/WH	ηδεισαν αυτον Χριστον ειναι "they knew him to be Christ" B L W Θ f[1] 28 33[vid] NASBmg NETmg
variant 2	ηδεισαν αυτον τον Χριστον ειναι "they knew him to be the Christ" ℵ[2] (C) f[13] 700 none

Although the expansions in the variant readings are probably the result of scribal conformity to Luke 4:41, it seems odd that not one scribe made an insertion from a Markan parallel, such as 1:24 (where the demons call him "Holy One of God") or 3:11 and 5:7 (where the demons call him "the Son of God"). In any case, it is within the scope of Mark's presentation for the demons to know Jesus' divine identity and for Jesus to silence them. This is part of the "messianic secret" motif that recurs in this gospel. Westcott and Hort adopted the first variant due to their preference for B, although it is bracketed. All English versions follow TR or NU.

Mark 1:38

Excellent testimony (ℵ B C L Θ 33) supports the reading, εις τουτο γαρ εξηλθον, which literally reads, "for this purpose I came out." Other variants on the verb are (1) εληλυθα ("I came") in W Δ f[13] 565 and (2) εξεληλυθα ("I came out") in A D f[1] 700. In context, Jesus was primarily referring to the fact that he left Capernaum to go to the neighboring towns to preach the gospel (1:35). But he could also be speaking about "coming from God" as the sent one (see NJBmg). In light of this, it is possible that any of the variants could have been scribal adjustments.

Mark 1:39

The scribe of W again (see 1:32) omitted a phrase about demons: και τα δαιμονια εκβαλλων ("he was casting out demons"). Was this accidental or did the scribe purposely excise statements about exorcism? Since such omissions are not evident throughout the rest of Mark, it must be judged that the omissions were the result of haplography—the eye of the scribe passing from και to και.

Mark 1:40

A significant combination of manuscripts (B D W) omits και γονυπετων ("and kneeling down") from the text. It is possible that other scribes, influenced by the descriptions in Matt 8:2 (where the leper is said to "worship" Jesus) and Luke 5:12 (where he is said to "fall on his face" before Jesus), added "and kneeling" to give color to Mark's account. It is unlikely that the words were dropped due to homoeoteleuton because the word αυτον, following παρακαλων, would have also been dropped.

Mark 1:41

TR WH NU	σπλαγχνισθεὶς ἐκτείνας τὴν χεῖρα αὐτοῦ ἥψατο "being compassionate he stretched out his hand and touched [the man]" ℵ A B C L W f[1,13] 33 565 700 syr cop Diatessaron KJV NKJV RSV NRSV ESV NASB NIV TNIVmg NEBmg REBmg NJB NAB NLT HCSB NET
variant	οργισθεις εκτεινας την χειρα αυτου ηψατο "being angry he stretched out his hand and touched [the man]" D it[a] NRSVmg TNIV NEB REB NLTmg NETmg

Most scholars believe this to be a significant textual dilemma because the variant is such an obviously difficult reading, while TR WH NU have such exceedingly strong documentation. The argument runs as thus: If σπλαγχνισθεις ("being compassionate") had originally been in the text, why would any scribe want to change it to οργισθεις ("being angry")? Thus, οργισθεις must have been original, which was then changed to σπλαγχνισθεις. But we must remember that the scribe who wrote οργισθεις was the scribe of D. This scribe (or a predecessor) was a literary editor who had a propensity for making significant changes in the text. At this point, he may have decided to make Jesus angry with the leper for wanting a miracle—in keeping with the tone of voice Jesus used in 1:43 when he sternly warned the leper. But this was not a warning about seeking a miracle; it was a warning about keeping the miracle a secret so as to protect Jesus' identity.

Therefore, it would have to be said that, though it is possible Mark wrote οργισθεις, nearly all the documents line up against this. This is not to say that Jesus never got angry or exasperated with people; he did (see Mark 7:34; 9:19; John 11:33, 38). It simply seems unwise to take the testimony of D in this instance when good arguments can be made against it, according to both external and internal criteria.

Mark 2:2

WH NU	συνήχθησαν πολλοί "many were gathered together" 𝔓[88vid] ℵ B L W Θ 33 700 NKJVmg RSV NRSV ESV NASB NIV TNIV NEB REB NJB NAB NLT HCSB NET
variant/TR	ευθεως συνηχθησαν πολλοι "immediately many were gathered together" A C D f[1,13] Maj KJV NKJV

Since ευθεως ("immediately") is a favorite Markan expression, it could be argued that it originally stood in the text and was then deleted because scribes thought it strange that a whole crowd could immediately gather together. Nonetheless, the documentary evidence strongly favors its exclusion.

Mark 2:4

WH NU	μὴ δυνάμενοι προσενέγκαι αὐτῷ "they could not bring [the paralyzed man] to him" 𝔓[88] ℵ B L Θ 33 NRSV NASB NIV TNIV NJB NLT HCSB NET
variant 1/TR	μη δυναμενοι προσεγγισαι αυτω "they could not come near to him" A C D f[1,13] Maj KJV NKJV RSV ESV NEB REB NAB HCSBmg
variant 2	μη δυναμενοι προσελθειν αυτω "they were not able to come to him" W none

𝔓[88] (early fourth century) joins with ℵ and B in giving the earliest witness to the shortest reading. It was impossible for the men to bring the paralyzed man to Jesus because a crowd swarmed the entrance to the house. The first variant is probably a scribal attempt to clarify that the reason they could not bring him in was because the large crowd presented an obstacle to getting him near enough to Jesus for Jesus to heal him. The second variant may be attempting the same.

Mark 2:10

According to Metzger (TCGNT), B and Θ represent the primitive Aramaic order of words: αφιεναι αμαρτιας επι της γης ("to forgive sins on earth"); the word transpositions in other manuscripts may reflect subtle exegetical changes. However, most English versions prefer the order found in 𝔓[88] ℵ C D L: επι της γης αφιεναι αμαρτιας, translated as "[the Son of Man has authority] on earth to forgive sins."

Mark 2:14

The son of Alphaeus is named Λευιν ("Levi") in ℵ[2] B C L W. A slightly different spelling occurs in 𝔓[88] (Λευειν), and yet another spelling (Λευι) of the same name appears in ℵ* A K Δ 28. A very different variant is found in D Θ f[13] 565 it Diatessaron Origen: Ιακωβον ("James"). This variant is an attempt to align this disciple with the one mentioned in 3:18, "James the son of Alphaeus." (See note on 3:18 and Lindars 1958, 220-222.)

Mark 2:16a

WH NU	οἱ γραμματεῖς τῶν Φαρισαίων "the scribes of the Pharisees" $\mathfrak{P}^{88}$ א B L W 33 NKJVmg RSV NRSV ESV NASB NIV TNIV NEB REB NJB NAB NLT HCSB
variant/TR	οι γραμματεις και οι Φαρισαιοι "the scribes and the Pharisees" A C D Maj (also P.Oxy. 1224) KJV NKJV RSVmg NRSVmg ESVmg HCSBmg NET

P.Oxy. 1224, a fourth-century fragment of an unidentified gospel, reads "scribes and Pharisees" in a strikingly similar passage (folio 2 verso, col. 2). The first reading is the more difficult of the two and the one with better attestation among the manuscripts. Mark was speaking of certain scribes who were also Pharisees. Quite interestingly, the punctuation in א and B indicates that the scribes of the Pharisees (i.e., the scribes who were Pharisees) were following Jesus (Lane 1974, 102). This does not mean that they were disciples, but simply that they were among the crowd that followed Jesus to Matthew's house.

Mark 2:16b

WH NU	ἐσθίει μετὰ τῶν ἁμαρτωλῶν καὶ τελωνῶν "he eats with sinners and tax collectors" B D W RSV NRSV ESV NIV TNIV NEB REB NJB NAB NLT HCSB NET
variant 1/TR	εσθιει και πινει μετα των αμαρτωλων και τελωνων "he eats and drinks with sinners and tax collectors" $\mathfrak{P}^{88}$ A f^1 33 Maj KJV NKJV RSVmg NRSVmg ESVmg NASB HCSBmg
variant 2	εσθιει ο διδασκαλος υμων μετα των αμαρτωλων και τελωνων "your teacher eats with sinners and tax collectors" א none
variant 3	εσθιει και πινει ο διδασκαλος υμων μετα των αμαρτωλων και τελωνων "your teacher eats and drinks with sinners and tax collectors" (C) L Δ none

Unless it is the result of scribal harmonization to Matt 9:11, the shorter reading, found in B D W, is probably the one from which all the others diverged. The first variant was adapted from the parallel passage in Luke 5:30. The second and third variants are scribal expansions of the WH NU reading and first variant, respectively.

Mark 2:17

WH NU οὐκ ἦλθον καλέσαι δικαίους ἀλλὰ ἁμαρτωλούς
"I did not come to call [the] righteous but sinners"
א A B C L Maj
NKJVmg RSV NRSV ESV NASB NIV TNIV NEB REB NJB NAB NLT HCSB NET

variant/TR ουκ ηλθον καλεσαι δικαιους αλλα αμαρτωλους εις μετανοιαν
"I did not come to call [the] righteous but sinners to repentance"
1^{mg} 33
KJV NKJV

The longer text demonstrates scribal gap-filling inasmuch as it fills out what certain scribes thought—namely, that sinners had been called to repent. The point of the text, however, is that Jesus came to call sinners—that is, to invite them to be with him. TR (note the reading in 1^{mg}, a manuscript used by Erasmus) exhibits the longer text, followed by KJV and NKJV.

Mark 2:22a

WH NU ὁ οἶνος ἀπόλλυται καὶ οἱ ἀσκοί
"the wine will be ruined and the wineskins"
$\mathfrak{P}^{88}$ B 892
RSV NRSV ESV NASB NIV TNIV NEB REB NJB NAB NLT HCSB NET

variant/TR ο οινος εκχειται και οι ασκοι απολλυται
"the wine will be spilled out and the wineskins ruined"
א A C D L (W Θ) $f^{1,13}$ 33 Maj
KJV NKJV HCSBmg

The WH NU reading has the earliest support (from $\mathfrak{P}^{88}$ and B) and is likely the reading from which the others diverged. Mark used one verb, απολλυται, to describe the ruin of both the new wine and old wine skins if the new is put into the old.

Mark 2:22b

WH NU ἀλλὰ οἶνον νέον εἰς ἀσκοὺς καινούς
"but new wine [is] for fresh wineskins"
א* B
RSV ESV NEB REB NJB NAB NLT HCSB

variant 1/TR αλλα οινον νεον εις ασκους καινους βλητεον
"but new wine is put into fresh wineskins"
$\mathfrak{P}^{88}$ $א^{1}$ A C L Θ $f^{1,13}$ 33 Maj
KJV NKJV NIV NET

variant 2 αλλα οινον νεον εις ασκους καινους βαλλουσιν
"but they put new wine into fresh wineskins"
W ($it^{e,f}$) $syr^{p,s}$
NRSV NASB TNIV

variant 3 omit
D it
RSVmg NRSVmg

Scribes (as well as modern translators) supplied one of two verbs to complete a statement lacking a predicate. Thus, the reading in ℵ* B likely displays the original text. The omission in D is probably not accidental, but the result of editorial trimming.

Mark 2:26

All three editions (TR WH NU) indicate that David entered into the house of God "during [the time] of Abiathar, high priest" (επι Αβιαθαρ αρχιερεως). This is the reading of all manuscripts (some of which add the definite article του before αρχιερεως) except D W it syr[s]. The reading of the three editions has excellent support, including the earliest evidence coming from 𝔓[88]. But once this reading is accepted, there is an obvious problem: Ahimelech, Abiathar's father, was the high priest when David entered into the house of God and took the showbread (see 1 Sam 21:1-8); Abiathar does not come on the scene until 1 Sam 22:20, and even then he is not the high priest. Both Matthew (12:3) and Luke (6:3) deleted this statement, avoiding the mistake—as did the scribes of D and W, most Old Latin translators (including Jerome, *Epist.* 57.9), and syr[s] here in Mark. Nonetheless, many ancient scribes, remaining faithful to their exemplars and ultimately to the original text, retained the reading "Abiathar."

The addition of the article could perhaps allow for the translation, "in the time of Abiathar, the one who [later] became high priest." Another possibility is that it means "in the account of Abiathar the high priest" (as is done in Mark 12:26—"in the account of the bush") or "in the passage dealing with Abiathar the high priest" (Wessel 1984, 638). The scribes who inserted the article may have had such adjustments in mind or were simply adding an article before the title "high priest." In this light, it appears that the interpretations pertaining to the definite article are modern attempts to resolve a difficult problem. Suffice it to say, the OT itself seems to confuse Ahimelech and Abiathar. In 1 Sam 22:20, Abiathar is presented as the son of Ahimilech; whereas 2 Sam 8:17 and 1 Chr 24:6 refer to Ahimelech as the son of Abiathar and priest under David (Hurtado 1989, 54).

Mark 2:27-28

Verse 27 is omitted in D it[a,c,e]; these manuscripts read "But I say to you," followed by 2:28. W (with it[b] syr[s]) omits the last part of 2:27, thereby creating the reading, "the Sabbath was not made for man, so that the Son of Man is master of the Sabbath."

Mark 3:4

The verb αποκτειναι ("to kill"), found in ℵ A B C D Maj, was changed to απολεσαι ("to destroy"), found in L W f[1,13]. This change represents scribal harmonization to Luke 6:9.

Mark 3:5

WH NU ἀπεκατεστάθη ἡ χεὶρ αὐτοῦ
"his hand was restored"
ℵ A B C* D P
NKJVmg RSV NRSV ESV NASB NIV TNIV NEB REB NJB NAB NLT HCSB NET

variant/TR απεκατεσταθη η χειρ αυτου υιγης ως η αλλη
"his hand was restored as healthy [whole] as the other"
C[3] L M
KJV NKJV

The addition, found in a few late manuscripts (note the third corrector of C), reflects scribal coloring and gap-filling. This was adopted by TR and made popular by its presence in KJV and NKJV.

Mark 3:8

Some important manuscripts (א* W Θ f[1] syr[s]) omit και απο της Ιδουμαιας ("and from Idumea")—probably due to confusion with απο της Ιουδαιας ("from Judea") in the same sentence or perhaps due to harmonization with Matt 4:25.

Mark 3:14

WH NU ἐποίησεν δώδεκα [οὓς καὶ ἀποστόλους ὠνόμασεν]
"he appointed twelve, whom he also designated apostles"
א B (C*) Θ f[13] 28 cop
NKJVmg RSVmg NRSV ESV NASBmg NIV TNIVmg NAB NLT HCSB NET

variant/TR εποιησεν δωδεκα
"he appointed twelve"
A C[2] (D) L f[1] 33 Maj
KJV NKJV RSV NRSVmg NASB NIVmg TNIV NEB REB NJB NLTmg HCSBmg NETmg

Scholars have been suspicious that the longer reading may have been taken from Luke 6:13. Indeed, many translators have followed the shorter text (note the change in TNIV from NIV). However, the longer text cannot be easily dismissed, because it has excellent documentary support and because Mark elsewhere used the term "apostles" to describe the Twelve (6:30). The justification for the term αποστολους (literally "sent ones") comes from the following statement: αποστελλη αυτους κηρυσσειν ("he sent them to preach"). The apostles are the ones sent to proclaim the gospel.

Mark 3:15

WH NU καὶ ἔχειν ἐξουσίαν ἐκβάλλειν τὰ δαιμόνια
"and to have authority to cast out demons"
א B L
NKJVmg RSV NRSV ESV NASB NIV TNIV NEB REB NJB NAB NLT HCSB NET

variant 1 το ευαγγελιον και εδωκεν αυτοις εξουσιαν εκβαλλειν τα δαιμονια
"[to proclaim] the gospel and he gave them authority to cast out demons"
D W (it)
none

variant 2/TR και εχειν εξουσιαν θεραπευειν τας νοσους και εκβαλλειν τα δαιμονια
"and to have authority to heal diseases and to cast out demons"
A C[2] D W Θ f[1,13] 33 Maj
KJV NKJV HCSBmg

According to D and W (the first variant), Jesus commissioned the Twelve to proclaim the gospel and cast out demons. According to TR, the disciples were also given the authority to "heal diseases." This was borrowed from Matt 10:1. It seems that scribes took this passage (3:14-16) as the constitution for the Twelve, a passage in which all their "offices and duties" had to be included.

Mark 3:16

WH NU	[καὶ ἐποίησεν τοὺς δώδεκα]
	"and he appointed the Twelve"
	ℵ B C* Δ 565
	NKJVmg RSVmg NRSV ESV NASB NIV TNIV NEB REB NJB NAB NLT HCSB NET
variant 1/TR	omit
	A C^2 D L Θ f^1 33 Maj syr cop^{bo}
	KJV NKJV RSV NRSVmg HCSBmg NETmg
variant 2	και περιαγοντας κηρυσσειν το ευαγγελιον
	"and to proclaim the gospel as they traveled"
	W $it^{a,c,e}$
	none
variant 3	πρωτον Σιμωνα
	"first Simon"
	f^{13} cop^{saMSS}
	none

Although it could be argued that the words of WH NU were repeated accidentally from 3:14 due to dittography, it is just as likely that Mark wrote them to pick up where he left off in 3:14 (3:14b-15 being parenthetical). The addition in the second variant is a scribal innovation begun in 3:15 (see note). The third variant is probably an attempt to give prominence to Simon Peter (although this is done in the very next clause anyway).

Mark 3:18a

Most manuscripts read Θαδδαιον ("Thaddaeus"), followed by all English versions. But there are three variants on this: (1) Λεββαιον ("Lebbaeus") in D it; (2) omit name in W it^e; (3) Λευες ("Levi") in $MSS^{according\ to\ Origen}$.

By comparing the listings of apostles, Thaddaeus must be Judas son of James or Judas brother of James, possibly the author of Jude (see comments on Matt 10:4). In Matt 10:4, "Thaddaeus" is also called "Lebbeaus," according to several manuscripts. This accounts for the change in the first variant. The scribe of W omitted Thaddaeus, thereby listing only eleven apostles as follows: "Simon and Andrew, James and John, Philip and Bartholomew, Matthew and Thomas, James the son of Alphaeus and Simon the Cananean, and Judas Iscariot." Origen (*Cels.* 367) says that Λευες was a tax collector who followed Jesus, "but he was in no way of the number of the apostles except according to some copies of the Gospel of Mark."

Mark 3:18b

WH NU Σίμωνα τὸν Καναναῖον
"Simon the Cananean" (or, "Simon the Zealot")
א B C D L[vid] (W) Δ 33 565
RSV NRSV ESV NASB NIV TNIV NEB REB NJB NAB NLT HCSB NET

variant/TR Σιμωνα τον Κανανιτην
"Simon the Cananite"
A Θ $f^{1,13}$ Maj
KJV NKJV

The variant reading is a scribal attempt to make it perfectly clear that this Simon was known by his locality, Cana. However, the WH NU reading, "Cananean," is a Greek transliteration of an Aramaic word meaning "zeal" or "zealot." Thus, this Simon may not have just been known for this locality but for his religious or political zeal. Luke plainly calls him "Simon the Zealot" (Luke 6:15; Acts 1:13).

Mark 3:19

WH NU 'Ιούδαν 'Ισκαριώθ
"Judas Iscariot"
א B C L Δ Θ 33 565
all

variant 1/TR Ιουδαν Ισκαιωτην
"Judas of Kerioth"
A (W) $f^{1,13}$ Maj cop
none

variant 2 Ιουδαν Σκαριωτης
"Judas Scarioth"
D it
none

See note on Matt 10:4b.

Mark 3:20 (3:19b in TR and KJV)

WH NU ἔρχεται εἰς οἶκον
"he goes into a house"
א* B W Γ cop
RSV NRSV ESV NASB NIV (TNIV) NEB REB NJB NAB NLT HCSB (NET)

variant 1/TR ερχονται εις οικον
"they go into a house"
א[2] A C (D εισερχονται) L Θ $f^{1,13}$ 33 Maj
KJV NKJV

The WH NU reading has the best support and is the most difficult reading because the next clause (which has a plural subject) clearly indicates that Jesus had entered the house with his disciples.

Mark 3:21

Instead of Jesus' family (οι παρ αυτου) thinking that Jesus "had lost his mind" (εξεστη) because he never stopped ministering to others, D W and Old Latin MSS have "the scribes and the rest [of the leaders]" (οι γραμματεις και οι λοιποι) responding to him. According to D, they wanted to seize Jesus because "he had escaped from them" (εξεσταται αυτους). According to W, they wanted to take him because they said they were "his adherents" (εξηρτηνται αυτου). Both these readings are the creations of scribes who wanted to avoid saying that Jesus was insane (Lane 1974, 138).

Mark 3:22

TR NU	Βεελζεβούλ "Beelzebul" א A C D L W Θ $f^{1,13}$ 33 Maj NKJVmg RSV NRSV ESV NASB NIVmg TNIV REB NJB NAB (NLT) HCSB NET
variant 1/WH	Βεεζεβουλ "Beezebul" B NKJV NIVmg
variant 2	*Beelzebub* Vulgate $syr^{p,s}$ KJV NIV NEB

See note on Matt 10:25.

Mark 3:29

Several manuscripts, mostly Caesarean (D W Θ 1 28 565 700), omit εις τον αιωνα ("into the age"—i.e., forever). Perhaps the scribes made this excision to lessen the severity of Jesus' statement: "whoever blasphemes the Holy Spirit will not be forgiven" versus "whoever blasphemes the Holy Spirit will not be forgiven forever." Nonetheless, the next clause in all these same manuscripts calls this sin "an eternal sin."

Mark 3:32

NU	ἡ μήτηρ σου καὶ οἱ ἀδελφοί σου [καὶ αἱ ἀδελφαί σου] ἔξω ζητοῦσιν σε "Your mother and your brothers and your sisters are outside looking for you." A D Γ 700 NKJVmg RSVmg NRSV ESV NASBmg NJB NAB NLTmg HCSB NET
variant/TR WH	η μητηρ σου και οι αδελφοι σου εξω ζητουσιν σε "Your mother and your brothers are outside looking for you." א B C L W Δ Θ $f^{1,13}$ 33 565 lat syr KJV NKJV RSV NRSVmg ESVmg NASB NIV TNIV NEB REB NLT HCSBmg NETmg

Although it could be argued that the variant is the result of scribal harmonization to Matt 12:47 and Luke 8:20 or that the phrase was accidentally dropped (there are three occurrences of σου), the shorter reading has, by far, superior documentary support. Disagreeing with the decision of the majority of NU editors, Metzger (TCGNT) wrote: "The shorter text should be adopted;

the longer reading, perhaps of Western origin, crept into the text through mechanical expansion. From a historical point of view, it is extremely unlikely that Jesus' sisters would have joined in publicly seeking to check him in his ministry." Consequently, many modern versions part ways with NU here by following the shorter reading.

In all of this, it should be pointed out that the omission of "and his sisters" does not indicate that the Bible says that Jesus did not have sisters; he did (see Matt 13:56; Mark 6:3). Of course, this is not taught in Roman Catholic and Eastern Orthodox dogma, which posits the perpetual virginity of Mary and therefore denies that Jesus had any sisters or brothers. Those called "brothers and sisters" of Jesus in the Gospels are said to be children of Joseph by a former marriage or Jesus' cousins. This dogma arose in the early centuries of the church "when the emphasis on asceticism (celibacy, poverty, etc.) was developing into a movement in the church and became official teaching of Roman and Eastern bodies centuries later" (Hurtado 1989, 69-70). Scribes, affected by this dogma, may have tried to obscure the fact that Jesus had brothers and sisters, but this kind of censoring—if done at all (see notes on Matt 1:25 and 13:55)—was not done with any kind of consistency throughout the Gospels.

Mark 4:12

At the end of the quotation, after αφεθη αυτοις ("it will be forgiven them"), several manuscripts (A D Θ f^{13} Maj—so TR) add τα αμαρτηματα ("their sins"). This is clearly a scribal gloss, which is not drawn from the Hebrew text or the Septuagint of Isa 6:9-10, both of which read "I will heal them," nor is it drawn from the parallel passages in the NT (Matt 13:14-15; John 12:40; Acts 28:26-27), all of which read "I will heal them." Mark's citation is his own creative condensation and rendition of Isa 6:9-10.

Mark 4:15

WH NU αἴρει τὸν λόγον τὸν ἐσπαρμένον εἰς αὐτούς
"he [Satan] takes away the word having been sown into them"
B W $f^{1,13}$
RSV NRSV ESV NASB NIV TNIV NEB REB NJB NAB NLT HCSB NET

variant 1/TR αιρει τον λογον τον εσπαρμενον εν ταις καρδιαις αυτων
"he [Satan] takes away the word having been sown in their hearts"
D Θ 33 Maj
KJV NKJV HCSBmg

variant 2 αιρει τον λογον τον εσπαρμενον απο της καρδιας αυτων
"he [Satan] takes away from their heart the word having been sown"
A
none

variant 3 αιρει τον λογον τον εσπαρμενον εν αυτοις
"he [Satan] takes away the word having been sown in them"
א C L Δ
none

According to the manuscript evidence, Mark wrote either the WH NU reading or the third variant. The addition of "their hearts" (found in TR and KJV NKJV) was adopted from parallel accounts in Matt 13:18-23 and Luke 8:11-15. The second variant places the emphasis on the taking away of that which had been sown.

Mark 4:19

A few manuscripts (D W Θ f[1]) omit και αι περι τα λοιπα επιθυμιαι ("and the desire for any other things") due to scribal conformity to Matt 13:22.

Mark 4:20

With regard to the preposition ἐν ("in") or the cardinal number ἕν ("one"), the same textual variations occur here as in 4:8. The unaccented word appears in ℵ A C[2] D, the cardinal number "one" appears in L Θ and some ancient versions (it cop), and the preposition "in" appears in f[1,13] 28 33 565 700.

Mark 4:24

The words και προστεθησεται υμιν ("and will be added to you") are lacking in D W 565 it[b,e]; the excision is the result of scribal conformity to Matt 7:2.

Mark 4:26

Several manuscripts (ℵ B D L Δ 33) read, Ουτως εστιν η βασιλεια του θεου ως ανθρωπος βαλη τον σποροον επι της γης ("so is the kingdom of God as a man might throw seed on the earth"). The awkwardness of the comparison led certain scribes to make adjustments: (1) ως ανθρωπος οταν ("as when a man") in W f[1]; (2) ως εαν ανθρωπος ("as if a man") in A C Maj (so TR); (3) ωσπερ ανθρωπος ("just as when a man") in Θ f[13] 28 565 700. English versions make the same kinds of adjustments.

Mark 4:28

The NU editors followed the opinion of Westcott and Hort (1882, 24) in adopting the wording πληρης σιτον εν τω σταχυι ("full wheat in the head"), found in C*[vid] 28. Even though WH reads πληρη, Hort argued for πληρης as the original reading, saying that it was "similarly used as an indeclinable in the accusative in all good MSS of Acts 6:5 except B, and has good authority in the LXX."

Mark 4:40

WH NU τί δειλοί ἐστε; οὔπω ἔχετε πίστιν;
"Why are you fearful? Do you still not have faith?"
ℵ B D L Δ Θ 565 700 cop
NKJVmg RSV NRSV ESV NIV TNIV NEB REB NJB NAB NLT HCSB NET

variant 1/TR Τι δειλοι εστε ουτως; πως ουκ εχετε πιστιν;
"Why are you fearful in this way? How can you not have faith?"
A C 33 Maj
KJV NKJV NASB

variant 2 Τι δειλοι εστε ουτως; εχετε πιστιν;
"Why are you fearful in this way? Do you have faith?"
W it[e,q]
none

variant 3 Τι ουτως δειλοι εστε; ουπω εχετε πιστιν;
"Why are you fearful in this way? Do you still not have faith?"
𝔓[45vid] f[1,13]
none

It is difficult to determine which wording is original. The WH NU reading has the best external support and accords with Markan style (see 8:17, 21), but the first variant is the barest and boldest of all the readings. The second is a variation of the first, and the third is a variation of WH NU. Though the extant portion of 𝔓[45] shows only τι ου, it is legitimate to assume that it supported the reading as present in variant 3, inasmuch as it would not coincide with any of the other variants—unless ουπω followed τι, but that would be unusual (see *Text of Earliest MSS*, 165).

Mark 5:1a

A few scribes (ℵ[cvid] C L f[13]) changed ηλθον ("they came") to ηλθεν ("he came") to put the emphasis on Jesus at the beginning of this pericope.

Mark 5:1b

WH NU χώραν τῶν Γερασηνῶν
"region of the Gerasenes"
ℵ* B D
NKJVmg RSV NRSV ESV NASB NIV TNIV NEB REB NJB NAB NLT HCSB NET

variant 1/TR χωραν των Γαδαρηνων
"region of the Gadarenes"
A C f[13] Maj
KJV NKJV RSVmg NRSVmg ESVmg NIVmg TNIVmg NJBmg NLTmg HCSBmg NETmg

variant 2 χωραν των Γεργεσηνων
"region of the Gergesenes"
ℵ[2] L Δ Θ f[1] 28 33 565 700 (W Γεργυστηνων)
RSVmg NRSVmg ESVmg NIVmg TNIVmg NJBmg NLTmg HCSBmg NETmg

This place name appears in a variety of forms in the Synoptic Gospels. For Mark, the reading "Gerasenes" has the best witnesses, followed by modern English versions. This variant unit is discussed in the note at Matt 8:28.

Mark 5:13

WH NU καὶ ἐπέτρεψεν αὐτοῖς
"and he allowed them"
ℵ B C L W Δ f[1] it[b,e] syr[p,s] cop[bo]
NKJVmg RSV NRSV ESV NASB NIV TNIV NEB REB NJB NAB NLT HCSB NET

variant 1/TR καιεπετρεψεν αυτοις ευθεως ο Ιησους
"and immediately Jesus allowed them"
A f[13] 33 Maj
KJV NKJV

variant 2 και επεμψεν αυτους
"and he sent them"
Θ (565 700 add ο Ιησους)
none

variant 3 και ευθεως κυριος Ιησους επεμψεν αυτους εις τους χοιρους
"and immediately the Lord Jesus sent them into the pigs"
D it[MSS]
none

The simple statement of WH NU (with good documentary support) was changed in three ways. The first change, in TR, is a typical expansion. Interestingly, the expansion has one of Mark's favorite words, ευθεως ("immediately"). Thus, the canon that the reading which suits the author's style is most likely original is overruled here by documentary evidence. Variant 2 is Caesarean, and variant 3 displays typical embellishment.

Mark 5:19

According to א B C Δ Θ, the man healed by Jesus was ordered "to tell" (απαγγειλον) his friends and relatives what Jesus had done for him. According to several Caesarean witnesses (𝔓[45] W f[1,13] 28 700) and D, the verb is διαγγελιον—a word that describes missionary activity in Luke 9:60; Acts 21:26; Rom 9:17 (Lane 1974, 188).

Mark 5:21a

TR WH NU διαπεράσαντος τοῦ 'Ιησοῦ [ἐν τῷ πλοίῳ]
"Jesus crossed over in the boat"
א A B C L 0132 f[13] 33 Maj
all

variant διαπερασαντος του Ιησου
"Jesus crossed over"
(𝔓[45vid]) D Θ f[1] 28 565 700 it syr[s]
NRSVmg

The text of 𝔓[45] must have supported the shorter reading (see *Text of Earliest MSS,* 166). Given the fact that the scribe of 𝔓[45] had a proclivity for omitting words (especially those he considered superfluous), it could be argued that the words "in the boat" are original. However, several other witnesses also retain the short version. Thus, it could be argued that the words were added by scribes to fill out the sense. To signal the editors' indecision (or doubt), the prepositional phrase is bracketed in NU. This doubt has not affected any English versions and has prompted only one note—in the NRSV.

Mark 5:21b

The three editions (TR WH NU) read παλιν εις το περαν ("again to the other side"), with excellent support: א[1] A B C L W 0132 f[1] 33 Maj. There are three variants on this: (1) εις το περαν παλιν ("to the other side, again") in ℵ* D 565 700; (2) παλιν ("again") in 𝔓45; (3) εις το περαν ("to the other side") in Θ. The first and second variants are scribal adjustments linking παλιν ("again") with what follows: "again a large crowd gathered" (with reference to 4:1, 34). The third variant eliminates παλιν completely and thereby avoids the problem of where to place it.

Mark 5:22

The name of the synagogue leader, "Jairus" (Ιαιρος), is found in many excellent witnesses, including 𝔓45vid ℵ A B C L Δ. The Caesarean manuscripts W Θ 565 700 also include the name, but with the typical dative formula: ονοματι Ιαιρος (literally, "name to him—Jairus"). This name, however, is absent in D and Latin witnesses. Since names are usually not given to the people healed by Jesus in the gospel accounts, various scholars have thought that the naming of this synagogue leader is a secondary development, probably adapted from Luke 8:41. Gospel writers, however, did name some of the people healed by Jesus, such as blind Bartimaeus (Mark 10:46) and Lazarus (John 11). So, it is not unusual for Mark to have recorded the name of the man in this miracle story involving a resurrection. The name was dropped in D by accident or by purposeful assimilation to Matt 9:18, where the man is not named in any manuscript.

Mark 5:36

As Metzger said (TCGNT), "the ambiguity of παρακούσας ('ignoring' or 'overhearing') led to its replacement in ℵ[2] A C D K Θ *et al.* by the Lukan parallel ἀκούσας (Luke 8:50)." Though both renderings work well in this context, Jesus ignored the report about the death of Jairus's daughter by telling him to have faith and then by raising his daughter from the dead.

Mark 5:41

WH NU	ταλιθα κουμ *"Talitha koum"* ℵ B C L f[1] 33 RSV NRSV NASB NIV TNIV NEB REB NJB NAB NLT HCSB NET
variant 1/TR	ταλιθα κουμι *"Talitha koumi"* A Θ 0126 f[13] Maj KJV NKJV ESV
variant 2	Ταβιθα *"Tabitha"* W it[a] none
variant 3	ραββι θαβιτα κουμι *"Rabbi thabita koumi"* D none

The WH NU reading is a Greek transliteration of an Aramaic phrase, meaning "little girl, rise." The Aramaic verb in this reading is masculine but was often used without reference to sex; it was changed to the feminine form in the first variant. The second variant presents scribal assimilation to Acts 9:40, and the third variant is a corruption of ραβιθα κουμι meaning "girl, rise up."

Mark 5:42

WH NU ἐξέστησαν [εὐθύς]
"they were amazed immediately"
ℵ B C L Δ 33
RSV ESV NASB

variant 1/TR εξεστησαν
"they were amazed"
𝔓45 A W Θ f1,13 Maj
KJV NKJV NRSV NIV TNIV NEB REB NJB NAB NLT HCSB NET

variant 2 παντες εξεστησαν
"all were amazed"
D it
none

Since ευθυς ("immediately") is a favorite Markan term and has good textual support, it is possible that Mark wrote it. If so, scribes likely deleted it because it already appeared in the first clause of the verse. Most English translators have followed suit. The second variant is typical for Codex Bezae, whose scribe was fond of using παντες (TCGNT).

Mark 6:3

TR WH NU ὁ τέκτων, ὁ υἱὸς τῆς Μαρίας
"the carpenter, the son of Mary"
ℵ A B C D L W Δ Θ f1 syrh,p copsa Celsusaccording to Origen
all

variant 1 του τεκτονος υιος και της Μαριας
"son of the carpenter and of Mary"
f13 33vid (565) 700 Origen
NRSVmg NEBmg REBmg NLTmg NETmg

variant 2 υιος του τεκτονος, ο υιος της Μαριας
"the carpenter's son, the son of Mary"
𝔓45vid
NETmg

Both NA27 and UBS4 cite 𝔓45vid as supporting the first variant, but they place it in parentheses to show that it does not exactly read this way. In fact, the extant portion of 𝔓45 shows [τεκτον]ος ο υ[ς] (see *Text of Earliest MSS,* 166). This reading could perhaps support the first variant if ο υιος is attached to του τεκτονος = "the son of the carpenter." However, since 𝔓45 appears to show υιος as a nomen sacrum (there is an overbar showing over the first letter of υιος), it seems just as likely that the scribe wrote what is indicated in the second variant—inasmuch as Jesus' divine status was attached to his virgin birth through Mary.

The scribes who created the first variant did so to harmonize Mark 6:3 with Matt 13:55 or to obfuscate what some might consider an offensive statement—i.e., Jesus was here said to be not just the son of a carpenter but a carpenter himself! For example, Origen countered Celsus, a second-century antagonist of Christianity who attacked its founder as being nothing but "a carpenter by trade." Origen argued that "in none of the Gospels current in the churches is Jesus himself ever described as a carpenter" (*Cels.* 6.34 and 36). Origen must have forgotten Mark 6:3, or the text he knew of was like that found in the first variant.

There is nothing demeaning about Jesus being a carpenter. The Greek term describes a person who works in wood or stone. According to a second-century tradition (Justin, *Dial.* 88), Jesus constructed farm implements such as plows and yokes (cf. Jesus' statement in Matt 11:29). But he could have been a stone mason or house builder in nearby Sepphoris. Prior to beginning his ministry at the age of thirty, he supported himself and his family by the trade he had learned from his father (see Matt 13:55).

Some scholars have argued that the first variant is original because the reading of the text represents a dogmatic correction in the interest of the virgin birth. But the first variant is probably a scribal attempt to avoid directly saying that Jesus was "the son of Mary," which is an unusual way of identifying Jesus. Some scholars say that this was a disparaging remark because "it was contrary to Jewish usage to describe a man as the son of his mother, even when she was a widow, except in insulting terms. Rumors to the effect that Jesus was illegitimate appear to have circulated in his own lifetime and may lie behind this reference as well" (Lane 1974, 202-203). But McArthur (1973, 55) argues that the expression "son of Mary" represents an "informal descriptive" rather than a "formal genealogical" way of identifying Jesus by his well-known mother. In other words, these words in the mouths of the Galileans were not pejorative or theologically loaded.

Mark 6:11a

WH NU ὃς ἂν τόπος μὴ δέξηται ὑμᾶς
"whatever place does not welcome you"
ℵ B C*vid L W f13
NKJVmg RSV NRSV ESV NASB NIV TNIV NEB REB NJB NAB NLT HCSB NET

variant/TR οσοι αν μη δεξωνται υμας
"whoever does not welcome you"
A C2 D Θ 0167vid 33 Maj
KJV NKJV

The textual evidence and context affirm the reading that designates the place ("a house") as rejecting the disciples, not the people who rejected them. Of course, it is the people in the house who do the rejecting, so scribes changed "whatever" to "whoever" (so TR, followed by KJV and NKJV).

Mark 6:11b

WH NU εἰς μαρτύριον αὐτοῖς
"for a testimony to them"
ℵ B C D L W Δ Θ 28* 565
NKJVmg RSV NRSV ESV NASB NIV TNIV NEB REB NJB NAB NLT HCSB NET

variant/TR εις μαρτυριν αυτοις. αμην λεγω υμιν, ανεκτοτερον εσται Σοδομοις η Γομορροις εν ημερα κρισεως η τη πολει εκεινη
"for a testimony to them. Truly I say to you, 'It will be more tolerable for Sodom or Gomorrah on the day of judgment than for that city.'"
A (33) f1,13 Maj
KJV NKJV HCSBmg

The WH NU reading has early and diverse documentary support. The expanded reading is unquestionably a scribal interpolation taken almost verbatim from the parallel passage, Matt 10:15. (This addition lacks only one Matthean word, namely γη—"land".) TR includes the expanded reading, which is rendered in KJV and NKJV.

Mark 6:14

WH NU ἔλεγον ὅτι Ἰωάννης ὁ βαπτίζων ἐγήγερται ἐκ νεκρῶν
"they were saying that John the Baptist had risen from the dead"
B (D) W it[a,b]
RSV NRSV ESV NASB NIV TNIV NEB REB NJB NAB NLT HCSB NET

variant/TR ελεγεν οτι Ιωαννης ο Βαπτιζων εγηγερται εκ νεκρων
"he was saying that John the Baptist had risen from the dead"
ℵ A C L Θ $f^{1,13}$ 33 Maj
KJV NKJV RSVmg NRSVmg ESVmg NIVmg TNIVmg NEBmg REBmg NJBmg NLTmg HCSBmg

The variant (noted in all modern English versions) was created to achieve continuity with the previous singular verb ηκουσεν ("he heard"—i.e., Herod heard). But this clause and on to the end of 6:15 is a detached segment providing three samplings of what the people (i.e., "they") were saying about Jesus. The first part of 6:14 continues in 6:16 with what Herod had to say about Jesus, which coincidentally matched the first opinion of the populace: Jesus was John the Baptist risen from the dead.

Mark 6:17

Misreading Kenyon's transcription of 𝔓[45] (1933, 5), scholars cite 𝔓[45] for the omission of Φιλιππου ("Philip's") in this verse, but this manuscript shows only αυτου γυν[αικα] ("his wife")—with the lacuna continuing up until the word Ηρωδηι ("Herod") in 6:18. The lacuna is far too large to determine whether or not the scribe wrote Φιλιππου.

Mark 6:20

WH NU ἀκούσας αὐτοῦ πολλὰ ἠπόρει
"hearing him [John the Baptist], he [Herod] was greatly perplexed" (or, "hearing him often, he was perplexed")
ℵ B L (W) Θ cop
RSV NRSV ESV NASB NIV TNIV NEB REB NJB NAB NLT HCSB NET

variant/TR ακουσας αυτου πολλα εποιει
"hearing him [John the Baptist], he [Herod] did many things"
A C D f^{1} 33 Maj it syr
KJV NKJV NRSVmg NIVmg TNIVmg NLTmg HCSBmg NETmg

According to Greek usage, the adverbial position of πολλα ("often") almost always follows the verb, thereby putting the WH NU reading into question. Furthermore, the banality of the statement "he [Herod] did many things," may have led scribes to change verbs. But in defense of the WH NU reading, it can be argued that (1) a scribe or scribes mistakenly wrote εποιει for ηπορει, and the mistake was perpetuated in successive copies, (2) πολλα should be joined with the previous verb ηκουσας = "he heard him often," and (3) ηπορει ("was perplexed") perfectly describes Herod's condition, given the stress he was experiencing by listening to John the Baptist. The fourth point in favor of WH NU is that it has the best documentation.

Mark 6:22

WH NU τῆς θυγατρὸς αὐτοῦ Ἡρῳδιάδος
"his daughter, Herodias"
א B D L Δ 565
NRSV TNIVmg NLT HCSBmg NET

variant/TR της θυγατρος αυτης της Ηρωδιαδος
"the daughter of Herodias herself"
A C Θ f^{13} 33 Maj
KJV NKJV RSV NRSVmg ESV NASB NIV TNIV NEB REB NJB NAB NLTmg HCSB NETmg

According to WH NU, the girl who danced before Herod had the same name as her mother, Herodias, and she is described as being the daughter of Herod. But 6:24 says that she is the daughter of Herodias (so also Matt 14:6), and her name was Salome, according to Josephus (*J.W.* 18.136). Therefore, many commentators and translators consider the variant reading to be more accurate, both historically and contextually. However, the documentary evidence strongly favors the WH NU reading and is thereby followed by NRSV, NLT, and NET. If this is what Mark wrote, then his designation "daughter" of Herod must be equivalent to "step-daughter."

Mark 6:23

NU ὤμοσεν αὐτῇ [πολλά]
"he swore to her vehemently"
(𝔓[45vid]) D Θ 565 700 (C[*vid] W f^1)
NRSV NETmg

variant/TR WH ωμοσεν αυτη
"he swore to her"
א A B C[2vid] f^{13} 33 Maj
KJV NKJV RSV ESV NASB NIV TNIV NEB REB NJB NAB NLT HCSB NET

The Greek word πολλα is bracketed in NU because the word is not present in several reliable witnesses, yet it is retained because it accords with Markan style and because of its presence in 𝔓[45], the earliest witness. TR WH exclude the word, as do all English versions except the NRSV, which shows its usual loyalty to NU.

Mark 6:33

The last clause of the verse correctly reads προηλθον αυτους ("they arrived ahead of them"), supported by א B (0187) cop it. But various scribes, finding it difficult to imagine that a crowd running on foot could move more quickly than a boat, changed the verb to προσηλθον or to συνηλθον. Both these verbs indicate that the crowd arrived there at the same time Jesus and the disciples did. In TR (supported by 𝔓[84vid] A f^{13} Maj), the reading is conflated: προηλθον αυτους και συνηλθον προς αυτον ("They arrived before them and came together to Him"—NKJV). Westcott and Hort (1882, 95-99) have a lengthy discussion on how this conflation came into being.

Mark 6:36

WH NU — ἀγοράσωσιν ἑαυτοῖς τί φάγωσιν
"they may buy themselves something to eat"
𝔓[45vid] ℵ B
NKJVmg RSV NRSV ESV NASB NIV TNIV NEB REB NJB NAB NLT HCSB NET

variant/TR — αγορασωσιν εαυτοις αρτους τι γαρ φαγωσιν ουκ εχουσιν
"they may buy for themselves some bread, for they have nothing to eat"
(1) Vulgate
KJV NKJV

The expansion in TR is likely the result of scribal gap-filling. But the reader, following the context, can do this for himself. The variant is not cited in NU, perhaps because it is difficult to discover its manuscript support.

Mark 6:41

TR NU have the reading τοις μαθηταις αυτου ("to his disciples"), based on 𝔓[45] A D W Θ $f^{1,13}$ Maj. WH omits αυτου. Probably "his disciples" reflects an earlier stage in the transmission of the gospel tradition than "the disciples," by which they would be known later among the Christian community (TCGNT). If so, τοις μαθηταις ("to the disciples"), found in ℵ B L 33, could reflect Alexandrian polishing.

Mark 6:44

(TR) WH NU — καὶ ἦσαν οἱ φαγόντες [τοὺς ἄρτους] πεντακισχίλιοι ἄνδρες.
"And those who ate the loaves were five thousand men."
A B L 33 (Maj add ωσει—"about [five thousand men]"—so TR)
KJV NKJV RSV NRSV ESV NASB NEB REB NJB NAB HCSB NET

variant — και ησαν οι φαγοντες πεντακισχιλιοι ανδρες
"And those who ate were five thousand men."
𝔓[45] ℵ D W Θ $f^{1,13}$ 565 700
NIV TNIV NLT NETmg

The Greek words τους αρτους ("the bread") are bracketed in NU in deference to their omission in 𝔓[45] (which should not be listed as "vid" because the text is clearly visible here—see *Text of Earliest MSS,* 167) and because D and W, which usually have a longer text, have a shorter text here. But we have to be careful about adopting the variant reading just because it is shorter, for the scribe of 𝔓[45] had a proclivity for excision, and the other scribes may have thought "the loaves" should be omitted from 6:44 since "the fish" were not included in 6:43. Thus, bracketing the words is a safe decision. One final note: TR's addition of ωσει ("about") before πεντακισχιλιοι ("five thousand") came as the result of harmonization to Matt 14:21, a parallel passage.

Mark 6:45

The scribes of W f^1 syr[s] omitted εις το περαν ("to the other side") so as to have the text not say that the disciples made it all the way across the Sea of Galilee to Bethsaida, when, in fact, they landed at Gennesaret (6:53). But while Jesus had sent them out "toward Bethsaida" (προς Βηθσαιδαν), they never went there.

NA[27] and UBS[4] cite 𝔓[45vid] as supporting the omission. However, the number of letters required to fill the lacuna on the left side of the page seems to require that at least part of the word περαν precede προς (see *Text of Earliest MSS,* 167). As such, 𝔓[45] may very well have included the prepositional phrase.

Mark 6:47

A few manuscripts (𝔓[45] D f[1]) add παλαι (meaning "already" or "for a long time") to the words "when evening came, the boat was [already] in the middle of the lake." Most likely this is a scribal addition, influenced by Matt 14:24.

Mark 6:48

Some manuscripts (W Θ f[13]) have the addition σφορδα και ("strongly and"), thereby creating the reading, "for the wind was against them strongly, and about the fourth watch of the night he came to them." NA[27] also lists 𝔓[45vid] in support of this addition, but that is unlikely. Furthermore, NA[27] lists 𝔓[45vid] as omitting της νυκτος, but that also is unlikely. See the reconstruction of this verse in the *Text of Earliest MSS,* 167.

Mark 6:51

The expression και λιαν εκ περισσου εν εαυτοις εξισταντο ("and they were exceedingly, extremely amazed in themselves") is found in A f[13] Maj and adopted by TR NU. Perhaps the NU editors chose this longer reading over the shorter text (which omits εκ περισσου and is found in ℵ B (L)—so WH) on the basis that Alexandrian scribes were pruning excessive modification. (The TCGNT provides no explanation for this part of the verse.) By contrast, it should be noted that in the next part of the verse, the editors adopted the shorter reading εξισταντο ("they were amazed"), found in ℵ B L, as opposed to the expanded reading εξισταντο και εθαυμαζον ("they were amazed and marveled"), found in A D W Θ f[13] Maj (so TR—followed by KJV and NKJV). This is a prime example of atomized eclecticism: The reading of ℵ B L is rejected in the first part of the verse, and then accepted in the next part of the verse. Given a documentary emphasis, it is more consistent to judge that ℵ B L present the original text in both instances (as in WH), and that both longer readings are scribal expansions intended to accentuate the disciples' amazement over the miracle they just witnessed.

Mark 6:53

The final two words of the verse, και προσωρμισθησαν ("and anchored"), were omitted from D W Θ f[1,13] 565 700, probably because the scribes conformed this verse to Matt 14:34. Burkitt (1916, 19-21) argues that the words were original, were dropped by almost all texts at a very early time, and were then restored by the textual critic Origen in the third century. The Caesarean manuscripts do not support this theory, however.

Mark 7:2

WH NU — at end of verse omit εμεμψαντο ("they found fault")
ℵ A B L Γ Δ 0274
RSV NRSV ESV NASB NIV TNIV NEB REB NJB NAB NLT HCSB NET

variant/TR — at end of verse include εμεμψαντο ("they found fault")
K N W Θ 0278 f[1,13]
KJV NKJV

At the end of this verse, TR (following Maj) adds the verb εμεμψαντο ("they [the Pharisees] found fault"). This addition is a scribal correction of the anacoluthon in this verse. However, 7:3-4 is parenthetical; the thought begun in 7:2 is continued and completed in 7:5. Modern English versions, following the text, deal with the anacoluthon by turning the participle ιδοντες into a predicate, such as "they [the Pharisees] saw" or "they noticed."

Mark 7:3

TR WH NU — ἐὰν μὴ πυγμῇ νίψωνται τὰς χεῖρας
"unless they wash their hands with a fist"
A B (D) L Θ 0131 0274 f[1,13] Maj it syr[hmg] Origen
NKJVmg (ESV NASB NIV TNIV) NEBmg REBmg (NJB NLT HCSB NET)

variant 1 — εαν μη πυκνα νιψωνται τας χειρας
"unless they wash their hands often"
ℵ W it[f] syr[h,p] cop[bo]
KJV NEBmg REBmg NAB

variant 2 — εαν μη νιψωνται τας χειρας
"unless they wash their hands"
Δ syr[s] cop[sa] Diatessaron
(RSV NRSV) NEB REB

It is extremely difficult to explain what it meant for the Jewish people to wash "with a fist." The expression, known to the people of Jesus' time, refers to a Jewish cleansing ritual—perhaps pouring water over cupped hands (i.e., "fists"). Scribes, unable to make sense of πυγμη ("with fist"), changed it to πυκνα ("often") or omitted it altogether. Translators throughout the ages have had difficulty with this expression; for example, the NRSVmg admits that the meaning of the Greek is uncertain. The RSVmg indicates that they left the word untranslated. Furthermore, not one modern translation renders the text literally, even those that intend to follow NU. The closest functional equivalent translation is that found in the NLT: "they pour water over cupped hands." Other versions try a different approach: "wash their hands ritually" (HCSB) and "give their hands a ceremonial washing" (TNIV).

Mark 7:4a

TR NU — ἐὰν μὴ βαπτίσωνται
"unless they wash [themselves]"
A D W Θ f[1,13] 33 Maj
KJV NKJV RSVmg (NRSV) ESV NASB NIV TNIV NEB REB NAB NLT HCSB NET

variant 1	εαν μη βαπτιζωνται "unless it is immersed" L Δ (RSVmg)
variant 2/WH	εαν μη ραντισωνται "unless they sprinkle [themselves]" א B (RSV NRSVmg ESVmg) NJB NLTmg

The verb in TR NU, βαπτισωνται, is in the middle voice; this usage indicates that the Pharisees washed themselves. The first variant is in the passive voice; it suggests that the Pharisees washed whatever they bought from the marketplace before eating it. The second variant could be the result of Alexandrian scribal adjustment attempting to avoid the use of βαπτιζω ("baptize") in any context beside that of Christian baptism. But this verb was commonly used to describe normal washing (see Luke 11:38; and see Luke 16:24; John 13:26; Rev 19:13 for the use of the cognate verb βαπτω); so it does not follow that the scribes of א and B would have necessarily changed it to preserve it as a descriptor of the Christian rite. Rather, it is just as likely that ραντισωνται was the more unusual word that was changed to βαπτιζωνται.

Finally, it should be noted that some manuscripts (D W it) add οταν ελθωσιν ("whenever they come") after απ αγορας ("from the marketplace") in order to fill out the meaning: "whenever they come from the marketplace." The shorter text is preserved in 𝔓[45vid] א A B L etc.

Mark 7:4b

TR NU	βαπτισμοὺς ποτηρίων καὶ ξεστῶν καὶ χαλκίων [καὶ κλινῶν] "washing of cups and pitchers and bronze vessels and dining couches" A D W Θ f[1,13] 33 Maj KJV NKJV RSVmg NRSVmg ESV NIVmg TNIVmg NAB NLTmg HCSB NET
variant/WH	βαπτισμους ποτηριων και ξεστων και χαλκιων "washing of cups and pitchers and bronze vessels" 𝔓[45vid] א B L Δ RSV NRSV ESVmg NASB NIV TNIV NEB REB NJB NLT HCSBmg NETmg

If 𝔓[45] were the only early manuscript to contain the shorter reading, it could be dismissed as 𝔓[45]'s typical trimming of the text; but the words και κλινων are also lacking in several other significant manuscripts, including א and B. Perhaps the words were omitted accidentally due to homoeoteleuton (χαλκιων and κλινων end in the same two letters), or they may have been purposely excised because the scribes may have thought that κλινων meant "beds" and therefore deleted it as incongruous with the other items. But in context it has to mean "dining couches" because the passage speaks of the legalistic requirements pertaining to eating utensils. This word could not have been added under the influence of Lev 15, as Metzger suggests (TCGNT), because "the bed" in Lev 15 is the conjugal bed, which is never said to be washed. If it was added by scribes, it was done so as to include the largest of dining fixtures—the dining couch. Most modern translations (including the NRSV, which usually follows NU) adhere to the shorter text lacking the words "and beds."

Mark 7:5

WH NU κοιναῖς χερσίν
"impure hands"
ℵ* B (D W) Θ f[1] 33 cop
RSV NRSV ESV NASB NIV TNIV NEB REB NJB NAB (NLT) HCSB

variant 1/TR ανιπτοις χερσιν
"unwashed hands"
ℵ[2] A L Maj syr
KJV NKJV HCSBmg NET

variant 2 κοιναις χερσιν και ανιπτοις
"impure hands, that is, unwashed"
𝔓[45]
none

The first variant is the result of harmonization to a parallel passage, Matt 15:2. The second variant in 𝔓[45] probably does not reflect direct or conscious harmonization; rather, it shows the scribe's desire to help his readers understand Jewish tradition. Thus, he keeps the traditional terminology (κοιναις χερσιν—"common [or, impure] hands") with an added explanation (και ανιπτοις—"that is, unwashed"). This change shows that the scribe of 𝔓[45] was probably influenced by the usual textual construction in Mark, wherein the gospel writer presented a Jewish tradition, followed by a short gloss for the sake of his Roman readers (see 7:2; 14:12; 15:42). It also shows that he was prompted by the wording in 7:2, which has the same kind of gloss, to add the gloss here.

Mark 7:6

Instead of the phrase, "this people honors [τιμα] me with their lips," D W it[a,b,c] read "this people loves [αγαπα] me with their lips." This variant, though not original (based on its inferior manuscript support), expresses the intent of this passage: The people loved God in word only, not in heart or deed.

Mark 7:8

WH NU κρατεῖτε τὴν παράδοσιν τῶν ἀνθρώπων
"you hold to the traditions of men"
𝔓[45] ℵ B L W Δ 0274 f[1]
NKJVmg RSV NRSV ESV NASB NIV TNIV NEB REB NJB NAB NLT HCSB NET

variant/TR κρατειτε την παραδοσιν των ανθρωπων, βαπτισμους ξεστων και ποτηριων, και αλλα παρομοια τοιαυτα πολλα ποιειτε
"you hold to the traditions of men—the washing of pitchers and cups—and many other such things you do"
(A D Θ 0131[vid] 28 565) f[13] 33 Maj
KJV NKJV HCSBmg NETmg

WH NU are backed by early and diverse manuscripts. The variant is the result of scribal expansion, borrowing from the immediate context: first 7:4, then 7:13.

Mark 7:9

Rejecting the testimony of excellent documentation (א A B L f[13] 33 Maj syr[h] cop), the editors of NA[26] made a change from NA[25], from the verb τηρησητε ("you keep") to στησητε ("you establish"), supported by inferior witnesses (D W Θ f[1] 28 565 it syr[p,s]). As can be seen by Metzger's discussion (TCGNT), the committee was guessing what scribes may have done here. The safest approach, therefore, is to select the reading with the best documentation (so WH).

Mark 7:16

WH NU	omit verse א B L Δ* 0274 NKJVmg RSV NRSV ESV NASBmg NIV TNIV NEB REB NJBmg NAB NLT HCSBmg NET
variant/TR	add verse Ει τις εχει ωτα ακουειν ακουετω. "If any one has ears to hear, let him hear." A D W Θ f[1,13] 33 Maj KJV NKJV RSVmg NRSVmg NASB NIVmg NEBmg REBmg NJB NABmg NLTmg HCSB NETmg

The WH NU reading has the earliest support among the manuscripts. The extra verse was added by scribes, borrowing it directly from 4:23 (see also 4:9) to provide an ending to an otherwise very short pericope, 7:14-15. This addition was included in TR and made popular by KJV. NKJV, NASB, NJB, and HCSB also include this extra verse.

Mark 7:24

NU	ἀπῆλθεν εἰς τὰ ὅρια Τύρου "he departed to the district of Tyre" D L W Δ Θ 28 565 it syr[s] NKJVmg RSVmg NRSV ESVmg NASB NIV TNIV NEB REB NJB NAB NLT HCSBmg NET
variant/TR WH	απηλθεν εις τα ορια Τυρου και Σιδωνος "he departed to the district of Tyre and Sidon" א A B f[1,13] 33 Maj syr[h,p] cop KJV NKJV RSV NRSVmg ESV NASBmg NIVmg TNIVmg NJBmg NLTmg HCSB NETmg

In this verse the maxim that "the shorter reading is most likely original" was followed by the NU editors. Added to this is the argument that the longer reading may have been conformed to Matt 15:21 and Mark 7:31. If this is true, then this is a rare instance when א and B show signs of harmonization, whereas D and W do not.

A closer look shows that the shorter reading is most likely the result of harmonization to 7:31, which says that Jesus left the region of Tyre and went through Sidon. Scribes surmised: "How, then, could Jesus have come into Tyre and Sidon, if, when he left Tyre, he entered into Sidon?" The easiest fix was to drop "and Sidon" from 7:24. The verse, however, does not need fixing because the one district had two major cities—Tyre and Sidon (see note on 7:31). The English versions display the split opinion over this textual variant unit.

Mark 7:26

The woman healed by Jesus is identified in a variety of ways in the various manuscripts: (1) Συροφοινικισσα ("Syrophoenician") in 𝔓[45] ℵ A L Δ Θ f[1] 28 565 (which is the original wording); (2) Συρα Φοινικισσα ("a Phoenician from Syrus") in B N W f[13] 700; (3) Φοινισσα ("Phoenician"); in D it[i]. The variants (2-3) are all the result of scribes trying to clarify for their readers this woman's identity. Mark described this woman as a Syrophoenician because this refers to her political background. His Roman audience would easily identify her by the part of the empire that was her home. She was probably a Greek-speaking native of the Phoenician area.

Mark 7:28

NU λέγει αὐτῷ· κύριε, και
"she says to him, 'Lord, and [or, even] . . .'"
𝔓[45] W Θ f[13] 565 700 syr[s]
NRSV TNIV NEB REB NAB (NLT) HCSB

variant 1/WH λεγει αυτω, ναι κυριε και
"she says to him, 'Yes, Lord, and [or, even] . . .'"
ℵ B Δ 28 33
NRSVmg

variant 2/TR λεγει αυτω, ναι κυριε και γαρ
"she says to him, 'Yes, Lord, for even . . .'"
A L f[1] Maj
KJV NKJV RSV NRSVmg ESV NASB NIV NJB NET

variant 3 λεγει αυτω, κυριε, αλλα και
"she says to him, 'Lord, but even . . .'"
D it
none

In all of the variants, the woman's statement finishes out as "the dogs underneath the table eat of the crumbs of the children." The variation pertains to how her response begins. In the first and second variant, the Syrophoenician woman agrees with Jesus' statement ("Let the children be fed first, for it is not right to take the children's food and throw it to dogs.") by first saying "yes" (ναι). In NU (and the third variant), there is no such word. However, the third variant and the second add some extra verbiage to set up the contrast that follows. In particular, the second variant, the reading of TR, is the result of harmonization to Matt 15:27. Thus, the original text is the NU reading or the first variant. This reading constitutes a change in the Nestle text, which prior to NA[26] retained the word ναι ("yes"). The early witness of 𝔓[45] helped to produce the change.

Several English versions (such as RSV ESV NIV) include both "yes" with the following contrastive "but even." The scribe of 𝔓[45] chose to indicate that the woman addressed Jesus as "Lord" by writing κυριε as a nomen sacrum (see *Text of Earliest MSS*, 168). The scribe of B did the same. Had these scribes written out the word in full, it would indicate a non-sacral designation—i.e., "sir." Modern English versions are divided between using "sir" and "Lord."

Mark 7:31

WH NU	πάλιν ἐξελθὼν ἐκ τῶν ὁρίων Τύρου ἦλθεν διὰ Σιδῶνος εἰς τὴν θάλασσαν τῆς Γαλιλαίας "coming again out of the region of Tyre, he went through Sidon to the Sea of Galilee" א B D L Δ Θ 33 565 700 RSV NRSV ESV NASB NIV TNIV NEB REB NJB NAB NLT HCSB NET
variant/TR	παλιν εξελθων εκ των οριων Τυρου και Σιδωνος ηλθεν εις την θαλασσαν της Γαλιλαιας "coming again out of the region of Tyre and Sidon, he went to the Sea of Galilee" 𝔓45 A W 0131 $f^{1,13}$ Maj syr KJV NKJV

The WH NU reading indicates that Jesus left the region of Tyre and passed through Sidon (which is in the same region) on the way to the Sea of Galilee. Apparently, Mark called this area "the region of Tyre and Sidon" in 7:24 (see note above), then "the region of Tyre" in this verse. The scribes of א and B were content to leave it as is, whereas other scribes wanted to make them verbally equivalent in both instances. Thus, both verses in A $f^{1,13}$ Maj read "the region of Tyre and Sidon."

Mark 7:35

TR NU	[εὐθέως] ἠνοίγησαν αὐτοῦ αἱ ἀκοαί "immediately his ears were opened" 𝔓45 A W Θ 0131c $f^{1,13}$ Maj syr KJV NKJV NRSV NAB NLT HCSB NET
variant/WH	ηνοιγησαν αυτου αι ακοαι "his ears were opened" א B D L Δ 0131* 0274 33 it RSV ESV NASB NIV TNIV NEB REB NJB

The Greek word ευθεως ("immediately") is bracketed in NU because the external testimony against its inclusion is quite impressive. Its interpolation into the text, therefore, can be explained as the work of scribes adding one of Mark's favorite words to increase the drama of the miracle. (One of the weaknesses of this argument is that the scribe of 𝔓45 rarely added words.) However, the word may have come from Mark's pen and was then deleted by stylists attempting to trim the excessive use of ευθεως in Mark.

Mark 8:1

According to superior manuscript evidence (א B D L Δ 33), the text reads παλιν πολλου οχλου οντος ("again a large crowd was [there]"), but this was changed to παμπολλου οχλου οντος ("a very large crowd was [there]") in A K 0131 700 Maj (so TR, KJV). The change likely came as the result of a scribe mistaking ΠΑΛΙΝΠΟΛΛΟΥ for ΠΑΜΠΟΛΛΟΥ, which is a word that occurs nowhere else in the Greek New Testament.

Mark 8:7

WH NU
εὐλογήσας αὐτά
"having blessed them"
ℵ B C L Δ Θ
KJV NKJV RSV NRSV ESV NASB REB NJB NAB NLT HCSB

variant 1
ταυτα ευλογησας
"these things having blessed"
A K
none

variant 2/TR
ευλογησας
"having blessed"
N Γ 700 33
none

variant 3
ευχαριστησας
"having given thanks"
D
NIV TNIV NEB NET

The WH NU reading appears to be the original because it has early testimony among the manuscripts. The first variant is a natural change from the text, the second reflects the Jewish practice of blessing God rather than the food (Guelich 1989, 400), and the third is scribal conformity to 8:6.

Mark 8:10

TR WH NU
Δαλμανουθά
"Dalmanoutha"
ℵ A (B) C L 0274 Maj
all

variant 1
Δαλμουναι
"Dalmounai"
W
none

variant 2
Μαγαδα
"Magada"
D[c] it[c,k] syr[s]
RSVmg NRSVmg ESVmg NASBmg NEBmg REBmg NJBmg

variant 3
Μαγδαλα
"Magdala"
Θ f[1,13]
RSVmg NRSVmg NEBmg REBmg

variant 4
Μαγεδαν [or Μαγαδαν]
"Magedan"
𝔓[45vid]
none

The uncertainty of the location mentioned in this verse led to many textual variants. The first is a spelling variant, the second variant represents scribal conformity to the text of Matt 15:39

(with a slightly different spelling), the third variant displays scribal conformity to a variant of Matt 15:39, and the fourth also represents scribal conformity to the text of Matt 15:39 (with the closest spelling). 𝔓[45vid] is not cited in NA[27] or UBS[4], but the text, though broken, shows [μαγεδ]αν (see *Text of Earliest MSS*, 169). The Gospel of Matthew, as the first gospel in canonical order, was quite influential in the mind of the scribe of 𝔓[45]; nearly all gospel harmonization in 𝔓[45] is to Matthew. In this case, we know it was Matthew's text that provided the impetus for change and not some other independent nonbiblical document, because "Magedan" (or "Magadan") in no way helps to identify the location; it is just as obscure as "Dalmanutha." This obscurity prompted scribes in both Matt 15:39 (see note) and Mark 8:10 to substitute the name "Magdala," which was a well-known city on the coast of the Sea of Galilee.

Mark 8:13

The position of the word παλιν ("again") is ambiguous; it can mean "they left again" or "they got into the boat again." The ambiguity is preserved in manuscripts like ℵ B C L 0274 33. But other scribes wanted to make it perfectly clear that they got into the boat again. This is made explicit by the addition in A f[1] 0131 Maj (so TR), εμβας παλιν εις το πλοιον ("they entered again into the boat"), and by the transposition in D W Θ f[13], εμβας παλιν ("again they embarked"). (NA[27] incorrectly cites 𝔓[45] as supporting this transposition.)

Mark 8:14

Several Caesarean manuscripts (𝔓[45vid] W Θ f[1,13] 565 700) smooth out the awkward και ει μη αρτον ουκ ειχον ("and except one loaf they did not have") to ενα μονον αρτον εχοντες ("having only one loaf").

Mark 8:15

TR WH NU	τῆς ζύμης τῶν Φαρισαίων καὶ τῆς ζύμης Ἡρῴδου "the leaven of the Pharisees and the leaven of Herod" ℵ A B C D L 0131 33 all
variant	της ζυμης των Φαρισαιων και της ζυμης των Ηρωδιανων "the leaven of the Pharisees and the leaven of the Herodians" 𝔓[45] W Θ f[1,13] 28 565 RSVmg NRSVmg ESVmg

Several Caesarean witnesses changed "Herod" to "the Herodians" to align this verse with 3:6 and 12:13. The Herodians, mentioned only in Matthew (22:16) and Mark (here, 3:6, and 12:13), were an influential group of men who had political affiliations with the Herodian household and religious affiliations with the Sadducees.

The translators of the RSV, influenced by the testimony of 𝔓[45] and W (two manuscripts discovered after the publication of the ASV), provided the alternative reading in the margin. The NRSV followed suit, but no version has adopted this reading.

Mark 8:17

According to excellent documentary support (𝔓[45vid] ℵ B C L W Δ f[1,13] 33), the text reads πεπωρωμενην εχετε την καρδιαν υμων ("have your hearts been hardened?"). This question was intensified in several manuscripts (A Maj—so TR) with the addition of ετι ("still/yet"), yielding the variant, "are your hearts still hardened?" (see KJV NKJV).

Mark 8:26

WH NU μηδὲ εἰς τὴν κώμην εἰσέλθῃς.
"Do not enter the village."
(ℵ*) B L (W) f[1] syr[s] cop
NKJVmg RSV NRSV ESV NASB NIV TNIV REB NJB NAB NLT HCSB NET

variant 1/TR μηδε εις την κωμην εισελθης, μηδε ειπης τινι εν τη κωμη.
"Do not enter the village, neither speak to anyone in the village."
A C Maj syr[h,p]
KJV NKJV NRSVmg NIVmg TNIVmg NEBmg HCSBmg NETmg

variant 2 υπαγε εις τον οικον σου και μηδενι ειπης εις την κωμην
"Go into your house and do not speak in the village."
D it[q]
NEB REBmg

variant 3 υπαγε εις τον οικον σου, και εαν εις την κωμην εισελθης μηδενι ειπης μηδε εν τη κωμη.
"Go into your house; and if you go into the village, do not speak to anyone in the village."
(Θ f[13] 28 565)
none

This verse presents a textual difficulty that is not easy to solve. While the WH and NU editors chose the tersest reading, several other critics have argued that the original text must have been longer, as in the first or second variant (which is argued for by Ross 1987, 97-99). In any event, the common thrust of all the variants is that they intensify the secrecy motif that is prevalent in the Gospel of Mark. In this gospel, Jesus commands those who are healed not to tell others about their healing (see 1:44-45; 5:43; 7:36) because Jesus did not want to gain a reputation of being a thaumaturgist.

Mark 8:29

TR WH NU σὺ εἶ ὁ χριστός.
"You are the Christ."
A B C D Origen
all

variant 1 συ ει ο χριστος, ο υιος του θεου.
"You are the Christ, the Son of God."
ℵ L
none

variant 2 σu ει ο χριστος, ο υιος του θεου του ζωντος.
"You are the Christ, the Son of the living God."
W f^{13} it^{b} syr^{p}
none

The second variant presents scribal conformity of Mark to Matthew's account verbatim; in Matt 16:16 Peter tells Jesus, "You are the Christ, the son of the living God." The first variant is not an exact harmonization from any of the other parallel accounts, because in Luke 9:20 it is "the Christ of God" and in John 6:69, "the Holy One of God." Both of these passages also have their variant readings, many of which conform to Matt 16:16 and one (in Luke 9:20) that reads "the Christ, the Son of God." Thus, it was typical of scribes to include in Peter's confession that Jesus was not just the Christ, but also the Son of God. This is also important for Markan theology, which emphasizes that Jesus is the Christ and the Son of God (see 1:1 and note; 15:39). In any case, these kind of scribal changes reflect the ecclesiastical use of Peter's confession to promote a standard personal confession (as was done in Acts 8:37).

Mark 8:31-32

An interesting and ancient variant appears in it^{k} syr^{s} and the Arabic Diatessaron: "the Son of Man . . . will be killed, will rise again after three days, and then he will speak the word openly." This variant contributes to the predominant secrecy motif of Mark's gospel—it would not be until after Christ's resurrection that he would boldly and openly proclaim the word.

Mark 8:35

According to good textual evidence (א A B C), Jesus called upon people to forsake their lives "for the sake of me and the gospel" (ενεκεν εμου και του ευαγγελιου). However, this is abbreviated in $\mathfrak{P}^{45}$ D 28 700 it (syr^{s}) to "for the sake of the gospel" (ενεκεν του ευαγγελιου).

Mark 8:38a

TR WH NU ὃς γὰρ ἐὰν ἐπαισχυνθῇ με καὶ τοὺς ἐμοὺς λόγους
"for whoever is ashamed of me and my words"
א A B C D L 33 Maj
KJV NKJV RSV NRSV ESV NASB NIV TNIV NEBmg REB NJB NAB NLT HCSB NET

variant ος γαρ εαν επαισχυνθη με και τους εμους
"for whoever is ashamed of me and mine [i.e., my disciples]"
W it^{k} cop^{sa} Tertullian
NRSVmg NEB REBmg

$\mathfrak{P}^{45vid}$ is cited by NA^{27} as supporting the variant, but this is unfounded, given the fact that at this point in the manuscript, the left and right margins are uncertain and therefore defy reconstruction of the lacunae (see *Text of the Earliest MSS,* 170).The variant reading is attractive because it is the shorter and more difficult of the two readings. In the parallel passage, Luke 9:26, "words" is also lacking in some witnesses (see note). Perhaps λογους ("words") was a later addition made by scribes attempting to make the text more applicable to contemporary needs—for it is more relevant in later centuries to speak of being ashamed of Jesus' words than of Jesus' disciples. However, the textual evidence supports the longer reading, and the shorter reading does not have the support of $\mathfrak{P}^{45}$. Nonetheless, the translators of the NEB followed the shorter reading because they "considered that the reference in context is more likely to be to Jesus and his followers than to Jesus and his words" (Tasker 1964, 415). The REB, however, was changed to the longer text.

Mark 8:38b

TR WH NU ὅταν ἔλθῃ ἐν τῇ δόξῃ τοῦ πατρὸς αὐτοῦ μετὰ τῶν ἀγγέλων τῶν ἁγίων
"when he comes in the glory of his Father with his holy angels"
ℵ A B C D L W 33
KJV NKJV RSV NRSV ESV NASB NIV TNIV NEBmg REB NJB NAB NLT HCSB NET

variant οταν ελθη εν τη δοξη του πατρος αυτου και των αγγελων των αγιων
"when he comes in the glory of his Father and his holy angels"
𝔓45 W syrs
NEB REBmg

Both readings could be the product of harmonization: The TR WH NU reading to Matt 16:27, and the variant to Luke 9:26. Tasker (1964, 415), defending the NEB, argued for the variant, saying the other reading was the product of assimilation to Matt 16:27. Just the opposite, however, can be argued by citing Luke 9:26.

The meaning of the passage is different in each variant. TR WH NU indicate that when Jesus comes, the angels come with him. The variant indicates that the glory belongs to both the Father and the angels. The former is easier to understand because elsewhere the NT speaks of the angels coming with (μετα) Jesus in the parousia (Matt 25:31; 2 Thess 1:7; cf. Mark 13:26-27). The variant is more difficult to understand because it indicates that the angels, Jesus, and the Father share the same glory.

Mark 9:2

All three editions (TR WH NU) read μετεμορφωθη εμπροσθεν αυτων ("he was transformed before them"), following ℵ A B D. A variant reading, found in 𝔓45vid W Θ f13 (28 565), adds the preceding phrase, εν τω προσυεχεσθαι αυτους ("while they were praying"). This variant reading, found in Caesarean manuscripts, says the disciples were praying when they saw Jesus transfigured.

Mark 9:7

Following the support of 𝔓45vid ℵ* A B C D, all three editions (TR WH NU) read ουτος εστιν ο υιος μου ο αγαπητος ("this is my beloved Son"). Two additions were made to this: εν ω ευδοκησα ("in whom I am well pleased") in ℵ1 Δ; and ον εξελεξαμην ("whom I have chosen") in 0131.

The first variant presents verbatim scribal conformity to Matt 17:5, and the second variant is scribal conformity to Luke 9:35, which reads, "This is my Son, the chosen one." Throughout the Gospels there is a great variety of textual variation as to what the Father said about his Son at both Jesus' baptism and transfiguration. Some witnesses indicate that the Father affirmed Jesus as "his Son," others as "the chosen one," and still others as both "his Son, the chosen one." Both titles are extremely important; the "Son" asserts Jesus' divine relationship with the Father, and "the chosen one" points to Jesus as the one selected by God to be the Messiah and Savior. Since

Mark emphasizes Jesus' sonship, it is fitting for the affirmation to simply be "this is my beloved Son."

Mark 9:11

According to most manuscripts, it is only "the scribes" (οι γραμματεις) who said that Elijah had to precede the coming of the Messiah. A few manuscripts (including ℵ) also include "the Pharisees" (οι Φαρισαοι), a natural expansion, since Pharisees and scribes are often paired together in the Gospels.

Mark 9:19

By way of harmonization to Matt 17:17 and Luke 9:41, a few scribes (𝔓[45vid] W f[13]) added και διεστραμμενη ("and perverse") after γενεα απιστος ("faithless generation").

Mark 9:20

The verb συνεσπαραξεν ("convulsed"), in ℵ B C L Δ 33, may have been borrowed from Luke 9:42. If so, εσπαραξεν ("shook"), in 𝔓[45] A W Θ Ψ 067 f[1,13] Maj, could be original.

Mark 9:23

WH NU — τὸ εἰ δύνῃ
"[as to] the 'if you are able'"
ℵ B C* N* Δ f[1] it[k]
NKJVmg RSV NRSV ESV NASB NIV TNIV NEB REB NJB NAB NLT HCSB NET

variant 1/TR — το ει δυνασαι πιστευσαι
"[as to] the 'if you are able to believe'"
A C[3] Maj
(KJV NKJV) HCSBmg NETmg

variant 2 — ει δυνη πιστευσαι
"if you are able to believe"
D K Θ f[13] 28 565 700[c]
none

variant 3 — τουτο ει δυνη
"[as to] this [word] 'if you are able'"
W
none

variant 4 — ει δυνη
"if you are able"
𝔓[45]
(see commentary)

The WH NU reading has solid early and diverse testimony from the manuscripts. In the previous verse (9:22), the father of the demon-possessed boy had said to Jesus, "If you are able (ει τι δυνη), help us." In this verse, Jesus used the man's words in order to show that the man needed to have faith. ("Jesus said to him, 'As to the "if you are able," all things are possible to the one who believes.'") Wanting to make this perfectly clear in the first clause, several scribes added πιστευσαι ("to believe"), as in the first and second variants. The other variants, avoiding the addition of πιστευσαι, are attempts to clarify the awkwardness of the expression, το ει δυνη. Although most English versions are probably following the WH NU reading, the resultant translations reflect the same editorial trimming as done by the scribe of 𝔓45.

Mark 9:24

WH NU κράξας ὁ πατὴρ τοῦ παιδίου
"the father of the child cried out"
𝔓45 ℵ A* B C* L (W)
RSV NRSV ESV NASB NIV TNIV NEB REB NJB NAB NLT HCSB NET

variant/TR κραξας μετα δακρυων ο πατηρ του παιδιου
"the father of the child cried out with tears"
A2 C3 D Θ f1,13 33 Maj
KJV NKJV RSVmg NRSVmg ESVmg

The WH NU reading has superior testimony than that of the variant. The variant reading is likely the result of scribal coloring, which found its way into TR, followed by KJV and NKJV.

Mark 9:29

WH NU εἰ μὴ ἐν προσευχῇ.
"This kind does not come out except by prayer."
ℵ* B 0274 itk
NKJVmg RSV NRSV ESV NASB NIV TNIV NEB REB NJB NAB NLT HCSBmg NET

variant/TR ει μη εν προσευχη και νηστεια
"This kind does not come out except by prayer and fasting."
𝔓45vid? ℵ2 A C D L W Θ Ψ f1,13 33 Maj
KJV NKJV RSVmg NRSVmg ESVmg NASBmg NIVmg TNIVmg NEBmg REBmg NJBmg NABmg NLTmg HCSB NETmg

The shorter reading is supported by two reliable manuscripts, ℵ* B, and one noteworthy versional witness, itk. Had the words "and fasting" been in their exemplars, there is no good reason to explain why these scribes would have deleted them. The variant reading appears to be supported by 𝔓45, but it must be noted that this manuscript has a lacuna after προσ[ευχη], which may or may not have been filled in with και νηστεια ("and fasting"). Given the independent proclivities of the scribe of 𝔓45, one cannot dogmatically say this is what was there. In any event, the words "and fasting" were probably added by scribes who were influenced by the early church's strong emphasis on fasting. (See also note on Matt 17:21; Acts 10:30; 1 Cor 7:5 for the same kind of addition.) The KJV tradition retains the longer text, followed by NKJV and HCSB (set in brackets).

Mark 9:31

WH NU μετὰ τρεῖς ἡμέρας ἀναστήσεται
"after three days he will rise again"
ℵ B C* D L Ψ cop
RSV NRSV ESV NASB NIV TNIV NEB REB NJB NAB NLT HCSB NET

variant/TR τη τριτη ημερα αναστησεται
"on the third day he will rise again"
A C[3] W Θ $f^{1,13}$ Maj
KJV NKJV

The WH NU reading has the best documentary support and is the more difficult reading—especially since it says that Jesus would rise from the dead after three days when Jesus' actual entombment lasted only from Friday evening to Sunday morning. Thus, it is easier to say that he arose "on the third day." This was likely the motivation behind the variant, unless it was a harmonization to Matt 17:23, a parallel passage.

Mark 9:33

WH NU ἦλθον εἰς Καφαρναούμ
"they came into Capernaum"
א B D W 0274
RSV NRSV ESV NASB NIV TNIV NEB REB NJB NAB NLT HCSB NET

variant/TR ηλθεν εις Καφαρναουμ
"he [Jesus] came into Capernaum"
A C L Θ Ψ Maj
KJV NKJV

The WH NU reading, which has early and diverse testimony, was followed by all modern versions. The variant in TR (followed by KJV and NKJV) is a typical scribal alteration in the Gospels to focus the narrative on Jesus alone.

Mark 9:35

Two witnesses (D it[k]) omit the second part of this verse—from και λεγει ("and he says") to the end. This omission could have been accidental—the eye of the scribe passing from the και in 9:35 to the και that begins 9:36—or purposeful trimming. The resultant text, lacking the omitted portion, makes good sense: "And having sat down, he called the Twelve [omitted text], and taking a child he set him in the middle of them; and taking him into his arms he said, 'Whoever welcomes one such child in my name, welcomes me, and whoever welcomes me does not welcome me but him who sent me.'"

Mark 9:38

There are several variant readings of the statement John made to Jesus. According to excellent documentary support (א B C L Δ Θ 0274), it reads: ειδομεν τινα εν τω ονοματι σου εκβαλλοντα δαιμονια, και εκωλυομεν αυτον, οτι ουκ ηκολουθει ημιν ("We saw someone casting out demons in your name, and we forbade him because he does not follow with us"). In Caesarean manuscripts (W $f^{1,13}$ 28 565 700) and D, the phrase "who does not follow with us" is transposed to follow "someone"; in A and Maj, the phrase appears twice. The emphasis in the Caesarean manuscripts is "the man's apparent lack of authorization rather than merely a narrow sectarianism on the disciples' part" (Lane 1974, 341).

Mark 9:40

The reading ος γαρ ουκ εστιν καθ ημων υπερ ημων εστιν ("the person who is not against us is for us") is supported by ℵ B C W Δ Θ Ψ f[1,13] 28 565 it[k] cop. In this statement, Jesus is speaking of himself and the disciples. Several other manuscripts (A D Maj—so TR) twice substitute υμων ("you") for ημων ("us"), creating the reading, "the person who is not against you is for you." This reading is also found in P.Oxy. 1224 (folio 2 recto, column 1). This statement refers just to the disciples.

Mark 9:41

WH NU	ἐν ὀνόματι ὅτι Χριστοῦ ἐστε "in the name [= by the fact] that you are Christ's" ℵ[2] A B C* L Ψ f[1] syr NRSV ESV REB NLT NET
variant 1/TR	εν ονοματι μου οτι χριστου εστε "in my name because you are Christ's" C[3] (D Θ) f[13] Maj KJV NKJV RSV NASB NIV TNIV NEB NJB NAB HCSB
variant 2	εν ονοματι μου οτι εμον εστε "in my name because you are [for] me" ℵ* none

This verse presents a difficult textual problem. At the heart of the problem is the unusualness of Jesus using the term "Christ" when speaking of himself in this way, for it seems contrary to his usage elsewhere in the Synoptic Gospels (Lane 1974, 342). But this kind of usage appears in John's gospel, where Jesus in his prayer requested "that they may know you, the only true God, and Jesus Christ, whom you have sent" (John 17:3). The addition of μου ("my") in the first variant is a scribal attempt to fix a difficult statement, which probably means "on the grounds that you are Christ's." The reading in ℵ* (not listed correctly in NA[27]) has prompted certain scholars to conjecture that Mark originally wrote εμοι and that εμον is a scribal error. As such, the statement would read, "because you are mine" (Wessel 1984, 708). This reading perfectly agrees with the variant in 8:38, "ashamed of me and mine" (see note). However, it is possible that the scribe of ℵ was trying to avoid the use of χριστου ("of Christ").

Mark 9:42

TR NU	τῶν μικρῶν τούτων, τῶν πιστευόντων [εἰς ἐμέ] "these little ones, the ones believing into me" A B C[2] L W Θ Ψ f[1,13] Maj KJV NKJV RSV NRSV ESV NIV TNIV NJBmg NAB NLT HCSB NET
variant 1/WH	των μικρων τουτων, των πιστευοντων "these little ones, the ones believing" ℵ C*[vid] Δ it NRSVmg NASB REB

variant 2	των μικρων τουτων, των πιστιν εχοντων "these little ones, the ones having faith" D it[a] NEB NJB

The manuscript evidence is nearly evenly divided between the TR NU reading and the first variant (WH), with TR NU having slightly more diversity. However, the words "into me," included in TR NU, could have been borrowed from Matt 18:6, a parallel passage. Several modern versions followed one of the two shorter readings.

Mark 9:44, 46

WH NU	omit verses 44 and 46 א B C L W Δ Ψ 0274 f[1] 28 565 it[k] syr[s] cop NKJVmg RSV NRSV ESV NASBmg NIV TNIV NEB REB NJB NAB NLT HCSBmg NET
variant/TR	add verses 44 and 46 (which are identical to 9:48 in NU) οπου ο σκωληξ αυτων ου τελευτα και το πυρ ου σβεννυται. "where the worm does not die and the fire is not extinguished" A D Θ f[13] Maj KJV NKJV RSVmg NRSVmg ESVmg NASB NIVmg NEBmg REBmg NJBmg NABmg NLTmg HCSB NETmg

Although it could be argued that these verses were omitted by scribes who considered the repetition to be unnecessary, such a deletion could hardly occur in manuscripts of such vast diversity as those that give witness to the absence of these verses. Contrarily, verses 44 and 46 were added as a sort of prophetic refrain that makes for good oral reading. Indeed, many textual variants entered the textual stream as the result of scribes enhancing the text for oral reading in the church. This is a classic example. Several modern English versions omit these verses and then note their inclusion for the sake of readers familiar with their place in the KJV tradition. By retaining the verses in the text, the HCSB retains the KJV tradition.

Mark 9:49

WH NU	πᾶς γὰρ πυρὶ ἁλισθήσεται "for everyone will be salted with fire" (א) B L (W) Δ 0274 f[1,13] 28* 565 700 syr[s] RSV NRSV ESV NASB NIV TNIV NEB REB NJB NAB NLT HCSB NET
variant 1	πασα γαρ θυσια αλι αλισθησεται "for every sacrifice will be salted with salt" D it NETmg
variant 2/TR	πας γαρ πυρι αλισθησεται και πασα θυσια αλι αλισθησεται "for everyone will be salted with fire and every sacrifice will be salted with salt" A C Θ (Ψ) Maj KJV NKJV RSVmg NRSVmg ESVmg NJBmg NABmg NLTmg HCSBmg NETmg

The difficulty of this verse led to the textual variants. Among the many interpretations of this text, one of the most acceptable proceeds from the assumption that the "everyone" refers to everyone who follows Jesus. The "fire" can then be understood as a trial or test that a Christian must endure in order to be refined and perfected (see Mal 3:2; 1 Cor 3:13, 15; 1 Pet 1:7; cf. Isa 33:14). But it is the expression, "salted with fire," that has created the most difficulty. The best explanation of the origin of this image lies in the Jewish practice of salting a sacrifice. The meal offering was first roasted and then sprinkled with salt to symbolize the perfection of the offering (Lev 2:13). Since salt made the grain good to eat, this act indicated, in a figurative way, that the sacrifice was acceptable to God. Jesus may have had this ritual in mind when he said that every one of his followers would have to be "salted with fire" in order to be made acceptable before God. With this understanding of the passage, one scribe (perhaps the scribe of D was the originator), borrowing from Lev 2:13, changed the verse to read, "for every sacrifice will be salted with salt." Other scribes (as in the second variant) simply appended the gloss with a και. Yet in order for this addition to be a helpful gloss, the και must be understood as functioning epexegetically: "for everyone will be salted with fire, even as every sacrifice will be salted with salt."

Mark 10:1

WH NU τὰ ὅρια τῆς Ἰουδαίας [καὶ] πέραν τοῦ Ἰορδάνου
"the region of Judea and beyond the Jordan [= Transjordan]"
ℵ B C* L Ψ 0274 cop
RSV NRSV ESV NASB NIV TNIV NEB REB NJB NAB NLT HCSB NET

variant 1 τα ορια της Ιουδαιας περαν του Ιορδανου
"the region of Judea beyond the Jordan"
C² D W Δ Θ $f^{1,13}$ 28 565 $syr^{p,s}$
NRSVmg NETmg

variant 2/TR τα ορια της Ιουδαιας δια του περαν του Ιορδανου
"the region of Judea by the other side of the Jordan"
A Maj syr^h
KJV NKJV NETmg

The WH NU reading, supported by excellent authority, is ambiguous: It could mean (1) that Jesus came into two regions, Judea and the eastern side of the Jordan (= Transjordan), or (2) that the region of Judea extended eastward beyond the Jordan. But the latter understanding does not coincide with geographical history; the region to the east of Judea beyond the Jordan was Perea. Therefore, various copyists tried to emend Mark's geography (Wessel 1984, 712). The first variant, the result of harmonization to Matt 19:1, implies that Jesus entered Judea from the eastern side of the Jordan River. The second variant (in TR) indicates that Jesus traveled on the east side of the Jordan before entering Judea—a typical route for Jews wishing to avoid Samaria.

Mark 10:2

A few witnesses (D it syr^s) omit Φαρισαιοι ("Pharisees") from the text; the resultant reading leaves Jesus' critics unnamed. Hurtado has remarked, "it is highly likely, but not absolutely certain that the original text contained this reference to Pharisees" (1989, 166).

Mark 10:6

WH NU ἄρσεν καὶ θῆλυ ἐποίησεν αὐτούς
"he made them male and female"
ℵ B C L Δ cop
HCSBmg NET

variant 1 αρσεν και θηλυ εποιησεν ο θεος
"God made male and female"
D W
none

variant 2/TR αρσεν και θηλυ εποιησεν αυτους ο θεος
"God made them male and female"
A Θ Ψ f[1,13] Maj syr
KJV NKJV RSV NRSV ESV NASB NIV TNIV NEB REB NJB NAB HCSB NETmg

The WH NU reading is a direct quotation of the Septuagint (Gen 1:27). The two variants make the subject explicit by saying it was God who made them male and female. All English versions except NET have done likewise.

Mark 10:7

TR NU ἕνεκεν τούτου καταλείψει ἄνθρωπος τὸν πατέρα αὐτοῦ καὶ τὴν μητέρα [καὶ προσκολληθήσεται πρὸς τὴν γυναῖκα αὐτοῦ].
"For this cause a man will leave his father and mother and be joined to his wife."
D W Θ f[13] Maj (A C L Δ f[1] τη γυναικι)
KJV NKJV RSV NRSV ESV NASBmg NIV TNIV NEB REB NJBmg NAB NLT HCSB NETmg

variant/WH ενεκεν τουτο καταλειψει ανθρωπος τον πατερα και την μητερα.
"For this cause a man will leave his father and mother."
ℵ B Ψ 892* syr[s]
RSVmg NRSVmg ESVmg NASB NIVmg TNIVmg NEBmg NJB NLTmg HCSBmg NET

It is possible that the clause "and will be joined to his wife" was accidentally omitted by scribes whose eyes passed from the και that begins this clause to the και that begins the next verse. But it seems unlikely that this could have happened in several manuscripts, especially ℵ and B. Rather, it is more likely that the clause was added by scribes to conform Mark to either Matt 19:5 or Gen 2:24 (or both). The two forms of the text also make it suspect as an addition. Without this clause, the quotation reads, "That is why a man leaves his father and mother, and the two will become one flesh" (NJB). Admittedly, this is a harder reading because it lacks the transitional clause that brings the man to the woman. For this reason, not too many translators are willing to follow the shorter text. Nonetheless, it was characteristic of NT writers not to quote OT Scriptures in their entirety, because they were operating according to memory or intended eclecticism. Mark might have written the shorter rendition that was later filled in by Matthew in his gospel and by scribes working on Mark. The same kind of textual phenomenon has occurred in Eph 5:31, where Gen 2:24 is cited (see comments there).

Mark 10:12

WH NU — ἐὰν αὐτὴ ἀπολύσασα τὸν ἄνδρα αὐτῆς γαμήσῃ ἄλλον μοιχᾶται
"if she divorces her husband and marries another, she commits adultery"
א B (C) L (Δ Ψ) 892 cop
RSV NRSV ESV NASB NIV TNIV NEB REB NAB (NLT) HCSB NET

variant 1/TR — εαν γυνη απολυσασα τον ανδρα αυτης γαμηση αλλον μοιχαται
"if a woman divorces her husband and marries another, she commits adultery"
A Maj
KJV NKJV NJB

variant 2 — εαν εξελθη απο του ανδρος και αλλον γαμηση μοιχαται
"if she separates from her husband and marries another, she commits adultery"
D (Θ) f^{13} (28) 565 (700) it[a,b,(k)] syr[s] Augustine
none

The WH NU reading (which is clarified in the first variant) has good documentary support among Alexandrian witnesses and is the more difficult reading because it is known that women, according to Jewish law, were not permitted to divorce their husbands. This right belonged only to the man. However, among the Gentiles, women could and did divorce their husbands. Perhaps Jesus was looking beyond Jewish customs at this time to that which was practiced in all the surrounding nations. Nonetheless, Lane (1974, 352) has argued that the reading in the Caesarean and Western witnesses (variant 2) preserves the original text because this reading "represents a textual tradition current at Antioch, Caesarea, Carthage, Italy, and Gaul as early as A.D. 150" and because it is particularly appropriate to the situation of Herodias and Herod Antipas (see 6:17-18). However, the early date ascribed by Lane cannot be attached to any particular manuscript—only to a manuscript tradition, and the same can be said of the Alexandrian witnesses, which have known archetypes that are also as early as the second century.

Mark 10:14

The Caesarean manuscripts W Θ $f^{1,13}$ 28 565 add επιτιμησας ("rebuking") before ειπεν αυτοις ("he said to them"); this is a carryover from the previous verse.

Mark 10:19a

WH NU — μὴ φονεύσῃς, μὴ μοιχεύσῃς
"Do not murder, do not commit adultery."
א[2] B C Δ Ψ 0274 syr[s] cop
RSV NRSV ESV NASB NIV TNIV NEB REB NJB NAB NLT HCSB NET

variant 1/TR — μη μοιχευσης, μη φονευσης
"Do not commit adultery, do not murder."
A W Θ f^{13} Maj
KJV NKJV

variant 2 μη φονευσης
"Do not murder"
ℵ*
none

variant 3 μη μοιχευσης
"Do not commit adultery."
f^1
none

variant 4 μη μοιχευσης, μη πορνευσης
"Do not commit adultery, do not fornicate."
D (Γ) it^k
none

The usual order of commandments, as found in the Masoretic Text of Exod 20:12-16 and Deut 5:16-20 (also $LXX^{A,F}$), is preserved in the WH NU reading, which has outstanding textual support. The reverse order (the seventh commandment before the sixth) in the first variant agrees with the order in Luke 18:20, Exod 20:12-16 (LXX^B), and the Nash Papyrus. The questions are, did Mark alter the usual OT order for the sake of his narrative, did he follow the order in the Septuagint of B, or was this the work of scribes such as A W Θ f^{13} Maj? The placement of adultery first in the list fits well in Mark 10 because the preceding pericope deals with divorce and adultery. However, the first variant is probably the result of scribes harmonizing to Luke 18:20, without thinking about context or exegesis. The second and third variants are shorter renditions of the text and first variant, respectively, whereas the fourth variant is the creation of D's editorialization.

Mark 10:19b

ℵ A B^2 C D Θ 0274 Maj include μη αποστερησης ("do not defraud"). Several other manuscripts (B* K W Δ Ψ $f^{1,13}$ 28 700 syr^s) omit the phrase. According to the fuller text, Mark is the only gospel writer to include a prohibition against fraud, as a substitute for coveting, in the list of the Ten Commandments (see Exod 20:17); the other gospel parallels do not list the prohibition against coveting (cf. Matt 19:18; Luke 18:20). Evidently, Mark considered fraud to be a form of coveting because fraud often involves stealing what belongs to another. Indeed, the word is used in the Septuagint (Exod 21:10; Deut 24:14 [in A]; Sir 4:1) and in the NT (Jas 5:4) of people withholding wages from the poor. This would have been especially poignant in Jesus' address to a man who may have coveted wealth and even oppressed the poor in obtaining riches—this was likely Jesus' reason for commanding him to sell everything and distribute it to the poor.

The deletion of this prohibition (in the variant reading) was done by scribes who did not understand Mark's usage here or who thought they were correcting an error or interpolation created by a previous scribe.

Mark 10:21

WH NU δεῦρο ἀκολούθει μοι
"come, follow me"
ℵ B C D Δ Θ Ψ 0274
RSV NRSV ESV NASB NIV TNIV NEB REB NJB NAB NLT HCSB NET

variant/TR δευρο ακολουθει μοι, αρας τον σταυρον
"come, follow me, taking up the cross"
A W f[1,13] Maj
KJV NKJV HCSBmg

The WH NU reading has superior testimony among early and diverse manuscripts. At the end of this verse, several scribes add "take up the cross," borrowed from 8:34.

Mark 10:23, 25

Against all other documents, D it[a,b] have a transposition of verses 24 and 25, creating this order: 23, 25, 24, 26. This transposition is probably the editorial work of the scribe of Codex Bezae (or his predecessor), who wanted the aphorism in 10:25 (describing the impossibility of wealthy people entering the kingdom) to be juxtaposed with Jesus' statement in 10:23 about how difficult it is to enter the kingdom of God.

Mark 10:24

WH NU πῶς δύσκολον ἐστιν εἰς τὴν βασιλείαν τοῦ θεοῦ εἰσελθεῖν
"how difficult it is to enter the kingdom of God"
ℵ B (W) Δ Ψ it[k]
NKJVmg RSV NRSV ESV NASB NIV TNIV NEB REB NJB NAB NLT HCSB NET

variant/TR πως δυσκολον εστιν τους πεποιθοτας επι χρημασιν εις την βασιλεαιν του θεου εισελθειν
"how difficult it is for those who trust in riches to enter the kingdom of God"
A C D Θ f[1,13] Maj syr
KJV NKJV RSVmg NRSVmg NASBmg NIVmg NEBmg REBmg NLTmg HCSBmg NETmg

The variant reading is a scribal addition intended to clarify that it was the rich—not just everybody—who would have a difficult time entering the kingdom of God. The context warrants the validity of this exegesis, but textual criticism does not warrant the addition because the documentary evidence strongly supports the shorter reading.

Mark 10:25

As in Matt 19:24 (see note), the Greek word for "camel" (καμηλον) has been changed (in f[13] 28 arm geo) to καμιλον, meaning "rope" or "ship's cable"—creating this rendering, "it is easier for a rope [or ship's cable] to go through an eye of the needle than for a rich person to enter the kingdom of God." This change tones down the extent of Jesus' hyperbole, but Jesus was using a well-known proverb to show the absolute impossibility of a rich person entering the kingdom.

Mark 10:26

According to TR NU, the disciples were "saying among themselves (λεγοντες προς εαυτους) who then can be saved?" Though this reading accords with Markan style (1:27; 11:31; 12:7; 16:13), it has inferior manuscript support (A D W Θ f[1,13] Maj). The variant reading is supported by ℵ B C Δ Ψ, λεγοντες προς αυτον ("saying to him"). On documentary grounds, this is just as likely the original reading (so WH).

Mark 10:29

WH NU	ὃς ἀφῆκεν οἰκίαν ἢ ἀδελφοὺς ἢ ἀδελφὰς ἢ μητέρα ἢ πατέρα ἢ τέκνα "who has left houses or brothers or sisters or mother or father or children" ℵ B D W Δ Θ f[1] 565 700 syr[s] cop RSV NRSV ESV NASB NIV TNIV NEB REB NJB NAB NLT HCSB NET
variant/TR	ος αφηκεν οικιαν η αδελφους η αδελφας η μητερα η πατερα η γυναικα η τεκνα "who has left houses or brothers or sisters or mother or father or wife or children" A C Ψ f[13] Maj KJV NKJV HCSBmg

It is difficult to determine if Jesus included "wife" (γυναικα) in the list of what men had forsaken to follow him. Based on the manuscript evidence, it appears that it is a later addition; however, there are good reasons for its inclusion, each of which is discussed in the note on the parallel passage, Matt 19:29a.

Mark 10:29-30

The Western text (D it) compresses these two verses into a single statement: "whoever has left house and sisters and brothers and mother and children and fields with persecution, will receive eternal life in the age to come."

Mark 10:32

D K f[13] 28 700 omit the clause οι δε ακολουθουντες εφοβουντο ("and the ones following were afraid"). This clause created problems for scribes because it suggests that there was another group besides the disciples who were following Jesus and because there is no apparent reason for these people "to be afraid." The simplest solution was to delete the phrase. However, Mark may have intended to relate that two groups were following Jesus: (1) the disciples (the ones being led by Jesus) and (2) other followers—contrasted with the previously mentioned disciples by the use of οι δε (Wessel 1984, 719). These followers were probably afraid because they had just heard from Jesus how difficult it is to enter the kingdom of God and how those who follow him must be willing to forsake all (10:17-31). The mention of fear also anticipates the following verses wherein Jesus speaks of the upcoming trials that await him in Jerusalem (10:32b-34).

Mark 10:34

WH NU	μετὰ τρεῖς ἡμέρας ἀναστήσεται "after three days he will rise again" ℵ B C D L Δ Ψ it cop RSV NRSV ESV NASB NIV TNIV NEB REB NJB NAB NLT HCSB NET
variant/TR	τη τριτη ημερα αναστησεται "on the third day he will rise again" (A*) W Θ f[1,13] Maj KJV NKJV NETmg

The documentary evidence strongly supports the WH NU reading; the variant is the result of certain scribes attempting to synchronize the timing of Jesus' resurrection, which occurred on the third day (see comments on 9:31).

Mark 10:40

At the end of the verse, several witnesses (ℵ*,2 Θ f[1] it[a]) add the prepositional phrase υπο του πατρος μου ("by my Father") after αλλ οις ητοιμασται ("for the ones it has been prepared"). This addition was borrowed verbatim from Matt 20:23, a parallel passage. And a few manuscripts (225 it syr[c,s]) give witness to the reading αλλοις, meaning "for the others it has been prepared."

Mark 10:47-48

According to B L W Δ Θ Ψ f[1], the text reads Ιησους ο Ναζαρηνος ("Jesus the Nazarene"). This was Mark's typical way of writing this title (see 1:24; 14:67; 16:6). Other scribes (ℵ A C f[13] Maj—so TR) changed it to the way it more often appears in the rest of the NT: Ιησους ο Ναζαραιος ("Jesus, the one of Nazareth"). In place of the vocative Υιε Δαυιδ Ιησου ("son of David, Jesus"), found in ℵ B C L Δ Θ Ψ, there are several alternatives: (1) Υιος Δαυιδ Ιησου ("son of David, Jesus"—not vocative) in D K f[13]; (2) ο υιος Δαυιδ Ιησους ("the son of David, Jesus") in A W f[1] Maj; (3) Κυριε, υιος Δαυιδ Ιησου ("Lord, son of David, Jesus") in 28. The first two variants are the result of scribal conformity to Matt 20:30, a parallel passage. The third variant is scribal embellishment. The same kind of variations occurred in 10:48.

Verse 48 is not included in W and 1241, either due to scribal oversight (the eye of the scribe passing from the beginning και of 10:48 to the και of 10:49) or purposeful excision of a verse that seemed redundant.

Mark 10:51

In place of Ραββουνι ("Rabboni"), D and Old Latin manuscripts read Κυριε Ραββι ("Lord, Rabbi")—a conflated reading influenced by Matt 20:30 and Luke 18:41, both parallel passages.

Mark 11:8

WH NU — ἄλλοι δὲ στιβάδας κόψαντες ἐκ τῶν ἀγρῶν
"but others cut leafy branches from the trees"
ℵ B (C) L Δ Ψ it[k] cop[sa] Origen
RSV NRSV ESV NASB NIV TNIV NEB REB NJB NAB NLT HCSB NET

variant 1 — omit
W it[i] syr[s]
none

variant 2/TR — αλλοι δε στιβαδας εκοπτον εκ των δενδρων και εστρωννυον εις την οδον
"but others cut leafy branches from the trees and were spreading them on the road"
A D Θ f[1,13] Maj
KJV NKJV HCSBmg

The first variant can be explained in one of two ways: (1) The scribes had before them the fuller text of variant 2, but their eyes passed from εις την οδον at the end of 11:8a to the same words at the end of 11:8b and thereby skipped everything in between (due to homoeoteleuton); or (2) the clause was excised by scribes trying to avoid what they perceived to be an incomplete thought—that is, the text does not say what these people did with the branches after they cut them. Other scribes (variant 2) took a different approach: They added the words from Matt 21:8, a parallel passage, to complete the thought. This was followed by KJV and NKJV, while modern versions, following the text, carried over the verb "spread" from the first clause to the second.

Mark 11:9-10

In several Caesarean manuscripts (Θ f[13] 28 565 700) and it[k], the text reads Ωσαννα εν τοις υψιστοις ("Hosanna in the highest") instead of simply Ωσαννα ("Hosanna"), as in ℵ A B C. (D W omit Ωσαννα altogether.) The expanded reading is the result of scribes taking the wording from 11:10 and placing it at the beginning of the refrain in 11:9—"Hosanna in the highest! Blessed is he who comes in the name of the Lord!" Several of the same scribes and others then changed Ωσαννα εν τοις υψιστοις ("Hosanna in the highest") in 11:10 to ειρηνη εν τοις υψιστοις ("peace in the highest")—as in W 28 700 syr[s]—or to ειρηνη εν ουρανω και δοξα εν υψιστοις ("peace in heaven and glory in the highest")—as in Θ (f[1]) syr[h**]. These changes were influenced by the angelic anthems in Luke 2:13-14. TR repeats εν ονοματι κυριου ("in the name of the Lord") in 11:10, which is translated in KJV and NKJV.

Mark 11:19

WH NU	ἐξεπορεύοντο ἔξω τῆς πόλεως "they went out of the city" A B (W) Δ Ψ (28) 565 700 RSV NRSV ESV NASB NIV TNIV REB NAB NLT HCSB NET
variant/TR	εξεπορευετο εξω της πολεως "he went out of the city" ℵ C D Θ f[1,13] Maj cop KJV NKJV RSVmg NRSVmg ESVmg NIVmg TNIVmg NEB NJB NLTmg

According to the good textual evidence, Jesus and his disciples departed from the city. The verb was changed to the singular by scribes wanting to shift the focus to Jesus alone or by harmonization to the immediate context (see 11:18). Several versions, nevertheless, follow the variant or note it.

Mark 11:22

TR WH NU	ἔχετε πίστιν θεοῦ "have faith in God" A B C L W Δ Ψ f[1] 33* cop all
variant	ει εχετε πιστιν θεου "if you have faith in God" ℵ D Θ f[13] 28 33[c] 565 700 it[k] syr[s] NRSVmg NIVmg TNIVmg

Since the WH NU reading has excellent testimony, the variant is likely the result of scribal conformity to a parallel passage, Matt 21:21 (see also Luke 17:6). As such, the clause was turned into an "if" clause that introduces the statement in the next verse (although it does this very awkwardly).

Mark 11:26

WH NU — omit verse
ℵ B L W Δ Ψ 565 700 syr[s]
NKJVmg RSV NRSV ESV NASBmg NIV TNIV NEB REB NJB NAB NLT HCSBmg NET

variant/TR — add verse
Ει δε υμεις ουκ αφιετε, ουδε ο πατηρ υμων ο εν τοις ουρανοις αφησει τα παραπτωματα υμων.
"But if you do not forgive, neither will your Father in heaven forgive your trespasses."
A (C D) Θ (f[1,13] 33) Maj
KJV NKJV RSVmg NRSVmg NASB NIVmg NEBmg REBmg NJBmg NABmg NLTmg HCSB NETmg

Though it could be argued that verse 26 dropped out by a scribal mistake (both 11:25 and 11:26 end with the same three words), the WH NU reading has much better documentation than the variant. Thus, it is more likely that verse 26 is a natural scribal expansion of verse 25, borrowed from Matt 6:15, a parallel verse (cf. Matt 18:35). According to Mark's original text, Jesus was encouraging people to forgive others their trespasses against them before seeking forgiveness from God for their own trespasses. The addition makes God's forgiveness conditional. The extra verse is included in TR, followed by KJV, NKJV, as well as by NASB and HCSB, which persist in maintaining the KJV tradition. It is noted in modern versions out of deference to the KJV tradition.

Mark 11:28

The second sentence of this verse, "Or who gave you this authority to do these things?" is omitted in D it[k], probably because the scribes considered it a redundant question. However, the first question in the verse asks what kind of authority Jesus had, whereas the second asks who gave Jesus his authority.

Mark 12:4

WH NU — κακεῖνον ἐκεφαλίωσαν καὶ ἠτίμασαν
"and they struck that one on the head and treated him shamefully"
ℵ B (D) L Δ Ψ 33 cop
NKJVmg RSV NRSV ESV NASB NIV TNIV NEB REB NJB NAB NLT HCSB NET

variant/TR — κακεινον λιθοβολησαντες εκεφαλιωσαν και απεστειλαν ητιμωμενον
"and throwing stones, they struck that one in the head and they sent him away, shamefully treated"
A C Θ f[13] Maj
KJV NKJV HCSBmg

The WH NU reading has early and diverse support among the manuscripts. The expanded reading in the variant, drawing upon Matt 21:35 and Luke 20:10 (parallel passages), adds color to the description of what happened to one of the servants who were sent by the master to collect produce from those who were working his vineyard.

Mark 12:7

Probably influenced by Matt 21:38, the narrative was expanded in some Caesarean manuscripts (Θ f[13] 28 565 700) by adding θεασαμενοι αυτον ερχομενον ("seeing him coming").

Mark 12:14

D Θ 565 it[k] syr[s] read επικεφαλαιον ("poll tax") instead of the transliterated term κηνσον (from the Latin *census*) found in all other manuscripts. The transliterated term "reflects the impact made by the introduction of the Roman taxation into the Judean province in A.D. 6" (Lane 1974, 422). Matthew, a tax collector, used the same term (see Matt 22:19).

The last sentence of this verse, δωμεν η μη δωμεν; ("should we give or not give?"), was omitted in D it (syr[s]) probably because it was considered superfluous after the preceding question, "Is it lawful to pay the taxes to Caesar or not?"

Mark 12:15

In several Caesarean witnesses (𝔓[45] W Θ f[1,13] 28 565) the word υποκριται ("hypocrites") was added after Τι με πειραζετε; ("Why are you testing me?"). The addition was taken from Matt 22:18, a parallel passage.

Mark 12:23

TR NU — ἐν τῇ ἀναστάσει [ὅταν ἀναστῶσιν]
"in the resurrection, when they will rise"
A Θ f[1,(13)] Maj syr[h,s]
KJV NKJV NRSVmg ESV NASB NIVmg TNIVmg NEB REB NJB NAB HCSB NET

variant/WH — εν τη αναστασει
"in the resurrection"
א B C D L W Δ Ψ 33 it[c,k] syr[p] cop
RSV NRSV NASBmg NIV TNIV NLT HCSBmg NETmg

The NU editors selected the longer reading because it was hard for them "to imagine that a copyist would have been tempted to gloss ἐν τῇ ἀναστάσει, and the pleonasm is in accord with Mark's style" (TCGNT). Although this is a good internal argument against the shorter reading, the manuscript evidence overwhelmingly supports the shorter text, followed by several English versions (RSV NRSV NIV TNIV NLT) and noted in others.

Mark 12:27

WH NU — οὐκ ἔστιν θεὸς νεκρῶν ἀλλὰ ζώντων
"he is not God of dead ones but of living ones"
B D L W Δ 28
ESV HCSB

variant 1/TR	ουκ εστιν ο θεος νεκρων αλλα νεκρων "he is not the God of dead ones but of living ones" א A C Ψ f[1] Maj KJV NKJV RSV NRSV NASB NIV TNIV REB NJB NAB NLT NET
variant 2	ουκ εστιν ο θεος θεος νεκρων αλλα νεκρων "God is not the God of dead ones but of living ones." Θ f[13] 33 NEB

See comments on Matt 22:32.

Mark 12:30

According to most manuscripts in 12:30, Jesus says that the greatest commandment is "to love the Lord your God with all your heart and with all your soul and with all your mind and with all your might." This fourfold description does not coincide with Deut 6:5 (cf. 12:33, which does conform to Deut 6:5). D and it[c] conformed the quote to Deut 6:5 by omitting και εξ ολης της διανοιας σου ("and with all your mind").

Mark 12:30-31

WH NU	δευτέρα αὕτη "this [is] the second" א B L Δ Ψ NKJVmg RSV NRSV ESV NASB NIV TNIV NEB REB NJB NAB NLT HCSB NET
variant/TR	αυτη πρωτη εντολη. δευτερα δε ομοια αυτη "this is the first commandment; and the second is like it" A (D W Θ) f[1,13] 33 Maj KJV NKJV

Since the WH NU reading has substantial testimony and is the shorter reading, the variant is likely the result of scribal harmonization to Matt 22:37-39. In Mark's text, the first commandment is not labeled, and the second is introduced with the terse expression, "this [is] the second."

Mark 12:33

Several manuscripts (A 087 f[13] Maj—so TR and KJV) add και εξ ολης της ισχυος ("and with all the strength") to make a fourfold description like that found in 12:30. The threefold description is preserved in א B L W Δ Θ Ψ 28 565.

Mark 12:36

Many manuscripts (א A L Θ Ψ 087 f[1,13] Maj—so TR) display conformity to the Septuagint version of Ps 110:1—the word υποκατω ("underneath") was changed to υποποδιον ("footstool"). The superior reading, υποκατω, is supported by B D W 28 syr[s] cop (so WH NU).

Mark 12:38

Instead of στολιας ("long robes"), found in all Greek manuscripts, the Old Syriac Gospels (syr[pal,s] in Mark 12:38 and syr[c,s] in Luke 20:46) support the reading στοαι ("cloisters"). The variant, though an interesting alternative, is probably the result of translators misreading the Greek text.

Mark 12:40

A few Caesarean and Western manuscripts (D W f[13] 28 565 it) add των ορφανων ("the orphans") after τας οικιας των χηρων ("the houses of widows"). On internal grounds, a case can be made for this reading on two counts: (1) the words των ορφανων were accidentally dropped in other manuscripts due to homoeoteleuton; (2) the words were dropped because it did not make sense to scribes that orphans could have homes. However, the manuscript evidence for the shorter reading is superior (א A B L Θ), and it is possible that the words "and orphans" were added by common association with the phrase "orphans and widows" (see Jas 1:27).

Mark 12:41

As is typical in many manuscripts, the subject ο Ιησους ("Jesus"), was added (in A D W Θ f[1,13] 28 565 Maj—so TR) because a new section begins with 12:41 and Jesus had not been named since 12:35.

Mark 13:2

At the end of this verse, a few witnesses (D W it Cyprian) add και δια τριων ημερων αλλος αναστησεται ανευ χειρων ("and in three days another will be raised without hands"). This interpolation (drawing upon Mark 14:58 and John 2:19) was made by scribes who, knowing the accusation made against Jesus in 14:58 ("we heard him say, 'I will destroy this temple made with human hands, and in three days I will build another, made without human hands'"), may have felt that Jesus should actually say what he was later accused of, because there would otherwise be no record of this in the Gospel of Mark. The scribes of D (often followed by Old Latin MSS) and W frequently took on this editorial function. The irony is that Jesus never said he would destroy the temple. In Mark 13:2, he predicted the destruction of the temple in Jerusalem; in John 2:19-21 he told the Jews that they would destroy him, the temple of God, but that he would raise it up in three days. Jesus, of course, was speaking metaphorically of his body being the temple of God.

Mark 13:6-7

In 13:6, א B L W Ψ read πολλοι ελευσονται επι τω ονοματι μου λεγοντες οτι Εγω ειμι ("many will come in my name saying, 'I am [the one]'"). Other scribes (A D Θ f[1,13] 33 Maj), harmonizing Mark to Matt 24:5 and Luke 21:8, logically connected this verse to the previous statement by adding γαρ ("for"): "Beware that no one deceives you, for many will come in my name saying, 'I am the one' and lead many astray." In 13:7, א[2] A D L Θ f[1,13] Maj, γαρ ("for") was added to the second clause to connect it more directly with the preceding clause: "when you hear of wars and rumors of wars, do not be alarmed, for this must take place." Lane

(1974, 455) argues that "logically the γαρ is necessary in these verses, for it indicates the reason for the warnings expressed in verse 5 and verse 7a."

Mark 13:8

WH NU ἔσονται λιμοί
"there will be famines"
ℵ[2] B D L Ψ
NKJVmg RSV NRSV ESV NASB NIV TNIV NEB REB NJB NAB NLT HCSB NET

variant/TR εσονται λιμοι και ταραχαι
"there will be famines and troubles"
A (W Θ) $f^{1,13}$ 33 Maj
KJV NKJV HCSBmg

Metzger (TCGNT) suggests that και ταραχαι may have been dropped accidentally because of the similarity with the following word, αρχη ("beginning"). Or the words may have been dropped so as to conform Mark to Matt 24:8. However, since the manuscripts with the longer text are known for scribal expansions, this is likely what happened here. Westcott and Hort (1882, 26) suggested that the insertion was made for the sake of rhythm in oral reading or it was derived from an extraneous source.

Mark 13:9-10

Several Caesarean and Western witnesses (D W Θ f^1 28 565 700 it syr^s) omit βλεπετε δε υμεις εαυτους ("as for yourselves, watch out"). To accommodate this omission, some of these manuscripts (W f^1 28 syr^s) begin the next clause with και ("and"), others (D Θ 565 700) with ειτα ("then").

Mark 13:11

WH NU μὴ προμεριμνᾶτε τί λαλήσητε
"do not worry beforehand what you might say"
ℵ A B C L W
NKJVmg RSV NRSV ESV NASB NIV TNIV NEB REB NJB NAB NLT HCSB NET

variant/TR μη προμεριμνατε τι λαλησητε μηδε μελετατε
"do not worry beforehand what you might say neither meditate"
33 (Maj)
KJV NKJV

The WH NU reading has superior attestation, both early and diverse. The variant is a harmonization to Luke 21:14, a parallel passage. It was included in TR, and so KJV and NKJV.

Mark 13:14

WH NU τὸ βδέλυγμα τῆς ἐρημώσεως
"the abomination of desolation"
ℵ B D L
NKJVmg RSV NRSV ESV NASB NIV TNIV NEB REB NJB NAB NLT HCSB NET

variant/TR το βδελυγμα της ερημωσεως, το ρηθεν υπο Δανιηλ του προφητου
"the abomination of desolation, that which was spoken through Daniel the prophet"
A Maj
KJV NKJV

The WH NU reading has the earliest documentary support (א B), along with D and L. The expansion in the variant is a verbatim harmonization to Matt 24:15. Throughout the course of textual transmission, many gospel harmonizations in Mark and Luke were made to be in accord with Matthew, the primary gospel.

Mark 13:19

According to excellent textual evidence (א A B W Maj), the three editions (TR WH NU) read απ αρχης κτισεως ην εκτισεν ο θεος ("from the beginning of creation, which God created"). Some Caesarean and Western witnesses (D Θ 565 it) have a shorter reading: απ αρχης κτισεως ("from the beginning of creation"). Although it is generally considered that a shorter reading is more likely original, in this case the shorter reading is the result of scribes eliminating what they likely perceived to be a superfluous repetition. (Many English versions also truncate the expression.) But the TR WH NU reading presents a Markan expansion that clarifies a biblical statement for Mark's "Gentile readers, who would not necessarily assume that the creation of the world was the act of God" (Lane 1974, 465).

Mark 13:22

D it[i,k], omitting the expression ψευδοχριστοι ("false christs"), speak only of the false prophets deceiving the people. This shorter reading conforms to Deut 13:2.

Mark 13:32

Codex X and one Vulgate manuscript omit ουδε ο υιος ("neither the Son"). This is explained in the note on Matt 24:36, where the same omission occurred in several manuscripts.

Mark 13:33

WH NU Βλέπετε, ἀγρυπνεῖτε
"beware, keep alert"
B D it[a,c,k]
RSV NRSV ESV NASB NIV TNIV NEB REB NJB NAB NLT HCSB NET

variant/TR Βλεπετε, αγρυπνειτε, και προσευχεσθε
"beware, keep alert, and pray"
א A C L W Θ Ψ $f^{1,13}$ Maj syr cop
KJV NKJV RSVmg NRSVmg ESVmg NIVmg TNIVmg NEBmg REBmg NLTmg HCSBmg NETmg

Although it is possible that the words και προσευχεσθε ("and pray") were accidentally omitted due to homoeoteleuton, it is more likely that the variant is the result of scribal conformity to Mark 14:38. Nonetheless, because of the substantial manuscript support for the variant, modern translators feel obligated to note it as a possible reading.

Mark 14:1

D it[a] omit και τα αζυμα ("and unleavened bread") from the statement "it was the Passover and [Feast of] Unleavened Bread." Perhaps the scribe of D thought his readers would be confused with the two names for the one event, but Jews typically interchanged one for the other, calling Passover the Feast of Unleavened Bread, and vice versa.

Mark 14:5

The descriptor επανω ("more than") before δηναριων τριακοσιων ("three hundred denarii") was omitted in some witnesses (954 it[c,k] syr[s] Origen) to bring Mark's text into conformity with John 12:5.

Mark 14:10

Judas's name and pedigree appear in a number of forms both here and throughout the Gospels. The options here are as follows: (1) Ιουδας Ισκαριωθ ("Judas, from Kerioth") in ℵ* B C*[vid]; (2) Ιουδας ο Ισκαριωτης ("Judas Iscariot") in A C[2] W $f^{1,13}$ Maj; (3) Ιουδας ο Ισκαριωθ ("Judas, the one from Kerioth") in ℵ[2] L Θ Ψ 565; (4) Ιουδας ο Σκαριωτης ("Judas the Scarioth") in D it. All English versions follow the second option. (See comments on Matt 10:4b for a discussion on this issue.)

Mark 14:19

WH NU μήτι ἐγω;
"'Surely, not I?'"
ℵ B C L W Δ Ψ syr cop
NKJVmg RSV NRSV ESV NASB NIV TNIV NEB REB NJB NAB NLT HCSB NET

variant 1/TR Μητι εγω; και αλλος Μητι εγω;
"'Surely, not I?' And another [said], 'Surely, not I?'"
D Θ f^1 Maj it
KJV NKJV

variant 2 Μητι εγω; ειμι, κυριε; και αλλος Μητιν εγω;
"'Surely, not I?' 'Am I, Lord?' And another [said], 'Surely, not I?'"
(A f^{13}) 28
none

The WH NU reading is strongly supported by the earliest and best manuscripts. The variants, perhaps borrowing from Matt 26:22, intensify the drama of the moment by having one disciple, then another, (and so on), ask if he was the betrayer.

Mark 14:20

TR NU ὁ ἐμβαπτόμενος μετ' ἐμοῦ εἰς τὸ τρύβλιον
"the one dipping [bread] with me into the bowl"
ℵ A C[2] D L W Ψ $f^{1,13}$ Maj
KJV NKJV RSV NRSV ESV NASB NIV TNIV NAB NLT HCSB NET

variant/WH ο εμβαπτομενος μετ εμου εις το ἕν τρυβλιον
"the one dipping [bread] with me into the one [= same] bowl"
B C* Θ 565
NRSVmg NEB REB NJB

The variant reading has good support and could very well be original; indeed, it is included in WH, though in brackets. A few modern versions follow this reading. The act of eating out of the same bowl should be a sign of friendship, but this is the irony—one of Jesus' companions (Judas) who ate bread with him would turn against him (see John 13:18).

Mark 14:22

Codex Bobiensis (it[k]) reads, "he took bread and pronounced the blessing and broke [it] and gave [it] to them, and they all ate of it; and he said to them, 'This is my body.'" TR WH NU lack "they all ate of it" and introduce the statement "This is my body" with the command "Take it." Since it[k] is regarded as a translation of a second-century papyrus (Metzger 1992, 73), it is possible that it preserves an early form of the Markan text, which emphasizes the proceedings of the meal (i.e., that they all ate) rather than the liturgical emphasis ("take it").

Mark 14:24a

WH NU τὸ αἷμα μου τῆς διαθήκης
"my blood of the covenant"
ℵ B C D[c] L Θ Ψ 565 it[k]
NKJVmg RSV NRSV ESV NASB NIV TNIV NEB REB NJB NAB NLT HCSB NET

variant/TR το αιμα μου της καινης διαθηκης
"my blood of the new covenant"
A $f^{1,13}$ Maj syr
KJV NKJV RSVmg NRSVmg ESVmg NIVmg TNIVmg NLTmg HCSBmg NETmg

The addition of "new" to "covenant" is a late, Byzantine expansion, borrowed from the liturgical texts, Luke 22:20 and 1 Cor 11:25. (See note on Matt 26:28.)

Mark 14:24b

After the expression εκχυννομενον υπερ πολλων ("poured out for many"), a few scribes (W f^{13}) added εις αφεσιν αμαρτιων ("for the forgiveness of sins")—transported verbatim from Matt 26:28. Several manuscripts (D W Δ Θ f^{13} 565 syr[s]) omit πολλων ("many") in the expression, "poured out for many"—probably in an effort to solve the problem of why Jesus would die for "many" and not "all." In Isa 53:11-12, Qumran usage, and rabbinic teaching, the word "many" is a key word that refers to the chosen people in God's kingdom.

Mark 14:27

WH NU πάντες σκανδαλισθήσεσθε
"Every one [of you] will stumble."
ℵ B C* D L Γ Δ Ψ*
NKJVmg RSV NRSV ESV NASB NIV TNIV NEB REB NJB NAB (NLT) HCSB NET

variant 1	παντες σκανδαλισθησεσθε εν εμοι "Every one [of you] will stumble because of me." Ψ[c] 28 it syr[s] none
variant 2	παντες σκανδαλισθησεσθε εν τη νυκτι ταυτη "Every one [of you] will stumble during this night." a few late MSS and some cop[boMSS] none
variant 3/TR	παντες σκανδαλισθησεσθε εν εμοι εν τη νυκτι ταυτη "Every one [of you] will stumble because of me during this night." A C[2] W Θ f[1,13] 565 700 KJV NKJV HCSBmg

The WH NU reading has excellent testimony and the shortest of all the readings. The expansions are the result of scribal harmonization to the parallel passage, Matt 26:31—the full expansion of which is presented in the third variant, a verbatim reproduction of Matthew. This reading found its way into TR and was popularized by KJV and NKJV.

Mark 14:30

The pleonastic expression σημερον ταυτη τη νυκτι ("today—this very night"), typical of Mark, was modified in Western and Caesarean witnesses (D Θ f[13] 565 700 it) by dropping σημερον ("today").

Mention of the rooster crowing "twice" (δις) was deleted in several manuscripts (א C[(2)] D W) in order to conform Mark's account to the other gospels (see Matt 26:34; Luke 22:34; John 13:38). The scribe of א was thorough in his excisions—ridding the text of any mention of the rooster crowing in 14:68 and the "second" rooster crowing in 14:72. (See comments on 14:68 and 14:72a, 72b.)

Mark 14:39

TR WH NU	ἀπελθὼν προσηύξατο τὸν αὐτὸν λόγον εἰπών "he went away [and] prayed, saying the same words" א A B C W Maj KJV NKJV RSV NRSV ESV NASB NIV TNIV NEBmg REB NJB NAB NLT HCSB NET
variant	απελθων προσηυξατο "he went away [and] prayed" D it NEB

Because the variant has such paltry support, the shorter text does not represent the original; rather, it is another example of how the scribe of D (or his predecessor) trimmed his text of whatever words he considered superfluous.

Mark 14:41

The Greek expression απεχει· ηλθεν η ωρα has excellent support (א A B C L f[1] 28 700), but the first verb, απεχει, is difficult to interpret in this context. According to its use in the common papyri, it meant "paid in full"—thereby suggesting that Jesus was speaking of accomplishing redemption (see NEBmg). This, then, could be interpreted to mean: "the account is settled; the hour has come." There are three variants on this: (1) απεχει το τελος· ηλθεν η ωρα ("the end is pressing [on me]; the hour has come"), supported by (W) Θ f[13] 565 it syr[s]; (2) απεχει το τελος και η ωρα ("the end—even the hour—has fully come") in D it[c,q]; (3) ηλθεν η ωρα ("the hour has come") in Ψ 892 (it[k]). The first variant is a harmonization to Luke 22:37. The second variant is a modification of that found in the first; the third avoids the problem completely by omitting απεχει.

Mark 14:51-52

The expression in 14:51, περιβεβλημενος σινδονα επι γυμνου ("clothed with a linen garment over his naked [body]"), was shortened in W f[1] it[c,k] to simply "clothed with a linen garment." But επι γυμνου was written by Mark in anticipation of the next verse, which says the young man fled away naked after escaping the soldiers' grasp. In 14:52, several manuscripts (A D W Θ f[1,13] Maj—so TR and KJV) add απ αυτων ("from them") after γυμνος εφυγεν ("he fled naked"). As in WH NU (supported by ℵ B C), the statement exactly parallels 14:50, which says that all the disciples fled. This parallelism could suggest that this young man was also among the many disciples following Jesus; certain traditions say this was Mark, the writer of this gospel.

Mark 14:61-62

According to most manuscripts, the high priest asks Jesus, Συ ει ο χριστος ο υιος του ευλογητου ("Are you the Christ, the son of the Blessed One?"). This is shortened in a few witnesses (Γ Θ it[k]) to "Are you the son of the Blessed One?"

According to most manuscripts, Jesus' response to the high priest is simply Εγω ειμι ("I am"). However, in some Caesarean witnesses (Θ f[13] 565 700 Origen), the response is συ ειπας οτι Εγω ειμι ("you say that I am"), thereby bringing Mark's account into conformity with Matt 26:64 and Luke 22:70. Mark's original wording is more pointed than in Matthew and Luke because Jesus boldly and plainly affirms that he is the Son of God.

Mark 14:65

The clause και περικαλυπτειν αυτου το προσωπον ("and to cover his face") was omitted in D it[a] syr[s], perhaps as an attempt to conform Mark's account to Matthew's, which does not speak of Jesus' face being covered. Luke's account, however, confirms Mark's in that Luke says that Jesus was blindfolded. It is also possible that the clause was deleted because it made no sense to the scribes. This detail, however, is important because there was a tradition (based on Isa 11:2-4) that the Messiah was supposed to be able to judge without sight—indeed, he was supposed to be able to judge by smell (Lane 1974, 539-540). The Jewish officials, who were probably aware of this interpretation and did not believe that Jesus was the Messiah, took the opportunity to ridicule Jesus in this regard.

Mark 14:68

TR NU [καὶ ἀλέκτωρ ἐφώνησεν]
"and a rooster crowed"
A C D Θ Ψ[c] 067 f[1,13] Maj
KJV NKJV RSVmg NRSV ESV NASBmg NIVmg NEBmg REBmg NJB NABmg NLT HCSB NET

variant/WH	omit ℵ B L W Ψ* it^c syr^s cop^{bo} RSV NRSVmg ESVmg NASB NIV TNIV NEB REB NAB NLTmg HCSBmg NETmg

Scholars have offered strong arguments both for and against the inclusion of this text on the basis of internal evidence. (The English versions display the dividedness on this issue.) Those who argue that it was originally written by Mark and then deleted later say that scribes deleted it (1) to harmonize Mark with the other gospels (Matt 26:74; Luke 22:60; John 18:26), who mention only one rooster crowing, or (2) because it did not make sense to various scribes why Peter would not have repented after hearing the rooster crow the first time. Those who argue that it was not originally written by Mark but added later say that scribes added it (1) because they wanted to emphasize the literal fulfillment of Jesus' prediction in 14:30, or (2) they wanted to account for a first rooster crowing because a second one is mentioned in 14:72. Because the internal arguments are equally persuasive, we have to turn to the external evidence. Clearly, the earlier evidence points to the exclusion of these words. (See notes on 14:30 and 14:72.)

Mark 14:72a

TR WH NU	ἐκ δευτέρου ἀλέκτωρ ἐφώνησεν "a rooster crowed a second time" A B C^{2vid} D W Maj all
variant	αλεκτωρ εφωνησεν "a rooster crowed" ℵ C^{*vid} L it^c NIVmg TNIVmg

According to NU, the rooster crowed once after Peter's first denial (14:68) and again after his third (14:71-72). However, it is possible that Mark only reports the second crowing at Peter's third denial (14:71-72). This sequence is supported throughout by B, which may preserve the true reading (so WH—see Westcott and Hort 1882, 27).

Mark 14:72b

Among other transpositional changes at the end of this verse, ℵ C^{*vid} W delete εκ δευτερου ("twice") after αλεκτορα φωνησαι ("a rooster crowed"). For the scribe of ℵ, this change appears to have been the result of complete excision in this chapter of any mention of how often the rooster would crow.

Mark 15:8

According to superior testimony (ℵ B W Δ cop), the text reads ο οχλος ηρξατο αιτεισθαι καθως εποιει αυτοις—which is literally rendered, "the crowd began to ask just as he [Pilate] was doing for them," but should be rendered, "the crowd began to ask for him [Pilate] to do for them according to custom." Wanting to make it explicit that the crowds were asking for something that was customary (i.e., the release of one prisoner at Passover), certain scribes (A C^{vid} D f^{1,13} Maj—so TR) added αει ("always") to the expression καθως εποιει αυτοις ("as he always did for them"). A few Caesarean witnesses (Θ 565 700), with an expanded reading, are even more explanatory: καθως εθος ην ινα τον βαραββαν απολυση αυτοις ("as it was the custom, that he should release Barabbas to them").

Mark 15:12

The word θελετε ("do you wish"), not found in ℵ B C W Δ Ψ f[1,13] 33, is included in NU (in brackets), because the editors could not determine if the word had been deleted in ℵ B C etc. by way of conformation to Matt 27:22 (a parallel passage) or added in other manuscripts (A D Θ 0250 Maj—so TR) by way of conformation to Mark 15:9 (in the immediate context) or to Matt 27:21 or Luke 23:20, also parallel passages (see TCGNT). Given the fact that gospel harmonization is far more prevalent in the later manuscripts than in the earlier, the best decision is to exclude θελετε, as in WH.

Mark 15:17

Borrowing from Matt 27:28, a few Caesarean witnesses (Θ f[13] 565 700) insert χλαμυδα κοκκινην και ("with a scarlet robe and") after ενδιδυσκουσιν αυτον ("they clothed him").

Mark 15:19

D and it[k], probably influenced by John 19:2, omit και τιθεντες τα γονατα προσεκυνουν αυτω ("and bending their knees they were worshiping him").

Mark 15:20

Borrowing from Matt 27:31, some Caesarean witnesses (Θ f[13] 565 700) insert την χλαμυδα και ("[of] the robe and") after εξεδυσαν αυτον ("they stripped him").

Mark 15:23

Conforming to Matt 27:34, several manuscripts (A C[2] D Θ 0250 f[1,13] Maj—so TR) add πιειν ("to drink") after εδιδουν αυτω ("they were giving him").

Mark 15:24

The last three words of the verse, τις τι αρη ("which one might take [them]"), were omitted in D it syr[s] by scribes who probably considered them a superfluous addition to the OT quotation (Ps 22:18 [verse 19 in Hebrew and LXX]).

Mark 15:25

The addition in D it, και εφυλασσον ("and they guarded [him]"), modeled after Matt 27:36, is an attempt to avoid duplication of 15:24 (Lane 1974, 561).

Mark 15:26

Harmonizing the text to Matt 27:37 and Luke 23:38, some scribes (D 33[s]) added ουτος εστιν ("this one is") before ο βασιλυες των Ιουδαιων ("the King of the Jews"). The placard nailed to Jesus' cross is deictic in itself; it does not need to say "this one is."

Mark 15:27

In one Old Latin manuscript (it[c]), the two men crucified with Jesus are given names: *Zoathan* and *Chammata* (see note on Matt 27:38).

Mark 15:28

WH NU omit verse
א A B C D Ψ it[k] syr[s] cop[sa]
NKJVmg RSV NRSV ESV NASBmg NIV TNIV NEB REB NJB NAB NLT HCSBmg NET

variant/TR add verse
Και επληρωθη η γραφη η λεγουσα· και μετα ανομων ελογισθη
"And the Scripture was fulfilled that says, 'He was counted among the lawless.'"
L Θ 083 0250 f[1,13] Maj syr[h,p]
KJV NKJV RSVmg NRSVmg ESVmg NASB NIVmg NEBmg REBmg NJBmg NABmg NLTmg HCSB NETmg

The documentary evidence decisively shows that this verse was not present in any Greek manuscript prior to the late sixth century (namely, 083—a manuscript discovered in the 1970s at St. Catherine's Monastery). Borrowing from a parallel passage, Luke 22:37 (which is a quotation of Isa 53:12), later scribes inserted this verse as a prophetic proof text for the phenomenon of Jesus' death with the lawless. Of all the gospel writers, Mark was by far the least concerned with showing prophetic fulfillment in the events of Jesus' life. No doubt, his Roman audience (hardly aware of the OT Scriptures) influenced this literary approach. In any event, the verse is retained in KJV and NKJV, as well as in NASB and HCSB, which usually follow KJV with respect to keeping verses in the text—in contrast to all other modern versions.

Mark 15:34

Jesus' cry of distress is reproduced in various forms in the extant witnesses. Some manuscripts (D Θ 059 565) read Ηλι Ηλι ("Eli, Eli") instead of Ελωι Ελωι ("Eloi, Eloi"), found in all other documents. The former represents the Hebrew expression for "my God"; the latter represents the Aramaic expression for "my God." It could be argued that the Hebrew expression is original because it sounds more like "Elijah"—the person whom the bystanders thought Jesus was crying out to, but the same can be argued for the three-syllable Aramaic word. In any case, the Hebrew is more likely the result of scribal conformity to Matt 27:46. The second part of Jesus' cry for distress, according to good documentary support (א C L Δ Θ Ψ 0112), is λεμα σαβαχθανι (*lema sabachthani*). *Lema* is Aramaic for "why," and *sabachthani* is Aramaic for "you have forsaken me." (See comments on Matt 27:46.)

D (supported by it[c,i,k] Porphyry) reads ωνειδισας με ("reproached me") instead of εγκατελιπες ("forsaken me"), found in all other witnesses. As usual, this reading shows the creative editorialization of the scribe of the D-text, who thought it too much for Jesus to have been forsaken by God. This is the thesis posited by Ehrman (1993, 143-145), who thinks that the word "reproached" was introduced to avoid an implication that Jesus had become separated from divinity and therefore could not himself be divine. Thus, the change would combat a gnostic separationist Christology which posited that "the Christ" left Jesus to die on his own. In making the change, the D-reviser may have been thinking of the prophetic word, "The reproaches of those who reproached you have fallen on me," taken from Ps 69:9 (this text is also cited by Paul in Rom 15:3).

Mark 15:39

WH NU — οὕτως ἐξέπνευσεν
"[he saw] how he expired"
ℵ B L Ψ
RSV NRSV ESV NASB NIVmg TNIV NEB REB NJB NAB NLT HCSB NET

variant 1/TR — ουτως κραξας εξεπνευσεν
"[he saw] how he, crying out, expired"
A C (W Θ) $f^{1,13}$ Maj syr
KJV NKJV RSVmg NRSVmg ESVmg NIV TNIVmg NEBmg NLTmg HCSBmg

variant 2 — ουτως αυτον κραξαντα και εξεπνευσεν
"[he saw] how he cried out and expired"
D
none

variant 3 — *quia sic exclamavit*
"that he so cried out"
it^k
none

All the variants, probably borrowing from Matt 27:50, have the additional detail that the centurion witnessed the way in which Jesus cried out when he died, not just the way he died (as in WH NU). Although this extra detail helps the reader understand what exactly caught the attention of the centurion, it misses the point. It was the entire crucifixion (which was under the centurion's watch) that moved him to declare that Jesus was God's Son.

Mark 15:41

A few manuscripts (C D Δ) omit και διηκονουν αυτω ("and were serving him"). The omission may have been accidental—the eye of a scribe passing from ηκολουθουν αυτω to διηκονουν αυτω. But it is possible that a certain scribe or scribes omitted the clause because they did not think it likely that these women following Jesus were actually serving him. However, Luke affirmed the same: several women not only followed Jesus but provided for him and his ministry (see Luke 8:1-3).

Mark 15:44

TR NU — ἐπηρώτησεν αὐτὸν εἰ πάλαι ἀπέθανεν
"he asked him if he had been dead for some time"
ℵ A C L Ψ $f^{1,13}$
KJV NKJV RSVmg NRSV NEB NJB

variant/WH — επηρωτησεν αυτον ει ηδη απεθανεν
"he asked him if he had already died"
B D W Θ
RSV ESV NASB NIV TNIV REB NJBmg NAB NLT HCSB NET

Since crucified victims were known to stay on the cross for as long as two or three days, Pilate was amazed to hear that Jesus had died within hours. Thus, it is far more likely that he asked the question as presented in the variant, which has good, diverse witness. The only argument against this testimony is that a scribe may have mistakenly copied ηδη from the first clause of this verse.

Mark 15:47 and 16:1

The reading Μαρια η Ιωσητος ("Mary the [mother] of Joses"), found in א[2] B L Δ Ψ*, was changed to (1) Μαρια η Ιακωβου ("Mary the mother of James") in D it syr[s] in order to harmonize 15:47 with 16:1, and to (2) Μαρια η Ιακωβου και Ιωσητος ("Mary, the [mother] of James and Joses") in some Caesarean witnesses (Θ f[13] 565) in order to harmonize 15:47 with 15:40. There are two Marys at the end of Mark's narrative. These two, Mary Magdalene and Mary the mother of James and Joses, witnessed Jesus' crucifixion and burial, and then came to Jesus' tomb on the morning of the resurrection (15:40, 47; 16:1). Salome was co-witness of the crucifixion and came with the two Marys on the morning of the resurrection.

By omitting the first part of 16:1 (except the initial και), D and it[k] join the end of 15:47 with 16:1 as follows: "Now Mary Magdalene and Mary the mother of Joses saw where he was buried, and they bought spices that they might go and anoint him." The omission is an editorial excision intended to simplify the text by having it say that the same two women who witnessed the burial came to anoint Jesus in the tomb.

Mark 16:3

One manuscript (it[k]) has an extended gloss at the end of this verse: "Suddenly, at the third hour of the day, there was darkness over the whole earth, and angels descended from heaven, and rising in the splendor of the living God they ascended with him [i.e., Jesus], and immediately it was light." This variant, which bears some resemblance to the *Gospel of Peter* (35-44), is noteworthy because it is the only attempt to describe the actual resurrection of Jesus. None of the canonical gospels provide such a description; the reader is simply told that Jesus arose and then the reader (in the other gospels) is given glimpses of Jesus' resurrection appearances. This variant is also significant in that it is found in one of the few manuscripts that conclude with the shorter ending after 16:8; thus, it is possible that the scribe of it[k] provided his own resolution to the Gospel by including a description of the resurrection in 16:3.

Mark 16:4

According to some witnesses (D Θ 565 it[c] syr[s] Eusebius), the last phrase of 16:4, ην γαρ μεγας σφοδρα ("for the stone was great"), is transposed to make it immediately follow the statement in 16:3, "Who will roll away the stone for us from the entrance to the tomb?" This is logical editorialization at work.

Mark 16:7

D and it[k] change καθως ειπεν υμιν ("as he told you") to καθως ειρηκα υμιν ("as I have told you"). Thus, instead of the angels telling the women to give a report to Peter and the disciples about Jesus' resurrection, it is Jesus (the "I") who does the speaking (perhaps through the angels as his agents). The change was intended to have Mark's gospel include an account of Jesus' personal appearance postresurrection.

The Endings of Mark

The Gospel of Mark concludes in five ways:

1. End at 16:8

καὶ ἐξελθοῦσαι ἔφυγον ἀπὸ τοῦ μνημείου, εἶχεν γὰρ αὐτὰς τρόμος καὶ ἔκστασις· καὶ οὐδενὶ οὐδὲν εἶπαν· ἐφοβοῦντο γάρ

"So they went out and fled from the tomb, seized with terror and amazement; and they said nothing to anyone, for they were afraid."

ℵ B 304 syr[s] cop[sa] (1 MS) arm geo (2 MSS) Hesychius Eusebian canons MSS[according to Eusebius] MSS[according to Jerome] MSS[according to Severus]

NKJVmg RSVmg NRSVmg ESVmg NASBmg NIVmg TNIVmg NEBmg REBmg NJBmg NABmg NLTmg HCSBmg NETmg

2. Shorter Ending

πάντα δὲ τὰ παρηγγελμένα τοῖς περὶ τὸν Πέτρον συντόμως ἐξήγγειλαν. Μετὰ δὲ ταῦτα καὶ αὐτὸς ὁ Ἰησοῦς ἀπὸ ἀνατολῆς καὶ ἄχρι δύσεως ἐξαπέστειλεν δι᾽ αὐτῶν τὸ ἱερὸν καὶ ἄφθαρτον κήρυγμα τῆς αἰωνίου σωτηρίας. ἀμήν.

"And all that had been commanded them they told briefly to those with Peter. And afterward Jesus himself sent out through them, from the east and as far as the west, the holy and imperishable proclamation of eternal salvation. Amen."

it[k] (see MSS supporting 5 below)

included in NRSV NASB NEB REB NAB NLT; noted in RSVmg ESVmg NJBmg HCSBmg

3. Traditional Longer Ending (Mark 16:9-20)/TR WH

9 Ἀναστὰς δὲ πρωῒ πρώτῃ σαββάτου ἐφάνη πρῶτον
Μαρίᾳ τῇ Μαγδαληνῇ, παρ᾽ ἧς ἐκβεβλήκει ἑπτὰ
δαιμόνια. 10 ἐκείνη πορευθεῖσα ἀπήγγειλεν τοῖς μετ᾽
αὐτοῦ γενομένοις πενθοῦσι καὶ κλαίουσιν· 11 κἀκεῖνοι
ἀκούσαντες ὅτι ζῇ καὶ ἐθεάθη ὑπ᾽ αὐτῆς ἠπίστησαν.
12 Μετὰ δὲ ταῦτα δυσὶν ἐξ αὐτῶν περιπατοῦσιν
ἐφανερώθη ἐν ἑτέρᾳ μορφῇ πορευομένοις εἰς
ἀγρόν· 13 κἀκεῖνοι ἀπελθόντες ἀπήγγειλαν τοῖς
λοιποῖς· οὐδὲ ἐκείνοις ἐπίστευσαν. 14 Ὕστερον [δε]
ἀνακειμένοις αὐτοῖς τοῖς ἕνδεκα ἐφανερώθη καὶ
ὠνείδισεν τὴν ἀπιστίαν αὐτῶν καὶ σκληροκαρδίαν
ὅτι τοῖς θεασαμένοις αὐτὸν ἐγηγερμένον οὐκ
ἐπίστευσαν. 15 καὶ εἶπεν αὐτοῖς· πορευθέντες εἰς
τὸν κόσμον ἅπαντα κηρύξατε τὸ εὐαγγέλιον πάσῃ
τῇ κτίσει. 16 ὁ πιστεύσας καὶ βαπτισθεὶς σωθήσεται,
ὁ δὲ ἀπιστήσας κατακριθήσεται. 17 σημεῖα δὲ τοῖς
πιστεύσασιν ταῦτα παρακολουθήσει· ἐν τῷ ὀνόματί
μου δαιμόνια ἐκβαλοῦσιν, γλώσσαις λαλήσουσιν
καιναῖς, 18 [καὶ ἐν ταῖς χερσὶν] ὄφεις ἀροῦσιν κἂν

θανάσιμόν τι πίωσιν οὐ μὴ αὐτοὺς βλάψῃ, ἐπὶ
ἀρρώστους χεῖρας ἐπιθήσουσιν καὶ καλῶς ἕξουσιν.
19 Ὁ μὲν οὖν κύριος Ἰησοῦς μετὰ τὸ λαλῆσαι
αὐτοῖς ἀνελήμφθη εἰς τὸν οὐρανὸν καὶ ἐκάθισεν ἐκ
δεξιῶν τοῦ θεοῦ. 20 ἐκεῖνοι δὲ ἐξελθόντες ἐκήρυξαν
πανταχοῦ, τοῦ κυρίου συνεργοῦντος καὶ τὸν λόγον
βεβαιοῦντος διὰ τῶν ἐπακολουθούντων σημείων.

"9 Now after he rose early on the first day of the week, he appeared first to
Mary Magdalene, from whom he had cast out seven demons. 10 She went
out and told those who had been with him, while they were mourning and
weeping. 11 But when they heard that he was alive and had been seen by her,
they would not believe it. 12 After this he appeared in another form to two of
them, as they were walking into the country. 13 And they went back and told
the rest, but they did not believe them. 14 Later he appeared to the eleven
themselves as they were sitting at the table; and he upbraided them for their
lack of faith and stubbornness, because they had not believed those who
saw him after he had risen. 15 And he said to them, 'Go into all the world and
proclaim the good news to the whole creation. 16 The one who believes and is
baptized will be saved; but the one who does not believe will be condemned.
17 And these signs will accompany those who believe: by using my name they
will cast out demons; they will speak in new tongues; 18 they will pick up
snakes in their hands, and if they drink any deadly thing, it will not hurt them;
they will lay their hands on the sick, and they will recover.' 19 So then the Lord
Jesus, after he had spoken to them, was taken up into heaven and sat down
at the right hand of God. 20 And they went out and proclaimed the good news
everywhere, while the Lord worked with them and confirmed the message by
the signs that accompanied it."

A C D Δ Θ f^{13} 33 Maj MSS[according to Eusebius] MSS[according to Jerome] MSS[according to Severus] Irenaeus Apostolic Constitutions (Epiphanius) Severian Nestorius Ambrose Augustine

all

4. Traditional Longer Ending with an Addition after 16:14, which reads,

κακεινοι απελογουντο λεγοντες οτι ο αιων ουτος της ανομιας και της απιστιας υπο τον σαταναν εστιν, ο μη εων τα υπο των πνευματων ακαθαρτα την αληθειαν του θεου καταλαβεσθαι δυναμιν· δια τουτο αποκαλυψον σου την δικαιοσυνην ηδη, εκεινοι ελεγον τω χριστω. και ο χριστος εκεινοις προσελεγεν οτι πεπληρωται ο ορος των ετων της εξουσιας του σατανα, αλλα εγγιζει αλλα δεινα· και υπερ ων εγω αμαρτησαντων παρεδοθην εις θανατον ινα υποστρεψωσιν εις την αληθειαν και μηκετι αμαρτησωσιν ινα την εν τω ουρανω πνευματικην και αφθαρτον της δικαιοσυνης δοξαν κληρονομησωσιν

"And they excused themselves, saying, 'This age of lawlessness and unbelief is under Satan, who does not allow the truth and power of God to prevail over the unclean things of the spirits. Therefore reveal your righteousness now'—thus they spoke to Christ. And Christ replied to them, 'The term of years of Satan's power has been fulfilled, but other terrible things draw near.

And for those who have sinned I was handed over to death, that they may return to the truth and sin no more, that they may inherit the spiritual and imperishable glory of righteousness that is in heaven.'" (from NRSVmg)
W (MSS[according to Jerome])
RSVmg NRSVmg NJBmg NABmg NLTmg

5. Both Shorter Ending and Traditional Longer Ending/NU

L Ψ 083 099 274[mg] 579 syr[hmg] cop[sa,boMSS]
RSVmg (NRSV NLT)

The citation of patristic witnesses was greatly revised from the third edition of UBS to the fourth. The patristic witnesses cited above are from the fourth edition. Furthermore, UBS[3] lists 0112 in support of the fifth reading noted above; it has been changed to 083 in UBS[4] (as in NA[27]) because 0112 belongs to the same manuscript as 083, discovered in the 1970s at St. Catherine's Monastery.

The ending to Mark's gospel presents an intriguing dilemma for textual scholars: Which of the five endings, as presented above, did Mark write? Or is it possible that the original ending to Mark's gospel was lost forever and that none of the above endings is the way the book originally ended?

The textual evidence for the first reading (stopping at verse 8) is the best. This reading is attested to by ℵ and B (the two earliest extant manuscripts that preserve this portion of Mark) and some early versions (Syriac, Coptic, Armenian, Georgian). Of the church fathers, Clement, Origen, Cyprian, and Cyril of Jerusalem show no knowledge of any verses beyond 16:8. Eusebius said that the accurate copies of Mark ended with verse 8, adding that 16:9-20 were missing from almost all manuscripts (*Quaest. Mar.* 1 [PG 22:937]). The pericope is also absent from the Eusebian canons. Jerome affirmed the same by saying that almost all the Greek codices did not have 16:9-20 (*Epist.* 120.3 *ad Hedibiam*). Several minuscule manuscripts (1, 20, 22, 137, 1216, 1582) that include 16:9-20 have scholia (marginal notes) indicating that the more ancient manuscripts do not include this section.

Other manuscripts mark off the longer reading with obeli to indicate its questionable status. The textual evidence, therefore, shows that Mark's gospel circulated in many ancient copies with an ending at verse 8. But this ending seemed to be too abrupt for many readers—both ancient and modern! As a result, various endings were appended. One short ending was appended to round off verse 8 and to indicate that the women had followed the angels' orders in bringing the report to Peter and the disciples. But in order to make this addition, it is necessary to delete the words "and said nothing to no one" from verse 8—which is exactly what was done in it[k].

The most well-known ending is the longer, traditional ending of 16:9-20. The earliest witnesses to this ending come from Irenaeus (via a Latin translation of his work). The other patristic witnesses cited above are no earlier than the fourth century (MSS[according to Eusebius] MSS[according to Jerome] MSS[according to Severus] Apostolic Constitutions [Epiphanius] Severian Nestorius Ambrose Augustine). Thus, we know that this ending was probably in circulation in the third century. It became the most popular of the endings after the fourth century, and was copied again and again in many uncial manuscripts. Eventually, it was accepted as canonical by the Council of Trent.

But the longer ending is stylistically incongruous with 16:1-8. Any fair-minded reader can detect the non-Markan flavor of the style, tone, and vocabulary of 16:9-20. This is apparent in the very first word in 16:9. The Greek verb αναστας ("having risen") is an active aorist participle; it conveys the thought that Jesus himself rose from the dead. But almost everywhere else in the Gospels, the passive verb is used with respect to Jesus' resurrection. Furthermore, the additions are all narratively noncontiguous. This is especially apparent in the connection between verses 8 and 9. The subject of verse 8 is the women, whereas the presumed subject of verse 9 is Jesus. And Mary Magdalene is introduced as if she was not mentioned before or was not among the women of 15:47–16:8.

This longer ending was made even longer in W (the Freer Gospels, Codex W) with an addition after 16:14. Prior to the discovery of W, we had the record from Jerome that there was another similar ending:

> In certain exemplars and especially in the Greek manuscripts [of the Gospel] according to Mark, at the end of his Gospel, there is written, "Afterward, when the Eleven reclined at meal, Jesus appeared to them and upbraided them for their unbelief and hardness of heart because they had not believed those who had seen him after his resurrection. And they made excuse, saying, 'This age of iniquity and unbelief is under Satan who, through unclean spirits, does not permit the true power of God to be apprehended. Therefore, reveal your righteousness now.'"

The Freer Logion is an expansion of what was known to Jerome inasmuch as Jesus gives a response to their excuse concerning unbelief. The disciples, blaming Satan for the unbelief, made an appeal to Jesus for his parousia, which will bring the full revelation of his vindicating righteousness. In response, Jesus declares that Satan's time has already come to its end, but before he (Jesus) can reveal his righteous kingdom, there will a time "of terrible things." This terrible time—of apostasy and judgment—would be the prelude to the second coming (Lane 1974, 606-611).

Finally, some manuscripts include both the shorter reading and the traditional longer reading. The earliest evidence for these is in two eighth-century manuscripts, L and Ψ. Some ancient versions (syr^{hmg} cop^{sa,boMSS}) also have both endings. This is clearly the result of scribal ambiguity—the same kind that is manifest in several modern English versions that print both endings in the text.

What then do we make of the evidence? Scholarly consensus is that Mark did not write any of the endings (2-5 above); all are the work of other hands. Farmer's (1974) attempt to defend the view that Mark 16:9-20 was originally part of Mark's gospel, which was later deleted by Alexandrian scribes, is not convincing. Farmer argues that Alexandrian scribes were troubled by the references to picking up snakes and drinking poison and therefore deleted the passage. If they had been troubled by these references, they would have deleted only those verses, not the entire passage! No one else has made a good case for the originality of any of the various additions. The historical fact appears to be that various readers, bothered that Mark ended so abruptly, completed the Gospel with a variety of additions. According to Aland (1969, 157-180), the shorter and longer endings were composed independently in different geographical locations, and both were probably circulating in the second century. Metzger says that the longer ending displays some vocabulary (particularly ανιστημι for εγειρω) which "suggests that the composition of the ending is appropriately located at the end of the first century or in the middle of the second century" (1992, 297).

The reason the shorter ending was created has already been explained. The longer ending was composed afresh or taken verbatim from some other source so as to fill up what was perceived to be a gap in the text of Mark. This writer provided an extended conclusion derived from various sources, including the other gospels and Acts, inserting his own theological peculiarities. The reason the longer ending has become so popular is that it is a collage of events found in the other gospels and the book of Acts.

Jesus' appearance to Mary Magdalene (16:9) was adapted from John 20:11-17. Her report to the disciples (16:10) was taken from Luke 24:10 and John 20:18. However, the writer of the longer ending has this report concerning Jesus' appearance, whereas Mary's report in John comes after she has seen the empty tomb. John's account is affirmed by the account in Luke 24:11. In both John and Luke the disciples do not believe the report concerning the angelic appearance and the empty tomb; there was no mention yet of any appearance made by Jesus. The change of story in the longer ending to Mark was contrived because Mark 16:8 says that the women said nothing to anybody after seeing the empty tomb and the angelic messenger. The writer could not controvert this blatantly (by saying that Mary or any of the other women then went to the disciples and told them about the empty tomb), so the writer has Jesus appearing to Mary Magdalene, then Mary telling the disciples, who do not believe. Since this particular account contradicts the authentic gospels, it should be dismissed.

After this, the writer of the longer ending relates Jesus' appearance to two disciples as they were walking from Jerusalem into the country (16:12); this clearly was taken from Luke 24:13-35. The report of further unbelief (16:13) was the interpretation of the composer; Luke does not tell us that the report of the two disciples was disbelieved. Jesus' first resurrection appearance to the disciples (16:14) was borrowed from Luke 24:36-49—with an added emphasis on their unbelief (perhaps adapted from Matt 28:16-20). Jesus' great commission (16:15-16) is loosely based on Matt 28:19-20—with an emphasis on baptism as a prerequisite to salvation. The promise of signs accompanying the believers (16:17-18) comes from the record of what happened in Acts—including the speaking in tongues (Acts 2:4; 10:46) and protection against snakes (Acts 28:3-6). The ascension (16:19) is adapted from Luke 24:50-53, and the final verse (16:20) seems to be a summary of the book of Acts, which seems to be preemptively out of place for inclusion in a gospel and is another indication of its spuriousness. (None of the other gospels tell us anything about the disciples' work after Jesus' resurrection and ascension.)

Even though much of this longer ending was drawn from other gospels and Acts, the composer had an unusual emphasis on the disciples' unbelief in the resurrection of Christ. In this regard, the composer may have been following through on the Markan theme of identifying the unbelief and stubbornness of the disciples. Indeed, this gospel, more than any other, focuses on the disciples' repeated failures to believe Jesus and follow him (see Osborne 1992, 679). The composer of the longer ending also had a preference for belief and baptism as a requisite for salvation, as well as an exalted view of signs. Christians need to be warned against using this text for Christian doctrine because it is not on the same par as verifiable New Testament Scripture. Nothing in it should be used to establish Christian doctrine or practice. Unfortunately, certain churches have used Mark 16:16 to affirm dogmatically that one must believe and be baptized in order to be saved, and other churches have used Mark 16:18 to promote the practice of snake-handling. (Even some boxes that keep the rattlesnakes are marked with "Mark 16:18.") Those who are bitten by rattlesnakes, they believe, will not be harmed if they are true followers of Christ. The writer of the longer ending also emphasized what we would call charismatic experiences—speaking in tongues, performing healings, protection from snakes and poison. Although the book of Acts affirms these experiences for certain believers, they are not necessarily the norm for all.

The longer ending of W (noted also by Jerome) was probably a marginal gloss written in the third century that found its way into the text of some manuscripts prior to the fourth century. This gloss was likely created by a scribe who wanted to provide a reason for the unbelief that is prevalent in the longer ending. Satan is blamed for the faithlessness, and an appeal is made for Jesus to reveal his righteousness immediately. But this revelation would be postponed until after a time of terrible things. This interpolation may have been drawn from several sources, including Acts 1:6-7; 3:19-21; and *Barnabas* 4:9; 15:7. In any case, it is quite clear that Mark did not write it. The style is blatantly non-Markan.

Having concluded that Mark did not write any of the endings, we are still left with the question: Did Mark originally conclude his gospel with verse 8 or was an original extended ending lost?

In defense of the view that Mark originally ended his gospel at verse 8, four arguments can be posited: (1) As is, the Gospel ends with an announcement of Christ's resurrection. Jesus does not need to actually appear in resurrection to validate the announcement. Our demand that the Gospel must record this appearance comes from our knowledge of the other gospels. Mark did not have to end his gospel the way the others did. (2) Mark, as a creative writer, may have purposely ended abruptly in order to force his readers to fill in the gap with their own imaginations. Perhaps Mark did not want to describe—or think himself capable of describing—the resurrection of Christ and the risen Christ; thus, he left it to the readers to imagine how the risen Christ appeared to Peter and the other disciples. (3) Throughout this gospel, Mark presented a secrecy motif concerning Jesus being the Messiah (see note on 8:26). The final verse is the culmination of this motif: The women "said nothing to anyone." Of course, the reader knows that this silence would not last; indeed, the very opposite will happen—the word of Christ's resurrection will be announced to the disciples, and the disciples will proclaim this to the world. Thus, the ending was calculated by Mark to be the irony of ironies; perhaps he thought it would bring a smile to the face of the Christians reading or hearing this gospel for the first time, for they knew how the word had gone out! (4) Guelich (1989, 524) adds yet another reason for the short ending: It ends on a note of failure—the women's failure to go to Peter and the other disciples—because this is consistent with discipleship failure, another major theme in Mark's gospel. All these four reasons could account for Mark purposely concluding the Gospel at 16:8.

However, many readers are not satisfied with these reasons—primarily because they, having read the other gospels, have a different horizon of expectation for the conclusion of Mark. Thus, many readers have questioned whether it was Mark's original design to conclude with verse 8. Why conclude with merely an announcement of Jesus' resurrection and a description of the women's fear and bewilderment? In the Gospel of Mark, a pattern is set in which every one of Jesus' predictions is actually fulfilled in narrative form. According to Gundry (1993, 1009), the predictions that were fulfilled were as follows: God's kingdom having come with power at the transfiguration, the finding of a colt, the disciples' being met by a man carrying a jar of water, the showing of the upper room, the betrayal of Jesus by one of the Twelve, the scattering of the rest of the Twelve, the denials of Jesus by Peter, the passion, and the resurrection. Thus, since Jesus announced that he would see his disciples in Galilee (14:28), the narrative should have depicted an actual appearance of the risen Christ to his disciples in Galilee.

Since there is not such a record (even in the additions), some readers have thought that an original extended ending got lost in the early phase of textual transmission—probably because it was written on the last leaf of a papyrus codex and was torn away from the rest of the manuscript. The codex was in use by the end of the first century (see discussion in Comfort 2005, 27-39). The last part of Mark could not have been lost earlier if it was written on a scroll because this portion would have been rolled into the innermost part. The codex form of Mark could have contained just the Gospel of Mark or all four gospels set in the typical Western order: Matthew, John, Luke, Mark (which is the case for 𝔓[45]). In both scenarios, Mark 16 would have been the last sheet. However, it seems very odd and most unusual that this ending would not have survived in some manuscript somewhere. The history of textual transmission is characterized by tenacity; once a reading enters the textual stream, it will usually be preserved in some manuscript and show up somewhere down the line. Thus, this imagined ending to Mark must have been lost very soon after the composition of the Gospel, if there was such an ending.

It is possible that 16:7 was intended to be the concluding verse of the first paragraph of Mark's original last chapter (inasmuch as it concludes with the glorious angelic announcement of Christ's resurrection) and that 16:8 was the first sentence of the next paragraph. It seems that the last two words of 16:8, εφοβουντο γαρ ("for they were afraid"), could have been the first two words of a new sentence. Indeed, it is highly unusual for a sentence, let alone an entire gospel, to end with the conjunctive γαρ; so it is likely that some word or words followed, such as εφοβουντο γαρ λαλειν ("for they were afraid to speak"). After this, Mark's narrative would have continued to relate, most likely, that Jesus appeared to the women (as in Matthew and John), and that the women, no longer afraid, then went and told the disciples what they saw. This would have probably been followed by Jesus appearing to his disciples in Jerusalem and then in Galilee. This is the basic pattern found in the other gospels. And since Mark was probably used by the other gospel writers, it stands to reason that their narrative pattern reflects Mark's original work.

With respect to the inclusion of the various endings of Mark in WH NU, it would be better if the editions more accurately reflected the evidence of the earliest manuscripts and did, in fact, conclude the Gospel at 16:8. All the endings, then, should be placed in the textual apparatus. English translators should do the same: conclude the Gospel at 16:8 and then place all the endings in an extended footnote or endnote.

Mark 16:20

WH NU	omit αμην ("amen")
	A C^2 f^1 33 it syr cop^{sa}
	RSV NRSV ESV NASB NIV TNIV NEB REB NJB NAB NLT HCSB NET
variant/TR	include αμην ("amen")
	C* D^s L W Θ Ψ f^{13} Maj cop^{bo}
	KJV NKJV

Because the books of the NT were read out loud in church meetings, it became customary to end the reading with an "amen." Gradually, this spoken word was added onto the printed page of many late manuscripts. This addition took place in all four gospels and Acts. The exclusion of "amen" is attested to by several manuscripts which also include the longer ending. Those with a shorter ending (at 16:8), such as ℵ and B, do not include "amen."

Subscription

TR appends a subscription to the Gospel, as follows: Το κατα Μαρκον ευαγγελιον ("the Gospel according to Mark"). The codices ℵ and B also have subscriptions following 16:8. Codex Sinaiticus reads ευαγγελιον κατα Μαρκον ("Gospel according to Mark"), and B reads κατα Μαρκον ("According to Mark"). (For comments on this, see note on the Inscription to Mark.) The placement of the subscription immediately following 16:8 in ℵ and B affirms the conclusion of this gospel at this point in these codices.

Gospel according to LUKE

Inscription (Title)

WH NU	Κατα Λουκαν "According to Luke" א B (NIV TNIV NLT NET)
variant 1	Ευαγγελιον κατα Λουκαν "Gospel according to Luke" (A) D L W Θ Ξ Ψ 33 Maj NKJV RSV NRSV ESV NASB NEB REB NJB NAB HCSB
variant 2/TR	Το κατα Λουκαν Αγιον Ευαγγελιον "The Holy Gospel according to Luke" (Or, "The Gospel according to Saint Luke") 209 579 KJV
variant 3	Αρχη του κατα Λουκαν Αγιον Ευαγγελιον "The beginning of the Holy Gospel according to Luke" 1241 none

In its original composition, the Gospel of Luke was probably untitled. The first four verses, which served as the introduction or preface to the book, are far more descriptive of the content of the book than any title could be. Interestingly, three of the four Gospels have unique incipits signaled by the word αρχη ("beginning"): Mark commences with "The beginning of the gospel of Jesus Christ, the Son of God"; Luke traces his story from those who were "with Jesus from the beginning"; and John starts his gospel with the expression, "In the beginning was the Word."

Variant 1 represents the first stage in giving inscriptions to the Gospels. Each gospel was titled separately because each gospel often was a book by itself (see comments on the title to John). The WH NU reading reflects the second stage in titling the Gospels, a stage when all four gospels were placed together in one codex and were titled under one head: The Gospel—According to Matthew, According to Mark, According to Luke, According to John. This titling was mostly influenced by Codex Vaticanus, which has κατα μαθθαιον, κατα μαρκον, κατα λουκαν, κατα ιωαννην written for both the inscription and subscription in each gospel. Codex Sinaiticus has the same titling for the inscription, but in the subscription for Mark, Luke, and John the word ευαγγελιον ("Gospel") comes first (see comments on

Matthew's subscription). This reflects the fact that each gospel was titled separately in the earlier history of textual transmission.

Luke 1:3

Borrowing from Acts 15:28, a few Old Latin manuscripts (it[b,q]) expand the text to read, "it seemed good to me and the Holy Spirit."

Luke 1:9

In Luke 1–2, there is a strong Semitic element of naming God as "the Lord"; "the Lord" in this verse is not "the Lord Jesus Christ" but "Yahweh." Some scribes (C* D Ψ) wanted to make it absolutely clear that the "Lord" here was "God." Thus, they changed τον ναον του κυριου ("the temple of the Lord"), found in most manuscripts, to τον ναον του θεου ("the temple of God").

Luke 1:15

The best manuscript evidence (א A B C D L W f[1] 33) affirms the statement that John would be great before the "Lord" (κυριου). (This accords perfectly with 1 Sam 2:21.) As in 1:9 (see note), some scribes (Θ Ψ f[13] 700) changed κυριου ("Lord") to θεου ("God") in order to make it clear that—according to their interpretation—the Lord here is Yahweh, not the Lord Jesus Christ.

Luke 1:26

According to א B L W and other witnesses, the angel Gabriel was sent from (απο) God. The preposition was changed in A C D Θ 33 Maj (so TR) to υπο ("by"). This adjustment obfuscates the spatial imagery of Gabriel having come *from* God to earth.

Luke 1:27

Superior external evidence (A B D W) supports the reading εξ οικου Δαυιδ ("of the house of David"). Borrowing from 2:4, a few manuscripts (א C L f[1] 700) expand it to εξ οικου και πατριας Δαυιδ ("of the house and lineage of David").

Luke 1:28a

The subject of the first clause (assumed to be the angel Gabriel) is left unspecified in B L W Θ and other manuscripts. This subject, ο αγγελος ("the angel"), is supplied in A C D f[13] 33 Maj. The shorter reading is likely original.

Luke 1:28b

WH NU ὁ κύριος μετὰ σοῦ.
"The Lord is with you."
א B L W Ψ f[1] 565 700 cop
NKJVmg RSV NRSV ESV NASB NIV TNIV NEB REB NJB NAB NLT HCSB NET

variant/TR ο κυριος μετα σου. ευλογημενη συ εν γυναιξιν.
"The Lord is with you. You are blessed among women."
A C D Θ f^{13} 33 Maj
KJV NKJV RSVmg NRSVmg ESVmg NASBmg NJBmg NLTmg HCSBmg NETmg

The variant reading is an expansion borrowed from 1:42, where it is Elizabeth who says that Mary is "blessed among women." KJV and NKJV reflect the expansion of TR, whereas the modern versions do not. (It is only out of respect to the KJV tradition that the variant is noted in many of the modern versions.)

Luke 1:29

WH NU ἡ δὲ ἐπὶ τῷ λόγῳ διεταράχθη
"but she was troubled by his message"
א B D L W Ψ f^{1}
NKJVmg RSV NRSV ESV NASB NIV TNIV NEB REB NJB NAB NLT HCSB NET

variant 1/TR η δε ιδουσα επι τω λογω διεταραχθη
"but seeing [him] she was troubled by his message"
A C Θ 0130 f^{13} 33 Maj
KJV NKJV NETmg

variant 2 η δε ακουσασα επι τω λογω διεταραχθη
"but hearing [him] she was troubled by his message"
1194
none

The WH NU reading has superior documentation. The two variants are narrative gap-fillers, the first of which found its way into the majority of manuscripts, TR, and the KJV tradition.

Luke 1:35

TR WH NU τὸ γεννώμενον
"the one being born"
א A B D
NKJV RSV NRSV ESV NASB NIV TNIV NEB REB NJB NAB NLT HCSB NET

variant το γεννωμενον εκ σου
"the one being born of you"
C* Θ f^{1} 33 Diatessaron
KJV NKJVmg RSVmg NRSVmg NETmg

It is possible that the addition of εκ σου ("of you") was prompted only by stylistic concerns—to achieve balance with the two previous occurrences of the second person pronoun in this verse. However, it is just as likely that the addition was produced by Tatian (in the Diatessaron), who wanted to emphasize Mary's role in the birthing of the Son of God (see TCGNT). In TR WH NU, Mary's participation is limited: The Holy Spirit came upon her and the power of the Most High overshadowed her (like a tabernacle), resulting in the birth of the holy one, the Son of God. Only one version, the KJV, followed the variant, and not by following TR. A few other versions, however, note the inclusion of the phrase "of you."

Luke 1:37

WH NU	οὐκ ἀδυνατήσει παρὰ τοῦ θεοῦ πᾶν ῥῆμα "no word from God can ever fail" א* B (D) L W 565 TNIV NEB REB
variant/TR	ουκ αδυνατησει παρα τω θεω παν ρημα "nothing will be impossible with God" א² A C Θ f(1),13 33 Maj KJV NKJV (RSV NRSV ESV NASB NIV) NEBmg REBmg (NJB NAB NLT HCSB NET)

The variant is probably the result of a grammatical adjustment, changing a Semitic genitive (του θεου) to a more usual dative, τω θεω (Nolland 1989, 40); or the variant may be the result of scribal harmonization to Gen 18:14 in the Septuagint. The text can be rendered in two ways, based on whether ρημα is translated as "word" or "thing." For the former, the idea is that God is able to do whatever he says he will do—literally, "no word from God will be powerless." Mary will conceive and give birth to the Son of God. For the latter, the idea is that "nothing will be impossible for God" (lit. "nothing from God is impossible"). Since this latter translation is basically equivalent to the variant reading, it is not entirely clear which reading the various English translations were following. However, since the NEB and REB translators note the variant reading in the margin, they made it clear they were following WH NU. Note also the change from NIV to TNIV.

Luke 1:41

A few witnesses (א* 565c) harmonized this verse to 1:44 by adding that the baby in Elizabeth's womb leaped "with joy" (εν αγαλλιασει) when Mary came to her house.

Luke 1:46

According to several Old Latin witnesses (ita,b,l Irenaeuslat) and Origenaccording to Jerome, the woman who speaks the *Magnificat* is Elizabeth, not Mary (see NJBmg NABmg). Although "Elizabeth" is the more difficult reading, the textual evidence is slim. The Old Latin witnesses are from the fourth, fifth, and seventh centuries respectively. Irenaeus's support is gathered from Armenian and Latin translations of *Against Heresies* 4.7.1, and Origen's attestation comes from Jerome's translation of *Homilies in Luke* 7. As such, there is not one Greek manuscript that has the reading "Elizabeth." Thus, according to documentary evidence, the reading would have to be "Mary."

Nonetheless, it has been argued on internal grounds that the text originally read "Elizabeth" and was changed to "Mary" because of the deep respect that Christians have given to Mary. Those who argue for Elizabeth say that the hymn provides a parallel to Zechariah's *Benedictus* (1:67-79) and that Elizabeth, a childless woman, is a better antitype to Hannah (whose song this one follows) than is Mary (see Burkitt 1905, 220-227).

Others have argued that the text originally did not have any one named, so scribes later added "Mary" or "Elizabeth." Those who added "Elizabeth" carried over the subject/speaker from 1:41-45, and those who added "Mary" assumed it from 1:56. However, 1:56 is very ambiguous in that it could be used to argue for Mary or Elizabeth as the speaker of the *Magnificat*. (For a thorough discussion, see Laurentin 1957, 15-23.)

Luke 1:66

The last sentence of this verse in WH NU, και γαρ χειρ κυριου ην μετ αυτου ("for the hand of the Lord was with him"), has excellent support: 𝔓[4] ℵ B C* L W Ψ. But it was problematic for various scribes. Several copyists (A C[2] Θ f[1,13] Maj—so TR), finding it difficult to see the direct connection between the people's comment ("what then will this child become?") and the following statement, dropped γαρ ("for"). Other scribes (D it) dropped the verb ην ("was") in an attempt to make the last sentence part of the people's remark: "what then will this child be, for the Lord's hand [is] with him?"

Luke 1:68

TR WH NU	Εὐλογητὸς κύριος ὁ θεὸς τοῦ Ἰσραήλ "Blessed be [the] Lord, the God of Israel" ℵ A B C D KJV NKJV RSV NRSV ESV NASB NIV TNIV REB NJB NAB NLT HCSB NET
variant	Ευλογητος ο θεος του Ισραηλ "Blessed be the God of Israel" 𝔓[4] W it syr[s] cop[saMSS] NEB

Although it could be argued that κυριος ("Lord") was dropped due to homoeoteleuton (ευλογητος/κυριος), in ancient manuscripts κυριος was written as a nomen sacrum, KC. Thus, this is not likely to have happened. It is more likely that κυριος was added in order to make the quotation conform to the Septuagint (Pss 41:13 [40:14]; 106:48 [105:48]). Nonetheless, the expression "the Lord God" is typically Lukan (see 1:16, 32, 68; 4:12; 10:27; 20:37) and has good attestation.

Luke 1:78

WH NU	ἐπισκέψεται ἡμᾶς ἀνατολη "the dayspring will visit us" 𝔓[4vid] ℵ* B L W Θ 0177 NKJVmg RSV NRSV ESV NASB NIV TNIV NEB REB NAB NLT HCSB NET
variant/TR	επεσκεψατο ημας ανατολη "the dayspring has visited us" ℵ[2] A C D Ξ Ψ 0130 f[1,13] 33 Maj KJV NKJV RSVmg NRSVmg NEBmg NJB

𝔓[4vid] is not listed in NA[27] or UBS[4], probably because the manuscript is very difficult to read in this place. My examination of the actual manuscript shows that the word in 𝔓[4] is επισκεψεται ("will visit"), not επεσκεψατο ("has visited") because the letter before the lacuna is a broken *iota* (επι), not a broken *epsilon* (επε).

The change from the future tense to the aorist (past) is more probable than vice versa because the same verb is aorist in Luke 1:68. Even though the verb is future, the expression in context points to Christ's first advent—his visitation as the sunrise or dayspring from the heavens to the earth. The word ανατολη has a secondary meaning: branch or shoot (see BDAG 74), which was used in the Septuagint to translate the Hebrew word for "Branch" (Isa 11:11; Jer 23:5; 33:15; Zech 3:8; 6:12). The dual image celebrates Christ's coming as the dayspring and Branch. In fact, this is the only NT reference to the OT messianic title, "Branch."

Luke 1:80

By writing the nomen sacrum for πνευματι ($\overline{\text{ΠΝΙ}}$), the scribes of 𝔓4 C L W Θ Ψ made it clear that, according to their interpretation, John the Baptist was strengthened by the divine Spirit. This contrasts with English versions, which put the emphasis on his human spirit: "he grew strong in spirit."

Luke 2:2

All manuscripts except two support this translation of the verse: "this was the first registration while Quirinius was governor of Syria." Two manuscripts, ℵ* and D, reorder the words αυτη απογραφη πρωτη εγενετο ("this was the first registration") to αυτη απογραφη εγενετο πρωτη ("this registration occurred before"). A fuller translation of this variant is: "This registration occurred before Quirinius was governor of Syria" (see Turner 1965, 23-24, who defends this translation). This reading indicates that Luke was referring to a registration (census) conducted prior to Quirinius's well-known census in A.D. 6–7, referred to in Acts 5:37 (Fitzmeyer 1981, 401). The variant is obviously an attempt to get around the difficulty of coinciding the date of this registration (census) with the more likely date of Jesus' birth, 6–5 B.C. Nonetheless, it is possible that Quirinius enacted a previous census around 6 B.C., of which we have no other historical record (DJG 68).

Luke 2:3

Nearly all the manuscripts indicate that, in response to the census, everyone traveled to his own city (πολιν). However, there are two variants: (1) χωραν ("region") in C* and (2) πατριδι ("native land") in D. These variants are scribal attempts to deal with the problem of saying that Joseph and Mary had to return to Bethlehem as their "own city," when 2:39 clearly says that Nazareth was their "own city." Apparently, the Jews were required in this census to return to their primary place of residence, which would have been ancestrally determined (Nolland 1989, 104). Joseph, being descended from the line of David, would have regarded Bethlehem as his ancestral city.

Luke 2:9

The expression δοξα κυριου ("glory of the Lord") has excellent testimony from ℵ A B C etc. But as occasionally happened in the first chapters of Luke, κυριου ("Lord") was changed to θεου ("God")—see ℵ2 Ξ Ψ 892. (See notes on 2:38a; 3:6.)

Luke 2:11

The unusual expression Χριστος κυριος ("Christ Lord"), which appears only here in the NT, was changed to the more usual κυριος Χριστος ("Lord Christ") in W syr^{p,s} and rendered as "the Lord's Christ" in a few Old Latin texts. Strictly speaking, the grammar indicates two nominative titles, Χριστος and κυριος. Based on Acts 2:36, it is likely that Luke intended that readers understand that Jesus was to be both "Christ" and "Lord." However, the anarthrous expression allows for the rendering, "anointed Lord" (as in Lam 4:20 LXX).

Luke 2:14

WH NU   ἐπὶ γῆς εἰρήνη ἐν ἀνθρώποις εὐδοκίας
"on earth peace among men of [God's] pleasure"
א* A B* D W cop[sa]
NKJVmg RSV NRSV ESV NASB NIV TNIV NEB REB NJB NAB NLT HCSB NET

variant/TR   επι γης ειρηνη εν ανθρωποις ευδοκια
"on earth peace, good pleasure [= will] among [= toward] men"
א[2] B[2] L Θ Ξ Ψ f[1,13] Maj Eusebius
KJV NKJV RSVmg NRSVmg NEBmg NJBmg NABmg HCSBmg NETmg

The WH NU reading has excellent documentary support. Westcott and Hort (1882, 54) wrote, "the agreement, not only of א with B, but of D and all the Latins with both, and of A with them all, supported by Origen in at least one work, and that in a certified text, affords a peculiarly strong presumption in favor of ευδοκιας."

The orthographic difference between the two readings is simply one letter: ευδοκιας/ ευδοκια. The first is genitive for "good pleasure/good will," the second is nominative. The genitive expression reflects a Semitic expression meaning "good pleasure of God." The entire clause means that peace is given on earth to those in whom God takes pleasure. Another way to say this is that God's peace rests on those whom he has chosen—i.e., it was God's good pleasure to select certain people to be the recipients of his peace that came with the coming of the Savior, Jesus Christ. Various documents among the Dead Sea Scrolls affirm this Semitic expression, such as "the sons of God's good pleasure" (1QH[a] 4:32-33) and "the elect of God's good pleasure" (1QH 11:9). The Coptic Sahidic translation of Luke 2:14 also affirms this reading: "peace among men of his pleasure."

Unaware of this Semitism or uncomfortable with ευδοκιας, scribes corrected it to ευδοκια. Indeed, two separate correctors emended א and B in this fashion. (In this light, it is quite unlikely that the final sigma was accidentally dropped.) The resultant text yields the well-known triplet: "glory to God in the highest, and peace on earth, good will toward men." Even though this sounds poetic, the couplet (joined by και) is far more balanced poetry. Furthermore, the expression "good will toward men" can be misleading, because Jesus did not come to promote a kind of good will among human beings (often associated with Christmas cheer). Jesus was sent by God to those whom God had chosen according to his good pleasure. This is close to Eph 1:3-6, 9, wherein Paul reveals that God's election was motivated by his good pleasure (ευδοκιαν).

Luke 2:22

TR WH NU   τοῦ καθαρισμοῦ αὐτῶν
"their purification"
א A B L W Θ f[1,13] Maj
RSV NRSV ESV NASB NIV NEB NJB NAB NLT HCSB NET

variant 1   του καθαρισμου αυτου
"his purification"
D syr[s]
none

variant 2   του καθαρισμου
"the purification"
435 cop[bo]
TNIV (REB)

variant 3 του καθαρισμου αυτης
"her purification"
76
KJV NKJV NJBmg NETmg

The TR WH NU reading, though strongly supported, is puzzling because the law of Moses called for the purification of only the woman who gave birth (see Lev 12:6), not the husband or child. This problem prompted the variants listed above. The first indicates that the baby Jesus was purified, the second leaves the matter ambiguous, and the third specifically identifies Mary. The third reading, supported by one late cursive manuscript (76), was adopted in the Complutensian Polyglot Bible (1514) and several of Beza's editions, which was followed by KJV. "It is a remarkable instance of a reading which had almost no authority becoming widely adopted" (Plummer 1896, 63).

In defense of the TR WH NU reading, Luke may have considered the purification a family matter, involving both Mary and Joseph (the grammatical subjects of the verse). But commentators since Origen have tried to make "their" refer to Mary and Jesus (Fitzmeyer 1981, 424), arguing that the purification of Mary and the presentation of Jesus were considered as two aspects of one "cleansing" (Marshall 1978, 116).

Luke 2:33

WH NU ὁ πατὴρ αὐτοῦ καὶ ἡ μήτηρ
"his father and the (= his) mother"
א[1] B D W f[1] cop[sa,bo] Origen
NKJVmg RSV NRSV ESV NASB NIV TNIV NEB REB NJB NAB NLT HCSB NET

variant 1 ο πατηρ αυτου και η μητηρ αυτου
"his father and his mother"
א* L syr[s]
(same as above)

variant 2/TR Ιωσηφ και η μητηρ αυτου
"Joseph and his mother"
(A) Θ (Ψ) f[13] 33 Maj it syr
KJV NKJV HCSBmg NETmg

These are the three principal variants of this text; there are several others (especially among the ancient versions), but none significantly vary from these. The first variant reading is simply lexical balancing (i.e., making sure αυτου follows both nouns—modern English translators do the same). The second is a calculated recension. The natural description of Joseph and Mary as the father and mother of Jesus caused offense to various scribes and led to this alteration (Marshall 1978, 121) in TR and KJV.

Luke 2:37

WH NU αὐτὴ χήρα ἕως ἐτῶν ὀγδοήκοντα τεσσάρων
"she was a widow [up] until eighty-four years"
א* A B L N Ξ Ψ 0130 33
NKJVmg RSV NRSV ESV NASB NIV TNIVmg REB NAB NLT

variant 1/TR αυτη χηρα ως ετων ογδοηκοντα τεσσαρων
"she was a widow about eighty-four years"
ℵ[2] W Θ f[1,13] Maj
KJV NKJV

variant 2 αυτη χηρα ετων ογδοηκοντα τεσσαρων
"she was a widow eighty-four years"
D it
ESVmg NIVmg TNIV NLTmg HCSB NET

Exegetes and translators alike have been baffled as to what to make of Luke's description of the widow. Was she an eighty-four-year-old woman who also happened to be a widow? Or had she been widowed for eighty-four years? The problem is with the word εως, which means "until." The Greek is literally translated in the NIV: "she was a widow until she was eighty-four." This leaves open several possible interpretations: (1) she was an eighty-four-year-old widow; (2) she lived until she was eighty-four and was a widow ever since her husband died seven years into the marriage; (3) she was a widow to the age of eighty-four but not anymore. Of the three possibilities, the second seems most likely. Luke, from his perspective (writing in the A.D. 60s or 70s) was simply stating how long the woman lived—eighty-four years. She lived most of those years as a widow serving God. Thus, Luke was not necessarily saying that the woman was an eighty-four-year-old widow at the time she saw the baby Jesus in the temple. In any event, various scribes saw the polyvalence of the text and tried to cure it in one of two ways: (1) change εως ("until") to ως ("about") so as to make her a widow "about" eighty-four years old; (2) get rid of εως so as to make her an eighty-four-year-old widow. Some modern English versions bypass the problem by making two statements: She was a widow, and she was eighty-four years old (so NEB NJB NLT).

Luke 2:38a

WH NU ἀνθωμολογεῖτο τῷ θεῷ
"praising God"
all Greek MSS
NKJVmg RSV NRSV ESV NASB NIV TNIV NEB REB NJB NAB NLT HCSB NET

variant/TR ανθωμολογειτο τω κυριω
"praising the Lord"
Vulgate
KJV NKJV

With no Greek manuscript support, TR, following the Vulgate, has "Lord" instead of "God." The Vulgate may represent a christological interpretation, in the sense that "Lord" would convey "Lord Jesus" (see notes on 2:9; 3:6).

Luke 2:38b

WH NU λύτρωσιν 'Ιερουσαλήμ
redemption of Jerusalem
ℵ B W Ξ 565* syr[p,s] cop
RSV NRSV ESV NASB NIV TNIV NEB REB NJB NAB NLT HCSB NET

variant 1/TR λυτρωσιν εν Ιερουσαλημ
"redemption in Jerusalem"
A D L Θ Ψ 0130 33 f[13] Maj
KJV NKJV HCSBmg NETmg

variant 2 λυτρωσιν Ισραηλ
"redemption of Israel"
1216 it[a,r]
NETmg

The WH NU reading, which has the best documentary support, signifies that people in Jerusalem were anticipating that Jerusalem would be delivered by the Messiah from Roman rule (see Isa 52:9). "Redemption" (also translated as "deliverance") signified total deliverance from Roman rule. Indeed, during the second revolt of the Palestinian Jews against Rome (A.D. 132–135), documents were sometimes dated to the years of "the Redemption of Israel" (Fitzmeyer 1981, 432). This conception of redemption accords well with the general tenor of Luke's opening chapters, wherein there are great expectations expressed for military deliverance by the mighty hand of the Messiah (see 1:51-52, 68-71, 74; 2:11, 30-31, 34). But the reading of the text was altered by later scribes (see first variant) in the direction of spiritualizing the redemption—i.e., Jesus' redemption for sins took place on a cross in Jerusalem. Other scribes changed "Jerusalem" to "Israel," thereby enlarging the recipient of redemption to include the whole nation, not just the residents of the capital city, Jerusalem.

Luke 2:39

Noting that the verse says that Jesus' parents took him back to Nazareth, the scribe of D (also it[a]) could not resist adding an adaptation of Matt 2:23 here—καθως ερρεθη δια του προφητου οτι Ναζαωραιος κληθησεται ("as it was said through the prophet, 'he will be called a Nazarene' ").

Luke 2:40

WH NU ηὔξανεν καὶ ἐκραταιοῦτο
"he grew and was strengthened"
ℵ B D L N W syr[s] cop
NKJVmg RSV NRSV ESV NASB NIV TNIV NEB REB NJB NAB NLT HCSB NET

variant/TR ηυξανεν και εκραταιουτο πνευματι
"he grew and was strengthened in spirit"
A Θ Ψ f[1,13] 33 Maj
KJV NKJV NETmg

The variant is the result of scribal conformity to Luke 1:80, which says that John the Baptist was εκραταιουτο πνευματι ("strengthened in spirit/by the Spirit"). (See note on 1:80.)

Luke 2:41, 43, 48

In these verses (as in 2:33), various scribes, trying to preserve the doctrine of the virgin birth, altered the text so that it would not say that Joseph and Mary were the parents of Jesus. In 2:41, the expression γονεις αυτου ("his parents") were changed to "Joseph and Mary" in many Old Latin manuscripts. In 2:43, again, the expression οι γονεις αυτου ("his parents"), found in ℵ B D L W Θ f[1] 33, was changed in many later manuscripts (A C Ψ 0130 Maj—so TR) to Ιωσηφ και η μητηρ αυτου ("Joseph and his [Jesus'] mother"). In 2:48, the words ο πατηρ σου καγω ("your father and I") were altered to "we" in it[a,b,l] syr[s].

Luke 3:6

D syr[c,s] substituted το σωτηριον του κυριου ("the salvation of the Lord") for το σωτηριον του θεου ("the salvation of God"). As occasionally happened in the early chapters of Luke (see notes on 2:9; 2:38a), scribes "christianized" the text by changing "God" to "Lord" (i.e., the Lord Jesus Christ).

Luke 3:9

All three editions (TR WH NU) read καρπον καλον ("good fruit"), with the solid testimony of ℵ A B C L W f[1,13]. A few witnesses, however, have the shorter καρπον ("fruit"): 𝔓[4] it[a,aur,ff2] Origen Irenaeus. The expression is plural (καρπους καλους) in D syr[c,p,s]. Although the text has excellent documentary support, it is possible that this reading was harmonized to the parallel passage, Matt 3:10. Indeed, the earliest reading (found in 𝔓[4] and supported by Origen and Irenaeus) lacks the adjective. (Compare Matt 3:10, where the adjective καλον is lacking in syr[s] and Irenaeus). The second variant, which pluralizes the text, is the result of Western editorialization.

Luke 3:10

At the end of this verse, several scribes made additions to the question the people asked John the Baptist, Τι ουν ποιησωμεν; ("what then should we do?"). Borrowing from Acts 16:30, D and some cop[sa] manuscripts have the expansion, "What then should we do that we may be saved?" whereas other cop[sa] manuscripts and some Old Latin manuscripts (it[b,q]) read, "What then should we do that we may live?"

Luke 3:16

Borrowing from Matt 3:11, some scribes (C D) added εις μετανοιαν ("unto repentance") after εγω μεν υδατι βαπτιζω υμας ("I baptize you with water").

A few witnesses (64 Tertullian) omit αγιω ("holy") from the expression βαπτισει εν πνευματι αγιω και πυρι. The absence of αγιω allows for the translation "he will baptize you in wind and fire." This is an interesting rendering inasmuch as the following image (in 3:17) depicts chaff being blown away by the wind (as the result of winnowing) and then consumed by the fire. English translations cannot effectively reflect the double meaning of πνευμα as wind and spirit.

Luke 3:19

Several manuscripts (A C W Ψ 33 565), showing conformity to Matt 14:3 and Mark 6:17, add Φιλιππου ("Philip") to the identification of Herod's brother. (See notes on Matt 14:3 and Mark 6:17).

Luke 3:22a

Most manuscripts read το πνευμα το αγιον σωματικω ("the Holy Spirit in bodily form [descended]"). 𝔓[75] lacks the article before πνευμα, and 𝔓[4] reads το $\overline{\text{ΠΝΑ}}$ το αγιον $\overline{\text{ΠΝΙ}}$. The editor for the text of 𝔓[4] (Merell 1938) explained $\overline{\text{ΠΝΙ}}$ as a simple case of dittography. But if that had been so, why did the scribe not write $\overline{\text{ΠΝΑ}}$ again? Rather, he seems to have intentionally changed to the dative, ΠΝΙ = πνευματι. As such, 𝔓[4] has this interesting variation that can be rendered in at least two ways: (1) "the Holy Spirit descended in spiritual form," or (2) "the Holy Spirit descended as spirit." The first option provides a creative alternative to the difficult idea of the Spirit descending in bodily form.

Luke 3:22b

TR WH NU	σὺ εἶ ὁ υἱός μου ὁ ἀγαπητός, ἐν σοὶ εὐδόκησα. "You are my Son, the beloved, in whom I am well pleased." 𝔓[4] ℵ A B L W 070 33 MSS[according to Augustine] KJV NKJV RSV NRSV ESV NASB NIV TNIV NEB REB NJBmg NAB NLT HCSB NET
variant	υιος μου ει συ, εγω σημερον γεγεννηκα σε "You are my Son; this day I have begotten you." D it Justin (Clement) Hilary MSS[according to Augustine] RSVmg NRSVmg ESVmg NEBmg REBmg NJB NABmg NLTmg NETmg

The TR WH NU reading has the earliest and most diverse documentary support. The variant reading is later and more localized (in the west)—a true "Western" reading. Augustine knew of both readings, although he made it clear that the variant reading was "not found in the more ancient manuscripts" (*Cons.* 2.14).

In spite of the documentary evidence, many scholars have defended the variant reading as being the more difficult reading and therefore more likely original. They argue that the reading was originally a full quotation of Ps 2:7, which (in the words of the NJB translators) shows Jesus to be "the King-Messiah of the Ps [2:7] enthroned at the Baptism to establish the rule of God in the world." This reading was then harmonized to the baptism accounts in Matt 3:17 and Mark 1:11 by orthodox scribes trying to avoid having the text say that Jesus was "begotten" on the day of his baptism—an erroneous view held by the Adoptionists. (For a full discussion of this issue, see Ehrman 1993, 62-67.) However, it can be argued the scribe of D (known for his creative editorialization) changed the text to replicate Ps 2:7 or was himself influenced by adoptionist views. Indeed, the variant reading was included in the second-century *Gospel of the Ebionites,* who were chief among the Adoptionists. "They regarded Jesus as the son of Joseph and Mary, but elected Son of God at his baptism when he was united with the eternal Christ" (NIDCC).

In any case, Ps 2:7 appears to have been used exclusively by NT writers with reference to Jesus' resurrection from the dead (Acts 13:33; Heb 1:5; 5:5). Since in Luke's book of Acts it is explicitly used to affirm the prophetic word about Jesus' resurrection, it would seem odd that he would use it to affirm Jesus' baptism. Given the TR WH NU reading, it seems more likely that Luke was thinking of Ps 2:7 for the first part of the statement ("this is my beloved Son") and Isa 42:1 for the second part ("in whom I am well pleased"). The Isaiah passage is especially fitting given its connection with the Messiah's reception of the Spirit.

Luke 3:23-38

Who reads genealogies? Evidently, not the scribe of W, who omitted this section entirely! Perhaps he thought he was producing a reader's Bible; therefore, trying to serve his readers' best interest, he omitted a passage that would not be read orally to a congregation. The scribe of D was also at work with Luke's genealogy. He conformed Luke 3:23-31 to Matt 1:6-16—in reverse order!

Other harmonizations to Matthew's genealogy are present in various manuscripts. In Luke 3:32, several manuscripts (ℵ[2] A D L Θ Ψ 0102 33 Maj—so TR) read Σαλμον ("Salmon"), harmonized from Matt 1:4-5, as opposed to Σαλα ("Sala"), found in the earliest manuscripts, 𝔓[4] ℵ* B (so WH NU).

In Luke 3:33 there are many variations on the reading του Αμιναδαβ του Αδμιν του Αρνι ("[the son] of Amminadab, [the son] of Admin, [the son] of Arni"), supported by 𝔓[4vid] ℵ[2] L f^{13} cop[bo]. The critical apparatus of NA[27] indicates that 𝔓[4vid] (along with ℵ* 1241) reads του Αδαμ του Αδμιν του Αρνι, ("[the son] of Adam, [the son] of Admin, [the son] of Arni"). This is a possible reconstruction of 𝔓[4], but the first reading is also possible—the only letter that clearly shows for the first name is the initial *alpha,* whether for Αμιναδαβ or Αδαμ. Codex B omits του Αμινιδαβ. The manuscripts A D 33 565 read του Αμιναδαβ του Αραμ ("[the son] of Amminidab, [the son] of Ram"—see Matt 1:4). Other manuscripts (Δ Ψ 700 it[b,e]) replace Αρνι with Ιωραμ ("Joram"). Codex A omits του Φαρες ("[the son] of Phares").

Luke 4:1

WH NU ἤγετο ἐν τῷ πνεύματι ἐν τῇ ἐρήμῳ
"he was led by the Spirit in the wilderness"
𝔓[4] 𝔓[7] 𝔓[75] ℵ B D L W
RSV NRSV ESV TNIV NEB REB NLT HCSB NET

variant/TR ηγετο εν τω πνευματι εις την ερημον
"he was led by the Spirit into the wilderness"
A Θ Ξ Ψ 0102 $f^{1,13}$ 33 Maj
KJV NKJV NASB NIV NJB NAB NETmg

The WH NU reading has early and diverse support. The variant reading is the result of scribal conformity to Matt 4:1 and Mark 1:12, a reading that was followed by several English versions. The Lukan account, according to the best witnesses, allows for the interpretation that the Spirit's leading was durative—not just directional (into the wilderness). Whereas Matthew and Mark emphasize that the Spirit led Jesus (after his baptism) from the Jordan River into the wilderness, Luke's account relates that the Spirit was leading Jesus every day he was in the wilderness.

Luke 4:2

The word διαβολου ("devil"), found in most manuscripts, was changed to Σατανα ("Satan") in D it[e] syr[s], by way of conformity to Mark 1:13, a parallel verse.

Luke 4:4

WH NU οὐκ ἐπ' ἄρτῳ μόνῳ ζήσεται ὁ ἄνθρωπος.
"A person does not live by bread alone."
ℵ B L W syr[s] cop[sa]
RSV NRSV ESV NASB NIV TNIV NEB REB NJB NAB NLT HCSB NET

variant/TR ουκ επ αρτω μονω ζησεται ο ανθρωπος αλλ επι παντι ρηματι θεου.
"A person does not live by bread alone but by every word of God."
A (D) Θ Ψ $f^{1,13}$ 33 Maj
KJV NKJV HCSBmg NETmg

The expanded reading in the variant is the result of scribal conformity to Matt 4:4, the parallel passage. Such harmonizations fill TR, which is followed by KJV and NKJV.

Luke 4:5-12

Many Old Latin manuscripts and Ambrose in his commentary on Luke transposed Luke 4:5-8 with 4:9-12 in order to make Luke's account of Jesus' temptation conform to Matthew's account.

Luke 4:5

WH NU καὶ ἀναγαγὼν αὐτόν
"and having led him up"
א* B L
(RSV NRSV ESV NASB NIV TNIV) NEB (NJB) NAB (NLT) HCSB (NET)

variant/TR και αναγαγων αυτον ο διαβολος εις ορος υψηλον
"and the devil, having led him up to a high mountain"
A Θ Ψ 0102 (f[13]) 33 Maj it (omit ο διαβολος א[1] D W f[1])
KJV NKJV HCSBmg NETmg

Again, the expanded reading in the variant is the result of scribal conformity to Matt 4:8, the parallel passage. And, again, this harmonization found its way into TR, followed by KJV and NKJV. According to Luke, it is left unclear where Satan led Jesus to show him all the kingdoms of the world. Perhaps Luke dropped the detail about the mountain because he realized it must be metaphorical, inasmuch as "there is no literal mountain from which one may see the whole world" (Marshall 1978, 171). Many English versions substitute "devil" for "he" for the sake of clarity.

Luke 4:8

WH NU omit Υπαγε οπισω μου Σατανα ("get behind me Satan")
א B D L W f[1] 33
RSV NRSV ESV NASB NIV TNIV NEB REB NJB NAB NLT HCSB NET

variant/TR include
A Θ Ψ 0102 f[13] Maj it
KJV NKJV HCSBmg NETmg

The WH NU reading has early and diverse testimony. The variant reading is the result of scribal conformity to Matt 4:10 (the parallel passage), expanded further by Matt 16:23.

Luke 4:12

Instead of ειρηται ("it is said"), found in most manuscripts, D and W read γεγραπται ("it is written"). This change is the result of scribal harmonization to the immediate context, wherein γεγραπται was previously used to introduce biblical citations (see 4:4, 8, 10).

Luke 4:17

TR NU ἀναπτύξας τὸ βιβλίον
"having unrolled the book"
א (D*) Θ Ψ f[1,13] Maj
NRSV ESV NIV TNIV NJB NAB NLT HCSB NET

variant/WH ανοιξας το βιβλιον
"having opened the book"
A B L W Ξ 33
KJV NKJV RSV NASB NEB REB

The documentary support for the two readings is evenly divided. Thus, we turn to internal considerations to determine the most likely original reading. The verb for unrolling a scroll is usually αναπτυσσω (see BDAG 71). This is the verb in NU that is used to describe what Jesus did with the scroll of Isaiah before reading a portion of it to his hometown congregation in Nazareth: "he unrolled [αναπτυξας] the scroll." The other verb, ανοιξας, is the generic term for "opening"; it could be used for opening a scroll or a codex. It is possible that Christian scribes in later generations would be more familiar with the Scriptures being in codex form (i.e., a book with leaves stitched together at the spine). Thus, it would have been natural for some of these scribes to change the verb αναπτυξας ("unroll") to ανοιξας ("open"). In any case, it seems that Luke wrote "unrolled" because the antonym πτυξας ("rolled up") is used in 4:20, uncontested by any variant readings.

Luke 4:18

WH NU κηρύξαι αἰχμαλώτοις ἄφεσιν
"to proclaim release to the captives"
ℵ B D L W f^{13} 33 syr^{s} cop Origen Eusebius Didymus
NKJVmg RSV NRSV ESV NASB NIV TNIV NEB REB NJB NAB NLT HCSB NET

variant/TR ιασασθαι τους συντετριμμενους την καρδιαν, κηρυξαι αιχμαλωτοις αφεσιν
"to heal the brokenhearted, to proclaim release to the captives"
A Θ Ψ 0102 f^{1} Maj
KJV NKJV NJBmg HCSBmg NETmg

This textual variant is troublesome for some people because it involves the reading of OT Scriptures (Isa 61:1-2) by Jesus, who—it is presumed—would not have omitted a line of text. Thus, the scribes are blamed for omitting the phrase "to heal the brokenhearted." But there is no reason why scribes would have done this if the words appeared in their exemplars. The only conclusion is that the omission was the work of Luke.

First of all, it must be said that Jesus was reading the Hebrew Scriptures. Luke does not make any attempt to replicate them in Greek. Rather, his source was the Septuagint, from which he omitted the clause, "to heal the brokenhearted," perhaps because he viewed Jesus' healing ministry as dealing with physical sickness only. Luke did not consider it his obligation to quote the entire passage verbatim; indeed, most scholars recognize that he omitted Isa 61:2b ("the day of vengeance of our God") because this phrase was also not within the scope of Jesus' ministry.

Above all these considerations, the WH NU reading has to be accepted as original because it is supported by early and diverse witnesses. The variant reading, which has poorer support, must be deemed a scribal interpolation that brings Luke's text into conformity with Isa 61:1-2 (LXX). (The scribe of A, especially, had a habit of conforming OT citations to the LXX.)

Luke 4:31

In order to harmonize Luke's account with Matthew's (see Matt 4:12-16), the scribe of D added την παραθαλασσιον εν οριοις Ζαβουλων και Νεφθαλιμ ("beside the sea in the territory of Zebulun and Naphtali").

Luke 4:41

WH NU — σὺ εἶ ὁ υἱὸς τοῦ θεοῦ
"You are the Son of God."
𝔓[75vid] ℵ B C D L W 33 700 syr[s] cop[sa] Marcion Origen
NKJVmg RSV NRSV ESV NASB NIV TNIV NEB REB NJB NAB NLT HCSB NET

variant/TR — συ ει ο Χριστος, ο υιος του θεου
"You are the Christ, the Son of God."
A Q Θ Ψ 0102 f[1,13] Maj
KJV NKJV NETmg

𝔓[75] is not listed in NA[27], but it supports the WH NU reading (see *Text of Earliest MSS,* 508). The variant is a scribal expansion that occurred in almost every gospel text where Jesus is identified by others as "the Son of God." Influenced by Matt 16:16 and other passages, scribes could not resist adding "the Christ." The expansion became part of TR and KJV tradition.

Luke 4:44

WH NU — συναγωγὰς τῆς 'Ιουδαίας
"synagogues of Judea"
𝔓[75] ℵ B (C L) Q
RSV NRSV ESV NASB NIV TNIV NEB REB NJB NAB NLT HCSBmg NET

variant 1/TR — συναγωγαις της Γαλιλαιας
"synagogues of Galilee"
A D Θ Ψ f[13] 33 Maj
KJV NKJV RSVmg NRSVmg ESVmg NASBmg NIVmg NEBmg NJBmg NLTmg HCSB NETmg

variant 2 — συναγωγας των Ιουδαιων
"synagogues of the Jews"
W (1424)
NETmg

The WH NU reading, having the more difficult and better attested wording (especially from 𝔓[75] ℵ B), is most likely original. Scribes harmonized Luke's account to Matt 4:23 and Mark 1:39, or they fixed what they believed to be a contradiction of facts in Luke's account (Luke 4:14 and 5:1 indicate that Jesus was in Galilee). However, Luke probably used "Judea" to cover all of Palestine, which includes Galilee (see Luke 1:5; 6:17; 7:17; 23:5; Acts 10:37). Whereas most modern translations adopt the more difficult reading, Today's English Version (TEV) avoided the problem altogether by translating this verse, "So he preached in the synagogues all over the country."

Luke 5:2

The expression δυο πλοια ("two boats"), found in 𝔓[75] ℵ[c] C[3] D Θ f[1,13] Maj, is the reading in TR NU. Other manuscripts (B W) have the words in reverse order (so WH), one (ℵ*) lacks δυο ("two"), and several (A C* L Q Ψ 33) read δυο πλοιαρια ("two small boats"). The last two readings could be the result of scribal conformity to Mark 3:9, whereas the TR NU reading may be the result of scribal conformity to the immediate context (see 5:3-4).

Luke 5:10-11

D and it[e] changed these verses to make them conform to Matthew and Mark, so that Jesus' call would not be to Peter alone, but to James and John as well. As it turns out, in Luke's account James and John also respond to Jesus' call—even though it is specifically directed toward Peter.

Luke 5:14

The pronoun in the expression εις μαρτυριον αυτοις ("for a testimony to them"), found in most manuscripts, was changed to υμιν ("you") in D it (Marcion). And at the end of this verse D has a lengthy addition, adapted from Mark 1:45: "But he went out and began to talk freely about it and to spread the news, so that he [Jesus] could no longer openly enter a town, but was out in wilderness places. People came to him, and he went back to Capernaum." This is another instance of D's editorial liberty and harmonization.

Luke 5:17a

As TR WH NU read, it is the scribes and teachers of the law who had come there from every village of Galilee and Judea and Jerusalem. D (it[e]) syr[s] adjusted this as follows: "It occurred on one of those days when he was teaching that the scribes and teachers of the law came together. But when they were together, people came from every village of Galilee and Judea and Jerusalem."

Luke 5:17b

WH NU δύναμις κυρίου ἦν εἰς τὸ ἰᾶσθαι αὐτόν
"the power of the Lord was there for him to heal"
ℵ B L W Ξ syr[s] cop[sa] Didymus
NKJVmg RSV NRSV ESV NASB (NIV TNIV NEB) REB NJB NAB NLT HCSB NET

variant/TR δυναμις κυριου ην εις το ιασθαι αυτους
"the power of the Lord was present to heal them"
A C D Θ Ψ f[1,13] 33 Maj cop[bo]
KJV NKJV RSVmg NRSVmg ESVmg NETmg

The WH NU reading, having early and diverse support, is likely original. The variant probably arose when scribes were unable to make sense of αυτον ("him") as a direct object of ιασθαι ("to heal"); so they changed αυτον to αυτους ("them"). In fact, αυτον is the subject of the infinitive phrase το ιασθαι. The text does not emphasize who Jesus was healing (that comes in the next verse), but that he had the Lord God's power to heal.

Luke 5:21

D and it, borrowing from Mark 2:8, add εν ταις καρδιαις αυτων ("in their hearts") after ηρξαντο διαλογιζεσθαι ("began to reason").

Luke 5:26

D W Ψ it[e] dropped the words και εκστασις ελαβεν απαντας και εδοξαζον τον θεον ("and terror seized everyone and they were glorifying God") due to homoeoteleuton, that is, the eye of a scribe passing from δοξαζων τον θεον in 5:25 to the following και in 5:26.

Luke 5:30

WH NU read οι Φαρισαιοι και οι γραμματεις αυτων ("the Pharisees and their scribes") with the support of B C L W Ξ 33. TR reorders the words to οι γραμματεις αυτων και οι Φαρισαιοι ("their scribes and the Pharisees"), with the support of A Θ Ψ f[13] Maj. The transposition was probably created to avoid the notion of Pharisees having scribes.

Luke 5:33

WH NU — οἱ μαθηταὶ Ἰωάννου νηστεύουσιν
"the disciples of John fast"
𝔓[4] א[1] B L W Ξ 33
NKJVmg RSV NRSV ESV NASB NIV TNIV NEB REB NJB NAB NLT HCSB NET

variant/TR — δια τι οι μαθηται Ιωαννου νηστευουσιν
"why do the disciples of John fast?"
א[*,2] A C D Θ Ψ f[1,13] Maj
KJV NKJV HCSBmg

The variant, having inferior documentary support, is likely the result of scribal conformity to Mark 2:18, a parallel verse.

Luke 5:38

WH NU — οἶνον νέον εἰς ἀσκοὺς καινοὺς βλητέον
"new wine must be put into new wineskins"
𝔓[4] 𝔓[75vid] א B L W f[1] 33 cop
RSV NRSV ESV NASB NIV TNIV NEB REB NJB NAB NLT HCSB NET

variant/TR — οινον νεον εις ασκους καινους βλητεον και αμφοτεροι συντηρουνται
"but new wine must be put into new wineskins, and both are preserved"
A C (D) Θ Ψ f[13] Maj
KJV NKJV HCSBmg NETmg

The documentary evidence in favor of the shorter reading is extremely strong. The expansion in the variant reading is clearly taken from Matt 9:17, a parallel passage. Again, TR incorporates this expansion, which is reflected in KJV and NKJV.

Luke 5:39

All three editions (TR WH NU) retain this verse, as do all English versions, which render it something like: "And no one drinking the old desires the new, for he says, 'the old is better.'" The documentary evidence supporting the inclusion of this verse is impressive: 𝔓[4] 𝔓[75vid] א A B C W Maj. However, the verse is excluded in the following witnesses: D it Marcion Eusebius Irenaeus. Marcion may have deleted it because he thought it validated the authority of the OT. It is also possible that it was deleted to conform the pericope to the parallel passages in Matthew and Mark, which have no such verse. Or it is possible that it was deleted by scribes who took offense at Jesus speaking about wine-drinking with such candor and knowledgeable detail. Westcott and Hort bracketed this verse, perhaps thinking it might be a "Western non-interpolation" (though they left no note on this). The documentation favoring the text is so impressive that all doubt should be removed, as well as the brackets.

Luke 6:1

WH NU	ἐν σαββάτῳ "on the Sabbath" 𝔓4 𝔓75vid ℵ B L W f1 33 cop NKJVmg RSV NRSV ESV NASB NIV TNIV NEB REB NJB NAB NLT HCSB NET
variant 1/TR	εν σαββατω δευτεροπρωτω "on the second-first Sabbath" A C D Θ Ψ f13 Maj KJV NKJV RSVmg NRSVmg ESVmg NASBmg HCSBmg NETmg
variant 2	εν σαββατω δευτερω πρωτω "second Sabbath [of] the first [month]" f13 28 none
variant 3	*sabbato mane* "early Sabbath" it[e] none

𝔓75vid is not cited in NA27 or UBS4, but a reconstruction of the text shows that the manuscript did not contain any of the extra words in the variants (see *Text of Earliest MSS,* 510). The problem with determining the original wording here is that the WH NU reading has the best external testimony, whereas the first variant reading is clearly more difficult. If the text originally read simply "Sabbath," why would scribes add the difficult modifier, δευτεροπρωτω, which appears nowhere else in the NT? Westcott and Hort (1882, 58) suggest that some copyist added πρωτω as a correlative to the "other Sabbath" mentioned in 6:5, which was then changed to δευτερω by another scribe in light of 4:31. Both words were retained and combined in subsequent copies; hence TR contains a pure scribal blunder (see Skeat 1988). It is also likely that some scribe considered that "the second sabbath of the first month (the time of first ripening barley) was the correct date for this episode" (Nolland 1989, 255), and therefore he made the insertion. This reading is reflected in the second variant: "the second Sabbath of the first month."

Luke 6:5, 10

Marcion and D place 6:5 after 6:10; and instead of 6:5, D reads the following: "That same day he saw a man working on the Sabbath and said to him, 'Man, if you know what you are doing, you are fortunate; but if you do not, then you are accursed and a violator of the law'" (see NJBmg). This saying, similar to a number of sayings in the *Gospel of Thomas,* comes from an apocryphal tradition (Fitzmyer 1981, 610). Westcott and Hort (1882, 59) conjectured that this saying came from the same source as the pericope of the adulteress (John 7:52–8:11), but they do not say why. Metzger explains that the change in D "makes Luke enumerate three incidents concerning Jesus and the sabbath, and climaxes the series with the pronouncement concerning the sovereignty of the Son of Man over the sabbath" (TCGNT).

In 6:5 several manuscripts (A D L Θ Ψ f[1,13] 33 Maj—so TR) conform Luke's reading κυριος εστιν του σαββατου ο υιος του ανθρωπου ("the Son of Man is Lord of the Sabbath") to Mark 2:28 by adding και: "the Son of Man is Lord even of the Sabbath." The shorter reading is preserved in א B W.

In 6:10 several manuscripts (A D Q Δ Θ Ψ 565 it) add ως η αλλη ("as the other") or υγιης ως η αλλη ("healthy as the other"—f[13] Maj—so TR) or simply υγιης ("healthy"—W). These additions conform Luke to Matt 12:13, a parallel passage. The shorter text is preserved in 𝔓[4] א B L 33 (so WH NU).

Luke 6:14-16

The scribe of D adjusted the list of twelve apostles in Luke according to the lists found in Matt 10:2-4 and Mark 3:17-19. Borrowing from Matt 10:2, he added πρωτον ("first") before the naming of Peter; and borrowing from Mark 3:17, he made an addition after Ιακωβον και Ιωαννην ("James and John")—τον αδελφον αυτου, ους επωνομασεν Βοανηργες ο εστιν υιοι Βροντης ("his brother, whom [plural] he named Boanerges, which is 'sons of thunder'"). The scribe of D also borrowed from John 11:16 in identifying Thomas as the one called Διδυμον ("Didymus"). For a discussion on the textual variants for the name Judas Iscariot, see note on Matt 10:4b. The best-attested spelling for his name in Luke 6:16 is Ιουδαν Ισκαριωθ, as found in 𝔓[4] א* B L 33.

Luke 6:17

A few manuscripts (א* W) have the additional words και τη Περαιας ("and to Perea") among the list of localities from which people came to see Jesus. This is the only place in the entire NT where the region Perea is specifically named. Perea was the territory in Palestine on the eastern side of the Jordan River; it is described as "beyond the Jordan" in the synoptic parallel passages (Matt 4:25; Mark 3:8). Thus, the addition in Luke 6:17 was made by scribes who wanted to harmonize Luke with Matthew and Mark and did so by providing the specific place name.

Luke 6:20

Several copyists (א[2] Q Θ f[1,13] 33) conformed Luke's wording, μακαριοι οι πτωχοι ("blessed are the poor"), to Matthew's, μακαριοι οι πτωχοι τω πνευματι ("blessed are the poor in spirit"). Whereas Matthew emphasizes spiritual poverty as a prerequisite for the kingdom's blessings, Luke emphasizes social poverty. This is in keeping with the entire tenor of Luke, which presents Jesus as the deliverer of the poor (see 4:18; 6:20; 7:22; 14:13, 21; 16:20-25; 18:22; 21:3).

Luke 6:26

Several witnesses (D L Δ syr[p,s] cop[bo]) omit παντες ("all") from the expression "beware when all men speak well of you"—probably because the statement seemed too global. The words οι πατερες αυτων ("their fathers"), omitted in 𝔓[75vid] B 700* syr[s] cop[sa], are probably not original.

Luke 6:31

Several scribes (א A D L W Θ Ξ Ψ $f^{1,13}$ Maj—so TR) conformed this verse to a parallel one, Matt 7:12, by adding και υμεις ("you also") to the second clause. The shorter reading is supported by 𝔓^{75vid} B 700.

Luke 6:35

WH NU — μηδὲν ἀπελπίζοντες
"expecting [in return] nothing"
A B D L P $f^{1,13}$ it cop
all

variant/TR — μηδενα απελπιζοντες
"despairing of no one"
א W Ξ syr^{p,s}
RSVmg NRSVmg NEBmg NJBmg

The textual variant is the result of scribal perplexity concerning the verb απελπιζοντες, which usually means "despair." However, we know that from as early as the fourth century it was used with the meaning "to hope for some return" (Marshall 1978, 264). Luke must have employed it in the same way: A person must lend to others without expecting anything in return.

Luke 6:48

WH NU — διὰ τὸ καλῶς οἰκοδομῆσθαι αὐτήν
"because it was well built"
𝔓^{75vid} א B L W Ξ 33
NKJVmg RSV NRSV ESV NASB NIV TNIV NEB REB NJB NAB NLT HCSB NET

variant 1/TR — τεθεμελιωτο γαρ επι την πετραν
"for it was founded upon the rock"
A C D Θ Ψ $f^{1,13}$ Maj
KJV NKJV RSVmg NRSVmg ESVmg NETmg

variant 2 — omit
𝔓^{45vid} 700* syr^{s}
none

The second variant, although the shorter reading, is probably not original because the scribe of 𝔓^{45} is known for concision and brevity. The first variant is the result of scribal harmonization to Matt 7:25, a parallel passage. The first reading (supported by 𝔓^{75vid} etc.) was the obvious choice for the editors of the WH NU Greek editions and modern English translators. KJV and NKJV follow TR's harmonized text.

Luke 6:49

WH NU have the verb συνεπεσεν ("collapsed"), with the excellent support of 𝔓^{45} 𝔓^{75} א B D L etc. This was changed to the more common verb, επεσεν ("fell") in A C W Ψ Maj (so TR).

Luke 7:7

The first sentence of this verse is omitted in D 700* it syr[s] by way of conformity to Matt 8:8, a parallel verse. Scribal conformity to the same verse is responsible for the verb ιαθησεται ("he will be healed"), appearing in ℵ A C D W Θ Ψ f[1,13] 33 Maj (so TR) versus ιαθητω ("let him be healed") found in 𝔓[75vid] B L (so WH NU).

Luke 7:10

WH NU — εὗρον τὸν δοῦλον ὑγιαίνοντα
"he found the servant healed"
𝔓[75] ℵ B L W f[1] it cop
NKJVmg RSV NRSV ESV NASB NIV TNIV NEB REB NJB NAB NLT HCSB NET

variant/TR — ευρον τον δουλον ασθενουντα υγιαινοντα
"he found the servant, who had been sick, healed"
A C (D) Θ Ψ f[13] 33 Maj
KJV NKJV NETmg

The variant is a typical scribal expansion found in inferior manuscripts. This was incorporated in TR and reflected in KJV and NKJV.

Luke 7:11a

WH NU — ἐγένετο ἐν τῷ ἑξῆς
"it came about afterward"
𝔓[75] ℵ[c] A B L 33
RSV NRSV NASB NIV TNIV NEB REB NJB NAB NLT HCSB NET

variant/TR — εγενετο εν τη εξης
"it came about on the next [day]"
ℵ* C (W) 28 565
KJV NKJV RSVmg ESVmg NEBmg NETmg

Although both idioms noted above could have been written by Luke, the WH NU reading has the best testimony, which was followed by all modern versions.

Luke 7:11b

The best manuscript evidence (𝔓[75] ℵ B D L W—so WH NU) indicates that Jesus' "disciples and a great crowd" (οι μαθηται αυτου και οχλος πολυς) accompanied him as he traveled. However, other manuscripts (A C Θ Ψ f[1,13] 33 Maj—so TR) have the added word ικανοι, borrowed from 7:12, yielding the translation, "a great number of disciples and a great crowd."

Luke 7:13

This is the first instance in this gospel where the articular expression ο κυριος ("the Lord") is used to describe Jesus. (Luke wrote ο κυριος with reference to "the Lord God" and κυριος to describe Jesus as Lord.) Perhaps to retain Luke's previous stylistic pattern, several scribes (D W f[1] 700 it[f] syr[p,s] cop[bo]) changed ο κυριος to Ιησους ("Jesus").

Luke 7:19a

WH NU ἔπεμψεν πρὸς τὸν κύριον
"he sent to the Lord"
B L Ξ f^{13} 33
NKJVmg RSV NRSV ESV NASB NIV TNIV NEB REB NJB NAB NLT HCSB NETmg

variant/TR επεμψεν προς τον Ιησουν
"he sent to Jesus"
א A W Θ Ψ f^1 it syr cop^{bo}
KJV NKJV NET

Although the manuscript evidence is divided, the same reason expressed in 7:13 (see note) probably accounts for the variant here.

Luke 7:19b-20

Συ ει ο ερχομενος η αλλον προσδοκωμεν; ("are you the coming one or should we be expecting another?"). This question (occurring twice) was posed by John's disciples to Jesus. Two differing words appear in the extant manuscripts: αλλον (usually meaning "another of the same kind") and ετερον (usually meaning "another of a different kind"). If there was an authorial-intended difference, then the nuance is clear: Would someone just like Jesus be coming? Or someone altogether different? The evidence is as follows for 7:19: αλλον in A D Θ $f^{1,13}$ Maj (so TR NU); ετερον in א B L W Ξ Ψ 33 (so WH). The evidence is as follows for 7:20: αλλον in $\mathfrak{P}^{75}$ A B Θ f^{13} Maj (so TR WH NU); ετερον in א D L W Ξ Ψ f^1 33. Various manuscripts shift variant readings from one verse to the next. The shift may reflect scribal uncertainty. More likely, Luke varied two words he perceived to be synonymous. As such, ετερον is the more likely reading for 7:19, followed by αλλον in 7:20.

Luke 7:22

D and it^e begin this verse with the wording, "Tell John what your eyes saw and your ears heard."

Luke 7:26 and 7:28a

D and it^a move the first sentence of 7:28 to the end of 7:26. Thus, the expression "and among those born of women, no one is greater than John" appears after "Yes, I say to you, and he is more than a prophet." As such, John becomes the greatest prophet.

Luke 7:27

The last two words of the verse, εμπροσθεν σου ("before you") are omitted in D and it, probably to conform Luke's quote with Mark 1:2, which also contains a conflated quotation of Exod 23:20 and Mal 3:1.

Luke 7:28

WH NU — Ἰωάννου
"John"
𝔓[75] א B L W
NKJVmg RSV NRSV ESV NASB NIV TNIV NEB REB NJB NAB NLT HCSB NET

variant 1 — Ιωαννου του Βαπτιστου
"John the Baptist"
K 33 565 it
NETmg

variant 2 — προφητης Ιωαννου
"[the] prophet John"
Ψ 700 syr[s]
NETmg

variant 3/TR — προφητης Ιωαννου του Βαπτιστου
"[the] prophet John the Baptist"
A (D) Θ f[13] Maj
KJV NKJV HCSBmg

The simple name "John" was expanded in various manuscripts by adding "the Baptist" or "[the] prophet" or both as in the majority of manuscripts. TR has this expanded reading, so KJV and NKJV.

Luke 7:31

Without any Greek manuscript evidence, TR adds ειπεν δε ο κυριος ("and the Lord said") to the beginning of the verse.

Luke 7:35

As the result of scribal harmonization to Matt 11:19, א[2], against all other witnesses, reads εργων ("works") instead of τεκνων ("children"). The emphasis in Matthew is on the works and actions of the Messiah (see Matt 11:2)—hence, the expression, "Wisdom is vindicated by her works." In Luke the focus is on those who respond to Wisdom and thereby become her children (cf. 7:32). As the children of wisdom, they allow themselves to be formed by her and thereby prove her rightness (see Prov 8:32).

Luke 7:39

Two manuscripts (B* Ξ) prefix a definite article before προφητης, thereby creating the reading, "the Prophet." As often happened in the NT text (see note on John 7:52), such an addition was intended to show that Jesus was "the Prophet" like Moses (Deut 18:15; Acts 3:22-23; 7:37).

Luke 7:42

WH NU have the reading τις ουν αυτων πλειον αγαπησει αυτον; ("which of them will love him more?") This has the testimony of 𝔓[3] א B L W Ξ Ψ. Some manuscripts (A Θ 079 f[13] Maj) have the addition ειπε ("tell"), yielding the reading, "tell [me], which of them will love him more"?) This is the reading of TR, followed by KJV and NKJV.

Luke 8:3

WH NU	δϊηκόνουν αὐτοῖς "[the women] were providing for them" B D K W Γ Δ Θ f[13] NKJVmg RSV NRSV ESV NASB NIV TNIV NEB REB NJB NAB NLT HCSB NET
variant/TR	διηκονουν αυτω "[the women] were providing for him" ℵ A L Ψ f[1] 33 it cop KJV NKJV RSVmg NRSVmg ESVmg NETmg

Although the manuscript evidence is nearly evenly divided for this textual variant, it seems more likely that αυτοις was changed to αυτω than vice versa, because the variant is probably the result of harmonization to Matt 27:55 and Mark 15:41. According to Luke, the women in Jesus' company (Mary Magdalene, Joanna, and Susanna) financially supported Jesus and the Twelve—not just Jesus. This was no small undertaking; it was one that would require the financial means that Joanna (wife of Chuza, Herod's steward) probably had access to.

Luke 8:5

Some manuscripts (D W it syr) omit του ουρανου ("of heaven") as a descriptor of the birds (πετεινα). This is the result of harmonization to Matt 13:4 and Mark 4:4.

Luke 8:16

All three editions (TR WH NU) retain the final clause of this verse, ινα οι εισπορευομενοι βλεπωσιν το φως ("so that those entering may see the light.") The clause is included in all manuscripts except 𝔓[75] and B. One could argue that the scribe of 𝔓[75] (followed by the scribe of B) deleted the phrase in order to make Luke 8:16-17 conform to Mark 4:21-22. However, the scribe of 𝔓[75] is reputed for being a faithful copyist, and the shorter text of 𝔓[75] quite often reflects the original. Thus, it is far more likely that later scribes added this clause verbatim from Luke 11:33. Unfortunately, not one English version has noted the shorter reading, let alone adopted it.

Luke 8:19

The reference to Jesus' "mother and brothers" was deleted by Marcion, no doubt because he did not want it to appear that Jesus belonged to a human family (Bruce 1989, 138).

Luke 8:25

The words at the end of the verse, και υπακουουσιν αυτω ("and they obey him"), not present in 𝔓[75] B 700, were very likely added by later scribes (ℵ A C D W Maj) to make Luke conform to Matt 8:27 and Mark 4:41, which are parallel passages. Nonetheless, all three editions (TR WH NU) include the words, as do all English translations.

Luke 8:26

WH NU Γερασηνῶν
"Gerasenes"
𝔓[75] B D
NKJVmg RSV NRSV ESV NASB NIV TNIV NEBmg REB NJB NAB NLT HCSB NET

variant 1 Γεργεσηνων
"Gergesenes"
א L Θ Ξ f[1] 33
RSVmg NRSVmg ESVmg NIVmg TNIVmg NEB REBmg NJBmg NLTmg NETmg

variant 2/TR Γαδαρηνων
"Gadarenes"
A W Ψ f[13] Maj
KJV NKJV RSVmg NRSVmg ESVmg NIVmg TNIVmg NEBmg REBmg NJBmg NLTmg HCSBmg NETmg

In every instance in the Synoptic Gospels where the writer records Jesus' visit to the region on the eastern side of the Galilee (where he healed the demoniac), there is textual variation as to what this region is called. In Matt 8:28, Mark 5:1, and here all three readings occur: "Gerasenes," "Gergesenes," and "Gadarenes." In every instance, the NU editors adopted the reading with the earliest support. In Matt 8:28 that reading is "Gadarenes" (supported by א* B C); in Mark 5:1 (supported by א B D) and Luke 8:26 that reading is "Gerasenes," associated with the town of Jerash in modern Jordan, about thirty-five miles southeast of the Sea of Galilee. Most translations reflect the same kind of thinking. In this verse, the testimony of the earliest manuscripts (𝔓[75] and B) was followed by all modern versions except the NEB.

Luke 8:27

WH NU ἔχων δαιμόνια καὶ χρόνῳ ἱκανῷ οὐκ ἐνεδύσατο ἱμάτιον
"[a man] having demons and for a considerable time he wore no clothes"
𝔓[75] א*,2 B L Ξ 33
NKJVmg RSV NRSV ESV NASB NIV TNIV NEB REB NJB NAB NLT HCSB NET

variant/TR εχων δαιμονια εκ χρονων ικανων και ιματιον ουκ ενεδιδυσκετο
"[a man] having demons for a considerable time and he wore no clothes"
א[1] A (D) W Θ Ψ f[1,13] Maj
KJV NKJV

WH NU has the more difficult reading and superior documentary support. The variant reading was created by scribes to make the words εκ χρονων ικανων ("for a considerable time") describe the duration of the man's demon-possession, whereas in the WH NU reading the words "for a considerable time" describe the duration of his nakedness and homelessness.

Luke 8:37

WH NU Γερασηνῶν
"Gerasenes"
𝔓[75] B C* D 0279
NKJVmg RSV NRSV ESV NASB NIV TNIV NEBmg REB NJB NAB NLT HCSB NET

variant 1 Γεργεσηνων
"Gergesenes"
ℵ*,c (C²) L P Θ f1,13 33
RSVmg NRSVmg ESVmg NIVmg TNIVmg NEB REBmg NJBmg NLTmg NETmg

variant 2/TR Γαδαρηνων
"Gadarenes"
ℵ² A W Ψ Maj
KJV NKJV RSVmg NRSVmg ESVmg NIVmg TNIVmg NEBmg REBmg NJBmg NLTmg HCSBmg NETmg

See comments on 8:26.

Luke 8:43

TR NU ἥτις [ἰατροῖς προσαναλώσασα ὅλον τὸν βίον] οὐκ ἴσχυσεν ἀπ' οὐδενὸς θεραπευθῆναι
"who spent all her living on physicians and was not able to be healed by anyone"
ℵ A C L W Θ Ξ Ψ f1,13 33 Maj
KJV NKJV RSVmg NRSV ESV NASBmg NIVmg TNIVmg NEBmg REBmg NJBmg NAB NLTmg HCSB NETmg

variant/WH ητις ουκ ισχυσεν απ ουδενος θεραπευθηναι
"who was not able to be healed by anyone"
𝔓75 B (D) 0279 syrs copsa Origen
RSV NRSVmg ESVmg NASB NIV TNIV NEB REB NJB NLT HCSBmg NET

Though the above noted clause ("spent all her living on physicians") is included in NU, it has been bracketed in the text to show the editors' doubts about its inclusion. On one hand, it looks as though it could be a true Lukan condensation of Mark 5:26; on the other hand, it is just as likely that the clause was borrowed by scribes from Mark 5:26 and 12:44. If it had been original, it is difficult to explain why the clause would have been dropped by the scribes of 𝔓75 B D. Most modern translators thought the clause did not belong as part of Luke, and the testimony of 𝔓75 especially strengthens their position, as does 0279, a manuscript discovered at St. Catherine's Monastery in the 1970s. Here is one case where a strong majority of modern translators have made a better decision than the editors of NU; the extra clause does not belong in the text at all.

Luke 8:44

Conforming the text to Mark 5:27, D and it omit του κρασπεδου ("the hem") before του ιματιου αυτου ("his garment"). But these words, which have excellent documentary support (𝔓75 ℵ A B C W), highlight the intensity of the woman's faith.

Luke 8:45

WH NU εἶπεν ὁ Πέτρος· ἐπιστάτα, οἱ ὄχλοι συνέχουσίν σε καὶ ἀποθλίβουσιν.
"Peter said, 'Master, the crowds are surrounding you and pressing against you.'"
𝔓75 B Π 700* syrc,s copsa
NKJVmg RSV NRSV ESV NASB NIV TNIV NEB REB NJB NAB NLT HCSB NET

variant/TR ειπεν ο Πετρος και οι συν αυτω, επιστατα, οι οχλοι συνεχουσιν σε και αποθλιβουσιν, και λεγεις, τις ο αψαμενος μου;
"Peter and the ones with him said, 'Master, the crowds are surrounding you and pressing against you. And you say, "Who touched me?"' "
ℵ A C[3] D L W Θ Ξ $f^{1,13}$ 33 (C* Ψ Maj μετ αυτου)
KJV NKJV RSVmg NRSVmg ESVmg NASBmg HCSBmg

Other manuscripts besides those cited above are extant for this portion but provide a divided testimony. For example, ℵ and L include the first expansion but not the second one. Nonetheless, the WH NU reading has the support of the two earliest manuscripts (𝔓[75] B) and other diverse witnesses. Furthermore, the expansions in the variant reading appear to reflect scribal conformity to Mark 5:31.

Luke 8:48

Borrowing from Matt 9:22, several manuscripts (A C W Θ f^{13} Maj—so TR) add θαρσει ("be encouraged") to Jesus' address to the woman.

Luke 8:54

WH NU κρατήσας τῆς χειρὸς αὐτῆς
"he took her hand"
𝔓[75] ℵ B D L 0291
NKJVmg RSV NRSV ESV NASB NIV TNIV NEB REB NJB NAB NLT HCSB NET

variant/TR εκβαλων εξω παντας και κρατησας της χειρος αυτης
"he put [them] all outside and he took her hand"
(A C W Θ 33) Ψ Maj
KJV NKJV HCSBmg

The WH NU reading has superior testimony. The variant in TR is the result of scribal harmonization to Matt 9:25 and Mark 5:40, parallel passages.

Luke 9:1

WH NU τοὺς δώδεκα
"the Twelve"
𝔓[75] A B D W f^1 Maj Marcion
RSV NRSV ESV NASB NIV TNIV NEB REB NJB NAB (NLT) HCSB NET

variant 1 τους δωδεκα αποστολους
"the twelve apostles"
ℵ C* L Θ Ξ Ψ 070 0291 f^{13} 33
NETmg

variant 2/TR τους δεδεκα μαθητας αυτου
"his twelve disciples"
C[3] it Eusebius
KJV NKJV NETmg

Because of the excellent testimony for the WH NU reading, we can judge that it was probably Luke himself who used the Markan appellation, "the Twelve" (see Mark 6:7). Borrowing from Luke 6:13, scribes filled out the expression with "apostles" or "his disciples."

Luke 9:2

According to B and syr[c,s] (as well as Marcion), the Twelve are said to have been sent out to heal (ιασθαι). Other manuscripts (א A D L Ξ Ψ 070 f[1] 33—so NU) fill out this infinitive with τους ασθενεις ("the sick") or τους ασθενουντας (C W Θ f[13] Maj—so TR). Though it could be argued that the full expression (an infinitive followed by an object) accords with Lukan style, the presence of the fuller expression in two forms suggests scribal expansion in two different ways. Westcott and Hort, as such, were correct in going with the shorter text, and the NU editors were prudent to bracket τους ασθενεις.

Luke 9:7

WH NU τὰ γινόμενα πάντα
"all the things that had been done"
𝔓[75] א B C* D L Ξ f[13]
RSV NRSV ESV NASB NIV TNIV NEB REB NJB NAB NLT HCSB NET

variant/TR τα γινομενα υπ αυτου παντα
"all the things that had been done by him [Jesus]"
A C[3] W Θ Ψ f[1] 33 Maj
KJV NKJV

The variant reading, which has inferior support, is too limiting; Herod had not just heard about Jesus but about Jesus' ministry and its overall effect. Luke probably had in mind the spread of Jesus' fame (cf. Mark 6:14) "caused by the mission of the Twelve and the growth of the rumors about him" (Marshall 1978, 355). This is reflected in the WH NU reading.

Luke 9:10

WH NU πόλιν καλουμένην Βηθσαιδά
"town called Bethsaida"
(𝔓[75] βηδσαιδα) א[1] B L Ξ* 33 cop
RSV NRSV ESV NASB NIV TNIV NEB REB NJB NAB NLT HCSB NET

variant 1 κομη λεγομενην Βηδσαιδα
"village named Bedsaida"
D
NETmg

variant 2 τοπον ερημον
"desert place"
א*,2 syr[c]
NETmg

variant 3 κομη καλουμενην Βηδσαιδα εις τοπον ερημον
"village called Bedsaida in a desert place"
Θ
NETmg

variant 4/TR τοπον ερημον πολεως καλουμενης Βηθσαιδα
"a deserted place near the town called Bethsaida"
A C W Ξ[mg] f[(1),13] Maj
KJV NKJV HCSBmg NETmg

The textual tradition was greatly affected by the fact that Luke's account does not coincide with Matthew and Mark. According to Matt 14:13 and Mark 6:31, Jesus went with his disciples to a deserted place. According to Luke (per the best manuscript evidence), Jesus went to a town called Bethsaida. This is difficult because Luke 9:12 speaks of the locale of the feeding of the five thousand as being "a deserted place." Scribes, aware of this problem, tried to fix the text by calling Bethsaida a "village" or adding that Jesus went to a desert place. Evidently, Luke used the name Bethsaida here to identify the closest town to the wilderness site and to prepare for its mention in 10:13.

Luke 9:16

Most manuscripts say that Jesus blessed the bread and fish (ευλογησεν αυτους = "he blessed them"). This was changed in D it syr[c,(s)] and Marcion to ευλογησεν επ αυτους ("he said a blessing over them") probably because scribes found it difficult to imagine that food could be blessed. Usually blessings given before a meal ascribe the blessing to God, not the food. An ancient mealtime prayer recorded in the Mishnah says, "Blessed be you, O Lord our God, king of the world, who causes bread to come from the earth."

Luke 9:20

Peter's declaration of Jesus' divine identity is stated differently in each gospel. In Matt 16:16 Peter says, "You are the Christ, the Son of the living God." In Mark 8:29 he says, "You are the Christ." In John 6:69 he says, "You are the Holy One of God." In Luke's account, according to the best witnesses (𝔓[75] ℵ B etc.), Peter says, "You are the Christ of God." In all four instances certain scribes attempted to conform one gospel to another (see comments on each of the verses noted above). In this verse in Luke, D 892 it cop[boMS] have the additional "Son," producing the appellation, "the Christ, the Son of God." Luke's original expression, "the Christ of God," emphasizes the special role Jesus has as God's anointed to fulfill God's purpose on earth.

Luke 9:26

TR WH NU ὃς γὰρ ἂν ἐπαισχυνθῇ με καὶ τοὺς ἐμοὺς λόγους
"for whoever is ashamed of me and my words"
𝔓[45] 𝔓[75vid] A B C L W
KJV NKJV RSV NRSV ESV NASB NIV TNIV NEBmg REB NJB NAB NLT HCSB NET

variant ος γαρ αν επαισχυνθη με και τους εμους
"for whoever is ashamed of me and mine [i.e., my disciples]"
D it[a,e] syr[c]
NEB REBmg

As in Mark 8:38a (see note), so here the variant indicates that Jesus was speaking of himself and his disciples. If this is what Luke wrote, then the TR WH NU reading, which has λογους ("words"), is a scribal expansion attempting to make the text more contemporary—inasmuch as it is more relevant in later centuries to speak of being ashamed of Jesus' words than of Jesus' disciples. However, the textual evidence strongly favors the TR WH NU reading, which would have been pertinent in Jesus' time, as well as in later generations. Furthermore, it can be argued that λογους was accidentally dropped due to homoeoteleuton—the two previous words end with ους.

The translators of the NEB selected the variant reading because they thought it suited the context better (Tasker 1964, 419). The same thinking was behind the selection of the same variant reading in Mark 8:38a (see comments there). The REB translators revised the NEB.

Luke 9:28

According to several manuscripts (including ℵ and B), the names of the three disciples appear in this order: Πετρον και Ιωαννην και Ιακωβον ("Peter and John and James"). Other manuscripts (including 𝔓45 and 𝔓75vid) have this order: "Peter and James and John"—which is the more typical arrangement in the Gospels. It is difficult to determine which is original. Was the latter conformed to Luke 8:51, or was the former conformed to Matt 17:1 and Mark 9:2 (the parallel passages)?

Luke 9:35

WH NU	ὁ υἱός μου ὁ ἐκλελεγμένος "my Son, the chosen one" 𝔓45 𝔓75 ℵ B L Ξ it[a] syr[s] cop (Θ 1 εκλεκτος for last word) NKJVmg RSV NRSV ESV NASB NIV TNIV NEB REB NJB NAB NLT HCSB NET
variant 1/TR	ο υιος μου ο αγαπητος "my beloved Son" A C* W f[13] 33 Maj it Marcion KJV NKJV RSVmg NRSVmg ESVmg NJBmg NLTmg HCSBmg NETmg
variant 2	ο υιος μου ο αγαπητος, εν ω ευδοκησα "my beloved Son, in whom I am well pleased" C[3] D Ψ NETmg

As often happened in the textual transmission of the Gospels (especially from the end of the fourth century onward), divine proclamations about Jesus were harmonized. At Jesus' transfiguration, each of the Synoptic Gospels has different wording. Matthew 17:5 reads, "This is my beloved Son, in whom I am well pleased"; Mark 9:7 reads, "This is my beloved Son"; and Luke 9:35 reads, "This is the Son, the chosen one." The first variant is a harmonization to Mark, and the second to Matthew (or perhaps Luke 3:22).

The WH NU reading, supported by the four earliest manuscripts (𝔓45 𝔓75 ℵ B), is without question the one Luke wrote. The wording in Luke reveals the twofold position of Jesus as both God's Son and the chosen one—that is, the Father chose his Son to be the Messiah (see note on Luke 9:20). Luke's wording is reminiscent of Ps 2:7 and especially Isa 42:1 (LXX), which speaks of the messianic Servant. This chosen Servant was destined to carry out God's will by suffering death on the cross. This entirely suits the context which speaks of Jesus' "exodus from Jerusalem" (9:31). Indeed, as Jesus was making his exodus (via the cross), the religious leaders mockingly said, "He saved others. Let him save himself, if he is the Christ of God, the chosen one" (23:35). The irony is, they did not realize that Jesus had been chosen—not to be the conquering King-Messiah—but to be the suffering Servant-Messiah.

Luke 9:47

The WH NU editions have the word ειδως ("perceiving") in the statement "Jesus was perceiving the thoughts of their hearts." This has the support of 𝔓75vid ℵ B 700. (𝔓75vid is not listed in

NA[27] or UBS[4], but 𝔓[75vid], which reads ειδ [ως], favors WH NU.) TR has the word ιδων ("seeing"), with the support of A C D L W Θ Ξ Ψ 0115 f[13] Maj Origen. This is the more difficult reading because it is harder to understand how one could "see" the thoughts of others, as opposed to "perceive" the thoughts of others. However, the documentary evidence, including the earliest witness, 𝔓[75], favors WH NU.

Luke 9:54

WH NU	omit at end of verse: ως και Ηλιας εποιησεν ("as Elijah also did") 𝔓[45] 𝔓[75] ℵ B L Ξ NKJVmg RSV NRSV ESV NASB NIV TNIV NEB REB NJB NAB NLT HCSB NET
variant/TR	add at end of verse: ως και Ηλιας εποιησεν ("as Elijah also did") A C D W Θ Ψ f[1,13] 33 Maj KJV NKJV RSVmg NRSVmg ESVmg NIVmg TNIVmg NEBmg REBmg NJBmg NLTmg HCSBmg NETmg

According to WH NU, a full rendering of the verse is: "James and John said, 'Lord, do you want us to command fire to come down from heaven and destroy them?'" The words of James and John would easily bring to mind Elijah's action of calling down fire from heaven (see 2 Kgs 1:10). Thus, this allusion may have first been written as an explanatory marginal note, which was later inserted by a scribe into the text. If the words had originally been in the text, there is no good reason why they would have been deleted in the four earliest extant manuscripts (𝔓[45] 𝔓[75] ℵ B). Not one modern version includes the extra words, although many note it out of deference to the KJV tradition.

Luke 9:55

WH NU	στραφεὶς δὲ ἐπετίμησεν αὐτοῖς "But turning, he rebuked them." 𝔓[45] 𝔓[75] ℵ A B C L W Δ Ξ Ψ 33 NKJVmg RSV NRSV ESV NIV TNIV NEB REB NJB NAB NLT HCSB
variant 1	στραφεις δε επετιμησεν αυτοις και ειπεν, Ουκ οιδατε οιου πνευματος εστε υμεις "But turning, he rebuked them and he said, 'You do not know of what spirit you are.'" D it[d] (NETmg)
variant 2/TR	στραφεις δε επετιμησεν αυτοις και ειπεν, Ουκ οιδατε οιου πνευματος εστε υμεις [56]γαρ ο υιος του ανθρωπου ουκ ηλθεν ψυχας ανθρωπων απολεσαι αλλα σωσαι "But turning, he rebuked them and he said, 'You do not know of what spirit you are, [56] for the Son of Man did not come to destroy men's lives but to save them.'" K Γ Θ f[1,13] 700 it syr[c,h,p] KJV NKJV RSVmg NRSVmg ESVmg NASB NIVmg NEBmg REBmg NJBmg NLTmg HCSBmg NETmg

The WH NU reading, supported by an excellent array of witnesses, says only that Jesus rebuked them; the actual words of the rebuke are not recorded. Dissatisfied with this gap in the narrative, scribes provided two additions—a short one and a longer one (perhaps built on the other). Most likely, the longer addition was adapted from Luke 19:10. There is a similar addition to Matt 18:10, which suggests that this was a popular gloss. In this context, it was used to describe the difference between the disciples' spirit and Jesus' spirit. James and John, with a vengeful spirit, wanted to destroy the Samaritans for not receiving Jesus. Jesus' spirit, by contrast, was set on saving people's lives, not destroying them. In fact, that is why he had resolved to go to Jerusalem (9:51-53), and that is why the Samaritans did not receive him—for they perceived that he was a man with a mission. Thus, the additional words—though not written by Luke—are compatible with the text and Lukan theology.

All the modern versions follow the best authorities, and all of them include the variant reading(s) in the margin. Unfortunately, the marginal notes do not specify that the manuscripts which support the variant are all late manuscripts or that the reading of the text is supported by all the earliest and most reliable manuscripts. KJV and NKJV, following TR, display the expanded text, as does NASB (even though it is bracketed).

Luke 9:59

When called to follow Jesus, the second of three men said, "Lord, let me first go and bury my father." The word "Lord" (κυριε) is present in several witnesses (including 𝔓[45] 𝔓[75] ℵ A B[2] C L W Θ Ξ Ψ 0181), but not in B* D syr[s] (so WH). It is quite likely that it was dropped because it was perceived that this man had not recognized the lordship of Jesus in his life when he made an excuse for not following Jesus. Thus, it was thought that it was not fitting for the man to call Jesus "Lord."

Luke 9:62

TR WH NU	οὐδεὶς ἐπιβαλὼν τὴν χεῖρα ἐπ' ἄροτρον καὶ βλέπων εἰς τὰ ὀπίσω εὔθετος ἐστιν τῇ βασιλείᾳ τοῦ θεοῦ. "No one putting his hand to the plow and looking at what is behind is fit for the kingdom of God." (𝔓[75]) B 0181 (ℵ A C L W Θ Ξ f[13] 33 Maj add αυτου after χειρα) all
variant	ουδεις εις τα οπισω βλεπων και επιβαλων την χειρα αυτου επ αροτρον εστιν τη βασιλεια του θεου. "No one looking to what is behind and putting his hand to the plow is fit for the kingdom of God." 𝔓[45vid] D it Clement NEBmg

The variant reading reverses the actions but conveys the same message: One who constantly desires his past way of life cannot properly follow Jesus (see Phil 3:13; Heb 12:1). This variant was noted in the NEB because of the testimony of 𝔓[45], D, Old Latin manuscripts, and Clement (Tasker 1964, 420).

Luke 10:1

WH NU	ἑβδομήκοντα [δύο] "seventy-two" 𝔓[75] B D 0181 syr[c,s] cop[sa] NKJVmg RSVmg NRSVmg ESV NASBmg NIV TNIV NEB REB NJB NAB NLT HCSBmg NET

variant/TR ϵβδομηκοντα
"seventy"
ℵ A C L W Θ Ξ Ψ $f^{1,13}$ Maj
KJV NKJV RSV NRSV ESVmg NASB NIVmg TNIVmg NEBmg REBmg NJBmg NLTmg HCSB NETmg

See comments on Luke 10:17.

Luke 10:17

WH NU οἱ ἑβδομήκοντα [δύο]
"the seventy-two"
𝔓45 𝔓75 B D syr^s cop^{sa}
NKJVmg RSVmg NRSVmg ESV NIV TNIV NEB REB NJB NAB NLT HCSBmg NET

variant/TR οι ϵβδομηκοντα
"the seventy"
ℵ A C L W Θ Ξ Ψ 0115 $f^{1,13}$ 33 Maj
KJV NKJV RSV NRSV ESVmg NASB NIVmg TNIVmg NEBmg REBmg NJBmg NLTmg HCSB NETmg

The same variant reading occurs in 10:1 and 10:17, because the former describes Jesus' selection and sending out of these disciples, and the latter describes their return. Some manuscripts (including 𝔓75 B D) read "seventy-two," while others (including ℵ A C L W) read "seventy." Thus, the pattern is the same for Luke 10:1 and 10:17—with one exception: 𝔓45 has a lacuna at Luke 10:1. But it could easily be conjectured that it also read "seventy-two." Of the two readings, "seventy-two" has the earliest and most diverse support (Alexandrian, Western, Syriac). Furthermore, it is more difficult to imagine a scribe changing "seventy" to "seventy-two" than vice versa, inasmuch as "seventy" was a familiar numeral in expressions such as "the seventy elders" (Exod 24:1; Num 11:16, 24), "the seventy descendants of Jacob" (Exod 1:5; Deut 10:22), and the seventy members of the Sanhedrin. (See further arguments by Kurt Aland on Luke 10:1 in TCGNT.)

Although "seventy" appears to be more symbolically suggestive than "seventy-two" ("seventy" suggests perfection and completion), "seventy-two" also has its symbolism and perhaps practical application. Seventy-two, as a multiple of twelve, also suggests perfection and completion. It is possible that Jesus chose seventy-two disciples so that one apostle would oversee a group of six, thereby making seven in each group. Marshall (1978, 415) suggests that Luke was following Gen 10 (LXX), which lists seventy-two nations, because these disciples typified the gospel ministry to all the nations of the world.

Whatever the intrinsic reasons for selecting "seventy-two," it appears that most modern translations were influenced by the documentary testimony of 𝔓45 and 𝔓75. 𝔓45 (published in 1933) alone was not enough to convince the RSV translators, but 𝔓45 and 𝔓75 (published in 1961) must have influenced ESV, NIV, NEB, REB, NJB, NAB, NLT, and NET. Curiously, the NRSV did not follow the NU text here.

Luke 10:21a

WH NU τῷ πνεύματι τῷ ἁγίῳ
"in the Holy Spirit"
𝔓75 ℵ B C D L Ξ 33
RSV NRSV ESV NASB NIV TNIV NEB REB NJB NAB NLT HCSB NET

variant/TR τω πνευματι
"in the spirit"
𝔓45vid A W Ψ 0115 f13 Maj itq Clement
KJV NKJV NRSVmg NEBmg REBmg HCSBmg

In fuller context, a rendering of WH NU would be: "he [Jesus] rejoiced in the Holy Spirit." Prior to NA26, the Nestle text displayed the variant reading; then the editors of NA26 and UBS3 adopted the first reading. Metzger (TCGNT) provides the rationale for the change: "The strangeness of the expression 'exulted in the Holy Spirit' (for which there is no parallel in the Scriptures) may have led to the omission of τῷ ἁγίῳ from 𝔓45 A W [etc.]." Indeed, this is a strange expression. The gospel writers did not use the term "Holy Spirit" when speaking of an action that Jesus himself performed εν τω πνευματι ("in the spirit/Spirit") or of an emotion that emanated from his spirit. Jesus is said to have "perceived in his spirit" (Mark 2:8), "sighed deeply in his spirit" (Mark 8:12), "grown strong in spirit" (Luke 2:40 in some MSS), "groaned in the [or his] spirit" (John 11:33), and "was troubled in spirit" (John 13:21). In grammatical terms, there is no other instance in the Gospels in which the word πνευμα refers to the Holy Spirit when it is (1) in the dative case and (2) preceded by a verb in the active voice with Jesus as the subject (with the exception of the statement about Jesus baptizing "with [or, in] the Holy Spirit"—Matt 3:11). Whenever the gospel writers spoke about Jesus' mental or emotional activity related to the spirit/Spirit, they viewed it as an activity happening within his spirit. Thus, it would be unusual for Luke to say that Jesus "rejoiced in the Holy Spirit." But it is this unusualness, coupled with such good textual support, which seems to favor the reading of the text.

However, in defense of the variant reading, it can be said that τω αγιω ("the Holy") was added because (1) scribes had a propensity to add αγιω to πνευματι and (2) some scribes may have wanted to clearly distinguish the "spirit" (πνευμα) mentioned in Luke 10:21 from the "spirits" (πνευματα) mentioned in the previous verse (10:20, which says "do not rejoice in this, that the spirits are subject to you, but rejoice that your names are recorded in heaven"—NASB). If the second reading is original, the text could be read as Jesus rejoicing in the divine Spirit or in his spirit—the Greek can be taken either way. But it should be noted that all the scribes of the early centuries wrote πνευμα as a nomen sacrum ($\overline{\text{ΠΝΑ}}$) even when referring to what most exegetes would consider Jesus' human spirit. They could have written it in *plene*, but chose not to. As a point of fact, the scribe of 𝔓45 wrote the nomen sacrum $\overline{\text{ΠΝΙ}}$ in Luke 10:21. Thus, even though αγιω was not attached to this, it is clear in the manuscript 𝔓45 that Jesus was rejoicing in the divine Spirit.

Luke 10:21b

According to most manuscripts, Jesus addressed his Father as κυριε του ουρανου και της γης ("Lord of heaven and of earth"). In 𝔓45 and Marcion the expression is truncated to κυριε του ουρανου ("Lord of heaven"). (See Birdsall 1970, 331.)

Luke 10:22

WH NU omit at beginning of verse και στραφεις προς τους μαθητας ειπεν ("and turning to the disciples he said")
𝔓45vid 𝔓75 ℵ B D L Ξ 070 f1,13 33
KJV NKJV RSV NRSV ESV NASB NIV TNIV REB NJB NAB NLT HCSB NET

variant/TR add και στραφεις προς τους μαθητας ειπεν ("and turning to the disciples he said")
A (C[2]) W Θ Ψ (0115) Maj
NKJVmg NEB HCSBmg

Tasker (1964, 420), in defense of the NEB, argued that "the recurrence of the same words (but with the significant addition of κατ ιδιαν) in verse 23 may have led to their omission in verse 22." However, it is more likely that an addition was made by scribes who considered it strange for Jesus to address his Father directly in 10:21 ("I thank you, Father") and then shift to the third person in 10:22 ("all things have been handed over to me by my Father"). Thus, the words about Jesus turning to his disciples were added at the beginning of 10:22 to avoid the awkwardness of this verse being a continuation of Jesus' prayer in 10:21. This addition has its own awkwardness because the clause is repeated again as an introduction to 10:23. The KJV and NKJV translators did not follow TR here, and the REB translators revised the NEB.

Luke 10:24

A few witnesses (D it Marcion) omit "and kings" (και βασιλεις) from Jesus' statement, "many prophets and kings have wanted to see what you see and have not seen them." Since there is no transcriptional explanation for the omission, we can imagine that the scribes/editors of these manuscripts considered that only the prophets—not the kings—were visionaries expecting the coming of Christ.

The two earliest extant manuscripts for this portion, 𝔓[75] and B (𝔓[45] lacks 10:22-25), have an added μου after ακουσαι, producing the reading, "many prophets and kings wanted . . . to hear from me what you hear and did not hear [them]."

Luke 10:31

The expression κατα συγκυριαν, which occurs only here in the NT, means "by chance" or "by coincidence." The scribe of 𝔓[75] first wrote this as κατα συγκυριαν (as it appears in all other manuscripts except D, which reads κατα τυχα), but then wrote it as κατα συγ-τυχειαν (= κατα συντυχειαν) (see *Text of Earliest MSS,* 530). This expression, though nearly synonymous with κατα συγκυριαν, connotes "good fortune" (LSJ 1729), not just "coincidence." Furthermore, συντυχειαν is found primarily in Greek lyric poets and the writings of Herodotus (BDAG 976). The change in 𝔓[75] probably reveals the scribe's knowledge of Greek literature and thereby helps us understand some of his reading repertoire. The change also shows that the scribe was anticipating the good outcome of the following story and thereby gave his readers a clue by choosing a word that would suggest a fortunate outcome for the victim who was rescued by the Good Samaritan.

Luke 10:38

The NU edition indicates that Martha simply "received him [Jesus]" (υπεδεξατο αυτον). This has the support of 𝔓[45] 𝔓[75] B cop[sa]. WH adds εις την οικιαν ("into the house"), with the support of 𝔓[3vid] ℵ C L 33. TR adds εις τον οικον αυτης ("into her house") with the support of A D W Θ Ψ 070 f[1,13] Maj. Of the three, the NU reading is most likely original because it is found in the three earliest manuscripts and because it is quite apparent that the other two readings display scribal additions—inserted to fill out the sentence. The papyri with B caused the editors of NA[26] to adopt the first reading over the third, which used to be in previous editions of the Nestle text. However, all translators (following the majority of scribes) have felt obligated to expand the text.

Luke 10:39-41a

NU prints κυριου ("Lord"), based on 𝔓3 ℵ B2 D L Ξ syrc, whereas slightly better evidence supports the reading Ιησου ("Jesus"): 𝔓45 𝔓75 A B* C2 W Θ Ψ f1,13 Maj syrs. The reading κυριου may have been the result of scribal conformity to 10:40-41. In 10:41, the same variant appears: κυριος versus Ιησους, but in this instance Ιησους has the strong support of 𝔓3 (𝔓45) 𝔓75 ℵ B2 L.

Luke 10:41b-42

TR NU	μεριμνᾷς καὶ θορυβάζῃ περὶ πολλά, 42ἑνὸς δέ ἐστιν χρεία "you are worried and troubled about many things, 42 but one thing is needed" 𝔓45 𝔓75 C* W Θ* (τυρβαζη for θορυβαζη A Θc f13 Maj—so TR) KJV NKJV RSV NRSV ESV NASBmg NIV TNIVmg NEB REB NJBmg NAB NLT HCSB NET
variant 1/WH	μεριμνας και θορυβαζη περι πολλα 42ολιγων δε εστιν χρεια η ενος "you are worried and troubled about many things, 42 but few things are needed—or [only] one" 𝔓3 (ℵ B) C2 L f1 33 copbo RSVmg NRSVmg ESVmg NASB NIVmg TNIV NEBmg REBmg NJB NABmg NETmg
variant 2	θορυβαζη "you are troubled" D itd NEBmg
variant 3	omit ita,b,e syrs NEBmg

Among the many variants here, the shorter readings (variants 2-3) do not reflect a briefer, original text, because the manuscript support for these readings is inferior and because it is unlikely that such simple statements could produce either of the two longer, more complicated texts. Therefore, these variants should be dismissed as scribal simplifications or excisions of a difficult saying. Among the other readings, the TR NU reading has the best documentation and presents the clearest message. Unlike Martha, who was distracted from Jesus by doing many things (presumably for him), Mary's attention was riveted on one thing: Jesus and his teachings. But the problem with this reading is that if it were original, why would scribes change it? Shifting from "one thing is needful" to "few things are needful or only one" yields a more complex but comprehensible text: "Martha, Martha, you are worried and upset about many things. However, few things are really needed, or, if you will, only one; for that indeed is what Mary has chosen." Fee (1981, 75), who supports this reading, argues as follows: "The text is not so much a 'put down' of Martha, as it is a gentle rebuke for her anxiety. For a meal, Jesus says, there is no cause to fret over πολλα [many things], when only ολιγα [few things] are necessary. Then, having spoken of 'necessity,' he moves on to affirm Mary's 'outrageous' action. 'Indeed,' he says, 'in another sense only one thing is necessary. For this is indeed what Mary has chosen.'" Although Fee's argument has weight, the NU editors adopted the reading supported by 𝔓45 and 𝔓75 over against the one in previous editions of the Nestle edition and the WH edition. As such, the testimony of the two earliest manuscripts, 𝔓45 and 𝔓75, offset the testimony of 𝔓3 ℵ B. Many of the modern translations follow NU, while the first variant is noted in some.

Luke 11:2a

WH NU	Πάτερ "Father" 𝔓75 ℵ B syr[s] Marcion Origen NKJVmg RSV NRSV ESV NASB NIV TNIV NEB REB NJB NAB NLT HCSB NET
variant/TR	Πατερ ημων ο εν τοις ουρανοις "Our Father who is in heaven" A C D W Θ Ψ 070 f[13] 33[vid] Maj it syr[c,h,p] cop KJV NKJV NRSVmg NASBmg NIVmg TNIVmg NEBmg REBmg NLTmg HCSBmg NETmg

See comments on Luke 11:4b below.

Luke 11:2b

TR WH NU	ἐλθέτω ἡ βασιλεία σου "let your kingdom come" 𝔓75 ℵ A B C L W Δ Θ Ψ f[1,13] 33 it[a,b,c,e] syr cop all
variant 1	εφ ημας ελθετω σου η βασιλεια "let your kingdom come upon us" D it[d] NIVmg
variant 2	ελθετω το πνευμα σου το αγιον εφ ημας και καθαρισατω ημας "let your Holy Spirit come upon us and cleanse us" 700 Gregory of Nyssa (Tertullian) Maximus-Confessor NRSVmg NIVmg REBmg NJBmg NABmg
variant 3	ελθετω το αγιον πνευμα σου, ελθετω η βασιλεια σου "let your Holy Spirit come, let your kingdom come" Marcion[according to Tertullian] none

The TR WH NU reading is likely the one written by Luke. The first variant is a typical Bezaean expansion—whether εφ ημας ("upon us") goes with the previous clause ("let your name be sanctified upon us") or this one ("let your kingdom come upon us"). The third variant reading was current as early as the second century. Tertullian (*Marc.* 4.26), quoting either from his own text or Marcion's, made a petition to the Holy Spirit after invoking the Father. According to Westcott and Hort (1882, 60), an early Western text (Marcion's or Tertullian's) with another reading like this (second variant) must have been noticed by Gregory of Nyssa, whose comment on this was then noticed by Maximus the Confessor.

This reading, which showed up later in tenth- and eleventh-century manuscripts, was probably first created to accommodate the Lord's Prayer to a baptismal ceremony, wherein the person baptized asked for the Holy Spirit to come upon him and cleanse him (cf. Titus 3:5-6). If so, this is another example of how ecclesiastical practice influenced the text.

Luke 11:2c

WH NU	omit γενηθητω το θελημα σου ως εν ουρανω και επι της γης ("let your will be done on earth as it is in heaven") 𝔓[75] B L syr[c,s] Marcion Origen NKJVmg RSV NRSV ESV NASB NIV TNIV NEB REB NJB NAB NLT HCSB NET
variant/TR	add γενηθητω το θελημα σου ως εν ουρανω και επι γης ("let your will be done on earth as it is in heaven") ℵ A C D W Θ Ψ 070 f[13] 33[vid] Maj it syr[h,p] cop[bo] KJV NKJV NRSVmg NASBmg NIVmg TNIVmg NEBmg REBmg NLTmg HCSBmg NETmg

See comments on Luke 11:4b below.

Luke 11:4a

TR WH NU	καὶ ἄφες ἡμιν τὰς ἁμαρτίας ἡμῶν "and forgive us our sins" 𝔓[75] ℵ[1] A B C D W Maj all
variant	και αφες ημιν τα οφειληματα ημων "and forgive us our debts" D 2542 it[b,c] NJBmg

See comments on Luke 11:4b.

Luke 11:4b

WH NU	omit αλλα ρυσαι ημας απο του πονηρου ("but rescue us from evil") 𝔓[75] ℵ[*,2] B L syr[s] cop[sa] Origen NKJVmg RSV NRSV ESV NASB NIV TNIV NEB REB NJB NAB NLT HCSB NET
variant/TR	add αλλα ρυσαι ημας απο του πονηρου ("but rescue us from evil") ℵ[1] A C D W Θ Ψ 070 f[13] 33 Maj it syr[c,h,p] KJV NKJV NRSVmg NASBmg NIVmg TNIVmg NEBmg REBmg NLTmg HCSBmg NETmg

Evidently, Matthew's version of the Lord's Prayer must have been current in the churches he knew, and Luke's version must have been used in the churches he frequented. Both recorded the prayer with different verbiage. But many scribes (apparently from the fourth century onward) harmonized Luke's version of the Lord's Prayer to Matthew's. Interestingly, the harmonization did not go the other way—from Luke to Matthew—because Matthew was the more popular text. For both the Sermon on the Mount and Lord's Prayer, scribes conformed Luke to Matthew. All the major early fifth-century manuscripts (A C D W) display the harmonization. The harmonized text is reflected in TR.

In four instances noted above (Luke 11:2a, 2c, 4a, 4b), the longer readings are scribal expansions borrowed from the wording of the Lord's Prayer recorded in Matt 6:9-10, 13. In every instance, the modern translations followed the shorter reading, which is always supported by 𝔓^{75} and B (with other MSS). The expanded readings, however, are noted in several versions out of deference to the KJV tradition.

Luke 11:11

WH NU	αἰτήσει ὁ υἱὸς ἰχθύν, καὶ ἀντὶ ἰχθύος ὄφιν αὐτῷ ἐπιδώσει; "if a son asks for a fish, will he instead give him a serpent?" 𝔓^{45} (𝔓^{75}) B it^{i} syr^{s} cop^{sa} NKJVmg RSV NRSV ESV NASB NIV TNIV NEB REB NJB NAB NLT HCSB NET
variant/TR	αιτησει ο υιος αρτον μη λιθον επιδωσει αυτω, ιχθυν και αντι ιχθυος οφιν αυτω επιδωσει; "if a son asks for bread, will he give him a stone? [if] a fish, will he instead give him a serpent?" (א) A C (D) L W Θ Ψ f^{1,13} 33 Maj KJV NKJV RSVmg NRSVmg ESVmg TNIVmg NEBmg REBmg NJBmg NLTmg HCSBmg

According to Luke's original writing, which has excellent documentary support, there are two pairs mentioned in Jesus' analogy: fish/serpent and egg/scorpion. According to Matthew's account, there are also two pairs, which are different: bread/stone and fish/serpent. The variant reading is clearly a harmonization to Matt 7:9; it expands the text to three pairs: fish/serpent, bread/stone, and egg/scorpion. Two pairs are enough (in either gospel) to make the point, but Luke's pairs especially contrast two beneficial gifts (fish and egg) with two harmful ones (serpent and scorpion). If earthly fathers would not give their children harmful gifts, would the heavenly Father? On the contrary, he would give the best gift, the Holy Spirit (see following note on Luke 11:13).

KJV and NKJV reflect the traditional reading of TR, but not so with the modern versions, which must have been influenced by 𝔓^{45} and 𝔓^{75}.

Luke 11:13

TR WH NU	πνεῦμα ἅγιον "[the] Holy Spirit" 𝔓^{75} א A B C W f^{1,13} Maj all
variant 1	πνευμα αγαθον "[the] good Spirit" 𝔓^{45} L syr^{hmg} none
variant 2	αγαθον δομα "a good gift" D it NEBmg

variant 3 δοματα αγαθα
"good gifts"
Θ (syr[s])
NJBmg

The TR WH NU reading in full is rendered as, "the Father will give the Holy Spirit from heaven to those who ask him." This has excellent documentary support. The third variant is clearly the result of harmonization to Matt 7:11 or a conflation derived from Luke 11:12; the second is a slight modification. The first variant is either the result of scribal inadvertence (confusing αγιον for αγαθον) or an interesting combination of "good [gifts]" with "Spirit."

Luke 11:15, 18, 19

TR NU Βεελζεβούλ
"Beelzebul"
𝔓[45] 𝔓[75] A C D (L) W Θ Ψ f[1,13] 33 Maj it syr[h] cop
NKJVmg RSV NRSV ESV NASB NIVmg TNIV REB NJB NAB NLT HCSB NET

variant 1/WH Βεεζεβουλ
"Beezebul"
א B
NLTmg

variant 2 *Beelzebub*
it[c] syr[p,s]
KJV NKJV NIV NEB NLTmg

The same textual variations occur in Matt 10:25 (see note) and Mark 3:22.

Luke 11:23

TR WH NU καὶ ὁ μὴ συνάγων μετ' ἐμοῦ σκορπίζει
"the one not gathering with me scatters"
𝔓[45] (𝔓[75]) א[1] A B C* D W f[1,13] Maj syr[c]
all

variant και ο μη συναγων μετ εμου σκορπιζει με
"the one not gathering with me scatters me"
א*,2 C[2] L Θ Ψ 33 syr[s] cop[bo]
NEBmg

Metzger (TCGNT) readily dismisses the variant as a scribal blunder because the resultant text is "almost meaningless." But how could such a blunder occur in so many manuscripts of diverse origin and date? And why would correctors purposely add what is a blatant mistake or ancient translators translate it? The reading with "scatters me," though strange to our sensibilities, is not meaningless. The strangeness comes from the fact that we do not think of scattering the sheep as including the shepherd (Jesus), but he is so identified with his flock that to scatter Jesus' sheep is to scatter or divide Jesus himself, inasmuch as he is united to those who are his own. The idea is that of solidarity between the shepherd and the sheep. All this goes to say that the variant cannot be easily dismissed. And there is something to be said for the fact that both here and in Matt 12:30, the witnesses א 33 syr[s] cop[bo] display the reading "scatters me." Nonetheless, far superior documentary testimony supports the reading "scatters," and for that reason it would have to be adopted as the text.

Luke 11:29

WH NU	τὸ σημεῖον Ἰωνᾶ "the sign of Jonah" 𝔓45 𝔓75 ℵ B D L Ξ NKJVmg RSV NRSV ESV NASB NIV TNIV NEB REB NJB NAB NLT HCSB NET
variant/TR	το σημειον Ιωνα του προφητου "the sign of Jonah the prophet" A C W Θ Ψ 070 $f^{1,13}$ 33 Maj KJV NKJV HCSBmg

The variant reading, found in TR, exhibits harmonization to Matt 12:39. The additional title, "the prophet," is superfluous. Whereas Matthew is very interested in the messianic predictions of the prophets, Luke emphasizes the personal sign of Jonah to the Ninevites after his miraculous "resurrection" from the belly of a great fish.

Luke 11:30

At the end of this verse, D and some Old Latin versions add words borrowed from Matt 12:40, "and as Jonah was in the belly of the whale three days and three nights, so also will the Son of Man be in the earth."

Luke 11:31

All Greek manuscripts, including 𝔓75c, indicate that it is "the queen of the South" (βασιλισσα νοτου) who will be raised in the judgment against the generation that rejected Jesus. 𝔓75* simply calls her "the queen" (βασιλισσα). The word νοτου appears to have been added by another scribe because it is a superlinear correction in another hand (see *Text of Earliest MSS,* 534).

Luke 11:33a

TR WH NU	οὐδεὶς λύχνον ἅψας εἰς κρύπτην τίθησιν [οὐδὲ ὑπὸ τὸν μόδιον] "no one, lighting a lamp, puts it in hiding or under a basket" ℵ A B C D W Θ Ψ f^{13} Maj KJV NKJV RSV NRSVmg ESV NASB NIV TNIV NEBmg NJB NAB NLT HCSB NET
variant	ουδεις λυχνον αψας εις κρυπτην τιθησιν "no one, lighting a lamp, puts it in hiding" 𝔓45 𝔓75 L Γ Ξ 070 f^1 syr^s cop^{sa} NRSV NEB REB NLTmg HCSBmg NETmg

The Greek phrase ουδε υπο τον μοδιον, not appearing in the papyri and several other diverse witnesses, was most likely borrowed from Matt 5:15 or Mark 4:21, parallel passages. The shorter reading emphasizes the need to not hide the light so that it can benefit those desiring to be enlightened: "No one, lighting a lamp, puts it in hiding, but he places it on a lamp stand that the ones entering may see the light." The additional words, "under a basket," are a distraction from the central message. Interestingly, NRSV diverges from NU by not including this wording.

Luke 11:33b

𝔓[75] ℵ B C D Θ 070 read φως ("light"), whereas 𝔓[45] A L W Γ Δ Ψ read φεγγος ("radiance"). Marshall (1978, 488) indicates that the first reading may be the result of harmonization to Luke 8:16, but this could not be so for 𝔓[75] and B, neither of which have the final clause of 8:16 (see note above).

Luke 11:35-36

The difficulty of these verses led to textual adjustments. D and many Old Latin manuscripts substitute the wording of Matt 6:23, "If therefore the light in you is darkness, how great the darkness." The Curetonian Syriac uses the same wording to replace 11:35 and then retains 11:36. These changes may be the result of trying to replace an enigmatic expression with a transparent one, but Matthew's statement is nearly as difficult as Luke's: "Watch out that the light in you does not become darkness." In both Matthew and Luke, Jesus was warning his listeners that the "light" they had (i.e., knowledge of the Torah and the rabbinic writings) could prevent them from seeing the light of life, Jesus Christ. As such, their light would actually be darkness (cf. 2 Cor 3:12-15).

Luke 11:42

Jesus castigated the Pharisees for their observance of trifling rituals (such as cleaning their utensils and tithing every herb) while "neglecting justice and the love of God." He concluded by saying, "these you ought to have done, without neglecting the others." This sentence was omitted by Marcion because he could not tolerate Jesus encouraging any kind of ritualistic practice derived from the OT. The scribe of D, perhaps influenced by a Marcionite text, also omitted it. The NEBmg makes note of this omission in some witnesses.

Luke 11:43

Some manuscripts (C D f[13]) harmonize Luke 11:43 to Matt 23:6 by adding και ταις πρωτοκλισιας εν τοις δειπνοις ("and the places of honor at the banquets") at the end of the verse.

Luke 11:44

WH NU οὐαὶ ὑμῖν
"woe to you"
𝔓[45vid] 𝔓[75] ℵ B C L
NKJVmg RSV NRSV ESV NASB NIV TNIV NEB REB NJB NAB NLT HCSB NET

variant/TR ουαι υμιν γραμματεις και Φαρισαιοι υποκριται
"woe to you, scribes and Pharisees, hypocrites"
A D W Θ Ψ f[13] Maj
KJV NKJV HCSBmg NETmg

The WH NU reading has superior attestation. The expanded reading is the result of scribal harmonization to Matt 23:27, a parallel passage. Such harmonization is replete in TR, followed by KJV and NKJV.

Luke 11:48

Many manuscripts (A C W Θ Ψ 33 Maj—so TR) add αυτων τα μνημεια ("their tombs") after οικοδομειτε ("you build") in order to provide a direct object for this transitive verb.

Luke 11:49

According to Matt 23:34, it is Jesus who says, "I will send them prophets and sages and scribes." Luke, however, uses the expression "the wisdom of God" for the speaker: "The wisdom of God said, 'I will send them prophets and apostles, some of whom they will kill and persecute.'" The term "wisdom of God" may refer to Jesus, or it could mean "divine wisdom." Either way, the editor of D and translator of it[b] deleted the phrase, thereby bringing it into harmony with Matt 23:34.

Luke 11:51

Some witnesses (D it[a] syr[c,s]) conform Luke to Matt 23:35 by adding "son of Berachiah" after "Zechariah." But Luke purposely left off "son of Berachiah" to avoid a difficult, if not improbable, identification (see comments on Matt 23:35).

Luke 11:53a

WH NU	κακειθεν ἐξελθόντος αὐτους "and as he went away from there" 𝔓[45vid] (𝔓[75] εξελθοντες) ℵ B C L 33 cop NKJVmg RSV NRSV ESV NASB NIV TNIV NEB REB NJB NAB NLT HCSB NET
variant/TR	λεγοντος δε αυτου ταυτα προς αυτους "and as he was saying these things to them" A (D) W Θ Ψ f[1,13] Maj KJV NKJV HCSBmg

In full translation WH NU read, "And as he went away from there, the scribes and Pharisees began to press him hard, and to provoke him to say many things, lying in wait for him, to catch him at something he might say" (RSV). TR begins the verse differently so as to have Jesus still being in the presence of the scribes and Pharisees as he said these things. Documentary evidence strongly favors the WH NU reading.

Luke 11:53b-54

Some witnesses (D Θ it syr[c,s]) have a different variation for 11:53b-54: ενωπιον παντος του λαου ηρξαντο οι Φαρισαιοι και οι νομικοι δεινως εχειν και συμβαλλειν αυτω περι πλειονων ζητουντες αφορμην τινα λαβειν αυτου ινα ευρωσιν κατηγορησαι αυτου ("[and as he was saying these things to them] in the presence of all the people, the Pharisees and the lawyers began to react violently and to argue with him about many things, seeking some pretext to catch him so that they might accuse him.") This change has "lawyers" instead of "scribes" and specifies that they wanted to catch Jesus in some pretext (αφορμην).

Luke 11:54b

WH NU	omit at end of verse: ινα κατηγορησωσιν αυτου ("so that they might accuse him") 𝔓45 𝔓75 א B L cop NKJVmg RSV NRSV ESV NASB NIV TNIV NEB REB NJB NAB NLT HCSB NET
variant/TR	add at end of verse: ινα κατηγορησωσιν αυτου ("so that they might accuse him") A C (D) W Θ Ψ f1,13 33 Maj KJV NKJV HCSBmg

The WH NU reading has impressive support from all the earliest manuscripts. The addition in TR is scribal gap-filling, intended to help readers understand that the reason they wanted to catch Jesus in something he might say was so that they could bring formal accusations against him.

Luke 12:8-9

In both these verses א* and Marcion omit των αγγελων ("the angels") from the statements (1) ομολογησει εν αυτω εμπροσθεν των αγγελων του θεου ("he [the Son of Man] will confess him before the angels of God") and (2) απαρνηθησεται ενωπιον των αγγελων του θεου ("he will be denied before the angels of God"). These changes were made because it is easier to imagine Jesus making such a confession to God than to the angels of God. This presentation also accords with the parallel passage, Matt 10:32-33.

All of verse 9 was omitted in 𝔓45 it[e] syr[s] and one cop[bo] manuscript. The omission may have been accidental, due to haplography—the eye of a scribe passing from the last four words of 12:8 (which are the same at the end of 12:9—των αγγελων του θεου ["the angels of God"]) to the beginning of 12:10.

Luke 12:18

WH NU	πάντα τὸν σῖτον καὶ τὰ ἀγαθά μου "all the grain and my goods" 𝔓75c (𝔓75* has μου after σιτον) (א2) B L 070 f1 RSV NRSV ESV NASB NIV (TNIV) NEB NJB NAB (NLT) HCSB NET
variant 1	παντα τα γενηματα μου "all my produce" א* D it (syr[c,s]) none
variant 2/TR	παντα τα γενηματα μου και τα αγαθα μου "all my produce and my goods" A Q W Θ Ψ 33[vid] Maj KJV NKJV

It is difficult to determine which of the first two readings is original. The term γενηματα μου ("my goods") may have been borrowed from the Septuagint (Exod 23:10; Lev 25:20; Jer 8:13), or it may have been replaced by Alexandrian scribes who disliked γενημα (see Isa 65:21; LXX). The second variant is the result of scribal conflation of the first two. "'Other goods' refers to more than farm produce; it makes the story applicable to others than just farmers" (Fitzmyer 1985, 973).

Luke 12:21

This verse is omitted in D it[a,b]. Since there is no apparent reason for the omission on transcriptional grounds, it must be assumed that its excision was intentional. Perhaps the D-editor (so also it[a,b]) considered the question posed in 12:20 as providing a more dramatic conclusion to the pericope than does 12:21, which functions as the concluding moral to the story.

At the end of this pericope, a few scribes (U f[13] 892) added the formulaic concluding statement found frequently throughout the Gospels: ταυτα λεγων εφωνει· ο εχων ωτα ακουειν ακουετω ("having said these things, he called out, 'Let him who has ears to hear, hear'").

Luke 12:22

The testimony of the three earliest witnesses, 𝔓[45vid] 𝔓[75] B, attests to the reading τους μαθητας ("the disciples"), whereas all other manuscripts read τους μαθητας αυτου ("his disciples"). Metzger (TCGNT) argues that "his disciples" is Lukan. But the earliest testimony here favors the shorter reading, hence it is bracketed in NU.

Luke 12:27

TR WH NU πῶς αὐξάνει· οὐ κοπιᾷ οὐδὲ νήθει
"how it [the lily] grows; it neither labors nor spins"
𝔓[45] 𝔓[75] ℵ A B L W Maj
KJV NKJV RSV NRSV ESV NASB NIV TNIV NEBmg NJBmg NAB NLT HCSB NET

variant πως ουτε νηθει ουτε υφαινει
"how it [the lily] neither spins nor weaves"
D syr[c,s] (it[a] Marcion[according to Tertullian]) Clement
ESVmg NEB REB NJB

Similar variation occurred in Matt 6:28 (see note). The variant reading in this verse, which has almost exclusively Western support, conjoins two verbs that pertain to the making of clothing (spinning and weaving)—probably in anticipation of the following comparison to Solomon's clothing. Both the NEB and NJB adopted this Western reading, which is not an unusual practice for these two versions. It is somewhat uncharacteristic, however, that the REB did not follow the NU text here.

Luke 12:31

The wording ζητειτε την βασιλειαν αυτου ("seek his kingdom"), found in ℵ B D* L Ψ, is shortened to ζητειτε την βασιλειαν ("seek the kingdom") in 𝔓[75] and lengthened to ζητειτε την βασιλειαν του θεου ("seek the kingdom of God") in 𝔓[45] A D[1] Q W Θ 070 f[1,13] Maj (so TR)—by way of conformity to Matt 6:33. A few versions (vg[cl] eth) harmonize this completely to Matt 6:33, "seek the kingdom of God and his righteousness."

Luke 12:38

In place of the first clause of the text, D (basically followed by f[1] it syr[c]) reads, και εαν ελθη τη εσπερινη φυλακη και ευρησει ουτως ποιησει και εαν εν τη δευτερα και τη τριτη ("should he [the master] come during the evening watch and find them, he will do so—and even if it is in the second or third watch").

Luke 12:39

NU οὐκ ἂν ἀφῆκεν διορυχθῆναι τὸν οἶκον αὐτοῦ
"he would not have allowed his house to be broken into"
𝔓75 א* (D) ite,i syrc,s Marcionaccording to Tertullian
NKJVmg RSV NRSV ESV NASB NIV TNIV NEB REB NJB NAB NLT HCSB NET

variant/TR WH εγρηγορησεν αν και ουκ αν αφηκεν διορυχθηναι τον οικον αυτου
"he would have kept watch and not allowed his house to be broken into"
א1 (A) B L Q W Δ Θ Ψ 070 f1,13 33 Maj
KJV NKJV RSVmg NRSVmg ESVmg NETmg

Even though it has diverse documentation, the variant reading is the result of scribal harmonization to a parallel passage, Matt 24:43. All modern translations have followed the reading attested to by the earliest manuscript, 𝔓75.

Luke 12:47

WH NU καὶ μὴ ἑτοιμάσας ἢ ποιήσας πρὸς τὸ θέλημα αὐτοῦ
"and not preparing [for it] or doing his will"
𝔓75 א B Ψ 070 33
RSV NRSV ESV NASB NIV TNIV NJB NAB NLT HCSB NET

variant 1 και ποιησας προς το θελημα αυτου
"and doing his own will"
𝔓45
none

variant 2 και μη ετοιμασας προς το θελημα αυτου
"and not being prepared for his will"
L W f13 it syrc,s
none

variant 3 και μη ποιησας προς το θελημα αυτου
"and not doing his will"
D Marcion Irenaeus Origen
NEB REB

variant 4/TR και μη ετοιμασας μηδε ποιησας προς το θελημα αυτου
"and not preparing [for it] or even doing his will"
A Θ f1 Maj
KJV NKJV

The WH NU reading has solid documentary support and makes perfectly good sense: "the slave, knowing the will of his master and not preparing [for it] or doing his will, will be beaten with many blows." The second and third variants are truncations of the text, and the fourth has but a slight alteration. The variant in 𝔓45 cannot be easily explained as a scribal error because although either μη ετοιμασας or η ποιησας could have dropped out due to homoeoteleuton, not so for μη ετοιμασας η. Thus, if the change was intentional, it is possible that the scribe of 𝔓45 was thinking that the servant's sin was that of conspiring against the master's will (see Fitzmyer 1985, 992). This means the servant knew the master's will and yet went ahead to do his own will (cf. Jas 4:17). The last part of the verse—"he will receive many blows"—may have prompted this adjustment, inasmuch as nothing short of rebellion could have called for such severe punishment.

Luke 12:52-53

The first verb of 12:53 in all three editions (TR WH NU), διαμερισθησονται ("having been divided"), can be joined with the end of 12:52 ("three against two and two against three have been divided"). What follows in 12:53, therefore, is a list. Yet it is also possible to join it with the first part of 12:53 ("father divided against son and son against father," etc.). Interestingly, the two earliest manuscripts are divided on this: 𝔓45 (by means of punctuation) joins the verb with 12:52, and 𝔓75 (also by means of punctuation) joins it with 12:53.

Luke 12:56

WH NU — πῶς οὐκ οἴδατε δοκιμάζειν;
"why don't you know how to interpret?"
𝔓75 ℵ B L Θ 33
RSV NRSV ESV NIV TNIV NJB NAB NLT HCSB NET

variant 1/TR — πως ου δοκιμαζετε;
"why can't you interpret?"
𝔓45 A W $f^{1,13}$ Maj
KJV NKJV NASB NEB REB NETmg

variant 2 — ου δοκιμαζετε;
"can't you interpret?"
D it syr[c]
none

Because of the excellent testimony behind WH NU, it should be judged that the two variants are the result of scribal trimming. According to WH NU, Jesus was not only condemning their lack of perception of what was happening around them; he was condemning their inability to interpret at all.

Luke 13:3, 5

In both these verses the present subjunctive μετανοητε ("repent"), supported by 𝔓75 (ℵ) B W, was changed to an aorist subjunctive, μετανοσητε in A D Θ $f^{1,(13)}$, to emphasize an immediate, once-and-for-all repentance.

Luke 13:19

WH NU — ἐγένετο εἰς δένδρον
"became a tree"
𝔓75 ℵ B (D) L 070
NKJVmg RSV NRSV ESV NASB NIV TNIV NEB REB NJB (NAB) NLT HCSB NET

variant/TR — εγενετο εις μεγα δενδρον
"became a great tree"
𝔓45 A W Θ Ψ f^{13} 33 Maj
KJV NKJV

Although it could be argued that μεγα ("great") was deleted by scribes in order to conform this text to Matt 13:32 (the parallel passage), it is just as likely that the word was added to heighten the sense (TCGNT). Besides, the manuscripts with the shorter text (especially 𝔓[75] ℵ B) generally show far less harmonization in the Gospels than those that have the addition. All modern versions follow the shorter text.

Luke 13:24

Influenced by the parallel passage in Matt 7:13-14, scribes (A W Ψ f^{13} Maj—so TR) changed θυρας ("door") to πυλη ("gate"). But the Matthean image depicts a gate providing entry to a road, whereas the Lukan image depicts a door of the master's house.

Luke 13:25

Influenced by Matt 7:21-22 or Matt 25:11, some scribes (A D W Θ Ψ 070 $f^{1,13}$ Maj—so TR) doubled the vocative κυριε ("Lord") to κυριε κυριε ("Lord, Lord").

Luke 13:27

The beginning words of this verse were altered by various scribes, but the original text is preserved in 𝔓[75c] and B. It is clear that the wording ερει λεγων υμιν (literally "he will speak saying to you") appeared in the exemplar used by the scribe of 𝔓[75] because he first wrote ερει λεγω υμιν ("he will speak, 'I say to you . . .'"), then corrected it to ερει λεγων υμιν. This change also shows that the scribe copied his manuscript carefully; when he noted the difference between his text and his exemplar, he added a *nu* at the end of λεγω. The wording Luke used probably represents the construction of the Hebrew infinitive absolute: "he will indeed say to you" (TCGNT).

Luke 13:35

WH NU	ἀφίεται ὑμῖν ὁ οἶκος ὑμῶν "your house is left to you" 𝔓[45vid] 𝔓[75] ℵ A B L W syr[s] cop[sa] RSV NRSV ESV NEB REB NJB NLT HCSB NET
variant/TR	αφιεται υμιν ο οικος υμων ερημος "your house is left to you desolate" D N Δ Θ Ψ f^{13} 33 Maj it syr[c] KJV NKJV NASB NIV TNIV NAB

Whereas in Matt 23:38, the best documentation supports the inclusion of the word ερημος ("desolate"), in Luke it is just the opposite. It is quite likely that D Θ Ψ f^{13} Maj it syr[c] added ερημος to Luke from their text of Matt 23:38, so that in these manuscripts Matt 23:38 and Luke 13:35 perfectly harmonize. (See note on Matt 23:38.) Several modern English versions reflect the inferior reading probably because English style calls for "desolate" or "abandoned" after "is left to you."

Luke 14:5

WH NU υἱὸς ἢ βοῦς
"son or ox"
(𝔓45 adds η before υιος) 𝔓75 (A) B W Maj it[e] syr[h,p] cop[sa]
NKJVmg RSV NRSV ESV NASB NIV TNIV NEBmg REB NJB NAB NLT HCSB NET

variant 1/TR ονος η βους
"donkey or ox"
ℵ K L Ψ f[1,13] 33 cop[bo]
KJV NKJV RSVmg NRSVmg ESVmg NIVmg TNIVmg NEB REBmg NJBmg NLTmg NETmg

variant 2 βους η ονος
"ox or donkey"
syr[s]
none

variant 3 υιος η βους η ονος
"son or ox or donkey"
syr[c]
none

variant 4 ονος υιος η βους
"foal of a donkey or an ox"
Θ
none

variant 5 προβατον η βους
"sheep or ox"
D it[d]
none

A rendering of WH NU in full is as follows: "Which of you, having a son or an ox falling into a well, will not immediately pull him out on the Sabbath?" This reading is preferred because it has the best documentary support and is the reading that explains the origin of all the variants. This reading cannot necessarily be explained as a transcriptional error, wherein ονος was mistaken for υιος because in many ancient manuscripts υιος would have been contracted as $\overline{\Upsilon\Sigma}$. In fact, in 𝔓75 the word υιος is written as $\overline{\Upsilon\Sigma}$; as such, the scribe clearly knew he was writing the word for "son." And it is very unlikely that υιος ("son") is a corruption of οις ("sheep"), as was conjectured by Mill (1723, 44), because οις is a poetic word that rarely appears in Greek prose.

The fifth variant is the result of assimilation to Matt 12:11. The second, third, and fourth variants are poorly attested conflations of the WH NU reading or of the first variant. The first variant (and all those that follow) is the result of scribes fixing what appeared to be an incongruous collocation of two words: "son" and "ox." It would be natural to change this to "a donkey or an ox" in light of OT texts such as Exod 21:33; 22:4; Deut 22:4. But there was rabbinic and Qumranic teaching around the time of Christ that stipulated rules pertaining to the rescue of people and of animals on the Sabbath day (Marshall 1978, 580). Thus, Jesus' combination of "son and ox" would not have sounded incongruous to his Pharisaic listeners.

It should be noted that the variant in 𝔓45 reveals that the scribe may have had the first variant in his exemplar or that at least he knew of the reading, because the feminine article η does not coincide with masculine υιος; rather, it presupposes ονος, which—with the feminine article—designates a female donkey (cf. Matt 21:2). Perhaps he first intended to write ονος, but he wrote υιος in the end—leaving the η uncorrected. This duplicity shows that both readings were quite early, and that the scribe of 𝔓[45] was in the position to make a choice, one which was influenced by his reading of Matthew.

Luke 14:17

WH NU	ἕτοιμα ἐστιν "it is ready" B it RSV NRSV NASB NIV NEB REB NJB NLT
variant 1	ετοιμα εισιν "they are ready" 𝔓[75] ℵ*,2 L Θ none
variant 2/TR	ετοιμα εστιν παντα "everything is ready" A (D) W Ψ $f^{1,13}$ Maj KJV NKJV ESV TNIV NAB HCSB NET
variant 3	ετοιμα εισιν παντα "all things are ready" ℵ[1] same as variant 2

The addition of παντα (in the second and third variants) is probably a carryover assimilation to Matt 22:4, a parallel passage. This assimilation was included in TR and rendered in KJV and NKJV. Luke could have written either εστιν or εισιν, but the latter has better textual support.

Luke 14:24

At the end of this verse, several manuscripts (Γ f^{13} 28[mg] 700 892[mg] 1010[mg]) add (often in the margin), πολλοι γαρ εισιν κλητοι· ολιγοι δε εκλεκτοι ("for many are called but few are chosen"). This is clearly an interpolation taken from Matt 22:14.

Luke 14:27

This verse, which puts forth a call to follow Jesus in a path of self-denial, was accidentally omitted in some manuscripts (Γ syr[s] cop[boMS]) due to homoeoteleuton—the eye of a scribe passing over the words, ου δυναται ειναι μου μαθητης ("he is not able to be my disciple"), which appear at the end of 14:26 and 14:27.

Luke 14:32

Many manuscripts (ℵ[2] A D L W Θ Ψ $f^{1,13}$ Maj) read ερωτα τα προς ειρηνην ("he asked for the things pertaining to peace" = "he asked for the terms of peace"). This was shortened in ℵ* to ερωτα εις ειρηνη ("he asked for peace"), and shortened even further in 𝔓[75] to ερωτα ειρηνη ("he asked peace"). This redaction of the idiom may have been influenced by Acts 12:20 (Marshall 1978, 594), revealing the scribe's knowledge of Luke's sequel.

Luke 15:16

WH NU	ἐπεθύμει χορτασθῆναι "he desired to satisfy himself" 𝔓75 ℵ B D L f1,13 it^e (syr^c) cop^sa RSV NRSV ESV NEBmg NJB NLT HCSB NET
variant 1/TR	επεθυμει γεμισαι την κοιλιαν αυτου "he desired to fill his stomach" A Θ Ψ Maj syr^h,p,s cop^bo KJV NKJV RSVmg NRSVmg NASB NIV TNIV NEB REB NAB HCSBmg
variant 2	επεθυμει γεμισαι την κολιαν και χορτασθηναι "he desired to fill his stomach and satisfy himself" W none

Internal arguments can go either way on this reading. Uncomfortable with the crude expression, "fill his stomach," some scribes may have softened it; contrarily, other scribes may have colored the narrative with this expression. (The second variant is a conflation of the other two.) However, the softening cannot be charged to Alexandrian polishing because the manuscripts that show this reading go far beyond those of Alexandrian origin. Furthermore, the expression επεθυμει χορτασθηναι ("he desires to be satisfied") accords with Lukan style (see 16:21). Thus, it is more likely that the scribes have colored the text for greater narrative effectiveness; but this coloring misses the point. The prodigal son could have filled his stomach with pods, but he would not have been satisfied with them (Westcott and Hort 1882, 62). Nonetheless, the KJV tradition and several modern versions follow TR—either consciously or for the sake of coloring.

Luke 15:21

TR NU	οὐκέτι εἰμὶ ἄξιος κληθῆναι υἱός σου. "I am no longer worthy to be called your son." 𝔓75 A L W Θ Ψ f1,13 Maj syr^c,s cop all
variant/WH	ουκετι ειμι αξιος κληθηναι υιος σου. ποιησον με ως ενα των μισθιων σου. "I am no longer worthy to be called your son; make me like one of your hired men." ℵ B D 33 syr^h RSVmg NRSVmg ESVmg NIVmg NEBmg NLTmg

There are two factors that favor the TR NU reading: (1) it has earlier and more diverse testimony, and (2) the words in the variant were carried over from Luke 15:19 so that the son's actual speech would replicate the one he had planned. Not one translation includes these words; however, out of deference to the testimony of ℵ B D, several versions note them. WH includes the words in brackets to show doubt about their authenticity. In this case the testimony of ℵ and B (favored by WH) is overridden by 𝔓75 etc.

Luke 15:29

Instead of εριφον ("goat"), found in most manuscripts, 𝔓75 and B read εριφιον ("a young goat"), and D reads εριφον εξ αιγων ("kid of goats")—derived from Gen 38:20 (LXX).

Luke 15:32

In several later manuscripts, this verse is harmonized with 15:24 by changing the verb εζησεν ("he lived") to ανεζησεν ("he lived again"—as in א[2] A D Θ Ψ f[1,13] Maj—so TR), and by changing απολωλως ("having been lost") to ην απολωλως ("he was lost"—in Maj and TR).

Luke 16:6

Instead of the wording εκατον βατους ελαιου ("one hundred baths of oil"), found in most manuscripts, D* and 1241 read εκατον καδους ελαιου ("one hundred jars of oil"). Since one hundred baths of oil would be about nine hundred gallons, one hundred jars are significantly smaller.

Luke 16:9

WH NU	ὅταν ἐκλίπῃ "when it fails" 𝔓[75] B א* D L Ψ NKJVmg RSV NRSV ESV NASB NIV TNIV NEB REB NJB NAB NLT HCSB NET
variant/TR	οταν εκλιπητε "when you fail [or, when you give out]" Maj Vulgate KJV NKJV HCSBmg

According to the best manuscript evidence, the text speaks of the wealth of unrighteousness giving out. Instead of speaking of money running out, this variant speaks of one's life running out ("when you give out" is a euphemism for death). Of course, this scribal adjustment, which may reflect an early exegetical tradition, fits very nicely with the following statement: "when you die, they will receive you into the eternal dwellings." The Latin Vulgate and KJV (following TR) reflect this reading.

Luke 16:12

TR NU	τὸ ὑμέτερον τίς ὑμῖν δώσει; "who will give you what is your own?" 𝔓[75] א A D W Θ Ψ f[1,13] Maj syr cop all
variant 1/WH	το ημετερον τις υμιν δωσει; "who will give you what is ours?" B L NASBmg NJBmg
variant 2	το εμον τις υμιν δωσει; "who will give you what is mine?" 157 it[e,i] Marcion Tertullian none
variant 3	το αληθινον τις υμιν δωσει; "who will give you what is true?" 33[vid] none

In context, TR NU read, "And if you are not faithful with what belongs to another, who will give you what is your own?" The obscurity of the text gave rise to the different variants. The general idea seems to be that worldly wealth does not belong to the believers; their wealth is that which is given to them by God. In other words, they will be given the treasures of heaven. The third variant approximates this meaning, but it is a carryover from 16:11. The first variant is probably a transcriptional error; but if not, "ours" includes the Father and the Son—"who will give to you what belongs to the Father and the Son." The second variant includes only the Son—"who will give to you what belongs to me [the Son]."

Luke 16:14

According to excellent documentary evidence (𝔓[75] א B L Ψ syr[s] cop), the text reads ηκουον δε ταυτα παντα οι Φαρισαιοι ("and the Pharisees heard all these things"). This was slightly modified in A W Θ f[1,13] Maj (so TR) to ηκουον δε ταυτα παντα και οι Φαρισαιοι ("and the Pharisees also heard all these things"). This adds a contrast between them and the disciples of 16:1 (Fitzmyer 1985, 1112).

Luke 16:18

Several manuscripts (א A W Θ Ψ f[1,13] Maj—so TR) add πας ("everyone") before the second clause to retain a parallel expression with the first. D and syr[p,s] omit απο ανδρος ("by [her] husband"), but this does not alter the sense: "whoever marries a divorced woman commits adultery."

Luke 16:19

Codex D introduces the pericope of the rich man and Lazarus with the words ειπεν δε και ετεραν παραβολην ("and he spoke another parable"). This interpolation indicates that the D-reviser did not consider this to be a historical account. In like manner, modern interpreters tend to call it an illustration or an example story (see Bock 1996, 1362-1363).

This is the only parable told by Jesus in which one of the characters is given a name; the beggar is called Lazarus. Some witnesses provide testimony of scribal attempts (beginning as early as the second century) to give the rich man a name. The scribe of 𝔓[75] provided him a name, Νευης; and one Coptic Sahidic manuscript reads *Nineue*. Both of these names may be synonyms for Nineveh, the wealthy city that came under God's judgment. According to a pseudo-Cyprianic text (third century), the rich man is called *Finaeus*. Priscillian also gave him the name *Finees*, which is probably an alternate to Phinehas, Eleazar's son (Exod 6:25; Num 25:7, 11). Peter of Riga called him *Amonofis*, which is a form of "Amenophis," a name held by many Pharaohs (see TCGNT). These namings all exemplify the scribal desire to fill perceived gaps in the narrative text (for more on this see Comfort 2008).

Luke 16:21

The WH NU reading (supported by 𝔓[75] א* B L it syr[s]) was modified by later scribes (א[2] A D W Θ Ψ f[1,13] Maj—so TR), who added των ψιχων ("the crumbs") to απο των πιπτοντων ("from the things falling"), yielding the translation, "who desired to be fed with the crumbs falling from the master's table." The additional verbiage was probably borrowed from Matt 15:27. At the end of the first sentence, a few Latin witnesses and f[13] add και ουδεις εδιδου αυτω ("and no one was giving [anything] to him"). This addition came from Luke 15:16, which describes the abject condition of the prodigal son.

Luke 16:22-23

According to most witnesses, verse 22 ends with και εταφη ("and he was buried"), which is followed by a new sentence in verse 23: και εν τω αδη επαρας τους οφθαλμους ("and in Hades he lifted up his eyes"). A few witnesses (א* Old Latin MSS and Marcion), however, read και εταφη εν τω αδη ("and he was buried in Hades"). This reading, attractive at first glance, lacks sufficient documentary authority and says something that is nowhere else in the NT—i.e., that a person can be buried in Hades. The usual presentation is that people are buried in the earth and then go to Hades disembodied.

Luke 17:2

Instead of the expression λιθος μυλικος ("millstone"—literally "a stone belonging to a mill"), found in $\mathfrak{P}^{75}$ א B D L Θ $f^{1,13}$, other manuscripts (A Ψ Maj syr cop[bo]—so TR) read μυλος ονικος (literally "a mill turned by an ass"). This reading is the result of scribal harmonization to Matt 18:6 and Mark 9:42, parallel passages.

Luke 17:3

WH NU	ἐὰν ἁμάρτῃ ὁ ἀδελφός σου ἐπιτίμησον αὐτῷ "if your brother sins, rebuke him" א A B L W Θ f^1 syr cop RSV NRSV ESV NASB NIV REB NJB NAB NLT HCSB NET
variant/TR	εαν αμαρτη εις σε ο αδελφος σου επιτιμησον αυτω "if your brother sins against you, rebuke him" D Ψ f^{13} Maj KJV NKJV TNIV NEB HCSBmg

The variant is the result of scribal harmonization to Matt 18:15 (see comments there). As usual, TR picked up this harmonization, and KJV and NKJV translated it. So do TNIV and NEB, following the Western text.

Luke 17:4

As a carryover from the first part of the verse ("if he sins seven times during the day"), various scribes (A W Θ $f^{1,13}$ Maj) added της ημερας ("during the day") to επτακις επι-στρεψη ("he repents seven times").

Luke 17:6

Borrowing from Matt 17:20, the editor of D added, τω ορει τουτω· μεταβα εντευθεν εκει, και μετεβαινεν ("if you say to this [mountain], 'move from here to there,' it would move").

Luke 17:9

WH NU μὴ ἔχει χάριν τῷ δούλῳ ὅτι ἐποίησεν τὰ διαταχθέντα;
"Do you thank the slave for doing what was commanded?"
𝔓[75] ℵ[1] B L f^1 it[e]
RSV NRSV ESV NASB NIV TNIV NEB REB NJB NAB (NLT) HCSB NET

variant 1 μη εχει χαριν τω δουλω οτι εποιησεν τα διαταχθεντα; ου δοκω.
"Do you thank the slave for doing what was commanded? I don't think so."
A W Θ Ψ Maj
NKJVmg

variant 2/TR μη εχει χαριν τω δουλω οτι εποιησεν τα διαταχθεντα αυτω; ου δοκω.
"Do you thank the slave for doing what was commanded him? I don't think so."
D f^{13} it syr[p]
KJV NKJV HCSBmg

The two variants present two forms of scribal gap-filling. The first supplies an answer to the question. But according to Greek grammar, the initial μη sufficiently signals a negative response. The second variant supplies an object for διαταχθεντα ("commanded"), as well as an answer.

Luke 17:14

In the bottom margin of 𝔓[75], some writer other than the original scribe inserted θελω καθαρισθητε και ευθεως εκαθαρισθησαν ("'I will cleanse you,' and immediately he was cleansed") at the beginning of Jesus' speech to the ten men who had leprosy. This gloss was taken from Matt 8:2-3, where Jesus is said to have expressed his willingness to cleanse a man from his leprosy when he asked Jesus for healing. Evidently, a reader of 𝔓[75] considered it important to include a similar expression in Luke (Comfort 1997b, 241).

Luke 17:24

TR NU οὕτως ἔσται ὁ υἱὸς τοῦ ἀνθρώπου [ἐν τῇ ἡμέρᾳ αὐτοῦ]
"so will be the Son of Man in his day"
ℵ A L W Θ Ψ $f^{1,13}$ Maj
all

variant/WH ουτως εσται ο υιος του ανθρωπου
"so will be the Son of Man"
𝔓[75] B D it cop[sa]
RSVmg NRSVmg NIVmg TNIVmg NETmg

In a fuller context, a rendering of TR NU is, "For as the lightning flashes and lights up the sky from one end to the other, so will be the Son of Man in his day." The phrase εν τη ημερα αυτου ("in his day") is bracketed in NU to signal the editors' doubts about it being originally written by Luke, since the phrase is lacking in 𝔓[75] B D—which represents early and diverse testimony (see TCGNT). Internal arguments can go both ways. Scribes may have added "in his day" to make a parallel statement with 17:22 ("you will desire to see one of the days of the Son of Man"), or scribes could have dropped the phrase to make it conform to the Matthean parallel (Matt 24:27). However, since the scribes of 𝔓75 and B were rarely given to harmonization, it seems more likely that "in his day" was added later. This was the understanding of WH based on B, which is now supported by 𝔓75. Not one English version has yet followed this shorter reading, though several note it.

Luke 17:33

WH NU	ὃς ἐὰν ζητήσῃ τὴν ψυχὴν αὐτοῦ περιποιήσασθαι "whoever seeks to preserve his life" 𝔓75 B L RSV NRSV ESV NASB NIV TNIV REB NJB NAB NLT HCSB NET
variant 1/TR	ος εαν ζητηση την ψυχην αυτου σωσαι "whoever seeks to save his life" ℵ A W Θ Ψ f1,13 Maj KJV NKJV NEB HCSBmg
variant 2	ος αν θεληση ζωογονησαι "whoever wants to keep alive" D itd syrc,s copsa none

The WH NU reading has the earliest support (𝔓75 B) and is likely original. The first variant is the result of scribal conformity to Luke 9:24; the second is taken from the last clause of this verse, which has the verb ζωογονησει ("will keep [it] alive").

Luke 17:36

WH NU	omit verse 𝔓75 ℵ A B L W Δ Θ Ψ f1 33 copsa,bo NKJVmg RSV NRSV ESV NASBmg NIV TNIV NEB REB NJB NAB NLT HCSBmg NET
variant/TR	add verse Δυο εσονται εν τω αγρω, εἶς παραλημφθησεται και ο ετερος αφεθησεται "Two will be in the field; one will be taken and the other left." D f13 700 it syr KJV NKJV RSVmg NRSVmg ESVmg NASB NIVmg NEBmg REBmg NJBmg NABmg NLTmg HCSB NETmg

Although it is possible that the verse could have been omitted due to homoeoteleuton, it is hardly possible that the mistake would have occurred in so many manuscripts of such great diversity. Therefore, it is far more likely that the verse is a scribal interpolation borrowed from Matt 24:40, with harmonization to the style of Luke 17:35. Though the verse is not present in TR, it was included in KJV (perhaps under the influence of the Latin Vulgate), NKJV, and HCSB, which in deference to KJV has a pattern of including verses that are omitted by all other modern versions.

Luke 18:7

The last sentence of this verse is difficult to interpret because it is not readily apparent how και μακροθυμει επ αυτοις ("and he has patience with them") should be joined with what precedes this: "And will God not grant justice to his chosen ones who cry to him day and night?" (NRSV). In an attempt to combine the last clause with the previous part of the verse, scribes (W f[13] Maj—so TR) changed μακροθυμει (found in א A B D L etc.) to the participle μακροθυμων. The participle allows for this rendering: "And will God not grant justice to his chosen ones who cry to him day and night, even while being patient with them?"

Luke 18:11

TR NU	ὁ Φαρισαῖος σταθεὶς πρὸς ἑαυτὸν ταῦτα προσηύχετο "the Pharisee standing by himself [or, taking his stand] prayed these things" A W f[13] Maj NRSV ESV TNIV NEBmg NLT HCSB NETmg
variant 1/WH	ο Φαρισαιος σταθεις ταυτα προς εαυτον προσηυχετο "the Pharisee stood and prayed these things with [or, to] himself" 𝔓[75] א[2] B L T Θ Ψ f[1] KJV NKJV RSV NASB (NIV) NJB NAB NLTmg NET
variant 2	ο Φαρισαιος σταθεις ταυτα προσηυχετο "the Pharisee standing, prayed these things" א* it cop[sa] NEB REB
variant 3	ο Φαρισαιος σταθεις καθ εαυτον ταυτα προσηυχετο "the Pharisee stood and prayed these things privately" D NEBmg

The NU editors adopted their text because they considered the expression σταθεις προς εαυτον (which probably means "taking one's stand") to have been changed by scribes who had difficulty understanding it (TCGNT). However, the first variant is just as difficult to understand and has better attestation. The second variant eliminates the problem altogether, and the third variant is a clarification of the first variant. As is noted above, the English versions are divided on this verse, displaying some representation for each of the readings.

Luke 18:15

Instead of βρεφη ("babies"), found in all manuscripts, the scribe of D wrote παιδια ("children"), thereby harmonizing Luke's story with Mark 10:13.

Luke 18:24

TR NU	ἰδὼν δὲ αὐτὸν ὁ Ἰησοῦς [περίλυπον γενόμενον] εἶπεν "and Jesus, seeing him becoming very sad, said" A (D) W Θ Ψ 078 f[13] Maj syr KJV NKJV (ESV) NAB HCSB NETmg

variant/WH ιδων δε αυτον ο Ιησους ειπεν
"and Jesus, seeing him, said"
ℵ B L f^1 cop
RSV NRSV NASB NIV TNIV NEB REB NJB NLT HCSBmg NET

The TR NU reading has weak attestation and appears to be an expansion carried over from 18:23. The NU editors should have done more than bracket the words περιλυπον γενομενον; they should have omitted them. The two earliest witnesses, ℵ and B, very likely preserve the original text (so WH). Nearly all modern translators (except NAB and HCSB, which often preserves the KJV tradition) have been of the same opinion. The translators of the ESV connected the emotion of sadness not with the rich young ruler but with Jesus: "Jesus, looking at him with sadness."

Luke 18:25

Jesus' statement, "It is easier for a camel to go through an eye of a needle than for a rich man to enter the kingdom of God," was subject to textual variation in Matthew (19:24), Mark (10:25), and here in Luke. Ever since the second century, commentators (such as Origen, Cyril of Alexandria, and Theophylact) suggested that the *eta* in καμηλον ("camel") was mistaken for the *iōta* in καμιλον ("rope" or "ship's cable") because the two vowels were pronounced alike (Fitzmyer 1985, 1204). This interpretation is reflected in some witnesses (S f^{13}), where the Greek word for "camel" (καμηλον), found in all other manuscripts, was changed to καμιλον. (See note on Matt 19:24.)

Luke 18:28

WH NU ἡμεῖς ἀφέντες τὰ ἴδια ἠκολουθήσαμέν σοι
"we, having left our own, have followed you"
$ℵ^2$ B (D) L cop[bo]
NKJVmg NRSV ESV NASB NLT HCSB NET

variant/TR ημεις αφηκαμεν παντα και ηκολουθησαμεν σοι
"we have left everything and followed you"
ℵ* A W Ψ 33 Maj
KJV NKJV RSV NRSV NIV TNIV NEB REB NJB NAB

The textual evidence slightly favors the WH NU reading. The variant is probably the result of scribal harmonization to the parallel passages in Matthew (19:27) and Mark (10:28). Luke's terminology, αφεντες τα ιδια, includes the abandonment of whatever was dear to the disciples, each of which is itemized in the following verse.

Luke 18:30

Instead of πολλαπλασιονα ("many times as much"), found in most manuscripts, D it and one cop[sa] manuscript read επταπλασιονα ("seven times as much"), and 1241 syr[c,s] read εκατονταπλασιονα ("a hundred times as much")—a harmonization to Mark 10:30.

Luke 18:32

Unless it is a case of homoeoteleuton, a few manuscripts (D L 700 1241) harmonize this verse with Matt 20:19 and Mark 10:34 by dropping υβρισθησεται ("and will be insulted"). Luke's use of the word υβριζω would have been especially poignant to a Gentile audience because it is the Gentiles who are said to have insulted Jesus. This verb was typically used in the Greek world to denote outrageous abuse.

Luke 19:25

All three editions (TR WH NU) include this verse on the basis of excellent testimony: ℵ A (B) L Δ Θ Ψ 0233 f^{1,13} it^{a,c} cop^{sa}. All English versions also include it: "And they said to him, 'Lord, he has ten minas.'" The verse is omitted in D W it^{b,d,e} syr^{c,s}, probably because the verse seems obtrusive and perhaps unnecessary. Furthermore, it might have been deleted because (1) the verse is not found in Matthew's parallel account (Matt 25:28-29) and (2) it is difficult to identify who is speaking here: some of the ten servants or those listening to Jesus' parable? In either case, the objection posed by these people heightens the account in which the master gives one more mina to him who already had ten.

Luke 19:26

The expression και ο εχει ("even what he has") was changed to και ο δοκει εχειν ("even what he thinks he has") in Θ 69 syr^{c} Marcion, under the influence of Luke 8:18. Many other manuscripts (ℵ^{2} A D W Θ Ψ f^{1,13} Maj—so TR) add the prepositional phrase, απ αυτου ("from him") after αρθησεται ("will be taken")—as the result of a natural fill-in or as a harmonization to Matt 25:29, a parallel verse. The original text is preserved in ℵ* B L.

Luke 19:38

WH NU	εὐλογημένος ὁ ἐρχόμενος ὁ βασιλεὺς ἐν ὀνόματι κυρίου. "Blessed be the coming one, the King, in the name of the Lord." B NEB REB NJB
variant 1/TR	ευλογημενος ο ερχομενος βασιλευς εν ονοματι κυριου. "Blessed be the King coming in the name of the Lord." ℵ^{2} A L Θ Ψ f^{1,13} Maj KJV NKJV RSV NRSV ESV NASB NIV TNIV NAB NLT HCSB NET
variant 2	ευλογημενος ο βασιλευς εν ονοματι κυριου. "Blessed be the King in the name of the Lord." ℵ* Origen none
variant 3	ευλογημενος ο ερχομενος εν ονοματι κυριου. "Blessed be the one coming in the name of the Lord." W none
variant 4	ευλογημενος ο ερχομενος εν ονοματι κυριου. ευλογημενος ο βασιλευς. "Blessed be the one coming in the name of the Lord. Blessed be the King." D it none

Because of the difficult construction ο ερχομενος ο βασιλευς, the WH NU reading is most likely the one from which the others diverged. The first variant (found in TR) avoids the difficulty by omitting the second article, the second variant by omitting ο ερχομενος ("the one coming"), the third variant by omitting ο βασιλευς ("the king"). Most English versions follow TR because it is smoother. The fourth variant is an attempt to retain the wording of Ps 118:26 in the first sentence, and then it adds the exclamation about the king. As is, Luke's text does not follow Ps 118:26 (or Matt 21:9 and Mark 11:9) verbatim because he inserts "the king." This Lukan wording was foreshadowed in 1:32 and 18:38-40, and it parallels John 12:13-15, which cites Ps 118:25-26 and Zech 9:9 with reference to Jesus coming as the king. Thus, Luke's citation may be a composite of Ps 118:26 and Zech 9:9.

Luke 19:45

WH NU	ἤρξατο ἐκβάλλειν τοὺς πωλοῦντας "he began to throw out those who were selling [things]" א B L cop NKJVmg RSV NRSV ESV NASB NIV TNIV NEB REB NJB NAB NLT HCSB
variant 1/TR	ηρξατο εκβαλλειν τους πωλουντας εν αυτω και αγοραζοντας "he began to throw out those who were selling in it and buying" A (C) W Θ (Ψ f[13]) Maj KJV NKJV HCSBmg
variant 2	ηρξατο εκβαλλειν τους πωλουντας εν αυτω και αγοραζοντας και τας τραπεζας των κολλυβιστων εξεχεεν και τας καθεδρας των πωλουντων τας περιστερας "he began to throw out those who were selling in it and buying, and he poured out [= spilled?] the tables of the moneychangers and the chairs of the ones selling doves" D it syr[h] none

The WH NU reading is likely original because it has the earliest support (א B) and because the variants appear to be the work of scribal adjustment. The first variant is the result of scribes borrowing from Matt 21:12 and Mark 11:15 to fill out the sentence. The second variant is complete harmonization to Matt 21:12 and Mark 11:15—with one exception, the editor of D used the verb εξεχεεν, taken from John 2:15, instead of ατεστρεψεν. The result is odd because it is strange to describe tables and chairs as being poured out or spilled.

Luke 19:46

Instead of the wording, εσται ο οικος μου οικος προσευχης ("my house will be a house of prayer"), found in א[1] B L f[1,13], a few manuscripts (C[2] 1241) read κληθησεται ο οικος μου οικος προσευχης ("my house will be called a house of prayer"), thereby bringing the phrasing in harmony with Isa 56:7 in the Septuagint, as well as with Matt 21:13 and Mark 11:17.

Luke 20:9

TR NU, following A W Θ f[13], read ανθρωπος τις ("a certain man"), instead of ανθρωπος ("a man"), as found in ℵ B L Ψ f[1] 33 Maj (so WH). Since the same witnesses (A W Θ f[13]) have this wording in Mark 12:1, it is very likely a case of harmonization. Or since Luke set up a pattern for this wording throughout his gospel (10:30; 12:16; 14:16; 15:11; 16:1; 19:12), it could have been easily transferred by a scribe to this verse as well. The more likely original text is found in WH. (The choice of NU reveals the eclectic method at work in that the readings of A and W were typically rejected in this portion of Luke—see critical apparatus of NA[27].)

Luke 20:20

In place of παρατηρησαντες ("having carefully watched"), a few manuscripts substitute αποχωρησαντες (D Θ) or υποχωρησαντες (W)—both of which mean "having departed"—while syr[c,s] replace it with "after these things." The participle was replaced because the text does not say what or who the religious leaders were watching, but it is implicit that they were looking for an opportunity to trap Jesus.

Luke 20:21-25

This section of text appeared in at least three different forms in the second century. An ancient version of this appears in the second-century Egerton Papyrus, which is translated as follows:

> "Coming to him, they began to tempt him with a question, saying, 'Master, Jesus, we know you are come from God, for what you are doing bears testimony beyond that of all the prophets. Tell us, then, is it lawful to pay kings what pertains to their rule? Shall we give it to them or not?' But Jesus, knowing their thoughts, said, 'Why do you call me with your mouth Master, when you hear not what I say. Well did Isaiah prophesy of you, saying, 'This people honors me with their lips, but their hearts are far from me. In vain they worship me; their precepts . . . .' "

This text is a type of "Diatessaron" in that it weaves together a gospel narrative from preexisting gospel accounts—in this case, probably from John 3:2; 10:25; Matt 22:17-18; Mark 12:14-15; Luke 20:22-23; 6:46; 18:19; Matt 15:7-9; Mark 7:6-7.

Another version of this passage is preserved in the writings of the second-century apologist, Justin Martyr (*1 Apol.* 1.17.2): "For about that time some people came up to him and asked him whether one ought to pay taxes to Caesar. And he answered, 'Tell me, whose image does the coin bear?' And they said, 'Caesar's.' And he replied, 'Pay, then, to Caesar what is Caesar's and to God what is God's.'" This account more closely follows the Gospels, especially Luke 20:24 and Matt 22:21. The apocryphal *Gospel of Thomas* (100), composed in the second century, has its own rendition: "They showed Jesus a gold coin and said to him, 'Caesar's agents demand of us taxes.' He said to them, 'Give Caesar the things of Caesar, give God the things of God, and give me what is mine.'"

Luke 20:23

WH NU εἶπεν πρὸς αὐτούς
"he said to them"
ℵ B L 0266[vid] f[1] it[e] cop
NKJVmg RSV NRSV ESV NASB NIV TNIV NEB REB NJB NAB NLT HCSB NET

variant/TR ειπεν προς αυτους, Τι με πειραζετε;
"he said to them, 'Why are you testing me?'"
A (C S add υποκριται —hypocrites) D W Θ Ψ f^{13} 33 Maj
KJV NKJV HCSBmg

The WH NU reading, which has early and diverse textual support, is the shorter reading and very likely original. The addition in the variant is the result of scribal harmonization to Matt 22:18 and Mark 12:15, parallel verses. TR invariably contains these harmonizations, followed by KJV and NKJV.

Luke 20:27

TR NU Σαδδουκαίων, οἱ ἀντιλέγοντες ἀνάστασιν μὴ εἶναι
"Sadducees, the ones denying there is a resurrection"
A W f^{13} Maj
KJV NKJV ESV REB NAB

variant/WH Σαδδουκαιων, οι λεγοντες αναστασιν μη ειναι
"Sadducees, the ones saying there is no resurrection"
א B C D L Θ f^{1} 33 565
RSV NRSV NASB NIV TNIV NEB NJB NLT HCSB NET

Because of the double negative, the TR NU reading was considered by the NU editors to be the more difficult. But the external evidence strongly favors the variant, which is followed by most modern versions. Either way, the meaning is not affected; both readings make it clear that the Sadducees did not believe in the resurrection of the dead.

Luke 20:30

WH NU καὶ ὁ δεύτερος
"and the second"
א B D L 0266 it^{e} cop
NKJVmg RSV NRSV ESV NASB NIV TNIV NEB REB NJB NAB (NLT) HCSB NET

variant/TR και ελαβεν ο δευτερος την γυναικα και ουτος απεθανεν ατεκνος
"and the second took the woman and this man died childless"
A W (Θ) Ψ $f^{1,13}$ 33 Maj
KJV NKJV HCSBmg NETmg

The expanded reading of the variant is a scribal adjustment intended to fill out the text (as in Matthew and Mark) or to avoid the grammatical problem of having a singular verb (ελαβεν) follow a plural subject, the second and third husbands.

Luke 20:34

D (it $syr^{c,s}$) add γεννωνται και γεννωσιν ("they are born and beget") before γαμουσιν και γαμισκονται ("they marry and are given in marriage"). The resultant text hardly has a claim to being original, since it has insufficient textual evidence and the parallelism has procreation preceding marriage—an unlikely order (Marshall 1978, 741).

Luke 20:36

Instead of ισαγγελοι γαρ εισιν και υιοι εισιν θεου ("for they are like angels and they are sons of God"), D (with it and syr[s]) has ισαγγελοι γαρ εισιν τω θεω ("for they are like angels to God"). This is a significant change because it completely eliminates "the sons of God."

Luke 21:4

WH NU — τὰ δῶρα
"the offerings (gifts)"
א B L f[1] syr[c,s] (cop)
NKJVmg RSV NRSV ESV NASB NIV TNIV NEB REB NJB NAB NLT HCSB NET

variant/TR — τα δωρα του θεου
"the offerings (gifts) of God"
A D W Θ Ψ 0102 f[13] 33 Maj
KJV NKJV

The WH NU reading, in full, could be translated as, "for all these people from their abundance have put something into the offerings" or "for all these people from their abundance have put in their gifts." The addition in the variant may be an attempt to avoid this ambiguity, but it creates another ambiguous statement, in that τα δωρα του θεου can mean "gifts for God" (NKJV) or "the gifts of God."

Luke 21:6

TR NU — λίθος ἐπὶ λίθῳ
"stone upon stone"
A W Θ Ψ 0102 Maj
KJV NKJV NRSV ESV NASB NIV TNIV NEB REB NJB NAB HCSB NET

variant 1/WH — λιθος επι λιθω ωδε
"stone upon a stone here"
א B L f[13]
RSV

variant 2 — λιθος επι λιθω εν τοιχω ωδε
"a stone upon a stone in a wall here"
D (it)
none

In full, TR NU could be rendered as "days will come in which there will not be a stone upon a stone that will not be thrown down." In an uncharacteristic manner, א B L, instead of A W Θ Ψ Maj, probably display harmonization to remote parallels, Matt 24:2 and Mark 13:2. The second variant is a typical Bezaean and Old Latin expansion.

Luke 21:11

There are several different word orders among the extant manuscripts, but the meaning is not affected thereby. A few witnesses (it syr[c,p]) add "and tempests" at the end of the verse. In a parallel passage (Mark 13:8), "and troubles" was added in many manuscripts. Since the source for these additions is unknown, it can be conjectured that translators and scribes added them to give extra color (see note on Mark 13:8).

Luke 21:18

This verse is omitted in syr[c] and Marcion, most likely because it is not present in the parallel passages, Matt 24:13 and Mark 13:13.

Luke 21:19

TR NU read κτησασθε ("you must gain"), on the authority of ℵ D L W Ψ f[1] Maj. WH reads κτησεσθε ("you will gain"), on the authority of A B Θ f[13] 33. Marcion supports the verb σωσετε ("you will save"). Even though the WH reading has decent documentary support, it is probably the work of scribes conforming it to the tense of the surrounding future tense verbs. Nonetheless, the future indicative gives forth more promise ("by your endurance you will gain your souls") than an aorist imperative. Marcion's rendition reflects harmonization to the parallel passages, Matt 24:13 and Mark 13:13.

Luke 21:34-35

WH NU ἐπιστῇ ἐφ' ὑμᾶς αἰφνίδιος ἡ ἡμέρα ἐκείνη [35]ὡς παγίς· ἐπεισελεύσεται γὰρ ἐπὶ πάντας
"that day may catch you suddenly [35] as a trap, for it will come upon all"
ℵ* B D (L) it cop
RSV NRSV ESV NASB NIV TNIV NEB REB NJB NAB NLT HCSB NET

variant/TR επιστη εφ υμας αιφνιδιος η ημερα εκεινη· [35]ως παγις γαρ επελευσεται επι παντας
"that day may catch you suddenly. [35] For, as a trap, it will come upon all"
A C W Θ Ψ f[1,13] 33 Maj syr
KJV NKJV

The crux of the problem is that ως παγις ("as a trap") can be joined with the end of 21:34 or the beginning of 21:35. It is doubtful—though not impossible—that the original manuscript had punctuation to make it clear. Thus, scribes felt free to make their own interpretation—some joining it with the end of verse 34, and others with the beginning of verse 35. According to the WH NU reading (which has good Alexandrian and Western support), the simile "as a trap" directly describes the suddenness of being caught unaware on that day. According to the variant, verse 35 confirms the statement that the day will come like a trap (or snare) on everybody.

Luke 21:36

WH NU δεόμενοι ἵνα κατισχύσητε ἐκφυγεῖν
"pray that you may have strength to escape"
ℵ B L T (W) Ψ 070 f[1] 33 cop
NKJVmg RSV NRSV NASB NIV TNIV NEB REB NJB NAB NLT HCSB NET

variant/TR δεομενοι ινα καταξιωθητε εκφυγειν
"pray that you may be found worthy to escape"
A C D Θ f[13] Maj
KJV NKJV HCSBmg

The WH NU reading has early and diverse documentary support. The variant reading, with inferior attestation, was probably carried over from 20:35. The difference in meaning is between having strength to escape the persecution and being worthy to escape.

Luke 21:37-38

According to eight manuscripts belonging to f^{13} (13 69 124 346 543 788 826 983), the pericope of the adulteress appears after Luke 21:37-38 (see also note on 24:53b). The insertion of this story (probably taken from an oral tradition) at this place in Luke's narrative is a much better fit than where it is typically placed in John's narrative (between 7:52 and 8:12). In John, it interrupts the connection between the Sanhedrin's rejection of Jesus (on the basis that he was a Galilean) and Jesus' following rejoinder. Chronologically, the story belongs in Jesus' last week in Jerusalem, at a time when he was going back and forth between the temple (to teach in the daytime) and the garden of Gethsemane (to sleep at night). Thematically, the story belongs with the others that show the religious leaders trying to trap Jesus into some kind of lawlessness and thereby have grounds to arrest him. These encounters, according to the Synoptic Gospels, also appear in Jesus' last days in Jerusalem.

The group of manuscripts, f^{13}, could represent the earliest positioning of the pericope of the adulteress, which was then transferred to the end of John 7, or it could represent an independent positioning. Westcott and Hort (1882, 63) said this passage was probably known to a scribe "exclusively as a church lesson, recently come into use, and placed by him here on account of the close resemblance between Luke 21:37-38 and John 7:53–8:2. Had he known it as part of a continuous text of St. John's Gospel, he was not likely to transpose it." It is also possible that the earliest scribe of a manuscript in the group of f^{13} (either the composer of the archetype in Calabria or the scribes of 124 or 788) made the editorial decision to move it from its usual spot at the end of John 7, to follow Luke 21. This transposition, which was a good editorial decision, affirms the transitory nature of the pericope of the adulteress—which is to say, it was not treated on the same par as fixed, inviolable Scripture. (See comments on John 7:53–8:11.)

Luke 22:6

The first two words of this verse, και εξωμολογησεν ("and he consented"), were omitted in ℵ* C it syr[s], to bring Luke into conformity with Matt 26:15-16 and Mark 14:11.

Luke 22:14

WH NU	οἱ ἀπόστολοι "the apostles" 𝔓[75] ℵ* B D it NKJVmg RSV NRSV ESV NASB NIV TNIV NEB REB NJB NAB NLT HCSB NET
variant 1	οι δωδεκα "the Twelve" ℵ[1] L none
variant 2/TR	οι δωδεκα αποστολοι "the twelve apostles" ℵ[2] A C W Θ Ψ $f^{1,13}$ Maj Marcion KJV NKJV

variant 3 "his disciples"
syr[s]
none

Luke avoided the term "the Twelve" probably because he did not want his account to imply that Judas was present at the Last Supper (see 22:6). Nevertheless, scribes harmonized Luke to Matt 26:20 and Mark 14:17 by making it "the Twelve," and the one Syriac translator avoided the problem by calling them "his disciples." The second variant, a conflation of WH NU and the first variant reading, became the most popular wording, finding its way into TR and KJV.

Luke 22:17-20

TR WH NU
17καὶ δεξάμενος ποτήριον εὐχαριστήσας εἶπεν·
λάβετε τοῦτο καὶ διαμερίσατε εἰς ἑαυτούς· 18λέγω
γὰρ ὑμῖν, [ὅτι] οὐ μὴ πίω ἀπὸ τοῦ νῦν ἀπὸ τοῦ
γενήματος τῆς ἀμπέλου ἕως οὗ ἡ βασιλεία τοῦ
θεοῦ ἔλθῃ. 19καὶ λαβὼν ἄρτον εὐχαριστήσας ἔκλασεν
καὶ ἔδωκεν αὐτοῖς λέγων· τοῦτό ἐστιν τὸ σῶμά
μου τὸ ὑπὲρ ὑμῶν διδόμενον· τοῦτο ποιεῖτε εἰς
τὴν ἐμὴν ἀνάμνησιν. 20καὶ τὸ ποτήριον ὡσαύτως
μετὰ τὸ δειπνῆσαι, λέγων· τοῦτο τὸ ποτήριον
ἡ καινὴ διαθήκη ἐν τῷ αἵματί μου τὸ ὑπὲρ ὑμῶν
ἐκχυννόμενον.
"17Then he took a cup, and when he had given thanks for it, he said, 'Take this
and share it among yourselves. 18For I tell you, I will not drink of the fruit of
the vine from now on until the Kingdom of God comes.' 19Then he took a loaf
of bread; and when he had given thanks for it, he broke it and gave it to them,
saying, 'This is my body, given for you. Do this in remembrance of me.' 20And
he did the same with the cup after supper, saying, 'This cup that is poured out
for you is the new covenant in my blood.'"
𝔓75 ℵ A B C L T[vid] W Δ Θ Ψ f[1,13] it[c] syr[p] cop[sa,bo]
KJV NKJV RSV NRSV ESV NASB NIV TNIV NEBmg REBmg NJB NAB NLT HCSB NET

variant 1
omit 22:19b-20, yielding this translation:
"17Then he took a cup, and when he had given thanks for it, he said, 'Take this
and share it among yourselves. 18For I tell you, I will not drink of the fruit of
the vine from now on until the Kingdom of God comes.' 19Then he took a loaf
of bread; and when he had given thanks for it, he broke it and gave it to them,
saying, 'This is my body.'"
D it[a,d,i,l] Didache
NKJVmg RSVmg NRSVmg ESVmg NASBmg NEB REB NABmg NLTmg HCSBmg NETmg

variant 2
transposed order (22:19a, 17, 18)
"19aThen he took a loaf of bread; and when he had given thanks for it, he
broke it and gave it to them, saying, 'This is my body.' 17Then he took a cup,
and when he had given thanks for it, he said, 'Take this and share it among
yourselves. 18For I tell you, I will not drink of the fruit of the vine from now on
until the Kingdom of God comes.'"
it[b,e]
none

variant 3 — transposed order (22:19, 17, 18)
"[19] Then he took a loaf of bread; and when he had given thanks for it, he broke it and gave it to them, saying, 'This is my body, given for you. Do this in remembrance of me.' [17] Then he took a cup, and when he had given thanks for it, he said, 'Take this and share it among yourselves. [18] For I tell you, I will not drink of the fruit of the vine from now on until the Kingdom of God comes.'"
syr[c]
none

variant 4 — transposed order (22:19, 20a, 17, 20b, 18)
"[19] Then he took a loaf of bread; and when he had given thanks for it, he broke it and gave it to them, saying, 'This is my body, given for you. Do this in remembrance of me.' [20a] And after supper, [17] he took a cup, and when he had given thanks for it, he said, 'Take this and share it among yourselves; [20b] this is my blood of the new covenant. [18] For I tell you, I will not drink of the fruit of the vine from now on until the Kingdom of God comes.'"
syr[s]
none

variant 5 — shortened version (22:19-20)
"[19] Then he took a loaf of bread; and when he had given thanks for it, he broke it and gave it to them, saying, 'This is my body, given for you. Do this in remembrance of me.' [20] And he did the same with the cup after supper, saying, 'This cup that is poured out for you is the new covenant in my blood.'"
syr[p]
none

All Greek manuscripts except D testify to the presence of Luke 22:19b-20 in the account of the Last Supper. Very likely, the Bezaean editor (D) was puzzled by the cup/bread/cup sequence, and therefore deleted this portion, but in so doing the text was left with the cup/bread sequence, contrary to Matt 26:26-28; Mark 14:22-24; and 1 Cor 11:23-26. As far as we know, the Bezaean order is found only in the *Didache* 9.2-3 and some Old Latin manuscripts. The other four variants show translators' attempts to resolve the same problem of cup/bread/cup, but their deletions and transpositions produce the more usual bread/cup sequence. The Bezaean editor, Latin translators, and Old Syriac translators must not have realized that the cup mentioned in 22:17 was the cup of the Passover celebration, occupying 22:15-18. Going back to 22:16, it seems clear that the food of the Passover is implied when Jesus speaks of never again eating it until the kingdom of God is realized. Then, according to 22:17-18, Jesus passed around a cup of wine, again saying that he would not drink of it until the kingdom of God came. Thus, 22:16-18 has its own bread/cup sequence as part of the Passover meal. Following this, 22:19-20 has the bread/cup sequence of the new covenant.

All the translations except the NEB and REB include this portion, though several provide a marginal note as to its omission. Tasker (1964, 422-423) provides a lengthy discussion as to why the translators of the NEB did not include Luke 22:19b-20. The REB persists in leaving the shorter reading in the text.

Luke 22:20

Marcion omitted καινη ("new") before διαθηκη ("covenant") because he did not recognize two covenants, an old one and a new one; he recognized only one covenant—the one established by Jesus.

Luke 22:31

WH NU	Σίμων Σίμων "Simon, Simon" 𝔓[75] B L T syr[c] cop NKJVmg RSV NRSV ESV NASB NIV TNIV NEB REB NJB NAB NLT HCSB NET
variant/TR	ειπεν δε ο κυριος, Σιμων, Σιμων "and the Lord said, 'Simon, Simon'" ℵ A D W Θ Ψ f[1,13] Maj KJV NKJV HCSBmg NETmg

The addition at the beginning of the verse reintroduces the main speaker at the beginning of a paragraph. The exclusion of these words, however, is well-attested.

Luke 22:43-44

TR WH NU	include verses, [43]ὤφθη δε αὐτῷ ἄγγελος ἀπ' οὐρανοῦ ἐνισχύων αὐτόν. [44]καὶ γενόμενος ἐν ἀγωνίᾳ ἐκτενέστερον προσηύχετο· καὶ ἐγένετο ὁ ἱδρὼς αὐτοῦ ὡσεὶ θρόμβοι αἵματος καταβαίνοντες ἐπὶ τὴν γῆν. "[43] And an angel from heaven appeared to him, strengthening him. [44] And being in agony, he prayed more earnestly, and his sweat became like great drops of blood falling down on the ground." ℵ[*,2] D L Θ Ψ 0171[vid] 0233 f[1] Maj (with asterisks or obeli: Δ[c] Π[c] 892[c] 1079 1195 1216 cop[boMSS]) most Greek MSS[according to Anastasius] MSS[according to Jerome] MSS[according to Epiphanius, Hilary] Justin Irenaeus Hippolytus Eusebius KJV NKJV RSVmg NRSV ESV NASB NIV TNIV NEB REB NJB NAB NLT HCSB NET
variant 1	place verses after Matt 26:39 f[13] (13*) and some lectionaries with additions none
variant 2	omit verses 𝔓[69vid] 𝔓[75] ℵ[1] A B N T W it[f] syr[s] cop[sa] some Greek MSS[according to Anastasius] MSS[according to Jerome] some Greek and Old Latin MSS[according to Hilary] Marcion Clement Origen (NKJVmg) RSV NRSVmg ESVmg NIVmg TNIVmg NEBmg REBmg NJBmg NABmg NLTmg HCSBmg NETmg

𝔓[69vid] was not cited in UBS[3] in support of the omission of Luke 22:43-44, but it is now noted in UBS[4] in parentheses. The editors of 𝔓[69] (P.Oxy. 2383) were fairly confident that the only way to account for the size of the lacuna in 𝔓[69] (from Luke 22:41 to Luke 22:45) is that the copyist's exemplar did not contain Luke 22:43-44 and that the scribe's eye moved from προσηυχετο in 22:41 to προσευχης in 22:45. The editors calculated that these two words would have been on the end of lines, four lines apart. The manuscript 0171 should be listed as "vid" (as in UBS[4]) inasmuch as it shows only a portion of 22:44; however, there are no obeli or asterisks as noted in UBS[4]. (For the reconstructions of 𝔓[69] and 0171 respectively, see *Text of Earliest MSS,* 471-472, 687-691).

The manuscript evidence for this textual variant is decidedly in favor of the exclusion of 22:43-44. The Greek manuscripts (dating from the second to fifth century) favoring the exclusion of these verses forms an impressive list: 𝔓[69vid] 𝔓[75] ℵ[1] B T W. (The first corrector of ℵ was a contemporary of the scribe who produced the manuscript of Luke; indeed, he was the diorthotes who worked on this manuscript before it left the scriptorium.) Other signs of its doubtfulness appear in manuscripts marking the passage with obeli or crossing out the passage (as was done by the first corrector of ℵ). Its transposition to Matt 26 in some manuscripts and lectionaries indicates that it was a free-floating passage that could be interjected into any of the passion narratives (see note on Matt 26:39).

The manuscript support for including the verses involves several witnesses, the earliest of which is 0171^{vid} (ca. 300). None of the other manuscripts are earlier than the fifth century. However, several early fathers (Justin, Irenaeus, Hippolytus, Dionysius, Eusebius) acknowledged this portion as part of Luke's gospel.

When we turn to the writings of other early church fathers, we discover that many noted both the presence and absence of the "bloody sweat" passage in the manuscripts known to them. We have notes on this from Jerome, Hilary, Anastasius, and Epiphanius. For example, Epiphanius (*Ancoratus* 31.4-5) indicated that the verses were found in some "uncorrected copies" of Luke (see Westcott and Hort 1882, 65-66). This tells us that in the early course of textual transmission, the Gospel of Luke (in this chapter) was being copied in two forms—one that lacked the "bloody sweat" passage (as in $\mathfrak{P}^{69vid}$ $\mathfrak{P}^{75}$ T W) and one that included it (as in 0171^{vid}). The question, then, is: Did Luke write these verses, which were later deleted, or did someone else add them later?

I affirm Metzger's view of this: "On grounds of transcriptional probability it is less likely that the verses were deleted in several different areas of the church by those who felt that the account of Jesus being overwhelmed with human weakness was incompatible with his sharing the divine omnipotence of the Father, than that they were added from an early source" (TCGNT). Westcott and Hort also considered the "bloody sweat" passage to be an early (second-century) interpolation, added from an oral tradition concerning the life of Jesus (see Westcott and Hort 1882, 64-67).

One would think, then, that the WH and NU editors would *not* have included the verses in a Greek text intending to represent the original writings. But both WH and NU include the bloody sweat passage (albeit in double brackets). Even though both groups of editors considered this passage to be a later addition to the text, it was retained because of its importance in the textual tradition. Westcott and Hort said, "these verses . . . may be safely called the most precious among the remains of this evangelic tradition which were rescued from oblivion by the scribes of the second century." The words of Metzger echo this: "they [these verses] were added from an early source, oral or written, of extra-canonical traditions concerning the life and passion of Jesus. Nevertheless, while acknowledging that the passage is a later addition to the text, in view of its evident antiquity and its importance in the textual tradition, a majority of the Committee decided to retain the words in the text but to enclose them within double square brackets" (TCGNT).

Luke 22:43-44 thereby shares a unique position with another passage, the pericope of the adulterous woman (John 7:53–8:11). Both stand in the NU text because of their place in tradition. But neither texts are part of the original writings and therefore should not be included in any modern edition of the Greek NT. The refusal to relegate these texts to the margin—indeed, the persistence to keep them in the text (even if they are double-bracketed) gives Bible translators the grounds to persist in keeping them in their translations, which (in turn) perpetuates their authenticity in the minds of most Christians who depend exclusively on translations.

The RSV translators were the only ones to exclude both passages (Luke 22:43-44 and John 7:53–8:11). Outside pressures forced them to place John 7:53–8:11 back into the text after its first printing (see comments on John 7:53–8:11), but they did not do so with Luke 22:43-44. All other versions have kept Luke 22:43-44 in the text, with many providing notes about its absence in ancient witnesses.

As to Luke 22:43-44, most Christians consider this detail about Jesus' passion to be authentic—in that it came from the hand of Luke as he received it from Jesus' eyewitnesses (Luke 1:1-4). However, it is often interpreted incorrectly to say that Jesus was in such agony that he was sweating blood (technically called *hematidrosis*); that is why the text is often called the "bloody sweat" passage. But the text says that he was sweating so "profusely that it looked like blood dripping from a wound" (Liefeld 1984, 1032), not that his sweat became dripping blood.

Luke 22:47

Instead of ο λεγομενος Ιουδας ("the one called Judas"), found in most manuscripts, D 0171[vid] f[1] read ο καλουμενος Ιουδας Ισκαριωθ ("the one called Judas Iscariot"). And borrowing from Mark 14:44, D Θ f[13] add τουτο γαρ σημειον δεδωκει αυτοις· ον αν φιλησω αυτος εστιν ("for this is the sign I will give them: whoever I kiss is he").

Luke 22:52

According to 𝔓[75] ℵ A B T Θ, the subject is explicitly stated as Ιησους ("Jesus")—without an article. Several manuscripts (L W Ψ f[13] Maj) add an article, but this is not needed because ο Ιησους appears in the previous verse. D f[1] it[e] syr[c,s] omit the subject altogether, probably as a perceived redundancy from the previous verse.

Luke 22:54

The words και εισηγαγον ("and brought [him]") were omitted from D Θ f[1] because they were considered redundant directly following αυτον ηγαγον ("they led him away").

Luke 22:61

According to 𝔓[69] 𝔓[75] ℵ B L T (so WH NU), Peter remembers του ρηματος του κυριου ("the spoken word of the Lord"). But according to A D W Θ Ψ 0250 f[1,13] Maj (so TR), Peter remembers του λογου του κυριου ("the word of the Lord"). The difference between ρημα and λογος is that the former emphasizes actual speech, while the latter emphasizes the message (whether oral or written). Though it is possible that ρηματος was assimilated to Matt 26:75 and Mark 14:72 (parallel passages), the textual evidence favors this reading, as does the fact that Luke elsewhere spoke of Peter remembering του ρηματος του κυριου (see Acts 11:16).

Luke 22:62

TR WH NU	include verse καὶ ἐξελθὼν ἔξω ἔκλαυσεν πικρῶς "and having gone outside, he cried bitterly" 𝔓[75] ℵ A B D L T W Maj KJV NKJV RSV NRSV ESV NASB NIV TNIV NEBmg REB NJB NAB NLT HCSB NET
variant	omit verse 0171[vid] it[a,b,e,i,l] NEB

Although it is possible that the verse could have been added from the Matthean parallel text (Matt 26:75), it is far more likely—given the textual evidence—that it was dropped in 0171[vid] and several Old Latin manuscripts by accident (the eye of the scribe passing from the beginning και of 22:62 to the και of 22:63) or on purpose—perhaps to make Luke like John in not making any mention of Peter's reaction after the denial (see John 18:27). (For a reconstruction of the text of 0171, not cited in NA[27], see *Text of Earliest MSS,* 691.) In any case, the NEB translators did not include this verse because they considered it to have been borrowed by scribes from Matt 26:75 or Mark 14:72 (see Tasker 1964, 423). This was completely reversed in the REB, without even a footnote indicating the omission of this verse from some manuscripts.

Luke 22:64

WH NU — περικαλύψαντες αὐτὸν ἐπηρώτων
"having blindfolded him, they were questioning [him]"
𝔓[75] (א) B L T cop[bo]
NKJVmg RSV NRSV ESV NASB NIV TNIV NEB REB NJB NAB NLT HCSB NET

variant 1/TR — περικαλυψαντες αυτον ετυπτον αυτου το προσωπον και επηρωτων αυτον
"having blindfolded him, they struck his face and they were questioning him"
(A* D) W Ψ f[13] Maj
KJV NKJV HCSBmg

variant 2 — περικαλυψαντες αυτου το προσωπον επηρωτων
"having blindfolded his face, they were questioning [him]"
070 f[1] it syr[c,p,s] cop[sa]
none

The WH NU reading, which has superior attestation, is followed by all modern English versions. The first variant, found in TR (and followed by KJV and NKJV), is the result of harmonization to parallel passages in Matt 26:67 and Mark 14:65. The second variant is a natural scribal expansion wherein a specific direct object ("his face") is supplied for the participle, περικαλυψαντες ("having covered/blindfolded"). The text sufficiently conveys the gruesome detail that the Roman soldiers were hitting Jesus while he was blindfolded, and in sheer mockery asked Jesus to be a clairvoyant.

Luke 22:68

WH NU — ἐὰν δὲ ἐρωτήσω, οὐ μὴ ἀποκριθῆτε
"And if I question [you], you will certainly not answer."
𝔓[75] א B L T cop[bo]
NKJVmg RSV NRSV ESV NASB NIV TNIV NEB REB NJB NAB NLT HCSB NET

variant 1/TR — εαν δε και ερωτησω ου μη αποκριθητε μοι η απολυσητε
"And even if I question [you], you will certainly not answer me or let me go."
A (D) W Θ Ψ f[1,13] Maj
KJV NKJV

variant 2 — omit verse
Marcion it[e]
none

The WH NU reading poses an exegetical problem: How can Jesus, who is being interrogated, say that he would like to interrogate his interrogators? But this is exactly the intended irony; the one being judged is actually the judge. Perplexed by this, several scribes expanded the text to give some understandable cause for Jesus making this statement (such as, even if Jesus asked what the charges were against him, the religious leaders would not answer him because they had made up their minds to convict him). Marcion and several Old Latin translators either (1) avoided the problem altogether by deleting the verse or (2) deleted the verse because they considered it unlikely that Jesus would make such a statement.

Luke 23:2

After διαστρεφοντα το εθνος ημων ("misleading our nation"), Marcion and several Old Latin manuscripts add "and destroying the law and the prophets." This interpolation affirms the core of the Marcionite heresy which espoused Jesus' complete rejection of the old covenant. After the second charge against Jesus, κωλουντα φορους Καισαρι διδοναι ("preventing [us] from paying taxes to Caesar"), Marcion added "and misleading our wives and our children."

Luke 23:5

At the end of this verse there are two forms of a gloss in two Old Latin manuscripts: (1) "and he turns our children and our wives away from us, because he is not baptized as we are" (it^{c}) and (2) "and he turns our children and our wives away from us, because they are not baptized as also we are, nor do they purify themselves" (it^{e}). These glosses, strange as they seem, were probably added by Christian scribes attempting to differentiate Christianity from Judaism on the basis of baptism.

Luke 23:6

WH NU Πιλᾶτος δὲ ἀκούσας ἐπηρώτησεν εἰ ὁ ἄνθρωπος Γαλιλαῖός ἐστιν.
"And Pilate, having heard, asked if the man is a Galilean."
$\mathfrak{P}^{75}$ ℵ B L T 070 cop^{bo}
NKJVmg RSV NRSV ESV NASB NIV TNIV NEB REB NJB NAB NLT HCSB NET

variant/TR Πιλατος δε ακουσας Γαλιλαιαν επηρωτησεν ει ο ανθπωπος Γαλιλαιος εστιν.
"And Pilate, having heard 'Galilee,' asked if the man is a Galilean."
A (D) W Θ Ψ $f^{1,13}$ Maj syr cop^{sa}
KJV NKJV HCSBmg

The WH NU reading has early and diverse documentation. The insertion of Γαλιλαιαν ("Galilee") is a typical scribal filler carried over from 23:5. This insertion became part of TR, followed by KJV and NKJV.

Luke 23:15

WH NU ἀνέπεμψεν γὰρ αὐτὸν πρὸς ἡμᾶς
"for he [Herod] sent him [Jesus] back to us"
$\mathfrak{P}^{75}$ ℵ B L T Θ cop
NKJVmg RSV NRSV ESV NASB NIV TNIV NEB REB NJB NAB NLT HCSB NET

variant 1 αvεπεμψα γαρ υμας προς αυτον
"for I [Pilate] sent you [plural] to him [Herod]"
A D W Ψ f[1] Maj syr[h]
KJV NKJV

variant 2 αvεπεμψα γαρ αυτον προς υμας
"I [Pilate] sent him [Jesus] to you [plural]"
f[13] syr[hmg]
none

The only reading that makes sense in the immediate context is the WH NU reading, which has excellent documentary support. The first variant only makes sense when it is connected to 23:7-10, wherein it is implied that the Jewish leaders must have accompanied Jesus to Herod when Pilate sent him there. The second variant is garbled.

Luke 23:17

WH NU omit verse
𝔓[75] A B L T 070 892[txt] it[a] cop[sa]
NKJVmg RSV NRSV ESV NASBmg NIV TNIV NEB REB NJB NAB NLT HCSBmg NET

variant/TR include verse
Αναγκην δε ειχεν απολυειν αυτοις κατα εορτην ενα
"it was necessary for him to release one [prisoner] for them at the festival"
א W (Θ Ψ) f[1,13] 892[mg] Maj (D syr[c,s] after 23:19)
KJV NKJV RSVmg NRSVmg NASB NIVmg NEBmg REBmg NJBmg NABmg NLTmg HCSB NETmg

Since this verse is absent from several significant manuscripts and is transposed in D syr[c,s], its presence in the other manuscripts is most likely the result of scribal interpolation—borrowing primarily from Mark 15:6, as well as Matt 27:15. The verse was probably added to provide a reason for the crowd's request that Pilate release Barabbas instead of Jesus (23:18). But the text reads contiguously from 23:16 to 23:18, joining Pilate's statement about releasing Jesus to an immediate plea from the crowd to release Barabbas instead. Modern versions exclude the verse, yet they note it out of deference to the KJV tradition. The NASB and HCSB persist in including verses that are excluded by all other modern versions.

Luke 23:23

WH NU κατίσχυον αἱ φωναὶ αὐτῶν
"their voices prevailed"
𝔓[75] א B L 070 cop
NKJVmg RSV NRSV ESV NASB NIV TNIV NEB REB NJB NAB NLT HCSB NET

variant/TR κατισχυον αι φωναι αυτων και των αρχιερεων
"their voices and those of the leading priests prevailed"
A D W Θ Ψ f[1,13] Maj syr
KJV NKJV HCSBmg

In context, a fuller rendering of WH NU is: "But they were insisting with loud voices, asking for him to be crucified, and their voices prevailed." Although it is possible that the last phrase was accidentally dropped due to homoeoteleuton (the eye of the scribe mistaking the ending of αρχιερεων for αυτων), it is more likely that the phrase was added to make it absolutely clear that the leading priests were eminently responsible for Jesus' death (see 23:13). The shorter text has early and diverse support; it is followed by all the modern versions.

Luke 23:34

TR (WH NU)	[[ὁ δε 'Ιησοῦς ἔλεγεν· πάτερ, ἄφες αὐτοῖς, οὐ γὰρ οἴδασιν τί ποιοῦσιν.]] "And Jesus said, 'Father, forgive them, for they do not know what they are doing.'" א*[,2] (A) C D[2] (E with obeli) L Ψ 0250 f[1,(13)] Maj syr[c,h,p] Diatessaron Hegesippus all
variant	omit 𝔓[75] א[1] B D* W Θ 070 it[a] syr[s] cop[sa] NKJVmg RSVmg NRSVmg ESVmg NIVmg TNIVmg NEBmg REBmg NJBmg NABmg NLTmg HCSBmg NETmg

The omission of these words in early and diverse manuscripts (the earliest being 𝔓[75]) cannot be explained as a scribal blunder. But were the words purposely excised? Westcott and Hort (1882, 68) considered willful excision to be absolutely unthinkable. But Marshall (1978, 867-868) can think of several reasons why scribes might have deleted the words—the most convincing of which is that scribes might have been influenced by an anti-Jewish polemic and therefore did not want the text saying that Jesus forgave the Jews who killed him. This would be especially true for Codex Bezae (D), whose scribe has been charged with having anti-Judaic tendencies (see Epp 1962, 51-62). However, there are four manuscripts—of diverse traditions—earlier than D (namely, 𝔓[75] B W it[a]), which do not include these words. Thus, D could not have been the first to eliminate the words. The primary argument against excision (on the basis of an anti-Judaic polemic) is that Jesus was forgiving his Roman executioners, not the Jewish leaders. The grammar affirms this; in 23:33 it says εσταυρωσαν αυτον ("they [the Roman execution squad] crucified him"), then in 23:34 Jesus says, αφες αυτοις ("forgive them")—i.e., the Roman execution squad. Furthermore, Jesus had already pronounced judgment on the Jewish leaders who would not believe in him and even worse who proclaimed that his works were empowered by Beelzebul, the prince of demons (Matt 12:24-32).

It is easier to explain that the words were not written by Luke but were added later (as early as the second century—for it is attested to by Hegesippus and the Diatessaron). If the words came from an oral tradition, many scholars are of the opinion that they are authentic. Indeed, Westcott and Hort (1882, 67) considered these words and 22:43-44 to be "the most precious among the remains of the evangelic tradition which were rescued from oblivion by the scribes of the second century."

But what if the words did not come from an oral tradition about Jesus' life and sayings? What would have inspired their inclusion? My guess is that the words were added to make Jesus the model for Christian martyrs—of offering forgiveness to one's executioners. Whoever first added the words may have drawn from Acts 7:60, where Stephen forgives his executioners. Since Stephen's final words parallel Jesus' final utterances (cf. Acts 7:56 to Luke 22:69; Acts 7:59 to Luke 23:46), it seemed appropriate to have Luke 23:34 emulate Acts 7:60. Or the words could have come from martyrdom stories, such as the account of the execution of James the Just, who is said to have forgiven his executioners (Eusebius, *Hist. eccl.* 2.23, 16). Thus, it can be imagined that church leaders told would-be martyrs to forgive their executors because Jesus had done the same.

Contrary to the external evidence and good internal arguments, the words appear in the three Greek editions (TR WH NU) and in all English translations because they have become so much a part of the traditional gospel text that editors of Greek texts and Bible translators alike are not willing to excise this classic statement from their text. The first known person to excise the sentence from the text was the first diorthotes of Codex Sinaiticus (corrector 1), who worked on the manuscript before it left the scriptorium. Evidently, this diorthotes used a different exemplar (which must have antedated the fourth century) that did not have these words. A second corrector, several centuries later, expunged the first corrector's deletion marks.

WH NU double-bracketed this text to show their strong doubts about its inclusion. All English versions include it, and all (with the exception of KJV which does not have marginal notes) have marginal notes about its omission in various manuscripts.

Luke 23:35

WH NU	εἰ οὗτός ἐστιν ὁ χριστὸς τοῦ θεοῦ ὁ ἐκλεκτός "if this one is the Christ of God, the chosen one" א[1] L W f[1] (א* ο before του θεου) RSV NRSV ESV NASB NIV TNIV NEB REB NJB NAB NLT HCSB NET
variant 1/TR	ει ουτος εστιν ο Χριστος ο του θεου εκλεκτος "if this one is the Christ, the chosen one of God" A C[3] Δ Θ Maj KJV NKJV
variant 2	ει ουτος εστιν ο Χριστος ο υιος του θεου ο εκλεκτος "if this one is the Christ, the Son of God, the chosen one" 𝔓[75] (070) f[13] syr[h] cop none
variant 3	ει ουτος υιος εστιν ο Χριστος του θεου ο εκλεκτος "if this one is [the] Son, the Christ of God, the chosen one" B none
variant 4	υιος ει του θεου, ει Χριστος, ει ο εκλεκτος "if you are [the] Son of God, if you are the Christ, if you are the chosen one" D none

Throughout the course of textual transmission, there is scarcely an instance where a title of Jesus or Christ has not been altered in one fashion or another by various scribes. The variants here are multiple. There is a double title (as in the WH NU reading and the first variant), which includes "Christ" and "chosen one." And there is a triple title (as in the other three variants), which includes "Christ," "Son of God," and "chosen one." The one title in question, then, is "Son of God."

The textual evidence for the inclusion of "Son of God" is solid, having the dual support of 𝔓[75] and B (which usually preserve the original wording in Luke), as well as D 070 f[13] syr[h] and Coptic manuscripts. This testimony is both early and diverse. With respect to internal considerations, it is noteworthy that according to Luke's account the Jewish leaders at Jesus' trial wanted to know if he was both "the Christ" and "the Son of God" (Luke 22:67-70). Thus, it is fitting for Luke to have both titles coming from the mouths of the same Jewish leaders who were taunting Jesus during his crucifixion. Furthermore, the inclusion of "Son of God" puts an emphasis on Jesus' divinity; as such, the Jewish leaders were asking Jesus to display his divine power by saving himself from death on the cross.

The textual evidence for the exclusion of "Son of God" is also diverse, but not as early. The argument in favor of the exclusion of "Son of God" is that scribes, in general, had a tendency to expand divine titles. However, the problem with wholeheartedly adopting this position here is that the scribes of 𝔓[75] and B are not known as those who expanded titles. Therefore, we must ask if somewhere in the textual tradition other scribes deleted "the Son of God"—and, if so, what would have been the motivation? It is possible that scribes altered Luke to conform to Mark's account where the Jewish leaders taunt Jesus with this statement: "If you are the Christ, the King of Israel, come down from the cross" (Mark 15:32). Given this alteration, the account in Luke would be more fitting with Mark in that both would have taunts against Jesus as "the Christ" (Mark 15:32; Luke 23:35) and "the King of Israel/the Jews" (Mark 15:32; Luke 23:38). However, there is a counterargument to this supposition of harmonization. In Matthew's gospel, the taunt of the Jewish leaders includes two titles: "the Son of God" and "the King of Israel." Thus, it can always be argued that the scribes of 𝔓[75] B D etc. added "Son of God" to harmonize Luke with Matthew.

In the end, both external and internal arguments offset each other. In such cases, translators have no choice but to decide on one reading and then note the other in the margin. All things being equal, I would tend to follow a reading supported by 𝔓[75] and B. It is evident that no other translators have thought the same because all have excluded "Son of God." Or could it be that no one has given any thought to this textual variant? It is not noted in the UBS editions, Metzger does not comment on it in TCGNT, and not even one translation has a marginal note indicating that other manuscripts include "the Son of God."

Luke 23:38

WH NU	ἐπιγραφὴ ἐπ' αὐτῷ "[there was] an inscription over him" 𝔓[75] א[1] B C* L 070 cop[sa] syr[c,s] NKJVmg RSV NRSV ESV NASB NIV TNIV NEB REB NJB NAB NLT HCSB NET
variant/TR	γεγραμμενη επ αυτω γραμμασιν Ελληνικοις και Ρωμαικοις και Εβραικοις "an inscription was written over him in Greek, Latin, and Hebrew." א*,c A C[3] D W Θ 0250 f[1,13] Maj KJV NKJV ESVmg HCSBmg

The WH NU reading, which has superior attestation, is followed by all modern English versions. Borrowing from John 19:20, several scribes added an expression naming the three languages written on the placard nailed to Jesus' cross. This addition does not follow John 19:20 exactly, because John's order is Hebrew, Latin, Greek. The variant appears in TR, followed by KJV and NKJV.

Luke 23:39

D (it[e]) have a truncated rendition of this verse: εις δε των κακουργων εβλασφημει αυτον ("one of the criminals blasphemed him"). This sort of excision is typical for the D text (see note on 24:52).

Luke 23:42-43

WH NU μνήσθητι μου ὅταν ἔλθῃς εἰς τὴν βασιλείαν σου
"remember me when you come into your kingdom"
𝔓[75] (א) B (C*) L
KJV NKJV RSV NRSV ESV NIV TNIV NEB REB NJB NAB NLT HCSB NETmg

variant 1/TR μνησθητι μου, κυριε, οταν ελθης εν τη βασιλεια σου
"remember me, Lord, when you come in [or, with] your kingdom"
A C[2] W Θ Ψ f[1,13] 33 Maj
NKJVmg RSVmg NRSVmg (NASB—excludes "Lord") (TNIVmg) NEBmg NJBmg (NET—excludes "Lord")

variant 2 μνησθητι μου εν τη ημρα τησ ελευσεωσ σου
remember me in the day of your coming
D
NETmg

The WH NU reading, having superior documentary attestation, speaks of an imminent kingdom, a kingdom into which Jesus was about to enter—according to the perception of the believing thief. The first variant, having inferior attestation, refers to a coming, future kingdom. The scribe of D (second variant) altered this passage significantly. In full it reads, "And turning to the Lord he says to him, 'Remember me in the day of your coming.' Jesus said to the one reproving him, 'Take heart.'" Thus, in the Bezaean rendition the unbelieving thief gets encouragement from Jesus!

Luke 23:45

WH NU τοῦ ἡλίου ἐκλιπόντος
"the sun's light failed"
𝔓[75]* א C*[vid] L 070 MSS[according to Origen]
(NKJVmg) RSV NRSV ESV NASB NIV TNIV NEB REB NJB NAB NLT HCSB NET

variant/TR και εσκοτισθη ο ηλιος
"and the sun was darkened"
A C[3] (D) W Θ Ψ f[1,13] Maj MSS[according to Origen]
KJV NKJV HCSBmg NETmg

The WH NU reading also allows for the translation, "the sun was eclipsed." However, since an eclipse during Passover is very unlikely, it probably refers to the sunlight being obfuscated by darkness. But to avoid the possibility of it being interpreted as an eclipse, the text was changed to "the sun was darkened." Origen (*Comm. Matt.* 134), aware of this textual problem, preferred the variant reading and thereby promoted its popularity, which was then secured by its inclusion in TR, followed by KJV and NKJV.

Luke 23:48

Several manuscripts display additions at the end of this verse. In addition to beating their chests, D and it[c] have the people also beating "their foreheads" as they lament Jesus' death. A few other manuscripts (it[g1] syr[c,s]) put words into the mouth of those lamenting: "woe to us for the sins we have committed this day, for the destruction of Jerusalem is imminent!" (cf. *Gos. Pet.* 7.25).

Luke 23:49

A fragment of Tatian's Diatessaron (0212) has the unusual reading (with some lacunae): αι γυναικες των συνακολουθησαντων αυτω απο της Γαλιλαιας ("the wives of the ones following him from Galilee"), instead of that printed in NU: γυναικες αι συνακολουθουσαι αυτω απο της Γαλιλαιας ("the women, the ones following with him from Galilee"). The implication of Tatian's text is that the disciples' wives accompanied them as they followed Jesus from Galilee to Jerusalem. But since there is no other indication of this in the NT, we have to assume this detail to be the product of Tatian's imagination or an oral tradition.

Luke 23:53

Borrowing from Matt 27:60 and Mark 15:46, a few manuscripts (f[13] 700 cop[bo]) add και προσεκλυλισεν λιθον μεγαν επι την θυραν του μνημειου ("and he rolled a big stone up across the entrance to the tomb"). Even more expansive, D it[c] add, "and after he had been laid there, he [Joseph of Arimathea] placed over the tomb a stone which he could barely roll."

Luke 24:1a

The reading μνημειον is to be preferred over μνημα (NU) because the former is supported by 𝔓[75] ℵ C* Δ (Fitzmyer 1985, 1544). Both words mean "tomb."

The D-text (D it syr[c,s]) omits αρωματα ("spices"), producing the reading, "they brought what they had prepared." This was a purposeful excision to make 24:1 not contradict the previous verse (23:56), which says that the women prepared both αρωματα και μυρα ("spices and ointments").

Luke 24:1b

WH NU	at end of verse omit και τινες συν αυταις ("and some other women with them") 𝔓[75] ℵ B C* L 33 NKJVmg RSV NRSV ESV NASB NIV TNIV NEB REB NJB NAB NLT HCSB NET
variant/TR	at end of verse add και τινες συν αυταις ("and some other women with them") A C[3] W Θ Ψ f[1,13] Maj KJV NKJV HCSBmg

This addition was made to bring the text into harmony with Luke 24:10, which speaks of other women beside Mary Magdalene, Joanna, and Mary the mother of James.

Borrowing from Mark 16:3, D (070) adds, ελογιζοντο δε εν εαυταις· τις αρα αποκυλισει τον λιθον; ("and they were discussing among themselves, 'Who will roll away the stone?' "). But Luke had not mentioned a stone being rolled before the entrance; this was an addition created by the editor of D (and other scribes in other forms) in Luke 23:53 (see note).

Luke 24:3

TR (WH) NU οὐχ εὗρον τὸ σῶμα τοῦ κυρίου Ἰησοῦ
"they did not find the body of the Lord Jesus"
𝔓[75] ℵ A B C L W Θ Ψ 070 cop (syr[c,s] "of Jesus")
KJV NKJV RSVmg NRSVmg ESV NASB NIV TNIV REB NJB NAB NLT HCSB NET

variant ουχ ευρον το σωμα
"they did not find the body"
D it
RSV NRSV NEB NETmg

Westcott and Hort (1882, 71) thought Codex Bezae (D) contained the original wording of Luke's gospel in 24:3, 6, 12, 36, 40, 51, and 52. (All these portions are double-bracketed in WH to show the editors' strong doubts about their inclusion in the text.) Calling the omissions in D "Western non-interpolations," they posited the theory that all the other manuscripts contain interpolations in these verses. This theory affected the Nestle text until its twenty-sixth edition, at which point this theory was abandoned—note the changes in Luke 24:3, 6, 12, 36, 40, 51, 52, where none of the portions are double-bracketed. This theory also affected several modern English versions—especially the RSV and NEB, which in nearly every one of these Luke 24 passages followed the testimony of D. The NASB was also affected by this theory, but not as much as the RSV and NEB. After all three of these translations were published, 𝔓[75] was discovered. In every instance, 𝔓[75] attests to the longer reading. 𝔓[75] impacted the Nestle text, which now in every verse noted above follows the testimony of 𝔓[75] etc. It also influenced the most recent versions (NIV NJB NAB NLT), which in every case followed its testimony to include those portions excluded by previous translations. The NRSV deviated from NU by following the shorter reading here, but went with the longer NU readings in 24:6, 12, 36, 40, 51, and 52. Just as curious is the fact that the REB went along with NU here, but followed all the so-called "Western non-interpolations" in 24:6, 12, 36, 40, 51, and 52. Added to this, the NASB (first edition) followed the longer NU reading here, but went with "Western non-interpolations" in 24:36, 51, and 52.

One wonders why Westcott and Hort were so taken with the evidence of D only in the latter part of Luke, when all throughout Luke D displays many omissions. In Luke, D displays at least 75 omissions that are two words or more—and frequently the excision is of a phrase, a clause, or an entire sentence. In chapter 24 alone, D has 13 such omissions. With respect to these omissions, D often stands alone among the witnesses, or has slim support from an Old Latin or Syriac manuscript. In nearly every case, the omission cannot be explained away as a transcriptional error; rather, the deletions are the careful work of an editor having a penchant for pruning (in the critical apparatus of NA[27] see Luke 1:26; 5:9, 12, 26, 30, 39; 6:12, 21, 34; 7:3, 7, 18, 27, 28, 30, 47; 8:5, 15, 24, 28a, 28b, 43, 44; 9:12, 15, 16, 23, 48; 10:19, 23, 24; 11:8, 31, 32, 46, 49;12:19, 41; 13:25; 16:6, 18; 17:24; 18:9, 40; 19:4, 25, 31, 36, 43, 44; 20:31, 36; 21:10, 24, 37; 22:19-20, 22, 54, 61; 23:39, 45, 56; 24:9, 12, 19, 22, 25, 30, 36, 40, 46, 49, 51, 52). The reviser usually displayed an opposite penchant in the book of Acts—that of expanding—but not always (see D-text subtractions in the textual commentary on Acts). The main point to realize about the D-reviser is that he was a redactor who both excised and enhanced.

In this verse, the longer text accords with Luke's style (see Acts 1:21; 4:33; 8:16). The shorter text is a Western excision, perhaps influenced by 24:23. What is most surprising is that the NRSV followed the D-text here.

Luke 24:6

TR (WH) NU οὐκ ἔστιν ὧδε, ἀλλὰ ἠγέρθη
"he is not here, but was raised"
𝔓[75] ℵ A B C[3] L (W) Δ Θ Ψ 070 f[1,13] syr[c,s] cop
KJV NKJV RSVmg NRSV ESV NASB NIV TNIV NEBmg REBmg NJB NAB NLT HCSB NET

variant omit
D it
RSV NRSVmg NEB REB NETmg

In favor of the variant is the argument that the longer text could be the result of harmonization to parallel passages, Matt 28:6 and Mark 16:6 (Westcott and Hort 1882, 71). But the wording in Luke does not exactly replicate Matthew or Mark and appears completely Lukan. Furthermore, textual support for the omission comes only from the Western witnesses, D and it, which hardly outweigh the diverse and early testimony for the longer reading. As noted before (see Luke 24:3), the RSV and NEB translators adopted Westcott and Hort's theory of Western non-interpolations in Luke 24. All modern versions, with the exception of REB, follow the superior attestation.

Luke 24:9

The TR WH NU editions have the wording υποστρεψασαι απο του μνημειου απηγγειλαν ταυτα παντα ("having returned from the tomb, they reported all these things"), impressively supported by 𝔓[75] ℵ A B C L W Δ Θ Ψ. D and Old Latin MSS have a shorter reading: υποστρεψασαι απηγγειλαν ταυτα παντα ("having returned, they reported all these things"). The shorter reading is either the result of scribal inattention or purposeful excision—as is typical for the editor of D in Luke 24 (see note on Luke 24:3). Curiously, Westcott and Hort ignored this so-called Western non-interpolation, and not one English version omits it—contra all the other so-called Western non-interpolations in Luke 24.

Luke 24:12

TR (WH) NU Ὁ δὲ Πέτρος ἀναστὰς ἔδραμεν ἐπὶ τὸ μνημεῖον καὶ παρακύψας βλέπει τὰ ὀθόνια μόνα, καὶ ἀπῆλθεν πρὸς ἑαυτὸν θαυμάζων τὸ γεγονός.
"Peter rose up, ran to the tomb, bent over, and saw the linen clothes lying there, and he departed, wondering what had happened."
𝔓[75] ℵ B W Δ 070 079 syr[c,s] cop (A L Θ Ψ f[1,13] Maj add κειμενα after οθονια—so TR)
KJV NKJV RSVmg NRSV ESV NASB NIV TNIV NEBmg REBmg NJB NAB NLT HCSB NET

variant omit
D it
RSV NRSVmg NASBmg NEB REB NJBmg NABmg NETmg

Westcott and Hort (1882, 71) argued that the verse is a consolidated interpolation from John 20:3-10. However, the scribe of 𝔓[75] rarely interpolated from remote parallels, and the scribe of B did so only occasionally. Whereas many other scribes (recognizing the resemblance between this verse and John 20:5-6) added κειμενα ("lying"—see A L Θ Ψ f[1,13] Maj—so TR), this was not done in 𝔓[75] ℵ B W syr[c,s] cop. Thus, it is far more likely that this is a Western excision intended to alleviate any bad impressions about Peter (D has a tendency in Acts to promote Peter).

Luke 24:13

TR WH NU σταδίους ἑξήκοντα ἀπὸ Ἰερουσαλήμ
"sixty stadia from Jerusalem"
𝔓[75] A B D L W 070 it syr[c,s] cop
all

variant εκατον σταδιους εξηκοντα απο Ιερουσαλημ
"one hundred sixty stadia from Jerusalem"
א N Θ 079[vid] Jerome
RSVmg NJBmg

According to Metzger (TCGNT), the variant reading "seems to have arisen in connection with patristic identification of Emmaus with 'Amwâs (mod. Nicopolis), about twenty-two Roman miles (176 stadia) from Jerusalem." Of course, this distance would have been far too great for the two disciples to have re-traversed the same evening (see 24:33). The distance according to TR WH NU is about seven miles.

Luke 24:32

TR NU οὐχὶ ἡ καρδία ἡμῶν καιομένη ἦν [ἐν ἡμῖν]
"were not our hearts burning within us"
א A L W 33 Maj
KJV NKJV RSV NRSV ESV NASB NIV TNIV NJB NAB HCSB NET

variant/WH ουχι η καρδια ημων καιομενη ην
"were not our hearts burning"
𝔓[75] B D syr[c,s]
RSVmg NRSVmg NEB REB NLT NETmg

The words "within us" are included in the NU text but within brackets—out of respect to the combined testimony of 𝔓[75] B D. WH exclude the words. Three modern versions (NEB REB NLT) also exclude these words. The expression καιομενη ("burning") was changed to κεκαλυμμενη ("veiled") in D, "blinded" in it[c], "obtuse" in it[l], "put out" in it[e], and "heavy" in syr. These Western emendations again show the creative effort put into the editorialization of Luke 24.

Luke 24:34

According to most manuscripts, the accusative plural λεγοντας indicates that it is the gathered group of disciples (the eleven plus the others) who say that Jesus has risen and appeared to Peter. The D-reviser changed this to λεγοντες, a nominative plural participle. This change then means that it is the two disciples returning from Emmaus who say that Jesus has risen and has appeared to Peter. Though the two knew that Jesus had risen, how could they know that he appeared to Peter?—unless, of course, the other unnamed disciple who was heading for Emmaus was Peter. This, in fact, was Origen's view (*Cels.* 2.62, 68), and may have been the view of the D-reviser. In any case, the accusative plural λεγοντας is original (as found in all other manuscripts) and entirely suitable to the context.

Luke 24:36

TR (WH) NU καὶ λέγει αὐτοῖς· εἰρήνη ὑμῖν
"and he says to them, 'Peace to you.'"
𝔓75 ℵ A B L Δ Θ Ψ cop syr^{c,s}
KJV NKJV RSVmg NRSV ESV NASB NIV TNIV NEBmg REBmg NJB NAB NLT HCSB NET

variant 1 και λεγει αυτοις, Ειρηνη υμιν. Εγω ειμι, μη φοβεισθε
"and he says to them, 'Peace to you. I am [here]; do not be afraid.'"
P (W) syr^{h,p} cop^{boMSS}
none

variant 2 omit
D it
RSV NRSVmg NEB REB NETmg

The first variant is a scribal addition borrowed from John 6:20. The statement εγω ειμι ("I am") statement adds a theophanic element to this christophany. The second variant was considered original by Westcott and Hort (1882, 72; see my note on Luke 24:3), who believed that the longer text was a scribal interpolation borrowed from John 20:19. (WH included the words, though in double brackets.) But Luke and John probably derived their accounts about the resurrection from many of the same sources; thus, this verbal equivalence is not unusual. Three translations are consistent in following the D-text throughout Luke 24—namely RSV NEB REB. The NASB translators also excluded the text here and in 24:51-52, then added the text back again in their updated version.

Luke 24:40

TR (WH) NU include verse
καὶ τοῦτο εἰπὼν ἔδειξεν αὐτοῖς τὰς χεῖρας καὶ τοὺς πόδας
"and having said this, he showed them his hands and feet"
𝔓75 ℵ A B L W Δ Θ Ψ cop
KJV NKJV RSVmg NRSV ESV NASB NIV TNIV NEBmg REBmg NJB NAB NLT HCSB NET

variant omit verse
D it syr^{c,s}
NKJVmg RSV NRSVmg NASBmg NEB REB NJBmg NETmg

Again, Westcott and Hort (1882, 72) considered the longer text to be a scribal interpolation (see note on 24:3) borrowed from John 20:20. But Luke and John seemed to have used many of the same sources for their resurrection narratives; thus, this verbal equivalence is not unusual.

Luke 24:42

WH NU ἰχθύος ὀπτοῦ μέρος
"a piece of cooked fish"
𝔓75 ℵ A B D L W it^{e} syr^{s} cop^{sa}
NKJVmg RSV NRSV ESV NASB NIV TNIV NEB REB NJB NAB NLT HCSB NET

variant/TR ιχθυος οπτου μερος και απο μελισσιου κηριου
"a piece of cooked fish and [a piece] of honeycomb"
(Θ) Ψ) f1,(13) 33 Maj syr[c,h**,p]
KJV NKJV ESVmg HCSBmg

The WH NU reading is likely original because it has superior documentation and because it presents the shorter reading. The variant adds "honeycomb." Since honey was used in the Lord's Supper and baptisms, it is quite likely that the words were added to provide scriptural sanction for an ecclesiastical practice (see Nestle 1911, 567-568).

Luke 24:46

WH NU οὕτως γέγραπται
"thus it is written"
𝔓75 ℵ B C* D L it
NKJVmg RSV NRSV ESV NASB NIV TNIV NEB REB NJB NAB NLT HCSB NET

variant/TR ουτως γεγραπτι και ουτως εδει
"thus it is written and thus it is necessary"
A C[2vid] W Θ Ψ f1,13 33 Maj
KJV NKJV HCSBmg

In fuller context, WH NU could be rendered: "thus it is written, the Christ [is] to suffer and to be raised from the dead on the third day." The variant displays a scribal expansion supplying the infinitives with a leading εδει, and thereby bringing the text into harmony with 24:26. This harmonization was included in TR and translated in KJV and NKJV.

Luke 24:51

TR (WH) NU διέστη ἀπ᾽ αὐτῶν καὶ ἀνεφέρετο εἰς τὸν οὐρανόν
"he departed from them and was taken up into heaven"
𝔓75 ℵ[c] A B C L W Δ Θ Ψ cop
KJV NKJV RSVmg NRSV ESV NASB NIV TNIV NEBmg REBmg NJB NAB NLT HCSB NET

variant διεστη απ αυτων
"he departed from them"
ℵ* D it syr[s]
RSV NRSVmg NEB REB NJBmg NLTmg NETmg

Westcott and Hort (1882, 73) considered the variant to be a Western non-interpolation (see note on 24:3). They argued that the longer reading "was evidently inserted from an assumption that a separation from the disciples at the close of a gospel must be the Ascension. The Ascension apparently did not lie within the proper scope of the Gospels, as seen in their genuine texts; its true place was at the head of the Acts of the Apostles, as the preparation for the Day of Pentecost, and thus the beginning of the history of the Church." Indeed, Jesus' separation from the disciples need not mean that he ascended, because after his resurrection Jesus intermittently appeared to his disciples in visible form, then disappeared. In this regard, the shorter text is exegetically defensible. But Westcott and Hort's next argument is weak because, in effect, they say that the longer text is the result of scribes attempting to harmonize Luke 24 with Acts 1 by adding a reference to the ascension. But it is far more likely that other scribes deleted the reference to the ascension in Luke so that it would not conflict with the chronology of the ascension recorded in Acts 1:3, 9-11. This is all the more apparent when we understand that the editor of

Codex Bezae (perhaps followed by other Western scribes) was determined to eliminate any mention of Jesus' bodily ascension in both Luke and Acts (see Epp 1981, 131-145). In Acts 1:2 and 1:9 (see notes), manuscripts belonging to the Western text omit the words about Jesus' ascension. In Acts 1:11 the ascension is retained, but it is modified in the Western text from "taken up into heaven" to simply "taken up" (see note); and in Acts 1:22 the Western text (with all other witnesses) refers to Jesus being "taken up." Never does the Western text portray an actual physical ascension.

In conclusion, let us consider one more point: If one were to accept the shorter reading as original, does this mean that there is no mention of the ascension in the Gospels, as posited by Westcott and Hort? For Matthew this is true. For Mark this is also true, if we accept that the original text ended with 16:8. For John this is not true, because Jesus clearly speaks of an ascension to the Father on the morning of the resurrection (John 20:17). Since this ascension occurred before the one recorded in Acts 1:3, 9-11, why is it not possible for Luke to speak of yet another ascension—or, better still, to be speaking of the same ascension as Acts but in general terms (lacking specific chronology)? Indeed, in Acts 1:2 Luke clearly indicates that his gospel covered the entire scope of Jesus' ministry up until the ascension. Thus, it is very likely that Luke spoke of Jesus' ascension in his gospel and then again in Acts. (See comments on Luke 24:3.)

In any event, three modern translations (RSV, NEB, and REB) show the shorter text. These translations are consistent in following the D-text throughout Luke 24. The NASB translators originally chose to do so only in 24:36, 51-52, exhibiting a methodological inconsistency. Then they corrected this in the updated version.

Luke 24:52

TR (WH) NU — προσκυνήσαντες αὐτὸν ὑπέστρεψαν εἰς Ἰερουσαλήμ
"having worshiped him, they returned to Jerusalem"
𝔓75 ℵ A B C L W Δ Θ Ψ cop
KJV NKJV RSVmg NRSV ESV NASB NIV TNIV NEBmg REBmg NJB NAB NLT HCSB NET

variant — υπεστρεψαν εις Ιερουσαλημ
"they returned to Jerusalem"
D it syr[s]
RSV NRSVmg NEB REB NJBmg NETmg

Again, Westcott and Hort (1882, 73) considered the shorter text to represent the original wording of Luke (see note on 24:3), but the textual evidence speaks against this. Luke waited until the very end of his gospel to speak of Jesus being worshiped, for his resurrection proved to the disciples that he was indeed God, worthy of their worship.

Four modern translations (RSV, NASB, NEB, and REB) show the shorter text. Three translations are consistent in following the D-text throughout Luke 24—namely RSV NEB REB. The NASB translators chose to do so only in 24:36, 51-52, exhibiting a methodological inconsistency, which was corrected in the updated version.

Luke 24:53a

The D-text (D it) changed the participle ευλογουντες ("blessing") to αινουντες ("praising") in order to avoid repeating the same word used in 24:51. "This does away with the offense that ευλογειν is applied to the disciples immediately after it has been ascribed to the ascending Lord" (Haenchen 1971, 57).

Luke 24:53b

WH NU	at end of verse omit αμην ("amen") 𝔓[75] ℵ C* D L W 33 it syr[s] cop NKJVmg RSV NRSV ESV NASB NIV TNIV NEB REB NJB NAB NLT HCSB NET
variant/TR	at end of verse add αμην ("amen") A B C[2] Θ Ψ f[13] Maj KJV NKJV HCSBmg NETmg

Because the NT books were read orally in church meetings, it became customary to end the reading with an "amen." Gradually, this spoken word was added to the printed page of many late manuscripts. This addition took place in all four gospels and Acts.

The manuscript 1333c adds the pericope of the adultress in a slightly shorter version (John 8:3-11) at the end of Luke. This is another sign that this story was a piece of floating oral tradition inserted into the Gospels in various places (see comments on Luke 21:38; John 7:53–8:11).

Subscription

TR appends a subscription to the Gospel, as follows: Το κατα Λουκαν ευαγγελιον ("the Gospel according to Luke"). The codices ℵ and B also have subscriptions. ℵ reads ευαγ-γελιον κατα Λουκαν ("Gospel according to Luke"), and B reads κατα Λουκαν ("According to Luke"). For comments on this, see note on Inscription to Luke.

Gospel according to JOHN

Inscription (Title)

WH NU	Κατα Ιωαννην "According to John" א B (NIV TNIV NLT NET)
variant 1	Ευαγγελιον κατα Ιωαννην "Gospel according to John" $\mathfrak{P}^{66}$ $\mathfrak{P}^{75}$ (A) C D L W^s Θ f^1 33 Maj NKJV RSV NRSV ESV NASB NEB REB NJB NAB HCSB
variant 2/TR	Αγιον Ευαγγελιον κατα Ιωαννην "Holy Gospel according to John" (or, "Gospel according to Saint John") (28) KJV

Since biblical authors usually did not title their works, scribes added titles to the manuscripts later. The very title "Gospel according to John" speaks volumes because this tells us that all the scribes considered the author to be John—and very likely the apostle John. The two earliest manuscripts, $\mathfrak{P}^{66}$ (containing John only) and $\mathfrak{P}^{75}$ (containing Luke and John) read "Gospel according to John," as do several other early manuscripts. The WH NU reading reflects the second stage in titling the Gospels, a stage when all four gospels were placed together in one codex and were titled under one head: The Gospel—According to Matthew, According to Mark, According to Luke, According to John. This titling in the WH NU texts was mostly influenced by Codex Vaticanus, which has κατα μαθθαιον, κατα μαρκον, κατα λουκαν, κατα ιωαννην written for both the inscription and subscription in each gospel. Codex Sinaiticus has the same titling for the inscription, but in the subscription for Mark, Luke, and John the word ευαγγελιον ("Gospel") comes first (see comments on Matthew's subscription). In later manuscripts the titles were further expanded, as in TR, where αγιον (= "holy" or "saint") could modify ευαγγελιον ("Gospel") or the writer Ιωαννης ("John"). Many English translations reflect the pattern set by $\mathfrak{P}^{66}$ and $\mathfrak{P}^{75}$; that is, they designate each gospel separately. But NIV TNIV NLT NET reflect the format used by the scribes of Vaticanus and Sinaiticus; that is, each gospel is titled as a part of the one, fourfold gospel collection.

John 1:3-4a

WH NU — [3]πάντα δι αὐτοῦ ἐγένετο, καὶ χωρὶς αὐτοῦ ἐγένετο οὐδὲ ἕν. ὃ γέγονεν [4]ἐν αὐτῷ ζωὴ ἦν
"[3] All things came into being through him, and without him not one thing came into being. What has come into being [4] in him was life"
𝔓[75c] C D L (W[s] omit ηυ) 050*
RSVmg NRSV ESVmg NEB REBmg NJB NAB NLT HCSBmg NETmg

variant 1/TR — [3]παντα δι αυτου εγενετο, και χωρις αυτου εγενετο ουδε ἕν ο γεγονεν. [4]εν αυτω ζωη ην
"[3] All things came into being through him, and without him not one thing came into being that has come into being. [4] In him was life"
א[c] Θ Ψ 050[c] f[1,13] 33 Maj
KJV NKJV RSV NRSVmg ESV NASB NIV TNIV NEBmg REB NJBmg NLTmg HCSB NET

variant 2 — [3]παντα δι αυτου εγενετο, και χωρις αυτου εγενετο ουδεν ο γεγονεν [4]αυτω ζωη ην
"[3] All things came into being through him, and without him not one thing came into being. What has come into being [4] by him was life"
𝔓[66]
none

The last phrase of 1:3 (ο γεγονεν—"that which has come into being") has been connected with 1:3 or with 1:4 by various ancient scribes and modern translators by means of punctuation. The earliest manuscripts (𝔓[66] 𝔓[75*] א* A B) do not have any punctuation in these verses. If John had read the passage out loud, the hearers would have known how he punctuated the text. Lacking his notations, all readers—from ancient to modern—have had to guess his intentions. Of course, it must also be said that, since the prologue is poetic, it is possible that John intended ambiguity; thus, it is not a question of which reading is correct. The earliest scribes, by not adding punctuation, left the text ambiguous; ancient readers could read it both ways and still make sense of it. A corrector of 𝔓[75] (or simply a later reader) punctuated 1:3-4 as in WH NU.

The majority of the early church fathers interpreted 1:3-4 according to the phrasing in WH NU. The passage was taken to mean that all created things were "life" by virtue of being in him. The statement is intended to affirm that the Word not only created the universe, he presently sustains it—all things are alive with his life (see Col 1:17; Heb 1:2-3). This idea is rendered quite well in the NLT: "He gives life to everything he created." The next phrase in the prologue, "and the life was the light of men," was then understood by several early interpreters to mean that the Word enlightened people—even prior to his incarnation. This was the view of Justin Martyr and the Christian philosophers of Alexandria.

However, the expression "what has come into being in him was life" could also be understood to mean that life had "come into being" in the Word (i.e., "that which came into being in him was life" or "life is that which came into being in him"—as in W[s]). This is a more difficult concept than the first interpretation discussed above. Certain fourth-century Arians took this to mean that the Son had undergone change and therefore was not truly equal with the Father (Brown 1966, 6). Thereafter, many church fathers supported the reading as it is in the first variant. This reading emphasizes the Word's impartation of life to men concurrent with the giving of light to men. In short, it speaks of Jesus' ministry on earth as the life-giver and light-giver. Even to the present day, many interpreters have followed this interpretation (see the discussion in Schnackenburg 1982, 1:239-240), while other scholars (e.g., Westcott 1881, 28-31; Brown 1966, 6-7; Beasley-Murray 1987, 2) support the WH NU reading.

One of the difficulties of the WH NU reading pertains to the function of the preposition εν in the expression ο γεγονεν εν αυτω ζωη ην, for it is difficult to understand how creation came to be life *in* him (especially when "in him" is read as a locative). It appears that the scribe of 𝔓^{66} confronted this problem and dealt with it by omitting the preposition (the second variant). Of course, it could be argued that the omission of εν was accidental, due to homoeoteleuton: γεγονεν εν. However, since this was left uncorrected, it is just as likely that it was a purposeful omission intended to rectify this exegetical problem. With εν gone, the phrase is clearly dative, which therefore points to agency: "What has come into being by him was life [or, was made life], and the life was the light of men."

It should also be noted that several witnesses (א D it MSS$^{\text{according to Origen}}$) read εστιν ("is") in the expression, εν αυτω ζωη εστιν ("in him is life"), against the testimony of 𝔓^{66} 𝔓^{75} A B C L, which read ην ("was"). The variant with the present tense, although a true statement and one that John himself would espouse (see 11:25; 14:6), appears to be the work of scribes wanting to affirm the "presentness" of life in the Word and thereby obviate any thought that life was no longer in him. Or perhaps scribes made the change to the present tense in an attempt to clarify the difficult statement, "that which was created in him was life." But John chose to use the imperfect ην throughout the first four verses of the prologue to indicate the past and continual presence of the Word.

In the final analysis, we need to see that John's prologue is poetry, which allows for polyvalence. As such, John may have wanted the phrase to connect with both 1:3 and 1:4, showing that the Word is life-giver in all creation, as well as life-giver in regeneration.

John 1:13

TR WH NU	οἳ οὐκ ἐξ αἱμάτων οὐδὲ ἐκ θελήματος σαρκὸς οὐδὲ ἐκ θελήματος ἀνδρὸς ἀλλ ἐκ θεοῦ ἐγεννήθησαν. "the ones who not of blood nor of the will of the flesh nor of the will of a husband but of God were born" 𝔓^{66} (𝔓^{75} A B* εγενηθησαν) א B^{2} C D^{c} L W^{s} Ψ f^{1,13} 33 Maj syr^{p,h} cop all
variant	ος ουκ εξ αιματων ουδε εκ θεληματος σαρκος ουδε εκ θεληματος ανδρος αλλ εκ θεου εγενηθη "[he] who not of blood nor of the will of the flesh nor of the will of a husband but of God was born" (D* omits ος) it^{b} syr^{c} Irenaeus Tertullian NJBmg NABmg

The TR WH NU reading has vastly superior external support than does the variant, which has the support of only one Greek manuscript, D*. The singular construction ("he who was born") in the variant reading indicates that it was the Son of God who was born—not of blood or of the will of the flesh or of the will of man—but of God. Obviously, the scribe of D* and one Latin translator were attempting to provide more description of Christ's incarnation. Tertullian also used the variant as a proof text for Jesus' true divinity and humanity—that is, Jesus' birth was both supernatural and a real physical event. In *The Flesh of Christ* (19) Tertullian argued that the Valentinian gnostics had altered the text to suit their own views. The Jerusalem Bible (a version produced by Roman Catholic scholars) adopted the singular reading, but this was changed to the plural in the New Jerusalem Bible with this marginal note: "there are strong arguments for reading the verb in the singular, 'who was born,' in which case the verse refers to Jesus' divine origin, not to the virgin birth." The New American Bible (an American Catholic translation) notes the variant as follows: "The variant 'He who was begotten,' asserting Jesus' virginal conception, is weakly attested in Old Latin and Syriac versions."

John 1:15

TR NU — λέγων· οὗτος ἦν ὃν εἶπον· ὁ ὀπίσω μου ἐρχόμενος ἔμπροσθεν μου γέγονεν
"saying, 'This was he of whom I said, "He who comes after me has become before me."'"
𝔓66 𝔓75 A D* Maj
all

variant 1/WH — λεγων· ουτος ην ο ειπων ο οπισω μου ερχομενος εμπροσθεν μου γεγονεν
"saying, 'This was he who said, "He who comes after me has become before me."'"
א1 B* C* Origen
none

variant 2 — λεγων· ουτος ην ο οπισω μου ερχομενος ος εμπροσθεν μου γεγονεν
"saying, 'This was the one who comes after me who has become before me.'"
א*
none

Both the TR NU reading and the first variant have ancient testimony—the papyri for TR NU and Origen (in two separate citations) for the first variant. The TR NU reading is difficult because it is grammatically awkward; hence, the creation of the two variants. Westcott and Hort adopted the first variant for their text. The scribe of א* made changes to straighten out the difficulties of having a quotation within a quotation.

John 1:16

WH NU — ὅτι ἐκ τοῦ πληρώματος αὐτοῦ ἡμεῖς πάντες ἐλάβομεν
"because from his fullness have we all received"
𝔓66 𝔓75 א B C* D L 33
NKJVmg NRSV ESV NASB NIV (TNIV) NEB REB NJB NAB (NLT) NET

variant/TR — και εκ του πληρωματος αυτου ημεις παντες ελαβομεν
"and of his fullness have we all received"
A C3 Ws Θ Ψ f1,13 Maj
KJV NKJV RSV HCSB

The replacement of και for οτι is a scribal adjustment intended to make a more logical connection between 1:15 and 1:16. However, οτι in 1:16 connects with 1:14 inasmuch as 1:15 is a parenthetical statement (usually set off by parentheses in English translations). Connecting the end of 1:14 with οτι at the beginning of 1:16 gives this reading: "we saw his glory, glory as of the only Son of the Father, full of grace and truth . . . because (οτι) from his fullness we have all received, even grace added to grace." John was saying that he (and the other apostles) knew by experience that the Son of God was full of grace and truth because they had continually been recipients of that full supply.

John 1:17

TR WH NU ὁ νόμος διὰ Μωϋσέως ἐδόθη, ἡ χάρις καὶ ἡ ἀλήθεια διὰ Ἰησοῦ Χριστοῦ ἐγένετο
"the law was given through Moses, the grace and the truth came through Jesus Christ"
𝔓[75] ℵ B D L Θ Ψ Maj
RSV NRSV ESV NASB NIV TNIV NEB NJB NAB HCSB

variant ο νομος δια Μωυσεως εδοθη, η χαρις δε και η αληθεια δια Ιησου χριστου εγεντο
"the law was given through Moses, but the grace and the truth came through Jesus Christ"
𝔓[66] (W[s]) it syr[h**] cop[bo]
KJV NKJV REB NLT NET

By adding the contrastive δε ("but"), the scribes and ancient translators producing the variant were signaling a contrast between the two dispensations: the law (given by Moses) and grace and truth (given by Jesus). Though there is no implication thus far in John's prologue (1:1-18) of any kind of contrast between the law and grace, this contrast is constantly made throughout the book of John and in many other books of the NT, especially in the Epistles of Paul, where grace is presented as superseding the law.

John 1:18

WH NU μονογενὴς θεός
"an only one, God" (or, "only begotten God")
𝔓[66] ℵ* B C* L syr[hmg,p]
NKJVmg RSVmg (NRSV) ESV NASB NIV (TNIV) NEBmg NJBmg NAB (NLT) HCSBmg NET

variant 1 ο μονογενης θεος
"the only begotten God"
𝔓[75] ℵ[1] 33 cop[bo]
NRSVmg NASBmg NIVmg NETmg

variant 2/TR ο μονογενης υιος
"the only begotten Son"
A C[3] (W[s]) Θ Ψ f[1,13] Maj syr[c]
KJV NKJV RSV ESVmg NASBmg NIVmg TNIVmg (NEB REB) NJB NLTmg HCSB NETmg

The two early papyri (𝔓[66] and 𝔓[75]), the earliest uncials (ℵ B C*), and some early versions (Coptic and Syriac) support the word θεος, and many church fathers (Irenaeus, Clement, Origen, Eusebius, Serapion, Basil, Didymus, Gregory-Nyssa, Epiphanius, Valentinians[according to Irenaeus], Clement) knew of this reading. The second variant with υιος was known by many early church fathers (Irenaeus, Clement, Hippolytus, Alexander, Eusebius, Eastathius, Serapion, Julian, Basil, and Gregory-Nazianzus) and was translated in some early versions (Old Latin and Syriac). However, the discovery of two second-century papyri, 𝔓[66] and 𝔓[75], both of which read θεος ("God"), tipped the balance. It is now clear that μονογενης θεος is the earlier—and preferred—reading. This was changed as early as the beginning of the third century, if not earlier, to the more ordinary reading, μονογενης υιος ("the only begotten Son").

Even without the knowledge of the two papyri (which were discovered in the 1950s and 1960s), Hort (1876, 1-26) argued extensively and convincingly for the reading μονογενης θεος. He argued that gnostics (such as Valentinus, the first known writer to have used this phrase) did not invent this phrase; rather, they simply quoted it. And he argued that this phrase is very suitable for the closing verse of the prologue, in which Christ has been called "God" (θεος—in 1:1) and "an only one" (μονογενης—in 1:14), and finally, "an only one, God" (μονογενης θεος), which combines the two titles into one. This masterfully concludes the prologue, for 1:18 then mirrors 1:1. Both verses have the following three corresponding phrases: (1) Christ as God's expression (the "Word" and "he has explained him"), (2) Christ as God ("the Word was God" and "an only one, God"), and (3) Christ as the one close to God ("the Word was face to face with God" [WILLIAMS] and "in the bosom of the Father").

After the discovery of the papyri, English translators started to adopt the reading "God." However, the entire phrase, μονογενης θεος, is very difficult to render, so translators have not known whether to treat μονογενης as an adjective alone or as an adjective functioning as a substantive. Should this be rendered, "an only begotten God" or "an only one, God" or "unique God"? Since the term μονογενης more likely speaks of "uniqueness" than "only one born," it probably functions as a substantive indicating Jesus' unique identity as being both God and near to God, as a Son in the bosom of his Father. This is made somewhat clear in NET: "the only one, himself God" or NIVmg—"God the Only Begotten." But note that even these translations add an article, and thereby follow the first variant. A literal translation as found in the NASB ("the only begotten God") could lead readers to think mistakenly that the Son is a begotten God. Other translations offer conflated readings, which include both "God" and "Son"—as in the first edition of the NIV and the NRSV, which both read "God the only Son," and the TNIV, which reads, "the one and only Son, who is himself God." Of course, these translations are rendering μονογενης as "only Son," but this rendering ends up reflecting the inferior textual variant. Several modern translations still follow the third reading: "the only Son" (NJB HCSB) and "God's only Son" (REB). To accurately reflect what John wrote, an English translation could read, "No one has see God at any time; a very unique one, who is God and who is in the bosom of the Father, has explained him."

What is important to note in this passage is that Jesus' deity is affirmed in the same manner as it is in 1:1. He is unique in that he is God and with God, his Father. Jesus' deity is a major theme in John's gospel, affirmed in 1:1; 5:17-18; 8:58; 10:30-36; 14:9-11; and 20:28. To these verses should be added 1:18, a profound conclusion to the prologue and a strong affirmation of Jesus' divine uniqueness. He alone who is God and near to God the Father is qualified to explain God to humanity (see Comfort 2005, 336).

John 1:19

WH NU — ἀπέστειλαν [πρὸς αὐτὸν] οἱ Ἰουδαῖοι ἐξ Ἱεροσολύμων ἱερεῖς καὶ Λευίτας
"the Jews from Jerusalem sent to him priests and Levites"
B C* 33 892[c] (𝔓[66cvid] A Θ Ψ f[13] lat syr[h] προς αυτον after Λευιτας)
NASB NAB NETmg

variant/TR — απεστειλαν οι Ιουδαιοι εξ Ιεροσολυμων ιερεις και Λευιτας
"the Jews from Jerusalem sent priests and Levites"
𝔓[66] 𝔓[75] ℵ C[3] L W[s] f[1] Maj
KJV NKJV RSV NRSV ESV NIV TNIV NEB REB NJB NLT HCSB NET

The documentary evidence shows clearly that the phrase προς αυτον ("to him") is a scribal addition, inserted by scribes to provide an indirect object after the verb απεστειλαν ("sent"). The transposition of this phrase in various manuscripts also makes the reading suspect as a scribal addition. The NU editors retained it in the text (in brackets) in deference to the testimony of B. Most English versions follow the superior variant reading.

John 1:24

WH NU read απεσταλμενοι ησαν εκ των Φαρισαιων, with excellent attestation from 𝔓66 𝔓75 ℵ* A* B C* L Ψ. A variant reading adds a definite article (οι) before απεσταλμενοι (ℵ2 Ac C3 Ws f1,13 Maj). The first reading, without the article, indicates that the envoy included some of the Pharisees (see NIV NEB). Beasley-Murray (1987, 24) argues that the variant is an attempt to indicate that the group of delegates (1:19) were sent by the Pharisees; he posits that this is very unlikely because Pharisees were generally laymen. Actually, either reading can be understood to mean that the delegates included Pharisees. However, many English versions (e.g., RSV NRSV NLT) understand the text to be saying that the delegates were sent by the Pharisees.

John 1:26

The perfect tense verb εστηκεν has more diverse documentary support (among the Greek manuscripts, 𝔓66 A C Tvid Ws Θ Ψ f13 Maj—so TR NU) than any of the other readings, each of which is a different tense of the same verb (pluperfect, present, imperfect): (1) ειστηκει ("had stood") 𝔓75 𝔓120vid (an early reading that could be original); (2) στηκει ("stands") B L 083 f1 ite syrs copsa,bo (so WH); (3) εστηκει ("was standing") ℵ. Metzger (TCGNT) said, "the perfect tense, so frequently employed with theological over-tones by the Fourth Evangelist, conveys a special force here (something like, 'there is One who has taken his stand in your midst')." In other words, "the hidden Messiah is present in Israel" (Beasley-Murray 1987, 24). Because the present tense captures this idea well, several early versions used a present tense verb in the translation. English versions do the same.

John 1:27a

In the first part of the verse there are two variants: ο οπισω μου ερχομενος ("the one coming after me"), supported by 𝔓66 𝔓75 𝔓120vid ℵ2 C* L T Ws (so NU), versus οπισω μου ερχομενος ("coming after me"), supported by ℵ* B (so WH). Barrett (1978, 174) argued that the article before ερχομενος may have been added to form the messianic title, "the Coming One." But it seems more likely that it was accidentally dropped due to haplography (note the correction in ℵ). TR adds ος εμπροσθεν μου γεγονεν ("the one having come before me") following A C3 f13 Maj.

John 1:27b

In John the Baptist's statement ("I am not worthy that I should untie the straps of his sandals"), the Greek word for "worthy" is αξιος according to the testimony of 𝔓119vid 𝔓120vid ℵ A B C D 33 Maj (so TR WH NU). A variant word is ικανος ("qualified"—"I am not qualified that I should untie the straps of his sandals"), found in two early manuscripts, 𝔓66 and 𝔓75. However, the reading does not show up again until the thirteenth century—in the minuscule 472. Thus, it is very likely that the scribes of 𝔓66 and 𝔓75, perhaps independently, conformed 1:27 to the wording in the parallel passages (Matt 3:11; Mark 1:7; Luke 3:16), where the word contained in all the manuscripts is ικανος ("qualified"). This shows that the other gospels' account of the Baptist's statement about his inferiority to Jesus had formed a horizon of expectation for the scribes of 𝔓66 and 𝔓75. Quite likely, they had this particular wording memorized. Thus, when John's wording challenged this horizon of expectation, they changed the wording.

John 1:27c

Another harmonization to another gospel, namely Matthew (see Matt 3:11), occurred in N and a few other manuscripts, which add αυτος υμας βαπτιζει εν πνευματι αγιω και πυρι ("he will baptize you in the Holy Spirit and fire") at the end of the verse.

John 1:28

WH NU Βηθανια
"Bethany"
𝔓66 𝔓75 ℵ B C W[s] MSS[according to Origen]
NKJVmg RSV NRSV ESV NASB NIV TNIV NEB REB NJB NAB NLT HCSB NET

variant 1/TR Βηθαβαρα
"Bethabara"
C[2] K T Ψ[c] 083 f[1,13] 33 syr[s,c] cop[sa] MSS[according to Origen]
KJV NKJV HCSBmg NETmg

variant 2 Βηθαραβα
"Betharaba"
ℵ[2] 892[mg]
none

UBS[3] cited 𝔓59vid as supporting Βηθανια but 𝔓59 shows only Βη[. . .]. Thus, 𝔓59 could support any of the readings. This was corrected in UBS[4]; 𝔓59 is not cited. The WH NU reading is very likely original. It was the reading that Origen (*Comm. Jo.* 6.24, 40) encountered in "nearly all the copies," and it was the reading Heracleon acknowledged (according to Origen). But Origen could not locate any "Bethany" by the Jordan when he traveled to Palestine. However, there was a town called Bethabara in the vicinity, which, according to local tradition, was the site of John's baptism. Origen, therefore, adopted the reading Βηθαβαρα (see Barrett 1978, 175). He was followed by Eusebius and by Jerome, who, however, let "Bethany" stand in the Vulgate (Schnackenburg 1982, 1:296). The second variant probably points to the Beth-arabah mentioned in Josh 15:6, 61; 18:22, located near Jericho and therefore near the traditional site of John's baptism of Jesus.

John 1:33

C* cop[sa] add και πυρι ("and fire") at end of verse—a harmonization to Matt 3:11 ("he will baptize you in the Holy Spirit and fire"). In 𝔓75, a later, second hand added κα[. . .] in the margin at the end of this verse. The rest of the wording cannot be read, but it can be presumed that the writer was intending to add και πυρι (see *Text of Earliest MSS,* 569).

John 1:34

TR WH NU	ὁ υἱὸς τοῦ θεοῦ "the Son of God" 𝔓66 𝔓75 𝔓120 ℵ2 A B C W Δ Θ Ψ 083 KJV NKJV RSV NRSV ESV NASB NIV TNIVmg NEBmg REBmg NJBmg NAB NLTmg HCSB NETmg
variant 1	ο εκλεκτος του θεου "the chosen one of God" 𝔓5vid 𝔓106vid ℵ* it[e] syr[c,s] NRSVmg TNIV NEB REB NJB NLT HCSBmg NET
variant 2	"chosen son of God" it[a] syr[pal] cop[sa] NETmg

Though both 𝔓5 and 𝔓106 are listed as "vid" in UBS4 (not cited in NA27) it is fairly certain that both manuscripts read εκλεκτος, not υιος. The transcription of 𝔓5 in Elliott and Parker 1995 showing [υιο]ς is incorrect. The spacing on the line calls for εκλεκτος, as judged by the original editors, Grenfell and Hunt. (See the Oxyrhynchus volumes on 𝔓5 and 𝔓106, and see *Text of Earliest MSS*, 75, 646.) The recently published 𝔓120 has the wording ο υιος ("the Son").

The TR WH NU reading has excellent external support among the papyri and early uncials, but so does the first variant. Indeed, it is supported by two early papyri (𝔓5 and 𝔓106), an early uncial (ℵ*), and two of the most reliable early Western witnesses (it[e] syr[s]). The presence of the conflated reading, "chosen Son of God" (variant 2), shows that both readings were present at an early stage of textual transmission. The second corrector of Codex Sinaiticus (sixth or seventh century) deleted εκλεκτος and wrote the nomen sacrum for υιος in the margin.

Several scholars have argued that it is more likely that the reading εκλεκτος ("chosen one") was changed to υιος ("Son") than vice versa. For example, Gordon Fee (1979, 431-432) thinks an orthodox scribe of the second century might have sensed "the possibility that the designation 'Chosen One' might be used to support adoptionism and so altered the text for orthodox reasons." Or the change could have happened because scribes thought "Son" conformed with the synoptic accounts of Jesus' baptism (where God calls Jesus "my Son") or suited John's gospel better than "chosen one." Indeed, "Son of God" frequently occurs in John's gospel, but not all who recognized Jesus' deity called him "the Son of God." For example, Peter called him "the holy one of God" (6:69). All these reasons strengthen the case for "chosen one" being the original reading (see Comfort 2005, 336-337). Furthermore, "chosen one" adds one more messianic title to the chain of witnesses in John 1, while "Son" is repetitive (see 1:14, 49; and see Williams 1974, 353). Christ as the Word is called God (1:1, 18; cf. Isa 9:6); and Jesus is called the Christ or Messiah (1:17, 41; cf. Ps 2:2; Dan 9:25), the Son of God (1:14, 49, cf. Ps 2:7), the Lamb of God (1:29, 36; cf. Isa 53), the one predicted by Moses (1:45; cf. Deut 18:16-18), the King of Israel (1:49; cf. Ps 2:6; Zeph 3:15), and the Son of Man (1:51; cf. Dan 7:13). If the title "the chosen one of God" also were included, there is yet another messianic witness—this one, referring to Isa 42:1 ("Behold, My Servant, whom I uphold; My chosen one in whom My soul delights," NASB).

A growing number of translators have decided to follow the reading "chosen one." The recent publication of 𝔓106 (early third century) has strengthened the case for the translators of TNIV NEB REB NJB NLT NET to choose this text. However, the even more recent publication of 𝔓120 (showing "the Son") shows that both readings were present early in the textual history.

John 1:36

The shorter text, Ιδε, ο αμνος του θεου ("Look, the Lamb of God") is supported by 𝔓^{5vid} 𝔓^{66c} 𝔓^{75} ℵ B etc. This is extended in other manuscripts (𝔓^{66*} C W it^{a}) with the addition of ο αιρων την αμαρτιαν του κοσμου ("the one taking away the sin of the world"). After making the expansion (to conform this verse to 1:29), the scribe of 𝔓^{66} himself, or another corrector, subsequently deleted it. Other scribes (C W) added the phrase permanently.

John 1:41

WH NU εὑρίσκει οὗτος πρῶτον τὸν ἀδελφόν
"this one [Andrew] first finds his brother"
𝔓^{66} 𝔓^{75} ℵ^{2} A B Θ Ψ 083
all

variant 1/TR ευρισκει ουτος πρωτος τον αδελφον
"this one [Andrew] was the first to find his brother"
ℵ* L W^{s} Maj
NETmg

variant 2 "in the morning this one [Andrew] finds his brother"
it^{b,e,j}
NEBmg NJBmg

The WH NU reading has superior testimony, especially from the papyri. The second variant reading, noted in NEB and NJB, represents an early interpretation found in a few Old Latin manuscripts. The Latin word *mane* ("in the morning") carries forward the narrative from 1:39, which speaks of the first evening the disciples stayed with Jesus.

John 1:42

WH NU Σίμων ὁ υἱὸς Ἰωάννου
"Simon, the son of John"
𝔓^{66} 𝔓^{75} 𝔓^{106vid} ℵ B* L W^{s} 33
NKJVmg RSV NRSV ESV NASB NIV TNIV NEB REB NJB NAB NLT HCSB NET

variant 1/TR Σιμων ο υιος Ιωνα
"Simon, the son of Jonah"
A B^{2} Ψ f^{1,13} Maj
KJV NKJV HCSBmg NETmg

variant 2 Σιμων ο υιος Ιωαννα
"Simon the son of Joanna"
Θ 1241 Vulgate
none

The WH NU reading has excellent documentation. The first variant is a scribal harmonization to Matt 16:17, where Peter is called "Simon, son of Jonah." The second variant is either a scribal mistake or an attempt to associate Peter with the Joanna of Luke 8:3; 24:10. But this identification is impossible inasmuch as Joanna was the wife of Chuza, Herod's steward.

John 1:51

WH NU	ὄψεσθε τὸν οὐρανὸν ἀνεῳγότα "you will see the heavens opened" $\mathfrak{P}^{66}$ $\mathfrak{P}^{75}$ ℵ B L W^s NKJVmg RSV NRSV ESV NASB NIV TNIV NEB REB NJB NAB NLT HCSB NET
variant/TR	απ αρτι οψεσθε τον ουρανον ανεωγοτα "hereafter you will see the heavens opened" A Θ Ψ $f^{1,13}$ Maj KJV NKJV

The addition of απ αρτι ("hereafter") was borrowed from Matt 26:64 (which reads, "Hereafter you will see the Son of Man sitting on the right hand of power and coming on the clouds of heaven"). Some commentators think the scribal addition of απ αρτι links 1:51 with Matt 26:64 exegetically, but this is not so. The promise in Matthew is eschatological; the promise in John was to be fulfilled in Jesus' lifetime. The prophetic promise in 1:51 is an allusion to Jacob's vision of the ladder connecting heaven to earth (see Gen 28:12-21). Jesus, as the Son of Man, was the real vehicle of communication between heaven and earth, divinity and humanity.

John 2:3

TR WH NU	οἶνον οὐκ ἔχουσιν "they have no wine" $\mathfrak{P}^{66}$ $\mathfrak{P}^{75}$ B C W^s KJV NKJV RSV NRSV ESV NASB NIV TNIV NEB REB NAB NLT HCSB NET
variant	οινον ουκ ειχον οτι συνετελεσθη ο οινος του γαμου· ειτα "they have no wine because the wine for the wedding was used up; then" ℵ* $it^{a,j}$ syr^{hmg} NJB

The addition is a scribal expansion intended to explain why the wine was used up. Though it has meager textual support, this reading was adopted by the NJB.

John 2:12

There is some textual variation with respect to the "brothers" and "disciples" in this verse. TR NU read οι αδελφοι αυτου και οι μαθηται αυτου ("his brothers and his disciples"), following the testimony of $\mathfrak{P}^{66c}$ A W^s Θ $f^{1,13}$ Maj. WH reads οι αδελφοι και οι μαθηται αυτου ("the brothers and his disciples"); this is supported by $\mathfrak{P}^{66*}$ $\mathfrak{P}^{75}$ B Ψ 0162. The latter is the preferred reading. However, since either reading can be rendered as "his brothers and his disciples," it is impossible to determine which reading a particular English version follows. Another variant reading (in ℵ it cop^{ach2}) excludes και οι μαθηται αυτου ("and his disciples"), which is a scribal attempt to have the text say that Jesus did not go to Capernaum with his disciples.

In the next part of the verse, excellent documentation ($\mathfrak{P}^{66*}$ $\mathfrak{P}^{75}$ ℵ B L 0162 etc.) affirms the reading εμειναν ("they remained"). A variant reading with slim support ($\mathfrak{P}^{66c}$ A f^1) reads εμεινεν ("he remained"). The variant was probably introduced, first by the corrector of $\mathfrak{P}^{66}$ (among the extant manuscripts), to make 2:12 conform with 2:13, which says that Jesus went up to Jerusalem—apparently alone, without his family or disciples. Thus, the corrector of

𝔓[66] thought the text should say that Jesus did not stay there many days but went on alone to Jerusalem. However, the following narrative indicates that his disciples were present with him (2:17).

John 2:15

All three texts (TR WH NU) say that Jesus made a whip out of cords (ποιησας φραγελλιον εκ σχοινιων), following ℵ A B Δ Θ Ψ f[13] Maj syr[p,h] cop. However, several other notable manuscripts (𝔓[66] 𝔓[75] L W[s] 0162 f[1] 33 it[a,e]) indicate that Jesus made "a kind of whip out of cords" (ποιησας ως φραγελλιον εκ σχοινιων). Although commentators generally argue that ως was added to soften the text, the variant reading has merit because it has excellent external support—from the three earliest manuscripts (𝔓[66] 𝔓[75] 0162) and other diverse witnesses—and because Jesus more than likely constructed something like a whip. Perhaps later scribes deleted the ως as unnecessary. In any event, not one English version adopted the reading with ως or even noted it.

TR NU, supported by 𝔓[66*] ℵ A Θ Ψ f[1,13] Maj, say that Jesus poured out "the money" (το κερμα) of the moneychangers. A different reading in 𝔓[66c2] 𝔓[59vid] (not listed in NA[27]) 𝔓[75] B L W[s] 083 0162 33 says he poured out "the coins" (τα κερματα). This reading, present in WH, has stronger attestation. Most English versions (except the KJV) use the word "coins" instead of "money," but it is not certain which reading they follow.

John 3:5a

A few witnesses (1023 syr[h] vg) omit υδατος και ("of water and") from the expression γεννηθη εκ υδατος και πνευματος ("be born of the water and the Spirit"). This deletion was either accidental or an attempt to rid the text of a difficult reading. Throughout the ages, commentators have struggled over what it means to be born of both water and Spirit. To be born of the Spirit is perfectly understandable—especially in the context of John 3; it is the added expression "of water" that causes difficulties for exegetes.

Some commentators have said that the "water" denotes physical birth (a baby is born in a sac of "water") and "the Spirit," spiritual birth—thus, Jesus was saying that a man has to have two births: one physical and the second, spiritual. Other commentators have said that the water symbolizes baptism and the Spirit, spiritual regeneration—thus, Jesus was saying that a person must be baptized (in accordance with John's water baptism) and receive the Spirit (the baptism Jesus gives) in order to enter the kingdom of God. According to the Greek text, there is only one preposition (εξ) before "water" and "Spirit." Had there been two prepositions, we could say that Jesus was speaking of two different experiences. But the construction in Greek seems to indicate that Jesus was speaking of one experience with two aspects. Thus, the water could signify the cleansing and life-giving action of the Spirit. This is substantiated by 7:37-39, where the Spirit is likened to flowing waters, and by Titus 3:5, where the Spirit is said to both cleanse and regenerate, and by Ezek 36:25-27, where the cleansing and regeneration of Israel are associated with the Spirit. However this passage is to be interpreted, it must be done with the inclusion of εξ υδατος, which is supported by all Greek witnesses. To conjecture (as do some modern exegetes) that it was added by scribes or a redactor wanting to supply a reference to water baptism is to decide against nearly all external testimony.

John 3:5b

The TR WH NU texts all read την βασιλειαν του θεου ("the kingdom of God") based on excellent testimony: 𝔓[66] 𝔓[75] ℵ[c] A L W[s] Θ syr[s] cop. All English versions follow this. But a variant reads την βασιλειαν των ουρανων ("the kingdom of heavens") in ℵ* 0141 it[e]. This adjustment of the text can be explained as an attempt to conform John's phraseology to Matthew's, who habitually spoke of "entering into the kingdom of heaven" (see Matt 5:20; 7:21; 18:3; 19:23).

John 3:6

In English, translators can distinguish between the divine Spirit and the human spirit (or any other kind of spirit) by capitalizing the former. This method could not be used in Greek manuscripts because the words were written in all capital letters. However, scribes could take advantage of a system of special contractions for nomina sacra (sacred names) to display their own interpretation. Normally, they wrote $\overline{\Pi NA}$ for πνευμα ("Spirit"). However, they could choose to write out the word πνευμα to indicate the human spirit. For example, in this verse the copyist of 𝔓[66] distinguished the divine Spirit from the human spirit by making the first word a nomen sacrum $\overline{\Pi NA}$ and by writing out the second (πνευμα)—thereby indicating that the divine Spirit is that which generates and the human spirit is that which is generated. This shows that scribes could demonstrate their own exegetical decisions without changing words. This sort of distinguishing of the divine Spirit from the human spirit was also done by the scribes of 𝔓[13] 𝔓[46] 𝔓[75] (Comfort 1984, 130-133).

John 3:8

The scribe of 𝔓[66] first started to write the word for "wind" (writing the first four letters πνευ for πνευμα) and immediately corrected it to $\overline{\Pi NA}$, the contracted form for the nomen sacrum, "the Spirit." This probably shows that the scribe of 𝔓[66] recognized that πνευμα required a different orthography for a different sense but then succumbed to the standard formula for designating nomina sacra. (See comments on 6:63.)

The scribe of 𝔓[75] also wrote πνευμα as a nomen sacrum, $\overline{\Pi NA}$, and even placed an overbar above the verb $\overline{\Pi NEI}$, marking the action of the πνευμα as sacred. Typically, exegetes see the πνευμα in 3:8 as describing the activity of the wind, which is symbolic of the activity of the Spirit. The scribe of 𝔓[75] emphasized the symbolism with nomina sacra.

John 3:13

WH NU οὐδεὶς ἀναβέβηκεν εἰς τὸν οὐρανὸν εἰ μὴ ὁ ἐκ τοῦ οὐρανοῦ καταβάς, ὁ υἱὸς τοῦ ἀνθρώπου
"no one has ascended into heaven except the one coming down from heaven, the Son of Man"
𝔓[66] 𝔓[75] ℵ B L T W[s] 083 086 cop Diatessaron
NKJVmg RSV NRSV ESV NASB NIV TNIV NEBmg NJB NAB NLT HCSB NET

variant/TR ουδεις αναβεβηκεν εις τον ουρανον ει μη ο εκ του ουρανου καταβας, ο υιος του ανθρωπου ο ων εν τω ουρανω
"no one has ascended into heaven except the one coming down from heaven, the Son of Man, the one being in heaven"
(A* omit ων) Θ Ψ 050 f[1,13] Maj
KJV NKJV RSVmg NRSVmg ESVmg NIVmg TNIVmg NEB REB NLTmg HCSBmg NETmg

There are two other variants on the longer reading: (1) "the Son of Man who was in heaven" it[e] syr[c]; (2) ο υιος του ανθρωπου ο ων εκ του ουρανου ("the Son of Man, the one being from heaven") 0141 syr[s]. It is difficult to determine if the words ο ων εν τω ουρανω ("the one being in heaven") were originally written by John or were added later by scribes. The shorter reading (WH NU) has excellent and early support—from the papyri, the early Alexandrian uncials, the Diatessaron, and Coptic versions. The shorter reading was also known to many church fathers, such as Origen, Didymus, and Jerome. The longer reading appears in some later Greek manuscripts, was known to many early church fathers (Hippolytus, Origen, Dionysius, Hesychius, Hilary, Lucifer, Jerome, Augustine), and was translated in some early versions (primarily Old Latin and Syriac). From a documentary perspective, the shorter reading is more trustworthy.

However, some critics have argued that this phrase was deleted in the Alexandrian manuscripts because of its enigmatic meaning—i.e., how could the Son of Man who was then and there on earth also be in heaven? In support of this view, it could be argued that other scribes attempted to adjust this existing, difficult expression (as in the two variants of the longer reading listed above) in lieu of deleting it (see Black 1985, 49-66). But other critics argue that the phrase was added by scribes who may have been thinking of the expression in 1:18, ο ων εις τον κολπον του πατρος ("the one being in the bosom of the Father"). For example, Wescott and Hort (1882, 75-76) argued that it was "a Western gloss, suggested perhaps by 1:18; it may have been inserted to correct any misunderstanding arising out of the position of αναβεβηκεν [has ascended], as coming before καταβας [having descended]." As is explained below, it seems that if any verse motivated scribes to make the addition, it was 1:18.

The English versions display the division on this issue—with KJV/NKJV and some modern versions (NEB REB) opting for the longer reading, and the rest of the modern versions presenting the shorter reading. Hence, it is necessary for the interpreter to understand and explain both variants. The shorter reading is Jesus' declaration of his exclusive ability to reveal the God of heaven, who is God the Father, to men on earth. The declaration, "no one has ascended into heaven," is nearly equivalent to "no one has seen God at any time" in 1:18. He, the Son of Man, had come from heaven and would go back to heaven. The longer reading shows that Jesus' divine existence was not limited to just earth. He lives in heaven and earth simultaneously. Just as the Father who sent his Son to earth accompanied the Son he sent, so the Son who left heaven was still with his Father in heaven. As was noted earlier, this concept is also affirmed in 1:18, which describes Christ (in his deity) as always existing by the Father's side. The longer reading could also be understood from the historical perspective of John's readers who knew the post-resurrected Jesus as the one in heaven (Barrett 1978, 213); as such, the last phrase of the longer reading could be John's personal reflective statement (NETmg).

John 3:15

WH NU ἵνα πᾶς ὁ πιστεύων ἐν αὐτῷ ἔχῃ ζωὴν αἰώνιον
"so that everyone who believes, may have eternal life in him"
𝔓75 B T Ws 083
NIVmg TNIV NLTmg

variant 1 ινα πας ο πιστευων εις αυτον εχη ζωην αιωνιον
"so that everyone believing into [or, in] him may have eternal life"
א 086 f1 33 (𝔓66 L have επ αυτω = "on him")
NKJVmg RSV NRSV ESV NASB NIV NEB REB NJB NAB NLT HCSB NET

variant 2/TR ινα πας ο πιστευων εις αυτον μη αποληται αλλ εχη ζωην αιωνιον
"so that everyone believing into [or, in] him may not perish but have eternal life"
𝔓63 (A επ αυτον) Θ Ψ f13 Maj
KJV NKJV

Since John only used the prepositional phrase εις αυτον after the verb πιστευω, it is unusual that the scribes of 𝔓75 B Ws 083 would have changed a characteristically Johannine expression. Thus, those who argue for the WH NU reading point out that John often spoke of simply believing—without adding an object after believe (see 1:7; 3:12; 4:41, 53; 5:44; 6:36, 64; 11:15; 12:39; 16:31). As such, εν αυτω ("in him") must be syntactically joined with the last phrase; therefore, the expression means that those who believe have eternal life in him. However, all English versions except TNIV reflect the understanding of the first variant, while two (NIVmg NLTmg) note the rendering of the WH NU text. The TR adds the wording "may not perish," borrowed from the following verse (3:16).

John 3:17

NA26 cites 𝔓5vid in support of adding αυτου after τον υιον, but 𝔓5 does not have any part of John 3 (see Comfort 1990, 625-629). This has been corrected in NA27.

John 3:25

WH NU ζήτησις ἐκ τῶν μαθητῶν 'Ιωάννου μετὰ 'Ιουδαίου
"an argument between some of John's disciples and a Jew"
𝔓75 א2 A B L Ws Δ Ψ 070 086
RSV NRSV ESV NASB NIV TNIV NJB NAB NLT HCSB NET

variant/TR ζητησις εκ των μαθητων Ιωαννου μετα Ιουδαιων
"an argument between some of John's disciples and Jews"
𝔓66 א* Θ f1,13 ite syrc cop Origen
KJV NKJV NRSVmg NEB REB NLTmg HCSBmg NETmg

The WH NU reading is the preferred one because it is far more likely that the singular form of "Jew" (which appears only one other time in John—namely, 4:9) was changed to a plural than vice versa. However, both readings seem rather bare; one would expect τινος before Ιουδαιου (= "a certain Jew") and των before Ιουδαιων (= "the Jews"). This bareness of expression and the fact that the following narrative speaks about the comparative worth of John and Jesus, not baptism, has led scholars to think there was an ancient textual corruption here, and therefore they have conjectured that the text originally read Ιησους ("Jesus"): (1) "there was an argument [or, discussion] between the disciples of John and Jesus" or (2) των Ιησους ("the ones of Jesus"): "there was an argument [or, discussion] between the disciples of John and those of Jesus" (Barrett 1978, 221). But textual critics must avoid such conjectures if the actual documentary evidence preserves an understandable text. Furthermore, this particular conjecture fails to take into account that Ιησους would have been written as a nomen sacrum (ΙΣ̅) in all manuscripts beginning as early as A.D. 100. No scribe would have mistaken it for Ιουδαιου ("Jew").

John 3:31-32

TR WH NU ὁ ἐκ τοῦ οὐρανοῦ ἐρχόμενος [ἐπάνω πάντων ἐστίν]· ³²ὃ ἑώρακεν καὶ ἤκουσεν τοῦτο μαρτυρεῖ
"the one coming from heaven is above all. ³² What he sees and hears this he testifies."
𝔓[36vid] (𝔓[66*] omits ερχομενος) 𝔓[66c2] ℵ[2] B L W[s] Ψ 083 086 33 f[13] Maj syr[h,p,s] cop[bo] (A Δ Θ 063 add και at beginning of 3:32)
KJV NKJV RSV NRSV ESV NASB NIV TNIV NEBmg REBmg NJBmg NAB NLT HCSB NET

variant ο εκ του ουρανου ερχομενος ³²ο εωρακεν και ηκουσεν τουτο μαρτυρει.
"the one coming from heaven ³² testifies that which he has seen and heard."
𝔓[75] it syr[c] cop[sa] Origen (ℵ* D f[1] omit τουτο)
NEB REB NJB NLTmg NETmg

𝔓[36vid] was incorrectly cited as 𝔓[5vid] in NA[26] and UBS[3]; this is now corrected in NA[27] and UBS[4] (see Comfort 1990, 625-629). In the first part of 3:31, 𝔓[66*] did not include και εκ της γης λαλει ("and of the earth speaks") and ερχομενος ("coming") after ο εκ του ουρανου ("the one from heaven"). These were added by 𝔓[66c2] (see *Text of Earliest MSS*, 397).

The manuscript evidence for both readings is evenly split. The early papyri, 𝔓[66] and 𝔓[75], are divided, as are ℵ and B, and the ancient Syriac and Coptic versions; thus, they neutralize each other's testimony. Furthermore, good reasons could be given why scribes would be tempted to add the words επανω παντων εστιν ("is over all"), as a repeat from the first part of the verse, or delete the words because they seemed redundant. Because the first reading is the more difficult of the two, especially in respect to the syntactical connection between 3:31 and 3:32 (note the addition of και in certain MSS to solve this problem), it could be judged that this is the reading that was most likely changed. Furthermore, the repetition of επανω παντων εστιν conforms to Johannine repetitive style and forms an inclusio. However, it must always be noted that scribes were more prone to add clauses than delete them, and the shorter text has excellent testimony. With either reading the same basic meaning is conveyed, but if the second reading is accepted as original, the text and translation must present the end of 3:31 and the beginning of 3:32 as one syntactical unit.

John 3:34

WH NU οὐ γὰρ ἐκ μέτρου δίδωσιν τὸ πνεῦμα
"for he gives the Spirit without measure"
𝔓[36vid] 𝔓[66c] 𝔓[75] ℵ B[2] C* W[s]
RSV NRSV ESV NASB (TNIV) NJBmg NAB HCSB NET

variant/TR ου γαρ εκ μετρου διδωσιν ο θεος το πνευμα
"for God gives the Spirit without measure"
𝔓80vid A C2 D Θ Ψ 086 f13 Maj Origen
KJV NKJV NIV NEB REB NJB NLT HCSBmg

𝔓80vid is not cited in NA27 or UBS4, but the line lengths strongly suggest that the scribe wrote ο ΘC (see *Text of Earliest MSS*, 613). Furthermore, 𝔓66 should be listed as 𝔓66c because the scribe of 𝔓66 originally wrote ου γαρ εκ μερους διδωσιν το πνευμα ("for not in part he gives the Spirit"). He then corrected it to the WH NU reading (see *Text of Earliest MSS*, 398). This variant and its correction show that the scribe of 𝔓66 was uncomfortable with writing the expression ουκ εκ μετρου ("not from measure"). Indeed, this expression appears nowhere else in Greek literature (BDAG 644). The scribe was far more comfortable with writing ουκ εκ μερους, for this was a common idiom in Greek and in the NT; it means "not in part [i.e., fully]." However, this was not the expression in his exemplar, so he made the correction.

The addition of ο θεος ("God") is clearly a secondary development—very likely added to relieve the text of ambiguity. As is, the expression of the text could mean that God gives the immeasurable Spirit to his Son, or that Jesus gives the immeasurable Spirit when he speaks the words of God. Some scholars (e.g., Brown 1966, 161-162) favor the second option, for it can be argued that Jesus Christ dispensed the Spirit via his spoken word. John 6:63 says that his words are spirit. But most scholars favor the first option, primarily because the next verse speaks of the Father giving all things to the Son. As such, the Son was the recipient of the immeasurable Spirit for his prophetic ministry (see Isa 11:2).

John 4:1

NU ἔγνω ὁ Ἰησοῦς ὅτι ἤκουσαν οἱ Φαρισαῖοι ὅτι Ἰησοῦς πλείονας μαθητὰς ποιεῖ καὶ βαπτίζει ἢ Ἰωάννης
"Jesus realized that the Pharisees heard that Jesus was gaining and baptizing more disciples than John."
𝔓66* ℵ D Θ 086 f1
NRSV ESV (NIV TNIV) NEB REB NJB NAB NLT HCSB NET

variant/TR WH εγνω ο κυριος οτι ηκουσαν οι Φαρισαιοι οτι Ιησους πλειονας μαθητας ποιει και βαπτιζει η Ιωαννης
"the Lord realized that the Pharisees heard that Jesus was gaining and baptizing more disciples than John."
𝔓66c2 𝔓75 A B C L Ws 083 f13 Maj
KJV NKJV RSV NRSVmg NASB NLTmg HCSBmg NETmg

Upon close examination of 𝔓66 it appears that the manuscript originally read IC (the nomen sacrum for Ιησους—Jesus) and was changed to KC (the nomen sacrum for κυριος—Lord) by adding the < stroke to the I = I< (K). Since the resultant K does not look like the other *kappas* written by the original scribe (see Fee 1968b, 87), it is suspect as a correction made by the diorthotes, the second corrector (see *Text of Earliest MSS*, 398).

Most likely Ιησους ("Jesus") was changed to κυριος ("Lord") by scribes (such as the corrector of 𝔓66) because they wanted to alleviate the awkwardness of repeating Jesus' name. Indeed, this awkwardness is avoided in nearly every modern English version. Translations either use Jesus' name once, as in the NIV ("the Pharisees heard that Jesus was gaining and baptizing more disciples than John"), or turn the clause after the second οτι into a direct quotation, as in the NRSV: "Now when Jesus learned that the Pharisees had heard, 'Jesus is making and baptizing more disciples than John.'" However, κυριος has superior testimony and could be perceived to be just as awkward (see Comfort 2005, 337).

John 4:9

TR WH NU	οὐ γὰρ συγχρῶνται Ἰουδαῖοι Σαμαρίταις "for Jews do not share anything in common with Samaritans" 𝔓[63] 𝔓[66] 𝔓[75] 𝔓[76] ℵ[1] A B C L W[s] Δ Θ Ψ 083 086 33 f[1,13] all
variant	omit ℵ* D it[a,b,e,j] cop[fay] NRSVmg NEBmg REBmg NJBmg NLTmg HCSBmg

Though some scholars have argued that this statement is a gloss that found its way into the text, it is more likely that this expression was part of the original text—for it was customary for John to add such explanations for his Gentile readers. These are not the words of the Samaritan woman, but of John the gospel writer, who here provides his Gentile readers with an explanation about the relationship between Jews and Samaritans. The Greek word translated "associate" (συγχρωνται) literally means "to share the use of." It is thought, then, that John was saying that Jews would not share the same utensils or facilities that Samaritan women used because Jews considered Samaritan women and their utensils to be ceremonially unclean—inasmuch as one never knew when a Samaritan woman was menstruating (see Lev 15:19; Daube 1950, 137-147). This interpretation is reflected in the TEV: "Jews will not use the same dishes that Samaritans use" (see also NIVmg). But since the Greek word for "Samaritans" is masculine (not feminine—hence the statement is not directed to Samaritan women only), John's parenthetical expression may not be so specific; rather, it speaks generally of a strained relationship between Jews and Samaritans.

John 4:24

This verse can be understood in two ways: (1) "God is spirit, and those who worship him must worship him in spirit and in truth" or (2) "God is Spirit, and those who worship him must worship him in spirit and in truth." Most English translations read "God is spirit," so as to emphasize God's spiritual nature. The most ancient scribes (𝔓[66] 𝔓[75] ℵ) did not understand it this way. They used the nomen sacrum ($\overline{\text{ΠΝΑ}}$) to denote the person of the Spirit: "God is Spirit." Most exegetes and modern translators also understand the second πνευμα to refer to the human spirit (locative), but ancient scribes (𝔓[66] 𝔓[75] ℵ) understood it as the divine Spirit (instrumental) inasmuch as they wrote it as a nomen sacrum ($\overline{\text{ΠΝΙ}}$). Brown (1966, 172) and Schnackenburg (1982, 1:437-438) also take it as instrumental; as such, the phrase indicates the way in which one worships—God must be worshiped in and by the Spirit.

John 4:25

Excellent testimony (𝔓[66*] 𝔓[75] ℵ* A B C D W[s]) supports the reading in which the woman says, "I know [οιδα] that Messiah, the one called Christ, is coming." However, a few manuscripts (𝔓[66c2] ℵ[2] L N f[13] 33) read, "We know [οιδαμεν] that Messiah, the one called Christ, is coming." The variant reading, very likely a scribal emendation, has the Samaritan woman speaking on behalf of the Samaritans from start to finish—as opposed to just at the completion of the sentence where she says, "he will explain everything to us."

John 4:35-36

The final Greek word of 4:35, ηδη ("already"), could be joined with the end of 4:35 (giving the rendering "Look on the fields, that they are already white for harvest") or with the beginning of 4:36 (giving the rendering "Look on the fields, that they are white for harvest. He who reaps is already receiving wages . . ."). If we could have heard the author read the text out loud, his reading would have indicated where to place ηδη. But scribes, readers, and translators have had to guess.

Some of the earliest manuscripts ($\mathfrak{P}^{66}$ ℵ* A B) have no punctuation here at all. $\mathfrak{P}^{75}$ C^{3} and 083 have a punctuation mark after ηδη (thereby including it with 4:35); ℵ^{c} C* D L W have a punctuation mark before it (thereby including it with 4:36). There is no consensus among the modern English translations. For example, RSV NEB NLT include "already" with 4:35; whereas NRSV NASB NIV join it with 4:36. Good arguments, from an exegetical viewpoint, can be advanced for either position. Jesus could have been saying that the harvest was already white, or he could have been saying that the reapers were already reaping the harvest. Both were true.

John 4:37

$\mathfrak{P}^{75}$ omits this entire verse ("For in this the saying is true, 'one sows and another reaps'"). The usual explanation for the omission of this verse in $\mathfrak{P}^{75}$ is that it was accidental, due to homoeoteleuton—both 4:36 and 4:37 end with ο θεριζων ("the one reaping"). But the scribe of $\mathfrak{P}^{75}$ is not known for carelessness; quite the contrary, he was a meticulous copyist. Thus, there could be another reason for the omission. Perhaps the scribe purposely deleted the verse because he knew that it is not a direct quotation of any known biblical passage. This saying is somewhat like Deut 20:6; 28:30; Job 15:28 (LXX); 31:8; and Mic 6:15, but not exactly. The saying could have come from some Greek literary source, or it might have been a rural adage commonly quoted in the Galilean hill country. But in the gospel context, the words "the saying is true" usually allude to a biblical saying. Thus, the scribe may have deleted the statement to avoid the predicament of not being able to align it with a known text. Besides, the verse adds little to Jesus' thesis that sowers and reapers rejoice together over the fruits of their labor.

John 4:42

WH NU — ὁ σωτὴρ τοῦ κόσμου
"the Savior of the world"
$\mathfrak{P}^{66}$ $\mathfrak{P}^{75}$ ℵ B C* W^{s} syr^{c}
NKJVmg RSV NRSV ESV NASB NIV TNIV NEB REB NJB NAB NLT HCSB NET

variant/TR — ο σωτηρ του κοσμου, ο Χριστος
"the Savior of the world, the Christ"
A C^{3} D L Θ Ψ f^{1,13} Maj it^{e} syr^{h,p}
KJV NKJV HCSBmg

The expansion of Jesus' titles was a common practice among scribes. The addition of ο Χρσιτος ("the Christ") fills out the pericope nicely because Jesus had revealed to the Samaritans that he was the Christ they were expecting (4:25-26). However, the title ο σωτηρ του κοσμου ("the Savior of the world") is even more significant theologically because it speaks of how Jesus had come not just to be the Jews' Messiah but to be the world's Savior—the deliverer of all people, including the Samaritans—for it is they who say, "We know that he is truly the Savior of the world."

John 4:51

WH NU — οἱ δοῦλοι αὐτοῦ ὑπήντησαν αὐτῷ λέγοντες ὅτι ὁ παῖς αὐτοῦ ζῇ
"his slaves met him, saying that his child lives"
𝔓66* 𝔓75 A B Ws Origen
RSV NRSV ESV TNIV REB NAB (NLT) HCSB NET

variant 1/TR — οι δουλοι αυτου υπηντησαν αυτω λεγοντες οτι ο παις σου ζη
"his slaves met him, saying 'your child lives'"
Θ Ψ f1
KJV NKJV NASB NIV NEB NJB

variant 2 — οι δουλοι αυτου υπηντησαν αυτω λεγοντες οτι ο υιος σου ζη
"his slaves met him, saying 'your child lives'"
𝔓66c1 D L 33
none (or same versions following variant 1—see note below)

The WH NU reading has the best documentary support and is the one that was adjusted into the two variants (note the correction in 𝔓66). The first variant adjusts an awkward indirect comment, where one would expect a direct statement from the slaves to their master: "your child lives." Many modern versions also turn the slaves' words into direct speech (see REB NJB). The second variant also makes this adjustment and then changes the word παις ("child"), which appears only here in the Gospel of John, to υιος ("son"), a common word in John. But since παις can be rendered as "child" or "son" (see BDAG 750), it is difficult to be certain which variant these English versions followed.

John 5:1

TR WH NU — ἑορτὴ τῶν 'Ιουδαίων
"a feast of the Jews"
𝔓66 𝔓75 A B D Ws Θ 0125 f13
all

variant — η εορτη των Ιουδαιων
"the feast of the Jews"
א C L Δ Ψ f1 33
NASBmg NEBmg NJBmg NETmg

According to the earliest manuscripts (𝔓66 𝔓75 B), there is no article before "feast." Thus, the feast is unspecified. (The expression των Ιουδαιων ["of the Jews"] was written by John as a help to his Gentile readers.) Undoubtedly, certain scribes added the definite article before "feast" in an attempt to designate a specific feast (as either Passover, Pentecost, or Tabernacles) and thus provide the narrative of John with a more specific chronology.

When trying to determine the length of Jesus' ministry according to John's chronology, interpreters have proposed a two-year ministry (spanning three Passovers) and a three-year ministry (spanning four Passovers). In John's gospel there are three explicit references to Passover celebrations: John 2:13 mentions the first Passover, 6:4 the next Passover, and 11:55 the third and final Passover. If there were only three Passovers, then Jesus' ministry (which began just prior to the first Passover) lasted only two years—unless the time period prior to the first Passover (2:13) was an entire year (but this does not seem likely). If 5:1 is another Passover or Pentecost (which occurred 50 days after Passover), then Jesus' ministry lasted three years: 2:13–5:1 first year; 5:1–6:4 second year; 6:4–11:55 third year. If 5:1 is the Feast of Tabernacles, it would have occurred in between the first and second Passover, and then Jesus' ministry would have lasted two years: 2:13–6:4 first year (Passover–Tabernacles–Passover); 6:4–11:55 second year (Passover–Tabernacles–Passover). Against the two-year theory, 4:35 indicates that Jesus spoke of the harvest not coming for another four months. This tells us that Jesus was in Samaria, then Galilee, in early winter, which would have been after the Feast of Tabernacles (in October) and four months before Pentecost (the harvest festival). Therefore, the words μετα ταυτα ("after these things") in 5:1 speak of this interim between Jesus' Galilean ministry (4:43-54) and the next festival, which was probably Pentecost (see NJBmg). Many early Greek fathers (such as John Chrysostom and Cyril of Alexandria) believed it was Pentecost, which would help explain the references to Moses in the discourse (5:46-47), "for in that process which connected agricultural feasts to events in Israel's history, the Feast of Weeks (Pentecost) was identified with the celebration of Moses' receiving the Law on Mount Sinai" (Brown 1966, 206).

John 5:2a

TR WH NU	ἐν τοῖς Ἱεροσολύμοις ἐπὶ τῇ προβατικῇ κολυμβήθρα "in Jerusalem near the sheep [gate] a pool" 𝔓66c 𝔓75 B C T (Ws) 0125 NIV TNIV NAB NLT
variant 1	εν τοις Ιεροσολυμοις εν τη προβατικη κολυμβηθρα "in Jerusalem by the sheep [gate] a pool" א2 A D L Θ KJV NKJV RSV NRSV ESV NASB REB HCSB NET
variant 2	εν τοις Ιεροσολυμοις προβατικη κολυμβηθρα "in Jerusalem at the Sheep Pool" א* ite NEB NJB

The TR WH NU reading has the best documentation and is the most difficult of all the variants. The difficulty this reading presents is that there is no substantive specified after επι τη προβατικη, literally, "pertaining to the sheep." Very likely the ancient readers familiar with Jerusalem would have known that John was speaking about the Sheep Gate (mentioned in Neh 3:1, 32; 12:39). Thus, the word πυλη ("gate") must be understood or supplied. The substitution of εν (as in the first variant) for επι does not alleviate the problem, whereas the deletion of επι τη allows for an understandable statement: "Now at the Sheep Pool in Jerusalem there is a place called Bethesda" (NEB NJB). Those who defend this interpretation assert that all the ancient exegetes coupled together προβατικη and κολυμβηθρα to signify the "Sheep Pool." However, the scribe of 𝔓66 purposely separated προβατικη and κολυμβηθρα with a punctuation mark between them (see *Text of Earliest MSS*, 403), thereby affirming the TR WH NU reading.

John 5:2b

WH NU	Βηθζαθα "Bethzatha" א (L ite βηζαθα) 33 Eusebius NKJVmg RSV NRSV NIVmg TNIVmg NJBmg NABmg NLTmg HCSBmg NET

variant 1	Βηθσαιδα "Bethsaida" (𝔓[66c] Βηδσαιδα—𝔓[66*] Βηδσαιδαν) 𝔓[75] B W[s] RSVmg NRSVmg NIVmg TNIVmg NJBmg NABmg NLTmg NETmg
variant 2/TR	Βηθεσδα "Bethesda" A C Θ 078 $f^{1,13}$ Maj KJV NKJV RSVmg NRSVmg ESV NASB NIV TNIV NEB REB NJB NAB NLT HCSB NETmg
variant 3	Βελζεθα "Belzetha" D none

The name of the pool in Jerusalem appears with different spellings in various manuscripts. Βηθσαιδα (meaning "house of fish") has the best documentary support and cannot be easily dismissed as an assimilation to the name of the city on the Sea of Galilee. Indeed, the opposite could be argued: Scribes could have just as likely changed the name of a Jerusalem site to make it different from the Galilean city. The second variant, Βηθεσδα ("Bethesda"), meaning "house of mercy," has fair documentary support and is a popular choice of modern versions. "Bethesda" (which may be the Hebrew word for the Aramaic Βηθζαθα, the WH NU reading) was rejected by the NU editors because it was also "suspect as a scribal alteration originally introduced because of its edifying etymology" (TCGNT).

However, many scholars prefer the reading "Bethesda" because it is indirectly attested to by the Copper Scroll discovered in Qumran, which calls this place "Betheshdathayim" (3Q15, column 11, line 12), meaning "the place of the twin outpouring" (Bruce 1983, 122). Recent excavations show this site to have had two pools, with five colonnades (πεντε στοας). The name "house of mercy" accords well with the passage, for it is here that men and women sought mercy from God for their healing. Most English versions have also favored the reading "Bethesda."

The reading accepted for the NU text βηθζαθα is supported by Eusebius (*Onom.* 58.21-26) and is perhaps the same name (with a slightly different spelling) as that which Josephus used (Βηζηθα—"Bezetha") for describing the sector of Jerusalem just north of this pool (*J.W.* 2.15.5). This reading was selected by the NU committee because it was "the least unsatisfactory reading."

John 5:3b-4

WH NU	omit 5:3b-4 𝔓[66] 𝔓[75] א A* B C* L T cop NKJVmg RSV NRSV ESV NASBmg NIV TNIV NEB REB NJB NAB NLT HCSBmg NET
variant 1	include only 5:3b D W[s] 33 none
variant 2	include only 5:4 A* L none
variant 3/TR	include 5:3b-4, with different variations in later manuscripts—printed in TR thus: εκδεχομενων την του υδατος κινησιν [4]αγγελος

γαρ κατα καιρον κατεβαινεν εν τη κολυμβηθρα, και εταρασσεν το υδωρ· ο ουν πρωτος εμβας μετα την ταραχην του υδατος, υγιης εγινετο, ω δηποτε κατειχετο νοσηματι

"waiting for the movement of the water. [4] For an angel went down at a certain season into the pool and stirred up the water; whoever then first stepped in, after the stirring up of the water, was made well from whatever disease he was afflicted with."

A^2 C^3 L Θ Ψ 078[vid] Maj it

KJV NKJV RSVmg NRSVmg ESVmg NASB NIVmg TNIVmg NEBmg REBmg NJBmg NABmg NLTmg HCSB NETmg

This portion (5:3b-4) was probably not written by John, because it is not found in the earliest manuscripts (𝔓66 𝔓75 א B C* T), and where it does occur in later manuscripts it is often marked with obeli (marks like asterisks) to signal spuriousness (so Π 047 syr[h] marking 5:4). The passage was a later addition—even added to manuscripts, such as A and C, that did not originally contain the portion. This scribal gloss is characteristic of the expansions that occurred in gospel texts after the fourth century. The expansion happened in two phases: First came the addition of 5:3b—inserted to explain what the sick people were waiting for; and then came 5:4—inserted to provide an explanation about the troubling of the water mentioned in 5:7. Of course, the second expansion is fuller and more imaginative. Nearly all modern textual critics and translators will not accept the longer portion as part of the original text. NASB and HCSB, however, continue to retain verses in deference to the KJV tradition.

John 5:12

A* W syr[s] omit this verse probably due to homoeoteleuton—both 5:11 and 5:12 end with και περιπατει ("and walk").

John 5:16

WH NU — ἐδίωκον οἱ Ἰουδαῖοι τὸν Ἰησοῦν

"the Jews began to persecute Jesus"

𝔓66 𝔓75 א B C D L W 33

NKJVmg RSV NRSV ESV NASB NIV TNIV NEB REB NJB NAB NLT HCSB NET

variant/TR — εδιωκον οι Ιουδαιοι τον Ιησουν και εζητουν αυτον αποκτειναι

"the Jews began to persecute Jesus and were seeking to kill him"

A Θ Ψ (f^{13}) Maj

KJV NKJV HCSBmg

The addition in the variant reading is a harmonization to the immediate context (see 5:18), where nearly the same expression occurs. This harmonization was included in TR and then rendered in KJV and NKJV.

John 5:39

Papyrus Egerton 2 (dated A.D. 140–160) contains this verse in a slightly different form, which can be translated, "And turning to the rulers, he said this word, 'You search the Scriptures, in which you think you have life; these are [they] which testify concerning me.'" A few Old Latin manuscripts (it[a,b]) and one Syriac manuscript (syr[c]) read essentially, "You search the Scriptures; these writings in which you think to have life are those which bear testimony of me."

Thus, four witnesses provide this interesting variation on 5:39, all of which exclude the word αιωνιον ("eternal") that appears in all other witnesses after ζωη ("life"). Perhaps the word "eternal" was dropped by the scribe of the Egerton Papyrus because it was customary to think that Jews would have considered that Scripture reading would enrich one's spiritual life on earth, not give everlasting life. But several rabbis claimed that everlasting life could be found by studying the Scriptures. For example, Hillel said, "The more study of the law the more life, . . . if one has gained for himself words of the law he has gained for himself life in the age to come" (*'Abot* 2.7). It was perfectly fitting for Jesus to have used "eternal life" in his reproach to the religious leaders who thought biblical studies gave them an entrance into eternity.

John 5:44

TR WH NU τὴν δόξαν τὴν παρὰ τοῦ μόνου θεοῦ
"the glory from the only God"
𝔓[63vid] ℵ A D L Δ Θ Ψ 0210[vid] f[1,13] 33 it[e] syr Maj
all

variant τηv δοξαν την παρα του μονου
"the glory from the Only One"
𝔓[66] 𝔓[75] B W it[a,b] cop
NIVmg TNIVmg NJBmg NLTmg NETmg

The variant reading, supported by the earliest manuscripts (𝔓[66] 𝔓[75] B) and also by several early versions (Old Latin and Coptic), was, nevertheless, rejected by the editors of NA[26] and UBS[3] on the grounds that the word for "God" (θεου—contracted as ΘΥ) probably dropped from the text due to homoeoteleuton: ΤΟΥΜΟΝΟΥΘΥ (TCGNT).

But there are a few problems with this view. First, scribes would not have easily dropped a nomen sacrum, especially because of the obvious overbar: ΘΥ. Second, would this have occurred in so many diverse manuscripts? Third, certain ancient translators must have recognized the expression μονου as functional by itself, not needing the addition of θεου. But various Greek scribes were not of the same opinion; they added θεου to fill in what would otherwise seem incomplete. Scribes aware of the Jewish Shema (Deut 6:4) would have been inclined to add "God" to get the phrase, "the only God."

According to Abbott (1906) the expression του μονου is a titular substantive, which could be written του Μονου, translated as "the Only One" or "the Unique One." This reading suits the passage well. Since the Jews were seeking to receive glory from one another, they had neglected to seek the glory that comes from the unique one, the only one who gives glory (see Comfort 2005, 338). Unfortunately, not one modern translation has adopted this reading, though it is noted in NRSV NIV NLT NET.

John 6:1

Excellent testimony (𝔓[66c1] 𝔓[75vid] ℵ A B L W etc.) supports the reading which says, ο Ιησους περαν της θαλασσης της Γαλιλαιας της Τιβεριαδος ("Jesus crossed the Sea of Galilee, the Tiberias.") In this reading, της Τιβεριαδος is an appositive providing another name for the sea. The Sea of Galilee was given the name "Sea of Tiberias" by Herod Antipas in honor of the Emperor Tiberius in A.D. 20. A variant reading is ο Ιησους περαν της θαλασσης της Γαλιλαιας εις τα μερη της Τιβεριαδος ("Jesus crossed the Sea of Galilee into the region of Tiberias"), found in D Θ it[b,d,e,j]. This would place the miracle on the western shore near Tiberias. However, the superior reading indicates that Jesus crossed the sea to the eastern shore.

John 6:11

WH NU εὐχαριστήσας διέδωκεν τοῖς ἀνακειμένοις
"having blessed [the loaves], [Jesus] gave them to the ones reclining"
𝔓[28vid] 𝔓[66] 𝔓[75] ℵ* A B L N W f[13] 33
NKJVmg RSV NRSV ESV NASB NIV TNIV NEB REB NJB NAB NLT HCSB NET

variant/TR ευχαριστησας διεδωκεν τοις μαθηταις οι δε μαθηται τοις ανακειμενοις
"having blessed [the loaves], [Jesus] gave them to the disciples and the disciples to the ones reclining"
ℵ[2] D Θ Ψ f[13] Maj
KJV NKJV

The addition in the variant is the result of scribal harmonization to the synoptic accounts of this same event (see Matt 14:19; Mark 6:41; Luke 9:16). In John's account, however, the disciples are not said to have participated in the distribution of the multiplied loaves and fish. Typical of John's gospel, Jesus is the sole focus of the miraculous event.

Martin, the editor of the *editio princeps* of 𝔓[75], reconstructed a part of 6:11 (ελαβεν ουν τους αρτους ο Ιησους = "then Jesus took the loaves"), wherein he wrote [ι]η[σ]ου[ς], thereby signifying that Jesus' name was written in full. However, a better reconstruction of the lines shows that it should be αρ[τ]ου[ς ο ις] (a new reconstruction of the lines can be seen in *Text of Earliest MSS*, 582). What is significant about this is that the Martin reconstruction has the name Ιησους written in full, which would be the only such instance in all the early manuscripts. My reconstruction shows the name as a nomen sacrum, which was the standard way of writing Jesus' name.

John 6:14

TR NU ἰδόντες ὃ ἐποίησεν σημεῖον
"having seen the sign which he did"
ℵ D W syr[c,s] cop (add ο Ιησους A L Θ Ψ f[1,13] Maj)
all

variant/WH ιδοντες α εποιησεν σημεια
"having seen the signs he did"
𝔓[75] B 091 it[a]
HCSBmg

The TR NU reading has good manuscript support and seems to suit the context. But the variant is the more difficult reading and has the early and superior testimony of 𝔓[75] and B. The reading with the plural σημεια ("signs") is more difficult because in context Jesus had provided just one sign—the multiplication of the loaves and fishes. But elsewhere in John the plural σημεια is used with no accompanying description of specific miracles performed (2:23). Since this verse describes the first Jewish, public recognition of Jesus as the Prophet (the people said, "This is truly the prophet coming into the world")—even the Messiah-King (see 6:15), we must ask: Was it just this one miraculous display that made the people believe, or had it been accumulative? Recall that this chapter began with a description of how great crowds were following Jesus and seeing the miraculous signs that he did upon the sick (εθεωρουν τα σημεια α εποιει επι των ασθενουντων—the use of the imperfect tense for both the verbs indicates ongoing activity, 6:2). This same crowd was fed by a miracle. Not only did they see Jesus perform miracles on the sick, they partook of a miracle themselves. All this had a cumulative effect, causing them to embrace Jesus as their Messiah-King. It is for this reason John very likely wrote ιδοντες α εποιησεν σημεια ("seeing the signs which he did"). (The same kind of change from the plural to the singular occurred in 11:45-46. See note there.) Although Westcott and Hort selected this reading, not one English version has followed it. Only HCSB has noted it.

John 6:15

According to 𝔓75 B C W, the text says that Jesus "departed [ανεχωρησεν] again to the mountain by himself." The verb is different in ℵ* lat syr^c: φευγει ("flees"). Even though the first reading has superior testimony, some commentators (e.g., Brown 1966, 235) think ενεχωρησεν ("departed") is a scribal emendation intended to soften φευγει ("flees"). However, the testimony of ℵ, especially in the first eight chapters of John, is suspect inasmuch as its text displays many idiosyncrasies associated with the wildness of the Western text (Fee 1968a, 23-44). D adds that Jesus went there to pray: κακει προσηυχετο; this addition is a harmonization to Mark 6:46.

John 6:22

WH NU — πλοιάριον ἄλλο οὐκ ἦν ἐκεῖ εἰ μὴ ἕν
"there was no other boat there except one"
𝔓75 ℵ2 A B L N W
NKJVmg RSV NRSV ESV NASB NIV TNIV NEB REB NJB NAB NLT HCSB NET

variant/TR — πλοιαριον αλλο ουκ ην εκει ει μη ἓν εκεινο εις ο ενεβησαν οι μαθηται αυτου
"there was no other boat there except that one in which the disciples had embarked"
(ℵ* D^c f13 του Ιησου instead of αυτου) Θ Maj
KJV NKJV HCSBmg

The variant is a scribal gloss intended to clarify which one boat the crowd had observed. "The crowd knew that one boat only was at the place where the disciples had embarked and that Jesus did not go with them; hence, they were perplexed as to what had happened to Jesus" (Beasley-Murray 1987, 89-90).

John 6:23

One look at the critical apparatus of UBS4 and the reader will be overwhelmed by the number of variants in this verse. The first set of variants involves the expression αλλα ηλθεν πλοια εκ Τιβεριαδος ("but boats came from Tiberias"), a reading found in 𝔓75 and B (which adds της before Τιβεριαδος). The other readings most likely diverged from this one. Other manuscripts (A W Θ f13) read αλλα δε ηλθεν πλοιαρια εκ Τιβεριαδος ("but other boats came from Tiberias")—in this instance αλλα is taken to mean "other," not "but." And there are other textual variations, all of which show that various scribes were trying to make sense of a difficult passage—namely 6:22-25. The crux of the problem has to do with the location of where Jesus performed the miracle of feeding the five thousand. According to the reading of some manuscripts in 6:1, Jesus performed the miracle on the east side of Galilee near Tiberias. But this reading is probably a scribal emendation attempting to harmonize 6:1 with 6:23, which says the boats came from Tiberias.

The most likely scenario is as follows: Jesus performed the miracle of feeding the five thousand somewhere on the eastern shore of the Galilean sea. That evening his disciples had boarded a boat headed west toward Capernaum. Jesus came to them during the storm and together they arrived at Capernaum (presumably before dawn). The crowd had noticed that the disciples—without Jesus—boarded the one boat that was there. The next morning they saw that the boat was gone and that Jesus was gone; they knew he had not gone in that one boat. During the evening either the storm had blown in some boats from Tiberias (on the western shore) or manned boats had come there from Tiberias. The people in the crowd used these boats to cross the sea to Capernaum, searching after Jesus. When they found him in Capernaum in the synagogue (6:59), they did not ask him "how did you get here?" (which seems to be the right question)—but ωδε γεγονας ("when did you get here?"), for they would not have thought that he came any other way than by boat. Thus, when the variant text says "other boats," it is trying to distinguish these boats from the one boat the disciples used.

In the last part of 6:23 there is another significant variant. The expression ευχαριστησαντος του κυριου ("after the Lord had given thanks") does not appear in D 091 it[a,e] syr[c,s]. In view of the fact that John rarely referred to Jesus as "the Lord" in his gospel and that this phrase is absent in several "Western" manuscripts, it is thought by some textual scholars that this phrase may not have been written by John but was introduced later as a liturgical edition. The words are omitted from NJB and noted in NEBmg and NETmg. However, the documentary evidence (𝔓[75] א A B L W Δ Θ f[13] 33 syr[h,pal] cop) supporting the inclusion of these words attests to its early and widespread presence in the Gospel of John. Furthermore, it can be argued that the words were omitted because they appeared to be a cumbersome addition to an already difficult text.

John 6:29

D W Δ 0145 f[13] Maj read the aorist subjunctive πιστευσητε ("that you might believe"), whereas all the early manuscripts read the present subjunctive πιστευητε ("that you might continue to believe"). In most instances John used the aorist subjunctive with the ινα clause (see 1:7; 6:30; 9:36; 11:15, 42; 13:19); thus, it was natural for scribes to change the present tense to the aorist.

John 6:36

TR WH NU	ἑωράκατε [με] καὶ οὐ πιστεύετε "you have seen me and you do not believe" 𝔓[66] 𝔓[75vid] B D (T) W Δ Θ Ψ f[1,13] 33 Maj syr[p,h,pal] cop KJV NKJV RSV NRSV ESV NASB NIV TNIV NEBmg REBmg NJB NAB NLT HCSB NET
variant	εωρακατε και ου πιστευετε "you have seen and you do not believe" א A it[a,b,e] syr[c,s] NEB REB HCSBmg NETmg

The TR WH NU reading has superior testimony. At this point in the discourse Jesus was not speaking about the crowds having seen the sign (of the miraculous feeding), which is the meaning implicit in the variant; rather, he had just pointed to himself as "the bread of life" (6:35).

The very bread of life come down from heaven was standing before them, and yet they did not believe in him. Until they did, they would go on hungering and thirsting.

John 6:39

A few manuscripts (ℵ*,2 C 565) omit τουτο δε εστιν το θελημα του πεμψαντος με ("and this is the will of the one who sent me") due to homoeoteleuton or perceived redundancy—the previous clause in 6:38 has almost exactly the same wording.

John 6:42

According to excellent testimony (𝔓66 𝔓75 B C D etc.), the people ask, "Is this not Jesus, the son of Joseph, whose father and mother we know?" A variant reading in ℵ* W it[b] syr[s,c] does not include και την μητερα ("and his mother"), yielding the question, "Is this not Jesus, the son of Joseph, whose father we know?" The words were omitted probably because the verse speaks initially only of Jesus' father—Jesus was known as "the son of Joseph."

John 6:47

WH NU ὁ πιστεύων ἔχει ζωὴν αἰώνιον
"the one believing has eternal life"
𝔓66 𝔓75vid ℵ B C* L T W
NKJVmg RSV NRSV ESV NASB NIV TNIV NEB REB NJB NAB NLT HCSB NET

variant 1/TR ο πιστεων εις εμε εχει ζωην αιωνιον
"the one believing in me has eternal life"
A C2 D Ψ f1,13 33 Maj
KJV NKJV HCSBmg NETmg

variant 2 "the one believing in God has eternal life"
syr[s,c]
NETmg

Scribes could not resist adding εις εμε ("in me") after ο πιστεων ("the one believing"), inasmuch as this is a typical Johannine expression (see 6:35), or adding some other object (God). TR incorporated the first variant, which was then translated in KJV and NKJV.

John 6:63

It is interesting to note that the scribe of 𝔓66 first started to write the word for "spirit" (writing the first four letters πνευ for πνευμα) and immediately corrected it to $\overline{\text{ΠΝΑ}}$, the contraction for the nomen sacrum, the divine Spirit. This shows that the scribe of 𝔓66 probably thought πνευμα required a different orthography for a different sense in this context—namely, that the words Jesus spoke were spiritual words with spiritual significance. However, the scribe of 𝔓66 ultimately decided to use the standard formula for designating a nomen sacrum, which then yields the sense: "my words are Spirit and they are life." Supporting this view, Beasley-Murray (1987, 96) said, "The words of Jesus in the discourse are Spirit and life for those who receive them in faith, since they who accept them and believe in the Son receive the Spirit and the life of which he speaks." This means that the Spirit was transmitted through Jesus' words.

John 6:64

Most manuscripts preserve this statement in full: "for Jesus knew from the beginning who are the ones not believing and who is the one betraying him." But a few manuscripts (𝔓66* it^e syr^s,c) omit the phrase τινες εισιν οι μη πιστευοντες και ("who are the ones not believing and"). Since this error cannot be explained as a transcriptional mistake, it is possible that some ancient scribes were offended by the notion of Jesus' foreknowledge of "the unbelieving" (i.e., the damned). The primary scribe of 𝔓66 left the shortened text as is; another corrector, the diorthotes, added the words in the upper margin of the page (see *Text of Earliest MSS*, 411).

John 6:69

WH NU	ὁ ἅγιος τοῦ θεοῦ "the Holy One of God" 𝔓75 ℵ B C* D L W it^d NKJVmg RSV NRSV ESV NASB NIV TNIV NEB REB NJB NAB NLT HCSB NET
variant 1	ο Χριστος ο αγιος του θεου "the Christ, the Holy One of God" 𝔓66 cop^sa,bo,ach2 NLTmg NETmg
variant 2	"the Son of God" it^b syr^c NETmg
variant 3	ο Χριστος ο υιος του θεου "the Christ, the Son of God" C3 Θ* 0141 f1 33 it^a,c,e syr^s NLTmg HCSBmg NETmg
variant 4/TR	ο Χριστος ο υιος του θεου ζωντος "the Christ, the Son of the living God" Θ^c Ψ 0250 f13 syr^p,h,pal Maj KJV NKJV NRSVmg NLTmg NETmg

The WH NU reading is superior to all the other variant readings because of its excellent documentary support and because most of the other variant readings are obvious assimilations to Matt 16:16 ("the Christ, the Son of the living God") or some derivation thereof. The fourth variant replicates Matt 16:16 verbatim. It was included in TR and popularized by KJV and NKJV. But in each of the synoptic accounts, Peter's declaration is slightly different: "You are the Christ, the Son of the living God" (Matt 16:16); "You are the Christ" (Mark 8:29); "[You are] the Christ of God" (Luke 9:20). Though the title "Holy One of God" is rare in the New Testament (the only other occurrence is in Mark 1:24), Peter spoke of Jesus as being "the Holy One" on two other occasions (see Acts 2:27; 3:14). Quite interestingly, 𝔓66 and a few Coptic manuscripts display a conflated reading: "the Christ, the Holy One of God." This tells us that some manuscript prior to 𝔓66 (perhaps its exemplar) had the reading ο αγιος του θεου, but the scribe of 𝔓66, who was aware of the other gospels, wanted Peter also to say, "You are the Christ." Modern English versions follow the superior text. The NLT does likewise and lists three of the four variants.

John 6:71

WH NU — Ἰούδαν Σίμωνος Ἰσκαριώτου
"Judas [son of] Simon Iscariot"
𝔓66 𝔓75 א2 B C L W Ψ 33
RSV NRSV ESV NASB NIV TNIV NEB REB NJB NAB NLT HCSB NET

variant 1/TR — Ιουδαν Σιμωνος Ισκαριωτην
"Judas Iscariot son of Simon"
f[1] Maj
KJV NKJV HCSBmg

variant 2 — Ιουδαν Σιμωνος απο Καρυωτου
"Judas [son of] Simon from Kerioth"
א* Θ f[13]
none

variant 3 — Ιουδαν Σιμωνος Σκαριωθ
"Judas [son of] Simon, [the] Scarioth"
D it
none

There are several variants on the name of Jesus' betrayer. He is consistently presented as the son of Simon, but the next identifier is variable in the various manuscripts. See the note on Matt 10:4 for a discussion of these variants.

John 7:1

TR WH NU — οὐ γὰρ ἤθελεν ἐν τῇ Ἰουδαίᾳ περιπατεῖν
"for he did not want to walk in Judea"
𝔓66 𝔓75 א B C D L f[1,13] Maj it[c,d,e,f] cop syr[s]
KJV NKJV RSV NRSV ESV NASB NIV TNIV NEB REB NJBmg NAB NLT HCSB NET

variant — ου γαρ ειχεν εξουσιαν εν τη Ιουδαια περιπατειν
"for he did not have freedom to walk in Judea"
W it syr[c] Chrysostom
NRSVmg NJB

The variant reading, εχειν εξουσιαν (literally "to have authority," but can also be translated "was [not] free to") is the more difficult reading, and therefore is accepted as original by some scholars (see Barrett 1978, 309-310). One version (NJB) accepts this reading, and one version (NRSV) notes it. In these versions, the verse then reads, "And after these things Jesus walked in Galilee, for he did not have the freedom to walk in Judea because the Jewish leaders were seeking to kill him." However, the documentary support strongly favors the TR WH NU reading. Therefore, it is difficult to determine which one John wrote. If we accept the TR WH NU reading, the sense is that Jesus willfully chose not to stay in Judea, even though he could have if he so desired. The sense of the second reading is that Jesus could not have stayed in Judea even if he so desired. The expression is used in John to describe Jesus' control over his own life (see 10:18) and Pilate's political control or authority over other men's lives (19:10). To say that Jesus did not have control or authority over his life while in Judea seems to go against a major theme in John's gospel, which asserts Jesus' complete control over his life.

John 7:8

NU ἐγὼ οὐκ ἀναβαίνω εἰς τὴν ἑορτὴν ταύτην
"I am not going up to this feast"
ℵ D it $syr^{c,s}$ cop^{bo}
NKJVmg RSV NRSV ESV NASB NIVmg TNIV NEB REB NJB NAB NLT HCSBmg NET

variant/TR WH εγω ουπω αναβαινω εις την εορτην ταυτην
"I am not yet going up to this feast"
$\mathfrak{P}^{66}$ $\mathfrak{P}^{75}$ B L T W Θ Ψ 070 0105 0250 $f^{1,13}$ Maj $syr^{p,h}$ $cop^{sa,ach2}$
KJV NKJV RSVmg NRSVmg ESVmg NIV TNIVmg NEBmg REBmg NJBmg NLTmg HCSB NETmg

The NU editors selected the first reading on the basis of intrinsic probability versus documentary evidence, which strongly favors ουπω ("not yet"). Given the context of John 7, in which Jesus makes one of the above statements to his brothers and then later goes to the festival, it would make more sense if he said he was not *yet* going to the festival than that he was simply *not* going to the festival. The latter statement seems to be contradicted by his action (for 7:10 says he went to the feast). Thus, the first reading is seen to be the harder and therefore more likely original.

However, it should be noted that the NU reading does not necessarily present a contradiction, because the wording "I am not going up to the festival" could mean (1) "I am not going up to the festival the way you [my brothers] want me to go" (i.e., in open manifestation, proclaiming himself to be the Christ—see 7:10) or (2) "I am not going up to the festival until the Father tells me to do so"—which is implicit in the next statement: "because for me the right time has not yet come." In fact, Jesus could not be found during the first few days of the festival (see 7:11 and 14). In 7:6 Jesus had said, ο καιρος ο εμος ουπω παρεστιν ("my time has not yet come"). This seems to indicate that Jesus knew that it was not yet time for him to go to Jerusalem and die. He awaited the Father's command as to when he should go to Jerusalem and as to when that would be his last visit ending in crucifixion. Thus, to argue for the first reading on the basis that it is the more difficult is only superficially true. The documentary evidence, which is early and diverse, supports the variant.

John 7:9

NU ταῦτα δὲ εἰπὼν αὐτὸς ἔμεινεν ἐν τῇ Γαλιλαίᾳ
"and saying these things, he (himself) remained in Galilee"
$\mathfrak{P}^{66}$ ℵ D* L W 070 f^{1} cop
RSV NRSV ESV NIV TNIV NEB REB NJB NAB HCSB NET

variant/TR WH ταυτα δε ειπων αυτοις εμεινεν εν τη Γαλιλαια
"and saying these things to them, he remained in Galilee"
$\mathfrak{P}^{75}$ B D^{1} T Θ Ψ 0105 0250 f^{13} 33 Maj syr^{h}
KJV NKJV NASB NLT

Since there is only a one-letter difference (an *iota*) between the two readings—αυτος/αυτοις, a transcriptional error could have happened either way. Nonetheless, the variant reading has slightly stronger documentary support and is the more natural reading. The effect of the intensifier αυτος in the NU reading is that John would have been indicating that Jesus himself—that is, Jesus alone without his disciples—stayed in Galilee. And this seems to be the situation in the following narrative (7:9-44). The English versions that follow this reading, however, do not reflect the intensifier.

John 7:36

One manuscript (225) inserts the pericope of the adulteress (7:53–8:11) at the end of this verse. The place of this insertion is less disturbing to the narrative than at the end of 7:52 inasmuch as 7:37–8:20 comprises a narrative unit. (See comments on 7:53–8:11).

John 7:37-38

The first of two issues in these verses pertains to the inclusion or exclusion of the prepositional phrase προς με following ερχεσθω (= "come to me"). Most manuscripts include the phrase—manuscripts such as 𝔓[66c2] (𝔓[75] B read προς εμε) ℵ[2] L T W Δ Θ Ψ. A few manuscripts (𝔓[66*] ℵ* D it[b,d,e]) omit the phrase—either due to scribal oversight or to achieve a closer link between the two imperative verbs (ερχεσω and πινετω). But, as is explained below, the prepositional phrase προς με is needed for symmetrical balance with εις εμε.

The next issue pertains to punctuation. In NU these verses are punctuated as follows:

> εἱστήκει ὁ Ἰησοῦς καὶ ἔκραξεν λέγων· ἐάν τις διψᾷ ἐρχέσθω πρός με καὶ πινέτω. [38]ὁ πιστεύων εἰς ἐμέ, καθὼς εἶπεν ἡ γραφή, ποταμοὶ ἐκ τῆς κοιλίας αὐτοῦ ῥεύσουσιν ὕδατος ζῶντος.
>
> "Jesus stood and shouted out, 'If anyone is thirsty, let him come to me and drink. [38] He who believes in me, as the Scripture has said, will have streams of living water flowing from within him.'"

However, there is another way to punctuate it:

> ειστηκει ο Ιησους και εκραξεν λεγων· εαν τις διψα ερχεσθω προς με· και πινετω ο πιστευων εις εμε, καθως ειπεν η γραφη, ποταμοι εκ της κοιλιας αυτου ρευσουσιν υδατος ζωντος.
>
> "Jesus stood and shouted out, 'If anyone is thirsty, let him come to me; and let him drink [38]who believes in me. As the Scripture has said, streams of living water will flow from within him.'"

Jesus' words can be rendered in two ways: (1) the first has the believer being the one from whom the living waters flow; (2) the other way has Jesus being the source from which the living waters flow (as in RSVmg ESVmg NIVmg TNIVmg NEB REBmg NJB NLT NET). In the first rendering, the word αυτου ("his") before κοιλιας ("innermost being") refers to the believer; in the second, αυτου ("his") refers to Ιησους ("Jesus"). The second rendering seems more suitable, for it is Jesus who is the antitype of the rock or temple from which the waters flow, not the believer. The first reading has been called the "Eastern" interpretation because it has the support of Origen, Athanasius, and the Greek fathers. The second reading has been called the "Western" interpretation because it has the support of Justin, Hippolytus, Tertullian, and Irenaeus.

Some scholars have argued that the Greek more closely and naturally yields the first rendering, but F. F. Bruce (1983, 181-182) has argued that the second more closely corresponds to the original Aramaic utterance. And not only that, Burge (1987, 88-93) points out that this reading is purposely written in chiastic form:

A εαν τις διψα ("if anyone thirsts")

B ερχεσθω προς με ("let him come to me")

B′ και πινετω ("and let him drink")

A′ ο πιστευων εις εμε ("the one believing in me").

The scripture cited by Jesus does not help us determine if he was speaking about himself or the believer as the source because there is no single verse in the OT that exactly says "out his innermost being [lit. "belly"] will flow rivers of living water." Jesus may have been paraphrasing Ps 78:16, 20 (77:16, 20 in LXX) ("He brought forth streams also from the rock, and caused waters to run down like rivers . . . As he smote the rock and water flowed and streams overflowed"). As such, he is the fulfillment of the rock (cf. 1 Cor 10:4). Or Jesus may have been thinking of Zech 14:8, especially in reference to the idea of living water coming from the temple. We could also imagine that he was paraphrasing Ezek 47:1 and Joel 3:18, which both speak of the living waters flowing from the temple in Jerusalem. Since John presents Jesus as the antitype of the temple throughout this gospel (see 1:14; 2:19-22; 14:2-3), John could also be showing that Jesus, positioning himself in Jerusalem, was proclaiming that he was the true fulfillment of giving living waters to all those who would come to him and drink. Other verses in the OT generally speak of the believers' experience of receiving spiritual, living water (Isa 12:3; 44:3). Indeed, Isa 44:3 ties together the images of water and Spirit, as did Jesus. And there is one verse, Isa 58:11, that speaks of the believer having a living spring within.

It is interesting to note that the two earliest manuscripts (𝔓66 and 𝔓75) both indicate a full stop after the word πινετω ("drink") (see *Text of Earliest MSS,* 415, 588). This punctuation may reveal the Eastern interpretation and not at all be reflective of the original text. If, however, the full stop is reflective of the original, then John intended this statement to indicate that the believer who drinks of Christ as the waters flowing from the temple or from the rock will experience the living waters flowing out from him. Westcott (1881, 123) put it this way: "He who drinks of the Spiritual Rock becomes in turn himself a rock from within which the waters flow to slake the thirst of others."

John 7:39a

In the first part of this verse, there is textual variation concerning the gender of the pronoun following του πνευματος ("the Spirit"). In some manuscripts (𝔓75 B 0105—so NU), the pronoun is neuter (ο)—"the Spirit, which the ones who believed in him were about to receive." In other manuscripts (𝔓66 ℵ D L N T W Γ Δ Θ Ψ $f^{1,13}$ 33—so TR WH), the pronoun is masculine (ου)—"the Spirit, whom the ones who believed in him were about to receive." According to correct grammar, the neuter is right. But John may have used the masculine pronoun to signal the personality of the Spirit of Jesus—unless this was the work of later scribes. If the masculine is original, then the change to the neuter was the work of Alexandrian scribes (𝔓75 B) to correct the grammar. Interestingly, the same kind of variation occurs in other verses pertaining to the Spirit (see note on 14:17).

John 7:39b

WH NU	οὔπω γὰρ ἦν πνεῦμα "for the Spirit was not yet" 𝔓66c 𝔓75 ℵ K N* T Θ Ψ Origen NRSV NJB NAB NLTmg
variant 1/TR	ουπω γαρ ην πνευμα αγιον "for the Holy Spirit was not yet" 𝔓66* L W 0105 $f^{1,13}$ 33 Maj NLTmg HCSBmg

variant 2 οὔπω γὰρ ἦν πνεῦμα δεδομένον
"for the Spirit was not yet given"
it^{a,aur,b,c} syr^{c,s,p} Eusebius
NKJVmg RSV NRSVmg ESV NASB NIV TNIV NEB REB NJBmg NABmg NLT HCSB NET

variant 3 οὔπω γὰρ ἦν πνεῦμα ἅγιον δεδομένον
"for the Holy Spirit was not yet given"
B it^{e} syr^{h**}
KJV NKJV NRSVmg NLTmg HCSBmg

variant 4 οὔπω γὰρ ἦν τὸ πνεῦμα τὸ ἅγιον ἐπ' αὐτοῖς
"for the Holy Spirit was not yet upon them"
D* it^{d,f}
none

This verse is John's own gloss, inserted to provide an explanation of Jesus' declaration in 7:37-38. There are several textual variants in this explanation, but the most significant one pertains to the expression οὔπω γὰρ ἦν πνεῦμα ("[the] Spirit was not yet"), attested to by $\mathfrak{P}^{66c}$ $\mathfrak{P}^{75}$ ℵ T etc. Various scribes could not resist the temptation to add the word ἅγιον ("Holy") to πνεῦμα ("Spirit")—an addition that frequently happened throughout the course of the transmission of the New Testament text—or to add δεδομένον ("given") or both. The scribe of $\mathfrak{P}^{66}$ first wrote the word ἅγιον and then deleted it—to conform his text to his original exemplar or yet another one. Most translators (except those of NRSV, NASB, and NJB) have also felt compelled to add the word "given." But this addition slightly modifies the meaning of the original wording. According to the best manuscript evidence, the best rendering would be, "there was no Spirit as yet" (NJB).

In context, this statement was part of a parenthetical explanation provided by John, a statement providing the reader with the key to understanding Jesus' declaration in 7:37-38. Jesus had just promised that anyone who believes in him could come to him and drink of him and thereby experience an inner flow of living water. John's parenthetical remark makes it clear that Jesus was promising the believer an experience of the Spirit that could not happen until after Jesus was glorified and the Spirit was made available ("the Spirit was not yet because Jesus was not yet glorified"). John's word does not mean that the Spirit did not exist at the time Jesus spoke (cf. 1:33) or that believers had not received the spirit and life of Jesus' words (see 6:63, 68). John's note pointed to a time when the Spirit of the glorified Jesus would become available through a special dispensation to all who had believed in him. Thus, the availability of the Spirit is linked with the glorification of Jesus, for it was after Jesus' glorification via death and resurrection that the Spirit became available to the believers (see 20:22).

The early manuscripts shed light on another matter which pertains to the absence of the article before πνεῦμα and its implications for interpretation. Because of the absence of the article, this verse has been understood in two ways: (1) "for [the] Spirit was not yet because Jesus was not yet glorified" or (2) "for [a gift of the] spirit was not yet [available] because Jesus was not yet glorified."

The second interpretation is proposed by Westcott who said, "when *pneuma* occurs without the article, it marks an operation, or manifestation, a gift of the Spirit, and not the personal Spirit." But the scribes of $\mathfrak{P}^{66}$ and $\mathfrak{P}^{75}$ wrote the word *pneuma* as a nomen sacrum here ($\overline{\text{ΠΝΑ}}$), thereby showing that they thought of the Spirit here as being the divine Spirit.

Finally, it should be noted that many scribes (ℵ D Θ Ψ 0105 f^{1,13} Maj) changed the aorist participial phrase οἱ πιστεύσαντες ("the ones having believed"), found in $\mathfrak{P}^{66}$ B L T W, to a present participle πιστεύοντες ("the ones believing") in order to make Jesus' promise more present for the Christians of their own times. John, however, was speaking specifically of all those who had believed in Jesus prior to the glorification of his resurrection. Because of their belief, they would receive the Spirit of the glorified Jesus. This, then, would be a principle for all believers thereafter.

John 7:52

TR WH NU ἐκ τῆς Γαλιλαίας προφήτης οὐκ ἐγείρεται
"a prophet does not arise out of Galilee"
𝔓[66c] א A B Maj
all

variant εκ της Γαλιλαιας ο προφητης ουκ εγειρεται
"the prophet does not arise out of Galilee"
𝔓[66*] 𝔓[75vid?]
NIVmg NLTmg NETmg

One Greek manuscript, 𝔓[66*] (not cited in NA[26] or NA[27], but cited in UBS[4]), definitely reads ο προφητης ("the prophet"), which then was corrected to προφητης ([a] prophet). By looking at the photograph of 𝔓[66], it seems fairly certain that the scribe or corrector attempted to rid the text of the definite article ο; though the letter can still be read, it is distinctly lighter than the other letters on the page and bears the signs of attempted erasure. What makes it certain that the corrector was ridding the text of the definite article is that transposition marks stroked before εκ της γαλιλαιας and προφητης, excluding ο, indicate this corrected reading: προφητης εκ της γαλιλαιας (see *Text of Earliest MSS,* 417). Also, Martin and Kasser (1961, 48) wrote ο προφητης in the lacuna of their transcription of 𝔓[75]. But since the scribe of 𝔓[75] wrote very small *omicrons*, we cannot make a precise decision about how many letters it would take to fill the lacuna. This is reflected in *Text of Earliest MSS,* 589. Thus, one early manuscript (𝔓[66*]) and perhaps another (𝔓[75vid?]) read "the Prophet"—that is, the messianic Prophet predicted by Moses (see 1:21; Deut 18:15, 18). Many exegetes had affirmed this sense even before the discovery of the Bodmer papyri, 𝔓[66] and 𝔓[75]. The text could still convey the same sense with the reading προφητης ("a prophet"), if it is interpreted as: "If, according to the Scriptures, not even a prophet comes out of Galilee, how much less the Christ?"

John 7:53–8:11

This passage is included in NA[27] and UBS[4] but enclosed in double square brackets. In WH, it appears after John's gospel. It is included in TR as 7:53–8:11.

omit 7:53–8:11

𝔓[39vid] 𝔓[66] 𝔓[75] א A[vid] B C[vid] L N T W Δ Θ Ψ 0141 33 it[a,f] syr[c,s,p] cop[sa,bo,ach2] geo Diatessaron Origen Chrysostom Cyril Tertullian Cyprian MSS[according to Augustine]
NKJVmg RSVmg NRSVmg ESVmg NASBmg NIVmg TNIVmg NEBmg REB NJBmg NABmg NLTmg HCSBmg NETmg

include 7:53–8:11

D (F) G H K M U Γ it[aur,c,d,e] syr[h,pal] cop[boMSS] Maj MSS[according to Didymus]; E 8:2-11 with asterisks; Λ 8:3-11 with asterisks; f[1] after John 21:25; f[13] after Luke 21:38; 1333[c] 8:3-11 after Luke 24:53; 225 after John 7:36

English translations including the pericope after 7:52.

KJV NKJV RSV NRSV ESV NASB NIV TNIV NEB REBmg NJB NAB NLT HCSB NET

𝔓[39vid] is not noted in the critical apparatus of NA[27] or UBS[4] for the omission of 7:53–8:11. Nonetheless, it is quite likely that the manuscript did not contain this pericope, because extant pagination and uniform lettering allow for a reconstruction of the number of pages in the codex up to 8:14 (the first verse extant in 𝔓39), and this number does not allow for the inclusion of 7:53–8:11. (See my full discussion on 𝔓39 in Comfort 2005, 353-354.) As for the manuscripts A and C, though they both have lacunae in this portion of John, careful calculations make it unlikely that there was enough space in the original codices of both of these manuscripts to contain the story (TCGNT).

The pericope about the adulteress (7:53–8:11) is not included in any of the earliest manuscripts (second–fourth century), including the two earliest, 𝔓66 and 𝔓75, as well as 𝔓39vid of the early third century (see note above). The other witnesses to the exclusion of this passage are equally impressive, including all the fourth-century codices (א A B C T), Diatessaron, the early versions, and most of the early church fathers. Its first appearance in a Greek manuscript is in D (ca. 400), but it is not contained in other Greek manuscripts until the ninth century. (Didymus [died 398] indicates he knew of manuscripts containing the story.) When this story is inserted in later manuscripts, it appears in different places (after Luke 21:38; 24:53, John 7:36, 52, and at the end of John); and when it does appear it is often marked off by obeli or asterisks to signal its probable spuriousness. In most of the manuscripts that include this story, it appears at the beginning of John 8, probably because it provides an illustration of Jesus' resistance to pass judgment, which is spoken of in the following discourse (see 8:15-19). A marginal note in the NAB suggests that it fits more naturally after Luke 21:38 than after John 7:52 (see note in this commentary).

The inclusion of this story in the NT text is a prime example of how the oral tradition, originally not included in the text, eventually found its way into the written text. In its oral form the story may have been in circulation beginning in the early second century. Papias may have been speaking of this incident when he "expounded another story about a woman who was accused before the Lord of many sins, which the Gospel according to the Hebrews contains" (Eusebius, *Hist. eccl.* 3.39.17). However, in the pericope of the adulteress there is no mention of many "sins," only one—that of adultery (Bruce 1983, 417-418).

According to Ehrman (1988, 24-44), a story about a condemned woman being rescued by Jesus was extant in written form as early as the fourth century in three different versions: (1) as a story where the religious leaders were trying to trap Jesus as to whether or not he would uphold the Mosaic law and where he freely pardons a sinful woman—basically the story known to Papias and the author of the *Didascalia Apostolorum*; (2) the story of Jesus' intervention in an execution—an episode preserved in the *Gospel of the Hebrews* and retold by Didymus in his commentary on Ecclesiastes; (3) the popular version found in most of the later manuscripts of John, "a version which represents a conflation of the two earlier stories."

My conjecture is that the popular version was first inserted by the scribe of Codex Bezae—not only because this is the earliest extant Greek manuscript to include the story but also because the Bezaean editor had a proclivity for enlarging the text. (The book of Acts, for example, in D is one-tenth larger than the Alexandrian text.) The D-reviser was quite keen on filling in perceived gaps in the text. Perhaps he believed John's narrative was lacking an example of Jesus both upholding the law while simultaneously showing forth grace, and thus supplied this story. Or the story could have been inserted to demonstrate that the religious leaders were always too quick to judge others (7:51-52), while Jesus only judged as the Father directed him (3:17; 5:22, 30). Or it is possible that the D-reviser may have thought the entire fourfold gospel was lacking without this story, and therefore he inserted it wherever it was convenient. Quite specifically, it is characteristic for the Bezaean scribe to have added the words in 7:53, και επορευθησαν εκαστος εις τον οικον αυτου ("and each one went to his own home") because he made an almost identical addition at the end of Acts 5:18 (see note).

Not only is the external evidence against the Johannine authorship of the pericope about the adulteress (see above), so is the internal evidence. First of all, many scholars have pointed out that the vocabulary used in this pericope does not accord with the rest of John. Second, the insertion of the pericope about the adulteress at this point in John (after 7:52 and before 8:12) greatly disrupts the narrative flow. Westcott and Hort indicated that the setting of John 7–8 is at Jerusalem during the Feast of Tabernacles. During this feast, the Jews would customarily pour water over a rock (in commemoration of the water supply coming from the rock in the wilderness) and light lamps (in commemoration of the pillar of light that accompanied the Israelites in their wilderness journey). With reference to these two ritualistic enactments, Jesus presented himself as the true source of living water (7:37-39) and as the true light to be followed (8:12). Westcott and Hort's (1882, 87-88) argument is that the pericope about the adulteress disrupts the continuity between the events. Wallace (1993) shows that the pericope does not match John's linguistic style or literary pattern.

In addition to this argument, it can also be said that the pericope concerning the adulteress interrupts the connection between 7:40-52 and 8:12-20 (Comfort 1989, 145-147). John 8:12-20 is Jesus' response to 7:52. When the text says, "he spoke to them again," it is clear that he was speaking to the Pharisees (mentioned in 7:45 and 48, then 8:13). The NIV incorrectly says that "Jesus spoke to the people." Not so: he was addressing the Pharisees who had just met in the Sanhedrin, where they denounced Jesus for his Galilean origins after Nicodemus had asked them to give Jesus a fair hearing. John 8:20 reads, "He spoke these words while teaching in the temple area near the treasury." This area was part of the Court of the Women and very close to the hall where the Sanhedrin met.

John 8:12-20 contains Jesus' rebuttal to these Pharisees who had boldly told Nicodemus that the Scriptures make no mention of even a prophet (much less the Christ) being raised up in Galilee. With respect to this assertion, Jesus made a declaration in which he implied that the Scriptures did speak of the Christ coming from Galilee. He said, "I am the light of the world; he who follows me will not walk in darkness, but will have the light of life." This statement was probably drawn from Isa 9:1-2: "But there will be no more gloom for her who was in anguish; in earlier times he treated the land of Zebulun and the land of Naphtali with contempt, but later on he will make it glorious, by the way of the sea, on the other side of the Jordan, Galilee of the Gentiles. The people who walk in darkness will see a great light; those who live in a dark land, the light will shine on them" (NASB).

The passages contain parallel images. Both Isa 9:2 and John 8:12 speak about the Messiah coming to give the light of life among those who are walking in darkness and sitting under the shadow of death. This provides a reproof to the Pharisees' declaration in 7:52 that the Scriptures nowhere speak of a prophet (not to mention the Messiah) having come from Galilee. Indeed, Matthew also cited Isa 9:1-2 to affirm the prophetic validity of Jesus' presence in Galilee (see Matt 4:12-16). Jesus' Galilean origin was a stumbling block to many of his contemporaries. They could not believe that Jesus was the Messiah because he came from Galilee. They were correct in thinking that the Christ, as David's offspring, should come from Bethlehem (see 1 Sam 16:1; Pss 89:3-4; 132:11; Isa 9:6-7; 11:1; Mic 5:2). And, in fact, Jesus was David's son (see Matt 1:1-18; Rom 1:3-4) born in Bethlehem (see Matt 2:1-6; Luke 2:1-11). But soon after his birth, Jesus was taken to Egypt to escape the sword of Herod and then later was brought by his parents to Nazareth of Galilee (the hometown of Joseph and Mary), where he was reared. Once Jesus began his ministry, he suffered the opprobrium of being known as a Galilean and a Nazarene, not a Judean or a Bethlehemite. However, Jesus never once defended his Bethlehemic origin; rather, he always pointed to his divine, heavenly origin. If a person knew the one he came from, he would know that Jesus was the Christ.

In 8:14 Jesus again refers to the fact that the Pharisees did not know where he came from. They thought they knew that Jesus could not have been the Messiah because he was from Galilee, not Bethlehem. But even on this count they were wrong. Jesus' origin was both from

Bethlehem and heaven. This is implicit in Mic 5:2, which speaks of the Messiah's birthplace as being Bethlehem yet in the same breath declares that "his origins are from old, from eternity."

Having said all this, it is very disappointing to realize that the pericope of the adulteress woman is included in the NU text, even though it is set in double brackets to signify the editors' serious doubts about its place in the text. There can be little doubt that John never wrote it and that it has no place whatsoever being in the text. Of course, it is very difficult to rid the Bible of spurious texts once they have gained a place in what people consider to be Holy Scripture. When the RSV was first published, this pericope was taken out of the text and placed in a footnote, but the outcry against this was so vehement that it was placed back in the text in the next printing. The REB translators have moved the pericope to an appendix following the Gospel of John, just as was done by Westcott and Hort in their Greek text.

But most English readers of the NT will not see any of the connections mentioned above because the pericope of the adulteress is still printed in the text between 7:52 and 8:12. True, the passage has been bracketed, or marked off with single lines (similar to the practice of marking obeli employed by several ancient scribes to the same passage), or set in italics (see TNIV). But there it stands—an obstacle to reading the true narrative of John's gospel. Even worse, its presence in the text misrepresents the testimony of the extant manuscripts. And, as long as it appears in the text of Greek editions and modern translations, readers will continue to think it is part of John's original text, and preachers will continue to expound on it without differentiating it from the rest of authentic Scripture. This is illustrated in a note in the NABmg, which after explaining the spuriousness of the pericope, then concludes: "The Catholic Church accepts this passage as canonical scripture." However, it must be strongly stated that 7:53–8:11 was not part of the Gospel of John when this gospel was being canonized by the early church (second to fourth centuries).

John 8:16

TR WH NU μόνος οὐκ εἰμί, ἀλλ ἐγὼ καὶ ὁ πέμψας με πατήρ
"I am not alone—but I and the Father having sent me"
𝔓[39] 𝔓[66] 𝔓[75] ℵ[2] B L T W 070 f[1,13] 33 it syr[p,h,pal] cop
KJV NKJV RSVmg NRSV ESV NASB NIV TNIV NAB NLT HCSB NET

variant μονος ουκ ειμι, αλλ εγω και ο πεμψας με
"I am not alone—but I and the one having sent me"
ℵ* D it[d] syr[c,s]
RSV NRSVmg NEB REB NJB NLTmg

It could be argued that the variant reading is the shorter one and therefore more likely original because it is easier to imagine why scribes would add πατηρ ("Father") than delete it. It was for this reason, no doubt, that the variant reading was the one included in the Nestle text—until NA[26], when the other reading was adopted on the basis of superior documentary evidence (note especially the early papyri: 𝔓[39] 𝔓[66] 𝔓[75]). Very likely, πατηρ ("Father") was dropped from ℵ* D etc. due to its final position in the sentence or the influence of 7:28; 8:26 and 29, where the expression is ο πεμψας με ("the one who sent me").

John 8:25

There are two basic readings for Jesus' response in this verse: (1) "[I am] principally that which I also speak to you" or "[I am] what I have been telling you from the beginning"; (2) "Why do I speak to you at all?" The first reading, rendered in various ways, is based on a text that reads την αρχην ο τι και λαλω υμιν; the second, on the reading την αρχην οτι και λαλω υμιν. Because so many early Greek manuscripts did not leave any spaces between words, it is difficult to determine if the text is to be read as ο τι ("that which") or οτι ("why"). In the early manuscripts there was usually no spacing between words, and punctuation was sporadic. The corrector of 𝔓66 (𝔓66c2) added ειπον υμιν ("I told you") before the phrase noted above. This yields a very understandable translation: "I told you in the beginning that which I also speak to you." A few scholars favor this reading (for example, see Funk 1958, 95-100; Smothers 1958, 111-122), but its singularity makes it suspect.

John 8:34

A few manuscripts (D itb syrs) omit της αμαρτιας ("of sin") from the expression πας ο ποιων την αμαρτιαν δουλος εστιν της αμαρτιας ("everyone committing sin is a slave of sin"). Although some exegetes adopt the shorter reading, the full expression (supported by all other manuscripts) is necessary to complete the sense.

John 8:35

A few manuscripts (א W 33 copbo) omit the final clause of this verse, ο υιος μενει εις τον αιωνων ("the son remains forever"), due to homoeoteleuton—the previous clause ends with the same three words—εις τον αιωνα, or due to purposeful excision of a difficult statement. The manuscript evidence in favor of its inclusion is impressive: 𝔓66 𝔓75 B C D 070, and so is the fact that it is necessary to complete the full meaning of 8:35, which is a short parable that amplifies the difference between a slave and a son: "the slave does not stay in the household forever; the son stays forever." A slave has no permanent standing in his master's house; he can easily be sold to another. But a son always has a place in his father's house; once a son, always a son. The Jews had a false sense of security because they claimed to be sons of Abraham, when actually they were slaves of sin. As such, they had no permanent standing in the Father's house. The use of ο υιος ("the son") in this verse has double significance: (1) it refers to the son, as opposed to the slave, who has a permanent place in his father's house, and (2) it refers to the Son of God who has an eternal place in his Father's house (cf. 1 Chr 17:11-14). The definite article "the" before "Son" lends support to this view, and the next verse could be seen as affirming it: "If the Son makes you free, you are free indeed." The Son of God alone has the power and authority to liberate men from their bondage to sin.

Interestingly, two ancient scribes (those of 𝔓66 and 𝔓75) were divided as to how to write the two terms for υιος in verses 35 and 36. The scribe of 𝔓66 made them both nomina sacra; the scribe of 𝔓75 wrote out the first word (ΥΙΟϹ), and made the second a nomen sacrum ($\overline{\text{ΥϹ}}$), thereby indicating his interpretation: verse 35 concerns "a son" generically speaking and verse 36 pertains to "the Son."

John 8:38

For the sake of distinguishing the two "fathers" (the Father of Jesus and the Jewish leaders' father, the devil), various scribes (א Θ Ψ 0250 Maj—so TR) added μου to τω πατρι (= "my father) and υμων ("your") to του πατρος (= "your father"). There is good manuscript evidence (𝔓66 𝔓75 B L W) to show that John originally wrote both without pronouns in an intended wordplay: "I speak of what I have seen with the father, and you do what you have heard from the father." At this point in the discussion, Jesus was being purposely subtle. As the discourse continued, he distinguished between the two "fathers." Jesus' father is God, and their father is the devil (see 8:42-44).

John 8:39

NU τὰ ἔργα τοῦ ᾿Αβραὰμ ἐποιεῖτε
"you would be doing the works of Abraham"
𝔓75 ℵ* B2 D W Θ 070 0250 it
KJV NKJV RSV NRSV ESV NIV TNIV NEB REB NJBmg NAB NLT HCSB NET

variant 1/WH τα εργα του Αβρααμ ποιειτε
"do the works of Abraham"
𝔓66 B* syrs
NRSVmg NASB NIVmg TNIVmg NEBmg NJB NLTmg NETmg

variant 2/TR τα εργα του Αβρααμ εποιειτε αν
"you would have done the works of Abraham"
ℵ2 C L Δ Ψ f1,13
NETmg

The editors of NA26 chose the reading of 𝔓75 etc. over 𝔓66 and B—a change from previous editions of the Nestle text. According to these editors, the verse in the original text reads, Ει τεκνα του Αβρααμ εστε, τα εργα του Αβρααμ εποιειτε ("If you are the children of Abraham, you would be doing the works of Abraham")—a mixed conditional sentence, "with ει . . . εστε in the protasis, and εποιειτε in the apodosis" (TCGNT).

If this is the correct reading, then Jesus was not urging his Jewish audience, who claimed to be Abraham's children, to do the works of Abraham (as in WH); rather, he was exposing them for acting in complete contradiction to the Abrahamic nature they claimed to possess. Indeed, they were seeking to kill Jesus (8:40). Most English versions present this latter rendering, while a few versions (NASB NJB) affirm the imperative.

John 8:54

NU λέγετε ὅτι θεὸς ἡμῶν ἐστιν
"you say, 'he is our God'"
(𝔓66c adds ο before θεος) 𝔓75 A B2 C W Θ 070 f1,13 33 Maj
NKJVmg NRSV ESV NASB NEB REB NJB NAB NLT HCSB NET

variant/TR WH λεγετε οτι θεος υμων εστιν
"you say that he is your God"
(𝔓66* L add ο before θεος) ℵ B* D Ψ
KJV NKJV RSV ESVmg NIV TNIV

The textual evidence supports the NU reading (NA27 does not show 𝔓66c as supporting the text, but UBS4 does, which is correct.) According to this reading, the word οτι should be viewed as introducing a direct quotation. The variant reading has the statement positioned as being indirect. The versions are divided on this issue, with the more recent ones favoring NU.

John 8:57

TR WH NU πεντήκοντα ἔτη οὔπω ἔχεις καὶ ᾿Αβραὰμ ἑώρακας;
"You are not yet fifty years old, and you have seen Abraham?"
𝔓66 ℵ2 A (B) C D L (W) Δ (Θ) Ψ f1,13 it syrp,h,pal
all

variant πεντακοντα ετη ουπω εχεις και Αβρααμ εωρακεν σε;
"You are not yet fifty years old, and Abraham has seen you?"
𝔓[75] ℵ* 070 syr[s] cop[sa,ach2]
RSVmg NRSVmg ESVmg NEBmg NLTmg HCSBmg

The variant reading in 𝔓[75] (which is known for its accuracy) and ℵ* (which is not Western beyond 8:38—see Fee 1968a, 23-44) is entirely consistent with the tenor of the passage, wherein Jesus has just said that Abraham had rejoiced to see his day (8:56). Jesus had not claimed to be a contemporary with Abraham or that he had seen Abraham; he had indicated that Abraham had prophetic foresight about the coming of the Messiah. (According to rabbinic tradition, Abraham was supposed to have been given foresight into future events pertaining to his descendants.) The variant reading has the religious leaders asking Jesus, "has Abraham seen you?" This is a more natural question than them asking Jesus, "have you seen Abraham?" But it is for this very reason that various commentators are suspicious that the variant reading appears to be an assimilation to the preceding verse (TCGNT)—plus, the TR WH NU reading has early and diverse support. This reading addresses the issue of Jesus' longevity—to which Jesus responds: "before Abraham came into being I am" (8:59). Whichever reading is original, this shows that scribes struggled with the meaning of the text and in both cases produced plausibly intelligible readings (see Comfort 2005, 338-339). All English versions follow the text, while a few note the alternative (as did WH).

One final thought: The comment about Jesus being not yet fifty years old is a roundabout way of saying that he was not yet an old man. It is very unlikely that John was supporting another tradition for the age of Jesus, which said that Jesus was between forty and fifty years old during his ministry (see Irenaeus, *Haer.* 2.22.5).

John 8:58

A few Western witnesses (D it) omit γενεσθαι from the statement πριν Αβρααμ γενεσθαι εγω ειμι, thereby creating the rendering "before Abraham I am." But since the point of the statement is to contrast Abraham's finite existence (a coming into being at some point in time—hence the verb γενεσθαι) with Jesus' eternal existence, both verbs are necessary. In one breath, Jesus asserted his eternal preexistence and his absolute deity. Abraham, as with all mortals, came into existence at one point in time. But Jesus, unlike all mortals, never had a beginning. He was eternal, and he was God. This is evident in the words εγω ειμι ("I AM"), for this statement refers to the Septuagint translation of Exod 3:14, in which God unveiled his identity as "I AM THAT I AM." Thus, Jesus was claiming to be the ever-existing, self-existent God.

John 8:59

WH NU Ἰησοῦς δὲ ἐκρύβη καὶ ἐξῆλθεν ἐκ τοῦ ἱεροῦ
"Jesus was hidden and went out of the temple."
𝔓[66] 𝔓[75] ℵ* B D W Θ* syr[s] cop
NKJVmg RSV NRSV ESV NASB NIV TNIV NEB REB NJB NAB NLT HCSB NET

variant/TR Ιησους δε εκρυβη και εξηλθεν εκ του ιερου και διελθων δια μεσου αυτων επορευετο και παρηγεν ουτως.
"Jesus was hidden and went out of the temple, and passing through the midst of them he went away, and so passed by."
ℵ[1] (A) C L N (Θ[c]) Ψ 070 33 f[1,13] Maj
KJV NKJV HCSBmg NETmg

All the earliest manuscripts attest to the shorter reading. Later scribes could not resist adding a little extra drama to the narrative, and so they borrowed from Luke 4:30 to show that Jesus did not just leave the temple but passed unharmed through the midst of his enemies. This extra verbiage, added to TR, has been popularized by KJV and NKJV.

John 9:4

There are two significant textual variants in this passage, both involving the two pronouns, as follows:

WH NU (1a) ἡμᾶς δεῖ
"it is necessary for us"
𝔓[66] 𝔓[75] ℵ* B D L W
NKJVmg RSV NRSV ESV NASB NIV TNIV NEB REB NAB NLT HCSB NET

variant/TR (1b) εμε διε
"it is necessary for me"
ℵ[1] A C Θ Ψ f[1,13] Maj
KJV NKJV NRSVmg NEBmg REBmg NJB NLTmg HCSBmg

TR WH NU (2a) του πεμψαντος με
"the one having sent me"
ℵ[1] A C Θ Ψ f[1,13] Maj
KJV NKJV RSV NRSV ESV NASB NIV TNIV NEB REB NJB NAB NLTmg HCSB NET

variant (2b) του πεμψαντος ημας
"the one having sent us"
𝔓[66] 𝔓[75] ℵ* L W
NRSVmg NLT HCSBmg

It seems most likely that John wrote, ημας δει εργαζεσθαι τα εργα του πεμψαντος ημας ("it is necessary for us to do the work of him who sent us"), which was then changed in various manuscripts. According to early and excellent manuscript support, the first pronoun is ημας and the last pronoun is ημας, whereas other manuscripts read εμε and με. WH NU followed B here in using ημας ("us") first and με ("me") second, thereby producing the sentence, "It is necessary for us to do the works of him who sent me." This is a mixed sentence, evidently created by scribes who were used to seeing the common Johannine expression "[the Father] who sent me" (5:37; 6:44; 8:16, 18; 12:49), not "sent us." The two earliest manuscripts (𝔓[66] 𝔓[75]), with three others (ℵ* L W), present a more consistent external testimony. Evidently, Jesus was speaking of himself and his disciples as coworkers. They were to learn from him because they would continue his work as his sent ones (see 20:21). He included the disciples in this work (although they did nothing for this blind man) because they would continue to shine forth his light after Jesus' departure (see Phil 2:15).

John 9:4 provides a telling example of how uneven the documentary presentation can be in NU. In the first part of this verse, the testimony of 𝔓[66] 𝔓[75] ℵ B L W is accepted, but in the next part of the very same clause, the testimony of 𝔓[66] 𝔓[75] ℵ* L W is rejected. This is the result of atomistic eclecticism.

John 9:6

Instead of the word επεχρισεν (which means "anointed" or "applied"), which is supported by 𝔓[66] 𝔓[75] ℵ A C D L W Maj, Codex Vaticanus (B) and the Diatessaron read επεθηκεν ("put").

The change may have arisen because the scribes considered it impossible to anoint with mud. Curiously, the same scribes did not alter the word επεχρισεν in 9:11.

John 9:35

WH NU	σὺ πιστεύεις εἰς τὸν υἱὸν τοῦ ἀνθρώπου; "Do you believe in the Son of Man?" 𝔓66 𝔓75 ℵ B D W it[d] syr[s] cop NKJVmg RSV NRSV ESV NASB NIV TNIV NEB REB NJB NAB NLT HCSB NET
variant/TR	συ πιστευεις εις τον υιον του θεου; "Do you believe in the Son of God?" A L Θ Ψ 070 0250 f[1,13] Maj syr[p,h] KJV NKJV RSVmg NRSVmg ESVmg NEBmg REBmg NLTmg HCSBmg NETmg

It is far more likely that ανθρωπου ("man") was changed to θεου ("God") than vice versa. Later in history, the church sought confession of Jesus' divine sonship—hence, the change from "the Son of Man" to "the Son of God" in later manuscripts (see comments on 9:38-39). Readers continue to be more comfortable with "the Son of God" than with "the Son of Man" because the term "Son of God" seems to be what is required after the verb "believe." Indeed, "the Son of Man" is never used elsewhere in John as the object of the verb "believe." (This unusualness may provide one of the reasons why the text was changed.)

In Jesus' day, it was important that people recognize him as "the Son of Man," and there are several good reasons why "Son of Man" completely suits the text. First, this passage ends with Jesus affirming his role as the judge (9:39-41), and it so happens that the title "Son of Man" is used for Jesus as the judge of all men (5:27; cf. Dan 7:13-14; Acts 17:31). Second, the Son of Man is also the one who gives eternal life (6:27), which the blind man received when he believed in Jesus. Third, since "Son of Man" was a surrogate title for "Messiah," Jesus was asking the blind man (now healed) if he believed in the Messiah—knowing full well that this confession would affirm his expulsion from the synagogue (see 9:22). Fourth, for the blind man to realize that Jesus was "the Son of Man" was for him to realize that Jesus was the revelation of God to man. This is important to chapter 9, in which we are presented with the gradual spiritual enlightenment of the blind man, culminating in this realization. The more the Pharisees questioned the man who received his sight, the clearer he became about Jesus. Their blind obstinacy augmented his clarity. At first, the man recognized him simply as "the man called Jesus" (9:11), then as "a prophet" (9:17), then as one who was "from God" and who had performed a miracle never done before (9:32-33), and then finally, when confronted by Jesus, as "the Son of Man"— the Messiah (9:35).

John 9:38-39a

TR WH NU	ὁ δὲ ἔφη· πιστεύω, κύριε· καὶ προσεκύνησεν αὐτῷ. [39]Καὶ εἶπεν ὁ Ἰησοῦς· "And he said, 'I believe, Lord.' And he worshiped him. [39] And Jesus said," 𝔓66 ℵ[2] A B D L Δ Θ Ψ Maj all
variant	omit 𝔓75 ℵ* W it[b] cop[ach2,saMS] TNIVmg NLTmg NETmg

The evidence for the omission of 9:38-39a is impressive, inasmuch as the manuscripts that do not include it are early and geographically dispersed. The three early Greek manuscripts (𝔓[75] א* W) would be impressive enough, even without the testimony of the early translations (Old Latin and Coptic).

It is usually argued that the omission was the result of a transcriptional error, but there is nothing in the text to suggest the usual kinds of error, such as homoeoteleuton or homoeoarchton. And even if it was an error, how could this have occurred in so many diverse manuscripts? Furthermore, εφη ("I said") is rarely used in John (only in 1:23), and the exact verbal form πιστευω ("I believe") occurs nowhere else in John (except in the singular reading of 𝔓[66] in 11:27). These factors point to a non-Johannine origin.

If John did not write these words, why were they added? Brown (1966, 380-381) suggests that "the words were an addition stemming from the association of John 9 with the baptismal liturgy and catechesis." He then elaborates: "When the catechumens passed their examinations and were judged worthy of Baptism, lessons from the OT concerning cleansing water were read to them. Then came the solemn opening of the Gospel book and the reading of John 9, with the confession of the blind man, 'I do believe, Lord' (38), serving as the climax. . . . After this the catechumens recited the creed." To affirm Brown, it could be pointed out that many Christian teachers in the early church (such as Irenaeus, Ambrose, and Augustine) taught that the blind man's action of "washing at the pool of Siloam" depicted baptism. Furthermore, Beasley-Murray (1987, 151) notes that in early lectionary usage the lesson extended from 9:1 to 9:38, and that 9:38 constituted the confession made at baptism.

Porter (1967, 387-394) argues that a similar interpolation found its way into Acts 8:37, which is clearly a baptismal confession inserted into the text. Prior to his baptism, the Ethiopian eunuch says: "I believe that Jesus Christ is the Son of God." But these words are not found in any of the early manuscripts (see comments on Acts 8:37). The same kind of interpolation found its way into John 9, but at a very early date, for it is present in 𝔓[66], a second-century manuscript. Interestingly, several second-century depictions in Roman catacombs about baptism include the blind man's washing at the pool of Siloam. Therefore, it is not unlikely that certain manuscripts of the Gospel of John were affected by this addition by the middle of the second century, if not earlier. Thus, this passage is a prime example of how the New Testament text was affected by ecclesiastical practices such as baptismal confession.

Without this portion, the text in 9:35-39 reads as follows:

> [35] Jesus heard that they threw him out. He found him and said, "Do you believe in the Son of Man?" [36] The man replied, "And who is he, sir, that I might believe in him?"
> [37] Jesus answered, "You have seen him and he is the one speaking with you. [39b] I came into the world to bring judgment—so that those who don't see could see and that those who see would become blind."

The text, without 9:38-39a, presents a continuous statement from Jesus' lips. However, it does not show how the blind man responded to Jesus' question. Of course, this is disappointing for the reader and could very likely be the prime factor that motivated scribes or redactors to insert the addition and thereby fill the gap. The reader wants to know if the blind man became a believer. Indeed, he did, but this is not readily apparent in the shorter text. Yet in saying that "those who don't see could see," Jesus was implying that the blind man had come to see that Jesus was the Messiah (see discussion on 9:35 above and see Comfort 2005, 339).

Having argued for the shorter reading, it is disappointing to observe that not one English version has adopted it. The NET translators were inclined to do so (see note in NET), but they decided to keep the verses in the text. Its omission is noted in NLT and TNIV.

John 10:7

All Greek manuscripts but one ($\mathfrak{P}^{75}$) read εγω ειμι η θυρα των προβατων ("I am the gate for the sheep"). The reader, however, would have expected Jesus to say here, ο ποιμην των προβατων ("the shepherd of the sheep"), which is the reading in $\mathfrak{P}^{75}$ and a few Coptic manuscripts. Thus, we see here the scribe of $\mathfrak{P}^{75}$ breaking his rigid pattern of copying his exemplar verbatim—unless, of course, he thought his predecessor had made a mistake. If not, we see here a "thinking" scribe who considered it odd for Jesus, in a parable about him being the shepherd of the sheep, to say "I am the gate," rather than "I am the shepherd."

Jesus thought it first necessary to explain the symbolic meaning of "the gate" (mentioned in 10:2a) before identifying the "shepherd of the sheep" (mentioned in10:2b). The meaning of "the gate for the sheep" is expounded in 10:7-10, and the meaning of "the shepherd of the sheep" in 10:11-18. The gate represents the "messiahship"—i.e., the office of the Messiah. Only one person could qualify for entering into that position. As the gate for the sheep, Jesus was the one uniquely qualified to fulfill the role of Messiah, and he is the way to salvation (10:9; cf. 14:6).

John 10:8

TR WH NU	πάντες ὅσοι ἦλθον [πρὸ ἐμοῦ] κλέπται εἰσὶν καὶ λῃσταί "all who came before me are thieves and bandits (revolutionaries)" $\mathfrak{P}^{66}$ ℵ² A B D L W Ψ f¹³ 33 syr^h** all
variant	παντες οσοι ηλθον κλεπται εισιν και λησται "all who came are thieves and bandits (revolutionaries)" $\mathfrak{P}^{45vid}$ $\mathfrak{P}^{75}$ ℵ* Γ Δ Maj it syr^s,p cop Augustine NKJVmg NJBmg NLTmg HCSBmg

The words προ εμου ("before me") may not have been written by John because they are not present in $\mathfrak{P}^{45vid}$ $\mathfrak{P}^{75}$ ℵ* and several other witnesses. On one hand, it can be argued that these words were added (in some manuscripts before the verb and in others after it) in an attempt to clarify an otherwise mysterious statement: "All who came are thieves and bandits." On the other hand, it can be argued that the words προ εμου were dropped "in order to lessen the possibility of taking the passage as a blanket condemnation of all Old Testament worthies" (TCGNT), or they were deleted because they were considered superfluous (the scribe of $\mathfrak{P}^{45}$ is well known for such deletions). But the statement was probably not directed at OT saints and prophets—rather, at those who came on the scene pretending to be the Christ (see 5:43). The emphasis is on the word ηλθον—to come as if one were the Christ. All such pretenders were actually thieves and bandits (or more likely, "revolutionaries" in this context). Such terms could depict evil Jewish religious leaders (see Matt 23:13) or false messiahs, especially those posing as revolutionaries against Rome (see Matt 24:5). But the sheep did not listen to them because none of them possessed the authentic voice of the Shepherd.

John 10:11

According to $\mathfrak{P}^{66}$ $\mathfrak{P}^{75}$ ℵ^c A B L W, the text says the shepherd την ψυχην αυτου τιθησιν ("lays down his life"). A variant in $\mathfrak{P}^{45}$ ℵ* D says την ψυχην αυτου διδωσιν ("gives his life"). Four times in this passage Jesus says that he would sacrifice his life for the sheep (10:11, 15, 17, 18). According to the imagery in this chapter, this statement indicates that the true shepherd would risk his life to save his sheep from the wolf. By saying this, Jesus was alluding to his substitutionary death, in which he would sacrifice his soul, his life (ψυχη), so that the sheep might enjoy the abundant, divine life. Isaiah 53:10 says the Messiah would offer "his soul as a sacrifice for sins." It is possible that John always used the verb τιθησιν to describe this heroic act, but the manuscript evidence in this verse (as well as 10:15—see next note) displays two verbs— τιθησιν ("lays down") and διδωσιν ("gives"). Since John was fond of using synonyms, perhaps he used διδωσιν in 10:11 and 15, then τιθησιν in 10:17 and 18, to describe the same act of giving one's life for the sake of others. If so, then certain scribes made the verbs uniform; if not, then other scribes created the synonyms themselves for the sake of variety. (See note on 10:15.)

John 10:15

As was discussed in the note on 10:11, two verbs were used to indicate Jesus' act of sacrificing his life. 𝔓45 𝔓66 ℵ* D W read διδωμι; ℵc A B L read τιθημι. It is difficult to determine if John wrote διδωμι ("I give [my life]") or τιθημι ("I lay down [my life]"). Quite possibly, certain copyists changed διδωμι to τιθημι because they were influenced by 10:11 (see comments on 10:11 above). However, it is equally possible that the other scribes were influenced by the expression "give [one's life]" found in the Synoptic Gospels (Matt 20:28; Mark 10:45) and therefore changed τιθημι to διδωμι. Finally, it should be said that it is difficult to determine which English version followed which reading (so also for 10:11) because both verbs can be translated in such a way as to denote sacrifice.

John 10:16

In this verse, there are two textual variants. The first pertains to the verb. WH NU read γενησονται μια ποιμνη ("they will be one flock"), based on the evidence of 𝔓45 ℵ2 B D L W Θ Ψ 33 supporting the plural verb. The verb is singular in TR—γενησεται μια ποιμνη ("there will be one flock"). This reading has excellent support: 𝔓66 𝔓75vid ℵ* A f13 Maj. 𝔓75vid is not listed in NA26/UBS3 or NA27/UBS4, but it supports the variant reading inasmuch as the four letters εται are preserved after the lacuna, and therefore the word must have been γενησεται (see *Text of Earliest MSS*, 597). As such, documentary evidence favors this verb. The testimony of 𝔓75vid in favor of the variant was not considered by the editors of the NA26/UBS3. Had it been, the twenty-fifth edition of the Nestle text (which read γενησεται) might not have been changed. But the argument for the change was based on stylistic considerations—as Metzger said, "the singular number appears to be a stylistic correction" (TCGNT). The other variant pertains to the translation of ποιμνη. There is no textual support for the rendering "fold" in the KJV translation, "there shall be one fold, and one shepherd." All the manuscripts read ποιμνη ("flock"). The error goes back to Jerome's Latin Vulgate translation.

John 10:18

TR NU οὐδεὶς αἴρει αὐτὴν ἀπ' ἐμοῦ
"no one takes it [my life] from me"
𝔓66 ℵ2 A D L W Δ Θ Ψ f1,13 Maj
KJV NKJV RSV NRSV ESV NASBmg NIV TNIV REB NJB NAB NLT HCSB NET

variant/WH ουδεις ηρεν αυτην απ εμου
"no one took it [my life] from me"
𝔓45 ℵ* B
NRSVmg NASB NEB NLTmg

The present tense αιρει was selected for the text of NA26/UBS3 (the previous editions of the Nestle text read ηρεν); this accords with the other present tense verbs in this sentence. However, John often used the proleptic aorist (in this verse ηρεν) when Jesus spoke about the certainty of significant, future events in his life—especially his death and resurrection (see 13:31-32), as in this case. Thus, it is possible that ηρεν was harmonized to the present to better suit the context.

John 10:29

WH NU ὁ πατήρ μου ὃ δέδωκεν μοι πάντων μεῖζον ἐστιν
"that which my Father has given me is greater than all"
B* (it) cop^bo
RSVmg NRSV ESVmg NASBmg NIVmg NEBmg REBmg NJBmg NABmg NLTmg

variant 1/TR ο πατηρ μου ος δεδωκεν μοι μειζων παντων εστιν
"my Father who has given them to me is greater than all"
𝔓66c (𝔓66* 𝔓75vid εδωκεν) f1,13 33 Maj
KJV NKJV RSV NRSVmg ESV NASB NIV TNIV NEB REB NAB NLT HCSB NET

variant 2 ο πατηρ μου ο δεδωκεν μοι παντων μειζων εστιν
"my Father, as to that which he has given me, is greater than all"
ℵ (D) L W Ψ
RSVmg NEBmg NJB NABmg NLTmg

𝔓75 clearly reads ὃς (with even a rough breathing mark over the word), but deterioration has marred the word μειζων/μειζον (see *Text of Earliest MSS*, 597). Perhaps this lack is why neither NA27 nor UBS4 cite 𝔓75 for this set of variants.

WH NU has a combination of the neuter relative pronoun ο and neuter μειζον; the first variant reading comes from a combination of the masculine relative pronoun ος and masculine μειζων; the second variant from ο and μειζων. (Other variants have ος with μειζον.) Of all the readings, the first variant makes the most sense and seems to be characteristically Johannine (i.e., the Son often spoke of the Father as the one who had given various things to him—see 5:26-27; 6:37, 39; 17:2). However, the simplicity of this reading (as compared to the others) has caused it to be suspect—what scribe would have changed a simple, direct reading to a very difficult one? Thus, it is quite possible that John wrote this verse with the combination ο and μειζον. Elsewhere in his gospel, John used the neuter singular to designate the corporate entity of believers (which encompasses all Christians as one unit) which was given to him as a gift from the Father (see 6:37, 39; 17:2, 24). Given the context of John 10, Jesus would be saying that this one corporate entity (which could be called the church), which was given to the Son by the Father and was under the protective care of the Father's hand and the Son's hand, would be invincible to the attack of the enemy (see 10:1, 5, 8, 10, 12) and therefore would be greater than all (i.e., greater than all the enemies mentioned in John 10). The second variant reading noted above seems to be impossible Greek (so Metzger, TCGNT), but some scholars favor it (Birdsall 1960; Barrett 1978, 381-382) and translators have made sense of it as, "My Father, as to that which he has given me, is greater than all" (see NJB; see also RSVmg NIVmg NEBmg REBmg NABmg NLTmg). But most English versions go with the easier-to-read variant, as in TR.

John 10:33

The scribe of 𝔓[66] wrote συ ανθρωπος ων ποιεις σεαυτον τον θεον, which has the effect of saying, "you, being human, make yourself the very God." This is the only manuscript to have a definite article before θεον—the article giving the force of personalization. Without the article, the rendering is "you being human make yourself divine" or "you being human make yourself deity." The article was then deleted, either by the scribe himself or a second corrector (see *Text of Earliest MSS*, 428).

John 10:34

TR WH NU οὐκ ἔστιν γεγραμμένον ἐν τῷ νόμῳ ὑμῶν;
"Is it not written in your law?"
𝔓[66] 𝔓[75] ℵ[2] A B L W f[1,13] 33 cop Maj
all

variant ουκ εστιν γεγραμμενον εν τω νομω;
"Is it not written in the law?"
𝔓[45] ℵ* D Θ it
NRSVmg HCSBmg

Scribes must have found it difficult that Jesus, when speaking to the Jews, spoke of the Scriptures as "your law," not "our law" or simply "the law." Hence, they dropped the pronoun υμων ("your")—a noted tendency for the scribe of 𝔓[45]. The inclusion of the pronoun has good support from the manuscripts and accords with Johannine style (8:17).

John 10:35

As is typical in 𝔓[45], this verse is significantly shorter than in all other manuscripts: ει εκειvους ειπεν θεους, και ου δυναται λυθηναι ("if he [God] called those ones 'gods'—and it [= the law] cannot be broken"). The pruning was purposeful, not accidental, trimming off any excess that might distract from Jesus' main proposition: If God calls mortals "gods," then Jesus can call himself the Son of God because he is heavenly.

John 10:38

WH NU ἵνα γνῶτε καὶ γινώσκητε ὅτι ἐν ἐμοὶ ὁ πατὴρ καγὼ ἐν τῷ πατρί
"that you may know and continue to know that the Father is in me and I in the Father"
𝔓[45] 𝔓[66] 𝔓[75] B L W Θ f[1] 33 cop
RSV NRSV ESV NASB NIV TNIV NEB REB NJB (NAB) NLT HCSB NET

variant 1/TR ινα γνωτε και πιστευσητε οτι εν εμοι ο πατηρ καγω εν τω πατρι
"that you may know and you may believe that the Father is in me and I in the Father"
(ℵ πιστευητε) A Ψ f[13] Maj
KJV NKJV NRSVmg HCSBmg

variant 2 ινα γνωτε οτι εν εμοι ο πατηρ καγω εν τω πατρι
"that you may know that the Father is in me and I in the Father"
D it[a,b,c,d,e] syr[s]
none

According to excellent documentary support (the four earliest manuscripts), the verse contains the Greek word γινωσκω twice, in two tenses: aorist and present, suggesting inceptive knowledge and continuous knowledge. In certain manuscripts it was changed to πιστευσητε for the sake of immediate conformity; in other manuscripts it was dropped because the scribes thought it was redundant.

John 11:2

In keeping with Jesus' prediction (Matt 26:13), Mary was well known in the Christian community because of her display of love and devotion to Christ (Matt 26:6-13; Mark 14:3-9). Therefore, John identified her with this event even before he described it (12:1-7): "And Mary was the one who anointed the Lord with perfume and wiped his feet with her hair; it was her brother Lazarus who was sick." John's original readers would have known of this woman and of the event. But the scribe of 𝔓[45] (as well as subsequent translators—it[e] syr[p,s] cop) wanted to help the readers of his own generation with this identification; so he added a deictic pronoun and an article for added specificity: αυτη η Μαριαμ ("this same Mary").

John 11:25

TR WH NU ἐγώ εἰμι ἡ ἀνάστασις καὶ ἡ ζωή
"I am the resurrection and the life."
𝔓[66] 𝔓[75] ℵ A B C D L W Δ Θ 0250 f[1,13] 33 cop
KJV NKJV RSV NRSV ESV NASB NIV TNIV NEB REB NJBmg NAB NLT HCSB NET

variant εγω ειμι η αναστασις
"I am the resurrection"
𝔓[45] it[l] syr[s] Cyprian
RSVmg NRSVmg ESVmg NEBmg REBmg NJB NLTmg

Though it is usually argued that scribes tended to expand the text rather than shorten it, this argument does not generally apply to the early period of textual transmission. The scribe of 𝔓[45], whose proclivity for excision is well known, abbreviated Jesus' self-declaration. The testimony of the two other versions and Cyprian in favor of the shorter reading is overpowered by the support for the longer reading. Nonetheless, the shorter text was adopted by NJB and noted in several versions.

Both expressions ("resurrection" and "life") are necessary to complete Jesus' self-affirmation. In context, Jesus was speaking with Martha about how he would raise Lazarus from the dead (11:23). But Martha thought Jesus was speaking of an eschatological event—the resurrection of the dead at the end of the age (11:24). Jesus revealed that he, a person, is the resurrection and the life. Life that is truly life (1 Tim 6:19) is by its very nature resurrection-life because it can stand the trial of death. Only one kind of life—the life of God (Eph 4:18), the indissoluble life (Heb 7:16), designated ζωη in the NT—is truly life. All else that is called "life" eventually dies. Jesus is this life; therefore, he is also the resurrection (cf. Rev 1:18). Thus, in making the statement εγω ειμι η αναστασις και η ζωη, he was saying "I am the resurrection because I am the life." Thus, both expressions are necessary to complete Jesus' self-declaration.

John 11:33

The original scribe of 𝔓[66] wrote εβριμησατο τω πνευματι και εταραξεν εαυτον ("he was agitated in [or, by] the spirit and troubled in himself"). This was corrected by the diorthotes (𝔓[66c2]) to read εταραχθη τω πνευματι ως εμβριμωμενος ("he was troubled in [or, by] the spirit as if agitated") (see *Text of Earliest MSS,* 432). This is also the reading in 𝔓[45vid] D and some other witnesses. The correction undoubtedly represents an attempt to soften the statement about Jesus' agitation and anger. Indeed, the Greek word ενεβριμησατο (also used in 11:38) is consistently used in the Septuagint and NT to express anger or agitation (see Lam 2:6; Dan 11:30 LXX; Matt 9:30; Mark 1:43; 14:5). Jesus may have been angered and agitated by the mourners' excessive sorrow, Martha's lack of understanding, Mary's faithlessness, the general unbelief that surrounded him, and the reality of death.

John 11:45-46

TR NU	θεασάμενοι ἃ ἐποίησεν ἐπίστευσαν εἰς αὐτόν "seeing the things he did, they believed in him" 𝔓[6] (𝔓[45]) ℵ A* L W Θ Ψ 0250 f[13] 33 Maj KJV NKJV NAB NET
variant 1	θεασαμενοι οσα εποιησεν επιστευσαν εις αυτον "seeing whatever he did, they believed in him" (𝔓[66c2]) 0141 none
variant 2/WH	θεασαμενοι ὃ εποιησεν επιστευσαν εις αυτον "seeing what he did, they believed in him" (𝔓[66*]) A[c] B C (D) RSV NRSV ESV NASB NIV TNIV NEB REB NJB NLT HCSB

It should be first noted that 𝔓[45] 𝔓[66] and D have the participle εωρακοτες instead of θεασαμενοι. The textual variants here pertain to the relative pronoun and thereby present the dilemma: Did the people believe in Jesus based on one sign (the raising of Lazarus) or many signs? The textual evidence is divided, as are the internal arguments. It could be argued that the scribes conformed 11:45 to 11:46, which reads α in most ancient manuscripts. However, it could be argued just as easily that the scribes of 𝔓[66*] et al. changed the plural to the singular because the crowd saw Jesus perform only one sign—i.e., the raising of Lazarus. NU aligns with TR here, followed by KJV and NKJV, but not followed by any modern version except the NAB. In 11:46 α εποιησεν was changed again to ο εποιησεν in C and D, and to οσα εποιησεν in A and f[13].

John 11:50

WH NU	συμφέρει ὑμῖν ἵνα εἷς ἄνθρωπος ἀποθάνῃ ὑπὲρ τοῦ λαοῦ "it is better for you that one man should die on behalf of the people" 𝔓[45] 𝔓[66] B D L NKJVmg RSV NRSV ESV NASB NIV TNIV NEB REB NJB NAB NLT HCSB NET

variant 1/TR σῠμφερει ημιν ινα εις ανθρωπος αποθανη υπερ λαου
"it is better for us that one man should die on behalf of the people"
A W Θ Ψ 0250 f[1,13] 33 Maj Origen
KJV NKJV HCSBmg

variant 2 συμφερει ινα εις ανθρωπος αποθανη υπερ λαου
"it is better that one man should die on behalf of the people"
ℵ cop[sa,bo]
none

It seems odd that Caiaphas, the high priest, would address the Sanhedrin as if he were an outsider—telling them, "it is better for you that one man should die." This reading, therefore, was changed by substituting ημιν ("us") for υμιν ("you") or dropping the pronoun completely. However, the reading of the text is poignant, for in it we do, in fact, see that Caiaphas was an outsider, for he had been appointed by the Romans to be the high priest and therefore was considered by many Jews not to be the true high priest. As is typical, KJV and NKJV follow TR, while modern versions follow WH NU.

John 11:54

Based on the evidence of 𝔓66* 𝔓75 ℵ B L W, NU has the verb εμεινεν ("he [Jesus] remained"). Other manuscripts (𝔓45 𝔓66c A D Θ Ψ 0250 f[1,13] Maj) read διετριβεν ("he [Jesus] spent time with [them]"). Because the manuscript evidence is so evenly divided, it is very difficult to determine which verb John wrote. (The fact that 𝔓66 was corrected from εμεινεν to διετριβεν shows that both readings existed in the second century.) Since εμεινεν (from μενω) is a very common verb in John, it could be argued that the text conforms to Johannine style and is original, or it could be argued that scribes conformed the text to Johannine style and therefore it is not original. The verb διατριβω is used only one other time in John, in a similar statement concerning Jesus spending time alone with his disciples (3:22). This verb, which literally means "to wear away," suggests "passing away the hours"; whereas μενω suggests living in a dwelling place. Thus, the word διετριβεν is more conducive to companionship in wilderness solitude. Yet it could then be argued that scribes conformed 11:54 to 3:22, where the textual evidence for διετριβεν is solid.

John 12:1

WH NU ὅπου ἦν Λάζαρος, ὃν ἤγειρεν ἐκ νεκρῶν Ἰησοῦς
"where Lazarus was, whom Jesus had raised from the dead"
ℵ B L W it[a,c,e] syr[p] cop[sa]
NKJVmg RSV NRSV ESV NASB NIV TNIV NEB REB NJB NAB NLT HCSB NET

variant/TR οπου ην Λαζαρος ο τεθνηκως ον ηγειρεν εκ νεκρων Ιησους
"where Lazarus, the dead one, was, whom Jesus had raised from the dead"
𝔓66 A D Θ Ψ 0217[vid] 0250 f[1,13] 33 Maj it[b,d] syr[s,h] cop[ac]
KJV NKJV HCSBmg

Since the documentary evidence is evenly divided between the two readings, we need to consider internal factors. It seems more likely that the expression ο τεθνηκως ("the dead one") was deleted rather than added, because it would have seemed unnecessary in light of the following statement "whom he raised from the dead." In the Gospels those people who receive a miracle from Jesus are frequently identified by their pre-healed condition even after the miracle has taken place. For example, the man who was healed of his blindness is still called "the blind man" (9:17); and Simon, who hosted the meal at Bethany and was evidently healed of leprosy, is still called "Simon the leper" (Mark 14:3).

John 12:4

WH NU Ιουδας ο Ισκαριωτης
"Judas Iscariot"
𝔓66 𝔓75vid ℵ B L W 33
RSV NRSV ESV NASB NIV TNIV NEB REB NJB NAB NLT HCSB NET

variant 1/TR Ιουδας Σιμωνος Ισκαριωτης
"Judas son of Simon Iscariot"
A Θ (Ψ) f1,13 Maj
KJV NKJV

variant 2 Ιουδας απο Καρυωτου
"Judas from Kerioth"
D itd
none

The same kind of variations on Judas's name occur in 6:71 (see comments there).

John 12:7

According to the best manuscript evidence, this verse reads, Αφες αυτην, ινα εις την ημεραν του ενταφιασμου μου τηρηση αυτο ("Leave her alone, so that she might keep it for the day of my burial"). The Greek text is difficult. Something needs to be supplied before the ινα clause. The NRSV adds "she bought it," and the NIV adds "it was intended." Confronted with the difficulty of the ινα clause, some scribes (A f1,13 Maj) dropped the word ινα and switched to the perfect tense τετηρεκεν, yielding the translation, "Let her alone; she has kept this for the day of my burial" (so TR and NKJV).

John 12:11

The best textual evidence (𝔓75 ℵ A B C) states πολλοι δι αυτον υπηγον των Ιουδαιων και επιστευον εις τον Ιησουν, which can be rendered "because of him [Lazarus], many of the Jews left and were believing in Jesus" or "because of him [Lazarus], many left the Jews and were believing in Jesus" (taken as a partitive genitive). With either rendering, the statement means that many Jews were "going over" or "going away" (i.e., leaving their allegiance to Judaism and to the Jewish religious leaders) and "were believing in Jesus" (or, "were beginning to put their faith in him"). But this abandonment of Judaism for Jesus is completely absent in 𝔓66 (which lacks υπηγον και—"went away and"). Why? It would be tempting to answer that it was never part of John's gospel and that it was added later in an attempt to emphasize the split between Judaism and Christianity. But the words are present in 𝔓75, which is not much older than 𝔓66; therefore, this cannot be stated with absolute certainty. So, if the words were in the exemplar for 𝔓66, it is possible that the scribe deleted them because he thought his readers would not understand the expression υπηγον ("were leaving"). However, it must be noted that the corrector of 𝔓66 (who normally supplied accidental deletions) had no problem with this omission, thereby leaving the possibility that these words were not in their exemplars.

John 12:17

TR WH NU ἐμαρτύρει οὖν ὁ ὄχλος ὁ ὢν μετ' αὐτοῦ ὅτε τὸν Λάζαρον ἐφώνησεν ἐκ τοῦ μνημείου καὶ ἤγειρεν αὐτὸν ἐκ νεκρῶν.
"So the crowd that had been with him when he called Lazarus out of the tomb and raised him from the dead continued to testify."
א A B W Δ Θ Ψ 0250 f[1,13] Maj
KJV NKJV RSV NRSV ESV NASB NIVmg TNIV NEB REB NJB NAB NLT HCSB NET

variant εμαρτυρει ουν ο οχλος ο ων μετ αυτου οτι τον Λαζαρον εφωνησεν εκ του μνημειου και ηγειρεν αυτον εκ νεκρων
"So the crowd that had been with him continued to testify that he called Lazarus out of the tomb and raised him from the dead."
𝔓[66] D L it syr[p] cop
NRSVmg NIV HCSBmg

Since there is only a one-letter difference between the two readings: οτε ("when")/οτι ("that"), scribal error could account for either reading. If the change was intentional, the variant probably arose as "an attempt to smooth out the difficulty concerning the mention of the various crowds in this narrative" (Newman and Nida 1980, 400-401). The crowd mentioned in this verse was composed of people who had witnessed Lazarus's resurrection. The crowd mentioned in the next verse was composed of both those who had witnessed the resurrection and those who had heard about it from the eyewitnesses. Nearly all the English versions follow the TR WH NU reading, with two (NRSV and HCSB) noting the variant. The TNIV diverged from the NIV.

John 12:28

In some later manuscripts Jesus' prayer here was conformed to the prayer he made in chapter 17. In 12:28 Jesus begins by saying to the Father, δοξασον σου το ονομα ("glorify your name"). This was harmonized in L X f[1,13] to δοξασον σου τον υιον ("glorify your son"), taken from 17:1. D adds to this from 17:5, εν τη δοξη η ειχον παρα σοι προ του τον κοσμον γενεσθαι ("with the glory I had with you before the world was").

John 12:32

TR WH NU πάντας ἑλκύσω πρὸς ἐμαυτόν
"I will draw all [people] to myself"
𝔓[75vid] א[2] A B L W (Δ) Θ Ψ 0250 f[1,13]
all

variant παντα ελκυσω προς εμαυτον
"I will draw every [person or everything] to myself"
𝔓[66] א* (D)
NRSVmg

An analysis of the length of the lacuna in 𝔓[75] indicates that it reads παντας (see *Text of Earliest MSS,* 604). The TR WH NU reading, παντας, is accusative plural masculine ("all men"), whereas the variant, παντα, could be accusative singular masculine ("every man") or accusative plural neuter ("everything"). Because of this ambiguity, scribes may have added a *sigma* to παντα. In either case, it seems that Jesus had people in mind when he spoke of drawing all to himself by being lifted up on the cross. Of course, this drawing could suggest a kind of universal reconciliation of all things, as in Col 1:20. But the major focus of the metaphor in context is that Jesus would attract all kinds of people (Jews and Gentiles) to himself by his death on the cross and subsequent glorification.

John 12:34

𝔓[75] and 2211 omit τις εστιν ουτος ο υιος του ανθρωπου; ("who is this Son of Man?")—probably due to homoeoteleuton (the previous sentence ends with ο υιος του ανθρωπου).

John 12:41

WH NU — ταῦτα εἶπεν 'Ησαίας ὅτι εἶδεν τὴν δόξαν αὐτοῦ
"Isaiah said these things because he saw his glory"
𝔓[66] 𝔓[75] א A B L Θ Ψ 33 it[e] cop
NKJVmg RSV NRSV ESV NASB NIV TNIV NEB REB NJB NAB NLT HCSB NET

variant/TR — ταυτα ειπεν Ησαιας οτε ειδεν την δοξαν αυτου
"Isaiah said these things when he saw his glory"
D f[13] Maj syr Eusebius
KJV NKJV NRSVmg NEBmg NJBmg HCSBmg

The textual variation in this verse involves a one-letter difference: οτι ("because")/οτε ("when"). The WH NU reading, which has the best external support, is likely the one John wrote. Isaiah had seen the Lord of glory, and because of his vision Isaiah predicted the blindness to come (see Isa 6:1-10). Later scribes obfuscated the causal (οτι) by using the temporal (οτε), which makes for an easier reading needing little explanation.

John 13:2a

WH NU — καὶ δείπνου γινομένου
"and supper happening" (= "and during supper")
א* B L W Ψ
NKJVmg RSV NRSV ESV NASB NIV TNIV NEB REB NJB NAB NLT HCSB NET

variant/TR — και δειπνου γενομενου
"and supper having happened" (= "and after supper")
𝔓[66] א[2] A D Θ f[1,13] Maj
KJV NKJV

In the beginning of this verse there is a significant textual variant, which involves a single letter in the Greek (*iota/epsilon*): γινομενου/γενομενου. Unless the variant reading is understood as an ingressive aorist ("supper having been served"), the statement contradicts the context, which clearly indicates that the supper was in progress (13:26, 30). Since scribes would have wanted to make this absolutely clear, it seems likely that the more difficult γενομενου was changed to γινομενου, rather than vice versa.

John 13:2b

WH NU τοῦ διαβόλου ἤδη βεβληκότος εἰς τὴν καρδίαν ἵνα παραδοῖ αὐτὸν Ἰούδας

"the devil already had it in his heart [i.e., had resolved] that Judas would betray him [Jesus]"

($\mathfrak{P}^{66}$ ℵ[2] L W Ψ 070 παραδω) ℵ B

NJBmg NLT

variant/TR του διαβολου ηδη βεβληκοτος εις την καρδιαν ινα παραδω αυτον Ιουδα

"the devil had already put it into the heart of Judas to betray him [Jesus]"

A Θ $f^{1,13}$ 33 Maj

KJV NKJV RSV NRSV ESV NASB NIV TNIV NEB REB NJB NAB NLTmg HCSB

Ιουδας is nominative in the earliest and best manuscripts, and genitive (Ιουδα) in later and inferior manuscripts. The change to the genitive was intended to show that it was Judas's heart, not the devil's heart, that was affected with the satanic design. But according to the best manuscript evidence, this verse indicates that the devil decided in his heart to instigate the actual events of betrayal at that moment. Judas had already been in league with the devil and was ready to do his bidding (see 6:70-71). This idea is conveyed in NLT and NJBmg; the rest of the English versions follow the easier reading, which has inferior support.

John 13:2c

NU, following L Ψ 070, reads Ιουδας Σιμωνος Ισκαριωτου ("Judas, son of Simon Iscariot"). WH, supported by $\mathfrak{P}^{66}$ $\mathfrak{P}^{75vid}$ ℵ B, reads Ιουδας Σιμωνος Ισκαριωτης ("Judas, son of Simon Iscariot"). $\mathfrak{P}^{75vid}$ is cited in UBS[4] but not in NA[27]. We have no way to verify this reading because this leaf of $\mathfrak{P}^{75}$, initially stuck to the cover of the codex, has not yet been published. TR, supported by A Θ f^1 33 Maj, reads Ιουδα Σιμωνος Ισκαριωτου ("Judas Iscariot, son of Simon"—so KJV).

John 13:5

The scribe of $\mathfrak{P}^{66}$ added some descriptive color to his text by changing the generic word νιπτηρα ("basin") to the specific ποδονιπτηρα ("foot pan"). The νιπτηρα was used for all kinds of washing; the ποδονιπτηρα was used specifically to describe a foot pan or basin for foot washing. The latter word was in existence as early as the third century B.C., spelled as ποδανιπτηρ (BDAG 838). The spelling used by the scribe of $\mathfrak{P}^{66}$ is a later form, appearing in works in the first to third centuries A.D. (LSJ 1426).

John 13:10

WH NU ὁ λελουμένος οὐκ ἔχει χρείαν εἰ μὴ τοὺς πόδας νίψασθαι

"the one having been bathed has no need except to wash the feet [= needs only to wash the feet]"

B C* (L) W Ψ f^{13} ($\mathfrak{P}^{66}$ Θ $syr^{s,p}$ add μονον [only] after ποδας)

RSV NRSV ESV NASB NIV TNIV NEBmg REBmg NJBmg NLT HCSB NET

variant 1 ο λελουμενος ουκ εχει χρειαν νιψασθαι
"the one having been bathed does not need to wash"
א Origen
RSVmg NRSVmg ESVmg NEB REB NJB NAB NLTmg

variant 2 ο λελουμενος ου χρειαν εχει την κεφαλην νιψασθαι ει μη τους ποδας μονον
"the one being bathed does not need to wash the head, only the feet"
D
none

variant 3/TR ο λελουμενος ου χρειαν εχει η τους ποδας νιψασθαι
"the one being bathed has no [other] need than to wash the feet"
(𝔓[75] A ουκ εχει χρειαν) C[3] Δ Maj
KJV NKJV

The reading for 𝔓[75] is cited in both NA[27] and UBS[4], and not in previous editions. This reading cannot be verified, however, because this leaf of 𝔓[75], initially stuck to the cover of the codex, has not yet been published. The first variant is the most significant because it is the shortest reading and excludes any mention of the feet; the second variant (in D) adds the idea that the head does not need to be washed; and the third variant is only slightly different from the text. The primary focus is whether or not the expression ει μη τους ποδας ("except the feet") is part of the original writing.

If the phrase belongs to the original text, then Jesus was speaking of two kinds of bathing—the first, a bath of the whole body, and the second, a washing of the feet. In speaking to Peter, Jesus used two different Greek words (νιπτω and λουω) to convey two different kinds of washing. The Greek word νιπτω appearing in 13:5, 6, 8, and in the last part of 13:10, is used throughout the Septuagint and NT to indicate the washing of the extremities (i.e., the hands and the feet). The Greek word λουω (from which is formed the perfect participle λελουμενος in 13:10) specifically means bathing. According to the customs of those times, once a person had bathed his body, he needed only to wash his feet before partaking of a meal. In his response to Peter, Jesus used both words in order to advance a precious truth: As he who has been bathed needs only to wash his feet daily, so he who has been bathed by the Lord (through baptism or regeneration) needs only to wash himself daily (by confession or spiritual renewal) from the filth and defilement he accumulates by his contact with the world. If the Gospel originally did not include the phrase ει μη τους ποδας ("except the feet"), then Jesus was telling Peter that the initial bath was sufficient; there was no further need for cleansing. In spiritual terms, this could mean that one's regenerative cleansing is a once-and-for-all event that never need be repeated.

It is difficult to determine which position is right. Scholars have offered cogent arguments for the inclusion of the phrase and for its exclusion (see Beasley-Murray 1987, 229). The manuscript evidence favors its inclusion: 𝔓[66] 𝔓[75] B C* W. However, Origen knew of Greek manuscripts that did not include it, as is the case with א. If it was added, the addition occurred as early as the late second century (the date for 𝔓[66]). The insertion may have been generated by a scribe (or scribes) trying to explain why Jesus was giving the disciples a foot washing and not a complete bath. If it was deleted, it was done so to make things simple: The person who has been washed has no need of further cleansing.

John 13:18

WH NU — ὁ τρώγων μου τὸν ἄρτον ἐπῆρεν ἐπ᾽ ἐμὲ τὴν πτέρναν αὐτοῦ
"the one eating my bread has lifted up his heel against me"
B C L Origen
NKJVmg RSV NRSV ESV NASB NIV TNIV NJB NAB NLT HCSB NET

variant/TR — ο τρωγων μετ εμου τον αρτον επηρεν επ εμε την πτερναν αυτου
"the one eating bread with me has lifted up his heel against me"
$\mathfrak{P}^{66}$ ℵ A D W Θ Ψ f^{1,13} Maj
KJV NKJV NRSVmg NEB REB HCSBmg

The verse is a quotation from Ps 41:9 (translated from the Hebrew). Psalm 41 is a very fitting portion of Scripture for Jesus to reference regarding his betrayal because it describes how one of David's companions, perhaps Ahithophel, had turned against him. In Ps 41:9, David laments the actions of one he calls "my close friend, in whom I trusted" (NASB); but this part of the verse was not cited by Jesus because Jesus had not trusted Judas, knowing all along that Judas would betray him (see 6:64, 70-71; Matt 17:22, 23; 20:17-19). Nonetheless, Judas was in Jesus' circle and was one of those who ate bread with the Messiah. Thus, internally speaking, the variant reading makes better sense because it places the emphasis on the companionship: "he who eats bread with me," not on the bread itself. However, critics have used this against the variant reading and said that it represents a harmonization to the Septuagint, which reads ο τρωγων μετ εμου τον αρτον ("the one eating bread with me"). If so, then scribes as early as $\mathfrak{P}^{66}$ made a conscious effort to make this harmonization. If not, then the variant reading represents the original—and this is certainly possible because the NT writers often cited the Septuagint over against the Hebrew text.

John 13:24

TR NU — πυθέσθαι τίς ἂν εἴη περὶ οὗ λέγει.
"to ask who it is he was speaking about"
($\mathfrak{P}^{66c3}$ ειπεν instead of λεγει) A (D) W (Θ) f^{1,13} Maj
KJV NKJV NRSV ESV NAB NLT HCSB NET

variant/WH — και λεγει αυτω ειπε τις εστιν περι ου λεγει
"and he says to him, 'tell [us] who is the one he's speaking about'"
($\mathfrak{P}^{66*vid}$) B C L 33
RSV NASB NIV TNIV NEB REB NJB

A slight variation of the verse is found in $\mathfrak{P}^{66c3}$, which reads πυθεσθαι τις αν ειη περι ου ειπεν ("to ask who it is he spoke about"). The apparatus of NA^{27} indicates that $\mathfrak{P}^{66*}$ is illegible. Though it is very difficult to decipher, most likely it reads κ/ [= και] λεγει αυτω ειπε (see Fee 1968b, 96), which was then corrected by the second corrector (designated as $\mathfrak{P}^{66c3}$; c1 = original scribe; c2 = first corrector). As such, the reading of $\mathfrak{P}^{66*}$ agrees with the reading found in B C L 33.

The variant reading has better documentary support than TR NU, and it accords with Johannine style—nowhere else does John use the verb πυθεσθαι. Thus, it is curious why a corrector of $\mathfrak{P}^{66}$ would have adjusted this. However, this corrector was not the diorthotes but another reader who made several notations in chapter 13 for the sake of oral reading.

John 13:32

TR NU [εἰ ὁ θεὸς ἐδοξάσθη ἐν αὐτῷ]
"if God is glorified in him"
ℵ[2] A C[2] Δ Θ Ψ f[13] 33 Maj it syr[p] cop[sa] Origen
all

variant/WH omit phrase
𝔓[66] ℵ* B C* D L W syr[s,h] cop[ach]
NRSVmg NIVmg TNIVmg NEBmg REBmg NJBmg NLTmg HCSBmg

The majority of later manuscripts begin with the phrase ει ο θεος εδοξασθη εν αυτω ("if God is [lit. "was"] glorified in him"), but the phrase is not present in the earliest witnesses and in other diverse witnesses. However, many scholars think the phrase is an intrinsic part of John's original writing—and that it was omitted from many manuscripts because of homoeoteleuton or deliberate deletion of perceived redundancy (see 13:31). Indeed, its inclusion makes for a nice chiasm or step parallelism in 13:31-32 (see TCGNT). But it is difficult to explain how the omission could have occurred in so many early and diverse manuscripts. Besides, it could be argued that the words were added to create a protasis—note the late corrections in ℵ and C.

In this case, therefore, documentary evidence should be given preference over internal considerations. Barrett (1978, 450) said, "it seems inevitable to follow the majority of the early authorities and accept the short text. The longer probably owes its popularity to Origen." Thus, we see how the text was changed later in its transmission (after the end of the fourth century) due to the influence of an earlier expositor, Origen. This influence stuck, because not one modern English version has followed the shorter reading.

Given either reading, the message it conveys is not appreciably altered. Jesus looked past the cross to his coming glorification in resurrection. Anticipating his glorification, Jesus made the proleptic proclamation, "Now is [lit. "was"] the Son of Man glorified, and God is [lit. "was"] glorified in him" (13:21). In other words, Jesus viewed his glorification as an accomplished fact; and he also believed that his glorification would glorify the Father (see Comfort 2005, 340).

John 14:4

WH NU καὶ ὅπου [ἐγὼ] ὑπάγω οἴδατε τὴν ὁδόν.
"And where I go you know the way."
𝔓[66c] ℵ B C* L Q (omit εγω 𝔓[66] W) it[a] cop[bo]
RSV NRSV ESV NASB NIV TNIV NEB REB NJB NAB NLT HCSB NET

variant/TR και οπου εγω υπαγω οιδατε και την οδον οιδατε.
"And where I go you know and the way you know."
𝔓[66*] A C[3] D Θ Ψ f[1,13] Maj it syr
KJV NKJV RSVmg NRSVmg ESVmg NASBmg NEBmg REBmg HCSBmg NETmg

The shorter reading, having the best support among the manuscripts, is most likely the true reading. The copyist of 𝔓[66] first wrote the longer reading and then he himself or another scribe corrected it to the shorter one. Evidently, the corrector made the emendation according to a different exemplar. Jesus was not assuming that the disciples knew both where he was going and the way to get there. Rather, Jesus' emphasis is on the way. However, the shorter statement may have seemed too abrupt and was therefore expanded to conform to 14:5.

John 14:7

NU — εἰ ἐγνώκατε με, καὶ τὸν πατέρα μου γνώσεσθε
"if you have known me, you will know my Father also"
𝔓^{66} ℵ D* W
NRSV ESVmg NIVmg TNIV NEBmg REBmg NJB NAB NLTmg HCSB NET

variant/TR WH — ει εγνωκειτε με, και τον πατερα μου αν ηδειτε
"if you had known me, you would have known my Father also"
A B C D^{1} L Θ Ψ f^{1,13} Maj
KJV NKJV RSV NRSVmg ESV NASB NIV TNIVmg NEB REB NJBmg NLT HCSBmg NETmg

The documentary evidence is divided: Scribes opted for verbs that presented a promise of future knowledge (as is the NU reading) or that presented a reproof (as is the reading of the variant). Internal arguments can be offered for both readings (see note in NET). The English versions display this split. Many scholars defend the variant reading because it seems more likely that Jesus was reproving the disciples than promising them (see 14:9)—that is, Jesus was not promising the disciples that they would come to know the Father as they had known the Son but that they should have already known the Father as manifest in the Son. Other scholars defend the NU reading by saying that the variant is an assimilation to 8:19 and that Jesus was promising the disciples that they would know the Father even as they had come to know the Son. This view seems to be affirmed by the next statement in 14:7, "and from now on you know him and have seen him." Though exegesis of the passage depends on which reading is accepted, both readings are contextually defensible and make good sense.

John 14:14

WH NU — ἐάν τι αἰτήσητε με ἐν τῷ ὀνόματι μου
"whatever you ask me in my name"
𝔓^{66} 𝔓^{75vid} ℵ B W Δ Θ 060 f^{13} 33
NKJVmg RSVmg NRSV ESV NASB NIV TNIV NEBmg NAB NLT HCSB NET

variant/TR — εαν τι αιτησητε εν τω ονοματι μου
"whatever you ask in my name"
A D L Q Ψ
KJV NKJV RSV NRSVmg ESVmg NEB REB NJB HCSBmg

The WH NU reading has the support of the earliest manuscripts. The word με ("me") was probably omitted to bring 14:14 in conformity with 14:13. Some witnesses (X f^{1} 565 it^{b} syr^{s,pal} arm geo) omit this verse entirely. The cause of the omission could have been accidental—the eye of the scribe may have passed over the word εαν in 14:14 to εαν in 14:15. Or the omission could have been intentional inasmuch as 14:14 repeats 14:13. It would have been especially tempting in ancient versions to omit a repetitive statement. The verse must be considered part of the original work because of its excellent testimony (𝔓^{66} 𝔓^{75} ℵ A B D L W Θ it cop).

John 14:17

There are two significant textual variants in this verse. The first pertains to the pronominal reference to πνευμα, whether it is αυτον or αυτο. According to grammatical correctness, the pronoun should be the neuter αυτο, as in 𝔓^{66c} 𝔓^{75} ℵ* B D^{c}; however, in 𝔓^{66*} ℵ^{2} D* L W Ψ, the pronoun is the masculine αυτον. The masculine pronoun serves to emphasize the personality of the Spirit—namely, this Spirit of truth is the Spirit of Jesus—his invisible, spiritual presence (see discussion below).

John may have written the masculine pronoun to emphasize the Spirit's personal existence, as he did in 16:13-14, using the masculine pronoun εκεινος, when it should have been neuter. If so, grammar-conscious scribes (such as 𝔓[66c2]) changed the masculine to the neuter. If John did not write the masculine pronoun, then the scribes of 𝔓[66*] D L et al. were making an exegetical point: the Spirit is a personal being just as Jesus is.

The second significant textual difference in this verse concerns the tenses of the two verbs in the second clause:

> παρ υμιν μένει/μενεῖ και εν υμιν εσται/εστιν
> "[the Spirit of truth] abides/will abide with you and will be/is in you."

The first verb is present tense when written as μένει, and future tense when written as μενεῖ. However, many of the earliest manuscripts do not exhibit accent marks, so the tense of this verb is uncertain. The second verb in 𝔓[66c2] 𝔓[75] א A D L Q is εσται ("will be"), and in 𝔓[66*] B D* W is εστιν ("is"). There are three possible translations: (1) because he abides with you and will be in you; (2) because he will abide with you and will be in you; and (3) because he abides with you and is in you. 𝔓[66c2] 𝔓[75] א A D L Q can support the first two renderings; 𝔓[66*] B D* W can support the third rendering. It is quite significant that the second corrector to 𝔓[66] changed the verb εστιν to εσται in order to produce a different meaning (either the first or the second). (For a transcription of 𝔓[66], see *Text of Earliest MSS,* 446.)

As it stands, the documentary evidence for both readings is impressive—with the testimony of 𝔓[66c2] 𝔓[75] א offsetting that of 𝔓[66*] B D*. Therefore, it is difficult to determine the most probable reading. In context, Jesus was telling his disciples that he would send them the Spirit as the παρακλετος ("the Encourager"). Jesus added that they should know who the Paraclete is because "he abides with you and will be (or, is) in you." If the text originally had two present verbs, this statement could be understood to describe, proleptically, the twofold location of the Spirit in relationship to the believer. In other words, the Spirit is viewed in his future state as present with and in the believer. (A text with both verbs in the future tense gives the same sense.) If the text originally had a present tense verb and a future tense verb, then Jesus probably meant that the Spirit as present with Jesus (then and there) was with the disciples, and, in the future, would be in the disciples.

Notice the shift of pronouns from 14:17 to 14:18—"He [the Spirit] will be in you. . . . I [Jesus] am coming to you." This implies that Jesus through the Spirit would be coming to the disciples and indwelling them. (Note that in 14:20 Jesus says "I am in you." Compare this with 14:17 where Jesus says that the Spirit "will be in you.") When we put these statements together, it should be clear that the coming of the Paraclete is none other than the coming of the Lord in the Spirit. Several commentators have remarked on this essential truth. Morris writes, "It is true, as many commentators point out, that He [Jesus] comes in the coming of the Spirit" (1971, 651). R. E. Brown indicated that Jesus' presence after his return to the Father was fulfilled in and through the Paraclete (1970, 644).

John 15:4

NU has two present subjunctives in this verse for the verb μενω—μενη, based on the testimony of א B L. The variant reading has the aorist, μεινη, based on the testimony of 𝔓[66vid] A D Θ 0250 f[1,13] Maj. (𝔓[66] clearly shows μει[ν]η for the second verb—see *Text of Earliest MSS,* 448.) Though English versions do not bring out the distinctions, the difference in rendering is that the present tense yields this: "as the branch cannot bear fruit of itself unless it continues to abide in the vine neither can you unless you continue to abide in me." The aorist yields this: "as the branch cannot bear fruit of itself unless it begins to abide in the vine neither can you unless you begin to abide in me."

John 15:8

NU has the verb γενησθε (an aorist subjunctive—"may become") based on B D L Θ, contra the verb γενησεσθε (future indicative—"will become"), following ℵ A Ψ 33 (so Nestle[25] and WHmg). NA[27] cites 𝔓[66vid] in support of its text, but 𝔓[66] actually reads γεν[ησ]θαι (an aorist infinitive)—see *Text of Earliest MSS*, 448. The difference between text and variant is slight: "that you bear much fruit and may become my disciples" or "that you bear much fruit and will become my disciples."

John 15:25

According to NU, following the testimony of 𝔓[22vid] 𝔓[66c3vid] ℵ B D L Ψ, the phrase is εν τω νομω αυτων γεγραμμενος ("it is written in their law"). The word order differs in A Θ f[13] Maj (so TR), but does not change the meaning. The singular variant in 𝔓[66*], however, is significant, because the original scribe wrote εν τω νομω γεγραμμενος ("it is written in the law"). The scribe may have done this because he perceived Jesus naming the Scriptures as "their law" to be a pejorative statement, wherein Jesus was disassociating himself from the Jews and their Scriptures. Indeed, Jesus had previously used the same kind of language when he labeled the Scriptures as "your law" when speaking to the Jewish leaders (see 8:17 and 10:34 where other scribes deleted "your"). A second corrector (designated as "c3" in *Text of Earliest MSS*, 450; distinct from the primary corrector, designated as "c2") added αυτων ("their").

John 16:7

The scribe of 𝔓[66] omitted εαν δε πορευθω, πεμψω αυτον προς υμας ("but if I go, I will send him to you"). The corrector (𝔓[66c2]) added the missing wording in the upper margin of the page (see *Text of Earliest MSS*, 450-451). The omission could have been accidental, due to homoeoteleuton (the previous clause ends with υμας), or intentional. If the latter, the scribe saw this expression as superfluous and redundant; it hinders the syntactical flow: "I tell you the truth: it is better for you that I go away. For if I do not go away, the Comforter will not come to you; [but if I go, I will send him to you.] And when he comes, he will judge the world." Thus, the deletion, if intentional, was made for the ease of reading.

John 16:15

𝔓[66] does not include this entire verse. Because the manuscript page is mutilated on the top and bottom portions of the page and is damaged where one might expect to see an insert mark after 16:14, it cannot be determined if the corrector added this verse in one of the margins. It is possible that the entire verse was accidentally excluded due to homoeoteleuton—both 16:14 and 16:15 end with the same three words, και αναγγελει υμιν ("and announce to you"). In fact, this was what occurred in ℵ*, which was then corrected. The verse is completely absent in several Coptic Bohairic manuscripts—perhaps for the same reason. Thus, the omission is likely accidental.

John 16:21

NA^{26} indicates that 𝔓^{5vid} supports ημερα, but the transcription in *Oxyrhynchus Papyri IV* reads η ωρα. 𝔓^{5vid} was subsequently removed from the critical apparatus in NA^{27} (see Comfort 1990, 625-629).

John 16:23

TR NU — ἄν τι αἰτήσητε τὸν πατέρα ἐν τῷ ὀνόματι μου δώσει ὑμῖν
"whatever you ask the Father in my name he will give it to you"
𝔓^{22vid} A C^{3vid} D W Θ Ψ f^{13}
KJV NKJV RSV NRSV ESV NIV TNIV NEB REB NAB (NLT) HCSB NET

variant/WH — αν τι αιτησητε τον πατερα δωσει υμιν εν τω ονοματι μου
"whatever you ask the Father he will give it to you in my name"
𝔓^{5vid} ℵ B C* L Δ
NRSVmg NASB NEBmg REBmg NJB

Both readings have support from early manuscripts; however, the variant reading has the earliest collective testimony and is the harder reading. Because Jesus usually spoke of making petition to the Father in his own name (see 14:13-14; 15:16; 16:24, 26), it would have been quite natural for scribes to conform this clause to the more usual order. Furthermore, it would be difficult to imagine why so many early scribes would have rearranged the syntax to the more difficult reading. But both Metzger (TCGNT) and Tasker (1964, 428) argue that the TR NU reading is more suitable to this context that deals with praying in the Lord's name. Many ancient scribes must have thought so, too; so they made a change to produce a more readable text to an audience that had become accustomed to asking (or praying) in the name of Jesus (see Comfort 2005, 341).

John 16:26

At the end of this verse, 𝔓^{5vid} and 𝔓^{66vid} (not cited in NA^{27} but see *Text of Earliest MSS*, 452) omit περι υμων ("concerning you"). The words may have been added later in order to complete the sense. However, the sentence can stand without this prepositional phrase: "I do not say to you that I will ask the Father." What Jesus will ask is left unspecified.

John 16:27

TR NU — ἐγὼ παρὰ [τοῦ] θεοῦ ἐξῆλθον
"I came from God"
𝔓^{5} 𝔓^{66vid} ℵ^{*,2} A Θ 33 (C^{3} W f^{1,13} Maj add του before θεου)
KJV NKJV NRSV ESV NIV TNIV NEB REB NJB NAB NLT HCSB NET

variant/WH — εγω παρα του πατρος εξηλθον
"I came from the Father"
ℵ^{1} B C D L cop
RSV NRSVmg ESVmg NASB HCSBmg NETmg

𝔓^{66vid}, though not in the apparatus of NA^{27} and UBS^{4}, supports θεου (see *Text of Earliest MSS*, 452). The TR NU reading (without the article) has earlier and more diverse support than the reading with πατρος ("Father")—which was probably assimilated from the next verse or is a modification intended to make the disciples' revelation more elevated. After all, Nicodemus had believed that Jesus came "from God" (3:2), as did the man who was healed of his blindness (9:33)—when both these men had just encountered Jesus. The disciples, who had been with Jesus for three years, should have realized that Jesus was the visible manifestation of the Father (see 14:7-9). Thus, it is likely that scribes found it more natural to change θεου ("God") to πατρου ("Father").

John 16:28

NU reads εξηλθον παρα του πατρος ("I came from the Father"), following the testimony of 𝔓^{5} 𝔓^{22} ℵ A C^{2} Θ f^{1,13} Maj (so also TR). WH reads εξηλθον εκ του πατρος ("I came out from the Father"), following the testimony of B C* L Ψ. The evidence of the papyri with ℵ is slightly stronger than that of B C*, which Westcott and Hort followed.

The complete clause is lacking in a few manuscripts (D W it^{d} syr^{s}). The omission was either accidental, influenced by the phrase παρα του πατρος εξηλθον in the previous verse, or intentional because Jesus had just said the same thing in the previous verse. The documentary evidence affirms these words as belonging to the text. 𝔓^{66vid}, though not cited above because the preposition is not extant, nevertheless contains the clause (see *Text of Earliest MSS,* 452).

John 17:1

WH NU	ὁ υἱὸς δοξάσῃ σέ "the Son may glorify you" 𝔓^{60vid} 𝔓^{66vid} ℵ B C* W 0109 0301 RSV NRSV ESV NASB NEB REB NLT HCSB NETmg
variant 1	ο υιος σου δοξαση σε "your Son may glorify you" A D Θ 0250 NIV TNIV NJB NAB NET
variant 2/TR	και ο υιος σου δοξαση σε "your Son also may glorify you" C^{3} L Δ Ψ f^{13} 33 Maj KJV NKJV

The WH NU reading is supported by early and diverse testimony. The embellishments in the two variants, spawned by the first clause ("Father, glorify your Son"), are unnecessary additions. Most manuscripts have these extra words, as contained in TR and perpetuated in KJV and NKJV, as well as in other English versions.

John 17:8

Excellent testimony (𝔓^{60vid} 𝔓^{66vid} B C) supports the inclusion of the words και εγνωσαν ("and knew") in the expression, "they received them [the words] and knew truly that I came from you." These two words, however, are absent from ℵ* A D W it^{a,e} cop^{ach2,bo}, producing the rendering, "they received them [the words] in truth that I came from you." Some scholars have suggested that the words και εγνωσαν ("and knew") were dropped because scribes thought they might contradict 6:69 (Beasley-Murray 1987, 293). But 6:69 affirms that the disciples both knew and believed that Jesus was God's Holy One, so this argument seems unconvincing.

Furthermore, in 16:30 the disciples had verbalized their realization that Jesus had come from God.

John 17:11

WH NU τήρησον αὐτοὺς ἐν τῷ ὀνόματι σου ᾧ δέδωκας μοι
"keep them in your name which you have given me"
𝔓[60] 𝔓[66vid] 𝔓[107] A B C (א L W εδωκας) Δ Θ Ψ f[1,13] Maj
NKJVmg RSV NRSV ESV NASB NIV TNIV NEBmg REB NJBmg NAB NLT HCSB NET

variant/TR τηρησον αυτους εν τω ονοματι σου ους δεδωκας μοι
"keep them in your name—those whom you have given me"
D[1] cop[sa] Hesychius Jerome Augustine
KJV NKJV NRSVmg NEB REBmg NJB NLTmg

Both NA[27] and UBS[4] cite 𝔓[66vid] as reading εδωκας, but a reconstruction of the lacuna could just as easily allow for δεδωκας. 𝔓[66] shows that a corrector made an insert mark after ω δεδωκας μοι and then very likely added the phrase ινα ωσιν εν καθως ημεις on the bottom of the page, but the correction is not extant. Furthermore, 𝔓[107] can now be added in support of the reading ω δεδωκας μοι (see *Text of Earliest MSS,* 454 for 𝔓[66], 648-649 for 𝔓[107]). The variant reading aligns the phrase δεδωκας μοι ("have given me") with αυτους ("them") by changing ω to ους, thereby creating the more natural reading: "keep in your name those whom you have given me." (The same change occurred in 17:12—see note below.) But the earliest manuscripts indicate that Jesus had been given the Father's name. Westcott (1881, 243) said, "These passages [17:11-12] suggest the idea that the 'giving of the Father's name' to Christ expresses the fullness of his commission as the Incarnate Word to reveal God. . . . And all spiritual truth is gathered up in the 'name' of God, the perfect expression (for men) of what God is, which 'name' the Father gave to the Son to declare when he took man's nature upon him."

John 17:12

WH NU ἐγὼ ἐτήρουν αὐτοὺς ἐν τῷ ὀνόματι σου ᾧ δέδωκας μοι
"I was keeping them in your name which you have given me"
𝔓[66cvid] (א[2]) B (C* W εδωκας) L 33
NKJVmg RSV NRSV ESV NASB NIV TNIV NEBmg REB NJBmg NAB NLT HCSB NET

variant/TR εγω ετηρουν αυτους εν τω ονοματι σου ους δεδωκας μοι
"I was keeping them in your name—those whom you have given me"
A (C[3]) D Δ Θ Ψ f[1,13] Maj
KJV NKJV NRSVmg NEB REBmg NJB NLTmg

A note in NA[27] indicates that 𝔓[66cvid] inserts ω δεδωκας μοι, whereas a note in UBS[4] says 𝔓[66] is mutilated here. But 𝔓[66] reveals an insert mark after σου, with one partially visible superlinear letter—either an *omega* or a *delta*. Hence, it can be presumed that the correction reads ω δεδωκας μοι. The WH NU reading has early and diverse textual support (𝔓[66cvid] B C* L W). The variant appears in later manuscripts for the same reasons explained in 17:11 (see above). In both instances, TR adopted the variant reading, which has been popularized by KJV.

John 17:14-18

There are several omissions in this section among the extant manuscripts, as follows:

1. 𝔓[66*] D f[13] it syr[s] omit καθως εγω ουκ ειμι εκ του κοσμου ("as I am not of this world") in 17:14.
2. 33 cop[bo] omit all of 17:15.
3. 𝔓[66c2] 33 cop[bo] omit all of 17:16.
4. 𝔓[66] omits the second clause of 17:18—καγω απεστειλα αυτους εις τον κοσμον ("and I have sent them into the world").

If any of these omissions were theologically motivated, it could be said that the scribe of 𝔓[66] did not want Jesus saying anything about his or the disciples' relationship to this world. However, it seems more likely that the omissions were accidental. The second corrector of 𝔓[66] added the phrase καθως εγω ειμι εκ του κοσμου back into 17:14, and then this corrector (or another one) deleted all of 17:16, perhaps thinking that the original scribe had misplaced the statement (17:14b and 17:16 say nearly the same thing). The scribe of 33 and various Coptic Bohairic manuscripts must have omitted 17:15-16 due to homoeoteleuton—the endings of 17:14 and 17:16 are similar.

John 17:21

WH NU	ἵνα καὶ αὐτοὶ ἐν ἡμῖν ὦσιν "that they also may be in us" 𝔓[66vid] B C* D W it cop RSV NRSV ESV NASB NIV TNIV NEB REB NJB NAB NLT HCSBmg NET
variant/TR	ινα και αυτοι εν ημιν ἓν ωσιν "that they also may be one in us" ℵ A C[3] L Δ Θ Ψ f[1,13] Maj KJV NKJV NRSVmg HCSB

The WH NU reading has the best support and is essential for providing the full meaning of the passage. There are three requests in this verse, each beginning with the word ινα ("in order that"). The three clauses are as follows: (1) "in order that they all may be one, as you, Father, are in me and I in you"; (2) "in order that they also may be in us"; (3) "in order that the world may believe you have sent me."

All the requests are sequential: (2) depends upon (1), and (3) depends on both. In the first request, Jesus asked that all the believers may be one. This all-encompassing petition includes all the believers throughout time. Then the first request is qualified by an astounding fact: The oneness among the believers is to be as the co-inherent oneness of the Father and the Son. In other words, as the Father and Son's oneness is that of mutual indwelling (10:30, 38; 14:9-11), so the believers are to have oneness with another by virtue of the mutual indwelling between each believer and the triune God. The variant reading (found in TR) obscures this request by simply becoming another request for oneness.

John 17:24

WH NU read ο δεδωκας μοι ("that which you have given me"), with the support of 𝔓[60] ℵ B D W it[d] syr[s] cop[bo]. The variant reading in TR is ους δεδωκας μοι ("those whom you have given me"), with the support of A C L Δ (Θ) Ψ f[1,13] Maj syr[p] cop[sa].

The WH NU reading has the best documentary support and is the reading that was most likely changed because it is more difficult. The neuter ο designates all the believers as the one collective entity given as a gift to Jesus from the Father; it is used by John in 6:37, 39; 10:29; and 17:2. This is the same group referred to in 17:2; it includes all the ones who have received and will receive the gift of eternal life. This corporate whole is the universal church, the one body composed of many members. The variant in later manuscripts makes for easier reading (which may also be the motivation for making this the reading in all English versions), but in so doing it obscures the corporate emphasis.

John 18:5

TR WH NU have Jesus responding with the simple εγω ειμι ("I am") when asked by those coming to arrest him if he was Jesus the Nazarene. This reading has the testimony of 𝔓[60] D syr[s,pal] cop[bo] Origen. However, many other manuscripts add ο Ιησους ("Jesus") either before or after εγω ειμι—א A B C L W Δ Θ Ψ f[1,13] 33 Maj it syr[p,h] cop[sa,ach2]. The addition seems to be the work of scribes attempting to clarify Jesus' self-identification: "I am Jesus." But the bare statement εγω ειμι affirms at once Jesus' human and divine identity: "I am [the Nazarene] you are seeking and I am that I am." The reaction Jesus' answer produced in those who had come to arrest him indicates that Jesus' words must have been charged with some kind of supernatural power—for they drew back and fell to the ground.

Surprisingly, TR resisted the addition of ο Ιησους, as did all English versions. However, most English versions add "he," after "I am." Although this makes for better English, it spoils the potency of the divine revelation, "I AM."

John 18:11

After Jesus' statement to Peter, "put the sword into the sheath," one manuscript (Θ) adds παντες γαρ οι λαμβοντες μαχαιραν εν μαχαιρη απολουνται ("for all who take the sword will die by the sword")—an obvious harmonization to Matt 26:52.

John 18:13-24

These verses have been rearranged in various manuscripts, as follows:

225 (A.D. 1192): 18:13a, 24, 13b, 14-23 (18:24 is inserted in the middle of 18:13)

1195 (A.D. 1123): 18:13, 24, 14-24 (also in Harclean Syriac[mg], Codex A of Palestinian Syriac Lectionary, and Cyril of Alexandria; see NEBmg)

Sinaiticus Syriac: 18:13, 24, 14-15, 19-23, 16-18, 25-27

The reason for this rearrangement of verses is that the usual sequence of verses has been problematic for many readers in that 18:13 speaks of Jesus being brought to Annas before Jesus is questioned, and then 18:24 speaks of Jesus being brought before Caiaphas with no mention of any subsequent trial. To confuse matters, the reader is not really sure who the high priest is, Annas or Caiaphas—for both are called such: Caiaphas (18:13, 24) and Annas (18:15, 19, 22). Thus, certain scribes and exegetes (such as Luther—who produced an order much like Sinaiticus Syriac) have tried to rearrange the verses so that Jesus would be seen as having been tried by Caiaphas (which would also accord with the synoptic accounts).

Knowledge of history helps us out of this dilemma. Annas had been deposed as the Jewish high priest by the Romans in A.D. 15, but he still exerted great influence over the ruling high priest, his son-in-law, Caiaphas. And he still retained the title "high priest" as an emeritus title.

Very likely, Annas had asked to interrogate Jesus and was given the first rights to do so (see 18:19-23). Then Jesus was tried by Caiaphas, the acting high priest. Thus, there is no real need to rearrange the verses.

John 18:24

With respect to the problem of historical sequencing discussed in the previous note, various scribes tried to alter 18:24 by changing the conjunction ουν ("then"), which has the best manuscript support (B C* L N W Δ Θ Ψ f[1] 33) and indicates that Jesus went to Annas and then to Caiaphas. Some scribes (א f[13]) changed ουν to δε (to signal contrast), and others (A C[3] D[s] Maj) deleted it. One English version (NIVmg) attempts to solve the problem by using "now" and a pluperfect verb: "Now Annas had sent him, still bound, to Caiaphas the high priest."

John 18:37-38

Pilate's words (ουκουν βασιλευς ει συ) are treated as a question in NA[27]/UBS[4] and by nearly all translations. The NIV, however, translates this, "You are a king, then!" This rendering may be supported by one second-century manuscript, 𝔓[90], which has συ ει (the inversion suggesting an emphatic declaration) instead of ει συ (which is more suggestive of interrogation). Jesus' following response suggests that Pilate was not asking a question but making a declaration—whether sincere or sarcastic. In effect Jesus was saying "you said it" when he answered, Συ λεγεις οτι βασιλευς ειμι ("you said it—I am a king"). This is similar to his response in Matt 26:64 (συ ειπας—"you said [it]"). Jesus then went on to explain that his kingly mission was to conquer by proclaiming truth.

John 19:5

Most manuscripts (such as 𝔓[90] א A C Maj) include the sentence και λεγει αυτοις Ιδου ο ανθρωπος ("and he says to them, 'Behold, the man'"). 𝔓[66*] it cop[ach2] omit the entire sentence. The corrector of 𝔓[66] probably intended to add these words into the text, for there is an insert symbol where this sentence should go. But the words themselves, probably written in the lower margin, are not extant.

John 19:14

A few manuscripts (א[2] D[s] L Δ Ψ) change the "sixth" (εκτη) hour to the "third" (τριτη) hour in an attempt to conform John's account to Mark 15:25. The same change in reverse order occurred in some manuscripts in Mark 15:25. According to John's account, Jesus was led away to be crucified around noon. Since this was the day of the preparation for the Passover (the day in which people prepared for the Passover meal), Jesus was being crucified (as the Lamb of God) at the same time the Passover lambs were being slaughtered. Thus, John's timing is significant.

John 19:16b-17

(WH) NU παρέλαβον οὖν τὸν Ἰησοῦν καὶ βαστάζων ἑαυτῷ τὸν σταυρὸν ἐξῆλθεν εἰς τὸν λεγόμενον Κρανίου Τόπον
"Then they took Jesus. And carrying the cross by himself, he departed to the Place of the Skull."
B L Ψ 33 it
NKJVmg RSV NRSV ESV NASB NIV TNIV NEB REB NJB NAB NLT HCSB NET

variant 1/TR παρελαβον δε τον Ιησουν και ηγαγον, και βασταζων εαυτω τον σταυρον εξηλθεν εις τον λεγομενον Κρανιου Τοπον
"And they took Jesus and led him away. And carrying the cross by himself, he departed to the Place of the Skull."
A D[s] Θ Maj
KJV NKJV HCSBmg

variant 2 οι δε παραλαβοντες τον Ιησουν απηγαγον και βασταζων εαυτω τον σταυρον εξηλθεν εις τον λεγομενον Κρανιου Τοπον
"And the ones taking Jesus led him away. And carrying the cross by himself, he departed to the Place of the Skull."
𝔓[60vid] (א add αυτον) N W f[1] 565
none

variant 3 παραλαβοντες αυτον απηγαγον εις τοπον λεγομενον Κρανιου
"Taking him they led him away to the place called the Skull."
𝔓[66*]
none

variant 4 παραλαβοντες αυτον απηγαγον και βασταζων εαυτω τον σταυρον εξηλθεν εις τοπον λεγομενον Κρανιου
"Taking him they led him away, and carrying the cross by himself he went out to the place called the Skull."
𝔓[66c2]
none

There are a host of other variants in this verse, but the ones listed above represent the basic forms. The shorter reading in WH NU is the best, for it is the one that accounts for the first two expansions. These expansions are attempts to say that it was the Roman soldiers who led Jesus away to be crucified, whereas the barer text is ambiguous—the "they" could refer to the Jewish priests or the Romans. Strictly speaking, the pronoun αυτοις ("them") in the first part of 19:16 (παρεδωκαν αυτον αυτοις—"he delivered him to them") refers to the "chief priests" in 19:15. But it was the Roman soldiers who actually carried out the crucifixion. The ambiguity was probably intentional. John wanted his readers to realize that it was the Jewish leaders who were ultimately responsible for Jesus' death, even though the Romans performed the execution. This idea is captured in the NEB: "Then at last, to satisfy them [the chief priests], he handed over Jesus to be crucified." (The same idea is expressed in Luke 23:25—"he delivered Jesus to their will.")

The reading in 𝔓[66*] is the barest of all the variants. And since there is no way to explain the shortness as coming from a scribal error, it must be assumed that the short text was intentional. This reading still retains the ambiguity but also leaves out the fact that Jesus carried the cross by himself. This must be seen as a deletion that came about as the result of the scribe's knowledge of the other three gospels, where it is made clear that Jesus himself did not carry his cross. According to the Synoptics, the Roman soldiers forced Simon of Cyrene to carry his cross (Matt 27:32; Mark 15:21; Luke 23:26). However, the corrector (𝔓[66c2]) noted the omission and dutifully filled it in (see *Text of Earliest MSS*, 461).

John 19:20

WH NU γεγραμμένον Ἑβραϊστί, Ῥωμαϊστί, Ἑλληνιστί
"written in Hebrew [or, Aramaic], Latin, Greek"
𝔓66vid ℵ1 B L N Ψ 33
RSV NRSV ESV NASB NIV TNIV NEB REB NJB NAB NLT HCSB NET

variant/TR γεγραμμενον Εβραιστι Ελληνιστι Ρωμαιστι
"written in Hebrew [or, Aramaic], Greek, Latin"
A Ds Θ f1 Maj
KJV NKJV

𝔓66vid was not cited in NA26, but is now cited in NA27. The reading of 𝔓66 is certain because a publication of new fragments of 𝔓66 (Comfort 1999, 229) shows that 𝔓66 reads Εβ[ραιστι Ρ]ω[μαιστι Ελ]ληνιστι. Prior to this publication, it could not be said that 𝔓66vid preserved this order, for the first two words were completely missing. 𝔓66 now provides the earliest testimony for the reading of the text.

Pilate provided a tribute to Jesus' kingship in a trilingual placard that everyone in Palestine could read, for it was written in the three major languages of the day: Hebrew (or, Aramaic—the language of the Jews), Latin (the Roman language, the official language) and Greek (the lingua franca, the common tongue). A change in the order was made, perhaps as Metzger (TCGNT) said, to "accord with a geographical order going from East to West."

John 19:29

One minuscule manuscript (476*) reads υσσω ("javelin"), a reading adopted by NEB, instead of υσσωπω ("hyssop" or "hyssop branch"). The reading υσσω is either the result of haplography or a deliberate change, inasmuch as it is difficult to imagine a hyssop branch being used to lift a wine-soaked sponge to Jesus' mouth. One commentator, Camerarius, had conjectured that the original reading was υσσω, and many commentators since have been tempted to embrace this conjecture. One Latin manuscript (itb) reads *perticae* (pole). Several modern one-man translations read "javelin" (MOFFAT, GOODSPEED, PHILLIPS, WILLIAMS). "Hyssop" is by far the best attested reading and may also have symbolic signification inasmuch as hyssop was a metonymy for cleansing. The Jews had used hyssop branches for smearing blood on the doorposts for their salvation from the destroying angel (Exod 12:22), and Moses enacted the old covenant by using a hyssop branch to sprinkle the book and the people with blood (Exod 24:6-8; Heb 9:19). Later, David used hyssop as a metonymy for cleansing from sin, when he called out to God, saying, "cleanse me with hyssop" (Ps 51:7). Thus, the appearance of hyssop in the crucifixion scene reminds readers of their need for spiritual cleansing.

John 19:30

Most commentators see the words παρεδωκαν το πνευμα ("he handed over the Spirit") as depicting Jesus committing his spirit into the hands of God the Father. This interpretation, however, is influenced by Luke 23:46, which explicitly states that Jesus committed his spirit into his Father's hands. John does not say to whom Jesus gave the Spirit. Brown (1970, 911, 931) suggests that Jesus passed on the Spirit to those who were standing at the foot of the cross, as a kind of symbolic action, resulting from Jesus' glorification (see 7:37-39) and preceding the real impartation of the Spirit in 20:22. If so, then the word πνευμα here would denote the divine Spirit, as opposed to Jesus' human spirit. Scribes had the option of showing their exegetical choice between the divine Spirit and the human spirit by writing $\overline{\text{ΠΝΑ}}$ (a nomen sacrum) or πνευμα (just as English translators can do so by writing "Spirit" with a capital "S" or "spirit" with a small "s"). The scribe of 𝔓[66] exercised his interpretive option by writing ΠΝΑ, perhaps denoting that he considered Jesus to have been handing over the divine Spirit. (Since, on other occasions, this same scribe wrote out the word πνευμα, in *plene*, we know he exercised both options depending on his interpretation (for example, see note on 3:6.)

John 19:35

TR NU	ἵνα καὶ ὑμεῖς πιστεύσητε "that you also may believe" ℵ[2] A D[s] L W Θ f[1,13] 33 Maj all
variant/WH	ινα και υμεις πιστευητε "that you may continue to believe" ℵ* B Ψ Origen NLTmg

It is important to see this statement in context: "And the one who has seen it has given testimony, and his testimony is true; that one knows that he tells the truth, that you may believe/that you may continue to believe." The earliest manuscripts read the present tense; later manuscripts read the aorist tense. The editors of NU included the reading with the aorist tense, but signaled their doubt about it by bracketing the sigma: πιστευ[σ]ητε. In most instances John used the aorist subjunctive with the ινα clause (see 1:7; 6:30; 9:36; 11:15, 42; 13:19); thus, it was natural for scribes to change the present tense to the aorist. The present subjunctive πιστευητε suggests a continual believing—as opposed to the aorist, which suggests initial faith. The same variant occurs in 20:31, where there is a similar affirmation. John's intent is to encourage ongoing faith (see 20:30-31).

Two Old Latin manuscripts omit this verse entirely: it[e] and Codex Fuldensis, an important manuscript of the Vulgate. Barrett (1978, 558), with hesitation, suggests that the whole verse may not have been in the first edition and was added later to secure the book's authority because of the eyewitness testimony affirmed herein. This suggestion is far too conjectural in light of the fact that all known Greek manuscripts contain the verse.

John 19:38

All Greek manuscripts except 𝔓[66vid] include the sentence, και επετρεψεν ο Πιλατος ("And Pilate gave permission"). In examining the shorter text of 𝔓[66], it is helpful to see this short statement in context: "Joseph of Arimathea (being a disciple of Jesus, but a secret one, for fear of the Jewish leaders), asked that he might take the body of Jesus. And Pilate gave permission. Then he came and took the body of Jesus." There is no apparent reason in the Greek text why the scribe would have omitted this short sentence accidentally. Thus, we have to look for other reasons for the omission, of which two emerge as possibilities. First, he thought it was nonessential to the meaning of the whole verse. Obviously, if Joseph had asked Pilate for Jesus' body and then went to take Jesus' body, it only follows that Pilate had given him permission. Second, the scribe may have omitted the sentence so as to harmonize this verse with Luke 23:52-53, a parallel text, which says, "This man went to Pilate and asked for the body of Jesus. Then he took it down." Given the scribe's propensity to harmonize John with the Synoptic Gospels, it seems that the second motivation was more prominent than the first. But it must also be noted that the corrector of 𝔓[66] may have inserted this missing sentence. Yet we have no way of knowing this because the line is not completely extant for this page of the manuscript, nor are the upper or lower margins, where a correction would have been written.

John 19:39

TR NU read μιγμα σμυρνης και αλοης ("a mixture of myrrh and aloes"), with the early and diverse support of 𝔓[66vid] ℵ[c] A D[s] L Θ $f^{1,13}$ Maj. All English versions follow this reading. However, there are three variant readings on this: (1) ελιγμα σμυρνης και αλοης ("a packet of myrrh and aloes") in ℵ* B W (so WH); (2) σμιγμα σμυρνης και αλοης ("mixture of myrrh and aloes") in Ψ 892[s]; (3) σμηγμα σμυρνης και αλοης ("ointment of myrrh and aloes") in 1242* syr[p]. The first variant is the most difficult reading of them all, and one that has good testimony. It is possible, therefore, that John said that Nicodemus was carrying some kind of "packet" (the definition given in LSJ 533 for ελιγμα) containing myrrh and aloes. However, the reading μιγμα has excellent support and is also difficult. In ancient times Jews used myrrh for a burial unguent, but not aloes; thus, certain scribes may have been perplexed as to why Nicodemus would have had a mixture of the two, and therefore changed it to ελιγμα. No matter which reading is selected, it must be recognized that this was an extraordinarily large amount of burial unguent (over seventy pounds), which must have cost Nicodemus a great sum. Such a lavish amount of ointment was offered only to kings at the time of burial; so with King Asa (2 Chr 16:14).

John 20:23

WH NU	τὰς ἁμαρτίας ἀφέωνται "the sins have been forgiven" ℵ[2] (B* Ψ αφιονται) A D (L) $f^{1,13}$ 33[vid] NASB NAB
variant 1/TR	τας αμαρτιας αφιενται "the sins are forgiven" B[2] W Δ Θ 078 KJV NKJV RSV NRSV ESV NIV TNIV NEB REB NJB NLT HCSB NET
variant 2	τας αμαρτιας αφεθησεται "the sins will be forgiven" ℵ* cop none

This verse, with its parallel passages in Matt 16:19 and 18:18, has been understood differently by various grammarians and exegetes throughout the centuries. And the tense of verbs is the focus of the disagreement. Thus, the textual variants are not insignificant and very likely represent different interpretations of the passage by various scribes.

Those who argue for the perfect tense (αφιενται) affirm the usual force of the perfect: It signals a past action with a present result. When the church on earth forgives someone's sins, the church is simply affirming a previous divine act. In this verse, as in the Matthean passages, the perfect passive is taken to be a divine passive. The church's actions display the present effect of God's actions (Mantey 1939, 243-249). The present tense and future tense give a different hermeneutic. As the church forgives, God also forgives—or will forgive. In this case, God follows the decision of the church.

There are scholars, however, who argue that there is no appreciable difference in meaning among any of the verbal variations. The strongest argument was presented by Cadbury (1939, 251-254) who, in responding to Mantey, argued that the verbs in the perfect tense in 20:23

(αφεωνται and κεκρατηνται) and Matt 16:19 and 18:18 are in the apodosis of a general condition and should not be limited to time—whether past, present, or future.

John 20:31

TR NU ἵνα πιστεύσητε
"that you may believe"
ℵ[2] A C D L W Δ Ψ $f^{1,13}$ 33 Maj
KJV NKJV RSV NRSV ESV NASB NIV NEBmg REB NJB NAB NLTmg HCSB NET

variant/WH ινα πιστευητε
"that you may continue to believe"
𝔓[66vid] ℵ* B Θ 0250
NRSVmg NIVmg TNIVmg NEB REBmg NABmg NLT NETmg

The full verse reads, "But these have been written that you may believe [or, "may continue to believe"] that Jesus is the Christ, the Son of God, and that by believing you may have life in his name." The earliest manuscripts read the present subjunctive πιστευητε ("may continue to believe"). Later manuscripts read the aorist, πιστευσητε. The editors of NU followed this reading, but signaled their doubt about the aorist verb by bracketing the sigma: πιστευ[σ]ητε (as was done in 19:35). In most instances John used the aorist subjunctive with the ινα clause (see 1:7; 6:30; 9:36; 11:15, 42; 13:19); thus, it was natural for scribes to change the present tense to the aorist. The aorist would have suggested initial belief, but the present suggests continual belief. If John used the present tense originally, we can infer that he considered his readers to already be believers, who needed encouragement in their faith. He was certifying the trustworthiness of his testimony so that the readers would continue to believe the veracity of the gospel. This does not mean, however, that the Gospel was not intended to create new faith. Indeed, history has shown that John's gospel is a powerful tool for evangelism.

Two English versions, NEB and NLT, follow the present tense, while several others make a point of noting the present tense.

John 21:6

The best manuscript support (ℵ* A B C D) indicates that the disciples did not verbally respond to Jesus after he said, "Cast to the right side of the boat, and you will find [fish]." In a few manuscripts, however, the sentence is added: οι δε ειπον δι ολης της νυκτος εκοπιασαμεν και ουδεν ελαβομεν· επι δε τω σω ρηματι βαλουμεν ("But they said, 'Throughout the whole night we labored and caught nothing, but at your word we will cast'"). These manuscripts are 𝔓[66vid] (ονοματι instead of ρηματι) ℵ[1] Ψ (κοπιασαντες) cop[sa].

This story is so similar to the one where Jesus first encountered Peter that it would be difficult for any reader not to think of the two as paralleling each other. In Luke 5:1-11, as well as in John 21:1-19, the scene shows Peter fishing, catching nothing, receiving a visitation from Jesus, and then witnessing a miraculous catch of fish. When Jesus appeared to Peter the first time, Peter fell on his knees before him and, realizing he was a sinful man, asked Jesus to depart from him. Jesus would not depart. He had come to Peter to make him his disciple. In this appearance, Peter is again exposed. But Jesus restores him.

As often happened with parallel passages, scribes could not resist the temptation to conform them verbally. Thus, the scribe of 𝔓[66], who had some propensity for gospel harmonization, added a portion of Luke 5:5 to John 21:6. As such, he allowed his horizon of expectation to interfere with the horizon of the text. The narrative in John 21 does not need this insertion and is, in fact, hindered by it. The disciples' response, "At your designation we will let down the nets," presumes that they had recognized that it was Jesus who was speaking to them. But in John's narrative this recognition does not come until after the fish are caught—when the beloved disciple says, "It is the Lord!" (21:7). Thus, the insertion spoils the timing of the epiphany.

ℵ[1] duplicates Luke 5:5 nearly verbatim, especially with respect to the expression τω σω ρηματι ("at your word"), whereas 𝔓[66] differs in using τω σω ονοματι ("at your designation/at your naming"), an extremely unusual expression.

John 21:18

TR (WH) NU	ἄλλος σε ζώσει καὶ οἴσει "another will gird you and he will carry [you]" A Θ Ψ f[13] Maj all
variant	αλλοι σε ζωσουσιν και αποισουσιν "others will gird you and they will carry [you] off" 𝔓[59vid] 𝔓[109vid] (ℵ C[2]) D W 33 NLTmg

The entire verse reads, "When you grow old, you will stretch out your hands, and another/others will gird you and carry you where you do not want to go." The image depicts Peter's death by crucifixion (see *1 Clem.* 5.4). Tertullian (*Scorp.* 15, written A.D. 211), referring to John 21:18, said that Peter was "girded by another" when his arms were stretched out and fastened to the cross. The TR WH NU reading indicates that only "one" would be responsible for taking Peter to this death—and that "one" perhaps could be the Lord who was in control of Peter's life and death (see 2 Pet 1:13-15). Or that "one" could simply be a vague reference to an executioner. However, the plural has better textual support; 𝔓[109] (ca. 200) gives the earliest testimony to the reading with the plural subject and plural verbs. 𝔓[109] shows αλλοι on one line and . . .]ουσιν σε on another line. Though the lacuna on the second line does not allow for a precise reconstruction, it does support a plural verb (see *Text of Earliest MSS*, 653). And a diversity of other manuscripts affirm the plural (see Comfort 2005, 341-342). This variant, relegated to the margin of NA[27], challenges the reading with the singular subject and verb. However, not one English version has adopted the reading with the plurals, though it is noted in NLT.

John 21:23

A few manuscripts (ℵ* C[2vid] it[a,e] syr[s]) omit the phrase τι προς σε ("what [is that] to you?"). Perhaps it was added later to conform the statement in 21:23 to 21:22. However, since the inclusion of the phrase is well attested (𝔓[109vid] ℵ[1] A B C* W Θ Ψ f[13] 33 Maj), it should be considered original.

John 21:25

It was detected by Milne and Skeat (1938, 12) that the scribe of ℵ originally concluded his gospel with 21:24, following it with a flourish and a subscription. Then, later, he washed out the flourish and subscription, and added 21:25, followed by another flourish and subscription. Either his exemplar stopped at 21:24 or he made an error by concluding his gospel too soon. If his exemplar stopped at 21:24, he made the addition of 21:25 on the basis of some other manuscript.

Addition of John 7:53–8:11 as an appendix

A few late Greek minuscules (f[1]) and Armenian manuscripts add the pericope of the adulteress (7:53–8:11) after 21:25, thereby indicating that this portion was considered an appendix to the Gospel of John. (See note on 7:53–8:11 for commentary on this text.)

In their edition of the Greek New Testament, Westcott and Hort place 7:53–8:11 as an appendix immediately following the last chapter of John. The REB also prints the pericope as an appendix. This is an appropriate way of showing the secondary nature of this text.

Subscription

The codices ℵ and B have subscriptions to this gospel. ℵ reads ευαγγελιον κατα Ιωαννην ("Gospel according to John"), and B reads κατα Ιωανην ("According to John"). For comments on this, see Inscription to John.

ACTS OF THE APOSTLES

Special treatment has been given to the Western text and Codex Bezae's text (D) in the book of Acts because of their distinct textual difference from other manuscript traditions. In every verse where the Western text (and specifically the D-text, a particular form of the Western text), differs from NU, there is an English translation (see Wilson 1923). (The D-text in the books of Acts is discussed in the Introduction, pp. xviii-xix.) This translation shows how the Western text differs from the NU text by (1) putting the Western text in bold type where it differs or has an interpolation, and (2) placing square brackets around words not included in the Western text. Those who read Greek can refer to the critical apparatus of NA[27] to see the corresponding Greek text of D and other Western manuscripts. Significant differences will receive comment. Codex Bezae (D) is extant up to Acts 22:29. Thereafter, other manuscripts display the Western text.

Those who are familiar with the New Jerusalem Bible (NJB) should take note of how often this translation follows or gives recognition (in marginal notes) to the "Western text" in the book of Acts. The New English Bible (NEB), on occasion, also follows the Western text. (See Introduction for a discussion of the manuscripts of Acts and the revision work produced by the scribe I call the "D-reviser.")

Inscription (Title)

WH NU	Πραξεις Αποστολων "Acts of Apostles" (𝔓[74] א B as subscription) (D) Ψ NEB REB NJB HCSB
variant 1	Πραξεις "Acts" 1175 NIV TNIV NLT NET
variant 2	Αι Πραξεις των Αποστολων "The Acts of the Apostles" 323[s] 945 KJV NKJV RSV NRSV ESV NASB NAB
variant 3/TR	Πραξεις των Αγιων Αποστολων "Acts of the Holy Apostles" 453 (1739[s]) 1884 none

variant 4 Λουκα Ευαγγελιστου Πραξεις των Αγιων Αποστολων
"Luke [the] Evangelist's Acts of the Apostles"
33 2344
none

It is very doubtful that this book was originally titled by the author, especially since it was published as a sequel to Luke's Gospel (see Acts 1:1-2). We do not know who first entitled it "Acts of the Apostles." We do know that the book was referred to as "the acts of all the apostles" in the Muratorian Canon (dated late second c.). None of the early manuscripts (prior to ca. 300) preserve the first page of this book. In any event, this title stuck and was subsequently embellished by successive scribes—as shown in variants 2-4. The shorter title in variant 1 could be more primitive than WH NU or simply a truncation of it.

Acts 1:1-2

Western text (D syr^{hmg}) reads:

> "In the first book, Theophilus, I wrote about all that Jesus began to do and teach until the day when he was received up, after giving instructions through the Holy Spirit to the apostles whom he had chosen **and commanded to proclaim the gospel.**"

Another form of the Western text (it^{gig,t} syr^{p,hmg}) reads:

> "In the first book, Theophilus, I wrote about all that Jesus began to do and teach **on the day when he chose the apostles** through the Holy Spirit and commanded them to proclaim the gospel."

The additional clause in the first variant listed above is a typical Western expansion, drawn from texts like Matt 28:19-20. The omission of the word ανελημφθη ("he was taken up") in the second form of the Western text is significant inasmuch as the Western text omits the mention of Jesus' ascension in Luke 24:51 (see note). These scribes made the harmonization complete between Luke and Acts by omitting reference to Jesus' ascension in both books. In Luke 24:51 the words "and he was taken up into heaven" were omitted; subsequently in it^{gig,t} syr^{p,hmg} "he was taken up" was deleted from Acts 1:2. In contrast to this errant consistency, WH is inconsistent in that it allows for the omission in Luke, calling it a Western noninterpolation, but it includes it here, as well as in 1:9 and 1:11 (see notes).

Acts 1:4-6

Western text (D Augustine) reads:

> "While eating with them, he ordered them not to leave Jerusalem, but to wait there for the promise of the Father. 'This,' he said, 'is what you have heard from **my mouth.** For John baptized with water, but you will be baptized with the Holy Spirit **and that which you are about to receive** after these not many days **until the Pentecost.**'"

This expansion anticipates the outpouring of the Spirit on the day of Pentecost (Acts 2:1). Jesus, however, did not tell the disciples exactly when they would receive the Holy Spirit, much less that it would occur on the day of Pentecost.

In addition, the participle συναλιζομενος ("eating together with") was changed to συναυλιζομενος ("lodging together") in several minuscule manuscripts (614 1241 1739^{s}). The first hand of D wrote συναλισκομενος μετ αυτων, which is nonsense, for it means "being taken captive with them." A second hand corrected it to συναλιζομενος μετ αυτων ("eating together with them").

Acts 1:9

Following excellent testimony (א[1] A B C E Ψ 1739[s]), the three editions (TR WH NU) indicate that Jesus was lifted up and taken away in a cloud as the disciples were watching: και ταυτα ειπων βλεποντων αυτων επηρθη, και νεφελη υπελαβεν αυτον απο των οφθαλμων αυτων ("and as he was saying these things, while they were watching, he was lifted up, and a cloud took him out of their sight"). The D-text reads, και ταυτα ειποντος αυτου νεφελη υπεβαλεν αυτον και απηρθη απο των οφθαλμων αυτων ("and as he was saying this, a cloud took him over and lifted him out of their sight").

The lack of the expression, "as they were watching," could suggest that the ascension, according to the D-text, was not an observable event. However, this text does not eliminate the final words "out of their sight," thereby leaving open the possibility that the disciples were watching Jesus ascend. What is clearly different about this Western text, however, is that they did not see a bodily ascension—only a cloud enveloping Jesus while he was still on the ground and then taking him away. It is possible, as Plooij suggests (1929, 53), that an early reviser was trying to avoid a bodily ascension (see note on Acts 1:11). Perhaps the reviser's view of the ascension was more like the transfiguration, where Jesus was enveloped with the cloud of God's glory (see Mark 9:7).

Acts 1:11

A Western text (D it[d,gig] Augustine Vigilus) omits εις τον ουρανον ("into heaven") from the first clause, producing the rendering, "This Jesus, who has been taken up from you, will come in the same way as you saw him go into heaven." The words εις τον ουρανον are found in א A B C E Ψ 1739[s] syr.

The omission in this Western text could be part of the continuing process of an early reviser to eliminate mention of Jesus' ascension into heaven. However, the elimination is not thorough, for the text still says that the disciples saw Jesus go into heaven. Thus, it is safe to say that this Western text (both in Luke and Acts) attempted to diminish the description of Jesus' bodily ascension. Epp's summary of the situation (1981, 141) is worth quoting: "Had the 'Western' text carried through its tendency here with full rigor, and were the 'Western' text to be adjudged the original Lukan text, the ascension as an observable incident would all but disappear from the NT. Alternatively, were the standard (i.e., the 'Neutral') Lukan text to be taken as original—which seems more likely—an argument could be made (with only slightly some rough edges) that the 'Western' text assumed for itself the task of reducing if not eliminating the observable, objectifying aspects from the Gospels and Acts."

Christ's ascension is taken as a fact in many NT passages that speak of the risen Christ as having been exalted to the right hand of God, and there are Scriptures about Christ being taken up into glory (see 1 Tim 3:16). But it is only in Luke and Acts that we have an account of Jesus' bodily ascension into heaven. These verses, as preserved in many ancient witnesses, provide the eyewitness verification of this extraordinary, climactic event in Christ's life, and these verses are the foundation for the Christian belief in Christ's bodily ascension into heaven and his return in like manner.

Acts 1:14a

WH NU ὁμοθυμαδὸν τῇ προσευχῇ
"with one accord in prayer"
𝔓[74] ℵ A B C* D E Ψ
NKJVmg RSV NRSV ESV NASB NIV TNIV NEB REB NJB NAB NLT HCSB NET

variant/TR ομοθυμαδον τη προσευχη και τη δεησει
"with one accord in prayer and supplication"
C[3] 33 1739[s] Maj
KJV NKJV HCSBmg

This addition, taken from Phil 4:6, found its way into the majority of manuscripts and TR, and is followed by KJV and NKJV.

Acts 1:14b

In place of συν γυναιξιν ("with [the] women"), D reads συν γυναιξιν και τεκνοις ("with [the] women and children"). This addition probably came about as the result of a natural tendency for scribes to complete pairs, such as "eating and drinking" (see note on Mark 2:16b) and "prayer and fasting" (see notes on Mark 9:29 and 1 Cor 7:5). It is also possible that the D-reviser was thinking of the wives of the apostles and their children.

Acts 1:15

WH NU ἐν μέσῳ τῶν ἀδελφῶν
"in the midst of the brothers"
ℵ A B C* 33[vid] cop
NKJVmg RSV NRSV ESV NASB NIV (TNIV) NEB REB NJB NAB (NLT) HCSB (NET)

variant 1/TR εν τω μεσω των μαθητων
"in the midst of the disciples"
(C[3]) D E Ψ 1739[s] Maj it syr
KJV NKJV HCSBmg

variant 2 εν τω μεσω των αποστολων
"in the midst of the apostles"
𝔓[74vid]
none

The two variants are the result of scribes trying to relieve the text of any misunderstanding: The "brothers" are not the brothers of Jesus mentioned in 1:14 but the group of Christians who had come to Jerusalem. TNIV NLT and NET translate "brothers" as "believers" so as to be inclusive.

Acts 1:18

The description of Judas's death is obscure: πρηνης γενομενος ελακησεν μεσος και εξεχυθη παντα τα σπλαγχνα αυτου ("falling headlong, he burst open in the middle and all his inward parts were poured out"). Ancient translators ascribed various interpretations to πρηνης γενομενος (literally "having become prone"). Several Latin versions harmonized this description with Matt 27:5, which says that Judas "went out and hanged himself." Augustine (*Fel.* 1.4) said that Judas "bound himself around the neck and, having fallen on his face, burst open in the middle and all his inward parts were poured out." The

Latin Vulgate says "being hanged, he burst open in the middle and all his inward parts were poured out." The Armenian and Old Georgian versions say Judas "being swollen up, burst open in the middle and all his inward parts were poured out." This translation indicates that the translators must have understood πρηνης as being connected with πρηθω ("to swell out"). (This is the basis for Eberhard Nestle's conjectured πεπρησμενος, cited in the Nestle text.) According to Papias (*Exegeses of the Lord's Oracles* 4), there was an early tradition that Judas swelled up to monstrous proportions.

None of these changes are substantiated by the evidence of Greek manuscripts. This shows that Greek scribes were content to copy the text as is, without attempting harmonization to Matt 27:5 or adjusting the text to oral tradition. The text as is, however, does not preclude the idea that Judas's fall could have come after he hanged himself.

Acts 1:21

Western text (D syr[h]) reads:

> "So choose one of the men who have accompanied us during all the time that the Lord Jesus **Christ** went in and out among us."

The addition of "Christ" to the Lord Jesus' name is typical for the scribe of D (see 3:13; 4:33; 8:16; 11:20; 15:11; 16:31; 19:5; 21:13), thereby exposing the expansive nature of the Western text (Bruce 1990, 111).

Acts 1:23

Instead of the group of Christians proposing the two men as candidates for the apostolic office (as is indicated by the plural verb εστησαν—"they put forward"), a Western text (D it[gig] Augustine) reads εστησεν ("he [Peter] put forward"). Thus, in this variant it is Peter alone who takes the action of selecting Joseph and Matthias. "Here and elsewhere in the Western text, one recognizes clearly the later point of view, according to which Peter rules the church with the authority of the monarchial episcopate" (Metzger 1992, 249). The D-reviser gave preference to Peter in his editorialization of the text (see notes on 2:14; 3:17; 5:29).

In a Western text (D it), Joseph is surnamed Βαρναββαν ("Barnabbas"), by confusion with Acts 4:36, instead of Βαρσαββαν ("Barsabbas"), which means "son of the Sabbath" (or "born on the Sabbath").

Acts 1:25

WH NU λαβεῖν τὸν τόπον τῆς διακονίας ταύτης
"to take the place of this ministry"
𝔓[74] A B C* D Ψ syr[hmg] cop
RSV NRSV ESV NIV TNIV NEB REB NJB NAB NLT HCSB NET

variant/TR λαβειν τον κληρον της διακονιας ταυτης
"to take the share of this ministry"
א C[3] E Maj 33 1739[s]
KJV NKJV NRSVmg NASB HCSBmg

By way of assimilation to 1:17 and perhaps 1:26, τοπον ("place") was changed to κληρον ("share"). The word τοπον is rarely used to indicate a religious office (see John 11:48, where the allusion could be to the Jews' religious office or to the temple, and see *1 Clem.* 40:5). This rarity would have also prompted a change. This change found its way into the majority of manuscripts, TR, and into versions such as KJV, NKJV, and NASB.

Acts 1:26

TR WH NU τῶν ἕνδεκα ἀποστόλων
"the eleven apostles"
𝔓74 ℵ A B C
KJV NKJV RSV NRSV ESV NASB NIV TNIV NEBmg REB NAB NLT HCSB NET

variant των δωδεκα αποστολων
"the twelve apostles"
D it[d] Eusebius
NEB NJB

Although the translators of the NEB considered the numeration "eleven" to have been a correction of a pedantic editor (Tasker 1964, 429), it is more likely that we see the work of a "Western" reviser wanting to show that Matthias had become part of the famed "Twelve."

Acts 2:1-2

Western text (D) reads:

> "And **it came to pass in those days** of the arrival of the day of Pentecost, that while they were all together, behold there came a sound from heaven like the rush of a violent wind, and it filled the entire house where they were sitting."

This is a narrative filler between the end of Acts 1 and Acts 2; such fillers are frequently found in the Western text.

Acts 2:5

TR WH NU Ἰουδαῖοι, ἄνδρες εὐλαβεῖς
"Jews, devout men"
A B (C D E) Ψ 1739[s]
KJV NKJV RSV NRSV ESV NASB NIV TNIV NEB REB NJBmg NAB NLT HCSB NET

variant ανδρες ευλαβεις
"devout men"
ℵ a few Old Latin MSS
NEBmg NJB

The TR WH NU reading, as is, could refer to the Jews and proselytes from many nations who were visiting Jerusalem for Pentecost, but it is more likely that Luke was referring "to the residents of Jerusalem who had returned from Diaspora lands ('from every nation under heaven') at some earlier time to settle down in the homeland" (Longenecker 1981, 272). Luke's use of the participle κατοικουντες in Acts shows that he was thinking of those who were residents. The omission of "Jews" (Ιουδαιοι) could have been a scribal attempt to steer the text in the direction of the first interpretation—i.e., those dwelling in Jerusalem were visitors to Jerusalem, not native Judeans. This interpretation helps explain why the early church in Jerusalem was pressed into immediate communal living: Far too many of the first converts were visitors to Jerusalem, who, having become Christians and members of the new community, needed food and shelter. Following the other interpretation, many resident Jerusalemites became the first members of the church, who voluntarily decided to practice communal living.

Acts 2:7

Two insertions occurred in this verse: (1) παντες ("all") was inserted after εξισταντο δε ("and they were amazed") in א* A C E Ψ 33 (so TR and KJV), and (2) προς αλληλους ("to one another") was appended to λεγοντες ("speaking") in C³ D E (so TR and KJV).

Acts 2:9

It is difficult to explain why Ιουδαιαν ("Judea") would appear among the list of countries occupied by the Jewish Diaspora. Ancient writers, such as Tertullian and Augustine, substituted *Armeniam;* Jerome replaced it with *Syria.* Not one Greek scribe altered it.

Acts 2:12

Western text (D syr^hmg) reads:

> "All were amazed and perplexed, saying to one another **about what had taken place,** 'What does this mean?'"

This is a typical Western expansion.

Acts 2:14

Western text (D) reads:

> "Then Peter, standing up with the **ten apostles,** raised his voice **first** and **said to** them, 'Men of Judea and all who live in Jerusalem, let this be known to you, and listen to what I say.'"

The reviser excluded Matthias as the newly appointed twelfth apostle, and, as is typical, he gave Peter prominence by adding the word "first." Finally, D substitutes the plain Greek word ειπεν ("said") for απεφθεγζατο, which means "declared" or, more specifically in this context, "uttered inspired speech."

Acts 2:16

TR WH NU δὶα τοῦ προφήτου Ἰωήλ
"through the prophet Joel"
א A B C E Ψ 076 33
KJV NKJV RSV NRSV ESV NASB NIV TNIV NJBmg NAB NLT HCSB NET

variant δια του προφητου
"through the prophet"
D it^d,r Irenaeus Augustine
NEB REB NJB

It is possible that the Western text here preserves the original text; in other words, it may be a Western "noninterpolation." Elsewhere in Acts, the words of the Minor Prophets are quoted without mentioning the prophet by name: 7:42 (Amos); 13:40 (Habakkuk); 15:15 (Amos). But this can be an argument both for and against the inclusion of Joel here: Western scribes may have deleted "Joel" to conform 2:16 to the other passages, or Alexandrian scribes may have added "Joel" contrary to Luke's style. A few English versions (NEB REB NJB) followed the Western text.

Acts 2:17-21

Western text (D it[d]) reads:

> "[17] In the last days it will be, **the Lord** declares, that I will pour out my Spirit upon all flesh, and **their** sons and **their** daughters shall prophesy, and **the** young men shall see visions, and **the** old men shall dream dreams. [18] Even upon my slaves, both men and women, [in those days] I will pour out my Spirit; [and they shall prophesy.] [19] And I will show portents in the heaven above and signs on the earth below, [blood, and fire, and smoky mist.] [20] The sun shall be turned to darkness and the moon to blood, before the coming of the Lord's great [and glorious] day. [21] Then everyone who calls on the name of the Lord shall be saved."

The Western text citation of Joel 2:28-32 (adopted by NJB) is abbreviated by comparison to the text that is printed in NU, which is supported by a host of witnesses (𝔓74 א A B C E Ψ syr cop etc.) and which generally accords with the Septuagint (in LXX Joel 2:28-32 is numbered 3:1-5). Given this excellent external testimony and the fact that Luke usually followed the Septuagint closely when making OT citations, it is very likely that the Western text is a recension. However, it must be noted that Luke probably did not follow the Septuagint verbatim. Luke introduced the quotation with εσται εν ταις εσχαταις ημεραις ("it will be in the last days") to make it suitable to Peter's emphasis on fulfilled eschatology. But a few scribes (B C 076 cop[sa]) changed it to the Septuagint wording, μετα ταυτα ("after these things"). And Luke added και προφητευσουσιν ("and they shall prophesy") at the end of 2:18, which was deleted by Western scribes who, in this instance alone, may have wanted to conform the citation to the OT text (both LXX and Hebrew).

The other changes in the Western text can be explained as having been motivated by the reviser's desire to have Joel's prophesy speak to all people ("all flesh")—not just the Jews. Hence, "your sons, your daughters, your old men, your young men" (as addressed to a Jewish audience) become "their sons, their daughters, the old men, the young men" (as addressed to a universal audience) in the Western text. The words "blood, and fire, and smoky mist" were deleted probably because there were no such signs on the day of Pentecost. Peter's hearers may have associated this phenomenon with the darkness that occurred on Good Friday (Bruce 1990, 121).

Acts 2:22

Western text (D* 1241) reads:

> "You that are Israelites, listen to what I have to say: Jesus of Nazareth [was] a man attested to **us** by God with deeds of power, wonders, and signs that God did through him among you, as you yourselves know."

Unless it was a transcriptional accident, D* has ημας ("us") for υμας ("you") because "only the disciples, not the men of Jerusalem, have experienced these miracles" (Haenchen 1971, 180). D was subsequently corrected.

Acts 2:23

Several later manuscripts (א[2] C[3] D E Ψ Maj) add λαβοντες ("taken") before δια χειρος ανομων ("by the hands of lawless men"); this addition is found in TR. The testimony for its omission is strong: 𝔓74 א* A B C 1739.

Acts 2:24

Western text (D it^{d,e,gig} syr^{p} Augustine) reads:

> "But God raised him up, having freed him from the pains of **Hades** because it was impossible for him to be held in its power."

The Western text shows the change of θανατου ("death") to αδου ("Hades") and thereby conforms 2:24 to the wording of 2:27, 31. It is also possible that a reviser wanted to make it clear that Jesus did not suffer detainment in Hades.

Acts 2:30a

Instead of οσφους ("loins"), found in nearly all Greek manuscripts, it^{gig,r} syr^{p} support the reading κοιλιας ("belly"). This is probably an attempt to replicate the Septuagint (Ps 132:11 [131:11]). D*, which reads καρδιας ("heart"), could be an archetypal corruption of κοιλιας.

Acts 2:30b

WH NU καθίσαι ἐπὶ τὸν θρόνον αὐτοῦ
"[from David] he would seat one on the throne"
א A B C cop^{bo,sa}
NKJVmg RSV NRSV ESV NASB NIV TNIV NEB REB NJB NAB NLT HCSB NET

variant/TR το κατα σαρκα αναστησειν τον Χριστον καθισαι επι τον θρονον αυτου
"[from David] according to the flesh he would raise up the Christ to sit on the throne"
(D) P 049 056 0142 (Ψ 33) Maj
KJV NKJV HCSBmg

There are other variants with minor word differences than the ones listed above (see UBS^{4}). The variant is an expansion most likely derived from 2 Sam 7:12-13 and Rom 1:3-4; it serves to make it clear that Jesus Christ was the earthly descendant of David. This variant was incorporated in TR and perpetuated by KJV and NKJV.

Acts 2:31a

Western text (D* it^{d}) reads:

> "[He, foreseeing this, spoke of the] resurrection of the Christ, saying, 'He was not abandoned to Hades, nor did his flesh experience corruption.'"

The bracketed words were accidentally omitted in D's copy, then restored by D^{2}, who wrote προειδως ("foreknowing") for προιδων ("foreseeing").

Acts 2:31b

WH NU οὔτε ἐγκατελείφθη εἰς ᾅδην
"neither was he abandoned in Hades"
𝔓^{74} 𝔓^{91vid} א A B C* D syr^{p} cop Origen
RSV NRSV ESV NASB NIV TNIV NEB REB NJB NAB NLT HCSB NET

variant/TR οὐτε εγκατελειφθη η ψυχη αυτου εις αδην
"neither was his soul abandoned in Hades"
C[3] E Ψ 33 1739 Maj syr[h]
KJV NKJV HCSBmg

The WH NU reading has excellent documentary support (𝔓[91], dated third century, provides the earliest witness). The variant is scribal harmonization to 2:27.

Acts 2:37

Western text (D and syr[hmg] in part) reads:

> "**Then all who had come together,** when they heard this, were cut to the heart, and **some of them** said to Peter and to [the rest of] the apostles, 'Men and brothers, what **therefore** should we do? **Show us.**'"

The editing of the reviser demonstrates his freedom with the text. With an eye for circumstantial accuracy, he made sure it was not "all" who spoke to Peter but only "some." The word λοιπους ("the rest") is omitted in D (as well as in it[d,gig] Augustine). The translators of the NEB considered λοιπους to be a pedantic scribal addition inasmuch as "the tendency of D in Acts is to expand rather than abbreviate" (Tasker 1964, 429). But the D-text shows many omissions. Besides, the omission here is probably accidental, due to homoeoteleuton, inasmuch as the words both before and after λοιπους (τους and αποστολους) have the same ending (TCGNT).

Acts 2:38

Divine names were often expanded in the transmission of the text. In this case, Ιησου Χριστου ("Jesus Christ"), found in ℵ A B C, was expanded to του κυριου Ιησου Χριστου ("the Lord Jesus Christ") in D E 614 945 1739.

Acts 2:41-42

Western text (D) reads:

> "So those who **believed** were baptized, and that day about three thousand persons were added. [42] They devoted themselves to the apostles' teaching **in Jerusalem,** and fellowship, in the breaking of bread and the prayers."

The reviser substituted πιστευσαντες ("having believed") for αποδεξαμενοι ("having received [the message]"), probably because he considered faith to be the prerequisite to baptism, not just reception of the word. The reviser also added "in Jerusalem" in keeping with an editorial design to furnish the text with circumstantial details.

Acts 2:43

TR WH NU πολλά τε τέρατα καὶ σημεῖα διὰ τῶν ἀποστόλων ἐγίνετο
"many signs and wonders through the apostles were occurring"
B (D) Maj 1739 syr[h] cop[sa]
all

variant 1 — add at end of verse: εν Ιερουσαλημ ("in Jerusalem")
E 33 syr[p]
none

variant 2 — add at end of verse: εν Ιερουσαλημ, φοβος τε ην μεγας επι παντας και
"in Jerusalem, and great fear was upon all and"
𝔓[74] ℵ (A C) Ψ cop[bo]
NASBmg NJBmg

The addition of "in Jerusalem" in both variants helps readers identify the specific setting of the event. The extra clause in the second variant heightens the description concerning the impact the believers were having on the people of Jerusalem. If the clause is original, scribes may have deleted it because it seemed a redundancy of the first clause in the verse; but if not, it was likely added (from Acts 5:5, 11) to intensify the sense of fear and awe.

Acts 2:44

The present participle οι πιστευοντες ("the ones believing"), found in most manuscripts, is normally used in Acts to designate the ones who have ongoing faith in Jesus—the Christians. The aorist participle πιστευσαντες, found in ℵ B, usually designates initial faith. In this case, either would suit the context, but since the passage is speaking of the neophyte church it is possible that Luke was speaking of the newly converted.

The expression επι το αυτο is an idiom used in the NT to indicate the togetherness of the believers. The expression suggests both church unity and a church gathering in one place (see 1 Cor 11:18, 20; 14:23). In Acts the expression was used to indicate the one place where the believers had gathered (1:15; 2:1), as well the unity they experienced once gathered (2:44, 47). A similar expression was used by the Qumran community: the *yakhad*—"the gathered fellowship" (Longenecker 1981, 292). If ℵ and B preserve the original text, Luke was saying, "the new believers, in gathered fellowship, shared all things in common."

Acts 2:45-46

Western text (D) reads:

> "45 **As many as those who** had properties and possessions, they were selling them and distributing them **daily** to all, as many as who had need. 46 And [daily] they **all** spent much time [together] in the temple, breaking bread from house to house."

The Western text adds οσοι ("those who") to indicate that not all property owners sold their possessions for distribution. This text also moves καθ ημεραν ("daily") from describing temple attendance (2:46) to characterizing the distribution in 2:45.

Acts 2:47a

In place of τον λαον ("the people"), D reads τον κοσμον ("the world"), so as to heighten the account: "they had favor with the whole world."

Acts 2:47b–3:1

WH NU ὁ δὲ κύριος προσετίθει τοὺς σῳζομένους καθ ἡμέραν ἐπὶ τὸ αὐτό. Πέτρος δὲ καὶ Ἰωάννης ἀνέβαινον εἰς τὸ ἱερόν

"Day by day the Lord was adding those being saved to the gathered fellowship. Now Peter and John were going up to the temple."

𝔓74vid 𝔓91vid ℵ A B C 095 cop[bo,sa]

NKJVmg RSV NRSV ESV NASB NIV TNIV NEB REB NJB NAB NLT HCSB NET

variant 1/TR ο δε κυριος προσετιθει τους σωζομενους καθ ημεραν τη εκκλησια. Επι το αυτο δε Πετρος και Ιωαννης ανεβαινον εις το ιερον

"Day by day the Lord was adding those being saved to the church. Together Peter and John went up to the temple."

E P Ψ 33 Maj it[e] syr[h]

KJV NKJV HCSBmg

variant 2 ο δε κυριος προσετιθει τους σωζομενους καθ ημεραν επι το αυτο εν τη εκκλησια. Εν δε ταις ημεραις ταυταις Πετρος δε και Ιωαννης ανεβαινον εις το ιερον το δειλινον

"Day by day the Lord was adding those being saved together in the church. Now in these days Peter and John were going up to the temple toward evening."

D

none

The first variant was likely created by a scribe who did not understand the special meaning of επι το αυτο (see note on 2:44) and therefore inserted "the church" and then connected επι το αυτο with John and Peter's action of going up to the temple. This change was included in TR and translated in KJV and NKJV. The Western reviser made a similar adjustment, and then he added circumstantial details to 3:1 which describe Peter and John's activity of going up to the temple for evening devotion as a regular event in those days. The Western text's addition, "in these days," also provides a narrative connective between chapters.

Acts 3:2-5

Western text (D) reads:

> "And **behold** a man [who was] lame from birth was being carried in. People would lay him daily at the gate of the temple called the Beautiful Gate so that he could ask for alms from those entering the temple. [3] **He, fixing intently his eyes and** seeing Peter and John about to go into the temple, begged [to receive] alms. [4] Peter looked intently at him, as did John, and said, 'Look **intently** at us.' [5] And he fixed his attention on them, expecting to receive something from them."

The adjustments made by the reviser are mixed: Some trim the text of perceived nonessential words (such as υπαρχων and λαβειν), and others add to the text more description, such as the addition in 3:3.

Acts 3:6

TR NU [ἔγειρε καὶ] περιπάτει
"rise up and walk"
A C E Ψ 095[vid] 33 1739 Maj it syr cop[bo]
KJV NKJV ESV REB NJBmg NAB NLT HCSB NET

variant/WH περιπατει
"walk"
א B D it[d] cop[sa]
RSV NRSV NASB NIV TNIV NEB NJB NETmg

The TR NU reading appears to be a scribal expansion borrowed from the Gospels where the formula "arise and walk" is common (see Matt 9:5; Mark 2:9; Luke 5:23; and John 5:8). The variant has the best attestation—especially with the combination of א and B with D. But eclecticism (based on vague internal criteria) overruled proper consideration for the documentary evidence when the NU committee adopted the longer reading (see TCGNT). Modern English versions are divided.

Acts 3:8

Western text (D it[h]) reads:

> "Jumping up, he stood and began to walk, **rejoicing,** and he entered the temple with them, [walking and leaping and] praising God."

The D-reviser, who had a habit of paraphrasing the text, modified it by replacing a concrete description of joy ("walking and leaping") with an abstraction ("rejoicing").

Acts 3:11

Western text (D) reads:

> "And **as Peter and John went out,** he **went out with them, and** held them; and [all the people ran together to them and] **stood** wondering in the colonnade called Solomon's, astonished."

By contrast, the Alexandrian text reads, "While he clung to Peter and John, all the people ran together to them in the colonnade called Solomon's, astonished." According to Bruce (1990, 138), "the Western text makes explicit what is implicit in the B-text, as though the readers could not be trusted to draw the correct inference for themselves." In other words, this is a classic case of gap-filling. The function readers should perform in their minds has been supplied by the reviser in actual words. The healed man must have accompanied the apostles into the temple and then returned with them to the outer court, where the people were waiting at Solomon's colonnade. Jesus used to teach in the colonnade (see John 10:23), and then it became a gathering place for the early Christians (Acts 5:12).

Acts 3:12

A few ancient versions (it[h,p] syr[p] arm) incorrectly translate the text as though it read δυναμει η εξουσια ("power or authority") instead of δυναμει η ευσεβεια ("power or godliness")—a very rare combination in the NT.

Acts 3:13a

NU	ὁ θεὸς ᾽Αβραὰμ καὶ [ὁ θεὸς] ᾽Ισαὰκ καὶ [ὁ θεὸς] ᾽Ιακώβ "the God of Abraham and the God of Isaac and the God of Jacob" 𝔓[74] ℵ C (A D omit ο before second and third θεος) NRSV ESV NAB NETmg
variant/TR WH	ο θεος Αβρααμ και Ισαακ και Ιακωβ "the God of Abraham and of Isaac and of Jacob" B E Ψ 0236[vid] 33 1739 Maj KJV NKJV RSV NASB NIV TNIV NEB REB NJB NLT HCSB NET

The documentary evidence is nearly evenly divided. When we look at internal factors, it must be judged that the fuller form of this OT citation (Exod 3:6) is most likely the result of scribal conformity to the Septuagint or the gospel citations of the same verse (Matt 22:32; Mark 12:26; Luke 20:37), which all have "God" in triple form. The variation in A and D is also a telltale sign of an addition. The NU editors accepted the longer version here, while adopting the shorter one in 7:32 (see note). Most English versions follow the variant, while NRSV, ESV, and NAB remain faithful to the NU text.

Acts 3:13b-14

Western text (D) reads:

> "The God of our ancestors has glorified his servant Jesus, whom you handed over **to judgment** and rejected in the presence of Pilate, when he had **judged and wanted** to release him. [14] But you **oppressed** the Holy and Righteous One and asked to have a murderer given to you."

The changes in 3:13 may show anti-Semitism in the sense that D heightens the Jews' responsibility in killing Jesus. In 3:13, D adds that Jesus was handed over "for judgment" (εις κρισιν). The D reading also indicates that Pilate wanted to release Jesus (απολυειν αυτον θελοντος). The change in 3:14 from ηρνησασθε ("you rejected") to ηβαρυνατε ("you oppressed") probably arose as an attempt to avoid repeating the same verb as in 3:13.

Acts 3:16

Western text (D) reads:

> "And by faith in his name **you see this man and know that his name made him strong,** and the faith that is through him has given this man perfect health in the presence of all of you."

The adjustment in the Western text was aimed at relieving the text of the awkward positioning of the double mention of Jesus' name in the Greek text: επι τη πιστει του ονοματος αυτου τουτον ον θεωρειτε και οιδατε, εστερεωσεν το ονομα αυτου ("and by faith in his name, this man whom you see and know has been made strong by his name"). The clumsiness can be eased by putting a midpoint after εστερεωσεν (as Lachmann did). This yields the rendering: "and by faith in his name, this man whom you see and know has made been made strong: by his name and faith through him, he was made whole in the presence of you all."

Acts 3:17

Western text (D and it syr^{hmg} for last change) reads:

> "And now, **men and** brothers, **we** know that you did **a wicked thing** in ignorance, as did also your rulers."

The Western text has some noteworthy modifications: (1) adding "men" to "brothers" so as to formalize the expression, (2) changing "I know" to "we know" so as to make Peter a representative for all the believers or apostles, and (3) adding "a wicked thing" lest the Jews be excused for killing Jesus on the basis that they acted only out of ignorance. Some scholars have made an argument that the D-text reviser who was responsible for deleting Jesus' utterance of forgiveness on the cross for those who acted in ignorance (see note on Luke 23:34 where I argue that the verse was most likely added) was consistent here in that this reviser did not want the Jews excused from crucifying Jesus on the basis that they did it in ignorance (see Epp 1962, 51). But Jesus' proclamation of forgiveness was for his Roman executioners, not the Jews who arrested him. After all, Jesus implicated Caiaphas as being worthy of greater judgment than Pilate (see John 19:11).

Acts 3:20

WH NU — ἀποστείλῃ τὸν προκεχειρισμένον ὑμῖν χριστόν Ἰησοῦν
"He will send you the previously proclaimed Christ, [namely] Jesus."
ℵ B D E 1241
NKJVmg RSV NRSV ESV NIV TNIV NEB REB NJB NAB NLT HCSB NET

variant/TR — αποστειλη τον προκεχειρισμενον υμιν, Ιησουν Χριστον
"He will send you the one previously proclaimed, Jesus Christ."
𝔓[74] A C Ψ 33 1739
KJV NKJV NASB

The WH NU reading has the best combination of witnesses and is the more difficult reading. The prophets proclaimed the coming Messiah; that Messiah, whom God sent to his people, was Jesus. This is different than saying that God was going to send Jesus Christ, who was proclaimed beforehand by the prophets. In other words, the prophets had no knowledge of Jesus, only of a coming Messiah. Jesus was that Messiah (Christ).

Acts 3:21

WH NU — τῶν ἁγίων ἀπ' αἰῶνος αὐτοῦ προφητῶν
"of the holy prophets long ago"
𝔓[74] ℵ* A B* C 1739
RSV NRSV ESV NASB NIV TNIV NEBmg REB NJBmg NAB NLT HCSB NET

variant 1 — των αγιων των απ αιωνος αυτου προφητων
"of his holy prophets from of old"
ℵ[2] B[2] E
none

variant 2/TR πάντων ἁγίων αὐτοῦ προφητῶν ἀπ αἰῶνος
"of all his holy prophets from of old"
(Ψ) Maj
KJV NKJV

variant 3 ἁγίων αὐτοῦ τῶν προφητῶν
"of his holy prophets"
D it Tertullian
NEB NJB

According to the WH NU text, the full reading is "he must remain in heaven until the times of restoration of all things, which God spoke through the mouth of the holy prophets long ago." In defense of the D-reading (variant 3), Tasker (1964, 430) argues that the absence of απ αιωνος in D and the various positions it assumes in the manuscript tradition marks it as a scribal insertion borrowed from Luke 1:70. But why would scribes add a difficult expression? It could just as easily be argued that the expression was originally in the text and various scribes moved it around or deleted it. Scribes were probably perplexed regarding whether απ αιωνος ("from ages" = "of old") describes the prophets as being ancient or whether it describes God's speaking as originating from long ago. The Bezaean scribe (contra Tasker) eliminated the complication by eliminating the expression. But the WH NU reading has good support and accords with Luke 1:70, where απ αιωνος expresses the timelessness of God's speaking through the ancient prophets. The English versions are divided on this issue, with NEB and NJB following the D-text. As noted before, NJB—of all the translations—has the greatest tendency to follow the D-text and/or Western text.

Acts 3:22a

WH NU Μωϋσῆς μὲν εἶπεν
"Moses indeed said"
𝔓74vid ℵ A B C
RSV NRSV ESV NASB NIV TNIV NEB REB NJB NAB NLT HCSB NET

variant 1/TR Μωυσης μεν γαρ προς τους πατερας ειπεν
"for Moses indeed said to the fathers"
Maj
KJV NKJV HCSBmg

variant 2 Μωυσης μεν ειπεν προς τους πατερας ημων
"Moses indeed said to our fathers"
D 33vid it
none

variant 3 Μωυσης μεν ειπεν προς τους πατερας
"Moses indeed said to the fathers"
Ψ 1739 syr^h
none

The WH NU reading has outstanding manuscript support. The expanded text, in whatever form, is a natural scribal extension, perhaps influenced by 3:13 and 3:25.

Acts 3:22b

TR NU	κύριος ὁ θεὸς ὑμῶν "the Lord your God" ℵ[2] A D 1739 KJV NKJV NRSV NIV TNIV NAB NLT HCSB NET
variant 1	κυριος ο θεος ημων "the Lord our God" ℵ* C E Ψ 33 syr[h] none
variant 2/WH	κυριος ο θεος "the Lord God" B it[h,p] Eusebius RSV ESV NASB NEB REB NJB

The Septuagint version of Deut 18:15 reads κυριος ο θεος σου ("the Lord your God"), which Luke has here pluralized—unless B preserves the original text. In any case, the two pronouns, ημων and υμων, were often confused in textual transmission because they sounded similar and looked nearly identical. Thus, it is difficult to determine which one Luke wrote—and in the final analysis, it is hardly significant.

Acts 4:1

TR NU	οἱ ἱερεῖς καὶ ὁ στρατηγὸς τοῦ ἱεροῦ "the priests and the captain of the temple" ℵ A E Ψ 0165 33 1739 it syr cop KJV NKJV RSV NRSV ESV NASB NIV TNIV NEBmg REBmg NJB NAB NLT HCSB NET
variant 1/WH	οι αρχιερεις και ο στρατηγος του ιερου "the chief priests and the captain of the temple" B C NEB REB
variant 2	οι ιερεις "the priests" D none

It is difficult to explain why "chief priests" would have been changed to "priests" if the former were originally in the text. Conversely, it is easier to explain why scribes would have changed "priests" to "chief priests": They did so to correlate 4:1 with 4:6, which mentions the chief priests, Annas and Caiaphas. NEB (followed by REB) adopted the reading "chief priests" on the grounds "that action by superior officials seems to be indicated" (Tasker 1964, 430). But it is precisely that reason that prompted scribes to make the change. Finally, the D-reviser, for some unknown reason, deleted mention of "the captain of the temple," who was second in rank to the high priest.

Acts 4:2

Western text (D) reads:

> "They were teaching the people and proclaiming **Jesus in [by] the resurrection of the dead.**"

The original text says, "that in Jesus there is the resurrection of the dead." The apostles were arguing with the Sadducees (who deny the resurrection) that there is a resurrection as evidenced by Jesus' resurrection. The D-reviser may have wanted to clarify this point, but the resultant text misses the mark.

Acts 4:4

According to good manuscript authority (𝔓[74] ℵ A), the verse says "five thousand" (χιλιαδες πεντε) men responded to the gospel. WH NU adopted the reading ως χιλιαδες πεντε ("about five thousand") on the basis of fairly good documentary support (B D 0165). Other manuscripts (E Ψ Maj—so TR) read ωσει χιλιαδες πεντε ("about five thousand"). It seems that the qualifying word ωσει ("about") is a scribal addition borrowed from 2:41.

Acts 4:6

TR WH NU — Ἰωάννης καὶ Ἀλέξανδρος
"John and Alexander"
𝔓[74] ℵ A B (E 33 1739) 0165 syr cop
KJV NKJV RSV NRSV ESV NASB NIV TNIV NEBmg REB NJBmg NAB NLT HCSB NET

variant — Ιωναθας και Αλεξανδρος
"Jonathan and Alexander"
D it[gig,p]
NRSVmg NEB REBmg NJB

It is not known who John and Alexander were. Annas was high priest from A.D. 6–15; and his son-in-law, Caiaphas, was high priest from A.D. 18–36. According to Josephus (*Ant.* 18.4.3), Jonathan was supposed to have succeeded Caiaphas, per Annas's appointment. Thus, the D-reviser was most likely supplying a historically known figure for an unknown. (This does not mean that Luke was wrong in naming John and Alexander, because each of these men could have been part of the priestly family without necessarily becoming the high priest.) Those who argue for the Western text as being original would have to satisfactorily explain why scribes would change "Jonathan"—if it had originally been in the text—to "John." Tasker's argument (1964, 430) that the familiar name "John" was substituted for an unfamiliar is not convincing.

Acts 4:8

WH NU — πρεσβύτεροι
"elders"
𝔓[74] ℵ A B 0165 cop
RSV NRSV ESV NASB NIV TNIV NEB REB NJB NAB (NLT) HCSB NET

variant/TR — πρεσβυτεροι του Ισραηλ
"elders of Israel"
D E Ψ 33 1739 Maj it syr[p]
KJV NKJV NETmg

The simpler wording in WH NU has excellent documentary support. The scribal addition, "of Israel," achieves symmetry with "of the people," producing "rulers of the people"/"elders of Israel." It also accords with 4:10, where Peter speaks to "the people of Israel."

Acts 4:10

At the end of this verse, a few witnesses (E it^{h} syr^{hmg}) add και εν αλλω ουδενι ("and in no other"), thereby producing the reading (as in the NJB): "you must know, all of you, and the whole people of Israel, that it is by the name of Jesus Christ the Nazarene, whom you crucified, and God raised from the dead, by this name *and by no other* that this man stands before you cured" (emphasis mine).

Acts 4:12-16

Western text (D) reads:

> "'There is [salvation] in no one else, for there is no other name under heaven given among **mortals by which we must be saved.'** 13 Now when they saw the boldness of Peter and John and realized that they were uneducated [and common] men, they were amazed and recognized them as companions of Jesus. 14 When they saw the man who had been cured standing beside them, they could **do or** say nothing in opposition. 15 So they ordered them to **be led out of** the council while they discussed the matter with one another. 16 They said, 'What will we do with them? For it is **more than** clear to all who live in Jerusalem that a notable sign has been done through them; we cannot deny it.'"

The D-reviser adjusted this portion with two deletions, one substitution, and two additions. He excised η σωτηρια ("salvation") as interfering with the final clause δει σωθηναι ημας ("for you to be saved"), and he excised ιδιωται ("common men"), perhaps because he considered the term too degrading for the apostles or because he took it as a synonym for the previous noun, αγραμματοι ("unlearned"). The term ιδιωται means nothing more than that they were laymen or unprofessionals. The additions in 4:14 and 4:16 serve to intensify the account, and the substitution of απαχθηναι ("to be led out") is more potent than απελθειν ("to leave"). And he intensified φανερον ("clear") by making it φανερωτερον ("more than clear").

Acts 4:18

Western text (D it^{gig,h} syr^{hmg}) reads:

> "So **when they had agreed to this decision,** they called them and ordered them not to speak or teach at all in the name of Jesus."

The Western text interpolation was intended to help the reader connect 4:17 with 4:18, but readers normally do this kind of narrative gap-filling automatically.

Acts 4:24a

Western text (D cop^{mae}) reads:

> "And when they heard it **and recognized the working of God,** with one accord they lifted up their voice to God."

This interpolation was added to help readers understand that the early believers recognized God's providential hand in the recent events (see 4:13-22; cf. 4:28).

Acts 4:24b

WH NU δέσποτα, σὺ ὁ ποιήσας τὸν οὐρανόν
"Master, you who made the heaven"
𝔓74 ℵ A B copbo
RSV NRSV ESV NASB NIV TNIV NEB REB NJB NAB NLT HCSB NET

variant 1/TR δεσποτα, συ ο θεος ο ποιησας τον ουρανον
"Master, you are the God who made heaven"
D E Ψ 1739 Maj syr copsa
KJV NKJV

variant 2 δεσποτα, συ κυριε ο θεος ο ποιησας τον ουρανον
"Master, you are the Lord God who made heaven"
33 (eth arm)
none

The first and second variants are scribal expansions, probably intended to heighten the believers' adoration in prayer or imitate prayers found in the OT, such as in Exod 20:11; Ps 146:6; Isa 37:16-20.

Acts 4:25

WH NU ὁ τοῦ πατρὸς ἡμῶν διὰ πνεύματος ἁγίου στόματος Δαυὶδ παιδός σου εἰπών
"the one speaking through the Holy Spirit by the mouth of your servant, our father David"
𝔓74 ℵ A B E Ψ 33 1739
NKJVmg RSV NRSV ESV NASB NIV TNIV NJB NAB NLT HCSB NET

variant 1 ος δια πνευματος αγιου του στοματος λαλησας Δαυιδ παιδος σου
"who spoke through the Holy Spirit by the mouth of your servant David"
D (itd syrp)
NEB REB

variant 2/TR ο δια στοματος Δαυιδ παιδος σου ειπων
"the one speaking through the mouth of your servant David"
181 614 Maj (itp arm geo) Chrysostom
KJV NKJV NEBmg

This verse, as it reads in the best manuscripts, is exceedingly difficult to translate because God's speaking is both through the Holy Spirit and David's mouth (simultaneously) and because David is called both God's servant and the Jews' father. The text would seem to be so much simpler if one of each of the options were written, not all four! Consequently, various scribes tried to relieve the text of this heavy load by getting rid of "our father" (as in the first variant) or both "through the Spirit" and "our father" (as in the second variant—so TR). However, most Greek scribes kept the text as is, and this presents the problem of understanding how God spoke through the Holy Spirit and David simultaneously, when it would seem more logical for David (as a prophet) to be the one speaking by the Holy Spirit. If this is what Luke intended (or actually wrote), then the text—as it has come down to us—does not say this. What the text says is that God spoke through the Holy Spirit and David's mouth as through a united oracle. Westcott and Hort (1881, 92) recognized that the mouth of David is represented as the mouth of the Holy Spirit. This can be affirmed because, according to the Greek, David's "mouth" is in apposition to the "Holy Spirit"; this indicates that David's prophetic utterance (in Ps 2:1-2) was the same as the Holy Spirit's.

Acts 4:27

WH NU	include ἐν τῇ πόλει ταύτῃ ("in this city") 𝔓74 א A B D Maj RSV NRSV ESV NASB NIV TNIV NEB REB NJB NAB NLT HCSB NET
variant/TR	omit 69 KJV NKJV

The omission in TR likely came about because the words are not represented in the passage from Ps 2, which Luke just quoted.

Acts 4:31

Western text (D E it[r] Irenaeus) reads:

> "When they had prayed, the place in which they were gathered together was shaken; and they were all filled with the Holy Spirit and spoke the word of God with boldness **to everyone who wanted to believe.**"

Curiously, the addition in the Western text specifies the audience as those who wanted to believe. But why would it take specially endowed boldness to proclaim the word of God to those who had a desire to believe? Rather, the believers were asking for boldness to preach the word even to their adversaries. Perhaps the Western text here reflects the influence of a predestination theology or of other passages in Acts such as 13:48, which says that it was those who had been foreordained to receive eternal life who believed the word when they heard it.

Acts 4:32

Western text (D E) reads:

> "Now the whole group of those who believed were of one heart and soul, **and there was no quarreling among them at all,** and no one claimed private ownership of any possessions, but everything they owned was held in common."

The D-text could also mean that there was no distinction (διακρισις) among the believers due to their practice of commonality. Manuscript E says there was no division (χωρισμος) among them. Either way, these are both scribal enhancements intended to magnify the unity of spirit that the church in Jerusalem enjoyed at that time.

Acts 4:33

All three editions (TR WH NU) read της αναστασεως του κυριου Ιησου ("the resurrection of the Lord Jesus"), with good support: 𝔓8 (B) Ψ Maj syr[h] cop[sa]. As often happened throughout the course of textual transmission, the divine title was expanded: (1) κυριου Ιησου Χριστου ("Lord Jesus Christ") in D E 1739; (2) Ιησου Χριστου του Κυριου ("Jesus Christ the Lord") in א A.

Acts 5:3

The verb επληρωσεν ("filled"), in the expression "why has Satan filled your heart," has excellent support: 𝔓[8] ℵ[2] A B D E Ψ 0189 33[vid] 1739. This verb is επηρωσεν ("maimed") in ℵ* and επειρασεν ("tempted") in 𝔓[74] (also reflected in the Vulgate). The first variant was hardly intentional; it was simply a scribal mistake of omitting the *lamda*, which was then corrected. The second variant was intentional: Either the scribe of 𝔓[74] thought his exemplar had a mistake or he presumed it more natural to speak of Satan "tempting" Ananias (see 5:9) than "filling" his heart.

Acts 5:4

The three editions (TR WH NU) read το πραγμα τουτο ("this thing") in the expression, "why have you conceived this thing in your heart?" This has the excellent support of 𝔓[8] ℵ A B C. A few other witnesses (𝔓[74] D* syr[p] cop[sa]) change this to ποιησαι το πονηρον το τουτο (𝔓[74] retains πραγμα). This yields the rendering, "Why have you conceived to do this evil thing in your heart?" This variant reading is a scribal amplification emphasizing the wickedness of Ananias's evil intentions.

Acts 5:8

Western text (D) reads:

> "Peter said to her, '**I will ask you if indeed you** sold the land for such and such a price.' And she said, 'Yes, that was the price.'"

This is a typical Western text expansion.

Acts 5:9

In place of the unusual expression το πνευμα κυριου ("the Spirit of the Lord"), found in early witnesses like 𝔓[8] 𝔓[57vid] ℵ B 0189, some later scribes (𝔓[74] 1838) wrote the more common, το πνευμα το αγιον ("the Holy Spirit"). These few scribes were probably influenced by 5:3, as well as by several other verses in Luke and Acts wherein it is apparent that Luke was fond of this expression. But Luke used other titles for the Spirit, especially to emphasize the union between Christ and the Spirit in the evangelistic activity of the believers: "the Spirit of the Lord" (8:39) and "the Spirit of Jesus" (16:7).

Acts 5:10

Western text (D syr[p]) reads:

> "Immediately she fell down at his feet and died. When the young men came in they found her dead; so they **wrapped her up and** carried her out and buried her beside her husband."

This addition reflects the reviser's penchant for adding circumstantial details to the text. The reader is well able to do this without its explicit mention in the text.

Acts 5:12

(Western text) (D cop^{G67,mae,sa}) reads:

> "Now many signs and wonders were done among the people through the apostles. And they were all together **in the temple** in Solomon's Colonnade."

This addition, again, shows the reviser's proclivity for adding circumstantial details to the text. Codex E adds εν τω ναω συνηγμενοι ("they were gathering in the temple").

Acts 5:14-15

Western text (D) reads:

> "Yet more than ever believers were added to the Lord, great numbers of both men and women, so that they even carried **their** sick into the streets, and laid them on cots and mats, in order that Peter's shadow might fall on some of them as he came by. **For they were set free from every sickness each of them had.**"

The reviser did some gap-filling by explaining that the sick people who were brought to Peter were healed if his shadow fell on them. This is not explicit in the text. It is possible that not everyone was healed when Peter's shadow passed over them, but that is the message the reviser wanted his readers to get. Other scribes (E it^{gig} vg^{MSS}) made a similar addition: "And they were delivered from whatever disease they had."

Acts 5:16

WH NU — συνήρχετο δὲ καὶ τὸ πλῆθος τῶν πέριξ πόλεων Ἰερουσαλήμ
"a great number of people gathered from the towns around Jerusalem"
𝔓74 ℵ A B 0189
RSV NRSV ESV NASB NIV TNIV NEB REB NJB NAB NLT HCSB NET

variant/TR — συνηρχετο δε και το πληθος των περιξ πολεων εις Ιερουσαλημ
"a great number of people gathered from surrounding towns into Jerusalem"
D E Ψ 1739 Maj
KJV NKJV

The preposition περιξ ("around"), appearing only here in the NT, conjoins with Ιερουσαλημ. As such, Luke was thinking of the townships of Judea near Jerusalem. Unaware of this geographical usage, scribes added the preposition εις ("into") and thereby make the text say that these people were gathering into Jerusalem.

Acts 5:17

TR WH NU — Ἀναστὰς δὲ ὁ ἀρχιερεύς
"the high priest arose"
𝔓45 𝔓74 ℵ A B D Ψ 0189
all

variant 1 Αννας δε ο αρχιερευς
"Annas the high priest"
it^{p}
NJBmg

variant 2 και ταυτα βλεπων αναστας δε ο αρχιερευς
"and seeing these things, the high priest arose"
E it^{e}
none

The first variant is a translator's error—mistaking ΑΝΑΣΤΑΣ ("arose") for ΑΝΝΑΣ ("Annas"), as influenced by 4:6. It should not be noted as a legitimate variant (as in NJBmg). The second variant is a scribal expansion that Bede observed in several Greek manuscripts.

Acts 5:18

Western text (D) reads:

> "They arrested the apostles and put them in the public prison. **And each one went to his own home.**"

This Western text addition is another case of narrative gap-filling, but readers can easily do this for themselves. What is noteworthy about this addition is that it is the same one that begins the pericope of the adulteress (John 7:53; compare the wording in the Greek). Inasmuch as D is the earliest extant Greek witness to include the pericope, it is possible that the Bezaean editor was the one responsible for first adding John 7:53–8:11.

Acts 5:21-22a

Western text (D and syr^{h**} for 5:22) reads:

> "When they heard this, they entered the temple at daybreak and went on with their teaching. When the high priest and those with him arrived, **having risen early** they called together the council and the whole body of the elders of Israel, and sent to the prison to have them brought. [22] But when the temple police came **and opened the prison,** they did not find them **inside.**"

The circumstantial detail added into 5:21 by the editor of D shows his tendency to perform gap-filling. The changes in 5:22 show his tendency to make explicit (i.e., opening prison doors) what is implicit in the text.

Acts 5:28

TR NU [οὐ] παραγγελίᾳ παρηγγείλαμεν ὑμῖν;
"did we not strictly charge you?"
א^{2} D E Ψ 1739 Maj
KJV NKJV NJBmg NAB HCSB NETmg

variant/WH παραγγελια παρηγγειλαμεν υμιν
"we strictly charged you"
𝔓^{74} א* A B
RSV NRSV ESV NASB NIV TNIV NEB REB NJB NLT NET

The majority of NU editors accepted the TR NU reading over against the variant on the basis that scribes altered the text to make it a rebuke rather than a question. Metzger (TCGNT), demurring, argued that the interrogatory format was created due to the influence of the verb επηρωτησεν ("he questioned") in the previous verse. The variant, with excellent testimony, is more likely original, which yields this translation: "we strictly charged you not to teach in this name." Most modern versions follow this variant reading. In the next part of the verse, the D-reviser heightens the caustic nature of the high priest's reference to Jesus by substituting εκεινου ("that") for τουτου ("this") (Longenecker 1981, 321). The Western text becomes βουλεσθε επαγαγειν εφ ημας το αιμα του ανθρωπου εκεινου ("you have determined to bring upon us the blood of that man").

Acts 5:29

Western text (D[c] syr[p]) reads:

> "But Peter [and the apostles] answered, 'We must obey God rather than men.'"

The reviser again (see notes on 1:23; 2:14; 3:17) reveals his preference for Peter as the prominent apostle by omitting Peter's co-apostles from the text.

Acts 5:31

Western text (D it[d] cop[sa] Irenaeus) reads:

> "God exalted him **for his glory** as Leader and Savior that he might give repentance to Israel and forgiveness of sins **in him.**"

The Western reading may have come about as a result of a scribe confusing δοξη ("glory") for δεξια ("right hand"), or of a scribe trying to avoid anthropomorphic language for deity.

Acts 5:32

WH NU
ἡμεῖς ἐσμεν μάρτυρες
"we are witnesses"
𝔓[74vid] ℵ (A) D* cop
RSV NRSV ESV NASB NIV TNIV NEB REB NJB NAB NLT HCSB NET

variant 1/TR
ημεις εσμεν αυτου μαρτυρες
"we are his witnesses"
D[c] E (Ψ) Maj
KJV NKJV

variant 2
εν αυτω εσμεν μαρτυρες
"in him we are witnesses"
(B) 1739
NASBmg

The WH NU reading, having good manuscript support, is likely original. If so, the first variant is a scribal enhancement attempting to make prominent the fact that the apostles were Jesus' witnesses (see 1:8). The second variant reveals a Pauline influence inasmuch as Paul is well known for his use of εν αυτω to mean "in union with Christ."

Acts 5:33

The verb εβουλοντο ("decided"), found in A B E Ψ, suits the context better than εβουλευοντο ("took council"), found in ℵ D Maj, because the scene depicts a rash action motivated by rage rather than a rational decision motivated by judiciousness.

Acts 5:34

WH NU τοὺς ἀνθρώπους
"the men"
𝔓[45vid] ℵ A B
RSV NRSV ESV NASB NIV TNIV NEB REB NJB NAB NLT HCSB NET

variant/TR τους αποστολους
"the apostles"
(D) E Ψ Maj 33[vid]
KJV NKJV HCSBmg

According to WH NU, which have excellent testimony, a full translation is, "He [Gamaliel] commanded the men to be put outside for awhile." Later scribes dignified the "men" on trial before the Sanhedrin by giving them their proper title: "apostles."

Acts 5:35

(Western text) (D cop[sa]) reads:

> "Then he said to **the rulers and those of the council,** 'Men, Israelites, consider carefully what you propose to do to these men.'"

Because the pronoun in the phrase ειπεν τε προς αυτους ("he said to them") could be misconstrued as referring to the apostles (5:34), the D-reviser substituted "them" with "the rulers and those of the council." This shows an editorial concern to make the text unambiguous for the reader.

Acts 5:36

Western text (D E it[gig,h] syr[p]; D only for "he destroyed himself") reads:

> "For some time ago Theudas rose up, claiming to be someone **great,** and a number of men, about four hundred, joined him; but he **destroyed himself,** and all who followed him were dispersed and disappeared."

The expression about Theudas, λεγων ειναι τινα εαυτον, is an idiom that means "claiming to be someone." It hardly requires the addition found in D etc.: μεγαν ("great"). The second change, found in D only, indicates either that Theudas's life ended in suicide or he brought about his own downfall, whereas Josephus said he was captured then decapitated (*Ant.* 20.5.1).

Acts 5:37

WH NU ἀπέστησεν λαόν
"he incited people to revolt"
𝔓[74] ℵ A* B
RSV NRSV ESV NASB NIV NEB REB NJB NAB NLT HCSB NET

variant 1/TR	απεστησεν λαον ικανον "he incited several people to revolt" A[c] (E Ψ 33) 1739 Maj KJV NKJV (TNIV)
variant 2	απεστησεν λαον πολυν "he incited many people to revolt" C[vid] D it none

According to WH NU, which have good documentary support, a full translation is: "he [Judas the Galilean] incited people to follow after him in revolt." The variants probably arose for one of two reasons: (1) scribes, understanding λαον to indicate "the people" (i.e., the whole of Israel), wanted to qualify the expression, or (2) scribes, understanding λαος to indicate only some people, purposely exaggerated the account. Since the TNIV says it was a "band of people," it appears that it follows the first variant, but this is not certain.

Acts 5:38-39

Western text (D syr[h**] and E in part) reads:

> "So in the present case, **brothers,** I tell you, keep away from these men and let them alone, **not defiling your hands;** because if this plan or this undertaking is of man, it will fail;
> 39 but if it is of God, you will not be able to overthrow them—**neither you nor kings nor tyrants. Keep away from these men** so that you won't be found fighting against God!"

According to Metzger (TCGNT) the interpolation in the Western text "shows the influence of a passage in the Wisdom of Solomon where the writer is dealing with the same problem as in Acts, namely the question whether it is safe to oppose God" (see Wis 12:13-14). The variant also promotes a concern for ritual purity (see NJBmg). Gamaliel warns the Sanhedrin not to interfere, for if these men are not from God, the members of the Sanhedrin would have defiled themselves by interacting with them.

Acts 5:41

WH NU	ὑπὲρ τοῦ ὀνόματος "for the sake of the Name" 𝔓[74] א A B C (D) 1739 NKJVmg RSV NRSV ESV NIV TNIV NEB REB NJB NAB (NLT) HCSB NET
variant 1	υπερ του ονοματος αυτου "for the sake of his name" 945 1175 KJV NKJV NASB
variant 2	υπερ του ονοματος Ιησου "for the sake of the name of Jesus" Ψ 33 Maj NJKVmg

variant 3 υπερ του ονοματος κυριου Ιησου
"for the sake of the name Lord Jesus"
E syr[h]
none

According to the superior documentary evidence, the absolute use of the term του ονοματος ("the Name"), referring to the all-inclusiveness of Jesus Christ's person, is spoiled here by the additions. The early Christians knew that "the Name" denoted "Jesus Christ." Other NT writers simply said "the Name" and expected their readers to know that this referred to Jesus Christ (see Heb 13:15; Jas 2:7; 3 John 7).

Acts 6:1

Western text (D it[h]) reads:

> "Now during those days, when the disciples were increasing in number, the Hellenists complained against the Hebrews because their widows were being neglected in the daily distribution, **in the distribution of the Hebrews.**"

This Bezaean addition is so clumsy that considerations other than stylistic ones must have motivated the interpolation. Evidently, the reviser wanted to make it clear that it was the "Hebrews" (the Hebraic Jews or Aramaic-speaking Jews) who were responsible for distributing food to the needy in the early Christian community, and it was the Hellenists (the Hellenistic Jews or Greek-speaking Jews) who were on the receiving end. Since the Hebrews were natives of Jerusalem or Judea, they assumed the responsibility for helping the Hellenists, who were Jews that returned to Jerusalem after the Diaspora. The reviser, having this knowledge, wanted to clarify this for his readers.

Acts 6:3a

Western text (D it[h,p] Marcion) reads:

> "**What is it then,** brothers, select from among yourselves seven men of good standing."

The additional words in the Western text serve little purpose. By contrast, a change in B—from επισκεψασθε ("you select") to επισκεψωμεθα ("let us select")—is a scribal effort to include the apostles in the act of selecting the seven deacons.

Acts 6:3b

WH NU πλήρεις πνεύματος καὶ σοφίας
"[men] full of the Spirit and wisdom"
𝔓8 𝔓74 א B C2 D
RSV NRSV ESV NASB NIV TNIV NEB REB NJB NAB NLT HCSB NET

variant/TR πληρεις πνευματος αγιου και σοφιας
"[men] full of the Holy Spirit and wisdom"
A C* E Ψ Maj
KJV NKJV

The WH NU reading has excellent manuscript support. Scribes frequently added the word αγιος ("holy") to the word πνευμα ("Spirit") in an attempt to clarify the identity of the Spirit. In this case, it was convenient for scribes to borrow the same terminology from 6:5.

Acts 6:5

Western text (D it^h) reads:

> "What they said pleased the multitude **of the disciples,** and they chose Stephen, a man full of faith and the Holy Spirit, together with Philip, Prochorus, Nicanor, Timon, Parmenas, and Nicolaus, a proselyte of Antioch."

This addition shows that the reviser wanted to make it clear that the "multitude" (πληθους) was not a multitude of unbelievers, but the whole congregation of believers.

Acts 6:7a

TR WH NU	ὁ λόγος τοῦ θεοῦ "the word of God" 𝔓74 א A B C 33 1739 cop KJV NKJV RSV NRSV ESV NASB NIV TNIV NEB REB NAB NLT HCSB NET
variant	ο λογος του κυριου "the word of the Lord" D E Ψ it syr^h NJB

Since Luke used both phrases—"the word of the Lord" and "the word of God"—in equal distribution throughout Acts, stylistic concerns cannot help us determine which wording Luke wrote. Thus, it is best to make a determination on the basis of the documentary evidence, which decidedly favors "the word of God"—even though it could be argued that "the word of God" was carried over from 6:2. NJB alone followed the Western text.

Acts 6:7b

Luke remarks that πολυς τε οχλος των ιερεων υπηκουον τη πιστει ("a great crowd of the priests were becoming obedient to the faith"). That so many Jewish priests would have become Christians seems to have perplexed a few scribes (א* 142 424 syr^p), who changed ιερεων ("priests") to Ιουδαιων ("Jews"). But Jeremias (1969, 198-213) indicates there were 8,000 priests and 10,000 Levites serving in Jerusalem at this time; thus, for a large group of priests to become believers is not extraordinary.

Acts 6:8a

WH NU	πλήρης χάριτος καὶ δυνάμεως "full of grace and power" 𝔓8 𝔓45 𝔓74 א A B D 0175 33 1739 NKJVmg RSV NRSV ESV NASB NIV TNIV NEB REB NJB NAB NLT HCSB NET
variant 1/TR	πληρης πιστεως και δυναμεως "full of faith and power" Maj syr^h KJV NKJV
variant 2	πληρης χαριτος και πιστεως και δυναμεως "full of grace and faith and power" E none

variant 3 πληρης πιστεως χαριτος πνευματος και δυναμεως
"full of faith, grace, Spirit, and power"
Ψ
none

The WH NU reading has extraordinarily good documentary support. (The support of 𝔓[45] for WH NU, though listed as "vid," is certain—see *Text of Earliest MSS,* 187). The variants are the result of scribal harmonization and expansion. Each of the three variants likely borrowed from 6:5, which speaks of Stephen being full of faith and the Holy Spirit. TR incorporated the first variant, which was then popularized by KJV.

Acts 6:8b

Western text (D E 33 it syr[h**]) reads:

> "[Stephen] did great wonders and signs among the people **through the name of the Lord Jesus Christ.**"

This expansion could reveal the tendency of "Western" scribes to expand the text based on lexical associations. In this case, the performance of "signs and wonders" evoked the appendage of "through the name of the Lord Jesus Christ," because a similar expression occurred in 4:30.

Acts 6:9

The name Λιβερτινων ("Libertines") seems out of place among a number of place-names (Cyrenians, Alexandrians, Cilicians, and Asians). Hence, it was conjectured by Theodore Beza (see critical apparatus of NA[27]) that it should have read Λιβυστινων ("Libyans"). This problem can be avoided if we read the text as speaking of only one synagogue—the Synagogue of the Libertines—comprised of Cyrenians, Alexandrians, Cilicians, and Asians, as opposed to five separate Hellenistic synagogues in Jerusalem. This "singular" treatment is supported by the reading της λεγομενης Λιβερτινων ("the one called 'Libertines'" in 𝔓[8] 𝔓[74] B C D E P etc.) versus των λεγομενων Λιβερτινων ("the ones being called 'Libertines'" in ℵ A 0175 33).

Acts 6:10-11

Western text (D E syr[hmg]) reads:

> "But they could not withstand the wisdom **that was in him** and the **Holy** Spirit with which he spoke**, because they were confuted by him with all boldness.** [11] **Being unable, therefore, to face up to the truth,** they secretly instigated some men to say, 'We have heard him speak blasphemous words against Moses and God.'"

The causal insertion in 6:10b intends to explain why the Jews could not withstand Stephen's wisdom. But this did not lead to humble acceptance of Stephen's message. Rather, they denied the truth and instigated a plot to murder Stephen (6:11). All this comes from reading in-between the lines—a task the reviser was very willing to do. Knowing what is ahead, he supplies a few hints about Stephen's boldness and the Jews' recalcitrance.

Acts 6:13

WH NU οὐ παύεται λαλῶν ῥήματα
"he never stops saying things"
𝔓8vid 𝔓45 𝔓74 א (A) B C (D)
NKJVmg RSV NRSV ESV NASB NIV TNIV NEB REB NJB NAB NLT NET

variant/TR ου παυεται ρηματα βλασφημα λαλων
"he never stops saying blasphemous things"
E Ψ (33) Maj
KJV NKJV HCSB

The scribal insertion in TR of the word "blasphemous" heightens the accusation against Stephen: "They set up false witnesses who said, 'This man never stops saying blasphemous things against the holy place.'" TR is followed here, as usual, by KJV and NKJV as well as the HCSB, which has a habit of following the KJV tradition.

Acts 6:15

Western text (D it[h]) reads:

> "And all who sat in the council looked intently at him, and they saw that his face was like the face of an angel **standing in their midst.**"

J. Rendell Harris (1894, 70-75) argued that the Bezaean expansion could belong at the beginning of 7:1, as follows: "**Standing in their midst,** the high priest then asked him, 'Are these things so?'" But he based his argument on the Latin text of D, not the Greek, whose genitive expression εστωτος εν μεσω αυτων ("standing in their midst") must agree with the genitive αγγελου ("angel").

Acts 7:1

Western text (D E it) reads:

> "And the high priest **said to Stephen, 'Is this thing** so?'"

Because this verse marks the beginning of a new chapter, some scribes thought it helpful to reintroduce Stephen's name into the text. Some modern English versions do the same (for example, see NLT and TEV).

Acts 7:4

Western text (D E syr[h**]) reads:

> "Then **Abraham** left the country of the Chaldeans and settled in Haran. And **there he was** until after his father died. Then God had him move from there to this country in which you are now living, **and our fathers who were before us.**"

The last addition, "and our fathers who were before us," provides Stephen's speech with a greater sense of identification with his audience.

Acts 7:13

Metzger (TCGNT), in defense of the selection of ανεγνωρισθη over against εγνωρισθη, argued that the former was changed to the latter because "the compound form seems to imply that Joseph had also made himself known to his brothers on their first visit to Egypt." But the verb ανεγνωρισθη is not used to mean "was made known again—a second time" but simply, "was recognized." Joseph was recognized by his brothers on their second visit. Thus, it is far more likely that ανεγνωρισθη, found in 𝔓74 א C D E Ψ Maj, is a scribal modification based on the Septuagint (Gen 45:1). A and B probably preserve the original wording, εγνωρισθη (so WH).

Acts 7:16

WH NU	τῶν υἱῶν Ἐμμὼρ ἐν Συχέμ "the sons of Hamor in Shechem" א* B C 1739 RSV NRSV ESV NASB NIV TNIV NEB REB NJBmg NAB NLT HCSB NET
variant 1	των υιων Εμμωρ του εν Συχεμ "the sons of Hamor, the one in Shechem" א2 A E NJBmg
variant 2/TR	των υιων Εμμωρ του Συχεμ "the sons of Hamor, the [father] of Shechem" 𝔓74 D Ψ Maj KJV NKJV NJB
variant 3	"the sons of Hamor" syrp none

According to WH NU, the verse is rendered: "And they were brought back to Shechem and laid in the tomb that Abraham had bought for a sum of silver from the sons of Hamor in Shechem." The second variant makes Shechem a person, not a place. If this was true, then the place mentioned in the first part of the verse was named after the person, Shechem. But it seems odd that a place would be named after a living grandson of Hamor. Thus, it seems more likely that the first variant arose as a slight adjustment of the text, and subsequently the second variant was the result of scribal inadvertence, wherein the word εν ("in") was accidentally omitted. The third variant solves the problem by omitting the name altogether.

Acts 7:17

WH NU, with the support of 𝔓74 א A B C, have the verb ωμολογησεν, meaning "he promised" or "he assured" in this context. But there are two variants on this: (1) επηγγειλατο ("he promised") in 𝔓45 D E; (2) ωμοσεν ("he swore") in Ψ 1739 Maj (so TR). The verb ομολογεω was changed by scribes, probably because it had taken on a technical meaning in the early church: to make confession. But in NT usage it conveyed the idea of making a serious promise (see Matt 14:7). The second variant reflects this, while the first is a natural carryover from the previous words.

Acts 7:18

WH NU ἀνέστη βασιλεὺς ἕτερος [ἐπ' Αἴγυπτον]
"a different king arose over Egypt"
𝔓33vid 𝔓74 א A B C Ψ 1739 cop syr^p,hmg
RSV NRSV ESV NASB NIV TNIV NEB REB NJB NAB NLT HCSB NET

variant/TR ανεστη βασιλευς ετερος
"a different king arose"
𝔓45vid D E Maj syr^h
KJV NKJV HCSBmg

Despite the contrary reading of 𝔓45, the manuscript evidence for the WH NU reading is early and diverse. Although it is possible that the WH NU reading is the result of scribal conformity to the Septuagint rendering of Exod 1:8, it is just as likely that "in Egypt" was dropped in the variant because it was perceived to be redundant. (The previous verse says, "our people in Egypt increased and multiplied.") This is all the more likely when one takes note of the fact that the scribe of 𝔓45 had a proclivity for trimming the text.

Acts 7:21

Western text (D E syr^h**) reads:

> "When he was abandoned **by the riverside,** Pharaoh's daughter adopted him and brought him up as her own son."

This is another example of a Western addition that adds color to the text by supplying some narrative details.

Acts 7:24

Western text (D) reads:

> "When he saw one of **his race** being wronged, he defended the oppressed man and avenged him by striking down the Egyptian**, and hid him in the sand.**"

The D-reviser drew upon his knowledge of the OT account (Exod 2:11-12 LXX) to insert some historical details. The last clause finishes out the Septuagint wording of Exod 2:12 verbatim.

Acts 7:26

Western text (D) reads:

> "And **then** on the next day he came to some of them as they were quarreling, **and saw them doing injustice,** and tried to reconcile them, saying, '**What are you doing,** men and brothers? Why do you wrong each other?'"

The D-reviser, reflecting the Septuagint use of the expression τω αδικουντι ("the one doing injustice") in Exod 2:13, incorporated this notion (along with other details) into the text.

Acts 7:30

WH NU ἄγγελος
"angel"
𝔓74 א A B C
NKJVmg RSV NRSV ESV NASB NIV TNIV NEB REB NJB NAB NLT HCSB NET

variant/TR αγγελος κυριου
"angel of the Lord"
D E Ψ 33 1739 Maj syr
KJV NKJV HCSBmg

A full rendering, according to WH NU, is as follows: "And when forty years had passed, an angel appeared to him in the wilderness of Mount Sinai, in the flame of a burning bush." The textual variant is the result of scribes conforming the text to Exod 3:2, which in the Hebrew text is "the angel of Yahweh," and in the Septuagint, "the angel of the Lord." Scribes were motivated to make this title "the angel of the Lord" because this was God's special representative in making divine communications with humanity. In Exod 3, this angel is so linked with Yahweh that he speaks as the voice of Yahweh. The same connections are made in Acts 7:30-32, where we see the angel coming as "the voice of the Lord," speaking for God and even as God.

Acts 7:31

Western text (D syr^{p}) reads:

> "When Moses saw it, he was amazed at the sight; and as he approached to look, **the Lord spoke to him.**"

As was discussed in the previous note, the passage speaks of the angel coming from God, accompanied by "the voice of the Lord" resonating from the burning bush. The D-reviser changed "the voice of the Lord came" to "the Lord spoke to him" to avoid the idea of a voice coming.

Acts 7:32

WH NU ὁ θεὸς 'Αβραὰμ καὶ 'Ισαὰκ καὶ 'Ιακώβ
"the God of Abraham and of Isaac and of Jacob"
𝔓74 א A B C Ψ
RSV NRSV ESV NASB NIV TNIV NEB REB NJB NAB NLT HCSB NET

variant/TR ο θεος Αβρααμ και ο θεος Ισαακ και ο θεος Ιακωβ
"the God of Abraham and the God of Isaac and the God of Jacob"
D E 33 1739 Maj cop
KJV NKJV

The fuller form of this OT citation (Exod 3:6) is most likely the result of scribal conformity to the Septuagint or the gospel citations of the same verse (Matt 22:32; Mark 12:26; Luke 20:37), all of which have "God" in triple form.

Acts 7:37

WH NU at end of verse, omit αυτου ακουσεσθε ("hear him")
𝔓45 א A B Ψ Maj
NKJVmg RSV NRSV ESV NASB NIV TNIV NEB REB NJB NAB NLT HCSB NET

variant/TR	at end of verse, add αυτου ακουσεσθε ("hear him") C D E 33 1739 syr cop[bo] KJV NKJV

The WH NU reading has the support of the four earliest manuscripts (𝔓[45] א A B), as well as the majority of manuscripts. 𝔓[45] does not have to be listed as 𝔓[45vid] (as in NA[27]), because the manuscript shows the last word of 7:37 immediately followed by the first words of 7:38. (For reconstruction, see *Text of Earliest MSS,* 190.) The variant reading is the result of scribes filling out an OT citation to bring it into conformity with Deut 18:15, as well as Acts 3:22, which has the same quotation. The filled-out reading is as follows: "This is the Moses who said to the sons of Israel, 'the Lord God will raise up a prophet for you from your own brothers, as he raised me up. Hear him.'" TR adds "Lord" (supported by C E H P and other MSS) before "God."

Acts 7:38

TR NU	ὃς ἐδέξατο λόγια ζῶντα δοῦναι ἡμῖν "who received living words to give to us" A C D E Ψ 33 1739 Maj syr KJV NKJV RSV NRSV ESV NASB NIV TNIV NEB REB NJB NAB NLT HCSB NETmg
variant/WH	ος εδεξατο λογια ζωντα δουναι υμιν "who received living words to give to you" 𝔓[74] א B cop NASB NLTmg NET

Pronouns are often altered in the course of textual transmission, and in this case, the documentary evidence slightly favors the variant reading, having support from solid Alexandrian witnesses. The NU editors, however, argued for their reading on internal grounds: "It appears from the context that what is needed is ημιν . . . for Stephen does not wish to disassociate himself from those who received God's revelation in the past, but only from those who misinterpreted and disobeyed that revelation" (TCGNT). The translators of the NET argue contrarily that the variant has better external support and is the harder reading and therefore original (see NETmg).

Acts 7:43a

TR NU	τοῦ θεοῦ [ὑμῶν] Ῥαιφάν "your god Rephan" 𝔓[74] א A C E Maj syr[h] cop[bo] (with variations on the spelling for Ραιφαν) KJV NKJV NRSV ESV NIV TNIV NAB NLT HCSB NETmg
variant/WH	του θεου Ραιφαν "the god Rephan" B D syr[p] cop[sa] Irenaeus Origen (with variations on the spelling for Ραιφαν) RSV NASB NEB REB NJB NET

According to TR NU, a full rendering of this verse is: "you took up the tabernacle of Moloch and the star of your god Rephan." The variant looks like a scribal attempt to avoid saying that Rephan (the god of the planet Saturn) had become the god of the Israelites, but this is precisely the message of Amos (5:25-27), here repeated by Stephen—to the chagrin of his listeners. However, it could be that υμων ("your") was added by the scribes of 𝔓[74] א A C etc., to bring the text into conformity with Amos 5:26 (LXX). The English versions are divided on this.

Acts 7:43b

Western text (D* it[gig]) reads:

"I will carry you away **into the parts of** Babylon."

Instead of the reading, "I will carry you beyond Babylon," found in all other manuscripts, the reviser changed the text to "I will carry you into the parts of Babylon," probably to make it clear that this was speaking of the captivity that took the Israelites to Babylon, not to some region beyond Babylon. But the expression "I will carry you beyond Babylon" means, "I will carry you beyond—to Babylon."

Acts 7:46

NU τῷ οἴκῳ 'Ιακώβ
"the house of Jacob"
𝔓74 ℵ* B D H 049
NRSV ESVmg NASBmg NIVmg TNIVmg NEBmg REBmg NJB NAB NLTmg HCSBmg NET

variant/TR WH τω θεω Ιακωβ
"the God of Jacob"
ℵ2 A C E Ψ 33 1739 Maj syr cop
KJV NKJV RSV NRSVmg ESV NASB NIV TNIV NEB REB NJBmg NLT HCSB NETmg

A full rendering of the NU text is as follows: "[David] found grace before God and asked that he might find a dwelling place for the house of Jacob." The variant has "the God of Jacob" for the last words. This is a difficult textual problem. The reading of the NU text, "the house of Jacob," has the best documentary support but makes the least sense. The variant reading has inferior documentary support, but makes the best sense. The arguments for the reading of the NU text are: (1) it has the best combination of witnesses (especially B with D); (2) it is the more difficult reading and therefore was subject to change; and (3) it varies from the Septuagint (Ps 132:5), which is often a sign of originality. The arguments for the variant are: (1) it has a wide variety of witnesses; (2) it suits the context thematically (David wanted to build a tabernacle for God) and grammatically (the following οικοδομησεν αυτω—"built for him"—in 7:47 accords with τω θεω); and (3) it perfectly agrees with the Septuagint (Ps 132:5). The conflicting criteria for making a sure textual decision is displayed in the English versions. The translators who adopt the variant reading probably do so on the basis that it more naturally fits the context. Those who accept "the house of Jacob" as original could interpret the passage to mean that David was asking God if he could seek out or find for the Israelites (i.e., "the house of Jacob") a permanent sanctuary wherein God would dwell; then Solomon fulfilled David's desire by building a temple. Another interpretation, proposed by Klijn (1957), is that David was seeking to establish a spiritual house within the house of Jacob. In any event, this textual variant is a good place for translators to tell readers that both variants could be original. One simple way to do this is to use the word "Or" before citing the reading in other manuscripts. For example, a translation which has "the house of Jacob" in the text would have a note that reads: "Or, as in other manuscripts, 'the God of Jacob.'"

Acts 7:55

Western text (D it^h,p^) reads:

> "But filled with the Holy Spirit, he gazed into heaven and saw the glory of God and Jesus **the Lord** standing at the right hand of God."

The D-reviser had a penchant for adding names to "Jesus"—sometimes he added "Lord," and sometimes "Christ."

Acts 7:56

As often happened in the transmission of the New Testament text (for example, see John 9:35), some scribes could not resist changing υιον του ανθρωπου ("Son of Man") to υιον του θεου ("Son of God"). Here this change was made in 𝔓[74vid] 614 and some cop[bo] manuscripts.

Acts 8:1

Western text (D) reads:

> "And there arose that day a great persecution **and affliction** against the church in Jerusalem, and all were scattered throughout the countryside of Judea and Samaria, except the apostles, **who remained in Jerusalem.**"

This expanded text shows the work of the D-reviser, who enjoyed multiplying words (adding "and affliction"), as well as inserting circumstantial details ("who remained in Jerusalem"). Again, this addition supplies in actual words what is implicit in the text.

Acts 8:4

Several Western witnesses (E it[t,w] vg syr[p]) add του θεου ("of God") after τον λογον ("the word").

Acts 8:5

WH NU	[τὴν] πόλιν τῆς Σαμαρείας "the city of Samaria" 𝔓[74] ℵ A B KJV NKJV NRSV ESV NASB NJBmg NAB NLT HCSBmg (NET)
variant/TR	πολιν της Σαμαρειας "a city of Samaria" C D E Ψ 33 1739 Maj NKJVmg RSV NRSVmg ESVmg NIV TNIV NEB REB NJB HCSB

The WH NU reading has the testimony of four very reliable manuscripts. Given this reading, was Luke referring to the actual city that was called Samaria in Old Testament times and then changed to Sebaste by Herod the Great? Or was he referring to Shechem, the main city of the region of Samaria (see note in NET), which was known as the religious headquarters for the Samaritans? This ambiguity probably prompted scribal change to "a city of Samaria" (cf. Matt 10:5). Nonetheless, several modern English versions follow this variant reading likely because the wording in WH NU ("the city of Samaria") is vague in that there were a number of cities in Samaria.

Acts 8:16

Western text (D) reads:

> "For as yet the Spirit had not fallen upon any of them; they had only been baptized in the name of the Lord Jesus **Christ.**"

The D-reviser had a habit of expanding Jesus' name to either "Lord Jesus" or "Lord Jesus Christ." For examples, see 1:21; 3:13; 4:33; 11:20; 15:11; 16:31; 19:5; 21:13.

Acts 8:18

WH NU τὸ πνεῦμα
"the Spirit"
א A^c B cop[sa] Apostolic Constitutions
RSV NRSV ESV NASB NIV TNIV NEB REB NJB NAB NLT HCSBmg NET

variant/TR πνευμα το αγιον
"the Holy Spirit"
𝔓[45] 𝔓[74] A* C D E 33 1739
KJV NKJV HCSB NETmg

The WH NU reading in fuller translation is as follows: "when Simon saw that the Spirit was given through the laying on of the apostles' hands, he offered them money." The shorter title, "the Spirit," would more likely be changed to the longer than vice versa because scribes would be inclined to make the account of the Samaritans' Spirit Baptism conform to all the other accounts in Acts (i.e., the disciples on Pentecost, Saul of Tarsus, the Gentiles with Cornelius), each of which says that the believers received the Holy Spirit (see Acts 2:4; 9:17; 11:15). Furthermore, scribes would have been inclined to conform this verse to the previous one, which has πνευμα αγιον in all manuscripts. Thus, the slim but early testimony of א A^c B most likely attests to the original wording.

Acts 8:19

Western text (D it[gig,p]) reads:

> "He was **exhorting and** saying, 'Give me also this power so that anyone on whom I **also** lay my hands may receive the Holy Spirit.'"

These are Western text additions intended to enhance the force of Simon's request.

Acts 8:24

Western text (D and syr[hmg] in part) reads:

> "Simon answered **and said to them, 'I beseech you,** pray for me to **God,** that none of these **evils** of which you have said may happen to me.' **And he ceased not to shed many tears.**"

This verse displays some of the reviser's most ambitious, but superfluous, additions. The last addition is a colorful but clumsy one, intended to show that Simon repented with great remorse. But all of these changes are simply imaginative gap-filling. Others, such as the Pseudo-Clementines (*Homilies* 20.21), pictured Simon as weeping tears of rage and disappointment.

Acts 8:27

According to the best manuscript evidence (𝔓50 א A B C Dc E), the text identifies the Ethiopian eunuch as δυναστης Κανδακης βασιλισσης Αιθιοπων ("a court official of Candace, queen of the Ethiopians"). In this context, "Candace" is not the proper name of the queen, but the title for a woman ruler (as was customarily used in the Hellenistic period). This is made clear in certain versions by printing it as "a court official of the Candace, queen of the Ethiopians" (NRSV) or "a high official of Kandake, or Queen, of Ethiopia" (NEB). Later manuscripts (Ψ Maj 33 1739) reflect an attempt to identify the eunuch as belonging to a person named Candace, the queen of Ethiopia. This was achieved by adding a definite article: Κανδακης της βασιλισσης ("Candace the queen"). The reviser (D*), changed the text to δυναστης Κανδακης βασιλισσης τινος Αιθιοπων ("an official of Candace, a certain one of the queen of the Ethiopians").

Acts 8:37

WH NU	omit verse 𝔓45 𝔓74 א A B C Ψ 33vid syrp copbo,sa Chrysostom Ambrose NKJVmg RSV NRSV ESV NASBmg NIV TNIV NEB REB NJB NAB NLT HCSBmg NET
variant/TR	add verse Ειπεν δε ο Φιλιππος, Ει πιστευεις εξ ολης της καρδιας, εξεστιν. Αποκριθεις δε ειπεν, Πιστευω τον υιον του θεου ειναι τον Ιησουν Χριστον. "And Philip said, 'If you believe with all your heart, you may.' And he replied, 'I believe that Jesus Christ is the Son of God.'" 4mg (E 1739 it syrh** Irenaeus Cyprian) KJV NKJV RSVmg NRSVmg ESVmg NASB NIVmg TNIVmg NEBmg REBmg NJBmg NABmg NLTmg HCSB NETmg

If the verse was an original part of Luke's text, there is no good reason for explaining why it would have been omitted in so many ancient manuscripts and versions. Rather, this verse is a classic example of scribal gap-filling, in that it supplied the apparent gap left by the unanswered question of the previous verse ("The eunuch said, 'Look, here is water! What is to prevent me from being baptized?'"). The interpolation puts an answer on Philip's lips that is derived from ancient Christian baptismal practices. Before being baptized, the new believer had to make a confession of his or her faith in Jesus as the Son of God. A similar addition also worked its way into the text of John 9:38-39 (see note).

There is nothing doctrinally wrong with this interpolation; it affirms belief with the heart (in accordance with verses like Rom 10:9-10) and elicits the response of faith in Jesus Christ as the Son of God (in accordance with verses like John 20:31). But it is not essential that one make such a verbatim confession before being baptized. In fact, the eunuch had made no such confession, but it was obvious to Philip that he believed Jesus was the Messiah when the eunuch said, "Look, here is water. What prevents me from being baptized?" This is part of the beauty of the book of Acts: Many individuals come to faith in Christ in a variety of ways. The church throughout history has had a habit of standardizing the way people express their faith in Christ.

It is difficult to know when this interpolation first entered the text, but it could have been as early as the second century, since Irenaeus (*Haer.* 3.12.8) quoted part of it. The earliest extant Greek manuscript to include it is E, of the sixth century. Erasmus included the verse in his edition of the Greek New Testament because—even though it was not present in many of the manuscripts he knew—he considered it to have been omitted by the carelessness of scribes. He based its inclusion on a marginal reading in codex 4 (see TCGNT). From Erasmus's edition it worked its way into TR and subsequently KJV. The only reason it is printed in the margins of all the other versions is that translations invariably inform the reader about instances in which the text omits a verse that is often included in other prominent versions, especially KJV. The NASB and HCSB, with typical sensitivity to the KJV tradition, include the verse, though it is set in brackets.

Acts 8:39

TR WH NU πνεῦμα κυρίου ἥρπασεν τὸν Φίλιππον
"the Spirit of the Lord carried away Philip"
𝔓45 𝔓74 ℵ A* B C E Ψ 33vid
all

variant πνευμα αγιον επεπεσεν επι τον ευνουχον, αγγελος δε ηρπασεν τον Φιλιππον
"the Holy Spirit fell on the eunuch, and an angel carried away Philip"
Ac 1739 itw (syrh**) arm geo
NJBmg

The documentary evidence firmly establishes the TR WH NU reading as original. But this reading may have presented an exegetical problem to a certain scribe (or scribes) because it seems to say that Philip was suddenly snatched away (ηρπασεν) by the Lord's Spirit and transported to Azotus. Apparently it seemed more likely to the scribe that the Holy Spirit fell on the eunuch, and that an angel carried Philip away. These assumptions were based on (1) a pattern in the book of Acts in which the Holy Spirit fell on believers after they were baptized (see 2:38; 19:5-6), and (2) the fact that an angel was with Philip at the beginning of this episode (8:26) and would have transported him to his next destination. This Western text (D is lacking here) presents one more Spirit Baptism in the book of Acts than does the Alexandrian text.

The positioning of this Spirit Baptism is significant because, according to the Alexandrian text, Jews first received the Spirit Baptism (2:4, 38), then Samaritans (8:17), then Saul, the future apostle to the Gentiles (9:17), then Gentiles (i.e., Cornelius, 10:44). In the Western textual tradition, the order was Jews (2:4, 38), Samaritans (8:17), a eunuch (8:39 variant reading), Saul (9:17), Gentiles (10:44). If the eunuch was a Gentile "God-fearer" (a proselyte to Judaism), his Spirit Baptism would have come before Cornelius's (also a God-fearer) and without the preaching of Peter or the laying on of his hands.

Acts 9:4 (see also 9:6)

Excellent testimony (𝔓45vid 𝔓74 ℵ A B C) affirms that the verse ends with τι με διωκεις; ("Why do you persecute me?"). Other witnesses (E 431 syrp,h**) add σκληρον σοι προς κεντρα λακτιζειν ("it hurts you to kick against the goads"). The variant reading is the result of scribes wanting to harmonize the three accounts of Paul's conversion recorded in Acts: here (the actual event) and two retellings of it by Paul (22:6-16 and 26:12-18). In each pericope different details are presented, but the scribe of E and the translator of syrh conformed both 9:4 and 22:7 to 26:14 by adding the statement, "it hurts you to kick against the goads," to both verses. This kind of harmonization is similar to what occurred in the Gospels: Scribes felt obligated to make parallel passages verbally equivalent. Luke, however, had no such constraints. He recorded three different versions of Paul's conversion experience; the second and third are noticeably different because Paul presented two re-creations of the event for the sake of two different audiences: (1) a Jewish audience in Jerusalem which wanted to kill him (22:6-16), and (2) Agrippa, who listened to Paul's legal defense (26:12-18). In this final defense, Paul says that

Jesus told him, "It hurts you to kick against the goads." In the Greek world this was a well-known expression for opposition to deity (Euripides, *Bacchanals* 794-795; Aeschylus, *Prometheus Bound* 324-325; Pindar, *Pythian Odes* 2.94-95). Longenecker (1981, 552-553) elaborates: "Lest [Paul] be misunderstood as proclaiming only a Galilean prophet he had formerly opposed, he pointed out to his hearers what was obvious to any Jew: correction by a voice from heaven meant opposition to God himself. So he used a current expression familiar to Agrippa and the others."

Acts 9:5-6

WH NU — ἀλλὰ ἀνάστηθι καὶ εἴσελθε εἰς τὴν πόλιν.
"But get up and enter into the city."
𝔓45vid 𝔓74 א A B C E P Ψ 33 1739 Maj
NKJVmg RSV NRSV ESV NASB NIV TNIV NEB REB NJB NAB NLT HCSB NET

variant/TR — σκληρον σοι προς κεντρα λακτιζειν. 6 τρεμων τε και θαμβων ειπεν, Τι με θελεις ποιησαι; και ο κυριος προς αυτον, αναστηθι και εσελθε εις την πολιν.
"'It hurts you to kick against the goads.' Trembling and astonished, he said, 'Lord, what do you want me to do?' And he said, 'Get up and enter the city.'"
(629 the first clause) it[h,p] syr[h**] vg
KJV NKJV

Though 𝔓45 is cited as vid, according to space allotment 𝔓45 could not have contained the extra words. (See reconstruction in *Text of Earliest MSS,* 192.) The expanded version, not found in any Greek witnesses (except the fourteenth-century minuscule 629—but only in part), is the result of ancient translators embellishing the text with their own coloring (such as adding "trembling and astonished") and harmonizing this account with the other records of Paul's conversion experience (namely, 22:10 and 26:14). (See discussion on 9:4 above.) What is noteworthy about this variant is that the full interpolation became part of TR without ever being in a Greek witness. According to Metzger (TCGNT), Erasmus translated this addition from the Latin Vulgate and incorporated it into the first edition of his Greek New Testament in 1516. From there it became part of TR, and was included in KJV.

Acts 9:12

(TR) WH NU — εἶδεν ἄνδρα [ἐν ὁράματι]
"he saw a man in a vision"
B C 1175 (E 33 1739 Maj transposed order—so TR)
KJV NKJV NRSV ESV NASB NIV TNIV NEB REB NAB NLT HCSB NET

variant 1 — ειδεν ανδρα
"he saw a man"
𝔓74 א A it cop
RSV NJB HCSBmg NETmg

variant 2 — ειδεν εν οραματι
"he saw in a vision"
Ψ
none

The documentary support for the TR WH NU reading is not as good as that for the first variant, which has the support of three excellent manuscripts (𝔓74 א A), as well as two ancient versions

(Old Latin and Coptic). Furthermore, the first variant is the shortest reading of the three, making it more likely original, since scribes had a habit of adding words for clarity. In this case, the words εν οραματι ("in a vision") appear to be a scribal insertion intended to help the reader understand that Saul saw Ananias only "in a vision"—not yet "in person." In other words, scribes made explicit what is implicit in the text. RSV and NJB follow the shortest reading. The translators of NET also argue for the shortest reading (see NETmg) but then include the words "in a vision" because of "contextual considerations." This is exactly what motivated ancient scribes to do the same.

Acts 9:17

TR WH NU ὁ κύριος ἀπέσταλκεν με, Ἰησοῦς
"the Lord has sent me, Jesus"
𝔓74 ℵ A B C E Ψ 1739
all

variant ο κυριος απεσταλκεν με
"the Lord has sent me"
Maj
NKJVmg

The manuscript evidence overwhelmingly supports the TR WH NU reading. The syntactical awkwardness of the appositional name, "Jesus," prompted its omission in the majority of later manuscripts. In English versions, the split of names is handled by joining them together: "the Lord Jesus has sent me."

Acts 9:18

WH NU ἀνέβλεψεν τε
"he saw again"
𝔓45 𝔓74 ℵ A B C* Ψ
RSV NRSV ESV NASB NIV TNIV NEB REB NJB NAB NLT HCSB NET

variant/TR ανεβλεψεν τε παρχρημα
"he saw again instantly"
C2 E L 33 1739 it^{p} syr^{h}
KJV NKJV

The manuscript evidence for the WH NU reading is vastly superior to that for TR. The scribal addition in the variant reading is an echoing of several gospel accounts where people were healed immediately from their diseases. But in this instance it is a case of overload to add παρχρημα ("instantly") after ευθεως ("immediately"). This addition was incorporated in TR and translated in KJV and NKJV.

Acts 9:20

WH NU ἐκήρυσσεν τὸν Ἰησοῦν
"he was preaching Jesus"
𝔓45 𝔓74 ℵ A B C E
NKJVmg RSV NRSV ESV NASB NIV TNIV NEB REB NJB NAB NLT HCSB NET

variant/TR εκηρυσσεν τον Χριστον
"he was preaching the Christ"
HLP
KJV NKJV

Supported by the testimony of six good manuscripts, the evidence for the WH NU reading is superior to that of TR. The reading in TR fails to convey Luke's message, who wanted to make it clear that Saul was identifying a specific man, Jesus, as the Son of God. He was not speaking abstractly about the Christ (the Messiah) being the Son of God, as if he wanted to persuade his listeners that the Messiah (as predicted in the OT) would be God's Son, not David's son. Although this is true and implicit in his words, Paul's primary purpose was to identify a man from Nazareth as being God's Son. His audience, who had heard of this man Jesus and knew that Saul was persecuting those who followed Jesus, was shocked to hear that Saul was now proclaiming Jesus to be "the Son of God."

Acts 9:22

Some scribes (C E it[h,p]) added the words εν τω λογω ("in the word") after Σαυλος δε μαλλον ενεδυναμουτο ("Saul was all the more strengthened") to make it clear that the passage was speaking of spiritual empowering to proclaim the word. Influenced by Matt 3:17 and/or Luke 3:22, a few Old Latin witnesses (it[gig,h,p]) add "in whom God is well pleased" after "this is the Christ."

Acts 9:25

The WH NU reading (supported by 𝔓[74] ℵ A B C) presents an interesting problem inasmuch as the words οι μαθηται αυτου ("his disciples") are spoken in reference to Saul. Could Paul have had disciples at this time? Some scholars think so. For example, Longenecker (1981, 377) said that this verse presented an exception to Luke's normal usage of "disciple" in that it was "used of followers of Saul and suggests that his proclamation of Jesus had a favorable response among at least some." Others completely disagree; they argue that Saul could not have had any disciples by this time. Consequently, they argue that αυτον was mistaken for αυτου at an early stage of textual transmission, which was then corrected in later manuscripts (E Ψ 1739 Maj—so TR). Haenchen (1971, 332) says, "the reading αυτον in the later MSS is thus a correction which—for once—is correct." With αυτον, the text reads, λαβοντες δε αυτον οι μαθηται ("the disciples took him").

Acts 9:29

A few witnesses (A 424) read Ελληνας instead of Ελληνιστας. The former means "Greeks" or "Gentiles"; the latter means "Greek-speaking Jews." But according to Haenchen (1971, 333), "Gentiles would not have plotted the murder of a Jewish missionary in Jerusalem, and Luke cannot have meant to relate anything of the kind."

Acts 9:31

WH NU Ἡ μὲν οὖν ἐκκλησία καθ ὅλης τῆς Ἰουδαίας καὶ Γαλιλαίας καὶ Σαμαρείας εἶχεν εἰρήνην

οἰκοδομουμένη καὶ πορευομένη τῷ φόβῳ τοῦ κυρίου καὶ τῇ παρακλήσει τοῦ ἁγίου πνεύματος ἐπληθύνετο.
"Meanwhile the church throughout all of Judea, Galilee, and Samaria had peace, was being built up, and, walking in the fear of the Lord and in the comfort of the Holy Spirit, was increasing."
𝔓74 ℵ A B C 1739 (syr^{p}) cop
NKJVmg RSV NRSV ESV NASB NIV TNIV NEB REB NJBmg NAB NLT HCSB NET

variant/TR Αι μεν ουν εκκλησιαι καθ ολης της Ιουδαιας και Γαλιλαιας και Σαμαρειας ειχον ειρηνην οικοδομουμεναι και πορευομεναι τω φοβω του κυριου και τη παρακλησει του αγιου πνευματος επληθυνοντο.
"Meanwhile the churches throughout all of Judea, Galilee, and Samaria had peace, were being built up, and, walking in the fear of the Lord and in the comfort of the Holy Spirit, were increasing."
(E) Maj it syr^{h}
KJV NKJV NJB

The reading that speaks of the church in the singular number, supported by the best witnesses, was changed to the plural in later manuscripts (so TR) under the influence of verses like 16:5 or the Pauline Epistles, which so often speak of individual churches. (The NJB followed the Western text and Antiochene text, versus the Alexandrian—see NJBmg.) The significance of speaking about the singular "church" throughout all Judea, Galilee, and Samaria is that it shows the unity of the one universal church at that time. All the Christians in these regions at that time were products of the Jerusalem church and therefore had solidarity with it and with one another. In time, as missionary efforts extended out from Antioch, churches would be designated by the locality (such as "the church in Philippi") or by the region (such as "the churches in Galatia").

Acts 9:34

WH NU Ἰησοῦς Χριστός
"Jesus Christ"
𝔓74 ℵ B* C Ψ Didymus
KJV RSV NRSV ESV NASB NIV TNIV NEB REB NJB NAB NLT HCSB NETmg

variant 1/TR Ιησους ο Χριστος
"Jesus the Christ"
B^{c} E 1739 Maj
NKJV NET

variant 2 ο κυριος Ιησους Χριστος
"the Lord Jesus Christ"
A it
none

variant 3 ο Χριστος
"the Christ"
614 1505
none

Among the various readings, the second and third variants do not commend themselves, due to weak attestation and excessive expansion (variant 2) or trimming (variant 3). The first variant could be original. In fact, the translators of NET argue that it was the uniqueness of the expression, "Jesus the Christ" (found nowhere else in the NT) that gave rise to the other variants and is therefore the original wording (see NETmg). Be that as it may, the WH NU reading has the best documentary support.

Acts 9:40

After Peter's command, ταβιθα, αναστηθι ("Tabitha, arise"), several Western witnesses (it[gig,p] syr[h**] arm) add, "in the name of our Lord Jesus Christ." This is a typical formula accompanying miracles (see 3:6; 4:10; 9:34; 16:18).

Acts 10:6

WH NU	conclude verse with ᾧ ἐστιν οἰκία παρὰ θάλασσαν ("who is in a house by the sea") 𝔓[74] א A B C 1739 Maj NKJVmg RSV NRSV ESV NASB NIV TNIV NEB REB NJB NAB NLT HCSB NET
variant 1/TR	add at end of verse: ουτος λαλησει σοι τι σε δει ποιειν "this one will tell you what to do" 69[mg] a few Old Latin MSS KJV NKJV
variant 2	add at end of verse all of 11:14 ος λαλησει ρηματα προς σε εν οις σωθηση συ και πας ο οικος σου "who will speak words to you by which you and all your household will be saved" 436 453 466 none

The manuscript evidence for the WH NU reading is vastly superior to that of the two variants. The first addition, with very little manuscript support, made its way into TR and was translated in KJV. The second variant is clearly a case of harmonizing this verse with 11:14, where Peter recounts the story of Cornelius's conversion.

Acts 10:12

WH NU	ἑρπετὰ τῆς γῆς καὶ πετεινά "reptiles of the earth and birds" 𝔓[45] 𝔓[74] א A B C[2vid] cop Clement Origen RSV NRSV ESV NASB NIV TNIV NEB REB NJB NAB NLT HCSB NET
variant/TR	ερπετα και τα θηρια και τα πετεινα "reptiles and beasts and birds" (E C*[vid] L) Ψ Maj KJV NKJV

The manuscript evidence for the WH NU reading is superior to that for TR. The insertion of "and beasts" in the variant reading (inserted in various positions in the manuscripts) is the result of scribal harmonization to 11:6, which has "beasts" in the list of animals Peter gave, as he recounted the story.

Acts 10:16

WH NU εὐθὺς ἀνελήμφθη τὸ σκεῦος
"the vessel was immediately taken up"
𝔓74 ℵ A B C E
RSV NRSV ESV NASB NIV TNIV NLT NET

variant 1 ανελημφθη το σκευος
"the vessel was taken up"
𝔓45 it[d] syr[p] cop[sa]
NEB REB NAB HCSB

variant 2/TR παλιν ανελημφθη το σκευος
"the vessel was immediately taken up again"
(D) Ψ 1739 Maj syr[h]
KJV NKJV NJB

The first variant is probably original because ευθυς ("immediately") is not a Lukan term. The other variant, containing παλιν ("again"), was probably added by way of assimilation to 11:10. Four modern versions (NEB, REB, NAB, and HCSB) follow the first variant. The KJV tradition, following TR, is joined by NJB, which follows the Western text here.

Acts 10:17

Western text (D) reads:

> "Now **when he came to himself,** Peter was greatly puzzled about what to make of the vision that he had seen; behold, the men sent from Cornelius appeared. They were asking about Simon's house and were standing by the gate."

This is a typical gap-filler in the Western text.

Acts 10:19

TR NU ἄνδρες τρεῖς ζητοῦντές σε
"three men are seeking you"
𝔓74 ℵ A C E 33 1739 syr[p,hmg] cop
KJV NKJV RSV NRSV ESV NASB NIV TNIV NEBmg NJBmg NAB NLT HCSB NET

variant 1/WH ανδρες δυο ζητουντες σε
"two men are seeking you"
B
NRSVmg NIVmg TNIVmg NEBmg

variant 2 ανδρες ζητουντες σε
"men are seeking you"
D Ψ Maj syr[h]
NIVmg TNIVmg NEB REB NJB

According to 10:7, Cornelius sent two of his slaves and one soldier, who had served him, to go to Joppa and find Peter. Thus, the reading with "three men" makes the most sense and has excellent documentary support. The second variant, though poorly supported, also makes sense; it is followed by NEB, REB, and NJB. The first variant (noted in several modern versions) is the most difficult but could still be plausible if we consider the two slaves to be the two men seeking Peter, excluding the Roman soldier, who must be considered as merely accompanying the messengers as an escort.

Acts 10:21-29

Western text (D, and E in part) reads:

> "**Then** Peter went down to the men and said, 'I am the one you are looking for. **What do you want?** What is the reason for your coming?' 22 And they said **to him, 'A certain** Cornelius, a centurion, an upright and God-fearing man, who is well spoken of by the whole Jewish nation, was directed by a holy angel to send for you to come to his house and to hear what you have to say.' 23 So **Peter** let them in and gave them lodging. The next day he got up and went with them, and some of the brothers from Joppa accompanied him. 24 The following day **he** came to Caesarea. Cornelius was expecting them and had called together his relatives and close friends. 25 **And as Peter was coming near to Caesarea, one of the servants ran forward and announced that he had come. And Cornelius sprang up and** met him, and falling at his feet, worshiped him. 26 But Peter made him get up, saying, '**What are you doing?** I also am a man **as you are.**' 27 And [as he talked with him,] he went in and found that many had assembled. 28 And he said to them, 'You yourselves know **very well** that it is unlawful for a Jew to associate with or to visit a Gentile; but God has shown me that I should not call anyone profane or unclean. 29 So when I was sent for **by you,** I came without objection. Now may I ask why you sent for me?'"

Most of the additions in the Western text are superfluous embellishments. The most substantial enhancement (at the beginning of 10:25) was created by the D-reviser to fill in a narrative gap because the text does not say how Cornelius could have known that Peter had come, yet he goes out and meets him on his arrival. Again, this is simply a matter of the reviser following the textual signals to make explicit what is implicit in the text.

Acts 10:30

WH NU
ἀπὸ τετάρτης ἡμέρας μέχρι ταύτης τῆς ὥρας ἤμην τὴν ἐνάτην προσευχόμενος
"from the fourth day until this [hour], I was praying at the ninth hour"
𝔓74 א A* B C 1739
NKJVmg RSV NRSV ESV NASB NIV TNIV NEB REB NAB NLT HCSB NET

variant 1/TR
απο τεταρτης ημερας μεχρι ταυτης της ωρας ημην νηστευων, και την ενατην προσευχομενος
"from the fourth day until this [hour], I was fasting and I was keeping the ninth hour of prayer"
𝔓50 A2 (D*) Ψ Maj it syr cop^sa
KJV NKJV NJBmg HCSBmg

variant 2
απο της τριτης ημερας μεχρι ταυτης της ωρας ημην νησευων, και την ενατην προσευχομενος
"from the third day until this hour I was fasting, and I was keeping the ninth hour of prayer"
D1
NJB

This is the only instance in which 𝔓50 is cited in UBS4. Unfortunately, it is given an unrepresentative showing because in this case it aligns with D and other Western manuscripts against B and other Alexandrian manuscripts, though 𝔓50 usually follows the Alexandrian text. Nonetheless, it provides the earliest extant evidence among the Greek witnesses for the inclusion of the words, "and fasting." On one hand, it could be argued that "fasting" was dropped in the Alexandrian witnesses because in the previous narrative no mention is made of Cornelius fasting—only that he prayed habitually. But, on the other hand, it is more convincing to argue that the words "and fasting" represent a pietistic expansion—for it often happened in later manuscripts that "fasting" was added to "prayer" (see notes on Mark 9:29 and 1 Cor 7:5). The D-reviser took it one step further by changing the length of days from "four" to "three" to accommodate the normal time span for a fast. In any event, none of the modern translations adopted the reading with "fasting," except the NJB, which is known for its attentiveness to the Western text.

Acts 10:32

WH NU	end verse with παρὰ θάλασσαν ("[house] by the sea") 𝔓45 𝔓74 ℵ A B NKJVmg RSV NRSV ESV NASB NIV TNIV NEB REB NJB NLT HCSB NET
variant/TR	add at end of verse ος παραγενομενος λαλησει σοι ("who, when he comes, will speak to you") C D E Ψ 1739 Maj it syr KJV NKJV HCSBmg

The WH NU reading has the support of five excellent manuscripts. The expanded reading (which became part of TR) is the result of scribal gap-filling. Some scribe apparently surmised that it was important for Cornelius to be told by the angel that Peter would speak to him. But the angel did not say this (see 10:5-6), and the reader does not need this to be said in order to figure out the intent of the angel's message.

Acts 10:33

Western text (D, with 𝔓74 Maj on the last word only) reads:

> "Therefore I sent for you immediately, **entreating you to come to us,** and you have done well to come to us **speedily.** So, **look,** all of us are here in **your** presence to hear **from you** all that has been commanded to you by **God.**"

The changes in the first sentence are typical Western text editorial embellishments. The changes in the second sentence are more significant inasmuch as ενωπιον σου ("before you"—i.e., "in Peter's presence") gives quite a different sense than ενωπιον του θεου ("before God"). Although Cornelius had great reverence for Peter—he even kneeled before him—his ultimate devotion went to God. Thus, though it was entirely fitting for Cornelius to have spoken either of these words, the words "before God" suit the solemnity of the occasion. Finally, since D is not alone in reading "God" instead of "Lord," it must be considered as a viable candidate for the original text. However, the weight of testimony strongly favors κυριος ("Lord"): 𝔓45 ℵ A B C E 1739.

Acts 10:40-41

Western text (D and E it in part) reads:

> "But God raised him up **after** the third day and allowed him to appear, 41 not to all the people but to us who were chosen by God as witnesses, and who ate and drank with him **and accompanied him** after he rose from the dead, **for forty days.**"

The D-reviser had a habit of speaking about Jesus' resurrection as occurring after three days (see notes on Matt 16:21; 17:23), perhaps because he wanted it to appear that Jesus had literally fulfilled the prophecy of being in the grave three days and three nights (see Jonah 1:17; Matt 12:40), or because the editor was influenced by the Latin translation of this codex, *post tertium diem* ("after the third day").

The changes in 10:41 reflect a conscious effort on the part of some scribe(s) to make it clear to readers that Jesus did not just eat and drink with his disciples after he rose from the dead, he also journeyed alongside them—for a period of forty days (see 1:3). But the point Peter was making is that Jesus' eating and drinking with the disciples was one of the most convincing proofs of his bodily resurrection (Bruce 1990, 263). This is an important point in Luke's presentation of the risen Christ (see Luke 24:41-43; Acts 1:4).

Acts 10:48

WH NU ἐν τῷ ὀνόματι Ἰησοῦ Χριστοῦ
"in the name of Jesus Christ"
𝔓74 א A B E (Ψ) 33 1739 syr[h] cop
RSV NRSV ESV NASB NIV TNIV NEB REB NJB NAB NLT HCSB NET

variant 1 εν τω ονοματι του κυριου
"in the name of the Lord"
H L P
KJV NKJV

variant 2 εν τω ονοματι του κυριου Ιησου
"in the name of the Lord Jesus"
436 1241
none

variant 3 εν τω ονοματι του κυριου Ιησου Χριστου
"in the name of the Lord Jesus Christ"
D 81* syr[p]
none

It was a common practice among scribes to expand divine titles—especially when they appear in connection with Christian baptism. Had we only the three variants listed above, it could be argued that "Lord" grew to "Lord Jesus" and then to "Lord Jesus Christ." While this may have happened some lines later in the textual transmission of this verse, the external evidence shows that the original wording was not "Lord," but "Jesus Christ"—from which the others diverged.

Acts 11:1-3

Western text (D it[d] syr[h**]) reads:

> "Now the apostles and the brothers who were in Judea heard that the Gentiles had also accepted the word of God. [2] Peter **therefore for a considerable time wanted to journey to Jerusalem, and he called to himself the brothers, and established them—speaking much throughout the countryside and teaching them. He also went to meet with them, and he reported to them the grace of God. But the brothers of** the circumcision criticized him, [3] saying, 'Why did you go to uncircumcised men and eat with them?'" (see NJBmg).

What motivated the D-reviser to make this extended insertion? There are two possibilities: (1) Perhaps he was disturbed that a controversy followed so closely after the conversion of

Cornelius, so he provided extra narrative details to make the transition more smooth (Bruce 1990, 266). (2) Not wanting Peter to look bad (which seems to be the tendency of the D-reviser), the revision makes it appear that Peter continued with his missionary activity and then went up, of his own volition, to Jerusalem to give a report of his missionary activity, which resulted in a confrontation with those of the circumcision (Crehan 1957, 596-603).

The truth of the matter is, the circumcision sector of the Jerusalem church was very strong, and they would confront anyone that offended their Jewish predilections—including the leading apostle, Peter. This was but the beginning of problems that would come from the circumcision party. Paul's missionary activity to the Gentiles would be forever harassed and hindered by these zealots. So the introduction of it at this point in Acts is critical because chapter 11 commences the greater missionary journey to the Gentiles by the gospel going out to the Greeks (11:20) and by connecting Paul with Antioch (11:25-26), the headquarters for the mission to the Gentiles. Peter led the way for Paul in bringing the gospel to the Gentiles, and both were persecuted for it by the Jewish Christians who adhered to their Judaism.

Acts 11:11

WH NU τὴν οἰκίαν ἐν ᾗ ἦμεν
"the house in which we were"
𝔓74 ℵ A B D
RSV NRSV ESV NASB NEBmg REBmg NJB NAB NLT HCSB NET

variant/TR την οικιαν εν η ημην
"the house in which I was"
𝔓45 E Ψ 33 1739 Maj syr cop
KJV NKJV NIV TNIV NEB REB

The variant in this verse could have easily occurred because one word might have been confused for the other—in written form (ημεν/ημην) or in oral (the two words were pronounced alike). If the change was not accidental, then it is possible that ημην ("I was") is a scribal assimilation to 11:5. The uncertainty is displayed in the translations, which are divided on this text.

Acts 11:12

WH NU μηδὲν διακρίναντα
"without making a distinction [i.e., a distinction between Gentiles and Jews]"
(ℵ*) A B (E Ψ) 33 1739
RSV NRSV ESV NEBmg NAB (NLT)

variant 1/TR μηδεν διακρινομενον
"without doubting [or, with no hesitation]"
Maj
KJV NKJV NASB NIV TNIV NJB HCSB NET

variant 2 μηδεν ανακριναντα
"without questioning"
𝔓74
none

variant 3 omit
𝔓45vid? D syr^{h}
NEB REB

There is a significant difference between the WH NU reading (which has good documentary support) and all the variants (which have inferior documentary support). The text indicates that Peter was being charged by the Spirit not to make a distinction between Jews and Gentiles (just as in the vision God had instructed Peter not to make a distinction between unclean food and clean); in other words, Peter was prompted by the Spirit to take the gospel to the Gentiles without prejudice (see 15:9, where the same verb is used). The first and second variants speak of hesitancy, and the third variant does not speak at all in this regard. The first variant probably reflects scribal assimilation to 10:20; the second variant is a slight adjustment of this. The third variant solves the problem entirely by omitting the expression. But it should be remembered that the copyist of 𝔓45 was given to excision. Nevertheless, the translators of the NEB (Tasker 1964, 431) adopted the text in D and 𝔓45 because they considered the other readings to be additions. The REB followed.

Acts 11:17

Western text (D with it^{p,w} syr^{h**} for second change) reads:

> "If then [God] gave them the same gift that he gave us when we believed in the Lord Jesus Christ, who was I that I could hinder God—**that he should not give them the Holy Spirit when they believed?**"

Ropes (1926, 105) argued that "God" was deleted because it was the "'Western' reviser's view that the Holy Spirit was the gift of Christ" (see also NJBmg). But if that is true, why did he append the clause about the gift of the Holy Spirit as coming from "God"? It is possible, however, that the reviser was thinking about Peter, not God, for the addition in D could also be rendered "that I [Peter] should not give them the Holy Spirit when they believed" (see Wilson 1923, 64).

Acts 11:20

TR WH NU	τοὺς Ἑλληνιστάς "the Hellenists" B D² E Ψ 1739 Maj NKJV NRSV ESV (NLT) HCSB
variant	τους Ελληνας "the Greeks [or, the Gentiles]" 𝔓74 ℵ² A D* KJV RSV NRSVmg NASB NIV TNIV NEB REB NJB NAB NLTmg HCSBmg NET

Presuming that Ελληνιστας (literally "Hellenists") means "Greek-speaking Jews" (BDAG 318), the TR WH NU reading does not seem to make sense, because this verse seems to call for a contrast between those who preached only to the Jews (11:19) and the Cypriotes and Cyrenians who also preached to Greeks or Gentiles. The way out of this dilemma is to argue that Ελληνιστας means anyone given to Greek culture or language, which, as Metzger (TCGNT) puts it, could refer to "the mixed population of Antioch in contrast to the Ἰουδαῖοι [Jews] of ver. 19." The other way out of the dilemma is to accept the variant reading as original, which is what many scholars do (for example, see Bruce 1990, 272). But Westcott and Hort (1882, 93-94) argue strongly that the common word Ελληνας would never have been purposely changed to the uncommon one, Ελληνιστας, which appears only three times in the New Testament (Acts 6:1; 9:29; and here in 11:20).

It should be noted that ℵ* reads ευαγγελιστας—a strange scribal error combining the last part of Ελληνιστας with the first part of the next word, ευαγγελιζομενοι.

This most likely reveals that Ελληνιστας stood in the exemplar manuscript that the scribe of א was copying.

Acts 11:25-26

Western text (D^2) reads:

> "**And having heard that Saul was at Tarsus,** Barnabas went out to seek him, [26] and when he had found him, he **encouraged** him to come to Antioch. **When they had come,** for an entire year a great many people **were stirred up;** and **then** for the first time the disciples were called 'Christians' in Antioch."

The D-reviser (with one defective line filled in by a second corrector) added some circumstantial details to the narrative that are hardly necessary. The most curious change is where he omitted the words (probably accidentally) that speak of Saul and Barnabas "teaching in the church," and supplying a description of the people being stirred up. Apparently, it was important to the reviser to show the great enthusiasm and fervor that Saul and Barnabas created in Antioch (see 11:28).

Acts 11:28

Western text (D $it^{d,p}$ Augustine) reads:

> "**And there was much rejoicing, and when we were gathered together,** one of them named Agabus stood up, signifying by the Spirit that there would be a severe famine over all the world." (see NJBmg)

The variant in the Western text is unique in that it includes Luke (the author of the book) as among the believers present at Antioch. This interpolation probably came as a result of the reviser's knowledge of the Eusebian tradition that Luke was a native of Syrian Antioch. All other manuscripts do not have a "we" passage until 16:10-17. The other additions in D show the reviser's touch of heightening the narrative with a sense of joy among the early believers in Antioch (see note on 11:25-26).

Acts 12:1-3

Western text (D it^{p} syr^{h**}) reads:

> "About that time King Herod laid violent hands upon some who belonged to the church **in Judea.** [2] He had James, the brother of John, killed with the sword. [3] After he saw that **his laying hands upon the faithful** pleased the Jews, he proceeded to arrest Peter also. (This was during the festival of Unleavened Bread.)"

Again, the reviser added circumstantial details to orient his readers to the geography of the next event (12:1), and then reiterated (12:3) that Herod pleased the Jewish leaders with his violent attacks on the faithful.

Acts 12:5

Western text (D^2) reads:

> "While Peter was kept in prison, **much** prayer **about him** was made earnestly by the church of God for him."

The additions in the Western text are as awkward and unnecessary in the Greek text as they are in this English translation.

Acts 12:7

Western text (D) reads:

> "Suddenly an angel of the Lord stood by **Peter** and a light shone **upon [him]** in the jail room. He **nudged** Peter on his side and woke him, saying, 'Get up quickly.' And the chains fell off his wrists."

The D-reviser colored the text with the addition of Peter's name, a more defined positioning of the shining light (i.e., it shined on Peter), and a less forceful action by the angel (he "nudged" Peter instead of "striking" him).

Acts 12:10

Western text (D) reads:

> "After they had passed the first and the second guard, they came before the iron gate leading to the city. It opened for them of its own accord; and they went out **and went down the seven steps,** and walked along a street, when suddenly the angel left him."

The additional detail about descending seven steps could indicate that the reviser had knowledge about Jerusalem's buildings prior to their destruction or was simply adding a detail derived from some unknown tradition. We do not know if Peter was imprisoned in Herod's palace or the fortress of Antonia, and we do not know if either of these places had steps leading down to the city and, if so, how many. But whether historically accurate or not, this addition gives the text a nice touch of local color.

Acts 12:17

Western text (D^{c} it^{p} syr^{h**}) reads:

> "He motioned to them with his hand to be quiet; **he came in and** told them how the Lord had brought him out of the prison. And he said, 'Tell these things to James and to the brothers.' Then he left and went to another place."

Again, the reviser added a circumstantial detail in order to get Peter inside the room before he recounted his miraculous escape from prison. This sort of gap-filling is entirely unnecessary because readers do this automatically.

Acts 12:19b-23

Western text (D) reads:

> "Then he went down from Judea to Caesarea and stayed there. [20] **For** Herod was angry with the people of Tyre and Sidon. **But** they came to **the king from both the cities** in one accord. And after winning over Blastus, the king's chamberlain, they asked for peace, because their country depended on the king's country for food. [21] On an appointed day Herod put on his royal robes, took his seat on the throne, and made an oration to them, **after being reconciled with the Tyrians.** [22] And the people kept shouting, 'It is the voice of a god, and not of a man!' [23] And immediately an angel of the Lord struck him because he

had not given God the glory. **And he came down from the throne, and while he was still living** he was eaten by worms and **so** he died."

The D-reviser expanded the account of Herod Agrippa's death in an attempt to provide his readers with causal connections and historical details. The addition of "for" (γαρ) in 12:20 supposedly helps readers understand why Herod left Jerusalem to go to Caesarea (12:19), but no connection can readily be made between going to Caesarea and a conflict with Tyre and Sidon (both of which were incorporated into the Roman Empire in 20 B.C.). To hazard a guess, it could be that there was some conflict between these two port cities and the port city of Caesarea over trading.

The addition in 12:21 lets the reader know that the reconciliation was successful, but this is implicit in the text. The expansion in 12:23 helps the reader understand that Agrippa did not die on the spot as a result of being eaten by worms. In fact, the reviser's expansion coincides with Josephus's account (*Ant.* 19.343-350), who related that Agrippa did not renounce the acclamation that he was a god. Contrarily, having accepted this accolade, he was smitten by God with excruciating pain in his stomach that lasted for five days until he died.

Acts 12:24

The phrase λογος του θεου ("word of God") has excellent support: 𝔓74 ℵ A D E Ψ 33 1739 Maj (so TR NU). WH show their preference for B by reading λογος του κυριου ("word of the Lord").

Acts 12:25

WH NU — Βαρναβᾶς δὲ καὶ Σαῦλος ὑπέστρεψαν εἰς Ἰερουσαλὴμ πληρώσαντες τὴν διακονίαν
"Barnabas and Saul returned to Jerusalem, having completed their ministry" (or, "Barnabas and Saul returned, having completed their ministry in Jerusalem")
ℵ B Maj
NKJVmg RSVmg NRSV ESVmg NIVmg TNIVmg NEBmg REBmg NJB NAB NLT HCSB NET

variant 1/TR — Βαρναβας δε και Σαυλος υπεστρεψαν εξ Ιερουσαλημ πληρωσαντες την διακονιαν
"Barnabas and Saul returned from Jerusalem, having completed their ministry"
𝔓74 A 33 (D Ψ απο instead of εξ)
KJV NKJV RSV NRSVmg ESV NASB NIV TNIV NEB REB NJBmg NABmg NLTmg HCSBmg NETmg

variant 2 — Βαρναβας δε και Σαυλος υπεστρεψαν εξ Ιερουσαλημ εις Αντιοχειαν πληρωσαντες την διακονιαν
"Barnabas and Saul returned from Jerusalem to Antioch, having completed their ministry"
(E) 1739 it^{e,p,w} syr^{p} cop^{sa}
NLTmg NETmg

There is an obvious exegetical and logistical problem if we accept the WH NU reading as original (if translated literally), because Barnabas and Saul were actually returning *from* Jerusalem to Antioch after completing the delivery of the relief fund to the Christians in Jerusalem. As such, several scholars are convinced that απο ("from") or εξ ("out from") must have originally been in the text, and that εις accidentally replaced one of these prepositions (see Longenecker 1981, 417 and Tasker 1964, 431). But this sort of accident is very unlikely, and scribes usually did not make changes that made the text more difficult. Therefore, it is far more likely that scribes, noticing the difficulty with εις, made a change of prepositions. Other scribes made the change, either to απο or εξ, both of which mean "from" (see variants 1 and 2). A few scribes (including the reviser) and ancient translators, wanting to leave no doubt in the mind of their readers, made it clear that Barnabas and Saul "returned from Jerusalem to Antioch."

All these changes suggest that εις, though difficult, is original. As such, it is the exegete's and translator's task to make sense of it without straining grammar or syntax. The best solution is to recognize that Luke must have placed the phrase εις Ιερουσαλημ ahead of the participial phrase to which it belongs (Haenchen 1971, 387), thereby yielding a perfectly acceptable translation: "Barnabas and Saul returned [to Antioch], having completed their ministry in Jerusalem." (See NJB NLT NEBmg for similar renderings.)

Acts 13:3

Western text (D) reads:

> "After they had **all** fasted and prayed, they laid their hands on them, [sending them off]."

The D-reviser's addition of "all" probably reflects the true historical situation because in the early church all the believers often participated in commissioning people for special ministries (see 6:2-4). Aware of this, the reviser made this clarification. Later in church history, it was the task of only the leaders to lay hands on people for special ministry. The omission of απελυσαν ("sending them off") in D was probably an error.

Acts 13:5

Western text (D) reads:

> "When they arrived at Salamis, they proclaimed the word of **the Lord** in the synagogues of the Jews. And they had John also **assisting them.**"

While all other Greek manuscripts speak of "the word of God," the D-reviser changed the text to reflect the Christianization of the traditional expression (TCGNT). According to most Greek manuscripts, John Mark is called an "assistant" or "attendant" (υπηρετην) to Barnabas and Saul. The D-reviser avoids using this as a title for John Mark and replaces it with a descriptive function: υπηρετουντα αυτοις ("assisting them").

Acts 13:6

Western text (D $it^{d,gig}$) reads:

> "When they had gone **around** the whole island as far as Paphos, they met a certain magician, a Jewish false prophet, named Bar-Jesus."

According to most manuscripts, Barnabas and Saul traveled the length of Cyprus, from Salamis to Paphos, without mention of any intermediate stops. Attempting to adjust this scenario, the reviser has the missionaries sail south from Salamis around the island until they reach Paphos (Haenchen 1971, 397).

Acts 13:8

Western text (D*) reads:

> "But **Etoimas** the sorcerer (for that is the translation of his name) opposed them and tried to turn the proconsul away from the faith, **since he was hearing them with the greatest pleasure.**"

In 13:6 the Jewish magician was called Bar-Jesus. Here his name suddenly changes to "Elymas" (in all manuscripts except D)—with the added explanation that this is the translation of his name. "Elymas" is not a translation of the name "Bar-Jesus" (which means "son of Joshua" or "son of Jesus"). "Elymas" means "wise" or "learned," which Luke says is a translation of ο μαγος ("the magician" or "the sorcerer"). But the D-reviser gives this sorcerer a completely different name: "Etoimas." It is possible that he was thinking of the same Jewish magician that Josephus identified as "Atomos" (*Ant.* 20.142), who was active during the same time period in Cyprus.

The addition at the end of the verse (also found in E syr^{h**}) is a typical case of gap-filling which attempts to help the reader understand that Elymas tried to prevent the proconsul from believing because he could tell that the proconsul was readily receiving the gospel message from Barnabas and Saul.

Acts 13:12

Western text (D) reads:

> "When the proconsul saw what had happened, **he marveled and** believed **in God,** being astonished at the teaching about the Lord."

The first addition shows that the proconsul was so awestruck by seeing Bar-Jesus blinded by Paul's command that he became a believer. This detracts from the message that it was preeminently the teaching about the Lord that amazed him. The second addition is a typical scribal filler of a direct object after the verb for "believe."

Acts 13:14

The TR reading Αντιοχειαν της Πισιδιας ("Antioch of Pisidia") has the support of later manuscripts: D E Ψ 33 1739 Maj. It reflects a later boundary under Diocletian, after 295 (Barrett 1994, 627). The better reading (in WH NU) is Αντιοχειαν την Πισιδιαν, which means "Antioch toward Pisidia." This reading, which has the excellent support of $\mathfrak{P}^{45}$ $\mathfrak{P}^{74}$ ℵ A B C, distinguishes this Antioch from another Phyrgian Antioch on the Menander River.

Acts 13:18

TR WH NU	ἐτροποφόρησεν αὐτοὺς ἐν τῇ ἐρήμῳ "he put up with them in the wilderness" ℵ B C² D Maj KJV NKJV RSV NRSV ESV NASB NIV TNIV NEB REB NJBmg NAB NLT HCSB NET
variant	ετροφοφορησεν αυτους εν τη ερημω "he cared for them in the wilderness" $\mathfrak{P}^{74}$ A C* E Ψ 33^{vid} it^{d} syr cop RSVmg NRSVmg ESVmg NIVmg TNIVmg NEBmg REBmg NJB NLTmg HCSBmg

The documentary evidence is evenly divided, although the combination of ℵ B D is impressive. However, it is quite possible that one word was mistaken for the other because there is only a one-letter difference (π/φ) in the two Greek words: ετροποφορησεν ("put up with") and ετροφοφορησεν ("cared for"). The same variation occurred in Deut 1:31 (LXX), the passage here cited by Paul; but τροποφορεω in Deut 1:31 has clearly superior attestation. The variation in the Septuagint, as well as in the New Testament, could stem from the fact that the Hebrew word *nasa'* in Deut 1:31 can mean "carry" or "endure" (Bruce 1990, 304). Although our sentimental preference may be for the more positive divine action (i.e., God cared for them), both words work in this context because God both carried his people along (as a nurturing nurse) and endured their stubborn unbelief. Thus, translators and exegetes alike can defensibly choose either word, while giving due respect to the other in a marginal note. However, all English versions except the NJB reflect ετροποφορησεν ("put up with") in the text.

Acts 13:19b-20

WH NU κατεκληρονόμησεν τὴν γῆν αὐτῶν [20]ὡς ἔτεσιν τετρακοσίοις καὶ πεντήκοντα. καὶ μετὰ ταῦτα ἔδωκεν κριτὰς ἕως Σαμουήλ
"He gave the land [of Canaan] for their inheritance [20] for about four hundred fifty years. After these things he gave them judges until the time of Samuel."
𝔓74 ℵ A B C 33
RSV NRSV ESV NASB NIV TNIV NEB REB NJB NAB NLT HCSB NET

variant/(TR) κατεκληρονομησεν αυτοις την γην αυτων. [20]και μετα ταυτα ως ετεσιν τετρακοσιοις και πεντηκοντα, εδωκεν κριτας εως Σαμουηλ.
"He gave to them the land [of Canaan] for their inheritance. [20] And after these things, for about four hundred fifty years, he gave them judges until the time of Samuel."
D1 E Ψ Maj
KJV NKJV NJBmg

The variant reading was probably created to avoid the problem of ascribing a time period of four hundred fifty years for Israel to possess the land. Generally speaking, Israel's sojourning lasted four hundred years (13:17), followed by forty years in the wilderness (13:18), followed by another ten years of conquering Canaan and distributing the land to the twelve tribes.

Acts 13:27-29

Western text (D) reads:

> "Because the ones living in Jerusalem and their leaders [did not recognize him] or understand the **writings** of the prophets that are read every Sabbath, they fulfilled those words by condemning him. [28] Even though they found no cause to sentence him to death, **after judging him they gave him over to** Pilate to have him killed. [29] When they had carried out everything that was written about him, **they asked Pilate to crucify him. And when they had obtained this also,** they took him down from the tree and laid him in a tomb."

The additions in the D text are anti-Judaic in that they squarely place the blame of Jesus' judgment and crucifixion upon the Jewish leaders and not on Rome (see Epp 1962, 57-59; 1966, 41-51).

Acts 13:33a (13:32b in TR)

TR NU τοῖς τέκνοις [αὐτῶν] ἡμῖν
"for us, their children"
C³ E 33 1739 Maj syr
KJV NKJV RSV NRSV ESV NIV TNIV NEBmg REBmg NAB NLT HCSB NET

variant 1/WH τοις τεκνοις ημων
"for our children"
𝔓⁷⁴ א A B C* D
NASB NEBmg NJBmg

variant 2 τοις τεκνοις αυτων
"for their children"
1175 it^{gig}
NEB (REB) NJB

variant 3 τοις τεκνοις ημιν
"to us, the children"
142
none

All the readings are problematic. The first variant, though well attested, seems ill suited for this context: How could God's promises be for Paul's children and/or the children of his listeners? The TR NU reading and the second variant, though they make better sense, are scribal corrections. Westcott and Hort (1882, 95), judging the original text to have suffered some primitive corruption, suggested that τοις τεκνοις ημιν ("to us, the children") is what Luke originally wrote. This reading is found in one eleventh-century manuscript, 142 (see TCGNT); but it is probably the work of emendation. In the final analysis, the text critic would have to judge that the first variant, with the best attestation, is what Luke wrote, unless (of course) the original text suffered early corruption. Translators can avoid the problem by rendering it, "God has fulfilled [the promises] for their children by raising Jesus for us" (see NLT).

Acts 13:33b

TR WH NU ἐν τῷ ψαλμῷ γέγραπται τῷ δευτέρῳ
"it has been written in the second psalm"
𝔓⁷⁴ א A B C (E) Ψ 33
KJV NKJV RSV NRSV ESV NASB NIV TNIV NEB REB NJBmg NAB NLT HCSB NET

variant 1 εν πρωτω ψαλμω γεγραπται
"in the first psalm it has been written"
D it^{d,gig}
NEBmg NJBmg

variant 2 εν τοις ψαλμοις γεγραπται
"in the psalms it has been written"
𝔓^{45vid}
NJB

The scribe of D, in changing "the second psalm" to "the first psalm," displayed his knowledge of Hebrew manuscripts that joined the first two psalms into one. Origen (commenting on Ps 2 in *Psalms;* cited in Bruce 1990, 309), said he had seen two Hebrew manuscripts in which the first two psalms were coupled together as one. Justin, Tertullian, and Cyprian also acknowledged this coupling. Since these are "Western" fathers, it is altogether likely that the "Western" reviser of D was familiar with the Psalms in the same format. The translators of the NJB preferred the testimony of 𝔓[45] against all the other manuscripts perhaps because the original may have indeed just read "psalms," before scribes appended one numeral or the other. However, it is just as likely that the scribe of 𝔓[45] was avoiding the problem of specificity by using the generic "psalms."

Acts 13:33c

Western text (D syr[hmg]) reads:

> "You are my Son; today I have begotten you. **Ask of me and I will give you the Gentiles for your inheritance, and the ends of the earth for your possession.**"

The scribe of D continued the Psalm quotation (see previous note) by adding the next verse (Ps 2:8). This enhances Paul's mission to the Gentiles because it emphasizes that the Gentiles would come under the lordship of Jesus Christ. (See 13:26, where Paul includes the "God-fearing Gentiles" as being members of his audience.)

Acts 13:38-39

Western text (D syr[hmg]) reads:

> "Let it be known to you therefore, my brothers, that through this man forgiveness of sins is proclaimed **and repentance** from all things from which you could not be justified by the law of Moses. In him **therefore** everyone who believes is justified **before God.**"

The addition of "and repentance," intending to smooth out the sentence, actually produces a more complex statement. The other additions are typical embellishments.

Acts 13:41

Western text (D with E Maj on omission of "a work") reads:

> "'Look, you scoffers! Be amazed and perish, for in your days I am doing a work, [a work] that you will never believe, even if someone tells you.' **And they were silent.**"

The reviser dropped the second occurrence of εργον ("work") either because he perceived it to be redundant or because he was conforming the text to the Septuagint (Hab 1:5). The additional last sentence provides a bridge to the next paragraph and produces the impression that Paul's speech overwhelmed his listeners.

Acts 13:42

WH NU	ἐξιόντων δὲ αὐτῶν παρεκάλουν "and when they left, they were urging" 𝔓[74] ℵ A (B) C Ψ 33 1739 NKJVmg RSV NRSV ESV NASB NIV TNIV NEB REB NJB NAB (NLT) HCSB NET
variant/TR	εξιοντων δε εκ της συναγωγης των Ιουδαιων παρεκαλουν τα εθνη "and when they left the synagogue of the Jews, the Gentiles were urging" Maj KJV NKJV HCSBmg

The WH NU reading has the backing of early and diverse documentary evidence. The additions in TR clarify for the reader that the Gentiles outside the Jews' synagogue wanted to hear the word from Paul.

Acts 13:43

Western text (D syr^{hmg}, also E with slightly different wording) reads:

> "When the meeting of the synagogue broke up, many Jews and devout converts to Judaism followed Paul and Barnabas, who spoke to them and urged them to continue in the grace of God. **And it came to pass that the word of God went throughout the whole city.**"

The addition was made to fill in a perceived gap between 13:43 and 13:44—that is, some account must be given to explain why the whole city would assemble together to hear Paul and Barnabas preach on the next Sabbath. Not wanting to leave this gap-filling to the reader's imagination, the D-reviser inserted a plausible explanation: The word was preached between the intervening Sabbaths, thereby arousing the whole city to come hear the message on the following Sabbath (see NJBmg).

Acts 13:44

NU — ἀκοῦσαι τὸν λόγον τοῦ κυρίου
"to hear the word of the Lord"
𝔓^{74} א A B^{2} 33 1739
NRSV ESV NASB NIV TNIV NJBmg NAB NLT HCSB NET

variant 1/TR WH — ακουσαι τον λογον του θεου
"to hear the word of God"
B* C E Ψ Maj
KJV NKJV RSV NRSVmg NEB REB NJB HCSBmg

variant 2 — ακουσαι Παυλου πολυν τε λογον ποιησαμενου περι του κυριου
"to hear Paul telling about the Lord in many words"
D it^{d}
none

The NU text has slightly stronger documentary support than the first variant. Furthermore, since it was more common for the NT writers to use the expression "the word of God" rather than "the word of the Lord," it is likely that scribes changed the latter to the former in this instance. The first variant could likely be the result of scribal assimilation to 13:46. Nevertheless, many modern versions concur with TR WH in reading "the word of God." The expansion in the second variant is a typical Western paraphrase.

Acts 13:45

WH NU — βλασφημοῦντες
"speaking evil"
𝔓^{74} א A B C L Ψ 33 1739
RSV NRSV (ESV) NASB NIV (TNIV) NEB REB NJB NAB NLT HCSB NET

variant 1/TR	αντιλεγοντες και βλασφημουντες "contradicting and speaking evil" D 097 Maj syr[h] (E εναντιουμενοι) KJV NKJV

The WH NU reading has superior documentary support. The bareness and brashness of ending the verse with βλασφημουντες ("speaking evil") prompted two kinds of similar additions. As usual, TR incorporates the addition, which was then translated in KJV and NKJV.

Acts 13:48

TR NU	ἐδόξαζον τὸν λόγον τοῦ κυρίου "they were glorifying the word of the Lord" 𝔓[45] 𝔓[74] ℵ A C 33 KJV NKJV NRSV ESV NASB NIV TNIV NEB REB NJB NAB NLT HCSB NET
variant 1/WH	εδοξαζον τον λογον του θεου "they were glorifying the word of God" B E 049 RSV NJBmg
variant 2	εδεξαντο τον λογον του θεου "they were receiving the word of God" D it[gig] none
variant 3	εδοξαζον τον θεον "they were glorifying God" 614 syr none

The TR NU reading has excellent support, followed by all the English versions except the RSV. The change to "word of God" represents scribal conformity to the more ordinary expression or to 13:46. Nonetheless, WH again shows its preference for B, followed here by RSV. Although the reading in D may have occurred as a result of error—the scribe confusing εδοξαζον for εδεξαντο—it is more likely a purposeful modification of the unique expression, "glorifying the word of the Lord" (i.e., giving glory to the Lord for being able to hear and respond to his word). The third variant conveys the idea of glorifying God but says nothing of exulting in the word.

Acts 13:49

𝔓[45] alone has the barer expression, ο λογος ("the word"), instead of ο λογος του κυριου ("the word of the Lord"), found in other manuscripts. Although it is tempting to say the shorter reading is original, caution against this is warranted because the scribe of 𝔓[45] is known for trimming.

Acts 13:50

Western text (D E) reads:

> "But the Jews incited the God-fearing women of high standing and the leading men of the city, and stirred up **great affliction and** persecution against Paul and Barnabas, and drove them out of their region."

The extra verbiage hardly helps and may not even be true. A similar addition was made by the D-reviser in 8:1.

Acts 14:2-7

Western text (D) reads:

> "But the **leading men of the synagogue of the Jews and the rulers of the synagogue stirred up a persecution against the righteous** and poisoned the minds of the Gentiles against the brothers. **But the Lord quickly gave them peace.** [3] So they remained for a long time, speaking boldly for the Lord, who testified to the word of his grace by granting signs and wonders to be done through them. [4] But the residents of the city were divided; some sided with the Jews, and some with the apostles, **clinging to them on account of the word of God.** [5] And when an attempt was made by both Gentiles and Jews, with their rulers, to mistreat them and to stone them, [6] they learned of it and fled to Lystra and Derbe, cities of Lycaonia, and to the **entire** surrounding country; [7] and there they preached the gospel. **And the whole multitude was moved by the teaching. And Paul and Barnabas spent some time in Lystra.**"

There is an obvious problem between verses 2 and 3: Why would Paul and Barnabas stay in Iconium for a long time if there was such persecution against them? Consequently, some scholars tried to fix the problem by transposing the verses (see, for example, MOFFATT). The reviser fixed the problem by patching up the hostility with peace. The reviser also specifically identified the leading men of the Jewish synagogue as being the perpetrators of the persecution. This is probably an accurate conjecture. He made other additions (in 14:4 and 14:7), both promoting the efficacy of the apostles' teaching. Again, the reviser is responsible for producing a text that robs the reader of doing his own gap-filling. F. F. Bruce (1990, 317-318) put it well when he said, "It requires no excess of imagination to suppose that the Jewish authorities of Pisidian Antioch communicated with those of Iconium, who proceeded at once to prejudice the civic leaders against Paul and Barnabas; v. 2 will then indicate the immediate Jewish hostility, v. 5 the success of the attempt to stir up the magistrates and populace. But until the Gentile opposition broke out, the missionaries ignored the Jewish hostility and carried on the work of evangelization for a considerable time."

Acts 14:9-10

Western text (D syr^{hmg} with C E on longer addition in 14:10) reads:

> "He, **being in fear,** listened to Paul as he was speaking. **And Paul,** looking at him intently and seeing that he had faith to be healed, [10] said in a loud voice, '**I say to you in the name of the Lord Jesus Christ,** stand upright on your feet **and walk.**' And he **immediately** sprang up and began to walk."

The additions in 14:9 are typical Western text embellishments. The interpolation in 14:10 is a common expansion in later manuscripts. Later scribes felt obligated to make healing pronouncements formulaic and therefore added "in the name of the Lord Jesus Christ" in imitation of such verses as 3:6 (see notes on 6:8b and 9:40).

Acts 14:13-14

Western text (D) reads:

> "The **priests** of Zeus, whose temple was just outside the city, brought oxen and garlands to the gates; **they** with the crowds wanted to offer sacrifice. [14] When [the apostles] Barnabas and Paul heard of it, they tore their clothes and rushed out to the crowd."

Exercising his knowledge of Hellenstic temple practices, wherein it was common for each temple to have a group of priests, the D-reviser made the number of priests plural. But the Lystran temple of Zeus may have been modest, being attended to by only one priest, or Luke may have chosen to mention only one priest. In the next verse, the reviser omitted "the apostles," perhaps because he did not consider it appropriate for Barnabas to be called an apostle.

Acts 14:18

Not satisfied with the conclusion to this pericope (14:1-18), various scribes (C 6 33 614 syr[hmg]) added αλλα πορευεσθαι εκαστον εις τα ιδια ("but each went to his own home"). This same kind of addition was made by the scribe of D in 5:18 and by many scribes in John 7:53 (see notes). Longenecker (1981, 437) incorrectly lists 𝔓[45] in support of the addition, but correctly observes that this addition is "a rounding off of the section for lectionary purposes."

Acts 14:19

Western text (C D E) reads:

> "[But] **while they were spending some time there and teaching, certain** Jews came there from Antioch and Iconium and they persuaded the crowds **to withdraw from them, saying they were not telling the truth at all, but were nothing but liars.** Then they stoned Paul and dragged him out of the city, supposing him to be dead."

The Western text supplies a transition from the end of the previous pericope to this one. Following this, the Western text (extant in C but not D) enhances the narrative by providing a more defined cause for the stoning that occurred. Admittedly, the gap in the Alexandrian text between the first and second sentences is big: It shifts from the crowd being won over to Paul being stoned. Nevertheless, a reader can normally navigate this gap for himself.

Acts 14:20

Instead of "the disciples," a few manuscripts (𝔓[45] D E) read των μαθητων αυτου ("his disciples"), meaning "Paul's disciples." If this wording was original, we could easily explain the change because it is customary to see the term "the disciples" (i.e., Jesus' disciples or the Christians) in the book of Acts. (See note on 9:25 for a similar textual problem.)

Acts 14:25a

TR WH NU	τὸν λόγον "the word" B D 1739 Maj cop KJV NKJV RSV NRSV ESV NASB NIV TNIV REB NJB NAB NLT HCSB NET
variant 1	τον λογον του κυριου "the word of the Lord" ℵ A C Ψ 33 NEB
variant 2	τον λογον του θεου "the word of God" 𝔓74 E none

The TR WH NU reading and the first variant have equally good testimony. However, the fact that there are two variant readings with expansions—both common expressions—is a good indication that the text originally contained the unadorned expression "the word." Indeed, "the word" was often expanded to the "word of God" or "the word of the Lord" in Acts.

Acts 14:25b

Western text (D syr^{h**}) reads:

> "When they had spoken the word in Perga, they went down to Attalia, **preaching the gospel to them.**"

The reviser made the assumption that Paul and Barnabas preached the gospel when they went to Attalia, but these missionaries did not necessarily preach in every city they went to.

Acts 15:1-5

Western text (D syr^{hmg}) reads:

> "Then certain individuals came down from Judea and were teaching the brothers, 'Unless you are circumcised **and walk** according to the custom of Moses, you cannot be saved.' [2] And Paul and Barnabas had no small dissension and debate with them, **for Paul spoke strongly, maintaining that they [the Gentiles] should remain the same as when they believed. But those who had come from Jerusalem ordered** Paul and Barnabas and some of the others to go up to Jerusalem to discuss this question with the apostles and the elders **that they might be judged before them.** [3] So they were sent on their way by the church, and as they passed through both Phoenicia and Samaria, they reported the conversion of the Gentiles, and brought great joy to all the brothers. [4] When they came to Jerusalem, they were welcomed by the church and the apostles and the elders, and they reported all that God had done with them. [5] But **those who had charged them to go up to the elders, being** certain ones of the sect of the Pharisees who believed, stood up and said, 'It is necessary for them to be circumcised and ordered to keep the law of Moses.'"

According to the Alexandrian text, Paul and Barnabas were sent (presumably by the church in Antioch) to go to Jerusalem to settle the Gentile issue. According to the Western text, Paul and Barnabas were ordered (by the Jewish Pharisaic Christians from Jerusalem) to go to Jerusalem so that they might be judged by the Jerusalem church. This is a significant difference insofar as it asserts Jerusalem's ecclesiastical authority over other churches. Haenchen (1971, 443) said it well: "The D text evidences the developing tendency to have ecclesiastical controversies settled by higher authority; this procedure is seen as justified by the example of Jerusalem."

Furthermore, the Western text (or D text) strongly suggests that the Jewish Christians from Jerusalem considered themselves superior to all other believers—including Paul and Barnabas—and that they alone decided what was orthodox and what was not. The secondary nature of the Western text here is clearly manifest by these prejudices and by the fact that the expanded verbiage of 15:2 was borrowed from 1 Cor 7:20, 24.

Acts 15:7

WH NU — ἐν ὑμῖν ἐξελέξατο ὁ θεός
"God made a choice among you"
𝔓74 א A B C 0294 33 1739
RSV NRSV ESV NASB NIV TNIV NEB REB NJB NAB NLT HCSB NET

variant/TR — εν ημιν εξελεξατο ο θεος
"God made a choice among us"
D E Ψ Maj
KJV NKJV HCSBmg

According to the WH NU reading, which has excellent testimony, Peter said: "you know that in the early days God made a choice among you, that I should be the one through whom the Gentiles would hear the message of the good news." The change of pronoun from υμιν ("you") to ημιν ("us") is significant in that "you" represents the entire church (see note on 15:5), whereas "us" represents just the apostles. Evidently, it seemed more appropriate to certain scribes to have the selection of the man who would be God's oracle as coming exclusively from the apostles. It may be noted that the scribe of 𝔓45 accidentally copied 15:2 in the middle of this verse (see *Text of Earliest MSS,* 198-199).

Acts 15:12

Western text (D syr^{h**}) reads:

> "**And when the elders agreed to what had been spoken by Peter,** the whole assembly kept silence, and listened to Barnabas and Paul."

As often happens in the Western text, Peter is given prominence by expansions such as these (see notes on 1:23; 2:14; 3:17; 4:29; 5:29).

Acts 15:17-18

WH NU — λέγει κύριος ποιῶν ταῦτα [18]γνωστὰ ἀπ' αἰῶνος.
"says the Lord, doing these things [18] known from long ago."
א B C Ψ 33
NKJVmg RSV NRSV ESV NASB NIV TNIV NEB REB NJB NAB NLT HCSB NET

variant 1 — λεγει κυριος ποιων ταυτα· [18]γνωστον απ αιωνος εστιν τω κυριω το εργον αυτου
"says the Lord, doing these things. [18] Known to the Lord from long ago is his work."
𝔓74 A (D) it
NIVmg TNIVmg NJBmg

variant 2/TR λεγει κυριος ποιων ταυτα παντα· [18]γνωστα απ αιωνος εστιν τω θεω παντα τα εργα αυτου
"says the Lord doing all these things. [18] Known to God from long ago are all his works."
(E) Maj syr
KJV NKJV HCSBmg

According to WH NU, a full rendering of 15:15-18 is: "[15] And this fulfills the words of the prophets, as it is written [16]'After this I will return, and I will rebuild the tabernacle of David, which has fallen; from its ruins I will rebuild it, and I will restore it, [17] so that all other people may seek the Lord—even all the Gentiles over whom my name has been called, says the Lord, doing these things [18] known from long ago.'" The textual issue pertains to the last words: "says the Lord, doing these things known from long ago."

The textual issue is complicated by the fact that it is difficult to determine if James was (1) citing only and all of Amos 9:11-12 in Acts 15:16-18, (2) citing Amos 9:11-12 in 15:16-17—with 5:18 being James's own remark—or (3) citing Amos 9:11-12 in 15:16-17 and then alluding to Isa 45:21 in 15:18. In favor of the last proposition is the fact that James introduced his quotation by saying that the prophets (plural) spoke of these things, which would allow for him to draw from both Amos and Isaiah. But it is also possible that James mentioned "the prophets" as being equivalent to the book of the Prophets (cf. Luke 24:44), from which he cited only one passage—from Amos. As such, the last words (in 15:18) are James's.

But what does the expression, γνωστα απ αιωνος ("known from long ago") mean? According to the WH NU reading, it is likely that James was saying that prophets such as Amos knew long ago about the events that were occurring in James's day—namely, that Jesus had come to restore the true house of Israel (even if it were composed of a remnant of Jews), and that in so doing he had provided Gentiles everywhere access to God. The two variant readings display the work of scribes trying to make sense of this terse, cryptic expression and thereby expanding it. These expansions place the emphasis on God's foreknowledge of the events unfolding in the church. As such, James was saying that the church leaders should not stand in "opposition to the expressed will of God, as evidenced by Peter's testimony and the prophets' words—but only God himself knows for certain how everything fits together and is to be fully understood" (Longenecker 1981, 447).

Acts 15:20a

TR WH NU include και της πορνειας ("and from sexual immorality")
𝔓[74] א A B C D E Maj
all

variant omit
𝔓[45] Origen
NEBmg REBmg

See comments below on 15:20c.

Acts 15:20b

TR WH NU include και του πνικτου ("and from what is strangled")
𝔓[45] 𝔓[74] א A B C E 33 Maj
all

variant omit
D it^gig Irenaeus
none

See comments below on 15:20c.

Acts 15:20c

TR WH NU καὶ τοῦ αἵματος
"and from blood"
𝔓45 𝔓74 A B C E 33 Maj
all

variant και του αιματος και οσα αν μη θελωσιν αυτοις γινεσθαι ετεροις μη ποιειν
"and from blood and [to refrain] from doing to others whatsoever they would not like done to themselves"
(D) 1739 cop^sa Irenaeus^1739mg Eusebius^1739mg
NEBmg REBmg NJBmg

The Jerusalem decree to the Gentile believers, though intended to promote compromise, is weighted with Jewish sensitivities. In other words, the Gentiles—in exchange for not having to be circumcised—are still asked to refrain from doing things that would offend their Jewish Christian brothers. All of these restraints, it could be said, deal with practices related to pagan idolatry, which heads the list, and is followed by sexual immorality (related to temple prostitution), not eating blood or things strangled (as done in pagan festivals). These restraints would also help the Jews to associate with the Gentiles in table fellowship, inasmuch as Jews are repulsed by eating what is unclean or not drained of blood.

The TR WH NU reading of 15:20a, 20b, 20c has excellent textual support, which is both early and diverse. The changes in the Western text appear to steer the text away from pagan idolatry and Jewish observances to ethical issues. The omission of "and from what is strangled" in the Western text seems to have been made in the interest of making the Jerusalem decree completely ethical; the Gentile believers are to abstain from idolatry, fornication, blood (which could be interpreted as "bloodshed"). To round off this list of ethical prohibitions, the reviser added the negative Golden Rule: "Do not do to others what you would not want done to yourself." He may have borrowed this from Matt 7:12 and Luke 6:31, which have the positive Golden Rule ("do to others what you would want done to yourself"), or he may have taken this from the *Didache* (1.2). The omission of "and from fornication" in 𝔓45 and Origen (*Cels.* 8.29) appears to be a change that makes the Jerusalem decree deal only with ceremonial issues. The final expansion was early inasmuch as 1739^mg notes that Irenaeus and Eusebius knew the reading.

Acts 15:23a

WH NU read γραψαντες δια χειρος αυτων ("having written with their hands"), with the excellent support of 𝔓33vid? 𝔓45 𝔓74 ℵ* A B cop^bo. TR adds ταδε ("thus" = "having written with their hands thus"), following ℵ2 E 33 1739 Maj. All English versions do the same, many with the statement, "the following letter." Other manuscripts expand the statement as γραψαντες επιστολην δια χειρος αυτων περιεχουσαν ταδε ("having written a letter with their hands containing thus")—so (C) D it^gig (syr^p,hmg cop^sa). The reading γραψαντες επιστολην δια χειρος αυτων εχουσαν τον τυπον τουτον ("having written a letter with their hands containing this message") is found in Ψ.

Acts 15:23b

WH NU οἱ ἀπόστολοι καὶ οἱ πρεσβύτεροι ἀδελφοί
"the apostles and the elders, brothers"
𝔓33 𝔓74 ℵ* A B C D 33
RSV NRSV ESV NASB NIV TNIV NEB REB NJB NAB NLT HCSB NET

variant 1/TR οι αποστολοι και οι πρεσβυτεροι και οι αδελφοι
"the apostles and the elders and the brothers"
ℵ2 E Ψ 1739 Maj syr
KJV NKJV

variant 2 οι αποστολοι και οι πρεσβυτεροι
"the apostles and the elders"
copsa Origen
none

The difficulty of making sense of αδελφοι ("brothers") immediately following πρεσβυτεροι ("elders") in the identification of the authors of the Jerusalem decree prompted two changes: one that made "the brothers" an additional identification, and another that dropped it completely. The first variant allows for the entire church at Jerusalem to be co-participants in the authorship of the decree, but the authors were exclusively the apostles and elders. The WH NU reading, which has excellent testimony, is best rendered in the NIV and NLT: "the apostles and the elders, your brothers." As such, it is written by the brothers (who are elders and apostles) to the brothers in Antioch, Syria, and Cilicia, thereby acknowledging brotherhood and promoting solidarity between Jerusalem and the Gentile churches.

Acts 15:24

WH NU ἀνασκευάζοντες τὰς ψυχὰς ὑμῶν
"unsettling your souls"
𝔓33 𝔓45vid 𝔓74 ℵ A B D 33 cop
NKJVmg RSV NRSV ESV NASB NIV TNIV NEB REB NJB NAB NLT HCSB NET

variant/TR ανασκευαζοντες τας ψυχας υμων λεγοντες περιτεμνεσθαι και τηρειν τον νομον
"unsettling your souls by saying [it is necessary] to be circumcised and to keep the law"
C E Ψ 1739 Maj syr
KJV NKJV HCSBmg

The expanded reading, assimilating 15:5, provides an explanation for the readers of Acts (in later generations) as to why the Gentiles were unsettled. But the Gentile readers of the letter would have already known why they were unsettled. Thus, this is but another example of unnecessary gap-filling, which found its way into TR and KJV.

Acts 15:26

Western text (D E syrhmg) reads:

> "[Barnabas and Paul,] who have risked their lives for the sake of our Lord Jesus Christ **in every trial.**"

This is a typical Western text embellishment, intended to clarify the meaning of παραδεδωκοσι τας ψυχας αυτων, which could mean "committed their souls" or possibly "risked their lives."

Acts 15:29

Western text (D it[d] Irenaeus 1739[mg]) reads:

> "You must abstain from what has been sacrificed to idols and from blood [and from what is strangled] and from fornication, **and from whatever you would not want done to you, do not do to one another.** If you keep yourselves from these, you will do well, **being carried along by the Holy Spirit.** Farewell."

Since this verse recounts in writing what was decided in 15:20, we would expect to see some of the same textual variants. The Western text does not disappoint us; it displays the same omission as in 15:20—deleting "and from what is strangled," probably to make the text more ethically oriented. The Western text also has the negative Golden Rule (see note on 15:20c). The reviser then provides another addition to the conclusion of the letter, wherein the recipients of the letter are encouraged to do well as they are carried along by the Holy Spirit (see NJBmg). These words, very likely borrowed from 2 Pet 1:21, function to provide a spiritual stimulus to what would otherwise seem to be legalistic commands. They also provide a parallel to 15:28, which implicates the Spirit's involvement in the composing of the Jerusalem Decree; thus, they will be supplied the Spirit to carry out the demands of that decree.

Acts 15:30

Western text (D*) reads:

> "So they were sent off and **in a few days** went down to Antioch. When they gathered the congregation together, they delivered the letter."

Again, the scribe of D provides a circumstantial addition.

Acts 15:32

Western text (D) reads:

> "Judas and Silas, who were themselves prophets, **full of the Holy Spirit,** said much to encourage and strengthen the brothers."

The D-reviser, wherever possible, made interpolations concerning the empowering of the Holy Spirit (see 15:29; 19:1; 20:3). Indeed, it is a recurring motif in the book of Acts that the Holy Spirit empowers those who speak for God. Thus, it was correct for the reviser to think that Judas and Silas must have been filled with the Holy Spirit when they spoke to the church. However, by this time in the narrative (more than halfway through Acts), most readers would have understood this motif and imagined this by themselves.

Acts 15:34

WH NU	omit verse 𝔓[74] ℵ A B E Ψ Maj syr[p] cop[bo] NKJVmg RSV NRSV ESV NASBmg NIV TNIV NEB REB NJB NAB NLT HCSB NET
variant/TR	add verse in two forms: (1) εδοξε δε τω Σιλα επιμειναι αυτου

"But it seemed good to Silas to remain there."
(C) 33 614 1739 syr[h**] cop[sa] (so TR)
KJV NKJV RSVmg NRSVmg ESVmg NASB NIVmg NEBmg REBmg NJBmg NABmg NLTmg HCSBmg NETmg
(2) εδοξε δε τω Σιλα επιμειναι προς αυτους, μονος δε Ιουδας επορευθη
"But it seemed good to Silas to remain with them, so Judas traveled alone."
D it[d,w]
none

The extra verse, though it contradicts 15:33, was added to avoid the difficulty in 15:40, which indicates that Silas was still in Antioch. Thus, in trying to solve one problem, the reviser (and other scribes) created another.

We may wonder how a verse that was not included in the Byzantine text (Maj) was incorporated into TR. The verse (in form 1) was inserted by Erasmus into his Greek text, even though he found it only in the margin of the Greek manuscripts he was using. Erasmus, probably aware of its inclusion in the Latin Vulgate, supposed that it had been omitted in the Greek manuscripts by an error of the scribes (Westcott and Hort 1882, 96). From Erasmus's text it went into TR and was then translated in KJV. Most modern versions note the omission out of deference to the KJV tradition. NASB retains the verse with a note saying that early manuscripts do not contain it.

Acts 15:37-38

Western text (D) reads:

"Barnabas wanted to [also] take with them John called Mark. But Paul **was not willing, saying that** one who had deserted them in Pamphylia and had not gone with them to the work **for which they had been sent—this one should not be with them.**"

The reviser expanded the text here in an effort to clarify Paul's reasons for rejecting John Mark as a missionary companion. But the text does not need this help; rather, the interpolations are an encumbrance.

Acts 15:40

WH NU τῇ χάριτι τοῦ κυρίου
"the grace of the Lord"
𝔓[74] ℵ A B D 33 it[d] cop[sa]
RSV NRSV ESV NASB NIV TNIV NEB REB NJBmg NAB NLT HCSB NET

variant/TR τη χαριτι του θεου
"the grace of God"
𝔓[45] C E Ψ 1739 Maj syr cop[bo]
KJV NKJV NJB

Both readings have ancient and diverse attestation, and both readings make perfectly good sense. However, the variant reading could be the result of assimilation to 14:26, which speaks of the brothers in Antioch commending Paul and Barnabas to "the grace of God." All modern English versions, except the NJB, follow the WH NU text.

Acts 15:41

Western text (D syr^{hmg} adding "apostles and" before "elders") reads:

> "He went through Syria and Cilicia, strengthening the churches, **delivering [to them] the commands of the elders.**"

The D-reviser, again, did a bit of gap-filling for the sake of his readers. But anyone who has read 15:23 knows this. Or, if the reader goes on, this will be made explicit in 16:4.

Acts 16:1

Western text (D it^{gig} syr^{hmg}) reads:

> "**Having passed through these nations,** he went on also to Derbe and to Lystra, where there was a certain disciple named Timothy, the son of a Jewish woman who was a believer; but his father was a Greek."

As often occurs at the beginning of new sections, the reviser adds some circumstantial details to provide a link between episodes. The addition also shows that Derbe and Lystra (both cities) were not included in Paul's travel to the countries of Syria and Cilicia, mentioned in 15:41.

Acts 16:4-5

Western text (D) reads:

> "As they went through the cities, **they preached and delivered to them, with all boldness, the Lord Jesus Christ,** and **at the same time also** they delivered to them the decisions that had been reached by the apostles and elders who were in Jerusalem. [5] So the churches were established [in the faith] and increased in numbers daily."

The expansion in 16:4 may have been created to help explain the phenomenal growth in the churches. The awkwardness of this addition, however, is manifest in the double occurrence of παραδιδωμι ("to deliver"). Its second occurrence is fine, for it speaks of delivering the Jerusalem Decree to the Gentile churches, but its first occurrence is very odd because "delivering . . . the Lord Jesus" is an expression often used in the NT to convey Jesus' betrayal or Jesus being handed over to death. The omission in 16:5 could have been the result of the reviser not wanting the text to convey the strengthening of existing believers as much as the establishing of new Christians.

Acts 16:6

Western text (D it^{gig} syr^{p} cop^{bo}) reads:

> "They went through the region of Phrygia and Galatia, having been forbidden by the Holy Spirit to speak the word **of God** in Asia."

This is a typical Western expansion, which is also present in cop^{bo}.

Acts 16:7

WH NU τὸ πνεῦμα Ἰησοῦ
"the Spirit of Jesus"
𝔓^{74} ℵ A B C^{2} D E 33 1739 syr cop^{bo}
NKJVmg RSV NRSV ESV NASB NIV TNIV NEB REB NJB NAB NLT HCSB NET

variant 1 το πνευμα κυριου
"the Spirit of the Lord"
C* it[gig]
none

variant 2/TR το πνευμα
"the Spirit"
Maj
KJV NKJV NJBmg

The WH NU reading is backed by both early and diverse documentary evidence. The uniqueness of the expression, "the Spirit of Jesus," caused the two variants. In fact, this is the first and only place in the NT where the phrase "the Spirit of Jesus" occurs. Elsewhere, the Spirit is called "the Spirit of Christ" (Rom 8:9; 1 Pet 1:11) and "the Spirit of Jesus Christ" (Phil 1:19). The use of the title "Spirit of Jesus" in Acts shows the unity of action between Jesus and the Spirit that permeates this book. During the days of Jesus' earthly ministry, the disciples were directed by Jesus; now, after his resurrection and ascension, by "the Spirit of Jesus."

Acts 16:9-10

Western text (D) reads:

> "And **in** a vision during the night, there stood **as it were** a certain man of Macedonia pleading with him and saying, 'Come over to Macedonia and help us.' [10] When **therefore he had risen up, he related to us the vision,** and we perceived that **the Lord** had called us to proclaim the gospel to **those who were in Macedonia.**"

The addition of "as it were" in 16:9 is to help the reader understand that a real, flesh-and-blood man did not appear to Paul; it was just an appearance of one who looked like a man. Perhaps the reviser was thinking of an angel, for angels often assumed a human visage when they made their appearances to human beings. The additions in 16:10 are unnecessary gap-fillers. The reader can read in between the lines to ascertain that Paul's companions knew about Paul's vision because he must have told them.

Acts 16:12

NU πρώτης μερίδος τῆς Μακεδονίας πόλις
"a city of the first district of Macedonia"
it[c] vg[mss] slav
NRSVmg NETmg

variant 1/WH πρωτη της μεριδος Μακεδονιας πολις
"a leading city of the district of Macedonia"
𝔓[74] ℵ A C Ψ 33
RSV NRSV ESV NASB NIV TNIV NEB REB NAB NLT HCSB NET

variant 2/TR πρωτη της μεριδος της Μακεδονιας πολις
"the leading city of the district of Macedonia"
(B omits first της) P Maj
KJV NKJV NJB

variant 3 κεφαλη της μεριδος Μακεδονιας πολις
"capital city of the district of Macedonia"
D it[d] syr[p]
none

The majority of NU editors adopted a reading without any Greek manuscript support because historical evidence does not support the fact that Philippi was the principal city of Macedonia. Thessalonica could make these claims (see TCGNT). However, the Alexandrian manuscripts (whether in variant 1 or 2) are not implausible because Philippi was "a leading city of the district of Macedonia," though not *the* principal or capital city (there is no definite article in the Greek before πρωτης). Furthermore, Philippi could have been called "first city" as a matter of civic pride (so Ascough 1998). Metzger and Wikgren, two of five editors for the NU text, expressed their dissent to the majority vote in favor of the view just expressed (see Wikgren 1981). Not one English version has followed the NU text, and rightly so because it has no backing in any Greek manuscript.

Acts 16:13

WH NU ἐνομίζομεν προσευχὴν εἶναι
"we supposed there was [a place of] prayer"
(א) A[c] C Ψ 33 cop[bo] (A* B προσευχη = "they would be at prayer")
RSV NRSV ESV NASB NIV TNIV NEB REB NAB (NLT) HCSB NET

variant 2/TR ενομιζετο προσευχη ειναι
"prayer was customarily made"
(𝔓[74] ενομιζεν) E 1739 Maj
KJV NKJV NEBmg NJB

variant 3 εδοκει προσευχη ειναι
"prayer was thought to be made"
D
none

It is difficult to judge which reading is original because the manuscripts do not clearly line up with one reading against another. The WH NU reading and the first variant, however, yield a similar sense: Paul and his companions went to the place in Philippi where they supposed people would be praying. (The D-reading is a variation of this.) The Majority reading is slightly different in that it points to a place where prayer was customarily made—and this would most naturally be a synagogue. But there was not a synagogue in Philippi (which required the gathering of at least ten adult Jewish males); rather, Paul found a group of women praying beside a river.

Acts 16:15

Western text (D) reads:

> "When she and **all** her household were baptized, she urged us, saying, 'If you have judged me to be faithful to **God,** come and stay at my home.' And she prevailed upon us."

The D-reviser's addition of "all" is an exaggeration. The shift from "Lord" to "God" is unfortunate because it obfuscates Lydia's newfound obedience to the Lord Jesus Christ. Lydia had already been a "God-fearer" prior to hearing Paul's message (cf. 16:14); it was the "Lord" (Jesus) who opened her heart.

Acts 16:16

Several manuscripts (𝔓74 ℵ A B C* D*) read πνευμα πυθωνα, which literally translated is, "Python-spirit." The Python was a mythical serpent who guarded the temple of Apollos. Those possessed with the spirit of divination were thought to be inspired by Apollos. Hence, they were said to have the spirit of Python. To make this clearer to readers, various scribes changed the wording to πνευμα πυθωνος ("spirit of Python"), which equals "a spirit of divination" (so 𝔓45 C3 D1 E Ψ 1739 Maj—so TR).

Acts 16:17

WH NU καταγγέλλουσιν ὑμῖν
"they are proclaiming to you"
𝔓74 ℵ B E 1739
RSV NRSV ESV NASB NIV TNIV NEB REB NJB NAB NLT HCSB NET

variant 1/TR καταγγελλουσιν ημιν
"they are proclaiming to us"
A C Ψ 33 Maj
KJV NKJV HCSBmg

variant 2 ευαγγελιζονται υμιν
"they are preaching [the] gospel to us"
D
none

The two pronouns, υμιν and ημιν, were often confounded in the transcription of the text because they look alike and sound alike. Nonetheless, υμιν ("you") has the best attestation and suits the context well. The reading of TR is based on inferior manuscript support. The D-reading is a scribal editorialization.

Acts 16:18

Western text (D) reads:

> "But Paul, **in the Spirit,** turned and being disturbed said, 'I order you in the name of Jesus Christ to come out of her.' And **immediately** it came out that very hour."

The Western text has Paul acting "in the Spirit," rather than speaking to the evil spirit that possessed the woman. This is in keeping with the reviser's desire to intensify the apostles' actions as having been done "in the Spirit" (see note on 15:32). The insertion of "immediately" is also intended to heighten the narrative, but the exaggeration is unnecessary.

Acts 16:19

Western text (D) reads:

> "But when the masters **of the woman** saw that they **were deprived of the gain which they had through her,** they seized Paul and Silas and dragged them into the marketplace before the authorities."

The reviser introduced expansions to help improve the readability of the text—none of which are needed.

Acts 16:27

As often happened in the history of the transmission of the NT text, certain scribes gave names to the nameless. Here a few late manuscripts (614 1799 2147) ascribe the title "the faithful Stephanas" to the jailer. Some scribe may have confused this person with the one mentioned in 1 Corinthians, because Paul also baptized everyone in the household of Stephanas (cf. Acts 16:33 with 1 Cor 1:16; and see 1 Cor 16:15, 17).

Acts 16:29-30

Western text (D syr^p,h**^) reads:

> "He called for lights, and rushing in, fell down trembling before **the feet of** Paul and Silas. [30]Then, **after securing the rest,** he brought them outside and said, 'Sirs, what must I do to be saved?'"

In typical fashion, the reviser provided some gap-fillers that readers are well able to supply for themselves.

Acts 16:31

WH NU τὸν κύριον Ἰησοῦν
"the Lord Jesus"
𝔓74vid ℵ A B 33 cop^bo
RSV NRSV ESV NASB NIV TNIV NEB REB NJB NAB NLT HCSB NET

variant/TR τον κυριον Ιησουν Χριστον
"the Lord Jesus Christ"
C D E Ψ 1739 Maj syr
KJV NKJV NETmg

The expansion of Jesus' name is characteristic of later manuscripts, especially in creedal pronouncements, as in this one: "Believe in the Lord Jesus and you will be saved."

Acts 16:32

TR NU τὸν λόγον τοῦ κυρίου
"the word of the Lord"
𝔓45 𝔓74 ℵ2 A C D E Ψ 33 1739 Maj
all

variant/WH τον λογον του θεου
"the word of God"
ℵ* B
NEBmg NJBmg

Favoring the testimony of ℵ and B, WH adopted the variant reading. However, the testimony of 𝔓45 𝔓74 etc. is superior; this reading was adopted for the text of NA[26] (a change from previous editions of the Nestle text) and all the translations.

Acts 16:35-40

Western text (D, with syr[hmg] in part) reads:

> "When morning came, the magistrates **assembled together into the market place, and recollecting the earthquake that had happened, they were afraid; and they** sent the police, saying, 'Let those men go **whom you took in yesterday.'** [36] And the jailer **came in** and reported the message to Paul, saying, 'The magistrates sent word to let you go; therefore come out now and go [in peace].' [37] But Paul replied, 'They have beaten us in public, men who are **innocent** and Roman citizens, and have thrown us into prison; and now are they going to discharge us in secret? Certainly not! Let them come and take us out themselves.' [38] The police reported to the magistrates **themselves, these words which were spoken for the magistrates,** and they were afraid when they heard that they were Roman citizens. [39] So **having come with many friends to the prison,** they besought them to go, **saying, 'We did not know about you, that you are righteous men.'** And they took them out and asked them to leave the city, **lest they again assemble against us, crying out against you.** [40] And they went out of the prison and went to Lydia's [home]; and when they had seen the brothers there, **they reported all the things the Lord had done for them.** And having encouraged them, they departed."

The D-reviser must have sensed there was a narrative gap between 16:25-34 and 16:35 because the magistrates, for no apparent reason, suddenly decided to release Paul and Silas. It is the earthquake, according to the reviser, that caused this sudden change in attitude. Somehow it spoke to them that they were wrong in imprisoning righteous men. The reviser then made a number of other circumstantial additions and supplied a few more gap-fillers, none of which are really needed. The final addition in 16:40 has Paul and Silas "reporting the events at Lydia's house, not out of any historical interest, but as an edifying proof of what the Lord has done for them" (Haenchen 1971, 499).

The reviser also made one deletion; in 16:36 he excised "in peace," probably because it seemed odd to have this expression on the lips of a Gentile jailer. However, a few scholars and translators (see NEBmg NJBmg) think the Western text (D it[d,gig]) might be original because scribes would be more likely to add such words of farewell than delete them. But the preponderance of testimony in favor of their inclusion is hard to argue against: 𝔓[45vid] 𝔓[74] ℵ A B C E 33 1739 Maj syr cop.

Acts 17:1

Western text (D) reads:

> "After they had passed through Amphipolis, **they went down to** Apollonia, and **from there** to Thessalonica, where there was a synagogue of the Jews."

Instead of having Paul and Silas pass through Amphipolis and Apollonia on the way to Thessalonica, the Western text has them stopping in Apollonia before going on to Thessalonica.

Acts 17:3

WH NU, with the support of only B, read ουτος εστιν ο Χριστος ο Ιησους ον εγω καταγγελλω, yielding the translation, "this is the Christ, the Jesus whom I proclaim." TR (with the support of Ψ 1739 Maj) drops the article before Ιησους, yielding the translation, "this is the Christ Jesus whom I proclaim." Another variant (found in 𝔓[74] A D 33) omits both articles, yielding the translation, "this is Christ Jesus whom I proclaim." Another variant (in

ℵ) reads Ιησους Χριστος, hence, "this is Jesus Christ whom I proclaim." And yet another variant (in E) reads Ιησους ο Χριστος, yielding the translation, "this is Jesus the Christ whom I proclaim."

The reading in B is the one the other readings most likely diverged from. The sense of the text is that Paul was saying, "this one is the Messiah, this Jesus whom I am proclaiming to you." Paul argued first that the Messiah had to suffer then rise again from the dead—this was a new revelation for Jews who were expecting only a Davidic deliverer. Then Paul proclaimed that none other than Jesus could be the Messiah, for he had suffered on the cross then rose again from the dead. Most English versions, however, find it difficult, for stylistic reasons, to follow the superior text. But a good way to capture the WH NU text is to render it, "This Jesus I am telling you about is the Messiah" (so NLT).

Acts 17:4

TR WH NU	γυναικῶν τε τῶν πρώτων "and prominent women" 𝔓74 ℵ A B E Ψ Maj all
variant	και γυναικες των πρωτων "and women of prominent men" D it NEBmg NLTmg

The TR WH NU reading is well attested, but it is ambiguous because των πρωτων either directly modifies γυναικων (i.e., "the first women") or refers to their husbands (i.e., "women of the first"—that is, leading men). The Western text (D it) relieves the ambiguity by making it "women of prominent men." Not one translation follows this, however, though it is noted in two.

Furthermore, it should be noted that the list of new converts in 17:4 is different in the Western text; it is not simply God-fearing Greeks (σεβομενων Ελληνων) and prominent women (as in other manuscripts), but God-fearers, Greeks, and wives of prominent men in the city. These changes are significant because they include pagan Greeks (or Gentiles) to be among the first Thessalonian converts and because they identify the women as wives of the prominent men.

Acts 17:5

WH NU	οἱ 'Ιουδαῖοι "the Jews" 𝔓74 ℵ A B 33 1739 cop NKJVmg RSV NRSV ESV NASB NIV TNIV NEB REB NJB NAB NLT HCSB NET
variant/TR	οι Ιουδαιοι οι απειθουντες "the Jews not being obedient" (= "the unbelieving Jews") (D) E Maj KJV NKJV

The WH NU reading has the backing of six excellent manuscripts, as well as the Coptic. The variant shows a bit of pedantic gap-filling by letting the reader know that it was the unbelieving Jews who started the persecution against Paul and Silas.

Acts 17:11

A few Western witnesses (614 it^{gig} syr^{h**}), after "examining the Scriptures daily to see if these things were so," add "as Paul was proclaiming."

Acts 17:12

Western text (D 614) reads:

> "**Some** of them therefore believed, **but some did not believe, and many of the Greeks and men and women of high standing believed.**"

In place of "many of them believed," the reviser substitutes what is absolutely obvious—if many believed, it is obvious that others did not.

Acts 17:14

WH NU — πορεύεσθαι ἕως ἐπὶ τὴν θάλασσαν
"to go as far as to the sea" (= "go to the coast")
𝔓^{74} א A B E 33 1739
RSV NRSV ESV NASB NIV TNIV NEB REB NJB NAB NLT HCSB NET

variant 1/TR — πορευεσθαι ως επι την θαλασσαν
"to go, as it were, to the sea"
Ψ Maj syr^{h}
KJV

variant 2 — πορευεσθαι επι την θαλασσαν
"to go to the sea"
D 049 it^{gig} syr^{p}
NKJV

The WH NU reading implies that Paul took a route headed toward the coast, presumably from which he later veered—choosing to travel by land (through Thessaly) to Athens. The Majority text tries to make this more explicit by changing εως ("as far as") to ως ("as it were"); this gives the verse an added dimension, for it suggests that Paul was trying to trick any pursuing Jews. The Western text (variant 2) implies that Paul took a sea route to Athens—because Paul was forbidden to preach in Thessaly (see the note below on 17:15).

Acts 17:15

Western text (D) reads:

> "Those who conducted Paul brought him as far as Athens. **But he passed by Thessaly for he was forbidden to proclaim the word to them;** and after receiving instructions **from Paul** to have Silas and Timothy join him as soon as possible, they left him."

The addition was made to explain why Paul had not carried out any ministry between Berea and Athens, in the region called Thessaly (see note on 17:14). Borrowing from 16:6-8, the reviser says Paul was prevented from preaching in Thessaly. But whereas in 16:7, we are told that it was "the Spirit of Jesus" who prevented Paul from going into Mysia, the subject is left unspecified here. Perhaps we are to assume it was Jesus' Spirit who prevented Paul.

Acts 17:18

Western text (D it[gig]) reads:

> "Also some Epicurean and Stoic philosophers debated with him. Some said, 'What does this babbler want to say?' Others said, 'He seems to be a proclaimer of foreign divinities,' [because he preached Jesus and the resurrection]."

It is possible that the Athenians thought Paul was proclaiming two different divinities: Jesus and Anastasis (which means "Resurrection"). To avoid this misperception or to avoid calling Jesus δαιμονιων (which can be rendered as "demon" or "divinity"), the reviser omitted the final phrase.

Acts 17:26

WH NU	ἐποίησεν τε ἐξ ἑνός "he made from one" 𝔓74 א A B 33 1739 cop NKJVmg (RSV NRSV ESV) NASB (NIV TNIV NEB REB NJB) NAB (NLT HCSB NET)
variant 1/TR	εποιησεν τε εξ ενος αιματος "he made from one blood" D E Maj it[gig] syr KJV NKJV NRSVmg NASBmg NJBmg NLTmg HCSBmg
variant 2	εποιησεν τε εξ ενος στοματος "he made from one mouth" Ψ none

The one substance from which God made all people was not named by Paul, either because it is difficult to designate the one common element or because it was not pertinent to Paul's argument. In any event, scribes and translators alike have felt compelled to name the substance. Some ancient scribes supplied "blood" or "mouth"—a metonym for God's speaking all things into being (Gen 1). Various modern translators have supplied "man" (NLT, HCSB, and NET), "nation of men" (RSV), "ancestor" (NRSV), or "stock" (NIV, NEB, and NJB). Grammatically and contextually, the most appropriate word to have supplied is "man" because Paul was trying to promote a new concept for the Greeks: that all men and women came from one man, and this comprised the basis of human commonality.

Acts 17:27

WH NU	ζητεῖν τὸν θεόν "to seek God" 𝔓74 א A B L Ψ 33 1739 syr cop RSV NRSV ESV NASB NIV TNIV NEB REB NJB NAB NLT HCSB NET
variant 1/TR	ζητειν τον κυριον "to seek the Lord" E Maj KJV NKJV

variant 2 μαλιστα ζητειν το θειον εστιν
"to seek most of all that which is divine"
D (it^{gig})
none

The documentary evidence strongly favors the WH NU reading. The first variant reveals a Christianization of the text by changing "God" to "Lord" (i.e., the Lord Jesus Christ). But Paul's speech was deliberately general and inclusive; the use of "God" would have had far greater appeal to an Athenian audience. The second variant is the reviser's attempt to Hellenize the text in the sense of recasting the language for an Athenian audience, who might be better able to understand how one could seek and grope after that which is divine—as opposed to seeking a personal God.

Acts 17:28

TR WH NU ὡς καί τινες τῶν καθ ὑμᾶς ποιητῶν εἰρήκασιν
"even as some of your own poets have said"
ℵ A E Ψ 1739 cop syr
all

variant 1 ως και τινες των καθ ημας ποιητων ειρηκασιν
"even as some of our own poets have said"
𝔓^{74} B 614 (Didymus)
NLTmg

variant 2 το καθ ημεραν, ωσπερ και των καθ υμας τινες ειρηκασιν
"day by day, just as also some of your own have said"
D it^{d,gig}
none

A full rendering of the TR WH NU text is: "For in him we live and move and exist, even as some of your own poets have said, 'For we are his offspring.'" However, the first variant, found in 𝔓^{74} B etc., could very well be original because Paul, who was a Cilician from Tarsus, quoted a line from the poet Aratus (*Phaen.* 5), who was also a Cilician, born in Soloi or Tarsus in 310 B.C. (see Bruce 1990, 385). As such, Paul was identifying himself with Aratus and with his Greek listeners. Not knowing the common bond between Aratus and Paul or being uncomfortable with Paul identifying himself as a Greek, scribes changed ημας ποιητων ("our poets") to υμας ποιητων ("your poets").

The second variant, in the Western text, is an aberration. First, the scribe added "day by day" (one of his favorite expressions) to the end of the statement, "in him we live and move and exist day by day." Second, he deleted the word "poets," perhaps by mistake or because he had some objection to Paul quoting poets. This may have been the same reason why certain ancient translators (syr^{p} arm eth) rendered this as "sages" instead of "poets" (TCGNT).

Acts 17:31

Western text (D it^{d} Irenaeus) reads:

> "He has fixed a day on which he will have the world judged in righteousness by a man, **Jesus,** whom he has appointed, and of this he has given assurance to all by raising him from the dead."

Most witnesses (including 𝔓^{41} 𝔓^{74} ℵ A B E Ψ 33 1739) simply read εν ανδρι ("by a man"). But the reviser could not resist adding the man's name, "Jesus." This addition spoils the suspense of the message, for we can surmise that Paul purposely left this man unnamed so that his listeners would make inquiry about his identity.

Acts 17:34

Western text (D) reads:

> "But some of them joined him and became believers, including Dionysius **a certain** Areopagite [and a woman named Damaris] **of high standing,** and others with them."

The omission in the Western text could be the result of an accident in transcription (a whole line of twenty-one letters in the exemplar being skipped over) or a purposeful excision stemming from the editor's antifeminist tendencies. In whatever way the omission occurred, the Western text indicates that Dionysius is the man "of high standing" (ευσχημων—an addition that is hardly needed since he was already identified as an Areopagite, a member of the council of the Areopagus).

Acts 18:2-4

Western text (D with portions from it[h] syr[hmg]) reads:

> "There he found a Jew named Aquila, a native of Pontus, who had recently come from Italy with his wife Priscilla, because Claudius **Caesar** had ordered all Jews to leave Rome; **and they came to dwell in Greece. Paul** went to see them, [3] and, because he was of the same trade, he stayed with them, and they worked together—[by trade they were tentmakers]. [4] And **entering into** the synagogue each Sabbath, he would have a discussion, **introducing the name of the Lord Jesus,** and he was convincing **not only** Jews **but also** Greeks."

The D-reviser, as usual, supplied some circumstantial details to help the reader understand the historical context. Claudius is identified as Caesar, and Aquila and Priscilla are said to have settled down in Greece after being exiled from Rome. The deletion in 18:3 could have been the result of stylistic trimming, but it is just as likely that the reviser did not want his readers to think Paul was a tentmaker (or leather worker). However, Jewish rabbis often had such trades and were encouraged to combine a technical trade with their research of the Scripture.

The insertion in 18:4 suggests that Paul's method of debating was to use the OT Scriptures and insert (or put forward) the name of Jesus as being the one spoken about in the passage. By inserting the name of Jesus, Paul would read Isa 53:4-5 this way, "Surely [Jesus] bore our griefs, and carried our sorrows, yet we ourselves esteemed [Jesus] stricken, smitten of God and afflicted. But [Jesus] was pierced for our transgressions, and crushed for our iniquities. The punishment for our well-being fell on [Jesus], and by [Jesus'] scourging we are healed." This would be a convincing way to expound the Scriptures in presenting Jesus as the Messiah (see note on 18:6).

Acts 18:5

WH NU συνείχετο τῷ λόγῳ ὁ Παῦλος
"Paul was occupied with the word"
𝔓[74] א A B D E Ψ 33
RSV NRSV ESV NASB NIV TNIV NEB REB NJB NAB NLT HCSB NET

variant/TR συνειχετο τω πνευματι ο Παυλος
"Paul was occupied in the Spirit"
1739 Maj syr[hmg]
KJV NKJV HCSBmg

The documentary evidence strongly supports the WH NU reading, as does the context, which is focused on Paul's arduous efforts to show the Jews from the Scriptures that Jesus was the predicted Messiah. The variant reading is probably the result of a scribal gloss (as in syr[hmg]) that made its way into the mainstream of Byzantine manuscripts.

Acts 18:6-7a

Western text (D it[h]) (with a note on an omission in 𝔓[74]) reads:

> "**And after there had been much discussion and the Scriptures had been interpreted,** when they opposed and reviled him, he shook out his clothes and said to them, 'Your blood be on your own heads! I am clean **from you.** From now on I will go to the Gentiles.' [7] **And then he left Aquila.**"

The initial interpolation in 18:6 is the reviser's attempt to emphasize that Paul spent a great deal of energy interpreting the Scriptures and discussing them with the Jews before they rejected him. The second addition is a stylistic expansion. It should also be noted that the scribe of 𝔓[74] omitted και βλασφημουντων ("and blaspheming/reviling"), probably not accidentally but to avoid ambiguity, inasmuch as the phrase could refer to blasphemy against Jesus (see 18:5) or slander against Paul himself.

Acts 18:7b

WH NU Τιτίου 'Ιούστου
"Titius Justus"
B* D[2] syr[h]
NKJVmg RSV NRSV ESV NASB NIV TNIV NEB REB NJBmg NLT HCSB NET

variant 1 Τιτου Ιουστου
"Titus Justus"
א E 1739 cop
RSVmg NRSVmg NJBmg NAB

variant 2/TR Ιουστου
"Justus"
A B[2] D* Ψ 33 Maj
KJV NKJV NJB

In defense of the WH NU reading, it can be said that the first variant was created by scribes conforming "Titius" to the more common, "Titus"; and the second variant was the result of accidental homoeoteleuton (both words end with του) or purposeful excision. It is difficult to explain how, if one name was originally in the text (i.e., Justus), scribes would add another. In any event, this man's name suggests he was a Roman citizen.

Acts 18:12-13

Western text (D it[h]) reads:

> "But when Gallio was proconsul of Achaia, the Jews with one accord rose up, **having talked together among themselves** against Paul; **and they laid their hands on him** and brought him before the tribunal, 13 **crying out and** saying, 'This man is persuading people to worship God in ways that are contrary to the law.'"

In typical fashion, the reviser tried to fill perceived gaps in the narrative, leaving nothing to the imagination of the reader.

Acts 18:17a

WH NU	ἐπιλαβόμενοι δὲ πάντες Σωσθένην "but everyone seized Sosthenes" 𝔓74 ℵ A B cop[bo] NKJVmg RSV NRSV ESV NASB NIV TNIV NEB REB NJB NAB NLT HCSB NET
variant 1/TR	επιλαβομενοι δε παντες οι Ελληνες Σωσθενην "but all the Greeks seized Sosthenes" D E Ψ 33 1739 Maj syr cop[sa] KJV NKJV NRSVmg HCSBmg
variant 2	επιλαβομενοι δε παντες οι Ιουδαιοι Σωσθενην "but all the Jews seized Sosthenes" 36 453 none

Because it is left unsaid who beat Sosthenes, scribes took the liberty to identify them as being either Greeks or Jews. What can be inferred from the text is that it was the Gentiles in the crowd gathered before Gallio's tribunal who started beating Sosthenes—when they saw that Gallio snubbed the Jews.

Acts 18:17b

The Greek portion of Codex D (a diglot having Greek and Latin) is lacking at this point, but the Latin portion is still extant. It reads, "Then Gallio pretended not to see him." This contrasts with all other witnesses which say, "But Gallio paid no attention to any of these things." The Western text is a good interpretation; indeed, Gallio looked the other way while Sosthenes was being beaten, perhaps to teach the Jews a lesson for having wasted his time with such trivialities (Longenecker 1981, 486).

Acts 18:19

Western text (D it[h]) reads:

> "When **he** came to Ephesus, and **on the next Sabbath** he left them there, but he himself went into the synagogue and had a discussion with the Jews."

The first change is simply one of conforming the verb to the singular form (κατηντησας) of the surrounding verbs; a similar change (κατηντησεν) occurred in several late manuscripts (𝔓74 Ψ 1739 Maj). The next change allows for a time gap between the day of his arrival and his visitation to the synagogue, which, of course, would be on the Sabbath.

Acts 18:21

WH NU πάλιν ἀνακάμψω
"I will return again"
𝔓74 א A B E 33
NKJVmg RSV NRSV ESV NASB NIV TNIV NEB REB NJB NAB NLT HCSB NET

variant/TR δει με παντως την εορτην την ερχομενην ποιησαι εις Ιεροσολυμα. παλιν ανακαμψω
"I must by all means make the feast in Jerusalem. I will return again."
(D) Ψ Maj it[gig,w] syr
KJV NKJV NLTmg HCSBmg

The manuscript support for the WH NU reading far outweighs that of the variant. Some scholars, however, have argued that the longer reading was deleted to avoid granting Pauline authority to Jewish practices (Ross 1992, 349). However, it is far more likely that the variant is an insertion to explain Paul's hasty departure (TCGNT) or to help the reader understand that the church Paul visited after arriving at the port in Caesarea was Jerusalem (the text simply says "the church"). In any event, the interpolation in the variant, perhaps borrowed from 20:16, could very well provide the real reason for Paul's hasty departure. If the feast was Passover (which fell on April 4 that year—A.D. 52), Paul would have little time to sail there because the seas did not allow sailing prior to March 10 (Bruce 1990, 399).

Acts 18:24-25a

Western text (D) reads:

> "Now there came to Ephesus a Jew named **Apollonius,** a native of Alexandria. He was an eloquent man, well versed in the Scriptures. 25 He had been instructed **in his own country** in the **word** of the Lord."

The D-reviser provides the full name for "Apollos" here, and then adds that Apollos had been instructed while he was still in his country—thereby indicating that Christianity must have been in Egypt prior to A.D. 50. "Whether the statement of the Western reviser depends on personal knowledge or is based on inference, the implication of the statement no doubt accords with historical fact" (TCGNT). Then, the reviser changed "way of the Lord" to "word of the Lord," perhaps because he wanted to emphasize Apollos's training in the Scriptures or because he did not think he had been instructed in the way of the Lord if he needed Aquila and Priscilla to teach him.

Acts 18:25b

WH NU τοῦ Ἰησοῦ
"Jesus"
𝔓74vid א A B (D) E L Ψ (33) 1739
RSV NRSV ESV NASB NIV TNIV NEB REB NJB NAB NLT HCSB NET

variant 1 του Χριστου
"the Christ"
𝔓41vid
none

variant 2/TR τoυ κυριoυ
"the Lord"
Maj
KJV NKJV

A full rendering of the WH NU reading is: "He [Apollos] was speaking and teaching accurately the things about Jesus." The documentary evidence strongly favors the WH NU reading, as does the context, in which it is important to note that Apollos was familiar with the actual person, Jesus of Nazareth, not just the Messiah or the Lord as a biblical personage.

Acts 18:26

Western text (D it^{d,gig}, with Maj on first change) reads:

> "He began to speak boldly in the synagogue; but when **Aquila and Priscilla** heard him, they took him aside and explained the way [of God] to him more accurately."

The D-reviser (and the majority of witnesses, Maj—so KJV) reversed the order of "Priscilla and Aquila" so as to not give prominence to Priscilla. One would then expect that his revision would have been thoroughgoing, but he did not change the order of "Priscilla and Aquila" in 18:18. In any event, Priscilla was generally given prominence in the NT record by being mentioned first (see Rom 16:3; 2 Tim 4:19). The Western text's shorter reading, "the way," could be original, but it is more likely the result of conformity to the form in which this description of early Christianity appears elsewhere in Acts (see 9:2; 19:9, 23; 22:4; 24:14, 22).

Acts 18:27

Western text (D with 𝔓^{38vid} for changes in last sentence) reads:

> **"Now certain Corinthians were staying in Ephesus, and having heard him [Apollos], they encouraged him** to cross over **with them to their own country. And when they had agreed, the Ephesians** wrote to the disciples **in Corinth that they should** welcome **the man. And when he arrived in Achaia** he greatly helped **the churches.**"

The D-reviser greatly expanded this verse in a display of intelligent yet imaginative gap-filling. His expanded version attempts to explain more fully why Apollos went to Corinth: He came not of his own initiative but at the urging of certain Corinthians who heard him preaching in Ephesus. The reviser probably used his knowledge of 1 Corinthians to create this addition, because that letter indicates that several Corinthians were quite impressed with Apollos.

What is also noteworthy about this addition is that it is found in a third century manuscript, 𝔓^{38}. Presumably, if the entire verse was extant (only the last sentence is), we would see similar—if not the same—wording. This is the first documentary proof in Acts that the D-text antedated Codex Bezae.

Acts 18:28

Western text (𝔓^{38} D) reads:

> "He powerfully refuted the Jews, **discoursing** publicly and proving by the Scriptures that the Christ is Jesus."

This addition, which is typical of the Western text (and D-text), is noteworthy because it appears (in nearly the same form) in 𝔓^{38} (a third-century manuscript) before it shows up in D (a fifth-century manuscript).

Acts 19:1

Western text ($\mathfrak{P}^{38vid}$ D it^{d} syr^{hmg}) reads:

> "**When Paul, pursuing his own plan, wanted to set out for Jerusalem, the Spirit told him to go back to Asia.** And [while Apollos was in Corinth], Paul passed through the interior regions and came to Ephesus, where he found some disciples." (see NJBmg)

According to the Western text, Paul did not go up to the church in Jerusalem (as is implied in 18:22—see NRSV), but to the church in Caesarea. Thus, Paul still wanted to go to Jerusalem. According to the reviser, this was Paul's own plan, contrary to the wishes of the Spirit (see 16:6-7 and note on 17:15). Later in the Acts narrative, we will see the spiritual struggle Paul experienced as he determined to go to Jerusalem (see chs. 20–21). Perhaps this textual change anticipates this.

Acts 19:2a

$\mathfrak{P}^{38}$ (one of the earliest extant D-text manuscripts), without any support from any other manuscript, reads, και ειπεν τοις μαθηταις ει πνευμα αγιον ελαβετε πιστευσαντες το ιδιον του κυριου ειναι. No other manuscript contains the last five words, which even in this manuscript are very difficult to read. (Perhaps this accounts for this variant not being cited in NA[27]; for reconstruction, see *Text of Earliest MSS,* 146.) $\mathfrak{P}^{38}$ could be rendered, "And he said to the disciples, 'Have you received the Holy Spirit, having believed the same [Spirit] to be of the Lord?'" The last part of this question could also be translated as "having believed that it [the Holy Spirit] is the characteristic quality of the Lord" (this last rendering was provided by Sanders 1927, 18). The scribe of $\mathfrak{P}^{38}$ thought it necessary to show the identification of the Spirit with the Lord. In other words, the Ephesian disciples needed to know that they needed the Spirit of the Lord to have a complete experience of the Lord.

Acts 19:2b

The three editions (TR WH NU), followed by all English versions, read, ουδ ει πνευμα αγιον εστιν ηκουσαμεν ("we have not even heard that there is [a] Holy Spirit"), supported superiorly by $\mathfrak{P}^{74}$ ℵ A B D^{c} Ψ 33 1739 Maj. A variant reading on this is: ουδ ει πνευμα αγιον λαμβανουσιν τινες ηκουσαμεν ("we have not even heard that anyone receives [the] Holy Spirit"). This has the support of $\mathfrak{P}^{38}$ $\mathfrak{P}^{41}$ D* it^{d} syr^{hmg} cop^{sa}—nearly all Western witnesses.

The statement in the text—coming out of the mouth of the twelve Ephesian disciples—that they had never heard of the Holy Spirit's existence, must have seemed incredible to an early Western reviser, who changed it to speak of receiving the Holy Spirit. It is not unusual that this would have been transmitted in several Western versions, and even in one late papyrus manuscript, $\mathfrak{P}^{41}$. (A similar change occurred in John 7:39; see note).

Acts 19:5

Western text ($\mathfrak{P}^{38vid}$ D) reads:

> "On hearing this, they were baptized in the name of the Lord Jesus **Christ for the forgiveness of sins.**"

The expanded reading in the Western text reflects the typical baptismal formula of the church in the centuries after the apostolic age (see note on 8:37).

Acts 19:6

Western text (𝔓[38vid] for "fell" D) reads:

> "When Paul had laid his hands on them, the Holy Spirit **immediately fell** upon them, and they spoke in tongues and prophesied."

Conforming the text to 10:44, the reviser has the Spirit falling on the twelve Ephesian disciples. He also added one of his favorite words: "immediately."

Acts 19:8

Western text (D syr[hmg]) reads:

> "He entered the synagogue and for three months spoke out boldly **with great power,** and argued persuasively about the kingdom of God."

The addition is the kind of embellishment typically found in the Western text.

Acts 19:9

WH NU	διαλεγόμενος ἐν τῇ σχολῇ Τυράννου "he reasoned in the lecture hall of Tyrannus" 𝔓[74] א A B 1739 cop RSV NRSV ESV NASB NIV TNIV NEB REB NJB NAB NLT HCSB NET
variant 1/TR	διαλεγομενους εν τη σχολη Τυραννου τινος "he reasoned in the lecture hall of a certain Tyrannus" E Ψ Maj KJV NKJV
variant 2	διαλεγομενους εν τη σχολη Τυραννου τινος απο ωρας πεμπτης εως δεκατης "he reasoned in the lecture hall of a certain Tyrannus, from the fifth to the tenth hour" D it[d] syr[h**] NRSVmg ESVmg NJBmg

Perhaps the Western reviser drew upon an oral tradition to add the detail that Paul taught in Tyrannus's lecture hall from the fifth to the tenth hour (i.e., from eleven o'clock in the morning to four in the afternoon). Or the reviser could have used his intelligent imagination to create these hours because this would have been the time in Ephesus where people were not occupied with their labors and therefore could come and hear Paul. Presumably, Tyrannus (if he was the lecturer) used the lecture hall from dawn until 11 a.m.; thus, the hall was vacant thereafter for Paul's use. Paul probably labored in the morning and then lectured during the afternoon. And he did this for two years; as a result, people from all over the province of Asia heard the word, leading to the establishment of several churches (including Ephesus, Smyrna, Colossae, and Laodicea).

Acts 19:14 and 19:16

Western text (𝔓[38] D syr[hmg]) reads:

> "**Among whom were also** the [seven] sons of a [Jewish high] priest named Sceva, [who] **wanted to do the same thing, being accustomed to exorcise such people. And they**

approached one who was demon-possessed and began to invoke the Name, saying, 'We command you by Jesus, whom Paul preaches, to come out.'"

The D-reviser provides a lengthy portion that does hardly more than repeat the previous verse. In the rewrite, however, the reviser makes Sceva simply a priest, probably because it seemed inconceivable that Ephesian exorcists could have been related to one of the Jewish high priests. Indeed, it is not likely that they were really related to the priestly clan; it is more likely that they fabricated this title for self-aggrandizement. The reviser also got rid of "seven" before "sons" to avoid the potential conflict with 19:16, which can be interpreted to mean that there were only two sons. (For this reason, it[gig] changed "seven sons" to "two sons.") However, αμφοτερων is not limited to the meaning, "both of them"; as used in the Koine papyri, it can mean "all of them." Nevertheless, to avoid any contradiction, several scribes (Ψ 1739 Maj) changed αμφοτερων to αυτων ("them") and one scribe (E) dropped it altogether.

Acts 19:20

With the testimony of א* A B, the text in WH NU reads κατα κρατος του κυριου ο λογος ηυξανεν και ισχυεν, which can be translated, "by the power of the Lord the word grew and prevailed" or "with power the Lord's word grew." The reading in TR is: κατα κρατος ο λογος του κυριου ηυξανεν και ισχυεν ("with power the word of the Lord grew and prevailed"). This has the support of 𝔓[74] א[2] (E Ψ) 33 1739 Maj. The text of D reads ουτως κατα κρατος ενισχυσεν και η πιστις του θεου ηυξανεν και επληθυνε ("so mightily it prevailed, and the faith of God grew and multiplied").

Grammatically, του κυριου ("of the Lord") could align with κρατος ("power") or ο λογος ("the word"); therefore, the WH NU reading and the first variant can be semantically interchanged. However, since it is more natural for του κυριου to be joined with ο λογος, scribes inverted the word order to ensure this meaning (i.e., "the word of the Lord"). English translators follow suit. The D-reviser must have thought it was too abstract to speak of the word of the Lord growing and prevailing, so he changed it to "the faith of God." But this, too, is abstract. In modern terminology, we would say "the gospel grew and prevailed" or "Christianity grew and prevailed."

Acts 19:28

Western text (D it[d] syr[hmg]) reads:

"When they heard this, they were full of rage; and **running out to the street** they shouted, 'Great is Artemis of the Ephesians!'" (see NJBmg)

The reviser again did a bit of gap-filling by adding the detail that the crowd took their shouting to the streets.

Acts 19:33

Several good manuscripts (𝔓[74] א A B E 33 1739) read εκ δε του οχλου συνεβιβασαν Αλεξανδρον ("some of the crowd instructed Alexander"). This is difficult to understand; why would an Ephesian crowd be instructing Alexander? It could mean, as stated in the NEB, that they were explaining to him what the problem was. Nonetheless, various scribes had problems with the verb συνεβιβασαν, which was changed to προεβιβασαν ("they put [him] forward") in D[1] Ψ Maj (so TR) and κατεβιβασαν ("they took [him] down") in D* it[d].

Acts 19:37

WH NU τὴν θεὸν ἡμῶν
"our god[dess]"
𝔓[74] ℵ A B 1739 (D* E[c] την θεαν ημων our goddess)
NKJVmg RSV NRSV ESV NASB NIV TNIV NEB REB NJB NAB NLT HCSB NET

variant/TR την θεαν υμων
"your goddess"
E* Maj
KJV NKJV NRSVmg HCSBmg

The change from ημων ("our") to υμων ("your") was made by scribes who thought Alexander (the speaker here), as a Jew, would not be calling Artemis (Diana) his goddess. But he was probably speaking as an Ephesian citizen when he said "our goddess." (The feminine article την before θεον necessitates the translation "goddess." The change from θεον to θεαν in D and E assures this meaning.) It should be noted that scribes had a way of showing that θεον ("God") here does not signify the Deity, the God of the Jews and Christians. They could do this by not writing it as a nomen sacrum ($\overline{\Theta N}$); rather, they could write out the word in *plene* (θεον) and thereby show they did not consider the word to have divine titular status. English translators do the same by not capitalizing the first letter of "God"—hence, "god." The scribes of 𝔓[74] ℵ A B D E, who normally used the nomen sacrum for θεος, wrote the word out in full here (θεον) in order to show that it is not a divine title.

Acts 20:3b-4

Western text (D, syr[hmg] in part) reads:

> "And when he had spent three months there and a plot was made against him by the Jews, he **wanted** to sail for Syria. **But the Spirit told him** to return through Macedonia. [4] **Therefore, when he was about to go out,** he was accompanied **as far as Asia** by Sopater son of Pyrrhus from Beroea, by Aristarchus and Secundus from Thessalonica, by Gaius of **Douberios,** and by Timothy, as well as by **the Ephesians Eutychus** and Trophimus."

The reviser made a number of changes in this passage. He indicates that Paul decided to set sail for Syria because of the plot of the Jews against him. But, according to the reviser, "the Spirit" prevented Paul from going there. This interpolation of the Spirit's intervention occurs often in the Western text (see note on 19:1). Then he changed "Tychicus and Trophimus from Asia" to "the Ephesians Eutychus and Trophimus." The change from Asia (the province) to Ephesus (a city in Asia) could imply that the reviser "belonged to, or was closely associated with Ephesus" (TCGNT). The name "Eutychus" was mistakenly taken from 20:9.

One of the D readings in this section has been considered original by the NEB—namely, "Gaius of Douberios." Doberus, a Macedonian city 26 miles northwest of Philippi, was probably unknown to most scribes, who may have changed it to the more familiar, "Derbe." This is the reasoning that prompted the NEB translators to adopt "Gaius the Doberian" in their translation (see Tasker 1964, 433). However, it is also quite possible that the reviser made this change because "Gaius" in 19:29 is said to be of Macedonia.

Acts 20:12

Western text (D) reads:

> "Meanwhile, **as they were saying goodbye, he brought** [to them] the boy alive and they were not a little comforted."

The D-reviser did some gap-filling in order to (1) make it clear that Paul brought Eutychus to the people and (2) provide a fitting end to this vignette (20:7-12).

Acts 20:15

WH NU — παρεβάλομεν εἰς Σάμον
"we crossed over to Samos"
𝔓[74] א A B C E 33 1739
RSV NRSV ESV NASB NIV TNIV NEB REB NAB NLT HCSB NET

variant/TR — παρεβαλομεν εις Σαμον και μειναντες εν Τρωγυλλιω
"we crossed over to Samos and we stayed in Trogyllium"
𝔓[41vid] D (Ψ) Maj syr cop[sa]
KJV NKJV RSVmg NRSVmg ESVmg NEBmg NJB NLTmg HCSBmg

Since Trogyllium is a promontory jutting out into the sea between Samos and Miletus, it is not unlikely for the sailing vessel to have landed there for the evening. The question remains, however, if this came from the pen of Luke or the reviser. The documentary evidence favors the shorter text. (𝔓[41] is incorrectly cited in NA[27] and UBS[4] as supporting the WH NU reading, when according to the *editio princeps,* it supports the variant.)

Acts 20:16-18

Western text (D) reads:

> "For Paul had decided to sail past Ephesus, so that he might not have **to be detained** in Asia, he was eager to be in Jerusalem, [if possible,] on the day of Pentecost. [17] From Miletus he sent [a message] to Ephesus, **sending for** the elders of the church to meet him. [18] When they came to him **and were together,** he said to them: 'You yourselves know**, brothers,** how I lived among you the entire time from the first day that I set foot in Asia, **for three years and even more.**'"

The D-reviser made his characteristic additions to help fill in the text, the most substantial of which is the note about Paul having spent more than three years in Ephesus. This was clearly borrowed from 20:31.

Acts 20:21

WH NU — πίστιν εἰς τὸν κύριον ἡμῶν Ἰησοῦν
"faith in our Lord Jesus"
B H L P Ψ syr[h]
NRSV NIV TNIV NEB REB NJB NAB NLT HCSB NET

variant 1/TR	πιστιν εις τον κυριον ημων Ιησουν Χριστον "faith in our Lord Jesus Christ" 𝔓[74] ℵ A C (E) 33 1739 syr[p] KJV NKJV RSV ESV NASB NETmg
variant 2	πιστιν δια του κυριον ημων Ιησου Χριστου "faith through our Lord Jesus Christ" D none

It is difficult to determine which of the first two readings is original because the first variant has the best documentary support but is suspect because scribes are known to have expanded divine titles. That leaves the WH NU reading as being more likely original. The translations are nearly divided between the two readings. The second variant is a typical Western text variation.

Acts 20:24

Western text (D, with Maj on the first change and 𝔓[41vid] on the third) reads:

> "**But I take no account regarding myself nor do I value my own life as being precious to me,** if only I may finish my course and the ministry **of the word** that I received from the Lord Jesus, to testify **to Jews and Gentiles** the good news of God's grace."

This verse has several textual variants, two of which are reflected in the translation above. The changes in the Western text are editorial expansions intended to emphasize Paul's special apostolic commission of completing the word of God by preaching to Jews and Gentiles alike.

Acts 20:28a

TR WH NU	τὴν ἐκκλησίαν τοῦ θεοῦ "the church of God" ℵ B syr KJV NKJV RSV NRSV ESV NASB NIV TNIV NEBmg REBmg NJB NAB NLT HCSB NET
variant 1	την εκκλησιαν του κυριου "the church of the Lord" 𝔓[74] A C* D E Ψ 33 1739 RSVmg NRSVmg ESVmg NASBmg NIVmg TNIVmg NEB REB NJBmg HCSBmg NETmg
variant 2	την εκκλησιαν του κυριου και του θεου "the church of the Lord and God" C[3] Maj NKJVmg HCSBmg NETmg

See following note.

Acts 20:28b

WH NU ἣν περιεποιήσατο διὰ τοῦ αἵματος τοῦ ἰδίου
"which he [God] purchased with his own blood"
(or, "which he [God] purchased with the blood of his own [Son]")
𝔓[74] ℵ A B C E Ψ 33 1739 (𝔓[41vid] D add εαυτω after περιεποιησατο)
RSV NRSV ESV NASB NIV TNIV NEBmg REBmg NJB NAB NLT HCSB NET

variant/TR ην περιεποιησατο δια του ιδιου αιματος
"which he purchased with his own blood"
Maj
KJV NKJV NEB REB NETmg

The WH NU reading for 20:28a has two arguments in its favor: (1) It is found in ℵ and B, the two earliest extant manuscripts preserving this passage. (2) We can surmise that "God" was changed to "Lord" because the following clause speaks of the one who purchased the church with his own blood. Uncomfortable with the idea of God having blood, scribes changed "God" to "Lord." The first variant also has two arguments in its favor: (1) It is supported by a greater range of witnesses. (2) The expression "church of the Lord" appears nowhere else in the NT and therefore was subject to be changed to the more common title, "church of God" (used by Paul eleven times). Thus far, the evidence is inconclusive.

The dilemma is complicated further by the fact that the next clause appears in two ways in the manuscripts, the first of which can be interpreted in two ways. The expression του αιματος του ιδιου could simply mean "his own blood" and thereby refer to "the blood of the Lord" or "the blood of God," depending on which variant is selected. But the expression του ιδιου ("his own") was also used in Greek papyri to mean "one's own child" (MM 298). God's Son, the one dear to him, is perhaps called here "his own"—as elsewhere he is called his "one and only" (see John 1:14, 18; 3:16). Thus, the expression could mean "the blood of his own" (i.e., "the blood of his Son"—see ESVmg).

The textual evidence allows for several different renderings, as follows:

1. "take care of the church of God"
   a. "which he [God] purchased with his own blood"
   b. "which he [God] purchased with the blood of his own Son"
2. "take care of the church of the Lord"
   a. "which he [the Lord] purchased with his own blood"
   b. "which he [the Lord] purchased with the blood of his own Son"

Renderings 1a and 1b have the support of ℵ and B, and rendering 2a has the support of 𝔓[74] A C D E Ψ 33 1739. Rendering 2b is impossible since "the Lord" refers to Jesus. The rendering for 1a and for 1b requires "God" to be the presumed subject, which, in turn, suggests that "church of God" would be in the text. This could very well be the original text and original meaning. As such, it suggests that Paul was assuming Jesus' deity in speaking of the shed blood as being God's (as in rendering 1a).

Rendering 2a also has much to commend it—not only from documentary attestation but also from the perspective that "the church of the Lord" is both the more natural reading in the immediate context and the more unusual reading in the NT record (see Tregelles 1854, 233). As such, exegetes and translators have recognized the viability of both readings (1a/b, and 2a) and, while choosing one reading, have usually shown the alternate in a marginal reading. In the end, both readings are communicating the same essential message: The elders are to take care of the church as shepherds caring for their sheep because the church is God's possession, purchased by the blood of Jesus, God's Son.

Acts 20:32

The NU text reads παρατιθεμαι υμας τω θεω ("I commend you to God") with the excellent support of 𝔓74 ℵ A C D E Ψ 33 1739 Maj syr. It is followed by all the English versions. A variant in WH is παρατιθεμαι υμας τω κυριω ("I commend you to the Lord"), supported by B it^{gig} cop^{bo}. In this case, Westcott and Hort were too biased in their preference for B. The documentary evidence strongly supports the reading of the NU text.

Acts 21:1

TR WH NU Πάταρα
"Patara"
(𝔓74 A C Πατερα) ℵ B E Ψ 33 1739 Maj syr
all

variant Παταρα και Μυρα
"Patara and Myra"
𝔓41vid D
RSVmg NRSVmg ESVmg NEBmg NJBmg

The verse says, "we came to Cos, and from there to Rhodes, and from there to Patara." It could be argued that και Μυρα ("and Myra"), following Παταρα, dropped out due to homoeoteleuton. But it is far more likely that the Western reviser added "and Myra" because it was the normal transshipping port (cf. 27:5). However, the ship could not have reached Myra in one day because Myra is yet another fifty miles or so beyond Patara. "And so what we have in here [in the Western text] is no better and older text, but the old conjecture of Acts' earliest commentator" (Haenchen 1971, 53).

Acts 21:8

WH NU ἤλθομεν εἰς Καισάρειαν
"we came into Caesarea"
𝔓74 ℵ A B C E 33 1739 syr cop
NKJVmg RSV NRSV ESV NASB NIV TNIV NEB REB NJB NAB NLT HCSB NET

variant/TR οι περι τον Παυλον ηλθον εις Καισαρειαν
"they who were accompanying Paul came into Caesarea"
Maj
(KJV NKJV)

The words were added to the beginning of this verse in the majority of late manuscripts to identify the subject. This was done for the sake of oral reading or to help readers beginning with this verse in an ecclesiastical lesson. The addition, incorporated in TR, was rejected by all modern translators. Even the KJV and NKJV translators did not follow this reading precisely; instead of rendering it "they who were accompanying Paul came into Caesarea," they used the pronoun "we"—"we who were accompanying Paul came into Caesarea."

Acts 21:12-17

Western text (D) reads:

> "When we heard this, we and the people there urged **Paul** not to go up to Jerusalem. [13]Then Paul said **to us,** 'What are you doing, weeping and **disturbing** my heart? For I **desire** not only to be bound but even to die in Jerusalem for the name of the Lord Jesus **Christ.**' [14]Since he would not be persuaded, we remained silent except to say **to one another,** 'The Lord's will be done.' [15]After **some** days we **said farewell** and started to go up to Jerusalem. [16]Some of the disciples from Caesarea also came along and brought us to those with whom we were to lodge; **and when we arrived at a certain village, we stayed with** Mnason of Cyprus, an early disciple. [17]**Leaving from there** we came to Jerusalem, where the brothers welcomed us warmly."

The D-reviser made a number of adjustments in this section. Among these, certain variations in 21:13 and 21:15-16 are noteworthy. In 21:13 he changed the uncommon word συνθρυπτοντες ("breaking") to the more common, θορυβουντες ("disturbing"). But the word Paul used is picturesque and poignant; it suggests softening the heart by pounding on it. Paul wanted to remain firm in his decision to go to Jerusalem. The reviser heightens this determination by adding βουλομαι to the verse, thereby affirming that Paul chose and even desired to suffer in Jerusalem.

In 21:15-16 the reviser inserted a resting stop between Caesarea and Jerusalem—"at a certain village." The distance between the two cities is 67 miles; it cannot be traveled in a day. Thus, the reviser has Paul go from Caesarea to a certain village, where he stays with Mnason, and then on to Jerusalem the next day.

Acts 21:20a

WH NU	ἐδόξαζον τὸν θεόν "they were glorifying God" 𝔓[74] א A B C E L 33 1739 cop[bo] RSV NRSV ESV NASB NIV TNIV NEB REB NJB NAB NLT HCSB NET
variant/TR	εδοξαζον τον κυριον "they were glorifying the Lord" D Ψ Maj syr[h] cop[sa] KJV NKJV

Although the WH NU reading could be the result of scribal conformity to the immediate context (21:19 has θεος), this reading has far superior documentary support compared to the variant.

Acts 21:20b

With excellent support (A B C E 33 1739), WH NU read εισιν εν τοις Ιουδαιοις ("there are among the Jews"). This appears in James's statement to Paul: "You see, brother, how many thousands there are among the Jews who have believed, and all are zealots of the law." This is different in TR (with the support of Ψ Maj): εισιν Ιουδαιων, producing the rendering, "how many thousands of Jews there are who have believed." A different reading appears in D (so also it[gig] syr[p] cop[sa]): εισιν εν τη Ιουδαια ("there are in Judea")—"how many thousands there are in Judea who have believed." א has the shortest reading: εισιν ("there are"): "how many thousands there are who have believed."

The WH NU reading, though a bit awkward, has the best documentary support. The first variant relieves the awkwardness with a plural genitive. The second variant expands the territory to Judea—perhaps to account for the great number. The variant in ℵ could be accidental.

Acts 21:21

𝔓[74] A D* E 33 read "They have been told about you that you teach [all] the Jews living among the Gentiles to forsake Moses, and that you tell them not to circumcise their children or observe the customs." The word "all" was omitted in these manuscripts text probably to avoid perceived exaggeration.

Acts 21:22

WH NU πάντως ἀκούσονται ὅτι ἐλήλυθας.
"Certainly they will hear that you have come."
B C*vid 1739 cop
RSV NRSV ESV NASB NIV TNIV NEB REB NJBmg NAB NLT HCSB NET

variant/TR δει συνελθειν πληθος ακουσονται γαρ οτι εληλυθας.
"The multitude is sure to gather, for certainly they will hear that you have come."
𝔓[74] ℵ C[2] (D Ψ Maj)
KJV NKJV NJB HCSBmg

The variant reading cannot be easily dismissed because of its good textual support and its inherent ambiguity—which could have given rise to its deletion. The added phrase could mean that "the whole church will come together" or "a mob will gather." The variant reading signals James's fear that (1) the church would hear about Paul's coming and insist on meeting together to determine how to receive him, or that (2) a mob would form because of Paul's bad reputation among the Jews. Indeed, a mob does form—and one that nearly kills Paul (see 21:27-36). If the former is the correct interpretation, then one could argue that the words were deleted in B C* etc., because nothing is said of the entire church coming together at this time. However, if the latter is the correct interpretation, then one could argue that the words were added in 𝔓[74] ℵ etc., in anticipation of the mob forming.

Acts 21:25

Western text (D itgig first change; C D E Ψ Maj second change—so TR; D itgig third change) reads:

> "But as for the Gentiles who have become believers, **they [the Jewish believers] have nothing to say against you, for** we have sent a letter with our judgment **that they should observe nothing of this sort, except** to keep themselves from what has been sacrificed to idols and from blood [and from what is strangled] and from fornication."

The first change in the Western text is supposed to account for why James speaks of Gentile believers in a context that is dealing with Paul taking care of the sensitivities of Jewish Christians. The statement is intended to show that Paul had nothing to defend about his message to the Gentiles but that he only had to do something to counter the rumors that he was teaching Jews to abandon the law. The second change is a natural gap-filler, which gained wide circulation in later witnesses. The third change—the deletion of "and from what is strangled"—accords with D's omission of the same phrase in the Jerusalem Decree (see note on 15:20).

Acts 21:39

Western text (D) reads:

> "Paul replied, 'I am a Jew, **born in** Tarsus of Cilicia, [a citizen of an important city]; I beg you, let me speak to the people.'"

The Western text displays assimilation to 22:3.

Acts 22:5

Borrowing from 23:2 and 24:1, a few Western witnesses (614 syr^{h**}) add "Ananias" after "the high priest." But Ananias was not the high priest during the days Paul was persecuting the church; Caiaphas was.

Acts 22:7

A few Western witnesses (E it^{gig} vg syr^{hmg}) harmonize this verse to 26:14 by adding "it is hard for you to kick against the goads." (See notes on 9:4; 26:14-15.)

Acts 22:9

WH NU τὸ μὲν φῶς ἐθεάσαντο
"they saw the light"
𝔓^{74} (א) A B 049 33 syr^{p} cop^{bo}
NKJVmg RSV NRSV ESV NASB NIV TNIV NEB REB NJB NAB NLT HCSB NET

variant/TR το μεν φως εθεασαντο και εμφοβοι εγενετο
"they saw the light and they became afraid"
D E Ψ 1739 Maj it^{gig} syr^{h} cop^{sa}
KJV NKJV

It is possible, but not likely, that the clause και εμφοβοι εγενετο ("and they were afraid") dropped out of the text due to homoeoteleuton (following εθεασαντο), or that the clause was dropped because neither of the other conversion accounts mention Paul's companions being afraid (see 9:1-9; 26:12-18). However, since the documentary evidence favors the shorter reading, it is more likely that the clause is a natural scribal expansion influenced by 10:4; Luke 24:5, 37.

Acts 22:26-28

Western text (D) reads:

> "When the centurion heard that **he was a Roman,** he went to the tribune and said to him, '**Watch** what you are about to do. This man is a Roman.' 27 The tribune came and asked him, 'Tell me, are you a Roman citizen?' And he said, '**I am.**' 28 The tribune answered, '**I know** how much it cost me to get my citizenship.' Paul said, 'I was born a citizen.'"

As usual, the D-reviser took pains to fill in any perceived gaps—none of which are necessary in this passage. The addition of "I know" in 22:28 gives the tribune's statement a tinge of sarcasm.

Acts 22:29

A few witnesses (614 syr[h**] cop[sa]) end this verse with the additional words: "and at once he released him," thereby preempting the same statement in 22:30. This addition may have been made because once Paul revealed his Roman citizenship, he should have been let go immediately. Codex D, in its extant form, concludes with 22:29.

Acts 23:9

WH NU εἰ δὲ πνεῦμα ἐλάλησεν αὐτῷ ἢ ἄγγελος;
"And what if a spirit or an angel spoke to him?"
𝔓[74] א A B C E Ψ 33 1739 syr
NKJVmg RSV NRSV ESV NASB NIV TNIV NEB REB NJB NAB NLT HCSB NET

variant/TR ει δε πνευμα ελαλησεν αυτω η αγγελος; μη θεομαχωμεν.
"And what if a spirit or an angel spoke to him? Let us not fight against God."
Maj cop[sa]
KJV NKJV HCSBmg

Probably borrowing from 5:39, later scribes put an affirmative statement in the mouths of the Pharisees. This interpolation was included in TR and then translated in KJV and NKJV.

Acts 23:12

WH NU ποιήσαντες συστροφὴν οἱ Ἰουδαῖοι
"the Jews formed a conspiracy"
𝔓[74] א A B C E 33 1739
RSV NRSV ESV NASB NIV TNIV NEB REB NJB NAB (NLT) HCSB NET

variant/TR ποιησαντες συστροφην τινες των Ιουδαιων
"some of the Jews formed a conspiracy"
(𝔓[48] βοηθειαν συστραφεντες) Maj it syr[p] cop[saMSS]
KJV NKJV

The WH NU reading has excellent testimony, both early and diverse. The variant reading (found in TR) harmonizes with 23:13, which speaks of a group of forty Jews who had banded together in a plot against Paul.

Acts 23:13

𝔓[48] and it[h] read αναθεματισαντες εαυτους ("having put a curse on themselves") instead of ταυτην την συνωμοσιαν ποιησαμενοι ("having made this plot"), probably because the plot originated with the Jewish leaders, not the forty men who had merely vowed to carry out the plan (Haenchen 1971, 645).

Acts 23:15

Western text (it[h] syr[hmg] 𝔓[48] in part) reads:

> "**We ask that you would do this for us: gather the Sanhedrin together, and** notify the tribune with the Sanhedrin to bring him down to you on the pretext that you want to make

a more thorough examination of his case. And we are ready to do away with him before he arrives, **even if we must die for it.**"

Two other Western witnesses, 𝔓⁴⁸ and it^{gig}, begin in the same way and then delete "with the Sanhedrin." The first interpolation formalizes the request; the second intensifies it.

Acts 23:23-24

Western text (𝔓^{48vid} 614 2147 it^{gig,h} syr^{hmg}) reads:

> "Then he summoned two of the centurions and said, 'Get soldiers ready to go to Caesarea, **a hundred** horsemen with two hundred spearmen,' **and he commanded that they be ready to start** at the third hour of the night. [24] **And he ordered the centurions** to provide mounts for Paul to ride, and take him **by night** safely to Felix the governor, **for he was afraid that the Jews would seize him [Paul] and kill him, and afterwards he would incur the accusation of having taken a bribe.**"

Metzger (TCGNT) indicates this Western expansion but does not cite the support of 𝔓⁴⁸, which clearly has the long addition at the end of 23:24 (see NA[27]) and thereby supplies a reason for the tribune's swift action of sending Paul off to Caesarea.

Acts 23:29

Western text (𝔓^{48vid} 614 2147 it^{gig} syr^{hmg}) reads:

> "I found that the accusation concerned disputed points of their Law **of Moses and a certain one called Jesus,** but there was no charge deserving death or imprisonment. **I got him away with difficulty by [using military] force.**" (see NJBmg)

In NA[27] the variant is cited with the following support: 614 2147 it^{gig} syr^{hmg}. To this should be added 𝔓^{48vid}. According to the transcription provided by Vitelli and Mercati (1932, 116), the last part of the manuscript reads as follows: [ ]ω εωσκαι. According to Clark (1933, 412-413), Mercati later reconstructed this as μ]ω[υσ]εως και ("Moses and"). (For a complete reconstruction of this manuscript, see *Text of Earliest MSS,* 353-354.) This restoration indicates that 𝔓⁴⁸ must have also included the addition, "of Moses, and [a certain one called Jesus]." This is a typical Western expansion intended to explain that Paul was imprisoned for issues pertaining to the law *of Moses* (i.e., the Jewish law) and also for proclaiming a certain man called *Jesus*. The concluding interpolation, not found in 𝔓⁴⁸ because the manuscript is lacking here, is simply a reiteration of the military power Lysias used to take Paul safely from Jerusalem to Caesarea.

Acts 23:30a

WH NU — ἐπιβουλῆς εἰς τὸν ἄνδρα ἔσεσθαι
"[knowing] there to be a plot against this man"
𝔓⁷⁴ B Ψ
NKJVmg RSV NRSV ESV NASB NIV TNIV NEB REB NJB NAB NLT HCSB NET

variant 1 — επιβουλης εις τον ανδρα εσεσθαι εξ αυτων
"[knowing] there to be a plot against this man by them"
א A E 1739
none

variant 2/TR επιβουλης εις τον ανδρα μελλειν εσεσθαι υπο των Ιουδαιων
"[knowing] there about to be a plot against this man by the Jews"
Maj
KJV NKJV HCSBmg

The WH NU reading has good textual support, but none better than in the first variant. Nonetheless, WH NU probably reflect the original reading because the first variant, as well as the second, supply a prepositional phrase to help the reader understand who instigated the plot against Paul.

Acts 23:30b

WH NU omit ερρωσο ("farewell") at end of verse
𝔓[74vid] A B 33 it[gig] cop
RSV NRSV ESV NASB NIV TNIV NEB REB NJB NAB NLT HCSB NET

variant/TR add ερρωσο ("farewell") at end of verse
ℵ E Ψ 1739 Maj syr
KJV NKJV NRSVmg NJBmg HCSBmg

Probably borrowing from the conclusion to the letter written by the Jerusalem leaders to the Gentile churches (15:29), scribes added a concluding "farewell" to Claudius Lysias's letter to Felix. This concluding "farewell" is very common in the nonliterary Greek papyri dated in the centuries just prior to and after Christ.

Acts 24:6-8

WH NU omit 24:6b-8a (see below)
𝔓[74] ℵ A B H L P 049 cop
NKJVmg RSV NRSV ESV NASBmg NIV TNIV NEB REB NJB NAB NLT HCSBmg NET

variant/TR add 24:6b-8a
και κατα τον ημετερον νομον ηθελησαμεν κριναι. [7]παρελθων δε Λυσιας ο χιλιαρχος μετα πολλης βιας εκ των χειρων ημων απηγαγε [8]κελευσας τους κατηγορους αυτου ερχεσθαι επι σε
And we would have judged him according to our law. [7] But the chief captain Lysias came and with great violence took him out of our hands, [8] commanding his accusers to come before you.
(E) Ψ Maj 33 614 1739 it[gig] (syr[p])
KJV NKJV RSVmg NRSVmg ESVmg NASB NIVmg NEBmg REBmg NJBmg NABmg NLTmg HCSB NETmg

The expanded reading, found primarily in Western manuscripts, produces a rendering of these verses in TR such as this: "[6] He even tried to profane the temple, and so we seized him. And we would have judged him according to our law. [7] But the chief captain Lysias came and with great violence took him out of our hands, [8] commanding his accusers to come before you. By examining him yourself you will be able to learn from him concerning everything of which we accuse him."

The variant reading, which found its way into the majority of manuscripts and was included in TR, is another example of gap-filling. The words are included, of course, by KJV and NKJV as well as NASB and HCSB, which often include verses that all other modern translations exclude. The words were added because a scribe did not think it likely that Felix would have received the whole story from Paul. Therefore, he connected the relative pronoun in the phrase παρ ου ("from whom") to Lysias, the tribune who rescued Paul from the Jews plotting to kill him. The same idea of using military power or force (μετα πολλης βιας) to accomplish this rescue is found in the Western addition to 23:29 (see note). But Lysias was not present to give Felix an account of these things, so the expanded variant is wrong. The text, without the interpolation, is bare but understandable: Paul was arrested so that he could now be examined and tried by Felix.

Acts 24:10

Western text (syr[hmg]) reads:

> "When the governor motioned to him to **make a defense for himself,** Paul answered. **And having assumed a godlike attitude,** he said, 'I cheerfully make my defense, knowing that for many years you have been a judge over this nation.'"

According to Bruce (1990, 478), these words were added because it was important in public speaking to take on a godlike attitude.

Acts 24:15

WH NU ἀνάστασιν μέλλειν ἔσεσθαι
"there is about to be a resurrection"
𝔓[74] א A B C 33 1739 cop
NKJVmg RSV NRSV ESV NASB NIV TNIV NEB REB NJB NAB NLT HCSB NET

variant/TR αναστασιν μελλειν εσεσθαι νεκρων
"there is about to be a resurrection of the dead"
E Ψ Maj syr
KJV NKJV HCSBmg

The variant reading is a natural expansion, which found its way into TR, and from there into KJV and NKJV.

Acts 24:24a

Western text (syr[hmg]) reads:

> "Some days later when Felix came with his wife Drusilla, a Jewess, **who asked to see Paul and hear the word. So, wanting to satisfy her,** he summoned Paul."

The expansion is intended to help readers understand that Felix, a Gentile, was willing to give Paul a hearing because he wanted to please his wife, Drusilla, who was a Jew. And what better way to please her than to show some interest in Paul, a former Jew turned Christian. This addition is in keeping with our knowledge of Felix's relationship with Drusilla. Felix convinced her to leave her second husband, Azizuz, by promising her great happiness if she joined him (Josephus, *Ant.* 20.7.141-144).

Acts 24:24b

WH NU τῆς εἰς Χριστὸν Ἰησοῦν πίστεως
"the faith in Christ Jesus"
𝔓74 ℵ* B E L Ψ 049 33 1739 syr[h] cop[bo]
RSV NRSV ESV NASB NIV TNIV NEB REB NJB NAB NLT HCSB NET

variant/TR της εις Χριστον πιστεως
"the faith in Christ"
ℵ[1] A C[vid] H syr[p]
KJV NKJV

In most instances, readings with the longer divine title are considered to be scribal expansions, but in this instance the documentary evidence favors "Christ Jesus." This reading also suits the context well because Paul would not be preaching about the Messiah alone but that Jesus was the Messiah. Felix had heard about "the Way" (the movement created by the followers of Jesus), and Paul had been identified with this sect.

Acts 24:26

WH NU χρήματα δοθήσεται αὐτῷ ὑπὸ τοῦ Παύλου
"[hoping] money might be given to him by Paul"
ℵ A B C E Ψ 33 1739 syr
NKJVmg RSV NRSV ESV NASB NIV TNIV NEB REB NJB NAB NLT HCSB NET

variant/TR χρηματα δοθησεται αυτω υπο του Παυλου οπως λυση αυτον
"[hoping] money might be given to him by Paul so that he might release him"
Maj cop
KJV NKJV HCSBmg

The WH NU reading has vastly superior documentary support than that behind TR. The majority of manuscripts display a natural scribal expansion here. Most readers, however, will fill in this gap for themselves.

Acts 24:27

Western text (614 2147 syr[hmg]) reads:

> "After two years had passed, Felix was succeeded by Porcius Festus. But Felix left Paul in prison **on account of Drusilla.**"

Instead of Felix leaving Paul in prison in order to please the Jews, the Western text has Felix keeping Paul imprisoned for the sake of his wife. We would assume, then, that she must have felt threatened by Paul's preaching about righteousness, self-control, and the coming judgment (24:25). His message may have fully convicted her because she was a renegade Jew who left her former husband for a Gentile.

Acts 25:18

WH NU include last word πονηρῶν ("evils" = "crimes")
ℵ[c] B E (πονηραν 𝔓74 A C* 1739; πονηρα ℵ* C[2])
RSV NRSV ESV NASB NIV TNIV NJB NAB NLT HCSB NET

variant/TR omit
Maj
KJV NKJV NRSVmg NEB REB

The WH NU reading has good support and suits the context well; it would be translated as, "the accusers did not charge him with any of the crimes I was expecting." The variant appears to be the result of scribal stylization. It would be translated as, "the accusers did not charge him with anything I was expecting."

Acts 25:23

Western text (syr^hmg) reads:

> "So on the next day Agrippa and Bernice came with great pomp, and they entered the audience hall with the military tribunes, and the prominent men of the **province came down.** Then Festus gave the order and Paul was brought in."

Instead of the prominent men "of the city" (i.e., Caesarea) coming to the hearing, the Western text has prominent men from the whole province come. This enlarges the grandeur of the event.

Acts 25:24-25

Western text (syr^hmg) reads:

> "And Festus said, 'King Agrippa and all here present with us, you see this man about whom all the Jewish people petitioned me, both in Jerusalem and here, **that I should hand him over to them for punishment without any defense. But I could not hand him over because of the orders we have from the emperor. But if anyone was going to accuse him, I said he should follow me to Caesarea, where he [Paul] was in custody. And when they came,** they shouted that he should not live any longer. 25 **But when I heard both sides of the case,** I found that he had done nothing guilty of death. **But when I said, "Are you willing to be judged before them in Jerusalem?"** he appealed to Caesar.'"

A marginal reading in the Harclean Syriac displays the kind of extensive gap-filling that is found throughout the Western text. The extra words basically reiterate the events that led up to this hearing, as if to supply Agrippa with the background information he would need in order to understand Paul's case. But all this is unnecessary. Readers can fill in these gaps for themselves from the previous narrative.

Acts 26:1

Western text (syr^hmg) reads:

> "Agrippa said to Paul, 'You have permission to speak for yourself.' Then Paul, **being confident and encouraged by the Holy Spirit,** stretched out his hand and began to defend himself."

The Western text is known for its added emphasis on the influence of the Holy Spirit in the life of the apostles, especially Paul (see notes on 11:17, 29, 32; 16:18b; 19:1; 20:3-4a).

Acts 26:7-8

Some manuscripts (𝔓^29vid A Ψ) do not include the word Βασιλευ ("king"). This allows for a reconstruction of the syntax, which permits this translation: "the promise for which our twelve tribes assiduously worship God day and night in the hope of attaining it; it is for this that I am now being arraigned by the Jews; namely, that God raises the dead" (so NJBmg).

Acts 26:14-15

Western text (614 it[gig] syr[hmg]) reads:

> "When we had all fallen to the ground **because of fear, I alone** heard a voice saying to me in the Hebrew language, 'Saul, Saul, why are you persecuting me? It hurts you to kick against the goads.' [15] I asked, 'Who are you, Lord?' The Lord answered, 'I am Jesus **the Nazarene** whom you are persecuting.'"

The changes in the Western text are an attempt to conform this account of Paul's conversion to the one recorded in 22:6-11, where it indicates that only Paul (not his companions) heard the voice of Jesus, who identified himself as "Jesus the Nazarene."

Acts 26:16

WH NU	ὧν τε εἶδες [με] "the things wherein you have seen me" B C*vid 1739 syr cop[sa] RSV NRSV ESV NIV TNIV NEB REB NJB NAB HCSBmg NETmg
variant/TR	ων τε ειδες "the things you have seen" 𝔓74 ℵ A C2 E Ψ 096 Maj KJV NKJV NRSVmg NASB NLT HCSB NET

According to the WH NU reading, which is the more difficult reading, the emphasis is on Jesus' revelation of himself to Paul. This is rendered in full as: "for this purpose I appeared to you, to appoint you a servant and a witness both of the things [wherein] you have seen me and of the things wherein I will appear to you." It is not just that Jesus revealed many things (or, many items) to Paul. Jesus revealed himself in his fullness to Paul so that Paul could preach him among the nations (see Eph 3:8). The first appearance Jesus made to Paul was on the road to Damascus. It was at this time that Paul saw the risen Christ (see 1 Cor 15:8). Subsequent to this appearance, Paul received more revelations from Jesus concerning his commission.

Acts 26:28

The Greek expression εν ολιγω με πειθεις Χριστιανον ποιησαι has been interpreted in various ways by scribes, exegetes, and translators. Was Agrippa asking, "in such a short time can you persuade me to become a Christian?" (see NIV and NRSV), or was he conceding, "you almost persuaded me to become a Christian" (see KJV and NKJV). If the latter interpretation is accepted, then it can be inferred that Paul's preaching had a positive effect on Agrippa. But the expression εν ολιγω does not mean "almost"; it means "in a short time." This is affirmed by Paul's response in the next verse: "Whether short [εν ολιγω] or long, I would to God that not only you but also all who hear me this day might become such as I am—except for these chains." This indicates that Paul picked up on the same Greek term (εν ολιγω) with the same meaning. Thus, even though the rendering in KJV has become well known ("almost thou persuadest me to become a Christian"), it is not accurate.

Furthermore, it is likely that the verb ποιησαι means "to play the part"—as in theatrical acting. As such, the expression means, "Quickly you will persuade me to play the Christian"

(NRSVmg). Unaware of this technical meaning or uncomfortable with it, several scribes (E Ψ 1739 Maj syr—so TR) changed ποιησαι ("to play the part") to γενεσθαι ("to become").

Finally, it should be noted that the reading in A, which substitutes πειθη for πειθεις, means "You trust you can make me a Christian in a short while." Some scholars, such as Lachmann and Alford, accepted this as the original wording.

Acts 26:30

Western text (614 Maj syr[h**]) reads:

> "**And after he had said these things,** the king got up, and with him the governor and Bernice and those who had been seated with them."

This is a typical Western interpolation, supplying a circumstantial detail.

Acts 26:32 and 27:1

Western text (𝔓[112vid] for 26:32; it[h] syr[p,hmg]) reads:

> "Agrippa said to Festus, 'This man could have been set free if he had not appealed to Caesar.' **So then the governor decided to send him to Caesar. And the next day** [27:1] [when it was decided that we were to sail for Italy,] **he called** a centurion of the Augustan Cohort, named Julius, and handed Paul and the other prisoners over to him."

The reason for the changes in the Western text (to which can now be added the support of the fifth-century papyrus, 𝔓[112]) is that it must have seemed odd to various scribes that Paul's companions would have accompanied him on this journey. Thus, the explicit assertion is made that Agrippa sent Paul to Caesar, followed by a deletion of the "we" passage at the beginning of chapter 27. Some modern scholars have also had problems with the "we" passage in 27:1—and for the same reason (see Bruce 1990, 509-510 for a discussion on this). But it is not unusual for Luke and other companions to have been granted permission to accompany Paul to Italy.

Acts 27:2

Western text (614 syr[h]) reads:

> "Embarking on a ship of Adramyttium that was about to set sail to the ports along the coast of Asia, we put to sea, accompanied by Aristarchus **and Secundus,** Macedonians from Thessalonica."

Borrowing from 20:4, the Western text adds "Secundus" as another traveler.

Acts 27:5

Western text (614 it[h] syr[h**]) reads:

> "After we had sailed **for fifteen days** across the sea that is off Cilicia and Pamphylia, we came to Myra in Lycia."

The Western interpolation, aimed at providing yet another circumstantial detail, is a calculated guess. It usually took about two weeks to get from Caesarea to Myra. The name of the city "Myra" is Μυρα in Ψ 33 1739 Maj and Μυρρα in B; other manuscripts have the aberrations Σμυρναν ("Smyrna"—in 69) and Λυστραν ("Lystra"—in 𝔓[74] א A). Λυστραν ("Lystra") probably came from the subsidiary name of the city, Λιμυρα ("Limura") (Haenchen 1971, 698).

Acts 27:14

WH NU εὐρακύλων
"Euraquilon" (= "Northeaster")
𝔓74 ℵ A B* syr^pal cop^bo,sa
NKJVmg RSV NRSV ESV NASB NIV TNIV NEB REB NJB NAB NLT HCSB NET

variant/TR ευροκλυδων
"Euroclydon"
B2 Ψ Maj syr
KJV NKJV

The WH NU reading has a hybrid word, from Greek ευρος ("east wind") and Latin *aquilo* ("north wind")—hence, a "Northeaster." The variant reading has a compound word derived from two Greek words, ευρος ("east wind") and κλυδων ("surging waves")—suggesting a sea storm coming in from the east.

Acts 27:15

Western text (614 syr^h**) reads:

> "Since the ship was caught and could not face directly into the wind **that was blowing, we furled the sails and, as happens in such cases,** were driven before it."

As usual, the Western text provides some circumstantial details, in this instance to help readers understand the maneuverings of a ship struggling against a storm.

Acts 27:16

WH NU Καυδα
"Cauda"
𝔓74 ℵ2 B (Ψ) syr^p
NKJVmg RSV NRSV ESV NASBmg NIV TNIV NEB REB NJB NAB NLT HCSB NET

variant/(TR) Κλαυδα
"Clauda"
ℵ* A^vid 33 1739 syr^h (Κλαυδην Maj)
KJV NKJV RSVmg NRSVmg ESVmg NASB NLTmg HCSBmg

The name of this island appears in an Alexandrian form (Cauda) and a Latinized form (Clauda). In Modern Greek it is called Γαυδος; in Italian it is called *Gozzo.* Most of the modern versions, with the exception of the NASB (which has a marked tendency of following TR), read "Cauda." And a few note the variant out of deference to the KJV tradition.

Acts 27:19

WH NU τὴν σκευὴν τοῦ πλοίου ἔρριψαν
"they threw out the gear of the ship"
𝔓74vid ℵ A B C 33 1739
RSV NRSV ESV NASB NIV TNIV NEB REB NJB NAB NLT HCSB NET

variant 1/TR την σκυεην του πλοιου ερριψαμεν εις την θαλασσαν
"we threw out the gear of the ship into the sea"
Ψ Maj syr
KJV NKJV

variant 2 την σκυεην του πλοιου ερριψαν εις την θαλασσαν
"they threw out the gear of the ship into the sea"
614 it syr[h**] cop[sa]
none

The WH NU reading is supported by the best manuscripts. The first variant is a carryover from the "we" of the previous verse ("we were pounded by the storm"). Paul and his companions (one of whom was Luke, the author of Acts) would not have taken part in throwing out the ship's equipment. In fact, the sailors did all the tasks to keep the ship afloat during the storm; they secured it with ropes, and they threw out the grain and equipment to lighten its load. The second variant is a natural expansion.

Acts 27:27

Codex B has the verb προσαχειν ("to resound"), suggesting "the resounding surf," instead of προσαγειν ("to be approaching"—hence, "approaching surf"), found in 𝔓[74] א[2] A C Ψ 33 1739 Maj. The idea is that the sailors were hearing the resounding surf and therefore knew that land was near. The form of the word is Doric, and "may have been first used by sailors outside the Ionic-Attic area, from whom it passed into more general usage as a technical term" (Bruce 1990, 522). The Old Latin manuscripts, it[gig,s], reflect the same meaning with the word *resonare*.

Acts 27:29-30

Western text (it[gig] and some Vulgate MSS) reads:

> "Fearing that we might run on the rocks, they let down four anchors from the stern and prayed for day to come, **that we might know if we could be saved.** 30 But the sailors tried to escape from the ship. They lowered the boat into the sea, on the pretext of putting out anchors from the bow, **so that the ship might ride more safely.**"

The interpolations are typical Western expansions intending to fill perceived gaps in the narrative.

Acts 27:35

Western text (614 syr[h**] cop[sa]) reads:

> "After he [Paul] had said this, he took bread; and giving thanks to God in the presence of all, he broke it and began to eat, **giving [some] also to us.**"

This addition is hardly necessary because the next verse says, "Then all of them were encouraged, and took food for themselves."

Acts 27:37

The number of people on the ship varies in the manuscripts. Two Greek editions (TR NU) accept the reading διακοσιαι εβδομηκοντα εξ ("two hundred seventy-six"). This has good support: א C Ψ 33 1739 syr[p,h] cop[bo], and is followed by all the English versions. The three variant readings on this are as follows: (1) διακοσιαι εβδομηκοντα πεντε ("two hundred seventy-five") in A; (2) ως εβδομηκοντα εξ ("about seventy-six") in B cop[sa] (so WH); (3) εβδομηκοντα εξ ("seventy-six") in 69.

The first variant rounds off the number. The second variant is the result of a scribal error (see TCGNT). Furthermore, ως ("about") would not precede an exact number. The third variant is an aberration of the second. The TR NU reading has excellent support and is very probable—ships did carry that many people in those days. Josephus (*Life* 15) recounted the story of how six hundred people on board a ship to Rome experienced a shipwreck.

Acts 27:39

The verb εξωσαι ("to run aground") has good documentary support (א A B[2] Ψ 33 1739 it syr[p,h]) and is the natural expression for this context (see 27:41). The verb is different in B* C cop (so WH): εκσωσαι ("to get out safely"). Though this word can also work in this context, it is probably the result of a scribal error due to hearing (both words sound the same).

Acts 27:41

Decent textual support lies behind the reading της βιας των κυματων ("the force of the waves"): 𝔓[74] א[2] C 33 1739 Maj syr. However, των κυματων ("of the waves") is lacking in three principle Alexandrian witnesses: א* A B. Thus, these words are bracketed in the NU text and excluded from the WH text. On internal grounds, it is far easier to argue that the words would have been inserted (to clarify βιας) rather than deleted for the sake of trimming.

Acts 28:1

According to most manuscripts, the island is called Μελιτη —literally, "Melita," known today as Malta. In B* and other ancient versions (it syr[h] cop[bo]) it is Μελιτηνη (so WH). This could be an error of dittography or a variant spelling of Melita, but it is also possible that the scribe of B was identifying the island of Mljet (Meleda), which is off the Dalmatian coast in the Adriatic Sea. Ptolemy (*Geogr.* 2.16.9) called this island Μελιτηνη. If a scribe were to understand 27:27 to be speaking of the Adriatic Sea, then this identification is understandable. But 27:27 speaks of the Mediterranean Sea, and "the Northeaster" (27:14) would not have blown the ship into the Adriatic. In Paul's day, the name "Sea of Adria" was applied to the Adriatic as well as the Ionian Sea, which fits well with the story in Acts.

Acts 28:13

WH NU	περιελόντες κατηντήσαμεν εἰς Ῥήγιον "having cast off, we came to Rhegium" א* B Ψ NRSV NIV TNIV NJB NLT HCSBmg NET
variant/TR	περιελθοντες κατηντησαμεν εις Ρηγιον "having gone around, we came to Rhegium" 𝔓[74] א[c] A 048 066 Maj syr KJV NKJV RSV ESV NASB NEB REB NAB HCSB NETmg

Although the one-letter difference (*theta*) between the two verbs could be accidental, it is likely that περιελοντες, being misunderstood, was changed to the more common verb, περιελθοντες ("having gone around")—a translation adopted by many translators. The Greek word περιελοντες is probably a nautical term that means "casting off." This definition is affirmed by 27:40, where we see the expression, τας αγκυρας περιελοντες ("having cast off the anchors"). If in 27:40 περιελοντες suggests throwing off, then in 28:13 it can suggest "casting off" (see Westcott and Hort 1882, 226-227).

Acts 28:16

WH NU — Ὅτε δὲ εἰσήλθομεν εἰς Ῥώμην, ἐπετράπη τῷ Παύλῳ μένειν καθ ἑαυτόν
"When we came into Rome, Paul was allowed to live by himself"
𝔓74vid ℵ A B Ψ 048vid 066 33vid 1739
RSV NRSV ESV NASB NIV TNIV NEB REB NJB NAB NLT HCSB NET

variant/TR — οτε δε εισηλθομεν εις Ρωμην, ο εκατονταρχος παρεδωκεν τους δεσμιους τω στρατοπεδαρχω τω δε Παυλω επετραπη μενειν καθ εατον
"When we came into Rome, the centurion delivered the prisoners to the captain of the guard, but Paul was allowed to live by himself"
Maj itgig (syrh**) copsa
KJV NKJV HCSBmg

The expanded reading in the variant was probably a Western creation that found its way into the mainstream of the Byzantine manuscripts, and then into TR. This expansion may reflect history accurately inasmuch as the captain of the guard (literally "the stratopedarch") was probably the commander of the praetorian barracks. The Western text (but not Maj), according to 614 it (syrh**), adds εξω της παρεμβολης ("outside the barracks") after καθ εαυτον ("by himself") to make it clear that Paul was not imprisoned in the barracks.

Acts 28:18-19

Western text (614 syrh**) reads:

> "When they had examined me **concerning many things,** they wanted to release me, because there was no reason for the death penalty in my case. [19] But the Jews were objecting **and were crying out, 'Away with our enemy!'** So I was compelled to appeal to Caesar—even though I had no charge to bring against my nation—**but [I did so] that I might deliver my soul from death."**

The Western text, in typical fashion, expands the verbiage in an effort to make a fuller and presumably clearer text. The first addition in 28:19 is borrowed from 22:22. The second addition attributes fear of death as Paul's reason for appealing to Caesar. But the book of Acts never says this explicitly. In fact, Paul asserts just the opposite: He was ready to die for the sake of Christ (see 21:13; 25:11).

Acts 28:25

WH NU — τοὺς πατέρας ὑμῶν
"to your fathers"
𝔓74 ℵ A B Ψ 33 1739 syrp
NKJVmg RSV NRSV ESV NASB NIV TNIV NEB REB NJB NAB NLT HCSB NET

variant 1/TR τους πατερας ημων
"to our fathers"
Maj
KJV NKJV HCSBmg

variant 2 τους πατερας
"to the fathers"
syr[h]
none

According to WH NU, a full rendering of this verse is: "The Holy Spirit spoke correctly through Isaiah the prophet to your fathers." The best attestation strongly favors this reading, as does the tone of Paul's address. At this point, Paul was not showing solidarity with the Jews (as would be the case with the first variant); rather, he was condemning them for their lack of faith. The second variant is a Syriac translator's generalization of the relationship to "fathers."

Acts 28:29

WH NU omit verse
𝔓[74] ℵ A B E Ψ 048 33 1739 syr[p] cop
NKJVmg RSV NRSV ESV NASBmg NIV TNIV NEB REB NJB NAB NLT HCSBmg NET

variant/TR add verse
Και ταυτα αυτου ειποντος απηλθον οι Ιουδαιοι, πολλην εχοντες εν εαυτοις συζητησιν
"And after he said these things, the Jews went away, arguing greatly among themselves."
Maj it syr[h**]
KJV NKJV RSVmg NRSVmg ESVmg NASB NIVmg NEBmg REBmg NJBmg NABmg NLTmg HCSB NETmg

The additional verse passed from the Western text into the Byzantine text. It was added to fill in the narrative gap between 28:28 and 28:30. All modern versions except NASB and HCSB do not include it in the text. Most note it out of deference to the KJV tradition.

Acts 28:30-31

Western text (614 syr[h**] for 28:30 and it[p] syr[h] for 28:31) reads:

> "He lived there two whole years at his own rented house, and he welcomed all who came to him, **both Jews and Gentiles,** [31] proclaiming the kingdom of God and teaching about the Lord Jesus Christ with all boldness and without hindrance, **saying that this is Jesus the Son of God, through whom the whole world is to be judged. Amen.**"

The first change in the Western text is to show Paul's magnanimous spirit. He was always willing to preach the gospel to Jews and Gentiles, even though many Jews in Rome were unreceptive to his message. The second change is a typical Western expansion that is not needed. In fact, it detracts from the force of Luke's final words. Luke's words culminate a major theme in this book: The gospel is preached with boldness, and Paul's words open the way for the continuation of the acts of the apostles, who, unhindered, will continue to proclaim Jesus Christ and his kingdom.

The Epistle to the ROMANS

Inscription (Title)

ℵ and B have the inscription and subscription προσ ρωμαιους ("to the Romans"); see last note.

Romans 1:1

NU	δοῦλος Χριστοῦ 'Ιησοῦ "slave of Christ Jesus" 𝔓10 B 81 ESV NASB NIV TNIV NEB REB NJB NAB NLT HCSB NET
variant/TR WH	δουλος Ιησου Χριστου "slave of Jesus Christ" 𝔓26 ℵ A G Ψ 33 1739 Maj KJV NKJV RSV NRSV

It was Paul's habit when introducing himself in an epistle to call himself "an apostle of Christ Jesus" (see 1 Cor 1:1; 2 Cor 1:1; Eph 1:1; Col 1:1; 1 Tim 1:1; 2 Tim 1:1). The only exception is Titus 1:1, where he calls himself "an apostle of Jesus Christ" (according to several manuscripts). In the introduction to Philippians, Paul identifies himself and Timothy as "slaves of Christ Jesus." Therefore, the variant word order is most likely the result of scribal conformation to the immediate context, where "Jesus Christ" is the accepted reading in 1:4, 6, 7, 8. Although supported slimly, the reading of the NU text has the testimony of the two earliest witnesses: 𝔓10 (ca. 320) and B (ca. 350). Most English versions follow the reading "Christ Jesus." Interestingly, the NRSV did not follow the NU reading here, contrary to its usual custom.

Romans 1:7

The reading πασιν τοις ουσιν εν Ρωμη αγαπητοις θεου ("to all the ones in Rome, loved of God") is based on the excellent testimony of 𝔓10 𝔓26vid ℵ A B C 33 81 1739mg syr cop. Some witnesses omit εν Ρωμη ("in Rome")—namely, G itg Origen (according to 1739mg). The first variant reading is significant in that it does not include "in Rome." The margin of 1739 attests to the omission of "in Rome" from Origen's commentary on Romans. The Greco-Latin Codex G, a Western manuscript of the ninth century, also lacks "in Rome."

The omission of "in Rome" could not be accidental, especially in G where "in Rome" is also omitted from 1:15. The absence of the city's name in both a Western source and Egyptian (Origen) could suggest that at an early date there were two forms of Paul's Epistles: one addressed to the Romans and another to the believers in general as an encyclical. Most likely, certain compilers of Paul's Epistles (in one corpus), recognizing the nonoccasional and treatise-like nature of Romans, attempted to give it a catholic (church-wide) audience by deleting "in Rome." Romans, though lacking occasional material (i.e., specific solutions to particular local problems), was clearly written to a church that Paul had not yet been to and one that he was intending to visit (see 1:10-13; 15:22-24, 32 and see comments on 16:25-27).

Romans 1:15

A few witnesses (G it[g] Origen[lat]) omit τοις εν Ρωμη ("to the ones in Rome"), thereby making this epistle as one addressed to the church in general. The same witnesses do not include "in Rome" in 1:7 (see note).

Romans 1:16a

WH NU τὸ εὐαγγέλιον
"the gospel"
𝔓[26vid] ℵ A B C D* G 33 1739 it syr cop
NKJVmg RSV NRSV ESV NASB NIV TNIV NEB REB NJB NAB NLT HCSB NET

variant/TR το ευαγγελιον του Χριστου
"the gospel of Christ"
D[c] Ψ Maj
KJV NKJV HCSBmg

The WH NU reading has vastly superior documentary support (both early and diverse) than that of the variant. The variant reading is a natural scribal expansion (perhaps influenced by 2:16 and 15:19) that found its way into the majority of late manuscripts, then into TR, followed by the KJV and NKJV.

Romans 1:16b

Paul said that the gospel was "the power of God unto salvation, to the Jews first and also to the Gentiles." Marcion, not wanting to give the Jews priority over the Gentiles, omitted πρωτον ("first"). This omission appears also in B G cop[sa].

Romans 1:17

The scribe of C* added μου to the quote from Hab 2:4, producing the reading ο δε δικαιος μου εκ πιστεως ζησεται ("my righteous one will live by faith"). This wording exactly corresponds with that found in Heb 10:38, which does not agree with the Septuagint ("the righteous by my faith will live"), the Masoretic Text ("the righteous by his faith will live"), or Paul's rendering ("the righteous by faith will live"). A corrector of C deleted μου, bringing it into conformity with Paul's rendering.

Romans 1:20

The adjective αιδιος ("everlasting") was omitted by the scribes of L 1506*, perhaps by accident or more likely because it is an unusual word in the NT—occurring only here in Paul's writings and in Jude 6.

Romans 1:29

WH NU	πονηρίᾳ πλεονεξίᾳ κακίᾳ "wickedness, greediness, evil" B 0172vid 1739 1881 NKJVmg RSV NRSV NASB NEB REB NJB NAB NLT HCSB NET
variant 1	κακια πονηρια πλεονεξια "evil, wickedness, greediness" C Ds2 33 81 none
variant 2	πονηρια κακια πλεονεξια "wickedness, evil, greediness" א A ESV NIV TNIV
variant 3	κακια πορνεια πλεονεξια "evil, fornication, greediness" Ds* G none
variant 4/TR	πορνεια πονηρια πλεονεξια κακια "fornication, wickedness, greediness, evil" Ψ Maj KJV NKJV HCSBmg

These words in the list of vices were rearranged in several manuscripts, and it is possible that πορνεια ("fornication"), being mistaken for πονηρια ("wickedness"), was accidentally dropped. But the superior manuscript evidence (the WH NU reading, variants 1 and 2) attests to a list without "fornication" (or "sexual immorality")—probably because Paul was listing the evil deeds that come as a result of idolatry and sexual immorality (see 1:22-24; TCGNT).

Romans 1:31

WH NU	ἀστόργους ἀνελεήμονας "unaffectionate, merciless" א* A B D G 1739 it copbo NKJVmg RSV NRSV ESV NASB NIV TNIV NEB REB NJB NAB NLT HCSB NET
variant/TR	αστοργους ασπονδους ανελεημονας "unaffectionate, irreconcilable, merciless" א2 C Ψ (33) Maj syr KJV NKJV

Likely borrowing from a similar list of vices in 2 Tim 3:3, some scribe added ασπονδους, which means "irreconcilable" or "unforgiving." The scribe who added this word did not break Paul's string of alliteration. With the addition, there are five words in a row beginning with *alpha* and four in a row with *alpha* and *sigma*. Of course, this could be an argument in favor of accidental omission—due to homoeoarchton (like beginnings), but the manuscript evidence favors a shorter text.

Romans 1:32

The Old Latin text tradition has a different reading for this verse: "They know that God is just, and yet they do not understand that those who behave like this deserve to die, and not only those who do this but those who encourage them" (see NJBmg).

Romans 2:2

TR WH NU read οιδαμεν δε οτι το κριμα του θεου εστιν κατα αληθειαν ("but we know that the judgment of God is according to truth"), following the authority of A B D 81 1739. The variant reading is οιδαμεν γαρ οτι το κριμα του θεου εστιν κατα αληθειαν ("for we know that the judgment of God is according to truth") in ℵ C 33 it[d]. Though the manuscript evidence is evenly divided between the two readings, the variant is probably the result of scribes failing to realize that 2:2 is not intended as a causal explanation of 2:1, but is intended as a further explanation (Dunn 1988, 78).

Romans 2:16a

Many scholars point out that 2:16 logically follows 2:13, not 2:15. To fix the problem, some scholars are inclined to move 2:16 after 2:13. For example, Moffatt moved 2:16 to follow 2:13 in his translation of the NT. Pohlenz conjectured (see NA[27]'s critical apparatus) that the verse should have begun with και δικαιωθησονται ("and they will be justified"). But there is no textual evidence to warrant these changes. TR WH NU accurately reflect the results of dictation—in that Paul often diverged from the main grammatical development and then returned to it later. The NJB displays this anacoluthon by placing ellipses at the beginning of 2:16.

In this verse Paul uses the unique expression κατα το ευαγγελιον μου ("according to my gospel"). Paul considered the gospel he preached to be his gospel in the sense that he presented salvation as available by God's grace to Jew and Gentile alike through faith in Christ Jesus. This gospel was committed to him by a revelation from Jesus Christ (see 16:25; 1 Cor 15:1; 2 Cor 11:7; Gal 1:11-17; Eph 3:1-6). Therefore, he was sure that the gospel he preached was authentic, emboldening him to call it "my gospel." Perhaps taking offense to Paul personalizing the gospel, some scribes and ancient translators (69 it[d] cop[sa]) omitted μου, making it "according to the gospel."

Romans 2:16b

WH NU	διὰ Χριστοῦ Ἰησοῦ "through Christ Jesus" (ℵ*[vid]) B 81 RSV ESV NASB NEB REB NAB NLT HCSB NET
variant 1/TR	δια Ιησου Χριστου "through Jesus Christ" ℵ[1] A Ψ 1739 Maj KJV NKJV NRSV NIV TNIV NJB
variant 2	δια Ιησου Χριστου του κυριου ημων "through Jesus Christ our Lord" D it[b,d] none

At the end of the verse, most manuscripts have the Lord's name as "Jesus Christ." But this probably reflects later usage. Paul was more prone to write "Christ Jesus," as is attested in the two earliest extant witnesses (א*vid B). Per course, KJV and NKJV followed TR, but why did NRSV, NIV, and TNIV, which normally follow the NU text? Perhaps it was due to inadvertence or deliberate conformity to English style.

Romans 2:17

WH NU	εἰ δὲ σὺ Ἰουδαῖος ἐπονομάζῃ "but if you call yourself a Jew" א A B D* Ψ 81 syr^p cop Clement NKJVmg RSV NRSV ESV NASB NIV TNIV NEB REB NJB NAB NLT HCSB NET
variant/TR	ιδε συ Ιουδαιος επονομαζη "look, you are called a Jew" D[2] 33 1739 1881 Maj syr^h KJV NKJV HCSBmg

The variant reading is probably the result of a scribal error that found its way into the majority of Byzantine manuscripts and TR. A scribe mistakenly wrote ιδε instead of ει δε—perhaps by an error of hearing (the two expressions sound alike). This would especially be true during the Byzantine era because multiple copies were often produced by one reader dictating the text to several scribes at the same time.

Romans 2:29

The scribes of 𝔓[113] א A D used the nomen sacrum for πνευματι (ΠΝΙ = "the Spirit") in the expression, "circumcision is of the heart, in spirit [or, Spirit], not of the letter." The use of the nomen sacrum shows that the scribes interpreted this verse to mean that Paul was speaking of an inward change of heart as produced by the divine Spirit—as is stated in the NLT, "it is a change of heart produced by God's Spirit." Had the scribes written out the word (in *plene*), as in B, it would denote that which is "spiritual" (as is understood by most modern versions—see, for example, RSV and NRSV).

Romans 3:4

In Romans (9:13; 10:15; 11:8), Paul's usual formula for introducing OT Scriptures is καθως γεγραπται ("as it is written"). That expression in this verse, however, has inferior support (A D G Maj) by comparison to the variant that reads καθαπερ γεγραπται ("just as it is written"), found in א B Ψ (so WH contra NU).

Romans 3:9

TR WH NU	Τί οὖν; προεχόμεθα; οὐ πάντως. "What then? Do we excel? [Or, Why then do we excel?] Not at all." א B (D[2]) 0219vid 33 1739 Maj (A L προεχωμεθα) all

variant 1 Τι ουν προεχομεθα;
"What then can we offer?" [= "Are we worse off?"]
P
NJBmg

variant 2 τι ουν προκατεχομεν περισσον;
"Why then are we especially superior?"
D* G (Ψ)
none

Although the first three words could be joined together to form one question (as in the first variant), the answer given does not readily follow. Therefore, it is best to treat the text as having two questions (as in TR WH NU), followed by one answer. Dahl (1982, 184-204) argued that the first variant (which he translates as "what do we hold before us as a defense?") is quite early and may be original because it appears that ου παντως was added to satisfy the demand for an answer. However, it could be argued just as easily that ου παντως was dropped because it does not really answer the three-word question (τι ουν προεχομεθα) when it is understood to mean "why then do we excel?" Therefore, it is quite likely that the difficulty of the expression prompted an omission in the first variant and an expansion in the second.

Romans 3:22

WH NU πίστεως Ἰησοῦ Χριστοῦ εἰς πάντας τοὺς πιστεύοντας
"faith (or, faithfulness) in (or, of) Jesus Christ for all the ones believing"
(𝔓[40]) ℵ* A (B omits Ιησου) C Ψ 81 1739 Clement
NKJVmg RSV NRSV ESV NASB NIV TNIV NEB REB NJB NAB NLT HCSB NET

variant 1 πιστεως Ιησου Χριστου επι παντας τους πιστευοντας
"faith (or, faithfulness) in (or, of) Jesus Christ upon all the ones believing"
vg[st,ww] Ambrosiaster Pelagius
none

variant 2/TR πιστεως Ιησου Χριστου εις παντας και επι παντας τους πιστευοντας
"faith (or, faithfulness) in (or, of) Jesus Christ for all and upon all the ones believing"
ℵ[2] D F G 33 Maj it
KJV NKJV

The WH text, in deference to B, brackets Ιησου. The reading is quite certain, having the support of several MSS, including 𝔓[40] (of the third century), even though the scribe of 𝔓[40] mistakenly wrote $\overline{\text{ΥΙ ΧΥ}}$ instead of $\overline{\text{ΙΥ ΧΥ}}$ (see *Text of Earliest MSS*, 152). The expanded reading in the second variant is a conflation of the WH NU reading and the first variant. The Latin Vulgate was probably responsible for the conflation occurring in Western, then Byzantine texts. The conflated reading is a more emphatic way of saying that all believers, without distinction or exception, are put in possession of this gratuitous justification purely by faith placed in Christ Jesus. (For a good note on whether the translation should read "faith in Christ Jesus" (an objective genitive) or "faithfulness of Christ Jesus" (a subjective genitive), see NET. In this verse, most commentators recommend "faith in Christ Jesus.")

Romans 3:25

TR NU read δια της πιστεως εν τω αυτου αιματι ("through the faith in his blood"), following the testimony of 𝔓40vid B C3 D2 Ψ 33 Maj. A variant reading in ℵ C* D* F G 0219vid 1739, followed by WH, does not include the article της ("the") before πιστεως ("faith"). It is difficult to determine which reading is original. It is possible that the article was inserted later (note how it was added to C and D by later hands) to refer the reader to the "faith in Jesus Christ" mentioned in 3:22 (cf. 3:30 and 31, where the definite article is used in the same manner). As such, it has the effect of saying, "whom God put forth as a propitiation, effective through this kind of faith in his blood." Codex A omits δια της πιστεως completely—hence, the rendering, "whom God put forth as a propitiation by his blood."

Romans 3:26

TR WH NU end this verse with the words πιστεως Ιησου ("faith in Jesus," or "faithfulness of Jesus"), as supported by ℵ A B C Maj copsa. All English versions follow. However, there are some significant variants in the textual tradition: (1) πιστεως Ιησου Χριστου ("faith in Jesus Christ," or "faithfulness of Jesus Christ") in 629 it syrp copbo; (2) πιστεως ("faith") in F G; and (3) πιστεως Ιησουν ("faith in Jesus") D L Ψ 33. The first variant is a natural scribal expansion—divine titles were typically enlarged, especially Jesus' name. The second variant may be an attempt to avoid the ambiguity of the genitive Ιησου after πιστεως, which could mean "faith in Jesus" (an objective genitive) or "Jesus' faithfulness" (a subjective genitive). The third variant (the accusative Ιησουν) is either a scribal error or an attempt to avoid the ambiguity of the genitive.

Romans 4:1a

TR NU	Τί οὖν ἐροῦμεν εὑρηκέναι 'Αβραάμ; "What then shall we say Abraham to have found?" 𝔓40vid ℵ*,2 A C* (33 Maj) syr cop KJV NKJV RSVmg NRSV ESV NASB NIV TNIV NJBmg NAB NLT HCSB NET
variant/WH	Τι ουν ερουμεν Αβρααμ; "What then shall we say [about] Abraham?" B 1739 RSV NRSVmg ESVmg NEB REB NJB

𝔓40vid is not cited in NA27 or UBS4, but it shows the word ευ]ρηκεν[αι (see *Text of Earliest MSS,* 152). The verb ευρηκεναι ("to have found," "to have discovered") is not present in B and 1739, and it appears in different places in the manuscript tradition. As such, it could be argued that Paul did not write it. But it seems likely that it was originally part of the text—for several reasons. First, the word is present in the earliest witness, 𝔓40vid. Second, the verb was often used in the Septuagint in the context of finding grace or finding mercy from God (see Gen 18:3). Third, the grammar of the sentence requires an infinitive to complete the sense. In any event, several English versions adopted the variant and supplied "about" after "say" to give the sentence proper sense.

Romans 4:1b

WH NU	Ἀβραὰμ τὸν προπάτορα ἡμῶν "Abraham our forefather" ℵ* A B C* syr cop RSV ESV NASB NIV TNIV (NAB NLT) HCSB
variant/TR	Αβρααμ τον πατερα ημων "Abraham our father" ℵ[1] C[3] D F G Ψ (33) (Maj) KJV NKJV NRSV NEB REB NJB NET

The WH NU reading has solid support from the four earliest manuscripts. The Greek word προπατορα ("forefather"), a *hapax legomenon* in the NT, was changed in later manuscripts to the more common πατερα ("father"). Indeed, the NT often identifies Abraham as "our father," as in verse 12 of this chapter (see also John 8:53; Acts 7:2). The point of calling Abraham "our forefather" at this point is to designate Abraham as the pioneer of faith and prototypical believer for all who believe, whether Jew or Gentile. Some modern versions reflect the reading in TR by having the rendering "ancestor."

Romans 4:12

The last clause of this verse should refer to the same class of people as the first part—the circumcised who have been justified by faith are also those who walk in the same steps as faithful Abraham. However, the expression αλλα και τοις ("but also to the ones") points to another group. Westcott and Hort (1882, 108), following T. Beza, considered that there must have been a primitive error in transcription and that what should have been written was και αυτοις ("even to them").

Romans 4:18

Two Western witnesses (F G) expand the quotation of Gen 15:5 (ουτως εσται το σπερμα σου—"so will be your seed") by adding words from a parallel passage, Gen 22:17, ως οι αστερες του ουρανου και το αμμον της θαλασσης ("as the stars of heaven and the sand of the sea"). While this expansion augments the extent of God's promise to Abraham, it detracts from a major thrust of Paul's argument, which is to prove that Abraham was justified by God prior to his circumcision (see 4:4-12). A quotation from Gen 22:17 incorrectly places it after Abraham's circumcision (Gen 17).

Romans 4:19a

WH NU	κατενόησεν τὸ ἑαυτοῦ σῶμα "he considered his own body" ℵ A B C 81 1739 cop RSV NRSV ESV NASB NIV TNIV NEB REB NJB NAB NLT HCSB NET
variant/TR	ου κατενοησεν το εαυτου σωμα "he did not consider his own body" D F G Ψ 33 Maj it KJV NKJV HCSBmg NETmg

See next note.

Romans 4:19b

TR WH NU	[ἤδη] νενεκρωμένον "already dead" ℵ A C D Ψ 33 Maj all
variant	νενεκρωμενον "dead" B F G 1739 1881 NETmg

The manuscript evidence is mixed as to the exclusion or inclusion of ου ("not") and ηδη ("already"). ℵ A C say that Abraham "considered his own body to have died already." D Ψ Maj say that Abraham "did not consider his own body to have died already." B and 1739 say that Abraham "considered his own body to have died." This last reading is most likely original. The idea is that Abraham took account of his real situation. He knew that his own body was dead, as well as Sarah's womb, with respect to producing offspring; in spite of this, he believed God's promise that his seed would be multiplied into a great nation. The negation of the verb (he did *not* consider) has Abraham looking away or disregarding his situation. This appears to be a scribal adjustment, as is the addition of ηδη ("already"). All the modern English versions indicate that Abraham was giving his body consideration, yet not one English version simply says that he "considered his body dead." All modify it in some fashion or another—the most popular expression being, "he considered his body as good as dead."

Romans 5:1

TR NU	εἰρήνην ἔχομεν πρὸς τὸν θεόν "we have peace with God" ℵ[1] B[2] F G P Ψ 0220[vid] 1739[c] KJV NKJV RSV NRSV ESV NASB NIV TNIV NEBmg REB NJB NAB NLT HCSB NET
variant/WH	ειρηνην εχωμεν προς τον θεον "let us have peace with God" ℵ* A B* C D L 33 1739* Marcion NKJVmg RSVmg NRSVmg ESVmg NASBmg NIVmg TNIVmg NEB REBmg NJBmg HCSBmg NETmg

The variant reading, a subjunctive, has excellent textual support (ℵ* A B* C); as such it was the reading adopted by WH. However, an earlier manuscript, 0220 (late third century), was discovered in the middle of the twentieth century, having the reading εχομεν, an indicative. Manuscript 0220 provides the earliest testimony to the TR NU reading. However, it is listed as "vid" because the Greek verb has broken letters. Hatch (1952, 83) examined the manuscript and provided this observation:

> "The first three letters of the verb stood at the end of the line, and a small hole in the vellum has destroyed the χ and the letter which followed it. However, the letter after χ must have been an ο, because the above-mentioned hole does not occupy enough space to contain the letters χ and ω. On the other hand, this space would be completely filled by a χ and an ο. Moreover, a little ink can be seen at the top and right hand side of the hole, and this seems to be the remainder of a letter with a closed top. Hence, the letter must have been an ο and not an ω. [This] fragment is the earliest known witness for εχομεν in Romans 5:1, and thus the indicative in this verse is attested by a good text which antedates the earliest testimony for the subjunctive."

The reading with an indicative ("we have peace") suits the context better than the subjunctive ("let us have peace" or "let us be at peace"). Paul was speaking of what the believers have received as a result of being justified: They have peace with God and access to him through the Lord Jesus Christ. It does not seem likely that Paul was urging the believers to "be at peace with God" (see NJBmg). If so, it is more likely that he would have used a different verb, ποιησωμεν ("let us make").

However, the translators of the NEB adopted the variant reading because they viewed εχωμεν as introducing the first of three hortative clauses, followed by καυχωμεθα ("let us boast"—if taken as a subjunctive and not an indicative) in both 5:2 and 5:3 (see Tasker 1964, 434). However, it is more likely that all three predicates are indicatives, stating that we have peace with God and, as such, are boasting in the hope of glory and in our sufferings, which intensify our hope.

Romans 5:2

TR WH NU	προσαγωγὴν ἐσχήκαμεν [τῇ πίστει] "we have access by the faith" ℵ* C Ψ 33 1739 Maj KJV NKJV RSVmg NRSVmg ESV NASB NIV TNIV NJB NAB NLT HCSB NET
variant 1	προσαγωγην εσχηκαμεν "we have access" B D F G 0220 cop[sa] RSV NRSV ESVmg NEB REB HCSBmg
variant 2	προσαγωγην εσχηκαμεν εν τη πιστει "we have access in the faith" ℵ[1] A none

The textual evidence, early and diverse, supports the exclusion of τη πιστει. WH NU bracket the words to signal doubts about their inclusion. At any rate, the sense is not affected with or without the words "by faith" or "in faith," because Paul had previously made it clear that the Christian's new standing with God—in righteousness—is based on faith in Christ (5:1). It is likely that the phrase was added in 5:2 in order to maintain Paul's emphasis. Four versions (RSV, NRSV, NEB, and REB) render the verse without the phrase.

Romans 5:11

Most manuscripts (ℵ A C D F G Ψ 1881* Maj) read του κυριου ημων Ιησου Χριστου ("our Lord Jesus Christ"), but B 1739 1881[c] have the shortened form, του κυριου ημων Ιησου ("our Lord Jesus"). Since scribes had a tendency to expand divine titles, the shorter form is likely original. WH bracket Χριστου to signal their doubts about its inclusion.

Romans 5:12

In a few Western witnesses (D F G it), the words ο θανατος are excluded, thereby leaving it ambiguous as to what came to all men—sin or death. If the omission was purposeful, then the creator of this text (the D-reviser) wanted the text to say: "and so it [sin or death] came to all men, for all have sinned." All other witnesses (including ℵ A B C 0220[vid] 33 1739) include the specific subject, ο θανατος ("death"), producing the reading "and so death came to all men."

Romans 6:3

A few manuscripts do not have the double title, Χριστον Ιησουν ("Christ Jesus"). 𝔓[40vid] B 104[c] 326 read only Χριστον ("Christ"). Based on the testimony of B, WH bracketed the title Χριστον; to this testimony can now be added 𝔓[40vid], for which I have provided a newly reconstructed fragment (see *Text of Earliest MSS,* 153; Comfort 1999, 220-221).

Romans 6:11

WH NU Χριστῷ Ἰησοῦ
"Christ Jesus"
𝔓[46] A B D F G Ψ 1739*
RSV NRSV ESV NASB NIV TNIV NEB REB NJB NAB NLT HCSB NET

variant/TR Χριστω Ιησου τω κυριω ημων
"Christ Jesus our Lord"
𝔓[94vid] ℵ C 33 1739[c] Maj cop[bo]
KJV NKJV HCSBmg

The expansion of divine titles was a common phenomenon among scribes, especially in later stages of the history of textual transmission—as is reflected in Maj and TR (followed by KJV and NKJV). This expansion conforms to Paul's usage in 1:4; 4:24; 5:21; 6:23; 7:25; 8:39.

Romans 6:12

WH NU τὸ ὑπακούειν ταῖς ἐπιθυμίαις αὐτοῦ
"to obey its [the body's] desires"
𝔓[94] ℵ A B C* 1739 syr[p] cop
RSV NRSV ESV TNIV NEB REB NJB NAB NLT HCSB NET

variant 1 το υπακουειν αυτη
"to obey it [sin]"
𝔓[46] D F G it[b] Irenaeus Tertullian Ambrosiaster
NASB NIV

variant 2/TR το υπακουειν αυτη εν ταις επιθυμιαις αυτου
"to obey it [sin] in its [the body's] desires"
C[3] Ψ (33) Maj syr[h]
KJV NKJV HCSBmg

The discrepancy between the WH NU reading and the first variant is that the former says that Christians should avoid giving in to the desires of the body, whereas the latter says that Christians should avoid yielding to sin. With the respect to the exegetical development of the following verses, Paul's emphasis is clearly on the Christian's battle with indwelling sin, not with the body per se. But since the body is the dwelling place of sin (7:24), it is not unreasonable to imagine Paul telling Christians to not give in to bodily desires. However, this could be misconstrued as dualism.

In any event, both readings have good exegetical support and textual support. The second variant is clearly a conflation of the other two variants, thereby revealing that both readings were popular and persistent in the transmission of the text. The NIV translators made their translation ambiguous by allowing for the possibility that the pronoun "its" could refer to both "sin" and the "body": "Do not let sin reign in your mortal bodies so that you obey its evil desires."

Romans 6:16

A few manuscripts (D 1739* cop[sa]) omit εις θανατον ("resulting in death"), probably by accident (it was correctly inserted in 1739[c]).

Romans 6:17

Influenced by verses such as Matt 5:8; 2 Tim 2:22; and 1 Pet 1:22 (see note), the scribe of Codex Alexandrinus (A) added καθαρας ("pure") before καρδιας ("heart").

Romans 6:19

B and syr[p] omit εις την ανομιαν ("resulting in lawlessness"). The omission is not accidental; it is the result of scribal pruning, inasmuch as it seems tautologous for the text to say "you present your members as slaves to impurity and lawlessness resulting in lawlessness." In deference to the testimony of B, WH bracket the expression.

Romans 7:6

WH NU	κατηργήθημεν ἀπὸ τοῦ νόμου ἀποθανόντες ἐν ᾧ κατειχόμεθα "we were freed from the law, having died [to that] in which we were held" ℵ A B C Ψ 33 1739 cop syr NKJV RSV NRSV ESV NASB NIV TNIV NEB REB NJB NAB NLT HCSB NET
variant 1	κατηργηθημεν απο του θανατου εν ω κατειχομεθα "we were freed from the death in which we were held" D F G it Ambrosiaster none
variant 2/TR	κατηργηθημεν απο του νομου αποθανοντος εν ω κατειχομεθα "we were freed from the law—bringing death—in which were held" no MSS [but printed in Elzevir's Greek edition] KJV

The first variant is a scribal attempt to avoid coupling "the law" with "death." It is simpler to say that Christians are freed from "death" than "the law of death." The second variant was printed in Elzevir's Greek New Testament (1624), based on a conjecture of Beza, who misunderstood Chrysostom. It was then translated in the KJV, which seems to indicate that the law generates death: "We are delivered from the law, that being dead wherein we were held." The WH NU reading has the best support and perfectly suits the context, which indicates that the believers are freed from the tyranny of the law because they have died to the law in Christ's death.

Romans 7:14

Instead of the sentence beginning with οιδαμεν ("we know"), some scholars prefer the division of words, οιδα μεν ("I know, on the one hand"). In the early manuscripts letters were written continuously with no break between words (*scriptio continua*). Therefore, there is no way to know what Paul originally intended. Scribes of later manuscripts (such as the scribe of the ninth-century manuscript 33) divided the words as οιδα μεν. Though either reading works fine, οιδαμεν is a word Paul frequently used to include his readers.

Romans 7:17

The verb in the second clause of this verse should be ενοικουσα ("indwelling"), as in WH, instead of οικουσα, as printed in NU, because ενοικουσα has the support of ℵ and B and because the following expression εν εμοι ("in me") would have influenced scribes to drop the prefix εν. Paul spoke of indwelling sin with the same kind of verbiage as he spoke of the indwelling Spirit (see 8:9, 11).

Romans 7:18

WH NU	τὸ δὲ κατεργάζεσθαι τὸ καλὸν οὔ "the accomplishing of the good is not [present]" ℵ A B C 1739 cop RSV NRSV ESV NASB NIV TNIV NEB REB NJB NAB NLT HCSB NET
variant 1/TR	το δε κατεργαζεσθαι το καλον ουχ ευρισκω "the good I do not find [how] to accomplish" D F G Ψ Maj syr KJV NKJV
variant 2	το δε κατεργαζεσθαι το καλον ου γινισκω "the good I do not know [how] to accomplish" 2127 none

The sentence ends abruptly—but cogently—with ου. In effect, Paul was saying "the willingness to do what is right is always there, but the carrying out of it isn't." Scribes, uncomfortable with a sentence ending with a negative, added one of two verbs, both of which require the addition of "how" (in English) to make complete sense.

Romans 7:20

The word εγω ("I") is not found in B C D (so WH), nor is it necessary to the sentence. Of course, its superfluity could account for its omission by excision. It is included in NU on the support of ℵ A Ψ 33 1739 Maj.

Romans 7:22

The expression τω νομω του θεου ("the law of God") appears as τω νομω του νοος ("the law of the mind") in B—probably as the result of conformation to 7:23.

Romans 7:23-25

A few scholars have conjectured that the last sentence of 7:25 ("so then with my mind I serve the law of God, but with my flesh, the law of sin") belongs after 7:23. For example, Moffatt placed it before verse 24 in his translation, arguing that it "seems its original and logical position before the climax of verse 24." Zuntz (1953, 16) said it "may be an addition by Paul himself or a summing up by some early reader; in any case, its present position is unsuitable and suggests that a marginal gloss has been inserted into the text." A marginal note in the NJB has a similar position: "This sentence, which would come more naturally before v. 24, seems to have been added—perhaps by Paul himself." Indeed, since not one witness shows this sentence to precede 7:24, it must be judged that Paul himself added this sentence as a summary to the previous section (7:7-24).

Romans 7:25

WH NU	χάρις δὲ τῷ θεῷ "but thanks [be] to God" א[1] C[2] Ψ 33 (omit δε B cop[sa] Origen) RSV NRSV ESV NASB NIV TNIV NEB REB NJB NAB NLT HCSB NET
variant 1/TR	ευχαριστω τω θεω "I thank God" א* A 1739 1881 Maj syr KJV NKJV NETmg
variant 2	η χαρις του θεου "the grace of God" D it none
variant 3	η χαρις κυριου "the grace of [the] Lord" F G none

Exasperated with his wretched condition, Paul asked the rhetorical question, "Who will rescue me from this body of death?" The answers vary according to the variant readings. According to WH NU, Paul thanks God for the deliverance "through our Lord Jesus Christ." This thanks is made explicit in TR, the first variant. The answer, according to the second and third variants, is that the grace of God (or, the grace of the Lord) will rescue him.

Romans 8:1

WH NU	end verse at Χριστῷ Ἰησοῦ ("Christ Jesus") א* B C[2] D* (F G with space for addition) 1739 it[b,d*] cop NKJVmg RSV NRSV ESV NASB NIV TNIV NEB REB NJB NAB NLT HCSB NET
variant 1	add μη κατα σαρκα περιπατουσιν "not walking according to the flesh" A D[1] Ψ syr[p] none
variant 2/TR	add μη κατα σαρκα περιπατουσιν αλλα κατα πνευμα "not walking according to the flesh, but according to Spirit" א[2] D[2] 33[vid] Maj syr[h] KJV NKJV ESVmg NIVmg HCSBmg NETmg

According to the best manuscript evidence, followed by all modern versions, Paul simply states, "there is therefore no condemnation to those in Christ Jesus." This was then expanded in two phases—the latter being the more accretive and more recent. Both expansions were taken from 8:4, and both attempt to clarify how it is that believers are no longer under condemnation. But

Paul does not attempt to put any condition on our justification. The condition—"not according to flesh but according to spirit"—is placed in 8:4, which speaks of the righteous requirements of the law being fulfilled in those who do not live in the flesh but in the Spirit.

Romans 8:2

WH NU	ἠλευθέρωσεν σε "freed you" ℵ B (F) G 1739* NRSV ESV NASB TNIV NEB REB NJB NAB NLT HCSB NET
variant 1/TR	ηλευθερωσεν με "freed me" A D 1739[c] Maj syr[h] cop[sa] KJV NKJV RSV NRSVmg ESVmg NASBmg NIV TNIVmg NJBmg NLTmg HCSBmg NETmg
variant 2	ηλευθερωσεν ημας "freed us" Ψ cop[bo] NRSVmg NJBmg NLTmg

The manuscript evidence affirms the WH NU reading, as does the fact that it is the most difficult reading. The first variant is an attempt to conjoin the end of chapter 7 with the beginning of chapter 8 by making Paul the subject. The second variant exhibits scribal conformity to the immediate context, where Paul pluralizes his audience (see 8:4, 9 etc.). As such, it is evident that Paul's personal outcry concludes at 7:25 and that a new didactic discourse begins at 8:1. What is unusual is that he addresses a singular subject, which must be the local church in Rome, since we know of no other individual whom Paul would have addressed.

Romans 8:11a

NU	ὁ ἐγείρας Χριστὸν ἐκ νεκρῶν "the one having raised Christ from the dead" B D[2] F G cop[sa] Marcion KJV NKJV NRSV NIV TNIV NAB HCSB NET
variant 1/WH	ο εγειρας εκ νεκρων Χριστον Ιησουν "the one having raised Christ Jesus from the dead" ℵ* A (C) 1739 (D* with a transposition) RSV NRSVmg ESV NASB NEB REB NJB NLT NETmg
variant 2/TR	ο εγειρας τον Χριστον εκ νεκρων "the one having raised the Christ from the dead" ℵ[2] Ψ 33 Maj NRSVmg

The only merit to the reading of the NU text is that it is the shortest, thereby casting suspicion on the other readings as being products of scribal expansion. However, the editors of NU were categorically suspicious of a reading supported by B with D F G (see TCGNT on 8:11b); so it seems inconsistent that this reading would be accepted for the text on the basis of B D[2] F G. But this is the result of an atomistic eclectic method. In this light, it seems just as likely that Paul wrote what appears in WH, for this reading has good support and is the most difficult syntactically—inasmuch as Paul usually said it in this order: (1) having been raised, (2) Christ, (3) from the dead. The English versions are curiously diverse here. KJV and NKJV do not reflect the definite article before "Christ," even though it is almost certain that the translators had TR in front of them.

Romans 8:11b

WH NU — διὰ τοῦ ἐνοικοῦντος αὐτοῦ πνεύματος ἐν ὑμῖν
"through his Spirit dwelling in you"
ℵ A C P[c] syr[h]
KJV NKJV RSV NRSV ESV NASB NIV NEB REB NJB NAB NLT HCSB NET

variant/TR — δια τον ενοικουν αυτου πνευμα εν υμιν
"because of his Spirit dwelling in you"
B D F G Ψ 33 1739 Maj it
NRSVmg NASBmg TNIV HCSBmg NETmg

According to Pseudo-Athanasius (*Dial.* 3.20), this textual variant may have been influenced by early debates between the heretical Macedonians (who denied the deity of the Holy Spirit) and the orthodox (who affirmed the Holy Spirit's deity). The Macedonians preferred the variant reading because it indicates that God will act independently in giving resurrection life to all who are indwelt by the Spirit ("who will give life to your mortal bodies because of his Spirit dwelling in you"). This divine action does not happen with the Spirit's participation but because of (accusative case) the Spirit's indwelling. The orthodox preferred the WH NU reading because it includes the participation of the Spirit, who not only regenerates the spirits of believers but will also resurrect them. This affirms the Spirit's divine activity from the time of regeneration, continuing with his indwelling, to the time of resurrection.

All versions except TNIV follow the WH NU reading, including KJV and NKJV, which here deviate from TR.

Romans 8:13

Usually, "the body" is considered neutral in Pauline terminology, whereas the "flesh" is the fallen Adamic nature. But here Paul charges the believers to put to death the practices of the σωματος ("body"). Perhaps unsettled by this, some scribes (D F G) changed σωματος to σαρκος ("flesh").

Romans 8:20-21

TR WH NU — τὸν ὑποτάξαντα, ἐφ᾽ ἐλπίδι [21]ὅτι καὶ αὐτὴ ἡ κτίσις ἐλευθερωθήσεται
"the one subjecting [it], in hope [21] that the creation itself will be freed"
𝔓[27vid] 𝔓[46] A B C D[2] Ψ 0289 Maj
NRSV ESV NASB NIV TNIV NEBmg REB NAB NLT HCSB NET

variant — τον υποταξαντα εφ ελπιδι, [21]διοτι και αυτη η κτισις ελευθερωθησεται
"the one subjecting it in hope, [21] because the creation itself will be freed"
ℵ D* F G
KJV NKJV RSV NASBmg TNIVmg NEB NJB

𝔓[46] ℵ B* D* F G Ψ read εφ ελπιδι, whereas 𝔓[27] A B[2] C D[2] Maj read επ ελπιδι—with no change in meaning. The letter spacing of 𝔓[27] strongly suggests that it read οτι instead of διοτι (see *Text of Earliest MSS,* 120).

This is a difficult variant-unit to sort out because the word οτι (in the TR WH NU reading) and the word διοτι (in the variant) can both be translated "because." But only οτι can be rendered "that"—which permits the first rendering, a rendering that connects together the last two words of 8:20 with the beginning of 8:21 ("for the creation was subjected to futility, not willingly, but because of the one subjecting it, in hope that the creation itself will be freed from the slavery of corruption"). This reading indicates that God subjected creation to futility—but only for a time; in the end he will release creation from its bondage at the same time he releases his children from mortality.

The testimony of 𝔓[46] with A B C caused the editors of NA[26] to adopt the first reading over the second—a change from previous editions of the Nestle text. This reading is followed by several modern versions.

Romans 8:23

TR WH NU	include υἱοθεσίαν ("sonship") ℵ A B C 33 1739 Maj syr cop KJV NKJV RSV NRSV ESV NASB NIV TNIV NEB REB NJBmg NAB NLT HCSB NET
variant	exclude υιοθεσιαν ("sonship") 𝔓[27vid?] 𝔓[46vid] D F G NEBmg NJB

Even though there is a lacuna in 𝔓[27] for this verse, the average line lengths for 𝔓[27] strongly suggest that this manuscript did not include υιοθεσιαν (see *Text of Earliest MSS,* 120). Even though 𝔓[46] is listed as "vid," the spacing makes it certain that it did not include υιοθεσιαν (see *Text of Earliest MSS,* 210).

According to the printed text of TR WH NU, followed by nearly all English versions (except NJB), the verse reads, "we also groan in ourselves, eagerly expecting sonship [or, adoption], the redemption of our bodies." This reading has an appositive: "the redemption of our bodies" describes what the sonship or adoption is. The variant reading lacks the appositive: "we also groan in ourselves, eagerly expecting the redemption of our bodies." This variant has early support, especially if we add the testimony of 𝔓[27]. However, the omission of "sonship" in the variant is usually explained as a scribal effort to eliminate a seeming contradiction between Paul's statement here about sonship and the statement he made in 8:15 ("you have received a spirit of sonship"). But in 8:15 Paul spoke about the believers' initial reception of the Spirit of sonship; whereas in 8:23 he was speaking about the ultimate appropriation of each son's inheritance—i.e., the possession of a glorified body (see NJBmg). Thus, there is not really a contradiction. Nonetheless, it is imagined that certain scribes may have thought there was, so they eliminated the word. However, it is possible that certain scribes borrowed the word from 8:15 to make it clear that the ultimate redemption equals the consummation of υιοθεσιαν. In any event, the NJB was the only version to follow the shorter reading, while it is noted in the NEBmg (see Tasker's reason, 1964, 434).

Romans 8:24

Although there are several variant readings in this verse, they basically yield one of two statements. Some manuscripts (𝔓[46] B* 1739[mg]) read τις ("who"), while others (ℵ[2] B[2] A C) read τι ("why"); and some manuscripts (𝔓[46] ℵ[2] B C D) read ελπιζει ("hopes"), while others (ℵ* A

1739^{mg}) read υπομενει ("waits," "endures"). Thus, the text could read, "who hopes for what he sees" (as in RSV NASBmg NIV NEB NJB NLT) or "why wait for what he sees" (as in NASB NEBmg NLTmg). The first reading (both instances) was adopted by the NU editors because of the weight of 𝔓^{46} with B, and was followed by most modern versions.

Romans 8:26

WH NU τὸ πνεῦμα ὑπερεντυγχάνει
"the Spirit intercedes"
𝔓^{27vid} 𝔓$^{46vid?}$ ℵ* A B D F G 1739
NKJVmg NRSV HCSBmg

variant/TR το πνευμα υπερεντυγχανει υπερ ημων
"the Spirit intercedes on our behalf"
ℵ^{2} C Ψ 33 Maj it syr cop
KJV NKJV RSV NRSVmg ESV NASB NIV TNIV NEB REB NJB NAB NLT HCSB NET

𝔓^{27vid} is not cited in NA^{27} or UBS^{4}, but it supports the text. 𝔓^{27} shows the last part of the word υπερεντυγχανει with no room on the following line to fit υπερ ημων before the next visible word, καρδιας in 8:27 (see *Text of Earliest MSS,* 120). 𝔓^{46} has a lacuna at this point; however, a reconstruction of the text, according to the average line lengths, strongly suggests that it did not include υπερ ημων (see *Text of Earliest MSS,* 210).

The WH NU reading has excellent support, including 𝔓^{27vid} and probably 𝔓^{46}. The variant is a later scribal addition (found in TR) intended to make explicit what is already implicit in the text. Indeed, the prefix υπερ on υπερεντυγχανει signals intercessory benefaction. That is why ancient versions (Old Latin, Syriac, Coptic) and most modern English versions fill out the sentence with "for us," regardless of what textual variant they followed. The sentence can, however, make good sense in English without having to supply "for us," as in NRSV: "that very Spirit intercedes with sighs too deep for words."

Romans 8:28

TR NU πάντα συνεργεῖ εἰς ἀγαθόν
"everything works together for good" (or, "he works together everything for good")
ℵ C D F G Ψ 33 1739 Maj
KJV NKJV RSVmg NRSV ESV NASBmg NIVmg TNIVmg NEB REB NJBmg NAB NLTmg HCSB NET

variant/WH παντα συνεργει ο θεος εις αγαθον
"God works everything together for good"
(𝔓^{46} παν for παντα) A B cop^{sa}
RSV NRSVmg ESVmg NASB NIV TNIV NEBmg REBmg NJB NLT HCSBmg NETmg

This is not an easy textual decision because the earliest Greek manuscripts support the inclusion of ο θεος, whereas internal considerations would argue against its inclusion. As such, it can be argued that the scribes of 𝔓^{46} A and B added ο θεος ("God") to an existing text in order to clarify the ambiguity—παντα can be taken as nominative (= "everything works together") or an accusative (= "he works everything together"). In the context of Romans 8, it would seem that the subject is "God" or "the Spirit" (both mentioned in 8:27). God or the Spirit is the one who works all things together for good. Of the two, "God" is the more natural subject—and one that Paul very likely would have used or intended. Perhaps it is best to leave the words ο θεος in the text but inside brackets, so as to signal doubts about their originality (as in WH). The split among the translations also displays this uncertainty.

Romans 8:34a

WH NU	Χριστὸς [Ἰησοῦς] "Christ Jesus" 𝔓46vid? ℵ A C F G L Ψ 33 syr^h it cop^bo RSV NRSV ESV NASB NIV TNIV NJB NAB NLT HCSB NETmg
variant/TR	Χριστος "Christ" B D 0289 1739 Maj syr^p cop^sa KJV NKJV NEB REB NET

The testimony of 𝔓46vid in support of the WH NU reading is questionable because the lacuna is in the right-hand margin, wherein the scribe may or may not have fit the three-letter nomen sacrum form of Ιησους. The textual evidence slightly favors the full title, "Christ Jesus." However, since scribes had a tendency to expand divine titles, it could be argued that the simple title "Christ" is original. All things considered, it is best to retain Ιησους in brackets, as in WH NU.

Romans 8:34b

TR NU	ἐγερθείς "having been raised" 𝔓27vid 𝔓46 ℵ2 B D F G 33 Maj syr KJV NKJV NRSV ESV NASB NIV TNIV REB NAB NLT HCSB NET
variant/WH	εγερθεις εκ νεκρων "having been raised from the dead" ℵ* A C 0289vid cop RSV NASBmg NEB NJB

The first reading has strong external and internal support. The three earliest witnesses contain this shorter reading. Though there is a lacuna in 𝔓27, there is not enough space to fit εκ νεκρων ("from the dead") on the line (see *Text of Earliest MSS,* 120). Scribes would have easily been tempted to add the words "from the dead," as this reflects Pauline style (see 4:24; 6:4, 9; 7:4; 8:11; 10:9). The simple expression εγερθεις is parallel to the preceding ο αποθανων ("the one having died"). WH bracketed εκ νεκρων on the basis of B etc.; the additional evidence of the papyri would have probably caused them to omit these words. The translators of RSV, NEB, and NJB, who had the testimony of 𝔓27vid and 𝔓46 available at the time of translation, still added "from the dead," thinking it necessary to fill out the expression "whom he raised" with the usual formula "from the dead."

Romans 8:34c

TR NU	ὃς καί ἐστιν ἐν δεξιᾷ τοῦ θεοῦ "who is also at the right hand of God" 𝔓27 𝔓46 ℵ2 B D F G Ψ Maj (KJV) NKJV (NJB) NAB

variant/WH οσ εστιν εν δεξια του θεου
"who is at the right hand of God"
ℵ* A C 0289[vid] it cop[bo]
RSV NRSV ESV NASB NIV TNIV NEB REB NLT HCSB NET

The presence of και in the two early papyri (𝔓[27] 𝔓[46]) was sufficient cause for the editors of NA[26] to change their edition, which previously followed ℵ* A C. The word και was probably dropped in these manuscripts to avoid redundancy with the next clause, which includes και.

Romans 8:35

TR WH NU τῆς ἀγάπης τοῦ Χριστοῦ
"the love of Christ"
C D F G Ψ 33 1739 Maj it syr cop Tertullian
all

variant 1 της αγαπης του θεου
"the love of God"
ℵ cop[sa]
NASBmg

variant 2 της αγαπης του θεου εν Χριστω Ιησου
"the love of God in Christ Jesus"
B
none

The TR WH NU reading has sufficient testimony to warrant its acceptance. Unfortunately, both 𝔓[27] and 𝔓[46] have a lacuna in this part of the verse, but it is certain neither one had the longer reading of the second variant. Both variants are probably the result of scribal harmonization to 8:39—the first in short form and the second in longer form. Paul's subject in 8:34 is "Christ"; he is the one who died, rose from the dead, was exalted to God's right hand, and now makes intercession for us. Paul's proclamation in 8:35 is that nothing can separate us from Christ's love.

Romans 8:37

Most manuscripts (including 𝔓[27] and 𝔓[46]) read υπερνικωμεν δια του αγαπησαντος ημας ("we more than conquer through him who loved us"), but three Western manuscripts (D F G) read υπερνικωμεν δια τον αγαπησαντα ημας ("we more than conquer on account of him who loved us")—"thus narrowing the reference to a look back to the past event of Christ's death rather than maintaining the sense of a continuing flow of sustaining love" (Dunn 1988, 497).

Romans 9:4a

All three editions (TR WH NU) read αι διαθηκαι ("the covenants"), with the support of ℵ C Ψ 0285 33 1739 Maj it syr cop[bo]. This is reflected in all the English versions. A variant reading is η διαθηκη ("the covenant"), found in 𝔓[46] B D F G it[b] cop[sa]. None of the English versions reflect this reading or even note it. Scholars generally observe that it is much more likely that the scribes changed the plural reading to a singular than vice versa, because the plural reading is more difficult. The natural tendency is to think that God enacted only one covenant with Israel—that which came to be known in the New Testament as the old covenant. Actually, God initiated covenants with Abraham, with the nation of Israel at Sinai, and with David, and these may be the "covenants" referred to here. Alternatively, the plural "covenants" could refer to the one covenant made with Abraham (Gen 15), then renewed with Isaac (Gen 17), and then Jacob (Gen 28). Everett F. Harrison (1976, 102) said, "There is rather good manuscript evidence for 'covenant' rather than 'covenants,' but this reading can hardly be original, for it would most naturally suggest the Mosaic covenant (2 Cor 3:6, 14), which would render the next item [in Paul's list], the reception of the law, quite unnecessary."

Romans 9:4b

All three editions (TR WH NU) read αι επαγγελιαι ("the promises"), with the support of ℵ C Ψ 0285 33 Maj it syr. All the English versions follow this. However, other manuscripts (𝔓[46] D F G cop[boMSS]) read η επαγγελια ("the promise"). This variant is perhaps the result of scribal editorialization—making all the items in the list of Israel's privileges singular. Thus, in 𝔓[46], as well as in the Western witnesses D F G, the Jews have been given one covenant and one promise. But whereas it is not difficult to understand the change from "covenants" to "covenant" (see note above), it is more difficult to imagine why scribes would change "promises" to "promise," because the plural implicates all the promises God made to Abraham, Isaac, and Jacob (Gen 12:7; 13:14-17; 17:4-8; 22:16-18; 26:3; 28:13) and because the plural "promises" is more prevalent in the NT. The singular "promise" probably refers to the unique messianic promise: God would send the Messiah to the Jews (see 2 Sam 7:12, 16; Isa 9:6; Jer 23:5; 31:31; Ezek 34:23; 37:24). This provides a fitting platform for the next verse, wherein Paul extols the Messiah, who, being God, came in the flesh as a Jew, for the Jews.

Romans 9:5

The punctuation of this verse is critical to its exegesis. The punctuation functions to either conjoin the expression ο ων επι παντων θεος ευλογητος εις τους αιωνας ("the one being over all God blessed forever") with ο Χριστος το κατα σαρκα ("the Christ according to the flesh") or to separate it. Depending upon which punctuation is employed, Christ is said to be God or not to be God—obviously a crucial difference. One of the following two renderings represents the original thought:

> "whose are the fathers, and from whom is the Christ according to the flesh, who is over all, God[,] blessed forever. Amen." (KJV NKJV RSVmg NRSV ESV NASB NIV TNIV NEBmg REBmg NJB NABmg NLT HCSB NET).
>
> "whose are the fathers, and from whom is the Christ according to the flesh. God, who is over all, be blessed forever. Amen." (RSV NRSVmg NIVmg TNIVmg NEB REB NAB NLTmg HCSBmg NETmg)

In the first rendering the comma following "flesh" signals that the following words constitute appositional expressions; hence, "Christ" is (1) "over all," (2) "God," and (3) "blessed forever." This is rendered quite well in the RSVmg as "Christ, who is God over all, blessed forever." In the second rendering, the period following "flesh" separates "the Christ" from these expressions—which are, instead, turned into a sentence of their own by inserting a predicate: "God, who is over all, be blessed forever!" (A slight modification on the second rendering is "whose are the fathers, and from whom is the Christ according to the flesh, who is over all. God be blessed forever! Amen.")

When we look to the ancient authorities for some help on this matter, we discover that the earliest witness, 𝔓[46], has a lacuna after σαρκα, so we cannot be certain if it was punctuated or not; but it seems that the allotted space could not allow for a punctuation mark by the hand of the original scribe. There is no punctuation mark in ℵ and D. A midpoint colon follows σαρκα in F G Ψ 049 056. A high point colon occurs after σαρκα in L 0142 0151. A space is left following the point in 0151 and following σαρκα in C. It is also reported that B[2] (second corrector) added a midpoint after σαρκα (see Harris 1992, 149). This data tells us that some of the earliest scribes left the text ambiguous, and that later ones did not. The upshot is that it is the task of interpreters to determine whether Christ was being called God or God was being praised.

Westcott and Hort (1882, 109-110) indicated that most of the ante-Nicene and post-Nicene fathers understood the expression "God over all" to describe "Christ." The primary reason for this is that it naturally follows the syntax of the Greek, whereas the doxology ("God be praised!") is asyndetic and non-Pauline. It is highly unlikely that Paul would abruptly, even sporadically, insert a praise to God the Father at the end of his enumeration of the divine privileges and promises given to the Jews. To the contrary, he was culminating that list with the greatest blessing of all—that the Christ, who is God over all, blessed forever, would come from the Jewish race! How could the Jews then reject him? This created anguish in Paul's heart, which was all the more intensified by the fact that the Jews were rejecting God himself in the person of Christ. As John said, the Word who was God came to his very own people, but his very people did not recognize him—and, worse yet, did not receive him (see John 1:1, 10-11).

The conjecture proposed by some scholars (see NA[27]) that the text originally read ων ο instead of ο ων provides for an easy way out of the exegetical dilemma inasmuch as ων ο produces the translation, "whose are the fathers, and whose is the Christ according to the flesh, and whose is the God over all blessed forever. Amen." In this rendering Christ and God, as separate entities, are two possessions of the Israelites. But the conjecture is suspect as a means of obviating one of the few Pauline affirmations of Christ's deity. The other affirmations occur in Phil 2:6 (which says that Christ lives in the form of God, equal with God in all things); Col 2:9 (which says that all the fullness of the Godhead bodily dwells in Christ); and Titus 2:13 (wherein Christ is called God and Savior). (For a complete review of this issue, see Harris 1992, 143-172, who concludes that Paul was affirming Jesus' deity in this verse. Also see TCGNT for a lengthy discussion by Metzger).

As for English versions, several affirm the interpretation that Christ is God over all, eternally blessed (KJV NKJV NRSV ESV NASB NIV TNIV NJB NLT HCSB NET). And most of the versions that do not present this in the text do note it as an alternative (RSVmg NEBmg REBmg NABmg).

Romans 9:6

To relieve the expression παντες οι εξ Ισραηλ ουτοι Ισραηλ ("not all the ones of Israel are Israel") of any ambiguity, a few Western witnesses (D F G) changed the last word to Ισραηλιται ("Israelites").

Romans 9:27

Defending υπολειμμα ("remnant"), found in ℵ* A B 81 1739[c] (so WH NU), Dunn (1988, 569) argues that the reading καταλειμμα ("remnant"), found in 𝔓[46] ℵ[1] D F G 1739* Maj (so TR), is the result of scribal conformity to the Septuagint version of Isa 10:22 and Hos 1:10 [2:1 LXX], the text cited here. But we cannot be certain about this, because Paul originally took many of the OT citations in this chapter from the Septuagint, as opposed to the Masoretic Text. So Paul could be responsible for the Septuagint-like reading. The stronger argument for υπολειμμα is that it is a *hapax legomenon,* which scribes changed to the more ordinary word.

Romans 9:28

WH NU λόγον γὰρ συντελῶν καὶ συντέμνων ποιήσει κύριος ἐπὶ τῆς γῆς
"For the Lord will execute his word upon the earth, finishing it and cutting it short."
𝔓46 ℵ* A B 1739 1881 syrp copsa,bo
NKJVmg RSV NRSV ESV NASB NIV TNIV NEB REB NJB NAB NLT HCSB NET

variant/TR Λογον γαρ συντελων και συντεμων εν δικαιοσυνη οτι λογον συντετμημενον ποιησει κυριος επι της γης
"For the Lord will execute his word in righteousness, because the Lord will make a short matter [or, work] upon the earth."
ℵ2 D F G Ψ 33 Maj syrh
KJV NKJV NJBmg NETmg

It is slightly possible that the shorter reading of the text is the result of a scribal error—the eye of a scribe passing from συντεμνων to συντετμημενον, but it is more likely that the variant found in later manuscripts is the result of scribal conformity to the fuller text of the Septuagint (Isa 10:22-23).

Romans 9:31

WH NU εἰς νόμον οὐκ ἔφθασεν
"did not attain [that] law"
𝔓46vid ℵ* A B D G 1739 cop
NKJVmg RSV NRSV ESV NASB NIV TNIV NEB REB NJB NAB NLT HCSB NET

variant/TR εις νομον δικαιοσυνης ουκ εφθασεν
"did not attain [that] law of righteousness"
ℵ2 F Ψ Maj it syr
KJV NKJV HCSBmg

The WH NU reading has early and diverse documentary support. The clause prior to this one is διωκων νομον δικαιοσυνης ("pursuing a law of righteousness"). The slight accretion in the variant is the result of scribal expansion (found in TR), borrowing from the previous clause.

Romans 9:32

WH NU ἐξ ἔργων
"by works"
ℵ* A B F G 1739 cop
NKJVmg RSV NRSV ESV NASB NIV TNIV NEB REB NJB NAB (NLT) HCSB NET

variant/TR εξ εργων νομου
"by works of law"
ℵ2 D Ψ 33 Maj syr
KJV NKJV HCSBmg NETmg

The WH NU reading has excellent documentary support. The variant (printed in TR) is the result of scribal conformity to Paul's normal usage (see 3:20, 28; Gal 2:16).

Romans 9:33

By way of conformity to 10:11, the Majority Text (so TR) inserts πας ("everyone") before ο πιστευων ("believing"). But Paul's citation of Isa 28:16 in 9:33 differs from that in 10:11, thereby showing that Paul was not intent on quoting the OT verbatim.

Romans 10:1

WH NU ὑπὲρ αὐτῶν
"[my prayer] for them"
𝔓46 ℵ* A B D F G 1739 syr (ℵ2 P Ψ 33 add εστιν [is])
NKJVmg RSV NRSV ESV NASB NEB REB NJB NAB HCSB

variant/TR υπερ του Ισραηλ εστιν
"[my prayer] for Israel is"
Maj
KJV NKJV NIV TNIV NLT HCSBmg NET

The WH NU reading has excellent documentary support; the two variants are obvious scribal accretions. The variant supplies a verb (as do most English versions) and has an inserted subject, "Israel," because this verse begins a new section, and scribes felt that new sections required a reintroduction of the subject (see 9:31) for the sake of oral reading. Several English versions do likewise.

Romans 10:5

TR NU Μωϋσῆς γὰρ γράφει τὴν δικαιοσύνην τὴν ἐκ [του] νόμου ὅτι ὁ ποιήσας αὐτὰ ἄνθρωπος ζήσεται ἐν αὐτοῖς
"For Moses writes concerning the righteousness which is of the law, that 'the man who does them will live by them.'"
𝔓46 D2 F G Maj
KJV NKJV NRSV ESV NIV TNIV NEB REB NJB NAB NLT HCSB NET

variant/WH Μωυσης γαρ γραφει οτι την δικαιοσυνην την εκ του νομου ο ποιησας ανθρωπος ζησεται εν αυτη
"For Moses writes that, 'the man who does the righteousness which is based on the law will live by it.'"
ℵ* (A D* 33*) 1739 cop (ℵ2 B omit του)
RSV NASB

There are several other variants in this verse, but these two represent the most critical differences in the reading of the text. The positioning of οτι in the first reading has the function of introducing an OT quotation (Lev 18:5); the positioning of οτι in the second reading makes δικαιοσυνην ("righteousness") the object of ποιησας ("doing") (TCGNT). The TR NU reading follows the Septuagint in that it also has the αυτα/αυτοις combination. Uncomfortable with these plurals being used to describe "the law," scribes deleted the first and changed the second to a singular (αυτη). Some of these same scribes moved οτι to immediately follow γραφει (a more natural syntactical order) without realizing that Paul wanted to quote only "the man who does them will live by them." In this verse, the testimony of 𝔓46 offsets that of the Alexandrian witnesses, and thereby warrants a change from WH. Most English versions reflect this.

Romans 10:8

Some manuscripts (D F G 33) and versions (it[a] cop[bo]) add a subject, η γραφη ("the Scripture"), to the beginning of the sentence. But the subject is not "the Scripture" (though the Scripture is quoted); the subject is "the righteousness that comes from faith" (10:6). This righteousness, personified, makes the declaration found in Scripture that "the word is near you—in your mouth and in your heart."

Romans 10:9

TR NU	ἐὰν ὁμολογήσῃς ἐν τῷ στόματί σου κύριον Ἰησοῦν "if you confess with your mouth, 'Lord Jesus'" א D F G Ψ 33 1739 Maj it syr cop all
variant 1	εαν ομολογησης εν τω στοματι σου κυριου Ιησουν Χριστον "if you confess with your mouth, 'Lord Jesus Christ'" 𝔓[46] A NLTmg
variant 2/WH	εαν ομολογησης το ρημα εν τω στοματι σου κυριου Ιησουν "if you confess the word with your mouth [that] the Lord [is] Jesus" B (81) cop[sa] Clement ASVmg

UBS[3] attaches "vid" to 𝔓[46], probably based on Kenyon's reconstruction. However, the reading is definitely "Lord Jesus Christ," as can be seen in the reconstruction in *Text of Earliest MSS,* 213. This has been corrected in UBS[4].

The TR NU reading, which has marginally good documentary support, could reflect a scribal tendency to conform the Christian confession to that found in 1 Cor 12:3. But it is more likely that the first variant reflects the early Christians' tendency to name their Savior fully (as the Lord Jesus Christ) when making a confession of faith (see Phil 2:11). And the second variant carries over the term το ρημα ("the word" = "the confession") from the previous verse, which defines το ρημα as the gospel preached by Paul. As such, "to confess the word" is tantamount to ascribing faith in the gospel, which is a prerequisite to making the confession, "Jesus is Lord." Therefore, the second variant could also reflect the early church's practice of insisting on faith prior to oral proclamation.

Romans 10:15

WH NU	ὡς ὡραῖοι οἱ πόδες "how beautiful the feet" 𝔓[46] א* A B C 1739 cop NKJVmg RSV NRSV ESV NASB NIV TNIV NEB REB NJB NAB NLT HCSB NET
variant/TR	ως ωραιοι οι ποδες των ευαγγελιζομενων ειρηνην "how beautiful the feet of those preaching good news of peace" א[2] D F G Ψ Maj it syr KJV NKJV HCSBmg

After this passage, in both readings, the verse reads των ευαγγελιζομενων τα αγαθα ("the ones preaching good news of good things"). It is possible, but not likely (given the early dates and wide range of witnesses), that the shorter reading is the result of a scribal accident—the eye of a scribe passing over the first occurrence of των ευαγγελιζομενων to the second. It is more likely that the variant is the result of scribal conformity to the Septuagint. It was a common phenomenon for scribes to conform OT citations in the NT to the exact verbiage of the OT text. In this case, the variant shows conformity to Isa 52:7 (LXX) and Nah 1:15 (LXX).

Romans 10:17

WH NU	ῥήματος Χριστοῦ "[the] word of Christ" 𝔓[46vid] ℵ* B C D* 1739 it cop RSV NRSV ESV NASB NIV TNIV NEB REB NJB NAB NLT HCSB NET
variant 1/TR	ρηματος θεου "[the] word of God" ℵ[1] A D[1] Ψ 33 Maj syr Clement KJV NKJV NRSVmg NJBmg HCSBmg NETmg
variant 2	ρηματος "[the] word" F G none

Although the earliest manuscript, 𝔓[46], is listed as "vid," my examination of the actual papyrus affirms that the reading is the nomen sacrum for "Christ" (see *Text of Earliest MSS,* 214). The documentary evidence for the WH NU reading is early and diverse. The unique expression, "word of Christ" (appearing only here in the NT), was changed in many later manuscripts to "the word of God" by way of conformity to the more usual NT expression (see Luke 3:2; John 3:34; Eph 6:17; Heb 6:5); in other manuscripts (F G) it was reduced to the simple "word."

Romans 10:20

A few Western witnesses (D* F G) omit αποτολμα και ("is very bold and"), shortening the first sentence to Ησαιας δε λεγει ("but Isaiah says"). Since αποτολμα occurs only here in the whole Greek Bible, it would be most unusual that scribes would have added it. Rather, its unusualness caused its deletion, or it was deleted because scribes could not understand how Isaiah was being bold in his prediction. Nonetheless, the statement is bold because it declares that the Gentiles, who did not seek God or ask for God, were given a revelation of God.

Romans 10:21

A few Western witnesses (F G Ambrosiaster) omit και αντιλεγοντα ("and opposing"). The words may have been dropped accidentally, due to homoeoteleuton (απειθουντα/αντιλεγοντα), or purposefully because there are no corresponding words in the Hebrew text of Isa 65:2 (the verse cited here).

Romans 11:1

The three editions (TR WH NU) read τον λαον αυτου ("his people"), with the excellent support of ℵ B C Ψ 33 1739 syr cop. All English versions follow. However, there are three variants: (1) την κληρονομιαν αυτου ("his inheritance") in F G it[b]; (2) την κληρονομιαν αυτου ον προεγνω ("his inheritance whom he foreknew") in 𝔓[46]; (3) τον λαον αυτου ον προεγνω ("his people whom he foreknew") in ℵ[2] A D*.

There are two sets of variants here: one that identifies the direct object as God's "people" (with or without the qualifier "whom he foreknew") and another that identifies the object as God's "inheritance" (with or without the qualifier "whom he foreknew"). The qualifier, ον προεγνω ("whom he foreknew"), was probably added from 11:2, but it is more difficult to say where the term κληρονομιαν ("inheritance") came from. It may have been borrowed from Ps 94:14 (LXX, cited in 11:2), but it is also possible that "inheritance" was original and then changed to "people" because the latter is more understandable. God's people are often spoken of as being his inheritance (see, for example, Pss 33:12; 79:1; Isa 19:25). As such, it is far stronger to speak of God casting away what actually belongs to him than to simply speak of casting away his people. Furthermore, it is possible that had "inheritance" originally been in the text, scribes would have deleted the qualifier "whom he foreknew" because the two expressions do not naturally go together. Therefore, if a vote is to be given to the most difficult reading, 𝔓[46] wins. As such, the text could have originally read "his inheritance whom he foreknew." If so, the last three words were dropped in certain manuscripts, and then "inheritance" was changed to "people" in other manuscripts. But until other manuscripts are discovered that have this reading, the singular testimony of 𝔓[46] cannot be accepted.

Romans 11:6

WH NU — οὐκέτι γίνεται χάρις
"it [grace] would no longer be grace"
𝔓[46] ℵ* A C D F G 1739 cop
NKJVmg RSV NRSV ESV NASB NIV TNIV NEB REB NJB NAB NLT HCSB NET

variant/TR — ουκετι γινεται χαρις. ει δε εξ εργων ουκετι εστι χαρις, επει το εργον ουκετι εστιν εργον
"it [grace] would no longer be grace. But if it is of works, then it is no longer grace; otherwise work is no longer work."
(B omits εστι and replaces final εργον with χαρις) ℵ[2] Ψ 33[vid] Maj (syr)
KJV NKJV NRSVmg NIVmg HCSBmg

The textual evidence in favor of the shorter reading is impressive. Furthermore, there is no good reason to account for the omission of the second sentence (in the variant) had it been originally in the epistle. Thus, the variant is likely an interpolation created perhaps as early as the fourth century. But this gloss does not help elucidate the passage, which plainly depicts the nature of grace as being a free gift, not a reward for doing work. The gloss adds nothing to this, but rather detracts with the opaque statement, "otherwise work is no longer work."

Romans 11:17

WH NU — τῆς ῥίζης τῆς πιότητος τῆς ἐλαίας
"of the root of the richness (or, the root, the richness) of the olive tree"
ℵ* B C Ψ it[b]
RSVmg NRSV ESV NASB NIV TNIV NJB NAB HCSB

variant 1/TR της ριζης και της πιοτητος της ελαιας
"of the root and (= even) of the richness of the olive tree"
ℵ[2] A D[2] 33 1739 Maj syr
KJV NKJV NEB REB HCSBmg NET

variant 2 της πιοτητος της ελαιας
"of the richness of the olive tree"
𝔓[46] D* F G cop[bo]
RSV NRSVmg ESVmg NLT

In defense of the WH NU reading, it could be said that scribes wanted to break up the string of three genitives by adding και (variant 1) or dropping one of the items (variant 2). The και probably functions epexegetically—that is, to be a partaker of the root is to be a partaker of the olive tree's rich supply. The second variant simplifies the image. If this reading is original, then it has to be argued that της ριζης ("of the root") was added from the immediate context (11:16, 18).

Quite manifestly, the rendering in the RSV displays the influence of 𝔓[46]. However, translations since the RSV have, for the most part, adhered to the first reading. The NLT is an exception.

Romans 11:21

TR NU include μη πως ("perhaps"), having the testimony of 𝔓[46] D F G Ψ Maj. WH excludes it, with the testimony of ℵ A B C P 1739. The first reading yields the sense, "if God did not spare the natural branches, perhaps he will not spare you." The second reading is more straightforward: "if God did not spare the natural branches, he will not spare you."

It is difficult to determine if μη πως is a scribal addition or part of the original wording of the text. Did a scribe add it so as to soften the possibility of divine retribution against the Gentile believers (the unnatural branches grafted into the olive tree)? If so, we would expect a similar change to 11:23, but there was no such change. Thus, it seems that μη πως (a typical Pauline expression) functions as a double negative strengthening Paul's assertion: "neither will he in any way spare you." Given this meaning, it is not difficult to imagine how scribes would have deleted μη πως as being superfluous.

Romans 11:22

WH NU χρηστότης θεοῦ
"God's kindness"
𝔓[46] ℵ A B C D* 1739 cop
NKJVmg RSV NRSV ESV NASB (NIV) NEB REB NAB (NLT) HCSB NET

variant/TR χρηστοτητα
"kindness"
D[2] F G Ψ 33 Maj it syr
KJV NKJV TNIV (NJB)

The documentary evidence strongly favors the WH NU reading. The variant, showing up later in the manuscript tradition (so TR), is the result of scribes stylizing the text to achieve symmetry. The verse begins with "the kindness and severity of God," so it is a sharper chiasm to have "severity . . . kindness" rather than "severity . . . kindness of God."

Romans 11:31

WH NU	[νῦν] ἐλεηθῶσιν "now receive mercy" א B D* RSVmg NRSV ESV NASB NIV TNIV NEB REB NAB NLTmg HCSB NET
variant 1/TR	ελεηθωσιν "receive mercy" 𝔓46vid A D2 F G Ψ Maj KJV NKJV RSV NRSVmg ESVmg TNIVmg NJB NLT HCSBmg NETmg
variant 2	υστερον ελεηθωσιν "later receive mercy" 33 365 copsa NLTmg NETmg

Given the documentary evidence and internal considerations, it is quite likely that νυν ("now") never appeared in the original text; it was probably added as a natural scribal carryover from the two previous clauses, both of which have νυν. The temporal significance of νυν ("now") is also exegetically problematic inasmuch as it seems that Paul had been arguing that the Jews would receive God's mercy later—that is, after the full number of Gentiles had come into the kingdom, God would mercifully allow the Jews to come in (see 11:25). This accounts for the change in the second variant.

Romans 12:9

The rare and strong word αποστυγουντες ("abhorring") was changed in some Western witnesses (F G it syr) to the more ordinary and somewhat softer word, μισουντες ("hating").

Romans 12:11

TR WH NU	τῷ κυρίῳ δουλεύοντες "serving the Lord" 𝔓46 א A B D2 1739 Maj Greek MSSaccording to Origen and Ambrosiaster syr cop all
variant	τω καιρω δουλευοντες "serving the time" (or, "meeting the demands of the hour") D*,c F G Latin MSSaccording to Origen and Jerome NEBmg NJBmg

At first glance, it would seem that the word κυριω ("Lord") could easily be mistaken for καιρω ("time"). But this is only true in printed Greek editions. In ancient manuscripts κυριω was contracted as a nomen sacrum, $\overline{\kappa\omega}$, which hardly looks like καιρω. Metzger (TCGNT), however, thought καιρω could have been written as κ/ρω (κ/ = και). But the overbar on divine titles is a distinguishing feature that would be difficult to misread. Thus, the variant cannot be easily dismissed as a copyist's error.

The variant is likely the result of a scribe (or Latin translator—as evidenced by the comments of Origen and Jerome) attempting to make a general exhortation ("serving the Lord") more specific, especially since the surrounding exhortations are quite pointed. Indeed, the two prior exhortations (see above) evoke the images of zeal and fervency. What better way to continue the image than by adding a note about being opportunistic? This is, in fact, one of the ideas behind the idiom τω καιρω δουλευοντες—i.e., "taking advantage of the time" (cf. Eph 5:16).

The TR WH NU reading has the earliest and best documentary support; furthermore, it accords with Pauline thought (see 14:18; 16:18; 1 Thess 1:9). Paul calls the believers to serve the Lord with all spiritual zeal. In other words, having zeal and fervency in the Spirit is not an end to itself; the goal of a fervent spiritual life is to serve the Lord.

Romans 12:13

Instead of the expression, ταις χρειαις των αγιων κοινωνουντες ("contributing to the needs of the saints"), a few Western witnesses (D* F G) have the curious expression, ταις μνειαις των αγιων κοινωνουντες ("participating in the remembrance of the saints"). Westcott and Hort (1882, 110) surmised that the change could have been the result of a scribe mistaking one word for the other (χρειαις/μνειαις), but this seems unlikely. Rather, it seems more plausible that a scribe misconstrued Paul's exhortation to be one that urged prayer or intercession (μνειαις) for the saints (see 1:9; Eph 1:16; Phil 1:3; 1 Thess 1:2). But Paul never used μνειαις with κοινωνεω. More remotely, the change could possibly be a scribal attempt to reflect the practice of intercession for the dead (Dunn 1988, 737)—or, a little more likely, the practice (which began as early as the second century) of commemorating saints of the past, especially the martyrs (Cranfield 1979, 638).

Romans 12:14

TR NU	εὐλογεῖτε τοὺς διώκοντας [ὑμᾶς] "bless the ones persecuting you" ℵ A D Ψ Maj syr all
variant/WH	ευλογειτε τους διωκοντας "bless the ones persecuting" 𝔓46 B 1739 Clement NASBmg

The word υμας is bracketed in NA27/UBS4 to reflect the editors' indecision about its inclusion. (The word was not included in previous editions of the Nestle text.) It should not be included in the text, because superior documentary evidence favors its exclusion and because it would be natural for scribes (and translators) to supply an object after the verb. The addition also harmonizes this verse to verses such as Matt 5:44 and Luke 6:28.

Romans 12:17

Paul told his readers to take care of doing good "in the sight of all people" (ενωπιον παντων ανθρωπων). This has good support (𝔓46 ℵ A* B D), and is the reading found in TR WH NU. This was expanded to ενωπιον του θεου και ανθρωπων ("in the sight of God and in the sight of men") in A1, and to ου μονον ενωπιον του θεου αλλα και ανθρωπων ("not only in the sight of God but also in the sight of men") in F and G.

According to the TR WH NU reading, Paul was exhorting the believers to live exemplary lives in the presence of others. Perhaps this disturbed various scribes who considered it inappropriate for believers to display their spirituality only before men. Thus, they added the phrase which indicates that God is watching how Christians live. The first variant imitates Prov 3:4 (see LXX), and the second variant conforms to 2 Cor 8:21.

Romans 13:1

The TR WH NU reading is πασα ψυχη εξουσιαις υπερεχουσαις υποτασσεσθω ("let every person [soul] be subject to the governing authorities"), based on ℵ A B D[2] Ψ 33 1739 Maj. A variant reads πασαις εξουσιαις υπερεχουσαις υποτασσεσθε ("you [plural] be subject to all governing authorities"), found in 𝔓[46] D* F G. The TR WH NU reading reflects a Hebraism ("let every soul be subject"), and for this reason could be considered Pauline. The variant reading makes the command more directly personal (see comments on 13:5), and calls for submission to *all* governing authorities. This differs from the TR WH NU reading, which calls upon *everyone* to be submissive to the government.

Romans 13:9

WH NU — οὐ κλέψεις
"you shall not steal"
𝔓[46] A B D F G L Ψ 1739 syr[p] cop[sa]
NKJVmg RSV NRSV ESV NASB NIV TNIV NEB REB NJB NAB NLT HCSB NET

variant/TR — ου κλεψεις, ου ψευδομαρτυρησεις
"you shall not steal, you shall not bear false witness"
ℵ (P) 048 it[b] (syr[h]) cop[bo]
KJV NKJV NJBmg HCSBmg

According to early and diverse textual attestation, the commandments cited in this epistle are the seventh, sixth, eighth, and tenth of the Ten Commandments (in that order—see the MT of Exod 20:15-17 and Deut 5:19-21; the Nash Papyrus has it in the order Paul wrote). The ninth commandment ("you shall not bear false witness") was added later by scribes who wanted to complete the list. But Paul's intention was not to list all the commandments (note the following words: "and if there is any other commandment") but to call to mind that all the commandments that deal with interpersonal relationships are encapsulated in the one commandment, "love your neighbor as yourself" (Lev 19:18).

Romans 13:11

In the first part of this verse, NA[27] and UBS[4] cite 𝔓[46vid] in support of the variant reading ημας ("us") versus the reading of the text υμας ("you"), supported by ℵ* A B C P. However, it is just as likely that the transcription of 𝔓[46] should be υμας (see *Text of Earliest MSS*, 218).

Romans 13:12

The Greek verb αποθωμεθα ("let us put away") is printed in the NU text based on the authority of ℵ A B C D[1] 048 33 Maj. But the variant reading αποβαλωμεθα ("let us throw off"), found in 𝔓[46] D* F G, is just as likely the original reading because it is a *hapax legomenon* in the Pauline corpus—in contrast to αποτιθημι, which occurs in other Pauline writings in similar contexts (Eph 4:22, 25; Col 3:8). (See Cranfield 1979, 685 for a more detailed explanation.)

A few manuscripts (including A and D) change οπλα ("armor") to εργα ("works") in order to achieve verbal symmetry in the verse: "let us throw off the works of darkness, and put on the works of light." But Paul's use of οπλα has the dual image of weaponry (to fight against the works of darkness) and of protective clothing (to withstand the works of darkness).

Romans 13:14

TR WH NU τὸν κύριον Ἰησοῦν Χριστόν
"the Lord Jesus Christ"
ℵ A C D F G Ψ 0285[vid] 33 Maj syr
KJV NKJV RSV NRSV ESV NASB NIV TNIV NJB NAB NLT HCSB NET

variant 1 τον Χριστον Ιησουν
"the Christ, Jesus" (or, "Christ Jesus")
B Clement
NEB REB

variant 2 τον κυριον Ιησουν
"the Lord Jesus"
1739 1881
none

variant 3 Ιησουν Χριστον τον κυριον ημων
"Jesus Christ our Lord"
𝔓[46] it[a,t]
none

Variations on the name of Jesus appear all throughout the textual tradition. In most cases, the best rule of thumb is to give preference to the best documentary attestation. In this case, the widest range of witnesses support the TR WH NU reading.

Romans 14:4

WH NU ὁ κύριος
"the Lord" (or, "the Master")
𝔓[46] ℵ A B C P Ψ syr[p] cop
RSV NRSV ESV NASB NIV TNIV NEB REB NJB NAB NLT HCSB NET

variant/TR ο θεος
"God"
D F G 048 33 1739 Maj syr[h]
KJV NKJV NRSVmg HCSBmg NETmg

It is important to note that κυριος appears twice in this verse—with perhaps two different denotations. The verse in full context reads, as in the NEB, "Who are you to pass judgment on someone else's servant? Whether he stands or falls is his own Master's business; and stand he will, because his Master has power to enable him to stand." In this version, both occurrences of κυριος ("Master/Lord") are divine titles. According to other translations (see NIV NRSV NJB), the first κυριος is taken to denote a human master, and the second to denote the Lord—as in the NIV ("To his own master he stands or falls. And he will stand, for the Lord is able to make him stand.") The difference in interpretation has to do with whether one sees Paul addressing slaves or Christians in general. Nearly all scribes (as reflected in WH NU) made both occurrences of κυριος nomina sacra, thereby indicating the interpretation that the passage speaks about every Christian's relationship to their Lord. Codex C, however, has the first κυριος written in *plene,* and the second as a nomen sacrum (paralleling NIV NRSV NJB). As for the textual variant, the best documentary evidence favors κυριος, which could be rendered as "Lord" or as "Master." The substitution of θεος ("God") in later manuscripts was influenced by 14:3.

Romans 14:6

WH NU ὁ φρονῶν τὴν ἡμέραν κυρίῳ φρονεῖ
"the one regarding the day regards it to the Lord"
𝔓[46] א A B C[2vid] D F G 048 1739
NKJVmg RSV NRSV ESV NASB NIV TNIV NEB REB NJB NAB NLT HCSB NET

variant/TR ο φρονων την ημεραν κυριω φρονει και ο μη φρονων την ημεραν κυριω ου φρονει
"the one regarding the day regards it to the Lord, and the one not regarding the day, to the Lord regards it not"
C[3] Ψ 33 Maj syr
KJV NKJV HCSBmg

𝔓[46] is not cited in NA[26] or NA[27], but it clearly supports the text (see *Text of Earliest MSS,* 219). The earliest manuscripts (including 𝔓[46]) attest to the shorter text. To achieve balance with the second half of the verse, scribes added an antithetical statement. This change occurred late in the history of the transmission of the text and eventually found its way into TR, followed by KJV and NKJV, and noted in HCSB in deference to the KJV tradition.

Romans 14:9

WH NU Χριστὸς ἀπέθανεν καὶ ἔζησεν
"Christ died and lived"
א* A B C 1739 cop
NKJVmg RSV NRSV ESV NASB NIV TNIV NEB REB NJB NAB NLT HCSB NET

variant 1 Χριστος απεθανεν και ανεστη
"Christ died and rose"
F G Origen
none

variant 2/TR Χριστος και απεθανεν και ανεστη και εζησεν
"Christ also died and rose and lived"
א[2] (D*) Ψ 0209 33 Maj
KJV NKJV

The variants display scribal enhancements which attempt to elucidate the meaning of εζησεν, which obviously does not just mean that Christ "lived" but that he "lived again" after he rose from the dead.

Romans 14:10

WH NU τῷ βήματι τοῦ θεοῦ
"the judgment seat of God"
א* A B C* D F G 1739 cop
NKJVmg RSV NRSV ESV NASB NIV TNIV NEB REB NJB NAB NLT HCSB NET

variant/TR τω βηματι του Χριστου
"the judgment seat of Christ"
א[c] C[2] Ψ 048 0209 33 Maj
KJV NKJV HCSBmg

The WH NU reading has both early and diverse testimony. The change from "God" to "Christ" in TR was influenced by 14:9, where it speaks of Christ's death and resurrection. The natural follow-up would be to speak of Christ on the throne executing judgment. But Paul identifies "God" as the one who will execute the final judgment where, as it says in the next verse, "everyone will make confession to God."

Romans 14:12

A few manuscripts (B F G 1739 1881) have a shorter text here in that they do not include ουν ("therefore") and τω θεω ("to God")—the words are bracketed in WH NU. The resultant text would read: αρα εκαστος ημων περι εαυτου λογον δωσει ("so each of us will give an account concerning himself"). This shorter text could be original because the additional τω θεω looks like a scribal expansion influenced by 14:11.

Romans 14:18a

WH NU — ἐν τούτῳ
"in this [way]"
ℵ* A B C D* F G P 048 0209 1739
NKJVmg RSV NRSV ESV NASB NIV TNIV NEB REB NAB NLT HCSB NET

variant/TR — εν τουτοις
"in these things"
ℵ[1] D[2] Ψ 33 Maj syr
KJV NKJV NJB

In context, this statement has to do with "the one serving Christ" (ο δουλεων τω Χριστω). The vagueness of the passage prompted a correction in later manuscripts to make the deictic pronoun more inclusive.

Romans 14:18b

According to the NU text, the person serving Christ is said to be "well pleasing to God and approved by men" (ευαρεστος τω θεω και δοκιμος τοις ανθρωποις). Some scribes did not think it was right "that the approval of the general public should be a factor in weighing Christian conduct" (Dunn 1988, 816). Consequently, a slight correction was made in manuscripts B and G*: the addition of one *iota* to δοκιμος (δοκιμοις) altered the meaning to "well pleasing to God and to approved men."

Romans 14:19

Some Western witnesses (D* F G it) add φυλαζωμεν ("let us safeguard") to achieve balance with the first part of the verse.

Romans 14:20

By way of assimilation to Titus 1:15, the second corrector of ℵ expanded παντα μεν καθαρα ("all things are clean") to παντα μεν καθαρα τοις καθαροις ("all things are clean to the pure").

Romans 14:21

WH NU ὁ ἀδελφός σου προσκόπτει
"your brother stumbles"
(ℵ* λυπεται [is hurt] instead of προσκοπτει) A C 048 1739 syr[p] cop[bo]
NKJVmg RSV NRSV ESV NASB NIV TNIV NEB REB NAB NLT HCSB NET

variant/TR ο αδελφος σου προσκοπτει η σκανδαλιζεται η ασθενει
"your brother stumbles or is offended or is made weak"
𝔓[46vid] ℵ[2] B D F G Ψ 0209 33 Maj syr[h] cop[sa]
KJV NKJV ESVmg NJB HCSBmg NETmg

In defense of the WH NU reading, Metzger (TCGNT) said the variant was a Western expansion that gained wide circulation. The NJB per course followed the Western text here. But the variant reading can hardly be a Western invention when it appears in B and 𝔓[46vid]. Unfortunately, neither UBS[3] nor UBS[4] note that the earliest witness, 𝔓[46vid], supports the variant; but NA[26] does. (A letter count of the lacuna in 𝔓[46] affirms the citation in NA[26].) Thus, the variant reading has a slight advantage over the WH NU reading when it comes to documentary support. Furthermore, it is possible that the words η σκανδαλιζεται η ασθενει were accidentally dropped due to homoeoteleuton—the eye of the scribe passing from προσκοπτει to ασθενει; or the words may have been dropped because they were perceived as being superfluous. However, it is also possible that the words were added by scribes who were influenced by 1 Cor 8:11-13, a parallel passage.

Romans 14:22

WH NU σὺ πίστιν [ἣν] ἔχεις
"the faith which you have"
ℵ A B C 048
NKJVmg RSV NRSV ESV NASB NIV TNIV NEB REB NJB NAB NLT NET

variant/TR συ πιστιν εχεις;
"Do you have faith?"
D F G Ψ 1739 Maj it cop
KJV NKJV NJBmg HCSB NETmg

The omission of the relative pronoun ην ("which"), whether accidental or intentional, allows for the first clause to be read as a question (as in the variant). This creates better style, and is therefore suspect as a scribal improvement.

Romans 14:23

The doxology to the book of Romans, traditionally printed as 16:25-27 (the last three verses of the book), appears in various places in the extant manuscripts, including after 14:23. See note on 16:25-27 for a full discussion.

Romans 15:4

The unusual verb προεγραφη ("it was written before") was changed to the ordinary one, εγραφη ("it was written"), in B and some Old Latin manuscripts, thereby making it the same as the next verb in the verse. In other manuscripts (A Ψ 048 33 Maj) εγραφη, in the next phrase, was changed to προεγραφη to make it conform to the first verb.

A few manuscripts (B P Ψ 33) insert παντα ("all") before εις την ημετεραν διδασκαλιαν εγραφη ("was written for our instruction"), producing the rendering, "all was written for our instruction."

Romans 15:7

NU ὁ Χριστὸς προσελάβετο ὑμᾶς
"Christ received you"
ℵ A C D[2] F G Ψ 33 1739 Maj syr cop[bo]
NKJVmg RSV NRSV ESV NIV TNIV NJB NAB NLT HCSB NET

variant/TR WH ο Χριστος προσελαβετο ημας
"Christ received us"
B D* P 048 it[b] cop[sa]
KJV NKJV NASB NEB REB

The NU reading has diverse attestation and suits the context (see 15:5-7, where the second person plural pronoun is used). The lectionary use of the epistle would have likely prompted a change to the third person plural. Nonetheless, WH preferred the variant—probably on the basis of B and on the grounds that υμας could be scribal conformity to 15:5-7. The English versions are split on this issue.

Romans 15:9

Several witnesses (ℵ[2] 33 104 syr[h] cop[boMSS]) add κυριε ("Lord") after εξομολογησομαι σοι εν εθνεσιν ("I thank you among the Gentiles"), thereby conforming the text to the Septuagint version of Ps 17:49 (18:49 in English Bible) and 2 Sam 22:50.

Romans 15:11

WH NU read επαινεσατωσαν αυτον ("they were praising him") with the support of 𝔓[46] ℵ A B C D Ψ 1739. TR reads επαινεσατε αυτον ("praise him") with the support of F G 33 Maj syr. The change in TR (from a third person plural indicative verb to a second person plural imperative) is the result of scribal conformity to the Septuagint version of Ps 116:1 (117:1 in English Bible), the passage Paul cited here.

Romans 15:13

Several textual modifications occur in this verse (see note on 15:14). B F G heighten the expression πληρωσαι υμας πασης χαρας και ειρηνης ("fill you with all joy and peace") to πληροφορησαι υμας παση χαρα και ειρηνη ("you might be fully assured in all joy and peace"). D F G then omit εν τω πιστευειν ("in the believing"), and B omits the following phrase εις το περισσευειν ("in the abounding"). These omissions are probably accidental, due to haplography, the eye of a scribe passing over πιστευειν or περισσευειν.

Romans 15:14

There are numerous textual modifications beginning from this verse to the end of the epistle—perhaps revealing the textual fluidity of the latter part of Romans. If Paul published this epistle in two forms (see note on 14:23), then it is possible that Paul edited the final chapters himself; thus, some of the variants may not be the work of scribes but of the author himself. Of course, it is impossible to tell which is which without the autographs, so we have to resort to the usual craft of textual criticism of the extant manuscripts to determine the wording that is most likely original.

The earliest extant manuscript, 𝔓46, has a text that is significantly different from that printed in NU. In 15:14, for example, 𝔓46 has a considerably shorter text than that in the NU edition. 𝔓46 does not include μου ("my") after αδελφοι ("brothers"), και αυτοι ("also you"), and της ("the") before γνωσεως ("knowledge"). In most of these exclusions, 𝔓46 is supported by D F G, against ℵ and B, which include these words. Often, the shorter text is considered more likely to be original than the longer one, but in these instances the Alexandrian witness of ℵ B was deemed superior to that in 𝔓46 D F G—one proto-Alexandrian witness and three Western. However, the exclusion of της ("the") before γνωσεως ("knowledge") has more extensive support (𝔓46 A C D F G Maj) and could be original. One final note: The Majority Text reads αλλους ("others") instead of αλληλους ("one another"). This is a rare instance, however, when the Majority Text was not accepted by TR, KJV, or NKJV (see NKJVmg).

Romans 15:15

By virtue of having better documentary support (𝔓46 ℵ C D F G Ψ Maj), the reading τολμηροτερον ("boldly") ousted the reading which used to appear in the Nestle text prior to the twenty-sixth edition (also WH): τολμηροτερως (found in A B). Several manuscripts (𝔓46 ℵ2 D F G Ψ 33 Maj it syr) have an additional word, αδελφοι ("brothers"), after εγραψα υμιν ("I wrote to you"). This could be an addition for the sake of oral reading (TCGNT), but it does not seem necessary to add another αδελφοι when one appears in the previous verse. Therefore, it is quite possible that the second αδελφοι (in this verse) was deleted by many Alexandrian scribes (ℵ A B C) to avoid repetition.

Romans 15:17

𝔓46 has a singular variant at the beginning of the verse: ην εχω καυχησιν εν Χριστω ("which [offering] I have as a boast in Christ"). The scribe of 𝔓46 wanted to make it evidently clear that there is a connection between 15:17 and 15:16—Paul's boast is that the believing Gentiles had become an acceptable offering (προσφορα) to God. This same scribe wrote a shorter form of the messianic title, "Christ." This could have been accidental or a faithful copying of the original text, which became expanded with time—as was often the case with divine titles.

Romans 15:19

TR NU πνεύματος [θεοῦ]
"[the] Spirit of God"
𝔓46 ℵ D1 Ψ Maj syr
KJV NKJV NRSV ESV TNIV NJB NAB NLT HCSB NET

variant 1	πνευματος "[the] Spirit" B NRSVmg NASB NIV NLTmg
variant 2/WH	πνευματος αγιου "[the] Holy Spirit" A D*,2 F G 1739 1881 syr[hmg] cop RSV NRSVmg NEB REB NLTmg

Since scribes were known to expand titles of the divine Spirit, the reading in B could very well be original. The translators of the NIV must have thought so, and the editors of NU must have been inclined to this view because they bracketed θεου ("of God") after πνευματος ("Spirit"). They included θεου, however, in deference to the testimony of 𝔓46 with א and D versus B—a change from previous editions of the Nestle text which followed B, and is reflected in NIV and NASB. But one wonders why any translations would have adopted the second variant, for it has inferior external support and was most likely the work of scribes who had a proclivity for expanding the bare title "the Spirit" to "the Holy Spirit" and changing less usual titles of the Spirit to the more usual one, "the Holy Spirit" (Comfort 1996, 137).

Romans 15:24

WH NU	ὡς ἂν πορεύωμαι εἰς τὴν Σπανίαν "whenever I travel to Spain" 𝔓46 א* A B C D F G P Ψ 81 1739 syr[p] NKJVmg RSV NRSV ESV NASB NIV TNIV (NLT) HCSB NET
variant/TR	ως αν πορευωμαι εις την Σπανιαν, ελευσομαι προς υμας "whenever I travel to Spain, I will come to you" א2 33 Maj syr[h] KJV NKJV NEB REB NJB NAB HCSBmg

The WH NU reading is manifestly superior by virtue of the manuscript support. The variant is a scribal gloss attempting to fix a sentence that lacks a predicate. But Paul's original writings often have such anacoluthon. The verb is naturally supplied from 15:22.

Romans 15:29

WH NU	πληρώματι εὐλογίας Χριστοῦ "the fullness of Christ's blessing" 𝔓46 א* A B C 81 1739 cop NKJVmg RSV NRSV ESV NASB NIV TNIV NEB REB NJB NAB NLT HCSB NET
variant 1	πληροφορια ευλογιας Χριστου "the full assurance of Christ's blessing" (D*) F G none
variant 2/TR	πληρωματι ευλογιας του ευαγγελιου του Χριστου "the fullness of the blessing of the gospel of Christ" א2 Ψ 33 Maj syr KJV NKJV RSVmg NRSVmg ESVmg HCSBmg

The WH NU reading has the support of the five earliest manuscripts: 𝔓[46] א A B C. The first variant is a scribal attempt to avoid the abstractness that accompanies the word "fullness" or to specify that Paul's visit would give the Roman Christians full assurance and certainty about their blessings in Christ. The second variant is a late scribal gloss (eventually included in TR) intended to show that Paul wanted to give the Roman Christians the complete, full gospel (see 1:10-15). However, the passage is more inclusive than this; it conveys Paul's desire to share his full understanding of Christ and the Christian life with the Roman believers when he would be with them in person—just as he attempted to do in his written presentation.

Romans 15:30

TR WH NU	Παρακαλῶ δὲ ὑμᾶς[, ἀδελφοι,] "I encourage you, brothers" א A C D F G Ψ Maj KJV NKJV RSV NRSV ESV NASB NIV TNIV NJB NAB NLT HCSB NET
variant	Παρακαλω δε υμας "I encourage you" 𝔓[46] B NEB REB

The vocative αδελφοι ("brothers") was probably added by scribes for its lectionary effect. Its absence in the two earliest witnesses (𝔓[46] B) probably retains the original text—as reflected in NEB and REB.

Romans 15:31

TR WH NU	ἡ διακονία μου ἡ εἰς Ἰερουσαλήμ "my service which [is] for Jerusalem" 𝔓[46] א A C D[2] Ψ 33 1739 Maj syr cop KJV NKJV RSV NRSV ESV NASB NIV NEB REB NAB NLT HCSB NET
variant	η δωροφορια μου η εν Ιερουσαλημ "my gift which I am bringing to Jerusalem" B D* F G it TNIV NJB NLTmg

The TR WH NU reading has excellent manuscript support. Though the variant is supported by B, the combination of B with D F G in Paul's Epistles is usually not weighty testimony. The variant reading reflects a scribal attempt to clarify the kind of service Paul was bringing to Jerusalem—as it says in the NJB, which follows the variant, "pray . . . that the aid I carry to Jerusalem may be accepted by the saints."

Romans 15:32a

TR WH NU have the reading θεληματος θεου ("[the] will of God"), which has the support of 𝔓[46] א[2] A C D[2] Ψ Maj. The divine name, however, is different in several manuscripts, as follows: (1) κυριου Ιησου ("Lord Jesus") in B; (2) Χριστου Ιησου ("Christ Jesus") in D* F G it; and (3) Ιησου Χριστου ("Jesus Christ") in א*. The variants here are extremely unusual in that Paul always uses the phrase "the will of God," never "the will of Christ" or "the will of Jesus," etc. For this reason, one of the variants (especially 1 or 3) could very likely be original. However, earlier and more diverse documentary evidence supports the normal verbiage, "the will of God"—a reading accepted by all English translations.

Romans 15:32b

The words συναναπαυσωμαι υμιν ("I may rest with you") are not found in 𝔓^{46} and B. Metzger (TCGNT) suggested that the scribe of 𝔓^{46} accidentally omitted these words when his eyes passed from θεληματος ΘΥ to ο δε ΘϹ in 15:33—i.e., it was a case of homoeoteleuton. But this is not likely, because the nomen sacrum for Θεος does not look anything like the ending letters of θεληματος.

Furthermore, the scribe of 𝔓^{46} (and the scribe of B, who may have followed a text like that found in 𝔓^{46} here) may have changed the participle ελθων to a finite verb ελθω in order to get another predicate into the verse. In other words, these scribes purposely excised these words; they did this because the verb συναναπαυσωμαι can mean "to sleep with" (see Cranfield 1979, 779). Other scribes (D F G), sensing the problem, changed the expression to αναψυξω μεθ υμων ("I may be refreshed with you").

Romans 15:33

TR WH NU include αμην ("Amen"), with the support of ℵ B C D Ψ Maj it syr cop. All English versions do likewise. However, there is good documentary support for its exclusion: 𝔓^{46} A F G 1739 1881 it^{m,t} Ambrosiaster. These witnesses most likely reflect an early form—if not, original form—of the text, which likely concluded with chapter 15. At the end of this verse, 𝔓^{46} alone has the doxology usually placed at 16:25-27 (see note for full discussion). This doxology in 𝔓^{46} ends with αμην ("Amen"), thereby bringing the chapter to a close. It seems likely that Paul wrote chapters 1–15 as one epistle, and then perhaps sent a separate letter of commendation for Phoebe (with personal greetings); this short letter (which we now know as chapter 16) was later attached to the larger epistle. 𝔓^{46} bears witness to this twofold early form of the text. As such, chapter 15 is the concluding chapter of the first epistle; it ends appropriately with a benediction and final "amen." The sixteenth chapter is an appended letter of commendation. No translation, however, follows this form of the text, but it is noted in RSVmg NRSVmg NEBmg NJBmg.

It is possible that Romans 16 is actually a short letter to the Ephesian church that was attached to the end of Romans when the Pauline corpus was compiled. In defense of this hypothesis is the fact that Paul, by his own admission in the previous chapter, had never been to Rome. Therefore, the question of his having so many friends in a city which he had not visited has created a problem for many interpreters. Consequently, some reject this chapter as a portion of the initial Roman letter, suggesting that it is a mere fragment of a letter which the apostle addressed to the Ephesian church. Prior to 1935, this hypothesis remained a conjecture; but with the publication of the Chester Beatty Papyrus containing the Pauline Epistles (designated 𝔓^{46}, dated late second century), it became evident that the oldest known manuscript of Romans concluded Romans 15 with a doxology (see note on 16:25-27).

In spite of this evidence for a separate origin of chapter 16, F. F. Bruce (1989) opts for the position which retains this chapter as a portion of the original letter. His arguments are based chiefly on the large number of inscriptions discovered which contain personal names connected with Rome, and on the swiftness of travel due to the Roman roads and the *pax Romana*. The Babylonian exile had taken the Jews from the realm of meager agricultural activity to that of extensive commercialism. Surely the Jews of the first-century world were interested in commerce and trade; consequently they traveled along the well-used trade routes of his day. Paul, in this chapter, either commends or greets Christians who were living at Rome, or else were journeying to Rome. Approximately one-third of the names are those of women, revealing the prominent positions occupied by women in the Roman church.

Romans 16:1

The NU text reads Φοιβην την αδελφην ημων ("Phoebe our sister") based on ℵ B C D Ψ 33 1739 Maj syr. But other manuscripts (𝔓46 A F G P it) read φοιβην την αδελφην υμων ("Phoebe your sister"). Either this is simply a scribal slip or—if original—it indicates a different relationship between the church and Phoebe. According to the NU text, she needs to be freshly introduced by Paul to the Romans; according to the variant, she could very well have been known by the Roman church already.

Romans 16:3-5

The clause in 16:5, και την κατ οικον αυτων εκκλησιαν ("and the church in their house"), was moved to the end of 16:3 in some Western manuscripts (D*,2 F G) in order to get it closer to the main predicate, Ασπασασθε ("greet"). This rearrangement does not change the meaning, because it still indicates that the church met in the home of Priscilla and Aquila. (See notes on 16:16, 20.)

Romans 16:5

WH NU	ἀπαρχὴ τῆς ᾽Ασίας εἰς Χριστόν "firstfruit of Asia for Christ" ℵ A B C F G P 81 1739 NKJVmg RSV NRSV ESV NASB NIV TNIV NEB REB NJB NAB NLT HCSB NET
variant 1	απ αρχης της Ασιας εις Χριστον "one of the first of Asia for Christ" 𝔓46 (D* εν for εις) none
variant 2/TR	απαρχη της Αχαιας εις Χριστον "firstfruit of Achaia for Christ" D1 Ψ 33 Maj syr KJV NKJV HCSBmg
variant 3	απαρχη της Ασιας εν Χριστον "firstfruit of Asia in Christ" F G 1881 none

A few scribes (𝔓46 D*) wrote απ αρχης ("from the beginning") instead of απαρχη ("firstfruit[s]")—to describe Epaenetus as the first believer in the Roman province of Asia. Dunn (1988, 890) explains that this was "an understandable error through mishearing in transcription." But there are significant reasons to doubt that 𝔓46 was copied by a scribe listening to dictation. If it was copied by dictation, then this early manuscript was the product of a sizable scriptorium where it was normal for multiple manuscripts to be produced simultaneously by dictation. At this point in our understanding of early Christian scribal practices, it appears that most copies were produced one by one. The error could simply be one of visual misperception, since there is only a one-letter difference: απαρχης versus απαρχη. (See note on 2 Thess 2:13, where a similar error occurred.)

Other scribes (see variant 2), probably thinking of 1 Cor 16:15, wrote "Achaia" for "Asia." And others changed the preposition εις to the more natural εν.

Romans 16:7

TR, UBS[4], and NA[27] (up to the seventh printing) have the name Ἰουνιᾶν in their text. This name could be rendered as Junia (female name) or Junias (male name). Many manuscripts (א A B* C D* F G P) read Ιουνιαν with no accent mark. Other manuscripts (B[2] D[2] Ψ[vid] L 33 1739) accent the word as Ἰουνίαν (so WH and NA[27] in 8th printing).

Another variant reading is Ἰουλίαν ("Julia"), found in 𝔓[46] it[b] cop[bo] (noted in NRSVmg NEBmg NJBmg NLTmg). It is possible that this variant reading was the result of a transcriptional error—the Greek *nu* was made a *lambda*. The reverse error occurred in 16:15 in a few manuscripts (C* F G), where the name "Julia" appears. It is also possible that the scribe of 𝔓[46] and some ancient translators were influenced by 16:15. But whether the name is Junia or Julia, many commentators assert that this person was a woman. The thorough study of Cervin (1994) on this issue affirms that the name is feminine. Contrary to UBS[4], her name should not be accented as Ἰουνιᾶν (the accusative of Ιουνιας, a masculine name), but as Ἰουνίαν (the accusative of a common Roman female name). The English versions that read "Junia" (a female) are KJV NKJV NRSV ESV TNIV REB NAB NLT HCSB; those that read "Junias" (a male) are RSV NRSVmg ESVmg NASB NIV NEB REBmg NJB NABmg NLTmg HCSBmg.

Andronicus and Junia were probably husband and wife. These two, who became Christians before Paul did, were said to be επισημοι εν τοις αποστολοις, which could mean they were "outstanding among the apostles." This is a significant statement because it is the only one in the NT that accords apostolic status to a woman. However, others think the phrase more likely means that Andronicus and Junia were "well known to the apostles." According to Wallace (2001, 343-344), this is the meaning in nearly all Greek writings where επισμος was followed by a dative. As such, it means that Andronicus and Junia were well-reputed Christian servants. But this interpretation is not absolute.

Romans 16:9

Instead of εν Χριστω ("in Christ"), found in 𝔓[46] א A B 33 1739 Maj, some manuscripts (C D F G Ψ) read εν κυριω ("in the Lord"), thereby conforming this verse to the previous one.

Romans 16:15

The name Ιουλιαν ("Julia") was mistakenly written as Ιουνιαν ("Junia") in C* F G (see note on 16:7). The scribe of 𝔓[46] wrote Βηρεα και Αουλιαν ("Berea and Julia"[?]) for Ιουλιαν Νηρεα ("Julia, Nerea").

Romans 16:16

The Western manuscripts D F G moved the last sentence of this verse (Ασπαζονται υμας αι εκκλησιαι πασαι του Χριστου—"all the churches of Christ greet you") to the end of 16:21 in order to group together the verses that contain personal greetings from Paul's acquaintances. A similar transposition occurred in 16:3-5 (see note).

Romans 16:20

WH NU ῾Η χάρις τοῦ κυρίου ἡμῶν ᾿Ιησοῦ μεθ ὑμῶν
"The grace of our Lord Jesus be with you."
𝔓46 א B
NASB NIV TNIV NEB REB NAB NLT HCSB NET

variant 1/TR Η χαρις του κυριου ημων Ιησου Χριστου μεθ υμων
"The grace of our Lord Jesus Christ be with you."
A C Ψ 33 1739 Maj syr cop
KJV NKJV RSV NRSV ESV NJB NLTmg

variant 2 omit sentence
D F G
RSVmg NRSVmg NEBmg REBmg NJBmg

The first variant displays a typical scribal expansion of a divine name. Surprisingly, the expansion is followed by RSV NRSV NJB, even though it is based on inferior testimony. The WH NU reading has the best authority, even though it appears that this short benediction comes out of nowhere. It is perhaps for this reason that the scribes of D F G transposed this sentence to follow the postscript of 16:21-23 (comprising a whole new verse in TR and KJV—16:24), and the scribes of P 33 104 365 syr[p] and one cop[bo] manuscript repeated it at the end of the epistle (after 16:27). As was noted earlier, such transpositions reveal the textual fluidity of the last chapters of Romans. The omission is noted in the margins of several translations in connection with textual variation in 16:24 (see next note).

Romans 16:24

WH NU omit verse
𝔓46 𝔓61 א (A) B C 1739 it[b] cop
NKJVmg RSV NRSV ESV NASBmg NIV TNIV NEB REB NJB NAB NLT HCSBmg NET

variant/TR include verse (same as in 16:20—see note)
D (F G omit Ιησου Χριστου [Jesus Christ]) Ψ Maj syr[h]
KJV NKJV RSVmg NRSVmg ESVmg NASB NIVmg TNIVmg NEBmg REBmg NJBmg NABmg NLTmg HCSB NETmg

The omission of this verse is strongly supported by all the earliest manuscripts. The verse was copied from 16:20 by some scribe (or scribes) who thought it was also suited to follow the postscript (see note on 16:20). Since TR and Majority Text include this verse, so do KJV and NKJV. The Western manuscripts (D F G) add the benediction at 16:24 because they do not include 16:25-27. All modern translations, following superior testimony, do not include the verse. At the same time, these translations provide a textual note concerning this verse because of its place in traditional English translations. The textual situation of 16:24 must be considered along with 16:25-27 (see following note).

Romans 16:25-27

The doxology to Romans is as follows:

> Now to the one who is able to strengthen you, according to my gospel and the proclamation of Jesus Christ, according to the revelation of the mystery kept secret in times eternal, but is now manifested, and through the prophetic writings is made known to the Gentiles,

according to the command of the eternal God, to bring about the obedience of faith—to the only wise God, through Jesus Christ, to whom be the glory forever. Amen.

This doxology is found in several places in the manuscript tradition as follows:

1. 1:1–16:23 + doxology/WH NU (𝔓$^{61vid?}$ א B C D 1739 it^{d} syr^{p} cop RSV NRSV ESV NASB NIV TNIV NEB REB NJB NAB NLT HCSB NET). The first extant page of 𝔓^{61} exhibits portions of Rom 16:23, with 16:24 vacant, and 16:25-26. Thus, it is certain that the doxology immediately followed 16:23. What is not certain is whether or not 𝔓^{61} also had the doxology at the end of Rom 14 and/or 15.
2. 1:1–15:33 + doxology + 16:1-23 (𝔓^{46} NRSVmg NEBmg REBmg NLTmg HCSBmg NETmg). Each of these versions note that one manuscript has this placement; NLT calls it "one very early manuscript."
3. 1:1–14:23 + doxology + 15:1–16:23 + doxology (A P 33 ESVmg HCSBmg NETmg).
4. 1:1–14:23 + doxology + 15:1–16:24 (L Ψ 0209^{vid} syr^{h} MSS$^{\text{according to Origen}}$). Origen is said to have known manuscripts that included the doxology after 14:23.
5. 1:1–16:24 (F G MSS$^{\text{according to Jerome}}$). In Codex G, the scribe left a space after 14:23 large enough to contain the doxology, intimating that he knew of manuscripts that placed it after 14:23 but that it was not so in his exemplar. Jerome indicated he knew of various manuscripts that did not contain the doxology.
6. 1:1–14:23 (Marcion$^{\text{according to Origen}}$). According to Rufinus's translation of Origen's *Commentary on Romans* 8.453, Origen said Marcion not only deleted 16:25-27, but also all of chapters 15–16.
7. 1:1–14:23 + 16:24 + doxology(vg^{MSS} [1648 1792 2089] Codex Amiatinus^{vid})
8. 1:1–16:23 + 16:24 + doxology/TR (Maj KJV NKJV)
9. 1:1–14:23 + doxology + 15:1-33 + doxology + 16:1-23 (1506)

The various placements of the doxology in the last chapters of Romans, as well as the content of chapter 15 and especially chapter 16, have caused textual critics and biblical scholars to ask many questions about the arrangement of Paul's epistle to the Romans. Did it originally have only 14 chapters, to which two more were added? Or did it originally have only 15 chapters, to which the sixteenth was added? Or was it a 16-chapter epistle from the very beginning? And to which of these chapters does the doxology belong? As to the position that Romans was originally only fourteen chapters, there is no actual Greek manuscript evidence to support this. What we have is Origen's comment that Marcion's edition of Romans ended at chapter fourteen (reading 6 above), and there are some clues in a few Latin manuscripts that this may have been so (reading 7 and see comments below).

If Origen's words about Marcion's deletion can be trusted (see Westcott and Hort 1882, 111-113, who have their doubts that Origen meant that all of chapters 15–16 were deleted by Marcion), then it is possible that the purported manuscripts ending with 14:23 or having the doxology there (readings 4, 6, and 7) reflect Marcion's influence. (The readings 3 and 9 may also reflect this influence, but not fully.) Marcion would have been prone to delete chapter 15 because (1) it says that "whatever was written in former days was written for our instruction" (15:4); (2) it calls Christ "a servant to the circumcised to show God's truthfulness, to confirm the promises given to the patriarchs" (15:8); and (3) it is full of OT quotations (15:9-12). Bruce (1985, 29) said, "such a concentration of material offensive to Marcion can scarcely be paralleled in the Pauline writings." It is possible that Marcion would not need to delete chapter 16 because it might not have been known to him.

The chapter summaries or *capitula* in Codex Amiatinus suggest that 16:25-27 immediately followed 14:1-23 in archetypal manuscripts. *Capitulum* 50 reads "concerning the danger of grieving one's brother with one's food, and showing that the kingdom of God is not food and drink but righteousness and peace and joy in the Holy Spirit," followed by *Capitulum* 51: "concerning the mystery of God, which was kept in silence before the passion but has been revealed after his passion."

Gamble (1977, 123-132) argues for the original positioning of the doxology at 14:23 because putting the doxology at 16:23-25 would violate Paul's normal pattern of a grace benediction appearing at the close of the epistle. At the same time, Gamble argues for the inclusion of 16:24, but this has weak textual support (see reading 4 above and see note on 16:24).

Whatever one supposes about the epistle originally ending with chapter 14, the textual evidence stands against it. All extant Greek manuscripts have chapters 14, 15, and 16. Chapter 15 is completely contiguous with chapter 14, and it is replete with Pauline thought—the likes of which only Marcion would object to. Chapter 16 is different in intent and content. The epistle does not need it for any kind of completion inasmuch as Paul came to a natural conclusion in 15:30-33, where he asks the believers for their prayers, especially in anticipation of his coming to them, and then concludes with a benediction: "May the God of peace be with you all. Amen."

What we know as Romans 16 may have been sent as a separate letter of recommendation for Phoebe (with personal greetings included), which was later attached to the rest of the epistle. Or Paul may have made two copies of the epistle, one with chapter 16 (which may have gone to Ephesus) and one without chapter 16 (which would have gone to Rome). Interestingly, Codex G does not include "in Rome" in 1:7 and 15, and also has all 16 chapters without a doxology. Some have thought that this codex could be a witness to an earlier form of the epistle that would not have gone to the Romans (see reading 5 above). However, the subscription in G indicates that the letter was sent to the Romans.

$\mathfrak{P}^{46}$, with its doxology after 15:33 (see reading 2 above), probably reflects a form of the epistle that originally had only 15 chapters, to which chapter 16 (a separate, accompanying letter) was later appended. $\mathfrak{P}^{46}$, dated in the middle of the second century, shows a very primitive form of the Pauline text and corpus as a whole (see *Text of Earliest MSS*, 204-206). As to Romans, $\mathfrak{P}^{46}$ could very well reflect a form of the epistle as compiled by an early editor of Paul's Epistles—that is, one who placed and arranged Paul's Epistles in one codex. This compiler could have seamed together Paul's original complete epistle from 1:1—15:33 (which ends with his blessing of peace, followed by a doxology and a final "amen") and the accompanying letter of recommendation (chapter 16)—which in $\mathfrak{P}^{46}$ does not have a final benediction. Rather, it ends with a final greeting from Erastus and Quartus (16:23). So the arrangement in $\mathfrak{P}^{46}$ is as follows:

1. 1:1–15:33 (the last verse being "may the God of peace be with you all"—with no "amen");
2. 16:25-27 the doxology—concluded with an "amen";
3. 16:1-23 a short letter with recommendations for Phoebe and greetings from several believers.

The double presence of the doxology in certain manuscripts (A P 33, see reading 3)—both at the end of chapter 14 and of chapter 16—indicates that by the fifth century (and thereafter) some scribes were seeing the doxology at the end of both chapters in various exemplars and then copying it accordingly. The same holds true for the scribe of 1509, who must have seen the doxology at the end of chapter 15 (as in $\mathfrak{P}^{46}$) and at the end of chapter 16 (as in several MSS) in certain exemplars.

Some scholars think Paul wrote all sixteen chapters as one unit, which he concluded with his doxology at the end of chapter 16 (as in reading 1 above). This was then abridged to a 15-chapter epistle when it was circulated to other churches, because these churches would not need or be interested in the circumstantial details of chapter 16. But since there is not one extant manuscript that ends with chapter 15, this view has no textual support.

In conclusion, it seems to me that the presence of the doxology appearing at the end of chapter 14 only (as in reading 4) reflects the influence of Marcion. The presence of the doxology at the end of chapter 16 reflects the work of a compiler (or compilers) who moved it there when they added chapter 16 to the main body of the letter. The most likely original arrangement is reflected in 𝔓46 (the earliest manuscript), which has the blessing and doxology at the end of chapter 15, to which is appended an extra chapter, which probably was a short letter sent along to Rome with the major epistle (Romans 1–15)—much in the same way that Paul's letter to Philemon was sent along with his letter to the Colossians. Since this short letter begins with Paul's recommendation of Phoebe, it could very well be that Phoebe carried both epistles (chs 1–15, 16) to the leaders of the church in Rome. This letter of recommendation includes several personal greetings and its own short benediction: "the grace of our Lord Jesus be with you" (16:20). In keeping with his usual practice, Paul probably wrote this benediction in his own hand (see Comfort 2005, 7-8), as well as the next verse, where he passes on the greetings of "Timothy, my coworker" (16:21). Tertius, the amanuensis of this final chapter and probably of all of Romans, signed off in his own hand (16:22). He may have also passed along greetings from Gaius, Erastus, and Quartus—or, as is in keeping with ancient letter writing, each of these men gave their greeting in their own handwriting (16:23). As such, at the close of the original letter, the Roman Christians would see several different signatures. After this, they would not see the doxology; they would see blank papyrus.

Though a few English versions note the various positions of the doxology (see NRSVmg ESVmg NEBmg REBmg NLTmg HCSBmg NETmg), all modern versions follow the format printed in WH NU (see reading 1 above), which excludes 16:24, and is then followed by the doxology (16:25-27). KJV and NKJV follow TR in adding 16:24 after 16:23, before the doxology: 1:1–16:23 + 16:24 + doxology (see reading 8 above).

Within 16:25-27 itself, there are two significant textual variants. (1) According to Origen and according to Jerome (who noted this reading in several MSS), there is an addition in 16:26 after φανερωθεντος δε νυν δια τε γραφων προφητικων ("but now manifest through the writings of the prophets"). The addition is: και της επιφανειας του κυριου ημων Ιησου Χριστου ("and the appearing [epiphany] of our Lord Jesus Christ"). (2) The penultimate expression in the epistle is εις τους αιωνας ("into the age" = "forever"). This reading is supported by 𝔓46 B C Ψ 33 Maj. Other Greek MSS (𝔓61 ℵ A D) read εις τους αιωνας των αιωνων ("into the age of the ages" = "forever and ever"). This expansion frequently occurred throughout the course of textual transmission.

Subscription

Whereas scribes frequently added inscriptions (titles) to the Gospels, Acts, and Revelation, they did not usually do so for the Epistles. Instead, many scribes supplied subscriptions, which provide information about the writer, place of writing, sender, and recipient of the epistle. None of these subscriptions would have been part of the autographs; nonetheless, they are worth listing.

1. No subscription. Appears in 𝔓46 F 365 629 630 1505.
2. Προς Ρωμαιους ("To the Romans"). Appears in ℵ A B* C D* [G] Ψ 1739.
3. Προς Ρωμαιους εγραφη απο Κορινθου ("To the Romans written from Corinth") . Appears in B1 D1 (P).
4. Προς Ρωμαιους εγραφη απο Κορινθου δια Φοιβης της διακονου ("To the Romans written from Corinth through Phoebe the deacon"). Appears in 42 90 216 339 462 466* 642.

5. Προς Ρωμαιους εγραφη απο Κορινθου δια Φοιβης της διακονου της εν Κεγχρεαις εκκλησιας ("To the Romans written from Corinth through Phoebe the deacon of the church in Cenchrea"). Appears in 101 241 460 466[c] 469 602 603 1923 1927 1932 (so TR).

The above display is quite telling in that it provides a perfect example of how a text can become expanded throughout the course of its textual history. The earliest manuscript, 𝔓[46], preserving the original, has no subscription, though it probably had an inscription (initial title), given the fact that the other epistles in this codex have inscriptions. Then, beginning in the fourth century, manuscripts display a simple subscription, "to the Romans." Two of these manuscripts, B and D, were later emended with additional information about the place of writing ("from Corinth"). This was then expanded in still later witnesses to include more information about the envoy, "Phoebe" (or "Phoebe from Cenchrea"). One manuscript, 337 (not listed above), also noted that Tertius wrote the epistle (see 16:22). TR incorporated the fifth reading noted above, and in suit KJV prints an English translation of it at the end of Romans.

The First Epistle to the CORINTHIANS

Inscription (Title)

𝔓46 א and B title this epistle as Προς Κορινθιους Α ("To the Corinthians, A" = "1 Corinthians"). Several manuscripts (including א and B) have this title in the subscription (see last note for this book). Paul, however, would not have supplied a title. Inscriptions and subscriptions are the work of later scribes. (For more on this, see Comfort 2005, 9-10.)

1 Corinthians 1:1

NU ἀπόστολος Χριστοῦ Ἰησοῦ
"apostle of Christ Jesus"
𝔓46 B D F G 33
RSV NRSV ESV NIV TNIV NEB REB NJB NAB NLT HCSB NET

variant/TR WH αποστολος Ιησου Χριστου
"apostle of Jesus Christ"
א* A Ψ 1739 Maj
KJV NKJV NASB NETmg

The preferred word order is found in the NU text, supported by superior documentation and normal Pauline usage. Paul typically refers to "Christ Jesus" when speaking of his exalted state in glory, and to "Jesus Christ" when speaking of his earthly ministry or when speaking of "our Lord Jesus Christ."

1 Corinthians 1:4

TR NU Εὐχαριστῶ τῷ θεῷ μου
"I thank my God"
𝔓61vid א2 A C D F G Ψ 33 1739 Maj
KJV NKJV NRSV ESV NASB TNIV NAB NLTmg HCSB NET

variant/WH Ευχαριστω τω θεω
"I thank God"
א* B
RSV NRSVmg NIV NEB REB NJB NLT

It is quite possible that μου ("my") is a later scribal addition; it is equally possible that it was purposely omitted in ℵ and B—or in an archetype (unfortunately, 𝔓46 has a lacuna here). Either way, the meaning is not altered.

1 Corinthians 1:6

All three editions (TR WH NU) read το μαρτυριον του Χριστου ("the testimony of Christ"), with excellent documentation: 𝔓46 ℵ A B2 C D Ψ 33 1739 Maj it syr cop. All English versions follow. However, there is a variant in B* F G, which reads το μαρτυριον του θεου ("the testimony of God"). This variant is clearly the result of assimilation to a variant reading of 2:1, which has το μαρτυριον του θεου ("the testimony of God") in the very same manuscripts (B F G) and in others (ℵ2 D Ψ 33 1739 Maj). (See note on 2:1.)

1 Corinthians 1:8

All three editions (TR WH NU) read τη ημερα του κυριου ημων Ιησου Χριστου ("the day of our Lord Jesus Christ") based on the support of several witnesses: ℵ A C D F G Ψ 33 1739 Maj it syr cop. However, the two earliest manuscripts, 𝔓46 and B, do not include Χριστου ("Christ"). Although it could be argued that Χριστου was accidentally dropped after Ιησου, it seems more likely that the title was expanded, thereby conforming it to the preceding and following verses, both of which have "Jesus Christ." For a further discussion which argues for the shorter reading, see Zuntz (1953, 183-184).

1 Corinthians 1:13

TR WH NU μεμέρισται ὁ Χριστός;
"Has Christ been divided?"
ℵ A B C D 33 1739 Maj
KJV NKJV RSV NRSV ESV NASB NIV TNIV NJB NAB NLT HCSB NET

variant μη μεμερισται ο Χριστος;
"Christ cannot be divided, can he?"
𝔓46vid 2464* syrp copsa
NEB REB

The TR WH NU reading, which has excellent support, most likely preserves the original wording. According to the variant reading, which adds μη at the beginning of the sentence, Paul asked the first question expecting a negative answer. NEB and REB chose this reading. Other manuscripts do not have Paul asking a question that expects a negative answer until the second question: μη Παυλος εσταυρωθη υπερ υμων ("Paul wasn't crucified for you, was he?"). The scribe of 𝔓46 made μη govern both the first and second questions by placing it at the front and changing the second μη to η ("nor"): "Christ cannot be divided, can he? Nor was Paul crucified for you, was he?"

1 Corinthians 1:14

TR NU εὐχαριστῶ [τῷ θεῷ]
"I thank God"
ℵ2 C D F G Ψ Maj
KJV NKJV RSVmg NRSV ESV NASB TNIV NEB REB NAB NLT HCSB NET

variant 1 ευχαριστω τω θεω μου
"I thank my God"
A 33 81 syr[p,h**]
none

variant 2/WH ευχαριστω
"I am thankful"
ℵ* B 1739 Clement
RSV NRSVmg NIV NJB HCSBmg NETmg

The first variant is clearly a scribal expansion (as in 1:4—see note), and it is likely that the TR NU reading, which adds an object after the verb, is also an expansion. Since the absolute use of ευχαριστω ("I am thankful") is rare in the Pauline documents (Fee 1987, 51), scribes and translators could not help but add some kind of object after it. Thus, the second variant, supported by the earliest witnesses, is most likely original.

1 Corinthians 1:28

NU τὰ ἐξουθενημένα ἐξελέξατο ὁ θεός, τὰ μὴ ὄντα
"God chose the despised things—the things that are not"
𝔓[46] ℵ* A C* D* F G 33 1739
RSV NRSV ESV NASB NEB REB NJB NAB NLT HCSB NET

variant/TR WH τα εξουθενημενα εξελεξατο ο θεος και τα μη οντα
"God chose the despised things and the things that are not"
ℵ[2] B C[3] D[2] Ψ Maj syr
KJV NKJV NIV TNIV

According to 𝔓[46] etc., the expression "the things that are not" is in apposition to "the despised things." This is the best-attested reading, which was later emended (note the late corrections in ℵ C D) by the addition of και ("and").

1 Corinthians 2:1

WH NU τὸ μυστήριον τοῦ θεοῦ
"the mystery of God"
𝔓[46vid] ℵ* A C syr[p] cop[bo]
NKJVmg RSVmg NRSV ESVmg NASBmg NIVmg TNIVmg NEBmg REBmg NJB NAB NLT HCSBmg NETmg

variant/TR το μαρτυριον του θεου
"the testimony of God"
ℵ[2] B D F G Ψ 33 1739 Maj it[b] syr[h] cop[sa]
KJV NKJV RSV NRSVmg ESV NASB NIV TNIV NEB REB NJBmg HCSB NET

UBS[3] cites 𝔓[46vid?] in support of the NU text. The question mark follows "vid" because the editors were not sure that 𝔓[46] contains the word μυστηριον ("mystery"). Having examined the actual papyrus, I can affirm that the reading is μυστηριον ("mystery"), not μαρτυριον ("testimony"), because the Greek letter *eta*, though partially broken, is visible before the final four letters—which are also visible (ριον). The one letter makes all the difference in determining the reading. UBS[4] (as well as the Nestle text) now lists this papyrus as 𝔓[46vid].

WH NU have uncontestable support from the earliest extant document, 𝔓[46]. Several other witnesses, both early and diverse, also support WH NU. But the same can be said for the variant reading. So how then do we solve the problem? Competent textual critics such as Zuntz (1953,

101) and Fee (1987, 88; 1992, 5-8) have argued that μυστηριον is a scribal emendation influenced by 2:7. Other scholars, such as Brown (1968, 48-49) and Metzger (TCGNT), have argued that μαρτυριον is a scribal emendation influenced by 1:6. Actually, one can draw upon the context of 1 Cor 1–2 to support either word, because Paul's message in these chapters is that his mission was to testify only of Christ, who is the mystery of God. The immediate context seems to support "mystery," because chapter 2 focuses on the need for believers to receive revelation from the Spirit of God to truly understand all the hidden, secret riches of God that are in Christ Jesus (see 2:7-16). In summary, the internal and external evidence for this reading is divided, so it is not easy to make a decision of which variant is original. This indecision is displayed in the array of modern English versions. Though most versions follow "testimony," these same versions print "mystery" in the margin.

1 Corinthians 2:4

WH NU — οὐκ ἐν πειθοῖ[ς] σοφίας [λόγοις]
"not with persuasive words of wisdom"
(א*) B D 33 1739
RSV NRSV ESV NASB NIV TNIV NJB NAB NLT HCSB NET

variant 1/TR — ουκ εν πειθοις ανθρωπινης σοφιας λογοις
"not with persuasive words of human wisdom"
א² A C Ψ Maj
KJV NKJV HCSBmg

variant 2 — ουκ εν πειθοι ανθρωπινης σοφιας λογοις
"not with persuasiveness of words of human wisdom"
42 440
none

variant 3 — ουκ εν πειθοις σοφιας
"not with persuasion of wisdom"
𝔓46 F G
NEB REB

There are more variants than those listed here, but these present the basic alterations in this verse. The insertion of ανθρωπινης ("human") is very likely the result of scribal assimilation to 2:13, so the first variant is not original. The second variant displays a scribal attempt to fix the word πειθοις, which is never used as an adjective elsewhere in Greek literature. Without the final sigma, the word becomes a noun ("persuasiveness"). This may have been what Paul wrote; the WH NU reading could display a scribal error: the doubling of the initial sigma of σοφιας after πειθοι: πειθοισσοφιας. To this was added λογοις ("words") by way of conformity to 2:13. By a process of elimination, as Zuntz argues (1953, 23-25), the most likely reading lies behind that which is found in 𝔓46 F G—with the removal of the sigma after πειθοις. This is reflected by the brackets in NU.

1 Corinthians 2:10

TR NU — ἡμῖν δὲ ἀπεκάλυψεν ὁ θεὸς διὰ τοῦ πνεύματος
"but to us God has revealed them by the Spirit"
א A C (D F G Ψ Maj syr add αυτου after του πνευματος = "his Spirit")
KJV NKJV RSV NRSV ESV NIV NEB REB NLT HCSB

variant/WH ημιν γαρ απεκαλυψεν ο θεος δια του πνευματος
"for to us God has revealed them by the Spirit"
𝔓[46] B 1739 Clement
NASB TNIV NJB (NAB) NLTmg NET

The earliest witnesses, 𝔓[46] B (followed by 1739) Clement, support the variant reading; it is very likely original. The TR NU reading (with the contrastive δε) seems to be a scribal emendation, which attempts to avoid three γαρs in a row or which tries to make a contrast between 2:10 and 2:9. The contrast is as follows: "eye has not seen nor ear heard the things God has prepared for those who love him, but to us God has revealed them by the Spirit." The variant, however, conveys a different connection; other people cannot understand "the things that God has prepared for those who love him, for to us God has revealed them by the Spirit." The contrast is therefore not between unbelievers and believers per se but between not receiving revelation from the Spirit and receiving it (see Fee 1987, 109-110).

It should be noted that the atomized eclecticism of NU is quite manifest in this verse. In the first part of the verse, ℵ D F G Ψ Maj it syr are followed for selecting the word δε over γαρ, whereas in the second part of the verse they are all rejected for the insertion of αυτου after πνευματος. Obversely, 𝔓[46] B 1739 are rejected in the first part of the verse, and then accepted in the second. A and C remain the constant witnesses to the NU reading, but they are not the best witnesses in the Pauline Epistles.

1 Corinthians 2:13a

WH NU διδακτοῖς πνεύματος
"taught by [the] Spirit"
𝔓[46] ℵ A B C[vid] D F G Maj 0185 0289 33 1739 syr[p] cop
NKJVmg RSV NRSV ESV NASB NIV TNIV NEB REB NJB NAB NLT HCSB NET

variant/TR δικακτοις πνευματος αγιου
"taught by [the] Holy Spirit"
D[1] Maj syr[h]
KJV NKJV

The expansion of the bare title, "Spirit," to "Holy Spirit" was a common phenomenon in the transmission of the New Testament text. In this instance, the expansion found its way into the majority of manuscripts, TR, and was then translated in KJV and NKJV.

1 Corinthians 2:13-15; 3:1a

The expression πνευματικοις πνευματικα συγκρινοντες has troubled many a translator and exegete. Does this phrase mean "matching spiritual truths with corresponding spiritual words" or "explaining spiritual truths to spiritual people"? The manuscripts B and 33 provide a solution to the dilemma by slightly changing the wording to πνευματικως πνευματικα συγκρινοντες, which means "discerning spiritual things spiritually."

In 2:13–3:1, the scribe of 𝔓[46] decided in a few instances to designate πνευματικως and πνευματικος as nomina sacra in a way that is unique in the manuscript tradition. In 2:13 the scribe used the common nomen sacrum $\overline{\text{ΠΝC}}$ in the expression διδακτοις πνευματος ("taught by the Spirit"). Then the scribe wrote πνευματικοις πνευματικα συνκρεινοντες, which reveals his interpretation: "matching spiritual things with spiritual things (or, words)." Had the scribe intended πνευματικοις to convey "spiritual people," he could have written this as a nomen sacrum (which he did in 2:15 and 3:1), but his choice to write it in full (*plene*) indicates that he was probably not thinking of "spiritual ones." Then, in 2:14 the scribe of 𝔓[46] wrote the nomen sacrum ΠΝC for the adverbial word πνευματικως in the expression "they are spiritually discerned." No other manuscript does this; they either read πνικως or πνευματικως. Either 𝔓[46] has an early, unique nomen sacrum form, or the scribe of 𝔓[46] was providing a variant reading—namely, "they are discerned by the Spirit."

In 2:15 and 3:1 the scribe of 𝔓[46] again wrote the nomen sacrum ΠΝC for πνευματικος and πνευματικοις, whereas other manuscripts either have the words written in *plene* or written as πνικος or πνικοις (see Swanson 2003, 28-31) for "the one who is spiritual" and "the ones who are spiritual." The decision of the scribe of 𝔓[46] to write these with the nomen sacrum ΠΝC could have been the scribe's way of dignifying the identity of spiritual people by virtue of their union with the Holy Spirit. The "spiritual man" is "a person of the Spirit." But the nomen sacrum ΠΝC in 2:15 could be a textual variant—namely, πνευματος (genitive)—"the one of the Spirit discerns all things." But this does not work for 3:1, where the grammatical form has to be dative and therefore the nomen sacrum must represent πνευματικοις ("spiritual ones"). Thus, for both 2:15 and 3:1 the scribe of 𝔓[46] probably used this nomen sacrum for "spiritual people." As such, it is an example of an early form (ΠΝC) that became lengthened in the manuscript tradition, probably to avoid confusing πνευματικοις with πνευματος.

1 Corinthians 2:16

TR NU read ημεις δε νουν Χριστου εχομεν ("but we have the mind of Christ") with excellent support: 𝔓[46] ℵ A C D[1] Ψ 048 0289[vid] 33 1739 Maj syr cop. All English versions follow this. WH reads ημεις δε νουν Κυριου εχομεν ("but we have the mind of the Lord"), supported by B D* F G 81 it. This variant is likely the result of scribal conformity to the immediate context, in which Paul quotes Isa 40:13. However, Paul had no qualms about shifting from "Lord" (which is a title for God) to "Christ" because in Paul's thinking Christ is the Lord God.

1 Corinthians 3:1a

See note on 2:13-15 above.

1 Corinthians 3:1b, 3a

In 3:1b the best manuscript evidence (𝔓[46] ℵ A B C* D* 0289 33 1739) supports the reading σαρκινοις ("of the flesh") as opposed to σαρκικοις ("fleshly"), found in C[3] D[2] F G Ψ Maj as an adaptation to 3:3. In 3:3a the NU text prints σαρκικοι twice, alternating with σαρκινοι in the first instance by D* F G and also in the second by 𝔓[46] D* F G. Zuntz (1953, 99-100) argues that σαρκινοις is original because Paul consistently used this term when referring to human beings, whereas σαρκικοι refers to carnal behavior.

1 Corinthians 3:3b

WH NU ζῆλος καὶ ἔρις
"jealousy and strife"
𝔓[11] ℵ A B C P Ψ 0289 1739 1881 cop Clement Origen
RSV NRSV ESV NASB NIV TNIV NEB REB NJB NAB NLT HCSB NET

variant/TR ζηλος και ερις και διχοστασιαι
"jealousy and strife and divisions"
𝔓46 D F G Maj it[b] syr
KJV NKJV HCSBmg

The documentary evidence is evenly divided, with both readings having early and diverse attestation. However, it is difficult to account for the omission of και διχοστασιαι as a scribal error that affected so many witnesses. Thus, the only solution is to consider that the variant is the result of an early scribal interpolation influenced by Gal 5:20. Nevertheless, the additional words are not inaccurate, because the Corinthians were suffering divisions as the result of jealousy and strife.

1 Corinthians 3:4

WH NU οὐκ ἄνθρωποι ἐστε;
"are you not humans?"
𝔓46 ℵ* A B C 048 0289 33 1739
RSV NRSV ESV NASB NIV TNIV NEB REB NJB NAB (NLT) HCSB NET

variant/TR ουχι σαρκικοι εστε;
"are you not carnal?"
ℵ2 Ψ Maj syr
KJV NKJV HCSBmg

The WH NU reading has early and diverse manuscript support. The variant is a scribal emendation influenced by the previous verse. But Paul was not simply repeating his criticism against the Corinthians' carnality (3:1-3). Rather, he was pointing to their divisive behavior as being no different than that exhibited by all human beings. Nevertheless, as Christians they should have been different.

1 Corinthians 3:5

WH NU Τί οὖν ἐστιν 'Απολλως; τί δέ ἐστιν Παῦλος; οι διάκονοι δι' ὧν ἐπιστεύσατε.
"What then is Apollos? And what is Paul? Ministers through whom you believed."
ℵ* A B 0289 33 1739
RSV NRSV ESV NASB NIV TNIV NEB REB NJB NAB HCSB NET

variant 1 Τις ουν εστιν Απολλως; τις δε εστιν Παυλος; διακονοι δι ων επιστευσατε.
"Who then is Apollos? And who is Paul? Ministers through whom you believed."
𝔓46vid ℵ2 C D F G
NLT

variant 2/TR Τις ουν εστιν Παυλος τις δε Απολλως αλλ η διακονοι δι ων επιστευσατε;
"Who then is Paul and who is Apollos but ministers through whom you believed?"
D2 Ψ Maj syr
KJV NKJV

The first variant reading presents a normal scribal change: the replacement of a personal pronoun for an interrogative. However, Paul most likely used the word τι ("what") in order to emphasize his and Apollos's ministerial functions, not their personalities. In later manuscripts (see second variant), there is a reversal of Apollos and Paul in order to give Paul prominence. Paul would not likely have consciously tried to name himself before naming Apollos, though he sometimes did (see 3:6). In these later manuscripts, there was also an attempt to stylize the text by incorporating the second half of the sentence into the questions. But Paul's strategy was to ask two rhetorical questions and then answer them.

1 Corinthians 3:10a

All three editions (TR WH NU) have the full expression χαριν του θεου ("grace of God"), with the support of ℵ* A B C D F G 0289 33 1739. All English versions follow this. However, a few witnesses (𝔓[46] 81 it[b] Clement) support a shorter reading: χαριν ("grace"), yielding the rendering, "according to the grace given to me." Although the TR WH NU reading has good support, it is very possible that the words του θεου ("of God") were added as a natural scribal expansion. When Paul spoke of his gift (χαρις) of apostleship (see Rom 12:3; Gal 2:9), he did not speak of it as "the grace of God," for the latter term is used in connection with God's gracious gift of salvation given to all believers. Rather, Paul simply spoke of the special gift he was given to proclaim the gospel. Interestingly, the same insertion of του θεου ("of God") after χαριν ("grace") occurs in several manuscripts in Rom 12:3 (see Zuntz 1953, 47).

1 Corinthians 3:10b

The best textual evidence (𝔓[46] ℵ* A B C* 0289[vid] 33 1739 Didymus) indicates that Paul used the aorist tense (εθηκα) to speak of his work of laying the foundation for the church in Corinth. This action was given a durative quality in several manuscripts (ℵ[2] C[3] D Ψ Maj—so TR) by changing it to a perfect tense (τεθεικα).

1 Corinthians 3:13

WH NU include the word αυτο after το πυρ (= "the fire itself"), but the word αυτο, not found in 𝔓[46] ℵ D Ψ 0289 Maj Clement (so TR), is probably a scribal intensification.

1 Corinthians 3:20

According to excellent testimony (𝔓[46] ℵ A B C 1739), Paul cites the Septuagint version of Ps 94:11, with one important change—ανθρωπων ("men") was replaced with σοφων ("wise men"): "the Lord knows the reasonings of the wise." This change, by the hand of Paul, suits the context in which he had been arguing that human wisdom is foolishness in comparison to God's, who sent his Son to provide munificent salvation. However, in some late Greek manuscripts (33 630 1506) and a few versions (it[ar] cop[bo]), the verse was changed to conform to the exact wording of the Septuagint.

1 Corinthians 4:2

The three editions (TR WH NU) read ζητειται ("it is sought"), in the expression, "it is sought in stewards that one be found faithful." This indicative verb has the support of B Ψ Maj syr cop, and is followed by all the English versions. However, a variant reading, ζητειτε ("seek"), an imperative verb, is more likely original because it has much better support ($\mathfrak{P}^{46}$ ℵ A C D F G 33 1739 1881) and is seemingly the more difficult reading. But actually, it accords quite well with the following verse, in which Paul indicates that his stewardship was being judged by men. If the Corinthians were seeking such in Paul, they would discover that he was a faithful steward of God's mysteries.

1 Corinthians 4:6

The Greek expression μη υπερ α γεγραπται (literally, "not to go above [or, beyond] the things written") appears in all extant Greek manuscripts (with some manuscripts reading the singular ο instead of the plural α). NJBmg says that this was "perhaps a gloss deprecating some insertion by a scribe." Though this is an interesting conjecture, there is no documentation to substantiate it (see Fee 1987, 167-169). The expression, though obscure, means something like "do not live apart from the Scriptures" or "do not deviate from the Scriptures [I quoted] above" (see NLT).

1 Corinthians 4:13

The rare word δυσφημουμενοι ("being defamed"), found in $\mathfrak{P}^{46}$ ℵ* A C P 33 Clement, was replaced by the more common word, βλασφημουμενοι ("being slandered"), in $\mathfrak{P}^{68}$ ℵ^{2} B D F G Ψ 1739 Maj (so TR). In any event, the two words are nearly synonymous.

1 Corinthians 4:16

A few late manuscripts (104 614) and one version (it^{ar}) expand Paul's terse exhortation, μιμηται μου γινεσθε ("become imitators of me"), by adding καθως καγω Χριστου ("as I also am of Christ")—a phrase borrowed from 11:1.

1 Corinthians 4:17a

Early and diverse documentation ($\mathfrak{P}^{46}$ $\mathfrak{P}^{68}$ ℵ^{2} B C D F G Ψ 1739 Maj) supports the briefer wording, δια τουτο ("because of this"), over against the longer reading δια τουτο αυτο ("because of this very thing"), supported by decent but inferior attestation ($\mathfrak{P}^{11vid}$ ℵ* A P 33). According to Zuntz (1953, 63), Paul never used the idiom δια τουτο αυτο; rather, he preferred εις αυτο τουτο ("for this very reason").

1 Corinthians 4:17b

WH NU ἐν Χριστῷ [Ἰησοῦ]
"in Christ Jesus"
$\mathfrak{P}^{46}$ ℵ C D^{1} 33 1739 syr^{h} cop^{bo}
NRSV ESVmg NIV TNIV NAB NLT HCSB NETmg

variant 1/TR εν Χριστω
"in Christ"
A B D^{2} Ψ Maj it^{b} syr^{p} cop^{sa}
KJV NKJV RSV ESV NASB NEB REB NJB NET

variant 2 εν κυριω Ιησου
"in [the] Lord Jesus"
D* F G
none

In this verse, both the WH NU reading and the first variant could have been influenced by 4:15, which has both "Christ" and "Christ Jesus." The second variant suggests that it is a corruption of a text that once had "Jesus" in the title and therefore gives indirect witness to the reading "Christ Jesus." However, it is possible that the simple title "Christ" preceded the other two readings. But the manuscript evidence does not show that "Christ" is the earliest reading. Thus, it must be judged that the first variant is the result of scribal trimming. The scribe of B seemed to have had a habit of doing this in this epistle (see 4:15; cf. 2 Cor 4:6). Modern English versions (excluding KJV and NKJV) are split between the WH NU reading and the first variant.

1 Corinthians 5:1

WH NU τοιαύτη πορνεία ἥτις οὐδὲ ἐν τοῖς ἔθνεσιν
"such fornication as [is] not even among the Gentiles"
𝔓46 ℵ* A B C D F G 33 1739
NKJVmg RSV NRSV ESV NASB NIV TNIV NEB REB NJB NAB NLT HCSB NET

variant/TR τοιαυτη πορνεια ητις ουδε εν τοις εθνεσιν ονομαζεται
"such fornication as is not even named among the Gentiles"
𝔓68 ℵ2 Ψ Maj
KJV NKJV HCSBmg

The WH NU reading has early and diverse testimony. TR is supported by later manuscripts: 𝔓68 is seventh century, as is the work of the second corrector(s) of ℵ. Ψ is ninth century. The second clause of this verse, according to excellent testimony, is verbless. The verb, ονομαζεται ("is named"), was likely supplied later.

1 Corinthians 5:4a

WH NU τῷ ὀνόματι τοῦ κυρίου [ἡμῶν] 'Ιησοῦ
"the name of our Lord Jesus"
B D* 1739 it[b,d]
ESV NASB NIV TNIV NEB REB NJB NAB HCSB NET

variant 1 τω ονοματι του κυριου Ιησου
"the name of the Lord Jesus"
A Ψ
RSV NRSV NLT NETmg

variant 2 τω ονοματι του κυριου Ιησου Χριστου
"the name of the Lord Jesus Christ"
ℵ it[ar]
NETmg

variant 3/TR τω ονοματι του κυριου ημων Ιησου Χριστου
"the name of our Lord Jesus Christ"
𝔓46 D2 F G 33 Maj cop
KJV NKJV NETmg

It is difficult to determine which title is original. Frequently, scribes expanded divine titles. Thus, it could be argued that the title was "the Lord Jesus" (variant 1) or "our Lord Jesus" (WH NU), and then was expanded to "the Lord Jesus Christ" (variant 2) or "our Lord Jesus Christ." The varying witnesses make it impossible to determine with the current evidence.

1 Corinthians 5:4b

WH NU	δυνάμει τοῦ κυρίου ἡμῶν 'Ιησοῦ "power of our Lord Jesus" א A B D* cop[sa] RSV NRSV ESV NASB NIV TNIV NEB REB NJB NAB NLT HCSB NET
variant 1	δυναμει του κυριου Ιησου "power of the Lord Jesus" 𝔓[46] P Ψ syr[h] none
variant 2	δυναμει του κυριου "power of the Lord" 630 1739 none
variant 3/TR	δυναμει του κυριου ημων Ιησου Χριστου "power of our Lord Jesus Christ" F G Maj KJV NKJV

Since scribes had a tendency to add "our" to divine titles for the sake of audience inclusion, it is possible that either variant 1 or 2 is original, though evidence for either is slim. The third variant, in TR, displays a typical scribal expansion of a divine name.

1 Corinthians 5:5

WH NU	τῇ ἡμέρᾳ τοῦ κυρίου "the day of the Lord" 𝔓[46] B 1739 NKJVmg RSVmg NRSV ESV NASBmg NIV TNIV NEB REB NJB NAB NLT HCSB NET
variant 1/TR	τη ημερα του κυριου Ιησου "the day of the Lord Jesus" 𝔓[61vid] א Ψ Maj KJV NKJV RSV ESVmg NASB NLTmg NETmg
variant 2	τη ημερα του κυριου Ιησου Χριστου "the day of the Lord Jesus Christ" D it[d] NLTmg NETmg
variant 3	τη ημερα του κυριου ημων Ιησου Χριστου "the day of our Lord Jesus Christ" A F G P it[b] syr[h,p] cop NETmg

It appears that the divine title was expanded throughout the course of textual transmission. Under the influence of the previous verse, which has "Lord Jesus" or "Lord Jesus Christ" (depending on the manuscript), scribes added "Jesus" or "Jesus Christ." Paul used the phrase "the day of the Lord" when speaking of the eschaton (1 Thess 5:2; 2 Thess 2:2).

1 Corinthians 5:6

Instead of ζυμοι ("leavens"), the scribe of D wrote δολοι ("adulterates/falsifies"). Since he made the same change in a parallel passage (Gal 5:9), the change was probably intentional.

1 Corinthians 5:7

WH NU — ἐτύθη Χριστός
"Christ was sacrificed"
𝔓[11vid] 𝔓[46vid] א* A B C* D F G 33 1739 Clement
NKJVmg RSV NRSV ESV NASB NIV TNIV NEB REB NJB NAB (NLT) HCSB NET

variant/TR — υπερ ηωμν ετυθη Χριστος
"Christ was sacrificed on our behalf"
א[2] C[3] Ψ Maj syr cop[sa]
KJV NKJV HCSBmg

In NA[26] the only papyrus manuscript listed in support of the WH NU reading was 𝔓[11], but this has been correctly changed to 𝔓[11vid] 𝔓[46vid] in NA[27]. Though it has a lacuna, 𝔓[11] could not have fit υπερ ημων. The *editio princeps* of 𝔓[46] did not reconstruct this portion of the manuscript, but it is reconstructed in *Text of Earliest MSS,* 257. 𝔓[11] and 𝔓[46], plus a host of other manuscripts, attest to the shorter reading. The longer reading is the result of scribes wanting to supply a beneficiary for Christ's sacrifice.

1 Corinthians 5:10

According to excellent testimony (𝔓[61] א* A B C D* F G P 048 33 1739), the original text names three categories: fornicators, greedy ones and swindlers (= greedy swindlers), and idolaters. Some scribes, both early (𝔓[46]) and late (א[2] D[2] Ψ Maj), turned the list into a string of four evil personalities by changing πλεονεκταις και αρπαξιν ("greedy ones and swindlers") to πλεονεκταις η αρπαξιν ("greedy ones or swindlers").

1 Corinthians 5:13

Because there were no accents marking verb tenses in the early manuscripts, we do not know if Paul intended κρινει to be κρινεῖ ("will judge") or κρίνει ("judges"). The present tense was the choice of some later scribes (L Ψ 629—so TR WH), while the NU editors decided on the future tense, which intimates God's final judgment.

1 Corinthians 6:11

NU — ὀνόματι τοῦ κυρίου Ἰησοῦ Χριστοῦ
"name of the Lord Jesus Christ"
𝔓[11vid] 𝔓[46] א D*
RSV NRSV ESV NASB NIV TNIV NJB NAB NLT HCSB NET

variant 1/WH ονοματι του κυριου ημων Ιησου Χριστου
"name of our Lord Jesus Christ"
B C^{vid} P 33 1739
none

variant 2/TR ονοματι του κυριου Ιησου
"name of the Lord Jesus"
A D^{2} Ψ Maj
KJV NKJV NEB REB NETmg

Of the three readings, the first variant can be dismissed as the result of scribal assimilation to the next phrase, which reads, πνευματι του θεου ημων ("Spirit of our God"). But it is difficult to determine if scribes expanded the title or shortened it—whether accidentally or purposely. The textual evidence favors the NU reading, whereas the maxim that the shorter reading is more likely original (especially with respect to divine titles) favors the second variant, which is followed by TR, KJV, and NKJV. Evidently, this maxim was also operative for NEB and REB.

1 Corinthians 6:13

At the end of this verse, Marcion adds, "so that the temple is for God and God is for the temple." This addition anticipates Paul's own comment in 6:19 (Fee 1987, 249).

1 Corinthians 6:14

There are three verb tenses for the second occurrence of εξεγειρω in the extant manuscripts, as follows: (1) future: εξεγερει ("he will raise up") 𝔓^{46c1} ℵ C D^{2} Ψ Maj syr^{h} cop; (2) aorist: εξηγειρεν ("he raised up") 𝔓^{46c2} B 1739 it; and (3) present: εξεγειρει ("he raises up") 𝔓^{11} 𝔓^{46*} A D* P.

The manuscript 𝔓^{46} displays all three verbs. The original scribe wrote the present tense and then corrected it to the future. This was later changed by a different writer to the aorist tense (see *Text of Earliest MSS,* 259). The aorist tense could be the result of scribal conformity to the first part of the verse, where the tense is aorist: "God raised [ηγειρεν] the Lord." However, the resulting statement is more difficult in that it calls for a previous resurrection of the believers (concurrent with Christ's), not a future resurrection. For this very reason, the future tense is more natural. But the present tense is also functional if it is understood as a timeless present: "God, who raised the Lord, is also the one who raises us through his power." This calls for the believers' continuing experience of the resurrection power—from regeneration to transfiguration. Thus, all three of the readings are defensible from an exegetical perspective.

From a documentary perspective, it is likely that the verb was first written as a present tense, which was then changed to a future tense (by a scribe thinking a previous copyist had made an error of one letter); later, it was changed to the aorist tense to make it conform to the first part of the verse. This is exactly the process exhibited in the corrections of 𝔓^{46}.

1 Corinthians 6:17

The expression ο δε κολλωμενος τω κυριω ἕν πνευμα εστιν ("but the one joining himself to the Lord is one spirit") is generally understood to indicate spiritual union between the believer and Christ. As two bodies join to become one in sexual union, two spirits join to become one in spiritual union. It is a union of the divine Spirit with the human spirit; as such "spirit" should not be capitalized—for it is not just the divine Spirit. The scribes of 𝔓^{11} and

𝔓46 showed this interpretation by not writing πνευμα as a nomen sacrum (a divine title = the Spirit); rather, they wrote out the word in *plene*.

1 Corinthians 6:20

WH NU δοξάσατε δὴ τὸν θεὸν ἐν τῷ σώματι ὑμῶν
"glorify God in your body"
𝔓46 ℵ A B C* D* F G 33 1739*
NKJVmg RSV NRSV ESV NASB NIV TNIV NEB REB NJB NAB NLT HCSB NET

variant/TR δοξασατε δη τον θεον εν τω σωματι υμων και εν τω πνευματι υμων, ατινα εστιν του θεου
"glorify God in your body and in your spirit, which are God's"
C3 D2 Ψ Maj 1739mg syr
KJV NKJV HCSBmg

The expanded reading shows up later in the textual tradition. This addition most likely "reflects the influence of Greek dualism on the later church, which had great trouble with the body" (Fee 1987, 249). It is also possible that Paul's mention of our spiritual union with Christ (6:17) prompted the expansion. But the addition misses the whole point of the passage (6:12-20), in which Paul urged the Corinthians to not misuse their bodies, which belong to Christ, by having sexual relations with prostitutes.

1 Corinthians 7:1

WH NU περὶ δὲ ὧν ἐγράψατε
"concerning the things you wrote"
𝔓46 ℵ B C 33 1739
RSV NRSV ESV NASB NIV TNIV NEB REB NJB NAB NLT HCSB NET

variant/TR περι δε ων εγραψατε μοι
"concerning the things you wrote to me"
A D F G Ψ Maj
KJV NKJV HCSBmg

The WH NU reading has the testimony of the earliest manuscripts, as well as that of 33 and 1739. The addition in TR makes explicit what is implicit in the text—namely, that Paul was referring to a letter that the Corinthians had sent to him.

1 Corinthians 7:3

WH NU τῇ γυναικὶ ὁ ἀνὴρ τὴν ὀφειλὴν ἀποδιδότω
"the husband should fulfill his [marital] duty to his wife"
𝔓11 𝔓46 ℵ A B C D F G Ψ 33 1739 cop
RSV NRSV ESV NASB NIV TNIV NEB REB NJB NAB NLT HCSB NET

variant/TR τη γυναικι ο ανηρ την οφειλομενην ευνοιαν αποδιδοτω
"the husband should give his wife the kindness that is due [her]"
Maj syr
KJV NKJV

The WH NU reading is strongly supported by the manuscript evidence. The variant reveals that some translator or scribe tried to soften Paul's command that a husband had an obligation to satisfy his wife sexually.

1 Corinthians 7:5

WH NU σχολάσητε τῇ προσευχῇ
"you may devote yourselves to prayer"
𝔓11vid 𝔓46 א* A B C D F G Ψ 1739 cop
RSV NRSV ESV NASB NIV TNIV NEB REB NJB NAB NLT HCSB NET

variant/TR σχολασητε τη νηστεια και τη προσευχη
"you may devote yourselves to fasting and to prayer"
א2 Maj syr
KJV NKJV HCSBmg NETmg

The addition, which is late, reflects the ascetic tendencies of certain scribes influenced by the monastic movement. Paul would probably not be calling for one form of abstinence—fasting—in the same passage where he is clearly speaking against sexual abstinence. (See also note on Mark 9:29.)

1 Corinthians 7:7

Zuntz (1953, 52) argues that 𝔓46 (also א2 Ψ Maj) preserves the original wording of the last phrase, ος μεν ουτως, ος δε ουτως ("to one person this [gift] and to another that") instead of ο μεν ουτως, ο δε ουτως ("one to this and one to that"), found in א* A B C D F G P 33 1739. Zuntz's reason is that the latter reading is an atticism created by Alexandrian scribes.

1 Corinthians 7:9

TR NU have the aorist verb γαμησαι ("to marry") based on the testimony of 𝔓46 א2 B C2 D F G Ψ 1739 Maj. This is a change from previous editions of the Nestle text (and from WH), which read the present tense verb γαμειν, based on א* A C* 33. The latter word suggests "living in a state of marriage"; whereas the former connotes nothing more than "getting married." As such, γαμησαι is more natural in the immediate context: "it is better to get married than to burn."

1 Corinthians 7:14

All three editions (TR WH NU) read ηγιασται γαρ ο ανηρ ο απιστος εν τη γυναικι ("for the unbelieving husband is sanctified by the wife"). This is found in 𝔓46 א* A B C and in all English versions. Some Western witnesses (D F G syrh) add πιστη ("the believing") to "wife" to make explicit what is already implicit in the text: The wife has to be a believer in order to sanctify her unbelieving husband.

1 Corinthians 7:15

WH NU κέκληκεν ὑμᾶς ὁ θεός
"God has called you"
א* A C copbo
RSVmg NRSV ESV NEB REB NJB NAB NLT HCSB NET

variant/TR κεκληκεν ημας ο θεος
"God has called us"
𝔓46 ℵ2 B D F G Ψ 33 1739 Maj syr cop[sa]
KJV NKJV RSV NRSVmg ESVmg NASB NIV TNIV NJBmg NLTmg HCSBmg

Although the two pronouns υμας and ημας were often confused for one another in the course of textual transmission (because they look alike and were pronounced similarly), in this case ημας ("us") is the more difficult reading and better attested. It is more difficult to imagine Paul saying that God had called "us" to peace with respect to maintaining or breaking marital relations, when he himself was obviously excluded from such issues. But Paul had a habit of being inclusive in his exhortations.

1 Corinthians 7:17a

The scribe of 𝔓46 originally wrote the aorist verb, εμερισεν ("he apportioned"), which is also the reading in ℵ2 (A) C D F G Ψ Maj. Then the scribe himself corrected this word by changing the *sigma* to *kappa:* εμερικεν. He should have also added a *mu* at the beginning of the word to make it μεμερικεν, the perfect tense of this verb. (NA27 incorrectly cites 𝔓46 as reading μεμερικεν, although that was probably the scribe's intention.) This correction reveals that the scribe probably knew of both readings; thus, both variants are very early. The perfect tense was perpetuated in the Alexandrian tradition: ℵ* B 1739, while the aorist turned up in many later manuscripts. TR NU print the aorist, while WH preferred the perfect. The difference in meaning is that the aorist emphasizes the one-time action of God's distribution of gifts to the various members of the church, while the perfect emphasizes the long-lasting effect of this distribution.

1 Corinthians 7:17b

WH NU ἑκάστῳ ὡς ἐμέρισεν ὁ κύριος, ἕκαστον ὡς κέκληκεν ὁ θεός
"as the Lord has assigned to each one, as God has called each one"
𝔓46 ℵ A B C D F 33 1739 syr[p] cop
RSV NRSV ESV NASB NIV TNIV NEB REB NJB NAB NLT HCSB NET

variant 1/TR εσκατω ως εμερισεν ο θεος, εκαστον ως κεκληκεν ο κυριος
"as God has assigned to each one, as the Lord has called each one"
Maj syr[h]
KJV NKJV

variant 2 εσκατω ως εμερισεν ο θεος, εκαστον ως κεκληκεν ο θεος
"as God has assigned to each one, as God has called each one"
Ψ 1881
none

The manuscript evidence overwhelmingly supports the WH NU reading. The first variant, found in the majority of the manuscripts, is a change influenced by a similar passage, Rom 12:3. The second variant is an extension of the first. The first variant became part of TR, and so it was translated in KJV and NKJV.

1 Corinthians 7:28

A few Western manuscripts (D F G) changed the expression εαν δε και γαμησης ("but if indeed you marry"), supported by excellent witnesses ($\mathfrak{P}^{15}$ $\mathfrak{P}^{46}$ ℵ A B C etc.), to εαν δε και λαβης γυναικα ("but if indeed you take a wife").

1 Corinthians 7:33-34

WH NU

πῶς ἀρέσῃ τῇ γυναικί, [34]καὶ μεμέρισται. καὶ ἡ γυνὴ ἡ ἄγαμος καὶ ἡ παρθένος μεριμνᾷ τὰ τοῦ κυρίου.

"how he can please his wife, [34] and he is divided. And the unmarried woman or virgin is concerned about the things of the Lord."

$\mathfrak{P}^{15}$ B P cop^{sa}

RSV NRSV ESV NASB NIV TNIV NEB REB NJB NAB NLT HCSB NET

variant 1

πως αρεση τη γυναικι, [34]και μεμερισται. και η γυνη η αγαμος και η παρθενος η αγαμος μεριμνα τα του κυριου.

"how he can please his wife, [34] and he is divided. And the unmarried woman or unmarried virgin is concerned about the things of the Lord."

$\mathfrak{P}^{46}$ ℵ A 33 1739 1881 Origen$^{\text{according to 1739}}$

none

variant 2/TR

πως αρεση τη γυναικι. [34]μεμερισται η γυνη και η παρθενος. η αγαμος μεριμνα τα του κυριου.

"how he can please his wife. [34] There is a difference between the wife and the virgin; the unmarried woman is concerned about the things of the Lord."

D^2 F G Ψ Maj

KJV NKJV RSVmg NRSVmg NASBmg NEBmg REBmg NJBmg

The critical apparatus of NA^{27} and of UBS^4 lists a few more variants than the ones noted above, but these three readings represent the major textual differences. In context, a fuller rendering of the NU text is as follows: "But a married man is concerned about the affairs of this world—how he can please his wife—[34] and he is divided. And the unmarried woman or virgin is concerned about the Lord's affairs." The first variant has a repetition of η αγαμος ("the unmarried"); it is perhaps the result of scribal expansion. However, other scribes could have found it redundant and therefore deleted the second η αγαμος. Both of these readings, however, connect και μεμερισται ("and he is divided") with the end of 7:33. As such, the text means that a married man is divided in his interests—between the Lord and his wife. The second variant (in TR) alters the meaning significantly by bringing 7:33 to a close with the words "how he may please his wife" and then beginning 7:34 with a word about how there is a distinction of motives between a wife and a virgin.

1 Corinthians 7:38

WH NU

ὁ γαμίζων τὴν ἑαυτοῦ παρθένον

"the one marrying his own virgin"

$\mathfrak{P}^{15vid}$ ℵ* A P 33 1739 syr ($\mathfrak{P}^{46}$ B D αυτου instead of εαυτου)

NKJVmg RSV NRSV ESV NIV TNIV NEB REB NJB NAB NLT HCSB NET

variant/TR ο εκγαμιζων
"the one giving [her] in marriage"
א[2] Ψ Maj
KJV NKJV NASB NIVmg NEBmg REBmg NETmg

The WH NU reading is supported by the best manuscript evidence (with one variation of the pronoun). Nonetheless, this expression has been very problematic for interpreters, who have seen it either as way of saying that a fiancé marries his virgin fiancée or of saying that a father gives away his virgin daughter in marriage. The ambiguity is taken away in TR, which conveys the notion of a father giving away his virgin daughter in marriage. This is reflected in KJV and NKJV, as well as in NASB and margins of other modern versions.

1 Corinthians 7:39

WH NU γυνὴ δέδεται
"a woman is bound"
𝔓[15vid] 𝔓[46] א* A B D* 0278 33 1739
RSV NRSV ESV NASB NIV TNIV NEB REB NJB NAB (NLT) HCSB NET

variant 1/TR γυνη δεδεται νομω
"a woman is bound by law"
א[2] D[1] F G Ψ Maj syr
KJV NKJV HCSBmg

variant 2 γυνη δεδεται γαμω
"a woman is bound by marriage"
K cop[bo]
none

The WH NU reading is fully supported by a wide range of witnesses; in a fuller context it is rendered, "a woman is bound as long as her husband lives." Both variants are gap-fillers created by scribes who wanted to tell their readers just exactly how a woman was bound to her husband. The first variant was influenced by Rom 7:2; the second is a natural filler.

1 Corinthians 7:40

Most manuscripts read, δοκω δε καγω πνευμα θεου εχειν ("and I think I have the Spirit of God"). 𝔓[15] and 33, however, have a different title here: πνευμα Χριστου ("Spirit of Christ"). The title "Spirit of Christ" is far less common than "the Spirit of God"; the former appears only in Rom 8:9 and 1 Pet 1:11, the latter in many NT verses. It would be much more likely that scribes changed "the Spirit of Christ" to "the Spirit of God" than vice versa. In this chapter Paul has made the point of separating his advice from the Lord's directives (see 7:10, 25). Nonetheless, he claims that his advice concerning virgins and the unmarried is to be heeded because he has the Spirit of God/Christ. Having made the Lord (that is, the Lord Jesus Christ) the source of reference throughout this chapter, it would be natural for Paul to conclude with an affirmation of his possession of "the Spirit of Christ" rather than "the Spirit of God." But these arguments, based on internal evidence, cannot outweigh the fact that all other manuscripts read, "the Spirit of God" (Comfort 1996, 140-141).

1 Corinthians 8:3a

TR WH NU — εἰ δέ τις ἀγαπᾷ τὸν θεόν
"but if anyone loves God"
𝔓[15] ℵ[2] A B D F G Ψ
KJV NKJV RSV NRSV ESV NASB NIV TNIV NEBmg REB NJB NAB NLT HCSB NET

variant — ει δε τις αγαπα
"but if anyone loves"
𝔓[46] Clement
TNIVmg NEB NLTmg

See next note.

1 Corinthians 8:3b

TR WH NU — οὗτος ἔγνωσται ὑπ' αὐτοῦ
"this one is recognized by him"
𝔓[15vid] ℵ[2] A B D F G Ψ
all

variant — ουτος εγνωσται
"this one is recognized"
𝔓[46] ℵ* 33 Clement
TNIVmg NEBmg NLTmg

Zuntz (1953, 31-32) argues quite convincingly that the shorter reading found in 𝔓[46] preserves the original text. The context calls for the demonstration of love among Christians (as opposed to exercising judgment on the basis of superior spiritual knowledge), not love for God. The one who loves has true *gnosis* ("knowledge"); he will be recognized in the church and by God for having true spiritual knowledge. Scribes, however, could not resist adding a direct object after the first verb and a prepositional phrase after the second. (A similar addition occurred in 1 John 4:19—see note.) Nearly all translators followed suit in including the same additions. But the NEB translators preferred the reading of 𝔓[46] (in the first part of the verse) because they thought that the context calls for a statement about loving one's fellow Christians (Tasker 1964, 436). TNIV and NLT note the variants—quite specifically, the TNIV note indicates that "an early manuscript and another ancient witness" (i.e., 𝔓[46] and Clement) read "but whoever loves truly knows."

1 Corinthians 8:4

WH NU — οὐδεὶς θεὸς εἰ μὴ εἷς
"there is no God except one"
𝔓[46] ℵ* A B D F G Ψ
RSV NRSV ESV NASB NIV TNIV NEB REB NAB NLT HCSB NET

variant/TR — ουδεις θεος ετερος ει μη εἷς
"there is no other God except one"
ℵ[2] Maj syr
KJV NKJV (NJB)

The WH NU reading has excellent manuscript support. The addition of "other" in the majority of manuscripts exhibits the influence of a common OT motif that speaks against the worship of other gods (see Exod 20:3; Deut 5:7; 6:14; 28:14; Judg 10:13; 1 Sam 8:8).

1 Corinthians 8:6

At the end of this verse, a few late manuscripts (630 1881 0142) add και ἓν πνευμα αγιον, εν ω τα παντα και ημεις εν αυτω ("and one Holy Spirit, in whom are all things, and we in him"). The addition is clearly an attempt to make the verse a Trinitarian formula: "One God the Father . . . one Lord Jesus Christ . . . one Holy Spirit." This form of the verse may have been created as early as the fourth century, if not before, because Gregory Nazianzus (*Or. Bas.* 39.12) cites it.

1 Corinthians 8:7

WH NU τινὲς δὲ τῇ συνηθείᾳ ἕως ἄρτι τοῦ εἰδώλου
"but some being accustomed to the idol until now"
ℵ* A B P Ψ 33
RSV NRSV (ESV) NASB NIV TNIV NEB REB NJBmg NAB NLT HCSB NET

variant/TR τινες δε τη συνειδησει εως αρτι του ειδωλου
"but some having a conscience toward the idol until now"
ℵ[2] D F G Maj syr
KJV NKJV NEBmg NJB

The variant probably arose when a scribe confused συνηθεια ("accustomed") for συνειδησις ("conscience"), which appears in the next clause. Paul's point is that some of the Corinthians, prior to becoming Christians, had become so accustomed to thinking of idols as real gods that eating food purchased in the marketplace (which might have been offered to idols) was tantamount to participating in idolatry (Comfort 1993, 425). The variant reading, followed by KJV, NKJV, and NJB, affirms what the second part of the verse says: Such Christians have a sensitive conscience toward any association with idolatry.

1 Corinthians 8:8

WH NU οὔτε ἐὰν μὴ φάγωμεν ὑστερούμεθα, οὔτε ἐὰν φάγωμεν περισσεύομεν
"we are no worse off if we don't eat, and we are no better if we do eat"
𝔓[46] B 81 (1739) cop
RSV NRSV ESV NASB NIV TNIV NEB REB NJB NAB NLT HCSB NET

variant/TR γαρ ουτε εαν φαγωμεν περισσευομεν, ουτε εαν μη φαγωμεν υστερουμεθα
"for we are no better if we do eat, and we are no worse off if we do not eat"
D F G Ψ Maj (ℵ A[c] 33 lack γαρ)
KJV NKJV

The word order in WH NU, though supported only by Egyptian manuscripts, is the more difficult reading in that it places the negative statement first. This probably gave occasion for scribes to adjust the syntax so that the positive statement would come first.

1 Corinthians 8:12

TR WH NU τύπτοντες αὐτῶν τὴν συνείδησιν ἀσθενοῦσαν
"wounding their conscience when it is weak"
ℵ A B D 33 1739 Maj
RSV NRSV ESV NASB NIV TNIV NEBmg REB NJB NAB NLT HCSB NET

variant τυπτοντες αυτων συνειδησιν
"wounding their conscience"
𝔓[46] Clement
KJV NKJV NEB REBmg

Tasker (1964, 436) argued for the reading in NEB (supported by 𝔓[46]) by saying that the longer reading "was considered an addition to the text, natural in view of the general context, but less effective at this point, where to wound a brother's conscience seems to be regarded as a sin against Christ, whether that conscience is 'weak' or not." The NU editors thought the scribe of 𝔓[46] either made a mistake of omission or modified the text (TCGNT)—perhaps for the very reason Tasker purported. The REB translators revised NEB in favor of the longer reading.

1 Corinthians 9:1

WH NU Οὐκ εἰμὶ ἐλεύθερος; οὐκ εἰμὶ ἀπόστολος;
"Am I not free? Am I not an apostle?"
𝔓[46] ℵ A B P 33 1739 cop Tertullian
RSV NRSV ESV NASB NIV TNIV NEB REB NJB NAB NLT HCSB NET

variant/TR Ουκ ειμι αποστολος; ουκ ειμι ελευθερος;
"Am I not an apostle? Am I not free?"
D F G Ψ Maj
KJV NKJV

The inversion of questions in later witnesses is an attempt to make Paul's apostleship the leading motif of this pericope. However, the entire section takes its keynote from Paul's declaration of his freedom to do whatever is necessary to carry out his apostolic functions. Furthermore, the transposition in TR causes a split between the questions "Am I not an apostle?" and "Have I not seen Jesus our Lord?" These two belong together since it was Paul's vision of the risen Christ that affirmed his apostleship (see 15:3-8).

1 Corinthians 9:9a

All three editions (TR WH NU) read εν γαρ τω Μωυσεως νομω γεγραπται ("for in the law of Moses it is written"), with the support of B* D* F G 1739. All English versions follow. There are two shorter variants on this: 𝔓[46] it[b] omit Μωυσεως, yielding the rendering, "for in the law it is written." A few Western manuscripts (D* F G) read simply γεγραπται γαρ ("for it is written"). It is not like Paul to introduce a quotation from the Pentateuch with the expression, "the law of Moses." In fact, this is the only instance. Therefore, we can question if scribes went against Paul's style when they wrote "of Moses." Or is it possible that the Western text in the second variant, as the shorter reading, preserved the original wording which was then expanded in two forms? Certainty eludes us.

1 Corinthians 9:9b

The NU text reads ου κημωσεις βουν αλοωντα ("you shall not muzzle an ox treading grain") based on B* D* F G 1739. There is a variant verb, φιμωσεις, which also means "muzzle," found in 𝔓[46] ℵ A B[2] C D[1] Ψ 33 Maj (so TR WH). The two verbs, which are synonymous, could have been confounded one for the other because there is only a two-letter difference (κη/φι). Or, if a scribe was being meticulous, he could have purposely changed κημωσεις to φιμωσεις in order to make it conform to the Septuagint version of Deut 25:4, the Scripture cited here. However, it seems more likely that the more common word, φιμωσεις (which has a range of meaning from "silence" to "muzzle"), was changed to the more text-specific word, κημωσεις (which is used only of muzzling animals). Indeed, the scribe of D made this very same change in 1 Tim 5:18, where Deut 25:4 is also quoted. Thus, the variant reading is more likely original—but not only on internal grounds. In this case, the manuscript evidence, being both early and diverse, also favors the variant reading.

1 Corinthians 9:10

WH NU	ὁ ἀλοῶν ἐπ' ἐλπίδι τοῦ μετέχειν "the one threshing ought [to thresh] in hope of partaking" 𝔓46 ℵ* A B C P 33 1739 syr RSV NRSV ESV NASB NIV TNIV NEB REB NJB NAB NLT HCSB NET
variant 1	ο αλοων της ελπιδος αυτου μετεχειν "the one threshing ought to share his [the plowman's] hope of partaking" D* F G none
variant 2/TR	ο αλοων της ελπιδος αυτου μετεχειν επ ελπιδι "the one threshing in hope ought to share his [the plowman's] hope of partaking" ℵ2 D1 Ψ Maj KJV NKJV

According to WH NU, which have superior documentation to that of either of the variants, a full rendering is: "For it is written for us, 'the one plowing ought to plow in hope, and the one threshing ought [to thresh] in hope of partaking [of the crop].'" From the start, it should be noted that this does not come from any known OT quotation. Thus, we are left with these three variants of some unknown text that Paul was citing. It looks as if the elliptical expression in the WH NU reading was expanded to the way we see it in the first variant, which was then conflated with the text in the majority of manuscripts. In the WH NU reading, the hope is set on partaking of the crop—for both the plowman and thresher. In the variant readings, the thresher wants to participate in the plowman's hope of partaking in the crop. The WH NU reading suits the context, where Paul is focusing on the rights of a worker to receive his due reward. The variant is seemingly more logical in that it is the plowman who has to have the hope of partaking of the crop because he does not see the mature grain, whereas the thresher, who sees the grain, will soon partake of what the plowman had to hope for. But this is beside the point for Paul, who was not here teaching about hope; rather, he was arguing that all workers do their work anticipating a benefit for their labor.

1 Corinthians 9:16

All three editions (TR WH NU) have the word καυχημα ("boast") in the expression, "for when I preach the gospel, there is no boast for me." This has excellent support: 𝔓46 ℵ2 A B C D2 Ψ Maj syr cop, and is followed by all the English versions. A variant reading, found in ℵ* D* F G, has χαρις ("thanks/grace"): "for when I preach the gospel, there is no thanks (or, grace) for me." This variant reading could not have been a scribal error; rather, it was an attempt to anticipate Paul's following expression, "for woe to me if I do not preach the gospel," wherein the expression "woe to me" means "I will be damned." In other words, he would not receive any thanks or grace from God if he failed to fulfill his divinely appointed task of preaching the gospel; rather, he would receive judgment. But Paul's point is that he did not preach the gospel so that he could boast about it; he did it in response to an inner compulsion that was directed by the divine will.

1 Corinthians 9:20

WH NU τοῖς ὑπὸ νόμον ὡς ὑπὸ νόμον, μὴ ὢν αὐτὸς ὑπὸ νόμον
"to those under law, as [one] under law, not being myself under law"
𝔓46vid ℵ A B C D* F G P 33 1739
NKJVmg RSV NRSV ESV NASB NIV TNIV NEB REB NJB NAB NLT HCSB NET

variant/TR τοις υπο νομον ως υπο νομον
"to those under law, as [one] under law"
D² (L) Maj syrp
KJV NKJV HCSBmg NETmg

The WH NU reading has superior testimony including that of 𝔓46, which is not listed in either NA27 or UBS4. However, a reconstruction of the text shows that it must have included the full verbiage (see *Text of Earliest MSS*, 265). The omission of the last phrase in the majority of manuscripts probably arose as a scribal error of haplography (the eye of a scribe passing over the third υπο νομον—it appears four times in the verse).

1 Corinthians 9:22

WH NU ἐγενόμην τοῖς ἀσθενέσιν ἀσθενής
"to the weak I became weak"
𝔓46 ℵ* A B 1739 it
NKJVmg RSV NRSV ESV NASB NIV TNIV NEB REB NJB NAB NLT HCSB NET

variant/TR εγενομην τοις ασθενεσιν ως ασθενης
"to the weak I became as weak"
ℵ² C D F G Ψ 33 Maj syr cop
KJV NKJV

The WH NU reading has the testimony of the four earliest manuscripts, as well as 1739 and the Old Latin manuscripts. The reading in TR is a scribal carryover from the previous phrases, where Paul used the comparative ως ("as"). In this instance, however, Paul chose to declare his solidarity with those experiencing weakness (cf. 2 Cor 11:29).

1 Corinthians 9:23

WH NU πάντα δὲ ποιῶ διὰ τὸ εὐαγγέλιον
"I do all things on account of the gospel"
𝔓46 ℵ A B C D F G P 33 1739
RSV NRSV ESV NASB NIV TNIV NEB REB NJB NAB NLT HCSB NET

variant/TR τουτο δε ποιω δια το ευαγγελιον
"I do this on account of the gospel"
Ψ Maj syr
KJV NKJV

The change in the majority of manuscripts limits Paul's activities to those just previously mentioned, whereas the WH NU reading (with strong documentary support) indicates that Paul listed only some of the exemplary things he did for the sake of proclaiming the gospel.

1 Corinthians 10:2

NU πάντες εἰς τὸν Μωϋσῆν ἐβαπτίσθησαν
"all were baptized into Moses"
ℵ A C D F G Ψ 33
KJV NKJV RSV NRSV ESV NASB NIV TNIV NJB NAB NLT HCSB (NET)

variant/TR WH παντες εις τον Μωυσην εβαπτισαντο
"all had themselves baptized into Moses"
$\mathfrak{P}^{46c}$ ($\mathfrak{P}^{46*}$ εβαπτιζοντο) B 1739 Maj
NASBmg NEB REB (NETmg)

The original scribe of $\mathfrak{P}^{46}$ wrote εβαπτιζοντο ("they were having themselves baptized"—an imperfect middle verb), which was then changed by a later corrector to εβαπτισαντο (an aorist middle). The reading in NU is a passive voice verb; the variant is a middle voice. The reading for the NU text was adopted by the majority of NU editors, with Metzger and Wikgren voicing the minority view (see TCGNT). According to Metzger and Wikgren, the reading in $\mathfrak{P}^{46c}$ B and 1739 is more likely Pauline because the Jews baptized themselves (conveyed by the middle voice), whereas Christians were baptized by others (conveyed by the passive voice)—and Christian scribes would be more likely to change the middle voice to the passive than vice versa. The middle voice conveys the idea that the Jews "had themselves baptized" by the cloud and sea—or that they "immersed themselves" in the cloud and the sea when they joined Moses in the exodus. The NEB and REB translators, probably convinced by such arguments, followed the testimony of $\mathfrak{P}^{46c}$ with B, while the NASB translators noted the reading in deference to $\mathfrak{P}^{46c}$ with B. Though the NET translators agree with the minority view of Metzger and Wikgren (see note in NETmg), the actual translation in the text is no different than the majority view.

1 Corinthians 10:8

According to the text written by Paul, "23,000" (εικοσι τρεις χιλιαδες) Israelites died in one day as a result of their disobedience to God. But this number does not square with the number recorded in Num 25:9, which reads, "24,000." Consequently, some scribes (81 *pc*) and translators (vg^{MSS} syr^{h}) changed the number 23,000 to 24,000 so as to harmonize 1 Corinthians with Numbers.

1 Corinthians 10:9

TR NU μηδὲ ἐκπειράζωμεν τὸν Χριστόν
"neither let us test the Christ"
$\mathfrak{P}^{46}$ D F G Ψ 1739 Maj syr cop Irenaeus Origen$^{\text{according to 1739mg}}$
KJV NKJV RSVmg NRSV ESV TNIV NEBmg NJBmg NAB NLT HCSB NET

variant 1/WH μηδε εκπειραζωμεν τον κυριον
"neither let us test the Lord"
ℵ B C P 33 syr^{hmg}
RSV NRSVmg ESVmg NASB NIV TNIVmg NEB REB NJB NABmg NLTmg NETmg

variant 2 μηδε εκπειραζωμεν τον θεον
"neither let us test God"
A 81
NETmg

In a fuller context, the TR NU reading is rendered as: "neither let us test (or, tempt) the Christ as some of them tested [him] and were destroyed by serpents." This reading has early and diverse support, and it is the reading more likely to have been changed. It is far more likely that "Christ" was changed to "Lord" (or, "God") than vice versa. Given the context of 1 Cor 10, it was appropriate for Paul to speak of Christ being put to the test by the Israelites, for he had just previously mentioned that Christ was the spiritual rock that accompanied the Israelites in their wilderness wanderings (10:4). (Paul was probably aware of the OT calling God the "Rock" that accompanied the Jews in the wilderness. Indeed, in the Septuagint of Deut 32:4 and 15 the "Rock" is actually printed as θεος—that is, "the Rock" is another name for "God." Paul saw Christ, as God, being that spiritual Rock.) Paul twice spoke of Christ with respect to his presence with the Israelites. But some scribes had a theological or exegetical problem with the reading "Christ"—for one of two reasons: (1) they disagreed with any notion of a preincarnate presence of Christ, or (2) they did not want it to be said that Christ was the judge responsible for sending serpents to destroy several thousand Israelites. Thus, scribes tried to neutralize the text by changing "Christ" to "Lord" or "God." (A similar textual change occurred in Jude 4—see note.) The change to "Lord" occurred at least as early as the third century, per the testimony of the Letter of Hymenaeus (ca. 270). But the earliest extant manuscript, 𝔓[46], and some early church fathers (Irenaeus, Origen) attest to the reading "Christ"—a reading which persisted in later manuscripts (hence, its inclusion in TR, followed by KJV and NKJV).

Prior to NA[26], the reading in the Nestle text was κυριον ("Lord"). But now this has been changed to Χριστον ("Christ"). Most twentieth-century English versions follow "Lord." But this has changed as more recent versions (NRSV TNIV NAB NLT HCSB NET) have "Christ." (For a full discussion of this textual problem, see Osburn 1981, 201-212.)

1 Corinthians 10:11

WH NU	ταῦτα δὲ τυπικῶς συνέβαινεν "these things happened as examples" 𝔓[46vid] A B 33 1739 NKJVmg RSV NRSV ESV NASB NIV TNIV NEB NAB NLT HCSB NET
variant/TR	ταυτα δε παντα τυπικως συνεβαινεν "all these things happened as examples" C Ψ Maj it syr (ℵ D F G 81 παντα δε ταυτα) KJV NKJV REB NJB

The insertion of παντα ("all") in two different locations in the textual tradition exposes its secondary nature. Scribes added it in an attempt to have all the events noted by Paul in 10:1-10 be exemplary, whereas it is more likely that this summarizes only 10:7-10. Furthermore, it should be noted that 10:6 sufficiently summarizes 10:1-5 by pointing to those events as providing examples for the believers.

1 Corinthians 10:16

Instead of the expression, το ποτηριον της ευλογιας ("the cup of blessing"), found in nearly all manuscripts, a few Western manuscripts (F G 365) read το ποτηριον της ευχαριστιας ("the cup of the Eucharist").

1 Corinthians 10:17

The oneness of the church is here depicted as many members sharing one body, just as the many members share one loaf of bread during communion when each takes a piece. Thus, Paul chooses to speak only of the bread, not the cup. But several Western manuscripts (D F G it) add και του ενος ποτηριου ("and of the one cup") after ενος αρτου ("one bread").

1 Corinthians 10:19

All three editions (TR WH NU) include the clause, η οτι ειδωλον τι εστιν; ("or that an idol is anything?"). This has the support of א[c] B C[c] Maj. The clause is lacking in 𝔓[46] א* A C* 1881. This variant reading could be the result of homoeoteleuton: τι εστιν ends two clauses in a row. But would such an error have occurred in so many diverse witnesses? Thus, it is possible that the phrase "or that an idol is anything?" is an ancient gloss.

1 Corinthians 10:20

NU ἃ θύουσιν
"the things they sacrifice"
B D F G
NAB NLT HCSB NETmg

variant/TR WH α θυουσιν τα εθνη
"the things the Gentiles sacrifice"
𝔓[46vid] א A C P Ψ 33[vid] 1739 Maj
KJV NKJV RSV NRSV ESV NASB NIV TNIV NEB REB NJB HCSBmg NET

The difference among the variants pertains to the inclusion or exclusion of τα εθνη ("the Gentiles/the pagans"). Most likely it was added to clarify that it was not "Israel" that Paul was speaking about (10:18), but that he had shifted to a new subject—the Gentiles. Had τα εθνη ("the Gentiles") been original, there is no good reason why it would have been deleted. Most English versions reflect the variant because they add the subject for the sake of clarity.

1 Corinthians 10:23

WH NU πάντα ἔξεστιν . . . πάντα ἔξεστιν
"all things are lawful . . . all things are lawful"
𝔓[46] א* A B C* D F G (33) (1739[c])
NKJVmg RSV NRSV ESV NASB NIV NEB REB NJB NAB NLTmg HCSB NET

variant/TR παντα μοι εξεστιν . . . παντα μοι εξεστιν
"all things are lawful for me . . . all things are lawful for me"
א[2] C[3] H (P) Ψ Maj syr
KJV NKJV TNIV NLT HCSBmg

The manuscript evidence for the WH NU reading is early and diverse. The variant reading displays a scribal addition intended to particularize the statement, making it specific only to Paul: "all things are lawful for me but not all things are profitable; all things are lawful for me but not all things build up." Surely, Paul himself espoused this view (see 6:12), but the statement in this context is either a general maxim that describes Christian liberty and restraints or a quotation of what the Corinthians espoused about their freedom.

1 Corinthians 10:27

The Western text (D* F G it) exhibits typical scribal gap-filling by adding εις δειπνον ("to a meal") after ει τις καλει υμας των απιστων ("if any unbeliever invites you").

1 Corinthians 10:28a

The word ιεροθυτον ("a sacrifice offering"), found in 𝔓46 ℵ A B H 1739* (so WH NU), was changed to ειδωλοθυτον ("idolatrous sacrifice") in C D F G Ψ Maj (so TR) by way of conformity to 8:1, 4, 7.

1 Corinthians 10:28b

WH NU — μὴ ἐσθίετε δι' ἐκεῖνον τὸν μηνύσαντα καὶ τὴν συνείδησιν
"do not eat [it] for the sake of the one who told you and for conscience [sake]"
ℵ A B C D F G H* 33 1739
NKJVmg RSV NRSV ESV NASB NIV TNIV NEB REB NJB NAB NLT HCSB NET

variant 1 — μη εσθιετε δι εκεινον
"do not eat it because of this"
𝔓46
none

variant 2/TR — μη εσθιετε δι εκεινον τον μηνυσαντα και την συνειδησιν, του γαρ κυριου η γη και το πληρωμα αυτης
"do not eat [it] for the sake of the one who told you and for conscience [sake], for the earth is the Lord's and its fullness"
H[c] Ψ Maj syr[h]
KJV NKJV HCSBmg NETmg

The second variant, found in the majority of manuscripts, contains an added gloss, carried over from 10:26 (which has a citation of Ps 24:1). Fee (1987, 476) says "it appears to be a clumsy attempt to justify abstinence as well as indulgence on the basis of the same OT text." The first variant does not appear to be the result of any kind of scribal error. Either the scribe of 𝔓46 intentionally shortened his copy, or he preserved the original wording, to which was added the explanation found in ℵ A B H 1739*.

1 Corinthians 10:29

In an attempt to identify what kind of person Paul was imagining here, several Western witnesses (F G it[b,d]) replace αλλης συνειδησεως ("another man's conscience") with απιστου συνειδησεως ("an unbeliever's conscience").

1 Corinthians 11:1-2

The scribe of 𝔓46 made a clear break between the end of 11:1 and the beginning of 11:2. This spacing indicates that the scribe considered 11:1 to be the concluding sentence for the paragraph begun in 10:31, not the opening paragraph for chapter 11. The NU text has the same design, as do most modern translations. KJV, however, makes 11:1 the opening sentence for the eleventh chapter.

1 Corinthians 11:2

WH NU ἐπαινῶ δὲ ὑμᾶς
"now I praise you"
𝔓46 ℵ A B C 1739 cop
RSV NRSV ESV NASB NIV TNIV NEB REB NJB NAB NLT HCSB NET

variant/TR επαινω δε υμας, αδελφοι
"now I praise you, brothers"
D F G Ψ Maj syr
KJV NKJV HCSBmg NETmg

The WH NU reading has the support of the five earliest manuscripts, plus that of 1739 and Coptic manuscripts. Scribes may have also been prompted to add "brothers" because 11:2 opens a new section, and it is typical in Pauline epistles for new sections to begin with this vocative.

1 Corinthians 11:5

The text is ambiguous as to what "head" a woman shames if she shaves off her hair; the "head" could be her husband, Christ, or her own head. Some manuscripts (B D^{2}) relieve the ambiguity by changing καταισχυνει την κεφαλην αυτης ("shames her head") to καται-σχυνει την κεφαλην εαυτης ("shames her own head").

1 Corinthians 11:10

TR WH NU ὀφείλει ἡ γυνὴ ἐξουσίαν ἔχειν ἐπὶ τῆς κεφαλῆς
"the woman ought to have authority on her head"
all extant Greek MSS
all (see RSVmg NLTmg)

variant οφειλει η γυνη καλυμμα εχειν επι της κεφαλης
"the woman ought to have a veil on her head"
vg^{MSS} cop^{boMSS} MSS$^{according\ to\ Irenaeus}$
(see RSV NLT) NEBmg

All Greek manuscripts say that a woman should have "authority" (εξουσιαν) on her head. But the word "authority" was changed to "veil" because the latter was considered a metonym for the former. A marginal note in the RSV, which places "veil" in the text, explains that a "veil" is a symbol for the Greek word "authority." Those who argue that this passage is speaking of the subordination of women say that a woman has to wear a veil in deference to the angels because they were considered the guardians of order and decorum in public worship (see NJBmg, citing a Qumran interpretation of Deut 23:15). But this is the traditional view; the word εξουσιαν can also mean "the right to exercise one's freedom" (see 6:12; 8:9 for this usage). Thus, Paul could have been saying that a woman has the freedom to cover or not cover her head during public worship—"a woman ought to exercise her rights when it comes to her head."

1 Corinthians 11:24a

WH NU	τοῦτο μού ἐστιν τὸ σῶμα "this is my body" 𝔓46 ℵ A B C* D F G 0199 33 1739 cop NKJVmg RSV NRSV ESV NASB NIV TNIV NEB REB NJB NAB NLT HCSB NET
variant/TR	λαβετε, φαγετε, τουτο μου εστιν το σωμα "take, eat, this is my body" C3 Ψ Maj itt syr KJV NKJV HCSBmg

The WH NU reading is supported by vastly superior documentation to that of TR. The variant reading was created by those who wanted to harmonize Paul's version of the Eucharist with Matthew's (Matt 26:26). Evidently, it became increasingly important for the church to have harmonized accounts of the Eucharist for liturgical reasons. Thus, the majority of manuscripts display this change. The same harmonization occurred in the majority of manuscripts in Mark 14:22, a parallel passage. This harmonization was included in TR, followed by KJV and NKJV. (See next note.)

1 Corinthians 11:24b

WH NU	τὸ σῶμα τὸ ὑπὲρ ὑμῶν "my body for you" 𝔓46 ℵ* A B C* 1739* NKJVmg RSV NRSV ESV NASB NIV TNIV NEB REB NJB NAB (NLT) HCSB NET
variant 1/TR	το σωμα το υπερ υμων κλωμενον "my body broken for you" ℵ2 C3 D2 F G Ψ 1739mg Maj syr KJV NKJV RSVmg NRSVmg ESVmg NASBmg NJBmg HCSBmg
variant 2	το σωμα το υπερ υμων θρυπτομενον "this is my body sacrificed for you" D* none
variant 3	"this is my body given for you" cop NJBmg

The absence of a participle before το υπερ υμων elicited three supplements. The most natural, "given," is found in Coptic translations and many modern versions (variant 3). The scribe of D supplied his own invention: "sacrificed" (variant 2). And many manuscripts exhibit scribal conformity to the wording found in the gospel accounts of the Last Supper (see Matt 26:26-28; Mark 14:22-24; Luke 22:19-20). As was mentioned in the previous note, such changes were motivated by liturgical considerations. Church leaders did not want conflicting wording for the Eucharist. The change became so pervasive that two manuscripts (ℵ2 C3), which originally lacked any participle, were emended to include κλωμενον, and one manuscript (D2) was changed to κλωμενον. Most of these changes occurred in the sixth to the ninth centuries. The reading of the Majority Text was incorporated in TR in the sixteenth century and popularized by KJV and NKJV thereafter.

1 Corinthians 11:29

WH NU — ὁ γὰρ ἐσθίων καὶ πίνων κρίμα ἑαυτῷ ἐσθίει καὶ πίνει μὴ διακρίνων τὸ σῶμα
"for the one eating and drinking eats and drinks judgment to himself, not discerning the body"
𝔓46 ℵ* A B C* 33 1739 cop
NKJVmg RSV NRSV ESV NASB (TNIV) NEB REB NJB NAB (NLT) HCSB NET

variant/TR — ο γαρ εσθιων και πινων αναξιως κριμα εαυτω εσθιει και πινει, μη διακρινων το σωμα του κυριου
"for the one eating and drinking unworthily eats and drinks judgment to himself, not discerning the body of the Lord"
ℵ2 Cc D F G (Ψ) Maj syr
KJV NKJV NIV NLTmg HCSBmg

The WH NU reading has the support of the five earliest manuscripts, as well as of 1739 and Coptic manuscripts. The variant reading shows two scribal interpolations, both of which were intended to clarify the meaning of the text. The first addition makes it absolutely clear that a person can only be judged for eating and drinking the Eucharist if he does so in an unworthy manner. One imagines that the unworthiness would come from not being able to distinguish the Eucharist meal from common food. But this has already been made clear in 11:27. The second addition intends to specify "the body" as being the Lord Jesus' body (as represented by the bread), as opposed to the body of Christ, the church. TNIV and NLT identify the body as being "the body of Christ." But Paul probably intended a double meaning here—that is, "the body" is both the body of Jesus and the body which is the church. This goes back to 10:16-17, where the breaking-of-bread imagery symbolizes both Christ's sacrifice and the unity of the many members of the church. The one bread, Christ's body, eaten by all the members of the church, makes them one bread and one body.

1 Corinthians 12:3

On the authority of ℵ A B C 33 1739, WH NU indicate that no one speaking by the Holy Spirit can say Αναθεμα Ιησους, which literally is, "a curse [is] Jesus." This reads differently in other manuscripts (𝔓46 D G Ψ Maj—so TR): Αναθεμα Ιησουν; this can be translated "a curse on Jesus." This is the way it is rendered in NEB and TEV.

1 Corinthians 12:9

WH NU — χαρίσματα ἰαμάτων ἐν τῷ ἑνὶ πνεύματι
"gifts of healing[s] by the one Spirit"
A B 33 1739 it
NKJVmg RSV NRSV ESV NASB NIV TNIV NEB REB NJB NAB NLT HCSB NET

variant 1/TR — χαρισματα ιαματων εν τω αυτω πνευματι
"gifts of healing[s] by the same Spirit"
ℵ C3 D F G 0201 Maj syr
KJV NKJV

variant 2 χαρισματα ιαματων εν τω πνευματι
"gifts of healing[s] by the Spirit"
𝔓46
none

Most likely, the first variant displays scribal conformity to the two previous expressions. The second variant could be the result of a scribal slip or purposeful excision. Because it is the shortest reading, it could also be original. But we would expect to see this reading show up somewhere else in the textual tradition, and it does not.

1 Corinthians 12:10

All three texts (TR WH NU) read ενεργηματα δυναμεων ("workings of powers"), with the support of ℵ A B C Ψ 33 1739 Maj. The Western text (D F G) reads ενεργεια δυναμεως ("working of power"), and 𝔓46 alone reads ενεργηματα δυναμεως ("workings of power"). Zuntz (1953, 100) correctly observes that "the parallel between ενεργηματα δυναμεων [workings of miraculous powers] and the preceding χαρισματα ιαματων [gifts of healings] is so natural that δυναμεως [miraculous power] could have hardly gotten into the text unless it was there originally." Thus, the reading of the editions probably presents scribal conformity, whereas 𝔓46 preserves the original wording. (The Western text displays a conflation of the other two.) The reading in 𝔓46 indicates that the gift is called ενεργηματα and it emanates from δυναμεως. In other words, it is the gift of being able to do many supernatural works by the power that God gives.

1 Corinthians 12:12

WH NU πάντα δὲ τὰ μέλη τοῦ σώματος
"and all the members of the body"
𝔓46vid ℵ* A B C F G L 33vid 1739 syr copbo
RSV NRSV ESV NASB NIV NEB REB NJB NAB NLT HCSB NET

variant/TR παντα δε τα μελη του σωματος του ενος
"and all the members of the one body"
ℵ2 D Ψ Maj itb
KJV NKJV TNIV

The variant presents the work of some pedantic scribe(s) who unfortunately ruined the climax of the sentence, which starts with "many members" and leads up to "one body": "and all the members of the body, being many, are one body."

1 Corinthians 12:13

WH NU πάντες ἓν πνεῦμα ἐποτίσθημεν
"we all were given to drink one Spirit"
𝔓46 ℵ B C D* F G
NKJVmg RSV NRSV ESV NASB NIV TNIV NEB REB NJB NAB (NLT) HCSB NET

variant 1/TR παντες εις ἓν πνευμα εποτισθημεν
"we all were given to drink into one Spirit"
D2 L
KJV NKJV

variant 2 παντες ἓν πομα εποτισθημεν
"we all were given to drink one drink"
630 1881 syr[h] Clement
none

variant 3 παντες ἓν εσμεν σωμα
"we all are one body"
A
none

The first textual variant presents an exegetical problem: Just what does it mean to drink into one Spirit? Quite possibly, this problem never occurred to the scribe who made the change, for he probably mechanically added εις as a repetition of the previous clause: ημεις παντες εις ἓν σωμα εβαπτισθημεν ("we were all baptized into one body"). The second variant is an attempt to relate this passage to the drinking of the one eucharistic cup (see 11:25). The third variant is an accidental, truncated version. The point of the text is that the many members of the body of Christ are united by virtue of their participation in the Spirit. By the Spirit, the many are baptized into one body; so now the many can enjoy drinking the Spirit of life.

1 Corinthians 12:31

WH NU τὰ χαρίσματα τὰ μείζονα
"the greater gifts"
𝔓46 ℵ A B C 33 1739 cop
NKJVmg RSV NRSV ESV NASB NIV TNIV NEB REB NJB NAB NLT HCSB NET

variant/TR τα χαρισματα τα κρειττονα
"the better gifts"
D F G Ψ Maj it
KJV NKJV

The variant reading displays a word found nowhere else in Paul's writings, and it presents a statement contrary to Paul's presentation of the spiritual gifts. There is not one spiritual gift that is better than the others (12:4-11), but some gifts are of greater benefit to the community of believers (Zuntz 1953, 135). Among these "greater" gifts would be the gift of prophecy (speaking for God) because it builds up all the members of the church (see 14:1-5).

1 Corinthians 13:3

WH NU ἐὰν παραδῶ τὸ σῶμα μου ἵνα καυχήσωμαι
"if I give my body that I may boast"
𝔓46 ℵ A B 048 33 1739* cop MSS[according to Jerome]
NKJVmg RSVmg NRSV ESVmg NASBmg NIVmg TNIV NEBmg REBmg NJBmg NAB NLT HCSBmg NET

variant/TR εαν παραδω το σωμα μου ινα καυθησωμαι
"if I give my body that I may be burned"
Ψ 1739[c] Maj (C D F G L καυθησομαι)
KJV NKJV RSV NRSVmg ESV NASB NIV TNIVmg NEB REB NJB NLTmg HCSB NETmg

In Greek, the words καυχησωμαι ("I may boast") and καυθησωμαι ("I may be burned"—a future subjunctive) are quite similar. There is only a one-letter difference: χ/θ. Therefore, either word could have been mistaken for the other. But it is highly unlikely that such a mistake would have occurred in so many manuscripts. Furthermore, it is evident that the WH NU reading has superior testimony, and it is the more likely reading on the basis of internal evidence (see Petzer 1989, 229-253). Thus, it is reasonable to think that καυχησωμαι ("I may boast") was originally in the text and that it was purposely changed in later manuscripts to καυθησωμαι ("I may be burned")—either because (1) scribes assimilated this verse to Dan 3:28 (LXX), which speaks of Shadrach, Meshach, and Abednego giving their bodies over to the fire (παρεδωκαν τα σωματα αυτων εις πυρ), or (2) Christian scribes had become so accustomed to associating martyrdom with the giving over of one's body to the flames that they thought Paul could not have written anything but καυθησωμαι. However, martyrdom by burning was a phenomenon yet unknown to Paul or the original readers of this epistle.

In context, Paul was speaking about religious acts which seem to display faith in God but actually are done in ostentation. The first act mentioned in this verse is that of giving away one's possessions; the second is that of giving over one's body. This would not have necessarily meant martyrdom. More likely, the act of giving over one's body would be displayed in selling oneself as a slave to obtain food for others or exchanging places with a prisoner (Westcott and Hort 1882, 116). In Clement's Epistle to the Corinthians (written ca. 96), he spoke of those who delivered (παραδεδωκοτας) themselves to bondage in order to ransom others (*1 Clem.* 55:2). Thus, it is very likely that Paul was speaking about giving one's body for the sake of others. However, if this act was done so that the giver could boast about it, the giver did not act out of love. Indeed, the rebuke against boasting was pertinent for the Corinthians, who had a real problem with boasting about things that had no spiritual value (see 1:29, 31; 3:21; 4:7; 5:6). They needed to be reminded that acts of self-sacrifice should not be a cause for boasting but a demonstration of love.

Remarkably, English translations prior to the NAB (1986), NRSV (1990), NLT (1996), NET (2000), and TNIV (2001) did not follow the superior reading—either because it was too difficult to break with the traditional rendering or because the translators thought the variant reading would be more understandable to an audience who is generally familiar with the history of Christian martyrdom by fire. Even several recent English versions, including some in the twenty-first century (ESV and HCSB) retain the reading "that I may be burned"—probably for the sake of keeping the tradition.

1 Corinthians 13:4

TR NU	[ἡ ἀγάπη] οὐ περπερεύεται, οὐ φυσιοῦται "love does not brag, is not puffed up" ℵ A C D F G Ψ 048 0243 1739 Maj KJV NKJV NET
variant 1/WH	ου περπερευεται, ου φυσιουται "[it] does not brag, is not puffed up" B 33 it cop Clement RSV NRSV ESV NASB NIV TNIV NEB REB NJB NAB NLT HCSB
variant 2	ου περπερευεται, η αγαπη ου φυσιουται "[it] does not brag, love is not puffed up" 𝔓46 none

The subject of this poetic pericope, η αγαπη ("love"), is written three times at the onset, according to most manuscripts. However, it appears only twice in manuscripts such as B and 33. According to Zuntz (1953, 67-68), these manuscripts preserve true poetic rhythm. The third variant, found in the earliest witness (𝔓46), shows that η αγαπη was inserted at various junctures. Without the third instance of η αγαπη, the sentence can be rendered in two ways:

(1) love is long-suffering, is kind; love is not jealous, does not brag, is not puffed up; (2) love is long-suffering, love is kind, is not jealous, does not brag, is not puffed up.

1 Corinthians 13:5

Instead of the wording ουκ ασχημονει ("does not behave disgracefully"), 𝔓[46] alone reads ουκ ευσχημονει. This could be original because it is a very difficult reading inasmuch as it was probably taken to mean "does not behave with dignity or decorum." But the word can also mean "to behave in an affected manner, to play the gentleman or lady" (BDAG 413). If Paul originally wrote this, then his point is that true Christian love should not be affected, but genuine and sincere. In the next part of the verse most manuscripts read, ου ζητει τα εαυτης ("does not seek her own things"). 𝔓[46*] reads ου ζητει το εαυτης ("does not seek that which is her own"), which was then corrected to ου ζητει το μη εαυτης ("does not seek that which is not her own"). Since B alone reads the same, it is possible that this corrector of 𝔓[46] followed the same textual tradition as B.

1 Corinthians 13:8

WH NU — ἀγάπη οὐδέποτε πίπτει
"love never falls" (or, "love never ends")
𝔓[46] ℵ* A B C* 048 0243 33 1739
RSV NRSV ESV NEB REB NJB NLT HCSB NET

variant/TR — αγαπη ουδεποτε εκπιπτει
"love never fails"
ℵ[2] C[3] D F G Ψ Maj it
KJV NKJV NASB NIV TNIV NAB

The text probably means that "love never ends" (see NRSV), whereas the variant means that love can always be counted on—it never fails. The variant is almost certainly a scribal adjustment, probably created by a scribe who was baffled by the depiction of love as being that which cannot fall (πιπτει).

1 Corinthians 14:2

Instead of the expression πνευματι δε λαλει μυστηρια, which can be rendered "but in spirit he speaks mysteries" or "but in the Spirit he speaks mysteries," a few Western manuscripts (F G it[b] vg[MSS]) read πνευμα δε λαλει μυστηρια ("but the Spirit speaks mysteries"). Paul, however, was not talking about the utterances of the Spirit but those of the tongue speaker while he or she is in the Spirit.

1 Corinthians 14:12

Most manuscripts read ζηλωται εστε πνευματων, which literally is "you are zealous of spirits." Modern translators interpret this to mean "you are zealous of spiritual gifts." This interpretation was made explicit in certain manuscripts (P 1175), which read πνευματικων—"spiritual gifts," and in some ancient translations (it[r] syr[p] cop).

1 Corinthians 14:16

The expression εν πνευματι (or simply πνευματι, as it is in some manuscripts) has troubled scribe and translator. Does this mean "in spirit" (the human spirit) or "in the Spirit" (the Holy Spirit)? Scribes had a way of differentiating the human spirit from the divine Spirit by writing out the former in *plene* (πνευμα) and abbreviating the latter as a nomen sacrum, $\overline{\Pi NA}$ (Comfort 1984). On occasion, some scribes did this, including the scribe of $\mathfrak{P}^{46}$ (see note on 2:13-15). In this case, the scribe of $\mathfrak{P}^{46}$ wrote the word $\overline{\Pi NA}$ to designate the divine Spirit: "I will praise in the Spirit." (Other scribes did the same—see ℵ A 33). The scribes of F and G wrote out the word in *plene* (πνευματι), thereby indicating the human spirit. In later manuscripts (Ψ 1739 Maj—so TR), the divine Spirit is explicitly indicated by the addition of the definite article τω ("the") before πνευματι ("Spirit") = "the Spirit." It is better that the text be left ambiguous, because Paul could be speaking of the human spirit (see 14:15), or of the divine Spirit, or of both.

1 Corinthians 14:21

WH NU read εν χειλεσιν ετερων λαλησω τω λαω τουτω ("with lips of others I will speak to this people"), with the support of ℵ A B Ψ 0201 0243 33 1739. TR reads εν χειλεσιν ετεροις λαλησω τω λαω τουτω ("with other lips I will speak to this people"), with the support of $\mathfrak{P}^{46}$ D^{s} F G Maj it cop.

Paul adapted a passage from Isa 28:11-12 to introduce his thesis that tongue speaking functions only as a sign to the unbelievers, not to the believers (14:22-23). But it is difficult to see how this passage directly relates, unless we are to imagine that Paul was making some kind of parallel between God trying to communicate to the Israelites through prophets (and failing) and the believers trying to communicate to unbelievers through tongues (and also failing). If this is so, then the χειλεσιν ετερων ("lips of others") would be the Corinthians' lips. In any event, this text is difficult; so it prompted a scribal adjustment. The variant reading was an early scribal emendation (as evidenced in $\mathfrak{P}^{46}$), carried on in later manuscripts, which attempts to make "other lips" an equivalent expression to "other tongues." This creates a smooth and sensible reading: "in other tongues and with other lips I will speak to this people."

1 Corinthians 14:32

Several Western manuscripts (D F G it^{b} syr^{p}) show a change from πνευματα προφητων ("the spirits of prophets") to πνευμα προφητων ("the spirit of prophets"). The expression in most manuscripts conveys collective individuality—i.e., each prophet has a spirit. The Western text might convey the same, or it could connote that each prophet has the one divine Spirit.

1 Corinthians 14:33

The second part of this verse, ως εν πασαις ταις εκκλησιαις των αγιων ("as in all the churches of the saints"), can be conjoined with the first part of 14:33 or the first part of 14:34. It is a decision with exegetical consequences. Paul could be saying (1) "God is not the author of confusion but of harmony, as in all the churches of the saints" or (2) "As in all the churches of the saints, the women are to keep silent in the church meetings." The former speaks of God's presiding presence bringing order to all the churches. The latter speaks of the universal truth that women did not speak in any church meetings. But we know that women did speak in church meetings; indeed, Corinthian women even prayed and prophesied in church meetings (see 11:5). So, the second part of 14:33 is more suitable as a conclusion to 14:33. This is the way it is presented in TR (followed by KJV and NKJV) and WH (followed by NLT and TNIV). However, NU not only conjoins 14:33b with 14:34 but starts a new paragraph at 14:33b. Most modern translations follow suit (see NRSV ESV NIV NEB NJB HCSB NET). This makes the statement "as in all the churches of the saints" a maxim for all that follows. In my view, this creates serious exegetical problems—especially for the exposition of 14:34-35 (see next note).

1 Corinthians 14:34-35

TR WH NU	retain verses after 14:33 𝔓46 ℵ A B Ψ 0243 33 81 88mg 1739 Maj syr cop Origen Pelagius all
variant	place verses after 14:40 D F G 88* itb Ambrosiaster NRSVmg TNIVmg NLTmg NETmg

In the interest of the argument that follows, it is important to see 14:34-35 in a full rendering: "[34] The women are to keep silent in the church meetings, for it is not permitted for them to speak; but they must be submissive, even as the law says. [35] And if they desire to learn anything, let them ask their own husbands at home, for it is a shame for a woman to speak in the church meeting."

In addition to the textual evidence cited above, it must also be said that Payne (1995, 240-262) has noted that both B and itf (Old Latin Codex Fuldensis) have marginal markings or readings which suggest that their scribes knew of the textual problem pertaining to 14:34-35. In Codex Vaticanus, there is a marginal umlaut by the line that contains the end of 14:33, which, in Payne's view, indicates awareness of the textual problem regarding 14:34-35. As for Codex Fuldensis (produced in 546/547), it seems certain that Victor of Capua (the editor and reader of the manuscript) asked the original scribe to rewrite 14:36-40 in the margin. Payne argues that this rewrite was done so as to exclude 14:34-35. However, it must be said that there are no clear sigla in the manuscript which indicate such an omission. Finally, Payne conjectures that manuscript 88 must have originally been copied from an exemplar that did not contain 14:34-35 (see Payne 1998, 152-158). Niccum (1997, 242-255) presents a thorough case against Payne's observations and concludes that there is no textual evidence for the omission of 14:34-35. Miller (2003, 217-236) also sees other reasons for the presence of the umlaut in Codex B than signaling inauthenticity.

Even prior to Payne's observations about B, itf, and 88, certain scholars were convinced that 14:34-35 was a marginal gloss that found its way into the main text of other manuscripts. Fee (1987, 696-708) makes a strong and thorough argument for this position, which rests on one challenge: If the verses were originally part of Paul's discourse at this juncture, why would any scribe have moved them after 14:40, where they are obviously out of place? Granted this transposition occurred in Western manuscripts only—and the Western text is known for textual transposition (see notes on Matt 5:4-5; Luke 4:5-10)—but in this case (contra the other verses just noted), the transposition spoils the sense. Thus, Fee's conclusion is that the words were written as a marginal gloss, which was later inserted after 14:33 in several manuscripts and after 14:40 in others. It is possible that some scribe, influenced by 1 Tim 2:9-15, wanted to make it clear that women were not to speak at all during church meetings. However, since these verses appear in 𝔓46 (which dates to the second century), the gloss must have been made quite early.

Ellis (1981, 219-220), therefore, suggests that the gloss was written by Paul himself. It is also possible that the compiler of the Pauline corpus added this gloss.

Without these verses, the passage reads:

> "[33] God is not the author of confusion but of harmony, as in all the churches of the saints.
> [36] Or from you did the word of God go forth? Or to you only did it reach?"

The connection between these verses is not readily apparent but is clear enough. Paul argues that peace and order reigns in all the churches—should it be any different at Corinth? Were the Corinthians the only ones to have believed the word—did not the same word reach all the churches? So why should the Corinthian meetings be any different from what was going on in all the churches? Thus, Paul was contending that the Corinthians' meeting behavior should coincide with what was occurring in all the other churches.

With the verses included, the text reads:

> "[33] God is not the author of confusion but of harmony, as in all the churches of the saints. [34] The women are to keep silent in the church meetings, for it is not permitted for them to speak; but they must be submissive, even as the law says. [35] And if they desire to learn anything, let them ask their own husbands at home, for it is a shame for a woman to speak in the church meeting. [36] Or from you did the word of God go forth? Or to you only did it reach?"

As was discussed in the note on 14:33, the adverbial phrase "As in all the churches of the saints" (14:33b) could begin a new paragraph, modifying the following verses rather than the preceding.

The inclusion of 14:34-35 creates a number of exegetical concerns, the chief of which pertains to the issue of women's verbal participation in church meetings. If Paul prohibited women from speaking in church meetings, why would he have indicated in 11:5 and 13 that women who pray and prophesy must do so with their heads covered? Obviously, these women were performing these verbal functions during a church meeting (see 11:17). So why would Paul later censure their speech? The only plausible answer is that he was not prohibiting them from functioning spiritually during the meeting; rather, he was prohibiting them from talking during the part of the meeting where the Scriptures were taught. In other words, the women had a right to participate in the prayers and prophecies, but they did not have a right to participate orally in the public discussions which arose from the teaching of Scripture. Indeed, it would be shameful to the men taking the lead in the church for them to be challenged by a woman or for a woman to assume mastery over the situation. (This is probably the situation that is addressed in 1 Tim 2:11-15.) Thus, women (or, wives) were commanded to learn from their husbands at home. Furthermore, it is possible that certain women at Corinth believed they were oracles for God or that they had some special insight into God's word. If so, then Paul's words could be a rebuke aimed specifically at them: "Did the word of God originate from you?"

In summary, it seems fair to consider that 14:34-35 might be a gloss. If so, the point of Paul's passage is to urge the Corinthians to emulate the meeting behavior of the other churches (cf. 11:16). But if 14:34-35 is not a gloss—and there is no clear extant textual evidence to prove that it is—then we are faced with the challenge of exegeting the passage within the context of 1 Corinthians itself and the rest of the NT epistles. As such, it seems fair to say that Paul was not prohibiting all speech during a church meeting; rather, he was prohibiting female participation in the teaching of Scriptures in the church at Corinth, for this was a role designated to the male apostles and elders.

1 Corinthians 14:37

WH NU κυρίου ἐστὶν ἐντολή
"they are the Lord's commandment"
𝔓46 ℵ2 B 048 0243 33 1739*
RSV NRSV ESV NASB NIV TNIV NEB REB NJB NAB NLT HCSB NET

variant 1/TR κυριου εστιν εντολαι
"they are the Lord's commandments"
D2 Ψ Maj it syr copsa
KJV NKJV

variant 2 θεου εστιν εντολην
"they are God's commandment"
A 1739c
none

variant 3 κυριου εστιν
"they are of the Lord"
D* F G itb
none

Most likely, the first variant and the third variant (a Western reading) were created as an attempt to deal with the grammatical inconsistency between the plural α γραφω ("the things I write") and the singular εντολη ("commandment"). In the first variant, the object was made plural; in the third it was omitted. The second variant is easily explained as the result of some scribe associating the word "commandment" with the name "God" over against "Lord."

1 Corinthians 14:38

WH NU εἰ δέ τις ἀγνοεῖ, ἀγνοεῖται
"but if anyone ignores [or, does not recognize] this, he himself is ignored [or, not recognized]"
ℵ* A*vid D (F G) 048 0243 33 1739
RSV NRSV ESV NASB NIV TNIV NEB REB NJB NAB NLT HCSB NET

variant/TR ει δε τις αγνοει, αγνοειτω
"but if anyone ignores this, let him ignore this [or, if he is ignorant, let him be ignorant]"
𝔓46 ℵ2 Ac B D2 Ψ Maj
KJV NKJV NASBmg NIVmg TNIVmg NEBmg REBmg NJBmg NLTmg HCSBmg

The WH NU reading does not necessarily have better documentary support than the variant. Furthermore, the WH NU reading makes it sound as if the person who does not recognize Paul's words as being authoritative or divinely inspired is a person who will be ignored—perhaps by the church or by God (Paul does not specify). In any event, such a curse seems too harsh for this context. Zuntz (1953, 108) said, "this exposition credits Paul with an unbelievable recklessness in cursing his adversaries (3:15 is mild by comparison): the refusal to acknowledge his claim *ipso facto* excludes the doubters from the grace of God!" For these reasons, one should not be too hasty in abandoning the variant reading, which has early and diverse support, and which makes good sense. However, all modern English versions favor the WH NU reading over the variant, while many note the alternative reading.

1 Corinthians 15:2

The expression, τινι λογω ευηγγελισαμην υμιν ει κατεχετε, is difficult Greek. Most translations make it out to be, "if you hold fast to that word I preached to you," but it literally reads, "with what word I preached to you, if you hold it fast." Some ancient scribes and translators also had difficulty with this wording, so they changed it to τινι λογω ευηγγελισαμην υμιν οφειλετε κατεχειν ("you ought to hold fast to any word I preached to you"). This is the reading in several Western witnesses (D*[,c] F G it[b]), and appears to have been in an exemplar known to the scribe of 𝔓[46], who first wrote κατεχειν and then deleted it. (For a reconstruction of this, see *Text of Earliest MSS*, 277.) And so, in the end, 𝔓[46] supports the TR WH NU reading; at the same time, it displays that the variant was very early and existed as a conflated reading before 𝔓[46] was produced (see Zuntz 1953, 254-255).

1 Corinthians 15:3

All Greek manuscripts read παρεδωκα γαρ υμιν εν πρωτοις, ο και παρελαβον ("for I handed on to you, among the first things, that which I also received"). Perhaps uncomfortable with the notion of Paul having to receive his gospel from others, a few witnesses (it[b] Ambrosiaster) delete ο και παρελαβον ("that which I also received").

1 Corinthians 15:5

The three editions (TR WH NU) read ωφθη Κηφα ειτα τοις δωδεκα ("he was seen by Cephas and then by the twelve") supported by 𝔓[46vid] (ℵ A) B D[2] Ψ 0243 Maj, found in all translations. The Western text (D* F G it) substitutes τοις ενδεκα ("the eleven") for τοις δωδεκα ("the twelve"). This reading could have been initiated by a scribe attempting to clarify that, since Judas Iscariot was not with the disciples when Jesus appeared to them, there were only eleven present (see Luke 24:33). The variant could also suggest that Peter received a special visitation from the risen Christ, and then the eleven (without Peter) received another visitation. Though this could be implied in the Lukan account (Luke 24:34-36), John's account makes it clear that Peter was with the disciples when Jesus appeared to the disciples on the evening of his resurrection (John 20:19-24).

1 Corinthians 15:10

Most manuscripts read η χαρις αυτου η εις εμε ου κενη εγενηθη ("his grace to me has not been in vain"). This reads differently in some Western manuscripts (D* F G): η χαρις αυτου η εις εμε πτωχη ουκ εγενηθη ("his grace to me has not been poor"). Though probably not original, it makes for a nice contrast: God's rich grace was not poor in Paul's case (Fee 1987, 718).

1 Corinthians 15:15

Some Western witnesses (D it[a,b] syr[p] Irenaeus Tertullian) lack the last phrase of this verse, ειπερ αρα νεκροι ουκ εγειρονται ("if then the dead are not raised"). The omission is probably accidental inasmuch as the next phrase in the following verse is nearly identical. But if it was an intentional omission, the resulting expression is quite difficult: "we witness for God that he raised Christ, whom he did not raise."

1 Corinthians 15:20

WH NU Χριστὸς ἐγήγερται ἐκ νεκρῶν ἀπαρχὴ τῶν κεκοιμημένων
"Christ has been raised from the dead, [the] firstfruit[s] of the ones having slept"
𝔓46 א A B D* F G 0243 33 1739 it cop
RSV NRSV ESV NASB NIV TNIV NEB REB NJB NAB NLT HCSB NET

variant/TR Χριστος εγηγερται εκ νεκρων, απαρχη των κεκοιμημενων εγενετο
"Christ has been raised from the dead; he became the firstfruit[s] of the ones having slept"
D² Ψ Maj syr
KJV NKJV

According to superior manuscript evidence, the WH NU reading has an appositional expression: "the firstfruit[s] of the ones having slept" is a further description of Christ who was raised from dead. The expression "the firstfruits" indicates that more fruit is yet to come—that is, after Christ's resurrection others will be resurrected.

1 Corinthians 15:29

WH NU τί καὶ βαπτίζονται ὑπὲρ αὐτῶν;
"why indeed are they baptized on their behalf?"
𝔓46 א A B D* F G 075 0243 33 1739 it syr^h cop
RSV NRSV ESV NASB NIV TNIV NEB REB NJB NAB NLT HCSB NET

variant/TR τι και βαπτιζονται υπερ των νεκρων;
"why indeed are they baptized on behalf of the dead?"
D² Maj syr^p
KJV NKJV HCSBmg

The WH NU reading (in the last part of the verse) has outstanding documentary support. Furthermore, it is quite evident that the variant reading is a scribal clarification, which made its way into TR, followed by KJV and NKJV.

1 Corinthians 15:31a

WH NU νὴ τὴν ὑμετέραν καύχησιν, [ἀδελφοί,]
"I swear by the boasting of you, brothers"
א B P 33 it syr cop
RSV NRSV ESV NASB NIV NEB REB NJB NAB NLT

variant 1/TR νη την υμετεραν καυχησιν
"I swear by the boasting of you"
𝔓46 D F G Ψ 075 0243 Maj
KJV NKJV TNIV HCSB NET

variant 2 νη την ημετεραν καυχησιν, αδελφοι
"I swear by our boasting, brothers"
A 1881
none

As for textual support, the manuscripts are almost evenly divided between the WH NU reading and that of TR. The expression νη την υμετεραν καυχησιν gave scribes problems because it could mean "I swear by the boasting you [the Corinthians] give me [Paul]" or "I swear by my [Paul's] boasting about you [the Corinthians]." Both meanings are plausible, but it is likely that the second rendering is more appropriate. As such, one can imagine that the vocative αδελφοι ("brothers") was added to affirm this meaning. Thus, the first variant is possibly original, while the second variant is clearly an attempt to relieve the text of ambiguity.

1 Corinthians 15:31b

All three editions (TR WH NU), followed by all English versions, read εν Χριστω Ιησου τω κυριω ημων ("in Christ Jesus our Lord"), with the support of 𝔓[46] ℵ A B F G Maj. There is one textual variant here: εν κυριω ("in the Lord") in D* it[b]. It is possible that the divine title was expanded throughout the course of textual transmission, but the textual evidence does not support this in this case.

1 Corinthians 15:45

It is interesting to note that nearly all English versions translate the last part of this verse as saying that the last Adam (Jesus) became a "life-giving spirit" (lower case)—probably to designate Jesus' spiritual condition postresurrection. By contrast, most Greek manuscripts have the word πνευμα as a nomen sacrum, $\overline{\Pi NA}$ (see 𝔓[46] ℵ A C D etc.; the exception, B, never uses a nomen sacrum for πνευμα). This indicates that Jesus became the Spirit (divine title) that gives life, as in the TEV: "the last Adam is the life-giving Spirit" (see also NLT).

1 Corinthians 15:47

WH NU	ὁ δεύτερος ἄνθρωπος ἐξ οὐρανοῦ "the second man [is] from heaven" ℵ* B C D* 0243 33 1739* cop[bo] NKJVmg RSV NRSV ESV NASB NIV TNIV NEB REB NJB NAB NLT HCSB NET
variant 1	ο δευτερος ο κυριος εξ ουρανου "the second, the Lord from heaven" 630 Marcion none
variant 2/TR	ο δευτερος ανθρωπος ο κυριος εξ ουρανου "the second man, the Lord from heaven" ℵ[2] A D[1] Ψ 075 1739[mg] Maj syr KJV NKJV HCSBmg
variant 3	ο δευτερος ανθρωπος πνευματικος εξ ουρανου "the second man, a spiritual one from heaven" 𝔓[46] none
variant 4	ο δευτερος ανθρωπος εξ ουρανου ο ουρανιος "the second man, the heavenly one from heaven" F G none

The textual picture here shows that many scribes were trying to clarify just what kind of "man" Jesus was, for he was no ordinary human being. Marcion obscured Jesus' humanity altogether by substituting "Lord" for "man." Most other manuscripts kept "man," to which was added "Lord" in some manuscripts. The scribe of 𝔓[46], as a carryover from the two previous verses (where the scribe designated Jesus as ΠΝΑ ζωοποιουν = "life-giving Spirit" [15:45] and ΠΝΚΟΝ/ΠΝΙΚΟΝ = "the Spirit-One" or "the spiritual [body of Christ]" [15:46]), here also designated Jesus as "the Spirit-One" or "the Spiritual One" by writing the nomen sacrum το ΠΝΙΚΟΝ. Other scribes, borrowing from 15:48-49, called Jesus "the heavenly man." The language of the WH NU reading, however, is sufficient; it depicts Jesus as being made of heavenly stuff and coming from a heavenly origin (εξ ουρανου), as compared to the first man who was made of earthly stuff, even the dust of the ground.

1 Corinthians 15:49

WH NU φορέσομεν καὶ τὴν εἰκόνα τοῦ ἐπουρανίου
"we will also bear the image of the heavenly man"
B I 630 1881 cop[sa]
all

variant/TR φορεσωμεν και την εικονα του επουρανιου
"let us also bear the image of the heavenly man"
𝔓[46] ℵ A C D F G Ψ 075 0243 1739 Maj cop[bo] Clement Origen
NKJVmg RSVmg NRSVmg ESVmg NASBmg NIVmg TNIVmg NJBmg NLTmg

In a fuller context, a rendering of the WH NU is as follows: "as we bore the image of the man of dust, we will also bear the image of the heavenly man." Despite its slender documentary support, this reading has been taken by most scholars to be the one that best suits the context—which is didactic, not hortatory (TCGNT). But the textual evidence for the variant reading is far more extensive and earlier than for the WH NU reading. Thus, it is likely that a few scribes changed the hortatory ("let us bear") to the future ("we will bear") to make for easier reading or to conform the verb tense to the prevailing future, as evidenced in 15:51-54. Therefore, Fee (1987, 787) argues that the second reading "must be the original, and if original it must be intentional on Paul's part as a way of calling them [the Corinthians] to prepare now for the future that is to be." Not one English version has gone with this reading, though many note it.

1 Corinthians 15:51

All three editions (TR WH NU) read παντες ου κοιμηθησομεθα, παντες δε αλλαγησομεθα ("we all will not sleep, but we all will be changed"), with the support of B D[2] Ψ 075 0243[c] Maj MSS[according to Jerome] syr cop. There are four variants on this: (1) ℵ C F G 0243* 1739 MSS[according to Jerome] read παντες κοιμηθησομεθα, ου παντες δε αλλαγησομεθα ("we all will sleep, but we all will not be changed"); (2) 𝔓[46] and A[c] read παντες ου κοιμηθησομεθα, ου παντες δε αλλαγησομεθα ("we all will not sleep, and we all will not be changed"); (3) A* reads παντες κοιμηθησομεθα, οι παντες δε αλλαγησομεθα ("we all will sleep, and we all will be changed"); and (4) D* it[b,d] read παντες αναστησομεθα ου παντες δε αλλαγησομεθα ("we all will be raised, but we all will not be changed").

This is a difficult textual problem because there is such an assortment of readings, each presenting a different thesis about the resurrection. Most of these readings were known to Jerome, who commented on them (*Epist.* 119). The most satisfactory solution is to say that the TR WH NU reading (followed by all English versions) is the reading from which all the others diverged, whether accidentally or intentionally. The first statement of the TR WH NU texts certainly accords with Paul's presentation of the resurrection—that is, not all the believers will have died by the time Christ returns (see 1 Thess 4:15-17). The second statement is affirmed in the very next verse: "we will be changed."

However, since Paul himself died, some scribe(s) may have thought it necessary to make an adjustment to the text: "we all will sleep, but we all will not be changed" (variant 1). This could be interpreted to mean that all human beings will die but only Christians will be transformed. The fourth variant, borrowing language from 1 Thess 4:16, presents the same thesis.

The second variant is very curious. Zuntz (1953, 255-256) sees it as a conflation of the TR WH NU reading and the first variant. If so, that means both of these readings must have been very early. The third variant was the original reading of A, which was corrected in two stages: The second οι was changed to ου and another ου was added to the first clause, resulting in the reading of the second variant.

1 Corinthians 15:52

The expression εν ριπη οφθαλμου ("in the wink of an eye") is supported by ℵ A B C D[2] Ψ 33 Maj and printed in TR WH NU. However, other manuscripts (𝔓[46] D* F G 0243 1739) read εν ροπη οφθαλμου ("in the movement of an eye"). It is difficult to know if ροπη was originally in the text and was confused for ριπη (there is only one letter difference: ω/ι), or if it was the other way around. The word ριπη denotes the rapid movement of the eye—the casting of a glance or a wink. The word ροπη was used in Greek writings to describe the movement of a scale, especially when the scales are about to turn. Hence, it came to denote the critical moment, and was used in expressions like "the last moment of life" (see 3 Macc 5:49) and "in one moment" (Wis 18:12). In the greater context of 1 Cor 15, this meaning is quite appropriate, for it coincides with the most critical moment in the eschaton: the resurrection of the dead. However, the connection of ροπη with οφθαλμου is problematic because it is nonsensical to speak of "the decisive moment of the eye." But it does make sense to speak of the downward movement of an eye (BDAG 907), like a wink.

1 Corinthians 15:54

TR NU	ὅταν δὲ τὸ φθαρτὸν τοῦτο ἐνδύσηται ἀφθαρσίαν καὶ τὸ θνητὸν τοῦτο ἐνδύσηται ἀθανασίαν "when this perishable [nature] has been clothed with the imperishable, and this mortal [nature] puts on immortality" ℵ[2] (A) B C[2vid] D Ψ 075 (33) 1739[c] Maj KJV NKJV RSV NRSV ESV NASB NIV TNIV NEBmg REB NJB NAB NLTmg HCSB NET
variant 1/WH	οταν δε το θνητον τουτο ενδυσηται αθανασιαν "but when this mortal [nature] puts on immortality" 𝔓[46] ℵ* 088 0243 1739* it cop[bo] NEB REBmg NJBmg NLT
variant 2	omit F G none

Some textual critics would say that the variant reading was the result of haplography—the eye of a scribe skipping from the first ενδυσηται to the second ενδυσηται (see TCGNT); others would argue that the reading in TR NU is an expansion contrived by scribes attempting to make 15:54 parallel in structure with 15:53 (so Tasker 1964, 437, defending NEB). The second variant, which omits the words entirely, is definitely a scribal error due to homoeoteleuton with the previous verse—both end with αθανασιαν. The shorter reading (variant 1) has good testimony and could likely be original (so WH).

1 Corinthians 15:55

WH NU	ποῦ σου, θάνατε, τὸ νῖκος; ποῦ σου, θάνατε, τὸ κέντρον; "Where, O death, is your victory? Where, O death, is your sting?" (𝔓[46] B 088 νεικος) ℵ* C 1739* it cop NKJVmg RSV NRSV ESV NASB NIV TNIV NEB REB NJB NAB NLT HCSB NET
variant 1	που σου, θανατε, το κεντρον; που σου, θανατε, το νικος; "Where, O death, is your sting? Where, O death, is your victory?" (D[c]) F G none
variant 2/TR	που σου, θανατε, το κεντρον; που σου, αδη, το νικος; "Where, O death, is your sting? Where, Hades, is your victory?" ℵ[2] A[c] Ψ 075 Maj KJV NKJV
variant 3	που σου, θανατε, το νικος; που σου, αδη, το κεντρον; "Where, O death, is your victory? Where, Hades, is your sting?" 0121 0243 33 81 1739[c] none

Although there are several variants in this verse, they involve two changes: (1) the transposition of νικος ("victory") with κεντρον ("sting") and (2) the substitution of αδη ("Hades") for θανατε ("death") in the second clause. The changes reflect scribal conformity to Hos 13:14 (LXX), the passage Paul was paraphrasing here. Paul took the liberty to make "Hades" equivalent to "death," and thereby deride death for its double defeat. Since Christ had conquered death by his resurrection, death—which had always been victorious before—lost the victory. And in being defeated, it lost its power (which is the sting).

1 Corinthians 16:6

Several manuscripts (𝔓[34] B 0121 0243 1739[c]—so WH) have the verb καταμενω (which means "settle down") instead of παραμενω (which means "stay for awhile"), found in 𝔓[46] ℵ A C D (F G) Ψ 075 088 33 1739* Maj (so TR NU). Prior to the twenty-sixth edition of the Nestle text, καταμενω was in the text—probably because of its support from B and presence in WH. It was relegated to the margin thereafter because παραμενω has superior attestation (especially from 𝔓[46]) and suits the context better.

1 Corinthians 16:12

A few Western witnesses (D* F G it[a]) and ℵ* add δηλω υμιν οτι ("I make it clear to you that") at the beginning of the second phrase in order to improve the style of the sentence or to emphasize Paul's unswerving intentions to recommend Apollos to the Corinthians.

1 Corinthians 16:15

According to the best evidence (𝔓46 ℵ* A B C2 Ψ 075 0121 0243 33 1739 Maj), only the "household of Stephanas" (οικιαν Στεφανα) is mentioned in 16:15. But several other manuscripts reveal scribal attempts to make this verse include the same people that are mentioned in 16:17. Some manuscripts (ℵ2 D itb copbo) add και Φορτουνατου ("and Fortunatus"); other manuscripts (C*vid F G syrh**) add και Φορτουνατου και Αχαικου ("and Fortunatus and Achaicus"). It is possible that Fortunatus and Achaicus were, in fact, members of Stephanas's household, but we are not sure of this nor if they were "first-fruits" (i.e., among the first believers in Corinth).

1 Corinthians 16:19a

The entire verse was omitted by A, probably due to haplography (the next verse begins with the same two words). The scribe of 𝔓46 (and a few other manuscripts, including 69) left out αι εκκλησιαι της Ασιας ασπαζεται υμας (. . . the churches of Asia. Greet you . . .) due to haplography—the eye of the scribe passing from the first υμας to the second.

1 Corinthians 16:19b

WH NU	Ἀκύλας καὶ Πρίσκα "Aquila and Prisca" 𝔓46 ℵ B P 0243 33 1739 1881* RSV NRSV ESV NASB NEB REB NJB NAB NET
variant/TR	Ακυλας και Πρισκιλλα "Aquila and Priscilla" C D F G Ψ 075 Maj KJV NKJV NIV TNIV NLT HCSB

According to the best attestation, the text names Aquila's wife as Πρισκα ("Prisca"). Influenced by Acts 18, this name was changed to Πρισκιλλα ("Priscilla"), the full form of the name, in other manuscripts. Paul used the short form in his epistles (Rom 16:3; 2 Tim 4:19).

1 Corinthians 16:19c

After the mention of "Aquila and Prisca," some Western witnesses (D* F G it) add παρ οις και ξενιζομαι ("with whom also I am lodging"). If it were true that Paul was lodging with Aquila and Prisca, this would mean that this couple's home provided the meeting place for the church in Ephesus and lodging for Paul. As was so often commented upon in the book of Acts, the Western text is known for its propensity to supply historical details—few of which can be verified, as in this case.

1 Corinthians 16:22

The final expression of this verse, taken from the Aramaic, is μαραναθα. The earliest manuscripts (𝔓46 ℵ A B* C D*), written in *scriptio continua,* have no space between the letters. But it can be written as Μαρανα θα, which means "Our Lord, come," or it can be written as Μαραν αθα, which means "our Lord has come." The manuscripts B2 D2 G*vid K L Ψ have it written as Μαραν αθα, and this is the way it appears in TR WH. No known manuscript has it written as Μαρανα θα, which is the way it is printed in NU.

In context, both interpretations can work. Paul had pronounced a curse (αναθεμα) on anyone who does not love the Lord Jesus. Having said this, he could have said "our Lord has come"—the implication being "you need to recognize this Lord and love him, or else be cursed." Or Paul could have been invoking the Lord to come—much in the same way that the book of Revelation (Rev 22:20) concludes with the invocation: "Come, Lord Jesus!" As such, this invocation can stand apart from the curse, or signal Paul's desire for the Lord to come and affirm it.

1 Corinthians 16:23

WH NU — χάρις τοῦ κυρίου 'Ιησοῦ
"grace of the Lord Jesus"
א* B 33 cop^{sa}
RSV NRSV ESV NASB NIV TNIV REB NAB NLT HCSB NET

variant/TR — χαρις του κυριου Ιησου Χριστου
"grace of the Lord Jesus Christ"
𝔓$^{46vid?}$ א^{2} A C D F G Ψ 075 0243 Maj it syr cop^{bo}
KJV NKJV NEB NJB

A reconstruction of the last line of 𝔓^{46} on leaf 60 (recto) could indicate that the manuscript contained the longer title (for reconstruction, see *Text of Earliest MSS,* 282). Even though the documentary evidence is evenly divided, one would have to judge that the shorter reading is more likely original because scribes had a tendency to lengthen divine titles: especially "Lord Jesus" to "Lord Jesus Christ"—and especially in doxologies. Two modern English versions, NEB and NJB, reflect the longer title.

1 Corinthians 16:24

WH NU — omit αμην ("Amen") at end of verse
B F 0121 0243 33 1739* syr^{p} cop^{sa}
NRSV TNIV REB NJB NLT HCSB NET

variant/TR — include αμην ("Amen") at end of verse
א A C D Ψ 075 1739^{c} Maj it syr^{h}
KJV NKJV RSV NRSVmg ESV NASB NIV TNIVmg NEB NAB NLTmg NETmg

By looking at the textual evidence above, it is difficult to determine whether or not Paul concluded this epistle with an "amen," or if this was a scribal addition made in the interest of giving this epistle a nice liturgical ending. A study of the concluding verses of the NT epistles reveals that in nearly every instance, the "amen" is a scribal addition. Only three epistles (Romans, Galatians, Jude) appear to have a genuine "amen" for the last word. In the other epistles it seems evident that an "amen" was added. An "amen" was often inserted by later correctors in manuscripts that did not originally have an "amen" (as in 1739). In later manuscripts, the concluding "amen" is always there. This is true in Ψ and Maj. But other manuscripts hardly ever have the concluding "amen"—notably, 𝔓^{46} (except in Philippians), B, א*, and 1739*. Their testimony reflects the original state of the epistles, before they became liturgical documents. As these letters were read more and more in church meetings, it would only be natural for scribes to append a concluding "amen" to give the book closure. But when Paul wrote these epistles, he would not have felt the same need; indeed, it would have been awkward for Paul, in most instances, to have concluded his epistles with an "amen." It was natural for Paul to use the word at the end of some of his prayers (see Rom 11:36; Gal 1:5; Eph 3:21; Phil 4:20; 1 Tim 1:17; 6:16; 2 Tim 4:18), but not at the end of his letters.

Subscription

Whereas scribes frequently added inscriptions (titles) to the Gospels, Acts, and Revelation, they did not usually do so for the Epistles. Instead, many scribes supplied subscriptions, which provide information about the writer, place of writing, sender, and recipient of the epistle. None of these subscriptions would have been penned by the author; nonetheless, they are worth noting.

1. No subscription—but placed as an inscription: Προς Κορινθιους Α ("First to the Corinthians"). Appears in 𝔓[46].
2. No subscription. Appears in 0121 629 630 1505 2464.
3. Προς Κορινθιους Α ("First to the Corinthians"). Appears in ℵ A B* C (D* F G Ψ) 33.
4. Προς Κορινθιους Α εγραφη απο Εφεσου ("First to the Corinthians, written from Ephesus"). Appears in B[1] P.
5. Προς Κορινθιους Α εγραφη απο Φιλιππων δια Στεφανα και Φορτουνατου και Αχαικου και Τιμοθεου ("First to the Corinthians, written from Philippi through Stephanas and Fortunatus and Achaicus and Timothy"). Appears in D[2] 075 1739 1881 Maj (so TR).

This textual picture provides a good example of how a subscription became expanded throughout the course of its textual history. The simple subscription, "To the Corinthians A" (= "First Corinthians"), was subsequently loaded with additional information—first about the place of writing and then about those who participated in the writing. The designation of the place as being "Ephesus" (in the third reading) is correct, but not "Philippi," as noted in the fifth reading. Unfortunately, TR includes this reading, and KJV prints an English translation of it at the end of 1 Corinthians.

The Second Epistle to the CORINTHIANS

Inscription (Title)

𝔓46 ℵ and B title this epistle as Προς Κορινθιους Β ("To the Corinthians B" = "2 Corinthians"). Several manuscripts (including ℵ and B) also have this title in the subscription (see last note for this book). Paul, however, would not have titled this epistle in its original composition. Inscriptions and subscriptions are the work of later scribes (see Comfort 2005, 9-10). But it is interesting to note that the earliest extant collection of the Pauline Epistles (𝔓46) included only two letters to the Corinthians, though we are quite certain Paul wrote four (see standard commentaries on 2 Corinthians).

2 Corinthians 1:1

WH NU ἀπόστολος Χριστοῦ Ἰησοῦ
"apostle of Christ Jesus"
𝔓46 ℵ B 33
RSV NRSV ESV NASB NIV TNIV NEB REB NJB NAB NLT HCSB NET

variant/TR αποστολος Ιησου Χριστου
"apostle of Jesus Christ"
A D G L Ψ Maj
KJV NKJV

The WH NU reading is likely the original, being supported by superior documentation and normative Pauline usage. Paul typically refers to "Christ Jesus" when speaking of his exalted state, and to "Jesus Christ" when speaking of his earthly ministry or when speaking of "our Lord Jesus Christ."

2 Corinthians 1:6b-7a

WH NU ὑμῶν παρακλήσεως καὶ σωτηρίας· εἴτε παρακαλούμεθα, ὑπὲρ τῆς ὑμῶν παρακλήσεως τῆς ἐνεργουμένης ἐν ὑπομονῇ τῶν αὐτῶν παθημάτων ὧν καὶ ἡμεῖς πάσχομεν. 7καὶ ἡ ἐλπὶς ἡμῶν βεβαία ὑπὲρ ὑμῶν
"[it is for] your encouragement and salvation; or if we are encouraged, it is for

your encouragement, producing in you an endurance of the same sufferings which we also suffer. 7 And our hope for you is firm"
ℵ A C P Ψ 0243 1739 it[r] syr[p] cop[sa,bo]
RSV NRSV ESV NASB NIV TNIV NEB REB NJB NAB NLT HCSB NET

variant 1 υμων παρακλησεως και σωτηριας της ενεργουμενης εν υπομονη των αυτων παθηματων ων και ημεις πασχομεν 7και η ελπις ημων βεβαια υπερ υμων. Ειτε παρακαλουμεθα, υπερ της υμων παρακλησεως και σωτηριας
"[it is for] your encouragement and salvation, producing in [you] an endurance of the same sufferings which we also suffer. 7 And our hope for you is firm. Whether we are encouraged, it is for your encouragement and salvation."
(B 33 omit first και σωτηριας) D F G 0209 Maj it[a,b]
NEBmg

variant 2/TR υμων παρακλησεως και σωτηριας της ενεργουμενης εν υπομονη των αυτων παθηματων ων και ημεις πασχομεν ειτε παρακαλουμεθα, υπερ της υμων παρακλησεως και σωτηριας, 7και η ελπις ημων βεβαια υπερ υμων
"[it is for] your encouragement and salvation, producing in you an endurance of the same sufferings which also we suffer. Whether we are encouraged, it is for your encouragement and salvation. 7 And our hope for you is firm."
(K L)
KJV NKJV NEBmg

The WH NU reading has excellent documentation. The first variant, found in a variety of witnesses (especially Western), displays a syntactical rearrangement attempting to affirm that both Paul's sufferings and his times of encouragement were for the Corinthians' "encouragement and salvation." The last variant, found in TR (but not in any manuscript with this exact wording), retains the same syntactical arrangement as the WH NU reading yet also emphasizes that both Paul's sufferings and his times of encouragement were for the Corinthians' "encouragement and salvation." 𝔓[46] is not cited for any reading because the scribe accidentally skipped over παθηματων ("sufferings") in 1:6 to παθηματων ("sufferings") in 1:7, omitting all the words in between (see *Text of Earliest MSS,* 283).

2 Corinthians 1:10a

All three editions (TR WH NU) have the wording ος εκ τηλικουτου θανατου ερρυσατο ημας ("who from so great a death rescued us"). This has the support of ℵ A B C D F G Ψ 33 1739* Clement, and is followed by all modern versions (except TEV). A significant variation on this is that some manuscripts have the plural θανατων ("deaths"): "who from such great deaths rescued us." The witnesses to this reading are 𝔓[46] 1739[mg] it[d] syr[h,p] Origen. The manuscript 1739 preserves both readings: the singular in the text and the plural as an alternative rendering (presumably coming from Origen).

Those who favor the TR WH NU reading argue that Paul was probably speaking of a particular encounter with death (as recorded in Acts 19:23-41)—hence, the singular reading. They argue that the plural "deaths" was created to cover the dual action in the statement "he has rescued and will rescue" (see next note). However, not all have agreed that Paul used the singular. For example, Zuntz (1953, 104) favored the reading in 𝔓[46] "because it bears the stamp of genuine Pauline diction." According to Zuntz, the variant reading "could never have come about either by a scribe's slip or by intentional alteration." Contrarily, the TR WH NU reading, in the singular, "clearly arose from the pedantic idea that no one could risk more than one death." To reflect the force of the plural θανατων, Zuntz translates the phrase "out of such tremendous, mortal dangers." Bratcher (1983, 11), who translated the TEV, also supports the plural; he renders the phrase, "such terrible dangers of death."

2 Corinthians 1:10b

WH NU ἐρρύσατο ἡμᾶς καὶ ῥύσεται
"he rescued us and he will rescue"
𝔓46 ℵ B C P 0209vid 33 cop
NKJVmg RSV NRSV ESV NASB NIV TNIV NEB REB NJB NAB NLT HCSB NET

variant 1/TR ερρυσατο ημας και ρυεται
"he rescued us and he rescues"
D2 F G 1739 Maj
KJV NKJV NEBmg NJBmg

variant 2 ερρυσατο ημας
"he rescued us"
A D* Ψ itb syrp
none

The WH NU reading, which is well supported by early Alexandrian and other witnesses, indicates that Paul was thinking of a specific time or times in which he was rescued from death (see note above) and of the ultimate deliverance from final death—through resurrection. The first variant conveys the idea of God's ongoing ability to rescue the believers from death. The second variant is limited to a specific, past occurrence. As the shortest reading, it could be original, but it is more likely that at one point the text was purposely pruned.

2 Corinthians 1:11

TR WH NU εὐχαριστηθῇ ὑπὲρ ἡμῶν
"thanks may be given for us"
𝔓46c ℵ A C D* Maj
all

variant ευχαριστηθη υπερ υμων
"thanks may be given for you"
𝔓46* B D2 P
NKJVmg NIVmg NJBmg HCSBmg

The first reading has good textual support and is best suited for the context, in which Paul speaks of prayers and thanksgiving offered by many people for himself and his coworkers. All the translations, accordingly, reflect this reading. But NIV and NJB noted the variant probably out of respect for the combined testimony of 𝔓46* and B. According to the variant, the thanksgiving would be *for* the Corinthians (υπερ υμων—"for you") *from* the many people who had prayed for Paul and his coworkers. This is a possible construction, but not likely. The variant is probably the result of a common scribal error—confusing υμων for ημων.

2 Corinthians 1:12

TR NU — ἐν ἁπλότητι καὶ εἰλικρινείᾳ
"in simplicity and sincerity"
ℵ[2] D F G Maj syr
KJV NKJV NRSV ESV TNIV NEBmg REBmg NJBmg NLTmg HCSB NET

variant/WH — εν αγιοτητι και ελικρινεαι
"in sanctity and sincerity"
𝔓[46] ℵ* A B C 33 1739 cop
RSV NRSVmg ESVmg NASB NIV TNIVmg NEB REB NJB NAB NLT NETMG

According to NU, the verse reads, "in the simplicity and sincerity of God, and not in fleshly wisdom but in God's grace, we behaved ourselves in the world." The variant has "sanctity" instead of "sincerity." In Greek, one word could have easily been confused for the other because the two words differ in only two letters: απλοτητι ("simplicity") and αγιοτητι ("sanctity" or "holiness").

The manuscript evidence (𝔓[46] etc.) strongly favors the variant reading, and that is the reading followed by most modern translations. The first reading, adopted for the text of NA[26] (a change from previous editions of the Nestle text) and UBS[3], was selected because the context seems to call for a word that describes Paul's forthrightness in handling the contribution from the Gentile churches to the saints in Jerusalem (see 1:11). (See Martin's arguments [1986, 18] on behalf of απολτητι.) However, the word αγιοτητι ("holiness") also suits the context, for Paul was speaking of having a sanctified behavior "in this world" (see Thrall 1981, 371-372). Furthermore, αγιοτητι is a word Paul never uses elsewhere; thus, scribes would be inclined to change it to απλοτητι, which is used elsewhere a number of times in 2 Corinthians (8:2; 9:11, 13; 11:3). In the end, most modern English versions follow the variant—for any number of the reasons presented above.

2 Corinthians 1:13

All three editions (TR WH NU) include the words η και επιγινωσκετε ("or already know") supported by most manuscripts. In a fuller context, this yields the rendering: "for we did not write to you anything other than what you read or already know." A variant reading omits the three words, as supported by 𝔓[46] B 104 cop[boMS]. It is possible that the variant is the result of homoeoteleuton: αναγινωσκετε η και επιγινωσκετε. But it also possible that the text displays a scribal addition intended to make a logical connection between 1:13 and 1:14 (from "already know" to "fully know"). According to the variant, Paul goes from αναγινωσκετε ("you read") to επιγνωσεσθε ("you will know"), knowing that his Greek readers will understand his play on words (αναγινωσκετε means "to know by reading").

2 Corinthians 1:15

TR NU have the reading χαριν ("favor"), found in most Greek manuscripts: ℵ* A C D F G Ψ Maj. A variant reading has the word χαραν ("joy"), found in ℵ[c] B L P (so WH). Either one of these words could have been confused for the other in the process of transcription because there is only a one-letter difference (α/ι). But χαριν has the better attestation.

2 Corinthians 1:16

Two variants occur in this verse, both of which manifest a scribal intention to note that Paul would be departing from Corinth. Thus, διελθειν ("to go through") was changed to απελθειν ("to depart") in A D* F G, and the preposition υφ ("by") was changed to αφ ("from") in 𝔓46 D F G.

2 Corinthians 1:17

The expression το Ναι ναι και το Ου ου ("the Yes, yes, and the No, no") was shortened to το Ναι και το Ου ("the Yes and the No") in 𝔓46 0243 1739 (Origen in 1739mg), but the longer form shows Paul's purposeful intensification. His "yes" really meant "yes," and his "no" meant "no."

2 Corinthians 1:19

TR NU ὁ τοῦ θεοῦ γὰρ υἱὸς 'Ιησοῦς Χριστός
"for the Son of God, Jesus Christ"
𝔓46 א2 B D F G Ψ 1739 Maj
KJV NKJV RSV NRSV ESV NIV TNIV NJB NAB NLT HCSB NET

variant/WH ο του θεου γαρ υιος Χριστος Ιησους
"for the Son of God, Christ Jesus"
א* A C 0223
NASB NEB REB

Based on normative Pauline usage, one would usually think that the preferred word order is "Christ Jesus." However, in this case, earlier and diverse textual attestation affirms the order "Jesus Christ," which also accords with special Pauline usage, whereby "Jesus Christ" follows titles like "Son" (see 1 Cor 1:9) and "Lord" (see 1:1-2; 8:9; 13:14).

2 Corinthians 2:1

WH NU εκρινα γὰρ ἐμαυτῷ τοῦτο
"for I myself decided this"
𝔓46 B 0223 0243 33
RSV NRSV ESV NIV TNIV NEB REB NJB NAB NLT HCSB NET

variant/TR εκρινα δε εμαυτω τουτο
"but I myself decided this"
א A C D1 F G Ψ Maj
KJV NKJV NASB

According to the context, the reading with "for" (γαρ) must connect with 1:23 ("to spare you, I did not come to Corinth . . . for I determined that I would not come to you again in heaviness"), 1:24 being parenthetical. The reading with "but" (δε) would mark a change of direction from the preceding discourse. However, Paul had been trying to explain why he had not come to Corinth (that he did not want to come to them in heaviness so as to burden them), so γαρ is appropriate. This reading, having the earliest textual support, is the one followed by most translators.

2 Corinthians 2:3

Influenced by Phil 2:27, several witnesses (D F G Ψ 1739 syr[h**]) expand the phrase λυπην ("grief") to λυπην επι λυπην ("grief upon grief").

2 Corinthians 2:17

TR WH NU οὐ γάρ ἐσμεν ὡς οἱ πολλοὶ καπηλεύοντες τὸν λόγον τοῦ θεοῦ
"for we are not as the many who peddle the word of God"
ℵ A B C Ψ 33 1739 Maj cop
all

variant ου γαρ εσμεν ως οι λοιποι καπηλευοντες τον λογον του θεου
"for we are not as the rest who peddle the word of God"
𝔓46 D F G L syr
NKJVmg NRSVmg NJBmg HCSBmg

The manuscript evidence slightly favors the TR WH NU reading because it has the testimony of four outstanding Alexandrian manuscripts (ℵ A B C), as well as other support. However, the earliest manuscript, 𝔓46, supports the variant, as do some Western manuscripts (D F G), one later Alexandrian manuscript (L), and the Syriac. Internal considerations slightly favor the variant. If οι πολλοι ("the many") was originally in the text, what would have prompted scribes to change it to οι λοιποι ("the rest")? It does not seem likely that scribes would want to make Paul say something so extreme—i.e., Paul would be condemning all the rest of the Christian workers as being those who hawk the word of God. Thus, it is quite possible that the word λοιποι was changed to πολλοι ("many") because it was perceived as being too offensive. However, not one English version has followed the variant reading, though it has been noted in several. The note in the NKJV wrongly says that the M-text (Maj) supports the variant.

2 Corinthians 3:2

TR WH NU ἡ ἐπιστολὴ ἡμῶν ὑμεῖς ἐστε, ἐγγεγραμμένη ἐν ταῖς καρδίαις ἡμῶν
"you are our epistle, written in our hearts"
𝔓46 A B C D 33 1739 Maj
KJV NKJV RSVmg NRSV ESV NASB NIV TNIV NEB REB NJB NAB NLT HCSB NET

variant η επιστολη ημων υμεις εστε, εγγραμμενη εν ταις καρδιαις υμων
"you are our epistle, written in your hearts"
ℵ 33 1881
RSV NRSVmg ESVmg NJBmg NLTmg

The TR WH NU reading has, by far, the best documentary support and is the more difficult of the two. The variant is far easier to understand because it seems as if Paul was telling the Corinthians that they themselves were his letter of recommendation—i.e., his work among them was evidence of his apostleship. As such, he did not need anyone else to write a letter of recommendation for him; the Corinthian church was that letter. However, in the previous verse Paul spoke of two different kinds of letters—those "to you" and those "from you." The letter "to you" corresponds to the variant reading, which speaks of how Paul had written a letter in the

Corinthians' hearts. The letter "from you" corresponds to the TR WH NU reading, because Paul was speaking of a letter from the Corinthians to Paul. This probably means that the Corinthian church had made such an impression on Paul that he (as their father) carried them with him wherever he went (see 7:3) and spoke of them to others as a father bragging about his children (see 7:14; 8:24). As such, Paul himself was the Corinthians' letter. In the next verse (3:3), Paul speaks of how the Corinthians were a letter of Christ prepared by the apostles. Thus, the two letters mentioned in 3:1 are explained in the next two verses, in chiastic order (to you + from you . . . from you + to you). If the reading of the variant were genuine, there would be no further mention of a letter *from* the Corinthians to Paul.

Most modern versions follow the TR WH NU reading, whereas the translators of RSV, contrary to their usual practice of following 𝔓46 with other good testimony—especially B—followed the variant, probably for exegetical reasons. NRSV follows the superior testimony.

2 Corinthians 3:6

The scribe of 𝔓46 revealed his understanding of this verse by the way he wrote the word πνευμα ("spirit"), which appears twice in this verse. He could have written them both as divine titles but he chose not to designate the spirit as a nomen sacrum in its first instance, only in the second: διακονους καινης διαθηκης, ου γραμματος αλλα πνευματος· το γαρ γραμμα αποκτεννει το δε $\overline{\text{ΠΝΑ}}$ ζωοποιει ("ministers of a new covenant, not of letter but of spirit, for the letter kills but the Spirit gives life"). This way of writing the verse suggests that he understood the first occurrence of πνευμα ("spirit"), in its anarthrous form, to denote the spiritual manner in which the new covenant is ministered—in contrast to the legalism of the old covenant. In its arthrous form, το πνευμα ("the Spirit") designates the divine person and power who gives life to all who participate in the new covenant. A few English translators have made the same kind of distinction (see NEB REB).

2 Corinthians 3:9

NU has the wording ει γαρ τη διακονια της κατακρισεως δοξα ("for if there was glory in the ministry of condemnation"). This has excellent testimony: 𝔓46 ℵ A C D* F G 33 1739. TR WH, with the support of B D[2] Maj, read η διακονια instead of τη διακονια, yielding the rendering: "for if the ministry of condemnation was glory." TR followed Maj, and WH followed B.

The difference between the first reading and the second in the Greek is that the first is a dative, and the second a nominative. The variant is probably the result of scribal assimilation to the preceding and the following nominative, η διακονια. The resultant reading is slightly bolder in that it equates the ministry of condemnation with glory, whereas the NU reading indicates that there was an element of glory in the ministry of condemnation.

2 Corinthians 3:17

As often happened in the NT, unique titles of the Spirit were changed by scribes to more usual titles. In this case, το πνευμα κυριου ("the Spirit of the Lord") was changed to το πνευμα αγιον ("the Holy Spirit") in L and to το πνευμα ("the Spirit") in 323. The expression "the Spirit of the Lord" reveals a unification of identity between the Lord and the Spirit; in effect, it is a reiteration of the previous clause: ο δε κυριος το πνευμα εστιν ("the Lord is the Spirit"). This is not the same as saying the Lord is spirit, ontologically speaking (as in John 4:24, which says "God is spirit"); rather, this asserts the Lord's present reality as the Spirit who liberates people from bondage. In other words, we do not translate this "the Lord is spirit" but "the Lord is the Spirit." This is what the scribe of 𝔓46 was most likely thinking when he inscribed the nomen sacrum for πνευμα as ΠΝΑ.

2 Corinthians 4:1

WH NU have the idiom ουκ εγκακουμεν, which means "we do not lose heart," following 𝔓46 ℵ A B D* F G 33 cop. The variant reading is very similar: ουκ εκκακουμεν ("we do not grow weary"), found in C D[2] Ψ 0243 1739 1881 Maj (so TR). Because of the excellent testimony for the first reading, it is almost certain that the variant was a scribal mistake—there is only a one-letter difference (γ/κ) and the two words are pronounced similarly. (The same change occurred in 4:16—see note.) But the change hardly affects the meaning of the verse because both words work in context: Paul could have lost heart and grown weary if it had not been for the Lord's mercy reviving and encouraging him.

2 Corinthians 4:5a

NU — Ἰησοῦν Χριστόν
"Jesus Christ"
𝔓46 ℵ A C D it syr[h]
RSV NRSV ESV NIV TNIV NAB NLT HCSB NET

variant/TR WH — Χριστον Ιησουν
"Christ Jesus"
B H Ψ 0186 0243 33 1739 Maj
KJV NKJV NASB NEB REB NJB

The NU reading has good documentation and presents an unusual formation of Christ's name. Paul normally used the wording "Christ Jesus [the] Lord" or "the Lord Jesus Christ." The variant reading is likely the result of scribal assimilation to the more ordinary formation. In any event, English translations are divided on this.

2 Corinthians 4:5b

The three editions (TR WH NU) read δουλους υμων δια Ιησουν ("your servants because of Jesus"), with the support of A*[vid] B D F G H Ψ Maj. There are four textual variants on the prepositional phrase: (1) δια Ιησου ("through Jesus") in 𝔓46 ℵ* A[c] C 0243 33 1739 cop; (2) δια Χριστου ("through Christ") in ℵ[1] it[r]; (3) δια Χριστον ("because of Christ") in 326 1241[s]; (4) δια Ιησουν Χριστου ("because of Jesus Christ") in 629 630 it[b]. The second, third, and fourth variants are slimly supported and are obvious scribal assimilations to the first part of the verse. Thus, the true reading is found either in TR WH NU or in the first variant, both of which have early and diverse documentation. But the TR WH NU reading could be the result of assimilation to the previous accusative, Ιησουν. By contrast, the first variant (in the genitive) is unique, and it relates Paul's complete dependency on Jesus, which is the key theme of this chapter.

2 Corinthians 4:6a

The three editions (TR WH NU) read της γνωσεως της δοξης του θεου ("the knowledge of the glory of God"), with good documentation: ℵ A B C[3] D[2] Ψ 1739 1881 Maj it[r] syr cop. (In a fuller context, this yields the rendering: "he shone in our hearts for an illumination of the knowledge of the glory of God.") There are two variants on this: (1) της γνωσεως του θεου ("the knowledge of God") in 33; and (2) της γνωσεως της δοξης αυτου ("the knowledge of his glory") in 𝔓46 C* D* F G it^{b,r}. Because of its slim attestation, the first variant is likely the result of trimming, but the second variant could be original. It is difficult to determine if the text was originally long and then editorially shortened or originally short and then expanded. It should be noted that C and D originally contained the shorter reading, and then they were lengthened by correctors. Scribes could have perceived that του θεου ("of God") was redundant and thereby replaced it with a pronoun, or scribes may have wanted to distinguish "God" from "Christ," so they specified the person.

2 Corinthians 4:6b

TR NU — προσώπῳ ['Ιησοῦ] Χριστοῦ
"face of Jesus Christ"
𝔓46 ℵ C H Ψ 0209 1739^{c} Maj syr
KJV NKJV NRSV ESV NEB REB NAB NLT HCSB NETmg

variant 1/WH — προσωπω Χριστου
"face of Christ"
A B 33
RSV NASB NIV TNIV NJB NET

variant 2 — προσωπω Χριστου Ιησου
"face of Christ Jesus"
D F G 0243 1739*
NETmg

The manuscript support for the TR NU reading is both early and diverse. Westcott and Hort followed A and B (Codex Vaticanus)—their favorite manuscript. Had they known of the testimony of 𝔓46, which was discovered after their time, they probably would have decided otherwise. In line with the reasoning presented in the note on 4:5a, the wording "face of Jesus Christ" is both unique and possibly original. Giving Christ's earthly name first emphasizes his humanity and prompts the reader to think of a real man with an actual face. Paul's point is that as God's glory was seen in an actual man, Jesus Christ, so God's glory continues to shine through real people (such as Paul), who are nothing but earthen vessels. The single title "Christ" (the WH reading) points to Christ's risen presence. It is now, through the risen Christ, that God enlightens the hearts of men with divine knowledge. This could be Paul's original wording and intended thought (see Zuntz 1953, 181-182). But we cannot be absolutely certain, because there is the possibility that scribes were influenced by 2:10 to drop the word "Jesus."

2 Corinthians 4:14a

TR WH NU — ὁ ἐγείρας τὸν κύριον 'Ιησοῦν
"the one having raised the Lord Jesus"
ℵ C D F G Ψ Maj it^{b} syr cop^{bo}
KJV NKJV RSV NRSV ESV NASB NIV TNIV NEB REB NJB NAB NLT HCSB NETmg

variant — ο εγειρας τον Ιησουν
"the one having raised Jesus"
𝔓46 B (0243 33 1739 omit τον) it^{r} cop^{sa}
NLTmg NET

Although it is possible that the variant is the result of scribal assimilation to Rom 8:11, it is far more likely that the TR WH NU reading is an expansion because scribes had a habit of expanding the name "Jesus" to "Jesus Christ" or "Lord Jesus Christ." But Paul was purposely using only Jesus' name in this chapter (4:5, 6, 10, 11, 14) to underscore Jesus' human identification with the sufferings of people (see note on 4:6b). Disagreeing with the NU committee's majority decision to accept the TR WH NU reading, Metzger argued that the variant has more diverse attestation, while the TR WH NU reading was the work of a pious scribe expanding Jesus' name (TCGNT). All English versions, however, have followed the fuller text. Only the NLT notes the variant.

2 Corinthians 4:14b

WH NU ἡμᾶς σὺν Ἰησοῦ ἐγερεῖ
"he will raise us with Jesus"
𝔓46 ℵ* B C D* F G 0243 33 1739 cop
NKJV RSV NRSV ESV NASB NIV TNIV NEB REB NJB NAB NLT HCSB NET

variant/TR ημας δια Ιησου εγερει
"he will raise us through Jesus"
ℵ2 D1 Ψ Maj syr
KJV

The WH NU reading, which has superior attestation, poses an interesting exegetical problem: How will the believers (in the future) be raised with Jesus if he has already been raised? This problem may have prompted a correction in two manuscripts (ℵ2 D1), which was later propagated in the majority of manuscripts. The corrected text makes Jesus the agent of the resurrection, not the co-participant. But Paul is viewing the believers' union with Christ as realized eschatology; by virtue of Jesus' resurrection, those joined to Jesus will be raised with him.

2 Corinthians 4:16

WH NU οὐκ ἐγκακοῦμεν
"we do not lose heart"
𝔓46 ℵ A B D* F G cop
NKJV RSV NRSV ESV NASB NIV TNIV NEB REB NJB NAB NLT HCSB NET

variant/TR ουκ εκκακουμεν
"we do not grow weary"
C D2 Ψ 0243 33 1739 Maj
KJV

Almost all the same manuscripts line up in support of one or the other reading as they did in 4:1 (see note). It is almost certain that the variant was a scribal mistake. But the change hardly affects the meaning inasmuch as Paul was relating that he would not get discouraged with his trials because, as his outward man was decaying day by day, his inward person was being renewed.

2 Corinthians 5:3

NU εἴ γε καὶ ἐκδυσάμενοι οὐ γυμνοὶ εὑρεθησόμεθα
"for if indeed having been unclothed we will not be found naked"
D*,c ita Marcion Tertullian
NRSV ESVmg NASB HCSBmg NETmg

variant/TR WH ει γε και ενδυσαμενοι ου γυμνοι ευρεθησομεθα
"for if indeed having been clothed we will not be found naked"
𝔓46 ℵ B D2 Ψ 0243 33 1739 1881 Maj it syr cop Clement
KJV NKJV RSV NRSVmg ESV NIV TNIV NEB REB NJB NAB NLT HCSB NET

Paul's statement here must be understood in context. He is using a double metaphor to describe the death of our bodies: It is a putting off of old clothes and a departure from a temporary habitation (a tabernacle or tent). The permanent house represents our resurrected bodies, while the earthly tabernacle represents our present, earthly bodies. Christians long to be released from earthly bodies—not to become spirits without bodies (see NLT)—but to have new bodies, dwelling places that will come from heaven and will be brought to us when Christ returns (1 Thess 4:16). Thus, speaking of this future body Paul says, "having been clothed we will not be found naked" (according to the variant). Some scribes must have thought it was tautological, so they changed it to "having been unclothed we will not be found naked." But the variant reading is not a trite statement or tautological; it is a prophetic affirmation of a Christian's future state of being. Furthermore, this statement sets the stage for the next verse, where Paul affirms that his desire is "to be clothed." And since a great array of witnesses attest to this reading, the variant should be adopted as the original reading; this happened to be the personal opinion of Metzger, who disagreed with the decision of the committee (see TCGNT). Most translators, also, have followed the variant.

2 Corinthians 5:12

All three editions (TR WH NU) read καυχηματος υπερ ημων ("to boast for us"), with the testimony of C D Ψ 33 1739 Maj. However, good documentation supports the reading καυχηματος υπερ υμων ("to boast for you[rselves]")—so 𝔓46 ℵ B 33. According to the three editions, the full statement reads, "we are not commending ourselves to you again, but giving you an opportunity to boast for us." Though the TR WH NU reading has inferior documentation, it makes very good sense. It speaks of how Paul had been trying to give the Corinthians reason to boast about Paul to the dissidents who were strongly against Paul. The variant reading, found in the three earliest witnesses, is very difficult but not impossible. Martin (1986, 117) said, "it is possible that υπερ υμων could be interpreted to show that because of what Paul has done for the Corinthians they had reason to boast on their own account." The usual practice in textual criticism is to accept the reading that is more difficult—if it is not impossible—especially if the documentary evidence favors it. Thus, it would seem that the variant is the more likely reading.

2 Corinthians 5:17

WH NU γέγονεν καινά
"they have become new"
𝔓46 ℵ B C D* F G 048 0243 1739 cop Clement
RSV ESV NIV TNIV NEB REB NJB NAB NLT HCSB NET

variant/TR γεγονεν καινα τα παντα
"all things have become new"
D2 L P Ψ (075 33) Marcion[according to Tertullian]
KJV NKJV NRSV NASB HCSBmg NETmg

According to WH NU, a rendering of the full passage is: "if anyone is in Christ he is a new creation; old things have passed away, behold they have become new." The variant has "all things" becoming new. The variant reading could have first been created by a scribal error, due to dittography—τα and παντα occur at the beginning of the next verse. But the sequence τα δε παντα (with the δε interrupting τα and παντα) makes this unlikely. Thus, the variant reading is more likely a scribal assimilation to Rev 21:5, in which God says, "I make all things new." Marcion would have promoted the expansion because it shows the full superiority of the new covenant over the old. Whether intentional or not, both NASB and NRSV reflect TR, whereas the KJV and NKJV do so by design.

2 Corinthians 5:19

All three editions (TR WH NU) read τον λογον της καταλλαγης ("the message of reconciliation"). One variant (in 𝔓[46]) reads τον ευαγγελιον της καταλλαγης ("the gospel of reconciliation"). Another variant, found in Western texts (D* F G it[a]), reads ευαγγελιου τον λογον της καταλλαγης ("the gospel's message of reconciliation"). The first variant may have come from 4:1-4, where Paul speaks of his ministry and the gospel in one breath. Paul's message was the gospel. Thus, it would be natural for the scribe of 𝔓[46] to substitute "gospel" for "message." The second variant is a conflation of the TR WH NU reading and the first variant.

2 Corinthians 6:9

All three texts (TR WH NU) read παιδευομενοι και μη θανατουμενοι ("being punished and yet not being put to death") with the support of 𝔓[46] ℵ A B C Maj. A Western variant (D* F G it) reads πειραζομενοι και μη θανατουμενοι ("being tried and yet not being put to death"). This variant may be an attempt to make a more understandable semantic link between the two participles, inasmuch as it is easier to think of a trial leading to death than to think of punishment leading to death. But the word παιδευω was used by Luke, for example, to describe a very severe form of punishment—the "whipping" or "scourging" of Jesus before his crucifixion (see Luke 23:16, 22), and such scourging could also lead to death. According to statements made later in this epistle, Paul must have experienced similar whippings (see 11:24-25).

2 Corinthians 6:15

The name βελιαρ ("Beliar") is printed in the NU text, as supported by 𝔓[46] ℵ B C and many other manuscripts. Other manuscripts (D K Ψ) read Βελιαν ("Belian"), other manuscripts (F G) read Βελιαβ ("Beliab"), and others (it Tertullian) read βελιαλ ("Belial"). The spelling "Belial" is very popular with modern versions (see RSV ESV NIV NEB) probably because of its edifying etymology—it comes from a Hebrew word (*beliyya'al*) meaning "worthlessness" or perhaps "the place from which there is no ascent" (i.e., the abyss or Sheol). Furthermore, the name was used in Jewish literature as an appellation of the devil (Harris 1976, 361). Thus, Paul was contrasting Christ with the devil, and thereby urging that as Christ has no companionship with the devil, so a believer should not have any unity with an unbeliever.

2 Corinthians 6:16

WH NU	ἡμεῖς γὰρ ναὸς θεοῦ ἐσμεν ζῶντος "for we are the temple of the living God" B D* L P 33 cop NKJVmg RSV NRSV ESV NASB NIV TNIV NEB REB NJB NAB NLT HCSB NET

variant 1/TR υμεις γαρ ναος θεου εστε ζωντος
"for you are the temple of the living God"
𝔓46 (א2) C D2 F G Ψ (0209) Maj it syr
KJV NKJV HCSBmg

variant 2 ημεις γαρ ναοι θεου εστε ζωντος
"for we are temples of the living God"
א* 0243 1739
none

It is possible that the first variant is the result of scribal assimilation to 1 Cor 3:16, where Paul asked the Corinthians, "don't you know that you are God's temple?" But it is also possible that scribes shifted to the first person plural under the influence of 2 Cor 5:1-7, where Paul uses "we" to speak of the believers' longing for their heavenly home. In any event, both the WH NU reading and the first variant convey the thought that the church as a corporate unit is the temple of the living God. The second variant misses the mark, for it presents the notion that each believer is a temple of the living God. This probably shows the influence of 1 Cor 6:19.

2 Corinthians 7:1

All Greek manuscripts, except one, read καθαρισωμεν εαυτους απο παντος μολυσμου σαρκος και πνευματος ("let us cleanse ourselves from every defilement of flesh and spirit"). The one exception is 𝔓46, which substitutes πνευματι for πνευματος, thereby allowing the rendering, "let us cleanse ourselves from every defilement of flesh—even by the Spirit." (In 𝔓46 the word πνευματι is written as a nomen sacrum, $\overline{\Pi NI}$, thereby indicating "the Spirit.") This change makes the Spirit the agent of the cleansing; it avoids the exegetical problem of explaining how a Christian's spirit can become defiled.

Again, all Greek manuscripts, except one, read επιτελουντες αγιωσυνην εν φοβω θεου ("perfecting holiness in the fear of God"). The one exception is 𝔓46, which replaces φοβω with αγαπη, thereby producing the translation, "perfecting holiness in the love of God." This change is remarkable, for it displays the scribe's desire to show that one's love for God is the motivation for perfecting holiness, not one's fear of God (cf. 1 John 3:1-3).

2 Corinthians 7:8a

Most witnesses read ελυπησα υμας εν τη επιστολη ("I grieved you by the letter"). This was modified in a few manuscripts (1505 syr[h]) to ελυπησα υμας εν τη προτερα επιστολη ("I grieved you by the former letter")—making explicit reference to Paul's previous letter, which most scholars assume to be the third letter Paul wrote to the Corinthians. This "sorrowful" letter was written to rectify the rebellion against Paul in the Corinthian church. Other manuscripts (D* F G) read ελυπησα υμας εν τη επιστολη επ εμου ("I grieved you by the letter from me").

2 Corinthians 7:8b

TR NU βλέπω [γάρ]
"for I see"
א C D1 F G Ψ 0243 33 1739 Maj syr cop[bo]
KJV NKJV RSV NRSV ESV NASB REB NJB NAB (NLT) HCSB NET

variant 1 βλεπων
"seeing"
𝔓46* (vg)
NEB NETmg

variant 2/WH βλεπω
"I see"
𝔓46c B D* it cop[sa]
NIV TNIV NETmg

In a fuller context, the TR NU reading could be rendered: "Because even if I grieved you with the letter, I do not regret it, though indeed I did regret it, for I see that that letter—if even for an hour—grieved you." In the nineteenth century both Lachman and Hort considered the Latin Vulgate to have preserved the original reading—as evidenced by the participle *videns* ("seeing"). Westcott and Hort (1882, 120) argued that the word βλεπων could have easily been mistaken for βλεπω (especially if a superscript dash was used at the end of the line to signal a *nu*). The second-century manuscript 𝔓46, discovered in the twentieth century, affirms this reading. A corrector of 𝔓46 struck out the final *nu* (as in the second variant; see *Text of Earliest MSS*, 292). But this creates a kind of anacoluthon between the two sentences, which explains why other scribes felt obligated to add γαρ ("for"). Thus, the evolution of the text probably went from βλεπων ("seeing") to βλεπω ("I see") to βλεπω γαρ ("for I see").

2 Corinthians 7:10

Several manuscripts (𝔓99 ℵ2 F G Ψ 1739 Maj), followed by TR, have both predicates in this verse as κατεργαζεται ("produces"). This is the result of scribal assimilation. Superior documentation (𝔓46 ℵ* B C D) has εργαζεται ("brings") first, then κατεργαζεται ("produces"), to display intensification: "for godly grief brings repentance that leads to salvation with no regret, but worldly grief produces death."

2 Corinthians 7:12

TR WH NU τὴν σπουδὴν ὑμῶν τὴν ὑπὲρ ἡμῶν
"your zeal for us"
𝔓46 A B C
RSV NRSV ESV NASB NIV TNIV NEB REB NJB NAB NLT HCSB NET

variant 1 την σπουδην ημων την υπερ υμων
"our zeal for you"
323 945
KJV NKJV

variant 2 την σπουδην υμων την υπερ υμων
"your zeal for yourselves"
ℵ D*,c F 0243
none

variant 3 την σπουδην ημων την υπερ ημων
"our zeal for ourselves"
D1 G
none

According to TR WH NU, the verse would be rendered: "So although I wrote to you, it was not because of the one who did the wrong, nor because of the one who was wronged, but that your zeal for us might be made known to you before God." The issue in the textual variants pertains to who has zeal for whom. This is a classic example of how the pronouns ημων ("our") and υμων ("your") were easily mixed up in textual transmission. In this case, the first variant reverses the idea entirely, and the third variant makes no sense whatsoever. The second variant possibly conveys the notion that the Corinthians should be zealous for clearing up the problems among themselves.

2 Corinthians 8:4

WH NU — τῆς διακονίας τῆς εἰς τοὺς ἁγίους
"the ministry to the saints"
𝔓[46] א B C D L Maj
NKJVmg RSV NRSV ESV NASB NIV TNIV NEB REB NJB NAB NLT HCSB NET

variant/TR — της διακονιας της εις τους αγιους δεξασθαι ημας
"for us to receive the ministry to the saints"
6 945
KJV NKJV

A few late manuscripts have the added gloss δεξασθαι ημας ("for us to receive"), which is a scribal attempt to improve the grammar and sense of the sentence. One scribe inserted the gloss on the justification that "it was thus found in many copies" (εν πολλοις των αντιγραφων ουτως ευρηται)—written in a marginal note. Another scribe carelessly copied this marginal note into the text, as if it were part of Paul's epistle (see Metzger 1992, 194).

2 Corinthians 8:5

Most manuscripts read εδωκαν πρωτον τω κυριω και ημιν δια θεληματος θεου ("they first gave themselves to the Lord and to us through the will of God"). A few witnesses (𝔓[46] it[f,r]), however, read εδωκαν πρωτον τω θεω και ημιν δια θεληματος θεου ("they first gave themselves to God and to us through the will of God"). This change probably arose by way of assimilation to the immediate context.

2 Corinthians 8:7

WH NU — τῇ ἐξ ἡμῶν ἐν ὑμῖν ἀγάπῃ
"in love from us to you"
𝔓[46] B 0243 1739 it[r] syr[p] cop
NRSV ESV NASB NIVmg TNIV NEBmg REBmg NJBmg NAB NLT HCSBmg NET

variant 1/TR — τη εξ υμων εν ημιν αγαπη
"in your love for us"
א C D F G Ψ 33 Maj syr[h]
KJV NKJV RSV NRSVmg ESVmg NASBmg NIV TNIVmg NEB REB NJB NLTmg HCSB NETmg

variant 2 — τη εξ υμων εν υμιν αγαπη
"in your love among yourselves"
326 629 2464
none

According to WH NU, this portion of the verse reads, "but as in everything you abound, in faith and in word and in knowledge and in all zeal and in love from us to you." The WH NU reading has the earliest support and is seemingly the more difficult reading, but its meaning is clear enough: Paul was saying that the Corinthians had been blessed with an abundance of love from Paul and his coworkers. Or Paul could have been saying that he and his coworkers had kindled this love in their hearts (see NEBmg).

The first variant is apparently more natural in context because it praises the Corinthians for their love of the apostles. This reading is the one found in the majority of manuscripts and followed by most translators. However, the testimony of 𝔓[46] with B must have caused the change from the reading in the ASV (which follows the first variant) to that of the NASB and motivated the NIV and NEB translators to at least put the WH NU reading in a marginal note. The second variant is a scribal error, which only makes sense if it is understood as connoting corporate love.

2 Corinthians 8:19

TR NU — πρὸς τὴν [αὐτοῦ] τοῦ κυρίου δόξαν
"to his—the Lord's—glory" (or, "to the glory of the Lord himself")
א D[1] Ψ 1881* Maj syr
KJV NKJV NRSV ESV NASB TNIV NEB REB HCSB NET

variant 1 — προς την αυτην του κυριου δοξαν
"to the very glory of the Lord"
P 0243 1739 1881[c]
none

variant 2/WH — προς την του κυριου δοξαν
"to the glory of the Lord"
B C D* F G L it cop
RSV NRSVmg NIV NJB NAB NLT

The TR NU reading could also be rendered, "being administered by us for the glory of the Lord himself" (see NRSV), but the rendering cited above comes from Barrett's (1973, 217) suggestion that Paul wrote αυτου and then added του κυριου as an explanatory aside: "his—I mean, the Lord's." If this is what actually occurred in the original composition, then the other readings are scribal attempts to make the statement more intelligible. The first variant is a failed attempt because it aligns the pronoun with δοξαν and makes for an odd expression, "the very glory." The second variant is a successful alteration (in that it makes sense), which has appealed to many translators.

2 Corinthians 8:21

Most manuscripts read ενωπιον κυριου ("before the Lord"), but a few other witnesses (𝔓[46] it syr[p]) read ενωπιον του θεου ("before God"). This change could have been made in order to achieve a balance in the final expression of this verse: "not only before *God* but also before *men*."

2 Corinthians 9:4

WH NU — ἐν τῇ ὑποστάσει ταύτῃ
"in this confidence"
𝔓[46] א* B C* D F G 048
NKJVmg RSV NRSV ESV NASB NIV TNIV NEB REB NJB NAB (NLT HCSB) NET

variant/TR εν τη υποστασει ταυτη της καυχησεως
"in this confidence of boasting"
א[2] D[2] (Ψ) 0209 Maj
KJV NKJV NRSVmg

The manuscript evidence for the WH NU reading is very impressive. The expansion in the majority of manuscripts is a carryover from such verses as 7:4, 14; 8:24; 11:17, where Paul openly expresses his boasting in the Corinthians.

2 Corinthians 9:9

As often happened throughout the course of textual transmission, the expression εις τον αιωνα ("into the age" = "forever") was expanded to εις τον αιωνα του αιωνος ("into the age of the age" = "forever and ever") in later manuscripts (F G 0243 1739 1881).

2 Corinthians 9:10

WH NU χορηγήσει καὶ πληθυνεῖ τὸν σπόρον ὑμῶν καὶ αὐξήσει
"he will supply and he will multiply your seed and he will increase"
א* B C D* 33
NKJVmg RSV NRSV ESV NASB NIV TNIV NEB REB NJB NAB NLT HCSB NET

variant 1/TR χορηγησαι και πληθυναι τον σπορον υμων και αυξησαι
"may he supply and may he multiply your seed and may he increase"
א[2] D[2] Ψ 0209 0243 1739 1881 Maj
KJV NKJV

variant 2 χορηγησει και πληθυνει τον σπορον υμων και αυξησαι
"he will supply and he will multiply your seed and may he increase"
𝔓[46] 104
none

variant 3 χορηγησαι και πληθυναι τον σπορον υμων και αυξησει
"may he supply and may he multiply your seed and he will increase"
F G
none

The three verbs in this verse appear with varying morphology in various manuscripts: all future tense (WH NU); all optative mood (TR); or a combination of the two (variants 2 and 3). The manuscript evidence supports the future tense, as does the context. Paul was promising the Corinthians that God would bless them for their generous giving; Paul was not merely hoping or wishing for this (as would be conveyed by the optative mood). All modern versions reflect the promissory aspect by using the future tense.

2 Corinthians 9:14

Instead of the wording αυτων δεησει υπερ υμων ("their supplication for you"), found in most witnesses, a few important manuscripts (א* B) read αυτων δεησει υπερ ημων ("their supplication for us"). The original wording of 𝔓[46], in like manner, had the next phrase as επιποθουντων ημας ("having great affection for us"). But a corrector of 𝔓[46] (probably the original scribe) changed the incorrect wording to επιποθουντων υμας ("having great affection for you"). (For 𝔓[46], see *Text of Earliest MSS,* 296.) Paul was not talking about how the Jerusalem saints would be praying for the apostles, but for the Corinthians, who had contributed to their welfare.

2 Corinthians 10:7a

Most manuscripts read ει τις πεποιθεν εαυτω Χριστου ειναι ("if anyone has persuaded himself to be Christ's"). This was embellished in Western witnesses (D* F G) to ει τις πεποιθεν εαυτω Χριστου δουλος ειναι ("if anyone has persuaded himself to be Christ's slave").

2 Corinthians 10:7b

WH NU	καθὼς αὐτὸς Χριστοῦ, οὕτως καὶ ἡμεῖς "just as he is Christ's, so are we" א B C D* Maj NKJVmg RSV NRSV ESV NASB NIV TNIV NEB REB NJB NAB NLT HCSB NET
variant 1/TR	καθως αυτος Χριστου, ουτως και ημεις Χριστου "just as he is Christ's, so are we Christ's" D[c] K KJV NKJV
variant 2	καθως αυτος ο Χριστος, ουτως και ημεις "just as he is the Christ, so are we" 𝔓[46] none

The first variant is a natural scribal interpolation. The second cannot easily be dismissed as a transcriptional error where the scribe wrote χριστος instead of χριστου, because the scribe also wrote the nominative article. The wording could be intentional. If so, the uniqueness of the statement is that Paul was claiming that he was just as much "Christ" as anyone else who claimed to be so. The interloper at Corinth may have made grand claims for himself, but even if he claimed to be "the Christ," Paul would have just as much right to make the same claim (see 2:10, 15; 4:5; 5:20), even though he would not actually do so.

2 Corinthians 10:12b-13a

TR WH NU	ἀλλὰ αὐτοὶ ἐν ἑαυτοῖς ἑαυτοὺς μετροῦντες καὶ συγκρίνοντες ἑαυτοὺς ἑαυτοῖς οὐ συνιᾶσιν. [13]ἡμεῖς δὲ οὐκ εἰς τὰ ἄμετρα καυχησόμεθα "but they, measuring themselves with one another and comparing themselves with one another, are not wise. [13] But we will not boast beyond our limits" 𝔓[46] א[1] B H[vid] 0243 33 1739 all
variant 1	αλλα αυτοι εν εαυτοις εαυτους μετρουντες και

σvγκρινοντες εαυτους εαυτοις [13]ουκ εις τα αμετρα καυχησομεθα
"but they, measuring themselves with one another and comparing themselves with one another, [13]will not boast beyond our limits"
(D*) F G it[b]
NJBmg [see the rendering below]

variant 2 αλλα αυτοι εν εαυτοις εαυτους μετρουντες και συγκρινοντες εαυτους εαυτοις ου συνισασιν. [13]ημεις δε ουκ εις τα αμετρα καυχησομεθα
"but they, measuring themselves with one another and comparing themselves with one another, are not aware [of this]. [13]But we will not boast beyond our limits."
ℵ* 88
none

Tasker (1964, 437) says, "If the Western text [variant 1] were original, the longer text might have arisen as an attempt to avoid the suggestion that an apostle would have said that he measured himself by own standard of measurement." However, the only way to make sense of the variant reading in the Western text is to accommodate the participles to a first person plural usage (see Martin 1986, 315). This is done in NJBmg, which notes the Western variant as reading: "By measuring ourselves against ourselves and comparing ourselves with our own selves, we shall be doing no unmeasured boasting." But this is a stretch because this rendering does not account for the word αυτοι ("they"). Thus, the omission is likely the result of an accident—the eye of a scribe passing over from ου to ουκ. The second variant is also the result of a scribal error (which was corrected in ℵ), especially since it is very unlikely that Paul would have conceded that his opposers were not aware of what they were doing.

2 Corinthians 11:3

WH NU τῆς ἁπλότητος [καὶ τῆς ἁγνότητος] τῆς εἰς τὸν Χριστόν
"the simplicity and the purity in Christ"
𝔓[46] ℵ* B D* F G 33 syr[h**] cop Pelagius
NKJVmg RSV NRSV ESV NASB NIV TNIV NEBmg REBmg NJBmg NAB NLT HCSB NET

variant/TR της απλοτητος της εις τον Χριστον
"the simplicity in Christ"
ℵ[2] D[2vid] H Ψ 0121 0243 1739 Maj syr[p] Julius Cassianus[according to Clement]
KJV NKJV NEB REB NJB HCSBmg NETmg

According to WH NU, the rendering in full is: "I fear lest somehow, as the serpent deceived Eve with his cunning, your thoughts would be led away from the simplicity and purity of Christ." The variant reading is shorter in that it lacks "and the purity." The testimony for both readings is diverse, but the reading for WH NU has earlier documentation (𝔓[46] ℵ* B)—with the exception of the second-century witness of Julius Cassianus. The omission of the Greek words και της αγνοτητος is very likely the result of homoeoteleuton—απλοτητος and αγνοτητος have the same endings. Therefore, the words were most likely written by Paul and then later deleted accidentally. Some scholars, however, have thought that they were a later addition influenced by the word αγνη ("pure") in 11:2 (see Tasker 1964, 438). However, the believers' "purity" is just as important to be retained as their "simplicity." The "purity" speaks of the believers' chaste devotion to Christ as in a marriage relationship, while the "simplicity" speaks of being guileless and pristine.

2 Corinthians 11:4

WH NU καλῶς ἀνέχεσθε
"you put up with it well enough"
𝔓46 B D* 33 cop[sa]
NKJV RSV NRSV ESV NASB NIV TNIV NEB REB NJB NAB NLT HCSB NET

variant/TR καλως ανειχεσθε
"you would put up with it well enough"
𝔓34 ℵ D2 F G H 0121 0243 0278 1739 Maj it syr
KJV

According to WH NU, the phrase could be rendered, "if another comes preaching another Jesus, . . . you put up with it well enough." Although the variant could be nothing more than an accidental scribal slip (the insertion of an *iota*), it is more likely an intended change, attempting to present this sentence as conditional, not actual. But Paul had no doubt that the Corinthians had, in fact, received and even welcomed false teachers. All versions except the KJV reflect this.

2 Corinthians 11:17

All Greek manuscripts read κατα κυριον ("according to the Lord"), but several Latin manuscripts (it[ar,f,r,t]) read "according to God."

2 Corinthians 11:28

The WH NU editions read η επιστασις μοι η καθ ημεραν ("my daily presure"), based on excellent testimony: 𝔓46 𝔓99 ℵ B F G H 0278 33. The variant (in TR) reads η επισυστασις μοι η καθ ημεραν ("my daily disturbance") based on inferior testimony: (H[c] I[vid]) Ψ 0121 Maj. Nonetheless, the variant suggests that Paul was experiencing disturbance every day in his anxious care of all the churches (BDAG 380).

2 Corinthians 12:7a

WH NU include διο ("wherefore")
ℵ A B F G 0243 33 1739 syr[h] cop[bo]
RSV NRSV NASB NIV TNIV NEBmg REBmg NJB NAB NLT HCSB NET

variant/TR omit διο ("wherefore")
𝔓46 D Ψ 1881 Maj it cop[sa]
KJV NKJV NRSVmg ESV NEB REB NETmg

The omission/inclusion of one small word, διο ("wherefore"), makes a difference in how these two verses are construed. With the word, the verses can be rendered:

> "But I will spare [you this boasting], lest anyone gives me credit beyond what he sees or hears anything to be in me—[7] especially by the excess of my revelations. Wherefore, lest I should be too exalted, a thorn in the flesh was given to me, a messenger of Satan, that he might beat me."

Without the word, the verses can be rendered:

"But I will spare [you this boasting], lest anyone gives me credit beyond what he sees or hears anything to be in me. [7] And by the excess of my revelations, that I should not be too exalted, a thorn in the flesh was given to me, a messenger of Satan, that he might beat me."

According to the WH NU reading, "the excess of revelations" is connected with how other people perceive Paul. According to the variant, "the excess of revelations" is the cause for Paul receiving a thorn in the flesh—that is, God permitted a messenger of Satan to deflate him, lest he be too puffed up with pride from having received such glorious revelations. In the end, the textual critic would seem compelled to go with the WH NU reading because it has superior testimony. The majority of modern translations have done likewise. Nonetheless, the few others who have followed the variant have decent support.

2 Corinthians 12:7b

TR WH NU	ἵνα μὴ ὑπεραίρωμαι "lest I be too exalted" 𝔓[46] ℵ[2] B I[vid] Ψ 0243 1739 Maj syr cop all
variant	omit ℵ* A D F G 33 NRSVmg

It is likely that some scribe(s) omitted this phrase because it was considered redundant and therefore superfluous.

2 Corinthians 12:9

WH NU	ἡ γὰρ δύναμις ἐν ἀσθενείᾳ τελεῖται "for the power is perfected in weakness" 𝔓[46vid] 𝔓[99vid] ℵ* A* B D* F G NRSV NASB NEB REB NJB NAB HCSB NETmg
variant/TR	η γαρ δυναμις μου εν ασθενεια τελειουται "for my power has been perfected in weakness" ℵ[2] (A[c]) D[1] Ψ 0243 0278 33 1739 Maj KJV NKJV RSV NRSVmg ESV NASBmg NIV TNIV NLT HCSBmg NET

The addition of the pronoun μου ("my") is clearly a later scribal addition that found its way into many manuscripts (and TR), several of which originally lacked it (ℵ* A* D*). It was added to personalize "power," just as "grace" had been previously personalized. But it is obvious that both grace and power come from God. Many English translators added the pronoun for the same reasons that scribes added it.

2 Corinthians 12:11

WH NU	γέγονα ἄφρων "I became a fool" 𝔓[46] ℵ A B D F G 33 1739 it cop NKJVmg RSV NRSV ESV NASB NIV TNIV NEB REB NJB NAB NLTmg HCSB NET

variant/TR γενομα αφρων καυχωμενος
"I became a fool by boasting"
Ψ 0243 1881 Maj
KJV NKJV NLT

The addition, characteristic of what is found in the Majority Text, is intended to clarify in what way Paul had become a fool. But anyone who reads the last two chapters would not need this clarification (see 11:1, 16-17, 21; 12:1, 6).

2 Corinthians 12:19

WH NU πάλαι δοκεῖτε
"have you been thinking all along?"
א* A B F G 0243 33 1739 it
NKJVmg RSV NRSV ESV NASB NIV TNIV NEB REB (NJB) NAB (NLT) HCSB NET

variant 1 ου παλαι δοκειτε
"you haven't been thinking all along, have you?"
𝔓46
NETmg

variant 2/TR παλιν δοκειτε
"again, do you think?"
א2 D Ψ 0278 Maj syr cop^bo
KJV NKJV NETmg

A rendering of the WH NU reading in full is: "Have you been thinking all along that we have been making a defense to you?" This clause could also be rendered as a statement (see NA27 and NJB NLT). Either way, as statement or question, the meaning is not affected. Perhaps influenced by the previous verse, where there are two questions expecting negative answers, the scribe of 𝔓46 also posed this question to expect a negative answer. The next variant was created by some scribe(s) who wanted to avoid the difficulty that παλαι with the present tense presents (note: above it has been translated with the English perfect tense). Drawing on verses such as 3:1 and 5:12, the scribe changed the opening word to "again." This implies that Paul was asking them to consider afresh if they thought he was defending himself. This is in contrast to the context, which indicates that the Corinthians were thinking all along that he was defending himself before them.

2 Corinthians 13:2

WH NU ἀπὼν νῦν
"now being absent"
𝔓46 א A B D* F G I 0243 33 1739
NKJVmg RSV NRSV ESV NASB NIV TNIV NEB REB NJB NAB NLT HCSB NET

variant/TR απων νυν γραφω
"now being absent I write"
D1 Ψ Maj syr cop^sa
KJV NKJV

The insertion of γραφω in later witnesses is a scribal attempt to show that Paul was now speaking, via this written letter, to those who had previously rebelled. The astute reader will already infer this.

2 Corinthians 13:4a

WH NU	καὶ γὰρ ἐσταυρώθη ἐξ ἀσθενείας "for indeed he was crucified out of weakness" 𝔓[46vid] ℵ* B D* F G 0243 1739 cop RSV NRSV ESV NASB NIV TNIV NEB REB NJB NAB NLT HCSB NET
variant/TR	και γαρ ει εσταυρωθη εξ ασθενειας "for if indeed he was crucified out of weakness" ℵ[2] A D[1] Ψ Maj KJV NKJV

See following two notes.

2 Corinthians 13:4b

TR WH NU	ἡμεῖς ἀσθενοῦμεν ἐν αὐτῷ "for indeed we are weak in him" B D Ψ 0243 1739 Maj syr[h] cop[sa] all
variant	ημεις ασθενουμεν συν αυτω "we are weak with him" ℵ A F G NRSVmg NASBmg

See following note.

2 Corinthians 13:4c

WH NU	ζήσομεν σὺν αὐτῷ "we will live together with him" ℵ A B D* F G 0243 1739 all
variant 1	ζησομεν εν αυτω "we will live in him" D*,c 33 none
variant 2/TR	ζησομεθα συν αυτω "we will live with him" D[2] Ψ Maj none
variant 3	ζωμεν αυτω "we live in him" 𝔓[46vid] none

The reading in 𝔓[46] (cited afresh in NA[27]) is the only witness to affirm the present tense statement, ζωμεν αυτω. Kenyon (1936, 118) wrote this incorrectly in his transcription as ζων εν; it should read ζωμεν (see *Text of Earliest MSS*, 302).

The first change in this verse (13:4a) involves the insertion of ει, which makes the statement conditional rather than actual. But the assertion "he was crucified in weakness" is poignant, especially as it is set against the following statement, "but he lives by the power of God." The second and third changes (13:4b and 13:4c) involve a shift in tense (from present to future or vice versa) and a change of preposition from εν ("in") to συν ("with"). Since Paul was fond of speaking about the believers being incorporated in Christ—in union with his death and resurrection—it is likely that here also Paul spoke of the believers' being weak *in* Christ's weakness (as displayed in his death on the cross) and of the believers having new life *in* Christ (by virtue of their union with Christ's resurrection). However, it must be admitted that this union can also be conveyed by the preposition of συν; so either preposition works well. The same is true for the verb tense, because the believers' participation in the new life is in both the present and the future.

2 Corinthians 13:5

According to the testimony of B D Ψ 33 Maj (so all three editions: TR WH NU), Paul asks the Corinthians: η ουκ επιγινωσκετε εαυτους οτι Ιησους Χριστος εν υμιν; ("don't you yourselves know that Jesus Christ [is] in you?") The name is written as Χριστος Ιησους ("Christ Jesus") in several other manuscripts (א A F G P 0243 1739 1881). Since the textual evidence is evenly divided and interna l arguments can go either way, it is difficult to determine which reading is original. (WH notes "Christ Jesus" as an alternative reading.)

2 Corinthians 13:13a

In the three editions (TR WH NU), the Trinitarian blessing is: η χαρις του κυριου Ιησου Χριστου και η αγαπη του θεου και η κοινωνια του αγιου πνευματος μετα παντων υμων ("the grace of the Lord Jesus Christ and the love of God and the fellowship of the Holy Spirit be with you all"). This has the testimony of א A D Maj. There are two variants on this: (1) instead of κυριου Ιησου Χριστου ("Lord Jesus Christ"), B Ψ 1881 read κυριου Ιησου ("Lord Jesus"); (2) instead of αγιου πνευματος ("Holy Spirit"), 𝔓[46] reads πνευματος ("Spirit"). According to TR WH NU, the Trinity in this benediction is presented as "the Lord Jesus Christ," "God," and "the Holy Spirit." In a few manuscripts, however, two of these titles are shorter: "the Lord Jesus" and "the Spirit." Although it could be argued that the titles were accidentally trimmed, it is just as likely that the titles for Jesus and the Spirit started out short and were then expanded.

2 Corinthians 13:13b

WH NU	omit αμην ("Amen") 𝔓[46] א* A B F G 0243 1739 cop[sa] RSV NRSV ESV NASB NIV TNIV NEB REB NJB NAB NLT HCSB NET
variant/TR	include αμην א[2] D Ψ Maj it syr cop[bo] KJV NKJV NETmg

A study of the concluding verses of the New Testament epistles reveals that in nearly every instance, the "amen" is a scribal addition. (See note on 1 Cor 16:24.) Only three epistles (Romans, Galatians, Jude) appear to have a genuine "amen" for the last word.

Subscription

Whereas scribes frequently added inscriptions (titles) to the Gospels, Acts, and Revelation, they did not usually do so for the Epistles. Instead, many scribes supplied subscriptions, which provide information about the writer, place of writing, sender, and recipient of the epistle. None of these subscriptions would have been penned by the author (Comfort 2005, 9-10), but they are worth noting:

1. No subscription—but placed as an inscription: Προς Κορινθιους Β ("Second to the Corinthians"). Appears in 𝔓[46].
2. No subscription. Appears in 629 630 1505 2464.
3. Προς Κορινθιους Β ("Second to the Corinthians"). Appears in ℵ A B* (D* F G Ψ) 33.
4. Προς Κορινθιους Β εγραφη απο Φιλιππων ("Second to the Corinthians, written from Philippi"). Appears in B[1] P.
5. Προς Κορινθιους Β εγραφη απο Φιλιππων δια Τιτου και Λουκα ("Second to the Corinthians, written from Philippi through Titus and Luke"). Appears in (1739[c]) 1881 Maj.
6. Προς Κορινθιους Β εγραφη απο Φιλιππων της Μακεδονιας δια Τιτου και Λουκα ("Second to the Corinthians, written from Philippi of Macedonia through Titus and Luke"). Appears in K 81 104 (TR).

This textual scenario is a good example of how a subscription became expanded throughout the course of its textual history. To the simple subscription "To the Corinthians B" (= "2 Corinthians") was appended additional information—first about the place of writing and then about those who participated in the writing. The designation of the place as being "Philippi" may be correct, inasmuch as Philippi was an important city in Macedonia (as in TR), the place of writing (see 2:13; 7:5; 8:1; 9:2). It also correct to say that Titus was with Paul, but there is no mention of Luke in this epistle.

The Epistle to the GALATIANS

Inscription

𝔓[46] א and B title this epistle as Προς Γαλατας ("To the Galatians"). Several manuscripts (including א and B) also have this title in the subscription (see last note for this book). Paul, however, would not have entitled this epistle in its original composition. Inscriptions and subscriptions are the work of later scribes. (For more on this, see Comfort 2005, 9-10.)

Galatians 1:1

According to Jerome, Marcion made a significant change in this verse: Ιησου Χριστου του εγειραντος αυτον εκ νεκρων ("Jesus Christ, the one raising him[self] from the dead"). This replaces the normal reading that indicates that God the Father raised Jesus from the dead. Marcion's change reveals his intentions to show that Jesus rose from the dead of his own accord, without the assistance of his Father.

Galatians 1:3

WH NU θεοῦ πατρὸς ἡμῶν καὶ κυρίου Ἰησοῦ Χριστοῦ
"God our Father and Lord Jesus Christ"
א A P Ψ 33 it[b]
NRSV ESV NASB NIV TNIV NEBmg NLT HCSBmg NETmg

variant 1/TR θεου πατρος και κυριου ημων Ιησου Χριστου
"God [the] Father and our Lord Jesus Christ"
𝔓[46] 𝔓[51vid] B D F G H 1739 Maj syr cop[bo,sa]
KJV NKJV RSV NEB REB NJB NAB NLTmg HCSB NET

variant 2 θεου πατρος και κυριου Ιησου Χριστου
"God [the] Father and Lord Jesus Christ"
0278 1877
none

The NU editors adopted the WH NU reading because it accords with Paul's usual style (cf. Rom 1:7; 1 Cor 1:3; 2 Cor 1:2; Eph 1:2; Phil 1:2; see TCGNT). However, it has to be noted that Paul did not always use the formula "God our Father and Lord Jesus Christ"; in three other instances, Paul wrote "God the Father and our Lord Jesus Christ" (Eph 1:3; 2 Tim 1:2; Titus 1:4). Thus, the textual decision here should not be made on the basis of Pauline style. Documentation, both early and diverse, supports the first variant.

Galatians 1:6

TR WH NU χάριτι [Χριστοῦ]
"grace of Christ"
𝔓51 ℵ A B F[c] Ψ 33 1739 1881 Maj syr[p] cop[bo]
KJV NKJV RSV NRSV ESV NASB NIV TNIV NEBmg REBmg NJB NAB NLT HCSB NET

variant 1 χαριτι
"grace"
𝔓46vid F* G H[vid] it[b] Tertullian Cyprian Pelagius
NEB REB NLTmg NETmg

variant 2 χαριτι Ιησου Χριστου
"grace of Jesus Christ"
D 326 syr[h**]
NETmg

variant 3 χαριτι θεου
"grace of God"
327
NETmg

If "Christ" or "Jesus Christ" or "God" had originally been in the text, why would any scribe have deleted them? Thus, it is likely that the shorter reading, having early (𝔓46) and diverse support, is original and that scribes adorned χαριτι ("grace") with one of these divine titles. For similar reasons, the shorter reading was adopted for the NEB (see Tasker 1964, 438) and REB.

Galatians 1:9

Kenyon (1936, 131) indicated that 𝔓46 lacked five lines at the bottom of the sheet that displays the first part of Galatians. But given the format on all the other sheets of 𝔓46, this is very unlikely. Rather, it is probable that the scribe did not include all of verse 9 or significantly shortened this verse—which would more appropriately allow three missing lines at the bottom of the page, not five (see *Text of Earliest MSS,* 313). This omission could have been accidental, due to homoeoteleuton (both 1:8 and 1:9 end with the same word, εστω), or it could have been a purposeful excision of what was perceived to be redundant.

Galatians 1:11

WH NU Γνωρίζω γὰρ ὑμῖν
"for I want you to know"
ℵ[1] B D*,c F G 33 it cop[sa]
RSV NRSV ESV NASB NIV TNIV NEB REB NJB (NLT) NETmg

variant/TR Γνωριζω δε υμιν
"now I want you to know"
𝔓46 ℵ*,2 A D[1] Ψ 1739 1881 Maj syr cop[bo]
KJV NKJV NAB HCSB NET

The textual evidence for both readings is divided, as are the internal reasons for them. On one hand, it can be argued that 1:11 provides a summary (hence, γαρ ["for"] is appropriate); on the other hand, it can be argued that 1:11 both summarizes and begins a new thought (hence, δε ["now"] is appropriate as a resumptive conjunction and mild contrastive).

Galatians 1:15a

TR WH NU εὐδόκησεν [ὁ θεός]
"God was pleased"
ℵ A D Ψ 0278 33 1739 Maj cop
KJV NKJV NRSV NASB NIV TNIV NEB REB NJB NAB HCSB NETmg

variant ευδοκησεν
"he was pleased"
𝔓46 B F G it syrp
RSV ESV NLT NET

The title ο θεος ("God") is bracketed in WH NU to signal the editors' doubts about its inclusion in the text. Indeed, it was probably added by scribes to clarify the subject, which is obviously "God," for it is God who revealed Christ to and in Paul. The testimony of the two earliest witnesses, 𝔓46 and B, is sufficient to show that the text originally lacked this title.

Galatians 1:15b

TR WH NU include και καλεσας δια της χαριτος αυτου ("and having called me by his grace"), with good documentary support from ℵ A B D Maj. However, 𝔓46 1739 1881 do not include this phrase. Perhaps the phrase was accidentally omitted due to homoeoteleuton—the eye of a scribe passing from μου to αυτου. Or it could have been intentionally deleted because it was seen as an extra intrusion into the main thought of 1:15-16—"God was pleased . . . to reveal his Son in me." However, it cannot be ruled out that the variant preserves the original text. If so, the clause "and having called me by his grace" was borrowed from 1:6 and added here to emphasize that Paul's election—just as the Galatians' election—was by grace, not by works.

Galatians 1:17

According to ℵ A Ψ 33 1739 Maj, the text says ουδε ανηλθον εις Ιεροσολυμα ("nor did I go up to Jerusalem"). Travel to Jerusalem was customarily seen as a "going up" because of its higher altitude in comparison to the surrounding area. In any event, this reading could have been borrowed from 1:18. Other manuscripts (𝔓51 B D F G) have the verb απηλθον ("go away"). This statement, perhaps an assimilation to the next part of the verse, indicates that Paul did not depart Damascus for Jerusalem after his conversion. 𝔓46 alone has the common verb, ηλθον, yielding the translation, "nor did I leave for Jerusalem."

Galatians 1:18

WH NU Κηφαν
"Cephas"
𝔓46 𝔓51 ℵ* A B 33 1739* syrhmg cop
NKJVmg RSV NRSV ESV NASB (NIV) TNIV NEB REB NJB NAB (NLT) HCSB NET

variant/TR Πετρον
"Peter"
ℵ[2] D F G Ψ 0278 1739[mg] 1881 Maj
KJV NKJV HCSBmg

Having early and diverse support, the WH NU reading is decidedly superior. Scribes substituted the more familiar name, "Peter," for the Aramaic surname, "Cephas." This reading, found in TR, was popularized by KJV and NKJV. For the sake of modern readers, the NIV and NLT have "Peter" in the text, while noting that the Greek text reads "Cephas."

Galatians 2:5

TR WH NU οἷς οὐδὲ πρὸς ὥραν εἴξαμεν
"to whom we did not yield for a moment"
𝔓[46] ℵ A B C D[c] 1739
all

variant 1 ουδε προς ωραν ειξαμεν
"we did not yield for a moment"
Marcion
none

variant 2 οις προς ωραν ειξαμεν
"to whom we did yield for a moment"
D* it[b] Tertullian Ambrosiaster MSS[according to Jerome]
NEBmg REBmg NJBmg

The first variant is Marcion's attempt to show that Paul never subjected himself to anyone—not to the other apostles nor to the false brothers, whom Marcion might have thought were one and the same (Longenecker 1990, 52). The second variant (noted in NEB REB NJB) probably arose as an error and then was perpetuated because it coincided with the view that Paul was willing to accommodate others for the sake of the gospel (see 1 Cor 9:20-23)—in this case, allowing Titus to be circumcised. But this runs contrary to Paul's entire argument—that he would not yield to the demands of the legalists and have Titus circumcised, so that he might defend the gospel of liberty.

Galatians 2:9

TR WH NU Ἰάκωβος καὶ Κηφᾶς καὶ Ἰωάννης
"James and Cephas and John"
ℵ B C I[vid] Ψ 0278 33 1739 Maj syr cop
KJV NKJV RSV NRSV ESV NASB (NIV) TNIV NEB REB NJB NAB (NLT) HCSB NET

variant 1 Ιακωβος και Ιωαννης
"James and John"
A
NJBmg

variant 2 Ιακωβος και Πετρος και Ιωαννης
"James and Peter and John"
𝔓[46] it[r]
NJBmg

variant 3 Πετρος και Ιακωβος και Ιωαννης
"Peter and James and John"
D F G it[b] Tertullian Ambrosiaster Pelagius
none

The first variant, which is curious, could display the Alexandrian scribe's attempt to make two pairs: James and John with Paul and Barnabas. But why would he delete Cephas? Other scribes changed the Aramaic name "Cephas" to the Greek "Peter," and/or rearranged the order of the names to put Peter first to show his prominence. However, it is apparent that James, the brother of Jesus, had taken the leading role in Jerusalem at this point in the history of the church. This is evident by his decisive role at the Jerusalem council in A.D. 50 (see Acts 15), which occurred around the same time this epistle was written and which dealt with the same issues addressed in this epistle. This supports the placement of James at the beginning of the names here.

Nearly all versions have "Cephas" here, with the exception of NIV and NLT, which read "Peter" in the text (for the sake of modern readers), but note "Cephas" in the margin as being the word in Greek. The same occurs in 2:11.

Galatians 2:11

WH NU Κεφας
"Cephas"
ℵ A B C H P Ψ 0278 33 1739
NKJVmg RSV NRSV ESV NASB (NIV) TNIV NEB REB NJB NAB (NLT) HCSB NET

variant/TR Πετρος
"Peter"
D F G Maj it syr[h]
KJV NKJV HCSBmg

Having early and diverse support, the WH NU reading is superior. Scribes substituted the more familiar Greek name, "Peter," for the Aramaic surname, "Cephas." (See comments on 2:9.)

Galatians 2:12a

TR WH NU τινας ἀπὸ 'Ιακώβου
"certain ones [came] from James"
ℵ A B C D F G H Maj
all

variant τινα απο Ιακωβου
"a certain one [came] from James"
𝔓[46] it[d,r] Irenaeus
NEBmg

The NEBmg notes a variant reading here, saying that "some witnesses read *a certain person*." Only one extant Greek manuscript, 𝔓[46], reads this way. It is possible that the scribe of 𝔓[46] was thinking of the one Judaizer (from Jerusalem) who was negatively influencing the believers in Antioch—and perhaps in Galatia, as well. This one individual is alluded to in 3:1; 5:7-10 (note the singular "who" and "he"); he may have been the leader of the Judaizers that visited Galatia (compare 5:12 where the plural "they" is used). See comments on 2:12b.

Galatians 2:12b

TR WH NU ἦλθον
"they came"
A C D^2 H Ψ 0278 1739 1881 Maj
all

variant ηλθεν
"he came"
𝔓46 ℵ B D* F G 33 it^{b,d,g} Irenaeus
NEBmg

Metzger believes the variant is the result of scribal error (see his comments in TCGNT). But in so many diverse manuscripts? The singular, ηλθεν, in 𝔓46 is no mistake, for the scribe was writing of a particular individual who, having come from James, caused problems in the church at Antioch. It seems more likely that ηλθεν, in so many good witnesses, is not a mistake but rather points to an original τινα in 2:12a (see note), as in 𝔓46 (and it^{d,g} Irenaeus). If so, then Paul was speaking of a particular individual who disturbed the unity among Jewish and Gentile Christians in Galatia.

Galatians 2:14

WH NU Κηφα
"Cephas"
𝔓46 ℵ A B C H Ψ 0278 33 1739 cop
RSV NRSV ESV NASB (NIV) TNIV NEB REB NJB NAB (NLT) HCSB NET

variant/TR Πετρος
"Peter"
D F G Maj it
KJV NKJV HCSBmg

Having early and diverse support, the WH NU reading is superior. Later scribes substituted the more familiar name, "Peter" (see comments on 2:9 and 11).

Galatians 2:16a

TR NU πίστεως Ἰησοῦ Χριστοῦ
"faith of Jesus Christ" (or, "faithfulness of Jesus Christ")
𝔓46 ℵ C D F G H Ψ 1739 Maj it syr
KJV NKJV RSV NRSV ESV NIV TNIV NJB NAB NLT HCSB NET

variant/WH πιστεως Χριστου Ιησου
"faith of Christ Jesus" (or, "faithfulness of Christ Jesus")
A B 33
NASB NEB REB

See comments on 2:16b.

Galatians 2:16b

TR WH NU	εἰς Χριστὸν Ἰησοῦν ἐπιστεύσαμεν "in Christ Jesus we believed" ℵ A C D F G I[vid] Ψ Maj NKJV RSV NRSV ESV NASB NIV TNIV REB NJB NAB NLT HCSB NET
variant	εις Ιησουν Χριστον επιστευσαμεν "in Jesus Christ we believed" 𝔓46 B H 33 1739 1881 it[d] syr KJV NEB

On the basis of superior documentation and parallel usage in 3:22, we have to judge that Paul wrote "faith of Jesus Christ" in the first part of the verse. The expression "faith of Jesus Christ" is usually taken to mean "faith in Jesus Christ" (an objective genitive), but it can also mean "Jesus Christ's faith" or "Jesus Christ's trustworthiness" (see the excellent note in NET). The latter means that Christians have been justified by Jesus Christ's faithfulness in obeying the Father, which is the implicit message of 2:20.

The testimony in the second part of the verse is somewhat divided. Either reading can be attributed to assimilation to the first part of the verse. Most English versions follow the text in all three editions, but KJV deviates from TR and NEB again shows its independence.

Galatians 2:20

All the Greek editions and English versions follow the reading which says πιστει ζω τη του υιου του θεου ("I live by faith of [in] the Son of God"), supported by ℵ A C D[1] Ψ 0278 33 1739 1881 it syr cop Clement. However, early and diverse testimony (𝔓46 B D* F G) supports the reading πιστει ζω τη του θεου και Χριστου, which can be rendered as, "I live by faith of (in) God and Christ" or "I live by faith of (in) God, even Christ." Of course, all of these could also be rendered, "I live by the faithfulness of the Son of God," etc. (see note on 2:16b).

The variant reading could possibly be explained as a scribal error, wherein a scribe accidentally deleted του υιου ("the Son") before του θεου ("of God"), due to the eye passing from the first του to the second του (so Metzger in TCGNT), and then added και Χριστου ("and Christ") for the sake of what follows: "who loved me and gave himself for me." Metzger further adds that the variant reading "could scarcely be original since Paul nowhere else expressly speaks of God as the object of a Christian's faith." But it is just as plausible that some scribe(s), knowing that Paul normally spoke of having faith in "God's Son, Jesus Christ," not in "God," was perplexed by a statement professing faith in God and consequently changed it to "the Son of God" (perhaps under the influence of 1:16; 4:4; Eph 4:13).

However, the reading in the variant can be taken to mean that Paul was speaking of having faith in Christ, who is God (και functioning epexegetically). It can also mean that Christians live (1) by God's and Christ's faithfulness (see note on 2:16) or (2) by faith in God and in Christ. It was not extraordinary for Paul to speak of having faith in God (see 1 Thess 1:8), as well as in Christ. If the variant is original, then Paul was proclaiming that he had put his trust in Christ, who as God revealed his love by his sacrifice (cf. Phil 2:5-11).

Galatians 3:1a

WH NU τίς ὑμᾶς ἐβάσκανεν
"who bewitched you?"
ℵ A B D* F G 33* 1739 it cop
NKJVmg RSV NRSV ESV NASB NIV TNIV NEB REB NJB NAB NLT HCSB NET

variant/TR τις υμας εβασκανεν τη αληθεια μη πειθεσθαι
"who bewitched you that you should not obey the truth?"
C D² Ψ 0278 33ᶜ 1881 Maj
KJV NKJV

The WH NU reading has better manuscript support than what is behind TR. The addition in the variant, which found its way into the majority of manuscripts, was borrowed from 5:7, which presents a similar rebuke. In both instances, Paul was rebuking the Galatians for veering from the truth of the gospel.

Galatians 3:1b

WH NU Χριστὸς προεγράφη ἐσταυρωμένος
"Christ was portrayed as having been crucified"
ℵ A B C P Ψ 0278 33* 1739 cop
NKJVmg RSV NRSV ESV NASB NIV TNIV NEB REB NJB NAB (NLT) HCSB NET

variant/TR Χριστος προεγραφη εσταυρωμενος εν υμιν
"Christ was portrayed as having been crucified among you"
D F G 33ᶜ Maj it
KJV NKJV

The manuscript evidence (both early and diverse) for the WH NU reading is vastly superior to that for TR. The extra fill-in (εν υμιν = "among you") found in the majority of manuscripts is a scribal attempt to clarify that the portrayal of the crucified Jesus Christ took place among the Galatians. In his preaching to the Galatians and his life among them, Paul "portrayed" or "placarded" (as in a public display or poster) the dying Jesus. This vivid picture should have been enough to counteract all their fascination with the Judaizers.

Galatians 3:6-9

According to Tertullian (*Marc.* 5.3), Marcion omitted these verses because he did not want to make a spiritual connection between the faith of the NT believers and the faith of Abraham of the OT.

Galatians 3:14a

The WH text follows ℵ and B in reading Ιησου Χριστω ("Jesus Christ") instead of Χριστω Ιησου ("Christ Jesus"), found in all other Greek manuscripts (so TR NU).

Galatians 3:14b

TR WH NU	τὴν ἐπαγγελίαν τοῦ πνεύματος "the promise of the Spirit" 𝔓[99] ℵ A B C D[2] Ψ 0278 33 1739 Maj syr cop all
variant	την ευλογιαν του πνευματος "the blessing of the Spirit" 𝔓[46] D*,c F G it[b] Marcion NLTmg

It is possible that the variant is the result of some scribe(s) accidentally copying the word ευλογιαν from the first part of the verse. But it is also possible that some scribe(s) introduced the word επαγγελιαν ("promise") in anticipation of the following verses, which focus on the promise made to Abraham now received by all who believe in Christ. However, the documentary evidence slightly favors the TR WH NU reading.

Galatians 3:17

WH NU	διαθήκην προκεκυρωμένην ὑπὸ τοῦ θεοῦ "a covenant previously confirmed by God" 𝔓[46] ℵ A B C P Ψ 33 1739 cop NKJVmg RSV NRSV ESV NASB NIV TNIV NEB REB NJB NAB NLT HCSB NET
variant/TR	διαθηκην προκεκυρωμενην υπο του θεου εις Χριστον "a covenant previously confirmed by God in Christ" D F G I 0176 0278 Maj it syr KJV NKJV HCSBmg NETmg

The manuscript evidence for the WH NU reading is very good, having support from the four earliest manuscripts (the first four listed above), as well as others. The manuscript evidence for TR is fairly good, but not as early. Influenced by the previous verse and by 3:22-29, where Christ figures significantly in the new covenant, it is likely that some scribe(s) thought it helpful to elucidate that, though the covenant was confirmed by God, it was done so in Christ.

Galatians 3:19

TR WH NU read τι ουν ο νομος; των παραβασεων χαριν προσετεθη, αχρις ου ελθη το σπερμα ("Why then the law? It was added for the sake of transgressions until the seed should come."), supported by ℵ A B C D[2] Ψ 0176[vid] 33 1739 Maj, and followed by all English versions. However, there are some noteworthy textual variants:

1. τι ουν ο νομος; των παραδοσεων χαριν ετεθη, αχρις ου ελθη το σπερμα ("Why then the law? It was established on account of the traditions, until the seed should come"). Appears in D*.
2. τι ουν ο νομος των πραξεων; ετεθη αχρις ου ελθη το σπερμα ("Why then the law of deeds? It was established until the seed should come"). Appears in F G it.
3. τι ουν ο νομος των πραξεων αχρις ου ελθη το σπερμα ("Why then the law of deeds[? It was] until the seed should come"). Appears in 𝔓[46].

In the earliest manuscripts of the NT there were no question marks (so 𝔓[46]). Therefore, a scribe copying this verse could read the first words as Τι ουν ο νομος; ("Why then the law?") or as Τι ουν ο νομος των παραβασεων; ("Why then the law of transgressions?"). Since the latter makes little sense, scribes changed παραβασεων ("transgressions") to πραξεων ("deeds"), as in the second and third variants. Although the resultant change is nearly as difficult, it connotes the law requiring one's deeds or actions to fulfill it. The original scribe of D made an interesting change—from "transgressions" to "traditions," which was later corrected.

Galatians 3:21

TR WH NU τῶν ἐπαγγελιῶν [τοῦ θεοῦ]
"the promises of God"
ℵ A C D (F G) Ψ 33 1739 Maj it syr cop
KJV NKJV RSV NRSV ESV NASB NIV TNIV NJB NAB NLT HCSB NET

variant 1 των επαγγελιων
"the promises"
𝔓[46] B it[d]
NEB REB NLTmg

variant 2 των επαγγελιων του Χριστου
"the promises of Christ"
104
none

Though the TR WH NU reading has solid manuscript support, it lacks the evidence of the two earliest manuscripts (𝔓[46] B). Therefore, it is quite possible that the shorter wording, in the first variant, is original, which was then expanded in two forms: (1) "the promises of God" (probably influenced by Rom 4:20 and 2 Cor 1:20) and (2) "the promises of Christ." The translators of NEB and REB favored the shorter reading, and NLT notes it out of respect for the ancient testimony of 𝔓[46] B.

Galatians 3:26

TR WH NU read της πιστεως εν Χριστω Ιησου ("the faith in Christ Jesus"), as supported by ℵ B C D Maj and followed by all English versions. However, one variant is πιστεως του Χριστου Ιησου ("faith[fulness] of Christ Jesus") in 𝔓[46] cop[sa] 6, and another variant is της πιστεως του Ιησου Χριστου ("the faith[fulness] of Jesus Christ") in 1739 1881. The first variant is unusual in that it does not exactly repeat any other similar phrase in Galatians. Previously, Paul used the expressions "faith of Jesus Christ" (2:16; 3:22) and "faith of Christ" (2:16), but never "faith of Christ Jesus." Furthermore, the reading in 𝔓[46] lacks the article before πιστεως ("faith"), which would seem to convey the meaning "Christ Jesus' faith" or "Christ Jesus' faithfulness" (see note on 2:16b). This unusualness could speak for the originality of the reading, from which the others deviated. However, the scantiness of evidence cannot warrant an adoption of this reading. The second variant appears to be scribal assimilation to 2:16 and 3:22.

Galatians 4:6a

TR WH NU read εξαπεστειλεν ο θεος το πνευμα του υιου αυτου ("God sent forth the Spirit of his Son"), supported by ℵ A C D etc., and followed by all the English versions.

However, there are two shorter versions of this: (1) B 1739 and cop[sa] exclude ο θεος ("God"), hence the rendering "he sent forth the Spirit of his Son"; (2) 𝔓[46] excludes του υιου ("Son"), hence the rendering "God sent forth his Spirit."

Since the first omission cannot be accounted for on transcriptional grounds, and since scribes had a propensity for adding subjects, it could be original. The second variant could possibly be accounted for on transcriptional grounds: the eye of the scribe passed from του υιου to αυτου due to homoeoteleuton. But it is more likely that the scribe of 𝔓[46], when confronted with the unique expression "the Spirit of his Son" (it appears nowhere else in the NT), decided to change it to the more ordinary one, "his Spirit." But the title "the Spirit of his Son" is perfect in the context, for it denotes that believers share in Christ's sonship because they are indwelt by the Spirit of God's Son.

Galatians 4:6b

WH NU τὰς καρδίας ἡμῶν
"our hearts"
𝔓[46] ℵ A B C D* F G 1739 it cop[sa]
RSV NRSV ESV NASB NIV TNIV NEB REB NJB NAB NLT HCSB NET

variant/TR τας καρδιας υμων
"your hearts"
D[2] Ψ 33 Maj syr
KJV NKJV NRSVmg HCSBmg

As often happened in the transmission of the NT text, the two pronouns ημων and υμων, so similar in sight and sound, were confounded for one another. In this case, however, it is easy to detect which is original, because ημων has superior documentation and υμων is an obvious assimilation to the immediate context.

Galatians 4:7

WH NU κληρονόμος διὰ θεοῦ
"an heir through God"
𝔓[46] ℵ* A B C* 33 1739*[vid] it cop[bo]
NKJVmg RSV NRSV ESV NASB NIV TNIV NEB REB NJB NAB NLT HCSB NET

variant 1 κληρονομος δια θεον
"an heir because of God"
F G 1881
NETmg

variant 2 κληρονομος δια Χριστου
"an heir through Christ"
81 630 cop[sa]
NETmg

variant 3 κληρονομος δια Ιησου Χριστου
"an heir through Jesus Christ"
1739[c]
NETmg

variant 4/TR κληρονομος θεου δια Χριστου
"an heir of God through Christ"
ℵ² C³ D Maj syr
KJV NKJV NRSVmg NETmg

variant 5 κληρονομος μεν θεου, συγκληρονομος δε Χριστου
"heir of God, coheir of Christ"
Ψ
NETmg

The manuscript evidence, both early and diverse, favors the wording found in WH NU. The several changes to the ending of this verse reveal the perplexity scribes experienced with the expression "an heir through God." It is much easier to understand how believers become heirs because of what God did for them in regeneration or through Jesus Christ's work of salvation—thus, the changes in variants 1-3. The fourth variant arose either as a transposed conflation (θεου/Χριστου) or as an attempt to unpack the expression "heir through God" (note the corrections in ℵ and C). The fifth variant is a gloss borrowed verbatim from Rom 8:17, a parallel verse.

Galatians 4:14

WH NU τὸν πειρασμὸν ὑμῶν
"the trial to you"
ℵ* A B C² D* F G 33 cop[bo]
RSV NRSV ESV NASB NIV TNIV NEB REB NJB NAB NLT HCSB NET

variant 1/TR τον πειρασμον μου
"the trial to me"
𝔓[46] C*[vid] D¹ Ψ Maj syr[h] cop[sa]
KJV NKJV HCSBmg

variant 2 τον πειρασμον
"the trial"
ℵ² 0278 81
none

The variant readings display the problems scribes experienced with interpreting the awkward expression τον πειρασμον υμων εν τη σαρκι μου, which when paraphrased means something like "the problems you had with my physical condition." If this is the original text, then Paul was saying that the Galatians might have been tempted to reject Paul because of his physical maladies—but they did not because they considered him a messenger sent from God. However, this expression causes considerable grammatical problems inasmuch as the sentence says that the Galatians did not despise or loathe their "temptation" to reject Paul. We would expect that the sentence would say that they did not loathe or despise Paul with his illness. Hence, scribes made various changes, all to indicate this very thought. Finally, it should be noted that 𝔓[46] excludes the final two words of the clause: ουδε εξεπτυσατε, as the result of homoeoteleuton.

Galatians 4:17

At the end of this verse, some Western manuscripts (D* F G it[b]) add ζηλουτε δε τα κρειττω χαρισματα ("but be zealous of the greater gifts"). This is an expansion taken from 1 Cor 12:31. But this admonition hardly fits, especially since the context has nothing to do with spiritual gifts and because Paul goes on in the next verse to say that the Galatians should be "zealous for good things." The Judaizers wanted to alienate the Galatians from Paul and make them more zealous for them than for him. Paul did not ask them to have zeal for him but to have zeal for what is good.

Galatians 4:19

Some manuscripts (א[2] A C D[1] Ψ 33 Maj—so TR WH) read τεκνια ("little children") here rather than τεκνα ("children"), as in NU (following א* B D* F G 1739). The change to τεκνια probably shows the influence of Johannine phraseology (cf., for example, John 13:33; 1 John 2:1, 12, 28, etc., but nowhere else in Paul).

Galatians 4:25

WH NU τὸ δὲ ˋ Ἀγὰρ Σινᾶ ὄρος ἐστὶν ἐν τῇ Ἀραβίᾳ
"now Hagar is Mount Sinai in Arabia"
A B D 0278
RSV NRSV ESV NASB NIV TNIV REB NJBmg NAB NLT HCSB NET

variant 1/TR το γαρ Αγαρ Σινα ορος εστιν εν τη Αραβια
"for Hagar is Mount Sinai in Arabia"
Ψ 062[vid] 33 1881 Maj syr
KJV NKJV

variant 2 το γαρ Σινα ορος εστιν εν τη Αραβια
"for Sinai is a mountain in Arabia"
(𝔓[46] δε for γαρ) א C F G 1739 it
RSVmg NRSVmg NEB NJB NLTmg

The various readings involve an alteration of conjunctions (δε and γαρ) and the presence or absence of the name Hagar. Concerning the latter alteration, the weight of documentation (𝔓[46] א C F G 1739 versus A B D 062[vid] 33 1881 Maj) is evenly divided. If the name Hagar was not originally in the text, it is assumed to be a carryover from the previous verse. This is handled nicely in the NEB: "The two women stand for two covenants. The one bearing children into slavery is the covenant that comes from Mount Sinai: that is Hagar. [25] Sinai is a mountain in Arabia and it represents the Jerusalem of today, for she and her children are in slavery." If this was the original text, dittography could account for the addition of Αγαρ: γαραγαρ. Contrarily, if Αγαρ was originally in the text, it could have been deleted due to homoeoteleuton. The four-layered allegory of the two covenants is retained:

[old covenant] Hagar = Mt. Sinai = present city of Jerusalem = slavery

[new covenant] our mother = [Mt. Zion] = the Jerusalem above = freedom

Galatians 4:26

WH NU μήτηρ ἡμῶν
"our mother"
𝔓[46] א* B C* D F G Ψ 1739 cop Origen
RSV NRSV ESV NASB NIV TNIV NEB REB NJB NAB NLT HCSB NET

variant/TR μητηρ παντων ημων
"mother of us all"
ℵ[2] A C[3] 0261[vid] 0278 Maj it[b,t] syr[h]
KJV NKJV

The documentation behind the WH NU reading is impressive, having support from the four earliest manuscripts (the first four listed above), as well as the so-called "Western" trio (D F G). In context, Paul was speaking of "the Jerusalem above," which is "free"—i.e., not in slavery (see previous note). Then, Paul calls this heavenly Jerusalem "our mother." Some scribes decided to make the term more inclusive and therefore added παντων ("all")—hence, "mother of us all."

Galatians 4:28

NU ὑμεῖς δέ, ἀδελφοί ... ἐστέ
"but you, brothers . . . are"
𝔓[46] B D* F G 0261[vid] 0278 33 it[b] cop[sa]
RSVmg NRSV ESV NASB NIV TNIV NEB REB NJB NAB NLT HCSB NET

variant/TR WH ημεις δε, αδελπφοι ... εσμεν
"but we, brothers . . . are"
ℵ A C D[2] Ψ 062 Maj syr cop[bo]
KJV NKJV RSV NRSVmg NETmg

The two pronouns υμεις ("you") and ημεις ("we") were often confused for one another (see comments on Eph 4:32). Nonetheless, the testimony of 𝔓[46] B D* is sufficiently weighty to show that the reading of the NU text is original, whereas the variant is probably the result of scribes attempting to retain the unity with the first person plural in 4:26, 31.

Galatians 4:30

In this verse Paul cited Gen 21:10 (LXX) almost verbatim except in the last two words, where Paul wrote του υιου της ελευθερας ("the son of the free woman") instead of "my son Isaac," in order to make it fit his argument about a free woman versus a slave woman. As often happened, some Western reviser(s) (D* F G it Ambrosiaster) changed Paul's wording to make it conform verbatim with the OT text—by changing "the son of the free woman" to "my son Isaac" (του υιου μου Ισαακ).

Galatians 5:1

WH NU Τῇ ἐλευθερίᾳ ἡμᾶς Χριστὸς ἠλευθέρωσεν· στήκετε οὖν
"for freedom Christ freed us; stand therefore"
ℵ* A B (D*) P 33 (ℵ[2] C* Ψ 0278 1739 with word transposition)
NKJVmg RSV NRSV ESV NASB NIV TNIV NEB REB NJB NAB NLT HCSB NET

variant 1 η ελευθερια ημας Χριστος ηλευθερωσεν· στηκετε ουν
"in which freedom Christ freed us, stand therefore"
F G it[r]
none

variant 2/TR τῃ ελευθερια ουν η Χριστος ημας ηλευθερωσεν, στηκετε
"therefore, in the freedom wherein Christ freed us, stand"
D[1] Maj
KJV NKJV

The WH NU text has the bold assertion that Christ freed the believers for them to experience freedom. In other words, Christians were not freed from slavery to the law to become entangled in it again. The other two variants underscore the truth that Christians should not lose the freedom that was given to them. Thus, there is only a slight difference in the readings; the same basic proclamation rings forth: "keep the freedom Christ gave you!"

Galatians 5:9

Instead of ζυμοι, some Western witnesses (D* it Marcion Lucifer) read δολοι ("adulterates"/ "falsifies")—"a little leaven adulterates all the lump." The scribe of D made the same change in a parallel passage, 1 Cor 5:6.

Galatians 5:13

TR WH NU read δια της αγαπης δουλευετε αλληλους ("through love serve one another"), supported by excellent testimony: 𝔓[46] ℵ A B C Maj. This was expanded in primarily Western witnesses (D F G it) to τῃ αγαπῃ του πνευματος δουλευετε αλληλους ("in love of the Spirit [= in the Spirit's love] serve one another"). The expansion assimilates the thought of 5:22, wherein love is depicted as being a fruit of the Spirit.

Galatians 5:19

WH NU πορνεία
"fornication" (or, "sexual immorality")
ℵ* A B C P 33 1739* syr[p] cop
NKJVmg RSV NRSV ESV NASB NIV TNIV NEB REB NJB NAB NLT HCSB NET

variant/TR μοιχεια, πορνεια
"adultery, fornication"
ℵ[2] D (F G) Ψ 1739[mg] Maj syr[h]
KJV NKJV HCSBmg

Although it could be argued that μοιχεια ("adultery") was accidentally deleted due to homoeoteleuton (the next word, πορνεια, has the same last three letters), the manuscript evidence speaks against this. The addition of "adultery" to this list of the works of the flesh most likely exhibits a scribal attempt to harmonize Paul's list with Jesus' list of vices, as recorded in Mark 7:21-22. This insertion found its way into the majority of manuscripts and into TR, followed by KJV and NKJV (see next note).

Galatians 5:21

WN NU φθόνοι, μέθαι
"envyings, drunkennesses"
𝔓[46] ℵ B 33 cop[sa] Irenaeus Clement
NKJVmg RSV NRSV ESV NASB NIV TNIV NEB REB NJB NAB NLT HCSB NETmg

variant/TR φθονοι, φονοι, μεθαι
"envyings, murders, drunkennesses"
A C D F G Ψ 1739 1881 Maj it cop^bo
KJV NKJV RSVmg NRSVmg NET

Although it could be argued that φονοι ("murders") was accidentally deleted due to homoeoteleuton (the previous word, φθονοι, has the same last four letters), the manuscript evidence speaks against this. The addition of "murders" to this list most likely exhibits some scribe's attempt to harmonize Paul's list with Jesus' list of vices, as recorded in Mark 7:21-22, or with Paul's list of vices in Rom 1:29-31. As in 5:19 (see note), this insertion found its way into the majority of manuscripts.

Galatians 5:23

TR WH NU ἐγκράτεια
"self-control"
𝔓46 ℵ A B C P 33 1739* cop
all

variant εγκρατεια, αγνεια
"self-control, purity"
D* F G it
NJBmg

Several Western witnesses add another virtue to Paul's list, that of "purity" or "chastity." This interpolation may have been influenced by 1 Tim 4:12, which includes αγνεια ("purity") in a list of virtues. Or it may have been added to provide an antidote to the sexual impurities listed in 5:19. Showing its respect for the Western text, NJB notes the variant.

Galatians 5:24

WH NU Χριστοῦ ['Ιησοῦ]
"Christ Jesus"
ℵ A B C P Ψ 0122[1] 33 1739 cop
RSV NRSV ESV NASB NIV TNIV NEB REB NJB NAB NLT HCSB NETmg

variant/TR Χριστου
"Christ"
𝔓46 D F G 0122*,2 Maj it syr
KJV NKJV NET

Since the names "Jesus" or "Christ" were often expanded throughout the course of textual transmission, it is likely that "Christ" originally stood in the text. There is early and diverse textual evidence for the one term, "Christ," here, which explains why Ιησου ("Jesus") is bracketed in NU.

Galatians 6:2

NU ἀναπληρώσετε
"you will fulfill" (future tense)
(𝔓46 αποπληρωσετε) B F G it cop
NRSV ESV NIV TNIV NEB REB NJBmg NAB NLT HCSB NET

variant/TR WH αναπληρωσατε
"fulfill" (imperative)
ℵ A C D 33 1739 Maj
KJV NKJV RSV NRSVmg NASB NJB

The editors of NU preferred the first reading because it was more likely that scribes changed a future tense verb ("you will fulfill the law of Christ") to an imperative ("fulfill the law of Christ") than vice versa, because the preceding verse has two imperative verbs (see TCGNT). Furthermore, the evidence of 𝔓46 (which has a synonymous verb in the future tense) with B strengthens the case for adopting the first reading.

Galatians 6:4

Several important witnesses (𝔓46 B syrp copsa) omit εκαστος ("each one"), making its presence in the text suspect. WH rightly brackets the word.

Galatians 6:7

All manuscripts read μη πλανασθε ("do not be misled/deceived"). Marcion dropped the μη, with the resultant reading being "you are misled/deceived."

Galatians 6:9

Good manuscript evidence (ℵ A B D* 33 cop) supports the reading μη εγκακωμεν ("let us not get weary"), as opposed to μη εκκακωμεν ("let us not lose heart"), found in C D2 (F G) Ψ 1739* 1881 Maj (so TR). It is possible that either word could have been confounded for the other because there is only a one-letter difference (γ/κ) and because the two words are synonymous (cf. similar textual alterations in Luke 18:1; 2 Cor 4:1, 16). Nonetheless, the best documentation affirms the WH NU reading.

Galatians 6:11

Most manuscripts read Ιδετε πηλικοις υμιν γραμμασιν εγραψα ("see what large letters I wrote to you"). But a few important manuscripts (𝔓46 B* 33) have the adjective ηλικοις, which has the same meaning as the word πηλικοις. The manuscripts 0278 and 642 have the adjective ποικιλοις, which means "variegated" or simply "different." Whichever adjective Paul originally used, the point is that there was an extraordinary difference between Paul's handwriting and that of the amanuensis. As was typical in ancient times, the author of a document usually dictated the body of the epistle to an amanuensis and then took stylus in hand to personally write out the concluding remarks. We know that Paul used an amanuensis for the epistle to the Romans, namely Tertius (see Rom 16:22), and it can be assumed that he did so for at least four other epistles, because he specifically mentions that he provided the concluding salutation in his own handwriting: 1 Cor 16:21; here (Gal 6:11); Col 4:18; and 2 Thess 3:17.

Galatians 6:12

Most manuscripts (ℵ A C D F G Ψ 33 Maj—so TR NU) read τω σταυρω του Χριστου ("the cross of Christ"), but a few important manuscripts (𝔓46 B 1175—so WH) read τω σταυρω του Χριστου Ιησου ("the cross of Jesus Christ"). This variant could display the influence of 6:14 (which has the expression "the cross of our Lord Jesus Christ"). On the other hand, it could be argued that scribes omitted "Jesus" from the title to make it conform with other Pauline passages (1 Cor 1:17; Phil 3:18—both of which have the wording "the cross of Christ").

Galatians 6:13

TR WH NU οἱ περιτεμνόμενοι
"the ones being circumcised"
ℵ A C D 33 1739 cop[bo]
all

variant οι περιτετμημενοι
"the ones having been circumcised"
𝔓[46] B (F G) L Ψ
ASVmg NASBmg

The TR WH NU reading has the most diverse support and therefore was followed by all the translations. But in deference to B, ASV added the variant in a marginal note, and NASB also added a note—probably following ASV and influenced by 𝔓[46] and B.

Galatians 6:15

WH NU οὔτε γὰρ περιτομή τί ἐστιν
"for neither is circumcision anything"
𝔓[46] B 33 1739* (Ψ ισχυει for εστιν)
RSV NRSV ESV NASB NIV TNIV NEB REB NJB NAB NLT HCSB NET

variant/TR εν γαρ Χριστω Ιησου ουτε περιτομη τι ισχυει
"for in Christ Jesus neither is circumcision of any force"
(ℵ* A C D* F G) 1881 Maj (ℵ[2] D[2] 1881 Maj read ισχυει; ℵ* A C D* F G read εστιν)
KJV NKJV HCSBmg NETmg

The WH NU reading has sufficient documentary support. The variant reading is a scribal expansion borrowed from 5:6. As such, the insertion is fully Pauline, though not written by him in this verse. In both the shorter and longer reading, several later scribes substituted ισχυει ("have force") for εστιν ("is").

Galatians 6:17

WH NU τὰ στίγματα τοῦ 'Ιησοῦ
"the stigmata [marks] of Jesus"
𝔓[46] A B C* 33 it[f,t]
RSV NRSV ESV NASB NIV TNIV NEB REB NJB NAB NLT HCSB NET

variant 1 τα στιγματα του Χριστου
"the stigmata [marks] of the Christ"
P Ψ 0278 cop[bo]
none

variant 2/TR τα στιγματα του κυριου Ιησου
"the stigmata [marks] of the Lord Jesus"
C^3 D^2 (1739) 1881 Maj
KJV NKJV

variant 3 τα στιγματα του κυριου ημων Ιησου Χριστου
"the stigmata [marks] of our Lord Jesus Christ"
(ℵ D*) F G it
none

The WH NU reading has solid documentary support and is superior on internal grounds inasmuch as Paul is here identifying with the human sufferings of Jesus and therefore uses only Jesus' human name. The first variant is poorly supported; the next two variants, though having better support, are scribal expansions, probably influenced by 6:18.

Subscription

Whereas scribes frequently added inscriptions (titles) to the Gospels, Acts, and Revelation, they did not usually do so for the Epistles. Instead, many scribes supplied subscriptions, which provide information about the writer, place of writing, sender, and recipient of the epistle. None of these subscriptions would have been penned by the author; nonetheless, they are worth noting.

1. No subscription—but placed as an inscription (so WH NU): Προς Γαλατας ("To the Galatians"). Appears in $\mathfrak{P}^{46}$.
2. No subscription. Appears in 323 365 629 2464.
3. Προς Γαλατας ("To the Galatians"). Appears in ℵ A B* Ψ 33.
4. ετελεσθη επιστολη προς Γαλατας ("End of the Epistle to the Galatians"). Appears in F G.
5. Προς Γαλατας εγραφη απο Ρωμης ("To the Galatians written from Rome"). Appears in B^1 0278 1739 1881 Maj (so TR).

It is certain that no book of the NT originally had a title (inscription) or a subscription. (For more on this, see Comfort 2005, 9-10.) This is especially true for the Epistles, because their original purpose was to be an apostolic letter, not a literary work per se. Thus, all inscriptions and subscriptions are scribal addenda. The simplest form, Προς Γαλατας ("To the Galatians") appears in the earliest witnesses: in $\mathfrak{P}^{46}$ at the head of the epistle; in ℵ A B* at the end. As is typical, the subscription was expanded to include the place of writing—which, in this case, is cited as Rome. However, this location does not coincide with any modern scholarly ideas about the date and place of writing of the Epistle to the Galatians, which was either written ca. A.D. 49 or ca. 57—years before Paul was in Rome (ca. 60–62).

The Epistle to the EPHESIANS

Inscription (Title)

𝔓46 א and B title this epistle as Προς Εφεσιους ("To the Ephesians"). Several manuscripts (including א and B) also have this title in the subscription (see last note for this book). Paul, however, would not have entitled this epistle in its original composition. Inscriptions are the work of later scribes. (For more on this, see Comfort 2005, 9-10.)

Ephesians 1:1a

WH NU ἀπόστολος Χριστοῦ Ἰησοῦ
"apostle of Christ Jesus"
𝔓46 B D P 33 syr[h]
RSV NRSV ESV NASB NIV TNIV NEB REB NJB NAB NLT HCSB NET

variant/TR αποστολος Ιησου Χριστου
"apostle of Jesus Christ"
א A F G Ψ 1739 Maj it syr[p]
KJV NKJV

Several manuscripts (followed by TR) transpose "Christ Jesus" to "Jesus Christ," but this order is not characteristic of Paul. When identifying his position in the opening verses of his epistles, he calls himself an apostle of "Christ Jesus" (see 1 Cor 1:1; 2 Cor 1:1; Gal 1:1; Col 1:1; 1 Tim 1:1; 2 Tim 1:1; Titus 1:1). The WH NU text has the support of the two earliest witnesses (𝔓46 B), as well as other diverse attestation.

Ephesians 1:1b

TR WH NU τοῖς ἁγίοις τοῖς οὖσιν [ἐν Ἐφέσῳ] καὶ πιστοῖς ἐν Χριστῷ Ἰησοῦ
"to the saints being in Ephesus and faithful in Christ Jesus"
B[2] D F G Ψ 33 Maj syr cop[sa]
KJV NKJV RSVmg NRSV ESV NASB NIV TNIV NEB REB NJBmg NAB NLT NET

variant 1 τοις αγιοις πασιν τοις ουσιν εν Εφεσω και πιστοις εν Χριστω Ιησου
"to all the saints being in Ephesus and faithful in Christ Jesus"
א[2] A P it[b] cop[bo]
none

variant 2 τοις αγιοις τοις ουσιν και πιστοις εν Χριστω Ιησου
"to the saints being ________ and faithful in Christ Jesus"
𝔓46 א* B* 1739 Marcion
RSV NRSVmg ESVmg NASBmg NIVmg TNIVmg NEBmg REBmg NJB NABmg NLTmg NETmg

The insertion of πασιν ("all") in the first variant is clearly a scribal attempt to harmonize this opening verse with several other opening verses in Paul's Epistles, where Paul addresses "all" the saints in a particular locality (see Rom 1:7; 1 Cor 1:2; 2 Cor 1:1).

The second variant represents the original text as it was written by Paul. There are three good reasons why we can be confident about this: (1) This reading has the support of the three earliest manuscripts (𝔓46 א B), as well as 1739—a manuscript known for its textual integrity in the Pauline Epistles. None of these manuscripts include the words εν Εφεσω ("in Ephesus"). (2) If the text had originally included εν Εφεσω, there is no reason to explain why the words would have been deleted. In fact, the absence of εν Εφεσω makes for a very difficult sentence, grammatically speaking, because something has to follow the participial phrase τοις ουσιν. (3) The scribes of 𝔓46 א 1739 could have done something to fix this grammatical problem, but they stayed true to their exemplars, which retained the original form as it left the hand of Paul's amanuensis. Thus, in the original document (supported by 𝔓46 א B 1739 Marcion) a blank space was likely left between τοις ουσιν ("the ones being") and και πιστοις εν Χριστω Ιησου ("and faithful ones in Christ Jesus"). The blank would be filled in with the name of each local church ("in Ephesus," "in Laodicea," "in Colossae," etc.) as the epistle circulated from city to city. Later manuscripts reflect the insertion of "in Ephesus" because Ephesus was the leading city in that region.

Paul intended this epistle to be a general encyclical sent to the churches in Asia, of which Ephesus was one of the leading churches. No doubt, the epistle would have gone to Ephesus (perhaps first) and then on to other churches. Each time the epistle went to another church, the name of the locality would be supplied after the expression "to the saints in ________." Zuntz (1953, 228) indicated that this procedure also occurred with some multiple copies of royal letters during the Hellenistic period; the master copy would have a blank for the addressee and would be filled in for each copy. Zuntz considered the blank space in the address to the Ephesians to go back to the original. In the later textual tradition, certain scribes identified this epistle with Ephesus and therefore inserted "in Ephesus." In his own NT canon, Marcion listed this letter as the Epistle to the Laodiceans. But this designation was never inserted into any manuscript that we know of. However, Marcion's designation signals that the epistle had probably gone to Laodicea. This epistle is probably one and the same as the letter Paul mentions in Col 4:16, where he tells the Colossians, "see to it that you also read the letter *from Laodicea.*" This language indicates that a letter (presumably written by Paul) would be coming to the Colossians from Laodicea. Since it is fairly certain that Ephesians was written and sent at the same time as Colossians (Tychicus carried both epistles—Eph 6:21; Col 4:7-9), it can be assumed that Paul would expect that the encyclical epistle now known as Ephesians would eventually circulate from Colossae to Laodicea. Coming from Rome, Tychicus would have first arrived at Ephesus along the coast, then traveled north to Smyrna and Pergamum, then turned southeast to Thyatira, Sardis, Philadelphia, Laodicea—and then on to Colossae (as perhaps the last stop). We can surmise that this circulation route would have been similar to the one for the book of Revelation (Rev 1:11), which was also sent to the churches in Asia Minor. (The book of Revelation was circulated from Ephesus to Smyrna to Pergamum to Thyatira to Sardis to Philadelphia to Laodicea.) Just to the southeast of Laodicea was Colossae, thereby making it the next logical stop.

The content of this epistle affirms its general nature, for it lacks the usual references to local situations and persons as found in Paul's other epistles. Paul had lived with the Christians at Ephesus for three years (Acts 20:31). He knew them intimately; and yet in this epistle there are no personal greetings or specific exhortations. When we consider Paul's manner in many of his other epistles (see the conclusions to Romans, 1 Corinthians, Philippians, and Colossians), it would be quite unlike him to have excluded these personal expressions.

Thus, the position that Ephesians was an encyclical helps to substantiate Pauline authorship of Ephesians. Those who doubt Paul's authorship argue that Ephesians has wording which makes it sound as if Paul did not know his readers. For example, in 1:15, Paul wrote, "ever since I heard about your faith," and in 3:2, "surely you have heard about my stewardship." But this epistle was intended for an audience much greater than Ephesus. Paul was addressing those believers who had never had face-to-face contact with him.

In the end it must be said that this textual variant has significant import on the exegesis of this book. If the addressee is assumed to be a particular local church (Ephesus), then this church is called upon to be far more than any local church could ever hope to be. If the addressee is assumed to be the church at large, then it is easier to view this epistle as Paul's treatise on the universal church, the body of Christ. As such, it is not encumbered with local problems. It soars high above any mundane affairs and takes us into heaven, where we are presented with a heavenly view of the church as it fits into God's eternal plan. In this epistle Paul paints the church with multifarious splendor. He depicts her as God's inheritance (1:11, see NRSVmg NLTmg), Christ's body, his fullness (1:22-23), God's masterpiece (2:10), the one new person (2:15), the household of God (2:19), the habitation of God (2:21-22), the joint body comprised of Jewish and Gentile believers (3:6), the vessel for God to display his multifarious wisdom (3:10), the body equaling Christ's full stature (4:12-13), the full-grown, perfect person (4:13), the body growing into a building (4:16), the bride of Christ (5:23-32), the object of Christ's love (5:25), the very members of Christ's body (5:30), and God's warrior against Satan (6:11-18). The church he pictured with words was the church in ideal perfection, the church as seen from heaven—but not yet manifested on earth in fullness. There is not one local church throughout all history that has ever come close to matching this ideal. This is the goal of the universal church.

Two translations (RSV and NJB) attempted to follow the shorter, original superior reading. But in order to make good English they had to render the last part of the verse as "to the saints who are faithful in Christ Jesus." However, this rendering skips και and becomes a translation of τοις αγιοις τοις ουσιν πιστοις εν Χριστω Ιησου, literally translated as "to the saints, the ones being faithful in Christ Jesus." Paul's original document addressed two groups: (1) the saints being in ______, *and* (2) the faithful ones in Christ Jesus. Of course, the και could function epexegetically ("the saints in ______, even the faithful in Christ Jesus"). Either way, the entire Greek text as it stands in the earliest witnesses (𝔓[46] ℵ B) has not been accurately rendered in any English translation. I would suggest the following:

> "Paul, an apostle of Christ Jesus through God's will to the saints living in __________ and faithful in Christ Jesus."

Ephesians 1:4

Most manuscripts read εξελεξατο ημας εν αυτω ("he chose us in him"). Two manuscripts (F G) change this to εξελεξατο ημας εαυτω ("he chose us in [by] himself"). The difference could have been accidental (the omission of one letter, *nu*) or intentional (in order to make God the Father both the elector and the source of election). But as it is in the text, the Father is the elector and Christ is the source and sphere of election.

Ephesians 1:6a

WH NU read της χαριτος αυτου ης εχαριτωσεν ημας ("his grace of which he graced us"), according to 𝔓46 ℵ* A B P 33 1739. This was adjusted in later manuscripts (ℵ2 D F G Ψ Maj—so TR) to της χαριτος αυτου εν η εχαριτωσεν ημας ("his grace in which he graced us") in order to avoid the difficulty of the genitive ης ("of which").

Ephesians 1:6b

The expression, εν τω ηγαπημενω ("in the beloved one"), was expanded in many Western witnesses (D* F G it syrh**) and copsa to εν τω ηγαπημενω υιω αυτου ("in his beloved son").

Ephesians 1:7

A few manuscripts (ℵ* D* Ψ) changed the present tense, εχομεν ("we have [redemption]"), to the past tense εσχομεν ("we had [redemption]"). Although Christ's accomplishment of redemption was a past act, it is a present possession for believers; thus the present tense here is appropriate. Influenced by Rom 2:4, a few other witnesses (A copbo) changed χαριτος ("grace") to χρηστοτητος ("kindness").

Ephesians 1:10

Good documentation (𝔓46 ℵ* B D L) supports the reading επι τοις ουρανοις ("the things on the heavens"). Thus, this is the text of WH NU. TR, however, follows the reading with the preposition εν ("in"), based on the testimony of ℵ2 A F G P Ψ 33 1739 syrh. This reading was a scribal change motivated by one of two reasons: (1) it sounds odd to speak of things being "on/upon [επι] the heavens"; or (2) the text was conformed to Col 1:20, a parallel passage. The first factor motivated all English translators to make the phrase read, "the things in heaven."

Ephesians 1:11

All three editions (TR WH NU) have the reading εν ω και εκληρωθημεν, which can be rendered in two ways: (1) "in whom also we were made an inheritance" or (2) "in whom also we have obtained an inheritance" (see NLT). This reading, followed by most English versions (although variously rendered), has excellent testimony: 𝔓46 𝔓92 ℵ A B C. A variant reading is εν ω και εκληθωμεν ("in [by] whom also we were called"), found in A D (F*) G. The earliest manuscripts, including 𝔓46 and 𝔓92, affirm the reading εκληρωθημεν. As just noted, this Greek word in this context has been interpreted to mean (1) believers have become God's inheritance or (2) believers have been given a portion of God's inheritance. The first meaning accords with the passive voice, but it is more difficult to imagine the believers being God's inheritance than vice versa. For this reason, no doubt, the text was changed to the more common expression, εκληθωμεν ("we were called"). A few modern versions reflect this amelioration—notably the NIV, which reads, "we were chosen."

Ephesians 1:13

In 1:12 Paul was speaking of the Jewish believers when he said, "we who were the first to set our hope in Christ." But then the pronoun shifts in 1:13 to "you" plural, because Paul spoke of the

Gentile believers when he said, "and you also were included in Christ, when you heard the word of the truth, the gospel of your salvation" (NIV). Thus, the shift in pronouns (from ημας in 1:12 to υμεις and υμων in 1:13) is critical to the exegesis. However, the shift is completely absent in certain manuscripts, where the pronoun continues to be first person plural: ημεις ("we") in ℵ[2] A K L Ψ and ημων ("our") in K Ψ.

Ephesians 1:14

WH NU ὅ ἐστιν ἀρραβών
"which is a guarantee"
𝔓[46] A B F G L P 1739 it[b,d] syr[p]
KJV NKJVmg RSV NRSV (NEB REB) NAB (NLT)

variant/TR ος εστιν αρραβων
"who is a guarantee"
ℵ D Ψ 33 Maj
NKJV NRSVmg ESV NASB NIV TNIV NJB HCSB NET

In context, Paul was speaking of the promised Holy Spirit, which/who is the guarantee (or, "down payment"; αρραβων) of the believers' inheritance. With few exceptions, the Greek pronominal reference to the Spirit in the Greek NT is in the neuter because the Greek word for "Spirit" (πνευμα) is neuter. Two reasons can be given for the variation in 1:14: (1) Paul originally wrote the masculine pronoun, which was changed to the more common neuter; or (2) Paul originally wrote the neuter pronoun, which was later changed to the masculine by scribes who wanted to personalize the Spirit. The manuscript evidence seems to favor the second view, for the two earliest manuscripts (𝔓[46] B) contain the neuter, as well as several other diverse witnesses. The textual evidence of 𝔓[46] with B influenced the editors of NA[26] to make a change from previous editions of the Nestle text. Since translators also tend to personalize the Spirit, referring to the Spirit as "him" or "who" rather than "it" or "which," we cannot be absolutely sure whether or not the translators strictly adhered to one variant reading over the other.

Ephesians 1:15

TR NU ὑμᾶς πίστιν ἐν τῷ κυρίῳ Ἰησοῦ καὶ τὴν ἀγάπην τὴν εἰς πάντας τοὺς ἁγίους
"your faith in the Lord Jesus and love to all the saints"
ℵ[2] D[1] Ψ Maj syr[h] cop[sa] (D* F G omit second την)
all

variant/WH υμας πιστιν εν τω κυριω Ιησου και την εις παντας τους αγιους
"your faith (trust) in the Lord Jesus and in all the saints"
𝔓[46] ℵ* A B 33 1739 1881 Jerome
RSVmg NRSVmg ESVmg NASBmg NJBmg NLTmg NETmg

Metzger (TCGNT) reasoned that the variant was the result of a scribal error; the words were dropped due to homoeoarchton—the eye of the scribe passing from the την before αγαπην to the την before εις παντας. However, it is difficult to imagine that this error would have been present in so many diverse witnesses. On the contrary, the variant has the best attestation and is the most difficult of the readings. If the variant was the original text, Paul was saying that he had heard of the believers' "trust in the Lord Jesus and in all the saints." The only passage close to this is Phlm 5, which says, "having heard of your love and faith in the Lord Jesus and in all the saints." But this statement is usually understood to be a chiasm; hence, it is translated: "your faith in the Lord Jesus and love for all the saints." The variant in 1:15 is not chiastic; it has to be understood to mean that the believers trusted in Christ and in the saints. Since Paul emphasizes the universal solidarity of the church in this epistle and encourages mutual edification, it is not out of the question for him to have declared that they trusted Jesus *and* all the saints. Thus, it could be argued that all the other variants are merely attempts to fix what seemed incomplete or to make 1:15 conform to Col 1:4, a parallel passage. However, not one translation has adopted the shorter text, though some (probably influenced by the strong testimony of 𝔓46 ℵ* A B) provide a marginal note about the omission.

Ephesians 1:18

WH NU τοὺς ὀφθαλμοὺς τῆς καρδίας [ὑμῶν]
"the eyes of your hearts"
ℵ A D F G Ψ Maj syr
NKJVmg RSV NRSV ESV NASB NIV TNIV NEB REB NJBmg NAB NLT HCSB NET

variant 1 τους οφθαλμους της καρδιας
"the eyes of the hearts"
𝔓46 B 33 1739 1881
none

variant 2/TR τους οφθαλμους της διανοιας υμων
"the eyes of your mind"
it[d] Cyril Theodoret
KJV NKJV NJB

The reading of the WH NU text seems to include a scribal filler (υμων), which is not necessary to complete the meaning of the statement, since the article can function as a possessive. Thus, the first variant, which has better textual support, is likely original. By contrast, the second variant, which has little manuscript support, is the invention of someone who wanted to make it clear that spiritual enlightenment takes place in one's "mind." This reading, not found in the majority of manuscripts, made its way into TR, and was thereby rendered in KJV and NKJV. The NJB translators may have followed this reading or simply substituted "mind" for "heart" in the interest of understandability.

Ephesians 1:20

In the first part of the verse, A B (so WH) read the perfect tense verb ενηργηκεν ("he has exerted") instead of the aorist ενεργησεν ("he exerted"), found in ℵ D F G Ψ Maj (so NU). Either verb could have been confused for the other because there is only a one-letter difference (κ/σ), and either verb suits the context.

Ephesians 2:4

Instead of the words ηγαπησεν ημας ("he loved us"), found in most Greek manuscripts, 𝔓46 reads ηλεησεν ημας ("he had mercy on us"). This variation did not occur in 𝔓46 alone because this reading is reflected in it[b,d] and Ambrosiaster. Probably the change was influenced by the wording at the beginning of the verse, which says that God is "rich in mercy" (Ramaroson 1977, 389-390).

Ephesians 2:5a

TR WH NU	νεκροὺς τοῖς παραπτώμασιν "dead in the [= our] trespasses" ℵ A D² 0278 33 1739 Maj cop Clement NKJV RSV NRSV ESV NASB NIV TNIV NAB (NLT) HCSB NET
variant 1	νεκρους τοις σωμασιν "dead in the [= our] bodies" 𝔓46 none
variant 2	νεκρους ταις αμαρτιαις "dead in the [=our] sins" D* (F G) KJV NEB REB NJB
variant 3	νεκρους τοις παραπτωμασιν και ταις αμαρτιαις "dead in the [=our] trespasses and the [=our] sins" Ψ none
variant 4	νεκρους εν τοις παραπτωμασιν και ταις επιθυμιαις "dead in the [=our] trespasses and the [=our] lusts" B none

The second, third, and fourth variants can easily be explained. The second and third show the influence of 2:1, which speaks of "trespasses and sins." The fourth shows the influence of 2:3, which speaks of "lusts." (In 2:1, B also has επιθυμιαις instead of αμαρτιαις.) But the first variant cannot be tied to any verse in Ephesians. Perhaps the scribe of 𝔓46 was influenced by Rom 8:10, the only verse which speaks of the body being dead because of sin. Or perhaps this scribe simply made a transcriptional error, mistaking παραπτωμασιν for σωμασιν (both of which have the same last six letters).

Ephesians 2:5b

TR WH NU	συνεζωοποίησεν τῷ Χριστῷ "he made us alive together with Christ" ℵ A D F G Ψ 1739 all
variant	συνεζωοποιησεν εν τω Χριστω "he made us alive together in Christ" 𝔓46 B 33 cop NRSVmg NASBmg NJBmg

Metzger (TCGNT) suggests the variant reading was the result of accidental dittography (the first two words end in εν) or deliberate assimilation to Eph 2:6, εν Χριστω Ιησου ("in Christ Jesus"). But the variant has good documentation and therefore cannot be easily dismissed. Indeed, homoeoteleuton could account for the omission of εν after συνεζωοποιησεν. Furthermore, there is a difference in meaning between the two readings. The TR WH NU text indicates that the believers were made alive when Christ was vivified; the variant indicates that the Jewish and Gentile believers were made alive together by virtue of their union with Christ.

The latter is a more fitting prelude to Paul's following assertions about Christ's work to unify Jewish and Gentile believers (2:11-22).

Ephesians 2:15a

NU has the phrasing ινα τους δυο κτιση εν αὐτω, yielding the rendering "that he might create the two in him." WH makes the final pronoun reflexive by use of a rough breathing mark. This produces the rendering, "that he might create the two in himself." The manuscripts 𝔓[46] א* A B support αυτω without any breathing mark—thus, either reading is possible. In Hellenistic Greek, this pronoun could be understood according to its normal usage ("him") or according to reflexive usage ("himself"). Other manuscripts (א[2] D G Ψ Maj—so TR) clearly show the reflexive pronoun εαυτω, and therefore have the reading, "that he might create the two in himself." Of course, the context does call for the reflexive usage, for Christ created the one new man in himself—via his death and resurrection. As such, all translations display the reflexive usage regardless of the textual tradition being followed.

Ephesians 2:15b

All texts and translations have the reading ενα καινον ανθρωπον ("one new person"), with the support of א A B C D Maj. However, K has the reading ενα και μονον ανθρωπον ("one and only person"), and 𝔓[46] F G offer an interesting variant: ενα κοινον ανθρωπον ("one common/shared person"). This expression aptly describes the new humanity Christ created, because it speaks of the believers' solidarity and fellowship with each other as a result of their common union in Christ. In Christ, as a new creation, Jewish and Gentile believers are one "common" humanity. Of course, they are also a "new" (καινον) humanity because of their participation in a new creation. So, it is hard to say which word was mistaken for the other—there is only a one-letter difference (α/ο). It is possible that κοινον originally stood in the text but was changed under the influence of Col 3:9-10, a parallel passage that contrasts the "old nature" and the "new nature." But in Ephesians 2, the emphasis is not on new versus old per se, but on the unification of divergent groups by virtue of their union in Christ. It is also possible that some scribe (perhaps the scribe of 𝔓[46] was the first) simply mistook καινον for κοινον—and the mistake, which makes good sense, was perpetuated in later manuscripts such as F and G.

Ephesians 2:17

WH NU εἰρήνην τοῖς ἐγγύς
"peace to the ones near"
𝔓[46] א A B D F G P 33 1739 it cop
RSV NRSV ESV NASB NIV TNIV NEB REB NJB NAB NLT HCSB NET

variant/TR τοις εγγυς
"to the ones near"
Ψ Maj syr[h] Marcion
KJV NKJV

In context, the entire expression reads, "he preached peace to you, the ones far off, and [peace] to the ones near." The textual question pertains to whether ειρηνη ("peace") is repeated. The documentary evidence in support of WH NU is superior to that for the variant, which was perpetuated in most later manuscripts, TR, and KJV. Furthermore, it is likely that Paul reproduced the twofold reference to peace from the underlying OT text (Isa 57:19 LXX) but gave it a different sequence (Lincoln 1990, 124).

Ephesians 2:20

In an effort to help readers understand that ακρογωνιαιου, which literally means "at the extreme corner," denotes a corner*stone,* some scribes (see D* F G) added λιθου ("stone").

Ephesians 2:21

WH NU read εν ω πασα οικοδομη ("in whom every building"), with the support of א* B D F G Ψ 33 1739* Maj. TR has the reading εν ω η πασα οικοδομη ("in whom the whole building"), with the support of א[1] A C P 1739[c]. The anarthrous expression πασα οικοδομη could mean "every building" and thereby suggest that Paul had a multitude of individual local churches in mind. As such, it could be that Paul meant that each local church was a building for God's habitation fit together with all the other buildings to comprise one dwelling place for God. But since this does not readily fit with the general character of Ephesians, which emphasizes the unity of the universal church (not the local), scribes added the article—thereby making it "the whole building." However, this addition was not necessary because πασα οικοδομη is a Hebraism which has affected Koine usage and should be understood to mean "all the building" or "the whole building" (Lincoln 1990, 156). (See 1 Chr 28:8 and Amos 3:1 LXX; cf. Moule 1953, 94-95.) All English versions have the definite article.

Ephesians 3:1

The phrase Παυλος ο δεσμιος του Χριστου Ιησου ("Paul the prisoner of Christ Jesus"), found in 𝔓[46] א[1] A B (C) D[1] Ψ 1739 Maj Origen, is shorter in א* D* F G (which lack Ιησου ["Jesus"]). Although it could be argued that the longer form may have been influenced by the wording in Philemon, where Paul thrice calls himself a "prisoner of Christ Jesus" (Phlm 1, 9, 23), superior documentation supports the longer reading.

This verse is noticeably incomplete: "For this cause I, Paul, the prisoner of Christ Jesus for you Gentiles. . . ." Paul then breaks off into a digression for another twelve verses (from 3:2 to 3:13), and does not return to his beginning thought until 3:14, where he repeats the words of 3:1 ("For this cause") and then puts forth a predicate: "I bend my knees to the Father." Various scribes, impatient with this digression, felt obligated to complete verse 1 by adding a verb. D and 104* add πρεσβευω ("I am an ambassador") and 2464 adds κεκαυχημαι ("I have given laudatory testimony").

Ephesians 3:5

B and it[b] omit αποστολοις ("apostles") with the resultant text being τοις αγιοις αυτου και προφηταις ("his saints and prophets"). It is possible that αποστολοις was intentionally dropped to make this verse conform to Col 1:26, a parallel verse; however, it is just as likely that it was accidentally omitted due to homoeoteleuton: τοις αγιοις αποστολοις.

Ephesians 3:9a

TR NU — φωτίσαι [πάντας]
"to enlighten everyone"
𝔓46 ℵ2 B C D F G Ψ 33 Maj it syr cop
KJV NKJV RSV NRSV ESV NIV TNIV NLT HCSB NET

variant/WH — φωτισαι
"to bring to light"
ℵ* A 1739 1881
NASB NEB REB NJB NAB NLTmg

The TR NU reading has early and diverse support. The variant, though shorter, is probably the result of scribal deletion, and not original. The word παντας ("all") could have been deleted because scribes might have thought it contradicted Paul's previous statement that his commission was to take the gospel to the Gentiles (3:8). But the "all" here probably refers to all the Gentiles, for whom he was an apostle. And, indeed, he had the desire to reach them all (see Rom 1:5; 16:26; 2 Tim 4:17). Another argument as to why scribes would have excluded παντας is that some might have thought it was too bold for Paul to say he wanted to *enlighten everyone*. However, Paul had been appointed by God to open the eyes of both Jews and Gentiles through the proclamation of the gospel (see Acts 26:17-18).

Ephesians 3:9b

WH NU — ἡ οἰκονομία τοῦ μυστηρίου
"the stewardship [administration] of the mystery"
𝔓46 ℵ A B C D F G 33 1739 Ψ Maj it syr cop
NKJVmg RSV NRSV ESV NASB NIV TNIV NEB REB NJB NAB NLT HCSB NET

variant/TR — η κοινωνια του μυστηριου
"the fellowship of the mystery"
31mg and a few late miniscules
KJV NKJV

The reading in TR is remarkable for its slim documentary support—a few very late cursive manuscripts. (Perhaps a dyslexic scribe mistook οικονομια for κοινωνια!) At any rate, it was included in TR and has been perpetuated in both KJV and NKJV. But Paul was not speaking about "the fellowship of mystery" (whatever that is supposed to mean); rather, he was speaking about his stewardship (or administration, economy) of God's secret plan. Paul had been entrusted with the mystery concerning Christ and the church; his responsibility was to proclaim the unsearchable riches of Christ for the establishment and edification of the church, Christ's body.

Ephesians 3:9c

WH NU — θεῷ τῷ τὰ πάντα κτίσαντι
"God who created all things"
𝔓46 ℵ A B C D* F G P Ψ 33 1739 syrp cop
NKJVmg RSV NRSV ESV NASB NIV TNIV NEB REB NJB NAB NLT HCSB NET

variant/TR — θεω τω τα παντα κτισαντι δια Ιησου Χριστου
"God who created all things through Jesus Christ"
D2 (0278) Maj syrh**
KJV NKJV

Since the textual evidence strongly favors the shorter reading and since there is no good reason to explain why the phrase "through Jesus Christ" would have been omitted if it was originally in the text, we must reason that the phrase was added to emphasize Christ's role in creation (which accords with Pauline thought—see 1 Cor 8:6 and Col 1:16, which have some ideas that are similar to Eph 3:9-10).

Ephesians 3:14

WH NU τὸν πατέρα
"the Father"
𝔓46 ℵ* A B C P 33 1739 cop
NKJVmg RSV NRSV ESV NASB NIV TNIV NEB REB NJB NAB NLT HCSB NET

variant/TR τον πατερα του κυριου ημων Ιησου Χριστου
"the Father of our Lord Jesus Christ"
ℵ2 D F G Ψ 0278 Maj it syr
KJV NKJV NLTmg HCSBmg

The documentary support for the shorter reading far exceeds that for the longer reading. It was typical for scribes to expand divine titles, especially in identifying the Father as being the Father "of the Lord Christ Jesus" (or some such expression—see 1:3). Such expanded titles enhance oral reading.

Ephesians 3:19

TR WH NU ἵνα πληρωθῆτε εἰς πᾶν τὸ πλήρωμα τοῦ θεοῦ
"that you may be filled to all the fullness of God"
ℵ A C D F G Ψ 1739 Maj syr cop
all

variant 1 ινα πληρωθητε εις παν το πληρωμα του Χριστου
"that you may be filled to all the fullness of Christ"
1881
none

variant 2 ινα πληρωθη εις παν το πληρωμα του θεου
"that all the fullness of God may be filled"
𝔓46 B 0278 cop^sa
NJBmg

variant 3 ινα πληρωθη εις παν το πληρωμα του θεου εις υμας
"that all the fullness of God may be filled up in you"
33
none

Although there are four variants listed here, there are essentially two major differences—as represented by (1) the TR WH NU reading and the first variant (which substitutes "Christ" for "God") and (2) the second and third variants (which add "in you"). Both TR WH NU and the second variant have good documentary support and both make sense.

The TR WH NU reading indicates that the believers are filled up to the extent that they have the same measure as the fullness of God. It does not say that they are filled with all the fullness of God; this interpretation misreads the preposition εις, which signals result. The idea is similar to that in 4:13, which speaks of the believers attaining the measure of the stature of the fullness of Christ.

The second variant, which has excellent documentary support (including 𝔓46 B), is the more difficult reading (and perhaps original). In order to make sense of it, we must surmise that the expression "all the fullness of God" is tantamount to Christ's body, his fullness (1:23). This "fullness" needs to be filled with spiritual reality in order to be true fullness. Or "all the fullness of God" could be "Christ" (see Col 1:19; 2:9), who is fully expressed in his body when all the members fully express him. In similar fashion, it could mean that all of God's fullness (in its breadth, length, depth, and height—3:18) needs to be fully experienced by all the believers to thereby attain spiritual completion and fulfillment.

Ephesians 3:21

WH NU δόξα ἐν τῇ ἐκκλησίᾳ καὶ ἐν Χριστῷ Ἰησοῦ
"glory in the church and in Christ Jesus"
𝔓46 ℵ A B C (D* F G) 0278 33 1739
RSV NRSV ESV NASB NIV TNIV NEB REB NJB NAB NLT HCSB NET

variant/TR δοξα εν τη εκκλησια εν Χριστω Ιησου
"glory in the church in (by) Christ Jesus"
D2 Ψ Maj syr copsa
KJV NKJV

The omission of και ("and") in the majority of later witnesses (and TR) makes "Christ Jesus" the agent through whom God gains glory in the church. But the point of the statement, as found in early and diverse witnesses, is that God is glorified as equally in the church as in Christ Jesus, because the church is Christ's full expression on earth.

Ephesians 4:6

WH NU καὶ ἐν πᾶσιν
"and in all"
𝔓46 ℵ A B C P 082 33 1739* cop
NKJVmg RSV NRSV ESV NASB NIV TNIV NEB REB NJB NAB NLT HCSB NET

variant 1 και εν πασιν ημιν
"and in us all"
D F G Ψ (1739c) 0278 Maj it syr
NKJVmg

variant 2/TR και εν πασιν υμιν
"and in you all"
itk Theodoret Chrysostom
KJV NKJV

In context, Paul was affirming that there is "one God and Father of all, the one over all and through all and in all" (per the WH NU reading). Both variant readings were created by scribes who were trying to make the text not sound pantheistic or were attempting to restrict the "all" to believers. "You" is carried over from 4:4, and "us" aligns with the following verse (4:7). Of the two, "us" has better attestation, for it is found in several Western witnesses and in the majority of late manuscripts. By comparison, "you" is barely supported (appearing in no Greek manuscripts), yet it found its way into TR and has been perpetuated in KJV and NKJV.

Ephesians 4:8

NU	ἔδωκεν δόματα "he gave gifts" 𝔓46 ℵ* A C2 D* F G 33 NRSV NEB REB NJB HCSB
variant/TR WH	και εδωκεν δοματα "and he gave gifts" ℵ2 B C*,3 D2 Ψ 1739 Maj syr KJV NKJV RSV ESV NASB NIV TNIV NAB NLT NET

The reading with και ("and") is quite obviously a later addition—even a correction in several manuscripts—intended to relieve an unidiomatic Greek expression or to distinguish that Christ gave out the gifts *after* he led captivity captive in his ascent. The translators of KJV followed the variant reading, whether consciously or unconsciously, for syntactical reasons. So did several modern versions.

Ephesians 4:9a

WH NU	κατέβη "he descended" 𝔓46 ℵ* A C* D F G Ivid 082 33 1739 it copbo NKJVmg RSV NRSV ESV NASB NIV TNIV NEB REB NJB NAB NLT HCSB NET
variant/TR	κατεβη πρωτον "he descended first" ℵ2 B C3 Ψ syr KJV NKJV HCSBmg

The full statement is, "Now as to the 'he ascended,' what is it except that also he descended." According to the WH NU reading, we cannot tell if the ascension preceded the descent or vice versa. The WH NU text simply says that Christ ascended and descended. Many scribes, however, presumed that a descent preceded an ascension because they believed the text was talking about Christ's descent to earth (via incarnation) or to Hades (post-death and pre-resurrection) prior to his ascension to heaven. This accounts for the addition of "first." In any event, the manuscript evidence supports the WH NU reading, which is followed by all modern versions.

Ephesians 4:9b

Several manuscripts (ℵ A B C D2 I Ψ Maj) and the major Greek editions (TR WH NU), read τα κατωτερα μερη της γης ("the lower parts of the earth"). Other manuscripts (𝔓46 D* F G it) do not include μερη ("parts"). This variant reading can also be rendered, "into the realms below, the earth" because της γης could be an epexegetical expression. In other words, της γης is a genitive of definition: The regions below (τα κατωτερα) are the same as the earth. The same can be said for the TR WH NU reading, but it is not as easy to expound it this way because the addition of μερη more strongly connotes subterranean habitations. And it is for this reason that this reading is suspect—that is, it seems that scribes wanted to make certain that readers understood this as a descent beneath the earth (into Hades), not just a descent to earth (via incarnation). Of course, the other scribes could have deleted μερη in an effort to obscure this exegesis, but the doctrine of Christ's descent into Hades was not generally questioned in early centuries, as it has been in recent times.

Ephesians 4:13

According to most manuscripts, the text says that Christians are to aspire to grow in their "knowledge of the Son of God" (επιγνωσεως του υιου του θεου). But in a few Western witnesses (F G it[b]), this is shortened to "the knowledge of God" (επιγνωσεως του θεου), perhaps under the influence of Col 1:10, a similar verse. But Paul emphasized the knowledge of the Son of God because he is the one through whom we know the Father.

Ephesians 4:15

Several good manuscripts (followed by WH NU) read η κεφαλη, Χριστος ("the head, Christ"): so ℵ* A B C. However, TR (following ℵ[2] D F G Ψ Maj) has the reading, η κεφαλη ο Χριστος ("the head, the Christ"). 𝔓[46] has the interesting reading, κεφαλη του Χριστου ("the head of the Christ"). According to 𝔓[46], "the head of [the] Christ" would have to be "God" (see 1 Cor 11:3). As such, the verse indicates that the members of the body are growing up into God, who is Christ's head. (Of course, it is quite possible that the reading of 𝔓[46] is accidental.)

Ephesians 4:16

Two expressions in this verse seem to have troubled scribes. The first one, κατ ενεργειαν ("according to [the] working"), was changed in 𝔓[46] to a genitive complement of επιχορηγιας ("supply")—namely, ενεργειας. The phrase was deleted altogether in some Western witnesses (F G it). Second, the word μερους, which is a general word for "part" (whether of a body, a territory, or any other matter), was changed to a more logical surrogate, μελους, which specifically means "body member" or "limb." The change was made by scribes (A C Ψ) who wanted the more natural word or who may have thought a previous copyist mistakenly wrote μερους for μελους.

Ephesians 4:17

WH NU	τὰ ἔθνη "the Gentiles" 𝔓[46] 𝔓[49] ℵ* A B D* F G 082 33 1739 NKJVmg RSV NRSV ESV NASB NIV TNIV NEB REB NJB NAB NLT HCSB NET
variant/TR	τα λοιπα εθνη "the other Gentiles" ℵ[2] D[1] Ψ Maj syr KJV NKJV

The full statement is, "you must no longer live as also the [other] Gentiles live." The WH NU reading has superior documentation to that of the variant, which is evidenced in some later corrected manuscripts and in later Byzantine witnesses. The insertion of λοιπα was a scribal attempt to clearly show that Paul's Gentile audience, now Christian, was distinct from other Gentiles—or from "the rest of the Gentiles," as it is worded in NKJV.

Ephesians 4:19

Instead of the word απηλγηκοτες, which means "having put away a feeling of remorse," several Western witnesses (D F G it) and 𝔓[99] have απηλπικοτες, which means "despairing."

This reading could have been the result of a scribal error (there is only a two-letter difference between the words: γη/πι) or a scribal interpretation of the Gentile's condition (cf. 2:12).

Ephesians 4:23

TR WH NU ἀνανεοῦσθαι δὲ τῷ πνεύματι τοῦ νοὸς ὑμῶν
"to be renewed in the spirit of your mind"
ℵ A C Maj (𝔓[49] B 33 1739 add εν before τω)
NKJV NRSV ESV NASB NIV TNIV NAB NLT HCSB NET

variant ανανεουσθε δε τω πνευματι του νοος υμων
"you must be renewed in the spirit of your mind"
𝔓[46] D[1] K 33 it
KJV RSV NEB REB NJB

According to the textual evidence, it would seem that the infinitive ανανεουσθαι was changed to the imperative ανανεουσθε to make this statement more obviously a command. (But see next note.) Other scribes added the preposition εν to imprint a particular interpretation: renewal occurs *in* (locative) the spirit, not *by* (dative) the spirit. The TR WH NU text, without the preposition, allows for either interpretation, but most translators read it as a dative; as such, most renderings speak of spiritual renewal as occurring with respect to the spirit of the mind. What is noteworthy is that modern translators understand the "spirit" here to be a kind of spiritual attitude of mind (see NIV), whereas the ancient scribes (𝔓[46] and 𝔓[49] particularly) designated the "spirit" as the divine Spirit by writing it as a nomen sacrum ($\overline{\text{ΠΝΑ}}$). As such, their interpretation must have been that spiritual renewal occurs by the Spirit transforming the mind. However, it is often difficult in Paul's Epistles to distinguish between the divine Spirit and the human spirit because the spirit of a Christian is the human spirit regenerated by the divine Spirit (Rom 8:16) guiding and renewing the mind.

Ephesians 4:24a

TR WH NU ἐνδύσασθαι τὸν καινὸν ἄνθρωπον
"to put on the new person"
𝔓[49vid] A D* F G Ψ 33 1739 Maj
RSV NRSV ESV NIV TNIV NJB NAB NET

variant ενδυσασθε τον καινον ανθρωπον
"put on the new person"
𝔓[46] ℵ B* D[1] K 1881 it
KJV NKJV NASB NEB REB NLT HCSB

Contrary to 4:23 (see note), the textual evidence supports the variant reading having the imperative ενδυσασθε, instead of the infinitive ενδυσασθαι. Thus, there are basically three options for the grammatical structuring of 4:21-24. One option links three infinitives (to put off, to be renewed, to put on) with the main verb "you were taught" (in 4:21). Another option links two infinitives (to put off, to be renewed) with the main verb "you were taught"—followed by an imperative, "put on." A third option (in 𝔓[46]) links one infinitive (to put off) with the verbal "you were taught"—followed by two imperatives, "be renewed" and "put on." The first order is the most structured and that which is followed by NU. However, the textual support for the third infinitive, ενδυσασθαι, is fairly good, having the support of 𝔓[49] (not cited in NA[27], but see *Text of Earliest MSS*, 359).

Ephesians 4:24b

TR WH NU read εν δικαιοσυνη και οσιοτητι της αληθειας ("in righteousness and holiness of the truth") based on the excellent testimony of 𝔓46 𝔓49vid ℵ A B C. The variant reads εν δικαιοσυνη και οσιοτητι και αληθεια ("in righteousness and holiness and the truth") in Western manuscripts (D* F G it) in order to avoid the difficult expression οσιοτητι της αληθειας (which probably means "the holiness that comes from knowing the truth").

Ephesians 4:28

NU	ἐργαζόμενος ταῖς [ἰδίαις] χερσίν "working with his own hands" ℵ* A D F G NRSV ESV NASB NIV TNIV NEB REB NJB NAB HCSB NET
variant 1/TR WH	εργαζομενος ταις χερσιν "working with the [= his] hands" 𝔓46 𝔓49vid ℵ2 B (L Ψ) KJV NKJV RSV NLT
variant 2	εργαζομενος "working" P 33 1739 1881 none

The Greek word ιδιαις ("own") has been bracketed in NU to show the editors' doubts about its right to be in the text. Nevertheless, the editors included it on the grounds that it represents Koine usage (see TCGNT). However, the documentary evidence (𝔓46 𝔓49 B) strongly favors the first variant. The article ταις in and of itself conveys the possessive function: "his hands."

The second variant (which produces the rendering "working the good") is a scribal adjustment that hopes to avoid the connection between manual labor and achieving good (Lincoln 1990, 292).

Ephesians 4:29

TR WH NU	οἰκοδομὴν τῆς χρείας "edification of what is needed" 𝔓46 ℵ A B D2 Ivid Ψ 075 33 1739 Maj syr cop all
variant	οικοδομην της πιστεως "edification of the faith" D* F G it NRSVmg

The difficult and unusual idiom, οικοδομην της χρειας, means something like "edifying others according to their needs." This was changed in Western witnesses to get the more common idiom, οικοδομην της πιστεως, which means "edification of one's faith" or "edifying others in the faith" (cf. 1 Tim 1:4).

Ephesians 4:32

TR WH NU	ἐχαρίσατο ὑμῖν "he forgave you" 𝔓46 ℵ A F G P it cop all
variant	εχαρισατο ημιν "he forgave us" 𝔓49vid B D Ψ 0278 33 1739 Maj syr NRSVmg NASBmg NJBmg

The textual evidence is equally divided for the two readings. Nonetheless, of the two pronouns, υμιν ("you") is the better choice because in the previous sentence Paul uses υμων ("your"). Furthermore, the precious truth conveyed in this statement, "God in Christ forgave you," would probably prompt scribes to make it more inclusive and pertinent to their respective generation (see 5:2).

Ephesians 5:2a

TR NU	ὁ Χριστὸς ἠγάπησεν ἡμᾶς "Christ loved us" 𝔓46 𝔓49vid ℵ2 D F G Maj syr KJV NKJV RSV NRSV ESV NASBmg NIV TNIV NAB NLT HCSB NET
variant/WH	ο Χριστος ηγαπησεν υμας "Christ loved you" ℵ* A B P 0159 it cop NRSVmg NASB NEB REB NJB NLTmg NETmg

There are too many factors involved here to make a definitive judgment between the readings. Since the pronouns look alike and sound alike in Greek, they were easily confused for one another. Furthermore, it seems that Paul himself had a habit of shifting back and forth from second person plural to first person plural. In 4:32, he could have used either pronoun, though it seems more probable that he used the second person plural (see note). Here, he could have used either as well, but it seems likely that he used the second person plural again, because Paul was speaking in the command mode (note the imperative verbs in 5:1-3). But, as we have said, we cannot be absolutely certain about this—especially because it appears that he used the first person plural in the very next phrase (see next note).

Ephesians 5:2b

Most Greek manuscripts (including 𝔓46 𝔓49vid ℵ A D) read παρεδωκαν εαυτον υπερ ημων ("he gave himself up on our behalf"). Some witnesses (B it[b] cop) have this in the second person plural: υπερ υμων ("on your behalf"). In accordance with what has been noted above (4:32; 5:2a), it would be tempting for scribes and translators to keep the pronouns uniform. Indeed, this is what happened in some Old Latin and Coptic versions, where all the pronouns in 4:32 and 5:2 are "you" plural. But in this instance the textual evidence is too slim to support the second person plural.

Ephesians 5:5a

WH NU — ἢ πλεονέκτης, ὅ ἐστιν εἰδωλολάτρης
"a covetous person—that is, an idolater"
𝔓46 𝔓49vid ℵ B F G Ψ 33 1739
RSV NRSV ESV TNIV NEB REB NJB NAB NLT HCSB NET

variant/TR — η πλεονεκτης, ος εστιν ειδωλολατρης
"a covetous person, who is an idolater"
A D Maj
KJV NKJV NASB NIV

The WH NU reading has excellent documentary support. The variant displays a change from the relative pronoun to the personal; this makes the pronoun agree with the previous noun, πλε-ονεκτης ("covetous person"), and provides a subordinate clause.

Ephesians 5:5b

WH NU — τῇ βασιλείᾳ τοῦ Χριστοῦ καὶ θεοῦ
"the kingdom of Christ and God"
𝔓49 ℵ A B Maj
KJV NKJV RSV NRSV ESV NASB NIV TNIV NEB REB NAB NLT HCSB NET

variant 1 — η βασιλεια του θεου
"the kingdom of God"
𝔓46
NJB

variant 2 — η βασιλεια του θεου και Χριστου
"the kingdom of God and Christ"
F G Ambrosiaster
none

variant 3 — η βασιλεια του Χριστου του θεου
"the kingdom of the Christ of God"
1739*
none

The unique expression "kingdom of Christ and God," found in a vast array of witnesses, was adjusted in several ways. The scribe of 𝔓46 trimmed it to the ordinary expression, "the kingdom of God"; other Western witnesses reveal a transposition, which puts "God" before "Christ"; and still others also made "Christ" subservient to "God" by changing the και to του. All of these changes display a discomfort with having "Christ" prior to "God" or even having "Christ" present at all. But the grammar of the WH NU reading indicates an equality of God and Christ, who both rule the kingdom.

Ephesians 5:9

WH NU — καρπὸς τοῦ φωτός
"fruit of the light"
𝔓49 ℵ A B D* F G 33 1739* it syr[p] cop
NKJVmg RSV NRSV ESV NASB NIV TNIV NEB REB NJB NAB NLT HCSB NET

variant/TR καρπος του πνευματος
"fruit of the Spirit"
𝔓46 D2 Ψ Maj syrh
KJV NKJV HCSBmg NETmg

Here is an instance in which the testimony of one papyrus manuscript, 𝔓49, is a great help to offset the testimony of another, 𝔓46, which in this verse contains an emendation. The scribe of 𝔓46 was probably among the first to harmonize this verse with Gal 5:22, which has the phrase, "the fruit of the Spirit." But the emphasis in Ephesians is on how Christians should be living enlightened lives. The "fruit of the light" is the natural outcome of living in the light, for such living produces goodness, righteousness, and truth.

Ephesians 5:10

The wording ευαρεστον τω κυριω ("well pleasing to the Lord"), found in most manuscripts, was changed in some Western witnesses (D* F G) to ευαρεστον τω θεω ("well pleasing to God")—probably under the influence of verses like Rom 8:8; 1 Thess 2:4; 4:1; Heb 11:6. The *editio princeps* of 𝔓49 incorrectly reads κυριω (ΚΩ), when the manuscript reads χριστω (ΧΩ); see *Text of Earliest MSS,* 360. It appears that the extant letter is a *chi,* not a *kappa*. The *chi* is shaped exactly the same as the *chi* in 𝔓65 (another portion of the same manuscript; see *Text of Earliest MSS,* 358), which is visible in two words: ΧΥ (1 Thess 1:3) and Αχαια (1 Thess 1:6).

Ephesians 5:14

TR WH NU ἐπιφαύσει σοι ὁ Χριστός
"the Christ will shine on you"
𝔓46 א A B D* G 33 1739* it syrp cop Origen
all

variant επιψαυσεις του Χριστου
"you will touch the Christ"
D* itb Ambrosiaster Victorinus Jerome MSSaccording to Chrysostom
NJBmg

According to TR WH NU, the full saying Paul cites is: "Rise, sleeping one, and arise from the dead, and the Christ will shine on you." It is difficult to find the origin of this quotation; the best guess is that it was adapted from Isa 60:1. Many commentators think it was part of a hymn which was sung at baptism ceremonies (see Lincoln 1990, 318-319). In the early church, baptism was considered an enlightenment (as in Heb 6:4; 10:32). The variant reading, which could not be original because of its slim support, is nonetheless quite remarkable. Jerome in his *Commentary on Ephesians* (PL 26, 559a) interprets the words as addressed by Christ to Adam when releasing him from Hades. This variant reading could also mean "you will have a part in the Christ"; it suggests that believers can partake of Christ and experience him in extraordinary ways once they enter into a realm of resurrection. This reading may somehow reflect the story of the newly risen Jesus telling Mary that she could not touch him (John 20:17). Had Mary also been in resurrection she could touch (i.e., experience) the risen Christ in his realm. Whatever scribe created this variant (it was not an accident) may have had some such association in mind.

Ephesians 5:19

TR WH NU ᾠδαῖς πνευματικαῖς
"spiritual songs"
ℵ D F G Ψ Maj syr cop
KJV NKJV RSV NRSV ESV NASB NIV TNIV NEBmg REBmg NJB NAB NLT HCSB NET

variant 1 ωδαις
"songs"
𝔓46 B it[b,d]
NEB REB

variant 2 ωδαις πνευματικαις εν χαριτι
"spiritual songs with grace"
A
none

Paul was encouraging the believers to engage in three kinds of singing—in psalms and hymns and [spiritual] songs. The issue is whether or not he used "spiritual" to describe the "songs." It is quite likely that both the TR WH NU reading and the second variant are the result of scribal conformity to Col 3:16, a parallel verse. The two earliest Greek manuscripts (𝔓46 B) and Old Latin manuscripts (it[b,d]) do not include either the adjective "spiritual" or the prepositional phrase "with grace." NEB and REB adhere to this shorter reading.

Had the word πνευματικαις originally been in the text, the only reason to account for its omission is homoeoteleuton: ωδαις πνευματικαις—both end with the same three letters. Royse (1983, 543) argues that the scribe of 𝔓46 was prone to make scribal leaps and that this is one of them. But this is not the only witness to have the shorter reading, so Royse's argument is not conclusive in this regard.

Ephesians 5:20

All the Greek editions (TR WH NU), supported by ℵ A B D[1] Ψ 33 1739 Maj, read τω θεω και πατρι ("the God and Father"); all English versions follow. However, other witnesses (𝔓46 D* F G it) read, τω πατρι και θεω ("the Father and God"). Of the two readings, the variant has the more unusual formation—inasmuch as when God the Father is addressed, the name "God" usually precedes "the Father": "God, the Father." For this reason alone, one could consider the variant to be more likely original. Either reading, however, connotes the same person: "God who is the Father" or "the Father who is God." The former gives emphasis to his fatherhood; the latter, to his deity.

Ephesians 5:21

WH NU φόβῳ Χριστοῦ
"fear of Christ"
𝔓46 ℵ A B C Maj
NKJVmg RSV NRSV ESV NASB NIV TNIV NEB REB NJB NAB NLT HCSB NET

variant 1/TR φοβω θεου
"fear of God"
6 81 1881 Clement MSS[according to Ambrosiaster]
KJV NKJV

variant 2 φοβω Ιησου Χριστου
"fear of Jesus Christ"
(D) F G
none

variant 3 φοβω κυριου
"fear of the Lord"
K
none

The documentary evidence strongly supports the WH NU reading. As typically happened in the transmission of the NT text, the divine name was expanded or altered. The expansion, "Jesus Christ," needs no explanation. The alterations are easily explainable as scribal conformity to a more usual expression—whether "fear of God" or "fear of the Lord." Indeed, the phrase "fear of Christ" occurs only here in the NT. TR, followed by KJV and NKJV, has very minimal and late support for its reading.

Ephesians 5:22

WH NU γυναῖκες τοῖς ἰδίοις ἀνδράσιν
"wives to their own husbands"
𝔓46 B Clement MSS[according to Jerome]
HCSBmg

variant 1 γυναικες τοις ιδιοις ανδρασιν υποτασσεσθωσαν
"wives submitting to their own husbands"
ℵ A I P Ψ 1739 it cop
none

variant 2/TR γυναικες τοις ιδιοις ανδρασιν υποτασσεσθε
"wives, submit to their own husbands"
(D F G) Maj syr
all

The text, according to the earliest manuscripts, relies upon the participle υποτασσομενοι ("being submissive") of the previous verse to complete the sense of this verse. But later scribes supplied the verbal, either as a participle (variant 1) or an imperative verb (variant 2). Translators, wanting to make things easy for their readers, follow suit—usually with the imperative verb.

Ephesians 5:29

WH NU ὁ Χριστὸς τὴν ἐκκλησίαν
"Christ to the church"
𝔓46 ℵ A B D* F G Ψ 048 0285 33 1739 1881 syr cop
RSV NRSV ESV NASB NIV TNIV NEB REB NJB NAB NLT HCSB NET

variant/TR ο κυριος την εκκλησιαν
"the Lord to the church"
D^2 Maj
KJV NKJV

According to the WH NU text, which has a powerful array of witnesses, Paul was speaking of how Christ nourishes and cherishes the church. The change from "Christ" to "Lord" in the majority of later witnesses was probably influenced by 5:22. The change has been perpetuated by TR, followed by KJV and NKJV.

Ephesians 5:30

WH NU	μέλη ἐσμὲν τοῦ σώματος αὐτοῦ "we are members of his body" 𝔓^{46} ℵ* A B 048 33 1739* cop Jerome NKJVmg RSV NRSV ESV NASB NIV TNIV NEB REB NJB NAB NLT HCSB NET
variant/TR	μελη εσμεν του σωματος αυτου, εκ της σαρκος αυτου και εκ των οστεων αυτου "we are members of his body, of his flesh and of his bones" ℵ^{2} D F G Ψ 0285^{vid} 1739^{mg} Maj it syr Irenaeus KJV NKJV NRSVmg HCSBmg NETmg

It could be argued that the second phrase was accidentally omitted due to homoeoteleuton causing a scribal leap (αυτου ... αυτου). However, it is far more likely that the variant reading is a scribal expansion created to make 5:30 reflect the OT quotation, Gen 2:23. Since Gen 2:24 is cited in the very next verse (5:31), scribes wanted 5:30-31 to be a citation of Gen 2:23-24. But the expansion creates an exegetical problem: How can Christians be Christ's "flesh and bones"? The believers, as members of the church, are united to Christ's spiritual existence (see 1 Cor 6:17), but they are not part of his physical body. A husband and wife can be united physically, but not Christ and the church. Not recognizing this exegetical problem, scribes added the words anyway—perhaps taking the opportunity to affirm Christ's physical existence as an antidote to Docetism. Indeed, Irenaeus (*Haer.* 5.2.3) quotes this fuller text in confronting Gnostics who denied Jesus Christ's real physical existence and bodily resurrection. Modern versions, having the shorter text, stand in sharp contrast to KJV and NKJV, which have the expansion.

Ephesians 5:31

All the Greek texts (TR WH NU), supported by ℵ^{2} B D^{2} Ψ 1739^{mg} Maj Origen, have the reading και προσκολληθησεται προς την γυναικα αυτου ("and will be joined to his wife"). A few witnesses (6 1739* Jerome) omit this clause, and several manuscripts (𝔓^{46} ℵ^{1} A P 0285 33) include the clause without the preposition προς. TR WH NU accords with the rendering of Gen 2:24 as it appears in most manuscripts of the Septuagint. The omission in the first variant could have happened accidentally, due to homoeoarchton causing a scribal leap (και ... και), or it could have been an intentional excision to conform this citation to the one in Mark 10:7, where the best-attested reading (ℵ B) also omits the clause. The second variant could be the result of conformity to Matt 19:5, where the citation of Gen 2:24 does not include a preposition. Nonetheless, because of its documentary support, it is just as likely to have been the original wording.

Ephesians 6:1

TR WH NU	ὑπακούετε τοῖς γονεῦσιν ὑμῶν [ἐν κυρίῳ] "obey your parents in the Lord" 𝔓^{46} ℵ A D^{1} I^{vid} 0285 33 1739 Maj syr cop KJV NKJV RSV NRSV ESV NASB NIV TNIV NJB NAB NLT HCSB NET

variant	υπακουετε τοις γονευσιν υμων "obey your parents" B D* F G it[b] Marcion NRSVmg NEB REB NJBmg NLTmg

The phrase εν κυριω ("in the Lord") is not present in several witnesses. It could be argued that it was added to conform this verse to Col 3:20, a parallel text. But in Colossians the phrase is joined with the statement, "for this is well pleasing in the Lord." Thus, we would imagine that an insertion of the phrase "in the Lord" would have been added to the next clause in this verse: "for this is right in the Lord." Consequently, it seems that the phrase is part of the original text—as is affirmed by superior attestation.

Marcion probably omitted "in the Lord" because he objected to an OT injunction being linked with a christological motivation (Lincoln 1990, 395). His omission may have influenced textual transmission thereafter. Or scribes may have thought it too ambiguous to leave it in the text, inasmuch as "in the Lord" can modify the action of children's obedience (i.e., the Lord motivates their obedience) or "in the Lord" can modify the parents (i.e., children should obey Christian parents). Of course, the latter interpretation leaves open the question: Can children disobey parents who are not Christians? From parallel expressions in 5:22 and 6:5, it seems that Paul meant "in the Lord" to indicate that children should obey their parents because of their (the children's) devotion to Jesus Christ the Lord.

Ephesians 6:9

WH NU	εἰδότες ὅτι καὶ αὐτῶν καὶ ὑμῶν ὁ κύριος ἐστιν ἐν οὐρανοῖς "knowing that both their master and yours is in heaven" 𝔓46 ℵ A B D F G NKJVmg RSV NRSV ESV NASB NIV TNIV NEB REB NJB NAB NLT HCSB NET
variant/TR	ειδοτες οτι και υμων αυτων ο κυριος εστιν εν ουρανοις "knowing that also your own master is in heaven" Maj KJV NKJV

The WH NU reading has superior documentation. The change in the majority of later manuscripts (and TR) was probably influenced by Col 4:1, a parallel verse.

Ephesians 6:12a

The TR WH NU editions read ημιν η παλη ("our battle"), with the support of ℵ A D[2] I Maj syr[h] cop Clement Origen. However, some significant witnesses (𝔓46 B D* F G Ψ it syr[p]) read υμιν η παλη ("your battle"). Since the rest of this pericope (6:12-20) is in the second person plural, it could be argued that the reading with "our" is the more difficult reading and therefore original. However, Christian scribes had a habit of turning memorable statements (such as this one—"(y)our battle is not against flesh and blood") into inclusive mottos which all Christians could own.

Ephesians 6:12b

WH NU κοσμοκράτορας τοῦ σκότους τούτου
"world powers of this darkness"
𝔓[46] ℵ* A B D* F G 33 1739* syr[p] cop Origen
NKJVmg RSV NRSV ESV NASB NIV TNIV NEB NJB NAB NLT NET

variant/TR κοσμοκρατορας του σκοτους του αιωνος τουτου
"world powers of the darkness of this age"
ℵ[2] D[2] Ψ 1739[mg] Maj syr[h**]
KJV NKJV (REB) HCSB

The WH NU reading has excellent documentation, both early and diverse. The change in later manuscripts is an expansion probably motivated by 2:2, which identifies the satanic ruler of this world as the one who rules this age. Furthermore, it may have been added to help readers concretize the abstract expression "this darkness."

Ephesians 6:19

TR WH NU τὸ μυστήριον τοῦ εὐαγγελίου
"the mystery of the gospel"
ℵ A D I Ψ 0278 33 1739 Maj syr cop
all

variant το μυστηριον
"the mystery"
𝔓[46vid?] B F G it[b]
NLTmg

Scholars such as Metzger (TCGNT) and Lincoln (1990, 430) argue for the longer reading on the basis that (1) the alignment of B with Western witnesses such as F G does not count for much because B has a Western strand in the Pauline Epistles, and (2) had the shorter reading been original, one would expect other additions such as "of Christ" or "of God" (as in Col 2:2); yet there are no other additions except "of the gospel." But both of these arguments could be countered with the simple dictum that the shorter reading is usually more likely original. Furthermore, in Ephesians, scribes (perhaps influenced by Rom 16:25) would be inclined to add "of the gospel" to give it an evangelistic flavor. But it is unlikely that this is exactly what Paul had in mind. His goal was to proclaim the mystery of Christ and his church, the mystery of the newly revealed truth that, in Christ, all believers—whether Jews or Gentiles—are one body with equal share in all of God's blessings and promises (see 3:1-6). This was *the* mystery Paul wanted to make known to the world. Thus, the wording is referential (see 5:32), and not limited to "the gospel."

Finally, the shorter reading very likely has the support of 𝔓[46] because the lacuna in this manuscript allows for about 99 to 100 letters (the average of 33 letters per line) following αγιων in 6:18 to the beginning of ινα in 6:20, exactly the number of letters in the shorter text. The addition of του ευαγγελιου would make 113 letters, or 37.6 letters per line, which is too long for the line lengths of 𝔓[46]. Thus, it is fairly certain that 𝔓[46] had the shorter reading (see *Text of Earliest MSS,* 2nd printing, 312). As such, the attestation for the shorter reading is strengthened by the testimony of the earliest extant manuscript. WH brackets του ευαγγελιου ("of the gospel"), and NLT notes this reading.

Ephesians 6:20

A few important manuscripts (𝔓46 B 1739) read ινα αυτο παρρησιασωμαι ("that I may boldly speak it"), referring to το μυστηριον ("the mystery"), instead of ινα εν αυτω παρρησιασωμαι ("that I may be bold in him"), found in other manuscripts.

Ephesians 6:21

The expression ειδητε και υμεις ("you also may know") has been transposed in some manuscripts (א A D F G I P) to και υμεις ειδητε, with no change in meaning. Other manuscripts (𝔓46 33) shorten it to ειδητε ("you know").

Ephesians 6:24

WH NU	omit αμην ("Amen") at end of verse 𝔓46 א* A B F G 33 1739* RSV NRSV ESV NASB NIV TNIV NEB REB NJB NAB NLT HCSB NET
variant/TR	include αμην ("Amen") at end of verse א2 D Ψ 1739c Maj it syr KJV NKJV NETmg

Only three epistles (Romans, Galatians, and Jude) appear to have a genuine "amen" for the last word of the document. In the other epistles it seems apparent that an "amen" was added for liturgical purposes. According to the textual evidence cited above, it is clear that the "amen" at the end of Ephesians is a scribal addition.

Subscription

1. No subscription—but placed as an inscription: Προς Εφεσιους ("To the Ephesians"). Appears in 𝔓46.
2. No subscription. Appears in365 630 1505 2464.
3. Προς Εφεσιους ("To the Ephesians"). Appears in א A B* D (F G) Ψ 33.
4. Προς Εφεσιους εγραφη απο Ρωμης ("To the Ephesians written from Rome"). Appears in B1 P.
5. Προς Εφεσιους εγραφη απο Ρωμης δια Τυχικου ("To the Ephesians written from Rome through Tychicus"). Appears in 0278 1739 1881 Maj (TR).

It is quite certain that no book of the New Testament originally had a title (inscription) or a subscription. (For more on this, see Comfort 2005, 9-10.) This is especially true for the epistles because their original purpose was to be an apostolic letter, not a literary work per se. Thus, all inscriptions and subscriptions are scribal addenda. The simplest form, Προς Εφεσιους, appears in the earliest witnesses: in 𝔓46 at the head of the epistle; in א A B* at the end. As is typical, the subscription was expanded to include the place of writing (Rome), and the carrier, Tychicus. The same kind of expansions occurred in the same manuscripts in Colossians (see note on subscription in Colossians).

The Epistle to the PHILIPPIANS

Inscription (Title)

𝔓⁴⁶ ℵ and B title this epistle as Προς Φιλιππησιους ("To the Philippians"). Several manuscripts (including ℵ and B) also have this title in the subscription (see last note for this book). Paul, however, would not have entitled this epistle in its original composition. Inscriptions and subscriptions are the work of later scribes. (For more on this, see Comfort 2005, 9-10.)

Philippians 1:1a

WH NU	δοῦλοι Χριστοῦ 'Ιησοῦ "servants of Christ Jesus" ℵ B D cop RSV NRSV ESV NASB NIV TNIV NEB REB NJB NAB NLT HCSB NET
variant/TR	δουλοι Ιησου Χριστου "servants of Jesus Christ" F G KJV NKJV

The WH NU reading has excellent documentary support. TR's transposition has an order that is not characteristic of Paul. When Paul introduces himself (and his other cowriters) at the beginning of epistles, he will typically call himself an apostle of Christ Jesus (see note on Eph 1:1) or a servant of Christ Jesus (see Rom 1:1), but not of "Jesus Christ."

Philippians 1:1b

After greeting "all the saints" in Philippi, Paul adds συν επισκοποις και διακονοις, which is translated "with the overseers and deacons." However, it is possible to join together the first two words and make them one word, συνεπισκοποις, which means "co-overseers" (or "co-bishops"). This is the reading in later manuscripts: B[2] D[2] 075 33 1739. Earlier manuscripts could have read either way because no spaces were left between words. However, the sense of the passage is that Paul was writing to the entire church in Philippi, which encompassed "all the saints," among whom were the overseers and deacons.

Philippians 1:3

Most manuscripts, including the most ancient, begin this verse with ευχαριστω τω θεω μου ("I thank my God"). Some Western witnesses (D* F G it[b]) change this to εγω μεν ευχαριστω τω κυριω ημων ("I, for my part, thank our Lord"). This language is non-Pauline, for Paul typically gives thanks to "God," not "the Lord."

Philippians 1:6

NU ἡμέρας Χριστοῦ Ἰησοῦ
"day of Christ Jesus"
𝔓[46] B D Ψ Maj
ESV NASB NIV TNIV NEB REB NAB NLT NET

variant/TR WH ημερας Ιησου Χριστου
"day of Jesus Christ"
ℵ A F G P 075 33 1739
KJV NKJV RSV NRSV NJB HCSB

The NU reading has good attestation and accords with Pauline phrasing in this epistle (see 1:10; 2:16). The variant also has good attestation, yet differs from Pauline style. The English versions are divided, as well. Interestingly, NRSV diverts from NU here.

Philippians 1:7

The expression συγκοινωνους μου της χαριτος παντας υμας οντας ("you are all sharers of my grace") seemed odd to Eberhard Nestle (see critical apparatus of NA[27]), who conjectured that it must have originally read συγκοινωνους μου της χρειας παντας υμας οντας ("you are all sharers in my need"). Although this makes good sense, there is no manuscript support for it. The reading with χαριτος ("grace") is appropriate because Paul was saying that, as he received God's grace in his struggles for the gospel, so the Philippians would share in the same grace as they experienced persecution for their proclamation of the gospel (see 1:5). They were co-partakers of the grace that accompanied its proclamation.

Philippians 1:11

The Greek editions (TR WH NU) read δοξαν και επαινον θεου ("glory and praise of God"), with good support: ℵ A B D[2] I Ψ Maj it syr cop. All English versions follow. There are a few interesting textual variants, however: (1) δοξαν και επαινον Χριστου ("glory and praise of Christ") in D* (which was later corrected); (2) δοξαν και επαινον μου ("my [Paul's] glory and praise") in F G; (3) δοξαν θεου και επαινον εμοι ("glory of God and my [Paul's] praise") in 𝔓[46] (it[g]). The first variant involves a simple change from "God" to "Christ." But the next two variants are difficult to explain—either on transcriptional grounds or exegetical. Thus, it is possible that Paul originally wrote what was in the second or third variants. But the second variant, which omits θεου, looks like a scribal attempt to avoid such a close juxtaposition between God and Paul (Silva 1992a, 64). The third variant, found in the earliest manuscript, 𝔓[46], may preserve the original—not only on transcriptional grounds but also on exegetical. It was characteristic of Paul, when speaking of the Lord's return (see 1:10), to mention that the believers' transformed lives would bring glory to God and honor to Paul. In 2 Cor 1:14 and Phil 2:16, Paul says that the believers would be his boast on the day of Christ. In 1 Thess 2:19-20, Paul says that the believers in Thessalonica will be his glory on that day. Thus, it would not be too much for Paul to say that the Philippians would bring God glory and Paul praise.

Philippians 1:14

TR NU	τὸν λόγον "the word" 𝔓46 D2 1739 Maj itr KJV NKJV NRSV ESV (TNIV) NJB NAB NLTmg HCSB NET
variant 1/WH	τον λογον του θεου "the word of God" א A B (D*) P Ψ 048vid 33 syrp,h** RSV NRSVmg ESVmg NASB NIV NEB REB NLT HCSBmg NETmg
variant 2	τον λογον του κυριου "the word of the Lord" F G NJBmg NETmg

The two variants appear to be scribal attempts to make clear just what "the word" ("the message") means. Of course, this word is the message about the Lord, and it is a message that came from God. But this did not have to be said by Paul for his readers to understand it. Many English translators, however, have been impressed with testimony of א A B D* in support of the first variant—and/or followed WH or earlier editions of the Nestle text (prior to NA26). But the editors of NA26 (and UBS3) considered the variant readings to be expansions of the first. They therefore chose the reading supported by 𝔓46 over τον λογον του θεου ("the word of God"), the reading in previous Nestle editions.

Philippians 1:16-17

WH NU	verse 16 before verse 17 𝔓46 א A B D* F G P 048 075 33 1739 it cop NKJVmg RSV NRSV ESV NASB NIV TNIV NEB REB NJB NAB NLT HCSB NET
variant/TR	verse 17 before verse 16 (with οι μεν at the beginning of 1:16 and οι δε at the beginning of 1:17) D1 Ψ Maj syrh KJV NKJV NASBmg

The manuscript evidence, both early and diverse, overwhelmingly supports the wording in WH NU. A transposition of verses was made in the majority of manuscripts so that 1:16-17 would follow the order put forth in 1:15, where Paul first mentions those who preach from envy and rivalry, and second, those who preach from goodwill. But the original text displays a chiastic order:

A. 15 preachers with envy and rivalry

  B. preachers with good will

  B′. 16 preachers [of goodwill] do so out of love, knowing that Paul is set for the defense of the gospel

A′. 17 preachers creating rivalry do so impurely, trying to increase Paul's suffering in prison

Such chiasms are typically Pauline; the reversal of these may promote clarity, but it destroys the poetry.

Philippians 1:20

The noun αποκαραδοκιαν, meaning "eager expectation," which is "found only in Christian writings, was returned to its earlier, better known form, καραδοκιαν, in only a few manuscripts [F G]" (Hawthorne 1983, 32).

Philippians 1:27

The expression εν ενι πνευματι ("in one spirit") is taken by most English translators to denote a unified spirit, a spiritual solidarity, a kind of *esprit de corps*. This interpretation is enhanced by the following phrase, μια ψυχη ("one mind"), which is taken as an appositive. Indeed, TEV collapses the two expressions into one with this translation: "with one common purpose." The scribe of 𝔓[46], however, saw this verse as pointing to the agency of the divine Spirit, for he wrote EN ENI $\overline{\Pi NI}$ (using the nomen sacrum $\overline{\Pi NI}$) which means "in one Spirit." Had he wanted to designate the human spirit or the *esprit de corps*, he could have written out πνευματι (in *plene*) as he did on other occasions (see note on 1 Cor 2:14).

Philippians 1:28

WH NU ἥτις ἐστὶν αὐτοῖς ἔνδειξις ἀπωλείας, ὑμῶν δὲ σωτηρίας
"which is to them a proof of destruction, but your salvation"
ℵ A B C[2] P Ψ 33 1739
NKJVmg RSV NRSV ESV NASB NIV TNIV NEB REB NJB NAB NLT HCSB NET

variant 1/TR ητις αυτοις μεν εστιν ενδειξις απωλειας, υμιν δε σωτηριας
"which to them, on one hand, is a proof of destruction, but to you, on the other hand, of salvation"
Maj
KJV NKJV

variant 2 ητις εστιν αυτοις ενδειξις απωλειας, ημιν δε σωτηριας
"which to them is a proof of destruction, but to us [is] salvation"
C* D* F G
none

The manuscript evidence decidedly supports the wording in WH NU. The first variant is a scribal alteration that balances the two statements. The second variant, essentially "Western," makes the second statement inclusive (i.e., Paul and the Philippians). According to Hawthorne (1983, 55-57), these changes were created to make the two statements parallel and thereby allow for the text to be interpreted as contrasting two perceptions: (1) the adversaries who perceive the willingness of the Philippians to fight for the faith of the gospel as an indication of their (the Philippians') destruction, and (2) the Philippians themselves, who see the opposition as a sure sign of their salvation. This, of course, goes against the traditional interpretation, which emphasizes the contrast between *their* destruction and *your* salvation. The traditional exegesis says that this verse affirms that the opposition against the believers provides a twofold sign of what will be manifested when Christ returns: the destruction of those who persecute and the salvation of those who persevere (see 2 Thess 1:6-10).

Philippians 2:2

TR WH NU τὸ ἓν φρονοῦντες
"thinking the one thing"
𝔓46 א2 B D F G 075 1739 Maj
KJV NKJV RSV NRSV ESV NASB NIV TNIV NJB NAB NLT

variant το αυτο φρονουντες
"thinking the same thing"
א* A C I Ψ 33
NEB REB HCSB NET

The variant reading is probably the result of scribes conforming this phrase to the first phrase of the clause. No matter how subtle the difference, it is likely that Paul was making a general appeal for unity at the beginning of the verse in saying το αυτο φρονητε ("think the same thing"). Then he provided one specific focus that would unite their minds when he said το εν φρονουντες ("thinking the one thing"). Later in the epistle, Paul elaborates on this one thing: "it is to pursue the goal of knowing Christ Jesus." If any believers had a different goal, Paul prayed that they would be enlightened (see 3:12-15). Like a team of athletes (see 1:27), the Philippians were called by Paul to focus on one goal only—that of knowing Christ. This kind of thinking would unite their minds.

Philippians 2:3

Instead of the participle ηγουμενοι ("esteeming"), found in most manuscripts, a few important manuscripts (𝔓46 D I 075 0278) have the participle προηγουμενοι, which literally means "leading the way." The word appears only one other place in the NT, Rom 12:10, which was translated in many ancient versions (it syr arm) as "trying to outdo one another in showing respect" (BDAG 869). As such, προηγουμενοι is an excellent word in the context of Phil 2:1-6, where Paul is promoting willful submission among the brothers and sisters.

Philippians 2:4

There is textual variation for the first and second occurrences of εκαστος/εκαστοι in this verse. TR has the singular εκαστος in both occurrences; WH has the plural εκαστοι in both occurrences. NU has the singular first, then the plural. Based on the testimony of 𝔓46 א C D 1739 Maj and on the fact that the rest of the words are plural in this verse, the NU editors chose the singular εκαστος ("each one") for the first occurrence—because this is the more difficult reading. However, Hawthorne (1983, 63) argues that Greek scribes were more comfortable with using the singular εκαστος, even with plural subjects, and therefore changed the plural to a singular. Thus, he contends that εσκατοι ("every one of you"), found in A B F G Ψ 33, is original. However, this argument loses its force when we consider that the scribes of 𝔓46 א C D did not change the plural to a singular in the very next occurrence. The second occurrence of εκαστος/εκαστοι in this verse also has textual variation. But in this case the singular has very weak support (Maj it[d] syr) in comparison to the plural, which is found in 𝔓46 א A B D P Ψ 33 1739. Some of these same manuscripts (א* A 33) conclude 2:4 with τα ετερων ("the things of others"), and join εκαστοι with the beginning of 2:5—εκαστοι τουτο φρονειτε εν υμιν ("let this thinking be in every one of you").

Philippians 2:9

WH NU τὸ ὄνομα τὸ ὑπὲρ πᾶν ὄνομα
"the name above every name"
𝔓46 ℵ A B C 33 1739
NKJV RSV NRSV ESV NASB NIV TNIV NEB REB NJB NAB NLT HCSB NET

variant/TR ονομα το υπερ παν ονομα
"a name above every name"
D F G Ψ 075 0278 Maj Clement
KJV

The four earliest manuscripts, as well as C 33 1739, support the wording in WH NU. The definite article το was omitted probably because in Greek usage the article usually functions to point back to a previously mentioned subject. In this case, it points forward with a sense of anticipation—to the next verse, where the name is identified: τω ονοματι Ιησου ("the name of Jesus").

Philippians 2:11

TR WH NU ἐξομολογήσηται
"should confess"
𝔓46 ℵ B F[c] Clement
all

variant εξομολογησεται
"will confess"
A C D F* G L P 33 1739
NJBmg

The difference between these two readings involves a difference of a single letter (η/ε). The verb of the TR WH NU text is aorist subjunctive (giving the rendering, "every tongue should confess"), and the verb of the variant is future indicative (giving the rendering, "every tongue will confess"). Usually, a distinction in tenses will not greatly impact the exegesis of a passage. But in this case it is critical. The aorist subjunctive indicates that all people could and should confess that Jesus Christ is Lord—not that they necessarily will do so. But the future is predictive: All people *will* confess that Jesus Christ is Lord. This prediction is typically rejected by many Christians who think the Scriptures reveal that not all people will be saved. Those who espouse universalism (i.e., that all will be saved) urge that this verse looks forward to the day when all will indeed recognize Jesus as Lord.

In this light, it is not easy to say what was originally written. Certainly, one word could have been easily confused for the other, so the change might have been purely accidental. But if it was intentional, it is possible that scribes changed the future to the subjunctive to avoid any notions of universalism or to make the verb parallel to the subjunctive verb of the previous verse, καμψη ("should bend"). However, it is possible that scribes changed the subjunctive to the future so as to conform Paul's wording to Isa 45:23, the OT passage he quoted here. If so, such scribes cannot be said to be universalists per se; rather, their intentions were to show the eschatological regency of Christ over all humanity, irrespective of identifying who is or is not saved.

Philippians 2:15a

TR WH NU ἵνα γένησθε ἄμεμπτοι
"that you may become blameless"
ℵ B C D² Ψ 075 0278 33 1739 Maj
NKJV NIV TNIV

variant ινα ητε αμεμπτοι
"that you may be blameless"
𝔓⁴⁶ A D* F G
KJV RSV NRSV ESV NASB NEB REB NJB NAB (NLT) HCSB NET

It is difficult to determine which reading is original based on manuscript support or even Pauline style. Both readings have testimony from early and diverse witnesses, and Paul used both the subjunctive form of ειμι and γινομαι in ινα clauses. Silva (1992a, 148) says that "some scribes may have thought that γινομαι would imply that the Philippians were not yet children of God, but it would be misleading to press the force of 'become' in this verb." Indeed, the word γινομαι describes the process of becoming blameless and pure, not the process of becoming a child of God.

Philippians 2:15b

The adjective αμωμα ("flawless"), found in 𝔓⁴⁶ ℵ A B C 33, was changed to αμωμητα ("blameless" or "flawless") in later witnesses (D F G Ψ Maj—so TR), under the influence of Deut 32:5 (LXX), the OT passage Paul alluded to here.

Philippians 2:19

Instead of κυριω Ιησου ("Lord Jesus"), found in most Greek manuscripts, some Greek copies (C D* F G 1739) read Χριστω Ιησου ("Christ Jesus"), the more familiar Pauline expression.

Philippians 2:21

Several witnesses (B 0278 Maj—so TR WH) transpose the expression Ιησου Χριστου ("Jesus Christ") to Χριστου Ιησου ("Christ Jesus"), the more familiar Pauline expression.

Philippians 2:26

TR NU ἐπιποθῶν ἦν πάντας ὑμᾶς
"he was yearning for you all"
ℵ² (B) F G Ψ 1739 Maj
KJV NKJV RSV NRSV ESV NASB NIV TNIV NEB REB NJB NAB HCSB NET

variant 1/WH επιποθων ην παντας υμας ιδειν
"he was yearning to see you all"
ℵ* A C D I^vid 33 81 syr cop^bo
NRSVmg NASBmg NLT

variant 2 επιποθων ην πεμψαι προς υμας
"he was yearning to send [word] to you"
𝔓^46vid
none

The first variant, which has good testimony, makes explicit what is already implicit in the text—namely, Epaphroditus wanted to see the Philippians so that they could be assured that he was no longer ill. Nonetheless, the resultant text reflects Pauline idiom (see Rom 1:11; 1 Thess 3:6). The second variant in 𝔓46 could be the result of dittography—the scribe accidentally recopied πεμψαι προς υμας from the previous verse. (Though listed as "vid," the reading in 𝔓46 is quite certain; see *Text of Earliest MSS,* 324). If this variant was not an error, it is possible that the scribe was thinking of Epaphroditus sending a message to the Philippians about his recovery. However, Paul felt there was no better way than to send Epaphroditus himself back to the Philippians.

Philippians 2:30a

(TR) NU	τὸ ἔργον Χριστοῦ "the work of Christ" 𝔓46 B F G (D Maj add του before Χριστου) all
variant 1	το εργον "the work" C NJBmg
variant 2/WH	το εργον κυριου "the work of the Lord" ℵ A P Ψ 33 syr[h] cop[bo] NRSVmg NJBmg

Nowhere else does Paul use the term "the work of Christ," but he does use the phrase "the work of the Lord" in 1 Cor 15:58; 16:10. Therefore, it is quite likely that the second variant is an assimilation (Hawthorne 1983, 114). Lightfoot (1903, 124) preferred the first variant because it is the shortest and thereby explains the other two variants. "[The] discovery of 𝔓46, however, makes this position no longer tenable, because the three-pronged support of (του) Χριστου by (proto-) Alexandrian (𝔓46 B 1739), 'Western' (D F G it vg), and Byzantine witnesses is overwhelming" (Silva 1992a, 163). All English versions affirm this, while some note the significant differences.

Philippians 2:30b

WH NU	παραβολευσάμενος τῇ ψυχῇ "having risked his life" 𝔓46 ℵ A B D F G cop[sa] RSV NRSV ESV NASB NIV TNIV NEB REB NJB NAB NLT HCSB NET
variant/TR	παραβουλευσαμενος τη ψυχη "having no regard for his life" C Ψ 33 1739 Maj syr KJV NKJV

There is only a one-letter difference between the two variants: the inclusion or omission of an *upsilon*. Both readings make good sense inasmuch as Epaphroditus risked his life for the work of Christ and in so doing showed that he did not care about his life. However, the word in WH NU (which has superior documentary support) is more colorful in that it means that Epaphroditus "gambled with his life" (Lightfoot 1903, 124). By comparison, the reading in the majority of manuscripts (followed by TR) connotes only self-sacrifice.

Philippians 3:3

WH NU	οἱ πνεύματι θεοῦ λατρεύοντες "the ones worshiping in (by) God's Spirit" ℵ* A B C D² F G 33 1739 Maj syr^hmg cop NKJVmg RSVmg NRSV ESV NASB NIV TNIV NEBmg REB NJB NABmg NLT HCSB NET
variant 1/TR	οι πνευματι θεω λατρευοντες "the ones worshiping God in spirit" ℵ² D* P Ψ it syr KJV NKJV RSV NRSVmg ESVmg NEBmg REBmg NJBmg NAB NLTmg NETmg
variant 2	οι πνευματι λατρευοντες "the ones worshiping in spirit" 𝔓46 NEB NLTmg NETmg

According to Greek grammar, the WH NU reading can be rendered, "the ones worshiping by God's Spirit" or "the ones worshiping God's Spirit." In Greek the verb λατρευω ("worship") is normally accompanied by the dative (in this verse, πνευματι—"Spirit"); hence, the Spirit becomes the recipient of the worship (see Hawthorne 1983, 122). Since the grammar allows a rendering that might be offensive to those who do not think the Spirit should be worshiped, some scribes added another object in the dative case, θεω ("God")—the first variant noted above. But it should be noted that Lightfoot (1903, 145) demonstrated that the verb λατρευοντες had acquired a technical sense referring to the worship of God, and therefore one does not have to understand the phrase "God's Spirit" as the object of the worship. Thus, the text does not have to include an object to convey the message that God is being worshiped in spirit.

In this light, it is not unreasonable to imagine that the original reading may have been preserved in 𝔓46, for it has no object after the participle, and yet it must mean "worship God in spirit" because "God" is always the object of worship. But scribes were uncomfortable with this bare expression and therefore filled it out with either θεου or θεω. It is for this reason that 𝔓46 explains the origin of the other variants, which is the reason its reading was adopted for the NEB (see Tasker 1964, 439). It is unlikely that the scribe of 𝔓46 accidentally dropped one of these objects. Contrarily, it seems that the scribe put some thought into this verse, because he wrote out the word πνευματι instead of contracting it as a nomen sacrum, $\overline{\Pi NA}$; this could indicate his perception that this "spirit" referred to the human spirit, not the divine Spirit. This corresponds with John 4:23-24, which reveals that worshipers should worship God (who is Spirit) in spirit and in reality.

Though most of the English versions follow WH NU, the first variant is noted frequently, and the second variant less so, followed only by NEB.

Philippians 3:6

In an attempt to harmonize this verse with Gal 1:13 (a parallel passage which speaks of Paul's persecution of the church prior to his conversion), a few Western witnesses (F G) expand the expression διωκων την εκκλησιαν ("persecuting the church") to διωκων την εκκλησιαν θεου ("persecuting the church of God").

Philippians 3:7

The insertion of αλλα ("but") at the beginning of this verse appears to be a scribal addition, intended to mark a contrast between Paul's behavior before becoming a Christian and his behavior afterwards. This conjunction, though printed in NU, is not found in $\mathfrak{P}^{46}$ $\mathfrak{P}^{61vid}$ ℵ* A G 0282 1739. This is stronger testimony than that which supports its inclusion: $\aleph^2$ B D F Ψ Maj syr cop. Silva (1992a, 182) argues that the corrector of ℵ worked in the same scriptorium as the original scribe of ℵ, and therefore would have added the conjunction to accord with the master text. But in this case it was a second corrector ($\aleph^2$) who made the adjustment; he was part of a group of correctors working in Caesarea in the sixth or seventh century who corrected the text by "bringing it into general conformity with the Byzantine texts" (Metzger 1981, 77).

Philippians 3:10

NU reads [την] κοινωνιαν [των] παθηματων αυτου ("the fellowship of his sufferings") with both articles being bracketed. The documentary evidence in favor of not having the articles ($\mathfrak{P}^{46}$ ℵ* B) is far better than that including them: $\aleph^2$ D F G Ψ Maj, which are Western or Byzantine. Again, Silva (1992a, 195) argues that the corrector of ℵ worked in the same scriptorium as the original scribe of ℵ, and therefore would have added the conjunction to accord with the master text. But in this case it is a second corrector of Codex Sinaiticus who made the adjustments—a scribe of the sixth or seventh century who conformed the manuscript to a Byzantine text type (see note on 3:7).

Philippians 3:12a

The TR WH NU editions read ουχ οτι ηδη ελαβον η ηδη τετελειωμαι ("not that I already attained or have already been perfected"), with the support of $\mathfrak{P}^{61vid}$ ℵ A B D^c P Ψ 33 1739 it^c syr cop. All English versions follow. Some other witnesses have an added, imbedded clause: η ηδη δεδικαιωμαι ("or already have been justified"): $\mathfrak{P}^{46}$ D* (F G) Irenaeus Tertullian.

Given Paul's penchant for proclaiming that justification is an accomplished fact which occurs concurrent with one's faith in Christ, the variant reading is astounding, for it declares that justification is yet to come. What scribe would have invented this addition? Kennedy (1979, 456) argues that some pious scribe added it because "the Divine side of sanctification was left too much out of sight." But if this is so, then a scribe surely would and could have used a term that denotes sanctification, not justification. Others (for example, see Hawthorne 1983, 148) have argued that the addition was drawn from 1 Cor 4:4 or was supplemented to compensate for the lack of a direct object. But the so-called addition does not supply a direct object, and one wonders if any scribe would have thought that this verse was incomplete without 1 Cor 4:4.

The variant reading has three things in its favor: (1) From a documentary perspective, it has early and somewhat diverse testimony; (2) from a transcriptional perspective, it is easy to see how the phrase could have been omitted accidentally, due to homoeoarchton (the eye of a scribe passing from η ηδη in the previous clause to the next η ηδη); and (3) it is the more difficult reading, fraught with exegetical difficulties—not the least of which is that it seems to contradict what Paul himself said a few verses earlier: "that I may gain Christ and be found in him, not having my own righteousness based on the law, but the righteousness which is through faith in Christ, the righteousness of God based on faith" (3:8-9). However, there is not really a contradiction between this statement and the statement that he has not yet been justified. In both instances, the clear implication is that neither has yet been attained. Paul wanted to have this righteousness when Christ returned and thereby be justified for having retained this faith.

Thus, it is a personal call to perseverance and maintenance: to keep that righteousness which he has been given because of his faith—not because of his works. The whole pericope exudes Paul's spiritual aspirations: He wants to gain Christ, he wants to be found with God's righteousness (not his own), he wants perfection, and he wants to attain to the resurrection of the dead. From a doctrinal perspective, one would think that Paul should have been assured of these blessings automatically. But from an experiential perspective, it seems that Paul wanted to own all these experiences prior to his death so that he could be assured existentially that he knew Jesus, was justified, had been perfected, and would participate in the resurrection of the dead. This is what motivated him in his pursuit of Christ.

Philippians 3:12b

The long form of the divine title, Χριστου Ιησου ("Christ Jesus"), appears in early and diverse witnesses: 𝔓[46] 𝔓[61] ℵ A Ψ 1739 Maj. The short form, Χριστου ("Christ"), also has early and diverse witness: B (D[2]) F G 33 Tertullian Clement. Given the scribal tendency to expand divine titles, it is possible that the short form is original. For this reason, Ιησου is bracketed in WH NU.

Philippians 3:13

TR NU	ἐγὼ ἐμαυτὸν οὐ λογίζομαι κατειληφέναι "I count myself not to have laid hold" 𝔓[46] B D[2] F G Ψ Maj syr[h] KJV NKJV RSV NRSV ESV NJB NAB NLT HCSB NET
variant/WH	εγω εμαυτον ουπω λογιζομια κατειληθεναι "I count myself not yet to have laid hold" 𝔓[61vid] ℵ A D* P 33 syr[h**] NRSVmg NASB NIV TNIV NEB REB NLTmg HCSBmg

Since the papyri and other early uncials (ℵ A B) are divided on this reading, textual critics and translators alike are hard-pressed to pick one reading against the other. Nevertheless, the first reading is a slightly better candidate because of the 𝔓[46] B D combination supporting that reading and because it is likely that scribes added "yet" in view of the fact that Paul later in his life claims to have finished the race and expected to receive the prize (see 2 Tim 4:7-8).

Philippians 3:14

TR WH NU read της ανω κλησεως του θεου εν Χριστω Ιησου ("the high calling of God in Christ Jesus"), supported by 𝔓[61vid] ℵ A B D[2] I Ψ 33 1739 Maj it cop, followed by all the English versions. However, there are five variations on this: (1) της ανω κλησεως του θεου εν Ιησου Χριστου ("the high calling of God in Jesus Christ") in 𝔓[16]; (2) της ανω κλησεως εν κυριω Ιησου Χριστου ("the high calling in the Lord Jesus Christ") in F G; (3) της ανω κλησεως του θεου εν κυριω Ιησου Χριστου ("the high calling of God in the Lord Jesus Christ") in D*; (4) της ανω κλησεως θεου ("God's high calling") in 𝔓[46] Ambrosiaster; (5) της ανεγκλησιας του θεου εν Χριστου Ιησου ("the blamelessness before God in Christ Jesus") in 1739[mg] Tertullian.

It is possible that Paul wrote the bare expression, ανω κλησεως θεου ("God's high calling"). This is so ambiguous that scribes would have felt compelled to add some kind of modifier which would describe what this high calling is. All of the scribes recognized from the context that the prize had to do with gaining Christ; so in one way or another a prepositional modifier referring to Christ was appended. Since the modifier occurs in four different ways, it is fair to judge all of them as being secondary. If not, then the added phrase simply reiterates what is clear from the context (see 3:7-13): Paul wanted to gain the prize of knowing Christ Jesus fully. This was Paul's goal ever since his encounter with Jesus on the road to Damascus.

The expression ανω κλησεως ("high calling") is difficult to explain: Is it a high (noble) calling or a calling from above or a calling to go above (i.e., to heaven)? Two witnesses (1739[mg] Tertullian), avoiding the uncertainty, give testimony to what is probably a conjectural surrogate: ανεγκλησιας ("blamelessness"); hence, the verse would read, "I pursue for the prize of being blameless before God in Christ Jesus."

Philippians 3:16

WH NU τῷ αὐτῷ στοιχεῖν
"let us adhere to the same"
𝔓16 𝔓46 ℵ* A B I[vid] 33 1739 cop
NKJVmg RSV NRSV ESV NASB NIV TNIV NEB REB NJB NAB NLT HCSB NET

variant 1/TR τω αυτω στοιχειν κανονι, το αυτο φρονειν
"let us adhere to the same rule, to think the same thing"
ℵ[2] Ψ Maj
KJV NKJV NJBmg NETmg

variant 2 τω αυτο φρονειν, τω αυτω στοιχειν
"let us think the same, to adhere to the same"
(D*) (F G συνστοιχειν)
NETmg

The manuscript evidence overwhelmingly supports the WH NU reading, having witness from the papyri and ℵ* A B I 33 1739 cop. Both variants are scribal expansions intended to elucidate the meaning of τω αυτω στοιχειν. Quite literally, this expression means "to keep step with the same"—as in military marching. In context it means that Christians should keep following those things that effectively work in their lives to promote spiritual transformation. The addition of κανονι ("rule") in the first variant comes from Gal 6:16, where Paul encouraged the believers "to keep in line with the rule (principle)" that in Christ Jesus neither circumcision nor uncircumcision means anything—but a new creation.

Philippians 3:21a

WH NU read συμμορφον τω σωματι της δοξης αυτου ("conforming [it] to his glorious body"), with the support of 𝔓46vid ℵ A B D* F G 1739 it cop. 𝔓46 is not cited in NA[27] in support of WH NU, but the manuscript could not have contained the extra verbiage found in the variant (see *Text of Earliest MSS*, 325). TR reads εις το γενεσθαι αυτο συμμορφον τω σωματι της δοξης αυτου ("so that it might become conformed to his glorious body"), supported by inferior testimony: D[1] Ψ 33 Maj syr. This variant is clearly a late scribal addition, attempting to alleviate Paul's terse syntax. All English versions follow suit.

Philippians 3:21b

NU reads υποταξαι αὐτω τα παντα ("subject to him all things") following the excellent testimony of ℵ* A B D F G P 33 1739 syr. WH makes the pronoun reflexive by reading a rough breathing mark over αὑτω (= "himself"). TR makes the reflexive pronoun more explicit by reading υποταξαι εαυτω τα παντα ("subject to himself all things"), with the support of א² D² L Ψ. But the pronoun αυτω (written with or without a breathing mark in the earliest manuscripts) could also have been read reflexively in ancient times. Hence, the idea, as captured in all English versions, is that Jesus Christ is able to subject all things to himself (a reflexive reading)—as opposed to the idea that Jesus Christ is able to subject all things to him (i.e., God).

Philippians 4:3a

Since the grammar indicates that Paul was speaking to one person, some translators (see NJB NRSVmg NIVmg NLTmg) have understood the expression ερωτω και σε γνησιε συζυγε (normally translated, "I also entreat you, true yokefellow") to refer to a particular individual named Συζυγος ("Syzygus"). Otherwise, the text leaves the "true yokefellow" unnamed. Since all the ancient manuscripts were written with uncials (capital letters), there is no way to determine if ancient scribes designated a proper name, although there is no such name known in the Greco-Roman world (Fee 1995, 393).

Philippians 4:3b

TR WH NU καὶ τῶν λοιπῶν συνεργῶν μου
"and the rest of my coworkers"
𝔓46 א1 A B D Ivid
all

variant και συνεργων μου και των λοιπων
"and my coworkers and the rest"
𝔓16vid א*
NEBmg

The two readings are significantly different. In context, the first reading yields this translation: "They [Euodia and Syntyche] have labored side by side with me in the gospel together with Clement and the rest of my coworkers, whose names are in the book of life." The second reading is as follows: "They [Euodia and Syntyche] have labored side by side with me in the gospel together with Clement and my coworkers and the rest, whose names are written in the book of life."

Some scholars (such as Metzger, see TCGNT) think the textual variant in 𝔓16vid and א* should not be taken seriously because it is the result of scribal error. Other scholars (such as Silva 1992a, 223) urge that it should not be easily dismissed as scribal error, because the evidence of 𝔓16 shows that "it was an early competing variant." And this variant appears to reflect "a different understanding of Paul's words (i.e., that the women and Clement are not included under the category of 'coworkers')." If so, this variant could reflect an antifeminist tendency to exclude women from among those who were considered apostles or co-laborers with the apostles.

In any event, it is possible to interpret both variants as indicating that *all* the ones mentioned have their names written in the book of life. To make this interpretation, one has to consider that the pronoun ων is generically inclusive; it is not restrictive to συνεργων or to λοιπων, but includes all those previously mentioned, including Euodia, Syntyche, Clement, the unnamed coworkers, and the rest.

Philippians 4:7

Most manuscripts say that the peace of God will guard "your hearts and your thoughts" (τας καρδιας υμων και τα νοηματα υμων). But this differs in some Western witnesses (F G it[d]), which read "your hearts and your bodies" (τας καρδιας υμων και τα σωματα υμων). This variant must have been early, because the third-century manuscript, 𝔓[16vid], has a conflated reading: "your hearts and minds and your bodies" (τας καρδιας υμων και τα νοηματα και τα σωματα υμων).

It is not easy to account for how νοηματα ("thoughts") became σωματα ("bodies"), unless, of course, it was miscopied by a scribe. But if it was not a scribal mistake, what would motivate a scribe to change νοηματα to σωματα or vice versa? Divine protection of heart and thoughts speaks of God's superintendence over a believer's psychological life, whereas divine protection of heart and body speaks of God's care over a believer's psychological and physical life. The context guides us to think that Paul was considering God's protection over the believers' thought-life. But in later times, especially when the church was undergoing persecution, it is easy to see how this verse could have been applied to God's complete protection of the believer and subsequently been altered from νοηματα ("thoughts") to σωματα ("bodies").

Philippians 4:13

WH NU	τῷ ἐνδυναμοῦντι με "the one empowering me" ℵ* A B D* I 33 1739 it cop NKJVmg RSV NRSV ESV NASB NIV TNIV NEB REB NJB NAB (NLT) HCSB NET
variant/TR	τω ενδυναμουντι με, Χριστω "the one empowering me, Christ" ℵ[2] D[2] (F G) Ψ Maj syr Jerome KJV NKJV HCSBmg NETmg

The variant is clearly a scribal addition (note the corrections in ℵ and D) intended to make it absolutely clear that it was Christ who empowered Paul (see 1 Tim 1:12). But Paul hardly had to say this. Furthermore, he may have been thinking of "the Spirit of Jesus Christ," because Paul had previously referred to him as the one who supplied all he needed (see 1:19, NEBmg).

Philippians 4:16

The three editions (TR WH NU) read εις την χρειαν μοι επεμψατε ("you sent to my need"), supported by ℵ B F G Ψ 33 1739 Maj. D[1] L P show a change from μοι ("to me") to μου ("my"), the more usual pronoun in this grammatical construction. Both of these readings are anomalous in that there is no object after "sent." 𝔓[46] A 81 correct this anomaly by reading την χρειαν μοι επεμψατε ("you sent money to me"). The variant reading drops the preposition εις, thereby making την χρειαν a direct object. This change could have been purposeful or accidental—due to homoeoteleuton (δις and εις end with the same two letters).

Philippians 4:19

TR WH NU	θεός μου πληρώσει "my God will supply" 𝔓[46] ℵ A B D[2] Maj cop all

variant θεος μου πληρωσαι
"may my God supply"
D* F G Ψ 33 1739 1881
NJBmg

According to TR WH NU, the full statement here is, "my God will supply all your needs according to his riches in glory in Christ Jesus." The variant reading expresses a wish: "May God supply all your needs according to his riches in glory in Christ Jesus." Although it could be argued that the variant is simply a scribal mistake wherein an *alpha* replaced an *eta*, it is not likely that the same mistake would have occurred in such diverse witnesses (both Alexandrian and Western). Rather, it appears that the change was motivated by some scribe (or scribes) who took issue with a statement which promises that God will take care of all our needs.

Since the promise does not always square with our perception, we can imagine why a scribe would want to change it from the future indicative (denoting promise) to the aorist optative (denoting wishfulness). Thus, according to the variant reading (which is noted in NJB), Paul is not promising the Philippians that God *will* supply all their needs; rather, he was praying that God *would* supply all their needs (see Hawthorne 1983, 207-208). But the TR WH NU reading does not have to mean that God gives every believer a carte blanche promissory note. Indeed, the context indicates that Paul promises that God will take care of the Philippians' spiritual needs in response to their taking care of Paul's physical needs.

Philippians 4:23a

WH NU μετὰ τοῦ πνεύματος ὑμῶν
"with your spirit"
𝔓46 ℵ* A B D F G P 1739 cop
NKJVmg RSV NRSV ESV NASB NIV TNIV NEB REB NJB NAB NLT HCSB NET

variant/TR μετα παντων υμων
"with you all"
ℵ2 Ψ Maj syr
KJV NKJV

According to WH NU, the benediction in full reads, "The grace of the Lord Jesus Christ be with your spirit." The variant changes this to "the grace of the Lord Jesus Christ be with you all." Harmonization to the benedictions of other Pauline epistles can be attributed to either variant: the WH NU reading with Gal 6:18 and Phlm 25; the variant with 1 Cor 16:24; 2 Cor 13:14; 2 Thess 3:18; Titus 3:15. Consequently, we must look to the documentary evidence for the original reading. In this case, the WH NU reading clearly has superior attestation. Paul, in his conclusion, emphasizes the need for the believers to experience grace in the spirit. This accords with his earlier exhortation for them to be one in spirit (see 2:1) and with his proclamation that Christians are those who worship God in Spirit (3:3).

Philippians 4:23b

WH NU omit αμην ("Amen") at end of verse
B F G 1739* it[b] cop[sa]
RSV NRSV ESV NASB NIVmg TNIVmg NEB REB NJB NAB NLT HCSB NET

variant/TR include αμην ("Amen") at end of verse
𝔓46 ℵ A D Ψ 33 1739[c] Maj syr cop[bo]
KJV NKJV NRSVmg NIV TNIV NJBmg HCSBmg

By looking at the textual evidence above, it is difficult to determine if Paul concluded this epistle with an "amen," or if this was a scribal addition made in the interest of giving this epistle a satisfactory liturgical ending. Only three epistles (Romans, Galatians, Jude) appear to have a genuine "amen" for the last word. In the other epistles it seems evident that "Amen" was added. But what is perplexing about the above documentation is that 𝔓46 includes the "amen" in Philippians, but not in any other epistles. This testimony probably influenced the NIV and TNIV to include "Amen." Codex Vaticanus, however, consistently excludes the "amen," and this testimony is probably right. (See note on 1 Cor 16:24.)

Subscription

1. No subscription—but placed as an inscription: Προς Φιλιππησιους ("To the Philippians"). Appears in 𝔓46.
2. No subscription. Appears in 365 629 630 1505 2464.
3. Προς Φιλιππησιους ("To the Philippians"). Appears in ℵ A B* (D F G) Ψ 33.
4. Προς Φιλιππησιους εγραφη απο Ρωμης ("To the Philippians written from Rome"). Appears in B[1] 6.
5. Προς Φιλιππησιους εγραφη απο Ρωμης δια Επαφροδιτου ("To the Philippians written from Rome through Epaphroditus"). Appears in 1739 1881 Maj (TR).

As with all the books of the NT, it is quite certain that no book had a title (inscription) or a subscription. (For more on this, see Comfort 2005, 9-10.) This is especially true for the Epistles because their original purpose was to be an apostolic letter, not a literary work per se. Thus, all inscriptions and subscriptions are scribal addenda. The simplest form, Προς Φιλλιππησιους, appears in the earliest witnesses: in 𝔓46 at the head of the epistle; in ℵ A B* at the end. As is typical, the subscription was expanded with the passage of time to include place of writing (Rome) and the amanuensis (Epaphroditus). Many scholars accept Rome as the place from which Paul wrote this epistle, but a few others have argued for Caesarea (see Hawthorne 1983, xxxvi-xliv). As for Epaphroditus, we do not know if he was the amanuensis. Paul did employ the services of secretaries for his letters (see Rom 16:22; 1 Cor 16:21; Gal 6:11; Col 4:18; 2 Thess 3:17), but in the epistle to the Philippians no such specification is given. At best, we can affirm that Epaphroditus delivered the epistle to the Philippians (see 2:25-30).

The Epistle to the COLOSSIANS

Inscription (Title)

𝔓[46] ℵ and B title this epistle as Προς Κολασσαεις ("To the Colossians"). Several other manuscripts (including ℵ and B) have the same title in the subscription (see last note for this book). Paul, however, would not have entitled this epistle in its original composition. Inscriptions and subscriptions are the work of later scribes. (For more on this, see Comfort 2005, 9-10.)

Colossians 1:2a

The earliest manuscripts (𝔓[46vid] ℵ B) read αδελφοις εν Χριστω ("brothers in Christ"), but this was expanded to αδελφοις εν Χριστω Ιησου ("brothers in Christ Jesus") in later manuscripts (A D* F G 33), as a carryover from 1:1 or by way of conformity to the beginnings of other epistles, where Paul uses the phrase "in Christ Jesus" to describe the believers (see 1 Cor 1:2; Eph 1:1; Phil 1:1).

Colossians 1:2b

WH NU	θεοῦ πατρὸς ἡμῶν "God our Father" B D K L Ψ 33 1739 it[a] syr[p] cop[sa] NKJVmg RSV NRSV ESV NASB NIV TNIV NEB REB NJB NAB NLT HCSB NET
variant/TR	θεου πατρος ημων και κυριου Ιησου Χριστου "God our Father and the Lord Jesus Christ" ℵ A C F G I Maj it (syr[h**]) cop[bo] Jerome KJV NKJV NIVmg TNIVmg NJBmg HCSBmg NETmg

Since the manuscript evidence is evenly divided, we have to look for internal evidence to determine the original wording. From a stylistic perspective, it could be convincingly argued that the longer form accords with Pauline style, for Paul almost always included "God the Father" and "the Lord Jesus Christ" when he proclaimed his opening blessings: "grace and peace from God our Father and Lord Jesus Christ" (see Rom 1:7; 1 Cor 1:3; 2 Cor 1:2; Gal 1:3; Eph 1:2; Phil 1:2; 2 Thess 1:2; 1 Tim 1:2; 2 Tim 1:2; Phlm 3). It seems odd that he would have mentioned only the Father here. However, if the epistle had originally included "the Lord Jesus Christ," it is difficult to explain why any scribe would have omitted it. Thus, these arguments cancel each other. In the final analysis, it is likely that Paul mentioned only the Father in this verse because in the next verse Paul extols God as "the Father of our Lord Jesus Christ." As such, he saved the expression "the Lord Jesus Christ" for the next verse, choosing not to use it in 1:2. (A comparable situation occurs in 1 Thess 1:1-2; see note there.)

Colossians 1:3

WH NU εὐχαριστοῦμεν τῷ θεῷ πατρὶ τοῦ κυρίου ἡμῶν
"we give thanks to God, father of our Lord"
𝔓61vid B C* 1739
none

variant 1 ευχαριστουμεν τω θεω τω πατρι του κυριου ημων
"we give thanks to God, the Father of our Lord"
D* F G
RSV NRSV ESV NASB NIV TNIV NEB REB NJB NAB NLT HCSB NET

variant 2/TR ευχαριστουμεν τω θεω και πατρι του κυριου ημων
"we give thanks to the God and Father of our Lord"
ℵ A C2 D1 I Ψ 33 Maj
KJV NKJV

The second variant is most likely scribal harmonizations to normative Pauline expression. (Note the corrections in C and D.) The WH NU reading is unusual in that it characterizes God as being "father of our Lord Jesus Christ," rather than ascribing him the title, "the Father of our Lord Jesus Christ," as in the variants. The first variant yields the title, "God the Father" (reflected in all modern versions because they place the article "the" before "Father"), and TR has God being both the God and Father of Jesus (see also 3:17).

Colossians 1:6

WH NU ἐστὶν καρποφορούμενον καὶ αὐξανόμενον
"it is bearing fruit and growing"
𝔓46 𝔓61vid ℵ A B C D* P 33 1739
NKJVmg RSV NRSV ESV NIV TNIV NEB REB NJB NAB (NLT) HCSB NET

variant 1 και εστιν καρποφορουμενον και αυξανομενον
"and it is bearing fruit and is growing"
D2 F G Ψ Maj syrh
NASB

variant 2/TR εστιν καρποφορουμενον
"it is bearing fruit"
D1 K
KJV NKJV

The manuscript evidence, both early and diverse, overwhelmingly supports the wording in WH NU. The first variant is a scribal adjustment of the syntax of the sentence, whereby the phrase "as also in all the world" is joined to the clause of 1:5, thus: "of which [hope] you heard before in the word of the truth of the gospel, which has come to you, as also in all the world." The second variant is probably the result of a scribal error—due to homoeoteleuton (καρποφορουμενον . . . αυξανομενον).

Colossians 1:7

TR NU	ὑπὲρ ὑμῶν διάκονος "a servant on your behalf" א² C D¹ Ψ 33 1739 Maj it syr cop KJV NKJV RSVmg NRSV ESV NASBmg NIVmg TNIVmg NEBmg REBmg NJBmg NAB NLT HCSB
variant/WH	υπερ ημων διακονος "a servant on our behalf" 𝔓⁴⁶ א* A B D* F G RSV NRSVmg ESVmg NASB NIV TNIV NEB REB NJB NLTmg HCSBmg NET

The NU editors selected the reading with inferior Greek manuscript support on the basis that υμων ("your") appears in many versions and patristic witnesses and that the variant ημων ("our") was probably an assimilation to the preceding pronoun. But the Greek documentary evidence for the variant reading is far superior to that for TR NU, and it is the more difficult reading because it was generally known that Epaphras was a servant to the Colossians. Most modern English versions favored the variant, while noting the other reading in the margin. Epaphras was probably the founder of the church in Colossae. But Paul was looking at his service from a different perspective; Paul saw Epaphras, who was then in Rome, as being one who ministered to him. Paul had the same view of Epaphroditus of Philippi; when Epaphroditus was in Rome, Paul appreciated him as one who ministered to his need (Phil 2:25).

Colossians 1:12a

All the Greek editions (TR WH NU) have the reading ευχαριστουντες τω πατρι ("giving thanks to the Father"), having good support: 𝔓⁶¹ A C* D I^vid Ψ Maj cop^bo,sa. All English versions follow. With respect to the divine title, א reads τω θεω πατρι ("to God, Father"); F and G read τω πατρι θεω ("to Father God"); C³ 075 1739^mg syr^h** support τω θεω και τω πατρι ("to God and the Father"). As was noted in 1:3, scribes were inclined to expand the single-word title "Father" to "God the Father" or "God and Father." In fact, some of the same manuscripts have the same expansions here (see note on 1:3).

All the Greek editions (followed by the English versions) have the following substantival participle: τω ικανωσαντι ("the one qualifying"). The support for this is overwhelming: 𝔓⁴⁶ 𝔓^61vid א A C D² Ψ Maj syr cop^bo. Some manuscripts have the reading τω καλεσαντι ("the one calling")—so D* F G 33 it cop^sa (see NRSVmg). Curiously, B includes both participles (= "the one calling and qualifying").

There is no doubt that Col 1:12-14 contains many allusions to the OT record of how the Israelites were rescued out of Egypt to come to Canaan, where each tribe was given an allotment of the good land. Thus, it is easy to see why scribes would have been more inclined to use the word "call" to represent the divine call to Israel to come out of Egypt into the good land of Canaan. This change was made before the fourth century at the latest because, although it appears in fifth-century Greek manuscripts (and beyond), the reading "calls" shows up in cop^sa, and the fourth-century Vaticanus (B) displays a conflated reading. Paul used "qualified" to indicate that God had made the believers authorized heirs of the inheritance by virtue of their deliverance from Satan's kingdom and transference into Christ's kingdom via redemption (1:13-14).

Colossians 1:12b

WH NU ὑμᾶς
"you"
ℵ B 1739 1881 syr[hmg] cop[sa]
RSVmg NRSV ESV NIV TNIV NEB REB NJB NAB NLT HCSB NET

variant/TR ημας
"us"
A C D F G Ψ 33 Maj it syr cop[bo]
KJV NKJV RSV NRSVmg ESVmg NASB NIVmg TNIVmg NJBmg HCSBmg NETmg

The manuscript evidence slightly favors the WH NU reading, which is followed by nearly all modern versions. The variant is probably the result of scribal conformity to the next verse. Therefore, Paul probably used υμας ("you" plural) to indicate that Gentile Christians had also—along with the Jews—been empowered to participate in the kingdom (cf. Eph 2:19). The "allotment of the saints" is the inheritance once reserved for Israel, now made available to the Gentiles (see Eph 1:11-13).

Colossians 1:14

WH NU τὴν ἀπολύτρωσιν
"the redemption"
ℵ A B C D F G Ψ 075 33 1739
NKJVmg RSV NRSV ESV NASB NIV TNIV NEB REB NJB NAB NLT HCSB NET

variant/TR την απολυτρωσιν δια του αιματος αυτου
"the redemption through his blood"
614 630 syr[h]
KJV NKJV NRSVmg NIVmg NLTmg NETmg

Though Ephesians and Colossians were written at about the same time, the wording in each, though similar in many instances, is rarely a verbatim replication of what is in the other epistle. The variant is an obvious scribal attempt to make Col 1:14 exactly the same as Eph 1:7, a parallel passage. It should be noted that this variant did not appear in a Greek manuscript until the ninth century. Nonetheless, TR has this reading, followed by KJV and NKJV.

Colossians 1:18

TR NU read ος εστιν αρχη ("who is beginning"), supported by ℵ[1] A C D. WH, however, reads ος εστιν η αρχη ("who is the beginning"), with the support of 𝔓[46] B 075 0278 1739. Nearly all manuscripts follow with πρωτοτοκος εκ των νεκρων ("firstborn from the dead"), but 𝔓[46] and ℵ* read πρωτοτοκος των νεκρων ("firstborn of the dead"). One group of witnesses (𝔓[46] B 1739 etc.) include the definite article before αρχη and thereby specify that Christ is the beginning—i.e., the church's beginning, in that he was the first of many to rise from the dead (as is affirmed in the next statement). Another group (ℵ A C D) lacks the article, thereby suggesting that Christ is not just the church's beginning and source, but he is the principal cause of all life, the *arche* of the universe. The manuscripts also vary as to whether the word εκ appears in the text. The reading that excludes it emphasizes that Christ is the first—of many others later—to rise from the dead. The reading that includes it emphasizes that Christ is distinct from all dead people in that he came *out from* their realm—as it says in NJB, "the first to be born from the dead" and in NEB, "the first to return from the dead."

Colossians 1:20a

Many exegetes and translators consider the expression αποκαταλλαξαι τα παντα εις αυτον to mean that God (through Christ) "reconciled all things to himself." They argue this in spite of the fact that αυτον is not reflexive; nonetheless, it is considered to be so by grammarians such as Moule (1953, 119) and was punctuated as reflexive in the critical editions of Griesbach and Scholz.

Colossians 1:20b

The three editions (TR WH NU) include δι αυτου ("through him") in its second occurrence, with the support of 𝔓46 ℵ A C D1 048 Maj syr copbo. But there is substantial support for excluding these words: B D* F G I L 1739 1881 it copsa. In context, the difference is as follows: (1) "having made peace through the blood of his cross, through him, whether the things on earth or the things in heaven"; or (2) "having made peace through the blood of his cross, whether the things on earth or the things in heaven."

The TR WH NU reading does not seem to be the kind of addition scribes would have been prone to make, because it is awkward and obscures the meaning of the verse. Of course, it is possible that it was mistakenly added due to dittography (either from δια του or δι αυτου—previously in the verse). But it is odd that this "mistake" was perpetuated in such a wide variety of witnesses and was never corrected. Thus, it seems that δι αυτου originally stood in the text (as a kind of oral carryover from the beginning of the verse—the product of dictation), and was then deleted by scribes who could not tolerate this redundancy.

Colossians 1:22

(TR) WH NU	ἀποκατήλλαξεν "he reconciled" ℵ A C D2 Ψ 048 (0278) 1739 Maj all
variant 1	αποκατηλλαγατε "you were reconciled" (𝔓46 αποκατηλλαγητε) B NRSVmg NETmg
variant 2	αποκαταλλαγεντες "the one having reconciled" D* F G NETmg
variant 3	αποκατηλλακται "to reconcile" 33 none

The first variant has early support and is the most difficult reading in that it creates anacoluthon between the accusative υμας ("you") with the following infinitive παραστησαι: "you were reconciled . . . to present you." The active voice verb, found in WH NU, assumes this direct object: "yet now he reconciled [you]." As such, it looks like a scribal attempt to correct the anacoluthon. The other two variants appear to be reactions to the passive voice (in the first variant), for had the active voice verb been in the scribes' exemplars, there would be little need to create a variant. Unfortunately, what may be the original reading was not adopted by any version and noted only in the NRSVmg and NETmg.

Colossians 1:23

According to most Greek manuscripts, Paul calls himself a "servant" (διακονος) of the gospel. This title, however, was changed to κηρυξ και αποστολος ("herald and apostle") in ℵ* P, κηρυξ και αποστολος και διακονος ("herald and apostle and servant") in A syr[hmg], and διακονος και αποστολος ("servant and apostle") in 81. These changes show the influence of 1 Tim 2:7 and 2 Tim 1:11.

Colossians 1:27a

The words το πλουτος της δοξης του μυστηριου τουτου ("the wealth of the glory of this mystery") have been shortened in 𝔓46 to το πλουτος του μυστηριου τουτου ("the wealth of this mystery")—probably to simplify a complex expression.

Colossians 1:27b

WH NU ὅ ἐστιν Χριστὸς ἐν ὑμῖν
"which is Christ in you"
𝔓46 A B F G P 33 1739 1881
all

variant/TR ὅς εστιν Χριστος εν υμιν
"who is Christ in you"
ℵ C D H I Ψ 0278 Maj
NKJVmg

The manuscript evidence favors the WH NU reading, which is followed by all versions. The change in the variant is due to respect for Christ's person—namely, that he should not be designated with a neuter pronoun. Hence, the neuter pronoun was replaced with a masculine pronoun. But the neuter is necessary to show that Christ is the wealth (το πλουτος—neuter) of this glorious mystery. He himself, as the fullness of God, provides all spiritual riches to his people.

Colossians 1:28a

The second occurrence of παντα ανθρωπον ("every man") is omitted in D* F G 33 it syr[p], due to homoeoteleuton.

Colossians 1:28b

WH NU τελειον εν Χριστω
"complete in Christ"
𝔓46 ℵ* A B C D* F G 33 1739 cop[bo]
RSV NRSV ESV NASB NIV TNIV NEB REB NJB NAB NLT HCSB NET

variant/TR τελειον εν Χριστω Ιησου
"complete in Christ Jesus"
ℵ[2] D[2] H Ψ 075 0278 Maj cop[sa]
KJV NKJV

The variant is a typical scribal expansion of Jesus' name. Early and diverse witnesses support the shorter form.

Colossians 2:1

A few late Greek manuscripts (104 424), one Vulgate manuscript, and syr[h**] add the words και των εν Ιεραπολει ("and the ones in Hierapolis") after των εν Λαοδικεια ("the ones in Laodicea"). This interpolation was influenced by 4:13, where Paul mentions the believers in Laodicea together with those in Hierapolis, inasmuch as they were neighboring towns and sister churches.

Colossians 2:2

WH NU τοῦ μυστηρίου τοῦ θεοῦ, Χριστοῦ
"the mystery of God, Christ"
𝔓[46] B
NKJVmg RSV NRSV ESV NASB NIV TNIV NEB REB NJBmg NAB NLT HCSB NET

variant 1 του μυστηριου του θεου, ο εστιν Χριστου
"the mystery of God, which is Christ"
D*
NETmg

variant 2 του μυστηριου του θεου
"the mystery of God"
D[1] H P 1881
NJB

variant 3 του μυστηριου του Χριστου
"the mystery of Christ"
81 (1739) it[b]
NJBmg NETmg

variant 4 του μυστηριου του θεου πατρος του Χριστου
"the mystery of God, Father of Christ"
ℵ* A C 048[vid]
NJBmg

variant 5 του μυστηριου του θεου και πατρος του Χριστου
"the mystery of God, even the Father of Christ"
ℵ[2] Ψ 0208
none

variant 6/TR του μυστηριου του θεου και πατρος και του Χριστου
"the mystery of God and of the Father and of Christ"
D[2] Maj syr[h**]
KJV NKJV NRSVmg NJBmg NETmg

The number of variants shows that this text gave scribes a good deal of trouble. (There are actually more variants than these, but the ones above are primary. For more, see Metzger 1992,

233-237.) It seems that the reading in 𝔓[46] and B is the one from which all the other readings deviated—either by clarification (variant 1), abbreviation (variants 2 and 3), or expansion (variants 4-6). Some scholars argue for the abbreviated readings on the basis that they account for all the expansions (so NJB), including the WH NU reading. But the documentary support for these readings is weak. The expansions reveal scribal attempts to make the syntactical relationship between "God" and "Christ" clear. As is, the WH NU reading could mean "the mystery of God, which mystery is Christ" or "the mystery of God, who is Christ," because Χριστου can stand in apposition to the whole phrase or just to θεου. As such, Paul was either affirming that Christ is God's mystery unveiled or that Christ is God. The phrase could also mean "the mystery of God's Christ." Thus, various scribes added "Father" to show that God was the Father of Christ or to show that mystery was both the Father's and Christ's. But this was carried too far in the majority of manuscripts. The point of the passage is that God's mystery is Christ, for he is the embodiment of all the fullness of the Godhead (2:9).

Colossians 2:7a

According to WH NU, the wording is βεβαιουμενοι τη πιστει, which can be rendered "being established in the faith" or "being established by the faith." This has good support: B D* H 0208 33 1881. This reading, whether original or not, indicates that believers are established in the tenets of the Christian faith via the apostolic teaching. In other manuscripts (א D[2] 1739 Maj—so TR), the locative is made explicit by the insertion of εν ("in"). The manuscripts A C I Ψ also have the preposition εν but lack the article before πιστει. These manuscripts indicate that the believers are established because they have an active faith. This reading may be original because its documentary support is as good and because scribes would be tempted, in this context (which deals with the truths of the Christian faith) to add an article rather than delete it. (See comments on next note.) Finally, it should be noted that two other manuscripts (P 048[vid]) read βεβαιουμενοι εν αυτω εν τη πιστει ("being established in him in the faith"). This variant makes the believers established (or firmly founded) in Christ and in the Christian faith.

Colossians 2:7b

NU	περισσεύοντες ἐν εὐχαριστίᾳ "abounding in thanksgiving" א* A C H* I[vid] 33 1739 NKJVmg RSV NRSV ESV NASB NIV TNIV NEB REB NJB NAB NLT HCSB NET
variant 1/TR WH	περισσευοντες εν αυτη εν ευχαριστια "abounding in it with thanksgiving" B D[2] H[c] Maj syr cop[bo] KJV NKJV
variant 2	περισσευοντες εν αυτη "abounding in it" P Ψ 048[vid] none
variant 3	περισσευοντες εν αυτω εν ευχαριστια "abounding in him in thanksgiving" א[2] D* it[b] syr[hmg] none

Curiously, the NU editors rejected a reading supported by A C I in the first part of the verse (see note above) and then accepted a reading supported by A C I here. Such obvious inconsistency reflects the shortcomings of the atomistic eclectic method. The resultant eclectic text was never read by anyone in ancient times. But in this case (as above), it seems likely that A C I (with ℵ* 33 1739) have preserved the original wording. The first variant, included in TR and in WH (with brackets), contains an expansion intended to make it very clear that the abounding is related to the faith (εν αυτη refers back to τη πιστει). The second variant is probably a mistake of a scribe miscopying the first variant and leaving out εν ευχαριστια (TCGNT). The third variant makes "Christ" the one in whom believers abound with thanksgiving.

Colossians 2:10

TR WH NU ὅς ἐστιν ἡ κεφαλή
"who is the head"
ℵ A C Ψ 075 0208 0278 33 1739 Maj
RSV NRSV ESV NASB NIV (TNIV) NEB REB NJB NAB NLT HCSB NET

variant ὅ εστιν η κεφαλη
"which is the head"
𝔓46 B D F G
KJV NKJV

It is far more likely that the neuter pronoun (ὅ) was replaced with a masculine pronoun (ὅς) than vice versa because scribes would want to give due respect to Christ's person. (Most English versions follow suit.) However, the neuter anticipates the identification of Christ as being "head" of the body. Interestingly, the NU editors accepted the neuter in 1:27, supported by several of the same manuscripts (𝔓46 B F G) but rejected it here. Again, this is the result of atomized eclecticism. (NA26 incorrectly listed 𝔓46 both for the text and variant; it is correct in NA27.)

Colossians 2:11

WH NU τοῦ σώματος τῆς σαρκός
"the body of the flesh"
𝔓46 ℵ * A C D* F G 33 1739
NKJVmg RSV NRSV ESV NASB NIV TNIV NEB REB NJB NAB (NLT) HCSB NET

variant/TR του σωματος των αμαρτιων της σαρκος
"the body of the sins of the flesh"
ℵ2 D1 Ψ Maj
KJV NKJV

The reading found in WH NU has the support of all the earliest manuscripts. Imagining that readers might think that Paul was talking about a physical event when speaking about "putting off the body of the flesh" or wishing to clarify what Paul meant by "the flesh," some scribe(s) considered it necessary to clarify the text with the insertion "of sins." But for Paul, the "flesh" is the entire fallen human nature, which has a proclivity to sin. The flesh of humans, which is linked with their body but is not their body, is prone to commit sins.

Colossians 2:12

It is quite likely that βαπτισμω (found in 𝔓46 ℵ2 B D* F G 1739—so NU) was replaced with βαπτισματι in ℵ* A C D2 Ψ 33 Maj (so TR WH) because the latter word is regularly used in the NT for Christian baptism, whereas the former can be used to denote Jewish ceremonial washing (Mark 7:4; Heb 9:10; see Bruce 1984, 102). Though both words mean "baptism," it is significant that Paul would have used a word with Jewish connotations, because in this passage Paul is exulting Christian realities over Jewish ceremony. In Christ, believers have the true circumcision and the true "washing" (ablution/baptism) via their union with Christ's death and burial.

Colossians 2:13

WH NU	συνεζωοποίησεν ὑμᾶς "he made you alive" ℵ* A C K L 1739 NRSV ESV NASB NIV TNIV NEB REB NJBmg NAB NLT HCSB NET
variant 1	συνεζωοποιησεν ημας "he made us alive" 𝔓46 B 33 Origen[according to 1739mg] NRSVmg NIVmg NJB
variant 2/TR	συνεζωοποιησεν "he made alive" ℵ2 D F G Ψ 075 0208 0278 Maj KJV NKJV RSV

Ordinarily, critics would consider the shortest reading (variant 2) to be original, but not in this case because it is obvious that the pronoun was dropped so as not to repeat the υμας at the beginning of the verse: "and you [υμας], who were dead in trespasses and the uncircumcision of your flesh, he made alive." It is difficult, however, to decide between the other two readings because either one of them could have been harmonized to the two other pronouns in this verse: υμας ("you") and ημιν ("us"). However, since ημιν was changed to υμιν in some of the same manuscripts that support WH NU (K L), it is likely that ημας was also changed to υμας. Thus, the first variant, supported by the two earliest manuscripts (𝔓46 B) is probably original. In any event, both readings affirm that God gave spiritual life to all the believers by virtue of their union with the risen Christ.

Colossians 2:18

WH NU	ἃ ἑόρακεν ἐμβατεύων "delving into things which he has seen" 𝔓46 ℵ* A B D* I 33 1739 itb cop Origen MSS[according to Jerome] NKJVmg RSV NRSV ESV NASB NIV TNIV NEB REB NJB NAB NLT HCSB NET
variant 1/TR	α μη εορακεν εμβατευων "delving into things which he has not seen" ℵ2 C D1 Ψ 075 0278 Maj MSS[according to Jerome] (F G ουκ instead of μη) KJV NKJV NJBmg

The WH NU reading has exceedingly superior documentary support and suits the context exactly, for Paul was arguing against the proto-gnostics who based their religion on visions they had seen. These visions of the supernatural—even of angels—puffed up their spiritual pride. Most likely, it was changed to "things which they have not seen" to make these spiritualists look ridiculous: "they delved into things they couldn't even see!" Though the sarcasm is effective for the reader, it misses Paul's point, which is equally sarcastic but more subtle: "they, who claim to be spiritual, base their claims on what they say they have seen—not on what cannot be seen, the true spiritual realities!"

Colossians 2:19

A few manuscripts (D* it^b syr^h) add Χριστον ("Christ") after the first clause, την κεφαλην ("the head"), so as to make it clear Christ is the head. The same addition of "Christ" is made in versions such as the NLT.

Colossians 2:20

WH NU εἰ ἀπεθάνετε σὺν Χριστῷ
"since you died with Christ"
A B C D 0278*
NKJVmg RSV NRSV ESV NASB NIV TNIV NEB REB NJB NAB (NLT) HCSB NET

variant/TR ει ουν απεθανετε συν Χριστω
"since, therefore, you died with Christ"
א^(*),2 0278^c syr^h
KJV NKJV

The manuscript evidence favors the WH NU reading. The addition of ουν presupposes that Paul already spoke of the believers' union with Christ in his death. Although this is implied in 2:11-13, it was not said so explicitly. Thus, Paul was justified in not using ουν here; he saves it for 3:1, where he affirms union with Christ in resurrection—a point he explicitly made before in 2:12-13.

Colossians 2:23

TR WH NU ταπεινοφροσύνῃ [καὶ] ἀφειδίᾳ σώματος
"humility and severe treatment of the body"
א A C D H Ψ 075 Maj syr
KJV NKJV RSV NRSV ESV NASB NIV TNIV NEB REB NAB NLT HCSB NET

variant 1 ταπεινοφροσυνη του νοος και αφειδια σωματος
"humility of the mind and severe treatment of the body"
F G it
none

variant 2 ταπεινοφροσυνη, αφειδια σωματος
"humility, severe treatment of the body"
𝔓46 B 1739
NJB

It is quite likely that the original reading is found in the second variant (supported by the Alexandrian trio, 𝔓46 B 1739), wherein the expression "severe treatment of the body" (as an instrumental dative) describes the prepositional phrase, "in self-imposed worship and false humility." This indicates that the self-imposed worship and resultant humility were carried out by means of the worshiper treating his body harshly (so the rendering in NJB: "a humility which takes no account of the body"). The TR WH NU reading has an additional και ("and") because some scribe(s) considered that there were three objects of the preposition εν ("in"). The first variant is a carryover from 2:18 in that it specifies that this was an "imagined" humility and therefore false.

Colossians 3:4

NU ἡ ζωὴ ὑμῶν
"your life"
𝔓46 ℵ C D* F G P Ψ 075 33
NRSV ESV NIV TNIV NJB NAB NLT HCSB NET

variant/TR WH η ζωη ημων
"our life"
B D[1] H 0278 1739 Maj syr cop[sa]
KJV NKJV RSV NRSVmg NASB NIVmg TNIVmg NEB REB NJBmg NLTmg HCSBmg NETmg

The two Greek pronouns (υμων and ημων) were often confused one for the other because of their similarity in pronunciation and spelling. The editors of NA[26] and UBS[3] adopted the reading supported by 𝔓46 etc. (a change from previous editions of the Nestle text). Several modern versions follow, giving the rendering, "when Christ, your life, is manifested, you will be manifested with him."

Colossians 3:6

TR NU ἔρχεται ἡ ὀργὴ τοῦ θεοῦ [ἐπὶ τοὺς υἱοὺς τῆς ἀπειθείας]
"the anger of God is coming on the sons of disobedience"
ℵ A C D F G H I Ψ 0278 33 1739 Maj syr cop[bo]
KJV NKJV RSVmg NRSV ESV NASB NIVmg TNIVmg NJB NAB NLTmg HCSB NET

variant/WH ερχεται η οργη του θεου
"the anger of God is coming"
𝔓46 B it[b] cop[sa] Clement
RSV NRSVmg ESVmg NASBmg NIV TNIV NEB REB NJBmg NLT HCSBmg NETmg

The variant has early documentary support, and there is no reason why the extra phrase would have been deleted if it originally stood in the text. Thus, it is very likely that the verse was filled out by scribes who thought there should be a direct object after ερχεται ("comes") or wanted this verse to conform to Eph 5:6, a parallel passage. The extra phrase was excluded from WH but was included in UBS[3] and NA[26] (a change from previous editions of the Nestle text), but set within brackets to show the editors' doubts about its authenticity. Most modern translations do not contain this phrase as part of the text; rather, it is listed in the margin. The shorter text conveys the message that God's wrath is coming in reaction to the fornication, uncleanness, passion, evil, desire, and covetousness on earth (4:5); it does not specify who is the object of that wrath, though it can be assumed it will be those who are disobedient to God.

Colossians 3:8

After εκ του στοματος υμων ("from your mouth"), a few Western witnesses (F G it) and the Coptic tradition add μη εκπορευεσθω ("should not proceed")—taken from Eph 4:29, a parallel passage.

Colossians 3:11

To the beginning of the list of the category of peoples that are no longer distinguished because of the creation of the new man (i.e., Greeks, Jews; circumcision, uncircumcision; Barbarian, Scythian; slave, free), some Western witnesses (D* F G it) add αρσεν και θηλυ ("male and female"). This addition, borrowed from Gal 3:28 (a parallel passage), adds completeness to Paul's list.

Colossians 3:13

WH NU ὁ κύριος
"the Lord"
𝔓[46] A B D* F G
RSV NRSV ESV NASB NIV TNIV NEB REB NJB NAB NLT HCSB NET

variant 1/TR ο Χριστος
"the Christ"
ℵ[2] C D[1] Ψ 1739 Maj syr cop
KJV NKJV NRSVmg

variant 2 ο θεος
"God"
ℵ*
none

variant 3 ο θεος εν Χριστω
"God in Christ"
33
none

The WH NU reading has excellent documentary support, producing the rendering: "Forgive one another, even as the Lord forgave you" (so all modern versions). The variants can be explained as follows: The first is a scribal interpretation of "Lord" as equaling "Christ." The second variant is the result of some scribe perceiving it as "God's" responsibility to forgive sins—probably influenced by Eph 4:32, a parallel passage. The third variant comes directly from Eph 4:32. Paul used "Lord" in Colossians to show that all spiritual blessings, including forgiveness, come from the Lord Jesus, for he is the Redeemer and Reconciler (1:14, 19-21).

Colossians 3:14

By way of conformity to Eph 4:3, a parallel passage, several Western witnesses (D* F G it) read συνδεσμος της ενοτητος ("bond of unity") instead of συνδεσμος της τελειοτητος ("bond of completion").

Colossians 3:15

WH NU ἡ εἰρήνη τοῦ Χριστοῦ
"the peace of Christ"
ℵ* A B C* D F G P 1739 it syr cop Clement
RSV NRSV ESV NASB NIV TNIV NEB REB NJB NAB NLT HCSB NET

variant/TR η ειρηνη του θεου
"the peace of God"
א² C² D² Ψ 33 Maj
KJV NKJV

By way of conformity to Phil 4:7, a parallel passage, several late manuscripts changed "peace of Christ" to "peace of God." The lateness of corrections in a number of manuscripts (none earlier than the sixth century) reveals the secondary nature of the variant reading. Throughout this epistle, Paul emphasizes the preeminence of Christ in all phases of the Christian life. Thus, Paul is here affirming that, when there are differences among the members of Christ's body, the peace of Christ is the arbiter.

Colossians 3:16a

TR WH NU ὁ λόγος τοῦ Χριστοῦ
"the word of Christ"
𝔓⁴⁶ א² B C² D F G Ψ 1739 Maj it cop^sa
all

variant 1 ο λογος του θεου
"the word of God"
A C* 33
NRSVmg NASBmg NJBmg NETmg

variant 2 ο λογος του κυριου
"the word of the Lord"
א* I cop^bo
NRSVmg NASBmg NJBmg NETmg

In the margin of NJB, the translators conjectured that "possibly the text reads simply 'the word.'" But there is no textual evidence for this shortened reading. Thus, we do not have a situation here where a simple expression, "the word," was expanded in three ways. Rather, it is far more likely that the more unusual expression, "the word [message] of Christ," was changed to one of two more ordinary expressions. The documentary evidence strongly favors "the word of Christ," as does the general tenor of the epistle, which is aimed at exalting Christ (see note on 3:15).

Colossians 3:16b

WH NU τῷ θεῷ
"to God"
𝔓⁴⁶ א A B C* D* F G Ψ^c 33 1739 it syr cop Clement
RSV NRSV ESV NASB NIV TNIV NEB REB NJB NAB NLT HCSB NET

variant/TR τω κυριω
"to the Lord"
C² D² Ψ* Maj
KJV NKJV NRSVmg NEBmg

At the end of this verse, Paul says, "singing in your hearts to God," according to superior documentary evidence. 𝔓⁴⁶, the earliest witness for the WH NU reading, was mistakenly transcribed by Kenyon (1936, 134) to read the nomen sacrum for "Lord" ($\overline{\text{K}\Omega}$), but the broken letters are *theta* and *omega* ($\overline{\Theta\Omega}$ = "God"; see *Text of Earliest MSS,* 331), not *kappa* and *omega* ($\overline{\text{K}\Omega}$). Tasker (1964, 439) followed Kenyon in thinking that 𝔓⁴⁶ supported the variant reading. But 𝔓⁴⁶ affirms the WH NU text. The variant reading is the result of scribal conformity to Eph 5:19, a parallel passage.

Colossians 3:17a

TR WH NU read κυριου Ιησου ("Lord Jesus"), with excellent support: 𝔓[46] B D[2] 075 (Ψ) 33 1739 Maj syr[h] cop[sa] Clement. All English versions follow this, yielding the rendering, "do all things in the name of the Lord Jesus." There are three variants on this name: (1) Ιησου Χριστου ("Jesus Christ") in A C D* F G; (2) κυριου Ιησου Χριστου ("Lord Jesus Christ") in (ℵ[2] it[b] syr[p]) cop; (3) κυριου ("Lord") in L and Jerome.

The name "Jesus" was subject to textual change all throughout the transmission of the NT text. It was either altered, expanded, inverted with other titles, or occasionally shortened. In most instances, the text critic has to determine which reading has the best documentation and then explain why the variant readings are aberrations. In this case, the TR WH NU reading has good testimony, as does the first variant; but the weight goes to TR WH NU because it has both early and more diverse support. The second variant is the result of scribal conformity to Eph 5:20, a parallel passage. The third variant, though the shorter reading, cannot be preferred because of its slim documentary support.

Colossians 3:17b

WH NU εὐχαριστοῦντες τῷ θεῷ πατρί
"giving thanks to father God [or, God the Father]"
𝔓[46vid] ℵ A B C 1739 it
NKJV RSV NRSV ESV NASB NIV TNIV NEB REB NJB NAB NLT HCSB NET

variant/TR ευχαριστουντες τω θεω και πατρι
"giving thanks to God and [the] Father"
D F G Ψ 33 Maj
KJV

The variant is the result of scribal conformity to Eph 5:20, a parallel passage. The WH NU reading has excellent documentation and is unusual, for we rarely see the words τω θεω πατρι as a title for "God the Father." As was explained in the note on 1:3, it is more likely that the expression means something like "Father God."

Colossians 3:18

WH NU ὑποτάσσεσθε τοῖς ἀνδράσιν
"be subject to the (= your) husbands"
𝔓[46] ℵ A B C (D* F G it syr add υμων = "your")
RSV NRSV ESV NASB NIV TNIV NEB REB NJB NAB NLT HCSB NET

variant/TR υποτασσεσθε τοις ιδιοις ανδρασιν
"be subject to your own husbands"
L 6 1881
KJV NKJV

The addition of υμων (in D* F G) and ιδιοις are attempts to clarify that τοις ανδρασιν really means "your husbands" or "your own husbands." Actually, the definite article τοις sufficiently indicates the possessive function. The variant, in TR, shows conformity to Eph 5:22, a parallel passage.

Colossians 3:19

Several scribes tried to clarify that ταϛ γυναικαϛ (found in 𝔓[46] א* A B C* D[2] Ψ Maj) means "your wives" by adding υμων (= "your"; so C[2] D* F G it syr) or εαυτων (= "your own"; so א[2] 075). The definite article ταϛ sufficiently indicates the possessive function (see note on 3:18). Similar variants occur in Eph 5:25, a parallel passage.

Colossians 3:21

All three Greek editions (TR WH NU) have the wording μη ερεθιζετε ("do not aggravate," "do not provoke"), with the support of 𝔓[46] B D[1] Ψ 1739 Maj Clement. All English versions follow. A variant on this is μη παροργιζετε ("do not anger"), found in a substantial number of manuscripts (א A C D* F G L 0198 0278 33). However, this variant reading is the result of scribal conformity to Eph 6:4, a parallel passage. The TR WH NU reading has a different word in Colossians than what appears in Ephesians. In Colossians Paul was urging the fathers not to "aggravate" their children—that is, they should not provoke them to the extent that they become bitter and subsequently disheartened. In Ephesians Paul was commanding the fathers not to make their children angry, for that also would lead to apathy. The difference is subtle but significant. Since the children are exhorted to be obedient to their parents, fathers could take advantage of this by making unreasonable demands on their children. Thus, children would be aggravated or irritated by these weighty demands and then give up trying to please their parents.

Colossians 3:22a

All three Greek editions (TR WH NU) have the wording υπακουετε κατα παντα ("obey in every way"), with the support of א A B C D Maj. All English versions follow. Some manuscripts, however, exclude κατα παντα ("in every way")—so 𝔓[46] 075 0278 cop[sa]. The variant is likely the result of scribal conformity to Eph 6:5, a parallel passage.

Colossians 3:22b

WH NU — φοβούμενοι τὸν κύριον
"fearing the Lord"
א* A B C D* F G L Ψ 048 33 1739 it syr cop Clement
RSV NRSV ESV NASB NIV TNIV NEB REB NJB NAB NLT HCSB NET

variant/TR — φοβουμενοι τον θεον
"fearing God"
𝔓[46] א[2] D[2] Maj it[d]
KJV NKJV

Although the WH NU reading has excellent documentary support, it is possible that it is the product of scribal assimilation to Eph 6:7 (a parallel passage), which speaks of "serving the Lord," or the result of scribal conformity to the following verse (3:23), which speaks of working for "the Lord." Given the pattern of textual harmonization of wording in Colossians to the wording of Ephesians (see above notes), it is not unreasonable to think the same happened here. If so, then the earliest witness (𝔓[46]) supports the original reading, "God," as well as two corrected manuscripts and the Majority Text.

Colossians 3:23

TR WH NU	τῷ κυρίῳ καὶ οὐκ ἀνθρώποις "to the Lord and not to men" א C D Maj KJV NKJV NRSV ESV NASB NEB REB NJB NAB NLT HCSB NET
variant 1	τω κυριω δουλευοντες και ουκ ανθρωποις "serving the Lord and not men" A 075 Clement RSV NIV TNIV
variant 2	τω κυριω, ουκ ανθρωποις "to the Lord, not to men" 𝔓46 B 1739 none

The first variant is the result of scribal conformity to Eph 6:7, a parallel passage. The TR WH NU reading, with an added και ("and"), is probably also the result of scribal conformity to Eph 6:7. If so, the original text has been preserved in the Alexandrian trio, 𝔓46 B 1739, even though it is not followed by one translation.

Colossians 3:24

WH NU	τῷ κυρίῳ Χριστῷ δουλεύετε "serve [or, you are serving] the Lord Christ" 𝔓46 א A B C D* 33 1739 NKJVmg RSV NRSV ESV NASB NIV TNIV NEB REB NJB NAB NLT HCSB NET
variant 1/TR	τω γαρ κυριω Χριστω δουλευετε "because you are serving the Lord Christ" D[1] Ψ Maj syr Clement KJV NKJV
variant 2	του κυριου ημων Ιησου Χριστου ω δουλευετε "our Lord Jesus Christ whom you serve" F G none

The first of the two variants emends the apparent abruptness created by the final clause ("serve the Lord Christ") by making it causal: "you will receive the recompense of the inheritance because you serve the Lord Christ." The second variant also emends the abruptness but in so doing creates its own strangeness: "*from the Lord* . . . you will receive an inheritance of *our Lord* Jesus Christ." Accepting the WH NU reading, the final clause can be taken as an imperative or as an indicative because δουλευετε can be parsed either way. The imperative helps the clause stand alone; at the same time, it forms a bridge between what precedes and what follows.

Colossians 3:25

All three editions (TR WH NU) have the reading ουκ εστιν προσωποληνψια ("there is no respect of persons") on the basis of good authority: 𝔓46 א A B C D Maj. A few manuscripts (F G I) add the clarification: παρα τω θεω ("with God") by way of conformity to Eph 6:9, a parallel verse. But it is implicit in the text that it is God who is no respecter of persons.

Colossians 4:3

By way of conforming this verse to the parallel verse in Ephesians (Eph 6:19), the scribe of A added εν παρρησια ("with boldness") before λαλησαι ("to speak"). Further assimilation occurred in B* L 614 and some Coptic Sahidic manuscripts, whereby the expression το μυστηριον του Χριστου ("the mystery of Christ") became το μυστηριον του θεου ("the mystery of God") under the influence of 2:2. But in 2:2 Christ is identified as "the mystery of God" because he is the very unveiling of God in the flesh, whereas here Paul speaks of proclaiming the mystery of the gospel, which is Christ himself. For Paul to preach the gospel was to preach Christ. This is especially pronounced in his Epistle to the Colossians, where Paul extols Christ above all.

One other slight change follows. In B F G the text reads δι ον και δεδεμαι ("for whom also I have been bound"), instead of δι ο και δεδεμαι ("for which also I have been bound"). The change in B F G links Paul's imprisonment with his service to God or Christ; the text links it with his service to the gospel. The latter has better textual ($\mathfrak{P}^{46vid}$ ℵ A C D Maj) and contextual support.

Colossians 4:8

WH NU	ἵνα γνῶτε τὰ περὶ ἡμῶν "that you might know the things concerning us" A B D* F G P 048 075 0278 33 it NKJVmg RSV NRSV ESV NASB NIV TNIV NEB REB NJB NAB NLT HCSB NET
variant 1	ινα γνωτε τα περι υμων "that you might know the things concerning you" ℵ* 1241[s] none
variant 2/TR	ινα γνω τα περι υμων "that I might know the things concerning you" $\mathfrak{P}^{46}$ ℵ[2] C D[1] Ψ 1739 Maj syr cop[bo,sa] NRSVmg NJBmg (KJV NKJV TNIVmg HCSBmg understand γνω to be "he might know")

In context, Paul was saying that he had sent Tychicus to the Colossians so that they could stay in communication with Paul. The textual issue pertains to an identification of pronouns. Metzger (TCGNT) argues that the two variants could in no way be original. The first is a scribal error (confusing ημων for υμων) that produced a nonsensical statement, and the second is a scribal adjustment to the first variant—wherein τε was dropped from γνωτε (see Lightfoot 1879, 255). However, it seems unlikely that this latter change would have occurred in such a vast array of witnesses and at such an early date (prior to $\mathfrak{P}^{46}$ of the second century). Furthermore, though the second variant is not as compatible to the context as the WH NU reading, the second variant still makes sense. This is illustrated in the alternative rendering in the NRSV: "I have sent him to you for this very purpose, that I may know how you are, and that he may encourage your hearts" (NRSVmg). Of course, the difficulty with this statement is that in the surrounding verses (4:7, 9) Paul said he was sending Tychicus to tell the Colossians how he (Paul) was doing. So we are at a crossroads: Do we accept the reading that makes sense but could also be a harmonization to Eph 6:22, a parallel verse? Or do we take the more difficult reading, which makes sense by itself but is jarring when read in context? Bruce (1984, 176) admits that this is a situation where the documentary evidence is evenly balanced, so it might be best to adopt the maxim that the "more difficult reading is to be preferred."

Finally, it should be noted that in the early manuscripts the word γνω would have been unaccented. In our present system, a circumflex over the vowel (γνῶ) makes it first person singular aorist (as in the translation above, "that I may know"), whereas a circumflex and an *iota* subscript with the vowel (γνῷ) makes it a third person singular variant (as in the KJV and NKJV translations, "that he [Tychicus] may know"; so also TNIVmg HCSBmg). If the latter reading was the intent of Paul, then the contextual problem is lessened: "I sent Tychicus so that he might know the things concerning you."

Colossians 4:12

WH NU	δοῦλος Χριστοῦ ['Ιησοῦ] "slave of Christ Jesus" א A B C I L 0278 33 RSV NRSV ESV NIV TNIV NJB NAB NLT HCSB NETmg
variant 1	δουλος Ιησου Χριστου "slave of Jesus Christ" P 1241[s] NASB
variant 2/TR	δουλος Χριστου "slave of Christ" 𝔓[46] D F G Ψ 1739 Maj it syr KJV NKJV NEB REB NET

Since the documentary evidence is almost evenly divided between WH NU and the second variant and since the tendency of scribes was to expand the name of Christ, it is likely that "Christ Jesus" and "Jesus Christ" are expansions. (Ιησου is bracketed in NU.) KJV and NKJV reflect their allegiance to TR; NEB, REB, and NET align with TR because of the testimony of 𝔓[46] and a score of other witnesses and because they considered the variants to be expansions. Curiously, NASB follows a reading with little support.

Colossians 4:13

WH NU	πόνον "labor" א A B C P RSV NRSV ESV NIV TNIV NEB REB NJB NAB NLT HCSB NET
variant 1	κοπον "travail" D* F G none
variant 2	αγωνα "struggle" 6 1739 1881 none
variant 3/TR	ζηλον "zeal" D[1] Ψ 075 33 Maj syr KJV NKJV NASB HCSBmg

All the variants are lexically viable but not good candidates for having originated from Paul, on the basis of the textual evidence. Paul's point is that the Colossians should appreciate Tychicus's hard labor (πονον) for them. The NKJVmg is misleading in that it indicates that the NU text says that Tychicus had "concern" for them (so NASB); πονος can mean either "hard labor" or "pain" or "distress" (see BDAG 852), but it does not mean "concern."

Colossians 4:15

WH NU	Νύμφαν καὶ τὴν κατ' οἶκον αὐτῆς ἐκκλησίαν "Nympha and the church in her house" B 0278 1739 1881 syr[h] cop[sa] NKJVmg RSV NRSV ESV NASB NIV TNIV NEB REB NJB NAB NLT HCSB NET
variant 1/TR	Νυμφᾶν και την κατ οικον αυτου εκκλησιαν "Nymphas and the church in his house" D (F G) Ψ Maj syr[p,hmg] KJV NKJV NASBmg NEBmg REBmg NETmg
variant 2	Νύμφαν και την κατ οικον αυτων εκκλησιαν "Nympha and the church in their house" א A C P 33 cop[bo] NETmg

The textual problem in this verse is complex. Paul first says, "the brothers in Laodicea greet you." According to Paul's terminology, "the brothers in Laodicea" equals "the church in Laodicea" (cf. Phil 1:1; 4:21) because all the Christians in a particular locality comprise the church in that locality. Then Paul adds, "and Nymphas." This is a special salutation: "Greet the church—and especially Nymphas." Then Paul adds, "and the church at (his, her, or their) house." Three different pronouns appear in the manuscripts: "her" in B etc., "his" in D Maj, and "their" in א A C. If Nymphas was a man, it is quite correct to say "the church in his house"; if Nymphas was a woman, it is of course correct to say "the church in her house." Unfortunately, Nymphas's gender cannot be determined from the earliest Greek manuscripts, which did not accent the name Νυμφας; later MSS (as those used for TR) would have accented it with a circumflex over the last vowel so as to indicate a masculine name. Modern Greek editions (WH NU) have an acute accent over the first vowel to indicate a feminine name (cf. a similar case in Rom 16:7 concerning Junias [masculine] or Junia [feminine]). Given this dilemma of determining the gender of the person so named, various scribes used different pronouns before "house."

It is far more likely that the pronoun "her" was changed to "his" than vice versa because it would be perceived that a man, not a woman, hosted the church. However, we know that women did host churches in their homes; Mary, the mother of John Mark, hosted an assembly of believers in Jerusalem (Acts 12:12). Avoiding the problem of "his" or "her," other manuscripts read, "their house." But this creates another problem because "the brothers in Laodicea" is equal to "the church in Laodicea"—and how could the church in Laodicea have the church in their house? It is to avoid this problem that scholars (see Alford 1852, 2:246) suggest that the Greek word for "their" (αυτων) refers only to the ones with Nymphas (i.e., the members of his household) and not to "the brothers in Laodicea."

Whether the reading was "her house" or "their house," a particular group of believers within the church of Laodicea met there. Their meeting could legitimately be called an *ekklesia,* an assembling together. In other words, this church meeting in Nymphas's house would probably be one of several home meetings—all part of the one local church in Laodicea. Paul was sending a greeting to the entire church at Laodicea and to a particular gathering of believers who met at Nymphas's house (see Rom 16:5; 1 Cor 16:19-20 for a similar kind of greeting to a particular assembly of Christians within a local church). If the entire church met at Nymphas's house, it would be redundant for Paul to say, "Greet the brothers in Laodicea and the church at Nymphas's house."

Colossians 4:18

WH NU	omit αμην ("Amen") at end of verse
	𝔓[46vid] א* A B C F G 048 33 1739* cop[sa]
	RSV NRSV ESV NASB NIV TNIV NEB REB NJB NAB NLT HCSB NET
variant/TR	include αμην ("Amen") at end of verse
	א[2] D Ψ 075 0278 1739[c] Maj it syr
	KJV NKJV NRSVmg NJBmg HCSBmg NETmg

𝔓[46] is not cited in NA[27] or UBS[4] in support of the exclusion of αμην at the end of the verse. A reconstruction of the last line of Colossians (which has some text showing) reveals that the line would not have allowed for the inclusion of αμην and that the word does not appear on the next line (see *Text of Earliest MSS,* 333). According to the textual evidence, it is obvious that "amen" is a later scribal addition. Only three epistles (Romans, Galatians, Jude) appear to have a genuine "amen" for the last word. In the other epistles, as here, it is evident that an "amen" was added for liturgical purposes.

Subscription

1. No subscription—but placed as an inscription: Προς Κολασσαεις ("To the Colossians"). Appears in 𝔓[46].
2. No subscription. Appears in 323 365 629 630 1505 2464.
3. Προς Κολοσσαεις ("To the Colossians"). Appears in א B* C (D F G) Ψ 048 33.
4. Προς Κολοσσαεις εγραφη απο Ρωμης ("To the Colossians written from Rome"). Appears in (A) B[1] P.
5. Προς Κολοσσαεις εγραφη απο Ρωμης δια Τυχικου και Ονησιμου ("To the Colossians written from Rome through Tychicus and Onesimus"). Appears in 075 1739 1881 Maj (so TR).
6. Παυλου αποστολου επιστολη προς Κολοσσαεις εγραφη απο Ρωμης δια Τυχικου ("Epistle of Paul the apostle to the Colossians written from Rome through Tychicus"). 0278.

As with all the books of the NT, it is quite certain that no book originally had an inscription or a subscription. This is especially true for the Epistles because their original purpose was to be an apostolic letter, not a literary work per se. Thus, all inscriptions and subscriptions are scribal addenda. The simplest form, "To the Colossians," appears in the earliest witnesses: in 𝔓[46] at the head of the epistle; in א (A) B* at the end. As is typical, the subscription was expanded to include the place of writing (Rome) and the carriers of the epistle (Tychicus and Onesimus—see 4:7-9).

The First Epistle to the THESSALONIANS

Inscription (Title)

𝔓[46] ℵ and B title this epistle as Προς Θεσσαλονικεις Α ("To the Thessalonians A" = "1 Thessalonians"). Several other manuscripts (including ℵ and B) have the same title in the subscription (see last note for this book). Paul, however, would not have entitled this epistle in its original composition. Inscriptions and subscriptions are the work of later scribes. (For more on this, see Comfort 2005, 9-10.)

1 Thessalonians 1:1

WH NU χάρις ὑμῖν καὶ εἰρήνη
"grace to you and peace"
B F G Ψ 0278 1739 it cop[sa]
NKJVmg RSV NRSV ESV NASB NIV TNIV NEB REB NJB NAB NLT HCSB NET

variant/TR χαρις υμιν και ειρηνη απο θεου πατρος ημων και κυριου Ιησου Χριστου
"grace to you and peace from God our Father and the Lord Jesus Christ"
ℵ A (D) I 33 Maj syr[h**] cop[bo]
KJV NKJV NIVmg HCSBmg NETmg

Had the phrase "from God our Father and the Lord Jesus Christ" originally been in the text, there is no good reason to explain why scribes would delete it. Rather, it is easier to understand why it was added. In the introduction to nearly all of his epistles, Paul gave the blessing of grace and peace as coming from God the Father and the Lord Jesus Christ (see Rom 1:7; 1 Cor 1:3; 2 Cor 1:2; Gal 1:3; Eph 1:2; Phil 1:2; 2 Thess 1:2; 1 Tim 1:2; 2 Tim 1:2; Phlm 3). Thus, it would seem very unusual to some scribes for it not to be the same here; consequently, the verse was conformed to Pauline style. But Paul chose not to use the expression "God the Father and Lord Jesus Christ" twice in a row (the first part of the verse reads, "to the church of the Thessalonians in God the Father and Lord Jesus Christ"), so he shortened the blessing to "Grace to you and peace." (See note on Col 1:2 for a similar change.)

1 Thessalonians 1:5

Most witnesses affirm the reading, το ευαγγελιον ημων ("our gospel"), an expression that appears only two other places in Paul's epistles—2 Cor 4:3; 2 Thess 2:14. Disturbed, perhaps, by Paul calling the gospel "our gospel," one scribe (C) changed it to το ευαγγελιον του θεου ("the gospel of God") and another (א*) to το ευαγγελιον του θεου ημων ("the gospel of our God"). But Paul also had a habit of calling the gospel "my gospel" or "the gospel I preach" in an effort to affirm the apostolic authority of his gospel message (Rom 2:16; Gal 1:11).

1 Thessalonians 1:6

Most manuscripts read μετα χαρας πνευματος αγιου ("with joy of the Holy Spirit" = "with joy that comes from the Holy Spirit"). B (and a few Vulgate MSS) reads μετα χαρας και πνευματος αγιου ("with joy and the Holy Spirit"), which produces the translation, "you received the word in much affliction with joy and with the Holy Spirit."

1 Thessalonians 1:7

WH NU γενέσθαι ὑμᾶς τύπον
"you [plural] became an example"
B D*,c 33 1739 it syr^p
RSV NRSV ESV NASB NIV TNIV NEB REB NJB NAB NLT HCSB NET

variant/TR γενεσθαι υμας τυπους
"you [plural] became examples"
א A C D² F G Ψ 0278 Maj syr^h
KJV NKJV NETmg

The textual evidence for the two readings is evenly divided. The WH NU reading affirms the truth that the Thessalonians as a corporate body were an example to be emulated by all the believers in Macedonia. The variant reading presents the view that the individual believers in Thessalonica were examples to all the believers in Macedonia.

1 Thessalonians 2:7

WH NU ἐγενήθημεν νήπιοι ἐν μέσῳ ὑμῶν
"we were infants in your midst"
𝔓65 א* B C* D* F G I Ψ* it cop^bo
RSVmg NRSVmg ESVmg NASBmg TNIV NJBmg NABmg NLT HCSBmg NET

variant/TR εγενηθημεν ηπιοι εν μεσω υμων
"we were gentle in your midst"
א^c A C² D² Ψ^c 0278 33 1739 Maj
KJV NKJV RSV NRSV ESV NASB NIV NEB REB NJB NAB NLTmg HCSB

There is a one-letter difference (*nu*) between the two readings: νηπιοι ("infants"); ηπιοι ("gentle"). Concerning transcriptional errors, it is difficult to know which reading produced the other. The first word (νηπιοι) could have been created by dittography—the preceding word (εγενηθημεν) ends in *nu;* or the second word (ηπιοι) could have been created by haplography—also influenced by the preceding word. The variant reading seems to be the most natural in context—especially in connection with the following metaphor: "we were gentle in your midst, like a nursing mother caring for her children."

However, there are several arguments against this. First, several manuscripts (א C D Ψ) originally had the first reading, but were later corrected. This strongly suggests that scribes and correctors had a problem with the meaning of the wording νηπιοι and then made an emendation. Second, the WH NU reading has early and diverse attestation, including 𝔓65 (third century). Third, Westcott and Hort (1882, 128) argue that the adjective ηπιοι ("gentle") is not compatible with the expression εν μεσω υμων ("in your midst"). The appropriate word should be a noun, not an adjective.

But none of these arguments overcome the obstacle that the WH NU reading seems to create a very contorted metaphor: "we were infants in your midst, like a nursing mother caring for her children." Yet it can be explained. Fowl (1990, 469-473) notes that such mixing of metaphors is consistent with Pauline style. And Morris (1984, 56-57) notes that in this very same chapter Paul likens himself to a father (2:11) and then an orphan (2:17 απορφανισθεντες = "made orphans by separation"). Indeed, this word, a *hapax legomenon* in the NT, suggests that Paul was thinking of himself (metaphorically) as being a child who had been separated from his loved ones. His brief time with the Thessalonians, cut short by persecution and subsequent forced departure, caused him (and his coworkers) to acutely sense their separation. Thus, he used an emotive image in which he pictured himself as a child who had been orphaned from his parents. In like manner, in 2:7-8 he pictured himself as an infant in their midst to show that he was guileless, innocent, and unpretentious (see 2:3-6). In other words, he had no intention to take advantage of them. As such, the image of a child works. (See Sailors 2000, 81-98, for further discussion on Paul's mixing of metaphors).

The majority of editors of UBS[3] and NA[26] decided to adopt the word νηπιοι because it has the earliest support (𝔓[65] providing the earliest witness) and because it is the more difficult reading. Consequently, the Nestle text was changed to read νηπιοι. But two of the editors, Metzger and Wikgren, did not agree with the choice. However, they suggested that if this reading must be in the text, the punctuation must be changed (see TCGNT). Perhaps a change in punctuation could justify the following kind of translation of 2:7-8:

> [7]As apostles of Christ, we could have made demands on you, but we were infants in your midst. We were as a nursing mother who cares for her children—[8]being so affectionately desirous of you, we were willing to impart to you not the gospel of God only, but also our own souls, because you became dear to us.

In this way, the two metaphors of 2:7 are separated. The statement in 2:7a summarizes the message of apostolic purity in 2:3-6, and the statement in 2:7b is appropriately connected with 2:8.

Three recently published English translations (NLT, TNIV, and NET) have followed the reading of the best text. Taking the lead were the translators of the NLT, which nicely separates the metaphors: "we were like children among you. We were like a mother feeding and caring for her own children." The NRSV deviates from the standard text at this point, under the influence of Metzger (head of the committee for the NRSV), who disagreed with the majority vote for the NU text (see above). Several translations provide a marginal note citing the reading "infants" out of deference to its presence in all the earliest MSS.

1 Thessalonians 2:10 and 2:12

Most manuscripts in 2:10 speak of the Thessalonians as τοις πιστευουσιν ("the ones believing")—the present tense denoting their ongoing faith in Christ. But the earliest extant manuscript for this verse, namely 𝔓[65vid], and most Old Latin manuscripts designate them as τοις πιστευσασιν ("the ones having believed")—the aorist tense denoting the point of conversion under Paul's ministry. In 2:12 good textual evidence (B D F G 33 1739) affirms the ongoing nature of God's call to the believers, for God is identified as "the one calling you into his own kingdom" (του καλουντος υμας εις την εαυτου βασιλειαν). But this was changed in some manuscripts (א A) and ancient versions (it syr cop) to an aorist participle, which then identifies God as "the one having called you" (του καλεσαντος υμας). This reading emphasizes God's initial call to salvation, whereas the present tense focuses on God's continual calling.

1 Thessalonians 2:15

WH NU τοὺς προφήτας
"the prophets"
א A B D* F G I 0278 33 1739 it cop Origen
RSV NRSV ESV NASB NIV TNIV NEB REB NJB NAB NLT HCSB NET

variant/TR τους ιδιους προφητας
"their own prophets"
D[1] Ψ Maj syr Marcion
KJV NKJV NRSVmg NEBmg NETmg

The fuller context helps us understand the significance of the textual variant. Paul was speaking of the Thessalonians being persecuted by the Jews, "who both killed the Lord Jesus and the prophets." According to Tertullian (*Marc.* 5.15.1), Marcion altered the reading, "the prophets" to "their own prophets"—probably in an attempt to make the Jews even more culpable: "they [the Jews] killed the Lord Jesus and their very own prophets." Marcion's interpolation had its effect on the textual tradition, as is evidenced by the same interpolation being in several later witnesses and by finding its way into TR (and so into KJV and NKJV).

1 Thessalonians 2:16

The aorist verb εφθασεν ("overtook"), found in א A D[2] F G 33 1739 Maj, appears as a perfect tense εφθακεν ("has overtaken") in B D*,c Ψ 0278. Either way, the verb denotes a sudden, unexpected coming; in this context, it suggests that the Jews who killed Jesus were already the recipients of God's wrath. This is made explicit in the Western text (D F G), where του θεου is added after η οργη producing the reading "the wrath of God," a typical Pauline expression (Rom 1:18; Eph 5:6; Col 3:6).

1 Thessalonians 2:19

Instead of στεφανος καυχησεως ("crown of boasting"), found in most manuscripts, Codex Alexandrinus (A) reads στεφανος αγαλλιασεως ("crown of exultation"). Tertullian (in *Res.* 24) attests to the same reading.

1 Thessalonians 3:2

NU τὸν ἀδελφὸν ἡμῶν καὶ συνεργὸν τοῦ θεοῦ
"our brother and coworker of God"
D* 33 it[b]
NRSV ESV NASB NIV (TNIV) NEB REB NJB NAB NLT HCSB NET

variant 1/WH τον αδελφον ημων και συνεργον
"our brother and coworker"
B
NIVmg NEBmg NLTmg NETmg

variant 2	του αδελφον ημων και διακονον του θεου "our brother and servant of God" א A P Ψ 0278 1739 cop RSV ESVmg NIVmg NEBmg NJBmg NLTmg HCSBmg NETmg
variant 3/TR	του αδελφον ημων και διακονον του θεου και συνεργον ημων "our brother and servant of God and our coworker" D^2 Maj syr KJV NKJV NJBmg NLTmg NETmg
variant 4	του αδελφον ημων και διακονον και συνεργον του θεου "our brother and servant and coworker of God" F G NLTmg NETmg

The third and fourth variants are obviously conflated readings. The true reading must be preserved in the NU reading or in one of the first two variants. After Paul called Timothy "our brother," he called him either (1) a coworker of God, or (2) a coworker, or (3) a servant of God. The third option has the best attestation, but it is suspect as a scribal adjustment because it avoids calling Timothy "God's coworker"—which is quite an acclamation. The second option has the testimony of B and is the shorter reading; as such, it could be considered the reading from which all the others deviated. However, scholars (see Metzger 1992, 240-242) argue that συν-εργον would not have been purposely expanded to συνεργον του θεου ("coworker of God") because the latter is the more difficult reading. But we know that the Bezaean reviser (D) had a propensity for expansion, and he may have understood του θεου to be an objective genitive, not subjective—hence, the rendering "a coworker for God," which is not at all offensive. Yet—and finally—it must be said that Paul could have been saying that Timothy was a worker with God. After all, Paul made similar assertions in 1 Cor 3:9 and 2 Cor 6:1.

1 Thessalonians 3:9

Influenced by the previous verse, where "Lord" (κυριω) is the subject of the sentence, some scribes (א*D* F G) and one translator (it[b]) changed "God" (D* F G only for θεω and א* for θεου) to "Lord" (κυριω and κυριου): "How can we thank the Lord enough for you in return for all the joy we have before our Lord for you?"

1 Thessalonians 3:13

NU	include αμην ("amen") at end of verse א* A D* it cop[bo] NJBmg NAB HCSB NETmg
variant/TR WH	omit αμην ("amen") at end of verse $א^2$ B D^2 F G Ψ 0278 1739 Maj it syr cop[sa] KJV NKJV RSV NRSV ESV NASB NIV TNIV NEB REB NJB NLT HCSBmg NET

If "amen" had originally been in the text, there is no good reason to account for its omission on transcriptional grounds. Furthermore, the same manuscripts that have an additional "amen" here also have one at the end of 5:28. In fact, the scribes of א A D had quite a propensity for appending an "amen" to the end of prayers (see 1 Cor 16:24; 2 Cor 13:13; Eph 6:24; Phil 4:23; Col 4:18). This is a sure sign of a scribal enhancement intended to mark the end of a prayer prior to further discourse (4:1–5:28). Interestingly, though the word αμην appears in NU, only two translations (NAB and HCSB) follow it.

1 Thessalonians 4:1

WH NU	include καθὼς καὶ περιπατεῖτε ("as also you walk") א A B D* F G 0183[vid] 0278 33 (1739 it syr[h]) cop RSV NRSV ESV NASB NIV TNIV NEB REB NJB NAB NLT HCSB NET
variant/TR	omit D[2] Ψ Maj syr[p] KJV NKJV

The variant reading, though shorter, is not original on two counts. First, its documentary attestation is far inferior to that of the WH NU reading. Second, the phrase was evidently deleted by some scribe(s) who considered it clumsy, obtrusive, or extraneous.

1 Thessalonians 4:3

According to most manuscripts, Paul asked the Thessalonians to abstain from πορνειας. But since πορνεια could mean fornication, prostitution, or any kind of sexual immorality, some scribes (א[2] Ψ F G[c]) added πασης ("every") so as to give the broader sense, "every kind of illicit sexuality" (cf. Eph 5:3).

1 Thessalonians 4:11

TR NU	ταῖς [ἰδίαις] χερσὶν ὑμῶν "your own hands" א* A D[2] 33 Maj KJV NKJV NAB HCSB
variant/WH	ταις χερσιν υμων "your hands" א[2] B D* F G Ψ 0278 1739 syr[h] RSV NRSV ESV NASB NIV TNIV NEB REB NJB NLT NET

The word ιδιας ("own") is bracketed in NU to show the editors' doubts about its right to be in the text. Nevertheless, the editors included it on the grounds that it may have dropped out due to homoeoteleuton: ταις ιδιαις (see TCGNT). In any event, the article ταις placed before a noun designating a body part conveys the possessive function: "your hands" (see comments on Eph 4:28). All modern versions except NAB follow the shorter version (as in WH), whereas KJV and NKJV go with TR.

1 Thessalonians 4:13

The WH NU editions read περι των κοιμωμενων ("concerning the ones sleeping"), with the support of א A B 0278 33 1739 Origen. TR reads περι των κεκοιμημενων ("concerning the ones having slept"), with the support of D (F G) Ψ Maj. The variant reading in TR is a scribal alteration intended to conform this idiom to the more familiar form, which usually appears in the perfect tense (see Matt 27:52; 1 Cor 15:20). But Paul's emphasis here is not on those who experienced death (which is conveyed by the idiom κοιμωμενων), but on those who are presently dead, for which the present tense is appropriate. These are the Christians who sleep (in death) until the advent of Christ and their subsequent resurrection.

1 Thessalonians 4:16

Instead of the wording οι νεκροι εν Χριστω αναστησονται πρωτον ("the dead in Christ will rise first"), a Western reading (D* F G it) changes the last word to πρωτοι, yielding the rendering, "the dead in Christ are the first to rise." This change alleviates a potential problem for any reader who may try to figure out what the dead in Christ will do *second*—but that is not the point. Quite simply, Paul is affirming that dead Christians will precede living Christians in the Rapture.

1 Thessalonians 4:17

The Western text presents some changes in this verse. Instead of identifying the living Christians as οι ζωντες οι περιλειπομενοι ("the living ones, the remaining ones"), F G it[a,b] identify them as simply οι ζωντες ("the living ones"). Perhaps some scribe(s) thought they were ridding the text of a tautological expression, inasmuch as "the remaining ones" are none other than "the living ones." And instead of απαντησιν ("a meeting"), a few other Western manuscripts (D* F G) read υπαντησιν (which also means "meeting"), probably under the influence of Matt 25:1.

1 Thessalonians 4:18

At the end of this verse, 1739[c] and a few other manuscripts expand the final expression from λογοις τουτοις ("these words") to λογοις τουτοις του πνευματος ("these words of the Spirit"). Perhaps some scribe thought it necessary to show that Paul's description of Christ's advent and the resurrection of the believers (4:13-17) was not something of his own imagination but was inspired by the Spirit.

1 Thessalonians 5:4

TR NU	ἵνα ἡ ἡμέρα ὑμᾶς ὡς κλέπτης καταλάβῃ "that the day should overtake you as a thief" ℵ D F G 0278 33 1739 Maj all
variant/WH	ινα η ημερα υμας ως κλεπτας καταλαβη "that the day should overtake you as thieves" A B cop[bo] NEBmg NLTmg

In full context, the NU reading could be rendered, "But you, brothers, are not in darkness that the day should overtake you as a thief." There is great diversity of opinion about the variant reading. For example, Metzger (TCGNT) considers it near nonsense, whereas Lightfoot (1904, 73-74) considers it the more probable reading because it is more difficult and because it is far more likely that a scribe would change κελπτας to κλεπτης in order to make it conform to 5:2. Indeed, it is not unlike Paul to display a turn of phrase—shifting the metaphor from "you know the day of the Lord comes as a thief in the night" (5:2) to "be careful that the day of the

Lord would not overtake you as if you were thieves" (5:4). The idea is that the Thessalonians were being warned not to be caught in the act of living in darkness, as if they were thieves caught in the act of stealing. The natural antithesis follows: "for you are all sons of light and sons of the day" (5:5). Thus, the variant reading, supported by A and B, is possibly original, as was thought by WH.

1 Thessalonians 5:9

𝔓[30] B and a few other manuscripts read σωτηριας δια του κυριου ημων Ιησου ("salvation through our Lord Jesus") versus all the other manuscripts, which have the divine title as κυριου ημων Ιησου Χριστου ("our Lord Jesus Christ"). All the Greek editions (TR WH NU) have the fuller reading, as do all English versions. But since we know that scribes tended to add names to divine titles and that the two earliest manuscripts do not contain the word "Christ," it is possible that 𝔓[30] and B contain the original reading and that the other manuscripts exhibit an expansion influenced by 1:1 and 5:28.

1 Thessalonians 5:13

All three Greek editions (TR WH NU) have the wording ειρηνευετε εν εαυτοις, which has to be rendered as "be at peace among yourselves." This is the reading found in A B D^2 L 33 1739 and accepted by all English versions. However, some other manuscripts (𝔓[30] ℵ D* F G P Ψ) read ειρηνευετε εν αυτοις, which should probably be rendered as "be at peace with them."

The textual evidence is evenly divided between the two readings, so it is difficult to determine which is original. The first reading presents a general call to corporate peace and unity among all the members of the church in Thessalonica. Though the second reading could mean the same thing, it also allows for the interpretation that Paul was calling the Thessalonians to be at peace with the leaders in their church (see 5:12, where προισταμενους ["the ones exercising leadership"] is the most natural reference for αυτοις ["them"]).

1 Thessalonians 5:25

WH NU προσεύχεσθε [καὶ] περὶ ἡμῶν
"pray also concerning us"
𝔓[30] B D* 0278 33 1739 it^b syr^h cop^{sa}
NASBmg NEB REB NAB HCSB NET

variant/TR προσευχεσθε περι υμων
"pray concerning us"
ℵ A D^1 F G I^{vid} Ψ Maj syr^p cop^{bo}
KJV NKJV RSV NRSV ESV NASB NIV TNIV NJB NLT

The testimony of the two earliest manuscripts (𝔓[30] and B) in favor of the WH NU reading is weighty. Furthermore, it is likely that some scribe(s) omitted και because it signals no immediate connection with a previous statement about prayer. The connection, though remote, is with 5:16, where Paul encouraged the believers to pray without ceasing.

1 Thessalonians 5:27

WH NU πᾶσιν τοῖς ἀδελφοῖς
"to all the brothers"
ℵ* B D F G 0278 it cop^sa
NKJVmg RSV NRSV ESV NASB NIV TNIV NEB REB NJB NAB NLT HCSB NET

variant/TR πασιν τοις αγιοις αδελφοις
"to all the holy brothers"
ℵ² A Ψ (33) 1739 Maj syr cop^bo
KJV NKJV NETmg

It is difficult to determine which reading is original. On one hand, it can be argued that αγιοις ("holy") was accidentally dropped out due to homoeoteleuton: τοις αγιοις αδελφοις. On the other hand, it can be argued that αγιοις was added by scribes who had taken notice that holiness was a key theme in this epistle and was therefore an appropriate descriptor of the believers. Since the textual evidence slightly favors the first reading and since later scribes had a propensity for interpolation, the WH NU reading is more likely original.

1 Thessalonians 5:28

WH NU omit αμην ("Amen") at end of verse
B D* F G 0278 33 1739* cop^sa
RSV NRSV ESV NASB NIV TNIV NEB REB NJB NAB NLT HCSB NET

variant/TR include αμην ("Amen") at end of verse
ℵ A D¹ Ψ 1739^c Maj syr cop^bo
KJV NKJV NRSVmg NETmg

Though the textual evidence is evenly divided, it is more likely than not that the final word "amen" was added by scribes for liturgical purposes. Only three epistles (Romans, Galatians, Jude) appear to have a genuine "amen" for the last word.

Subscription

1. No subscription—but placed as an inscription: Προς Θεσσαλονικεις Α ("First to the Thessalonians"). Appears in 𝔓^46vid.
2. No subscription. Found in 323 365 614 1505.
3. Προς Θεσσαλονικεις Α ("First to the Thessalonians"). Appears in 𝔓^30 ℵ B* (D F G) Ψ 33.
4. Προς Θεσσαλονικεις Α εγραφη απο Αθηνων ("First to the Thessalonians written from Athens"). Appears in A B¹ 0278 1739* Maj (so TR).
5. Προς Θεσσαλονικεις Α εγραφη απο Αθηνων δια Τιμοθεου ("First to the Thessalonians written from Athens through Timothy"). Appears in 1739^c.
6. Προς Θεσσαλονικεις Α εγραφη απο Κορινθου υπο Παυλου και Σιλουανου και Τιμοθεου ("First to the Thessalonians written from Corinth by Paul and Silvanus and Timothy"). Appears in 81.

As with all the books of the NT, it is quite certain that no book had a title (inscription) or a subscription. (For more on this, see Comfort 2005, 9-10.) This is especially true for the Epistles because their purpose was to be apostolic letters, not literary works per se. Thus, all inscriptions and subscriptions are scribal addenda. The simplest form, Προς Θεσσαλονικεις Α ("1 Thessalonians"), appears in the earliest witnesses: in 𝔓46 at the head of the epistle; in the three other earliest witnesses (𝔓30 א B*) at the end. (It can be presumed that 𝔓30 also had an inscription with the same title, because the second epistle to the Thessalonians, which follows immediately in 𝔓30, has the inscription Προς Θεσσαλονικεις Β.) As is typical, the subscription was expanded to include the place of writing (Athens or Corinth) and Paul's coauthors, Silvanus and Timothy (see 1:1).

The Second Epistle to the THESSALONIANS

Inscription (Title)

𝔓30 ℵ and B title this epistle as Προς Θεσσαλονεκεις Β ("To the Thessalonians B" = "2 Thessalonians"). Several other manuscripts (including ℵ and B) have the same title in the subscription (see last note for this book). Paul, however, would not have entitled this epistle in its original composition. Inscriptions and subscriptions are the work of later scribes. (For more on this, see Comfort 2005, 9-10.)

2 Thessalonians 1:1-2a

All manuscripts read κυριω Ιησου Χριστω, including 𝔓30vid, according to Grenfell and Hunt's reconstruction (see *editio princeps* of P.Oxy. 1598). However, it seems more likely that the manuscript reads [κω Ιηυ] χα[ρις] (see *Text of Earliest MSS,* 131), yielding the reading "grace of the Lord Jesus."

2 Thessalonians 1:2b

TR NU	θεοῦ πατρὸς [ἡμῶν] "God our Father" ℵ A F G I 0278 Maj it syr cop^sa KJV NKJV NRSV ESV TNIV NAB NLT HCSB NETmg
variant/WH	θεου πατρος "God [the] Father" B D 0111^vid 33 1739 RSV NRSVmg NASB NIV NEB REB NJB NLTmg NET

Since the manuscript evidence for the two readings is evenly distributed, it is difficult to make a decision on external grounds. Internal considerations are no less divided. On one hand, it could be argued that ημων ("our") was added to conform this verse to other Pauline introductions, where the formulaic expression nearly always is "God our Father." On the other hand, it could be argued that ημων was dropped to avoid repeating the wording of the first verse (θεω πατρι ημων).

2 Thessalonians 1:4

Superior attestation (א A B 0111 33—so WH NU) supports the reading εγκαυχασθαι ("to boast") over the reading καυχασθαι (found in TR and supported by D F G Ψ 0278 1881 Maj), which also means "to boast." But εγκαυχασθαι is a *hapax legomenon* in the NT, which would make it susceptible to scribal alteration.

2 Thessalonians 1:12

WH NU τὸ ὄνομα τοῦ κυρίου ἡμῶν 'Ιησοῦ
"the name of our Lord Jesus"
א B D L Ψ 0111 it[b] cop[sa]
RSV NRSV ESV NASB NIV TNIV NEB REB NAB NLT HCSB NET

variant/TR το ονομα του κυριου ημων Ιησου Χριστου
"the name of our Lord Jesus Christ"
A F G P 0278 33 1739 syr
KJV NKJV NJB

The documentary evidence for the WH NU reading is superior to that of the variant, not to mention that the variant is probably the result of scribal assimilation to the next clause of this verse, which reads "Lord Jesus Christ."

2 Thessalonians 2:2

WH NU ἡ ἡμέρα τοῦ κυρίου
"the day of the Lord"
א A B D* F G L P Ψ 0278 (33) 1739 it syr cop
NKJVmg RSV NRSV ESV NASB NIV TNIV NEB REB NJB NAB NLT HCSB NET

variant/TR η ημερα του Χριστου
"the day of Christ"
D^2 Maj
KJV NKJV HCSBmg

The documentary evidence strongly favors the WH NU reading. The variant is likely the result of scribal conformity to other Pauline texts that designate the eschaton as "the day of Christ" (see 1 Cor 1:8; Phil 1:10; 2:16). In the end, however, there is no difference in meaning—both terms denote the parousia.

2 Thessalonians 2:3

WH NU ὁ ἄνθρωπος τῆς ἀνομίας
"the man of lawlessness"
א B 0278 1739 cop
NKJVmg RSV NRSV ESV NASB NIV TNIV NEB REB NJB NAB NLT HCSB NET

variant/TR ο ανθρωπος της αμαρτιας
"the man of sin"
A D F G Ψ Maj it syr Eusebius
KJV NKJV RSVmg NRSVmg ESVmg NASBmg NIVmg TNIVmg NLTmg HCSBmg NETmg

The two earliest manuscripts (ℵ B), as well as some others, read, "the man of lawlessness" or "the man of rebellion" (NIV). This one is "the anarchist"—he is opposed to all moral, religious, and civil law. Just as Christ embodied righteousness, so the "man of lawlessness" will embody lawlessness and rebellion (see Dan 11:36). This one is probably the same as "the antichrist" (1 John 2:18; 4:3) and "the beast" (Rev 13). He will perpetrate the worst crime ever: that of claiming to be God and demanding worship from all human beings (see next note). In this regard, he is the worst of sinners; therefore, it is understandable why he came to be known as "the man of sin." However, the title "the man of lawlessness" not only has superior attestation, it aptly describes the one who incites the eschatological apostasy.

2 Thessalonians 2:4

WH NU — καθίσαι
"to sit"
ℵ A B D* Ψ 33 1739 it cop
NKJVmg RSV NRSV ESV NASB NIV TNIV NEB REB NJB NAB NLT HCSB NET

variant 1/TR — ως θεον καθισαι
"to sit as God"
D^2 G^c Maj syr
KJV NKJV HCSBmg

variant 2 — ινα θεον καθισαι
"so as to sit as God"
F G*
none

The two variants are scribal expansions which attempt to clarify the point that the lawless one will perform an activity that only God should do—i.e., occupy a place of worship in the temple. However, the additions are not needed inasmuch as the next expression in the verse ("presenting himself that he is God") makes it more than clear what the lawless one will attempt to do. Pretending to be God, he will desecrate the temple by setting up an image of himself and then demand others to worship him as God. This is what is otherwise known in Scripture as the abominable sacrilege that causes desolation (see Dan 9:26-27; 11:31; 12:11; Matt 24:15; Mark 13:14).

2 Thessalonians 2:8a

WH NU — ὁ κύριος ['Ιησοῦς]
"the Lord Jesus"
ℵ A D* F G L^c P Ψ 0278 33 it syr cop
RSV NRSV ESV NIV TNIV NEB REB NJBmg NAB NLT HCSB NETmg

variant/TR — ο κυριος
"the Lord"
B D^2 1739 Maj Irenaeus
KJV NKJV NRSVmg NASB NJB NET

In this verse, Paul was paraphrasing Isa 11:4 (see next note), which speaks of what the Lord (Yahweh) will do to his enemies in the day of judgment. Paul, however, applied this to the Lord Jesus, who has been given the authority as the Son of Man to execute God's judgment (see John 5:27). If Paul originally wrote "Lord Jesus," it could be argued that the variant displays scribal conformity to Isa 11:4 (see next note). In any case, it is difficult to make a determination on internal grounds or on external grounds, because the documentation is evenly divided.

2 Thessalonians 2:8b

WH NU ἀνελεῖ
"he will destroy"
A B P 0278 it Irenaeus
RSV NRSV ESV NIV TNIV NEB REB NJB NAB NLT HCSB NET

variant 1 ανελοι
"may he destroy"
א D*vid F G 33 1739 Didymus
NASB

variant 2/TR αναλωσει
"he will consume"
D^2 Ψ Maj cop
KJV NKJV NRSVmg

The documentary evidence is nearly evenly divided between the WH NU reading and the first variant. Lightfoot (1904, 115) considered the second variant more likely to be a scribal alteration than is ανελει ("he will destroy"). Furthermore, he considered the first variant to be original, because it explains the other two variants. If so, the verse reads, "May the Lord Jesus destroy him with the breath of his mouth—even as he will destroy him by the radiance of his coming." One point can be added to Lightfoot's argument: ανελει might be the result of scribal conformity to the Septuagint's rendering of Isa 11:4, the verse alluded to here.

2 Thessalonians 2:11

WH NU have the present tense verb πεμπει ("he sends") based on excellent authority: א* A B D* F G 33 1739. A variant of this in TR is πεμψει ("he will send"), based on inferior testimony: $א^2$ D^2 Ψ 0278 Maj. The prophetic or proleptic present tense was changed to the future tense by later scribes. This reading was multiplied in the majority of manuscripts, which was followed by TR (and so KJV and NKJV).

2 Thessalonians 2:13

NU εἵλατο ὑμᾶς ὁ θεὸς ἀπαρχήν
"God chose you firstfruit(s)"
B F G P 0278 33 1739 syr^h cop^{bo}
RSVmg NRSV ESV NASBmg NIVmg TNIV NEBmg REBmg NJBmg NAB NLT HCSBmg NETmg

variant/TR WH ειλατο υμας ο θεος απ αρχης
"God chose you from [the] beginning"
א D Ψ Maj it syr^p cop^{sa}
KJV NKJV RSV NRSVmg ESVmg NASB NIV TNIVmg NEB REB NJB NABmg NLTmg HCSB NET

The textual attestation for these two variants is divided, as is the internal evidence. In a Greek manuscript (written in continuous letters with no space between words), the word for "firstfruits" (απαρχην) could have easily been confused for the expression "from the beginning" (απ αρχης), or vice versa. The NU reading could be original because Paul had the habit of calling the first converts in a certain geographical region the "firstfruits" (see Rom 16:5; 1 Cor 16:15), and the Thessalonians were among Paul's first converts in Europe. But the variant reading also has legitimacy because it was customary for Paul to speak of God's selection of his elect before the foundation of the world (see Eph 1:4; 2 Tim 1:9). The split among English translations shows the difficulty of making a definitive decision. This would be a good place to use the marginal notes to indicate that the alternative reading is just as viable. If the translators select "from the beginning" as the text, the note would read: "Or, as in other manuscripts, 'firstfruits.'"

2 Thessalonians 3:3

All the Greek editions (TR WH NU) read πιστος δε εστιν ο κυριος ("the Lord is faithful") on good authority: ℵ B D[2] Ψ 0278 33 1739 Maj syr cop. A few manuscripts (A D*,c F G), however, change κυριος ("Lord") to θεος ("God"). This variant reading is likely the result of scribal conformity to a typical Pauline expression (see Rom 3:3; 1 Cor 1:9; 10:13).

2 Thessalonians 3:6

NU — τὴν παράδοσιν ἣν παρελάβοσαν
"the tradition which they received"
ℵ* A 0278 33 (παρελαβον ℵ[2] D[2] Ψ 1739 Maj)
NKJVmg NRSV NAB NLT HCSB NET

variant 1/WH — την παραδοσιν ην παρελαβετε
"the tradition which you received"
B F G syr[h] cop[sa]
RSV NRSVmg ESV NASB NIV TNIV NEB REB NJB NLTmg NETmg

variant 2/TR — την παραδοσιν ην παρελαβεν
"the tradition which he received"
1962 (syr)
KJV NKJV

The Hellenistic form παρελαβοσαν was changed to the classical form παρελαβον by various correctors. The first variant (accepted in WH and followed by many English versions) could be original, given its documentary support; if not, it is the result of scribal conformity to the immediate context in which the second person plural is predominant. The second variant (TR), which virtually no manuscript supports, specifies the recipient of the apostolic traditions as the brother who lived a lazy life.

2 Thessalonians 3:12

WH NU — ἐν κυρίῳ Ἰησοῦ Χριστῷ
"in the Lord Jesus Christ"
ℵ* A B (D*) F G 0278 33 1739
RSV NRSV ESV NASB NIV TNIV NEB REB NJB NAB NLT HCSB NET

variant/TR — δια του κυριου ημων Ιησου Χριστου
"through our Lord Jesus Christ"
ℵ[2] D[2] Ψ Maj
KJV NKJV

The WH NU reading has superior support and accords with Pauline usage (see 1 Thess 4:1; 5:12). The variant is a corrected reading, probably influenced by 1 Thess 4:2, which made its way into the majority of NT manuscripts and TR, and thus is followed by the KJV and NKJV.

2 Thessalonians 3:16

The three Greek editions (TR WH NU) conclude Paul's blessing here with the words, εν παντι τροπω ("in every way"): "may the Lord of peace himself always give you peace in every way." This reading has excellent support: ℵ A[c] B D[2] Ψ 0278 1739 Maj syr cop, and is followed by all English versions. A variant on this is εν παντι τοπω ("in every place"): "May the Lord of peace himself always give you peace in every place." This is the reading in A* D* F G 33 it.

These two words could have been easily mistaken for each other in the transcriptional process inasmuch as there is only a one-letter difference (*rho*) between them: τροπω and τοπω. Furthermore, both make good idiomatic sense—the blessing of peace should accompany the believers in every manner or wherever they are. But the TR WH NU reading has superior attestation, and the variant is probably the result of scribal conformation to the wording in verses such as 1 Cor 1:2; 2 Cor 2:14; 1 Thess 1:8; 1 Tim 2:8.

2 Thessalonians 3:18

WH NU	omit αμην ("Amen") at end of verse ℵ* B 0278 33 1739* 1881* cop[sa] RSV NRSV ESV NASB NIV TNIV NEB REB NJB NAB NLT HCSB NET
variant/TR	include αμην ("Amen") at end of verse ℵ[2] A D F G Ψ 1881[c] Maj it syr cop[bo] KJV NKJV NRSVmg

The documentary evidence for the WH NU reading is superior to that for the variant. It is likely that the final "amen" was added by scribes for liturgical purposes. Only three epistles (Romans, Galatians, Jude) appear to have a genuine "amen" for the last word.

Subscription

1. No subscription—but placed as an inscription: Προς Θεσσαλονεικεις Β ("Second to the Thessalonians"). Found in 𝔓[30vid].
2. No subscription. Found in 323 365 629 630 1505.
3. Προς Θεσσαλονικεις Β ("Second to the Thessalonians"). Appears in ℵ B* (D F G) Ψ 33.
4. Προς Θεσσαλονικεις Β εγραφη απο Αθηνων ("Second to the Thessalonians written from Athens"). Appears in A B[1] 0278 1739* Maj (so TR).
5. Προς Θεσσαλονικεις Β εγραφη απο Αθηνων υπο Παυλου και Σιλουανου και Τιμοθεου ("Second to the Thessalonians written from Athens by Paul and Silvanus and Timothy"). Appears in 81.
6. Προς Θεσσαλονικεις Β εγραφη απο Ρωμης ("Second to the Thessalonians written from Rome"). Appears in 6 614 1739[mg].

As with all the books of the NT, it is quite certain that no book had a title (inscription) or a subscription. (For more on this, see Comfort 2005, 9-10.) This is especially true for the

Epistles because their original purpose was to be apostolic letters, not literary works per se. Thus, all inscriptions and subscriptions are scribal addenda. The simplest form, Προς Θεσσαλονικεις Β (= "2 Thessalonians"), appears in the earliest witness, 𝔓[30], at the beginning of the epistle. The two other earliest witnesses (א B*) have the same wording. As is typical, the subscription was expanded to include the place of writing (Athens or Rome) and Paul's coauthors, Silvanus and Timothy (see 1:1). See note on subscription to 1 Thessalonians.

The First Epistle to TIMOTHY

1 Timothy 1:1

TR WH NU	ἐπιταγὴν θεοῦ "command of God" A D F G I Ψ 33 1739 cop all
variant	επαγγελιαν θεου "promise of God" א NJBmg

The scribe of א, probably influenced by 2 Tim 1:1, changed "command" to "promise." This suggests his knowledge of both epistles prior to copying 1 Timothy.

1 Timothy 1:4a

The word εκζητησεις ("speculations") appears only here in the NT; it has the support of א A 33. Other manuscripts (D F G Ψ 0285[vid] 1739) and the majority of manuscripts (so TR) have the more usual, ζητησεις ("questionings")—probably under the influence of other verses in the Pastoral Epistles (1 Tim 6:4; 2 Tim 2:23; Titus 3:9).

1 Timothy 1:4b

TR WH NU	οἰκονομίαν θεοῦ "stewardship of God" א A F G Ψ 075 33 1739 cop RSV NRSV ESV NASB NIV TNIV NEB REB NJB NAB NLT HCSB NET
variant	οικοδομην θεου "edification of God" (= "godly edification") D* it Irenaeus KJV NKJV NJBmg NETmg

The best documentary evidence supports the reading "the stewardship of God," which could also be rendered "the economy of God." This refers to the way God's heavenly "household plan" is carried out on earth in the church. (This is why many English versions use the word "plan" to translate οικονομια.) Paul was instructing Timothy to encourage the believers to be engaged in promoting God's economy by carrying out the divine stewardship. The variant reading arose either as a transcriptional mistake or a scribal attempt to avert a difficult concept—i.e., the notion of promoting God's economy. The NJBmg indicates that the variant could also be rendered as "the building-up of God's house." Unusually, KJV and NKJV deviate from TR.

1 Timothy 1:12

According to excellent authority (ℵ[c] A D H I Ψ 1739 it syr cop[bo]), the declaration of Paul's empowering as coming from Christ is expressed with an aorist participle: τω ενδυναμωσαντι με Χριστω ("the one having empowered me—Christ"). Prompted by the wording in Phil 4:13, some scribes and ancient translators (ℵ* 33 cop[sa]) changed this to a present participle: τω ενδυναμουντι με Χριστω ("the one empowering me—Christ"). But in this context Paul was not speaking of his daily, existential dependence on Christ, but of his being chosen by Christ and thrust into apostolic service. Thus, the aorist tense functions to signal this initiation.

1 Timothy 1:17a

The "king of the ages" (βασιλει των αιωνων) is described as αφθαρτω αορατω ("incorruptible, invisible"), according to good testimony (ℵ A H I Ψ 1739—so TR WH NU). These words vary in other manuscripts, as follows: (1) αθανατω αορατω ("immortal, invisible") in D*[,c] it syr[hmg]; (2) αφθαρτω αορατω αθανατω ("incorruptible, invisible, immortal") in F G. In short, the original text was marred by various Western alterations, in which "immortal" replaced "incorruptible" (variant 1) or was added (variant 2). These changes were influenced by 1 Tim 6:16, in which God is described as ο μονος εχων αθανασιαν ("the only one having immortality"). All English translations reflect the first variant ("immortal, invisible") because "immortal" is more communicative than "incorruptible" when used to describe God.

1 Timothy 1:17b

WH NU	μόνῳ θεῷ "[the] only God" ℵ* A D* F G H* 33 1739 it syr[p] cop NKJVmg RSV NRSV ESV NASB NIV TNIV NEB REB NJB NAB NLT HCSB NET
variant/TR	μονω σοφω θεω "[the] only wise God" ℵ[2] D[1] H[c] Ψ Maj KJV NKJV HCSBmg NETmg

Although it could be argued that μονω ("wise") was accidentally dropped due to homoeoteleuton (both words on either side also end with *omega*), it is far more likely that scribes were influenced by Rom 16:27, a similar verse, and then inserted it into this verse. The three corrected manuscripts (ℵ[2] D[1] H[c]) bear witness to this scribal interpolation. In a context that emphasizes the gift of eternal life (1:16), this verse eulogizes God's eternality, incorruptibility, and uniqueness. It need not say anything about his wisdom; such words are appropriate in verses like Rom 16:27, where Paul extols God's sagaciousness in making his eternal plan.

1 Timothy 2:1

TR WH NU	παρακαλῶ "I urge" א A H 33 1739 Maj it syr[p] cop all
variant	παρακαλει "[you] urge" D* F G it[b] NJBmg

Instead of the first person indicative παρακαλω ("I urge"), a few Western manuscripts (noted in NJB) read the imperative παρακαλει ("[you] urge"). This intensifies Paul's admonition to Timothy in that it becomes Timothy's task to urge the church to pray.

1 Timothy 2:7a

WH NU	ἀλήθειαν λέγω "I speak truth" א[2] A D* F G Ψ 1739 it syr cop NKJVmg RSV NRSV ESV NASB NIV TNIV NEB REB NJB NAB NLT HCSB NET
variant/TR	αληθειαν λεγω εν Χριστω "I speak truth in Christ" א* D[2] H 33[vid] Maj KJV NKJV NRSVmg HCSBmg NETmg

Had the words "in Christ" originally been in the text, there is no reasonable explanation for their omission. Rather, it is far more likely that the words were added by scribes who were familiar with similar Pauline expressions (Rom 9:1; 2 Cor 2:17) and thought they belonged here.

1 Timothy 2:7b

With good manuscript support, Paul declares that he was a teacher of the Gentiles "in faith and truth" (εν πιστει και αληθεια): D F G H Ψ 33 1739 Maj it syr cop—so all Greek editions and English translations. The word πιστει ("faith") is replaced with γνωσει ("knowledge") in א and with πνευματι ("spirit") in A. The unusual combination of "faith" with "truth" prompted these two scribal changes. The first change, probably influenced by 2:4, joins "knowledge" with "truth." Though this is a sensible association, it misses the point. Paul taught the Gentiles to both live in faith and by the truth, as a healthy balance. The second change points to the mode in which Paul taught—"in spirit" or "by [the] Spirit." Although this is true (see 1 Cor 2:4, 13; 2 Cor 3:3), it also misses the point.

1 Timothy 3:1

TR WH NU	πιστὸς ὁ λόγος "Faithful [is] the saying." א A D[2] F G Ψ 075 0150 33 1739 syr cop KJV NKJV RSV NRSV ESV NASB NIV TNIV REB NJB NAB NLT HCSB NET

variant	ανθρωπινος ο λογος
"It [is] a human saying."
D* it[b,g,m] Ambrosiaster
NRSVmg NEB

Various scholars have attempted to explain how πιστος was changed to ανθρωπινος in the process of transcription. Swete (1916, 1) conjectured that an ancient translator or scribe confused πιστος (at the beginning of the line) with πινος and considered it to be the final syllables of ανθρωπινος. However, it is far more likely that the change occurred because some scribe(s) thought it improper for the idiom πιστος ο λογος to introduce a common adage, when in other places in the Pastoral Epistles the same idiom accompanies creedal statements (see 1:15; 4:8-9; 2 Tim 2:11-13; Titus 3:6-8). (It is for this reason that some scholars have suggested that the idiom should be attached to 2:15; however, this is more problematic because the statement in 2:15 is notoriously difficult.) In each of the instances where the idiom "the saying is faithful" occurs, it affirms the churchwide acceptance of these sayings. As such, the variant reading is not exceedingly different, for it means something like "it is a popular saying" (NEB) or "the saying is commonly accepted" (NRSVmg).

1 Timothy 3:3

WH NU	μὴ πλήκτην
"not violent"
ℵ A D F G it cop syr
NKJVmg RSV NRSV ESV NASB NIV TNIV NEB REB NJB NAB NLT HCSB NET

variant/TR	μη πληκτην μη αισχροκερδη
"not violent, not greedy for money"
326 365 614 630
KJV NKJV

Not found in any of the earliest manuscripts, the variant is a late interpolation, taken from Titus 1:7, a parallel verse. Harmonization among parallel passages was an increasing phenomenon throughout the history of the transmission of the NT text—culminating in TR, as evidenced here.

1 Timothy 3:16

WH NU	ὃς ἐφανερώθη
"who was manifested"
ℵ* A* C* F G 33 Didymus
ASV NKJVmg RSV NRSV ESV NASB NIV TNIV NEB REB NJB NAB NLT HCSB NET

variant 1	ὃ εφανερωθη
"which was manifested"
D*
ASVmg RSVmg NRSVmg ESVmg NABmg NETmg

variant 2/TR	θεος εφανερωθη
"God was manifested"
ℵ[c] A[c] C[2] D[2] Ψ 1739 Maj
KJV ASVmg NKJV RSVmg NRSVmg ESVmg NASBmg NIVmg NLTmg HCSBmg NETmg

Few textual problems generated so much stir and controversy in the nineteenth century as this one did. Many scholars entered the debate—and not without good reason, inasmuch as this verse is related to the doctrine of the incarnation. When the reading in TR and KJV ("God was manifest in the flesh") was challenged by another reading ("he who was manifest in the flesh"), some thought the doctrine of God becoming man was being undermined. Not so. The scholars who defended the reading with ὅς ("he who") primarily did so because they realized that the second reading was clearly an emendation. The original scribes of ℵ* A* C* wrote ὅς, which was then changed by later scribes in all three manuscripts to θεος ("God"). The original scribe of D wrote ὅ ("which"), which was also then corrected to θεος ("God"). Scholars have conjectured that some scribe mistook the word ΟϹ (= ος) for Θ̅Ϲ̅ (the nomen sacrum for θεος). But it is difficult to imagine how several fourth- and fifth-century scribes, who had seen thousands of nomina sacra, would have made this mistake. It is more likely that the change was motivated by a desire to make the text say that it was "God" who was manifest in the flesh. But in the original text, the subject of the verse is simply "who"—which most translators render as "he" and which most commentators identify as Christ. Christ, the God-man, manifested his deity in and through his humanity. All English versions since the ASV (and ERV, its British predecessor) have reflected the superior text, and most show the variant(s) in marginal notes.

1 Timothy 4:10

WH NU ἀγωνιζόμεθα
"we struggle"
ℵ* A C F G Ψ 33
NKJVmg RSV NRSV ESV NASB NIV TNIV NEB REB NJB NAB NLT HCSB NET

variant/TR ονειδιζομεθα
"we suffer reproach"
ℵ[2] D 0241[vid] 1739 Maj it syr cop
KJV NKJV RSVmg NRSVmg ESVmg NEBmg NLTmg NETmg

Both variants can be explained on internal grounds. If "struggle" was original, some scribes might have thought it somewhat redundant (coming after "labor") and changed it to "suffer reproach"—perhaps, as Fee (1988, 110) suggests, under the influence of the ideas expressed in 2 Tim 1:8, 12; 2:9-10. If the expression "suffer reproach" was original, other scribes might have thought it foreign to a context which emphasizes spiritual training and therefore changed it to "struggle." The textual evidence slightly favors αγωνιζομεθα (a word used to speak of the activity of athletic contestants), as does the fact that it is the best word to correspond with γυμναζε and γυμνασια of 4:7-8. Both these words speak of spiritual exercise as if it were athletic training. When taken together with αγωνιζομεθα, the message is that Paul and his coworkers were extremely exercised in their spiritual pursuits. Nonetheless, the variant has good support (note all three early versions—it syr cop) and therefore is noted by several English versions.

1 Timothy 4:12

WH NU ἐν ἀγάπῃ, ἐν πίστει
"in love, in faith"
ℵ A C D F G I Ψ 33 1739 it syr cop
NKJVmg RSV NRSV ESV NASB NIV TNIV NEB REB NJB NAB NLT HCSB NET

variant/TR εν αγαπη, εν πνευματι, εν πιστει
"in love, in spirit, in faith"
Maj
KJV NKJV HCSBmg

The addition of "in spirit," found in the majority of late witnesses, is an obvious scribal expansion, perhaps influenced by 2 Tim 1:7.

1 Timothy 5:4

WH NU ἀπόδεκτον
"acceptable"
א A C D F G Ψ
NKJVmg RSV NRSV ESV NASB NIV TNIV NEB REB NJB NAB NLT HCSB NET

variant/TR καλον και αποδεκτον
"good and acceptable"
323 365 945 cop
KJV NKJV

The variant reading, having late and little support, is the result of scribal conformity to 2:3. This reading was adopted by TR and subsequently translated in KJV and NKJV: "for this is good and acceptable in the sight of God."

1 Timothy 5:5

In the expression ηλπικεν επι θεον ("she has set her hope on God"), some scribes (א* D*) substituted κυριον ("Lord") for θεον ("God"), which was subsequently emended by later correctors. The initial change shows that the scribes' horizon of expectations was probably formed by their reading of the other NT epistles, wherein the concept of Christian hope is stated as being hope in the Lord Jesus Christ (see, for example, Eph 1:12; Phil 2:19). But in 1 Timothy the hope is directed toward "God" (see 1:1; 4:10).

1 Timothy 5:16

WH NU εἴ τις πιστὴ ἔχει χήρας
"if any female believer has widows"
א A C F G P 048 33 1739 1881 cop
NKJVmg RSV NRSV ESV NASB NIV TNIV NEBmg REB NJB NAB NLT HCSB NET

variant/TR ει τις πιστος η πιστη εχει χηρας
"if any male or female believer has widows"
D Ψ Maj it^{b} syr
KJV NKJV RSVmg NRSVmg NEB HCSBmg

According to WH NU , the entire verse reads, "if any female believer has widows, let her take care of them and thereby not become a burden to the church, so that the church may assist those who are really widows." This reading, having the best documentary support, is followed by nearly all modern versions (note the change from NEB to REB).

In defense of the variant, however, it must be noted that it is possible that πιστος η was accidentally dropped due to a combination of homoeoarchton and homoeoteleuton—the eye of a scribe skipping over πιστος η to πιστη. However, this mistake would have had to happen a number of times because the evidence for πιστη is very diverse. Thus, it is far more likely that πιστος η was added to assure sexual equality in the role of believers caring for widows. With this change, readers would not perceive this function to be limited to women caring for women. But Paul had already exhorted Christian men to take care of their relatives, which would include widows (see 5:8). So there is no need to add "a male believer."

1 Timothy 5:18

There are two Scripture quotations in this verse, one from the OT and one from the Gospels. According to good testimony (א D[2] F G 1739 Maj), the first quotation (from Deut 25:4) reads βουν αλοωντα ου φιμωσεις ("you shall not muzzle an ox treading grain"). The wording is rearranged but not changed in A C I P Ψ 048 33 (in accordance with the LXX). And the scribe of D*, conforming this to the wording of 1 Cor 9:9, changed it to βουν αλοωντα ου κημωσεις, which also means "you shall not muzzle an ox treading grain."

The second quotation of Scripture is nowhere to be found in the OT. Rather, it is a saying of Jesus from the Gospels. As such, it is the only verse in the NT that ascribes scriptural status to the Gospels. But which Gospel does this quote come from? The wording in most manuscripts, αξιος ο εργατης του μισθου αυτου ("the worker is worthy of his wages"), is derived from Luke 10:7. But according to a few other witnesses (א*vid Clement), the wording is αξιος ο εργατης της τροφης αυτου ("the worker is worthy of his food")—a quotation from Matt 10:10. This reading evidences knowledge of Matthew and recognition that this was a gospel quotation.

1 Timothy 5:21

WH NU — Χριστοῦ Ἰησοῦ
"Christ Jesus"
א A D* G 33 it cop Clement
RSV NRSV ESV NASB NIV TNIV NEB REB NAB NLT HCSB NET

variant 1 — Ιησου Χριστου
"Jesus Christ"
F Ψ 1739
NJB

variant 2/TR — κυριου Ιησου Χριστου
"Lord Jesus Christ"
D[2] Maj syr
KJV NKJV

According to WH NU, the full quotation here is, "I testify before God and Christ Jesus." More often than not, Paul used the phrase "Christ Jesus" as opposed to "Jesus Christ." In this epistle, "Christ Jesus" appears 12 times (1:1, 2, 12, 14, 15, 16; 2:5; 3:13; 4:6; 5:21; 6:13), and "Jesus Christ" appears only twice—both following "Lord" (6:3, 14). Thus, the two variants are manifest scribal emendations—the first, a transposition; the second, an expansion (probably influenced by the wording of 6:3, 14). The best documentary evidence supports the WH NU reading, which is followed by all modern English versions except the NJB.

1 Timothy 6:3

Most manuscripts retain the wording, μη προσερχεται υγιαινουσιν λογοις. The problem is that προσερχεται usually means "come to" or "approach," which would be difficult in this context. So it has to mean something like "agree with"—"[if anyone] does not agree with healthy teaching." The scribe of א* (and several Old Latin translators) avoided the problem by changing προσερχεται to προσεχεται ("hold to"): "[if anyone] does not hold on to healthy teaching."

1 Timothy 6:5

WH NU	at end of verse omit αφιστασο απο των τοιουτων ("depart from such men") ℵ A D* F G 048 33 1739 it cop NKJVmg RSV NRSV ESV NASB NIV TNIV NEB REB NJB NAB NLT HCSB NET
variant/TR	include αφιστασο απο των τοιουτων ("depart from such men") D[2] Ψ Maj it[b] syr KJV NKJV NRSVmg HCSBmg NETmg

The appended, personal admonition from Paul to Timothy was probably created by some Greek scribe or Old Latin translator who was influenced by 2 Tim 2:19. The appendage took hold in the textual tradition, was incorporated in TR, and translated in KJV and NKJV. The earliest and best manuscripts support the WH NU reading, which is followed by all modern versions.

1 Timothy 6:7

WH NU	ὅτι "so that" ℵ* A F G 048 33 1739 NKJVmg (RSV) NRSV (ESV) NASB (NIV TNIV) NEB (REB) (NJB) NAB (NLT) HCSB NET
variant 1	αληθες οτι "it is true that" D* it[b] RSVmg NRSVmg
variant 2/TR	δηλον οτι "it is evident that" ℵ[2] D[2] Ψ Maj syr KJV NKJV NASBmg HCSBmg

According to WH NU, the entire clause reads something like, "so that neither are we able to carry anything out" or "because neither are we able to carry anything out." It is difficult to know the precise sense of the word οτι, which introduces the second clause. This difficulty prompted several rectifications, one of which found its way into TR and is reflected in KJV and NKJV. Most modern translators have treated it as a resumptive οτι and therefore do not translate it at all or simply render it as "and."

1 Timothy 6:9

Reflecting the influence of 3:7, several Western witnesses (D* F G it) expand the word παγιδα ("snare") to παγιδα του διαβολου ("snare of the devil").

1 Timothy 6:13

There are several small but significant variants in this verse. The first concerns the inclusion or exclusion of σοι in the opening words, παραγγελω σοι ("I charge you"). The pronoun "you" (referring to Timothy) is absent in ℵ* F G Ψ 33 1739 (so NA[25]) and present in ℵ[2] A D H Maj (so WH and NA[26]). It was probably added to provide an object for the predicate.

The second variation concerns the word ζωογονουντος, found in A D F G H Ψ 33 1739. This rare word was changed to the more common word ζωοποιουντος in ℵ and was then perpetuated in the majority of late manuscripts (Maj—so TR). Though the two words are nearly synonymous, the first is used for preserving life, while the second is used for giving life.

The third variation pertains to the title, Χριστου Ιησου ("Christ Jesus"), which appears in the TR WH NU editions following the evidence of A D Ψ 33 1739 Maj it syr[h]. But other manuscripts (ℵ F G) read Ιησου Χριστου ("Jesus Christ"). This inversion was a common phenomenon throughout the course of textual transmission (see 5:21).

1 Timothy 6:17

WH NU	ἐπὶ θεῷ "on God" ℵ F G Origen (A I P Ψ 33 1739 add τω before θεω) RSV NRSV ESV NASB NIV TNIV NEB REB NJB NAB NLT HCSB NET
variant/TR	εν τω θεω τω ζωντι "in the living God" D Maj syr KJV NKJV

According to WH NU, the full statement is: "not to have hope on the uncertainty of wealth but on God." The WH NU reading has superior attestation, whereas the variant has paltry support. The variant is clearly the result of a scribal adjustment, influenced by 3:15 and 4:10 (a parallel passage).

1 Timothy 6:19

WH NU	τῆς ὄντως ζωῆς "the life of being" (= "the real life") ℵ A D* F G Ψ 1739 it syr RSV NRSV ESV NASB NIV TNIV NEB REB NJB NAB NLT HCSB NET
variant 1/TR	της αιωνιου ζωης "the eternal life" D[2] Maj KJV NKJV
variant 2	της αιωνιου οντως "the eternal being (existence)" 69 1175 none

The first variant is a scribal assimilation to 6:12 (a parallel verse), and the second variant is a conflated reading. The WH NU reading has excellent documentary support, and it contains the more difficult reading. The expression της οντως ζωης is unusual in that it means "the life that is," "the existing life," "the life of being"—hence "the real life." This life is not just "eternal"; it is the divine life that Christians can appropriate and enjoy during their own lifetimes. Thus, it is disappointing to see that scribes made this wording synonymous with 6:12 and that the change was perpetuated in TR, followed by KJV and NKJV.

1 Timothy 6:21a

WH NU χάρις μεθ' ὑμῶν
"grace [be] with you [plural]"
א A F G P 33
NRSV ESV NIV TNIV NEB REB NJBmg NAB NLT HCSB NET

variant/TR χαρις μεθ σου
"grace [be] with you [singular]"
D Ψ 048 1739 Maj it syr
KJV NKJV (RSV) NRSVmg (NASB NJB)

Though the documentary evidence is nearly divided here, internal considerations favor the WH NU reading. Scribes would be prone to change the plural υμων to the singular σοι because this was an epistle addressed to an individual, Timothy. However, it was Paul's habit to address the final salutations to more people than the one noted as the addressee at the beginning of the epistle—probably because Paul considered his epistle to be received by a more inclusive audience (see 2 Tim 4:22; Titus 3:15; Phlm 25). Thus, the plural "you" indicates that Paul directed this epistle to Timothy and the members of the Ephesian church.

English versions wishing to show the plural render this as "Grace be with you all." As for the other versions that simply read "grace be with you," the reader will assume that the "you" is singular—with reference to Timothy.

1 Timothy 6:21b

WH NU omit αμην ("Amen") at end of verse
א* A D* F G 33 1739* it
RSV NRSV ESV NASB NIV TNIV NEB REB NJB NAB NLT HCSB NET

variant/TR include αμην ("Amen") at end of verse
א[2] D[1] Ψ 1739[c] Maj syr
KJV NKJV NRSVmg NJBmg

The documentary evidence for the WH NU reading is superior to that for the variant. It is likely that the final "amen" was added by scribes for liturgical purposes. Only three epistles (Romans, Galatians, Jude) appear to have a genuine "amen" for the last word.

Subscription

1. No subscription. Found in 323 365 629 630 1505.
2. Προς Τιμοθεον Α ("First to Timothy"). Appears in א 33.
3. Προς Τιμοθεον Α επληρωθη ("End of [the] First to Timothy"). Appears in D.
4. επληρωθη επιστολη προς Τιμοθεον Α ("End of the First Epistle to Timothy"). Appears in F G.
5. Προς Τιμοθεον Α εγραφη απο Νικοπολεως ("First to Timothy written from Nicopolis"). Appears in P.
6. Προς Τιμοθεον Α εγραφη απο Λαοδικειας ("First Timothy, written from Laodicea"). Appears in A.
7. Προς Τιμοθεον Α απο Λαοδικειας ητις μετροπολις Φρυγιας της Πακατιανης ("First to Timothy written from Laodicea which is a chief city of Phrygia of Pacatiana"). Appears in 1739[c] Maj (so TR).

As with all the books of the NT, it is fairly certain that no book had an inscription or a subscription (see Comfort 2005, 9-10). This is especially true for the Epistles because their original purpose was to be apostolic letters, not literary works per se. Thus, all inscriptions and subscriptions are scribal additions. In this case, several late minuscules do not include any subscription (which reflects the original). The simplest form of the subscription, Προς Τιμοθεον Α (= "1 Timothy"), appears in several of the earliest extant witnesses. The subscription was then expanded to include the place of writing—either, Nicopolis or Laodicea (with the descriptor, "which is a chief city of Phrygia of Pacatiana," in the majority of late manuscripts). This final, expanded subscription appears in TR. But this location does not coincide with the internal evidence of the epistle itself, which implies that Paul was in Macedonia when he wrote this epistle to Timothy (see 1:3). As such, "Nicopolis" (variant 3) is closer to the mark, for it was a town in Achaia bordering Macedonia, and it was the place from which Paul wrote his epistle to Titus (see Titus 3:12)—an epistle which seems contemporaneous with 1 Timothy.

The Second Epistle to TIMOTHY

2 Timothy 1:2

TR WH NU   Χριστοῦ Ἰησοῦ τοῦ κυρίου ἡμῶν
"Christ Jesus our Lord"
ℵ[2] A D F G I Ψ Maj it syr[h] cop[sa]
KJV NKJV RSV NRSV ESV NASB NIV TNIV REB NJB NAB NLT HCSB NET

variant 1   Ιησου Χριστου του κυριου ημων
"Jesus Christ our Lord"
1739 1881
none

variant 2   κυριου Ιησου Χριστου
"Lord Jesus Christ"
ℵ* 33
NEB

The manuscript evidence strongly favors the TR WH NU reading. As often occurred in the history of textual transmission, the name "Christ Jesus" was transposed to "Jesus Christ" (so the first variant). Paul typically used "Christ Jesus," especially in the introductions to each of his epistles. The second variant, followed by NEB, reveals alteration to a usual formulation: "Lord Jesus Christ."

2 Timothy 1:10

WH NU   τοῦ σωτῆρος ἡμῶν Χριστοῦ Ἰησοῦ
"our Savior, Christ Jesus"
ℵ* A D*
RSV NRSV ESV NASB NIV TNIV NJB NAB NLT HCSB NET

variant 1/TR   του σωτηρος ημων Ιησου Χριστου
"our Savior, Jesus Christ"
ℵ[2] C D[2] F G Ψ 33 1739 1881 Maj it syr cop
KJV NKJV NEB REB

variant 2   του σωτηρος ημων θεου
"our Savior, God"
I
none

Although the textual evidence for the variant is extensive, it is not overwhelming. In fact, some of the earliest manuscripts support the WH NU reading. Thus, it is likely that the first variant is the result of scribal conformity to other passages where the title "Savior" accompanies "Jesus Christ." In the Pastoral Epistles, this occurs in Titus 2:13; 3:6. The influence may have also come from verses like Phil 3:20; 2 Pet 1:1, 11; 2:20; 3:18. But Paul was more prone to use "Christ Jesus" than "Jesus Christ," even with the designation "Savior" (see Titus 1:4, where 1739 and 1881 have the variant transposition, "Jesus Christ"). The second variant in Codex I reveals scribal alteration to a typical phrase found in the Pastoral Epistles: "God our Savior" (see 1 Tim 1:1; 2:3; 4:10; Titus 1:3; 2:10, 13; 3:4).

2 Timothy 1:11

WH NU　διδάσκαλος
"teacher"
א* A I
NKJVmg RSV NRSV ESV NASB NIV TNIV NEB REB NJB NAB NLT HCSB NET

variant 1/TR　διδασκαλος εθνων
"teacher of [the] Gentiles"
א[2] C D F G Ψ 1739 Maj it syr cop
KJV NKJV NRSVmg NJBmg HCSBmg NETmg

variant 2　διακονος
"servant"
33
none

According to WH NU, Paul's full statement is, "I was appointed a herald and an apostle and teacher." This reading is challenged by the textual evidence for the first variant. However, this variant has to be discounted for three reasons: (1) three early and reliable Greek manuscripts have the shorter reading; (2) there is no easy way to explain the omission of εθνων had it originally been in the text; (3) the first variant is most likely the result of scribal conformity to 1 Tim 2:7, wherein Paul names himself "a teacher of the Gentiles." The second variant is also a scribal creation, reflecting assimilation to such verses as 1 Cor 3:5; 2 Cor 3:6; 6:4; 11:23; Eph 3:7; Col 1:23-25.

2 Timothy 1:18

WH NU　ἐν Ἐφέσῳ διηκόνησεν
"he ministered in Ephesus"
א A C D F G Ψ 1739
RSV NRSV ESV NASB NEB REB NAB NLT HCSB

variant/TR　εν Εφεσω διηκονησεν μοι
"he ministered to me in Ephesus"
104 365 (629) it syr
KJV NKJV NIV TNIV NJB NET

The manuscript evidence decidedly favors the WH NU reading. The pronoun μοι was added to specify that Onesiphorus's ministry was exclusively for Paul. Although this may be true and what Paul intended to say, it is just as likely that Onesiphorus's ministry included services rendered to others in Ephesus, as well as to Paul.

2 Timothy 2:3

WH NU συγκακοπάθησον
"take your share of hardship"
ℵ A C* D* F G H* I 33 1739 1881*vid syr^hmg cop^bo
NKJVmg RSV NRSV ESV NASB NIV TNIV NEB REB NJB NAB NLT HCSB NET

variant 1/TR συ ουν κακοπαθησον
"you therefore suffer hardship"
C^3 D^1 H^c Ψ 1881^c Maj syr^h
KJV NKJV

variant 2 κακοπαθησον
"suffer hardship"
1175 it
none

The WH NU reading, which has early and diverse documentary attestation, can mean "take your share of hardship" (as in NEB), or "suffer together with us" (as in the NIV), or "endure suffering along with me" (as in NLT). Paul was asking Timothy to take his share of suffering, or to join Paul and his coworkers in their hardships as they served Christ. It was probably this ambiguity that prompted some scribe(s) to change the verb to the non-prefixed verb, κακοπαθησον ("suffer hardship"), and to repeat the pronoun and particle (συ ουν) of 2:1. It is also possible that some scribe mistook συγκακοπαθησον for συουνκακοπαθησον, but this would be unusual. In any event, the change became popular in the textual tradition and engendered the emendation of several manuscripts (C^3 D^1 H^c 1881^c), which originally had the WH NU reading. TR adopted the variant, which has been perpetuated in KJV and NKJV.

2 Timothy 2:4

As a carryover from 2:3, several Western witnesses (F G it) clarify the spiritual meaning of στρατευομενος ("serving as a soldier") by adding τω θεω: "serving *God* as a soldier."

2 Timothy 2:14

WH NU ἐνώπιον τοῦ θεοῦ
"in the sight of God"
ℵ C F G I
RSVmg NRSV ESV NASB NIV TNIV NEB REB NJB NAB NLT HCSB NETmg

variant 1/TR ενωπιον του κυριου
"in the sight of the Lord"
A D Ψ 048 1739 Maj it^b syr
KJV NKJV RSV NRSVmg NJBmg HCSBmg NET

variant 2 ενωπιον του Χριστου
"in the sight of Christ"
206 429 1758
none

The textual evidence supports the WH NU reading, as does the fact that when Paul spoke of giving witness, he did so "in the sight of God" (ενωπιον του θεου)—see 1 Tim 5:21; 2 Tim 4:1. The first and second variants were probably created by some scribe(s) influenced by the previous verses (2:10-13), which speak of Christ Jesus and the believers' relationship to him.

2 Timothy 2:18

TR NU read τηυ αυαστασιυ ("the resurrection"); in the NU edition, the article is bracketed. With the support of A C D Ψ 1739 Maj, this yields the rendering: "they are saying the resurrection has already occurred and overthrown the faith of some." WH excludes the definite article on the basis of ℵ F G 048 33. The first reading, with the inclusion of the article, specifies an event—"the resurrection." The variant reading, without an article, denotes a phenomenon, "resurrection"—"they are saying resurrection has already occurred." Which of these were Hymenaeus and Philetus denying?

Given the TR NU reading, the idea is that Hymenaeus and Philetus denied the future resurrection by claiming that the resurrection had already happened. (See 2 Thess 2:2 for a similar heresy.) But the Scriptures make it very clear that the believers' future glory rests on the literal reality of the resurrection (see 1 Cor 15:12-34). To believe it to have already happened is to deny its true sense.

If the variant is original, then it is possible that Hymenaeus and Philetus denied any kind of future resurrection. In saying that "resurrection already occurred," they would be saying that the believers already experienced resurrection when they believed in Christ. They may have used Paul's own words (Rom 6:4; Eph 2:6; Col 2:12) to teach that the resurrection was merely the spiritual raising of souls from spiritual death or that resurrection was the release of the spirit from the body at the point of death—a prominent Greek notion.

Although it is possible that Paul could have written either τηυ αυαστασιυ ("the resurrection") or αυαστασιυ ("resurrection"), it is likely that scribes added the article to make it clear that the text refers to the eschatological resurrection. However, it is even more likely that after Hymenaeus's excommunication (see 1 Tim 1:20), he and Philetus troubled the church with false notions of resurrection. By way of example, the *Acts of Paul and Thecla* has Demas and Hermogenes say that the resurrection "has already taken place in the children whom we have, and that we are risen again in that we have come to know the true God" (14).

2 Timothy 2:24

TR WH NU read ηπιου ειυαι προς παυτας ("to be gentle to all") on the basis of good authority: ℵ A C D[2] Ψ 048 33 1739 Maj syr cop. A variant on this in D* F G replaces the first word with υηπιου ("infant")—hence, the rendering, "a servant of the Lord ought not to fight but ought to be an infant to all."

There is a one-letter difference (*nu*) between the variants: υηπιου ("infant"); ηποιυ ("gentle"). One word could have easily been confused for the other in the transcription process. The same textual variant occurred in 1 Thess 2:7, where the same manuscripts, D* F G, read υηπιου ("infant") instead of ηπιου ("gentle"). In both instances, the word υηπιου is the more difficult reading, but not so difficult that it is impossible. As in 1 Thess 2:7, where Paul claimed to have been an infant among the Thessalonians, so here he may have been encouraging Timothy to assume the same lowly position. Of course, ηπιου ("gentle") works just as well.

2 Timothy 3:8

TR WH NU Ἰάννης καὶ Ἰαμβρῆς
"Jannes and Jambres"
ℵ A C[1] D Maj
all

variant 1 Ιαννης και Μαμβρης
"Jannes and Mambres"
F G it vg
NJBmg

variant 2 Ιωαννης και Ιαμβρης
"John and Jambres"
C*
none

The magicians of Egypt, mentioned in Exod 7:11–9:11, are not named in the OT text. But they were given the names Jannes and Jambres (or Mambres—hence, the variant) in Jewish writings (see *CD* 5:18; *Tg. Ps.-J.* 1.3). Westcott and Hort (1882, 135) thought the Western text derived "Mambres" from a Palestinian source. The reading Ιωαννης ("John") agrees with the form of the name occurring in several Jewish writings.

2 Timothy 3:9-10

The scribe of A made two noteworthy changes in these verses. Instead of ανοια ("folly"), he wrote διανοια ("plan"). Thus, the text of A translates: "their plan will be plain to all" (speaking of the workings of the heretical subverters). This is opposed to TR WH NU, which read, "their folly will be plain to all." The change could have been accidental or intentional—perhaps the scribe thought his exemplar was in error. In the following verse (3:10), the scribe of A omitted τη αγαπη ("love"), probably due to homoeoteleuton (τη αγαπη τη υπομονη).

2 Timothy 3:11

In this verse, Paul notes the sufferings that he experienced in Antioch. To this statement, a marginal gloss was added by the scribe of the ninth-century manuscript, Codex Mosquensis (K^{mg}), which reads τουτεστιν α δια την Θεκλαν πεπονθεν· εξ Ιουδαιων πιστευσασι εις Χριστον ("that is, the things which he suffered because of Thecla—from the Jews to those who had believed in Christ"). A similar gloss appears in 181^{mg} and syr^{hmg}. Thecla appears in the apocryphal work, *Acts of Paul and Thecla*.

2 Timothy 3:14

According to WH NU, Paul reminds Timothy about those from whom (plural) he has learned the Christian truths: ειδως παρα τινων εμαθες ("knowing from whom you have learned"). This has good manuscript support from ℵ A C* F G 33 1739. TR has a singular pronoun, τινος, with the inferior support of C^3 D Ψ Maj. Since both Greek pronouns are translated as "whom" in English, it is impossible to discern any difference in English versions—unless the English translation makes a conscious effort to show the plural (as in NLT: "those who taught you"). The variant is obviously a scribal attempt to make the text say that Paul was pointing only to himself as Timothy's teacher (see 3:10). But Paul was neither egotistical nor exclusive. The plural indicates that Paul was reminding Timothy of the various teachers who had taught him—especially Lois and Eunice, who had taught him the Scriptures ever since he was a child (2 Tim 1:5; 3:15-16).

2 Timothy 3:15

Two Greek editions, TR NU, read τα ιερα γραμματα ("the sacred writings"), with the documentary support of A C* D[1] Ψ 1739 Maj. (NU brackets the definite article.) The WH edition, following other manuscripts (ℵ C[2vid] D* F G 33), does not include the definite article: ιερα γραμματα ("sacred writings"). The manuscript evidence for the two readings is nearly evenly divided—with the WH reading having a slight edge. Nonetheless, the genuine reading cannot be easily determined on external grounds. Judging on internal evidence, it is far more likely that the article was added than deleted, because scribes would want to make it clear that the wording ιερα γραμματα refers to *the* sacred writings—i.e., the holy Scriptures (Fee 1988, 281), which we now know as the Old Testament. But ιερα γραμματα without the article was also used in antiquity to refer to the sacred Scriptures (see Josephus, *Ant.* 10.210; Philo, *Moses* 2.292).

2 Timothy 3:16

According to all Greek manuscripts, the verse begins with the wording πασα γραφη θεοπνευστος και ωφελιμος προς διδασκαλιαν, which is usually rendered as "all Scripture is God-inspired and profitable for teaching." But several ancient translations (it syr[p] vg) show a modification of the first part of this verse, wherein the word και is omitted, thereby producing the rendering, "all Scripture inspired by God is profitable for teaching." The difference in meaning is significant. The Greek affirms the inspiration of all Scripture because it is "God-breathed" (θεοπνευστος). The translations indicate that one must teach only God-inspired Scripture, thereby allowing the interpretation that some Scriptures (or writings) are not inspired and therefore not worthy to be taught. Some modern translations also display this variation. NEB, for example, reads "every inspired scripture has its use for teaching" (see also NRSVmg). This rendering ignores και and makes θεοπνευστος attributive. In the Greek θεοπνευστος is most certainly predicative, thereby yielding the translation, "all Scripture is God-breathed."

2 Timothy 4:1a

WH NU	διαμαρτύρομαι "I solemnly charge" ℵ A C D* F G I P 33 1739 1881 NKJVmg RSV NRSV ESV NASB NIV TNIV NEB REB NJB NAB NLT HCSB NET
variant 1	διαμαρτυρομαι ουν "therefore I solemnly charge" Ψ 1505 none
variant 2	διαμαρτυρομαι εγω "I myself solemnly charge" 326* none
variant 3/TR	διαμαρτυρομαι ουν εγω "therefore I myself solemnly charge" D[1] Maj KJV NKJV

The manuscript evidence overwhelmingly favors the reading in WH NU. All the variants display scribal additions. The first makes the verse clearly mark the beginning of a conclusion; the second makes Paul's personal declaration more emphatic; the third combines both these elements. This third variant appears in the majority of manuscripts, and thus found its way into TR, followed by KJV and NKJV.

2 Timothy 4:1b

WH NU — καὶ τὴν ἐπιφάνειαν αὐτοῦ
"and by his appearing"
ℵ* A C D* F G 1739
NKJVmg RSV NRSV ESV NASB NIV TNIV NEB REB NJB NAB (NLT) HCSB NET

variant/TR — κατα την επιφανειαν αυτου
"according to his appearing"
ℵ[2] D[2] Ψ Maj
KJV NKJV

The WH NU reading, strongly supported by the manuscript evidence, is syntactically awkward. Evidently, the phrase is to be joined with the opening predicate: "I make this charge before God and Christ Jesus . . . and by his appearing and his coming." In other words, Paul's charge to Timothy is made in the presence of God and Christ *and* in view of Jesus' parousia. Nonetheless, the syntactical awkwardness prompted an emendation which, by simply changing και to κατα, produces a smoother reading: "I make this charge before God and Christ Jesus, the one who is about to judge the living and the dead at his appearing and his coming." The variant reading means that Jesus will execute judgment at the time of his parousia.

2 Timothy 4:8

In this verse, Paul declares his expectation of receiving a crown of righteousness after Christ's return, a crown that the Lord promised to Paul and to all who love his appearance (or epiphany). Several witnesses, primarily Western (D* 1739* 1881 it syr[p]) omit πασι ("all") from the expression, πασι τοις ηγαπηκοσι την επιφανειαν αυτου ("to all the ones having loved his appearing"). Since the omission cannot be easily explained on transcriptional grounds, it is possible that some scribe took exception with the statement that all would receive the same crown as Paul.

2 Timothy 4:10

TR WH NU — Κρήσκης εἰς Γαλατίαν
"Crescens [went] to Galatia"
A D F G L Ψ 33 1739
all

variant — Κρησκης εις Γαλλιαν
"Crescens [went] to Gallian (= Gaul)"
ℵ C 81 104 326 Eusebius
RSVmg NRSVmg NEBmg REBmg NJBmg

The variant reading, which can also be translated "Gaul," could be the result of a transcriptional error, because the two words are quite similar: Γαλατιαν/Γαλλιαν. But it is more likely that the variant is a scribal alteration, for in the early centuries of the Christian era the Roman province Galatia was commonly known as Gaul or Gallia—named after the Gallic mercenaries who settled there (see NJBmg).

2 Timothy 4:14

WH NU ἀποδώσει αὐτῷ ὁ κύριος
"the Lord will repay him"
ℵ A C D*,c F G 33 1739
RSV NRSV ESV NASB NIV TNIV NEB REB NJB NAB NLT HCSB NET

variant/TR αποδωη αυτω ο κυριος
"may the Lord repay him"
D² Ψ Maj
KJV NKJV

Paul was speaking of Alexander the coppersmith, who did much harm to him. Having been excommunicated by Paul (see 1 Tim 1:20), Alexander may have sought revenge by accusing Paul before the Roman judges, whether of insurrection or of introducing a new religion. As a result, Paul was imprisoned for the second time. The future tense of the WH NU reading indicates that Paul was sure that the Lord would judge Alexander the coppersmith for his evil deeds. The variant verb, in the subjunctive mood, suggests an imprecatory prayer. Though both readings are contextually plausible, the WH NU reading has superior documentation and must be considered original.

2 Timothy 4:19

After the words ασπασαι Πρισκα και Ακυλαν ("greet Prisca and Aquila"), two late minuscules (181 460) insert Λεκτραν την γυναικα αυτου και Σιμαιαν και Ζηνωνα τους υιους αυτου ("Lectra his wife and Simaias and Zeno his sons"). According to the apocryphal book, *Acts of Paul and Thecla* (§ 2), these are the names of the wife and children of Onesiphorus. This insertion should have been made after Ονησιφορου ("Onesiphorus"). Its incorrect placement, after Ακυλαν ("Aquila"), makes Aquila have two wives, Priscilla and Lektra (see TCGNT).

2 Timothy 4:22a

WH NU ὁ κύριος
"the Lord"
ℵ* F G 33 1739 cop^sa
RSV NRSV ESV NASB NIV TNIV NEB REB NJB NAB NLT HCSB NET

variant 1 ο κυριος Ιησους
"the Lord Jesus"
A 104 614
NETmg

variant 2/TR ο κυριος Ιησου Χριστου
"the Lord Jesus Christ"
ℵ² C D Ψ Maj it^b syr cop^bo
KJV NKJV NETmg

Accidental omission of divine names is rare in the history of textual transmission (see TCGNT). On the contrary, since scribes had a propensity for expanding sacred names, it is most likely that the text originally read "Lord," which was then expanded to "Lord Jesus" and to "Lord Jesus Christ."

2 Timothy 4:22b

WH NU	ἡ χάρις μεθ' ὑμῶν. "Grace be with you [plural]" ℵ* A C F G 33 1739* NRSV ESV TNIV NEB REB NAB NLT
variant 1	η χαρις μεθ σου "grace be with you [singular]" syr^{p} cop^{boMS,saMS} KJV NKJV (RSV NASB NIV NJB HCSB NET)
variant 2	η χαρις μεθ ημων "grace be with us" 460 614 cop^{boMS} none
variant 3	ερρωσο εν ειρηνη "enjoy good health with peace" D^{*,1} it^{b} none
variant 4	omit sentence cop^{saMSS} none

Some ancient translators carried over the singular pronoun from the previous clause (variant 1). Other scribes mistakenly wrote ημων for υμων, a common transcriptional error (variant 2). The third variant, from Western witnesses, presents a typical Hellenistic conclusion to a letter (see Acts 15:29; 23:30—see note) combined with a Judeo-Christian blessing, "in peace." The fourth variant, a complete omission of this blessing, could reflect the most primitive form of the epistle. However, the WH NU reading, on the basis of excellent testimony, retains a plural pronoun; this benediction was therefore directed to Timothy and the members of the Ephesian church. Paul expected that his epistles addressed to individuals would be read by others in the local church (see 2 Tim 4:22; Titus 3:15; Phlm 25). English versions wishing to show the plural render this as "Grace be with you all." As for the other versions that simply read "Grace be with you," the reader will think the "you" refers only to Timothy.

2 Timothy 4:22c

WH NU	omit αμην ("Amen") at end of verse ℵ* A C F G 33 1739* it^{b} cop^{sa} RSV NRSV ESV NASB NIV TNIV NEB REB NJB NAB NLT HCSB NET
variant/TR	include αμην ("Amen") at end of verse ℵ^{2} D Ψ 1739^{c} Maj it syr KJV NKJV NRSVmg NETmg

The documentary evidence for the WH NU reading is superior to that for the variant. The final "amen" was added by scribes for liturgical purposes. Only three epistles (Romans, Galatians, Jude) appear to have a genuine "amen" following the final benediction.

Subscription

1. No subscription. Found in 323 365 629 630 1505.
2. Προς Τιμοθεον ("To Timothy"). Appears in ℵ C 33.
3. Προς Τιμοθεον Β ("Second to Timothy"). Appears in (D F G).
4. Προς Τιμοθεον Β εγραφη απο Λαοδικειας ("Second to Timothy written from Laodicea"). Appears in A.
5. Προς Τιμοθεον Β εγραφη απο Ρωμης ("Second to Timothy written from Rome"). Appears in P 1739* 1881.
6. Προς Τιμοθεον Β της Εφεσιων εκκλησιας επισκοπον πρωτον χειροτονηθεντα εγραφη απο Ρωμης οτε εκ δευτερου παρεστη Παυλος τω Καισαρι Ρωμης Νερωνι ("Second to Timothy, the first hand-picked overseer of the Ephesian church, written from Rome when Paul was placed before Rome's Caesar Nero the second time"). Appears in 1739[c] Maj (so TR).

It is fairly certain that no book of the NT had a title (inscription) or a subscription (see Comfort 2005, 9-10). This is especially true for the Epistles because their original purpose was to be apostolic letters, not literary works per se. Thus, all inscriptions and subscriptions are scribal additions. In this case, several late minuscules do not include any subscription (which reflects the original). The simplest form of the subscription, Προς Τιμοθεον, appears in some ancient witnesses (ℵ C 33). The subscription was designated Προς Τιμοθεον Β in the twin Western manuscripts, F G, and it is slightly expanded in D with the added επληρωθη (= "the end" or "completed"). Two other variants include the place of writing—either Laodicea or Rome. Where the scribe of Codex A came up with "Laodicea" is not easy to discern. Perhaps he unwittingly copied it from the subscription to 1 Timothy (see note). Paul was most likely in Rome when he wrote this letter, because it was penned just prior to his execution during Nero's reign (see Eusebius, *Hist. eccl.* 2.22). (About five years had elapsed between Paul's first imprisonment in A.D. 63 and his martyrdom in A.D. 68, the last year of Nero's reign.) This information is reflected in the final, expanded subscription, which provides added details about Timothy's position in Ephesus. This extensive subscription appears in TR.

The Epistle to TITUS

Titus 1:1

According to TR WH NU, Paul introduces himself as δουλος θεου, αποστολος δε Ιησου Χριστου ("a slave of God, and an apostle of Jesus Christ"), with the testimony of ℵ C D^c 33 1739 Maj. This reading is followed by all English versions. However, there are two variants on the name Jesus Christ. The first is Χριστου Ιησου ("Christ Jesus") in A 1175 it^b syr^h; the second is Χριστου ("Christ") in D*. The first variant is easy to explain. Whenever Paul introduced himself as an apostle, he called himself "an apostle of Christ Jesus" (see 1 Cor 1:1; 2 Cor 1:1; Eph 1:1; Phil 1:1; Col 1:1; 1 Tim 1:1; 2 Tim 1:1). Expecting the same pattern, but not finding it in the introduction to Titus, some scribes and translators transposed the words to what they considered normal Pauline style. The second variant in D* reveals this scribe's independence.

Titus 1:4a

WH NU	χάρις καὶ εἰρήνη "grace and peace" ℵ C* D F G Ψ 088 it syr^p cop RSV NRSV ESV NASB NIV TNIV NEB REB NJB NAB NLT HCSB NET
variant 1/TR	χαρις ελεος ειρηνη "grace, mercy, peace" A C^2 Maj syr^h KJV NKJV NRSVmg
variant 2	χαρις υμιν και ειρηνη "grace to you [plural] and peace" 33 none
variant 3	χαρις ειρηνη "grace, peace" 1739 1881 none

Three of the earliest manuscripts (ℵ C* 088) do not have the word "mercy." Later copyists likely added "mercy" in an attempt to emulate the style of the two other Pastoral Epistles (see 1 Tim 1:2; 2 Tim 1:2). This reading became popular, finding its way into the majority of manuscripts and TR. The second variant reveals assimilation to other Pauline epistles (see Rom 1:7; 1 Cor 1:3, etc.). The third variant is the result of a scribal error or an intentional truncation.

Titus 1:4b

WH NU Χριστοῦ Ἰησοῦ
"Christ Jesus"
ℵ A C D* Ψ 088 0240 33 it
NKJVmg RSV NRSV ESV NASB NIV TNIV NEB NJB NAB NLT HCSB NET

variant 1 Ιησου Χριστου
"Jesus Christ"
1739 1881
REB

variant 2/TR κυριου Ιησου Χριστου
"Lord Jesus Christ"
D[2] F G Maj syr
KJV NKJV

As often happened in the course of textual transmission, the name "Christ Jesus" was transposed to "Jesus Christ" and/or enlarged to "Lord Jesus Christ." Paul habitually preferred "Christ Jesus," especially in the introductions to each of his epistles (see note on 1:1). This reading has the best manuscript evidence in this instance, and is followed by all modern English versions except REB.

Titus 1:9

At the end of this verse, the trilingual manuscript 406 (Greek, Latin, Arabic; thirteenth century) adds this admonition: "Do not appoint those who have married twice or make them deacons, and do not take wives in a second marriage; let them not come to serve the divine one at the altar. As God's servant, reprove the rulers who are unrighteous judges and robbers and liars and merciless." This interpolation provides Titus with qualifications for deacons. No doubt, 1 Tim 3:1-13 influenced this expansion because in 1 Timothy, qualifications for deacons follow qualifications for elders.

Interestingly, the first sentence in this addendum provides one explanation of the wording μιας γυναικος ανηρ ("a one-wife man") in 1:6. Thus, an elder and a deacon are not prohibited from polygamy, but from remarriage—according to this scribe's interpretation. The mention of service at the altar suggests that this scribe was thinking of a liturgical setting common in the thirteenth century.

Titus 1:11

At the end of the verse, the trilingual manuscript 406 (see note on 1:9) has the addition: "The children who ill-treat or hit their parents you must teach and reprove and admonish as a father does [his] children."

Titus 1:14

Influenced by 1 Tim 1:4, a parallel verse, a few scribes (075 1908) changed εντολαις ("commandments") to γενεαλογιαις ("genealogies"). The twin manuscripts F G display the surrogate ενταλμασιν ("charge"), perhaps influenced by 1 Tim 6:14.

Titus 2:5a

The Greek word οικουργους ("home-worker") is certainly original—on two counts: (1) It has superior documentation (ℵ* A C D* F G I Ψ 33), and (2) it is a rare word in Greek literature, appearing only elsewhere in Soranus (BDAG 700). A variant οικουρους ("home-keeper") has weaker attestation (ℵ[2] D[2] H 1739 Maj—so TR) and was far more common in Greek literature.

Titus 2:5b

As a carryover from 1 Tim 6:1, the expression ινα μη ο λογος του θεου βλασφημηται ("lest the word of God be blasphemed") was expanded with the addition, και η διδασκαλια (= "lest the word of God and the teaching be blasphemed") in one Greek manuscript (C) and a few ancient translations (one Vulgate MS and syr[h]).

Titus 2:7a

There are four variants on the word used to describe the attitude Titus should express in his teaching. WH NU follow the reading αφθοριαν (literally, "incorruption," meaning "soundness"), with good support from ℵ* A C D* 33 1739 1881 it cop. TR has the second variant: αδιαφθοριαν ("sincerity," "integrity"), with the inferior support of ℵ[2] D[1] Ψ Maj. The third variant is αφθονιαν ("without envy"), having good support from 𝔓[32] F G 1881 cop[sa]. The fourth variant, a scribal mistake, is αδιαφοριαν ("indifference"), found in a few late manuscripts: 35[c] 205 1905.

Among the four readings, the WH NU reading and the third variant are more likely to be original. Both readings have fairly good textual support, and both readings are difficult inasmuch as this is the only occurrence of either word in the NT. Thus, it is difficult to say which was written first and which was substituted for the other. Since there is only a one-letter difference between the words (ρ/ν), either could have been mistaken for the other in the transcription process. Furthermore, both words are difficult in this context and invite change. Nonetheless, the word αφθονιαν would cause the most problems—for why would Paul urge Titus to be "free from envy" in his teachings? It is more understandable that he would urge him to have no corruption (αφθοριαν) in his teaching. For this is tantamount to saying that Titus's teaching needed to be "sound and wholesome"—a constant admonition in the Pastoral Epistles. But the charge to be "free from envy" is one which calls upon Titus to exhibit purity in his teaching within a climate of opposition, where some would oppose Titus out of jealousy and envy (see 2:8). The TR reading, found in the majority of manuscripts, was probably first created by a scribe who wanted a more sensible word in this context or thought his exemplar was in error and consequently corrected αφθοριαν to αδιαφθοριαν (as in ℵ[2] D[1]).

Titus 2:7b

WH NU	σεμνότητα "with seriousness" 𝔓[32vid] ℵ A C D* F G 33 1739 1881 it cop NKJVmg RSV NRSV ESV NASB NIV TNIV NEB REB NJB NAB NLT HCSB NET
variant/TR	σεμνοτητα, αφθαρσιαν "with seriousness, with incorruptibility" D[2] Ψ Maj syr[h] KJV NKJV

The additional word in the variant reading may have been borrowed from 2 Tim 1:10. But it is more likely that when the word αφθοριαν was changed to αδιαφθοριαν (note that the manuscripts are the same for this variant as for TR in 2:7a), some scribe noticed αφθοριαν in his exemplar and then decided to add it at the end of the verse. But misunderstanding the rare word αφθοριαν, the scribe wrote the more common αφθαρσιαν (see BDAG 155-156). This reading took hold, was multiplied in the majority of manuscripts, was printed in TR, and then was translated in KJV and NKJV. Not one modern translation has followed this reading or even noted it.

Titus 2:8

WH NU λέγειν περὶ ἡμῶν φαῦλον
"to speak bad about us"
ℵ C D* F G 33 1739 Maj it cop
NKJVmg RSV NRSV ESV NASB NIV TNIV NEB REB NJB NAB NLT HCSB NET

variant/TR λεγειν περι υμων φαυλον
"to speak bad about you"
A vg
KJV NKJV

According to the WH NU reading, Paul was encouraging Titus to teach in a way that would not bring criticism, so that "the opposer should not have anything bad to say about us." The variant is a scribal attempt to provide the passage with a more readily understood pronoun. The second person plural found its way into TR (not through the Majority Text in this instance) and was translated in the KJV and NKJV. But Paul used the first person plural to show his solidarity with the Christian community at Crete. He considered himself to be a part of their testimony to the world.

Titus 2:11

WH NU ἡ χάρις τοῦ θεοῦ σωτήριος πᾶσιν ἀνθρώποις
"the grace of God, salvation to all people"
ℵ[2] A C* D* 0278 1739 Clement
RSV NRSV ESV NASB NIV TNIV NEB (REB) NJB NAB NLT HCSB NET

variant 1 η χαρις του θεου σωτηρος πασιν ανθρωποις
"the grace of God, Savior to all people"
ℵ* it[t]
none

variant 2 η χαρις του θεου σωτηρος ημων πασιν ανθρωποις
"the grace of God our Savior to all people"
F G it[b] cop
none

variant 3/TR η χαρις του θεου η σωτηριος πασιν ανθρωποις
"the grace of God which [is] salvation to all people"
(C[3]) D[2] Ψ 33 Maj
KJV NKJV

The first two variants display scribal conformity to the previous verse, wherein the expression σωτηρος ημων θεου ("God our Savior") appears. The third variant, in TR, is an attempt to clarify that the grace of God is the salvation brought to all people. The WH NU reading says the same thing by way of apposition—σωτηριος ("salvation") being a further description of η χαρις του θεου ("the grace of God"). In translation, the relationship of "salvation" to "all" can be understood in two ways: (1) God's grace has appeared, bringing salvation to all (so translated above), or (2) God's grace has appeared to all, bringing salvation (see NRSV and NRSVmg).

Titus 2:13

TR NU	τοῦ μεγάλου θεοῦ καὶ σωτῆρος ἡμῶν ᾿Ιησοῦ Χριστοῦ "our great God and Savior, Jesus Christ" ℵ[2] A C D Ψ 0278 33 Maj it syr KJV NKJV RSV NRSV ESV NIV TNIV NAB NLT HCSB NET
variant 1/WH	του μεγαλου θεου και σωτηρος ημων Χριστου Ιησου "our great God and Savior, Christ Jesus" ℵ* F G it[b] NASB NEB REB NJB
variant 2	του μεγαλου θεου και σωτηρος ημων Ιησου "our great God and Savior, Jesus" 1739 none

The TR NU reading can also be rendered "the glory of the great God and of our Savior, Jesus Christ"—that is, the glory belongs both to God and to the Savior Jesus Christ. But the Greek syntax favors the rendering "our great God and Savior, Jesus Christ." In the Greek, there is one article governing the two titles "God" and "Savior Jesus Christ" joined by the conjunction και ("and"). According to a Greek grammatical rule (called the "Granville Sharp Rule"—see Dana and Mantey 1927, 147), this structure indicates that the two nouns describe one person. In this case, Jesus Christ is both God and Savior. Furthermore, Paul never used the word "appearing" when speaking of God the Father (cf. 1 Tim 6:16). This refers only to Christ, with reference to his first coming (2 Tim 1:10) or his second coming (1 Tim 6:14; 2 Tim 4:1, 8). Several English versions affirm this interpretation by setting "Jesus Christ" in clear apposition to "our great God and Savior"— for example, see NRSV, NIV, and NLT. Neither of the variant readings alters this ascription of deity to Jesus. The first is a typical transposition (see notes on 1:1; 1:4b), and the second an atypical shortening of a sacred name.

Titus 3:9

Displaying harmonization to 1 Tim 6:4, the twin manuscripts F and G read ζητησεις και λογομαχιας ("controversies and disputes over words") instead of ζητησεις και γενεαλογιας ("controversies and genealogies"). See note on 1:14.

Titus 3:15a

TR WH NU read η χαρις μετα παντων υμων ("the grace be with you all"), with the excellent support of 𝔓[61vid] ℵ A C H Ψ 048 1739 Maj syr cop. This reading is followed by all English versions. There are several variants on this in the textual tradition: (1) η χαρις του θεου μετα παντων υμων ("the grace of God be with you all") in F G; (2) η χαρις του κυριου μετα παντων υμων ("the grace of the Lord be with you all") in D it[b]; (3) η χαρις μετα του πνευματος σου ("the grace be with your [singular] spirit") in 33;

(4) η χαρις μετα παντων υμων και μετα του πνευματος σου ("the grace be with you all and with your [singular] spirit") in 81.

The expansions in variants 1 and 2 append a divine name to "grace." The third and fourth variants show conformity to 2 Tim 4:22. The plural, found in all manuscripts except 33, indicates that Paul was addressing an audience greater than just Titus (cf. 1 Tim 6:21; 2 Tim 4:22; Phlm 25).

Titus 3:15b

WH NU	omit αμην ("Amen") at end of verse ℵ* A C D* 048 33 1739 it[b] cop[sa] RSV NRSV ESV NASB NIV TNIV NEB REB NJB NAB NLT HCSB NET
variant/TR	include αμην ("Amen") at end of verse ℵ[2] D[1] F G H Ψ 0278 Maj it syr cop[bo] KJV NKJV NRSVmg NJBmg NETmg

The documentary evidence for the WH NU reading is superior to that for the variant. The final "amen" was added by scribes for liturgical purposes. (Note the corrections by later hands in ℵ and D.)

Subscription

1. No subscription. 323 365 629 630 1505.
2. Προς Τιτον ("To Titus"). Appears in 𝔓[61vid] ℵ C (D F G) Ψ 33.
3. Προς Τιτον εγραφη απο Νικοπολεως ("To Titus written from Nicopolis"). Appears in A P[vid].
4. Παυλου αποστολου προς Τιτον της Κρητων εκκλησιας πρωτον επισκοπον χειροτονηθεντα εγραφη απο Νικοπολεως της Μακεδονιας ("Apostle Paul to Titus, the first hand-picked overseer of the Cretan church, written from Nicopolis of Macedonia"). Appears in H (1739 1881) Maj (so TR).

Since no NT book originally had a subscription, 2–4 are scribal additions (see Comfort 2005, 9-10). In this case, several late minuscules do not include any subscription (which reflects the original). The simplest form of the subscription, Προς Τιτον ("to Titus"), appears in several early witnesses (𝔓[61vid] ℵ C D F G Ψ 33). The subscription was then expanded to include the place of writing, Nicopolis. The final, elaborate subscription appears in TR, whose information can be substantiated by the text. Titus was in Crete (1:5), sent there by Paul on a pioneering apostolic mission to elect the elders there and to teach the truth (1:5–2:9), and Paul was writing from Nicopolis (3:12).

The Epistle to PHILEMON

Philemon 1

Instead of naming Paul as δεσμιος Χριστου Ιησου ("prisoner of Christ Jesus"), D* names him αποστολος Χριστου Ιησου ("apostle of Christ Jesus"). This is obviously an assimilation to the opening line of several of Paul's epistles. But in this epistle, where Paul was being more personal and/or did not feel obligated to affirm his authority, he did not mention his apostleship (cf. Phil 1:1). After τω αγαπητω ("the beloved"), D* it[b] add αδελφω ("brother").

Philemon 2

WH NU Ἀπφίᾳ τῇ ἀδελφῇ
"Apphia the [= our] sister"
ℵ A D* F G I P 048 0278 33 1739 cop[bo]
NKJVmg RSV NRSV ESV NASB NIV TNIV NEB REB NJB NAB NLT HCSB NET

variant 1/TR Απφια τη αγαπητη
"Apphia the [= our] beloved"
D[2] Ψ Maj syr[p]
KJV NKJV HCSBmg NETmg

variant 2 Απφια αδελφη τη αγαπητη
"Apphia beloved sister"
629 syr[h]
none

The manuscript evidence overwhelmingly supports the wording in WH NU. The first variant arose as an attempt to make Paul's address to Apphia parallel to his address to Philemon, who is called αγαπητω ("beloved") in v. 1. The second variant is a conflation of the other two readings.

Philemon 5

Some manuscripts (𝔓[61vid] D 1739) transpose the wording σου την αγαπην και την πιστιν ("your love and faith") to σου την πιστιν και την αγαπην ("your faith and love") because the latter is characteristically Pauline. However, in this epistle Paul himself reversed his usual words of greeting because he wanted to appeal to Philemon's love above all else (see vv. 7-9).

Philemon 6a

WH NU πάντὸς ἀγαθοῦ τοῦ ἐν ἡμῖν
"every good that [is] in us"
A C D Ψ 048vid Maj syrhmg
NKJVmg RSV NRSV ESV NASBmg NIV TNIV NEB REB NJB NAB NLT HCSB NETmg

variant 1/TR παντος αγαθου του εν υμιν
"every good that [is] in you [plural]"
𝔓61 א P 0278 33 1739 itb syr cop
KJV NKJV NRSVmg NASB NABmg HCSBmg NET

variant 2 παντος αγαθου εργου του εν υμιν
"every good work that [is] in you [plural]"
F G
none

Paul told Philemon that he was praying that his sharing with others, which comes from faith, may be effective in producing the realization "of every good" (παντος αγαθου). This reading has the support of א D[2] F G Ψ Maj. The abstractness of αγαθου prompted the scribes of F and G to add εργου ("work"), an addition influenced by other Pauline passages (see 2 Cor 9:8; Col 1:10; 2 Thess 2:17).

The idea Paul was trying to communicate is that Philemon needed to activate his sharing, his liberality (κοινωνια), and thereby discover all the good that is within "us" Christians. Christians have a rich resource in Christ, but it takes the "fellowship" to activate it. This fellowship (or sharing) encompasses both spiritual and material giving and receiving among the members of Christ's body. If the text says "in us," it refers to the common inheritance of all believers. If it says "in you [plural]," it is limited to the believers in Colossae (see next note.) This variant has good documentary support and could likely be original, which is why a few modern versions have followed it (NASB NET) or noted it (NRSV NAB HCSB).

Philemon 6b

WH NU εἰς Χριστόν
"for (or, in) Christ"
𝔓61 א* A C 33 cop
RSV NRSV ESV NASB NIV TNIV NEB REB NJB NAB NLT HCSB NET

variant/TR εις Χριστον Ιησουν
"for (or, in) Christ Jesus"
א[2] D F G Ψ 0278 1739 Maj
KJV NKJV

The final prepositional phrase of this verse can be understood as pointing to a result ("activate all the good we have *for* Christ"—i.e., for Christ's glory) or as locative ("activate all the good we have *in* Christ"). However it is understood, the shorter of the two readings is more likely original because (1) the manuscript evidence slightly favors this reading and (2) scribes had a tendency to expand divine names.

Philemon 7

WH NU	χαρὰν γὰρ πολλὴν ἔσχον "for I had much joy" 𝔓[61vid] ℵ A C F G 048 0278 33 1739 syr cop NKJV RSV NRSV ESV NASB NIV TNIV NEB REB NJB NAB NLT HCSB NET
variant 1/TR	χαριν γαρ εχομεν πολλην "for we have much thanksgiving" Ψ Maj syr KJV NKJVmg
variant 2	χαραν γαρ πολλην εχομεν "for we have great joy" D[2] none
variant 3	χαραν γαρ πολλην εσχομεν "for we had great joy" D* it[b] none

The documentary evidence for the WH NU reading is impressively superior to each of the variants. It was probably an accident that made χαραν become χαριν—an error that became perpetuated in the majority of manuscripts and found its way into TR. The change from the singular to the plural was made in the light of Paul's mention that "the saints" (not just Paul) had been refreshed by Philemon.

Philemon 9

The Greek word πρεσβυτης appears in all the manuscripts; it means "old man." However, some scholars (note the conjecture by Bentley cited in NA[27]) and translators (see RSV and TEV) have thought that the word should be πρεσβευτης, meaning "ambassador." For example, Lightfoot (1879, 338-339) argued that the two words were often confused for one another by scribes who made copies of the Septuagint, and therefore the same happened here. But this conjecture is unnecessary, because πρεσβυτης is in all the extant documents and admirably suits the tenor of the epistle, wherein Paul is appealing to Philemon's sympathies. What better way than for Paul to call himself "an old man."

Philemon 12

WH NU	ὃν ἀνέπεμψα σοι, αὐτόν, τοῦτ' ἔστιν τὰ ἐμὰ σπλάγχνα "whom I sent back to you—him, this one [who] is my very heart" ℵ* A (F G) 33 NKJVmg RSV NRSV ESV NASB NIV TNIV NEB REB NJB NAB NLT HCSB NET
variant 1/TR	ον ανεπεμψα. συ δε αυτον, τουτ εστιν τα εμα σπλαγχνα, προσλαβου "whom I sent back. Now you receive him, this one [who] is my very heart" ℵ[2] C[2] D Maj it (syr) (C* σοι instead of συ δε) KJV NKJV HCSBmg

variant 2 ον ανεπεμψα σοι. συ δε αυτον προσλαβου, τουτ εστιν τα εμα σπλαγχνα
"whom I sent back to you. Now you receive him, this one [who] is my very heart"
048 it[g]
none

The manuscript evidence slightly favors the WH NU reading, as does the fact that the textual variants appear to have been intended to fill out a terse statement. But in so doing, scribes prematurely put into the mouth of Paul his request: "receive him." The request does not come until verse 17, by which point Paul has fully prepared Philemon to comply with his request.

Philemon 19

In order to make this verse parallel with v. 20, the scribe of D* added εν κυριω ("in the Lord") after σεαυτον μοι προσοφειλεις ("you owe me yourself").

Philemon 20

WH NU ἐν Χριστῷ
"in Christ"
ℵ A C D* F G L P Ψ 33 1739 syr cop
RSV NRSV ESV NASB NIV TNIV NEB REB NJB NAB NLT HCSB NET

variant/TR εν κυριω
"in the Lord"
D[2] Maj
KJV NKJV

According to the WH NU reading, Paul says to Philemon: "Yes, brother, may I have profit from you in the Lord; refresh my heart in Christ." This WH NU reading is heavily supported by early and extensive documentation. The variant reading is the result of scribal conformity to the immediate context, where εν κυριω ("in the Lord") appears in the first clause.

Philemon 25a

WH NU Ἡ χάρις τοῦ κυρίου Ἰησοῦ Χριστοῦ μετὰ τοῦ πνεύματος ὑμῶν.
"The grace of the Lord Jesus Christ be with your spirit."
ℵ P 33 1739 it[b] syr[h]
RSV NRSV ESV NASB NIV TNIV NEB REB NAB NLT HCSB NET

variant 1/TR Η χαρις του κυριου ημων Ιησου Χριστου μετα του πνευματος υμων.
"The grace of our Lord Jesus Christ be with your spirit."
A C D Ψ 0278 Maj syr[p] cop
KJV NKJV NJB HCSBmg

variant 2 Η χαρις μεθ υμων.
"Grace be with you."
𝔓[87]
none

It should be noted that the short benediction of $\mathfrak{P}^{87}$ is not cited in NA^{27} or UBS^{4}. Instead, both these editions show only that $\mathfrak{P}^{87}$ excludes the final αμην ("Amen") (see next note). See *Text of Earliest MSS*, 617, for a transcription of $\mathfrak{P}^{87}$.

The first two readings have equally strong documentary support, but it can be surmised that the shorter of the two is more likely original, because scribes had a proclivity for expanding benedictions. But the shortest reading of all is found in the earliest manuscript—the second-century papyrus, $\mathfrak{P}^{87}$. This reading could very well be original; it is in full accord with Paul's other personal epistles (1 Timothy, 2 Timothy, Titus), all of which end with the short "grace be with you" (Titus 3:15 adds "all"). It is also in accord with the benediction to Colossians (Col 4:18), to which Philemon was likely originally appended—for the two were written at nearly the same time and were delivered together. If $\mathfrak{P}^{87}$ preserves the original ending, it suggests that many of the extant benedictions in the Pauline epistles were subject to scribal expansion. Such enlargements could have happened when an editor put together the Pauline corpus or soon thereafter by scribes eager to provide a liturgical ending to each NT epistle. Here in Philemon a scribe or scribes could have easily used the benediction in Phil 4:23 or Gal 6:18 as models for enlarging the one at the end of Philemon.

Although a good case can be made for the short benediction, $\mathfrak{P}^{87}$ is the only document to show this shortened reading. It cannot be said with absolute certainty that it preserves the original text. We await the discovery of more manuscripts.

Philemon 25b

WH NU — omit αμην ("Amen") at end of verse
$\mathfrak{P}^{87}$ A D* 048^{vid} 1739*
RSV NRSV ESV NASB NIV TNIV NEB REB NJB NAB NLT HCSB NET

variant/TR — include αμην ("Amen") at end of verse
ℵ C D^{1} Ψ 0278 1739^{c} Maj it syr cop^{bo}
KJV NKJV NRSVmg NASBmg NJBmg

Two of the earliest manuscripts containing Philemon (ℵ C) end the epistle with "amen." However, $\mathfrak{P}^{87}$, a much earlier manuscript (second century), provides the most ancient testimony to the absence of "Amen." (This is noted in NA^{27}.) Thus, we can conclude that scribes, who were fond of adding "amen" at the end of various epistles, also did so here.

Subscription

1. No subscription. Found in $\mathfrak{P}^{87}$ A 0278^{vid} 323 365 629 630 1505.
2. Προς Φιλημονα ("To Philemon"). Appears in (D) ℵ C Ψ 33.
3. Προς Φιλημονα εγραφη απο Ρωμης ("To Philemon written from Rome"). Appears in P 048^{vid}.
4. Προς Φιλημονα εγραφη απο Ρωμης, δια Ονησιμου οικετου ("To Philemon written from Rome through Onesimus, a house servant"). Appears in Maj (so TR).
5. Προς Φιλημονα εγραφη απο Ρωμης, δια Τυχικου και Ονησιμου οικετου ("To Philemon written from Rome through Tychicus and Onesimus, a house servant"). Appears in 1739 1881.
6. Προς Φιλημονα και Απφιαν δεσποτας του Ονησιμου και προς Αρχιππον τον διακονον της εν Κολοσσαις εκκλησιας

εγραφη απο Ρωμης δια Τυχικου και Ονησιμου οικετου ("To Philemon and Apphia, masters of Onesimus, and to Archippus, deacon of the Colossian church, written from Rome through Tychicus and Onesimus, a house servant"). Appears in L.

It is quite certain that no book of the NT had a title (inscription) or a subscription (see Comfort 2005, 9-10). This is especially true for Philemon because it was originally a personal letter, not a literary work. Thus, all inscriptions and subscriptions are scribal addenda. 𝔓[87], the earliest manuscript, has no subscription. The simplest form, Προς Φιλημονα ("To Philemon"), appears in the next earliest manuscripts: ℵ C (D). As is typical, the subscription was expanded to include the place of writing (Rome) and the carriers of the epistle (Tychicus and Onesimus—see Col 4:7-9). The sixth variant is fascinating in that it tells us that (1) both Apphia and Philemon were the masters of Onesimus, thereby implying that they were a married couple; and (2) that Archippus was a deacon (or minister) in the Colossian church (see Col 4:17).

The Epistle to the HEBREWS

Inscription (Title)

𝔓46 ℵ and B title this epistle as Προς Εβραιους ("To the Hebrews"). Several other manuscripts (including ℵ and B) have the same title in the subscription (see last note for this book). The author, however, would not have entitled this epistle in its original composition. Inscriptions and subscriptions are the work of later scribes. (For more on this, see Comfort 2005, 9-10.) TR entitles it Η Προς Εβραιους Επιστολη Παυλου ("The Epistle of Paul to the Hebrews")—so KJV (see last note).

Hebrews 1:1

According to the TR WH NU editions, the writer of Hebrews used the expression τοις πατρασιν ("to the fathers") when he opened his epistle with this statement: "In many passages and in many ways God spoke in times past to the fathers by the prophets." This has the support of 𝔓46* ℵ A B C D Maj. However, two early Greek manuscripts, 𝔓12vid 𝔓46c, read τοις πατρασιν ημων ("to our fathers"), and this is also supported by two ancient versions: it[a] and syr[p].

It is difficult to decide whether or not ημων ("our") was originally in the text. On one hand, it could be argued that this pronoun was added to clarify that the author of Hebrews belonged to the Jewish lineage. On the other hand, it could be argued that it was dropped for precisely the opposite reason. The resultant text allows for the possibility that the author could have been a Gentile or a Jew. The earliest manuscript, 𝔓46, lacked the pronoun, which was then inserted supralinearly by a later hand. Most English versions follow the variant reading—unless, of course, the translators understood the article τοις to function as a possessive and therefore saw no difference in meaning between the two readings.

Hebrews 1:3a

The text speaks of God's Son upholding (φερων) all things by the word of his power. This was changed in B*,2 to φανερων ("manifesting"). The original scribe may have thought his exemplar was in error (there is only a two-letter difference between φερων and φανερων), or he may have considered the concept of divine manifestation to be more palatable than divine sustaining—especially in light of the previous verse, which says that Jesus is the radiance of God's glory and express image of God's character. The first corrector deleted the letters αν. But another corrector (in the 13th century) changed it back to φανερων and then wrote a word of rebuke in the margin to the previous corrector: εμαθεστατε και κακε, αφες τον παλαιον, μη μεταποιει ("you fool and bad person, leave the old [reading]; do not change it").

Furthermore, the expression της δυναμεως αυτου ("his power"), as found in TR WH NU, is shorter in the manuscripts 𝔓[46] 0243 1739 1881*—it lacks αυτου. This shorter reading is probably original because it suits Greek poetic rhythm (see Zuntz 1953, 285).

Hebrews 1:3b

WH NU — καθαρισμὸν τῶν ἁμαρτιῶν ποιησάμενος
"having made purification of sins"
ℵ A B H* P Ψ 075 0150 33
NKJVmg RSV NRSV ESV NASB NIV TNIV NEB REB NJB NAB (NLT) HCSB NET

variant 1 — δι αυτου καθαρισμον των αμαρτιων ποιησαμενος
"by him having made purification of sins"
𝔓[46] D* 0278
none

variant 2 — δι εαυτου καθαρισμον των αμαρτιων ποιησαμενος
"by himself having made purification of sins"
D^2 H^c 0243 0278 1739 it^b syr cop
none

variant 3/TR — δι εαυτου καθαρισμον των αμαρτιων ημων ποιησαμενος
"by himself having made a purification of our sins"
$ℵ^2$ D^1 H (Maj inverted word order) syr
KJV NKJV HCSBmg

The words δι αυτου ("through him") may have been original and were subsequently deleted because scribes thought readers would misunderstand how the Son could make purification through him. Another way to fix this was to make the pronoun reflexive (εαυτου) and thereby underscore the effect of the middle voice, ποιησαμενος: "having made by himself." (𝔓[46] does not support the reflexive as cited in NA[27]; it reads αυτου.) Of course, it is just as likely that the original text had no prepositional phrase and that both variants display scribal emendations. The point is, the Son is superior on two counts: He upholds the universe by his word, and he made purification of sins. The addition of ημων ("our") in the third variant is clearly an interpolation, which found its way into TR and KJV, as well as NKJV.

Hebrews 1:8

TR NU — τῆς βασιλείας σου
"your kingdom"
A D Ψ 0243 0278 33 1739 Maj syr cop
KJV NKJV RSV NRSV ESV NASBmg NIV TNIV NEBmg REB NJBmg NAB NLT HCSB NET

variant/WH — της βασιλειας αυτου
"his kingdom"
𝔓[46] ℵ B
RSVmg NRSVmg NASB NEB NJB

The TR NU reading yields this translation of the verse: "But to the Son [he says]: 'Your throne, O God, is forever and ever, and the scepter of righteousness is the scepter of your kingdom.'" The variant yields one of two translations: (1) "But to the Son [he says]: 'Your throne, O God, is forever and ever, and the scepter of righteousness is the scepter of his kingdom'" or (2) "But to the Son [he says]: 'God is your throne forever and ever, and the scepter of righteousness is the scepter of his [God's] kingdom.'" The context makes it clear that God is speaking to his Son. Thus, God the Father addresses his Son as "God." This is the TR NU reading, where ο θεος must be understood as a vocative. The variant reading allows for two different renderings, the most unusual of which is noted above as a second option for the variant ("God is your throne, etc."; see RSVmg, NEBmg). But such a reading violates the natural sense of the Greek and obscures Christ's deity. God calls his Son "God" and then declares that his throne is everlasting because of his righteousness. The next verse substantiates this affirmation of the Son's deity, where again the Father addresses the Son with the vocative, "O God" (see NEB). As F. F. Bruce (1964, 19) puts it, "our author may well have understood 'God' in the vocative twice over in this quotation; the last clause could easily be construed 'Therefore, O God, thy God has anointed thee with the oil of gladness above thy fellows.'"

The other rendering of the variant is listed first. The problem with this reading is that it involves a strange shift of persons. But there is a way to compensate for this awkwardness if we understand that the author of Hebrews inserted και, which is not in the original text of Ps 45:6-7, in order to break apart the two parts of the quote, as follows:

"Your throne, O God, is forever and ever."

"The scepter of righteousness is the scepter of his kingdom."

This restructuring does not completely solve the problem of the shift in persons. Yet it supplies one argument for the variant. But there are two more arguments. First, the three earliest extant manuscripts (𝔓46 ℵ B) support the variant. Second, it is the more difficult reading. Why would scribes, seeing σου ("your") in the text, change it to αυτου ("his")? Contrarily, it is easy to understand why a scribe would change αυτου to σου—for this is the pronoun which appears four times in these two verses. Furthermore, this is the pronoun of the Septuagint reading of Ps 45:6, strongly suggesting that later scribes made the earliest reading conform to the Septuagint. Given that the variant has the support of 𝔓46 with ℵ and B and that it is the more difficult reading, it is likely the original reading, which is found in WH and is followed by some versions (NASB, NEB, NJB).

Hebrews 1:9

In place of ανομιαν ("lawlessness"), found in 𝔓46 B D2 Ψ 0243 0278 1739 Maj, a few manuscripts (ℵ A 33vid) read αδικιαν ("unrighteousness"). This was probably created by some scribe(s) trying to achieve parallelism with the previous δικαιοσυνην ("righteousness"). A similar change occurred in some Septuagint manuscripts of Ps 45:7, the verse quoted here.

Hebrews 1:12

WH NU ὡς ἱμάτιον καὶ ἀλλαγήσονται
"as a garment also they will be changed"
𝔓46 𝔓114vid ℵ A B 1739
RSVmg NRSV ESV NASB NIV TNIV NEB REB NJB NAB NLT HCSB NET

variant/TR	και αλλαγησονται "and they will be changed" D[1] Ψ 0243 0278 33 Maj it syr cop[bo] KJV NKJV RSV NRSVmg ESVmg HCSBmg

One of the standard canons of textual criticism is that the shorter reading is to be preferred over the longer reading. But not in this case, for two reasons: (1) The longer reading has superior documentation: the early papyri (𝔓46 𝔓114) and ℵ A B 1739. (The third-century papyrus 𝔓114, though fragmented in this verse, attests to the inclusion of ως ιματιον; see *Text of Earliest MSS*, 663, for reconstruction.) (2) The shorter reading is likely the result of scribal conformity to the Septuagint version of Ps 102:26, the verse quoted here, for the Septuagint does not include ως ιματιον. RSV, which usually followed the testimony of 𝔓46, went with the shorter reading here.

Hebrews 2:1

A few manuscripts (0243 1739 1881) omit the entire verse. Since there is no way to account for this on transcriptional grounds, it could be conjectured that these scribes had difficulty with this warning itself (the first in Hebrews of several) or the placement of it, inasmuch as 2:2 provides perfectly good continuation from 1:14.

Hebrews 2:6

TR WH NU read τι εστιν ανθρωπος οτι μιμνησκη αυτου; ("What is man that you are mindful of him?"), according to ℵ A B D 1739 Maj. A variant reading, supported by 𝔓46 C* P 81 it[d] cop[bo], has a different interrogative: τις ("who"). The neuter interrogative has better documentary support, and it is generally regarded as the right word in this context, which explores what it is about man that attracts God's special care. However, Zuntz (1953, 48-49) argues that the variant poses the question about which man God is specifically mindful of ("who is the man God is mindful of?"). This question is then answered by the next line, "Truly, the Son of Man, because you visited him." As such, the writer of Hebrews adjusted the Septuagint text to secure a christological interpretation of this verse. But it is just as possible that some scribe (perhaps the copyist of 𝔓46) made the change for the same reason.

Hebrews 2:7

NU	δόξῃ καὶ τιμῇ ἐστεφάνωσας αὐτόν "with glory and honor you crowned him" 𝔓46 B D[2] Maj NKJVmg RSV NRSV ESV NASBmg NIV TNIV NEB REB NJB NAB NLT HCSB NET
variant/TR WH	δοξη και τιμη εστεφανωσας αυτον, και κατεστησας αυτον επι τα εργα των χειρων σου "with glory and honor you crowned him, and you set him over the works of your hands" ℵ A C D* P Ψ 0243 0278 33 1739 it (syr) cop KJV NKJV RSVmg NRSVmg ESVmg NASB NLTmg HCSBmg NETmg

The two earliest manuscripts (𝔓46 B), as well as the majority of manuscripts, do not contain the complete quote of Ps 8:6, whereas the other manuscripts do. Is the shorter text the result of a transcriptional mistake, or is the longer text the result of scribal expansion? Since it is difficult to explain what would have caused a transcriptional error, the conclusion is that the longer reading must be a scribal expansion for the sake of harmonization with Ps 8:6 (LXX). Apparently, the writer of Hebrews did not think it necessary to quote the verse in its entirety in order to make the point that man, though lower than angels, has been appointed the federal head of creation. Indeed, the writer of Hebrews, though prone to quote from the Septuagint, was not committed to producing a verbatim replication (see Bruce 1964, xlix).

Hebrews 2:9

TR WH NU	χάριτι θεοῦ ὑπὲρ παντὸς γεύσηται θανάτου "by God's grace he might taste death on behalf of all" 𝔓46 ℵ A B C D Ψ 1739c Maj all
variant	χωρις θεου υπερ παντος γευσηται θανατου "apart from God he might taste death on behalf of all" 0243 1739* MSSaccording to Origen, Jerome NEBmg REBmg NJBmg

It is possible that the variant arose due to a transcriptional error. Some scribe may have mistaken χαριτι ("by grace") for χωρις ("apart from"), or some scribe may have mistakenly corrected the text of 2:9 in light of a marginal gloss in 2:8 explaining that "God" was excluded (χωρις) from everything that had been subjected to Jesus (see Bruce 1992, 28). This hypothetical marginal gloss could have been influenced by 1 Cor 15:27, which says that everything, except God, was subjected to Christ.

However, it is more likely that the variant was an intentional change motivated by the thought that Jesus was abandoned by God in his death (see Mark 15:34) and therefore died "apart from God." Such a change must have occurred as early as the second century, because Origen noted its presence in various manuscripts, as did Jerome and Ambrose in later centuries. Various christological heresies (such as Adoptionism and later, Nestorianism) were developed in the early centuries of the church by those who did not believe that the eternal God could be born, suffer, or die. To them, Jesus was not the incarnate God from birth or the dying God on the cross. They believed that the man Jesus was the adopted Son of God at baptism and an abandoned man in crucifixion. It is no surprise, then, that Theodore of Mopsuestia (the teacher of Nestorius) favored this reading, as did the Nestorians (Tasker 1964, 441). Thus, this is a clear example of the text being changed for theological reasons—in this case, from an orthodox reading to a heretical one. Not one translation has adopted this variant, though it is noted in NEB, REB, and NJB.

Hebrews 3:2

TR WH NU	ἐν [ὅλῳ] τῷ οἴκῳ αὐτοῦ "in all his house" ℵ A C D Ψ 0243 0278 33 1739 Maj syr KJV NKJV RSVmg NRSV ESV NASB NIV TNIV NJB NAB NLT HCSB NET
variant	εν τω οικω αυτου "in his house" 𝔓13 𝔓46vid B cop RSV NRSVmg NEB REB NLTmg

According to TR WH NU, the writer to the Hebrews said that Jesus was "faithful to the one having appointed him, as was Moses in all his house." The TR WH NU reading follows Num 12:7 in the Septuagint exactly and accords with 3:5. These two facts, however, can be used to defend the variant reading, for one can argue that some scribe(s) conformed the text to Num 12:7 (LXX) or to Heb 3:5. Added to this argument is that of documentation: The three earliest manuscripts (𝔓13 𝔓46 B) do not include ολω ("all"). In keeping with their goal to incorporate the new manuscript evidence in their revision, the RSV translators favored the variant reading as supported by the two early papyri and B. The NEB translators did likewise. (See note on 3:6.)

Hebrews 3:6

NU	κατάσχωμεν "if we hold" 𝔓13 𝔓46 B cop[sa] NKJVmg RSV NRSV ESV NIV TNIV NEB REB NJB NAB NLT HCSB NET
variant/TR WH	μεχρι τελους βεβαιαν κατασχωμεν "if we hold firm until the end" ℵ A C D Ψ 0243 0278 33 1739 Maj it syr cop[bo] KJV NKJV RSVmg NRSVmg NASB NJBmg NLTmg HCSBmg NETmg

The three earliest manuscripts (𝔓13 𝔓46 B) do not contain the phrase "firm to the end." Some later scribe(s), familiar with the wording of 3:14, sensed a gap here that needed filling; as a result, the wording of 3:14 was inserted into 3:6. The weight of 𝔓13 𝔓46 B was enough to convince the RSV translators to change the ASV text, but it was not enough for the NASB translators, who had a tendency to retain many ASV readings.

Hebrews 3:9

WH NU read ου επειρασαν οι πατερες υμων εν δοκιμασια ("where your fathers tried with testing"), having the excellent support of 𝔓13 𝔓46 ℵ* A B C D* 33. TR adds με (me) twice: ου επειρασαν με οι πατερες υμων εν δοκιμασια με ("where your fathers tried me in testing me"), with inferior documentation: ℵ2 D2 Ψ 0278 Maj. This variant reading is clearly a scribal emendation (note corrections in ℵ D) which fills in the natural direct object ("me" = "God," the speaker) and then conforms εν εδοκιμασαν to the wording of Ps 95:9 (94:9 in LXX), with an additional με. This expanded reading found its way into TR (so KJV and NKJV), and it is essentially followed by most modern versions, which also have the inserted, pronominal direct object "me."

Hebrews 3:18

Instead of τοις απειθησασιν ("the ones having disobeyed"), found in all Greek manuscripts, 𝔓46 alone reads τοις απιστησασιν ("the ones having disbelieved"). (The Old Latin tradition also has this reading.) It seems this change was influenced by 3:19, but the scope goes beyond the immediate context. It appears that the scribe of 𝔓46 was prone to change the wording "disobedience" to "disbelief." These changes are evident in 4:11 and 11:31, where only 𝔓46 reads "disbelief" instead of "disobedience," as well as in 4:6, where 𝔓46 is joined by ℵ cop[bo] in reading "disbelief" instead of "disobedience" (see notes on 4:6; 11:31). These changes show that the scribe had a particular horizon of expectation that he forced upon the text—that is, he saw unbelief as being the primary factor that kept the Israelites from entering the good land of Canaan and that prevents Christians from entering into spiritual rest.

Hebrews 4:2

WH NU ἐκείνους μὴ συγκεκερασμένους τῇ πίστει τοῖς ἀκούσασιν
"those were not united in faith with the ones who heard it [the message]"
𝔓13 𝔓46 A B C Ψ 0243 0278 33 1739 it[t,v] syr[h]
NKJVmg RSVmg NRSV ESV NIVmg TNIV NJB NLT HCSB NET

variant 1/TR εκεινους μη συγκεκερασμενος τη πιστει τοις ακουσασιν
"those who heard did not combine it [the message] with faith"
א it[b,d] syr[p]
KJV NKJV RSV NRSVmg ESVmg NASB NIV TNIVmg NEB REB NJBmg NAB NLTmg HCSBmg NETmg

variant 2 εκεινους μη συγκεκερασμενους τη πιστει τοις ακουσθεισιν
"they were not united by faith with the things they heard"
1912 Theodore of Mopsuestia
none

variant 3 εκεινους μη συγκεκερασμενους τη πιστει των ακουσαντων
"they were not united with the faith of those who heard it [the message]"
D* syr[hmg]
none

The WH NU reading is almost certainly the original wording, because it has better external attestation, and it is more difficult. (Both NA[27] and UBS[4] cite 𝔓[13vid], as opposed to simply 𝔓[13], as supporting the reading συγκεκερασμενους, because the last three letters of this word are faded. However, close study of the manuscript reveals that the last three letters of the word in 𝔓[13] are ους; see *Text of Earliest MSS,* 86.) According to 𝔓[13] 𝔓[46] etc., the Greek word for "united" or "combined" (συγκεκερασμενους) agrees grammatically with the first "those" (εκει-νους; as opposed to "those who heard"— τοις ακουσασιν). This verse is not talking about combining faith with the word, but about the fact that the majority of Israelites were not united in faith with those men who heard the good news about the promised land (i.e., Moses, Joshua, and Caleb). These men were "the original and immediate hearers . . . through whom the Divine word was conveyed to those who were hearers in the second degree" (Westcott and Hort 1882, 130). Moses, Joshua, and Caleb truly heard the word concerning the promise of entering Canaan, and they believed it. But the Israelites, who heard the word through these men, did not share their faith.

This reading, however, was not understood by several scribes. The first attempt at changing it was to change the participle to συγκεκερασμενος so as to make it agree with ο λογος ("the message"), thereby making the matter of mingling that which occurs between faith and the word. The second variant, which retains this meaning, is an attempt to smooth out the grammar. The third variant, though not original, conveys the same idea as the text.

A growing number of the most recent English versions (NRSV ESV TNIV NJB NLT HCSB NET) have followed the superior reading supported by the papyri, 𝔓[13] and 𝔓[46], with A B C D. All of the other versions followed the easier yet inferior reading, although some of them noted in the margin what appears to be the superior reading.

Hebrews 4:3a

Contra the TR WH NU editions, but probably preserving the original text, the earliest witnesses (𝔓46 𝔓13vid B) and D* do not include the article την ("the") before καταπαυσιν ("rest"). It was added in many later manuscripts (א A C D[1] Ψ 0243 0278 33 1739 Maj) to specify *the* particular rest, which is mentioned in the following OT citation: την καταπαυσιν μου ("my rest"). But the anarthrous expression ("for the ones entering into rest") suggests a spiritual condition of restfulness.

Hebrews 4:3c and 4:5

The conjunction ει ("if") was problematic to some scribes, especially the scribe of 𝔓13, who did not include it in both 4:3 and 4:5. The *editio princeps* of 𝔓13 (P.Oxy. 657) has the wording for 4:3 as ει ελευσοντε, when it should probably read ει[σ]ελευσονται (see *Text of Earliest MSS*, 86 and see critical apparatus of NA27). The omission indicates that readers should not understand this statement as conditional ("if they enter into my rest"), but as prohibitive: "they will never enter into my rest."

Hebrews 4:6 and 4:11

According to most manuscripts in 4:6, the text says that the Israelites did not enter into Canaan because of "disobedience" (απειθειαν). Under the influence of 3:19, this was changed to "unbelief" (απιστιαν) in 𝔓46 א* it. The same change occurred in 4:11; the text warns readers not to follow the Israelites' example of "disobedience" (απειθειαν). But this was changed in 𝔓46 it syr[h] to "unbelief" (απιστιαν). These changes show that the scribe of 𝔓46 and several Old Latin translators made a consistent effort to promote the doctrine that it was unbelief, not disobedience, that prevented the Israelites from entering the good land. Of course, unbelief leads to disobedience. (See note on 3:18.)

Hebrews 4:12

In B and in some manuscripts known to Jerome, a variant reading for ενεργης ("effective") is εναργης, which means "clear-shining" or "evident." The change may have been a transcriptional mistake (there is only a one-letter difference: ε/α), or an attempt to prepare the reader for the truth that the word of God discerns and exposes.

Hebrews 6:1-2

TR NU read βαπτισμων διδαχης ("of instruction about baptisms") with the support of א A C D I 33 1739. WH reads βαπτισμων διδαχην ("with instruction about baptisms"), supported by 𝔓46 B 0150 it[d].

Though there is only a one-letter difference between the two readings (ς/ν), the difference is significant. The word διδαχης is a genitive—it is translated as in the first citation above. The word διδαχην is an accusative; it stands in apposition to "foundation," translated as in the second citation. According to the first reading, the instruction about baptisms is but one of six elements of the foundation (repentance, faith, instruction about baptisms, the laying on of hands, the resurrection, and eternal judgment). According to the second reading, the foundation is equated with a fourfold instruction: namely, the instruction about baptisms, the laying on of hands, the resurrection, and eternal judgment. Lane, who accepts this reading as original, says "the significance of reading διδαχήν lies in the virtual equation of repentance from works that lead to death and faith in God with the catechetical instruction that undergirds baptism and laying on of hands, since διδαχήν is epexegetical of θεμέλιον, 'foundation'" (1991, 132). It is difficult to determine which word the writer of Hebrews originally wrote. The earliest testimony, that of 𝔓46 and B (so WH), favors the variant reading; but the TR NU reading has good and diverse testimony. However, it is far more likely that the word originally was the accusative διδαχην, which was then changed to the genitive, so as to conform to all the surrounding genitives.

Hebrews 6:3

TR WH NU τοῦτο ποιήσομεν
"we will do this"
𝔓46 ℵ B I L 0122 0278 33 1739 it cop
all

variant τουτο ποιησωμεν
"let us do this"
A C D P Ψ
NKJVmg RSVmg

The future tense of the TR WH NU reading has superior testimony to the subjunctive. The variant arose as the result of a scribal slip (*omega* mistaken for *omicron*) or scribal conformity to the subjunctive φερωμεθα ("let us go on") in 6:1.

Hebrews 6:9

This is the only occurrence in the book of Hebrews where the author addresses his readers as "beloved"—no doubt, to soften the blow of the warning he just dropped on them (6:1-8). But a few scribes and translators (ℵ* Ψ 0278 syr) substituted αδελφοι ("brothers") for αγαπητοι ("beloved ones"), under the influence of 3:1, 12; 10:19; 13:22.

Hebrews 6:10

WH NU τῆς ἀγάπης
"love"
𝔓46 A B C D* P Ψ 0278 33 1739
NKJVmg RSV NRSV ESV NASB NIV TNIV NEB REB NJB NAB NLT HCSB NET

variant/TR του κοπου της αγαπης
"the labor of love"
D2 Maj cop^bo
KJV NKJV

The variant reading is a scribal expansion created by some scribe or Coptic translator who was reminded of 1 Thess 1:3, which says, "remembering your work of faith and labor of love." The harmonization became popular, as evidenced by its presence in the majority of late Greek manuscripts, and was incorporated in TR and subsequently included in KJV and NKJV.

Hebrews 6:11

Most manuscripts read την πληροφοριαν της ελπιδος ("the full assurance of hope"). But a few witnesses (I 33 it[a]), showing the influence of the wording of 10:22, read την πληροφοριαν της πιστεως ("full assurance of faith"). This change shows that a few scribes knew the whole book of Hebrews before they began the copying process and allowed their horizon of expectation to interfere with making an accurate copy.

Hebrews 6:18

Adhering to the testimony of 𝔓[46] א* A C 0278 33 1739, NU reads αδυνατον ψευσασθαι τον θεον, which means "it is impossible for God to lie." Other manuscripts (א[2] B D Ψ Maj—so TR WH) do not include the article, thereby allowing the translation, "it is impossible for one who is God to lie." Zuntz (1953, 130) argued that the anarthrous expression is original in design and intent, whereas the variant is the result of scribal conformity to the immediate context (6:10, 13, 17).

Hebrews 7:1-2

All manuscripts except one indicate that Melchizedek was "the king of Salem" (βασιλευς Σαλημ). That one manuscript is 𝔓[46*], which reads βασιλευς Σαμουηλ ("king of Samuel") in both 7:1 and 7:2. A corrector, who was probably the paginator (see Kim 1988, 255) and therefore a contemporary of the original scribe, changed Σαμουηλ to Σαλημ in both verses. It is not clear why the scribe of 𝔓[46] originally wrote "Samuel." Was it a transcriptional error? Or if it was not an error, what would have motivated the scribe to call Melchizedek "the king of Samuel"? It was likely because the scribe did not think "king of Salem" would communicate anything to his readers, so he used the title "king of Samuel" as a surrogate for "God" inasmuch as Samuel had no king but God—as opposed to the rest of the Israelites, who wanted a human king (see 1 Sam 10:19-24; 12:12-14). As such, the scribe of 𝔓[46] may have been recognizing Melchizedek as divine.

Another interesting textual aberration appears in a thirteenth-century minuscule, 460, which has the addition οτε εδιωξεν τους αλλοφυλους και εξειλατο Λωτ μετα πασης αιχμαλωσιας ("when he pursued the foreigners and rescued Lot with all the captives") inserted after the mention of the slaughter of the kings (της κοπης των βασιλεων). This interpolation probably originated from a gloss in some other earlier manuscript gleaned from Gen 14.

Hebrews 7:4

Several manuscripts (א A C D[2] Ψ 0278 33 Maj) have the reading ῷ και ("whom also") in the expression "to whom also [or, even] Abraham the patriarch gave a tenth of the spoils." This reading is included in TR NU, but it should not be—on two counts: (1) 𝔓[46] B D* 1739 omit και, and (2) it was probably added by way of conformity to 7:2. WH excludes και.

Hebrews 7:13

The manuscript 𝔓[46] has the aorist tense μετεσχεν for the perfect tense μετεσχηκεν (in all other Greek manuscripts). 𝔓[46] (with A C 33 1739) also has the aorist προσεσχεν for the perfect προσεσχηκεν, found in א B D Ψ 0278 Maj and adopted in NU. But the perfect tense verb προσεσχηκεν is likely the result of scribal conformity to μετεσχηκεν. Thus, the original text probably had a perfect tense, followed by an aorist: "he [Jesus] never had a permanent share in the tribe of Judah, from which tribe no one ever officiated at the altar" (see Zuntz 1953, 79). The scribe of 𝔓[46] altered the first to make both verbs aorist, while the scribes of ℵ B D etc. altered the second to make both perfect.

Hebrews 7:14

WH NU ἱερέων
"priests"
𝔓[46] ℵ A B C* D* 33
NKJVmg RSV NRSV ESV NASB NIV TNIV NEB REB NJB NAB NLT HCSB NET

variant/TR ιερωσυνης
"priesthood"
C[3] D[2] Ψ Maj it[b]
KJV NKJV

According to WH NU, the entire phrase reads, "our Lord descended from Judah, concerning which Moses said nothing about priests." The variant reading is the result of a late scribal correction (note C[3] D[2]) influenced by 7:11, 24. This correction found its way into the majority of manuscripts, TR, and KJV.

Hebrews 7:17

WH NU μαρτυρεῖται
"it is testified"
𝔓[46] ℵ A B D* P Ψ 0278 33 1739 1881 cop
NKJVmg RSV NRSV ESV NASB NIV TNIV NEB REB NJB NAB NLT HCSB NET

variant/TR μαρτυρει
"he testifies"
C D[2] Maj syr
KJV NKJV

The change from the unspecific passive expression ("it is testified, 'you are a priest forever'") to a specific active expression ("he testifies") is a scribal change attempting to make this verse parallel with 7:21 (which continues the quotation of Ps 110:4), which identifies the speaker ("he") as the Lord.

Hebrews 7:21

WH NU σὺ ἱερεὺς εἰς τὸν αἰῶνα
"you are a priest forever"
𝔓[46] (ℵ*) B C 0278 33 it
NKJVmg RSV NRSV ESV NASB NIV TNIV NEB REB NJB NAB NLT HCSB NET

variant/TR συ ιερευς εις τον αιωνα κατα την ταξιν Μελχισεδεκ
"you are a priest forever according to the order of Melchizedek"
ℵ[2] A D Ψ 1739 Maj syr
KJV NKJV

The shorter reading could be the result of parablepsis and homoeoteleuton—the eye of a scribe passing over the κατα here to the κατα which begins the next verse. But the documentation for the shorter reading is too diverse to allow this explanation; several scribes at various locations and in different ages would have had to make the same error. It is more likely that the variant reading is the result of scribal harmonization to 7:17. Evidently, some scribe's horizon of expectations was disappointed when he read the same citation in 7:21 as in 7:17 (namely Ps 110:4) but did not see exact verbal redundancy. This prompted the expanded harmonization.

Hebrews 7:28

All three Greek editions read αρχιερεις ("high priests"), with the testimony of ℵ A B D^{c} Ψ 33 1739. All English versions follow, thus having renderings such as this: "for the law appoints men as high priests who have weaknesses." However, there is good testimony for the word ιερεις ("priests"): 𝔓^{46vid} D* I^{vid} syr^{p} cop^{sa}. This reading is documented too diversely to be considered a scribal accident or an isolated emendation. Indeed, it may very well be original inasmuch as it would be more tempting for scribes—influenced by the immediate context (7:26-27)—to change "priests" to "high priests" than vice versa. Chapter 7 of Hebrews is more about priests in general (see 7:3, 11-12, 20, 23) than it is about high priests specifically, who are so designated only in 7:26-27. So it is appropriate to conclude the chapter with a word about priests in general, who, being human, are mortal and fallible—unlike Jesus who is immortal and infallible.

Hebrews 8:4

In many late manuscripts (D^{2} Ψ Maj—so TR) the expression των προσφεροντων ("the ones making offerings") is fleshed out to των ιερεων των προσφεροντων ("the offerings of the priests"). Most English translations follow suit.

Hebrews 8:8

WH NU read μεμφομενος γαρ αυτους λεγει ("for, finding fault with them, he says"). This has the support of ℵ* A D* I P Ψ 33 it cop. However, there is a variant on the pronoun, which is αυτοις in 𝔓^{46} ℵ^{2} B D^{2} 0278 1739 Maj (so TR). It produces the rendering, "for, finding fault, he says to them." The difference in the readings comes down to one letter: υ/ι. Thus, one word could have easily been confused for the other in the transcription process. And because the testimony for each is solid, one cannot be dogmatic about which one is the original reading. The first reading indicates that God found fault with "them" (his people) in their inability to keep the first covenant, so he determined to institute another one. The second reading indicates that God found fault with the first covenant and then promised another one to "them" (his people). Thus, the following quotation of Jer 31:31-34 (in 8:8-12) is that which God says to them.

Hebrews 8:10

Displaying conformation to the Septuagint rendering of Jer 31:31-34 (= 38:31-34 LXX), some manuscripts (A D Ψ) add μου ("my") after διαθηκη ("covenant"). A few other manuscripts (𝔓^{46} B Ψ 0285*) have the word γραψω ("I will write") instead of επιγραψω ("I will inscribe"). This could also be the result of conformity to the Septuagint.

Hebrews 8:11a

WH NU read πολιτην ("citizen"), with the excellent support of 𝔓[46] ℵ A B D 0278 33 1739 Maj syr cop. TR reads πλησιον ("neighbor"), with inferior documentation (P 81 it syr[hmg]). The variant reading is probably the result of scribal harmonization to the Hebrew text of Jer 31:34 (the verse quoted here), which has "neighbor," or to one of several Septuagint manuscripts which also have "neighbor." The reading "fellow-citizen" has superior support among the NT manuscripts and is found in several manuscripts of the Septuagint.

Hebrews 8:11b

Instead of writing γνωθι τον κυριον ("know the Lord"), the scribe of 𝔓[46] wrote εγνω αυτον κυριος, which means "the Lord knew him." Kenyon, the editor of the *editio princeps* of 𝔓[46], incorrectly transcribed the line to read γνωθι τον κυριον (1936, 34). The corrected transcription appears in *Text of Earliest MSS,* 235. Presumably, the reading in 𝔓[46] means that the Lord knows each believer, so one does not have to teach his neighbor or brother that the Lord knows or recognizes him.

Hebrews 8:12

WH NU	τῶν ἁμαρτιῶν αὐτῶν "their sins" 𝔓[46] ℵ* B 1739 it syr[p] cop NKJVmg RSV NRSV ESV NASB NIV TNIV NEB REB NJB NAB NLT HCSB NET
variant 1/TR	των αμαρτιων αυτων και των ανομιων αυτων "their sins and their lawlessnesses (= iniquities)" ℵ[2] A D 0285[vid] Maj KJV NKJV HCSBmg
variant 2	των ανομιων αυτων "their lawlessnesses" 0278 33 none

The WH NU reading has the excellent support of the three earliest manuscripts (𝔓[46] ℵ* B), plus 1739 and three early versions. Both variants are the result of scribal assimilation to Heb 10:17, a parallel passage which is also a citation of Jer 31:34. However, the writer of Hebrews at 10:17 added και των ανομιων αυτων to the Jeremiah wording. Thus, the extra verbiage "and their lawlessness" is part of the original text of Heb 10:17, but not here in 8:12. Evidently, some scribe was disappointed that 8:12 did not verbally replicate 10:17 and thereby made the addition (as in variant 1). Other scribes, working with this expanded text, got rid of one of the two expressions (των αμαρτιων αυτων), but it was the wrong one (as in variant 2).

Hebrews 9:1

The three editions (TR WH NU) include και ("also") after ουν ("therefore"), yielding the rendering, "therefore also the first covenant had regulations of service." This has the support of ℵ A D 0278 0285 33 Maj. However, better documentation supports the omission of και: 𝔓[46] B 1739 syr[p] cop. The first reading suggests that the old order is described as parallel to the new—as is suggested by και ("also"). But the writer's point is that Jewish worship is superseded by the sacrifice of Christ (Zuntz 1953, 209-210). This is the reading of the variant.

Hebrews 9:2a and 9:4

The scribe of B and some Coptic Sahidic translators saw a problem with placing "the golden incense altar" (το χρυσουν θυμιατηριον) in the holy of holies (9:4) instead of in the holy place (see Exod 30:1-6). Thus, they moved it from 9:4 to 9:2. Some scholars have avoided this problem by saying that the θυμιατηριον is a "censer," which the high priest took with him into the holy of holies on the Day of Atonement (Lev 16:12-13).

Hebrews 9:2b

The three editions, TR WH NU, have the wording for the "holy place" as Αγια. This has the textual support of ℵ D[c] I 0278 33 1739 Maj. There are two variants on this: (1) τα Αγια ("the holy place") in B; (2) Αγια Αγιων ("holy of holies") in 𝔓[46] A D*. This is the only place in Hebrews where the writer uses the anarthrous Αγια (neuter plural) to denote the holy place. Elsewhere the writer uses the neuter plural with the article (Lane 1991, 215). This accounts for the change in B. Thus, the first variant is hardly significant. But the same cannot be said for the second, for it calls the first tent the holy of holies! Furthermore, the scribe of 𝔓[46] made the first tent "the holy of holies" and the second tent, "the holy place" (see note on 9:3). The scribes of A and D* made both the first tent and second tent "the holy of holies." As Bruce observed (1964, 181), these changes signal some primitive disturbance of the text. Perhaps various scribes were making emendations to the assignment of sacred instruments to one or the other holy place (see previous note).

Hebrews 9:3

The three editions (TR WH NU) have the wording for the "holy of holies" as Αγια Αγιων, with the support of ℵ* A D* I[vid] 33 1881 Maj. There are variants on this:

1. τα Αγια των Αγιων ("the holy of holies") in ℵ[2] B D[2] L 0278
2. Αγια των Αγιων ("holy of holies") in P 1739
3. Αγια ("Holy [place]") in 𝔓[46vid?]

The first two variants display the addition of one or of two articles—neither of which changes the meaning. The third variant is suppositional because the actual reading of 𝔓[46] is ΑΝΑ, which could have been a mistaken writing for ΑΓΙΑ—the *gamma* running into the *iota* at an angle, making it look like a *nu*. If this was what the scribe of 𝔓[46] intended, then we are given a unique text in which he calls the first tent "the holy of holies" and the second tent "the holy place." This variant and those in 9:2 (see note) suggest that the designations Αγια and Αγια Αγιων were not universally accepted as proper nouns describing the first and second sections of the inner sanctuary of the tabernacle (or temple). Rather, this entire area was generally known as being Αγια.

Hebrews 9:11

WH NU	τῶν γενομένων ἀγαθῶν "the good things having come" (𝔓[46] γεναμενων) B D* 1739 syr[p,h] NKJVmg RSV NRSV ESV NASBmg NIV TNIV NEB REB NJBmg NAB NLT HCSB NET

variant/TR τῶν μελλοντων αγαθων
"the good things about to come"
ℵ A D[2] I[vid] 0278 33 Maj
KJV NKJV RSVmg NRSVmg ESVmg NASB NIVmg TNIVmg NEBmg REBmg NJB NLTmg HCSBmg

According to WH NU, which have good documentation, the fuller rendering is, "now Christ has come, a high priest of the good things having come." The variant reading, displaying the influence of Heb 10:1 (see Bruce 1992, 31), is probably a scribal emendation, which misses the point of the passage. The benefits of Christ's priesthood are not stored away for the future; they are now. Because Christ has appeared, all the shadows are now replaced by the reality. He himself provides the means to access God both now and forever. All modern versions, except NASB and NJB, follow the better reading.

Hebrews 9:14a

TR WH NU πνεύματος αἰωνίου
"eternal spirit"
𝔓[17vid] 𝔓[46] ℵ* A B D[2] 0278 33 1739 Maj it[b] syr
all

variant πνευματος αγιου
"Holy Spirit"
ℵ[2] D* it[a] cop[bo]
NRSVmg NJBmg

In context, the phrase reads, "through eternal Spirit/spirit he offered himself without blemish to God." The expression πνευματος αιωνιου is a unique expression in the New Testament, which could have two meanings. It either designates the Holy Spirit who is eternal, or it denotes that which is spiritual (in contrast to that which is of the flesh) and therefore has eternal value. The phrase, as connected with the verb "offered," indicates the agency by which Christ offered himself on the cross—i.e., he did it through eternal spirit. Interestingly, the scribe of 𝔓[46] demonstrated some such understanding because he chose to write out πνευματος (in *plene*) instead of making it a nomen sacrum, the usual designation for the divine Spirit. In so doing, he may have wanted to highlight Christ's spirit. The variant exhibits that some scribes and ancient translators opted for the first meaning and unabashedly changed "eternal" to "holy" in order to designate the divine Spirit.

Hebrews 9:14b

After the words θεω ζωντι ("living God"), a few manuscripts (A P 0278) add και αληθινω ("and true")—under the influence of 1 Thess 1:9.

Hebrews 9:19

Most manuscripts, with three kinds of minor variation, speak of the blood of bulls and goats (μοσχων και τραγων): (1) των μοσχων και των τραγων (ℵ* A C it—so WH NU); (2) των μοσχων και τραγων (33 Maj—so TR); (3) των τραγων και των μοσχων (D). However, some significant manuscripts (𝔓[46] ℵ[2] K L Ψ 0278 1739) do not include "and of goats" (και τραγων). The longer reading is probably the product of scribal harmonization to 9:12. The fact that the expansion appears in three forms exposes its artificiality. According to Zuntz (1953, 54-55), this interpolation completely conquered the B-text and D-text and became the norm also in the Byzantine text. Yet the original wording lived on in a fair number of late manuscripts (ℵ^2 L Ψ 0278), to be finally vindicated by the most ancient of all, $\mathfrak{P}^{46}$. However, all the Greek editions go with the longer reading (in two forms), which is followed by all English versions.

Hebrews 9:28

After the words οφθησεται τοις αυτον απεκδεχομενοις εις σωτηριαν ("he will appear to the ones awaiting him for salvation"), some manuscripts (A P 0285) add δια πιστεως ("through faith"). This is a pedantic insertion intended to reinforce the doctrine that salvation comes by faith.

Hebrews 10:1a

According to the Greek editions (TR WH NU), the writer to the Hebrews says that "the law is a shadow of the good things to come, not the very image of the things" (ουκ αυτην την εικονα των πραγματων). This has good documentary support: ℵ A C D 33 1739 Maj. One interesting variant is found in $\mathfrak{P}^{46}$, which substitutes και ("and") for ουκ αυτην ("not the very"). This yields the translation, "the law contains but a shadow and likeness of the good things to come" (see NEBmg). The scribe of $\mathfrak{P}^{46}$ probably considered the contrast between σκιαν ("shadow") and εικονα ("image") to be unnatural (see Tasker 1964, 461) and therefore made the two terms synonymous (see Bruce 1992, 32-33). This change most likely reveals that the scribe was influenced by the Platonic contrast of σκια and εικων with reality itself (Zuntz 1953, 20-23). As such, it could be said that the scribe's Platonic understanding formed a horizon of expectation which interfered with the horizon of the text. He resolved the conflict by emending the text.

But the writer of Hebrews must have intended to contrast the "shadow" and the "image," as is evident by the structure of the sentence. As such, he must have considered σκια to connote an imperfect sketch and the εικων an exact replica. Perhaps he had in mind an outline which is sketched by an artist in preparation for a finished portrait. The finished product is the εικων, for it bears the likeness of that which is portrayed. Thus, the Law, as it pertains to the Levitical priesthood, was but a shadowy outline of the completed work of Christ the High Priest (see Bruce 1964, 226).

Hebrews 10:1b

There is a significant textual difference between the two verbs δυναται ("it is able") and δυνανται ("they are able"). According to good, diverse testimony ($\mathfrak{P}^{46}$ D^{*,2} H L^s 0285 1739—so TR NU), it is "the law" (ο νομος) that is not able (δυναται—third person singular) to perfect the priests. Other manuscripts (ℵ A C D^1 P 0278 33 syr—so WH), however, indicate that it was "sacrifices" (θυσιαις) that were not able (δυνανται—third person plural) to perfect the priests.

Hebrews 10:9

WH NU τοῦ ποιῆσαι τὸ θέλημά σου
"to do your will"
𝔓46 ℵ* A C D P Ψ 33
NKJVmg RSV NRSV ESV NASB NIV TNIV NEB REB NJB NAB NLT HCSB NET

variant/TR του ποιησαι το θελημα σου ο θεος
"to do your will, O God"
ℵ2 0278vid 1739 Maj syr
KJV NKJV HCSBmg

The insertion of ο θεος ("O God") is a carryover from 10:7; it produces the rendering, "He said, 'Behold, I have come, O God, to do your will.'"

Hebrews 10:11

All three Greek editions (TR WH NU) read ιερευς ("priest"), with excellent support: 𝔓13vid? 𝔓46 𝔓79vid ℵ D Ψ 33 1739 Maj copbo. (All English versions follow.) A few other manuscripts (A C P 0278 syr copsa) read αρχιερευς ("high priest"). 𝔓13vid is not cited in NA27, probably because there is enough room on the previous line, now broken, to have fit the prefix αρχ prior to ιερευς standing clearly on the next line. However, the prefix does not have to be supplied for the line lengths to be even (for reconstruction, see *Text of Earliest MSS,* 88). In any event, it stands to reason that 𝔓13 would concur with 𝔓46 and 1739 here, as it usually does.

The change from "priest" to "high priest" was stimulated by the constant reference in this book to the high priest, especially in chapters 7–9. However, this verse speaks of the regular activity of making sacrificial offerings. Thus, it is pointing to the activity of the Levitical priests, not the high priest. It was prescribed by law (Deut 18:5) that these priests had to stand while doing their duties.

Hebrews 10:14

Instead of the expression τους αγιαζομενους ("the ones being sanctified"), found in most Greek manuscripts, 𝔓46 reads τους ανασωζομενους ("the ones being saved anew"). Perhaps the scribe was motivated to make the change because 10:10 says that the believers have been sanctified once and for all by Christ's sacrifice. If sanctification is complete, he may have reasoned, then it cannot also be ongoing. Thus, he made "salvation," instead of sanctification, to be that which the believer continually experiences.

Hebrews 10:15

WH NU εἰρηκέναι
"he had said"
𝔓13 𝔓46 ℵ A C D P Ψ 33 1739 it cop
RSV NRSV ESV NASB NIV TNIV NEB REB NJB NAB NLT HCSB NET

variant/TR προειρηκεναι
"he had previously said" (or, "first he said")
Maj
KJV NKJV

The slight variation, which occurs in the majority of manuscripts, is intended to introduce the sequential quotations (in 10:16), followed by the one in 10:17.

Hebrews 10:22

TR WH NU — προσερχώμεθα
"let us draw near"
𝔓^{13} 𝔓^{46cvid} ℵ A C Ψ 33 1739 Maj it cop
KJV NKJV RSV NRSV ESV NASB NIV TNIV NEB REB NAB NLT HCSB NET

variant — προσερχομεθα
"we draw near"
(𝔓^{46*vid} with γαρ) D L P 1881
NJB

The writer of Hebrews has just concluded his marvelous presentation of the superiority of Jesus as high priest over all the Aaronic and Levitical priesthood. Thus, the hortatory subjunctive προσερχωμεθα, extremely well documented, is fitting for this context. The whole nature of this book is one of exhortation. Thus, the subjunctive is original, and the variant is likely the result of a scribal error—some copyist(s) mistaking an *omega* for an *omicron*. Evidently, this is what occurred in 𝔓^{46}, where it seems that some corrector placed an *omega* over the *omicron*. (See *Text of Earliest MSS,* 240 and notes b and c, for text and changes in 𝔓^{46}.) In any event, this variant was followed by NJB.

Hebrews 10:29

The scribe of A omitted εν ω ηγιασθη ("by which he was sanctified"), probably to avoid the idea that a sanctified person could subsequently be punished by God for falling away.

Hebrews 10:30

WH NU — ἐμοὶ ἐκδίκησις, ἐγὼ ἀνταποδώσω.
"Vengeance is mine; I will repay."
𝔓^{13vid} 𝔓^{46} ℵ* D* P Ψ 33 it syr^{p}
NKJVmg RSV NRSV ESV NASB NIV TNIV NEB REB NJB NAB NLT HCSB NET

variant/TR — εμοι εκδικησις, εγω ανταποδωσω, λεγει κυριος.
"'Vengeance is mine; I will repay,' says the Lord."
ℵ^{2} A D^{2} Maj syr
KJV NKJV HCSBmg

The shorter reading has early and diverse support. The variant displays a scribal interpolation (note the corrections in ℵ^{2} D^{2}), influenced by a parallel passage, Rom 12:19, which adds "says the Lord" to the OT quotation (Deut 32:35).

Hebrews 10:34

WH NU — τοῖς δεσμίοις συνεπαθήσατε
"you sympathized with prisoners"
A D* H 33 1739 it syr cop
NKJVmg RSV NRSV ESV NASB NIV TNIV NEB REB NJB NAB NLT HCSB NET

variant 1/TR	τοις δεσμοις μου συνεπαθησατε "you sympathized with my chains" ℵ D² 1881 Maj KJV NKJV HCSBmg NETmg
variant 2	τοις δεσμοις συνεπαθησατε "you sympathized with the chains" 𝔓⁴⁶ Ψ NETmg
variant 3	τοις δεσμοις αυτων συνεπαθησατε "you sympathized with their chains" it^d,z none

One *iota* makes the difference between "chains" (δεσμοις) and "prisoners" (δεσμιοις). But this small change makes a big difference in meaning—especially in light of the authorship of the book of Hebrews. The first variant in TR ("you sympathized with my chains") suggests that the writer could have been commending the readers for their compassion on him while he was chained in prison (see 13:19). Of course, this could imply that the writer was Paul, who used similar language (see Phil 1:7, 13-17). This is likely the intent of the second variant, which adds the pronoun "my." This variant, popularized by its presence in TR, has led many Christians to think that Paul wrote the book of Hebrews. The second variant in 𝔓⁴⁶ and Ψ can mean "you sympathized with the chains [of prisoners]" or (taking the definite article to be possessive) "you sympathized with my chains." The third variant is an attempt to clarify the meaning of the second variant and to take it in the direction of the text—that is, the writer was commending his readers for visiting prisoners (see 13:3). In the end, it is difficult to decide between the readings, δεσμιοις ("prisoners") and δεσμοις ("chains"). The first has diverse textual evidence; the second is the most difficult reading, which could have given rise to all the other variants. Against the second option, if τοις δεσμιοις ("the prisoners") were originally in the text, a scribe could have changed it to τοις δεσμοις ("the chains") to impress Pauline authorship on this book. The scribe of 𝔓⁴⁶ may have been part of a tradition which accepted Pauline authorship of Hebrews because in the 𝔓⁴⁶ codex Hebrews immediately follows Romans, the first epistle in the collection. On the other hand, if τοις δεσμοις ("the chains") were originally in the text, a scribe could have changed it to τοις δεσμιοις ("the prisoners") to make it conform to 13:3.

Hebrews 10:38

WH NU	ὁ δὲ δίκαιός μου ἐκ πίστεως ζήσεται "my righteous one will live by faith" 𝔓⁴⁶ ℵ A H* 33 1739 cop^sa NKJVmg RSV NRSV ESV NASB NIV TNIV NEB REB NJB NAB NLT HCSB NET
variant 1/TR	ο δε δικαιος εκ πιστεως ζησεται "the righteous one will live by faith" 𝔓¹³ D² H^c I Ψ 1881 Maj cop^bo KJV NKJV NIVmg TNIVmg
variant 2	ο δε δικαιος εκ πιστεως μου ζησεται "the righteous one will live by my faith(fulness)" D* syr none

The difference in the first two readings concerns the inclusion or omission of the Greek word μου ("my"). Metzger writes: "influenced by the citation of the same Old Testament quotation in Ro 1.17 and Ga 3.11, where Paul omits the personal pronoun, 𝔓13 and the majority of later witnesses . . . followed by the Textus Receptus, omit the word here. But it undoubtedly belongs in the text, being strongly supported by early and reliable witnesses" (TCGNT). The second variant displays the influence of Hab 2:4 (LXX), as it appears in Codex B.

All the versions except NKJV follow the WH NU reading, while the secondary reading is noted in the margin of NIV. The NIVmg and TNIVmg indicate that one early manuscript reads "the righteous one"; that manuscript is 𝔓13, dated to the third century. However, this is not the only manuscript supporting this reading.

Hebrews 11:1

Most manuscripts read εστιν δε πιστις ελπιζομενων υποστασις ("faith is the substance of things hoped for"). But in place of υποστασις ("substance"), NA27 cites 𝔓13 as reading πραγματων αποστασις. Contrarily, UBS4 lists πραγματων αναστασις as the reading for 𝔓13 (also supported by it[b] Origen[lat] Sedulius-Scottus[vid]). But UBS4 is incorrect because the extant text clearly has *pi* after the initial *alpha:* πραγματ[ω]ν απ[ο]στα[xxx]. The three lost letters (marked with three *x*'s) are probably σις (=αποστασις), as noted in NA27 (for reconstruction of lines, see *Text of Earliest MSS,* 89). One of several meanings of αποστασις that could fit this context is "place where something is put away, storehouse, repository" (see Liddell and Scott, 219). Thus, the text of 𝔓13 says "faith is the storehouse of things hoped for, the evidence of things not seen."

Hebrews 11:4

TR WH NU — προσήνεγκεν τῷ θεῷ
"he [Abel] offered to God"
א A D2 Ψ 33 1739 cop
KJV NKJV RSV NRSV ESV NASB NIV TNIV NJB NAB NLT HCSB NET

variant — προσηνεγκεν
"he [Abel] offered"
𝔓13 𝔓46vid Clement
NEB REB

The variant probably displays the original reading for two reasons: (1) It has the testimony of the two earliest manuscripts, 𝔓13 𝔓46vid. (𝔓46vid is not listed in NA27 or UBS4, but the lacuna would hardly permit the inclusion of τω θεω at the end of the line; see Kenyon 1936, 41 and *Text of Earliest MSS,* 241.) (2) The longer reading appears to be the result of a scribal interpolation influenced by 9:14 or a natural scribal expansion. The shorter reading can be rendered quite nicely as, "By faith Abel offered a better sacrifice than Cain's" (cf. NEB REB). It does not need to have "to God" to complete the sense.

Hebrews 11:11

NU Πίστει καὶ αὐτὴ Σάρρα στεῖρα δύναμιν εἰς καταβολὴν σπέρματος ἔλαβεν καὶ παρὰ καιρὸν ἡλικίας
"by faith he (Abraham), even though past age—and Sarah herself was barren—received power to beget" [see also translation in commentary below]
𝔓[46] D* Ψ it
NRSV NIV TNIVmg NAB NLT HCSBmg NET

variant 1/TR WH Πιστει και αυτη Σαρρα δυναμιν εις καταβολην σπερματος ελαβεν και παρα καιρον ηλικιας
"by faith even Sarah herself, though past age, received power to conceive [from] a seed"
𝔓[13vid] ℵ A D^2 33 Maj
KJV NKJV RSV NRSVmg ESV NASB TNIV NEB REB NJB HCSB NETmg

variant 2 Πιστει και αυτη Σαρρα η στειρα δυναμιν εις καταβολην σπερματος ελαβεν και παρα καιρον ηλικιας
"by faith even Sarah herself, the barren one, received power to conceive [from] a seed, though past age"
D^1 81 1739 1881
none

This verse is fraught with grammatical and textual difficulties. The first problem pertains to who is the subject of ελαβεν ("received")—Abraham or Sarah? When we consider that the wording καταβολην σπερματος is a Hellenistic idiom for the male act of procreation (literally "putting down sperm"), it does not fit that Sarah would be the subject. However, it hardly makes sense to exclude Sarah from being the subject, because the verse mentions her by name and speaks of her sterility. Thus, there are two ways to include both Sarah and Abraham as subjects of this verse: (1) "by faith he [Abraham], even though past age—and Sarah herself was barren—received power to beget," and (2) "by faith he [Abraham] also, together with barren Sarah, received power to beget, even though past age." The first rendering considers the words και αυτη Σαρρα στειρα to be a Hebraic circumstantial clause, allowing for Abraham to be the subject. The second rendering considers this phrase to be a dative of accompaniment (TCGNT).

The first variant is probably the result of scribal error—due to homoeoteleuton: σαρρα στειρα. But if στειρα was purposely omitted, it may have been done in the interest of avoiding redundancy, inasmuch as "barrenness" is tantamount to "being past age." This variant appears in the majority of manuscripts and in TR; hence, it is followed by KJV and NKJV. It appears that many other modern versions have also followed this reading. However, translators could have followed one reading or the other and still have needed to make a decision about who is the subject of the sentence—Abraham or Sarah or both.

Hebrews 11:12

𝔓[46*] D* Ψ have the short text η αμμος της θαλασσης ("the sand of the sea"), whereas all other manuscripts have the fuller text, η αμμος η παρα το χειλος της θαλασσης ("the sand along the shore of the sea"). A corrector of 𝔓[46], in cursive hand, added the words η παρα το χειλος to make the fuller text. The shorter reading demonstrates that a verse in Romans (Rom 9:27), which in 𝔓46 immediately precedes Hebrews, may have formed a horizon of expectation for the original scribe of 𝔓46 in his reading of Hebrews.

Hebrews 11:13

WH NU καὶ ἀσπασάμενοι
"and having welcomed them [the promises]"
𝔓13vid 𝔓46 ℵ D 33 1739 it syr cop
NKJVmg RSV NRSV ESV NASB NIV TNIV NEB REB NJB NAB NLT HCSB NET

variant/TR και πεισθεντες και ασπασαμενοι
"having been persuaded and having welcomed them [the promises]"
1518?
KJV NKJV

The WH NU reading has the support of nearly all Greek manuscripts and the early versions. The variant reading printed in TR has the support of a few Greek manuscripts. NA[27] lists 1518? (a manuscript of the 14th/15th century) with *pc* (meaning a few manuscripts). The additional wording indicates that the patriarch's acceptance of God's promises was that which persuaded them to live as expatriates.

Hebrews 11:17

𝔓46vid, alone among the manuscripts, has the shortest reading here: προσενηνοχεν Ισαακ πειραζομενος ("having been tested, he offered up Isaac"). Most other Greek versions include Abraham's name and an article before Ισαακ.

Hebrews 11:23

At the end of this verse, D* 1827 it[d] and one Vulgate manuscript add πιστει μεγας γενομενος Μωυσης ανειλεν τον Αιγυπτιον κατανοων την ταπεινωσιν των αδελφων αυτου ("by faith Moses, when he was grown up, destroyed the Egyptian when he observed the humiliation of his brothers"). This interpolation (noted in NRSVmg) was borrowed from Exod 2:11-12, which is cited by Stephen in Acts 7:24.

Hebrews 11:31

The word απειθησασιν ("having disobeyed") was replaced by απιστησασιν ("having disbelieved") in 𝔓46 because the scribe of this manuscript had a propensity for changing verbs conveying disobedience to verbs conveying unbelief (see notes on 3:18; 4:6).

Hebrews 11:37

NU ἐπρίσθησαν
"they were sawn in two"
𝔓46 1241[s] syr[p] cop[sa]
NKJVmg RSV NRSV ESV NASBmg NIV TNIV NEB REB NJB NAB NLT HCSB NET

variant 1/WH ϵπϵιρασθησαν, ϵπρισθησαν
"they were tested, they were sawn in two"
ℵ (D*) L P 048 33 syr[h]
NETmg

variant 2/TR ϵπρισθησαν, ϵπϵιρασθησαν
"they were sawn in two, they were tested"
𝔓[13vid] A D[c] Ψ 1739
KJV NKJV RSVmg NRSVmg ESVmg NASB NIVmg TNIVmg NEBmg REBmg NJBmg NLTmg HCSBmg NETmg

In defense of the longer readings in the variants, it could be argued that some scribe accidentally deleted ϵπϵιρασθησαν due to homoeoteleuton or to the perception that "testing" hardly fits in a string of cruel punishments. But in defense of the NU reading, it must be pointed out that the variation of word order in the manuscript tradition is probably an indication that the word was a later insertion. Some scribe(s) likely added it to propound the motif of testing, which occurs through this epistle (2:18; 3:8-9; 11:17).

The early witness of 𝔓[46] figures significantly here. Indeed, the Nestle text (from the twenty-fifth edition) was changed to align with 𝔓[46]. Nearly all modern versions (except NASB) follow this reading and note the second variant out of deference to the KJV tradition.

Hebrews 12:1

TR WH NU τὴν εὐπερίστατον ἁμαρτίαν
"the ensnaring sin"
𝔓[13] ℵ A D Maj it cop syr
all

variant την ευπερισπαστον αμαρτιαν
"the easily distracting sin"
𝔓[46] 1739
NRSVmg NEBmg REBmg

The TR WH NU reading has abundant testimony and seems to make good sense, if indeed ευπεριστατον means "ensnaring" or "constricting." The lexical problem stems from the fact that this word appears nowhere else in previous or contemporary Greek literature (Lane 1991, 398-399), so its meaning has to be conjectured. In this context, the sense seems to be that the Christian runner is called upon to free himself from the sin that ensnares him or clings to him.

The variant reading, though slimly supported, is found in the earliest witness, 𝔓[46], and its later ally, 1739. Zuntz (1953, 28) considered it unquestionably original because it supplies the perfect word for the metaphor: "as ογκος ("weight") is liable to hamper the Christian athlete, thus sin is liable to divert him from his goal." Indeed, the whole point of the passage is to encourage believers to run the race without distraction. Many scholars have favored this reading (see the list in Lane, op. cit.), but not one translation has adopted it. In deference to the antiquity of 𝔓[46], the NEB translators added a marginal note that says, "*one witness reads* the sin which too easily distracts us." The NRSV and REB translators also added a note.

Hebrews 12:3

NU ὑπὸ τῶν ἁμαρτωλῶν εἰς ἑαυτὸν ἀντιλογίαν
"opposition by sinners against himself"
A P 0150
KJV NKJV RSV NRSV ESV NASB NLT HCSB NET

variant 1/TR υπο των αμαρτωλων εις αυτον αντιλογιαν
"opposition by sinners against him"
D² Ψ* 1739ᶜ 1881 Maj
NIV TNIV NEB REB (NJB) NAB

variant 2/WH υπο των αμαρτωλων εις αυτους αντιλογιαν
"opposition by sinners against themselves"
𝔓13 𝔓46 ℵ² D (ℵ* D* εαυτους) Ψᶜ 33 1739*
NRSVmg NJBmg NLTmg

In a fuller context, the NU reading yields this rendering: "for consider the one having endured such opposition by sinners against himself." The NU reading and the first variant convey nearly the same meaning: The readers are being urged to consider how much opposition Jesus received from sinners. No doubt, the writer of Hebrews had in mind the abuse that Jesus received prior to and during his crucifixion. But these readings are poorly attested—especially by comparison to documentation supporting the second variant. However, this second variant has not been generally accepted by textual scholars or translators because scholars have been hard pressed to garner any meaning from the expression εις αυτους αντιλογιαν in this context (see Lane 1991, 400-401). There are scholars who accept this reading (so Westcott and Hort as well as Wikgren—see his note in TCGNT) on the grounds that it is the more difficult reading but does make sense—Jesus received "opposition from sinners against themselves"—i.e., sinners doing hurt to themselves by opposing Jesus. This idea is expressed generally in Prov 8:36 and more specifically in Num 17:2-3 (LXX; Num 16:37-38 in English Bible), where Korah, Dathan, and Abiram are said to have sanctified the censers of sinners at the cost of the sinners' very lives.

Hebrews 12:4

𝔓46* originally read οπου μεχρις αιματος αντικατεστησεν ("insofar as he resisted unto blood")—which, when joined with the previous clause, would read as follows: "lest you become weary and lose heart—insofar as he [Jesus] resisted to the point of shedding blood—in your struggle against sin." The original scribe of 𝔓46 corrected the verb αντικατεστησεν (aorist) to αντικατεστηκεν (perfect), and then another corrector changed οπου ("insofar as") to ουπω ("not yet"). But the corrector made no change in the verb, so it still remained third person singular. Thus, the final text of 𝔓46 reads ουπω μεχρι αιματος αντικατεστηκεν ("he has not yet resisted unto blood"). (For a complete reconstruction of 𝔓46, see *Text of Earliest MSS,* 245-246.) This final reading is more radical than the original in that it says that Jesus did not shed his blood.

Finally, it should be noted that 𝔓13 and 𝔓46 may preserve the original wording, αγωνιζομενοι ("the ones struggling"), which was then intensified to ανταγωνιζομενοι ("the ones struggling against") in later manuscripts.

Hebrews 12:9

The unique expression τω πατρι των πνευματων ("the father of spirits") was changed to τω πατρι των πνευματικων ("the father of spiritual ones") in 440 and τω πατρι των πατερων ("the father of fathers") in 1241[s]. The expression "the Father of spirits" connotes God the Father's guidance over the spirits of those who belong to him (cf. 12:23).

Hebrews 12:15

The word ενοχλη ("it may trouble") is certainly written in 𝔓[46] as εν χολη ("in gall")—see *Text of Earliest MSS,* 246, which differs from the *editio princeps.* (This adds documentation to the conjecture posed by P. Katz as noted in NA[27].) 𝔓[46] makes perfectly good sense: "lest some root of bitterness would be sprouting up with gall and many be defiled by it." This reading follows Deut 29:18 (LXX), which says "lest there be in you a root springing up with gall and bitterness"—as opposed to the Masoretic Text, "lest there be among you a root bearing poisonous fruit and wormwood." Given the writer's propensity for quoting the Septuagint, it is not unreasonable to suppose that 𝔓[46] may have preserved the original wording. If so, a simple transposition of two letters (*chi* and *omicron*) accounts for the change to ενοχλη in all the other witnesses. But if 𝔓[46] is in error, the opposite transposition must have occurred, perhaps to conform the text to the Septuagint.

Hebrews 12:18a

WH NU	ψηλαφωμένῳ "what can be touched" 𝔓[46] א A C 048 33 it syr[p] cop NKJVmg RSV NRSV ESV NJB NAB (NLT) HCSB NET
variant/TR	ψηλαφωμενω ορει "a mountain that can be touched" D Ψ 1739 Maj KJV NKJV NRSVmg NASB NIV TNIV NEB REB NJBmg

The insertion of ορει ("mountain") was adapted from 12:20-22. This interpolation at this juncture distracts from the point that the author is about to introduce a contrast between the physical features of the events pertaining to the inauguration of the old covenant (i.e., those things that can be touched) and the spiritual elements of the new covenant (see 12:22-24). It is too limiting to specify only the mountain as that which can be touched. Nonetheless, this has become the insertion in most translations.

Hebrews 12:18b

WH NU	ζόφῳ καὶ θυέλλῃ "gloom and storm" א* A C D* 048 33 NKJVmg RSV NRSV ESV NASB NIV TNIV NEB REB NJB NAB NLT HCSB NET
variant/TR	σκοτω και θυελλη "darkness and storm" (𝔓[46] σκοτει) א[2] D[1] 1739 Maj KJV NKJV

It is difficult to determine which reading here is original. The variant may be the result of scribal conformity to Deut 4:11 (LXX), which describes the storm cloud in which God was enshrouded on Mount Sinai as being σκοτος, γνοφος, θυελλα ("dark, black, stormy"). The WH NU reading could be the result of scribal conformity to the Hebrew text of Deut 4:11, which uses gloom. On balance, the WH NU reading has slightly better testimony.

Hebrews 12:20

WH NU λιθοβοληθήσεται
"it [the animal] will be stoned"
𝔓46 א A C D 048 33 Maj
NKJVmg RSV NRSV ESV NASB NIV TNIV NEB REB NJB NAB NLT HCSB NET

variant/TR λιθοβοληθησεται η βολιδι κατατοξευθησεται
"it [the animal] will be stoned or thrust through with an arrow"
2 and a few other late MSS
KJV NKJV

The variant reading, slimly supported and clearly spurious, displays scribal expansion borrowed from Exod 19:13 (LXX). This reading appears in the Basel minuscule 2 (twelfth century) and was included by Erasmus in his Greek text when he used this manuscript. Thereafter, it was included in TR, followed by KJV and NKJV.

Hebrews 12:23

The expression πνευμασι δικαιων ("spirits of just men") was changed to πνευματι δικαιων ("the Spirit of just men") in D* it[b] and some Vulgate manuscripts. This yields a Trinitarian passage: "you have come . . . to *God,* the Judge of all, to the *Spirit* of just men made perfect, and to *Jesus,* the Mediator of the new covenant." D* has the unusual reading δικαιων πεθεμελιωμενων ("just men having been established"), and א* has the reading τελειων δεδικαιωμενοις ("perfect ones having been justified"). Both manuscripts were corrected to the standard text, διακαιων τετελειωμενων ("just men made perfect/completed").

Hebrews 12:26

WH NU σείσω
"I will shake"
𝔓46 א A C I 048 0243 0285 33 1739 it cop
NKJVmg RSV NRSV ESV NASB NIV TNIV NEB REB NJB NAB NLT HCSB NET

variant/TR σειω
"I shake"
D Ψ Maj
KJV NKJV

According to WH NU, the full citation reads: "Once again I will shake not only the earth but also the heaven" (Hag 2:20). The change of verb tense (from future to present), which is found in some Western and Byzantine manuscripts, was probably made in the interest of conforming this verse to Hag 2:21 (LXX), the verse cited here.

Hebrews 12:28

Some manuscripts (including 𝔓46* א P) have a reading in the indicative mood, εχομεν χαριν ("we are thankful"). Other manuscripts (including 𝔓46c A C D 0243 1739 Maj) have a reading in the (hortatory) subjunctive mood, εχωμεν χαριν ("let us be thankful").

Hebrews 13:9

WH NU — μὴ παραφέρεσθε
"do not be carried away"
𝔓[46] א* A D* cop
NKJVmg RSV NRSV ESV NASB NIV TNIV NEB REB NJB NAB (NLT) HCSB NET

variant/TR — μη περιφερεσθε
"do not be carried about"
K L
KJV NKJV

According to WH NU, the full expression is, "do not be carried away with strange and diverse teachings." This reading has the best documentary support. The variant arose as a scribal aberration, influenced by Eph 4:14 ("carried about by every wind of doctrine").

Hebrews 13:12

Instead of saying that Jesus suffered "outside the gate" (εξω της πυλης), a few witnesses (𝔓[46] P 104 and one cop[bo] MS) say he suffered "outside the camp" (εξω της παρεμβολης). This is the result of scribal conformity to the next verse.

Hebrews 13:15

TR NU include ουν ("therefore") with the support of א[2] A C D[1] 1739 Maj it syr[h]. WH excludes it; this has the support of 𝔓[46] א* D* P Ψ. It is not likely that ουν was accidentally dropped due to homoeoteleuton (as argued by Zuntz 1953, 192), for this would be unlikely to occur in so many manuscripts of diverse origin. Rather, it is more likely that it was added to give resumptive force.

Hebrews 13:20

As often occurred throughout the history of textual transmission, the name "Lord Jesus" was expanded to "Lord Jesus Christ." In this verse, D* Ψ 33 syr cop[bo] bear witness to this expansion by adding Χριστον ("Christ") after Ιησουν ("Jesus").

Hebrews 13:21a

WH NU — ἀγαθῷ
"good [thing]"
(𝔓[46]) א D* Ψ it cop[bo]
RSV NRSV ESV NASB NIV TNIV NEB REB NAB NLT HCSB NET

variant 1/TR — εργω αγαθω
"good work"
C D[2] 0243 0285 33 1739 Maj syr cop[sa]
KJV NKJV NJB

variant 2 — εργω και λογω αγαθω
"good work and word"
A
none

According to WH NU, the expression is, "that he may equip you with every good [thing]"—the "good" is left unspecified and therefore is inclusive. The first variant is probably the result of some scribe wanting to clarify the meaning of αγαθω. The second variation is the result of scribal conformity to 2 Thess 2:17.

Hebrews 13:21b

WH NU ποιῶν ἐν ἡμῖν
"doing in us"
𝔓46 ℵ A Dvid 0243 0285 33 1739
NKJVmg RSVmg NRSV ESV NASB NIV TNIV NEB REB NJB NLTmg HCSB NET

variant/TR ποιων εν υμιν
"doing in you"
C P Ψ syrh
KJV NKJV RSV NRSVmg ESVmg NAB NLT NETmg

Since the pronoun in the preceding clause is υμιν ("you"), copyists would be inclined to make the next pronoun the same. But the two clauses can be separated by means of punctuation (see NIV). The RSV translators diverted from their usual course of following the reading in 𝔓46 or the earliest reading. Perhaps they did this for stylistic reasons—to keep the pronouns in the successive clauses the same. NLT did the same.

Hebrews 13:21c

All three Greek editions (TR WH NU) print δοξα εις τους αιωνας των αιωνων ("glory into the ages of the ages"). This reading has the support of ℵ A (C*) 0243 0285 33 1739 Maj, and is followed by all English versions with the rendering "glory forever and ever." However, in 𝔓46 C3 D Ψ syrh, the reading is shorter, excluding των αιωνων ("of the ages")—these two words are bracketed in NU.

The longer text is the predominant form used in doxologies throughout the Epistles. This phrasing or some similar form appears in such verses as Gal 1:5; Eph 3:21; Phil 4:20; 1 Tim 1:17; 2 Tim 4:8; 1 Pet 4:11; 5:11; Jude 25. The short form, εις τους αιωνας ("into the ages" = "forever"), appears in such verses as Rom 11:36; 16:27; 2 Cor 9:9; Heb 13:8; 1 Pet 1:25. There are instances in the textual tradition where both forms have been emended—by shortening (as in Gal 1:5; Phil 4:20; 1 Pet 4:11; 5:11) and by lengthening (as in Rom 16:27; 2 Cor 9:9). It is possible that certain scribes shortened the text here to make it conform to the quasi-doxology of Heb 13:8. But it is just as likely that the short form is original, because it accords with the style of the author of Hebrews (see 5:6; 6:20; 7:17, 21) and because the general tendency of scribes was to expand the verbiage in doxologies (see Zuntz 1953, 120-122). The second-century manuscript 𝔓46 may preserve the earliest extant form of the doxology (see notes on 13:24; 13:25a; 13:25b).

Hebrews 13:24

The original manuscript of 𝔓46 did not include και παντας τους αγιους ("and to all the saints"); it was inserted supralinearly by a later corrector. Since there is no apparent way to explain the omission as accidental, it is possible that the exemplar for 𝔓46 did not include these words. It is just as likely that the phrase was not in the original text; rather, it was a later addition which came into the text as the epistle circulated to more and more Christians. Thus, 𝔓46 may preserve the most primitive text, if not the original.

Hebrews 13:25a

All three editions (TR WH NU) read η χαρις μετα παντων υμων ("grace be with all of you"), with the support of 𝔓[46c] ℵ A C D[c] 33 1739 Maj, and followed by all English versions. There are two variants at the end of this expression: (1) D* reads παντων των αγιων ("all of the saints"); (2) 𝔓[46*] reads παντων ("all"). The first variant is a scribal carryover from the previous verse. The second variant may preserve the original text inasmuch as liturgical statements were typically expanded throughout the course of textual transmission. (The scribe of 𝔓[46] concluded his epistle with παντων, next to which another hand added υμων.)

Hebrews 13:25b

WH NU	omit αμην ("Amen") at end of verse 𝔓[46] ℵ* I[vid] 33 cop[sa] NRSV ESV NASB NIV TNIV NEB REB NJB NAB NLT HCSB NET
variant/TR	include αμην ("Amen") at end of verse ℵ[2] A C D H Ψ 0243 1739 Maj it syr cop[bo] KJV NKJV RSV NRSVmg NETmg

If "amen" had originally been in the text, there is no good way to explain its omission. Rather, it seems clear that an "amen" was added by scribes and translators for liturgical purposes. Only three epistles (Romans, Galatians, Jude) appear to have a genuine "amen" for the last word of the letter.

Subscription

1. No subscription—but placed as an inscription. Προς Εβραιους ("To the Hebrews"). Appears in 𝔓[46].
2. No subscription. Appears in D 0243 365 629 630 1505.
3. Προς Εβραιους ("To the Hebrews"). Appears in ℵ C I Ψ 33.
4. Προς Εβραιους εγραφη απο Ρωμης ("To the Hebrews written from Rome"). Appears in A.
5. Προς Εβραιους εγραφη απο Ιταλιας ("To the Hebrews written from Italy"). Appears in P.
6. Προς Εβραιους εγραφη απο Ιταλιας δια Τιμοθεου ("To the Hebrews written from Italy through Timothy"). Appears in 1739 1881 Maj (so TR).
7. Προς Εβραιους εγραφη απο Ρωμης υπο Παυλου τοις εν Ιερουσαλημ ("To the Hebrews written from Rome by Paul to the ones in Jerusalem"). Appears in 81.
8. Προς Εβραιους εγραφη Εβραιστι απο της Ιταλιας ανονυμως δια Τιμοθεου ("To the Hebrews written in Hebrew from Italy anonymously through Timothy"). Appears in 104.
9. Παυλου επιστολη προς Εβραιους απο της Ιταλιας δια Τιμοθεου ("Epistle of Paul to the Hebrews from Italy through Timothy"). Appears in 0285[vid].

It is quite certain that no book of the NT originally had an inscription or a subscription (see Comfort 2005, 9-10). This is especially true for the Epistles because their original purpose was to be apostolic letters, not literary works per se. Thus, all inscriptions and subscriptions are scribal addenda. The simplest form, Προς Εβραιους ("To the Hebrews"), appears in the earliest witnesses: in 𝔓[46] at the head of the epistle; in ℵ C I Ψ 33 at the end. This was then expanded to include the conjectured place of writing (Rome or Italy), and the carrier, Timothy (who is referred to in 13:23). Other late manuscripts also identify the specific recipients (those in Jerusalem) and the writer, Paul. Of course, these are conjectures. Many in the early church considered the author to be Paul, while others did not. The writer could have just as likely been Apollos, because the epistle bears the mark of one well versed in Alexandrian typology. But no one knows who wrote this epistle (see the succinct discussion by Morris 1981, 4-6), as noted by the word ανονυμως ("anonymously") in 104. And no one knows exactly where it was sent. Jerusalem is a good guess because the letter speaks to a group of Jewish Christians who had not yet broken away from practicing a form of cultic Judaism that was closely tied to the temple and temple sacrifices.

In any event, the title "To the Hebrews" is the simplest and most ancient of all ascriptions. It is attested to by Pantaenus (according to Eusebius in *Hist. eccl.* 6.14.4) and by Tertullian in the West (*Modesty* 20). It appears in the earliest witness, 𝔓[46] (of the second century), though as an inscription, and in manuscripts of the fourth and fifth century (ℵ C I). As Morris says, "we have no knowledge of any other title or any time when it lacked this one" (1981, 4).

The Epistle of JAMES

Inscription (Title)

WH NU	Ιακωβου Επιστολη "Epistle of James" (ℵ as subscription) B K (Ψ) 81 NKJV RSV NRSV NASB NIV NEB REB NJB NAB NLT
variant 1	no inscription 𝔓74vid none
variant 2/TR	Ιακωβου Επιστολη καθολικη "Catholic [= General] Epistle of James" (P) 33 1739 KJV
variant 3	Επιστολη καθολικη του αγιου αποστολου Ιακωβου "Catholic Epistle of the holy Apostle James" L (049 69) none

James is the first of the General Epistles (otherwise known as the Catholic Epistles), so called because this is an epistle addressed to a large audience (all Jewish Christians—see 1:1-2), as opposed to a specific local audience. This catholicity is noted in the two extended inscriptions listed above, whereas other witnesses simply note it as "Epistle of James." It is almost certain, however, that this letter never had any inscription in its original composition (as is evidenced in 𝔓74). (For more on this, see Comfort 2005, 9-10.)

James 1:3

Perhaps under the influence of a variant reading in 1 Pet 1:7, a few witnesses (110 1241 Didymus) read δοκιμον instead of δοκιμιον, found in all other manuscripts. James's text speaks of "the testing of one's faith" (το δοκιμιον υμων της πιστεως), while the variant in Peter's text speaks of the approval of one's faith after being tested.

James 1:12a

Interestingly, a few witnesses (A Ψ 1448 Cyril) read ανθρωπος, the generic term for human being, instead of ανηρ, the Greek term denoting a male. Since James was writing to Jewish Christians, who still met in synagogues (2:2), and since synagogues were attended only by males, it is very likely that James was addressing his comments specifically to men. Indeed, James specifically uses the masculine term ανηρ several times throughout this epistle (see 1:7-8, 19-20, 23; 2:2; 3:2).

James 1:12b

WH NU — ἐπηγγείλατο
"he promised"
𝔓23 א A B Ψ cop
NRSVmg NEB NJBmg NAB HCSB NETmg

variant 1/TR — ο κυριος επηγγειλατο
"the Lord promised"
C P 0246 Maj syrh
KJV NKJV NRSV NASB NJB HCSBmg NETmg

variant 2 — ο θεος επηγγειλατο
"God promised"
33vid 1739 syrp
RSV ESV NIV TNIV REB NLT NET

According to the best testimony, the subject is left unspecified in what would be rendered in full as, "having been approved, he will receive the crown of life which he promised to those loving him." Copyists and translators (both ancient and modern) took it upon themselves to supply a subject. Some chose "the Lord," and some "God."

James 1:17

TR WH NU — οὐκ ἔνι παραλλαγὴ ἢ τροπῆς ἀποσκίασμα
"there is no variation or shadow of turning"
א2 A C 1739 Maj
KJV NKJV RSV NRSV ESV NASB NEBmg REBmg NAB NLT HCSB NET

variant 1 — ουκ ενι παραλλαγη η τροπης αποσκιασματος
"there is no variation which consists in the turning of the shadow"
א* B
RSVmg NRSVmg ESVmg NIV TNIV NEB REB NJB NLTmg

variant 2 — ουκ ενι παραλλαγης η τροπης αποσκιασματος
"there is no variation or turning of the shadow"
𝔓23
none

variant 3 — ουκ ενι παραλλαγη η τροπης αποσκιασμα ουδε μεχρι υπονοιας τινος υποβολη αποσκιασματος
"there is no variation or shadow of turning, not even the least suspicion of a shadow"
1832 2138
none

According to TR WH NU, the full statement could be rendered as, "Every good and perfect gift is from above, coming down from the Father of lights with whom there is no variation or shadow of turning." Due to the complexity of the metaphor, different scribes attempted to clarify the sense, and it is not easy to determine which scribe emended what. The image seems to portray God as an unchanging orb of light—quite unlike the natural sun, which from our perspective shifts and thus causes shadows. Or the image could point to the movements of the celestial bodies, such as the phases of the moon, the shadow cast by an eclipse, or the constant alternation of night and day (Moo 1985, 76). The TR WH NU reading seems to indicate that the second phrase defines the first: The shifting shadow is the variation. The first variant simply links the expressions together so as to show that the variation is one and the same with "the shifting shadows." The reading in $\mathfrak{P}^{23}$ (the second variant) has two expressions to describe the Father's invariability: (1) no variation and (2) no turning of the shadow. The second image could possibly allude to the image of an ancient sundial (which told time by the turning of the shadow). If so, James would be indicating that God is changeless *and* timeless (Comfort 1996, 172). But the context appears to deal only with God's unchanging, steadfast nature. The gloss, which appears in some late manuscripts (variant 3), is an attempt to explain just what "the turning of the shadow" means. With God there is no variation, not even a hint of it. Modern translations are divided on this verse, several of them giving alternative readings in the margin and three of them (RSV NRSV NLT) specifically giving the reading in variant 1. The reading of the earliest witness, $\mathfrak{P}^{23}$, is at least worthy of a note, but no translation has granted it one.

James 1:19

WH NU	Ιστε "you know" ℵ B C 1739 NKJVmg RSV NRSV ESV NASB NIV TNIV NEB REB NJB NAB NLT HCSB NET
variant 1	Ιστε δε "but you know" $\mathfrak{P}^{74vid}$ A none
variant 2/TR	Ωστε "so then" P Ψ Maj KJV NKJV

The WH NU reading has the best documentary support—from the combined witness of ℵ B C 1739. Both the variants are scribal attempts to make a better transition between the end of 1:18 and the beginning of 1:19.

James 1:26

WH NU	τις δοκεῖ θρησκὸς εἶναι "anyone [who] considers [himself] to be religious" ℵ A B C P Ψ 0173 33 1739 it syr cop NKJVmg RSV NRSV ESV NASB NIV TNIV NEB REB NJB NAB NLT HCSB NET

variant/TR τις δοκει θρησκος ειναι εν υμιν
"anyone among you [who] considers [himself] to be religious"
049 Maj
KJV NKJV HCSBmg

The manuscript evidence overwhelmingly supports the WH NU reading. The variant is a scribal attempt to particularize James's comment about those who consider themselves to be religious.

James 1:27

All manuscripts read επισκεπτεσθαι ορφανους και χηρας ("to visit orphans and widows"), with the exception of 𝔓[74], which reads υπερασπιζειν αυτους ορφανους και χηρας, which must be rendered as, "to protect them, orphans and widows." Black (1964, 43-45) indicated that this reading, though probably not original, focuses on protecting the weak ones in this world, more than just visiting them.

James 2:3

NU σὺ στῆθι ἐκεῖ ἢ κάθου
"you stand there or sit"
A C* Ψ 33 syr[h] cop[sa]
RSV NRSV ESV NASB NIV TNIV NEBmg REBmg NJB NAB NLT HCSB NET

variant 1/WH σου στηθι η καθου εκει
"you stand or sit there"
B 1739
NEB

variant 2/TR σου στηθι εκει η καθου ωδε
"you stand there or sit here"
𝔓[74vid] ℵ (C[2]) P Maj syr[p] cop
KJV NKJV NEBmg REB

The second variant is the result of scribal carryover from the previous clause, which reads συ καθου ωδε ("you sit here"). The first variant adjusts the text so that there are only two places mentioned in the verse: "here" (with reference to the position of the speaker) and "there" (under the footstool); albeit, this reading is accepted by *The Editio Critica Maior.* The NU reading has good testimony from A and C, which are excellent in the General Epistles.

James 2:11

Instead of the expression γεγονας παραβατης νομου ("you have become a transgressor of the law"), 𝔓[74] and A read γεγενου αποστατης νομου ("you have become an apostate of the law"). Kilpatrick (1967, 433) defends this reading by arguing that "transgressor" is a carryover from 2:9. Martin (1988, 57), building on this, acknowledges there would then be "a progression in the author's thought, climaxing in the warning against apostasy."

James 2:18

With excellent support (ℵ A B C Ψ 33), WH NU read δειξον μοι πιστιν σου χωρις των εργων ("show me your faith apart from works"). By contrast, TR reads δειξον μοι πιστιν σου εκ των εργων ("show me your faith by your works"), with the support of

𝔓[54vid] Maj. Hodges (1963, 345) has argued that the variant reading is the more difficult reading and therefore original. But this reading is tautological. In other words, there is no apparent difference in the two statements made by James's hypothetical objector. (As such, KJV and NKJV, which usually follow TR, render the text "without your works.") So it seems likely that the variant is the result of a scribal error—the eye of a scribe jumping ahead to the next identical phrase (εκ των εργων). According to WH NU, the emphasis is on the collaboration of faith and works (see 2:22).

James 2:19

NU	εἷς ἐστιν ὁ θεός "God is one" 𝔓[74] א A RSV NRSV ESV NASB NLTmg NAB HCSB NET
variant 1/WH	εἷς θεος εστιν "there is one God" B 614 630 (C 33[vid] 81 with def. article before θεος) KJV NKJV NASBmg NIV TNIV NEB REB NJB NLT
variant 2/TR	ο θεος εἷς εστιν "God is one" Maj none (but see above)

The NU reading conforms to the prevailing formula of Jewish orthodoxy. Westcott and Hort followed the reading in B, but this reading may be the result of assimilation to 1 Cor 8:6; Eph 4:6; 1 Tim 2:5. Most English versions follow this reading because it provides for the smoothest style.

James 2:20

WH NU	ἀργή "useless" B C* 1739 cop[sa] NKJVmg RSV NRSV ESV NASB NIV TNIV NEB REB NJB NAB NLT HCSB NET
variant 1/TR	νεκρα "dead" א A C[2] P Ψ 33 Maj KJV NKJV NIVmg TNIVmg NETmg
variant 2	κενη "empty" 𝔓[74] NETmg

The textual variant pertains to what is the predicate adjective in the expression, "faith without works is (1) useless, (2) dead, or (3) empty." The first variant, though found in some important uncials and in the majority of manuscripts, appears to be the result of assimilation to similar statements in this chapter (2:17, 26). The second variant, though conveying the same idea as the WH NU reading, is probably the result of scribal harmonization to the preceding wording ανθρωπε κενε ("empty man"). The WH NU reading has good documentation and displays James's sensitivities to lexical variation and perhaps even wordplay—between the words εργων and αργη (*alpha* privative and εργη) (see TCGNT). James argues that faith without the demonstration of works is not only dead (2:17, 26), it is useless in that it is unproductive.

James 2:25

Most ancient witnesses speak of Rahab receiving αγγελους ("messengers"), which were sent by Joshua to Jericho. These messengers are specified as αγγελους του Ισραηλ ("messengers of Israel") in a few manuscripts (including 61) and as κατασκοπους ("spies") in other manuscripts (C K[mg] L 1739 cop[bo])—see Josh 2:4, 6; Heb 11:31.

James 3:5

WH NU read μεγαλα αυχει ("boasts great things"), with the support of 𝔓[74] A B C* P 33, as listed in NA[27]. TR has one word μεγαλαυχει, which means the same thing. NA[27] lists the following witnesses in support of this reading: (𝔓[20*]) ℵ C[2] Ψ 1739 Maj. 𝔓[20c] should be added in the support of the WH NU reading—even though the corrector did not quite get it right, he was trying to copy an exemplar that had the wording μεγαλα αυχει (see *Text of Earliest MSS,* 108, note a).

James 3:8

WH NU	ἀκατάστατον κακόν "a restless evil" ℵ A B P 1739* it syr[p] cop[bo] RSV NRSV ESV NASB NIV TNIV REB NJB NAB NLT HCSB NET
variant/TR	ακαταςχετον κακον "an uncontrollable evil" C Ψ 1739[c] Maj KJV NKJV NEB NETmg

The WH NU reading, which has superior documentation, describes the tongue as a restless evil—"a pest that will not keep still" (NJB). The variant probably shows the work of scribes attempting to make this statement dovetail with the preceding one, which speaks of how impossible it is for men to tame the tongue.

James 3:9

WH NU	τὸν κύριον καὶ πατέρα "the Lord and Father" 𝔓[20] ℵ A B C P Ψ 1739 RSV NRSV ESV NASB NIV TNIV NEB REB NJB NAB NLT HCSB NET
variant/TR	τον θεον και πατερα "the God and Father" Maj syr[h] cop[ach,sa] KJV NKJV NETmg

The Granville Sharp rule stipulates that when one article precedes two personal nouns joined by και, then the same person is so designated. In this instance, one person is both the Lord and Father. This could mean that Jesus is both Lord and Father, since James has elsewhere called Jesus "Lord" (1:1; 2:1; cf. 5:7-8, 14-15) or that God is both Lord and Father, since James has elsewhere identified God as "Lord" (5:4, 9-10). It is likely that James was referring to God as Father, but some scribes and translators wanted to make this absolutely certain, so they changed "Lord" to "God." Or the change could have been motivated by the fact that God is nowhere else called "Lord and Father" in the NT.

James 3:12

WH NU — οὔτε ἁλυκὸν γλυκὺ ποιῆσαι ὕδωρ
"nor can salt water produce fresh water"
A B C* (א Ψ C^2 33 1739 add ουτως)
NKJVmg RSV NRSV ESV NASB NIV TNIV NEB REB NJB NAB (NLT) HCSB NET

variant/TR — ουτως ουδεμια πηγη αλυκον και γλυκυ ποιησαι υδωρ
"thus no fountain is able to make salt and sweet water"
Maj syr^h
KJV NKJV

The point of the WH NU reading, which has excellent documentation, is that one element cannot produce another unlike itself. This is in complete concord with the other images in this verse: A fig tree cannot make olives and a grapevine cannot make figs. The point of the variant is that one source cannot produce two different products. This is in agreement with 3:10, to which the Majority Text has been assimilated.

James 4:4

WH NU — μοιχαλίδες
"adulteresses" (= "adulterous women")
$\mathfrak{P}^{100}$ א* A B 33 1739
NKJVmg (RSV NRSV ESV NASB NIV TNIV NEB REB NJB NAB NLT) HCSB (NET)

variant/TR — μοιχοι και μοιχαλιδες
"adulterers and adulteresses"
$א^2$ P Ψ Maj syr^h
KJV NKJV HCSBmg

The expression μοιχαλιδες (the feminine form of "adulterer") is unusual. Some commentators have thought that James, at this juncture, turned his attention to the women in the congregation, but this is unlikely because the epistle appears to be directed to the men of the congregation throughout (see note on 1:12a). Thus, it is likely that James was speaking of all those who, like Israel, had strayed from their faithfulness to God and thereby brought upon themselves the condemnation of being "adulteresses": "Adulteresses, do you not know that friendship with the world is enmity with God?" This kind of language, in the feminine form, depicting Israel, is found in Isa 50:1; Jer 13:27; Ezek 16:38. The WH NU reading has excellent support, its earliest witness coming from $\mathfrak{P}^{100}$.

Unaware of James's adaptation of this OT usage and subsequently uncomfortable with James singling out only female adulterers, some scribe(s) added the masculine "adulterers" as well. This change became popularized in the majority of manuscripts, was accepted in TR, and has been perpetuated in KJV and NKJV. All other modern versions follow the WH NU reading, even though they all (with the exception of HCSB) translate the single feminine word as "adulterers." The Jerusalem Bible does a good job of capturing the feminine form with the rendering, "you are as unfaithful as adulterous wives."

James 4:5

WH NU	τὸ πνεῦμα ὃ κατῴκισεν ἐν ἡμῖν "the Spirit which he caused to dwell in us" 𝔓74 ℵ B Ψ 049 1739 RSV NRSV ESV NASB NIV TNIV NEB REB NJB NAB NLT HCSB NET
variant/TR	το πνευμα ο κατωκησεν εν ημιν "the Spirit which dwells in us" P 33 Maj KJV NKJV

According to WH NU, the full verse reads, "Or do you think that the Scripture vainly says, 'The Spirit which he caused to dwell in us desires with jealousy'?" The variant indicates simply that the Spirit dwells in us. Though one word could have easily been confused for the other (there is only a one-letter difference: ι/η), the WH NU reading has better textual support and is slightly more complex in that it presupposes that God is the active subject. This could mean that God placed his Spirit within the believers because he wanted it to protect them from straying in their love for him (God). Thus, the Spirit is jealous for the believers' affection. The variant conveys nearly the same meaning, without saying that God put the Spirit within the believers for this purpose.

James 4:12a

NU	[ὁ] νομοθέτης καὶ κριτής "the lawgiver and judge" ℵ A Ψ 33 1739 NKJVmg RSV NRSV ESV NASB NIV TNIV NEB REB NJB NAB NLT HCSB NET
variant 1/WH	νομοθετης και κριτης "lawgiver and judge" 𝔓100vid B P none
variant 2/TR	ο νομοθετης "the lawgiver" (𝔓74 omit ο) 049 Maj KJV NKJV HCSBmg

The first variant, having the support of both 𝔓100 and B, is likely original. The second variant, though the shorter reading, is probably the result of homoeoteleuton—the eye of a scribe passing from νομοθετης to κριτης. But it is possible that some scribe deleted it because the rest of the verse pertains only to judgment, not lawgiving.

James 4:12b

WH NU	ὁ κρίνων τὸν πλησίον "the one judging the [= your] neighbor" 𝔓74 𝔓100vid ℵ A B Ψ 33 1739 syr cop NKJVmg RSV NRSV ESV NASB NIV TNIV NEB REB NJB NAB NLT HCSB NET

variant/TR ος κρινεις τον ετερον
"who judges the other"
Maj
KJV NKJV

The change in the majority of manuscripts may be explained as a scribal attempt to make James's admonition specifically applicable to the Christian community—the ετερον assumed to be "another brother" (cf. Rom 14:4, 10).

James 4:13

WH NU σήμερον ἢ αὔριον πορευσόμεθα εἰς τήνδε τὴν πόλιν καὶ ποιήσομεν ἐκεῖ ἐνιαυτὸν καὶ ἐμπορευσόμεθα καὶ κερδήσομεν
"Today or tomorrow we will go into this or that city and we will spend a year there and we will do business and we will make money."
(𝔓74 𝔓100 א) B 33 1739 it
RSV NRSV ESV NASB NIV TNIV NEB REB NJB NAB NLT HCSB NET

variant/TR σημερον και αυριον πορευσωμεθα εις τηνδε την πολιν και ποιησωμεν εκει ενιαυτον ενα και εμπορευσωμεθα και κερδησωμεν
"Today and tomorrow we could go into this or that city and we could spend one year there and we could do business and we could make money."
(A Ψ) Maj
KJV NKJV

The WH NU reading is well supported by the ancient documents, including the two most ancient, 𝔓100 and B. The variant reading is represented by the majority of manuscripts and is largely found in A and Ψ (with a few minor variations). It appears that the changes in verb tense (from future indicative to aorist subjunctive) were done so as to emphasize that the businessmen's plans were tentative. The WH NU reading, however, reveals that the businessmen were making definite plans for the future. And this is what troubled James and led to his admonition. Christians who participate in business must entrust their future to the Lord (see 4:14-15).

James 4:14a

WH NU ποία ἡ ζωὴ ὑμῶν
"what your life [will be]"
א* B syr[h] cop[bo]
NASB NJB HCSB

variant/TR ποια γαρ η ζωη υμων;
"for what is your life?"
𝔓74 (𝔓100vid omit η) א2 A P Ψ 33 1739 Maj
KJV NKJV RSV NRSV ESV NIV TNIV NEB REB NAB NLT NET

The variant reading is well supported by a variety of manuscripts, including 𝔓100, and is the reading that most English versions followed. However, the editors of NU considered this variant to be an editorial fix intended to relieve ambiguity or perceived anacoluthon, both created by the word ποια ("what"). But this word can be joined with the verb επιστασθε ("do you know") in the previous clause (as in the NU reading for 4:14a); it yields this kind of rendering: "you do not know what will be tomorrow, what your life will be like" (see Martin 1988, 158). Or, as the feminine form of ποιος, ποια can be joined with η ζωη. As such, the last phrase is an appositive: "you have no knowledge of tomorrow—what your life will be."

James 4:14b

The NU edition, with paltry support (81 614 syr[h]), reads ατμις γαρ εστε η προς ολιγον φαινομενη ("for you are mist, the one appearing for a little while"). The WH edition, following B 1739, omits η, yielding the rendering, "for you are mist, appearing for a little while." TR, following L 33, reads ατμις γαρ εστιν η προς ολιγον φαινομενη ("for it is mist, which appears for a little while"). Other manuscripts (A P Ψ Maj) have the verb as εσται. Though the NU reading is so poorly attested, the NU editors considered all the other readings to be scribal variations—whether the omission of γαρ ("for"), as unnecessary, or the switch to the third person (to accommodate the reply to James's question). But it is far more likely that the article η was added to introduce the following expression as an appositive, rather than deleted. Thus, it is likely that the true text has been preserved in WH.

James 5:4

TR NU have the verb απεστερημενος ("have been kept back by fraud"), with the support of A B[2] Ψ 33 Maj. WH, following א B*, reads αφυστερημενος ("have been withheld"). The original reading is very likely that which is presented in the WH text (and Nestle's 25th edition), even though the editors of the NU text considered it an Alexandrian refinement (against Metzger's demur; see his comment in TCGNT). The NU reading is probably the result of scribal assimilation to Mal 3:5, the verse alluded to here. Thus, James is castigating landowners for withholding wages from their workers, not for defrauding them per se.

James 5:5

WH NU	ἐθρέψατε τὰς καρδίας ὑμῶν ἐν ἡμέρᾳ σφαγῆς "you have fattened your hearts for a day of slaughter" א* A B P 33 it cop NKJVmg RSV NRSV ESV NASB NIV TNIV NEB REB NAB NLT HCSB NET
variant 1/TR	εθρεψατε τας καρδιας υμων ως εν ημερα σφαγης "you fattened your hearts as for a day of slaughter" א[2] 1739 Maj KJV NKJV NIVmg NJB
variant 2	εθρεψατε τας σαρκας υμων ως εν ημερα σφαγης "you fattened your flesh as for a day of slaughter" Ψ syr[p] none

The WH NU reading has excellent support. Both variants are scribal attempts to clarify James's image, in which he described wealthy persons' consumption of good living as being nothing less than a fattening-up for slaughter. (The NLT rendering is good here: "you have fattened yourselves for the day of slaughter.") The first variant, with the insertion of ως ("as"), emphasizes that this is a simile; the second variant makes it even more explicit by saying that one's "flesh" (not one's "heart") is being fattened for slaughter. But if ως is not present, as in the original text, the poetic image is still clear, as well as the allusion to the day of judgment.

James 5:7

WH NU	λάβῃ πρόϊμον καὶ ὄψιμον "it receives early and latter" 𝔓74 B 048 1739 cop^{sa} none
variant 1/TR	λαβη υετον προιμον και οψιμον "it receives early and latter rain" A P Ψ 33^{vid} Maj all
variant 2	λαβη καρπον προιμον και οψιμον "he receives early and latter fruit" (ℵ*) syr^{hmg} cop^{bo} none

The WH NU reading, which has good documentation, was emended in two ways. The first reading supplies the most obvious word to follow "early and latter"—namely, "rain" (ευτον). But to ancient readers, who knew of these two rains (one in the fall and one in the spring), these two words meant nothing other than "early rain" and "latter rain." English readers generally do not know this; so all English versions have also supplied "rain." A few scribes and ancient translators understood the text to be saying that the farmer (not the earth) was waiting for the early and latter fruit.

James 5:14

With the support of ℵ 33 1739 Maj, all three editions (TR WH NU) read εν τω ονοματι του κυριου ("in the name of the Lord"), which is followed by all English versions. WH, however, brackets του κυριου because these words are not found in B. The manuscripts A Ψ 81 omit the article του before κυριου, and a few other late manuscripts read κυριου Ιησου ("Lord Jesus") or Ιησου Χριστου ("Jesus Christ").

It is possible that B preserves the original reading, because all the early Christians knew that the title "the Name" was a surrogate for "the Lord Jesus Christ" (see Acts 4:12, 17; 26:9; 1 Pet 4:16; 3 John 7), whereas later readers would not necessarily know this. Thus, it would be tempting for scribes to specify that name. If B's reading is original, the name was supplied as "the Lord" (referring to Jesus Christ—1:1; 2:1; 5:7-8) or as "Lord Jesus" or "Jesus Christ." However, more documentary evidence is needed to affirm the shorter reading in B.

James 5:20a

TR NU	γινωσκέτω ὅτι "let him know that" ℵ A P 1739 Maj it syr^{p} KJV NKJV RSV NRSV ESV NASB NIV NEB NJB NAB HCSB NET
variant 1/WH	γινωσκετε οτι "you know that" B 69 1505 syr^{h} TNIV REB NJBmg NLT

variant 2	οτι "that" Ψ none
variant 3	omit 𝔓74 cop[sa] none

The first two words of this verse have been altered throughout the course of textual transmission. According to TR NU, the complete rendering is, "let him know that the one turning back a sinner from his wandering saves his soul from death." According to this reading, James was addressing the person who would set out to bring back the wanderer. In WH, it is cast in the second person plural, "you know that"—perhaps to conform it to 5:19. Other scribes shortened it, so that it dovetails with 5:19 (as in the second and third variants).

James 5:20b

WH NU	σώσει ψυχὴν αὐτοῦ ἐκ θανάτου "he will save his soul from death" ℵ A P 048[vid] 33 1739 syr RSV NRSV ESV NASB NIV TNIV NEB NJB NAB NLT HCSB NET
variant 1	σωσει ψυχην εκ θανατου αυτου "he will save a soul from death itself" (or, "he will save his soul from death") 𝔓74 B none
variant 2/TR	σωσει ψυχην εκ θανατου "he will save a soul from death" Ψ Maj cop[sa] KJV NKJV REB

Assuming the WH NU reading to be original, the second variant can be explained as an attempt to eliminate the ambiguity about whose soul would be saved—the converted or the converter. Thus, some scribe(s) deleted the pronoun αυτου. This became a very popular reading, as evidenced by its presence in the majority of manuscripts, and as perpetuated by the KJV and NKJV tradition. But it is also possible that the first variant is original. As such, the pronoun αυτου probably functions intensively (although the other rendering is possible—see above). Not recognizing this intensification, some scribes either deleted it (as in variant 1) or transposed it (as in variant 2).

James 5:20c

All three editions (TR WH NU) do not include αμην ("Amen") at end of verse. This has the support of A B C 048 33 Maj cop, and is followed by all English versions. Of course, some scribes could not resist adding αμην at the conclusion of the epistle (so 614 1505 1852 syr[h]). Only three epistles (Romans, Galatians, Jude) appear to have a genuine "amen" for the last word of the book. In the other epistles it seems evident that an "amen" was added for liturgical purposes. According to the textual evidence, it is absolutely certain that "amen" at the end of James is a scribal addition.

The First Epistle of PETER

Inscription (Title)

WH NU	Πετρου Α "First of Peter" B (א as subscription) NIV TNIV NLT NET
variant 1	no inscription 𝔓74vid none
variant 2	Πετρου Επιστολη Α "First Epistle of Peter" 𝔓72 א A 33 NKJV RSV NRSV ESV NASB NEB REB NJB NAB HCSB
variant 3/(TR)	Πετρου Επιστολη καθολικη Α "First Catholic [= General] Epistle of Peter" 323 1505 (1739 adds αποστολου) KJV
variant 4	Επιστολη καθολικη Α του αγιου και πανευφημου αποστολου Πετρου "First Catholic Epistle of the holy and all-praiseworthy Apostle Peter" L (049) none

First Peter is one of the General Epistles (otherwise known as the Catholic Epistles), so called because this is an epistle addressed to a large audience (the Christians in Pontus, Galatia, Cappadocia, Asia, and Bithynia—see 1:1), as opposed to a specific local audience. This catholicity is noted in the third and fourth variants, whereas other witnesses simply note it as "First Epistle of Peter" or even simpler as "First of Peter." In reality, this letter never had any inscription in its original composition (as is evidenced in 𝔓74).

1 Peter 1:1

Peter addressed this epistle to the Christians in Pontus, Galatia, Cappadocia, Asia, and Bithynia, most of whom were exiles from the Jerusalem persecution; other Christians had been converted in these regions as a result of this Diaspora. As a result, Peter was addressing both Jewish

Christians (those who came from Jerusalem) and Gentile Christians (those who were indigenous to Pontus, Galatia, Cappadocia, Asia, and Bithynia). The scribe of B* deleted Bithynia from the list, perhaps because he considered Pontus and Bithynia to be the same province. Other scribes (א* 048) deleted "Asia," probably because these copyists thought that Asia encompassed the entire area to which this epistle was addressed and was therefore redundant (Michaels 1988, 3). Here, however, "Asia" refers to the Roman province of Asia, which occupied only the western portion of Asia Minor.

1 Peter 1:7

A few manuscripts (𝔓72 429* 1852) read δοκιμον instead of δοκιμιον, found in all other manuscripts. The word δοκιμον denotes the testing of one's faith, while δοκιμιον speaks of the genuineness of one's faith after being tested (see note on Jas 1:3).

1 Peter 1:8

WH NU οὐκ ἰδόντες
"not having seen"
𝔓72 א B C 1739 it syr cop[sa]
all

variant/TR ουκ ειδοτες
"not having known"
A P Ψ 33 Maj cop[bo]
NKJVmg RSVmg

The WH NU reading has excellent documentation—both early and diverse—and makes sense in the context: "Jesus Christ, whom not having seen, you love." Whereas Peter had seen Jesus Christ with his very eyes (see 5:1; 2 Pet 1:16-18), he was speaking to second-generation Christians who had not seen Jesus in the flesh yet still believed in him. This belief brought them into a spiritual "knowing" of Jesus Christ. It would be illogical for Peter to say that the believers did not know Jesus. Thus, it must be judged that ειδοτες was a scribal mistake for ιδοντες (the words sound and look similar). Once this mistake was made, it is possible that ειδοτες was understood as a perfect participle with past meaning, allowing the translation, "once you did not know Jesus Christ, but now you love him." Interestingly, the KJV translators deviated from TR here, in order to have their translation make sense. The variant has not been adopted by English versions, though noted in a few.

1 Peter 1:11

In this verse all manuscripts except one (Codex B) read πνευμα Χριστου ("the Spirit of Christ"). The scribe of B shortened it to πνευμα ("the Spirit") perhaps because he may not have understood how Christ's Spirit could be present before Christ's incarnation in the OT prophets (who predicted the coming of Christ and his experiences of suffering and being glorified). Because the Son of God was to become the Christ, he revealed himself in the OT by his Spirit in and through the prophets. The title, "the Spirit of Christ," shows up one other time in the NT—in Rom 8:9, which identifies "the Spirit of Christ" with the indwelling Christ and the indwelling Holy Spirit; thus, it is "the Spirit of Christ." Acts 16:7 has a similar phrase, "the Spirit of Jesus," and Phil 1:19 has the phrase "Spirit of Jesus Christ."

1 Peter 1:12a

WH NU ὑμῖν δὲ διηκόνουν αὐτά
"but to you they were ministering these things"
𝔓72 ℵ A B C Ψ 048 33 1739 Maj
NKJVmg RSV NRSV ESV NASB NIV TNIV NEB REB NJB NAB NLT HCSB NET

variant/TR ημιν δε διηκονουν αυτα
"but to us they were ministering these things"
945 1241
KJV NKJV

A few scribes changed "you" to "us," either by mistake (υμιν and ημιν are easily confounded) or in an effort to elevate the apostles' role (identified by "us") as being those who received these revelations and then disseminated them to the believers. This change made its way into TR and from there into KJV and NKJV.

1 Peter 1:12b

The preposition εν ("in") before πνευματι αγιω ("Holy Spirit") should not be included in NU, because the omission has the strong support of 𝔓72 A B Ψ 33 (see Metzger's dissenting note in TCGNT).

1 Peter 1:16

There are several textual variants in this verse, only one of which affects the meaning. While several ancient manuscripts (𝔓72 ℵ A B C Ψ—so WH NU) read αγιοι εσεσθε ("you will be holy"), many late manuscripts (K P 049 1739 Maj—so TR) read αγιοι γενεσθε ("you will become holy"). Although both readings can allow for a process of sanctification, the text can be read as a command or as denoting a future promise, "you will be holy." Albeit in the Leviticus context, from which this is taken (see Lev 11:44; 19:2), the sense is a command.

1 Peter 1:19-20

Between these verses, several Latin Vulgate manuscripts (and Bede) insert this gloss: "Therefore, he himself, who also was known before the foundation of the world and was born in the last time and suffered, received the glory that God the Word always possessed, abiding without beginning in the Father." The interpolation is an interesting mix of Petrine and Johannine sayings concerning the Son of God's journey from pristine glory, to incarnation, to the cross, and then ultimately back to glory with the Father.

1 Peter 1:21

The rare expression πιστους ("believers"), found in A B (so WH NU), was probably replaced by one of two ordinary expressions: (1) πιστευοντας ("the ones believing") in 𝔓72 ℵ C P Ψ 1739 Maj (so TR), or (2) πιστευσαντας ("the ones having believed") in 33.

1 Peter 1:22a

WH NU — ὑπακοῇ τῆς ἀληθείας
"obedience to the truth"
𝔓72 ℵ A B C Ψ 33 1739 syr cop
NKJVmg RSV NRSV ESV NASB NIV TNIV NEB REB NJB NAB NLT HCSB NET

variant/TR — υπακοη της αληθειας δια πνευματος
"obedience to the truth through [the] Spirit"
P 1vid Maj
KJV NKJV NRSVmg HCSBmg NETmg

It is extremely doubtful that δια πνευματος could have been accidentally dropped from the text, especially in so many ancient witnesses. Rather, it is far more likely that this is a later addition made by some scribe(s) wanting to emphasize the Spirit's work in the believers' sanctification (see 1:2; also 2 Thess 2:13; Titus 3:5). This reading found its way into TR, and it has been popularized in KJV and NKJV.

1 Peter 1:22b

TR NU — ἐκ [καθαρᾶς] καρδίας
"from a pure heart"
𝔓72 ℵ* C P Ψ 33 1739 Maj syrh cop
KJV NKJV RSVmg NRSVmg ESV NASBmg NIVmg TNIVmg REB NJBmg NAB NLTmg HCSB NET

variant 1/WH — εκ καρδιας
"from [the] heart"
A B
RSV NRSV NASB NIV TNIV NEB NJB NLT HCSBmg NETmg

variant 2 — εκ αληθινης καρδιας
"from a true heart"
ℵ2
none

The majority of NU editors adopted the TR NU reading because they were influenced by the testimony of 𝔓72 ℵ* etc. But in deference to the minority of the editors who thought καθαρας ("pure") was an addition, the words are bracketed in NU (see TCGNT). Indeed, the presence of two different adjectives ("pure" and "true") in the textual tradition shows that the original text has probably been preserved by A and B (so WH). Many modern translators, evidently persuaded by the same reasoning, have not included "pure" or "true."

1 Peter 1:23

WH NU — λόγου ζῶντος θεοῦ καὶ μένοντος
"living and remaining word of God"
𝔓72 ℵ A B C Ψ 33 1739 syrh cop
NKJVmg RSV NRSV ESV NASB NIV TNIV NEB REB NJB NAB NLT HCSB NET

variant/TR — λογου ζωντος θεου και μενοντος εις τον αιωνα
"living word of God and remaining for ever"
P Maj
KJV NKJV

The manuscript support for WH NU is vastly superior to that for TR. The expanded reading, found in the majority of manuscripts and popularized by the KJV, is an assimilation to the wording of 1:25, ρημα κυριου μενει εις τον αιωνα ("the word of the Lord remains forever").

1 Peter 1:24a

A few minor changes in this verse are probably scribal attempts to conform Peter's quotation of Isa 40:6-8 more closely to the Septuagint. Peter's rendition says πασα σαρξ ως χορτος ("all flesh is as grass"), according to 𝔓72 ℵ* B C P 049 Maj. This was changed to πασα σαρξ χορτος ("all flesh is grass") in ℵ2 A Ψ 33 1739. (See next note.)

1 Peter 1:24b

WH NU	πᾶσα δόξα αὐτῆς "all its glory" 𝔓72 ℵ2 A B C 33 1739 it syr cop[bo] NKJVmg RSV NRSV ESV NASB NIV TNIV NEB (REB) NJB NAB (NLT) HCSB NET
variant 1	πασα δοξα αυτου "all of his glory" ℵ* none
variant 2/TR	πασα δοξα ανθρωπου "all human glory" P Ψ Maj KJV NKJV

The manuscript evidence strongly supports the WH NU reading. Both variants are obvious attempts to conform Peter's quotation of Isa 40:6-8 more closely to the Septuagint. But it need not be said explicitly that this statement is speaking of "human glory" or even "his glory," because the entire passage illustrates man's impermanence and frailty by using a simile of grass flowering in its glory and then fading: "all its glory as the flower of grass."

1 Peter 2:2

WH NU	αὐξηθῆτε εἰς σωτηρίαν "you may grow into salvation" 𝔓72 ℵ A B C Ψ 33 syr cop NKJVmg RSV NRSV ESV NASB NIV TNIV NEB REB NJB NAB NLT HCSB NET
variant/TR	αυξηθητε "you may grow" Maj KJV NKJV HCSBmg

According to WH NU, the full statement is: "desire the pure spiritual milk of the word, that by it you may grow into salvation." This reading is supported by an array of early and significant witnesses. The variant, which appears in the majority of manuscripts, is clearly a late, scribal deletion. At some point in the history of the text, scribes must have found it difficult to conceive of how one could "grow into salvation," because salvation is normally considered as an initial gift accompanying regeneration or an eschatological event accompanying the believer's resurrection.

But salvation is just as much a process as sanctification and transformation are, for as Christians are transformed, they are also delivered (saved) from the world and their fallen nature. It is the word of God that gives the believers the nourishment to grow into this kind of salvation.

1 Peter 2:3

All three editions (TR WH NU) read ει εγευσασθε οτι χρηστος ο κυριος ("if you have tasted that the Lord is good"), with the support of ℵ A B C Ψ 1739 syr. A few manuscripts (K L 049 33[s]) substituted Χριστος ("Christ") for χρηστος ("good")—yielding this rendering: "if you have tasted that the Lord is Christ." 𝔓[72] changes this text with the wording ει εγευσασθε επιστευσατε οτι Χριστος ο κυριος ("if in tasting you believed that Christ is the Lord").

Since there is only a one-letter difference between χρηστος and χριστος (η/ι), we could conjecture that one word could have easily been confused for the other. But in the early manuscripts, the name χριστος was almost always written as a nomen sacrum (XPC). Therefore, a scribe would not have mistaken it for χρηστος. (Of course, nonbelievers often mistook the two words, thinking that Jesus was the χρηστος = "the kind one," because the term Χριστος, "Christ," meant nothing to those unfamiliar with the Hebrew notion of the Anointed One. But this was not the case with Christians.) What happened here was that some scribe was determined to make this a confessional statement of faith: "the Lord is Christ" or "Christ is the Lord." This is revealed in the emendation in 𝔓[72], where επιστευσατε was inserted to explain that "tasting" the Lord is tantamount to believing in him.

1 Peter 2:5a

WH NU
οἰκοδομεῖσθε οἶκος πνευματικὸς εἰς ἱεράτευμα ἅγιον
"you are being built a spiritual house for a holy priesthood"
𝔓[72] A* B Ψ 33
RSV NRSV ESV NASB NIV TNIV NEB REB NJB NAB NLT HCSB NET

variant 1
εποικοδομεισθε οικος πνευματικος εις ιερατευμα αγιον
"you are being built upon a spiritual house for a holy priesthood"
ℵ A[c] C 1739
none

variant 2/TR
οικοδομεισθε οικος πνευματικος, ιερατευμα αγιον
"you are being built a spiritual house, a holy priesthood"
P Maj
KJV NKJV

The WH NU reading, which has early and solid documentary support, was adjusted in two ways. The first variant may reflect a scribal attempt to show that the believers are built upon a certain foundation—whether Christ or the apostles (see 1 Cor 3:10-17; Eph 2:20). The second variant indicates that the believers are built up as a spiritual house, which is a holy priesthood. But the WH NU reading, by retaining the word εις, says that the community of believers is a spiritual house that functions as a holy priesthood. In other words, the purpose for which the spiritual house exists is to be a holy priesthood.

1 Peter 2:5b

Most manuscripts read ανενεγκαι πνευματικας θυσιας ("to offer up spiritual sacrifices"). Two notable variations of this are as follows: 𝔓72 reads ανενεγκαι πνευματικας ("to offer up spiritual things"); א reads ανενεγκαι θυσιας ("to offer up sacrifices"). The change in 𝔓72 could have been influenced by Rom 15:27; 1 Cor 12:1; 14:1, or it could have been accidental, due to homoeoteleuton. The change in א could have also been due to homoeoteleuton.

1 Peter 2:7

WH NU	ἀπιστοῦσιν "[the] unbelieving" 𝔓72 א B C Ψ 1739 syr[h] cop NKJVmg RSV NRSV ESV NASB NIV TNIV NEB REB NJB NAB NLT HCSB NET
variant/TR	απειθουσιν "[the] disobedient" A P Maj KJV NKJV

The variant reading, which first appears in A and is found in the majority of manuscripts, is probably the result of scribal conformity to the next verse, which identifies those who reject Jesus Christ as being απειθουντες ("disobedient"). But the primary issue in this verse is belief versus unbelief.

1 Peter 2:8

The scribe of B conformed this verse to the previous one by changing απειθουντες ("being disobedient") to απιστουσιν ("unbelieving"). See note on 2:7.

1 Peter 2:12

The present participle εποπτευοντες ("observing") has the excellent support of 𝔓72 א B C 1739 (so WH NU). The variant reading in TR is the aorist participle εποπτευσαντες δοξασωσιν τον θεον ("having observed, they glorified God"), found in A P Ψ 33 Maj. Michaels (1988, 114) offers a good explanation for how the variant arose: "Possibly the aorist participle was introduced because it seemed obvious to scribes that the 'observing' of the good works of Christians by the Gentiles in Asia must precede, both logically and temporally, their 'glorifying' of God on the final day of judgment."

1 Peter 2:19

With the good documentary support of א A[c] B P 049 Maj it cop, all three editions (TR WH NU) read συνειδησιν θεου, which could be rendered "consciousness of God" or "conscience toward God." There are two variants on this: (1) συνειδησιν αγαθην ("good conscience") in C Ψ 1739; (2) συνειδησιν θεου αγαθην ("good consciousness of God" or "good conscience toward God") in 𝔓72 (A* 33). The expression in the TR WH NU reading cannot mean "God's conscience" (taken as a subjective genitive); it must mean something like "a conscience toward God" or, even better, "a conscious awareness of God" (both understood as objective genitives). The idea is that the believer who suffers unjustly and bears up under it patiently does so because he or she has made a conscious commitment to God. In any event, the difficulty of the expression συνειδησιν θεου was the catalyst for a few scribal changes. The first variant displays the usual NT idiom, "good conscience," and the second is a conflation.

1 Peter 2:20

With the good documentary support of ℵ* A B C 33 Maj syr[h] cop, all three editions (TR WH NU) read κολαφιζομενοι ("being beaten"). A variant on this is κολαζομενοι ("being punished"), as found in 𝔓[72] ℵ[2] P Ψ 1739. It is possible that one word was mistaken for the other in the transcription process because there is only a two-letter difference (φι) between them. Furthermore, the two words are nearly synonymous, for it was a punishment to be beaten. Nevertheless, κολαφιζομενοι ("being beaten") is probably original, because it has better textual support and because the tenor of this chapter speaks of inflicted physical suffering.

1 Peter 2:21

WH NU	Χριστὸς ἔπαθεν ὑπὲρ ὑμῶν "Christ suffered for you" (𝔓[72] A περι for υπερ) B C 1739 syr[h] cop NKJVmg RSV NRSV ESV NASB NIV TNIV NEB REB NJB NAB NLT HCSB NET
variant 1/TR	Χριστος επαθεν υπερ ημων "Christ suffered for us" P 33 Maj KJV NKJV
variant 2	Χριστος απεθανεν υπερ υμων "Christ died for you" 𝔓[81] ℵ Ψ syr[p] NEBmg REBmg NJBmg NLTmg

According to WH NU, the entire phrase reads: "Christ suffered for you, leaving you an example that you should follow in his steps." The textual variation in this verse concerns whether Christ "suffered" for sins or "died" for sins. 𝔓[81] (early fourth century) provides an early witness for the reading "died"—against the evidence of the papyrus, 𝔓[72]. This lines up 𝔓[72] B against 𝔓[81] ℵ—a virtual standoff. The same textual variant occurs in 3:18, where it seems certain that "died" is original. But we cannot be certain in this verse, not only because of the documentary split, but because it is possible that some scribe(s) changed "died" to "suffered" to suit the context, which speaks of suffering, or, on the other hand, made the opposite change to promote the more ordinary NT saying, "Christ died for you" (see Rom 5:6-8; 14:15; 2 Cor 5:14-15; 1 Thess 5:10). In one reading, Peter was calling upon the believers to emulate Christ's sufferings. In the variant, Peter was calling upon the believers to be ready for martyrdom. The latter is the more radical reading.

Given the WH NU reading, Peter was speaking of how Jesus suffered for the believers and thereby left them a pattern to follow. The Greek word for "pattern" (υπογραμμον) literally means "an underwriting"; it was a model of handwriting set up by masters for their pupils to copy—letter by letter, right underneath the exemplar. The word was used, as here, as a figure of speech for a model of conduct for imitation. Given the variant in 𝔓[81] etc., Peter was encouraging the believers to suffer even unto the death.

1 Peter 2:23

Greek manuscripts say that Christ "gave himself to the one who judges righteously" (παρεδιδου δε τω κρινοντι δικαιως—a reference to Christ's commitment of his soul to God). However, a few Latin witnesses (it[t] vg Clement[lat]) say that Christ "gave himself to the one who judges unrighteously." This would mean that Christ allowed himself to be judged by unrighteous Pilate. Such a change may have happened in a Greek manuscript under the influence of 2:19 and then was transmitted into some Latin versions.

1 Peter 2:25

WH NU read πλανωμενοι, with the support of ℵ A B, yielding the rendering, "for you were wandering as sheep." TR reads πλανωμενα and has good support (𝔓[72] C P Ψ 33 1739 Maj), yielding the rendering, "for you were as wandering sheep." The difference in meaning between the two readings is subtle, but not subtle enough to have escaped the notice of the NJB translators, who noted the variant in the margin.

1 Peter 3:3

The three editions (TR WH NU) read εμπλοκης τριχων ("braiding hair") with the excellent support of ℵ A B P 33 1739 Maj. A few manuscripts (𝔓[72] C Ψ cop[sa]), however, exclude τριχων. This omission can hardly be explained as accidental. Thus, if it is not original, then it can be explained as coming from some scribe who confused εμπλοκης with εμπλοκιον, used in the Septuagint to describe gold twisted (or fashioned) in jewelry (see Exod 35:22; 36:22-25 and see Michaels 1988, 155).

1 Peter 3:7a

NU — συγκληρονόμοις
"[they are] coheirs"
𝔓[72] 𝔓[81] ℵ[2] B 33 1739
NRSV ESV NASB NIV TNIV NEB REB NJB NAB NLT HCSB NET

variant 1/TR WH — συγκληρονομοι
"[you are] coheirs"
A C P Ψ Maj
KJV NKJV RSV ESVmg NJBmg

variant 2 — συγκληρονομους
"[you are] coheirs"
ℵ*
none

According to NU, the full rendering is: "The husbands likewise dwelling together with [them] according to knowledge as with a weaker vessel—the female—showing them honor as also they are coheirs." In the first variant, the rendering of the last part becomes, "showing them honor, as also you [the men] are coheirs with them." The second variant provides the same idea.

It is likely that scribes found the shift from the dative singular (γυναικειω = "wife") to the dative plural (συγκληρονομοις) to be awkward and therefore changed it to the accusative (variant 2) or the nominative (variant 1). These changes make the husbands (ανδρες) the coheirs. But the original dative, συγκληρονομοις, indicates that the wives are the coheirs. This means that the wives share with their husbands in being copartners of grace. The testimony of the papyri 𝔓72 and 𝔓81 (with B) is significant; the NU edition, in following them, has surpassed the WH edition here. Most modern English versions have done the same.

1 Peter 3:7b

The three editions (TR WH NU) read χαριτος ζωης ("grace of life"), with excellent testimony: 𝔓81vid B C* P Ψ 33 1739 Maj. All English versions follow. But there are interesting variants: (1) ποικιλης χαριτος ζωης ("multifarious grace of life") in א A (C2) syrh copbo, and (2) χαριτος ζωης αιωνιου ("grace of eternal life") in 𝔓72 syrp. The first variant displays scribal conformity to 4:10, which speaks of "the multifarious grace of God" parceled out as special gifts to the individual members of the church. The context here does not call for this adjective. But one scribe (𝔓72) and ancient translator (syrp) thought it called for the adjective "eternal" (variant 2), which they adopted from one of several places in the NT where "life" is described as being eternal. Christian wives and husbands are heirs together of God's grace and therefore have inherited God's life for their present enjoyment and eternal portion.

1 Peter 3:8

WH NU	ταπεινόφρονες "humble-minded" 𝔓72 א A B C Ψ 33 1739 syr cop NKJVmg RSV NRSV ESV NASB NIV TNIV NEB REB NJB NAB NLT HCSB NET
variant 1/TR	φιλοφρονες "courteous" P 049 Maj KJV NKJV HCSBmg
variant 2	φιλοφρονες ταπεινοφρονες "courteous, humble-minded" L (it) none

The WH NU reading is so well documented that its authenticity can hardly be doubted. However, the first variant is difficult to account for. The word φιλοφρονες (which literally means "loving-minded") could not have been borrowed from anywhere else in the NT, because it appears nowhere else. And it does not seem likely that a scribe would want to change φιλοφρονες to ταπεινοφρονες because the latter is almost as rare in the NT. The only explanation is that the first variant could have been the result of dittography—a scribe accidentally repeating the letters φιλα from φιλαδελφια (two words back) and then transforming the α to ο: φιλοφρονες. The second variant is easy to explain: It is the result of conflation. In any event, the change in verbiage only slightly alters the meaning of the text: Believers are called upon to have "humble minds" or "loving attitudes" for the good of the Christian community.

1 Peter 3:9

WH NU	ὅτι εἰς τοῦτο ἐκλήθητε "that to this you were called" 𝔓72 𝔓81 א A B C Ψ 33 1739 syr cop RSV NRSV ESV NASB NIV TNIV NEB REB NJB NAB NLT HCSB NET

variant/TR εἰδοτες οτι εις τουτο εκληθητε
"knowing that to this you were called"
P Maj syr[hmg]
KJV NKJV

The WH NU reading has strong manuscript support, which is both early and diverse. The insertion of ειδοτες ("knowing") is probably a carryover from 1:18 (cf. 5:9); it suggests that this was an item of Christian dogma that the believers should have known very well.

1 Peter 3:10-12

Most Greek manuscripts conclude Peter's citation of Ps 34:13-17 (LXX) with προσωπον δε κυριου επι ποιουντας κακα ("but the face of the Lord is against evil ones"). However, a few late manuscripts (614 630 1505) extend the quotation from the Septuagint further: του εξολοθρευσαι αυτους εκ γης ("to destroy them from the earth").

1 Peter 3:14

TR WH NU μὴ φοβηθῆτε μηδὲ ταραχθῆτε
"do not fear nor be afraid"
ℵ A C P Ψ 33 1739 Maj it
all

variant μη φοβηθητε
"do not fear"
𝔓72 B L
(NJBmg)

The shorter reading could be the result of homoeoteleuton—the eye of a scribe passing from φοβηθητε to ταραχθητε. But it is unlikely that this could have happened independently in three different manuscripts—unless, of course, they all trace to the same exemplar. But it is equally possible that the last two words (μηδε ταραχθητε) were not originally in the text and were subsequently added to complete the OT quotation of Isa 8:12-13, begun in 3:14 and continued in 3:15. Thus, it seems just as likely that the two earliest witnesses (𝔓72 B) and L have preserved the original text, which lacks the redundancy found in the longer version.

1 Peter 3:15

WH NU κύριον δὲ τὸν Χριστὸν ἁγιάσατε
"but sanctify the Lord Christ"
𝔓72 ℵ A B C 33 1739 it syr[h] cop
NKJVmg RSV NRSV ESV NASB NIV TNIV NEB REB NJB NAB NLT HCSB NET

variant/TR κυριον δε τον θεον αγιασατε
"but sanctify the Lord God"
P Maj
KJV NKJV HCSBmg NETmg

The WH NU reading, which has excellent documentary support, can also be rendered, "but sanctify Christ as Lord in your hearts." This means that a Christian should maintain his inward sanctity in the midst of persecution from unbelievers; he needs to look to the indwelling Christ to prepare him to give a defense for his faith. The identification of the persecuted believer's solidarity with Jesus Christ is obscured in the variant because it makes the divine indweller the

"Lord God," a typical OT designation of God. But if this variant could be rendered "sanctify the Lord [= Jesus] as God in your hearts," then it is possible to see it as a way of scribes exalting the Lord Jesus' deity. However, it is more probable that "Lord Christ" was changed to "Lord God" so as to make the verse conform to Isa 8:13 (LXX), the verse cited here by Peter, who himself substituted "Christ" for "God." All modern versions follow the superior reading here without even noting the variant. As usual, the NKJV has a note to show where its textual tradition differs from NU.

1 Peter 3:16

WH NU — καταλαλεῖσθε
"you are spoken against"
𝔓72 B Ψ 1739 cop[sa]
RSV NRSV ESV NASB NIV TNIV NEB REB NJB NAB (NLT) HCSB NET

variant/TR — καταλαλουσιν υμων ως κακοποιων
"they speak against you as evildoers"
א A C P 33 Maj it cop[bo]
KJV NKJV

Though the WH NU reading has less documentary support than the variant, it has early and diverse attestation. The reading in the variant is the result of scribal conformity to 2:12, a parallel verse. This expansion, made somewhat early in the history of textual transmission, spread to a number of manuscripts, and has been popularized by TR, followed by KJV and NKJV.

1 Peter 3:18a

TR NU — περὶ ἁμαρτιῶν ἔπαθεν
"for sins he suffered"
B P Maj
KJV NKJV RSVmg NRSV ESV TNIV NEBmg REB NAB NLT HCSB NET

variant 1/(WH) — περι αμαρτιων υπερ υμων απεθανεν
"for sins he died on your behalf"
𝔓72 A
ESVmg HCSBmg NETmg

variant 2 — περι αμαρτιων υπερ ημων απεθανεν
"for sins he died on our behalf"
(א*) C[2vid] L 33 1739 1881 cop[bo]
RSV NASB NIV NEB NJB NABmg NLTmg HCSBmg NETmg

variant 3 — περι υμων υπερ αμαρτιων απεθανεν
"for us he died on behalf of sins"
Ψ
none

variant 4 — περι αμαρτιων ημων απεθανεν
"for our sins he died"
C[*vid] syr[p]
HCSBmg NETmg

There are a few more variants than those listed above, but none of them presents anything significantly different. The essential difference is whether or not Christ "suffered" (επαθεν) for our sins or "died" (απεθανεν) for our sins. (The choice of pronoun—our/your—is minor, as is the insertion of υπερ.) As in 2:21, in which the context seems to favor the reading "suffered" instead of "died" (see comments above), it would seem natural for Peter (again speaking about suffering—see 3:14-18) to say that Christ "suffered for sins" rather than "died for sins." But it is possible that Peter spoke of Christ dying for sins in anticipation of speaking of Jesus' redemptive act (the righteous dying for the unrighteous) and his actual death on the cross. However, a scribe, carrying with him the message of previous verses (which is a message about suffering), would be tempted to change "died" to "suffered" if he saw "died" in his exemplar. Or it is likely that the scribes of B P Maj simply conformed this verse to 2:18, which has the reading "suffered" in these manuscripts. Thus, I am inclined to accept the evidence of 𝔓[72] ℵ A C etc. for απεθανεν ("died") over against επαθεν ("suffered"), minus the υπερ + ημων/υμων phrase (as in WH). However, since modern translations are divided over which verb to follow ("died" or "suffered"), this would be a good place to institute a footnote which says, "Or, as in other manuscripts. . . ."

1 Peter 3:18b-19a

All Greek manuscripts say that Christ ζωοποιηθεις δε πνευματι εν ω και τοις εν φυλακη πνευμασιν πορευθεις εκηρυξεν ("was made alive in spirit—by which spirit he also went to make a proclamation to the spirits in prison"). This statement is difficult to interpret. Some exegetes suggest that Christ died to his former mode of life, but lived on in another—"in spirit." The Greek expression εν ω ("in which") refers to "spirit" in 3:18; it means that Christ in spirit went to the spirits in prison. But when did he make this journey? Some scholars think it occurred after his death and prior to his resurrection—that is, during his descent into Hades. Other scholars think it occurred sometime before the flood. Just as Jesus "came and preached peace" by his Spirit in the apostles and ministers after his death and ascension, so, before his incarnation, he preached in the spirit through Noah to the antediluvians. Christ, who in our times came in the flesh, came in the spirit through Noah in his times. In 1:11, Peter spoke of the Spirit of Christ in the OT prophets—Noah was one of those prophets. Enoch may have been another one. In fact, a few scholars have conjectured that the text read Ενωχ και = "Enoch also" (J. Bowyer, see critical apparatus of NA[27]) or εν ω και Ενωχ = "in whom also Enoch" (J. R. Harris, see critical apparatus of NA[27]) instead of εν ω και ("in whom also"). The resultant texts are: (1) "he was made alive in spirit—in Enoch he also went to make a proclamation to the spirits in prison" or (2) "he was made alive in spirit—by which spirit Enoch also went to make a proclamation to the spirits in prison." These are ingenious conjectures but could not be considered as reconstructions of the original, because though the original is difficult to interpret, it is comprehensible Greek. Nonetheless, the conjecture of Harris was adopted by both Goodspeed and Moffat in their respective translations of the NT.

1 Peter 3:19b

A few manuscripts (C it[z]) identify the prisoners as "having been locked up" (κατακλεισμενοις), and a few other manuscripts (including 614) identify the prison as Hades (αδη). A few other manuscripts (𝔓[72] 614 1881) change πνευμασιν ("spirits") to πνευματι ("in spirit"). This change was probably made to underscore the idea that Jesus traveled "in spirit" to those who were in prison (see comments on 3:18b-19).

1 Peter 4:1a

WH NU — παθόντος σαρκί
"he suffered in [the] flesh"
𝔓72 B C Ψ 0285 1739
NKJVmg RSV NRSV ESV NASB NIV TNIV NEB REB NJB NAB NLT HCSB NET

variant 1/TR — παθοντος υπερ ημων σαρκι
"he suffered in [the] flesh for us"
א2 A P Maj syrh copbo
KJV NKJV RSVmg NRSVmg ESVmg HCSBmg NETmg

variant 2 — παθοντος υπερ υμων σαρκι
"he suffered in [the] flesh for you"
69 1505 syrp
RSVmg NRSVmg ESVmg NETmg

variant 3 — αποθανοντος υπερ υμων σαρκι
"he died in [the] flesh for you"
א*
NETmg

The addition of a beneficiary of Christ's suffering—whether "you" or "us"—is a carryover from 2:21 and 3:18. But the point of this passage is not to exalt Jesus' vicarious death but to display Jesus as a model of suffering to be emulated by the believers. The change from "suffered" to "died" in א* was also influenced by 2:21 and 3:18, where א* reads "died" instead "suffered" in both instances.

1 Peter 4:1b

TR NU — πέπαυται ἁμαρτίας
"he ceased with sin"
𝔓72 א* A C P 1739 Maj
NRSV NIV TNIV NEB REB NJB NAB NLT HCSB NET

variant 1/WH — πεπαυται αμαρτιαις
"he ceased with sins"
א2 B Ψ
none

variant 2 — πεπαυται απο αμαρτιας
"he ceased from sin"
049 1881 Jerome
KJV NKJV RSV ESV NASB

According to TR NU, the full reading is, "the one suffering in the flesh has ceased with sin" (referring to the believer or Jesus, see NLTmg). According to WH, the full reading is, "the one suffering in the flesh has ceased with sins." In English, there is only a one-letter difference (an *s*—sin/sins); in Greek, there is only one iota of a difference between the TR NU reading and the first variant. The *iota* could have been accidentally added or dropped, but if the change was intentional it is likely that scribes added the *iota* because they were trying to deal with the notion of how a Christian can be finished with sin just because he or she has suffered in the flesh. These scribes may have thought that "sin"—as an operative principle in the flesh—can never be eliminated in this lifetime and therefore changed "sin" to "sins" (as in the first variant). Other scribes and the translator Jerome added the preposition "from" to help the text say that one is freed or given rest from the power of sin (see Rom 6:7). Of course, this reasoning assumes that "the one suffering in the flesh" is a reference to a Christian; some interpreters see this as describing Christ (see Michaels 1988, 226-229). Because of his passion on the cross, whereby he became sin itself and then died for all the sins of the world, Jesus ceased with sin—he no longer has to deal with it (see Heb 9:28).

1 Peter 4:3

WH NU ὁ παρεληλυθὼς χρόνος
"the time having passed"
𝔓72 א A B C Ψ 33 1739
NKJVmg RSV NRSV ESV NASB NIV TNIV NEB REB NJB NAB NLT HCSB NET

variant/TR ο παρεληλυθως χρονος του βιου
"the lifetime having passed"
P 049 Maj
KJV NKJV

The manuscript support for WH NU is very strong. The change in the Majority Text was influenced by the previous verse, which has the wording βιωσαι χρονον ("to live out one's time").

1 Peter 4:8

WH NU ἀγάπη καλύπτει πλῆθος ἁμαρτιῶν
"love covers a multitude of sins"
A B Ψ 33 1739 it syr
RSV NRSV ESV NASB NIV TNIV NEB REB NJB NAB NLT HCSB NET

variant/TR αγαπη καλυψει πληθος αμαρτιων
"love will cover a multitude of sins"
𝔓72 א P 049 Maj
KJV NKJV

Though the documentary support is evenly divided, the variant in TR is likely the result of scribal conformity to the Septuagint's rendition of Prov 10:12, the verse cited here by Peter. It is likely that Peter adapted the verse to make a statement about the power love has to cover sins, without reference to a specific time.

1 Peter 4:11

Most Greek manuscripts have the expression η δοξα και το κρατος εις τους αιωνας των αιωνων, αμην ("the glory and power forever and ever, amen"). In some witnesses (69 1739 syr[h] cop[sa]) this is shorter: η δοξα και το κρατος εις τους αιωνας, αμην ("the glory and power forever, amen"). In 𝔓72 it is even shorter: δοξα και κρατος εις τους αιωνας, αμην ("glory and power forever, amen"). Since scribes had a tendency to lengthen benedictions and doxologies, 𝔓72 may well preserve the original reading.

1 Peter 4:14a

WH NU	τὸ τῆς δόξης καὶ τὸ τοῦ θεοῦ πνεῦμα "the Spirit of glory and of God" 𝔓72 B L Ψ 049 all
variant 1	το της δοξης και δυναμεως και το του θεου πνευμα "the Spirit of glory and of power and of God" א A P 33 1739 cop[bo] RSVmg NRSVmg ESVmg NJBmg NETmg
variant 2	το της δοξης και δυναμεως του θεου ονομα και πνευμα "the Spirit of glory and of God's powerful name" 614 630 1505 syr[h] none

If the first variant is the original wording, it is possible that some scribes wanted to trim an elongated expression: "the of-glory and of-power and of-God Spirit" to the more compact, "the of-glory and of-God Spirit." However, the presence of two different expansions in the textual tradition (variant 1 and 2) is usually a sign that the shorter reading is the one from which the others deviated. Thus, the reading found in the two earliest manuscripts, 𝔓72 and B, is likely original, and the variant readings are scribal additions. The first expansion was probably influenced by the appended doxology to the Lord's Prayer in Matt 6:13 (see note). The second expansion was influenced by the use of Christ's name in this verse and in 4:16. Not one version contains these additions, though the first one is noted in several versions (RSVmg NRSVmg ESVmg NJBmg NETmg). Peter's verbiage expresses the thought that God's glorious Spirit will imbue anyone who is being persecuted because he or she confesses the name of Christ.

1 Peter 4:14b

WH NU	conclude verse with αναπαυεται ("rests") א* B 049 (𝔓72 א2 A επαναπαυται) (33 1739 αναπεπαυται) syr[p] cop[bo] NKJVmg RSV NRSV ESV NASB NIV TNIV NEB REB NJB NAB NLT HCSB NET
variant/TR	add at end of verse, κατα μεν αυτους βλασφημειται, κατα δε υμας δοξαζεται "on their part he is blasphemed, but on your part he is glorified" P Ψ Maj it syr[h] cop[sa] KJV NKJV NRSVmg NLTmg HCSBmg

It is possible that the longer text was accidentally omitted due to homoeoteleuton: αναπαυεται . . . δοξαζεται. But if this were so, one would think that at least one early Greek manuscript would have escaped this corruption and preserved the longer text. Since this is not the case, it stands to reason that the longer text is a scribal gloss on verse 14: The persecutor of Christians is a blasphemer of Christ, whereas the persecuted Christian glorifies Christ.

1 Peter 4:16a

Most manuscripts have the name χριστιανος, which means "Christian—one belonging to Christ." Interestingly, א* reads χρηστιανος ("Chrestian"). This is a significant reading inasmuch as the same kind of change happened to the name Χριστος in antiquity. From what can be gathered from certain writings, Gentiles did not understand what Χριστος ("Christ") meant—viz., "the Anointed One." They thought Jesus was called Χρηστος (meaning "useful one" or "kind one"). Chrestus was a common Greek name, especially for slaves, who were "useful" to their owners (see, for example, Suetonius, *Claud.* 25.4). It could be that this is what the Roman historian Tacitus thought when he called Jesus "Chrestus" in his record of how Nero blamed the Christians for the great fire of Rome in A.D. 64 and how he persecuted them (*Ann.* 15.44.2-8). Significantly, this misunderstanding of the name carried over to the Christians, as being called by some *Chrestians* (ones belonging to the Kind One) instead of *Christians*. In fact, *Chrestian* was written in place of *Christian* in all three of its occurrences in the NT (4:16; Acts 11:26; 26:28) in the first hand of Codex Sinaiticus (א*), which were then corrected. (Codex 81 also has the spelling *Chrestian* in Acts 11:26.)

1 Peter 4:16b

WH NU	δοξαζέτω δὲ τὸν θεὸν ἐν τῷ ὀνόματι τούτῳ "let him glorify God by this name" 𝔓[72] א A B Ψ 33 1739 syr cop NKJVmg RSV NRSV ESV NASB NIV TNIV NEB REB NJB NAB NLT HCSB NET
variant/TR	δοξαζετω δε τον θεον εν τω μερει τουτω "let him glorify God in this matter" P 049 Maj KJV NKJV

The WH NU reading has the best documentary support and is poignant. The message of the passage (4:14-16) is that a believer brings glory to God by his or her identification with the name of Christ—especially when suffering for being identified as a "Christian"—one belonging to Christ. Indeed, history tells us that believers have suffered for simply being known as "Christians" (see previous note). The variant, with late manuscript support, obfuscates this.

1 Peter 5:2a

TR NU	include ἐπισκοποῦντες ("overseeing") 𝔓[72] א[2] A P Ψ 33 1739 Maj KJV NKJV RSVmg NRSV NASB NIV TNIV REB NJB NAB NLT HCSB NET
variant/WH	omit επισκοπουντες ("overseeing") א* B RSV NRSVmg ESVmg NEB NJBmg HCSBmg NETmg

WH excludes the word επισκοπουντες ("overseeing") due to their preference for א and B. The Nestle text, prior to NA[26], also excluded the word (as followed by RSV NEB). But the documentary evidence supporting its inclusion is both early and diversified and thereby supports its inclusion. Actually, א* and B are the only two Greek manuscripts that lack the word (and the word was inserted by a corrector of א in the seventh century). Perhaps, the scribes of א* and B omitted the word because they had the misconception that the elders ("presbytery"—1 Pet 5:1) could not function as overseers (see Alford 1857, 4:382). At that time in church history (fourth century), the offices of elder and overseer (i.e., bishop) were differentiated. The overseer or bishop had been elevated to a rank above an elder—though this deviates from the situation in the NT, in which the overseers and elders were two functions of the same individuals. For example, Paul told the elders at Ephesus that the Holy Spirit had made them overseers (bishops) of the flock (Acts 20:17, 28). And so also here in 5:1-2; Peter was charging the elders that they should shepherd the church of God by overseeing it (i.e., by functioning as bishops).

1 Peter 5:2b

NU ἑκουσίως κατὰ θεόν
"willingly, according to God"
𝔓72 ℵ A 33 1739 it cop^bo
NKJVmg RSVmg NRSV ESV NASB NIV TNIV NEB REB NJB NAB NLT HCSB NET

variant/TR WH εκουσιως
"willingly"
B Maj
KJV NKJV RSV NRSVmg NJBmg HCSBmg

Since many important manuscripts include the words κατα θεον ("according to God") and since it is easier to explain why scribes would delete the words (being deemed unnecessary or unclear) than add them, it is very likely that the first reading contains the original text. The expression εκουσιως κατα θεον means "to do it willingly, as God would want you to." All modern translations except RSV (probably influenced by B) reflect this reading, whereas KJV and NKJV are loyal to TR.

1 Peter 5:3

This entire verse is omitted by B. Since the omission cannot be explained on transcriptional grounds, it is possible that the scribe of B was perplexed with the description of what elders were not supposed to do.

1 Peter 5:6

The last words of this verse in all three editions (TR WH NU) are υψωση εν καιρω, usually translated as "you may be exalted in due time." This reading has the authority of 𝔓72 ℵ B L 0206 syr^p cop^sa. A variant reading changes the final expression to υψωση εν καιρω επισκοπης ("you may be exalted in the time of visitation"), with the support of A P (Ψ) 33 (it) syr^h** cop^bo. The TR WH NU reading, which has excellent documentary support, speaks of God's good timing in rewarding those who humble themselves before him. The variant, with inferior documentation, specifies the time of reward—it will come at the end of time, in the day of God's judgment (see 2:12).

1 Peter 5:8

NU ζητῶν [τινα] καταπιεῖν
"seeking someone to devour"
Maj
RSV NRSV ESV NASB NIV TNIV NEB REB NJB NAB NLT HCSB NET

variant 1/TR ζητων τίνα καταπιειν
"seeking whom he may devour"
L P 1739
KJV NKJV NETmg

variant 2/WH ζητων καταπιειν
"seeking to devour"
B Ψ 0206[vid]
NETmg

Certain manuscripts are not listed above—namely, 𝔓[72] א A, because the word τινα is unaccented in these manuscripts and therefore could have signaled either a definite or indefinite pronoun—the ancient reader would have made some determination. In the majority of later manuscripts this determination was made by accenting the word. It is possible that the second variant is original. It has the support of two fourth-century manuscripts (B 0206[vid]) and is the reading which likely gave rise to other variants, each of which supplies a substantive after ζητων ("seeking"). As such, the description is focused on the activity of the lionlike devil (i.e., he seeks to devour), not the object—which is to be assumed.

1 Peter 5:10a

WH NU ὁ καλέσας ὑμᾶς
"the one having called you"
𝔓[72] א A B Ψ 33 1739 Maj
NKJVmg RSV NRSV ESV NASB NIV TNIV NEB REB NJB NAB NLT HCSB NET

variant/TR ο καλεσας ημας
"the one having called us"
0206 1881 syr[p]
KJV NKJV

Frequently, υμας and ημας were confounded in the transcription process. But if the change was intentional, υμας was changed to ημας more often than not in the interest of including present readers. In short, it makes for a better lectionary text to say "us" than "you." Indeed, ημας is found in a number of lectionaries (422 592 809 921 938 1153 1364 1441).

1 Peter 5:10b

TR NU ἐν Χριστῷ ['Ιησοῦ]
"in Christ Jesus"
𝔓[72] A P 33 1739 Maj it syr[h**] cop
KJV NKJV NAB NLT HCSB NETmg

variant 1/WH εν Χριστω
"in Christ"
א (B adds τω) 0206[vid]
RSV NRSV ESV NASB NIV TNIV NEB REB NJB NET

The variant is likely original because: (1) the testimony of א B 0206 is strong; (2) the scribes tended to elongate divine titles; (3) Peter's normal practice was to write "Jesus Christ" when combining the two titles, never "Christ Jesus" (see 1:1, 2, 3, 7, 13; 2:5; 3:21; 4:11; 2 Pet 1:1, 8, 11, 14, 16; 2:20; 3:18). The phrase "Christ Jesus" is influenced by Paul (Rom 15:17; Eph 3:21).

1 Peter 5:10c

NU αὐτὸς καταρτίσει, στηρίξει, σθενώσει, θεμελιώσει
"he will perfect, confirm, strengthen, establish"
א 33vid 1739*
NKJVmg RSVmg NRSV ESV NASB NIV TNIV NJB NAB NLT HCSB NET

variant 1/TR αυτος καταρτισει υμας, στηριξει, σθενωσει, θεμελιωσει
"he will perfect you, confirm, strengthen, establish"
P (1739c) Maj
KJV NKJV

variant 2/WH αυτος καταρτισει, στηριξει, σθενωσει
"he will perfect, confirm, strengthen"
A B (Ψ 0206 καταρτιει)
RSV NASBmg NEB REB

variant 3 αυτος καταρτισει, στηριξει, θεμελιωσει
"he will perfect, confirm, establish"
𝔓72 81
none

It could be argued that the shorter readings came as the result of homoeoteleuton—four words in a row end with σ(ξ)ει; thus, it would be easy for a scribe to miss one. Or it could be argued that the longer reading is an expansion—often found in such benedictions. The translations (some with marginal notes) reflect the uncertainty. All things considered, the second variant (with the testimony of A B Ψ 0206) may likely preserve the original (so WH). However, it must be noted that the presence of only three verbs in 𝔓72 may indicate that the shorter form is even more primitive. More textual evidence could determine the matter.

1 Peter 5:11a

WH NU αὐτῷ τὸ κράτος
"to him [be] the power"
(𝔓72 0206vid omit το) A B Ψ
RSV NRSV ESV NASB NIV TNIV NEB REB NJB NAB NLT HCSB NET

variant 1/TR αυτω η δοξα και το κρατος
"to him [be] the glory and the power"
א P Maj copsa
KJV NKJV NJBmg HCSBmg NET

variant 2 αυτω το κρατος και η δοξα
"to him [be] the power and the glory"
33 1739 syrh copbo
HCSBmg

See comments on next note.

1 Peter 5:11b

WH NU τοὺς αἰῶνας, ἀμήν
"the ages (= forever), amen."
𝔓72 B cop^bo
NLT HCSB NET

variant/TR τους αιωνας των αιωνων, αμην
"the ages of the ages (= forever and ever), amen."
א A Ψ 0206^vid 33 1739
KJV NKJV RSV NRSV ESV NASB NIV TNIV NEB REB NJB NAB HCSBmg

All the variants in both parts of 5:11 can be attributed to scribal harmonization to 4:11, a parallel passage. Scribes loved to expand doxologies; they especially enjoyed extending εις τους αιωνας to εις τους αιωνας των αιωνων. Often, the αμην ("amen") is an additional flourish. But here there is no manuscript evidence against it, so it must be considered original. Most English versions go with the embellished "forever and ever" over against the simpler "forever."

1 Peter 5:13

TR WH NU ἡ ἐν Βαβυλῶνι
"she in Babylon"
𝔓72 A B Ψ 1739 syr^h cop
NKJV RSV ESV NASB NIV TNIV NEB NJB NAB (NLT) HCSB

variant 1 η εν Βαβυλωνι εκκλησια
"the church in Babylon"
א syr^p
KJV NRSV NASBmg REB NET

variant 2 η εν Ρωμη
"she in Rome"
2138
none

The first variant reading is an attempt by the scribe of א (and a few ancient translators) to specifically identify the one Peter called συνεκλεκτη (lit. "the co-chosen one," in the feminine gender). "Church" is a good conjecture as to this one's identity, but it is nothing more than a conjecture. The KJV translators did exactly what a few other ancient translators did; they gave an interpretative rendering: "the church that is at Babylon." NRSV, REB, and NLT identify the greeter as "your sister church." But it is possible that Peter was speaking of his wife. If so, the greeting comes from two individuals: his wife and Mark. Ancient and modern exegetes alike have considered that Peter was using "Babylon" as a code word for "Rome" because (1) according to early church tradition Peter was in Rome; (2) there is no evidence for Peter's having been in Babylon in Egypt, or Babylon in Mesopotamia; and (3) the reference may be cryptic because of persecution, or it may be an allusion to the exile of God's people on the pattern of the exile of ancient Israel in Babylon (Blum 1981, 253-254). This reasoning accounts for the change in a few late witnesses.

1 Peter 5:14a

Most manuscripts indicate that the recipients of the letter are encouraged to greet each other with "a kiss of love" (φιληματι αγαπης). Under the influence of Pauline terminology (see Rom 16:16; 1 Cor 16:20; 2 Cor 13:12; 1 Thess 5:26), this was changed in some late manuscripts and versions (623 2464 syr^{p} vg) to a greeting accompanied by "a holy kiss" (φιληματι αγιω).

1 Peter 5:14b

WH NU	Εἰρήνη ὑμῖν πᾶσιν τοῖς ἐν Χριστῷ. "Peace be to you, all the ones in Christ." A B Ψ 33^{vid} RSV NRSV ESV NASB NIV TNIV NEB REB NJB NAB NLT HCSB NET
variant 1/TR	Ειρηνη υμιν πασιν τοις εν Χριστω Ιησου. αμην. "Peace be to you, all the ones in Christ Jesus. Amen." ℵ P 1739 Maj KJV NKJV NRSVmg HCSBmg NETmg
variant 2	omit sentence 𝔓^{72} none

Since textual history reveals that concluding doxologies were expanded with time, it is very possible that 𝔓^{72} (first variant) presents the original state of the last verse. At some point in time, some scribe added a final word of blessing: "Peace be to you, all the ones in Christ," which was then extended to "Peace be to you, all the ones in Christ Jesus. Amen." If this was not the scenario, then it is exceedingly difficult to explain the omission in 𝔓^{72}.

The scribe of 𝔓^{72} concluded the epistle with the words ειρηνη τω γραψαντι και τω αναγινωσκοντι ("peace to the one having written and to the one reading"). By these words, the scribe was asking for a blessing of peace on himself and the one reading (i.e., the lector) this epistle out loud to other Christians. The same wording appears at the end of 2 Peter in 𝔓^{72}.

The Second Epistle of PETER

Inscription (Title)

WH NU	Πετρου Β "Second of Peter" (א A B inscription and subscription) NIV TNIV NLT NET
variant 1	no inscription 𝔓74vid none
variant 2	Πετρου Επιστολη Β "Second Epistle of Peter" 𝔓72 C K Pvid (Ψ) 33 1739 NKJV RSV NRSV ESV NASB NEB REB NJB NAB HCSB
variant 3/(TR)	Πετρου Επιστολη καθολικη Β "Second Catholic [= General] Epistle of Peter" a few late MSS KJV
variant 4	Επιστολη καθολικη Β του αγιου αποστολου Πετρου "Second Catholic Epistle of the holy Apostle Peter" L (049) none

Second Peter is one of the General Epistles (otherwise known as the Catholic Epistles), so called because this is an epistle addressed to a general audience of Christian believers (see 1:1). This catholicity is noted in the fourth and fifth inscriptions noted above, whereas other witnesses simply note it as "Second Epistle of Peter" or even simpler as "Second of Peter." This letter did not have an inscription originally (as is evidenced in 𝔓74).

2 Peter 1:1a

TR NU	Συμεὼν Πέτρος "Simeon Peter" א A 0209vid 1739 Maj RSV NRSV ESV NASBmg NEB REB NJB NAB (NLT) HCSB NET

variant/WH Σιμων Πετρος
"Simon Peter"
𝔓72 B Ψ cop
KJV NKJV RSVmg NRSVmg NASB NIV TNIV

Although the documentary evidence for both readings is evenly divided, it is more likely that "Simeon" was changed to "Simon" than vice versa for the obvious reason that "Simon" is the more common spelling of Peter's name. Indeed, Peter is called "Simeon" in only one other NT verse, Acts 15:14. The Hebraic spelling, Simeon, also suggests the authenticity of this epistle inasmuch as a forger would have more likely used "Simon" (see NETmg).

2 Peter 1:1b

All three editions (TR WH NU) read δικαιοσυνη του θεου ημων και σωτηρος Ιησου Χριστου ("righteousness of our God and Savior, Jesus Christ"), with excellent support: 𝔓72 B C Maj. Instead of θεου (God), a few witnesses (א Ψ vg[MSS] syr[ph] cop[sa]) read κυριου ("Lord"), yielding the rendering: "righteousness of our Lord and Savior, Jesus Christ." In the Greek, there is one definite article (του) governing the two titles θεου ("God") and σωτηρος ("Savior") joined by the conjunction και ("and"). According to a Greek grammatical rule called the "Granville Sharp Rule" (see Dana and Mantey 1927, 147; also Titus 2:13), this structure indicates that the two nouns describe one person—in this case, Jesus Christ. Thus, this statement indicates that Jesus Christ is both God and Savior. This is the view of the great majority of twentieth-century commentators, grammarians, and authors of general works on Christology or 2 Peter (see Harris 1992, 230-238 for a full discussion and bibliography).

2 Peter 1:2

TR WH NU ἐπιγνώσει τοῦ θεοῦ καὶ Ἰησοῦ τοῦ κυρίου ἡμῶν
"knowledge of God and Jesus our Lord"
B C Maj
(KJV NKJV RSV NRSV ESV NASB NIV TNIV NEB REB) NJBmg (NAB NLT HCSB NET)

variant 1 επιγνωσει του κυριου ημων
"knowledge of our Lord"
P Ψ vg[MSS]
NJB

variant 2 επιγνωσει του θεου Ιησου του κυριου ημων
"knowledge of God, Jesus our Lord"
𝔓72
none

variant 3 επιγνωσει του θεου και Ιησου Χριστου του κυριου ημων
"knowledge of God and Jesus Christ our Lord"
א A L 0209 (33[vid]) 1739
NJBmg

Applying the Granville Sharp rule to the TR WH NU reading permits the interpretation that "our Lord" is both "God and Jesus" (see note on 1:1). This should come as no surprise, because this was exactly what was indicated in the first verse of the epistle (see comments). The scribe of Ψ seems to have adjusted the text in 1:1 to obviate an affirmation of Jesus' deity; he may have had the same motivation here. Thus, the change in 1:2 was likely intentional, not just a scribal error of parablepsis (the eye of a scribe passing from του to του). Nonetheless, NJB, displaying its favoritism for the Western text and the Vulgate, followed the shorter reading. And all the other English versions, while following the TR WH NU reading, chose to separate "God" from "Jesus our Lord" by repeating the preposition "of": "knowledge of God and of Jesus our Lord." The variant in 𝔓72 is very interesting, for it shows that the scribe's change identifies "Jesus" as "God" by means of apposition. The scribe shows the same tendency in Jude 5, where Christ is clearly ascribed the title "God," also by means of apposition (see note on Jude 5).

2 Peter 1:3

NU καλέσαντος ἡμᾶς ἰδίᾳ δόξῃ καὶ ἀρετῇ
"he called us by [or, to] his own glory and virtue"
ℵ A C P Ψ 33 1739
RSVmg NRSV ESV NIV TNIV NEB REB NJB NAB NLT HCSB NET

variant/TR WH καλεσαντος ημας δια δοξης και αρετης
"he called us through his glory and virtue"
𝔓72 B 0209vid Maj
KJV NKJV RSV NRSVmg NASB NETmg

Both readings have good textual support and are theologically defensible inasmuch as God calls believers to participate in *his own* glory and virtue, and he enables this to happen by expressing his glory and virtue *through* his Son. Scribes could have had problems with either concept: How can believers participate in God's own glory and virtue? And how can people be called through glory and virtue? The first question is answered in the next verse, which indicates that believers can be partakers of the divine nature. The second question is somewhat answered by the previous verse, which indicates that God is known through Jesus Christ—that is, Jesus is the expression of God's glory and virtuous character.

2 Peter 1:10

According to 𝔓72 B C 0209 1739 and other witnesses, Peter exhorts the brothers to make their calling and election sure (βεβαιαν υμων την κλησιν και εκλογην ποιεισθαι). A gloss, explaining how one was supposed to do this, was inserted in ℵ (A) Ψ: δια των καλων εργων ("by your good works"). But this gloss misses the mark. The diligence Peter was asking for does not pertain to doing good things but to advancing one's faith by partaking of the divine nature and divine virtues (see 1:4-9).

2 Peter 1:17

The WH NU editions, with the support of 𝔓72 and B, read ο υιος μου ο αγαπητος μου ουτος εστιν ("my son, my beloved, this is"). TR reads ουτος εστιν ο υιος μου ο αγαπητος μου ("this is my son, my beloved"), with the support of ℵ A C1 Ψ 0209 33 1739 Maj it syr. TR's reading, though well documented, is likely the result of scribal conformity to the wording in Matt 17:5. Such conformity is understandable because scribes would want to line up Peter's wording exactly with the gospel account. Thus, the original wording is preserved in the two earliest manuscripts, 𝔓72 B.

2 Peter 1:19

Most manuscripts read φωσφορος, while a few witnesses (614 1852 syr[hmg]) read Εωσφορος, which means "Bringer of the morn"—"the Morning Star" (LSJ 752). The word Εωσφορος is a cognate of the Doric Αωσφορος, meaning "Star Aphrodite." Thus, the change from φωσφορος to Εωσφορος may be an attempt to emphasize that this is a deific description.

2 Peter 1:20

Instead of the expression προφητεια γραφης ("prophecy of Scripture" = "Scripture with prophecy"), found in most manuscripts, there are two variant readings: (1) προφητεια και γραφης ("prophecy and Scripture"), found in 𝔓72 and some Vulgate manuscripts; (2) γραφη προφητειας ("written prophecy"), in 614 630 1505 syr[h]. Both variants are attempts to simplify a terse combination of words. In any event, Peter was referring to the prophetic Scriptures—especially those that predicted the comings of Christ.

2 Peter 1:21

WH NU	ὑπὸ πνεύματος ἁγίου φερόμενοι ἐλάλησαν ἀπὸ θεοῦ ἄνθρωποι "men, being carried along by the Holy Spirit, spoke from God" 𝔓72 B P 1739 syr[h] NKJVmg RSV NRSV ESV NASB NIV TNIV NEB REB NJB NAB NLT HCSB NET
variant 1/TR	υπο πνευματος αγιου φερομενοι ελαλησαν αγιοι θεου ανθρωποι "holy men of God spoke as they were carried along by the Holy Spirit" א A Ψ 33 Maj syr[ph] KJV NKJV RSVmg NRSVmg
variant 2	υπο πνευματος αγιου φερομενοι ελαλησαν απο θεου αγιοι ανθρωποι "holy men spoke from God as they were carried along by the Holy Spirit" C (81) none

The WH NU reading has the earliest evidence (𝔓72 B) and diverse testimony. Furthermore, it is the most challenging yet most enlightening of the readings. The point it makes is that the prophetic Scripture did not originate with any person's will but originated from God. These are the key words: απο θεου ("from God"). Men spoke under the guiding influence of the Holy Spirit; as they did so, their words came from God. This is the point of the previous verse, when it says that no prophetic writing ever originated with any man, nor was it interpreted by the prophets themselves as they delivered the message. This verse substantiates this notion of divine origin. As such, the first variant misses the mark. It is not important to note that the men were "holy" (though they were); it is important to emphasize that the Scriptures, though spoken and written by man, came from God. The second variant, though a conflation of the other two readings, preserves the idea that the prophetic Scripture originates from God.

2 Peter 2:2

According to most manuscripts, Peter says that "the way of truth" (η οδος της αληθειας) was being blasphemed by certain false prophets. This expression becomes "the glory of the truth" (η δοξα της αληθειας) in ℵ[2] A (cop[sa]). This change was probably influenced by 1:17, where the word δοξα ("glory") is twice used to describe the revelation of Jesus' divine identity. This is the glorious truth passed on by the eyewitness apostles to the church. However, "the way of truth" is suitable to this chapter, which later addresses the opposite "way"—the way of error promoted by Balaam and followed by all false prophets (2:15).

2 Peter 2:4a

TR NU	σειραῖς ζόφου "chains of gloom" 𝔓[72] P Ψ 33 1739 Maj syr KJV NKJV NRSV ESV NIVmg TNIV NEBmg REBmg NAB NLTmg HCSB NET
variant/WH	σειροις ζοφου "pits of gloom" (ℵ σιροις) A B C RSV NRSVmg ESVmg NASB NIV NEB REB NJB NLT HCSBmg NETmg

The full phrase, according to TR NU, reads, "for if God did not spare the angels but delivered them to chains of gloom in Tartarus." The variant, instead, speaks of "pits of gloom." The two Greek words in dispute differ in only one letter, α/ο (σειραις/σειροις), and therefore could have been confused in the transcription process. However, it is just as likely that there was some intentional changing going on. Certain scribes could have changed σειροις ("pits") to σειραις ("chains") to make this wording parallel to Jude 6, which describes these angels as being kept in "bonds" (δεσμοις). But it is more likely that scribes made the opposite change because (1) they were familiar with the story of the Watchers in *1 Enoch* and their banishment to pits and/or (2) they were perplexed with the strange poetic expression, σειραις ζοφου ("chains of gloom").

The adoption of the reading σειραις marked a change from the Nestle text (25th edition), which previously followed the testimony of ℵ A B C. Most modern English versions, however, concur with WH and note the other reading.

2 Peter 2:4b

All three editions (TR WH NU) read εις κρισιν τηρουμενους ("being kept for judgment"), with the support of 𝔓[72] B C* P 049 1739 Maj. Other manuscripts (ℵ A C[2] Ψ 33 cop) support the reading εις κρισιν κολαζομενους τηρειν ("being punished while kept for judgment"). The variant appears to be the result of scribal harmonization to a similar verse (2:9). Both of these verses speak of the detainment of those awaiting final judgment, whether rebellious angels or the wicked. But there is a distinction: The angels are simply being kept until that day, while the wicked are experiencing some kind of punishment.

2 Peter 2:6a

TR NU — [καταστροφῇ] κατέκρινεν
"he condemned [them] to extinction"
א A C[2] Ψ 33 Maj it syr cop[sa]
KJV NKJV RSV NRSV ESV NASB NEB REB NJB NAB HCSB NET

variant 1/WH — κατεκρινεν
"he condemned [them]"
𝔓[72*] B C* 1739 1881 cop[bo]
NRSVmg NIV TNIV NLT HCSBmg NETmg

variant 2 — κατεπρησεν
"he completely burned up(?)"
𝔓[72mg]
none

variant 3 — κατεστρεψεν
"he overthrew"
P 1852
none

It could be argued that the first variant was caused by a transcriptional error (homoeoarchton)—the two words appearing side by side both begin with κατ (καταστροφη/κατεκρινεν). But would this have occurred in so many diverse witnesses? Thus, it is just as likely that καταστροφη was added to show that Sodom and Gomorrah were not just condemned by God, but annihilated. The reading in the margin of 𝔓[72] provides another interpretation—if κατεπρησεν means "to completely burn" (see LSJ 1463 on πρηθω). This reading accords with the first variant in 3:10. Most versions follow TR NU, while three (NIV TNIV NLT) follow WH and the earliest witnesses.

2 Peter 2:6b

WH NU — ὑπόδειγμα μελλόντων ἀσεβέσιν
"an example of the things about to occur to [the] ungodly"
𝔓[72] B P syr
NRSV ESV NIV TNIV NEB REB NJB NAB NLT HCSB NET

variant/TR — υποδειγμα μελλοντων ασεβειν
"an example to those about to act ungodly"
א A C Ψ 33 1739 Maj it
KJV NKJV RSV NRSVmg ESVmg NASB HCSBmg

The difference between the two readings involves only one letter—a *sigma*. But the first reading has earlier testimony in 𝔓[72] and B and is the more difficult reading in that one would normally expect an infinitive verb, not a noun, to follow μελλοντων. It was this very expectation that prompted the variant reading. The statement according to WH NU is that the destruction of Sodom and Gomorrah is a prophetic example for the ungodly.

2 Peter 2:11

NU παρὰ κυρίου βλάσφημον κρίσιν
"slanderous judgment from the Lord"
𝔓72 056 0142 1241 syr[ph,h**]
NRSV TNIV NAB NLT HCSBmg NETmg

variant 1/TR WH παρα κυριω βαλσφημον κρισιν
"slanderous judgment before the Lord" (= "in the Lord's presence")
א B C P 1739 Maj
KJV NKJV RSV NRSVmg ESV NASB NIV TNIVmg NEB REB NJB HCSB NET

variant 2 βαλσφημον κρισιν
"slanderous judgment"
A Ψ 33 81 1881 cop
NRSVmg NETmg

The NU reading is perhaps the most difficult of the readings because it conveys that the Lord is capable of pronouncing a slanderous judgment: "whereas angels, being greater in strength and power, do not bring against them [the glorious ones] a slanderous judgment from the Lord." Most likely, this wording was changed to say that angels do not bring these slanderous judgments into the Lord's presence in the heavenly courtroom (variant 1). Or the problem was dealt with by deleting any mention of the Lord (variant 2). The second change may have also been influenced by Jude 9, a parallel verse, where there is no mention of the Lord's presence. The NU reading affirms the Lord's prerogative to revile someone (cf. Jude 9). While a few versions follow NU, most English versions follow the first variant—either because of superior textual evidence or because it is the more readily understood reading.

2 Peter 2:13a

WH NU ἀδικούμενοι μισθὸν ἀδικίας
"suffering wrong as retribution for wrong"
𝔓72 א* B P Ψ
RSV NRSV ESV NASB NIV TNIV NEB REB NJB NAB (NLT) HCSB NET

variant/TR κομιουμενοι μισθον αδικιας
"receiving retribution for wrong"
א2 A C 33[vid] 1739 Maj it syr[h] cop
KJV NKJV NRSVmg NABmg

The manuscript support (note the three earliest witnesses: 𝔓72 א* B) for the WH NU reading is better than that of TR. The variant reading displays the work of scribes modifying a difficult combination of words. But this change destroys the wordplay between αδικουμενοι and αδικιας, which works out to something like this in English: "suffering wrong in recompense for the wrong they have done" or "being defrauded of the money earned by fraud." The first rendering speaks of the general retribution awaiting the false prophets who have damaged others. The second rendering takes αδικεω as reference to acting fraudulently and thus points the reader forward to Balaam (2:15), who received "the wages of unrighteousness" (see Bauckham 1983, 264-265).

2 Peter 2:13b

TR WH NU ἀπάταις
"deceptions"
𝔓72 ℵ A* C 33 Maj syrh copbo
KJV NKJV RSV NRSV ESV NASB NIV TNIV NEB REB NJB NAB NLT HCSB NET

variant 1 αγαπαις
"love feasts"
Ac B Ψ syrph
RSVmg NRSVmg ESVmg NASBmg NIVmg TNIVmg NEBmg NLTmg HCSBmg

variant 2 αγνοιαις
"ignorant ideas"
1739 1881
none

In context, the phrase (according to TR WH NU) reads, "they are spots and blemishes, reveling in their deceits while they dine with you." The two variants substitute either "love feasts" or "ignorant ideas" for "deceits." In Greek, the three words could have been easily confused in textual transmission because of their similar features. However, it seems quite likely that απαταις, which has the best documentary support (𝔓72 ℵ A* C), was purposefully changed to αγαπαις, which was also changed in some manuscripts to αγνοιαις. The first change is the result of scribal harmonization to the parallel passage in Jude 12. The second change is an attempt to make sense of the tautology in the first variant ("reveling in their love *feasts* while they *feast* with you"). The idea behind the TR WH NU reading is that certain false prophets had become a blot on the church because of their deceptive behavior in various gatherings of the church. Almost all the English translations followed the TR WH NU reading, while many note the first variant because of its textual support.

2 Peter 2:15

TR NU Βαλαὰμ τοῦ Βοσόρ
"Balaam [son] of Bosor"
𝔓72 ℵ2 A C P Ψ 048 33vid 1739 Maj syrh
KJV NRSV (TNIV) REB NJB NAB NLTmg HCSB NET

variant 1/WH Βαλααμ του Βεωρ
"Balaam [son] of Beor"
B vg syrph
NKJV RSV NRSVmg ESV NASB NIV NEB REBmg NJBmg NLT HCSBmg NETmg

variant 2 Βαλααμ του Βεωορσορ
"Balaam [son] of Beorsor"
ℵ*
none

"Bosor" is the earlier of the readings (in 𝔓72) and has the most diverse documentary support. But why would the author of 2 Peter change a well-known name into an unknown one? Scholars have surmised that "Bosor" reflects a Hebrew wordplay on "flesh." Thus, Balaam is called "the son of flesh" (see Bauckham 1983, 267-268). Nonetheless, because the name "Bosor" is not found anywhere else in Scripture, some scribes and ancient translators changed it to "Beor"—by way of conformity to the Septuagint (see Num 22:5; 24:3, 15; 31:8). Modern translators, as well, have continued to name Balaam as "the son of Beor." The name "Beorsor" in ℵ* (variant 2) is a conflation of both names; it reveals that both "Bosor" and "Beor" must have been current in the fourth century.

2 Peter 2:17a

WH NU πηγαὶ ἄνυδροι καὶ ὁμίχλαι
"waterless wells and mists"
𝔓72 ℵ A B C Ψ 1739
NKJVmg RSV NRSV ESV NASB NIV TNIV NEB REB NJB NAB NLT HCSB NET

variant/TR πηγαι ανυδροι νεφελαι
"waterless wells, clouds"
048vid 049 Maj syrph
KJV NKJV

Whereas the WH NU reading is supported by early and diverse witnesses, the variant has late support and appears to be the result of scribal conformity to Jude 12, a parallel verse.

2 Peter 2:17b

WH NU σκότους τετήρηται
"darkness has been reserved"
𝔓72 ℵ B Ψ 048vid it syr cop
NKJVmg RSV NRSV ESV NASB NIV TNIV NEB REB NJB NAB NLT HCSB NET

variant/TR σκοτους εις αιωνα τετηρηται
"darkness has been reserved forever"
A C L P 049 33 1739
KJV NKJV

The WH NU reading, which in full reads "for whom the gloom of darkness has been reserved," has early and diverse support among the Greek manuscripts and shows that many ancient translators resisted the temptation to conform this verse to Jude 13, a parallel verse. The variant shows this scribal harmonization in several witnesses, most of which are late.

2 Peter 2:18

WH NU τοὺς ὀλίγως ἀποφεύγοντας
"those who have scarcely escaped"
𝔓72 ℵ2 A B Ψ 33 it syr cop
RSV NRSV ESV NASB NIV TNIV NEB REB NJB NAB NLT HCSB NET

variant 1/TR τους οντως αποφευγοντες
"those who have actually escaped"
ℵ* C P 048vid 1739 Maj
KJV NKJV NRSVmg

variant 2 τους οντας αποφευγοντας
"those having escaped"
1241 1881
none

Since the word ολιγως is a *hapax legomenon* in the NT and since it is supported by an impressive array of early and diverse witnesses, it is very likely the original wording. (According to WH NU, the rendering in full is: "with licentious desires of the flesh, they entice those who have scarcely escaped from those who live in error.") The first variant has decent textual support but presents a dilemma: How could those who have actually (οντως) escaped the deceitful false prophets still be enticed by them? Of course, some would then argue that this discrepancy could have prompted the change that we now see in the WH NU reading. But such a change would have had to occur very early and globally (note the number of early versions that attest to the WH NU reading). The point behind the WH NU reading is that new converts—those who have escaped "to a small extent" (another way to render ολιγως) the lusts of the flesh—are the most sought-after prey of the false prophets because these new believers can still be easily enticed by fleshly desires.

2 Peter 2:20

NU	τοῦ κυρίου [ἡμῶν] καὶ σωτῆρος Ἰησοῦ Χριστοῦ "our Lord and Savior Jesus Christ" 𝔓72 ℵ A C P 048vid 1739 syrh RSV NRSV ESV NIV TNIV NEB REB NJB NAB NLT HCSB NET
variant 1/TR WH	του κυριου και σωτηρος Ιησου Χριστου "the Lord and Savior, Jesus Christ" B Maj KJV NKJV NASB
variant 2	του κυριου ημων Ιησου Χριστου "our Lord Jesus Christ" L 1881 copbo none

The testimony of 𝔓72 etc. is stronger than that of B, which is the testimony adhered to in editions of the Nestle text prior to the 26th edition. Nonetheless, the NU reading is not completely free of doubt, because it could be the result of assimilation to 3:18. The second variant, though the shortest reading, has the weakest attestation.

2 Peter 2:21

NU, following the good testimony of 𝔓72 B C P 1739, says that the false teachers "turned back from" (υποστρεψαι εκ) the holy commandment that had been passed on to them. The verbiage is slightly changed in Maj (so TR) to επιστρεψαι εκ ("to turn away from"), and is expanded in ℵ A Ψ 048vid 33vid to εις τα οπισω ανακαμψαι απο ("to return to what was before—away from"). The two variants are obviously scribal attempts to make sure the reader understands that this is speaking of reverting back to one's former way of life (prior to knowing Christ). The substitution of the verb επιστρεψαι carries with it all the negative connotations of a reconversion because it is often used to describe conversion to Christ (for example, see Acts 9:35; 11:21; 1 Thess 1:9). The same holds true for the verbiage found in the second variant; it harkens to some very serious statements in the NT about those who began to follow Christ and then returned to their former ways of life (see John 6:66).

2 Peter 3:5-6

The difficult expression in 3:5 about "land being created out of water and by water" (γη εξ υδατος και δι υδατος συνεστωσα) prompted a few interesting textual changes.

Some scribes (C P 0156) clarified that it was "the earth" (η γη) so spoken of, not just "land" (generically speaking). Nonetheless, both readings interpret Gen 1:6-10 as describing the creation of land/earth as that which came out of the water (εξ υδατος) and as that which came about as the result of God separating the waters (= "by the waters"—δι υδατος). A few other scribes (431 1241) superimposed their reading of the Genesis account on the text, for they changed εξ υδατος και δι υδατος ("out of water and by water") to εξ υδατος και πνευματος ("out of water and Spirit"). They saw the land as coming out of the water over which the Spirit was brooding (Gen 1:2).

An equally difficult expression begins 3:6 because it cannot be immediately determined what the reference is. The short prepositional phrase δι ὧν, meaning "through which things," can refer to (1) heaven and earth, (2) the heavens, (3) the two kinds of water (see above), or (4) the water and the word of God. Many commentators (see Bauckham 1983, 298-299) favor the fourth view because God's word is then seen to accompany the water of creation (3:5), the flood (3:6) and the ultimate destruction by fire (3:7). Nonetheless, the plural ὧν is still ambiguous; so it was changed to δι ου ("through which") in a few witnesses (P 69vid 945) to make it a clear reference to "the word": "by the word the world at that time was flooded with water and perished."

2 Peter 3:8

The following expression is puzzling: μια ημερα παρα κυριω ως χιλια ετη και χιλια ετη ως ημερα μια ("one day with the Lord is as a thousand years and a thousand years as one day"). One view is that it is a statement that equates "the day of the Lord" with the millennium. Another view is that it is an idiom which depicts God as one who does not view time in the same manner as humans do. The second interpretation accords with Ps 90:4 (LXX), which is here quoted in part. The first view is evident in a few manuscripts and in Irenaeus, which change ημερα παρα κυριω ("a day with the Lord") to ημερα κυριου ("day of the Lord"). The second view is evident in ℵ: ημερα παρα κυριου, which means "a day from the Lord's perspective." A few manuscripts (𝔓72 ℵ 1241) omit και χιλια ετη ("and a thousand years"), but the deletion seems to have been accidental—due to parablepsis (the eye of a scribe passing from ετη to ετη).

2 Peter 3:9

WH NU μακροθυμεῖ εἰς ὑμᾶς
"he is longsuffering toward you"
𝔓72 B C P 048vid 0156 1739
NKJVmg RSV NRSV ESV NASB NIV TNIV NEB REB NJB NAB NLT HCSB NET

variant 1/TR μακροθυμει εις ημας
"he is longsuffering toward us"
Maj
KJV NKJV

variant 2 μακροθυμει δι ημας
"he is longsuffering because of us"
ℵ A Ψ 33 it syr copsa
none

The reading in WH NU has strong documentation. The change from "you" to "us" in the first variant was intended to expand the audience to all humanity and prevent the text from implicating Christians as the potential objects of destruction. The second variant is stylistic.

2 Peter 3:10

WH NU	καὶ γῆ καὶ τὰ ἐν αὐτῇ ἔργα εὑρεθήσεται "and the earth and the works in it will be found out" ℵ B P 0156[vid] 1739[txt] NKJVmg NRSV ESV NASBmg NIV (TNIV) NEB REB NJBmg NAB (NLT) HCSB NET
variant 1/TR	και γη και τα εν αυτη εργα κατακαησεται "and the earth and the works in it will be burned up" A 048 33 1739[mg] KJV NKJV RSV NRSVmg ESVmg NASB NIVmg NEBmg NJB NABmg NLTmg HCSBmg NETmg
variant 2	και γη και τα εν αυτη εργα αφανισθησονται "and the earth and the works in it will disappear" C TEV
variant 3	και γη και τα εν αυτη εργα ευρεθησεται λυομενα "and the earth and the works in it will be found destroyed" 𝔓[72] TEVmg NLTmg NETmg
variant 4	omit Ψ 1891 vg[MSS] none

The last word of this verse is the focus of enormous textual variation. Several scholars, concluding that none of these variants preserve the original text, have proposed various conjectural emendations. Those listed in NA[27] are as follows: (1) Hort suggested ρευσεται ("will flow")—an emendation based on *1 Enoch* 1:6; (2) Naber proposed συρρυησεται ("will flow together"); (3) Olivier offered εκπυρωθησεται ("will be burnt to ashes"); (4) Mayor proposed αρθησεται ("will be taken away"); (5) Eberhard Nestle offered κριθησεται ("will be judged"). Mayor (1907) proposed yet another conjectural emendation, which is the simplest of them all. He imagined that the text originally had ουχ before ευρεθησεται, thus creating the reading: "the earth and the works in it will not be found." All of the extant readings would have to be rejected as impossible or as scribal emendations before we could resort to adopting any of these conjectural emendations.

The WH NU reading could very well be original. The awkwardness and opaqueness of the verb ευρεθησεται can be removed if it is understood as a divine passive: "will be found out by God." As such, the verse speaks of divine judgment (cf. Job 20:27). When all the universe melts away on the final day of judgment (see Rev 20:11), everything that has been done on earth will be exposed to God's judgment; all will be discovered as to its value (cf. 1 Cor 3:10-15). This concept suits the context, which speaks of what will occur on the final day of God's judgment (see 3:7). Various scribes, wanting to make this statement parallel to 3:7 or 3:11, changed the verb to κατακαησεται (variant 1) or αφανισθησονται (variant 2). Other scribes solved the problem by omitting the clause completely (variant 4) or filling out what they considered to be the object of ευρεθησεται (variant 3). But the true reading has probably been preserved in a good number of witnesses (ℵ B P 0156[vid] 1739[txt]) and is also indirectly attested to in 𝔓[72].

Several translations follow NU, while the first variant ("will be burned up") has been quite popular among English translators because it is more readily understandable. The TEV alone follows the second variant, and a few versions (TEV NLT NET) note the reading in 𝔓[72].

2 Peter 3:12

An unusual expression appears in this verse: την παρουσιαν της του θεου ημερας ("the coming of the day of God"). Its peculiarity is that την παρουσιαν ("the parousia") is almost always associated with Christ's coming, and the NT consistently speaks of "the day of the Lord," not "the day of God." Thus, some scribes and ancient translators (C P 1739 it[t] cop[bo]) changed this to την παρουσιαν της του κυριου ημερας ("the coming of the day of the Lord").

2 Peter 3:18a

This verse aptly summarizes the major thesis of this epistle: A Christian's growth in the experiential knowledge of the Lord Jesus Christ (1:2-3, 5-11) is the best antidote against the deceptions of false teachings. Thus, it is unfortunate that a few scribes (P 69) changed γνωσει ("knowledge") to πιστει ("faith"): "grow in grace and in the faith of our Lord and Savior, Jesus Christ."

Several other late minuscules display other typical scribal expansions: (1) the addition of και θεου πατρος ("and God the Father") after our Lord and Savior, Jesus Christ, and (2) the change of εις ημεραν αιωνος ("the day of the age" = "eternity") to τους αιωνας των αιωνων ("the age of the ages"). Both of these changes exhibit the influence of Paul on various scribes.

2 Peter 3:18b

TR NU	include αμην ("Amen") at end of verse 𝔓72 א A C P Ψ 33 1739[c] Maj syr cop KJV NKJV RSV NRSV ESV NASB NIV TNIV NJB NAB NLT HCSB NETmg
variant/WH	omit αμην ("Amen") at end of verse B 1739* 1881 NRSVmg NEB REB HCSBmg NET

Although the inclusion of "Amen" has diverse testimony, it is suspect as being a scribal addition because in the conclusion of most epistles it seems evident that "Amen" was added for liturgical purposes. Indeed, only three epistles (Romans, Galatians, Jude) appear to have a genuine "amen" for the last word; and if we had earlier sources, they might also show that "Amen" in these epistles was also an addition. Thus, in this verse it is likely that B 1739* 1881 preserve the original text. NU places the word in brackets to signal their doubts about its authenticity.

The scribe of 𝔓72 concluded the epistle with the words ειρηνη τω γραψαντι και τω αναγινωσκοντι ("Peace to the one having written and to the one reading"). By these words, the scribe was asking for a blessing of peace on himself and the one reading (i.e., the lector) this epistle out loud to other Christians. The same wording appears at the end of 1 Peter.

The First Epistle of JOHN

Inscription (Title)

(WH) NU	Ιωαννου Α "First of John" (א) (A B as inscription and subscription) NIV TNIV NLT NET
variant 1	Ιωαννου Επιστολη Α "First Epistle of John" Ψ 33 1739 NKJV RSV NRSV ESV NASB NEB REB NJB NAB HCSB
variant 2/(TR)	Ιωαννου Επιστολη καθολικη Α "First Catholic [= General] Epistle of John" 323 614 KJV
variant 3	Επιστολη καθολικη του αγιου αποστολου Ιωαννου "Catholic Epistle of the holy Apostle John" (L 049) none
variant 4	Ιωαννου ευαγγελιστου και αποστολου Επιστολη Α "First Epistle of the evangelist and Apostle John" P none

First John is one of the General Epistles (otherwise known as the Catholic Epistles), so called because the addressees are not specified. However, most scholars recognize that this letter was addressed to a specific audience—though one larger than just a single local church. This was the Johannine community of churches, a cluster of churches in the Roman province of Asia Minor, who were the recipients of John's ministry.

However, the presumed catholicity of the Epistle was inscribed in various manuscripts (second and third variants). The third variant and the fourth present the usual embellishments attributed to the apostles by pious scribes (see notes on the inscriptions to 1 and 2 Peter). The third variant omits a numerical signification, perhaps because this was the only epistle of John's three epistles that is "general." Other witnesses title it as "First Epistle of John." In reality, the original letter never had a title (see Comfort 2005, 9-10). However, it is worthy of note that all the inscriptions ascribe the work to John.

1 John 1:4a

WH NU	ταῦτα γράφομεν ἡμεῖς "these things we write" א A*vid B P Ψ 33 RSV NRSV ESV NASB NIV TNIV NEB REB NAB NLT HCSB NET
variant/TR	ταυτα γραφομεν υμιν "these things we write to you" A[c] C 1739 Maj KJV NKJV NJB HCSBmg

Though the manuscript evidence is good for both readings, the WH NU reading is more likely original. Some copyist naturally expected the dative υμιν ("to you") to follow γραφομεν ("we write"), not the nominative plural ημεις ("we"). Thus, a copyist may have thought his exemplar was in error and therefore corrected it. This variant reading, found in the majority of manuscripts, was popularized by TR and KJV.

1 John 1:4b

TR WH NU	ἵνα ἡ χαρὰ ἡμῶν ᾖ πεπληρωμένη "that our joy may be full" א B L Ψ 049 syr[p] cop[sa] NKJVmg RSV NRSV ESV NASB NIV TNIV NEB REB NJB NAB NLT HCSB NET
variant	ινα η χαρα υμων η πεπληρωμενη "that your joy may be full" A C P 33 1739 syr[h] cop[bo] KJV NKJV RSVmg NRSVmg ESVmg NIVmg TNIVmg NJBmg NLTmg HCSBmg NETmg

One would think that John was writing for the benefit of his readers; therefore, it sounds unnatural for the writer to say "we write these things to you for our joy." However, the writer was thinking of their mutual happiness. In other words, he wrote this letter to encourage the readers' participation in the fellowship that he (John) and the other believers were enjoying. Thus, "our joy" speaks of "the joy of us all"—John and the readers. This idea finds parallel expression in 2 John 12 (see note there).

1 John 1:5

TR WH NU texts read εστιν αυτη η αγγελια ην ακηκοαμεν απ αυτου ("this is the message we have heard from him") following א(*),1 A B Maj. One variant (in C P 33 cop[sa]—also the minuscules 69 81 323 614 630 945 1241 1505 1739) substitutes η επαγγελια ("the promise") for η αγγελια ("the message"). Another variant (in א[2] Ψ) reads η αγαπη της επαγγελιας ("the love of the promise"). The idea of "promise" is difficult in this context because the statement that follows can hardly be construed as being a promise: "God is light and in him there is no darkness at all." Of course, "the promise" could be referring back to 1:3-4, wherein John promised the readers that they would be communing with the Father and the Son if they (the readers) fellowship with the apostles—resulting in full joy for all. This connection would require 1:5 to be punctuated as follows:

"And this is the promise we have heard from him."

"And we announce to you, 'God is light and in him there is no darkness at all.'"

The textual evidence, however, speaks against the variant with "promise," for the variant appears in two forms in later manuscripts, while the TR WH NU reading has the combined support of three early witnesses (ℵ* A B). Thus, the TR WH NU reading speaks of the transmission of Christ's message. Just as Christ passed on the message he heard from the Father, so the apostles in turn passed on the same message they heard from the Son (see note on 3:11).

1 John 1:7

WH NU — τὸ αἷμα Ἰησοῦ τοῦ υἱοῦ αὐτοῦ
"the blood of Jesus his Son"
ℵ B C P Ψ 1739 syr[p] cop[sa]
RSV NRSV ESV NASB NIV TNIV NEB REB NJB NAB NLT HCSB NET

variant 1 — το αιμα του υιου αυτου
"the blood of his Son"
1243* Tertullian
none

variant 2/TR — το αιμα του Ιησου Χριστου του υιου αυτου
"the blood of Jesus Christ his Son"
A 33 Maj it[t,w,z] syr[h**] cop[bo]
KJV NKJV

Although the shortest reading (variant 1) would usually be deemed original (especially in the case of divine names, which were often expanded by scribes), the variant in this instance has too little evidence behind it. The WH NU reading, which has the single name "Jesus," is substantially supported and appears to be original. The name "Jesus" was then expanded to "Jesus Christ" in many later witnesses—under the influence of John's usual wording (see 1:3; 2:1, 22; 3:23; 4:2; 5:6, 20).

1 John 1:8 and 2:4

Both these verses speak of "the truth" (η αληθεια) as not residing in those who are deceived into thinking they are believers yet have no spiritual reality in their lives. In order to clarify just what this "truth" is, some scribes (in 1:8, some minuscules and syr[h]; in 2:4, ℵ) expanded the expression to "the truth of God" (η αληθεια του θεου). But it is hard to know what this fuller expression is supposed to mean, since John never used it (in the Gospel or the Epistles). Paul used it in Rom 1:25 to speak of God's undeniable reality and in Rom 15:8 in reference to the true revelation of God's gospel. When John speaks of "the truth" he is speaking of spiritual reality and veracity.

1 John 2:7a

WH NU — Ἀγαπητοί
"beloved"
ℵ A B C P Ψ 1739 syr cop
NKJVmg RSV NRSV ESV NASB NIV TNIV NEB REB NJB NAB NLT HCSB NET

variant/TR Αδελφοι
"brothers"
K L 049 Maj
KJV NKJV

The WH NU reading is adequately supported and suits a context which focuses on love. Some scribe(s) may have mistaken αγαπητοι for αδελφοι or substituted the more common nomenclature for the less common. In any event, the variant became popularized by TR and KJV.

1 John 2:7b

WH NU ὁ λόγος ὃν ἠκούσατε
"the word you heard"
ℵ A B C P Ψ 1739 it syr cop
NKJVmg RSV NRSV ESV NASB NIV TNIV NJB NAB NLT HCSB NET

variant/TR ο λογος ον ηκουσατε απ αρχης
"the word you heard from the beginning"
Maj
KJV NKJV (NEB REB)

The majority of manuscripts display a late change in the text, wherein the expression απ αρχης ("from the beginning") is repeated from the first part of the verse. In this context, "the beginning" refers to the time the disciples first heard Jesus' command to love one another (John 13:34). The phrase "from the beginning" need not be repeated.

1 John 2:14

Most manuscripts have the expression, εγνωκατε τον απ αρχης ("you have known the one from the beginning"). However, B and Ψ* read εγνωκατε το απ αρχης ("you have known that which was from the beginning"), thereby reflecting conformity to 1:1, a parallel verse. The masculine pronoun τον in this verse (2:14) tells us that John may have been thinking of a person in 1:1, but chose instead to use the relative pronoun το ("what" or "that which") because it is more inclusive—it encompasses everything about the Word of life the apostles had come to know. Codex B truncates ο λογος του θεου ("the word of God"), referring to the Scriptures, to simply ο λογος ("the word"). The shortened term can refer to the Scriptures or be a title of Christ—"the Word" (as in 1 John 1:1).

1 John 2:17

At the end of this verse some ancient versions and patristic witnesses (it^{t} vg^{MSS} cop^{saMSS} Cyprian Lucifer Augustine) add the phrase, "just as God abides forever." The addition was probably intended to underscore the eternal security of the believer (Smalley 1984, 66).

1 John 2:20

WH NU οἴδατε πάντες
"you all know"
ℵ B P Ψ cop^{sa}
NKJVmg RSV NRSV ESV NASB NIV TNIV NEB REB NJB NAB NLT HCSB NET

variant/TR οιδατε παντα
"you know everything"
A C (049) 33 1739 Maj it syr cop[bo]
KJV NKJV RSVmg NRSVmg ESVmg NIVmg TNIVmg NEBmg REBmg NJBmg HCSBmg NETmg

The two readings could have easily been confounded for each other in the transmission process inasmuch as there is only a two-letter difference (παντες/παντα) between the two. Furthermore, both readings have decent documentary support and are exegetically defensible. According to the WH NU reading, John was affirming that all the members of the church community know who is a genuine believer and who is not (see 2:19): "you have an anointing from the Holy One and you all know." The anointing that each and every one of the believers has received helps them to discern the false from the true. Thus, the emphasis is on shared, communal knowledge. According to the reading of the variant, the emphasis is on the anointing and how it enables believers to know everything: "you have an anointing from the Holy One and you know everything." The term "anointing" describes the impartation of the Holy Spirit (see Isa 61:1). Christians, indwelt by the Holy Spirit, are joined to Christ, "the Anointed One," and share in his anointing (2 Cor 1:21-22). Therefore, Christians can know all things with respect to truth and falsehood.

1 John 2:23

WH NU include the phrase ο ομολογων τον υιον και τον πατερα εχει ("everyone confessing the Son also has the Father"), with the excellent support of ℵ A B C P Ψ 33 1739 it syr cop. This is followed by all English versions. TR omits this phrase, with the support of Maj it[z] vg[MS] cop[boMS]. The omission is the result of homoeoteleuton: the last three words in both clauses in the verse are identical (τον πατερα εχει). KJV shows its independence from TR by printing this clause in italics (a sign that the words have been supplied by the translators). Evidently, the translators had access to Greek manuscripts which include the fuller expression. The WH NU reading, superbly supported, provides the full thought: Denial of the Son is tantamount to denying his Father, just as confessing the Son is tantamount to confessing the Father—for the two are one. This is an important theme in John's Epistles because he was combating those who claimed to know the Father apart from the Son.

1 John 2:24

The three editions (TR WH NU) read και υμεις εν τω υιω και εν τω πατρι μενειτε ("you will also remain in the Son and in the Father") based on good testimony: A C P Ψ 33 1739 Maj syr[h]. There are a few variations on this. B omits the second εν ("in"); and ℵ 623 syr transpose the divine names—to "Father" and "Son." And two late minuscules (69 945) read εν τω υιω και εν τω πνευματι ("in the Son and in the Spirit"). The third change is noteworthy because it anticipates the coming statements about the Spirit (2:27; 3:24; 4:2, 13; 5:6, 8). It also makes 2:23-24 a Trinitarian passage by providing mention of the Father, the Son, and the Spirit.

1 John 2:27a

There are two significant textual variants in the first part of this verse, each of which was prompted by a scribal desire to clarify just what "the anointing" (το χρισμα) is. The scribe of B (and 1505) changed το χρισμα ("the anointing") to το χαρισμα ("the gift"), which is often used in the NT in connection with a spiritual gift (see Rom 12:6; 1 Cor 12:4, 9, 28, 30). If the scribe made this change intentionally, he may have been attempting to say that the anointing is a spiritual gift. But since he did not make the same change for the next occurrence of the word in the same verse, it seems more likely that this was a transcriptional mistake. But not so for the original scribe of א; he changed this to read το αυτου πνευμα ("his Spirit") so as to make it clear that "the anointing" is none other than "the Spirit."

1 John 2:27b

WH NU — μένετε ἐν αὐτῷ
"you remain in him"
א A B C P Ψ 33 1739 it cop
NKJVmg RSV NRSV ESV NASB NIV TNIV NEB REB NJB NAB NLT HCSB NET

variant/TR — μενεῖτε εν αυτω
"you will remain in him"
049 Maj
KJV NKJV

The verb in the WH NU reading can be understood as a second person plural indicative or a second person plural imperative. As such, John was either stating a fact or making a command. Perhaps this ambiguity prompted a change to the future tense, which connotes a sense of promise. This reading was popularized by its presence in TR and KJV.

1 John 2:28

The first part of this verse is missing in א 69 630 and some Vulgate manuscripts. The omission is probably due to homoeoteleuton; the previous verse and the clause of this verse both end with the same words: μενετε εν αυτω ("remain in him").

1 John 3:1

WH NU — ἵνα τέκνα θεοῦ κληθῶμεν, καὶ ἐσμέν
"that we should be called God's children, and we are"
𝔓74vid א A B C 33 1739
NKJVmg RSV NRSV ESV NASB NIV TNIV NEB REB NJB NAB NLT HCSB NET

variant/TR — ινα τεκνα θεου κληθωμεν
"that we should be called God's children"
K L 049 69 Maj
KJV NKJV

A full rendering of WH NU is: "See what kind of love the Father has given us that we should be called God's children, and we are." Even though the WH NU reading has the short additional clause (και εσμεν—"and we are"), it cannot be easily dismissed as a scribal expansion, because it has such early and diverse testimony. Thus, it is likely that και εσμεν was dropped by some scribe(s) because it was perceived to be clumsy inasmuch as it seems to anticipate the following statement in 3:2—"now we are the children of God." But John's style is replete with intentional redundancy—one thought repeated with slight variation. John's point is that the believers are now the children of God even though they have not yet matured to the extent that they fully bear Christ's image.

1 John 3:5a

The word οιδατε ("you know") appears in most Greek manuscripts, including A B C L. It reads as οιδαμεν ("we know") in ℵ and many Coptic manuscripts—likely the result of assimilation to John's usual style of including his readers (see 2:3, 5, 18; 3:2, 24; 4:2, 6, 13; 5:2, 15, 18-20).

1 John 3:5b

The WH NU editions read ινα τας αμαρτιας αρη ("that he might take away the sins"), with good support: A B P 33 1739 it syr[h] cop[bo]. TR adds ημων after αμαρτιας, yielding the rendering: "that he might take away our sins." This has the support of (ℵ) C Ψ Maj syr[p] cop[sa]. The pronoun ημων ("our") was inserted to particularize the recipients of Christ's atonement. But the fact is: Christ died for the sins of the whole world (see 2:1-2). Some English versions (NIV NLT), though not following TR per se, also insert "our" for the sake of style or as a translation of the article τας.

1 John 3:7

According to ℵ B L, John addressed his readers as τεκνια; according to A P Ψ 33 1739, he called them παιδια. Since both words mean "young children" and seem to be used synonymously by John (see 2:12 and 14; 2:18 and 28), either suits the context.

1 John 3:11

TR WH NU have the word αγγελια ("message") in the clause "this is the message we have heard from the beginning." This has the support of A B 049 33 Maj. A variant reading is επαγγελια ("promise"), yielding the reading, "this is the promise we have heard from the beginning." This is found in ℵ C P cop (also 323 614 630 945 1241 1505 1739). As in 1:5 (see note), so here, nearly the same manuscripts exhibit the textual difference between αγγελια ("message") and επαγγελια ("promise"). It is possible that the two words were confused for each other because there is only a two-letter difference between them. However, "promise" hardly works in this context. What follows is not a promise but a command: "Love one another."

1 John 3:14

WH NU — ὁ μὴ ἀγαπῶν
"the one not loving"
ℵ A B 33 1739 it cop[bo]
NKJVmg RSV NRSV ESV NASB NIV TNIV NEB REB NJB NAB NLT HCSB NET

variant 1/TR — ο μη αγαπων τον αδελφον
"the one not loving the brother"
C Ψ Maj
KJV NKJV

variant 2 — ο μη αγαπων τον αδελφον αυτου
"the one not loving his brother"
P 1505 syr
none

The manuscript evidence decidedly favors the wording in WH NU. Both variants are scribal fillers, neither of which is necessary, because it is obvious from the context that John was speaking about brotherly love.

1 John 3:19

WH NU	γνωσόμεθα ὅτι ἐκ τῆς ἀληθείας ἐσμέν "we will know that we are of the truth" א A B C 33 1739 NKJVmg RSV NRSV ESV NASB (NEB) REB NJB NAB NLT HCSB NET
variant/TR	γινωσκομεν οτι εκ της αληθειας εσμεν "we know that we are of the truth" K L 049 Maj it KJV NKJV NIV TNIV

The variant reading displays scribal assimilation to the present plural verb, γινωσκομεν ("we know"), used predominately in this epistle (see 2:3, 18; 3:24; 4:6, 13; 5:2). But John deviated from the present tense in this instance because he wanted to include a notion of future accountability, as well as ongoing accountability.

1 John 3:20

According to most Greek manuscripts, the verse reads οτι εαν καταγινωσκη ημων η καρδια, οτι μειζων εστιν ο θεος της καρδιας ημων και γινωσκει παντα ("that if our heart condemns us, God is greater than our hearts and knows all things"). A variant reading in Ψ it[t,w] vg[MSS] adds μη ("not") before the word καταγινωσκη ("condemn"), yielding the rendering, "if our heart does not condemn us, God is greater than our hearts and knows all things." This change was intended to provide the text with a negative interpretation.

According to the better-attested reading, John's statement can be seen in positive light or negative—each depending on how the expression "God is greater than our hearts" is understood. The positive interpretation is that the believer can take consolation in God's graciousness (see Stott 1988, 150-152). The negative interpretation is that the believer should recognize that God, who is greater than us, would echo any condemnation and do so in greater fashion (see Alford 1857, 4:479-481). The variant reading, which could not be original because it is so poorly attested, takes sides with the second interpretation, for it indicates that God still knows everything about us, even if we are calloused to sin and choose to ignore it.

1 John 3:23a

All three editions (TR WH NU) read the aorist subjunctive πιστευσωμεν ("we should believe"), with the support of B and Maj. However, diverse documentation (א A C Ψ 0245 33 1739) supports the present subjunctive πιστευωμεν ("we should continue to believe"). In John's writings, he used both the aorist and present subjunctive forms for the verb πιστευω. The aorist usually points to initial belief or to belief at a particular time (punctiliar), whereas the present denotes ongoing belief. In this instance, the present subjunctive is to be preferred because it has both early and diverse documentation. As such, John was encouraging existing believers to continue in their faith. (See note on John 20:31 for a discussion on the same issue.)

1 John 3:23b

According to excellent documentation (ℵ B C 33 1739 Maj), the reader is instructed to believe "in the name of his Son, Jesus Christ" (τω ονοματι του υιου αυτου Ιησου Χρυστου). This was altered in a few witnesses (A 1846 vg[MSS]) to "in his name, Jesus Christ" (τω ονοματι αυτου Ιησου Χριστου).

1 John 3:23c

TR WH NU καθὼς ἔδωκεν ἐντολὴν ἡμῖν
"as he gave us commandment"
ℵ A B C Ψ 0245 33 1739 it syr cop
KJV NKJV RSV NRSV ESV NASB NIV TNIV REB NJB NAB NLT HCSB NET

variant καθως εδωκεν εντολην
"as he gave commandment"
049 Maj
NKJVmg NEB

The TR WH NU reading has excellent support and is followed by nearly all the English versions. Note here that the KJV and NKJV divert from the Majority Text (with a note in NKJVmg). The change in the variant could have been accidental—due to homoeoteleuton: εντολην/ημιν.

1 John 4:3a

TR WH NU πᾶν πνεῦμα ὃ μὴ ὁμολογεῖ
"every spirit that does not confess"
ℵ A B C 33 1739* Maj
all

variant παν πνευμα ὃ λυει
"every spirit that destroys"
1739[mg] it[c] vg (which reads *solvit* = "severs") Irenaeus Clement Origen[according to 1739mg] Augustine[MSS according to Socrates]
NRSVmg NJBmg

In this verse, the "spirit" is the spirit operating in the false prophets, through whom the spirit would make such a confession. This is the spirit of the antichrist (2:18) and the spirit of error (4:6). According to nearly every Greek manuscript, the spirit is identified as one that does not confess Jesus. Some ancient translators and commentators, however, saw an opportunity here to make an anti-gnostic statement by changing the text to read "every spirit that annuls Jesus" or "every spirit that severs Jesus" (as in the Vulgate). The annulling would be to destroy the orthodox teaching about Jesus' incarnation; the severing would be to divide "Jesus" from "the Christ," as was done by Docetists and Nestorians (see note on 4:3b).

1 John 4:3b

WH NU τὸν 'Ιησοῦν
"Jesus"
A B 1739 cop[bo] Origen
NKJVmg RSV NRSV ESV NASB NIV TNIV NEB REB NJB NAB NLT HCSB NET

variant 1 τον Ιησουν εν σαρκι εληλυθοτα
"Jesus having come in the flesh"
Ψ (33)
HCSBmg

variant 2 τον Ιησουν κυριον εν σαρκι εληλυθοτα
"Jesus [as] Lord having come in the flesh"
א
none

variant 3/TR τον Ιησουν Χριστον εν σαρκι εληλυθοτα
"Jesus [as] Christ having come in the flesh"
Maj vg[MS]
KJV NKJV

There are other minor variants in this part of the verse, but the four readings listed above are the primary ones. The WH NU reading, which has early documentary support, was expanded in two ways. First, the words "having come in the flesh" were either pedantically carried over from 4:2 or purposely added to make sure that the confession included an insertion of the orthodox position on the incarnation. Second, the name of "Jesus" was enlarged to "Jesus Lord" or "Jesus Christ." These could be normal expansions of nomina sacra, or the scribes may have been intending to clarify the orthodoxy of the confession. It was not Jesus who *came* to live in the flesh—since he did not have the human name Jesus until after his incarnation—it was "the Christ" or "the Lord" who came in the flesh and took on humanity in the man Jesus. In other words, all these changes were attempts to make it even clearer that John was refuting the heretical view that "the Christ" as a divine aeon descended into Jesus at the time of his baptism and then withdrew from him before he died on the cross. Stott (1988, 159) said it well: "The truth is not that Christ came 'into' the flesh of Jesus, but that Jesus was the Christ come 'in' the flesh." This is probably what motivated various ancient Latin translators to make the text condemn those who *separated* "Jesus" from "the Christ" (see note above on 4:3a).

The expanded reading, "Jesus Christ come in the flesh," was popularized by TR and KJV. But John needed only to write "and every spirit not confessing Jesus," because the preceding verses make it perfectly clear in what regard one is confessing Jesus—namely, as the incarnate one—the Word made flesh (see 1:1-3). Jesus did not merely appear to be a man; he actually became a man with a human body. John's "statement is directed against the gnostic error promulgated by Cerinthus, that the Christ descended into an already existing man" (Vine 1970, 75).

1 John 4:6

Good testimony supports the inclusion of the clause, ος ουκ εστιν εκ του θεου ουκ ακουει ημων ("the one who is not of God does not hear us"): א B 33 1739 Maj (so TR WH NU). A few manuscripts (A L 1241 1881) omit the clause. The omission could be due to homoeoteleuton—the last two words of the second and third clauses in this verse are identical (ακουει ημων). However, we cannot be certain that the change was accidental inasmuch as it occurred in four independent witnesses. Some scribe(s) may have purposely excised the third clause as being superfluous. But John had a penchant for antithetical restatement (see 1:5, 6, 8; 2:4, 27, 28; 4:7-8; 5:10, 12).

1 John 4:7

Most manuscripts have John saying πας ο αγαπων εκ του θεου γεγεννηται και γινωσκει τον θεον ("everyone who loves is born of God and knows God"). The statement in isolation could be taken to mean that all people who love are those who are born of God and know him. By adding τον θεον ("God") after αγαπων ("loving"), the scribe of A provided a corrective: Everyone loving *God* is born of God and knows God. But this misses the mark. John was speaking of brotherly love—love among believers.

1 John 4:15

As often happened in the course of textual transmission, scribes expanded the divine title in this verse. The scribe of B expanded the title Ιησους ("Jesus") to Ιησους Χριστος ("Jesus Christ"). This expansion, included in WH (showing its favoritism to B), was probably prompted by 4:2.

1 John 4:16

According to most Greek manuscripts (including the three earliest, 𝔓[9] ℵ B), there are two perfect tense verbs in this verse: εγνωκαμεν ("we have known") and πεπιστευκαμεν ("we have believed"). But A and 33 read the present tense πιστευομεν ("we believe"). The change was probably intended to counter any notion that "faith is simply a 'past' experience, although the perfect tense itself contains a 'continuous,' and thus perfect, reference" (Smalley 1984, 234).

According to all Greek manuscripts except 𝔓[9], the following expression is την αγαπην ην εχει ο θεος εν ημιν ("the love which God has in [toward] us"). In 𝔓[9], the divine name θεος, (normally written as the nomen sacrum $\overline{\text{ΘC}}$) is written as (1) $\overline{\text{XΘC}}$, where the scribe had mistakenly written X before the normal nomen sacrum, or as (2) $\overline{\text{XPC}}$, a special way of writing the nomen sacrum for Χριστος (Greenlee 1958, 187). If the latter is correct, then 𝔓[9] has a singular reading here: "Christ" instead of TR WH NU's "God." However, having examined the actual manuscript, I am not certain that the scribe intended to write a *rho*, which has an altogether different shape in another word in 𝔓[9] (see the first line of the recto in the misspelled word ταπρισεν). (For text and photo, see *Text of Earliest MSS*, 79-81.)

1 John 4:17

After John says that "we may have confidence in the day of judgment," nearly all Greek manuscripts read οτι καθως εκεινος εστιν και ημεις εσμεν εν τω κοσμω τουτω ("because as that one is, so are we in this world"). This causal explanation is perplexing because it seems to mean that Christians—without any maturation—are now even as Christ is, when experience speaks against this. Some scribes, seeing this problem, made two adjustments. The first is an interpolation, which adds προς τον ενανθρωπησαντα ("with respect to having put on human nature") before this clause (in 1505 1611 2138). This interpolation suggests that Christians will be judged as humans, which is a nature they share with Jesus Christ, and so they are said to be even as he is—i.e., both Jesus Christ and the believers are human. The second alteration appears in 2138 only; it adds the words ην εν τω κοσμω αμωμος και καθαρος ("he was blameless and pure in the world") in order to describe in what way Jesus was "in the world." The third alteration is not as drastic, but effective; it changes the present tense verb εσμεν ("we are") to a future tense, εσομεθα ("we will be"—so ℵ 2138), with the resultant rendering, "as that one is so we will be in this world." This change allows for the maturation process. All three changes occur in the eleventh-century manuscript 2138, which reads in full: "We may have confidence in the day of judgment, because just as that one is [was] blameless and pure in the world, so we, who [also] have human nature, will be in this world."

1 John 4:19

WH NU	ημεις αγαπωμεν "we love" A B 1739 NKJVmg RSV NRSV ESV NASB NIV TNIV NEB REB NJB NAB NLT HCSB NET
variant 1	ημεις αγαπωμεν τον θεον "we love God" א 048 33 syr cop[bo] NRSVmg NLTmg
variant 2/TR	ημεις αγαπωμεν αυτον "we love him" Ψ Maj KJV NKJV NRSVmg NLTmg HCSBmg

John's First Epistle is an exhortation to community love; he encourages the members of Christ's community to love one another as a demonstration of true spirituality. His epistle is not an exhortation to private mysticism or an appeal to the advancement of divine affections. Although these are worthy practices, they are outside of John's focus. In fact, those presuming to have personal affections for God must have those affections tested by their love for the community of believers (see 4:20).

Thus, both variant readings, which display scribal gap-filling, are misleading. John was not saying that we love God alone, as a result of him having first loved us; rather, he was saying that we are now able to truly love because God demonstrated what love is when he sent his Son to die for our sins. In other words, John purposely left out the object of "we love" because the object is not of primary importance—the action is.

1 John 4:20

WH NU	τὸν θεὸν ὃν οὐχ ἑώρακεν οὐ δύναται ἀγαπᾶν "he is not able to love God whom he has not seen" א B Ψ 1739 syr[h] cop[sa] NKJVmg RSV NRSV ESV NASB NIV TNIV NEB REB NJB NAB HCSB NET
variant/TR	τον θεον ον ουχ εωρακεν πως δυναται αγαπαν; "how is he able to love God whom he has not seen?" A 048 33 Maj syr[p] cop[bo] KJV NKJV RSVmg NLT HCSBmg

The variant reading positions the sentence as a rhetorical question, when John probably intended it to be a proclamation of a significant spiritual truth, which is the way the WH NU reading presents it (on the basis of superior documentation). Thus, the rendering found in most modern versions goes something like this: "He who does not love his brother whom he has seen, cannot love God whom he has not seen" (so RSV).

1 John 4:21

Most manuscripts read ταυτην την εντολην εχομεν απ αυτου ("this is the command we have from him"). Attempting to identify the pronoun, a few witnesses (A 048[vid] it[r]) change απ αυτου ("from him") to απο του θεου ("from God").

1 John 5:2

WH NU	τὰς ἐντολὰς αὐτοῦ ποιῶμεν "[when] we do (or, obey) his commandments" B Ψ 81 1739 RSV NRSV ESV NASB NIV TNIV NEB REB NJB NAB NLT HCSB NET
variant/TR	τας εντολας αυτου τηρωμεν "[when] we keep his commandments" א P (048) Maj KJV NKJV HCSBmg

Though the manuscript evidence is divided, the variant reading is likely the result of conformity to John's usual idiom (see 2:3-5; 3:22, 24; 5:3). The meaning of the verse, however, is not affected. What is noteworthy is that the reading of B Ψ 048 in the previous verse was rejected by the NU editors (see note), whereas here the testimony of B Ψ 048 was accepted. This disparity points out a problem in the atomistic eclectic method.

1 John 5:6a

With good authority (B Ψ 1739* Maj syr[p]), WH NU read ουτος εστιν ο ελθων δι υδατος και αιματος, Ιησους Χριστος ("This is the one coming through water and blood, Jesus Christ"). TR adds a definite article before Χριστος. There are three variants on the phrase υδατος και αιματος ("water and blood"):

1. υδατος και πνευματος ("water and Spirit"). Appears in 945 1241 1739[mg.]
2. υδατος και αιματος και πνευματος ("water and blood and Spirit"). Appears in א A 1739[c] syr[h] cop
3. υδατος και πνευματος και αιματος ("water and Spirit and blood"). Appears in P 0296 81

Among the three variants, the first and third would have to be dismissed on the grounds of having very slim textual support. That leaves the WH NU reading and the second variant, whose support is evenly divided. Thus, the original could say that Jesus came through "water and blood." In this context, this can mean one of two things: (1) The phrase takes us back to Christ's death on the cross, at which time he was pierced—and out flowed blood and water (John 19:34-35). John witnessed this and asserted the importance of this occurrence. Cerinthus and the Docetists had denied Christ's true and lasting humanity; but John saw Jesus shed blood and die. (2) The second possibility is that the phrase "water and blood" refers to Christ's baptism (water) and crucifixion (blood). F. F. Bruce (1970, 118-119) affirmed this: "The sequence 'water and blood' is not accidental, but corresponds to the historical sequence of our Lord's baptism and passion. Cerinthus, we recall, taught that 'the Christ' (a spiritual being) came down on the man Jesus when He was baptized but left Him before He died. The Christ, that is to say, came through *water* (baptism) but not through *blood* (death). To this misrepresentation of the truth John replies that the One whom believers acknowledge to be the Son of God (verse 5) came 'not with the water only but with the water and with the blood': the One who died on the cross was as truly the Christ, the Son of God, as the One who was baptized in Jordan."

This interpretation of the WH NU reading is solid. However, it must be acknowledged that John may have written what is printed as the second variant: "he came through water and blood and Spirit." This would mean that Christ was manifested as the Son of God at three critical moments: his baptism (= the water), his death (= the blood), and his resurrection (= the Spirit). In resurrection, Christ became life-giving Spirit, while still retaining a glorified body (1 Cor 15:44-45). In resurrection he appeared to his disciples and breathed into them the Holy Spirit (John 20:22). Thus, the apostles were not only eyewitnesses of the resurrection but participated in its life-giving effects. As such, the second variant does not contradict the WH NU reading; it simply adds another event in the apostles' eyewitness repertoire.

In the end, we cannot be sure which reading is more likely original. It is possible that some scribes deleted the reference to "the Spirit" in the interest of preserving John's emphasis on Jesus' humanity (4:2). It is equally possible that some scribes added "the Spirit" in anticipation of the next part of the verse, which speaks of the water, the blood, and the Spirit. (See next note.)

1 John 5:6b

All three editions (TR WH NU) read ουκ εν τω υδατι μονον αλλ εν τω υδατι και εν τω αιματι ("not in the water only but in the water and in the blood") with the support of (א) B[vid] L Ψ 33 (Maj). There are textual variations on the expression εν τω υδατι και εν τω αιματι ("in the water and in the blood"), as follows: (1) εν τω υδατι και εν τω πνευματι ("in the water and in the Spirit") A; (2) εν τω αιματι και εν τω πνευματι ("in the blood and in the Spirit") 424[c]; (3) εν τω αιματι και εν τω υδατι και πνευματι ("in the blood and in the water and in the Spirit") 1739[c] vg[MSS].

As was discussed in the previous note, "the Spirit" may or may not be part of the original text. Codex Alexandrinus (A) and 1739[c] retain "the Spirit" in 5:6a and 5:6b. But this is not quite strong enough testimony to validate a place in the text. Though it is less certain that "the Spirit" was added in the first part of the verse, it is quite certain—given the documentary evidence—that it was added here.

1 John 5:7b-8

WH NU

ὅτι τρεῖς εἰσιν οἱ μαρτυροῦντες, [8] τὸ πνεῦμα καὶ τὸ ὕδωρ καὶ τὸ αἷμα, καὶ οἱ τρεῖς εἰς τὸ ἕν εἰσιν.
"because there are three testifying: [8] the Spirit and the water and the blood, and the three are for one [testimony]."
א A B (Ψ) Maj syr cop arm eth it
NKJVmg RSV NRSV ESV NASB NIV TNIV NEB REB NJB NAB NLT HCSB NET

variant/TR

οτι τρεις εισεν οι μαρτυρουντες εν τω ουρανω, ο πατηρ, ο λογος και το αγιον πνευμα, και ουτοι οι τρεις ἕν εισιν. [8] και τρεις οι μαρτυρουντες εν τη γη, το πνευμα και το υδωρ και το αιμα, και οι τρεις εις το ἕν εισιν.
"because there are three testifying in heaven: the Father, the Word, and the

Holy Spirit, and these three are one. [8] And there are three that testify on earth: the Spirit and the water and the blood, and the three are for one [testimony]."
(61 629 omit και ουτοι οι τρεις ἕν εισιν) 88[v.r.] 221[v.r.] 429[v.r.] 636[v.r.] 918 2318 it[l,q] vg[MSS] Speculum (Priscillian Fulgentius)
KJV NKJV NRSVmg NIVmg TNIVmg NJBmg NLTmg HCSBmg

John never wrote the following words: "in heaven, the Father, the Word, and the Holy Spirit: and these three are one. And there are three that bear witness in earth." This famous passage, called "the heavenly witness" or *Comma Johanneum,* came from a gloss on 5:8 which explained that the three elements (water, blood, and Spirit) symbolize the Trinity (the Father, the Word [Son], and the Spirit).

This gloss had a Latin origin (as did the one in 5:20—see note). The first time this passage appears in the longer form (with the heavenly witness) is in the treatise *Liber Apologeticus,* written by the Spanish heretic Priscillian (died ca. 385) or his follower, Bishop Instantius. Metzger said, "apparently the gloss arose when the original passage was understood to symbolize the Trinity (through the mention of the three witnesses: the Spirit, the water, and the blood), an interpretation which may have been written first as a marginal note that afterwards found its way into the text" (TCGNT). The gloss showed up in the writings of Latin fathers in North Africa and Italy (as part of the text of the Epistle) from the fifth century onward, and it found its way into more and more copies of the Latin Vulgate. (The original translation of Jerome did not include it.) "The heavenly witnesses" passage has not been found in the text of any Greek manuscript prior to the fourteenth century, and it was never cited by any Greek father. Many of the Greek manuscripts listed above (in support of the variant reading) do not even include the extra verbiage in the text but rather record these words as a "variant reading" (v.r.) in the margin.

Erasmus did not include "the heavenly witnesses" passage in the first two editions of his Greek New Testament. He was criticized for this by defenders of the Latin Vulgate. Erasmus, in reply, said that he would include it if he could see it in any one Greek manuscript. In turn, a manuscript (most likely the Monfort Manuscript, 61, of the sixteenth century) was especially fabricated to contain the passage and thereby fool Erasmus. Erasmus kept his promise; he included it in the third edition. From there it became incorporated into TR and was translated in the KJV. Both KJV and NKJV have popularized this expanded passage. The NKJV translators included it in the text, knowing full well that it has no place there. This is evident in their footnote: "Only four or five very late manuscripts contain these words in Greek." Its inclusion in the text demonstrates their commitment to maintain the KJV heritage.

Without the intrusive words the text reads: "For there are three that testify: the Spirit, the water, and the blood; and the three are in agreement" (NIV). It has nothing to do with the Triune God, but with the three critical phases in Jesus' life where he was manifested as God incarnate, the Son of God in human form. This was made evident at his baptism (= the water), his death (= the blood), and his resurrection (= the Spirit). At his baptism, the man Jesus was declared God's beloved Son (see Matt 3:16-17). At his crucifixion, a man spilling blood was recognized by others as "God's Son" (see Mark 15:39). In resurrection, he was designated as the Son of God in power (see Rom 1:3-4). This threefold testimony is unified in one aspect: Each event demonstrated that the man Jesus was the divine Son of God.

1 John 5:10

Excellent Greek testimony (א B P Ψ 0296 1739[mg]) affirms the reading ο μη πιστευων τω θεω ("the one not believing God"). Some manuscripts, however, display assimilation to the previous clause, which speaks of believing in "the Son of God." Thus, A 1739* vg read ο μη πιστευων τω υιω ("the one not believing the Son"), and many Coptic manuscripts read "the one not believing the Son of God." These changes may obscure a critical point: To believe in the Son of God is to believe in God, because the Son of God is God (see 5:20).

1 John 5:13

WH NU — Ταῦτα ἔγραψα ὑμῖν ἵνα εἰδῆτε ὅτι ζωὴν ἔχετε αἰώνιον, τοῖς πιστεύουσιν εἰς τὸ ὄνομα τοῦ υἱοῦ τοῦ θεοῦ.
"These things I wrote to you that you may know that you have eternal life—to the ones believing in the name of the Son of God."
א* (A) B 0296
NKJVmg RSV NRSV ESV NASB NIV TNIV NEB REB NJB NAB NLT HCSB NET

variant/TR — Ταυτα εγραψα υμιν, τοις πιστευουσιν εις το ονομα του υιου του θεου, ινα ειδητε οτι ζωην εχετε αιωνιον, και ινα πιστευητε εις το ονομα του υιου του θεου
"These things I wrote to you, the ones believing in the name of the Son of God, that you may know that you have eternal life and that you may believe in the name of the Son of God."
P Maj
KJV NKJV

In this verse John explicitly states his purpose for writing: that his readers as believers in the Son of God may be sure that they have eternal life. This is perfectly clear in the WH NU reading, which has excellent documentary support. The majority of manuscripts have two alterations. The first is syntactical: some scribe(s) placed the appositive (τοις πιστευουσιν etc.) immediately after υμιν. The second change, probably influenced by John 20:31 (a parallel verse), fixed the vacancy left by the new positioning. As such, the final wording more closely parallels John 20:31, another verse that provides John's reason for writing what he did. But the verses, though parallel, are slightly different in the original text. The Gospel encourages the continuance of faith in the Son of God as the means to enjoying the divine life. The Epistle affirms the possession of divine life for all who believe in the Son of God.

1 John 5:18

WH NU — ὁ γεννηθεὶς ἐκ τοῦ θεοῦ τηρεῖ αὐτόν
"the One born of God keeps him"
A* B it
NKJVmg RSV NRSV ESV NASB NIV TNIV NEB REB NJB NAB NLT HCSB NET

variant/TR — ο γεννηθεις εκ του θεου τηρει εαυτον
"the one born of God keeps himself"
א A[c] P Ψ 33 1739 Maj Origen
KJV NKJV HCSBmg

A full rendering of WH NU is, "We know that everyone born of God does not continue sinning, but the One born of God keeps him and the evil one does not touch him." The variant is as follows: "We know that everyone born of God does not continue sinning, but the one born of God keeps himself and the evil one does not touch him."

The difference between the two readings revolves around the pronoun αυτον ("him"), which—in this context—produces a completely different sense when written as a reflexive pronoun, εαυτον ("himself"). The difference in meanings also stems from the interpretation of the phrase ο γεννηθεις εκ του θεου (the one born of God), which could be a reference to the Son of God (Christ) or to a son of God (a Christian).

The variant reading indicates that the believer, as a son of God, keeps himself from sin. The WH NU reading indicates that the Son of God, Christ, keeps the believer from sin. Many commentators favor this reading because (1) the first clause of this verse already mentions the believer who is born of God, (2) John consistently uses the perfect tense to describe the believer who has become a son of God (2:29; 3:9; 4:7; 5:1; 5:4; 5:18a), whereas here the aorist is used, and (3) there is little or no security in the fact that the believer must keep himself. Rather, it is the One begotten of God, the Son of God, who keeps each believer from the evil one. All modern versions favor this text and interpretation, whereas KJV and NKJV, following TR, present the variant reading and interpretation.

1 John 5:20a

After the words "the Son of God has come," several Latin witnesses (it[l] vg[MSS] Speculum) have this addition: "and was clothed with flesh for our sake, and suffered, and arose from the dead. He has adopted us." This creedal expansion may have supplied some sort of liturgical need.

1 John 5:20b

TR NU read ινα γινωσκωμεν ("that we may know"), supported by B[2] Ψ 1739 Maj. The variant reads ινα γινωσκομεν ("so that we will know"), found in ℵ A B* L 049 33 (so WH). The TR NU reading, though more grammatically correct than the variant, has inferior attestation. The variant reading, which has ινα with the future indicative, is common in the Koine Greek of the NT. For this reason, it is likely the reading that was changed.

1 John 5:20c

TR WH NU τὸν ἀληθινόν
"the true one"
ℵ[2] B 81 syr[p] Maj
KJV NKJV RSV NRSV ESV NASB NIV TNIV NEB NAB (NLT) HCSB NET

variant 1 τον αληθινον θεον
"the true God"
A Ψ 33 1739 vg
NRSVmg REB NJB HCSBmg

variant 2 το αληθινον
"that which is true"
ℵ* cop[sa]
none

The manuscript evidence slightly favors the text. Both variants appear to be scribal attempts to explain the referent of the adjective αληθινον. The first variant designates "the true" as "the true God," whereas the second variant points to that which is ontologically true. The TR WH NU reading expects the reader to understand that τον αληθινον is an adjectival surrogate for "the true one." This "true one" is God, as is supplied in the first variant. However, most readers will think this is identifying only God the Father, when it is really identifying both God the Father and God the Son. For, as John goes on to explain, the believers experience the reality of God the

Father by virtue of their union with God the Son. This is why John ultimately identifies Jesus as being "the true God and eternal life." In the Greek, the pronoun ουτος ("this one") in the expression ουτος εστιν ο αληθινος θεος και ζωη αιωνιος ("this one is the true God and eternal life") refers to the person just named—Ιησου Χριστω ("Jesus Christ").

1 John 5:21

WH NU	omit αμην ("Amen") at end of verse א A B Ψ 33 1739 syr cop RSV NRSV ESV NASB NIV TNIV NEB REB NJB NAB NLT HCSB NET
variant/TR	include αμην ("Amen") at end of verse P Maj KJV NKJV NETmg

Only three epistles (Romans, Galatians, Jude) appear to have a genuine "amen" for the last word of the document. In the other epistles it seems apparent that an "amen" was added for liturgical purposes. According to the textual evidence cited above, it is absolutely certain that the "amen" at the end of 1 John is a late, scribal addition.

The Second Epistle of JOHN

Inscription (Title)

(WH) NU	Ιωαννου Β "Second of John" (א A B inscription and subscription) 048 NIV TNIV NLT NET
variant 1	no inscription 0232[vid] none
variant 2/(TR)	Ιωαννου Επιστολη Β "Second Epistle of John" Ψ 33 1739 KJV NKJV RSV NRSV ESV NASB NEB REB NJB NAB HCSB
variant 3	του αυτου Επιστολου Β "His Second Epistle" 049 none
variant 4	του αγιου αποστολου Ιωαννου του θεολογου Επιστολη Β "Second Epistle of the holy Apostle John, the theologian" L none

Second John was placed among the General Epistles (otherwise known as the Catholic Epistles) by virtue of its association with 1 John. But this is not a general epistle; it was addressed either to a specific local church or a particular lady (with her children). But it is far more likely that John was using this address as a surrogate for a particular local church (as Peter also did in 1 Pet 5:13—referring to the church in Rome as "she who is in Babylon"). The nature of the epistle points to a corporate personality—the local assembly—rather than to a private individual (see verses 5, 6, 8, 10, 12). This was probably one of the churches in the Johannine community of churches, a cluster of churches in Asia Minor who were the recipients of John's apostolic ministry.

The WH NU reading presents the barest title, which was then expanded in various ways. The fourth variant is interesting in that it names John as a theologian. The fact of the matter is that this epistle, when originally written, was simply an untitled personal letter (as appears to be presented in 0232).

2 John 1

In ancient Greek the words εκλεκτη κυρια were written in all capital letters (ΕΚΛΕΚΤΗ ΚΥΡΙΑ), as were all other words. Therefore, one cannot tell from the printed page whether this referred to a specific woman (called either "a woman named Eclecta" or "the elect Kyria") or whether this denotes simply "a chosen lady." Clement of Alexandria thought her name was "Electa" (see *Fragments of Clemens Alexandrinus*, ANF 2.576-577). One modern English version (TLB) names her "Cyria." But most commentators and translators do not identify the recipient of the letter as an individual, since the Epistle does not speak of the woman with any particular details (in contrast to 3 John, which speaks specifically of Gaius, Diotrephes, and Demetrius). Thus, it seems likely that "the elect lady" was a corporate entity—a local church. Verses 6, 12, and 13 also point to a corporate recipient. Of course, it is possible that the church met in this woman's home, and thereby the epistle would have been written to a specific woman and the church meeting in her home.

2 John 2

The words δια την αληθειαν ("because of the truth") are absent from several witnesses (Ψ 614 1241 1505 1739 vg[MSS] syr[h]). The words could have been dropped accidentally due to homoeoteleuton (the previous clause ends with την αληθειαν), or the phrase may have been dropped intentionally to alleviate the first sentence (vv. 1-2) from having so many mentions of "the truth." This truncated version reads: "The elder to the chosen lady and her children, whom I love in the truth, and not only I but also all who know the truth abiding in us, and it will be with us forever."

2 John 3a

The wording χαρις ελεος ειρηνη ("grace, mercy, peace") occurs only here and in the greetings in 1 and 2 Timothy. Greetings in the NT epistles usually include "grace and peace." The unusualness of the expression prompted some copyists (81 vg[MS]) to drop ελεος ("mercy") from the list.

2 John 3b

WH NU	Ἰησοῦ Χριστοῦ τοῦ υἱοῦ τοῦ πατρός "Jesus Christ, the Son of the Father" A B 048 0232 81 1739 cop[sa] RSV NRSV ESV NASB NIV TNIV NEB REB NJB NAB NLT HCSB NET
variant 1/TR	κυριου Ιησου Χριστου του υιου του πατρος "Lord Jesus Christ, the Son of the Father" א P 33 Maj syr cop[bo] KJV NKJV NRSVmg

variant 2 Ιησου Χριστου του υιου
"Jesus Christ the Son"
945
none

variant 3 κυριου Ιησου Χριστου του υιου του θεου
"Lord Jesus Christ, the Son of God"
1881
none

Divine titles were habitually subjected to scribal tampering. In this case, "Jesus Christ" was expanded to "Lord Jesus Christ." This reading found its way into the majority of manuscripts, and was popularized by its inclusion in TR and translation in KJV and NKJV. Furthermore, some scribes, struck with the uniqueness of the expression "the Son of the Father" (it occurs only here in the NT), either shortened it to "the Son" or changed it to "the Son of God." But the title "Son of the Father" functions to show the unique relationship between the Son and his Father.

2 John 4

According to most Greek manuscripts (including A B C 0232[vid]), the text reads εντολην ελαβομεν παρα του πατρος ("a command we received from the Father"). But in א and 33 this reads εντολην ελαβον παρα του πατρος, which could be translated "a command I received from the Father" (first person singular) or "a command they received from the Father" (third person plural); the aorist verb could be parsed either way. In this case, it has to be a first person singular. As such, it agrees with the first part of the verse, where we see two first person singular verbs (εχαρην . . . ευρηκα = "I rejoiced . . . I have found"). What makes this variant interesting is that it says that John received a direct command from the Father. This is highly unusual because John always spoke of his apostolic commission as a corporate experience, not a private one (for example, see John 1:14 and 1 John 1:1-4).

2 John 8

WH NU βλέπετε ἑαυτούς, ἵνα μὴ ἀπολέσητε ἃ εἰργασάμεθα ἀλλὰ μισθὸν πλήρη ἀπολάβητε.
"watch yourselves, that you do not lose the things which we worked for, but that you receive a full reward"
B
NKJVmg RSVmg NRSV ESV NASB TNIV NEB REB NJB NAB NLT HCSB NET

variant 1 βλεπετε εαυτους ινα μη απολεσητε α ειργασασθε αλλα μισθον πληρη απολαβητε
"watch yourselves, that you do not lose the things which you worked for, but that you receive a full reward"
א A Ψ 0232[vid] 33 1739
RSV NRSVmg ESVmg NASBmg NIV TNIVmg NJBmg NLTmg HCSBmg

variant 2/TR βλεπετε εαυτους ινα μη απολεσωμεν α ειργασαμεθα αλλα μισθον πληρη απολαβωμεν
"watch out that we do not lose the things that we worked for, but that we receive a full reward"
P 049 056 0142 Maj
KJV NKJV

The textual evidence for this verse is complicated. It is simplified here for the sake of presenting the three major textual variants for the whole verse; see the critical apparatus of UBS[4] for a full presentation. In essence, there are two points of textual variation: (1) the subject of the two subjunctive verbs; and (2) the subject of the verb between them. For the two subjunctive verbs, the variants are:

1. μη απολεσητε . . . απολαβητε ("you might not lose . . . you might receive"). Appears in A B Ψ 0232[vid] 33 1739.
2. μη απολεσωμεν . . . απολαβωμεν ("we might not lose . . . we might receive"). Appears in P 049 056 0142 Maj.

For the verb in between, the variants are:

1. ειργασαμεθα ("we work"). Appears in B[c] P 049 056 0142 Maj.
2. ειργασασθε ("you work"). Appears in ℵ A Ψ 0232[vid] 33 1739.

In arguing for the editors' selection of the NU reading, Metzger (TCGNT) said that the shift from "you" to "we" is more likely "due to the author than to copyists." If so, then John was speaking of the labor that he, the apostles, and any other coworkers had done for the benefit of the believers. These laborers (the "we") proclaimed the truth, defined the truth, and defended the truth against heresy—all so that the church could get off to a good start and be built up. The believers, in turn, were admonished to exercise care in protecting that work from the destructive teachings of deceivers (v. 7). John feared that the apostatized deceivers would disrupt the community of faithful believers. (In Gal 4:11, Paul expresses a similar sentiment for the Galatian churches.)

It must be admitted, though, that the WH NU reading has very slim support: B in full, and later manuscripts in part. The array of witnesses supporting the first variant is impressive—so impressive that several modern versions adopted this reading, or at least noted it. The point of this reading is that it admonishes the believers to hold fast to the truths they know to be real and effective in their spiritual lives, and not to give in to any kind of deception that would rob them of their reward. (A similar sentiment is expressed by Paul in Col 2:18.) The second variant, which could provide evidence of an early presence of ειργασαμεθα in the textual tradition, is the result of a scribe creating verbal symmetry.

Finally, it should be noted that the expression βλεπετε εαυτους ("watch yourselves"), though found in most manuscripts, appears as βλεπετε αυτους in 0232 K L 1838 Irenaeus Lucifer. It means "watch them" or "beware of them"—with reference to πολλοι πλανοι ("many deceivers") in the previous verse. This reading is natural and could be original.

2 John 9a

WH NU	Πᾶς ὁ προάγων καὶ μὴ μένων ἐν τῇ διδαχῇ τοῦ Χριστοῦ θεὸν οὐκ ἔχει "Everyone going beyond and not staying in the teaching of Christ does not have God." ℵ A B 0232 cop NKJVmg RSV NRSV ESV NASB NIV TNIV NEB REB NJB NAB (NLT) HCSB NET
variant/TR	Πας ο παραβαινων και μη μενων εν τη διδαχη του Χριστου θεον ουκ εχει "Everyone transgressing and not staying in the teaching of Christ does not have God." P Ψ (33 substitutes αγαπη ["love"] for διδαχη ["teaching"]) 1739 Maj syr KJV NKJV

The *editio princeps* of the early fourth-century manuscript 0232 (see *P.Ant.* 12) shows the reading κυριου Χριστου ("Lord Christ") instead of Χριστου ("Christ"). According to my examination of the manuscript at the Ashmolean Museum, the reading should be Χριστου ("Christ"), which supports the WH NU reading. The WH NU reading, which has superior documentation and is likely the original wording, presents a different meaning than that which is found in the variant. When the WH NU reading speaks of πας ο προαγων (lit. "everyone going forward"), it is referring to those gnostics who considered themselves to be "the advanced ones"—the ones who thought they had "advanced" knowledge of God and spiritual truths. But this so-called advanced knowledge took them beyond the boundaries of true Christian orthodoxy—to the extent that they no longer stayed in the teaching concerning Christ (i.e., the teachings the apostles received from Christ). To remain in this teaching is to remain in the Son and the Father (see comments on 1 John 2:23). To depart from this teaching is a sign of apostasy.

The criticism against Gnosticism is missed in the variant reading, which simply conveys that the ones who have strayed from the teaching of Christ have transgressed. Some scribes must not have understood John's reference to gnostics claiming advanced knowledge and therefore changed προαγων to παραβαινων. This change was repeated in the majority of manuscripts (so TR and KJV).

2 John 9b

WH NU — ὁ μένων ἐν τῇ διδαχῇ
"the one remaining in the teaching"
ℵ A B Ψ 33 1739 cop
RSV NRSV ESV NASB NIV TNIV NEB REB (NJB) NAB NLT HCSB NET

variant/TR — ο μενων εν τη διδαχη του Χριστου
"the one remaining in the teaching of Christ"
P Maj vg^MSS cop^bo
KJV NKJV

The wording in WH NU has the best documentation, both early and diverse. The expanded reading in the variant is simply a carryover from the previous clause, wherein "the teaching" is explicitly identified as "the teaching of Christ" (see note on 9a).

2 John 11

At the end of the verse, several manuscripts of the Vulgate append this admonition: "Look, I have forewarned you so that in the Lord's day you may not be confounded."

2 John 12

TR NU — ἡ χαρὰ ἡμῶν πεπληρωμένη ᾖ
"our joy may be full"
ℵ K L P Ψ Maj
all

variant/WH — η χαρα υμων πεπληρωμενη η
"your joy may be full "
A B 33 1739 cop^bo
NJBmg NABmg

In spite of the fact that the variant has superior documentation, the NU editors adopted the TR NU reading on the basis that it "is quite in harmony with the author's generous spirit in associating himself with his readers (cf. ημων in 1 Jn 1.4)" (TCGNT). All translators have concurred. However, it must be noted that the wording in TR NU could be the result of scribes such as those of ℵ and Ψ harmonizing 2 John 12 to 1 John 1:4. In such cases, the documentary evidence must be given more weight, as was done here by WH.

2 John 13

WH NU
'Ασπάζεταί σε τὰ τέκνα τῆς ἀδελφῆς σου τῆς ἐκλεκτῆς.
"The children of your elect sister greet you."
ℵ A B P Ψ 33 1739 cop
RSV NRSV ESV NASB NIV TNIV NEB REB NJB NAB NLT HCSB NET

variant 1
Ασπαζεται σε τα τεκνα της αδελφης σου της εκκλησιας.
"The children of your sister church greet you."
307 vg^{MSS}
(NJBmg NLTmg)

variant 2/TR
Ασπαζεται σε τα τεκνα της αδελφης σου της εκλεκτης. αμην.
"The children of your elect sister greet you. Amen."
Maj vg^{MSS}
KJV NKJV NRSVmg NETmg

variant 3
Ασπαζεται σε τα τεκνα της αδελφης σου της εκλεκτης. Η χαρις μετα σου. αμην.
"The children of your elect sister greet you. Grace be with you. Amen."
442 1758 ($syr^{ph,h**}$) vg^{MSS}
none

The last verse of this epistle is busy with textual variants. Some scribes and Latin translators saw this as an opportunity to make it clear that this epistle was a communication from an apostle between sister churches (variant 1—see note on v. 1). Other scribes and translators appended one of two endings: (1) a concluding "amen" (variant 2—so TR); (2) a benediction of "grace and peace" followed by an "amen" (variant 3). Second John, in its original composition, is a typical letter of the Greco-Roman period. As such, it would have none of these embellishments, which show the influence of liturgical application.

The Third Epistle of JOHN

Inscription (Title)

(WH) NU	Ιωαννου Γ "Third of John" (א A B inscription and subscription) NIV TNIV NLT NET
variant 1/(TR)	Ιωαννου Επιστολη Γ "Third Epistle of John" Ψ 049 33 1739 KJV NKJV RSV NRSV ESV NASB NEB REB NJB NAB HCSB
variant 2	Επιστολη Γ του αγιου αποστολου Ιωαννου "Third Epistle of the holy Apostle John" L none
variant 3	του αγιου Ιωαννου επιστολη καθολικη "Catholic [= General] Epistle of the holy John" 1852 1881 none
variant 4	Ιωαννου προς Γαιον επιστολη "Epistle of John to Gaius" 1243 none

John's Third Epistle has been placed among the General Epistles (otherwise known as the Catholic Epistles) by virtue of its association with 1 John and 2 John. But this is not a general epistle; it was addressed to a specific individual, Gaius. As such, the fourth variant is the best title. But this inscription and all the others are scribal embellishments—from the simple "John's third" to "The Third Epistle of the holy apostle John." This letter was untitled in its original composition (see notes on the inscriptions to 1 and 2 John).

3 John 4

TR NU	χαράν "joy" א A C L P 1739 syr cop^{sa} all

variant/WH χαριν
"grace"
B 1243 2298 it cop[bo]
NJBmg

The TR NU reading produces the rendering, "I have no greater joy," whereas the variant reads, "I have no greater grace." Westcott (1886, 237) favored the variant reading. He said this reading was intrinsically superior because it "expresses the divine favour in concrete form." (NJBmg renders it "privilege.") However, it seems that Westcott selected this variant for external reasons—his preference for Codex Vaticanus. John was not speaking of "grace" here, but of his "joy" in seeing the believers live in the truth. Such joy is a key feature of the introductions to the Johannine epistles (see 1 John 1:4; 2 John 4).

3 John 8a

WH NU ὀφείλομεν ὑπολαμβάνειν τοὺς τοιούτους
"we ought to support such men"
ℵ A B C* Ψ 33 1739
NKJVmg RSV NRSV ESV NASB (NIV) TNIV NEB REB NAB NLT HCSB NET

variant/TR οφειλομεν απολαμβανειν τους τοιουτους
"we ought to receive such men"
C[2] P Maj
KJV NKJV (NJB)

Only a one-letter difference (υ/α) separates the two readings: υπολαμβανειν/απολαμβανειν. But there is a significant difference in meaning. The WH NU reading, which has superior attestation, provides an encouragement for the believers to support traveling teachers by giving them hospitality (see BDAG 1038) and an opportunity for ministry. The variant, which has inferior, late attestation, provides encouragement for the believers to welcome (see BDAG 115) the traveling teachers. The former speaks of greater commitment on the part of the believers.

3 John 8b

The three editions (TR WH NU) read ινα συνεργοι γινωμεθα τη αληθεια ("that we might become coworkers with the truth"), with the support of ℵ[c] B C Maj. Various manuscripts have alternative readings for the last two words: (1) της αληθειας, yielding the rendering, "that we might become coworkers of the truth" (so 614 1505); (2) τη εκκλησια, yielding the rendering "that we might become coworkers with the church" (so ℵ* A). The idea of the TR WH NU reading is that the believers can promote the propagation of the truth by supporting the traveling teachers who affirm and proclaim the orthodox, apostolic truth (see previous note). These missionaries, probably sent by John, would disseminate his message to the churches in Asia Minor. To receive them would be to complete the link between John and the churches, and thereby all would become co-laborers in advancing the cause of truth, which halts the spread of heresy. The first variant is a slight alteration of the text; it makes the people the coworkers with another, not with the truth. As such, it takes away the personification of truth. The second variant also obfuscates the personification of truth by substituting "the church" for "the truth." (The same change occurred in 3 John 12—see note.)

3 John 9

WH NU	⸀Εγραψα τι τῇ ἐκκλησίᾳ "I wrote something to the church" א* A 048vid 1739 (B reads εγραψας) RSV NRSV ESV NASB (NEB NJB NLT) HCSB NET
variant 1/TR	Εγραψα τη εκκλησια "I wrote to the church" C P Ψ Maj KJV NKJV NIV TNIV REB NAB
variant 2	Εγραψα αν τη εκκλησια "I would have written to the church" א² 33 vg syr none

The WH NU reading has strong documentation, both early and diverse. Both variant readings display the work of pedantic scribes. The first variant omits τι so that readers will not think to trivialize any writings of the apostles. The second variant is probably an attempt to circumvent any queries about why John's previous letter to the church is not extant. Of course, if 1 John or 2 John were that letter, then there would be no perceived problem. But it is a matter of conjecture whether or not this correspondence "to the church" (the only mention of εκκλησια in all of John's writings) refers to one of John's previous epistles or to some lost epistle. Many scholars (see Stott 1988, 228-229) reject 1 John as an option because, although it is a letter to the church or churches in the Johannine community, it says nothing about the reception or rejection of traveling teachers (the subject at hand in 3 John). And though 2 John is probably a letter to a specific church (see note on Inscription to 2 John), most scholars also reject it as an option because it, too, says nothing about traveling teachers. However, John does not explicitly say that his previous letter dealt with this issue; rather, he indicates that his letter to the church was not received by Diotrephes because he did not receive John and his coworkers. This situation perfectly coincides with a major theme in 1 John—namely, John's insistence that those who claim to have enlightened fellowship with God, while disdaining fellowship with the children of God, are liars. Such was Diotrephes. So, 1 John could very well be the previous correspondence to which John was referring Gaius. As such, the second variant could take on a whole new meaning. The wording, "I would have written to the church," means that John wrote to Gaius instead of to the church because he knew that Diotrephes would have interfered with his message to the church (Bruce 1970, 149-150).

3 John 12

The three editions (TR WH NU) read Δημητριω μεμαρτυρηται υπο παντων και υπο αυτης της αληθειας ("everyone has given testimony to Demetrius, and so has the truth itself"). This has excellent testimony (𝔓74c א Ac B P Ψ 049 33 1739 Maj), and is followed by all the English versions. However, there are two variants on the last part of this statement: (1) αυτης της εκκλησιας, yielding the rendering, "and so has the church itself" (so 𝔓74*vid A*vid); (2) αυτης της εκκλησιας και της αληθειας, yielding the rendering, "and so has the church itself and the truth" (so C syrph,hmg).

The TR WH NU reading is well attested and intrinsically superior to the other readings. As in verse 8, John personified "truth." In verse 8, the truth is depicted as a laborer, with whom the believers can cooperate for the advancement of orthodoxy. In this verse, the truth is depicted as a witness of the good works of Demetrius. This means that Demetrius advanced the cause of truth by being receptive to John and his emissaries—in contrast to Diotrephes, who opposed these and therefore hindered the truth.

The first variant shows that two scribes (of $\mathfrak{P}^{74}$ and A) were perhaps uncomfortable with "the truth" being personified in this way—thinking it more natural to say that "the church" gave witness to Demetrius's good works than to say "the truth" did. These two same scribes (or later correctors), noting their error, then corrected their manuscripts to read της αληθειας ("the truth"). The second variant is a conflated reading; its presence in the fifth-century manuscript C shows that both readings were present as early as the fourth century, if not earlier.

3 John 15

A common occurrence in the history of textual transmission was for an "amen" to be appended to the end of NT books, especially the epistles. Surprisingly, only a few scribes (L 614 1852) added an αμην ("Amen") at the end of 3 John. This letter, as with 2 John, is a typical letter of the Greco-Roman period. As such, it would never have ended with the word "amen."

The Epistle of JUDE

Inscription (Title)

WH NU Ιουδα
"Of Jude"
(א B inscription and subscription)
NIV TNIV NLT NET

variant 1 Ιουδα Επιστολη
"Epistle of Jude"
𝔓72 (A subscription) K Ψ 33 81
NKJV RSV NRSV ESV NASB NEB REB NJB NAB HCSB

variant 2/(TR) Ιουδα Επιστολη καθολικη
"Catholic [= General] Epistle of Jude"
614 1739
KJV

variant 3 Ιουδα αδελφου Ιακωβου Επιστολη καθολικη
"Catholic Epistle of Jude, brother of James"
1881
none

variant 4 Επιστολη του αγιου αποστολου Ιουδα
"Epistle of the holy Apostle Jude"
L (049)
none

Jude is one of the General Epistles (or Catholic Epistles), so called because it is an epistle addressed to a general audience, as opposed to a specific local audience. This catholicity is noted in the two extended inscriptions listed above, whereas other witnesses simply note it as "Epistle of Jude" or "Of Jude." Like the other epistles, this letter never had any inscription in the original.

Jude 1a

WH NU τοῖς ἐν θεῷ πατρὶ ἠγαπημένοις
"to the ones loved in God the Father"
𝔓72 א A B Ψ
RSV NRSV ESV NASB NIV TNIV NEB REB NJB NAB NLT HCSB NET

variant 1 τοις εθνεσιν εν θεω πατρι ηγαπημενοις
"to the nations loved in God the Father"
323 1505 1739 syr
NJBmg

variant 2/TR τοις εν θεω πατρι ηγιασμενοις
"to those sanctified in God the Father"
P Maj
KJV NKJV NRSVmg NJBmg HCSBmg

The WH NU reading is strongly supported by the earliest manuscripts. There are two basic changes in this verse: (1) the addition of εθνεσιν ("nations") in a few witnesses, and (2) the change from ηγαπημενοις ("loved ones") to ηγιασμενοις ("sanctified ones") in the majority of late manuscripts. The lack of identification of an audience for this epistle prompted the first variant, which identifies the recipients as the "nations" or "Gentiles." Of course, this was an attempt to make Jude conform to some of the other General Epistles (see Jas 1:1; 1 Pet 1:1). But Jude was probably not originally written as a general epistle. Rather, Jude was addressing a problem with Gnosticism in a specific local church.

The difficulty of the wording τοις εν θεω πατρι ηγαπημενοις prompted the second variant. The WH NU wording means that Christians are "loved ones" because they are in the heart of God the Father. But some scribes must have had difficulty understanding how one could be loved *in* God the Father and subsequently changed the participle to ηγιασμενοις—perhaps influenced by 1 Cor 1:2.

Jude 1b

A few witnesses (630 1505 syr[h]) omit και Ιησου Χριστω τετηρημενοις ("and kept by Jesus Christ"). This omission was accidental, due to homoeoteleuton—the eye of a scribe passing from ηγαπημενοις to κλητοις.

Jude 3

WH NU τῆς κοινῆς ἡμῶν σωτηρίας
"our common salvation"
𝔓72 A B 1739 syr cop[sa]
NKJV RSV NRSV ESV NASB NIV TNIV NEB REB NJB NAB NLT HCSB NET

variant 1 της κοινης υμων σωτηριας
"your common salvation"
1881 cop[bo]
none

variant 2/TR της κοινης σωτηριας
"the common salvation"
P Maj
KJV

variant 3 της κοινης υμων ζωης
"your common life"
1505 (syr)
none

variant 4 τηϛ κοινηϛ ημων σωτηριαϛ και ζωηϛ
"our common salvation and life"
א Ψ
none

The "common salvation" Jude was speaking about is the salvation shared by all believers. Since this was Jude's portion as well as his readers', it was natural for him to speak about it being "our common salvation" (i.e., the salvation experience we share in common). The change to "your" is slimly supported, and the omission of any pronoun, though found in the majority of manuscripts, was calculated to make the statement even more universal. The substitution or addition of "life" is an ingenious way of paraphrasing the text. Because of their common salvation, Christians share a common (or communal) life.

Jude 4a

TR NU have the indicative παρεισεδυσαν ("they crept in"), with the solid support of 𝔓72 א A P Ψ 33 1739 Maj. The WH reading, following B and C, has the subjunctive παρεισεδυησαν ("they might creep in"). The difference in meaning is significant. Jude was saying either that certain men had crept in among the believers or that they could creep in among them. The first is actual; the second, potential. Documentation favors the indicative.

Jude 4b

WH NU τὸν μόνον δεσπότην καὶ κύριον ἡμῶν 'Ιησοῦν Χριστὸν ἀρνούμενοι
"denying our only Master and Lord, Jesus Christ"
𝔓78 א A B C 33 1739 cop
NKJVmg RSV NRSV ESV NASB NIV TNIV NEB REB NJB NAB NLT HCSB NET

variant 1/TR τον μονον δεσποτην θεον και κυριον ημων Ιησουν Χριστον αρνουμενοι
"denying God, the only Master, and our Lord Jesus Christ"
P Ψ Maj syr
KJV NKJV RSVmg NRSVmg NEBmg NJBmg

variant 2 τον ημων δεσποτην και κυριον Ιησουν Χριστον ημων αρνουμενοι
"denying our Master and our Lord Jesus Christ"
𝔓72c
none

The reading in TR, poorly attested, is probably an attempt to avoid calling Jesus δεσποτην ("Master"), when this title is usually ascribed to God (Luke 2:29; Acts 4:24; Rev 6:10). Hence, θεοϛ ("God") was appended to δεσποτην. However, 2 Pet 2:1, a parallel passage, identifies the redeemer, Jesus Christ, as the δεσποτην. So here also, the WH NU reading, which is extremely well documented, shows that Jude considered Jesus to be the absolute sovereign. The scribe of 𝔓72 mistakenly wrote νομον instead of μονον, and then deleted νομον. This probably indicates that one exemplar known to him contained the word μονον.

Jude 5

(WH) NU	πάντα ὅτι [ὁ] κύριος ἅπαξ "[knowing that] the Lord having once for all" C* (א Ψ omit ο) syr^{h} RSVmg NRSV ESVmg NASB NIV TNIV NEB REB NJB NAB NLTmg HCSB
variant 1	απαξ παντα, οτι Ιησους "[knowing] once for all, that Jesus" A B 33 Cyril Jerome Bede RSVmg NRSVmg ESV NASBmg NIVmg TNIVmg NEBmg REBmg NJBmg NLT NET
variant 2	παντα, οτι Ιησους απαξ "[knowing] everything, that Jesus once" 1739 1881 Origen$^{\text{according to 1739mg}}$ cop none
variant 3	απαξ παντα, οτι θεος Χριστος "[knowing] once for all, that God [the] Messiah (or, Messiah God)" $\mathfrak{P}^{72c}$ ($\mathfrak{P}^{72*}$ παντας) NLTmg NETmg
variant 4	απαξ παντα, οτι ο θεος "[knowing] once for all, that God" C^{2} vg^{MS} RSVmg REBmg NLTmg NETmg
variant 5/TR	απαξ τουτο, οτι ο κυριος "once [you knew] this, that the Lord" (K L) Maj KJV NKJV NEBmg NLTmg

Among all the readings cited above, the first and second variants are the most remarkable, for they say that "Jesus delivered his people out of Egypt." This reading is found in A B 33 1739 1881 cop Origen Cyril Jerome Bede—an impressive collection of witnesses. $\mathfrak{P}^{72}$ may possibly be an indirect witness to the reading with "Jesus," because it shows that the scribe had before him in his exemplar a messianic title—"Christ" (= "Messiah"). At any rate, it is easier to argue (from a textual perspective) that the reading with "Jesus" is the one from which all the others deviated than to argue that the reading with "Lord" (or "God") was changed to "Jesus," because scribes were not known for fabricating difficult readings.

Some scholars, such as Wikgren (1967, 147-152), have argued that Jude may have written Ιησους in Jude 5 intending "Joshua" (see NEBmg), as in Heb 4:8. But this is very unlikely, because Joshua led the Israelites into the good land of Canaan, but not out of Egypt, and Joshua certainly did not destroy those who did not believe (Jude 5b). This was a divine activity. Thus, it is likely that Jesus is here being seen as Yahweh the Savior. In other words, from Jude's perspective, it was Jesus, the I Am (see John 8:58), who was present with the Israelites and operative in their deliverance from Egypt. Paul shared a similar view inasmuch as he proclaimed that "Christ" was the Rock that accompanied the Israelites in their desert journeys and that "Christ" was the one the Israelites constantly "tested" during these times (see 1 Cor 10:4, 9 and note on 1 Cor 10:9). Thus, the reading "Jesus," though difficult, is not impossible. As such, it should be accepted as the original reading (as it was by Eberhard Nestle [1901, 328-329] and F. F. Bruce [1964, 63]). The first edition of the United Bible Societies' *Greek New Testament* contained the reading "Jesus" in the text. But this was changed in the third edition, when a slim majority of the editors voted to put the reading with "Lord" in the text and the one with "Jesus" in the margin. (Metzger and Wikgren voted against this decision and stated their reasons for doing so in TCGNT.)

The first English translation to adopt the wording "Jesus" was NLT. (As the New Testament coordinator who proposed this reading to the NLT committee, I was glad to see them adopt it.) Two other recent versions have also adopted this reading: TNIV (a change from the NIV) and NET (see the note in NETmg). Otherwise, it has been relegated to the margin of all the other versions. NASB notes that "two early manuscripts read 'Jesus.'" Those manuscripts are A and B.

Jude 8

The TR WH NU editions speak of the false teachers categorically rejecting "lordship"; this is indicated by the Greek word κυριοτητα (supported by $\mathfrak{P}^{72}$ $\mathfrak{P}^{78}$ A B). But some scribes and translators (א Ψ cop[sa]) had difficulty with this kind of abstraction, so κυριοτητα was changed to κυριοτητας ("lords").

Most manuscripts indicate that the false prophets do not hesitate to blaspheme "glorious beings" (δοξας). The uncertainty of the identity of these beings (are they evil angels, God-sent angels, or demons?) prompted some scribes and ancient translators ($\mathfrak{P}^{78vid}$ vg[MSS] syr[ph]) to change δοξας to δοξαν—denoting "the Glorious One" (i.e., God).

Jude 9

In the expression, επιτιμησαι σοι κυριος ("[the] Lord rebuke you"), the last word in all three editions (TR WH NU) is κυριος ("Lord"), with good testimony: $\mathfrak{P}^{72}$ A C Maj. A few manuscripts ($\aleph^2$ 1505) add a definite article, and a few others (א* 1739 1881) change it to ο θεος ("God"). In B* Ψ the expression is επιτιμησαι εν σοι κυριος, showing scribal conformity to Zech 3:2 (LXX), the verse quoted here.

Jude 11

Instead of βαλααμ ("Balaam"), $\mathfrak{P}^{72}$ alone reads Βαλακ ("Balak"). If this was not an accidental mistake, the scribe of $\mathfrak{P}^{72}$ may have considered Balak (who hired Balaam to curse Israel) to be the figure Jude was using to make his point. But the text points to those who masquerade as prophets for the sake of making money.

Jude 12a

In a few manuscripts (א* C^2 cop[bo,sa]), the subject of the sentence (ουτοι—these ones) is identified as γογγυσται μεμψιμοιροι κατα τας [ιδιας—C^2]επιθυμιας αυτων πορευομενοι ("grumblers, complainers, ones who live according to their [own] desires"). This wording was borrowed almost verbatim from v. 16, a verse that describes the same false teachers.

Jude 12b

All three editions (TR WH NU) read αγαπαις ("love feasts"), with the support of $\mathfrak{P}^{72}$ א B Maj. All English versions follow. There are three variants on this: (1) απαταις ("deceptions") in A* C[vid]; (2) απαταις αυτων ("their deceptions") in A[c]; (3) ευωχιαις ("feasts") in 6. Some scribe(s) may have been troubled that false teachers were allowed into the Christians' love feasts (a weekly, Sunday meal which preceded communion). Influenced by 2 Pet 2:13, a parallel passage, they changed αγαπαις ("love feasts") to απαταις ("deceits"). However, the grammatical structure of Jude 12 hardly permits this change, even though the second variant tries to accommodate it. The third variant substitutes a common Greek synonym for the esoteric Christian term.

Jude 14

(TR) WH NU	ἁγίαις μυριάσιν αὐτοῦ "myriads of his holy ones" A B (C) 33 (1739) Maj KJV NKJV RSV NRSV ESV NASB NIV TNIV NJB NAB NLT HCSB NET
variant 1	αγιαις μυριασιν αγγελων "myriads of holy angels" Ψ NEB REB
variant 2	αγιων αγγελων μυριασιν "myriads of holy angels" 𝔓72 (א) none

In this verse, Jude cites *1 Enoch* 1:9 in an effort to exhibit a prophetic parousia of Christ (the verb "came" is a Semitic prophetic perfect). The event predicted is the coming of the Lord, who must be "the Lord Jesus" (see v. 5), accompanied by "thousands of holy ones." These holy ones are "the angels" who will accompany Jesus in his parousia (as in 1 Thess 3:13). Osburn (1976, 334-341) makes the case that 𝔓72's wording closely follows 4QEnoch 1:9 (first century B.C.) and may therefore be original—especially for a writer such as Jude, who was used to thinking in Aramaic and was consciously following *1 Enoch* as he wrote his epistle. If so, the manuscripts A B C present a later tradition.

Jude 15-16

Some manuscripts and ancient versions (א C 33 1739 syr cop[sa]) show that scribes felt compelled to fill out the meaning of των σκληρων ("the hard things") by adding λογων ("words"; hence, "the hard words"). The scribe of 𝔓72 accidentally left out two portions in these two verses (bracketed below)—both due to homoeoteleuton: (v. 15) περι παντων [των εργων ασεβειας αυτων ων ησεβησαν και περι παντων]; (v. 16) μεμψιμοιροι [κατα τας επιθυμιας εαυτων πορευομενοι]. A second-hand correction appears in the margin of 𝔓72, whereby the missing words of v. 16 are added.

Jude 19

WH NU	Οὗτοι εἰσιν οἱ ἀποδιορίζοντες. "These are the ones who cause divisions." 𝔓72 א A B NKJV RSV NRSV ESV NASB NIV TNIV NEBmg REB NJB NAB NLT HCSB NET
variant/TR	Ουτοι εισιν οι αποδιοριζοντες εαυτους. "These are the ones who separate themselves." C 1505 1739[mg] vg KJV NEB REBmg

The WH NU reading is strongly supported by the four earliest manuscripts (noted above). To the word αποδιοριζοντες, meaning "to separate," some scribe(s) felt compelled to add the reflexive εαυτους ("themselves"). But Jude was probably using this active verb to indicate that the false teachers were causing divisions. These people were not excluding themselves from the fellowship (so KJV); they were disrupting the fellowship.

Jude 22-23

This text appears in a variety of textual forms. Some manuscripts indicate three classes of people, as follows:

1a/NU

[22] Καὶ οὓς μὲν ἐλεᾶτε διακρινομένους,
[23] οὓς δὲ σῴζετε ἐκ πυρὸς ἁρπάζοντες,
οὓς δὲ ἐλεᾶτε ἐν φόβῳ
"[22] and show mercy to some who have doubts [or, who dispute];
[23] and save some, snatching them from fire;
and to some show mercy with fear"
א
NKJVmg RSV NRSV ESV NASB NIV TNIV NEBmg REB NJB NAB NLT HCSB NET

1b

και ους μεν ελεγχετε διακρινομενους
ους δε σωζετε εκ πυρος αρπαζοντες
ους δε ελεατε εν φοβω
"and reprove some who have doubts [or, who dispute];
and save some, snatching them from fire;
and to some show mercy with fear"
A
NKJVmg NEBmg REBmg NABmg NLTmg

Some manuscripts indicate two classes of people, as follows:

2a/WH

[22] και ους μεν ελεατε διακρινομενους σωζετε εκ πυρος αρπαζοντες
[23] ους δε ελεατε εν φοβω
"[22] and show mercy to some who have doubts—save them by snatching them from fire;
[23] and to some show mercy with fear"
B
NEB NJBmg NABmg NLTmg

2b/TR

[22] και ους μεν ελεγχετε διακρινομενους
[23] ους δε σωζετε εκ πυρος αρπαζοντες εν θοβω
"[22] and have mercy on some, making a difference,
[23] and others save with fear, pulling them out of the fire"
Maj
KJV NKJV

2c

και ους μεν ελεγχετε διακρινομενους
ους δε σωζετε εκ πυρος αρπαζοντες εν φοβω
"and reprove some who have doubts [or, who dispute],
and in fear save some from fire"
C*
NLTmg

2d ους μεν εκ πυρος αρπασατε
διακρινομενους δε ελεειτε εν φοβω
"and some snatch from fire,
and show mercy with fear to others who have doubts"
$\mathfrak{P}^{72}$
none

The textual problems in this passage are extremely complicated and require great effort to unravel. The essential textual distinctions involve the verb variation, ελεατε ("show mercy") and ελεγχετε ("reprove"), and the objects of these verbs. It is possible that Jude was speaking of certain people who needed reproof because they were causing disputes in the church, or he may have been speaking of other people who needed reproof because they were doubting the apostolic truths. It is equally possible that Jude was encouraging the church to show mercy to those who were having doubts (probably caused by the false teachers in their midst). If Jude was calling upon the church to reprove the disputers in verse 22 (as in 1b and 2c), then verse 23 is a call for Christians to rescue those who were contaminated by the erroneous teachings. The rescuers needed to do it with mercy and with fear—mercy toward the doubters and fear that the rescuers themselves would also be contaminated by their interaction with those who doubted. If Jude, in both verses, was calling for merciful action (as in 1a, 2a, 2b, and 2d), then all those mentioned in these verses had been contaminated—to one degree or another—by the false teachers.

Scholars have attempted to recover the original wording and form of this text with great difficulty. The work of one scholar in particular, Sakae Kubo (who did a major study on $\mathfrak{P}^{72}$), demonstrates this difficulty. Kubo (1965) first argued for the two-division form as found in $\mathfrak{P}^{72}$ or B, but then presented a new argument for the threefold division as found in א (1981, 239-253). All modern English versions except NEB follow this threefold presentation, and then several note that there is textual variation out of respect for the complexity of the manuscript tradition. The note in NRSV says, "the Greek text at verses 22-23 is uncertain at several points." The note in TNIV says, "The Greek manuscripts of these verses vary at several points." Uncertainty is one thing, variation is another. Either could be said of several passages in the NT; in this passage, we are faced with a lot of textual variation. Other versions provide actual wording of other textual variants, which is helpful. The fullest and clearest presentation is made in the second edition of NLT, which follows NU in having three categories of people (see above) and attaches this marginal note: "Some manuscripts have only two categories of people: (1) those whose faith is wavering and therefore need to be snatched from the flames of judgment, and (2) those who need to be shown mercy."

Jude 24

WH NU φυλάξαι ὑμᾶς
"to guard you"
א B C Ψ 33 1739
all

variant 1/TR φυλαξαι αυτους
"to guard them"
K P 049 Maj
NKJVmg

variant 2 φυλαξαι ημας
"to guard us"
A syr^{ph}
none

variant 3 στηριξαι ασπιλους αμωμους αγνευομενους απεναντι της δοξης αυτου
"to confirm [you] spotless, blameless, [and] pure to the praise of his glory with rejoicing"
𝔓72
none

The change reflected in the majority of manuscripts (so TR) identifies the recipients of the doxology as being either (1) those who need to be rescued from heresy or (2) the rescuers (see note on 22-23). But the doxology, as preserved in the WH NU reading (on good authority), is addressed to all the believers in general—the recipients of Jude's Epistle. The reading in 𝔓72, a singular variant, shows the scribe's creativity in producing a distinct doxology.

Jude 25a

WH NU μόνῳ θεῷ σωτῆρι ἡμῶν
"to [the] only God our Savior"
ℵ A B C Ψ 33 1739 it syr cop
NKJVmg RSV NRSV ESV NASB NIV TNIV NEB REB NJB NAB NLT HCSB NET

variant 1/TR μονω σοφω θεω σωτηρι ημων
"to [the] only wise God, our Savior"
P Maj
KJV NKJV

variant 2 μονω θεω ημων
"to our only God"
𝔓72 442c
none

The WH NU reading is solidly supported by a vast array of witnesses. The first variant displays scribal conformity to Rom 16:27, a parallel verse. The same addition occurred in 1 Tim 1:17, also a parallel verse. Both these additions were popularized in TR and KJV. The second variant, though the shortest reading and therefore potentially original, cannot be trusted, because the scribe of 𝔓72 was quite free in his copying of Jude.

Jude 25b

WH NU διὰ Ἰησοῦ Χριστοῦ τοῦ κυρίου ἡμῶν δόξα μεγαλωσύνη κράτος καὶ ἐξουσία πρὸ παντὸς τοῦ αἰῶνος
"[to God,] through Jesus Christ our Lord, be glory, greatness, might, and authority before all ages"
ℵ A B C (L Ψ) 33 (1739)
NKJVmg RSV NRSV ESV NASB NIV TNIV NEB REB NJB NAB NLT HCSB NET

variant 1/TR δοξα και μεγαλωσυνη κρατος και εξουσια
"[to God] be glory and greatness, might, and authority"
P Maj
KJV NKJV HCSBmg

variant 2 αυτω δοξα κρατος τιμη δια Ιησου Χριστου του κυριου ημων· αυτω δοξα και μεγαλωσυνη
"to him be glory, might, honor through Jesus Christ our Lord; to him be glory and greatness"
𝔓72
none

The first variant, found in the majority of manuscripts, is the shortest of the readings, lacking two phrases: "through Jesus Christ our Lord" and "before all ages." The second phrase is also absent in the earliest witness, 𝔓72. Since scribes had a penchant for expanding doxologies, it is possible that the first variant preserves the original text. However, it is also possible that some scribe(s) omitted one or both of these phrases because it was difficult to understand how God could be glorified through Jesus Christ before the ages began. Or it is possible that προ παντος του αιωνος ("before all the ages") was deleted in order to make Jude 25 conform to 2 Pet 3:18, a parallel verse.

The Book of REVELATION

Inscription (Title)

WH NU	Αποκαλυψις Ιωαννου "Revelation of John" (א inscription and subscription) (A subscription) RSV NRSV ESV NASB NEB REB NJB NAB
variant 1/TR	Αποκαλυψις Ιωαννου του θεολογου "Revelation of John the theologian" Maj KJV
variant 2	Αποκαλυψις Ιωαννου του θεολογου και ευαγγελιστου "Revelation of John the theologian and evangelist" 046 none

As elsewhere in the Greek NT, so here, inscriptions (titles) were not contained in the autographs. The inscription to the last book of the NT is simply "John's Revelation" in א and A. (B lacks the Revelation; otherwise, given its pattern, it would have probably had the same.) This title comes from a reading of the prologue (1:1-8), which clearly indicates that John received the revelation. The other titles assume this John to be "the theologian" (or "the divine" as it is in KJV) and/or "evangelist"—that is, the beloved disciple, John the apostle (see Inscriptions to 1 and 2 John, and comments). Besides the English versions noted above, others name the book simply "Revelation" (NIV TNIV NLT NET), whereas NKJV and HCSB title it "The Revelation of Jesus Christ."

Revelation 1:4

According to the rules of grammar, the preposition απο should be followed by the genitive case. Hence, the majority of manuscripts add θεου before the expression ο ων και ο ην και ο ερχομενος ("the one being and the one [who] was and the coming one"), supported by superior testimony ($\mathfrak{P}^{18vid}$ א A C P it syr cop).

Revelation 1:5

WH NU τῷ ἀγαπῶντι ἡμᾶς καὶ λύσαντι ἡμᾶς ἐκ τῶν ἁμαρτιῶν ἡμῶν
"to the one loving us and having freed us from our sins"
𝔓[18] א A C
NKJVmg RSV NRSV ESV NASB NIV TNIV NEB REB NJBmg NAB NLT HCSB NET

variant 1 τω αγαπωντι ημας και λουσαντι ημας εκ των αμαρτιων ημων
"to the one loving us and having washed us from our sins"
P Maj[K] it cop[bo]
NRSVmg NJB

variant 2/(TR) τω αγαπησαντι ημας και λουσαντι ημας εκ των αμαρτιων ημων
"to the one having loved us and having washed us from our sins"
Maj[A]
KJV NKJV HCSBmg NETmg

In the Greek there is only a one-letter difference (*omicron*) between the two readings. The first reading contains the Greek participle λυσαντι ("freeing"); the second reading contains the Greek participle λουσαντι ("washing"). The earliest and best witnesses attest to the first, more difficult reading. Uncomfortable with this wording, later scribes changed the word by adding an *omicron,* perhaps influenced by 7:14. TR has an additional change—turning both participles into aorists (αγαπησαντι . . . λουσαντι). All the modern English versions except NJB followed the superior reading, while KJV and NKJV adhere to TR.

Revelation 1:6a

WH NU ἐποίησεν ἡμᾶς βασιλείαν, ἱερεῖς τῷ θεῷ
"he made us a kingdom, priests to God"
𝔓[18c] (𝔓[18*] του θεου) A C Maj[K]
NKJVmg RSV NRSV ESV NASB NIV (TNIV) NEB REB NJB NAB NLT HCSB NET

variant 1/TR εποιησεν ημας βασιλεις και ιερεις τω θεω
"he made us kings and priests to God"
Maj[A]
KJV NKJV HCSBmg

variant 2 εποιησεν ημας βασιλειον, ιερεατευμα τω θεω
"he made us a kingdom, a priesthood to God"
2351
none

The WH NU reading has superior documentary support and is the most difficult reading of the three. (For the reconstruction of 𝔓[18], not cited in NA[27], see *Text of Earliest MSS,* 103-105.) The two variants are scribal attempts to make the direct objects parallel in construction. The wording in TR, popularized by KJV, says that the believers are "kings and priests." Although this reads nicely, it misses the point because it individualizes the believers' function. The message is that the priests, considered collectively, constitute God's kingdom (see Exod 19:6; 1 Pet 2:9). The Christians together comprise a kingdom of priests who serve God the Father. They are his kingdom by virtue of their priestly service to God.

Revelation 1:6b

TR NU τοὺς αἰῶνας [τῶν αἰώνων]
"the ages of the ages" (= "forever and ever")
ℵ C Maj it syr
all

variant/WH τους αιωνας
"the ages" (= "forever")
𝔓[18] A P (2344) cop[bo]
NETmg

Though the documentary evidence is almost evenly divided, the variant reading has the edge because it has both the testimony of the earliest extant manuscript (𝔓[18]) and the combined witness of A and 2344. Internal considerations also seem to favor the shorter reading because this is the only place in Revelation where the shorter form of the eternity expression occurs. The longer form appears twelve times in this book (1:18; 4:9, 10; 5:13; 7:12; 10:6; 11:15; 14:11; 15:7; 19:3; 20:10; 22:5). As such, scholars have argued that style should dictate our decision here (see TCGNT). But why, then, would the scribes of 𝔓[18] A P 2344 diverge from the normal style? There is no good explanation on transcriptional grounds. Thus, the shorter reading is probably original, which was then expanded. In light of the fact that other verses (see notes on 1:8 and 1:11) in the prologue were expanded to conform to later statements in Revelation, this line of reasoning seems plausible.

Revelation 1:8

WH NU τὸ ἄλφα καὶ τὸ ὦ
"the Alpha and the Omega"
ℵ[1] A C 2053 2062 Maj[K]
NKJVmg RSV NRSV ESV NASB NIV TNIV NEB REB NJB NAB NLT HCSB NET

variant/TR το αλφα και το ω, η αρχη και το τελος
"the Alpha and the Omega, the Beginning and the End"
ℵ[*,2] (2344) Maj[A] it cop[bo]
KJV NKJV NETmg

Throughout the book of Revelation, there are three similar divine self-descriptions, each of which extols the comprehensiveness of eternal deity: (1) "the Alpha and Omega" (the first and last letters of the Greek alphabet), (2) "the Beginning and the End," and (3) "the First and the Last." In each context (1:8, 17; 2:8; 21:6; 22:13), it is difficult to discern if the title applies to God (see Isa 41:4; 44:6) or to Jesus or to both. Most likely it can be attributed to the Godhead—God in Jesus Christ. Looking at the five verses (1:8, 17; 2:8; 21:6; 22:13), it is noteworthy that all three of these affirmations do not appear in each of these verses. Rather, there is an accumulation of titles as the book progresses: (1) I am the Alpha and the Omega (1:8); (2) I am the First and the Last (1:17; 2:8); (3) I am the Alpha and the Omega; the Beginning and the End (21:6); (4) I am the Alpha and the Omega; the First and the Last; the Beginning and the End (22:13—or I am the Alpha and the Omega; the Beginning and the End, the First and the Last, according to other manuscripts; see note on 22:13). To insert "the Beginning and the End" in the first proclamation ruins the build-up of titles. Scribes, insensitive to this, thought the expressions should be more parallel throughout. So they borrowed from 21:6 to fill out the divine proclamation here. (Another expansion occurs in 1:11—see note.)

Revelation 1:9a

WH NU ὑπομονῇ ἐν Ἰησοῦ
"endurance in Jesus"
א* C P 2053[vid]
RSV NRSV ESV NASB NIV TNIV NEB REB NJB NAB NLT HCSB NET

variant 1 υπομονη εν Χριστω
"endurance in Christ"
A
none

variant 2 υπομονη εν Χριστω Ιησου
"endurance in Christ Jesus"
(א[2]) Maj[K]
none

variant 3/TR υπομονη Ιησου Χριστου
"endurance of Jesus Christ"
2329 Maj[A] syr[h**]
KJV NKJV

Documentary evidence slightly favors the WH NU reading, as does the fact that scribes had a tendency to expand divine titles. The expansions in the third and second variants to "Jesus Christ" (or "Christ Jesus") were influenced by the prologue, where the title occurs three times (1:1-2, 5). Thereafter, the name is always simply "Jesus" (12:17; 14:12; 17:6; 19:10; 20:4; 22:16), until the end where "Lord Jesus" appears twice (22:20-21). Since "Christ" rarely appears alone in Revelation, the first variant (in A) is suspect.

Revelation 1:9b

WH NU τὴν μαρτυρίαν Ἰησοῦ
"the testimony of Jesus"
א* A C Maj[A]
RSV NRSV ESV NASB NIV TNIV NEB REB NJB NAB NLT HCSB NET

variant/TR την μαρτυριαν Ιησου Χριστου
"the testimony of Jesus Christ"
א[2] Maj[K] syr cop
KJV NKJV

Documentary evidence supports the WH NU reading. The expansion of Jesus' name, begun in 1:9a (see previous note), was carried on to the end of the verse.

Revelation 1:11a

WH NU ὃ βλέπεις γράψον εἰς βιβλίον
"Write in a book what you see."
א A C Maj[K] it syr cop[sa]
NKJVmg RSV NRSV ESV NASB NIV TNIV NEB REB NJB NAB NLT HCSB NET

variant/TR — Εγω ειμι το αλφα και το ω, ο πρωτος και ο εσχατος. και ο βλεπεις γραψον εις βιβλιον.
"I am the Alpha and the Omega, the First and the Last. And write in a book what you see."
Maj[A]
KJV NKJV

These extra words are present in only those manuscripts that follow the commentary of Andreas (Maj[A]). Evidently it was Andreas who interposed these words, borrowing from 22:13 (see note on 1:8). TR, followed by KJV and NKJV, has this expanded reading.

Revelation 1:11b

WH NU — ταῖς ἑπτὰ ἐκκλησίαις
"the seven churches"
all Greek MSS
NKJVmg RSV NRSV ESV NASB NIV TNIV NEB REB NJB NAB NLT HCSB NET

variant/TR — ταις επτα εκκλησιαις ταις εν Ασια
"the seven churches in Asia"
no Greek MSS vg (?)
KJV NKJV

With no textual support from any known Greek manuscript, TR, followed by KJV and NKJV, exhibits the expansion, "in Asia." Although this insertion is accurate (the seven churches listed thereafter were located in the Roman province of Asia), it is textually spurious.

Revelation 1:15

WH NU, supported by A and C, read οι ποδες αυτου ομοιοι χαλκολιβανω ως εν καμινω πεπυρωμενης. This could be rendered, "his feet like burnished bronze as if in a glowing furnace." However, πεπυρωμενης (a genitive singular participle) does not grammatically modify καμινω (a dative singular noun) or any other previous noun. If this was the original reading, scribes corrected this grammatical problem by changing the participle to πεπυρωμενω (a dative singular participle modifying καμινω ["furnace"] or χαλκολιβανω ["burnished bronze"])—as in ℵ 2053 2062, or to πεπυρωμενοι (a nominative plural masculine participle modifying οι ποδες αυτου ["his feet"])—as in Maj (so TR).

Revelation 1:17

The words μη φοβου ("do not fear") are not included in ℵ* 2053 2062, but are present in 𝔓[98] ℵ[c] A C. Since there is no reason to explain the omission on transcriptional grounds, it is possible that a scribe purposely deleted these words because he did not think John would have been afraid when he saw Jesus. All manuscripts except Codex Alexandrinus name Jesus here as ο πρωτος και ο εσχατος ("the First and the Last"). Alexandrinus names him ο πρωτοτοκος και ο εσχατος ("the Firstborn and the Last"). The context prompted this change inasmuch it speaks of Jesus as being the one who passed through death (1:18). As such, he is "the firstborn from the dead" (see Col 1:18). The same change appears in 2:8 in Codex Alexandrinus.

Revelation 1:18a

As noted in NA[27], a few ancient versions (it[gig] vg[MSS]) and Primasius did not include the words και ο ζων ("and the living one") at the beginning of this verse. What is not noted in NA[27] is that 𝔓[98vid] (with a high degree of certainty from my observation of the manuscript) should be added to the list (see *Text of Earliest MSS*, 631). Without the words, the text of 1:17-18 reads, "I am the First and the Last, who became dead, and behold I am alive forevermore."

Revelation 1:18b

WH NU ζῶν εἰμι εἰς τοὺς αἰῶνας τῶν αἰώνων
"I am living into the ages of the ages [= forever and ever]"
א* A C P 2053 2062
RSV NRSV ESV NASB NIV TNIV NEB REB NJB NAB NLT HCSB NET

variant/TR ζων ειμι εις τους αιωνας των αιωνων· αμην
"I am living into the ages of the ages [= forever and ever], amen."
א[1] Maj syr
KJV NKJV

The textual evidence strongly favors the exclusion of "amen." The doxological tone of Jesus' statement in 1:17-18 prompted the insertion of an "amen" by some enthusiastic scribe. Jesus would not have said "amen" to his own proclamation—the "amen" is a response that should come from others. However, Jesus does call himself "the Amen" (ο Αμην) in 3:14 because he is the one who faithfully attests to the truth of God's existence and purposes.

Revelation 1:20

WH NU αἱ λυχνίαι αἱ ἑπτά
"the seven lampstands"
(א*) A (C) 046 (2053 2062) it
NKJVmg RSV NRSV ESV NASB NIV TNIV NEB REB NJB NAB NLT HCSB NET

variant/TR αι επτα λυχνιαι ας ειδες
"the seven lampstands which you saw"
Maj[A] syr[ph] cop[bo]
KJV NKJV HCSBmg

The WH NU reading has the best documentation; it is followed by all modern versions. The interpolation appearing in the variant is a scribal carryover from the previous verse (1:19). TR has the extra words, followed by KJV and NKJV.

Revelation 2:5

WH NU ἔρχομαι σοι
"I am coming to you"
א A C P 2053
RSV NRSV ESV NASB NIV TNIV NEB REB NJB NAB NLT HCSB NET

variant/TR ερχομαι σοι ταχυ
"I am coming to you quickly"
Maj it[t] vg[MSS] syr[h]
KJV NKJV HCSBmg

The manuscript evidence (with the support of ℵ A C) decidedly favors the WH NU reading. In order to achieve verbal parity with similar statements in Jesus' proclamations to two other churches (Pergamum and Philadelphia—2:16; 3:11), scribes and ancient translators added "quickly" in this verse.

Revelation 2:7

All manuscripts, except A and C, read το πνευμα λεγει ταις εκκλησιαις ("the Spirit speaks to the churches"). These two manuscripts say the Spirit speaks to "the seven churches" (ταις επτα εκκλησιαις). The change was probably influenced by 1:4, 11, and 20.

Revelation 2:8

The scribe of A changed ο πρωτος ("the First") to ο πρωτοτοκος ("the Firstborn") here and in 1:17 (see note).

Revelation 2:9

WH NU — οἶδα σου τὴν θλῖψιν
"I know your affliction"
A C P 2053 it syr[ph] cop
RSV NRSV ESV NASB NIV TNIV NEB REB NJB NAB NLT HCSB NET

variant/TR — οιδα σου τα εργα και την θλιψιν
"I know your works and affliction"
ℵ Maj syr[h**]
KJV NKJV HCSBmg

The manuscript evidence (especially with the combined support of A C) supports the WH NU reading. In each of Jesus' declarations to the seven churches, he makes a statement concerning what he knows about them before he gives his assessment of their condition. In five of the seven addresses he begins by saying, "I know your works" (see 2:2, 19; 3:1, 8, 15). Scribes, bent on making the other two addresses the same as the other five, added "I know your works"—both here and in 2:13 (see note).

Revelation 2:13

WH NU — οἶδα ποῦ κατοικεῖς
"I know where you dwell"
ℵ A C P 2053 syr[ph] cop
RSV NRSV ESV NASB NIV TNIV NEB REB NJB NAB NLT HCSB NET

variant/TR — οιδα τα εργα σου και που κατοικεις
"I know your works and where you dwell"
Maj syr[h**]
KJV NKJV HCSBmg NETmg

The documentary evidence for the WH NU reading is early (ℵ A C) and diverse (note the early versions). This reading is followed by all modern English versions. As was mentioned in the previous note, scribes could not resist making all of Jesus' opening statements begin with the same formulaic statement, "I know your works." This expansion is in TR (so KJV and NKJV).

Revelation 2:15

WH NU ὁμοίως
"likewise"
א A C P
NKJVmg RSV NRSV ESV NASB NIV TNIV NEB REB NJB NAB NLT HCSB NET

variant/TR ο μισω
"which I hate"
Maj[A]
KJV NKJV

The last word of this verse is contested, producing either the rendering, "so you also have ones holding the teaching of the Nicolaitans likewise" (as in WH NU) or "so you also have ones holding the teaching of the Nicolaitans, which I hate" (the variant and TR). The variant reading displays conformity to 2:6, where Jesus said "I hate" the works of the Nicolaitans (a proto-gnostic group who syncretized pagan practices of idolatry with Christianity). The reading, though appearing only in manuscripts agreeing with the commentary of Andreas, was adopted in TR and popularized by KJV and NKJV.

Revelation 2:20a

WH NU ἔχω κατὰ σοῦ
"I have [this] against you"
A C P 2344
NKJVmg RSV NRSV ESV NASB NIV TNIV NEB REB NJB NAB NLT HCSB NET

variant 1 εχω κατα σου πολυ
"I have much against you"
א Maj[A] (it) syr[ph]
none

variant 2/TR εχω κατα σου ολιγα
"I have a few things against you"
vg[cl]
KJV NKJV

The absence of a direct object seems to leave a gap in the grammatical structure of the sentence. Various scribes filled the perceived gap by adding "much" or "a few things." The latter change, influenced by 2:14, does not appear in any Greek manuscripts; nevertheless, it found its way into TR and KJV (also NKJV).

Revelation 2:20b

Good manuscript support upholds the reading αφεις την γυναικα Ιεζαβελ ("you permit the woman Jezebel")—so א C P 2053 it cop. Other witnesses (A Maj[K] syr) add σου after γυναικα, yielding the reading, "you permit your wife Jezebel." This variant reading is unusual in that one can understand the "you" not to be the church in Thyatira but a human messenger of the church in Thyatira (2:18)—perhaps the leader of that church (see TCGNT)—and not an angel. (This could mean that the other "messengers" in chapters 2–3 were also human leaders, not angels.) As such, this leader was being rebuked for allowing his wife to teach in the assembly, because it is through teaching that one asserts authority over others. However, the word σου was probably inserted accidentally under the influence of σου appearing four times in the preceding words (2:19-20a). Thus, since this was probably not the leader's wife, it must have been some other woman whose actions resembled the wicked Jezebel, who had promoted idolatry throughout all Israel (cf. 1 Kgs 16:31-33; 2 Kgs 9:22). Whoever the woman in Thyatira was, she was to stop teaching.

Revelation 2:21

WH NU ἵνα μετανοήσῃ, καὶ οὐ θέλει μετανοῆσαι ἐκ τῆς πορνείας αὐτῆς
"that she might repent, and she did not want to repent of her fornication"
ℵ[c] A C Maj 2053 (ℵ* omits και θελει μετανοησαι, which was then corrected)
RSV NRSV ESV NASB NIV TNIV NEB REB NJB NAB (NLT) HCSB NET

variant/TR ινα μετανοηση εκ της πορνειας αυτης, και ου μετενοησεν
"that she might repent of her fornication, and she did not repent"
1 arm
KJV NKJV

The WH NU reading, which has the support of all known Greek manuscripts except the minuscule 1 (used by Erasmus), has a stronger message than the variant does in that it charges that Jezebel did not even want to repent of her fornication.

Revelation 2:22a

TR WH NU κλίνην
"bed"
ℵ C P 046 2053 2344 Maj syr[ph,h] cop[bo]
KJV NKJV RSV NRSV ESV (NASB) NIV (TNIV) NEB REB NJB NAB (NLT) HCSB (NET)

variant 1 κλιβανον
"furnace"
arm
NEBmg

variant 2 φυλακην
"prison"
A
none

variant 3 ασθενειαν
"sickness"
cop[sa]
none

variant 4 *luctum*
"sorrow"
MSS[according to Primasius]
none

As punishment to the woman, Jesus declares that he will cast her (and those who commit adultery with her) into "bed." Evidently, this language (with extremely good textual support) is an idiom for sickness (Louw and Nida 23.152). Various scribes and ancient translators did not think the term "bed" was sufficiently clear in denoting a place of punishment—thereby prompting various variants, the most creative of which is "furnace" (noted in NEBmg). Various English translators add some notion of sickness to clarify that it was a sickbed. For example, NASB calls it a "bed of sickness," while HCSB calls it a "sickbed" and NET has the colorful expression, "bed of violent illness." The change made by the scribe of A was probably influenced by 2:10.

Revelation 2:22b

WH NU — τῶν ἔργων αὐτῆς
"her deeds"
א C P 046 2053 Maj^K
NKJVmg RSV NRSV ESV NASB NIV TNIV NEB REB (NJBmg) NAB NLT HCSB NET

variant/TR — των εργων αυτων
"their deeds"
A 2344 Maj^A syr
KJV NKJV NASBmg NJB HCSBmg

WH NU present the followers of Jezebel as co-participants in her evil deeds—"unless they repent of her deeds." The variant isolates their actions from hers—"unless they repent of their deeds." But the WH NU reading, which has excellent documentation, views the church as being culpable for having participated in her evil deeds. (A similar scenario can be found in 1 Cor 5, where Paul blames the entire church in Corinth for the sexual misconduct of one man.) Most modern versions, except NJB, follow the WH NU reading, while—per course—KJV and NKJV follow TR. NJB has an error in its margin, in that it lists the same reading as a variant ("their practices") which had already been accepted for the text. Presumably, the NJB margin should read, "var. *her practices.*" NASB notes that one early manuscript (presumably Codex A) reads, "their deeds."

Revelation 3:2

WH NU — ἐνώπιον τοῦ θεοῦ μου
"in the sight of my God"
א A C Maj^K
NKJVmg RSV NRSV ESV NASB NIV TNIV NEB REB NJB NAB NLT HCSB NET

variant/TR — ενωπιον του θεου
"in the sight of God"
Maj^A syr^{ph}
KJV NKJV

A full rendering of the WH NU reading is, "strengthen the things that are about to die, for I [Jesus] have not found your works perfected in the sight of my God." The WH NU reading has strong manuscript support, especially from א A C; this reading is followed by all modern versions. The change in the variant was probably not accidental. Rather, it reflects a scribal redaction that attempts to avoid the theological problem inherent in Jesus (who is God) saying "my God." Of course, when one understands that the Son of God took a subservient position to God the Father in order to become the incarnate Christ (see Phil 2:5-6), there is no problem understanding how Jesus still calls the Father "my God." He did so on the cross (see Mark 15:34), after his resurrection (see John 20:17), and still does so in his exaltation.

Revelation 3:5

WH NU ὁ νικῶν οὕτως περιβαλεῖται ἐν ἱματίοις λευκοῖς
"the one overcoming, in similar manner, will be dressed in white garments"
ℵ* A C 2344 it syr cop
RSV NRSV ESV NASB NIV TNIV NEB REB NJB NAB NLT HCSB NET

variant/TR ο νικων ουτος περιβαλειται εν ιματιοις λευκοις
"the one overcoming, this one will be dressed in white garments"
ℵ[1] 2053 Maj
(KJV NKJV)

The two words in the readings could have easily been confused for each other because there is but a one-letter difference: ουτως/ουτος. Since the WH NU reading has superior documentation, it is generally regarded as original. This reading could indicate that the person who becomes an overcomer (a conqueror) will receive the same reward as those in Sardis who had already shown their purity and were promised a white garment as a reward (see 3:4).

Revelation 3:8

WH NU θύραν ἠνεῳγμένην, ἣν οὐδεὶς δύναται κλεῖσαι αὐτήν
"an open door, which no one is able to shut it"
A C 2053 Maj
none

variant 1 θυραν ηνεωγμενην, ην ουδεις δυναται κλεισαι
"an open door, which no one is able to shut"
ℵ 1006[c]
RSV NRSV ESV NASB NIV TNIV NEB REB NJB NAB NLT HCSB NET

variant 2/TR θυραν ηνεωγμενην, και ουδεις δυναται κλεισαι αυτην
"an open door, and no one is able to shut it"
1611
KJV NKJV

The WH NU reading has the support of A and C, two good witnesses in Revelation. Added to this is the fact that this reading is most difficult in that it has awkward grammar produced by the final word αυτην. This prompted two different corrections, as displayed above. TR solves the problem by changing ην to και—so KJV and NKJV. Modern English versions fix the grammar, as well, and thereby concur with the first variant.

Revelation 3:11

WH NU ἔρχομαι ταχύ
"I am coming quickly"
𝔓[115vid] ℵ A C Maj
NKJVmg RSV NRSV ESV NASB NIV TNIV NEB REB NJB NAB NLT HCSB NET

variant/TR Ιδου ερχομαι ταχυ
"Look, I am coming quickly"
2014
KJV NKJV

The insertion of ιδου ("look") was probably influenced by 1:7; it became popularized by its presence in TR and KJV. The WH NU reading has strong support, with 𝔓[115] (third century) supplying the earliest.

Revelation 3:14

WH NU τῷ ἀγγέλῳ τῆς ἐν Λαοδικείᾳ ἐκκλησίας
"to the messenger of the church in Laodicea"
א A C Maj
NKJVmg RSV NRSV ESV NASB NIV TNIV NEB REB NJB NAB NLT HCSB NET

variant/TR τω αγγελω της εκκλησιας Λαοδικεων
"to the messenger of the church of [the] Laodiceans"
1
KJV NKJV

All throughout chapters 2 and 3, the churches are designated by the formula "the church in" followed by the name of the locality ("the church in Ephesus," "the church in Smyrna," etc.). Thus, it would be highly unusual for there to be a change here whereby the church is named by the inhabitants of the city, "the church of the Laodiceans." Only one cursive, the minuscule 1 (used by Erasmus, listed by Alford and Tregelles) displays this change, which may have been influenced by verses such as 1 Thess 1:1; 2 Thess 1:1 ("the church of the Thessalonians"). This reading became popularized by TR and KJV.

Revelation 3:15

Codex A and 1006 omit the sentence οφελον ψυχρος ης η ζεστος ("I wish that you were cold or hot"). The omission was probably accidental—due to parablepsis and homoeoteleuton (the previous sentence ends with the same word, ζεστος). The scribe of Codex Alexandrinus may have been suffering from fatigue when he copied Revelation, because he made several omissions due to homoeoteleuton (see, for example, notes on 4:11b; 5:4a; 10:6a; 18:2; 22:11).

Revelation 4:3

The Majority Text (Maj) omits the first three words of 4:3, και ο καθημενος ("and the one sitting"). Strong testimony affirms their inclusion: א A P 046 0169 it syr cop. The Majority Text reading (not adopted by TR but noted in NKJVmg) is likely the result of parablepsis due to homoeoteleuton—the eye of a scribe passing from the first καθημενος in 4:2 to the second in 4:3. This change alters the meaning inasmuch as the description in 4:3 ("like in appearance to a jasper and carnelian stone") could be understood to be describing the throne, not the one sitting upon the throne.

Revelation 4:5

TR WH NU τὰ ἑπτὰ πνεύματα τοῦ θεοῦ
"the seven Spirits of God"
א A C Maj[A]
all

variant ⠀⠀ επτα πνευματα του θεου
"seven spirits of God"
1006 2344 Maj[K]
NKJVmg

The change in the variant is slight (the omission of an article) but significant because it conveys the thought that each of the seven lamps of fire represent a spirit ("the seven lamps burning before the throne, which are seven spirits of God"). In contrast, the TR WH NU reading conveys the idea that the seven lamps (as a unit) symbolize "the sevenfold Spirit of God" (as in NLT; see also NIVmg TNIVmg).

Revelation 4:8

According to most manuscripts, the chant of the four living creatures begins with the triad expression Αγιος αγιος αγιος ("Holy, holy, holy"). The Majority Text (Maj[K]) triples this (αγιος nine times—noted in NKJVmg), and ℵ* has αγιος eight times. The multiplication of this expression enhances the oral/aural effect.

Revelation 4:10

The idiom τους αιωνας των αιωνων ("the ages of the ages" = "forever and ever") habitually attracted the scribal addition of αμην ("amen"). In this case, the scribes of ℵ and 2329, as well as a couple of ancient translators (it[t] syr[ph]), added the final "amen" (see note on 15:7).

Revelation 4:11a

WH NU ⠀⠀ ὁ κύριος καὶ ὁ θεὸς ἡμῶν
"our Lord and God"
A (046*) syr
NKJVmg RSV NRSV ESV NASB NIV TNIV (NEB REB) NJB (NAB NLT) HCSB NET

variant 1 ⠀⠀ κυριε, ο κυριος και θεος ημων
"O Lord, our Lord and God"
ℵ
none

variant 2/TR ⠀⠀ κυριε
"O Lord"
1854 Maj[A] syr[h]
KJV NKJV HCSBmg

variant 3 ⠀⠀ ο κυριος και θεος ημων, ο αγιος
"our Lord and God, the Holy One"
1006 2351 Maj[K]
HCSBmg

Divine titles were rarely left alone in the process of textual transmission. This verse is no exception. Because the tendency was for scribes to expand titles, it could be argued that the shortest reading (in TR) is original. But this reading is suspect because it has poor manuscript support and because it looks as if scribes were troubled by a nominative being used in direct address and therefore substituted (or inserted—as in ℵ) the vocative, κυριε (usually translated as "O Lord"). NEB, REB, and NLT, though following the WH NU reading, also used the vocative, "O Lord our God." The addition of "the Holy One" was probably influenced by 3:7; 4:8; and 6:10.

Revelation 4:11b

WH NU ἦσαν καὶ ἐκτίσθησαν
"they existed and were created"
א 205 209 2053 MSS[according to Primasius]
NKJVmg RSV NRSV ESV NASB NEB REB NAB NET

variant 1 ουκ ησαν και εκτισθησαν
"they did not exist and were created"
046
NJB NETmg

variant 2/TR εισιν και εκτισθησαν
"they exist and were created"
P 1854 2050 2344 Maj[A] cop[sa]
KJV NKJV (NIV TNIV NLT) HCSB NETmg

variant 3 ησαν
"they existed"
A
NETmg

variant 4 εγενοντο
"they came into being"
2329
NETmg

The WH NU reading speaks of all created beings as having existed and having been created. To our way of thinking, this seems to not be chronological: Creation produces existence. But here it says that existence precedes creation. This could mean that creatures existed—as in the mind of God or as spirits—before they were actually physically created. Or the statement could be two ways of saying the same thing (the και being epexegetical): All creatures came into existence when they were created. However we interpret the WH NU reading, this wording troubled some scribes. One scribe (046) made the text say that the creatures did not exist until they were created (variant 1—so NJB). Other scribes made it clear that all creatures presently exist because they were created (variant 2). Several modern English versions went this way, as well—obviously for the sake of clarity; the textual evidence is not in their favor. The third variant is probably the result of parablepsis due to homoeoteleuton—after reading ησαν, the scribe of A passed over και εκτισθησαν (the last four letters also being ησαν). The fourth variant is obviously an attempt to simplify matters.

Revelation 5:1

TR WH NU βιβλίον γεγραμμένον ἔσωθεν καὶ ὄπισθεν
"a book written inside and back"
A 1 69 2344 syr[h]
KJV NKJV RSV NRSV ESV NASB NIV HCSB (NET)

variant 1 βιβλιον γεγραμμενον εσωθεν και εξωθεν
"a book written inside and outside"
Maj it syr[ph] cop[bo]
NEB (NAB NLT)

variant 2 βιβλιον γεγραμμενον εμπροσθεν και οπισθεν
"a book written front and back"
ℵ cop[sa] Origen
(TNIV REB NJB)

The textual differences here probably reflect different scribes' perspectives on the precise form of this "book" (βιβλιος)—a scroll or a codex? Most scholars have thought this book was a scroll, but it is just as likely that it was a codex—for three reasons: (1) The book is said to be located "on" (Greek, επι) God's right hand. This suggests a codex far more than a scroll, which would be grasped "in" (Greek, εν) one's hand. (2) The book is said to have writing on the inside and on the outside. Some scrolls did have writing on both sides; called opisthographs, they were usually private, nonsaleable documents, whereas scrolls with writing only on the inside were more official and valuable (Thompson 1912, 49-50). It is possible that the book in the right hand of God was an opisthograph; if so, scholars suggest that it connotes the fullness of the revelation. However, the codex form suits writing on both sides perfectly; in fact, that is what a codex was designed for. (3) A scroll hardly suits the scenario in which one broken seal after another (up to seven seals; see 6:1, 3, 5, 7, 9, 12; 8:1) reveals one revelation after another when each seal is broken (see Johnson 1981, 465; Comfort 2005, 27-30).

How, then, do the textual variants inform our view as to what form of book Jesus took from the right hand of God? The TR WH NU reading, with the wording "written on the inside and back," could indicate a codex or a scroll. The first variant, with the wording "written on the inside and outside," could also indicate a codex or a scroll. The wording of the second variant ("written on the front and back") probably denotes a codex, because this book form, by design, has a front and back.

Revelation 5:3

A few manuscripts (ℵ 1854 2344) omit ουδε υποκατω της γης ("neither under the earth"). The omission may have been accidental due to homoeoteleuton—the previous phrase ends with the same two words (ουδε επι της γης). It is also likely that the omission was intentional because the same manuscripts omit the same phrase in 5:13 (see note).

Revelation 5:4a

A few scribes (A 1854 2050 2329) omitted the entire verse accidentally—due to parablepsis caused by homoeoteleuton. The previous verse ends with exactly the same last six words as does 5:4 (ανοιξαι το βιβλιον ουτε βλεπειν αυτο).

Revelation 5:4b

WH NU ἀνοῖξαι τὸ βιβλίον οὔτε βλέπειν αὐτό
"to open the book or to look into it"
ℵ 046 2053 2344
NKJVmg RSV NRSV ESV NASB NIV TNIV NEB REB (NJB) NAB (NLT) HCSB NET

variant/TR ανοιξαι και αναγνωναι το βιβλιον ουτε βλεπειν αυτο
"to open and to read the book or to look into it"
1 2050
KJV NKJV HCSBmg

The addition is the product of scribal gap-filling—that opening a book should be followed by reading it. NJB and NLT use only two verbs, thereby following the WH NU reading, but the two verbs are "open" and "read" (this verb substituting for "look").

Revelation 5:5

WH NU ἀνοῖξαι τὸ βιβλίον καὶ τὰς ἑπτὰ σφραγῖδας αὐτοῦ
"to open the book and its seven seals"
A 2053 2062 Maj
NKJVmg RSV NRSV ESV NASB NIV TNIV REB NJB NAB HCSB NET

variant/TR ανοιξαι το βιβλιον και λυσαι τας επτα σφραγιδας αυτου
"to open the book and to break its seven seals"
א 2344 syr[ph]
KJV NKJV NEB NLT HCSBmg

Since the manuscript evidence is almost evenly divided here, we need to look at internal factors. On one hand, it could be argued that λυσαι ("to break") was added by scribes to help readers understand that a book cannot be opened until the seals are broken. (As such, the opening is seen as the result of the breaking—as in our modern idiom, "breaking open.") However, it could be argued that λυσαι was deleted because John was consistent in saying that Jesus "opened" each of the seven seals (see 6:1, 3, 5, 7, 9, 12; 8:1)—without ever mentioning that he also "broke" the seals. Therefore, we cannot be certain of the original text here, though textual critics would be more inclined to favor the shorter reading.

Revelation 5:6

TR WH NU τὰ [ἑπτὰ] πνεύματα τοῦ θεοῦ
"the seven Spirits of God"
𝔓[24] א 2053 2344 Maj[K] it syr
all

variant τα πνευματα του θεου
"the Spirits of God"
A Maj[A] vg
ASVmg

The word "seven" (επτα) has been bracketed in WH and in NU. The NU editors could not determine if certain copyists borrowed the word from 1:4, 3:1, or 4:5, or if other copyists accidentally dropped the word επτα ("seven") after having just written the same word twice (see TCGNT). All translators, however, have followed the TR WH NU reading.

It is instructive to note that the scribe of 𝔓[24] wrote the Greek expression for "the seven Spirits of God" as $\overline{\text{Z}}$ $\overline{\text{ΠΝΑ}}$ ΤΟΥ $\overline{\text{ΘΥ}}$ (with an overbar over all the words except του). By writing this expression as a nomen sacrum, the scribe of 𝔓[24] was indicating that he considered it to signify the divine Spirit. By contrast, several English translators have been hesitant to identify τα επτα πνευματα here with the divine Spirit. This is reflected in translations which render the expression in the lower case: "the seven spirits" (see RSV ESV NIV TNIV NEB HCSB), which would communicate to many readers that these spirits are angels (see note in NET). But how could τα επτα πνευματα ("the seven Spirits"), listed with the Father and the Son in 1:4-5 and identified with the Lord Jesus in 3:1 and 4:5, be anything other than the divine Spirit of God? Evidently, the scribe of 𝔓[24] thought this, or he would not have written the entire expression as a nomen sacrum. Other translators (see ASV NASB NJB) considered the title to be a description of the divine Spirit and therefore rendered it with a capital letter—"the seven Spirits." An ingenious way of rendering this title is found in NLT: "the sevenfold Spirit of God" (also noted in NIVmg TNIVmg). Many scholars would affirm that this is what the title means—God's one divine Spirit is called "seven" (a number symbolizing fullness) to express its full supply to the seven churches, inasmuch as the seven horns and seven eyes of the Lamb are the seven Spirits (or, the sevenfold Spirit) sent out to all the churches.

Revelation 5:9

WH NU — ἠγόρασας τῷ θεῷ ἐν τῷ αἵματί σου
"made a purchase for God with your blood"
$\mathfrak{P}^{115vid}$ A eth
KJV NKJV RSV (NRSV ESV) NASB (NIV TNIV) NEB REB NAB (NLT HCSB NET)

variant 1 — ηγορασας ημας εν τω αιματι σου
"purchased us with your blood"
1 2065*
NJB

variant 2/TR — ηγορασας τω θεω ημας εν τω αιματι σου
"purchased us for God with your blood"
א 2050 2344 Maj it
HCSBmg

While conceding that the evidence for the WH NU reading is slim (A eth), Metzger (TCGNT) argued for it on the basis that the absence of a direct object after the verb ηγορασας ("purchased") would have prompted scribes to add a direct object—either before or after the indirect object. Most English translators also supplied a direct object—often the word "people." The NU committee made this decision (as did WH) before the publication of $\mathfrak{P}^{115}$, which lends further support for this reading. Though there are lacunae in this verse, a reconstruction of the text, given acceptable margins, shows that the manuscript would not have included a direct object either before or after the verb ηγορασας (see *Text of Earliest MSS*, 667).

Revelation 5:10a

WH NU — βασιλείαν καὶ ἱερεῖς
"kingdom and priests"
A syr^{ph,hmg} cop
NKJVmg RSV NRSV ESV NASB NIV TNIV NEB REB NAB NLT HCSB NET

variant 1/TR — βασιλεις και ιερεις
"kings and priests"
it^{gig} vg^{cl}
KJV NKJV HCSBmg

variant 2 — βασιλειαν και ιερατειαν
"kingdom and priesthood"
א 2344
(NJB)

The same kind of textual changes occurred in 1:6a (see note). The first two variants are scribal attempts to make the direct objects parallel in construction. The wording in TR, popularized by

KJV, says that the believers are "kings and priests." Although this reads nicely, it misses the point that the priests, considered collectively, constitute God's kingdom (see Exod 19:6; 1 Pet 2:9).

Revelation 5:10b

NU — βασιλεύσουσιν ἐπὶ τῆς γῆς
"they will reign on the earth"
ℵ P 1 2053 2344 Maj[A] it cop
NKJVmg RSV NRSV ESV NASB NIV TNIV NEB REB NJB NAB NLT HCSB NET

variant 1/WH — βασιλευουσιν επι της γης
"they reign on the earth"
A 046 Maj[K]
TNIVmg NLTmg NETmg

variant 2/TR — βασιλευσομεν επι της γης
"we will reign on the earth"
2432 vg[cl]
KJV NKJV

There is only a one-letter difference between the NU reading and the first variant: a *sigma* in the verb, differentiating the future tense from the present tense. The tense change is significant, for the NU reading makes the prophetic prediction that God's people *will* eventually reign as kings on earth, while the variant makes this a present reality. The full reading of 5:10, according to NU, indicates that God has made his people a kingdom and priests (or, a kingdom of priests), and they will reign on the earth. The first variant (in WH) in 5:10b, taken together with 5:10a, indicates that God has made his people a kingdom of priests, and they are presently reigning on earth. This reading, presenting realized eschatology, has good support and is the more difficult reading. The second variant (in TR), with no Greek manuscript support, is a carryover from the change in 5:9.

Revelation 5:13

Several manuscripts (ℵ 1854 2050 2053 2329 2344) omit και υποκατω της γης ("and under the earth"). The omission may have been accidental due to homoeoteleuton—the previous phrase ends with the same two words (και επι της γης). But it is more likely that the omission was intentional, because several of the same scribes (ℵ 1854 2344) made the same omission in 5:3 (see note). It is possible that these scribes took exception to the idea that any subterranean being would even have the potential of opening up the book.

Revelation 6:1, 3, 5, 7

WH NU — ἔρχου
"come"
(𝔓[115]) A C 2053
RSV NRSV ESV NASB NIV TNIV NEB REB NJB NAB NLT HCSB NET

variant/TR — ερχου και ιδε
"come and see"
ℵ 2344 Maj[K] it syr[h**]
KJV NKJV HCSBmg NETmg

In 6:5, 𝔓[115] clearly supports the WH NU reading. Though 6:1, 3, and 7 are not extant in 𝔓[115], it would presumably support the WH NU reading in all these verses, because this is a formulaic statement. The extra verbiage in the variant is intended to identify John (ιδε is second person singular) as the direct object of the angel's command in all four verses (6:1, 3, 5, 7). But this is made explicit in the surrounding context, especially in the following words, και ειδον ("and I saw"), which appear in 6:2, 5, 8 (but see next note). It is also possible that the verb "come" is directed to each of the horsemen (so NETmg).

Revelation 6:2, 5, 8

Several witnesses do not include the words και ειδον ("and I saw") in these verses. In Maj[K] the words are omitted in all three verses; other manuscripts (1859 2329 2351 it[a]) omit the words in two of the three verses. However, the usually reliable witnesses (ℵ A C) include the words in all three places. In their respective extant portions, 𝔓[115] includes the words in 6:5, and 𝔓[24] includes the words in 6:8. Thus, the omission is probably secondary—either the result of haplography (the eye of a scribe passing from one και to the next: και ειδον και ιδου) or purposeful editorial trimming.

Revelation 6:9

Most manuscripts describe the souls underneath the altar as those who died "because of the word of God and the testimony which they held" (δια τον λογον του θεου και δια την μαρτυριαν ην ειχον). Some scribes (1611[c] 2351 Maj[K]) and one ancient translator (syr[h**]), deciding to specify this testimony, added του αρνιου ("of the Lamb"). In these manuscripts, it is made clear that these people were martyred because of their avowed allegiance to the Lamb, Jesus Christ (see 1:9; 12:11, 17; 19:10; 20:4). The nonspecificity of the TR WH NU reading concerning the testimony allows the reader to fill in the gap—undoubtedly imagining some kind of verbal confession of their faith in Jesus that brought about their martyrdom.

Revelation 6:13

Instead of the reading, οι αστερες του ουρανου ("the stars of heaven" = "the stars of the sky"), Codex Alexandrinus alone reads οι αστερες του θεου ("the stars of God"). This could have been a scribal error—mistaking ουρανου for θεου, but this seems unlikely inasmuch as θεου was always written in A in a unique format as a nomen sacrum ($\overline{\Theta\Upsilon}$). Thus, the scribe of A may have wanted to communicate that "the stars of God" falling from earth were evil supernatural beings (perhaps fallen angels) bringing supernatural calamities on the earth. Perhaps the scribe wanted to associate these "stars" with the star mentioned in 9:1 (i.e., the star who opens the abyss), which some commentators understand to be an angel (Johnson 1981, 492).

Revelation 6:15

WH NU οἱ χιλίαρχοι καὶ οἱ πλούσιοι καὶ οἱ ἰσχυροί
"the chiliarchs [= commanders] and the wealthy and the strong"
ℵ A C
NKJVmg RSV NRSV ESV NASB NIV TNIV NEB REB NJB NAB NLT HCSB NET

variant/TR οι πλουσιοι και οι χιλιαρχοι και οι δυνατοι
"the wealthy and the chiliarchs [= commanders] and the powerful"
Maj[A]
KJV NKJV

The syntactical change and slight lexical change (δυνατοι for ισχυροι) in TR barely alters the meaning of this verse, for both readings indicate that those who will suffer most are the high and the mighty. However, TR's change from ισχυροι to δυνατοι does not find support in any manuscript.

Revelation 6:17

WH NU τῆς ὀργῆς αὐτῶν
"their wrath"
ℵ C 2053 2344 it syr
RSV NRSV ESV NASB NIV TNIV NEB REB NJBmg NAB NLT HCSB NET

variant/TR της οργης αυτου
"his wrath"
A Maj cop
KJV NKJV TNIVmg NJB HCSBmg NETmg

The WH NU reading, which in context reads "the great day of their wrath has come," has better attestation than does the variant. Nonetheless, both readings can be explained as scribal redactions. Some scribes might think the WH NU reading would be speaking only of the Lamb's wrath coming on the earth; so they changed "their" to "his." Other scribes may have thought it odd that a singular genitive would be used with reference to two people, God and the Lamb—thereby prompting a change to the plural. Most modern English versions favor the WH NU reading, while some have noted the variant; NJB alone of the modern versions follows the variant.

Revelation 7:1

Codex Alexandrinus omits επι της γης ("upon the earth"). Since this is the third occurrence of this phrase in this verse, the omission was probably a transcriptional oversight.

Revelation 7:4

Codex Alexandrinus omits και ηκουσα τον αριθμον των εσφραγισμενων ("and I heard the number of the ones being sealed"). It is difficult to say why the scribe omitted this clause. There is no easy way to explain it as a transcriptional error or as a purposeful deletion. What is there to be gained by omitting this sentence? Thus, the only explanation is that the scribe of A seems to have been fatigued when he copied Revelation, for he made a number of omissions, including this one. (There are three significant omissions in Codex A just in this small chapter—see notes also on 7:1 and 7:12.)

Revelation 7:5-8

WH NU ἐσφραγισμένοι ("were sealed") appearing only twice—at the end of 7:5 and the end of 7:8
ℵ A C P
NKJVmg RSV NRSV ESV NASB NIV TNIV NEB REB NJB NAB NLT HCSB NET

variant/TR εσφραγισμενοι ("were sealed") appearing twelve times—at the end of each phrase from 7:5 to 7:8
1 vg
KJV NKJV HCSBmg

Erasmus followed an inferior codex (minuscule 1), according to Tregelles and Alford, in adding the word εσφραγισμενοι ("were sealed") after each name in the list of the twelve tribes. These additions have been perpetuated in the TR tradition as translated in KJV and NKJV, and noted in HCSB for KJV-friendly readers. According to the best manuscript evidence (namely א A C), the word appears twice—at the end of the first tribe (Judas) and the last tribe (Benjamin).

Revelation 7:7

א omits εκ φυλης Συμεων δωδεκα χιλιαδες ("of the tribe of Simeon, twelve thousand"). Since all the previous and following lines begin and end with the same words, it is easy to see how the scribe could have accidentally left out an entire line. But it is also possible that the scribe of א omitted the tribe of Simeon for the same reason the tribe was not included in the lists in Deut 33 and Judg 5—namely, his participation in the massacre of the men of Shechem following Dinah's rape and his participation in selling Joseph into slavery. But this omission leaves the list at only eleven tribes, which would make the total number 12,000 less than the 144,000 (see 7:4). This error was not amended by any of the correctors of א.

Revelation 7:10

At the end of the verse, א* adds εις τους αιωνας των αιωνων αμην ("into the ages of the ages, amen"). The addition is probably a scribal attempt to achieve parallelism with the praise recorded in 7:12, which ends with these very same words ("into the ages of the ages, amen"). A corrector of א subsequently deleted it.

Revelation 7:12

Codex Alexandrinus and it[t] omit και η σοφια ("and the wisdom")—either due to homoeoteleuton (the surrounding nouns end with α or ια) or to stylistic trimming. C and it[t] omit the final αμην, but א A P 046 2053 2344 syr cop include it. Therefore, though it is tempting to say that the final "amen" was a liturgical addition (as so often happened in the NT text), the textual evidence will not permit this judgment.

Revelation 7:14

WH NU κύριε μου, σὺ οἶδας
"my lord, you know"
א C 1611[c]
NKJVmg NASB NEB REB NAB (HCSB) NET

variant/TR κυριε, συ οιδας
"sir, you know"
A 1611*
KJV NKJV RSV NRSV ESV NIV TNIV NJB NLT

In context, John was responding to an elder who had asked him if he recognized the ones dressed in white. When John replies, he calls him κυριε. This can be interpreted to mean

"Lord" (as one who is divine), or as "lord" or "sir" (both terms of respect). Since the manuscript evidence slightly favors the WH NU reading, the textual variant may reflect scribal interpretation concerning John's attitude toward the one he was addressing. Since "the elder" was not "the Lord," to call him such may have been deemed inappropriate by various scribes and translators. Omission of μου seems to move the interpretation towards "sir" and not "lord" or "Lord" because "my Lord" is occasionally used in the NT in reference to deity (see John 20:28; Acts 2:34).

If we accept that the WH NU reading is original and signifies a divine "Lord," it leads us to the interpretation that John perceived all communications coming to him from the heavens, whether from angels or elders or Jesus or God, as being divine. In truth, it is even difficult for us, the readers, to distinguish the voices in the Apocalypse. Much more so for John, who was overwhelmed with a kaleidoscope of divine revelations. This is why, in one instance, John began to worship an angel, but he was prevented and then directed to worship Jesus instead (see 19:10).

However, not one English version uses the divine title, "Lord." The versions that follow WH NU read "my lord," and all of the English versions that follow the variant use the translation "sir." By contrast, the word κυριε is written as a nomen sacrum in ℵ, signifying a divine title.

Revelation 7:17

WH NU read ζωης πηγας υδατων, which is rendered as "fountains of living water." This has the support of three of the best witnesses in Revelation (ℵ A C). TR reads ζωσας πηγας υδατων ("living fountains of waters"). This is the reading in 2329 2344 and other MSS, which substitute the feminine participle ζωσας for the noun ζωης. This changes the reading from "fountains of waters of life" to "living fountains of waters." The change is smoother stylistically in Greek but takes the emphasis away from the primary word, ζωης ("life"). Consistent with the message of the Gospel of John, the book of Revelation also affirms that Christ had come to give ζωης ("divine life") to his believers (see 2:7; 21:6; 22:1-2, 14, 17, 19).

Revelation 8:7a

TR, with the support of 2329 Maj[A], adds αγγελος ("angel") after ο πρωτος ("the first"). This is a natural gloss, inserted by ancient translators (it cop[bo,sa]) and modern English translators (for example, see NRSV NIV NLT).

Revelation 8:7b

WH NU	include καὶ τὸ τρίτον τῶν δένδρων κατεκάη "and a third of the trees was burned up" 𝔓[115vid] ℵ A C 046[c] NKJVmg RSV NRSV ESV NASB NIV TNIV NEB REB NJB NAB NLT HCSB NET
variant/TR	omit 046* (2053) cop[sa] KJV NKJV

Though listed as "vid," 𝔓[115] must have contained this clause (see *Text of Earliest MSS,* 667), adding the earliest support to the WH NU reading. The omission of the clause was very likely accidental (note that 046 was corrected)—the result of three clauses ending with the same word, κατεκαη ("was burned up")— "and a third part of the earth was burned up [κατεκαη], and a third of the trees was burned up [κατεκαη], and a third of the grass was burned up [κατεκαη]." The truncated text was printed in TR and has been perpetuated by KJV and NKJV.

Revelation 8:10

The scribe of Codex Alexandrinus omitted the last phrase of this verse: και επι τας πηγας των υδατων ("and upon the springs of waters"). Again, the omission was probably accidental—due to homoeoteleuton. The previous phrase ends with a similar-looking word, ποταμων ("rivers").

Revelation 8:13

WH NU	ἀετοῦ "eagle" 𝔓115 א A 046 it syr cop NKJVmg RSV NRSV ESV NASB NIV TNIV NEB REB NJB NAB NLT HCSB NET
variant/TR	αγγελου "angel" P 1 Maj^A KJV NKJV HCSBmg NETmg

The difference between the readings is significant: Either John "heard one eagle flying in mid-air" or he "heard one angel flying in mid-air." The evidence strongly favors the WH NU reading, which has the support of 𝔓115 (not listed in NA27 or UBS4). The variant could be the result of a scribal mistake—confusing αετου for αγγελου—inasmuch as αγγελος appears eight other times in the same chapter. But it is just as likely that some scribe(s) changed "eagle" to "angel" because it seemed more appropriate that an angel would be making a proclamation of things to come, as happens in 14:6 (TCGNT).

The change in TR means that there are eight angels involved with the divine unveiling of events to come. This is inconsistent with the numerical coding in the book of Revelation, which typically has sevens, twelves, or their multiples.

Revelation 9:2

The opening clause of this verse is not present in several witnesses (א 1611 2053 Maj^K vg^MSS syr^ph cop): και ηνοιξεν το φρεαρ της αβυσσου ("and he opened the shaft of the abyss"). Most likely the clause was accidentally dropped due to homoeoteleuton—the previous clause ends with the same two words (της αβυσσου). The presence of this clause in 𝔓115vid A P 0207 provides the documentary evidence for its inclusion.

Revelation 9:11

Instead of the name Αβαδδων ("Abaddon"), found in most witnesses, 𝔓47 reads βαττων, a Coptic Sahidic translation of the same name.

Revelation 9:12-13a

(TR) WH NU — ἔρχεται ἔτι δύο οὐαὶ μετὰ ταῦτα. 13 Καὶ ὁ ἕκτος ἄγγελος ἐσάλπισεν
"two woes are yet coming after these things. 13 And the sixth angel trumpeted"
A P 1 1611 Maj[A] it syr[h]
all

variant 1 — ερχεται ετι δυο ουαι. 13 Μετα ταυτα ο εκτος αγγελος εσαλπισεν
"two woes are yet coming. 13 After these things the sixth angel trumpeted"
𝔓[47] ℵ 2344 syr[ph] cop
none

variant 2 — ερχεται ετι δυο ουαι. 13 Μετα ταυτα και ο εκτος αγγελος εσαλπισεν
"two woes are yet coming. 13 After these things also the sixth angel trumpeted"
(0207 μετα δε ταυτα και) (046) 1006 Maj[K]
none

Though it is difficult to determine which reading is original, the first variant appears to be the most likely candidate on the basis of superior textual support and Johannine style. The combination of 𝔓[47] ℵ 2344 syr[ph] cop is weighty, as well as the fact that 0207 046 also begin 9:13 with μετα ταυτα. Furthermore, John was more inclined to begin sequential statements with the phrase μετα ταυτα ("after these things") than to end with it. Whereas only two sentences end with μετα ταυτα (1:19; 4:1), seven sentences begin with it or with μετα τουτο (4:1; 7:1, 9; 15:5; 18:1; 19:1; 20:3). Despite these arguments, not one English version has followed the reading that places μετα ταυτα with the beginning of 9:13.

Revelation 9:13b

TR NU — τῶν [τεσσάρων] κεράτων τοῦ θυσιαστηρίου
"the four horns of the altar"
Maj vg[cl] syr[ph]
KJV NKJV RSV NRSV ESV NASB TNIV NJB NAB NLT HCSB NETmg

variant/WH — των κερατων του θυσιαστηριου
"the horns of the altar"
𝔓[47] (ℵ[1]) A 0207 2053 2344 it syr[h] cop
NRSVmg NIV NEB REB HCSBmg NET

The manuscript evidence strongly favors the variant reading (so WH), as does the fact that scribes had a propensity for adding descriptive details. The addition of τεσσαρων ("four") was probably motivated by the descriptions in Exod 27:2-4, 1 Kgs 7:30-34, or Ezek 45:19. Although the majority of English translations include the adjective, NIV NEB REB NET reflect what appears to be the superior reading.

Revelation 9:19

WH NU ἐξουσία τῶν ἵππων
"[the] power of the horses"
𝔓[115vid] 𝔓[47] ℵ A C Maj
NKJVmg RSV NRSV ESV NASB NIV TNIV NEB REB NJB NAB (NLT) HCSB NET

variant/TR εξουσιαι αυτων
"their powers"
1
KJV NKJV

According to Tregelles and Alford, Erasmus must have relied upon minuscule 1 for the change that was incorporated into his edition, which then became part of TR and then KJV and NKJV.

Revelation 9:21

WH NU read φαρμακων ("healing potions, magic potions"), with the support of 𝔓[47] ℵ C Maj[K]. TR reads φαρμακειων ("sorceries"), with the support of A 046 2053 2344 Maj[A]. The WH NU reading is more likely original than the variant because it has better textual support (𝔓[47] ℵ C) and because it is a *hapax legomenon* in the NT. The word φαρμακων was generally used in Hellenistic times to denote drugs, remedies, medicine, and healing potions (see BDAG 1050). When people used these drugs as magic potions, this was known as sorcery, which is the reading of the variant. Since φαρμακεια appears more frequently in the NT (see Gal 5:20; Rev 18:23), some scribes used it instead of φαρμακον. All English translators have also rendered the word denoting the practice of sorcery rather than the substance used by sorcerers.

Revelation 10:2, 8-10

In each of these verses there is a discrepancy among the manuscripts concerning "the book" the angel gave to John for him to eat. The variants are as follows:

1. βιβλαριδιον (TR WH NU for 10:2, 9-10) = "small book" or "small scroll." A (C) in 10:2, 9-10; ℵ P 2344 in 10:8 (so TR); 𝔓[85vid] 𝔓[115vid] in 10:9
2. βιβλιδαριον = "small book" or "small scroll." Maj in 10:8, 9
3. βιβλαριον = "small book" or "small scroll." 2329 in 10:2, 8-10
4. βιβλιον (WH NU for 10:8) = "book" or "scroll." 𝔓[47] in 10:2, 8-10; ℵ in 10:9-10; A C in 10:8
5. βιβλιδιον = "small book" or "small scroll." 𝔓[47] in 10:10

Other manuscripts could be cited in support of various readings, but the above list takes into account the most important ones. The WH and NU editors decided to follow the constant testimony of A and C, generally recognized as reliable manuscripts in Revelation (though A is given to accidental omission). 𝔓[85] and 𝔓[115], extant for only one word in 10:9, would have presumably had the same word (βιβλαριδιον) in the same places as A and C (also in 10:2, 10). This is especially more likely for 𝔓[115], which has more textual affinity with A and C than any other manuscript group. However, we cannot be certain about 𝔓[85] and 𝔓[115] for the other verses.

WH NU read βιβλαριδιον ("small scroll" or "small book") in 10:2, 9-10 and βιβλιον ("scroll" or "book") in 10:8. The reason for the shift in 10:8 can be explained as follows: This verse records God's command concerning the book, whereas the other verses record John's observations about the book. Thus, 10:8 is generic, whereas 10:2, 9-10 are descriptive/specific.

According to John's observations, this was a small book—small enough to put into his mouth. TR reads βιβλαριδιον for all four verses: 10:2, 8, 9, 10.

Revelation 10:5

WH NU	ἦρεν τὴν χεῖρα αὐτοῦ τὴν δεξιάν "he raised his right hand" 𝔓47 𝔓85 𝔓115 ℵ C NKJVmg RSV NRSV ESV NASB NIV TNIV NEB REB NJB NAB NLT HCSB NET
variant/TR	ηρεν την χειρα αυτου "he raised his hand" A Maj[A] vg syr[ph] cop[boMSS] KJV NKJV

The manuscript evidence (the three papyri, 𝔓47 𝔓85 𝔓115, with ℵ C) favors the inclusion of the adjective "right" before "hand." There is no easy way to explain the omission as an accidental error. Perhaps the word "right" was deleted because the expression "right hand" (a symbol of majestic power) is used in Revelation in descriptions of deity—whether of Christ (1:16-17, 20; 2:1) or of God on the throne (5:1, 7). Some scribes and translators may have thought the term should not be used in describing an angel.

Revelation 10:6a

Codex Alexandrinus and Maj[A] omit και την γην και τα εν αυτη ("and the earth and the things in it"). The omission was probably accidental—due to homoeoarchton in Maj[A] (the eye passing from the και before την γην to the και before την θαλασσαν). The omission in Codex A continues all the way through και την θαλασσαν και τα εν αυτη—perhaps due to homoeoteleuton (the eye passing from τα εν αυτω to τα εν αυτη)—see next note. The scribe of A often accidentally omitted text in the book of Revelation.

Revelation 10:6b

TR WH NU include και την θαλασσαν και τα εν αυτη ("and the sea and the things in it") with excellent support: 𝔓47 𝔓85vid 𝔓115 ℵ[c] C P. (The lacuna in 𝔓85 between 10:6a and 10:7b requires the above clause in order to be filled out properly—hence, 𝔓85vid.) But this phrase is omitted in ℵ* A 2344. The TR WH NU reading, though the longer of the two readings, has the best documentation. The omission was probably accidental, due to homoeoteleuton—the two successive clauses end with the same word (αυτη). The scribe of Codex Alexandrinus had a bad habit of omitting text in Revelation (see previous note). It appears that the same mistake was caught in ℵ and then corrected.

Revelation 10:7

WH NU read τους εαυτου δουλους, τους προφητας ("his own servants, the prophets"), with the support of A C 2053[com] Maj[A]. TR reads τοις εαυτου δουλοις τοις προφηταις ("his own servants, the prophets"), with the support of minuscule 1 and a few other minuscules. A second variant reads τους εαυτου δουλους και τους προφητας, which could be rendered "his own servants and the prophets" or "his own servants, even the prophets." This has the support of 𝔓47 𝔓85vid ℵ 2344 cop[sa]. The first variant, found in TR, is nothing more than a change from the accusative to the dative for grammatical correctness. The second variant was dismissed by the NU editors as (1) being inadequately supported and (2) as having been inadvertently inserted by copyists who were not familiar with the OT expression "his servants, the prophets," as in Jer 7:25; 25:4; Amos 3:7 (see TCGNT). The first argument is questionable, especially in light of the fact that two of the primary manuscripts (𝔓47 א), plus 𝔓85vid 2344 copsa, support this variant. As to the second argument, could not the same point be used to argue on behalf of the second variant? Scribes could have easily harmonized this WH NU reading to the OT passages; but, in fact, they did not have to look that far. In 11:18, the similar expression occurs: τοις δουλοις σου τοις προφηταις ("your servants, the prophets")—and this text remains unchanged in the manuscript tradition. Thus, it is just as likely that the original wording is preserved in what amounts to be the weightiest testimony. Nonetheless, it may not change the original meaning—especially if και functions epexegetically: "his own servants, even the prophets."

Revelation 10:11

WH NU — λέγουσιν μοι
"they say to me"
𝔓47 א A C
NKJVmg RSV NRSV (ESV) NASB (NIV TNIV) NEB REB (NJB NAB NLT HCSB) NET

variant/TR — λεγει μοι
"he says to me"
2053 MajA it syr cop
KJV NKJV

The WH NU reading is decidedly superior, having the support of the four earliest manuscripts (noted above). The change in the variant is easy to explain. Unable to identify the speakers (plural) here, various scribes and ancient translators found it much easier to make the speaker the same as the one speaking in the previous verses—namely, the angel (see 10:9). Thus, TR reads: "he [the angel] says to me, 'It is necessary for you to prophecy again.'" However, the book of Revelation presents a layering of messengers: from God to Jesus to an angel to the prophet(s) to the believers (see 1:1-2). As such, it is suitable for the speaker to be identified in the plural. Several modern English versions (noted above by parentheses) circumvent the textual issue by rendering the clause as a passive, "I was told." As such, the subject does not have to be identified. Readers of these versions will think the subject is the angel (10:9-10).

Revelation 11:1

TR WH NU — ἐδόθη μοι κάλαμος ὅμοιος ῥάβδῳ, λέγων· ἔγειρε καὶ μέτρησον τὸν ναόν
"a reed like a measuring rod was given to me, saying, 'Rise and measure the temple.'"
𝔓47 𝔓115vid א* A 2053 2344 cop
NKJVmg (RSV NRSV ESV NASB NIV TNIV NEB REB NJB NAB NLT) HCSB (NET)

variant — εδοθη μοι καλαμος ομοιος ραβδω, και ειστηκει ο αγγελος λεγων· εγειρε και μετρησον τον ναον
"a reed like a measuring rod was given to me, and the angel stood saying, 'Rise and measure the temple.'"
א2 046 syrph,h**
KJV NKJV NJBmg

Though 𝔓[115] has some lacunae in this verse, it is clear that the manuscript would not have contained the extra verbiage found in the variant (see *Text of Earliest MSS,* 670-671). The documentary evidence strongly favors the TR WH NU reading, as does the likelihood that scribes would want to emend the grammatical problem in the TR WH NU reading by making "the angel" the speaker. As is, the TR WH NU reading has καλαμος ("reed") as the nominal reference for the participle λεγων ("saying")—literally, "the reed was saying." Modern English translators fix this problem by making the subject "I" (John the seer) and rendering it in the passive voice: "I was told, 'Go and measure the temple.'" KJV diverts from TR by including "and the angel stood."

Revelation 11:2

The three editions (TR WH NU) read την αυλην την εξωθεν του ναου εκβαλε εξωθεν ("the outer court of the temple—leave it out"). The idea of "leaving it out" is then explained with the epexegetical expression: και μη αυτην μετρησης ("that is, do not measure it"). Several witnesses (including 𝔓[47] A 2053 Maj cop) support this reading. However, ℵ 2329 syr[ph] change the first εξωθεν to εσωθεν, thereby making it the inner court.

Revelation 11:4

WH NU — κυρίου τῆς γῆς
"Lord of the earth"
𝔓[47] ℵ A C cop syr
NKJVmg RSV NRSV ESV NASB NIV TNIV NEB REB NJB NAB NLT HCSB NET

variant/TR — θεου της γης
"God of the earth"
1 2053[txt] Maj[A]
KJV NKJV HCSBmg

The change from "Lord" to "God" may have been influenced by the immediate context, wherein "God" appears in 11:1 and 11:11. (The name "Lord" does not occur in the previous context since 7:14.) The title "Lord" is likely original—for two reasons: (1) It has solid documentary support, and (2) this is the name that occurs in Zech 4:14, of which Rev 11:4 is a close equivalent. In both Zechariah and Revelation the two "olive trees" are revealed as the anointed ones (i.e., the prophets) who "stand by the Lord of the earth"—ready to do his work on earth.

Revelation 11:8

WH NU — ὁ κύριος αὐτῶν ἐσταυρώθη
"their Lord was crucified"
ℵ[c] A C P syr
NKJVmg RSV NRSV ESV NASB NIV TNIV NEB REB NJB NAB NLT HCSB NET

variant 1/TR — ο κυριος ημων εσταυρωθη
"our Lord was crucified"
1
KJV NKJV

variant 2 — ο κυριος εσταυρωθη
"the Lord was crucified"
𝔓[47] ℵ*
none

The three textual differences display three scribal perspectives. The WH NU reading indicates that "the Lord" (who is the Lord Jesus) is the Lord of the two witnesses or the Lord of those in Jerusalem (which is symbolized by the names "Sodom and Egypt"). Thus, "their Lord" could be the two witnesses' Lord or Jerusalem's Lord. This was changed to "our Lord" (variant 1) in minuscule 1 and incorporated by Erasmus in his edition (so TR). This reading shows a scribal personalization of the text or an attempt to rectify what could have been perceived as a theological problem—that is, how could Jesus be the Lord of the city which crucified him? The third reading (variant 2) is neutral because it lacks a pronoun; it simply states where "the Lord" was crucified. It could be the original wording, having the support of the two earliest manuscripts (𝔓47 ℵ*). If not, it may exhibit an alteration of the text in the interest of removing the ambiguity of the expression, "their Lord." One final note of interest: The scribe of 𝔓47 wrote the verb "crucified" as a nomen sacrum with an unusual form: ϵσΤρω. Other early scribes (𝔓46 𝔓66 𝔓75) also used the nomen sacrum form for "cross" and "crucify," but this is the only instance of its use in Revelation among the extant papyri predating A.D. 300.

Revelation 11:12

TR WH NU — ἤκουσαν φωνῆς μεγάλης
"they heard a great voice"
ℵ* A C P 2053 syr
KJV NKJV RSV NRSV ESV NASB NIV TNIV NEB REB NJBmg NAB (NLT) HCSB NET

variant — ηκουσα φωνης μεγαλης
"I heard a great voice"
𝔓47 ℵc Maj cop
NKJVmg NJB HCSBmg

In the Greek there is only a one-letter difference (*nu*) between the two readings: ηκουσαν/ηκουσα. Thus, one word could have easily been confused for the other in the transcriptional process. The textual evidence, evenly divided, shows the disparity. The testimony of ℵ* A C is that the two witnesses heard the voice from heaven saying "come up here." The testimony of 𝔓47 etc., is that John heard the voice from heaven speaking to the two witnesses, commanding them to "come up here." This reading accords with the prevailing pattern set forth in this book that John is the one who hears all the heavenly oracles and then records them for the reader. In fact, the term ηκουσα ("I heard") appears 27 times in Revelation with reference to John's hearing a divine oracle or other heavenly messages.

Contrarily, the TR WH NU reading (ηκουσαν—"they heard") is a one-time occurrence in Revelation. Does this make it original because its uniqueness prompted scribal alteration? Or does this mean it was a mistake? Most translators took it to be original. The translators of NJB, however, followed the variant reading.

Revelation 11:15a

WH NU — ἐγένετο ἡ βασιλεία τοῦ κόσμου τοῦ κυρίου ἡμῶν
"the kingdom of the world has become our Lord's"
𝔓47 ℵ A C Maj
NKJVmg RSV NRSV ESV NASB NIV TNIV NEB REB NJB NAB NLT HCSB NET

variant/TR — εγενοντο αι βασιλειαι του κοσμου του κυριου ημων
"the kingdoms of the world have become our Lord's"
1
KJV NKJV

The pluralizing of "kingdom" in this verse was popularized because Erasmus followed the reading of the twelfth-century minuscule 1, which then became part of TR and was subsequently translated in KJV and NKJV. But the true reading is that the Lord, God's Anointed One, will take over the one kingdom that has ruled this world, which is the kingdom of the evil trinity of Satan, the beast, and the false prophet. This verse announces their imminent defeat.

Revelation 11:15b

Some witnesses (א 2344 cop^bo) have αμην ("amen") appended to the proclamation. Throughout the course of textual transmission, this was a common scribal addition to prayers, praises, and proclamations.

Revelation 11:17a

Most manuscripts have the ascription for God as follows:

κυριε ο θεος ο παντοκρατωρ
ο ων και ο ην
"Lord God the Almighty
the one who is and who was"

The scribe of 𝔓47 wrote ο θεος three times in a row. Either he or another corrector changed the first θεος to κυριος by writing a *kappa* in place of the *theta*, making $\overline{\text{ΘC}}$ become $\overline{\text{KC}}$. This change was not noted by the editor of the *editio princeps* of 𝔓47 (Kenyon 1934, 22), but it is noted in *Text of Earliest MSS*, 341. Kenyon did note that the second θεος was an error of dittography. But since the scribe of 𝔓47 first wrote θεος three times, it is very unlikely that this was an error. Rather, the line in 𝔓47* Ο $\overline{\text{ΘC}}$ Ο $\overline{\text{ΘC}}$ Ο $\overline{\text{ΘC}}$ was probably intentional. Broken in three lines, it reads:

ο θεος ο θεος
ο θεος ο παντοκρατωρ
ο ων και ο ην
"God, God,
God the Almighty
the one who is and who was"

𝔓47c reads:

ο κυριος ο θεος
ο θεος ο παντοκρατωρ
ο ων και ο ην
"the Lord, God
God the Almighty
the one who is and who was"

In both 𝔓47* and 𝔓47c there is no vocative. It is a nominative descriptor of God, rather than a praise in direct address.

Revelation 11:17b

WH NU — ὁ ὢν καὶ ὁ ἦν
"the one who is and the one who was"
𝔓47 א A C Maj
NKJVmg RSV NRSV ESV NASB NIV TNIV NEB REB NJB NAB NLT HCSB NET

variant/TR ο ων και ο ην και ο ερχομενος
"the one who is and the who was and the coming one"
051 1006
KJV NKJV HCSBmg

Having the testimony of the four earliest witnesses (noted above) and the majority of manuscripts, the WH NU reading is superior to that in TR. The variant in TR is the result of scribal harmonization, borrowed from the other refrains in Revelation which end with the expression "the coming one" (see 1:4, 8; 4:8). This is followed by KJV and NKJV, as well as noted in HCSB out of respect for the KJV tradition.

Revelation 11:19

All three editions (TR WH NU) read η κιβωτος της διαθηκης αυτου ("the ark of his covenant"), with the support of A C P. In context, this reads, "the temple of God was opened in heaven and the ark of his covenant in his temple was seen." There are two variants on this: (1) η κιβωτος της διαθηκης του κυριου ("the ark of the Lord's covenant") in 𝔓47 (2344) MajK syrhmg copsa; (2) η κιβωτος της διαθηκης του θεου ("the ark of God's covenant") in ℵ. The documentary evidence for the TR WH NU reading, though solid (with the combined testimony of A and C), is still not so substantial as to rule out the other readings, especially the first variant. Had the text originally read αυτου ("his"), as in A and C, or του θεου ("God's"), as in ℵ, it is difficult to explain why scribes would change it to κυριου (variant 1). Thus, one could argue that the text originally read "the covenant of the Lord" (variant 1), but this was seen to be at odds with the previous mention of "God." So it was either changed to αυτου ("his"—with reference to θεου) or to θεου itself. But even if the original wording were "the Lord," it is likely that this is a reference to "the Lord God"—a frequent appellation in the book of Revelation (1:8; 4:8; 11:15-17; 15:13; 16:7; 18:8; 19:6; 21:22).

Revelation 12:7

According to WH NU, following all known Greek manuscripts, the text reads Μιχαηλ και οι αγγελοι αυτου του πολεμησαι μετα του δρακοντος ("Michael and his angels had to fight with the dragon"). (𝔓47 ℵ omit του.) TR, probably following some Vulgate manuscript (so Alford 1857, 4:670), reads Μιχαηλ και οι αγγελοι αυτου επολεμησαν μετα του δρακοντος ("Michael and his angels fought with the dragon").

The infinitive phrase in the text (with or without the article as in 𝔓47 ℵ) is a Semitism which means "had to fight" (see Johnson 1981, 519). Erasmus either followed the Vulgate here or simply corrected what he thought was a mistake when he changed the infinitive πολεμησαι to επολεμησαν ("they fought"). This reading has no Greek manuscript support at all.

Revelation 12:8a

WH NU οὐκ ἴσχυσεν
"he was not strong enough"
A 1854 MajK copbo
ESV NIV TNIV REB NLT HCSB NET

variant/TR ουκ ισχυσαν
"they were not strong enough"
𝔓47 א C (046) 051 Maj[A] it syr
KJV NKJV RSV NRSV NASB NEB NJB NAB

See next note.

Revelation 12:8b

TR WH NU οὐδὲ τόπος εὑρέθη αὐτῶν
"nor was their place found"
𝔓47 A C Maj[A]
all

variant 1 ουδε τοπος ευρεθη αυτοις
"nor was a place found for them"
א[2] 051 syr[ph]
none

variant 2 ουδε τοπος ευρεθη αυτω
"nor was a place found for him"
Maj[K] cop[bo]
NKJVmg

variant 3 ουδε τοπος ευρεθη
"nor was a place found"
א*
none

The textual variants in this verse concern whether or not the focus is on the dragon alone (hence, the variants in the singular) or on the dragon and his angels (hence, the variants in the plural). The WH NU editions display a mixed text—first singular (12:8a), then plural (12:8b), on the basis of the testimony of A. This could be right, but it is risky to take the testimony of A over against 𝔓47 א C in 12:8a. Several English versions follow WH NU in 12:8a, each having first the singular then the plural: "But he [the dragon] was not strong enough, and they [the dragon and his angels] lost their place in heaven." Otherwise, the versions follow the plural throughout, thereby essentially following 𝔓47 א C.

Revelation 12:9

𝔓47 omits ο αρχαιος ("the ancient one"). This omission was probably accidental, due to homoeoteleuton—the subsequent nouns end with ος (ο καλουμενος Διαβολος). All other witnesses, including 𝔓115 א A C, retain the expression.

Revelation 12:10

On the authority of Codex Alexandrinus, the NU committee selected the reading ο κατηγωρ, against the testimony of 𝔓47 א C 051 Maj, which read ο κατηγορος (both words are translated as "the accuser"). Their reason for doing so: ο κατηγωρ is a *hapax legomenon* in the NT and therefore would likely be changed to ο κατηγορος (see TCGNT). But it is dangerous to adopt readings that have the support of only one manuscript.

Revelation 12:17a

WH NU τὴν μαρτυρίαν Ἰησοῦ
"the testimony of Jesus"
𝔓47 ℵc A C Maj
NKJVmg RSV NRSV ESV NASB NIV TNIV NEB REB NJB NAB NLT HCSB NET

variant 1/TR την μαρτυριαν Ιησου Χριστου
"the testimony of Jesus Christ"
vgMS?
KJV NKJV

variant 2 την μαρτυριαν του θεου
"the testimony of God"
ℵ*
none

The second variant is the result of scribal assimilation to the first clause, but this was corrected. The first variant, having no known Greek manuscript support, must be the work of Erasmus following a certain manuscript of the Vulgate (so Tregelles and Alford). His text, eventually becoming TR, has been popularized by KJV and NKJV. The same insertion occurred in 1:9 (see note).

Revelation 12:17b, 18; 13:1

WH NU Καὶ ἐστάθη ἐπὶ τὴν ἄμμον τῆς θαλάσσης.
"And he stood on the shore of the sea."
𝔓47 ℵ A C 2344 it syrh
NKJVmg RSV NRSV ESV NASB NIV TNIV NEB REB NJBmg NAB NLT HCSB NET

variant/TR Και εσταθην επι την αμμον της θαλασσης
"And I stood on the shore of the sea."
P 051 Maj vgMSS syrph cop
KJV NKJV RSVmg NRSVmg ESVmg NASBmg NIVmg TNIVmg NEBmg NJB NABmg NLTmg HCSBmg NETmg

The WH NU reading, having superior documentary support (𝔓47 ℵ A C 2344), indicates that "the dragon" (of 12:17) had taken up his position by the sea. The variant, with a less impressive array of witnesses, indicates that John (the seer) was standing by the sea. The expression "he stood" was changed to "I stood" so as to complement the next clause, which says "I saw a beast coming out of the sea" (13:1).

This textual variant has affected the way English versions arrange and versify the end of chapter 12 and the beginning of 13. Those versions that follow the variant reading join the statement "and I stood on the shore of the sea" with the beginning of 13:1 (see NJB) and have even eliminated the versification of 12:18 in the process (as in KJV and NKJV). Those versions that follow the WH NU reading keep the statement "and he stood on the shore of the sea" with chapter 12, as either the last part of 12:17 (as in RSV) or as a separate verse (as in NRSV). Nearly all the versions have a note on this textual variation, primarily because of its impact on the rearrangement of the versification for the end of Rev 12 and the beginning of Rev 13.

Revelation 13:5

TR WH NU — ἐδόθη αὐτῷ ἐξουσία ποιῆσαι
"he was given authority to act"
𝔓47 A C (א adds ο θελει after ποιησαι = "to do what he wills")
all

variant 1 — εδοθη αυτω εξουσια πολεμον ποιησαι
"he was given authority to make war"
051 2329 Maj[K]
NKJVmg HCSBmg

variant 2 — εδοθη αυτω εξουσια πολεμησαι
"he was given authority to make war"
2351
(NKJVmg)

The TR WH NU reading is strongly supported by the earliest manuscripts. The vagueness of the verb ποιησαι (it can mean "act," "continue," "make," etc.) prompted the changes, which indicate that the beast was given authority to make war (see 13:7).

Revelation 13:6

WH NU — τὴν σκηνὴν αὐτοῦ, τοὺς ἐν τῷ οὐρανῷ σκηνοῦντας
"his dwelling place—the ones dwelling in heaven"
(א*) A 046[c] 2053[com] 2344 Irenaeus
RSV NRSV ESV NASB NEBmg REB NLT HCSB NET

variant 1/TR — την σκηνην αυτου και τους εν τω ουρανω σκηνουντας
"his dwelling place and the ones dwelling in heaven"
א[2] 046* 2053[txt] Maj[A] it cop
KJV NKJV NIV TNIV NJB NAB NLTmg

variant 2 — την σκηνην αυτου εν τω ουρανω
"his dwelling place in heaven"
𝔓47
NEB

variant 3 — τους εν τω ουρανω σκηνουντας
"the ones dwelling in heaven"
C
none

The NEB translators considered the text of 𝔓47 to contain the original wording (see Tasker 1964, 444). However, the WH NU reading has better documentary support (especially the combined testimony of A with א*), is seemingly the most difficult reading, and is most likely the reading from which the others deviated. According to the syntax of this verse in Greek, the phrase "those who dwell [lit., 'tabernacle' as a verb] in heaven" is in direct apposition to "his dwelling place [lit., 'tabernacle' as a noun]." Thus, those who dwell in heaven are God's tabernacle in heaven; the people in heaven and the heavenly place are not two separate entities. This is made clear in versions like RSV NRSV NASB NLT HCSB and NET. The image of God's people being the same as God's habitation is presented again in 21:1-3, where the new Jerusalem is depicted as the people of God becoming God's habitation (see note on 21:3).

Revelation 13:7a

TR WH NU	include καὶ ἐδόθη αὐτῷ ποιῆσαι πόλεμον μετὰ τῶν ἁγίων καὶ νικῆσαι αὐτούς "and it [the beast] was allowed to war against the saints and to conquer them" 𝔓[115] ℵ 051 2344 Maj[K] all
variant	omit clause 𝔓[47] A C 2053 Maj[A] cop[sa] RSVmg NRSVmg ESVmg NEBmg

The TR WH NU reading, followed by all English versions, has good documentary support, including the early papyrus 𝔓[115] (third century). The variant reading can be explained as a scribal accident: A scribe's eyes passed over the first και εδοθη αυτω in the verse to the second και εδοθη αυτω, and therefore the scribe did not copy the first clause. But could this have happened independently in so many manuscripts—especially in three of the five leading witnesses to Revelation (𝔓[47] A C)? Unless all three manuscripts trace back to the same exemplar, this is unlikely. Therefore, we have to look for other reasons to explain the shorter reading. It is possible that the phrase about the beast's victory over the saints was deleted because various scribes thought it contrary to the whole message of Revelation—that is, the saints are victors and will triumph over evil. In fact, 15:2 speaks of the saints who had gotten the victory over the beast. But this is the irony: These believers were killed by the beast because they did not submit to him, and so in the end they become the conquerors. Revelation 12:11 says that they conquered him "by the blood of the Lamb, by the word of their testimony, and because they did not love their lives unto death."

Revelation 13:7b

WH NU	πᾶσαν φυλὴν καὶ λαὸν καὶ γλῶσσαν καὶ ἔθνος "every tribe and people and tongue and nation" 𝔓[115vid] ℵ A C NKJVmg RSV NRSV ESV NASB NIV TNIV NEB REB NJB NAB NLT HCSB NET
variant/TR	πασαν φυλην και γλωσσαν και εθνος "every tribe and tongue and nation" 𝔓[47] 051 1006 Maj[A] cop[bo] KJV NKJV

The weight of documentary evidence favors the fourfold list—with four important witnesses supporting it. Furthermore, in all the other occurrences of such lists in Revelation, all four are named: "tribe, people, tongue, and nation" (see 5:9; 7:9; 11:9; 14:6); thus, it appears to have been a fixed pattern. The variant is probably the result of a scribal error; when writing a string of nouns, a scribe could have easily skipped one (και λαον), especially since the preceding and following nouns also end with the same letter, *nu* (φυλην και γλωσσαν).

Revelation 13:8

NA[27] lists a number of textual variants for the reading οὗ οὐ γεγραπται το ονομα αυτου εν τω βιβλιω της ζωης ("each of whose names are not written in the book of life")—supported by C 1854 2053. The variants include a change from the singular pronouns οὗ and αυτου to the plurals, ων and αυτων—so 𝔓[47] ℵ P 051, also 𝔓[115vid] Maj, though they omit the second pronoun. All these changes are attempts to accommodate the previous expression παντες οι κατοικουντες επι της γης ("all the ones dwelling on earth"), of whom it is said that they are not written in the book of life. The singular form treats them collectively; the plural, individually. Finally, it should be noted that Codex A has the unusual reading: ουαι γεγραπται το ονομα αυτου εν τω βιβλιω της ζωης ("Woe! His name is written in the book of life"). This mistake—exchanging ουαι for ου ου—reveals the fatigue of the scribe of A in Revelation.

Revelation 13:10a

WH NU — εἴ τις εἰς αἰχμαλωσίαν, εἰς αἰχμαλωσίαν ὑπάγει
"if anyone [goes] into captivity, into captivity he goes"
A (syr cop^sa)
RSV NRSV ESV NASB NIV TNIV NEB REB NJB NAB NLT HCSB NET

variant 1/TR — ει τις αιχμαλωσιαν συναγει, εις αιχμαλωσιαν υπαγει
"if anyone gathers into captivity, into captivity he goes"
(1) 2059 2081
KJV NKJV

variant 2 — ει τις εις αιχμαλωσιαν υπαγει
"if anyone goes into captivity"
𝔓47 𝔓115vid ℵ C 046 051 2053 Maj cop^bo
none

There are several other variants for this portion of 13:10 (see critical apparatus of NA27 or UBS4), but these three variants are the most significant. There are three factors that favor variant 2: (1) It has superior documentation (especially with the fourfold testimony of 𝔓47 𝔓115vid ℵ C); (2) it is the shorter reading; (3) it does not conform to Jer 15:2, the OT passage alluded to here. (Though there is a lacuna in 𝔓115, it clearly supports the shortest variant reading, which must be that also found in 𝔓47 ℵ C. For a reconstruction of 𝔓115, see *Text of Earliest MSS*, 674.) It could be argued that the shorter reading is due to haplography caused by homoeoteleuton: the eye of a scribe passing from the first εις αιχμαλωσιαν to the second εις αιχμαλωσιαν. But would this error have occurred in so many diverse witnesses? If the shortness can be attributed to anything, it must be scribal trimming of what was perceived to be unnecessary words. But if the short reading is original, then the longer reading must be the result of scribal conformity to Jer 15:2 (LXX). All things being equal, documentation should probably be the determining factor.

Revelation 13:10b

NU — εἴ τις ἐν μαχαίρῃ ἀποκτανθῆναι, αὐτὸν ἐν μαχαίρῃ ἀποκτανθῆναι
"if anyone by a sword [is] to be killed, he by the sword [is] to be killed"
A
ESV NIV TNIV REB NJB NAB NLT HCSB NET

variant 1/TR WH ει τις εν μαχαιρη αποκτενεῖ δει αυτον εν μαχαιρη αποκτανθηναι
"if anyone will kill by a sword, it is necessary for him to be killed by a sword"
C P 051* 2053 Maj[A] it
NEB NETmg

variant 2 ει τις εν μαχαιρη αποκτενει δει αυτον εν μαχαιρη αποκτανθηναι
"if anyone kills by a sword, it is necessary for him to be killed by a sword"
ℵ 1611* syr[h]
KJV NKJV RSV NRSV NASB TNIVmg NJBmg HCSBmg NETmg

According to Codex A, both verbs are passive, and thus the second statement repeats the first: "If anyone is killed by the sword, he is killed by the sword." It speaks of destiny fulfilled (as in Jer 15:2, the basis for this verse). This reading provides promise to Christian martyrs that their death is the fulfillment of a divine appointment (see Westcott and Hort 1882, 138). NIV NJB NAB NLT and NET convey this idea of Christian martyrdom. In the other variants, the first verb is active, and either future tense (indicated by a circumflex over the final vowel) or present tense. According to these variant readings, retribution comes on those who kill with the sword. As Matt 26:52 says, "all who take up the sword die by the sword." This maxim is reflected in the rest of the English versions, even though all these versions use the present tense, as in the second variant.

Revelation 13:15a

WH reads αυτη ("to it"—fem.) with the support of A C, referring to εικονα ("image") in 13:14. TR NU read αυτω ("to him"), with the support of 𝔓[47] 𝔓[115] ℵ 051 Maj, referring to θηριου ("beast") in 13:14. The latter has superior support and makes good sense.

Revelation 13:15b

WH NU, following A P 2344, include ινα, producing the difficult expression, ποιηση ινα οσοι εαν μη προσκυνησωσιν τη εικονι του θηριου αποκτανθωσιν ("it [the image of the beast] might cause that as many as did not worship the image of the beast to be killed"). TR, with good support (𝔓[115vid] ℵ 1611 Maj), omits the word ινα, and thereby yields the translation: "It [the image of the beast] might cause as many as did not worship the image of the beast to be killed." 𝔓[47] (not cited in NA[27] or UBS[4]) solves the problem by substituting του ποιησαι for ινα, giving the translation: "to cause as many as did not worship the image of the beast to be killed."

Revelation 13:17

WH NU τὸ χάραγμα τὸ ὄνομα τοῦ θηρίου
"the mark, the name of the beast"
A 051 Maj
NKJVmg RSV NRSV ESV NASB NIV TNIV NEB REB NJB (NAB NLT) HCSB NET

variant 1 το χαραγμα του ονοματος του θηριου
"the mark of the name of the beast"
C
none

variant 2/TR το χαραγμα η του ονοματος του θηριου
"the mark or the name of the beast"
𝔓47 it[gig] (vg)
KJV NKJV

variant 3 το χαραγμα του θηριου η του ονοματος αυτου
"the mark of the beast or his name"
א cop
none

According to WH NU, "the name of the beast" is appositional to "the mark," which means that the mark bears the name of the beast. The variants, in one way or another, are adjustments to show the same relationship—especially if we understand that η ("or") signals interchangeability.

Revelation 13:18

TR WH NU ἑξακόσιοι ἑξήκοντα ἕξ [=χξς]
"666"
𝔓47 (א) A P Maj Irenaeus Hippolytus
all

variant 1 εξακοσιοι δεκα εξ [=χις]
"616"
𝔓115 C (5 11—no longer extant) MSS[according to Irenaeus]
RSVmg NRSVmg ESVmg NASBmg NJBmg NABmg NLTmg HCSBmg

variant 2 εξακοσια εξηκοντα πεντε [=χξε]
"665"
2344
none

Writing in the late second century, Irenaeus (*Haer.* 5.30) was aware of the reading "616" but denounced it as "heretical and deceptive." He claimed that "666" was found in "all the good and ancient copies" and was "attested to by those who had seen John face to face." Three significant witnesses (𝔓47 א A) must have their roots in those "good and ancient copies" because they read "666." However, the recently published 𝔓115 reads "616," as does Codex C. These are among the "good and ancient copies," and the number they contain, "616," is not heretical. Either "666" or "616" could be original inasmuch as both symbolize "Caesar Nero." In ancient times the letters of the Hebrew and Greek alphabets were used as numerals. The "number" of a name is the sum of its individual letters. The number "666," abbreviated in ancient manuscripts as χξς (χ = 600, ξ = 60, ς = 6), came from a Hebrew transliteration of the Greek for "Neron Caesar." The number "616," abbreviated in ancient manuscripts as χις, is either a Latin equivalent of the name "Nero Caesar" by way of gematria (see Aune 1998, 770-771; NETmg) or a different spelling of Neron Caesar, which drops the final "n" (Metzger 2003, 308). Both convey the same signification of the same person. As of yet, not one English translation prints "616" in the text, even though several note it. The note in HCSB says that one Greek manuscript plus other ancient evidence read "616." There are actually two ancient manuscripts, 𝔓115 and C.

Revelation 14:3a

TR WH NU	ᾄδουσιν [ὡς] ᾠδὴν καινήν "they sing, as it were, a new song" A C 051 Maj[A] KJV NKJV HCSBmg
variant	αδουσιν ωδην καινην "they sing a new song" 𝔓[47] 𝔓[115vid] ℵ P 046 2053 2344 RSV NRSV ESV NASB NIV TNIV NEB REB NJB NAB NLT HCSB NET

The Greek word for "as it were" (ως) has been bracketed in NA[27] and UBS[4] (it was not included in previous editions of the Nestle text). No doubt the word was included because of its presence in A and C but bracketed because of its absence in 𝔓[47] and ℵ. However, the word should not be included at all because it is a scribal carryover from 14:2, where it occurs three times. Furthermore, the added testimony of 𝔓[115] adds weight to the omission. All the modern English versions follow the variant.

Revelation 14:3b

C omits και των πρεσβυτερων ("and the elders")—probably due to homoeoteleuton. The three previous words end with the same letters.

Revelation 14:4a

TR WH NU	οὗτοι ἠγοράσθησαν ἀπὸ τῶν ἀνθρώπων "these ones were purchased from humanity" 𝔓[47vid] ℵ A all
variant 1	ουτοι ηγορασθησαν υπο Ιησου απο των ανθρωπων "these ones were purchased by Jesus from humanity" 051 1611 Maj[K] syr[h**] NKJVmg HCSBmg
variant 2	ουτοι ηγορασθησαν "these ones were purchased" C none

The TR WH NU reading has the support of the three earliest manuscripts (noted above). Each variant presents scribal editing. The first, an expansion, adds an agent ("Jesus") to the passive verb "were purchased." Most readers would have filled this gap easily. The second variant, a truncation, removes the interpretive obstacle of just what it means "to be purchased *from humanity*." Of course, this does not mean that 144,000 were sold by humanity, but that they were redeemed to become separate from all people (a partitive genitive)—a special heritage for the Lord who bought them with the price of his blood.

Revelation 14:4b

The three editions (TR WH NU) read απαρχη, which translates as "firstfruits." This has the support of A C Maj etc. However, 𝔓[47] and ℵ read απ αρχης ("from [the] beginning"). The *editio princeps* of 𝔓[47] mistakenly has απαρχη (see Kenyon 1934, 28), when it should be απ αρχης (see *Text of Earliest MSS,* 346). In context, a translation of A and C is, "they were purchased firstfruits to God and to the Lamb." In 47 and א it is "they were purchased from the beginning for God and the Lamb."

The textual attestation for these two variants is divided, as is the internal evidence. In the ancient Greek manuscripts, the word for "firstfruits" (απαρχην) could easily be confused for the expression "from the beginning" (απαρχης), or vice versa. In the early manuscripts no space was left between the words. The same textual problem occurred in 2 Thess 2:13 (see note).

Both readings are defensible exegetically. The notion of being redeemed or purchased as firstfruits points to the inestimable worth of these virgins in the sight of God. Christ paid the price for their purity with his own blood (1:5). But it is also possible that the text is speaking of their eternal worth insofar as Christ chose them from the beginning to be his very own special witnesses. Thus, the one who was from the beginning, who is himself the Alpha and Omega, chose these ones "from the beginning."

Revelation 14:5

WH NU — ἄμωμοι εἰσιν
"they are unblemished (= blameless)"
A C P 0253
NRSV NASB NIV TNIV NEB REB NJB NAB NLT HCSB NET

variant 1 — αμωμοι γαρ εισιν
"for they are unblemished (= blameless)"
𝔓[47] 𝔓[115vid] א Maj[K] it[a,t] cop Origen
RSV ESV NETmg

variant 2/TR — αμωμοι γαρ εισιν ενωπιον του θρονου του θεου
"for they are unblemished (= blameless) before the throne of God"
vg
KJV NKJV

The first variant, well supported, connects the clauses in an awkward fashion: "No lie was found in their mouths, for they are unblemished," when one would expect the opposite: "They are unblemished, for no lie was found in their mouths." As such, it is possible that the scribes of A and C dropped the causal γαρ. The second variant is spurious for two reasons: (1) It has no support from any Greek manuscripts, and (2) whereas the expression "before the throne" is common in Revelation (1:4; 4:5-6, 10; 7:9, 11; 14:3; 20:12), it never says "before the throne of God." However, Erasmus adopted this reading from the Latin Vulgate for his Greek edition, and it became part of TR.

Revelation 14:6

TR WH NU — εἶδον ἄλλον ἄγγελον
"I saw another angel"
𝔓[115vid] א[2] A C P 2053 it syr cop[bo]
KJV NKJV RSV NRSV ESV NASB NIV TNIV NJB NAB NLT HCSB NET

variant εἰδον αγγελον
"I saw an angel"
𝔓47 ℵ* Maj cop^sa
NEB REB

On one hand, the TR WH NU reading could be a scribal expansion intended to help readers realize that there has been a sequence of angelic appearances. On the other hand, the variant could also be a scribal editing inasmuch as the previous mention of an angel is far removed in the apocalyptic narrative (11:15). Since internal evidence is balanced, documentary evidence must decide in favor of the TR WH NU reading.

Revelation 14:8

NU ἄλλος ἄγγελος δεύτερος
"another angel, a second"
ℵ2 (C) 2053 2344 Maj^A
RSV NRSV ESV NASB NIV (TNIV) NEB REB NJB NAB (NLT HCSB) NET

variant 1/WH αλλος δευτερος αγγελος
"another, a second angel"
A Maj^K
NETmg

variant 2 αλλος δευτερος
"another, a second"
𝔓47 ℵ*
NETmg

variant 3/TR αλλος αγγελος
"another angel"
69 it^a vg
KJV NKJV NETmg

The manuscript evidence is not conclusive rendering a decision on any of the readings except that of TR, which is clearly not original. The difference between the first two variants and the NU reading is stylistic, whereas the third variant omits mention of the angel being the "second" one (see 14:6 for mention of the first one). Erasmus must have followed the Vulgate here (so TR), which was translated in KJV and NKJV.

Revelation 14:12

WH NU οἱ τηροῦντες τὰς ἐντολάς
"the ones keeping the commands"
𝔓47 ℵ A C
NKJVmg RSV NRSV ESV NASB NIV TNIV NEB REB NJB NAB NLT HCSB NET

variant/TR ωδε οι τηρουντες τας εντολας
"here are the ones keeping the commands"
051 Maj^A
KJV NKJV

The WH NU reading is supported by the four earliest manuscripts (noted above). The addition in TR is a scribal carryover from the first clause in the verse. According to WH NU, the entire second part of the sentence is appositional to "the saints." This means that there is only one category of people being described—the saints, who may be pictured here as the OT faithful (those who keep the commandments) and the NT faithful (those who have faith in Jesus).

Revelation 14:13a

The three editions (TR WH NU), with good authority (𝔓[47] ℵ A etc.), speak of those who have died "in the Lord" (εν κυριω). But as often occurred in the transmission of the text, divine names were altered. The name was changed in C P 1854 to Χριστω ("Christ") so as to clarify that the Lord is Christ or to indicate that they died as "Christians" (see NEB). A few other witnesses (1611 syr[h]) changed it to θεω ("God").

Revelation 14:13b

TR WH NU	ναί, λέγει τὸ πνεῦμα "'Yes,' says the Spirit" ℵ[c] A C P 2344 syr KJV NKJV RSV NRSV ESV NASB NIV TNIV NEBmg REBmg NJB NAB NLT HCSB NET
variant 1	λεγει το πνευμα "says the Spirit" 𝔓[47] ℵ* NEB REB
variant 2	και λεγει το πνευμα "and the Spirit says" 2053 none

The NEB and REB translators followed the first variant. They did so because they considered ναι ("yes"), not found in 𝔓[47] and ℵ*, to be secondary. As such, the previous phrase απ αρτι ("from now on") "must be construed with what follows" (Tasker 1964, 444). If this is the true text, the Spirit does not begin his speech with an affirmation of what the one from heaven said; rather, he goes on to append a promise: "'Blessed are the dead, the ones dying in the Lord. From now on,' says the Spirit, 'they may rest from their labors.'" This differs from the TR WH NU reading, which would be rendered as follows: "Blessed are the dead, the ones dying in the Lord from now on. Yes, says the Spirit, they may rest from their labors."

Revelation 14:15

WH NU	ἦλθεν ἡ ὥρα θερίσαι "the hour has come to reap" A C P Maj[K] NKJVmg RSV NRSV ESV NASB NIV TNIV NEB REB NJB NAB (NLT) HCSB NET
variant 1	ηλθεν σου η ωρα θερισαι "your hour has come to reap" 051 Maj[A] none
variant 2	ηλθεν η ωρα του θερισμου "the hour of reaping has come" ℵ none

variant 3 εξηλθεν ο θερισμος
"the harvest has come"
𝔓47
none

variant 4/TR ηλθεν σοι η ωρα του θερισαι
"the hour has come for you to reap"
(1)
KJV NKJV

It is possible that 𝔓47, having the shortest text, preserves the original wording. If not, it demonstrates that the scribe was simply interested in conveying the basic message. The WH NU reading has superior attestation, which is followed by all modern versions.

Revelation 14:19

The expression την ληνον του θυμου του θεου τον μεγαν (usually translated "the great winepress of the wrath of God") is grammatically incorrect because τον μεγαν does not agree with την ληνον ("the winepress") or του θεου ("of God"). Nonetheless, this is the reading in WH NU. If this is what John originally wrote, certain scribes (𝔓115 A C P 046) left it alone, others (𝔓47 1611) changed it to την ληνον του θυμου του θεου του μεγαλου ("the winepress of the wrath of the great God"), and others (א 1006 2053—so TR) changed it to the grammatically correct την ληνον του θυμου του θεου την μεγαλην (also translated "the great winepress of the wrath of God").

Revelation 14:20

The number of "stadia" (σταδια) in most manuscripts is listed as χιλιων εξακοσιων (= 1600), which equals about 200 miles. This appears as χιλιων εξακοσιων εξ (= 1606) in a few witnesses (2036 and other minuscules), as χιλιων διακοσιων (= 1200) in א* syr^{ph}, and as β'χ in 𝔓115 (= 2600).

Revelation 15:3

NU ὁ βασιλεὺς τῶν ἐθνῶν
"the king of the nations"
א1 A 051 Maj syr^{hmg} cop^{bo}
NKJVmg RSVmg NRSV ESV NASB TNIV NEBmg NJB NAB NLT HCSB NET

variant 1/WH ο βασιλευς των αιωνων
"the king of the ages"
𝔓47 א*,2 C vg syr^{ph,h} cop^{sa}
RSV NRSVmg ESVmg NASBmg NIV TNIVmg NEB REB NABmg NLTmg NETmg

variant 2/TR ο βασιλευς των αγιων
"the king of the saints"
269 2049
KJV NKJV

Those who prefer the NU reading can argue that the first variant was adopted from 1 Tim 1:17, whereas the NU reading is a unique expression in the NT. But it can also be argued that the words "the nations" in the next verse caused the scribes to change "ages" to "nations" (see Tasker 1964, 444). Thus, the internal considerations offset one another. With respect to the documentary evidence, the testimony of 𝔓[47] with א* and C demonstrates weightier external support than does א[1] and A. The divergence among the modern translations reveals that it is difficult to decide which word to follow: "nations" or "ages." But it takes no great text-critical skills to readily dismiss the word "saints" (αγιων), which somehow was adopted by Erasmus (despite the fact that he did not have access to the two manuscripts that support this reading—see TCGNT) and then found its way into TR. KJV and NKJV perpetuate this spurious reading.

Revelation 15:5

WH NU ἠνοίγη ὁ ναός
"the temple was opened"
א A C Maj
NKJVmg RSV NRSV ESV NASB NIV TNIV NEB REB NJB NAB NLT HCSB NET

variant/TR ιδου ηνοιγη ο ναος
"behold the temple was opened"
2344(?) some Old Latin MSS
KJV NKJV

The insertion of ιδου ("behold") was probably influenced by 14:1, 14 and became popularized by its presence in TR and KJV.

Revelation 15:6

TR NU ἐνδεδυμένοι λίνον
"clothed in linen"
P Maj syr
all

variant 1 ενδεδυμενοι λινουν
"clothed in linen garment[s]"
𝔓[47] א 046
NLTmg

variant 2/WH ενδεδυμενοι λιθον
"clothed in stone"
A C 2053 syr[hmg]
ASV NRSVmg NASBmg NLTmg

Are the angels covered in linen, linen garments, or stone? It is difficult to determine. The TR NU reading, having inferior attestation, is rarer because it is found only here in Revelation. It denotes linen material or flax, but never linen clothing in the Bible. "Fine linen clothing" is referred to in Revelation as βυσσινου (18:12, 16; 19:8, 14). The first variant, λινουν, not occurring elsewhere in the NT, is used in Greek literature to speak of linen clothing. (𝔓[47] and 046 read λινουν, meaning "made of linen"; א reads λινους, with the same meaning.) However, neither one of these readings might be original. The striking image, "clothed in stone," could have prompted changes to λινον or λινουν. Arguing for λιθον ("stone"), Westcott and Hort (1882, 139) said it perfectly accords with the imagery of Ezek 28:13, wherein the angel Lucifer is described as being covered with precious stones. Besides, it has the combined testimony of the two manuscripts (A and C) that are generally regarded as among the best witnesses in Revelation.

The ASV translators followed the best testimony available to them at the time—namely, A and C. But the subsequent discovery of 𝔓[47] and its reading in this verse (concurring with א)

seems to have offset the weight of A and C. Hence, all translations since ASV have followed the reading, "linen," with some noting "stone" in the margin. Whichever reading translators decide to adopt for the text, the other(s) should be noted in all versions because the evidence is so evenly divided.

Revelation 15:7

The idiom τους αιωνας των αιωνων ("the ages of the ages" = "forever and ever") attracted the scribal addition of αμην ("amen"). In this case, the scribe of ℵ, as well as a couple of ancient translators (syr^{ph} cop^{bo}) added it (see note on 4:10 and 7:10, where some of the same witnesses have the appended "amen").

Revelation 16:3, 4, 8, 10, 12, 17

In this chapter, there is a series of numbered angels that are identified as the first, the second, the third, the fourth, the fifth, the sixth, and the seventh. According to a number of reliable manuscripts (including 𝔓^{47} ℵ A C), the noun αγγελος ("angel") does not appear following the numeral. But certain scribes (051 2344), beginning with the second and continuing to the seventh, added the word αγγελος (so Maj^{A} and TR).

Revelation 16:4

TR WH NU ἐγένετο αἷμα
"it became blood"
ℵ C P Maj
ASV NASBmg

variant εγενοντο αιμα
"they became blood"
𝔓^{47} A 2053 it syr cop
KJV ASVmg NKJV RSV NRSV ESV NASB NIV TNIV NEB REB NJB NAB NLT HCSB NET

The TR WH NU reading is the more difficult one because the verb does not agree grammatically with the preceding nouns ("and the third [angel] poured out his vial on rivers and the fountains of the waters"). Thus, scribes would be prone to fix the grammar; and translators (both ancient and modern), desiring a polished rendering, would also follow the grammatically correct variant.

Revelation 16:5a

WH NU δίκαιος εἶ
"you are righteous"
all Greek MSS
NKJVmg RSV ESV NRSV NASB NIV TNIV NEB REB NJB NAB NLT HCSB NET

variant/TR δικαιος ει, κυριε
"you are righteous, Lord"
no Greek MSS; vg (?)
KJV NKJV

Without any Greek textual evidence whatsoever, Erasmus added the vocative Κυριε ("Lord"), which then was included in TR, and has been sustained by KJV and NKJV. The insertion may have been based on some Vulgate manuscript (so Tregelles).

Revelation 16:5b

According to the three editions (TR WH NU), the Lord is described as ο ων και ο ην, ο οσιος ("the one who is and the one who was, the holy one"), with the support of ℵ 051 Maj[A]. All English versions follow this. However, in the textual tradition, there are a number of variants following the και: (1) ος ην και οσιος ("the one who was and [is] holy") in 𝔓[47] 2329; (2) ος ην οσιος ("the one who was holy") in Maj[K]; (3) ο ην και ο οσιος ("the one who was and the holy one") in 1006 2053; (4) ο ην, οσιος ("the one who was, holy") in A C 1611 1854.

The variety of readings shows that scribes were struggling with how to attach the ascription οσιος ("holy") to the previous appellation. Is it a third description of God ("the one who is, the one who was, the one who is holy")? Or is it another adjective parallel to the first adjective in the sentence, δικαιος ("righteous")? If the latter is original, the Lord is ascribed two predicate adjectives ("righteous" and "holy"), on either side of the appellation ο ων και ο ην ("the one who is and the one who was"). The translation of this reading is: "Righteous are you, the one who is and the one who was, and holy." 𝔓[47] backs up this rendering exactly, but και ("and") may be an addition to help the sense. Therefore, it seems that A and C have preserved the original wording here, which translated in full would be, "righteous you are, the one who is and the one who was, holy." It was then changed by other scribes by adding a third article to make three substantive titles—as in ℵ 051 Maj[A] and in variant 3.

Revelation 16:7

WH NU ἤκουσα τοῦ θυσιαστηρίου λέγοντος
"I heard the altar saying"
𝔓[47] ℵ A C
NKJVmg RSV NRSV ESV NASB NIV TNIV NEB REB NJB NAB (NLT) HCSB NET

variant 1 ηκουσα εκ του θυσιαστηριου λεγοντος
"I heard from the altar [one] saying"
046 2329
none

variant 2/TR ηκουσα αλλου εκ του θυσιαστηριου λεγοντος
"I heard another from the altar saying"
vg (?)
KJV NKJV

Uncomfortable with the notion of an inanimate object (the altar) being able to speak, some scribes made some alterations to indicate that there was a person or angelic being behind this voice. Erasmus apparently followed some Vulgate manuscript (so Tregelles) in making the interpolation, αλλου εκ ("another from"). This was included in TR and has been perpetuated in KJV and NKJV.

Revelation 16:13

A few important witnesses (ℵ* C 2053) have some noticeable omissions in this verse, but these can be easily explained as the result of haplography due to homoeoarchton inasmuch as the phrase εκ του στοματος ("out of the mouth") appears three times in this verse: out of the mouth of the dragon, and out of the mouth of the beast, and out of the mouth of the false prophet. The scribe of ℵ skipped the first two (which were later inserted by a corrector), C skipped the first one, and 2053 skipped the second one.

Revelation 16:14

WH NU	τοὺς βασιλεῖς τῆς οἰκουμένης ὅλης "the kings of the entire inhabited world" 𝔓[47] א A C Maj NKJVmg RSV NRSV ESV NASB NIV TNIV NEB REB NJB NAB NLT HCSB NET
variant/TR	τους βασιλεις της γης και της οικουμενης ολης "the kings of the earth and of the entire inhabited world" 1[c] KJV NKJV

Erasmus followed one twelfth-century minuscule (Codex 1) in making a spurious addition (so Tregelles and Alford), which really does not help clarify anything.

Revelation 16:16

TR (WH) NU	῾Αρμαγεδών "Har-Magedon" (or, "Armageddon") א A C all
variant	Μαγεδδων "Mageddon" (= "Megiddo") 1611 2053 Maj[K] syr[ph,hmg] cop[boMSS] NKJVmg NJBmg HCSBmg

According to the TR WH NU reading, the term is derived from *Har*, which means a mountain, and *Megiddo*, a town that guards the mountain pass at the edge of the Jezreel Valley—hence, "Mountain of Megiddo." (This is made clear in WH which reads Ἁρ Μαγεδων). One primary variant reading, "Megiddo," lacks the word for "mountain." In this area God overthrew the Canaanite kings by miraculously aiding Deborah and Barak (Judg 5:19). But Josiah, the ally of Babylon, was also defeated and slain by Pharaoh Neco at Megiddo (2 Kgs 23:29) and thereby "made the place symbolise disaster for any armies assembling there" (NJBmg).

Revelation 16:17

WH NU	ἐξῆλθεν φωνὴ μεγάλη ἐκ τοῦ ναοῦ ἀπὸ τοῦ θρόνου "a great voice came out of the temple from the throne" 𝔓[47] A 0163[vid] 2053 it syr NKJVmg RSV NRSV ESV NASB NIV TNIV NEB REB NJBmg NAB NLT HCSB NET
variant 1	εξηλθεν φωνη μεγαλη εκ του ουρανου απο του θρονου "a great voice came out of heaven from the throne" Maj[A] none
variant 2/TR	εξηλθεν φωνη μεγαλη εκ του ναου του ουρανου απο του θρονου "a great voice came out of the temple of heaven from the throne" Maj[K] KJV NKJV HCSBmg

variant 3 εξηλθεν φωνη μεγαλη εκ του ναου του θεου
"a great voice came out of the temple of God"
א
none

The WH NU reading has the support of three early manuscripts: 𝔓[47] (third century), A and 0163 (both fifth century). All the variants display variations that were derived from other parts of Revelation. A divine voice is said to emanate "from heaven" (variant 1) in 10:4, 8; 11:12; 14:13. The temple is described as a heavenly temple (variant 2) in 14:17. And the throne is called "the throne of God" (variant 3) in 22:1, 3. NJB, not following any manuscripts, decided to go with a short reading: "a great voice boomed out from the sanctuary."

Revelation 16:18

NU ἀφ' οὗ ἄνθρωπος ἐγένετο ἐπὶ τῆς γῆς
"since humanity was on the earth"
(𝔓[47] εγενοντο) A
NRSV ESV NASB NIV TNIV (NEB REB NJB NAB NLT) HCSB NET

variant 1/TR (WH) αφ ου οι ανθρωποι εγενοντο επι της γης
"since human beings were on the earth"
1 2138 (א) 046 051 2053 2344 without οι)
KJV NKJV RSV

The NU reading has slim support—only Codex A. 𝔓[47] provides a mixed reading inasmuch as it has a singular subject, ανρθωπος, and a plural verb, εγενοντο. This combination indicates that the scribe of 𝔓[47] was probably thinking of collective humanity—which is the way it is rendered in many modern versions. The variant, which has fair attestation, reflects the same understanding by using plurals.

Revelation 17:4

TR WH NU τῆς πορνείας αὐτῆς
"her fornication"
A 051 2344 it[ar] syr[ph]
all

variant 1 της πορνειας της γης
"the fornication of the earth"
1611 2053 2062 Maj[K]
NKJVmg HCSBmg NETmg

variant 2 της πορνειας αυτης και της γης
"her fornication and the earth's"
א syr[h**] (cop)
NETmg

Metzger proposes that the first variant is the result of a scribal error, for it is not difficult to imagine a scribe writing της γης instead of αυτης (TCGNT). If this occurred in the course of textual transmission, it must have happened before the fourth century because א and the Coptic tradition (both from the fourth century) preserve a conflated reading. A more likely scenario is that της γης ("of the earth") was a purposeful substitution in light of the statement in 17:2, which says that the kings of the earth (οι βασιλεις της γης) had committed fornication with the great harlot. Thus, her cup overflowed with "the fornications of the earth."

Revelation 17:8

WH NU	καὶ παρέσται "and will be present" A P syr NKJVmg RSV NRSV ESV NASB NIV TNIV NEB REB NJB NAB NLT HCSB NET
variant 1	και παλιν παρεσται "and again will be present" ℵ* none
variant 2	και παρεστιν "and is present" ℵ[2] 1854 Maj[A] none
variant 3/TR	καιπερ εστιν "and yet is" no Greek MSS KJV NKJV

According to WH NU, the beast is described as follows: ην και ουκ εστιν και παρεσται ("it was and is not and will be present"). The last two words were changed in various manuscripts in an attempt to clarify an obscure statement about the existence of the beast. According to the WH NU reading and the first variant, the beast existed in the past, is presently (at the time of writing) not existing, but will (again) be present in the future. According to the second variant and the third (which was created by Erasmus), the beast existed in the past, then no longer existed, but is now (at the time of writing) present. These variants indicate the beast did not really die because he still exists. As such, ουκ εστιν και παρεστιν ("is not and is present") and ουκ εστιν καιπερ εστιν ("is not and yet is") are to be read as ontological statements, not as the second and third stages of the beast's existence. But this does not accord with the first part of this verse, which says that the beast "was and is not and is about to come up out of the abyss." In other words, it indicates that there will be some kind of beast redivivus. This is further developed in 17:10-11, where the beast incarnates himself in a king who once lived and later reappears. The time when the beast was not alive was the time during which it had the deadly wound. The healing of its wound corresponds to its ascending out of the bottomless pit. The beast (probably the antichrist or antichristian world-power) is predicted to return worse than ever, with satanic powers from the abyss.

Revelation 17:16

WH NU	τὰ δέκα κέρατα ἃ εἶδες καὶ τὸ θηρίον "the ten horns which you saw and the beast" all Greek MSS NKJVmg RSV NRSV ESV NASB NIV TNIV NEB REB NJB NAB NLT HCSB NET
variant/TR	τα δεκα κερατα α ειδες επι το θηριον "the ten horns which you saw on the beast" vg (?) it[e] KJV NKJV

The variant reading came from Erasmus, who must have followed the Vulgate here (so Alford, Tregelles) in making it only "the ten horns" which attack the harlot, instead of "the ten horns and the beast." TR's wording intensifies unity between the beast (= the antichrist) and the ten horns (= the ten kings).

Revelation 18:2

NU καὶ ἐγένετο κατοικητήριον δαιμονίων
καὶ φυλακὴ παντὸς πνεύματος ἀκαθάρτου
καὶ φυλακὴ παντὸς ὀρνέου ἀκαθάρτου
[καὶ φυλακὴ παντὸς θηρίου ἀκαθάρτου] καὶ μεμισημένου
"and she has become a habitation of demons
and a haunt of every unclean spirit
and a haunt of every unclean bird
and a haunt of every unclean and detestable beast"
2329 it[gig] syr[h] (A 1611—see comments below)
NRSV ESV TNIV NAB NLT HCSB NET

variant 1/TR WH omit bracketed words: [και φυλακη παντος θηριου ακαθαρτου] with the resulting translation:
"and she has become a habitation of demons
and a haunt of every unclean spirit
and a haunt of every unclean and detestable bird"
א C 051 2053 Maj it[a] vg syr[ph] cop[bo]
KJV NKJV RSV NASB NIV NEB REB NJB NLTmg HCSBmg NETmg

In addition to these two variants, it should be noted that one Greek manuscript (1611) does not include the second line, and several other manuscripts (A Maj[A] syr[ph]) do not include the third line. The variant excludes most of the fourth line. The cause for omission for either the second, third, or fourth lines could be attributed to haplography due to homoeoarchton (και φυλακη begins each line) and/or homoeoteleuton (ακαθαρτου at the end of the lines).

The critical apparatus of NA[27] cites A 1611 2329 it[gig] syr[h] in support of the inclusion of the bracketed clause. Although this is true, 1611 omits the second line, and A omits the third line. Not one of the significant Greek witnesses (א A C) has a text fully like that printed in NU. The English versions are divided on this verse—with several of the more recent versions following NU.

Revelation 18:3

TR NU πέπωκαν
"have drunk"
1006[c] 2329 it[MSS] syr[h]
KJV NKJV RSV NRSV ESV NASB NIV TNIV NEB REB NJB NAB NLTmg HCSB NETmg

variant/WH πεπτωκασιν (or πεπτωκαν)
"have fallen"
א A C 1006* 2053[c] syr[hmg]
RSVmg ESVmg NASBmg NEBmg NJBmg NLT HCSBmg NET

According to the TR NU editions, the full reading is "all the nations have drunk the wine of the wrath due to her fornication." But this reading has very slim support, especially from the Greek manuscripts. Nevertheless, the NU editors considered it the one reading from which the others diverged (see TCGNT). They blamed the divergence on mechanical assimilation to the previous mention of Babylon's *fall* (18:2), and argued that the context of 18:3 (speaking of wine) calls for the verb "have drunken," not "have fallen." These are strong arguments, but not strong enough to topple the testimony of the best three Greek witnesses in Revelation here: ℵ A C.

Assuming ℵ A C to have preserved the original wording, it is easy to see how scribes and ancient translators would have changed πεπτωκασιν ("have fallen") to πεπωκαν ("have drunk") in order to provide a clearer connection between wine and the action that follows. But the verse need not say that they drank the wine, for this is assumed; rather, the verse (according to the variant) says that the nations are now fallen as a result of their partaking of the wine (an assumed action, which means they have fallen because of their fornication with the harlot—or, they have been ruined by their fornication with the harlot (see NJBmg). Only two English versions (NLT NET) followed the variant reading.

Revelation 18:8a

Throughout the course of textual transmission divine names were often altered. In this verse, the divine title κυριος ο θεος ("Lord God"), found in ℵ[2] C 051 Maj (so TR WH NU), also appears in three different forms: (1) ο θεος ("God") in A 1006 2053[mg]; (2) ο κυριος ("the Lord") in 2053[txt] 2062; (3) ο θεος ο κυριος ("God the Lord") in ℵ*. The TR WH NU reading has good textual support and concurs with John's style (see 1:8; 4:8; 11:17; 15:3; 16:7; 19:6; 22:5).

Revelation 18:8b

WH NU	ὁ κρίνας αὐτήν "the one having judged her" A ℵ* C P NKJVmg ESV NEB REB NJB
variant/TR	ο κρινων αυτην "the one judging her" ℵ[c] 1 KJV NKJV RSV NRSV NASB NIV TNIV NAB NLT HCSB NET

The WH NU reading has the support of three early manuscripts (noted above), as well as P. The change from the aorist participle to the present was motivated by the context, wherein Babylon's destruction is being predicted as yet to happen. But prophetic Scripture is full of proleptic aorists to proclaim future judgment as accomplished fact. Most translators, however, have gone with the present tense because they, too, were thinking of the context. But an easy way to remain faithful to the best Greek text and not jar English readers is to render it the way it appears in NEB: "has pronounced her doom."

Revelation 18:12-13

In a list where many words have the same endings, it was easy for scribes to skip over words. This happened in ℵ to the words και μαρμαρου ("and of marble"), which immediately follow words with the same endings. Then the words και αμωμον ("and spice") were omitted in ℵ[2] 2053 Maj[K] because the previous two words are nearly identical: και κινναμωμον ("and cinnamon"). And the words και οινον ("and wine") were omitted in 046 2030 because of the similar-looking nearby words (και μυρον, και λιβανον, και ελαιον).

Revelation 18:17

WH NU read πας ο επι τοπον πλεων ("everyone sailing to a place"), having the support of A C 1006 1611. There are several variants on this: (1) πας ο επι τον τοπον πλεων ("everyone sailing to the place"), found in א 046 0229; (2) πας ο επι τον ποταμον πλεων ("everyone sailing to the river"), found in 2053 2062; (3) πας επι τον πλεων ("everyone sailing on the ships"), found in 051 Maj[A]; (4) πας ο επι των πλοιων ο ομιλος ("everyone in the company of ships"), found in 1 296 2049 (so TR and KJV). The unusualness of the expression in WH NU, which can be more freely rendered as "those who sail everywhere," prompted a number of changes. The change that became part of TR categorically includes any and all who work in the shipping industry, not just the sailors.

Revelation 18:20

WH NU   οἱ ἅγιοι καὶ οἱ ἀπόστολοι καὶ οἱ προφῆται
"the holy ones and the apostles and the prophets"
א A P syr
NKJVmg RSV NRSV ESV NASB NIV TNIV REB NJB NAB NLT HCSB NET

variant/TR   οι αγιοι αποστολοι και οι προφηται
"the holy apostles and the prophets"
C 051 2329 Maj[A]
KJV NKJV NEB

The manuscript evidence slightly favors the WH NU reading. The variant reading has the term αγιοι ("holy") function as an adjective rather than being one of three groups told to rejoice.

Revelation 18:22

The Greek expression και πας τεχνιτης πασης τεχνης ("and every craftsman of every craft"), found in C P 046 051 syr[h] cop[sa], is shortened in א A to και πας τεχνιτης ("and every craftsman") for stylistic reasons. Had the shorter text originally been in the exemplars of C P etc., there is little reason for these scribes to have lengthened it. A few witnesses (א syr[ph] cop[bo]) omit the last sentence of this verse. The omission must have come from homoeoteleuton—both sentences end with εν σοι ετι ("in you anymore").

Revelation 19:1a

WH NU   ἤκουσα ὡς φωνὴν μεγάλην
"I heard, as it were, a loud voice"
א A C P 2344
NKJVmg RSV NRSV ESV NASB NIV TNIV NEB REB NJB NAB NLT HCSB NET

variant/TR   ηκουσα φωνην μεγαλην
"I heard a loud voice"
051* 2053 Maj[A] syr
KJV NKJV

The documentary evidence favors the inclusion of ως ("as [it were]"). This is a word that John used repeatedly when recording his supernatural visions to indicate that the things he saw and heard were not exactly like the things we normally see and hear on earth. Thus, he continually said things such as "it was as if I heard a loud voice" or "it was as if I saw something that looked like a glassy sea," etc. (see 6:6; 8:8; 14:3; 15:2; 19:6 for good examples of this).

Revelation 19:1b

WH NU δύναμις τοῦ θεοῦ ἡμῶν
"power of (from) our God"
ℵ A C P Maj
NKJVmg RSV NRSV ESV NASB NIV TNIV NEB REB NJB NAB NLT HCSB NET

variant/TR δυναμις κυριω τω θεω ημων
"power to the Lord our God"
1
KJV NKJV

According to WH NU, the full rendering is: "the salvation and the glory and the power [come from] our God"—i.e., "belong to our God." The reading of the variant, found in only one manuscript and adopted by Erasmus (so Tregelles and Alford), displays grammatical alteration (to the dative case) and assimilation to verses such as 19:6 and 22:5.

Revelation 19:5a

TR NU αἰνεῖτε τῷ θεῷ ἡμῶν πάντες οἱ δοῦλοι αὐτοῦ [καὶ] οἱ φοβούμενοι αὐτόν
"praise our God, all his servants and the ones fearing him"
A 051 0229 Maj it syr
KJV NKJV NRSV NJB NAB NET

variant/WH αινετε τω θεω ημων παντες οι δουλοι αυτου, οι φοβουμενοι αυτου
"praise our God, all his servants, the ones fearing him"
ℵ C P cop
RSV ESV NASB NIV TNIV NEB REB NLT HCSB

The documentary evidence is evenly divided for the two readings. As to the TR NU reading, "the ones fearing him" could be a separate group (the God-fearers) if και is understood as "and"; alternatively, "the ones fearing him" must be considered as a further description of the same group if και is understood as "even." The ambiguity is eliminated in the variant; the servants are the ones who fear God.

Revelation 19:5b

WH NU οἱ μικροὶ καὶ οἱ μεγάλοι
"the small and the great"
ℵ A C P Maj
NKJVmg RSV NRSV ESV NASB NAB NLT

variant/TR και οι μικροι και οι μεγαλοι
"both the small and the great"
1
KJV NKJV NIV TNIV NEB REB NJB HCSB NET

The word καὶ, found in one minuscule used by Erasmus (Codex 1), according to Tregelles and Alford, was incorporated into his text (probably for stylistic reasons—as with several modern English versions) and from there became part of TR.

Revelation 19:6

(WH) NU κύριος ὁ θεὸς [ἡμῶν]
"Lord our God"
א[2] P 2053 2062 2344 Maj[K] syr[h]
RSV NRSV ESV NASB NEB REB NJB NAB NLT NET

variant 1/TR κυριος ο θεος
"Lord God"
A 1006 cop[bo]
KJV NKJV NLTmg NETmg

variant 2 ο θεος ημων
"our God"
051 (1) Maj[A]
NETmg

variant 3 ο θεος ο κυριος ημων
"God our Lord (or, our Lord God)"
א*
NKJVmg NIV TNIV HCSB NETmg

The documents display a variety of readings, which present two significant differences in exegesis. Is the all-powerful one (ο παντοκρατωρ) to be called "God" or is the all-powerful one called "Lord"? In other words, is this a reference to God or to Christ? In the book of Revelation, where the same or similar expression occurs ("the Lord God all-powerful"), the reference sometimes refers exclusively to God (4:8; 21:22), and sometimes to both God and Christ (1:8; 11:17; 15:3; 16:7). This appears to be one of those instances where the writer was thinking of both; as such, it cannot be determined on exegetical grounds which reading is most likely original. But it is probably the WH NU reading or the third variant. The first variant displays scribal conformity to 19:1 in TR (see note on 19:1b), and the second variant is probably the result of scribes removing ambiguity from the title.

Revelation 19:11

Jesus is here depicted as the one sitting on a white horse and NU describes him as καλουμενος πιστος και αληθινος ("the one being called faithful and true"). But the textual evidence for this wording is late: 1611 2053 2062 Maj[K]. Earlier witnesses either omit the word καλουμενος ("being called"), as in A 051 Maj[A], or they have it after πιστος ("faithful"), as in א (so WH). Dissenting from the majority view of his coeditors, Metzger (see TCGNT) presents convincing arguments for the reading in א.

Revelation 19:12

TR NU ὀφθαλμοὶ αὐτοῦ [ὡς] φλὸξ πυρός
"his eyes are like a flame of fire"
A 1006 it syr cop
KJV NKJV RSV NRSV ESV NIV TNIV NEB REB NAB NLT HCSB NET

variant/WH οφθαλμοι αυτου φλοξ πυρος
"his eyes are a flame of fire"
א 051 Maj
NASB NJB

The textual evidence and internal evidence for this variant-unit are evenly divided. Codex A and several versions support the TR NU reading; whereas some major uncials support the variant. Furthermore, John had a habit of using ως ("as") in describing various visions. Thus, the word could be original or the result of scribal assimilation to the author's style.

Revelation 19:13

TR NU ἱμάτιον βεβαμμένον αἵματι
"garment dipped in blood"
A 051 2344 Maj
all

variant 1/WH ιματιον ρεραντισμενον αιματι
"garment sprinkled [spattered] in blood"
P 2329 (ερραμμενον 2053 2062 Origen)
RSVmg NRSVmg ESVmg NEBmg NETmg

variant 2 ιματιον περιρεραμμενον αιματι
"garment sprinkled around [spattered about] in blood"
א* Tertullian
none

variant 3 ιματιον περιρεραντισμενον αιματι
"garment having been sprinkled around [spattered about] in blood"
(א^{2})
none

The documentary evidence is divided between two verbal roots. All the variants display some verbal form of ραινω or ραντιζω ("sprinkle"); these could be attempts to reflect the image in Isa 63:2-3, which presents the Messiah as being "sprinkled" with the blood (see LXX) of the enemies he has vanquished. The significance of the verbal form of the TR NU reading, being a derivative of βαπτιζω ("baptize," "immerse"), is that the Messiah is soaked in blood—perhaps his own.

Revelation 19:15

TR WH NU ῥομφαία
"sword"
A א 2053 2062
all

variant ρομφαια διστομος
"double-edged sword"
1006 2030 2039 Maj^{K} syr^{h**}
NKJVmg HCSBmg

The manuscript evidence supports the TR WH NU reading. The variant is the result of scribal conformity to 2:12, a previous parallel passage. The TR WH NU reading says, "out of his mouth goes a sharp sword."

Revelation 19:17

WH NU	τὸ δεῖπνον τὸ μέγα τοῦ θεοῦ "the great supper of God" A א 2053 2062 NKJVmg RSV NRSV ESV NASB NIV TNIV NEB REB NJB NAB NLT HCSB NET
variant/TR	το δειπνον του μεγαλου θεου "the supper of the great God" 051 Maj[A] KJV NKJV

The manuscript evidence supports the WH NU reading. The variant is probably the result of scribal metathesis, which then puts the emphasis on the greatness of God rather than the greatness of the supper.

Revelation 20:2

Among the several minor variants in this verse, the most noteworthy is the addition of the phrase ο πλανων την οικουμενην ολην ("the one deceiving the whole inhabited earth") in 051 2030 2377 Maj[K]. This interpolation brings this description of the evil one into harmony with that found in 12:9, which has a fivefold description: great dragon, ancient serpent, the devil, Satan, the one deceiving the whole inhabited earth.

Revelation 20:5

Several manuscripts (א 2030 2053 2062 Maj[K] syr[ph]) omit the first sentence of this verse: οι λοιποι των νεκρων ουκ εξησαν αχρι τελεσθη τα χιλια ετη ("the rest of the dead did not come out from the dead until the thousand years finished"). The omission may have been accidental, due to homoeoteleuton. The previous verse ends with the same last two words: χιλια ετη ("thousand years"). But it is also possible that the omission was intentional because it seems to interrupt a connection between 20:4 and 20:5b (assuming that αυτη η αναστασις η πρωτη ["this is the first resurrection"] is supposed to refer to 20:4b and not 20:5a). With the sentence deleted, there is a better syntactical connection: "And they came to life and reigned with Christ a thousand years [20:4]. This is the first resurrection [20:5b]."

Other scribes may have expunged the sentence for doctrinal reasons. Elimination of the sentence, "the rest of the dead did not come to life until the thousand years finished," eradicates the problem of having to explain how certain Christians (i.e., the martyrs of 20:4) are allowed to participate in the first resurrection and the millennial kingdom, while others (i.e., those who are not martyrs) have to wait until after the millennium to experience resurrection. If the witnesses א 2030 2053 2062 Maj[K] syr[ph] actually preserve the original text, then the sentence "the rest of the dead did not come out of the dead until the thousand years finished" could be seen as a scribal gloss (which eventually found its way into the text) that provides an explanation for what would happen to those Christians who did not get to participate in the millennium.

Revelation 20:9

WH NU	πῦρ ἐκ τοῦ οὐρανου "fire out of heaven" A 2053[com] cop[bo] Augustine RSV NRSV ESV NASB NIV TNIV NEB REB NJB NAB NLT HCSB NET

variant 1	πυρ απο του θεου "fire from God" 1854 none
variant 2/TR	πυρ απο του θεου εκ του ουρανου "fire from God out of heaven" ℵ[2] P 051 (Maj[A]) KJV NKJV RSVmg NRSVmg ESVmg HCSBmg

The first variant is slimly supported, and the second is probably the result of scribal harmonization to 21:2 and 10.

Revelation 20:12

WH NU	ἑστῶτας ἐνώπιον τοῦ θρόνου "standing before the throne" ℵ A P 051 2053 2062 syr NKJVmg RSV NRSV ESV NASB NIV TNIV NEB REB NJB NAB (NLT) HCSB NET
variant/TR	εστωτας ενωπιον του θεου "standing before God" 1 KJV NKJV

The change in TR, introduced by Erasmus from Codex 1 (according to Tregelles and Alford), personalizes the judgment: People stand before God himself, not just his throne. But the throne is used throughout Revelation as a metonymy for God's personal judgment.

Revelation 20:14

Several manuscripts (051 2053[txt] 2062[txt] Maj[A] cop[bo]) omit ουτος ο θανατος ο δευτερος εστιν, η λιμνη του πυρος ("this is the second death, the lake of fire"). The omission may have been accidental, due to homoeoteleuton. The previous clause ends with exactly the same last three words: λιμνη του πυρος ("lake of fire"). However, the omission could have been intentional. This seems likely for the scribes of 2053 and 2062 because these same scribes also omitted the sentence in 20:5 about the rest of the dead not coming back to life until the end of the millennium.

Revelation 21:2

WH NU	τὴν πόλιν τὴν ἁγίαν Ἰερουσαλὴμ καινὴν εἶδον "I saw the holy city, new Jerusalem" ℵ A 051 Maj NKJVmg RSV NRSV ESV NASB NIV TNIV NEB REB NJB NAB NLT HCSB NET
variant/TR	εγω Ιωαννης ειδον την αγιαν Ιεροσαλημ καινην "I, John, saw the holy city, new Jerusalem" no Greek MSS KJV NKJV

Erasmus did not use any Greek manuscript at this point when compiling his edition of the Greek text. Perhaps relying on some manuscript of the Latin Vulgate (so Tregelles), which he translated into Greek, he produced a textual aberration that conforms to 1:9 and 22:8, where the writer identifies himself as John. The interpolation has been sustained by its presence in KJV and NKJV.

Revelation 21:3a

WH NU	φωνῆς μεγάλης ἐκ τοῦ θρόνου "loud voice from the throne" א A it RSV NRSV ESV NASB NIV TNIV NEB REB NJB NAB NLT HCSB NET
variant/TR	φωνης μεγαλης εκ του ουρανου "loud voice from heaven" 051[s] Maj syr cop KJV NKJV HCSBmg

The variant exhibits conformity to 21:2—whether intentional or not. It is possible that some scribes mistook one word for the other: θρονου/ουρανου ("throne/heaven").

Revelation 21:3b

TR WH NU read η σκηνη του θεου μετα των ανθρωπων, και σκηνωσει μετ αυτων ("the tabernacle of God is with men, and he will tabernacle with them"). This statement is presented as a promise of God's personal, abiding presence with his people from that point forward into eternity. Other witnesses, however, have the aorist verb, εσκηνωσεν ("he tabernacled"): א* 2050 vg[MSS] syr[h]. This could be an allusion to Christ's incarnation, as depicted in John 1:14 ("he tabernacled [εσκηνωσεν] among us"), here seen as continuing into eternity (see note on 21:3d). Or it could be a proleptic aorist, which views the future reality of God living with his people as an accomplished fact.

Revelation 21:3c

TR NU	αὐτὸς ὁ θεὸς μετ' αὐτῶν ἔσται [αὐτῶν θεός] "God himself will be with them, their God" A 2030 2050 2053[txt] 2062 (051[s] Maj[A]) (KJV NKJV) RSVmg NRSVmg ESV NASBmg NIV TNIV NEBmg NJB NAB NLTmg HCSB NETmg
variant 1	αυτος ο θεος μετ αυτων εσται θεος "God himself will be with them [as] God" 1006 1611 1841 NETmg
variant 2/WH	αυτος ο θεος μετ αυτων εσται "God himself will be with them" (א) 1 RSV NRSV ESVmg NASB NEB REB NJB NLT HCSBmg NET

The wording of this part of the verse has been difficult for scribes and translators. Does the TR NU reading, with its complexities, represent the original wording or the redaction of scribes? Many modern translators considered the longer TR NU reading to be the result of scribal conformity to Isa 7:14; 8:8 (see Tasker 1964, 444). But it can also be argued that scribes were frustrated with the ambiguity of the longer wording and subsequently shortened it, as in the two variants. Either way, the idea of either reading is that the one called "God-with-us" (i.e.,

Immanuel) will be with his people. God will tabernacle with them (lit., "he will pitch his tent among them"). This is what God did when he became the man Christ Jesus; he tabernacled among men (John 1:14). God in the flesh actually walked among men. He could be seen, heard, and touched. In the future, God in Christ will live among and with his redeemed people in the same manner.

Revelation 21:8

TR WH NU ἀπίστοις
"unbelievers"
א A 2053 it cop
all

variant απιστοις και αμαρτωλος
"unbelievers and sinners"
1854 2329 M[k] syr[ph,h**]
NKJVmg HCSBmg

A few witnesses exhibit the addition of "sinners" to the list of those who will be excluded from participating in the new Jerusalem. But John put the emphasis where it should be: Unbelievers will be excluded, for unbelief is the greatest sin (see John 16:9).

Revelation 21:10

WH NU τὴν πόλιν τὴν ἁγίαν Ἰερουσαλήμ
"the holy city, Jerusalem"
א A 2053 it syr cop
NKJVmg RSV NRSV ESV NASB NIV TNIV NEB REB NJB NAB NLT HCSB NET

variant/(TR) την πολιν την μεγαλην και αγιαν Ιερουσαλημ
"the great and holy city, Jerusalem"
051[s] 1854 2030 2377 Maj[A]
(KJV NKJV)

The notion of "greatness" was added to the description of the new Jerusalem in several late manuscripts—perhaps to present parity with the other city in Revelation, the great Babylon (see 18:21). This addition was incorporated in TR (without και) and then popularized by KJV and NKJV. But the key descriptor for the new Jerusalem is "holy," for this adjective emphasizes that this city, as God's habitation with redeemed humanity, is distinct and separate from all that is contrary to his nature.

Revelation 21:12

A few manuscripts (A 051[s*] 2050) omit και επι τοις πυλωσιν αγγελους δωδεκα ("and at the gates twelve angels")—probably due to homoeoteleuton. The preceding phrase ends with the same word: δωδεκα.

Revelation 21:24a

WH NU περιπατήσουσιν τὰ ἔθνη διὰ τοῦ φωτὸς αὐτῆς
"the nations will walk by its light"
א A P
NKJVmg RSV NRSV ESV NASB NIV TNIV NEB REB NJB NAB NLT HCSB NET

variant/TR περιπατησουσιν τα εθνη των σωζομενων δια του φωτος αυτης
"the nations of the saved will walk by its light"
1
KJV NKJV HCSBmg

The words των σωζομενων ("of the saved ones") came from Codex 1 (according to Tregelles and Alford), which Erasmus used in making his Greek text. These words eventually became part of TR and were translated in KJV and NKJV. This interpolation may be the correct interpretation in the sense that these "nations" might be another description of the believers—for 21:27 says that none can enter into the city whose name is not in the Lamb's book of life. But it may not be the correct interpolation, if John was speaking of the "nations" as those people who live on the new earth and benefit from the new Jerusalem (see 22:2) but are not included among the redeemed. Either way, Erasmus's interpolation has had a long tradition because of its place in TR and KJV.

Revelation 21:24b

TR WH NU read οι βασιλεις της γης φερουσιν την δοξαν αυτων εις αυτην ("the kings of the earth will bring their glory into it") on the basis of excellent testimony: א A C. A variant on this is οι βασιλεις της γης φερουσιν αυτω δοξαν και τιμη των εθνων ("the kings of the earth will bring to him the nations' glory and honor"), based on inferior testimony: 1611 1854 Maj^{K}.

Revelation 21:26

At the end of this verse, some manuscripts (1611 1854 Maj^{K}) add ινα εισελθωσιν ("so that they may enter")—extending the verse to read, "and they will bring the glory and the honor of the nations into it, so that they may enter" (see NKJVmg). This addition reflects a scribal interpretation—namely, that one would only come to the city so as to enter in. This idea is made clear enough in the following verse.

Revelation 22:1

WH NU ποταμὸν ὕδατος ζωῆς
"river of water of life"
א A P
NKJVmg RSV NRSV ESV NASB NIV TNIV NEB REB NJB NAB NLT HCSB NET

variant/TR ποταμον καθαρον υδατος ζωης
"pure river of water of life"
051^{s} 2030 Maj^{A}
KJV NKJV

The addition in TR is the result of unnecessary scribal coloring. It is obvious to the reader that a river "bright as crystal" (λαμπρον ως κρυσταλλον) is "pure" (καθαρον).

Revelation 22:6

WH NU — ὁ κύριος ὁ θεὸς τῶν πνευμάτων τῶν προφητῶν
"the Lord God of the spirits of the prophets"
א A P
NKJVmg RSV NRSV ESV NASB NIV TNIV NEB REB NJB NAB NLT HCSB NET

variant/TR — ο κυριος ο θεος των αγιων προφητων
"the Lord God of the holy prophets"
051[s] Maj[A]
KJV NKJV HCSBmg

The manuscript evidence favors the WH NU reading. According to the book of Revelation's own record, the "spirit of prophecy" (i.e., the spirit of the prophet) is that which constitutes "the testimony of Jesus" (19:10). The revelation of Jesus was given by God through angels to the prophet John (see 1:1-2). The source of all prophecy is divine: God himself inspires the spirits of the prophets (see NLT) and gives them utterance (see 2 Pet 1:20-21). The variant misses the mark entirely by putting the emphasis on the prophets' holiness. The same kind of misguided change occurred in 2 Pet 1:21 (see note).

Revelation 22:11

A few manuscripts (A 2030 2050 2062[txt]) omit και ο ρυπαρος ρυπανθητω ετι ("and the one who is filthy let him be filthy still")—probably due to homoeoteleuton. The previous clause ends with the same word: ετι ("still"). The scribe of A had a proclivity for omissions in Revelation.

Revelation 22:13

WH NU — ἐγὼ τὸ ἄλφα καὶ τὸ ὦ, ὁ πρῶτος καὶ ὁ ἔσχατος, ἡ ἀρχὴ καὶ τὸ τέλος.
"I am the Alpha and the Omega, the First and the Last, the Beginning and the End."
א (A) P 051 (2053 2062)
NKJVmg RSV NRSV ESV NASB NIV TNIV NEB REB NJB NAB NLT HCSB NET

variant/TR — εγω το αλφα και το ω, αρχη και τελος, ο πρωτος και ο εσχατος.
"I am the Alpha and Omega, the Beginning and the End, the First and the Last."
2377 Maj[A]
KJV NKJV

The threefold divine appellation has an alternative order in TR, due to the influence of 21:6. In 1:8 and 21:6, God Almighty is called "the Alpha and Omega"; in 21:6, God is called "the Beginning and the End"; in 1:17, the Son of Man is called "the First and the Last." Here, at the consummation of Revelation, the Son of Man distinguishes himself with all three titles, thereby revealing his eternal deity.

Revelation 22:14

WH NU μακάριοι οἱ πλύνοντες τὰς στολὰς αὐτῶν
"blessed are the ones washing their robes"
ℵ A 1006 2050 2053 2062 cop[sa]
NKJVmg RSV NRSV ESV NASB NIV TNIV NEB REB NJB NAB NLT HCSB NET

variant/TR μακαριοι οι ποιουντες τας εντολας αυτου
"blessed are the ones doing his commandments"
Maj it[gig] syr cop[bo]
KJV NKJV RSVmg NRSVmg ESVmg HCSBmg

This statement has important soteriological consequences because the activity so described grants one to "have right to the tree of life." It is possible that some scribe or ancient translator misread πλυνοντες ("washing") as ποιουντες ("doing"), and τας στολας ("the robes") as τας εντολας ("the commandments"), but not so for the possessive pronoun (αυτου for αυτων). It is more likely that the change reflects a Pelagian influence—i.e., eternal life can be achieved by good works. The original reading points us in the opposite direction: Salvation comes from having one's "robes washed" in the Lamb's blood (7:14).

Revelation 22:19

WH NU τοῦ ξύλου τῆς ζωῆς
"the tree of life"
ℵ A P Maj
NKJVmg RSV NRSV ESV NASB NIV TNIV NEB REB NJB NAB NLT HCSB NET

variant/TR του βιβλιου της ζωης
"the book of life"
it[c] vg[MSS]
KJV NKJV NETmg

According to WH NU, a full rendering is as follows: "And if anyone takes words away from this book of prophecy, God will take away from him his share in the tree of life and in the holy city, which are written in this book." This verse was altered in the Greek text created by Erasmus, who did not have the last six verses of Revelation available to him in any Greek manuscript. Consequently, TR has several textual variants in the last six verses of Revelation with no Greek manuscript support. In this verse Erasmus followed the testimony of some Latin Vulgate manuscript. According to Metzger, some Latin copyist accidentally mistook *ligno* ("tree") for *libro* ("book") (see TCGNT). However, it is possible that the change in some Vulgate manuscript was deliberate because it makes for a nice turn of phrase: "if anyone takes away from this book, his part in the book of life will be taken away." However, an eminent promise in Revelation is that the faithful Christian will be allowed to enjoy the tree of life (see 2:7; 22:2, 14).

Revelation 22:20

WH NU 'Αμήν, ἔρχου κύριε 'Ιησοῦ
"Amen, come Lord Jesus"
ℵ A
RSV NRSV ESV NASB NIV TNIV NEB REB NJB NAB NLT HCSB NET

variant 1/TR Αμην, ναι, ερχου κυριε Ιησου
"Amen, yes, come Lord Jesus"
051[s] Maj[K]
KJV NKJV

variant 2 Αμην, ερχου κυριε Ιησου Χριστε
"Amen, come Lord Jesus Christ"
א[2] 1611 Maj[A]
none

After Jesus says, "I am coming soon," the believers give their response, which is poignant according to WH NU: "Amen, come Lord Jesus" (cf. 1 Cor 16:22). This was expanded with the addition of "yes" and the extension of the name to "Lord Jesus Christ."

Revelation 22:21a

NU ἡ χάρις τοῦ κυρίου 'Ιησοῦ
"the grace of the Lord Jesus"
א A 1611[s] 2053
RSV NRSV ESV NASB NIV TNIV NEB REB NJB NAB NLT HCSB NET

variant 1/WH η χαρις του κυριου Ιησου Χριστου
"the grace of the Lord Jesus Christ"
051[s] Maj syr[h]
HCSBmg

variant 2/TR η χαρις του κυριου ημων Ιησου Χριστου
"the grace of our Lord Jesus Christ"
2067 it syr[ph]
KJV NKJV

The title "Christ" is very rare in the book of Revelation, occurring only seven times (1:1, 2, 5; 11:15; 12:10; 20:4, 6). Thus, the "Lord Jesus" is more Johannine than "Lord Jesus Christ." As often happened throughout the course of textual transmission, Jesus' name was expanded and the possessive "our" was attached to it. Against their usual practice of following the best documentary evidence, WH included Χριστου.

Revelation 22:21b

NU μετὰ πάντων
"[be] with all"
A
NKJVmg RSVmg NRSVmg ESV NASB NEBmg REB NAB NET

variant 1/TR μετα παντων υμων
"[be] with you all"
296 (it) vg[MSS]
KJV NKJV NEB NJB

variant 2 μετα παντων ημων
"[be] with us all"
2050
none

variant 3/WH μετα των αγιων
"[be] with the saints"
א it[gig]
RSVmg NRSVmg NASBmg NIV TNIV NEBmg NJBmg (NLT)

variant 4 μετα παντων των αγιων
"[be] with all the saints"
051[s] 1611 Maj syr[h] cop[sa]
NKJVmg RSV NRSV ESVmg NJBmg HCSB

Although there are other variants here (see TCGNT), these are the primary ones. The NU reading, as the shortest one, is probably original because it has the support of Codex Alexandrinus and because benedictions were usually expanded throughout the course of textual transmission. Erasmus probably created the first variant when he translated from the Latin Vulgate into Greek to construct the last verses of Revelation for a printed edition. This reading became part of TR. The second variant is hardly different. The third and fourth include mention of "the saints" (so WH following א) or "all the saints"—perhaps to avoid a benediction being addressed to an unspecified audience. Several versions also mention "the saints," probably for the same reason.

Revelation 22:21c

WH NU omit αμην ("Amen") at end of verse
A 1006 1841 it[a,gig]
NRSVmg NEB REB NAB NLT HCSBmg NET

variant/TR include αμην ("Amen") at end of verse
א 051[s] 2050 Maj syr cop
KJV NKJV RSV NRSV ESV NASB NIV TNIV NEBmg NJB NLTmg HCSB NETmg

Although the inclusion of "Amen" has decent testimony, it is suspect as being a scribal addition because in most books of the NT it seems evident that an "amen" was added for liturgical purposes. Indeed, only three epistles (Romans, Galatians, Jude) appear to have a genuine "amen" for the last word; and if we had earlier sources, they might show that the "amen" in these epistles was also an addition. Tradition and liturgy must have also played some part in motivating several English translators to render the final "amen." Even the NRSV translators did so, against the NU reading.

APPENDIX A

Scribal Gap-Filling

It is my opinion that scribal gap-filling accounts for many of the textual variants (especially textual expansions) in the New Testament—particularly in the narrative books (the Four Gospels and Acts). Usually, textual critics examine textual variants as accidental deviations from the original text. However, some variants may be accounted for more accurately as individual "reader-receptions" of the text. By this, I mean variants created by individual scribes as they interpreted the text in the process of reading it. In the centuries prior to the production of copies via dictation (wherein many scribes in a scriptorium transcribed a text as it was dictated to them by one reader), all manuscript copies were made singly—each scribe working alone to produce a copy from an exemplar. The good scribe was expected not to have really processed the text internally but to have mechanically copied it word by word, even letter by letter. But no matter how meticulous or professional, a scribe would become subjectively involved with the text and—whether consciously or unconsciously—at times produce a transcription that differed from his exemplar, thereby leaving a written legacy of his individual reading of the text.

Even a scribe as meticulous as the one who produced 𝔓[75] could not refrain, on occasion, from filling in a perceived gap. This occurs in the parable in Luke 16:19-31 where the reader is told of an unnamed rich man and a beggar who has a name, Lazarus. Perceiving a gap in the story, the scribe gives the rich man a name: "Neues," perhaps meaning "Nineveh" (see note on Luke 16:19). Other scribes gave names to the two revolutionaries crucified with Jesus: Zoatham and Camma (in some manuscripts), or Joathas and Maggatras (in other manuscripts; see note on Matt 27:38). Many other scribes filled in bigger gaps, especially in narratives. In the story of the salvation of the Ethiopian eunuch recorded in Acts 8:26-40, some scribes added an entire verse so as to fill in a perceived gap of what one must confess before being baptized. Thus, we are given these extra words in Acts 8:37, "And Philip said, 'If you believe with all your heart, you may [be baptized].' And he [the eunuch] replied, 'I believe that Jesus Christ is the Son of God.'" (See note on Acts 8:37 for further discussion.)

The observations of certain literary theorists who focus on reader reception help us understand the dynamic interaction between the scribe (functioning as a true reader) and the text he or she was copying. Textual critics must take into account the historical situation of the scribes who produced the manuscripts we rely on for textual criticism. Textual critics must also realize that scribes were interactive readers. Indeed, as many literary critics in recent years have shifted their focus from the text itself to the readers of the text in an attempt to comprehend plurality of interpretation, so textual critics could analyze variant readings in the textual tradition as possibly being the products of different, personalized "readings" of the text created by the scribes who produced them.

The work of Wolfgang Iser is useful for understanding how scribes read and processed a text as they transcribed it. Iser is concerned not just with the question of what a literary text makes its readers do but with how readers participate in creating meaning. In other words, the meaning of a text is not inherent in the text but must be actualized by the reader. A reader must act as cocreator of the text by supplying that portion of it which is not written but only implied. Each reader uses his or her imagination to fill in the unwritten portions of the text, its "gaps" or areas of "indeterminacy." In other words, the meaning of a text is gradually actualized as the reader adopts the perspectives thrust on him or her by the text, experiences it sequentially, has expectations frustrated or modified, relates one part of the text to the other, and imagines and fills in all that the text leaves blank. The reader's reflection on the thwarting of his or her expectations, the negations of familiar values, the causes of their failure, and whatever potential solutions the text offers, require the reader to take an active part in formulating the meaning of the narrative.

While readers do this gap-filling in their imaginations only, scribes sometimes took the liberty to fill the unwritten gaps with written words. In other words, some scribes went beyond just imagining how the gaps should be filled and actually filled them. The historical evidence shows that each scribe who copied a text created a new written text. Although there are many factors that could have contributed to the making of this new text, one major factor is that the text constantly demands the reader to fill in the gaps.

A literary work is not autonomous but is an intensional object that depends on the cognition of the reader. As an intensional object, a literary work cannot fill in all the details; the reader is required to do this. During the reading process, the reader must concretize the gaps by using his or her imagination to give substance to textual omission and/or indefiniteness. Since this substantiation is a subjective and creative act, the concretization will assume many variations for different readers. For example, the Gospel of Luke says that the crowds who had watched Jesus' crucifixion "returned home, beating their breasts" (Luke 23:48). Although it would seem that most readers are given enough text to visualize this scene, the imaginations of various scribes were sparked to consider how extensive their grief was or to re-create what they might have been saying to one another as they walked home. A few scribes, imagining a more intense reaction, added, "they returned home, beating their breasts *and foreheads.*" Other scribes provided some dialogue: "they returned home beating their breasts, *and saying, 'Woe to us for the sins we have committed this day, for the destruction of Jerusalem is imminent!'* "

Iser calls the textual gaps "blanks"; each blank is a nothing that propels communication because the blank requires an act of ideation in order to be filled. "Blanks suspend connectibility of textual patterns, the resultant break in good continuation intensifies the acts of ideation on the reader's part, and in this respect the blank functions as an elementary function of communication" (Iser 1978, 189). According to Iser, the central factor in literary communication concerns the reader's filling in of these textual blanks. His theory of textual gaps is useful for understanding scribal reader-reception. Of course, his perception of gaps or blanks is far bigger and more demanding on the reader's imaginative powers than was usually the case for New Testament scribes. Nonetheless, scribes were confronted with gaps or blanks that begged for imaginative filling. Many scribes, when confronted with such textual gaps, took the liberty to fill in those gaps by adding extra words or changing the wording to provide what they thought would be a more communicative text. Indeed, the entire history of New Testament textual transmission shows the text getting longer and longer due to textual interpolations—i.e., the filling in of perceived gaps. We especially see the work of gap-filling in the substantial number of expansions in the D-text of the Gospels and Acts. Whoever edited this text had a propensity for filling in textual gaps, as he perceived them. Such gap-filling is especially pronounced in the book of Acts, where the D-reviser made countless interpolations (see introduction to Acts).

APPENDIX B[1]

Aland's Local-Genealogical Method

Kurt Aland (1979, 43) favors a type of textual criticism which he calls the local-genealogical method. He defines it as follows:

> It is impossible to proceed from the assumption of a manuscript stemma, and on the basis of a full review and analysis of the relationships obtaining among the variety of interrelated branches in the manuscript tradition, to undertake a recensio of the data as one would do with other Greek texts. Decisions must be made one by one, instance by instance. This method has been characterized as eclecticism, but wrongly so. After carefully establishing the variety of readings offered in a passage and the possibilities of their interpretation, it must always then be determined afresh on the basis of external and internal criteria which of these readings (and frequently they are quite numerous) is the original, from which the others may be regarded as derivative. From the perspective of our present knowledge, this local-genealogical method (if it must be given a name) is the only one which meets the requirements of the New Testament textual tradition.

The "local-genealogical" method assumes that for any given variation unit, any manuscript (or manuscripts) may have preserved the original text. The problem with doing textual criticism on the local-genealogical basis is that the editors must decide what the authors most likely wrote on a variant-unit by variant-unit basis, which leads to extensive eclecticism (despite Aland's protest to the contrary). The eclecticism is striking when we examine the selection process for variant readings within a single verse, such as Mark 6:51. In Mark 6:51, the expression και λιαν εκ περισσου εν εαυτοις εξισταντο ("and they were exceedingly, extremely amazed in themselves") is found in A f[13] Maj and was adopted as the text for the NU edition. Perhaps this longer reading was accepted over the shorter text (which omits εκ περισσου, "extremely"), found in ℵ B (L), on the supposition that the Alexandrian scribes of ℵ, B, and L were pruning excessive modifiers. However, in the next part of the verse, the shorter reading εξισταντο ("they were amazed"), found in ℵ B L, was adopted by NU, as opposed to the longer reading εξισταντο και εθαυμαζον ("they were amazed and marveled"), found in A D W f[13] Maj. This is a prime example of atomistic eclecticism (i.e., eclecticism on a variant-unit basis). Within one verse, the reading of ℵ B L was first rejected and then subsequently accepted. It is more consistent to judge that ℵ B L present the original text in both instances and that both longer readings are scribal expansions intended to accentuate the disciples' amazement over the miracle they just witnessed. This understanding is also consistent with what we know of the overall character of these manuscripts.

This kind of inconsistency is not uncommon. In Matthew 8:21, NU rejected the witness of ℵ B 33: ετερος δε των μαθητων ειπεν αυτω, κυριε, επιτρεψον μοι πρωτον

[1] Portions of appendices B–D are adapted from my book, *Encountering the Manuscripts*, pp. 298–306 (with permission of the publisher, Broadman & Holman).

απελθειν και θαψαι τον πατερα μου ("Another of the disciples said to him, 'Lord, let me first return and bury my father'"). Instead, NU favored the reading found in C L W Θ 0250, which adds αυτου ("his") after μαθητων ("disciples"). Metzger's comments in TCGNT reveal that most of the committee thought that αυτου was deleted by the scribes of ℵ B 33 to help readers understand that the scribe mentioned in 8:19 was not one of Jesus' disciples. The excellent documentary testimony of ℵ B 33 was thus rejected because of internal considerations. Four verses later (in 8:25), the testimony of the same manuscripts is accepted for the exclusion of οι μαθηται αυτου at the beginning of the verse.

Another occurrence of atomistic eclecticism occurs in the NU text of John 9:4. In the first part of the verse, NU reads ημας δει ("it is necessary for us"), following the testimony of $\mathfrak{P}^{66}$ $\mathfrak{P}^{75}$ ℵ* B D L W 0124. In the second part of the verse, NU reads του πεμψαντος με ("the one having sent me"), following the testimony of ℵ^{c} A B C D 0124 and rejecting the testimony of $\mathfrak{P}^{66}$ $\mathfrak{P}^{75}$ ℵ* L W, which read του πεμψαντος ημας ("the one having sent us"). In the first part of this verse, the testimony of $\mathfrak{P}^{66}$ $\mathfrak{P}^{75}$ ℵ B L W is accepted, but in the next part of the very same clause, the testimony of the $\mathfrak{P}^{66}$ $\mathfrak{P}^{75}$ ℵ* L W was rejected. This is the result of eclecticism, wherein internal evidence is given more weight than documentary evidence (see TCGNT).

In another case, in Romans 8:11, the reading ο εγειρας χριστον εκ νεκρων ("the one having raised Christ from the dead") is accepted into the NU text on the authority of B D^{2} F G. The only merit the NU reading has is that it is the shortest one. However, in general, the NU editors were categorically suspicious of a reading supported by B with D F G (see TCGNT on Rom 8:11b), so it seems inconsistent that this reading would be accepted on the basis of B D^{2} F G. But this is the result of the eclectic method.

These few examples show that many modern textual critics attempt to operate according to a syncretism of two conflicting theories: one that says the best readings are preserved in the best manuscripts and another that says the best readings are simply those that best fit the text, no matter what manuscripts they come from. As far as I am concerned, the best approach is to first establish which manuscripts (or groups of manuscripts) are the best authorities for each particular book or section (e.g., Paul's Epistles, General Epistles) of the New Testament. Once these are reckoned, the burden of proof for any textual variation is to show that these manuscripts do *not* have the original wording. As always, the critic must first look for transcriptional causes of error or variation. If transcriptional errors cannot account for the variation, then the critic has to look to the criteria for internal evidence. But one needs very strong arguments on internal grounds to overthrow strong documentary attestation. Of course, this means that the critic must know each manuscript well and have adequate knowledge about the workmanship and tendencies of the scribe who produced it.

APPENDIX C

Metzger's Judgment of Variant Readings according to Text-Types

Because there are so many individual manuscripts, textual critics are hard-pressed to know the individual characteristics of each manuscript. Consequently, many textual critics categorize the manuscripts into text-types, which they then use in their evaluation of textual variants. One of the foremost textual critics of our era, Bruce Metzger, exhibits this kind of evaluation. He placed the extant manuscripts into one of four text-types, usually called Alexandrian, Western, Caesarean, and Byzantine. Each of these requires some explanation. (More detailed explanations can be found in Metzger 1992, 211-219).

Alexandrian Manuscripts

The Alexandrian text is found in manuscripts produced by scribes trained in the Alexandrian scriptoral tradition, the best of its kind in Greco-Roman times. Such scribes were schooled in producing well-crafted, accurate copies. Among the New Testament manuscripts, it can be seen that there are several early Alexandrian manuscripts (sometimes called proto-Alexandrian) and later Alexandrian manuscripts. The earlier manuscripts are usually purer than the later ones in that the earlier are less polished and closer to the ruggedness of the original writings. In short, these manuscripts display the work of scribes who had the least creative interaction with the text; they were produced by scribes who stayed with their task of making faithful copies. Quite significantly, the text of several of the earlier or proto-Alexandrian manuscripts was transmitted quite faithfully. This is exemplified in the high percentage of textual agreement between 𝔓^{75} and B, thereby affirming Hort's theory that Codex Vaticanus traces back to an early, pure text. This textual relationship and others are detailed in my book, *The Quest for the Original Text of the New Testament* (1992, 101-118).

Metzger (1992, 216) lists the following Alexandrian witnesses, in the categories "Proto-Alexandrian" and "Later Alexandrian."

Proto-Alexandrian:

𝔓^{45} (in Acts) 𝔓^{46} 𝔓^{66} 𝔓^{75} א B Sahidic (in part), Clement of Alexandria, Origen (in part), and most of the papyrus fragments with Pauline text

Later Alexandrian:

Gospels: (C) L T W (in Luke 1:1–8:12 and John) (X) Z Δ (in Mark) Ξ Ψ (in Mark; partially in Luke and John) 33 579 892 1241 Bohairic

Acts: 𝔓^{50} A (C) Ψ 33 81 104 326

Pauline Epistles: A (C) H I Ψ 33 81 104 326 1739

Catholic Epistles: 𝔓^{20} 𝔓^{23} A (C) Ψ 33 81 104 326 1739

Revelation: A (C) 1006 1611 1854 2053 2344; less good 𝔓^{47} א

Western Manuscripts

The so-called "Western" text is a loose category. Actually, it is probably best to call it a kind of "popular" text inasmuch as most of the manuscripts that get put in this text-type share the common traits of scribal expansion, harmonization, and amelioration. Those who defend the cohesiveness of this text-type indicate that it seems to have developed at one point in history (mid- to late second century) and in a certain geographical region (Western Christendom). This form of the Gospels, Acts, and Paul's Epistles circulated in North Africa, Italy, and Gaul (which are geographically Western), but so-called "Western" manuscripts have also come from Egypt and other locations in the East. It is represented in the Old Latin manuscripts, Syriac manuscripts, and in the D-text (a special brand of the Western text—see discussion at the beginning of Acts). The Western text also prevails in the writings of Marcion, Tatian, Irenaeus, and Tertullian.

The "Western" witnesses listed by Metzger (1992, 214) are as follows:

Gospels: D W (in Mark 1:1–5:30) 0171 it syr^{s} syr^{c} (in part), early Latin fathers, Tatian's Diatessaron

Acts: $\mathfrak{P}^{29}$ $\mathfrak{P}^{38}$ $\mathfrak{P}^{48}$ D 383 614 syr^{hmg}, early Latin fathers

Paul's Epistles: The Greek-Latin diglots D E F G; Greek Fathers to the end of the third century; it and early Latin Fathers; Syrian Fathers to about A.D. 450

The Western text is not apparent in the General Epistles and Revelation. The recently published papyrus, $\mathfrak{P}^{112}$ (fifth century), is Western. And I would put a question mark next to $\mathfrak{P}^{29}$ because its text is too small to determine its textual affinities.

Caesarean Manuscripts

Another small group of manuscripts constitute a group known as the Caesarean text. Various scholars such as Streeter and Lake demonstrated that Origen brought a text with him from Egypt to Caesarea, which was then transported to Jerusalem. This text, showing a mixture of Alexandrian and Western readings, is apparent in the following manuscripts—only in the Gospels: $\mathfrak{P}^{45}$, W (in Mark 5:31–16:20), family 1 (f^{1}), family 13 (f^{13}), Θ, 565, and 700.

Byzantine Manuscripts

The Byzantine manuscripts constitute the largest group and are the furthest removed from the original text in most sections of the New Testament. The one notable exception is the book of Revelation, where several Byzantine manuscripts preserve a purer form of the text.

The Byzantine manuscripts are as follows:

Gospels: A E F G H K P S V W (in Matthew and Luke 8:13–24:53) Π Ψ (partially in Luke and John) Ω and most minuscules

Acts: H L P 049 and most minuscules

Epistles: L 049 and most minuscules

Revelation: 046 051 052 and many minuscules

Metzger argues that usually a variant reading "which is supported by a combination of Alexandrian and Western witnesses is superior to any other reading" (1992, 218). The observant reader will see that this kind of statement appears repeatedly throughout Metzger's textual commentary on the United Bible Societies' *Greek New Testament,* in support of the committee's decisions about certain readings. Metzger also made the following important observation:

> In the evaluation of readings which are supported by only one class of witnesses, the student will probably find that true readings survive frequently in the Alexandrian text alone, less frequently in the Western group alone, and very rarely only in Caesarean witnesses. As a rule of thumb, the beginner may ordinarily follow the Alexandrian text except in the case of readings contrary to the criteria which are responsible for its being given preference in general.

> Such a procedure, however, must not be allowed to degenerate into merely looking for the reading which is supported by B and ℵ (or even by B alone, as Hort was accused of doing); in every instance a full and careful evaluation is to be made of all the variant readings in the light of both transcriptional and intrinsic probabilities. The possibility must always be kept open that the original reading has been preserved alone in any one group of manuscripts, even, in extremely rare instances, in the Koine or Byzantine text. (1992, 218-219)

Metzger's observations are important, for they evolved from years of working with textual variants. But I would add one qualifier to the notion that a reading is likely original if it has support from several text-types. I would stipulate that the documentary support must be *early* and diverse. Diverse testimony among many later manuscripts (i.e., not the earliest ones), in my mind, signals only that the reading had been copied frequently in various sectors of the church; it does not necessarily validate a reading's originality.

APPENDIX D

The Importance of the Documentary Considerations

"Reasoned eclecticism" or the "local-genealogical" method in actual practice tend to give priority to internal evidence over external evidence, resulting in the atomistic eclecticism. I agree with Westcott and Hort that it has to be the other way around if we are going to recover the original text. In their compilation of *The New Testament in the Original Greek,* Hort wrote, "Documentary evidence has been in most cases allowed to confer the place of honour against internal evidence" (1881, 17).

Colwell was of the same mind when he wrote "Hort Redivivus: A Plea and a Program." In this article, Colwell decried the "growing tendency to rely entirely on the internal evidence of readings, without serious consideration of documentary evidence" (1969a, 152). Colwell called upon scholars to attempt a reconstruction of the history of the manuscript tradition. But very few scholars have followed Colwell's urgings because they believe (in agreement with Aland as quoted in appendix B) that it is impossible to reconstruct a stemma (a sort of manuscript "family tree") for the Greek New Testament. Perhaps they hold this line because they fear that some will attempt to make a stemma leading back to the original, and that such a reconstruction will involve a subjective determination of the best line of manuscripts. Westcott and Hort have been criticized for doing this when they posited the "Neutral" text, leading from B back to the original.

However, a reconstruction of the early manuscript tradition does not necessarily mandate a genealogical lineage back to the original text—although that is the ultimate purpose of making a stemma. The reconstruction can help us understand the relationships between various manuscripts and provide insights into origin and associations. In the process, it might also be discovered that, out of all the extant manuscripts, some of the earliest ones are, in fact, the closest replications of the original text.

One of the most compelling reasons for returning to a documentary approach is the evidence that the second-century papyrus $\mathfrak{P}^{75}$ provides. This is the gospel manuscript (containing Luke and John) that has changed—or should have changed—nearly everyone's mind about abandoning a historical-documentary approach. It is a well-known fact that the text produced by the scribe of $\mathfrak{P}^{75}$ is a very accurate manuscript. It is also well-known that a manuscript like $\mathfrak{P}^{75}$ was the exemplar for Codex Vaticanus; the texts of $\mathfrak{P}^{75}$ and B are remarkably similar, demonstrating 83-percent agreement (see Porter 1962, 363-376, a seminal article on this issue).

Prior to the discovery of $\mathfrak{P}^{75}$ (which was published in 1961), many textual scholars were convinced that the second- and third-century papyri displayed a text in flux, a text characterized only by individual independence. The Chester Beatty Papyrus, $\mathfrak{P}^{45}$, and the Bodmer Papyri, $\mathfrak{P}^{66}$ (uncorrected) and $\mathfrak{P}^{72}$ (in 2 Peter and Jude), show this kind of independence. Scholars thought that scribes at Alexandria must have used several such manuscripts to produce a good recension—as is exhibited in Codex Vaticanus. Kenyon conjectured:

> During the second and third centuries, a great variety of readings came into existence throughout the Christian world. In some quarters, considerable license was shown in dealing

> with the sacred text; in others, more respect was shown to the tradition. In Egypt this variety of texts existed, as elsewhere; but Egypt (and especially Alexandria) was a country of strong scholarship and with a knowledge of textual criticism. Here, therefore, a relatively faithful tradition was preserved. About the beginning of the fourth century, a scholar may well have set himself to compare the best accessible representatives of this tradition, and so have produced a text of which B is an early descendant. (1940, 250)

Much of what Kenyon said is accurate, especially about Alexandria preserving a relatively pure tradition. But Kenyon was wrong in thinking that Codex Vaticanus was the result of a "scholarly recension," resulting from "editorial selection" across the various textual histories (1949, 208). Kenyon cannot be faulted for this opinion, because $\mathfrak{P}^{75}$ had not yet been discovered when he wrote. However, the discovery of $\mathfrak{P}^{75}$ and Vaticanus's close textual relationship to it have caused textual critics to look at things differently, for it is now quite clear that Codex Vaticanus was a copy (with some modifications) of a manuscript much like the second-century papyrus $\mathfrak{P}^{75}$, not a copy of a fourth-century recension.

Zuntz held an opinion similar to Kenyon's, positing an Alexandrian recension. After studying $\mathfrak{P}^{46}$, Zuntz imagined that the Alexandrian scribes selected the best manuscripts and gradually produced a text that reflected what they considered to be the original. In other words, they functioned as the most ancient of the New Testament textual critics. Zuntz believed that, from at least the middle of the second century to the fourth century, the Alexandrian scribes worked to purify the text from textual corruption. Speaking of their efforts, Zuntz wrote:

> The Alexander correctors strove, in ever repeated efforts, to keep the text current in their sphere free from the many faults that had infected it in the previous period and which tended to crop up again even after they had been obelized [i.e., marked as spurious]. These labours must time and again have been checked by persecutions and the confiscation of Christian books, and counteracted by the continuing currency of manuscripts of the older type. Nonetheless they resulted in the emergence of a type of text (as distinct from a definite edition) which served as a norm for the correctors in provincial Egyptian scriptoria. The final result was the survival of a text far superior to that of the second century, even though the revisers, being fallible human beings, rejected some of its own correct readings and introduced some faults of their own. (1953, 271-272)

The point behind Zuntz's conjecture of a gradual Alexandrian recension was to prove that the Alexandrian text was the result of a process beginning in the second century and culminating in the fourth century with Codex Vaticanus. In this regard, Zuntz was incorrect. This, again, has been proven by the close textual affinity between $\mathfrak{P}^{75}$ and B. The "Alexandrian" text already existed in the late second century; it was not the culmination of a recension. In this regard, Haenchen wrote:

> In $\mathfrak{P}^{75}$, which may have been written around 200 A.D., the "neutral" readings are already practically all present, without any need for a long process of purification to bring them together *miro quodam modo* out of a multitude of manuscripts. . . . $\mathfrak{P}^{75}$ allows us rather to see the neutral text as already as good as finished, before that slow development could have started at all; it allows us the conclusion that such manuscripts as lay behind Vaticanus—even if not for all New Testament books—already existed for centuries. (1971, 59)

Kurt Aland's thinking was also changed by $\mathfrak{P}^{75}$. He used to speak of the second- and third-century manuscripts as exhibiting a text in flux or even a "mixed" text, but not after the discovery of $\mathfrak{P}^{75}$. He wrote, "$\mathfrak{P}^{75}$ shows such a close affinity with the Codex Vaticanus that the supposition of a recension of the text at Alexandria, in the fourth century, can no longer be held" (1965, 336).

The discovery of $\mathfrak{P}^{75}$ shows that Hort was basically right in his assertion that Codex Vaticanus must trace back to a very early and accurate copy. Hort (1882, 250-251) had written that Codex Vaticanus preserves "not only a very ancient text, but a very pure line of a very ancient text." But some scholars may point out that this does not automatically mean that $\mathfrak{P}^{75}$ and B preserve the original text. What it does mean, they say, is that we have a second-century manuscript showing great affinity with a fourth-century manuscript whose quality has been highly esteemed. However, Gordon Fee (1974, 19-43) has demonstrated that there was no Alexandrian recension before the time of $\mathfrak{P}^{75}$. In an article appropriately titled "$\mathfrak{P}^{75}$, $\mathfrak{P}^{66}$, and Origen: The Myth of Early Textual Recension in Alexandria," Fee posits that there was no Alexandrian recension before the time of $\mathfrak{P}^{75}$ (late second century) and Codex Vaticanus (early fourth) and that both these manuscripts "seem to represent a 'relatively pure' form of preservation of a 'relatively pure' line of descent from the original text." In other words, the original text of Luke and John is virtually preserved in $\mathfrak{P}^{75}$. Of course, $\mathfrak{P}^{75}$ is not perfect, but it is closer to perfect than Codex Vaticanus, partially because it is 125–150 years closer to the original text.

Some textual critics, however, are not convinced that the $\mathfrak{P}^{75}$/B type of text is superior to another type of early text, which has been called the "Western" text. The "Western" form of the text was early in that it appears to have been used by Marcion, Irenaeus, Tertullian, and Cyprian—all of whom were alive in the second century. The name "Western" was given to this type of text because it circulated primarily in western regions like North Africa, Gaul, and Italy, but it was also present in Syria and even in Egypt. Thus, most scholars recognize that the "Western" text is not really a text-type; rather, it is a loose categorization of early texts that were not Alexandrian (which is why "Western" is often put in quotation marks in the literature). Some scholars see it as a complete misnomer. Colwell, for example, states, "The so-called Western text or Delta type text is the uncontrolled, popular edition of the second century. It has no unity and should not be referred to as the 'Western text'" (1969b, 53). The Alands also see it to be nothing more than a loose association of manuscripts, arguing, "Wherever we look in the West, nowhere can we find a theological mind capable of developing and editing an independent 'Western text.'" (1987, 54).

These observations aside, some scholars are still skeptical that the $\mathfrak{P}^{75}$/B type of text is at all superior to the Western text. They argue that the preference given to B and $\mathfrak{P}^{75}$ is based on a subjective appreciation of the kind of text they contain (generally terser than the "Western" text), rather than on any kind of theoretical reconstruction of the early transmission of the text (see Epp 1974, 390-394). It is argued that this same subjective estimation was at work when Westcott and Hort decided that B was intrinsically superior to D (Westcott and Hort 1882, 32-42). However, the notion that manuscripts like $\mathfrak{P}^{75}$ and B represent the best of textual purity is persistent, particularly among textual critics who have worked with many actual manuscripts—both of the proto-Alexandrian type and the so-called Western type. In the task of compiling transcriptions and/or doing textual analysis these critics have seen firsthand the kind of errors, expansions, harmonizations, and interpolations that are far more present in Western manuscripts.

In conclusion, my preference for emphasizing the documentary method in making text-critical choices is revealed in the fact that I decide against many choices made by the editors of the NU text. The reader may see these decisions in the following notes:

Matthew 3:16; 4:24; 5:28; 8:21; 9:14, 26; 12:47; 13:35b; 14:16, 27, 30; 15:6b, 14; 17:9; 18:15; 19:22; 21:44; 25:6; 27:49
Mark 3:32; 6:51; 7:4; 15:12; 16:8 [ending to Mark]
Luke 3:22a; 8:43; 14:17; 17:24; 20:9; 22:43-44
John 1:34; 3:31-32; 5:44; 6:14; 7:9; 7:53–8:11; 9:4, 38-39a; 10:8, 16, 18; 11:45-46; 13:2a, 2c, 32; 16:23; 20:31; 21:18
Acts 3:6; 7:13, 38; 9:12; 16:12
Romans 3:4; 7:17; 8:11a, 23; 11:17; 12:14; 15:33 [placement of doxology]
1 Corinthians 1:14; 3:13; 4:2; 7:7, 15; 8:3a, 3b; 9:9b; 10:2; 12:10
2 Corinthians 4:5b; 5:3, 12
Galatians 1:3, 6, 15a; 2:12a, 12b; 3:21a

BIBLIOGRAPHY

Abbott, Edwin A.

1906. *Johannine Grammar.* Diatessarica 6. London: Black.

Aland, Barbara

1986–1993. *Das Neue Testament auf Papyrus.* 3 vols. Berlin: de Gruyter.

Aland, Barbara, Kurt Aland, Johannes Karavidopoulos, Carlo Martini, and Bruce Metzger

1993a. *The Greek New Testament.* 4th ed. New York: United Bible Societies.

1993b. *Novum Testamentum Graece.* 27th ed. Stuttgart: Deutsche Bibelstiftung.

Aland, Kurt

1963. *Kurzgefasste Liste der griechischen Handschriften des Neuen Testaments.* Berlin: de Gruyter.

1965. The Significance of the Papyri for New Testament Research. Pages 325–346 in *The Bible in Modern Scholarship.* Edited by J. P. Hyatt. Nashville: Abingdon.

1967. *Studien zur Überlieferung des Neuen Testaments und seines Textes.* Berlin: de Gruyter.

1969. Bemerkungen zum Schluss des Markusevangeliums. Pages 157–180 in *Neotestamentica et Semitica.* Edited by E. Earle Ellis and Max Wilcox. Edinburgh: T&T Clark.

1979. The Twentieth-century Interlude in New Testament Textual Criticism. Pages 1–14 in *Text and Interpretation: Studies in New Testament Presented to Matthew Black.* Edited by Ernest Best and Robert M. Wilson. Cambridge: Cambridge University Press.

1986. Der Text des Johannesevangeliums im 2. Jahrhundert. Pages 1–10 in *Studien zum Text und zur Ethik des Neuen Testaments.* Edited by Wolfgang Schrage. Berlin: de Gruyter.

Aland, Kurt, and Barbara Aland

1987. *The Text of the New Testament.* Grand Rapids: Eerdmans.

Albright, W. F., and C. S. Mann

1971. *Matthew.* Anchor Bible 26. Garden City, N. Y.: Doubleday.

Alford, Henry

1844–1857. *The Greek Testament.* 4 vols. London: Rivingtons.

Allen, Willoughby C.

1912. *A Critical and Exegetical Commentary on the Gospel according to St. Matthew.* Edinburgh: T&T Clark.

Ascough, Richard S.

1998. Civic Pride at Philippi: The Text-critical Problem of Acts 16.12. *New Testament Studies* 44:93–103.

Aune, David

1997–1998. *Revelation.* 3 vols. Word Biblical Commentary 52A–52C. Dallas: Word.

Baarda, Tjitze

1969. Gadarenes, Gerasenes, Gergesenes and the "Diatessaron" Traditions. Pages 181–197 in *Neotestamentica et Semitica*. Edited by E. Earle Ellis and Max Wilcox. Edinburgh: T&T Clark.

Barrett, C. K.

1973. *A Commentary on the Second Epistle to the Corinthians*. New York: Harper and Row.

1978. *The Gospel according to St. John*. Philadelphia: Westminster.

1994–1998. *A Critical and Exegetical Commentary on the Acts of the Apostles*. 2 vols. International Critical Commentary. Edinburgh: T&T Clark.

Bauckham, Richard J.

1983. *Jude, 2 Peter*. Word Biblical Commentary 50. Waco, Texas: Word.

Beasley-Murray, George R.

1987. *John*. Word Biblical Commentary 36. Waco, Texas: Word.

Bell, Harold I., and T. C. Skeat

1935. *Fragments of an Unknown Gospel and Other Early Christian Papyri*. London: British Library.

Bengel, Johannes Albert

1855. *Gnomon Novi Testamenti*. 3rd ed. Edited by J. Steudel. Tübingen.

Birdsall, J. Neville

1960. John x. 29. *Journal of Theological Studies* 11:342–344.

1970. The New Testament Text. Pages 308–377 in *From the Beginnings to Jerome*. Edited by Peter R. Ackroyd and Christopher F. Evans. Vol. 1 of *The Cambridge History of the Bible*. Cambridge: Cambridge University Press.

Black, David A.

1985. The Text of John 3:13. *Grace Theological Journal* 6:49–66.

2002. *Rethinking New Testament Textual Criticism*. Grand Rapids: Baker.

Black, Matthew

1964. Critical and Exegetical Notes on Three New Testament Texts: Hebrews xi. 11; Jude 5; James i. 27. Pages 39–45 in *Apophoreta*. Edited by W. Eltester and F. H. Kettler. Berlin: Töpelmann.

Blum, Edwin A.

1981. 1, 2 Peter, Jude. Pages 209–292, 381–398 in *Hebrews—Revelation*. Vol. 12 of *The Expositor's Bible Commentary*. Grand Rapids: Zondervan.

Bound, J. F.

1984. Who Are the "Virgins" Discussed in 1 Corinthians 7:25-38? *Evangelical Journal* 2:6–7.

Bratcher, R. G.

1983. *A Translator's Guide to Paul's Second Letter to the Corinthians*. New York: United Bible Societies.

Brown, Raymond E.

1966–1970. *The Gospel according to John*. 2 vols. Anchor Bible 29–29A. Garden City, N. Y.: Doubleday.

1968. *The Semitic Background of the Term "Mystery" in the New Testament*. Philadelphia: Fortress.

1977. *The Birth of the Messiah*. Garden City, N. Y.: Doubleday.

Bruce, Alexander B.

1979. *The Expositor's Greek New Testament: The Synoptic Gospels.* Repr., Grand Rapids: Eerdmans.

Bruce, F. F.

1964. *The Epistle to the Hebrews.* New International Commentary on the New Testament. Grand Rapids: Eerdmans.

1970. *The Epistles of John.* Grand Rapids: Eerdmans.

1982. *1 and 2 Thessalonians.* Word Biblical Commentary 45. Waco, Texas: Word.

1983. *The Gospel of John.* Grand Rapids: Eerdmans.

1984. *The Epistles to the Colossians, to Philemon, and to the Ephesians.* New International Commentary on the New Testament. Grand Rapids: Eerdmans.

1985. *The Letter of Paul to the Romans.* 2nd ed. Grand Rapids: Eerdmans.

1989. *The Canon of Scripture.* Grand Rapids: Eerdmans.

1990. *The Acts of the Apostles.* Grand Rapids: Eerdmans.

1992. Textual Problems in the Epistle to the Hebrews. Pages 27–39 in *Scribes and Scripture: New Testament Essays in Honor of J. Harold Greenlee.* Edited by David A. Black. Winona Lake: Eisenbrauns.

Bock, Darrell

1996. *Luke 9:51-24:53.* Baker Exegetical Commentary on the New Testament. Grand Rapids: Baker.

Burge, Gary

1987. *The Anointed Community: The Holy Spirit in the Johannine Tradition.* Grand Rapids: Eerdmans.

Burkitt, F. C.

1905. Who Spoke the Magnificat? *Journal of Theological Studies* 7:220–227.

1916. W and Θ: Studies in the Western Text of St. Mark. *Journal of Theological Studies* 17:19–21.

Cadbury, H. J.

1939. The Meaning of John 20:23; Matthew 16:19; and Matthew 18:18. *Journal of Biblical Literature* 58:251–254.

1962. A Proper Name for Dives. *Journal of Biblical Literature* 81:399–402.

Carson, D. A.

1984. Matthew. Pages 3–600 in *Matthew, Mark, Luke.* Vol. 8 of *The Expositor's Bible Commentary.* Grand Rapids: Zondervan.

1991. *The Gospel according to John.* Pillar New Testament Commentary. Grand Rapids: Eerdmans.

Cervin, Richard

1994. A Note Regarding the Name "Junia(s)" in Romans 16.7. *New Testament Studies* 40:464–470.

Clark, Albert Curtis

1933. *The Acts of the Apostles.* London: Clarendon.

Clark, Kenneth

1966. The Theological Relevance of Textual Variation in Current Criticism of the Greek New Testament. *Journal of Biblical Literature* 85:1–16.

Cole, R. Alan

1961. *The Gospel according to St. Mark.* Leicester: InterVarsity.

Colwell, E.

1965. Scribal Habits in Early Papyri: A Study in the Corruption of the Text. Pages 370–389 in *The Bible in Modern Scholarship.* Edited by J. P. Hyatt. Nashville: Abingdon. Repr. as Method in Evaluating Scribal Habits: A Study of $\mathfrak{P}^{45}$, $\mathfrak{P}^{66}$, $\mathfrak{P}^{75}$. Pages 106–124 in *Studies in Methodology in Textual Criticism of the New Testament.* New Testament Tools and Studies 9. Leiden: E. J. Brill, 1969.

1969a. Hort Redivivus: A Plea and a Program. Pages 148–171 in *Studies in Methodology in Textual Criticism of the New Testament.* Edited by E. Colwell. New Testament Tools and Studies 9. Leiden: E. J. Brill. (Orig. pub. as pages 131–155 in *Transitions in Biblical Scholarship.* Edited by J. Coert Rylaarsdam. Chicago: University of Chicago Press, 1968.)

1969b. Method in Establishing the Nature of Text-types of New Testament Manuscripts. Pages 45–55 in *Studies in Methodology in Textual Criticism of the New Testament.* Edited by E. Colwell. New Testament Tools and Studies 9. Leiden: E. J. Brill.

Colwell, E., and E. Tune

1964. Variant Readings: Classification and Use. *Journal of Biblical Literature* 83:253–261.

Comfort, Philip W.

1984. Light from the New Testament Papyri Concerning the Translation of πνευμα. *The Bible Translator* 35:130–133.

1989. The Pericope of the Adulteress. *The Bible Translator* 40:145–147.

1990. The Greek Text of the Gospel of John according to the Early Papyri (As Compared to Nestle-Aland's *Novum Testamentum Graece,* 26th edition—NA^{26}). *New Testament Studies* 36:625–629.

1992. *The Quest for the Original Text of the New Testament.* Grand Rapids: Baker.

1993. Idolatry. Pages 424–426 in *Dictionary of Paul and His Letters.* Edited by G. Hawthorne, R. Martin, and D. Reid. Downers Grove, Ill: InterVarsity.

1994. *I Am the Way: A Spiritual Journey through the Gospel of John.* Grand Rapids: Baker. Repr., Eugene, Oreg.: Wipf and Stock, 2001.

1995. Exploring the Common Identification of Three New Testament Manuscripts: $\mathfrak{P}^{4}$, $\mathfrak{P}^{64}$, $\mathfrak{P}^{67}$. *Tyndale Bulletin* 46.1:43–54.

1996. *Early Manuscripts and Modern Translations of the New Testament.* 2nd ed. Grand Rapids: Baker.

1997a. New Testament Textual Criticism. Pages 1171–1175 in *Dictionary of the Later New Testament and Its Developments.* Edited by Ralph Martin and Peter Davids. Downers Grove, Ill.: InterVarsity.

1997b. The Scribe as Interpreter: A New Look at New Testament Textual Criticism according to Reader Response Theory. D. Litt. et Phil. diss., University of South Africa.

1999. New Reconstructions and Identifications of New Testament Papyri. *Novum Testamentum* 41.3:214–230.

2000. *The Essential Guide to Bible Versions.* Wheaton: Tyndale.

2004. Scribes as Readers: Looking at New Testament Textual Variants according to Reader Reception Analysis. *Neotestamentica* 38.1:28–53.

2005. *Encountering the Manuscripts: An Introduction to New Testament Paleography and Textual Criticism.* Nashville: Broadman & Holman.

2008. The Significance of the Papyri in the New Testament Text and Translation. In *New Testament Text and Translation.* Edited by Stanley Porter and Mark Boda. Grand Rapids: Eerdmans.

Comfort, Philip, and David Barrett

2001. *The Text of the Earliest New Testament Greek Manuscripts.* Wheaton: Tyndale.

Cranfield, C. E. B.

1975–1979. *The Epistle to the Romans.* 2 vols. Edinburgh: T&T Clark.

Crehan, Joseph

1957. Peter according to the D-Text of Acts. *Theological Studies* 18:596–603.

Dahl, N. A.

1982. Romans 3:9: Text and Meaning. Pages 184–204 in *Paul and Paulinism.* Edited by C. K. Barrett, M. D. Hooker, S. G. Wilson. London: SPCK.

Dana, H. E., and Julius R. Mantey

1927. *A Manual Grammar of the Greek New Testament.* New York: Macmillan.

Daube, D.

1950. Jesus and the Samaritan Woman: The Meaning of συγχράομαι. *Journal of Biblical Literature* 69:137–147.

Dunn, J. D. G.

1988. *Romans.* 2 vols. Word Biblical Commentary 38A–38B. Dallas: Word.

Ehrman, Bart

1988. Jesus and the Adulteress. *New Testament Studies* 34:24–44.

1989. A Problem of Textual Circularity: The Alands on the Classification of New Testament Manuscripts. *Biblica* 70:377–388.

1993. *The Orthodox Corruption of Scripture.* Oxford: Oxford University Press.

Elliott, J. Keith

1989. *A Bibliography of Greek New Testament Manuscripts.* Cambridge: Cambridge University Press.

1999. The International Greek New Testament Project's Volumes on the Gospel of Luke: Prehistory and Aftermath. *New Testament Textual Research Update* 7:1–20.

2002. The Case for Thoroughgoing Eclecticism. Pages 101–124 in *Rethinking New Testament Textual Criticism.* Edited by David A. Black. Grand Rapids: Baker.

Elliott, W. J., and D. C. Parker

1995. *The Gospel according to St. John. Volume One: The Papyri.* Vol. IV of *The New Testament in Greek.* New Testament Tools and Studies 20. Edited by the American and British Committees of the International Greek New Testament Project. Leiden: E. J. Brill.

Ellis, E. Earle

1981. The Silenced Wives of Corinth: 1 Cor. 14:34–5. Pages 213–220 in *New Testament Textual Criticism: Its Significance for Exegesis.* Edited by Eldon Epp and Gordon Fee. Oxford: Clarendon.

Epp, Eldon J.

1962. The "Ignorance Motif" in Acts and the Antijudaic Tendencies in Codex Bezae. *Harvard Theological Review* 55:51–62.

1966. *The Theological Tendency of Codex Bezae Cantabrigiensis in Acts.* Cambridge: Cambridge University Press.

1974. The Twentieth Century Interlude in New Testament Textual Criticism. *Journal of Biblical Literature* 93:386–414.

1976. The Eclectic Method in New Testament Textual Criticism: Solution or Symptom? *Harvard Theological Review* 69:211–257.

1981. The Ascension in the Textual Tradition of Luke-Acts. Pages 131–145 in *New Testament Textual Criticism: Its Significance for Exegesis.* Edited by Eldon J. Epp and Gordon Fee. Oxford: Clarendon.

1989. The Significance of the Papyri for Determining the Nature of the New Testament Text in the Second Century: A Dynamic View of Textual Transmission. Pages 71–103 in *Gospel Traditions in the Second Century.* Edited by William J. Peterson. Notre Dame: University of Notre Dame Press.

Epp, Eldon J., and Gordon Fee

1981. *New Testament Textual Criticism: Its Significance for Exegesis.* Oxford: Clarendon.

1993. *Studies in the Theory and Method of New Testament Textual Criticism.* Grand Rapids: Eerdmans.

Erasmus, Desiderius

1516. *Novum Instrumentum Omne.* Basel: Johann Froben.

Farmer, William

1974. *The Last Twelve Verses of Mark.* Cambridge: Cambridge University Press.

Farstad, Arthur, and Zane Hodges

1982. *The Greek New Testament according to the Majority Text.* Nashville: Nelson.

Fee, Gordon

1965. The Corrections of Papyrus Bodmer II and Early Textual Transmission. *Novum Testamentum* 7:247–257.

1968a. Codex Sinaiticus in the Gospel of John: A Contribution to Methodology in Establishing Textual Relationships. *New Testament Studies* 15:23–44.

1968b. *Papyrus Bodmer II (P66): Its Textual Relationships and Scribal Characteristics.* Studies and Documents 34. Salt Lake City: University of Utah Press.

1974. $\mathfrak{P}^{75}$, $\mathfrak{P}^{66}$, and Origen: The Myth of the Early Textual Recension in Alexandria. Pages 19–45 in *New Dimensions in New Testament Study.* Edited by Richard N. Longenecker and Merrill C. Tenney. Grand Rapids: Zondervan.

1979. The Textual Criticism of the Greek New Testament. Pages 419–433 in *Introductory Articles.* Vol. 1 of *The Expositor's Bible Commentary.* Grand Rapids: Zondervan.

1981. "One Thing is Needful"? Luke 10:42. Pages 61–75 in *New Testament Textual Criticism: Its Significance for Exegesis.* Edited by Eldon J. Epp and Gordon Fee. Oxford: Clarendon.

1987. *The First Epistle to the Corinthians.* New International Commentary on the New Testament. Grand Rapids: Eerdmans.

1988. *1 and 2 Timothy, Titus.* New International Biblical Commentary. Peabody, Mass.: Hendrickson.

1992. Textual-Exegetical Observations on 1 Corinthians 1:2; 2:1, and 2:10. Pages 1–13 in *Scribes and Scripture: New Testament Essays in Honor of J. Harold Greenlee.* Edited by David A. Black. Winona Lake: Eisenbrauns.

1995. *Paul's Letter to the Philippians.* New International Commentary on the New Testament. Grand Rapids: Eerdmans.

Fitzmyer, Joseph

1981–1985. *The Gospel according to Luke.* 2 vols. Anchor Bible 28–28A. Garden City, N. Y.: Doubleday.

Fowl, S.

1990. A Metaphor in Distress: A Reading of νηπιοι in 1 Thessalonians 2:7. *New Testament Studies* 36:469–473.

Funk, R. W.

1958. Papyrus Bodmer II (𝔓[66]) and John 8, 25. *Harvard Theological Review* 51:95–100.

Gamble, Harry

1977. *The Textual History of the Letter to the Romans.* Studies and Documents 42. Grand Rapids: Eerdmans.

1995. *Books and Readers in the Early Church.* New Haven: Yale University Press.

Green, H. B.

1975. *The Gospel according to Matthew.* New York: Oxford.

Greenlee, J. Harold

1958. A Misinterpreted Nomen Sacrum in 𝔓[9]. *Harvard Theological Review* 51:187.

Grenfell, Bernard P.

1897. Oxyrhynchus and Its Papyri. Pages 1–12 in *Egypt Exploration Fund: Archaeological Report 1896–1897.* Edited by F. L. Griffith. London: Egypt Exploration Fund.

Grenfell, Bernard P., and Arthur S. Hunt

1903. *The Oxyrhynchus Papyri, Part III.* London: Egypt Exploration Fund.

Griesbach, J. J.

1796. *Novum Testamentum Graece.* London.

Grobel, K.

1964. Whose Name Was Neves. *New Testament Studies* 10:373–382.

Guelich, Robert

1989. *Mark 1–8:26.* Word Biblical Commentary 34. Waco, Texas: Word.

Gundry, Robert H.

1993. *Mark: A Commentary on His Apology for the Cross.* Grand Rapids: Eerdmans.

Haenchen, Ernst

1971. *The Acts of the Apostles.* Philadelphia: Westminster.

Hanson, R. P. C.

1965. The Provenance of the Interpolator in the "Western" Text of Acts and of Acts Itself. *New Testament Studies* 12:211–230.

Harris, J. R.

1894. *Four Lectures on the Western Text.* London.

Harris, Murray J.

1976. 2 Corinthians. Pages 299–406 in *Romans—Galatians.* Vol. 10 of *The Expositor's Bible Commentary.* Grand Rapids: Zondervan.

1992. *Jesus as God.* Grand Rapids: Baker.

Harrison, Everett F.

1976. Romans. Pages 1–172 in *Romans—Galatians.* Vol. 10 of *The Expositor's Bible Commentary.* Grand Rapids: Zondervan.

Hatch, William H. P.

1952. A Recently Discovered Fragment of the Epistle to the Romans. *Harvard Theological Review* 45:81-85.

Hawthorne, Gerald F.

1983. *Philippians.* Word Biblical Commentary 43. Waco, Texas: Word.

Head, Peter

1990. Observations on Early Papyri of the Synoptic Gospels. *Biblica* 71:240–247.

Hill, David

1972. *The Gospel of Matthew.* Grand Rapids: Eerdmans.

Hirunuma, Toshio

1981. Matthew 16:2b-3. Pages 35–45, 131–145 in *New Testament Textual Criticism: Its Significance for Exegesis.* Edited by Eldon J. Epp and Gordon Fee. Oxford: Clarendon.

Hodges, Zane

1963. Light on James Two from Textual Criticism. *Bibliotheca Sacra* 120:341–350.

Holmes, Michael

1986. The Text of Matthew 5.11. *New Testament Studies* 32:283–286.

1989. New Testament Textual Criticism. Pages 53–74 in *Introducing New Testament Interpretation.* Edited by Scot McKnight. Guides to New Testament Exegesis. Grand Rapids: Baker.

2002. The Case for Reasoned Eclecticism. Pages 77–100 in *Rethinking New Testament Textual Criticism.* Edited by David A. Black. Grand Rapids: Baker.

Hort, Fenton

1876. *Two Dissertations.* Cambridge: Macmillan.

Hunger, Herbert

1960. Zur Datierung des Papyrus Bodmer II ($\mathfrak{P}^{66}$). *Anzieger der österreichischen Akademie der Wissenschaften,* Philologisch-Historischen Klasse 4:12–23.

Hurtado, Larry

1981. The Doxology at the End of Romans. Pages 185–199 in *New Testament Textual Criticism: Its Significance for Exegesis.* Edited by Eldon J. Epp and Gordon Fee. Oxford: Clarendon.

1989. *Mark.* New International Bible Commentary. Peabody, Mass.: Hendrickson.

Iser, Wolfgang

1974. *The Implied Reader.* Baltimore: Johns Hopkins University Press.

1978. *The Act of Reading.* Baltimore: Johns Hopkins University Press.

James, M. R.

1955. *The Apocryphal New Testament.* 2nd ed. Oxford: Oxford University Press.

Jeremias, Joachim

1969. *Jerusalem in the Time of Jesus.* Translated by F. H. Cave and C. H. Cave. Philadelphia: Fortress.

Johnson, Alan F.

1981. Revelation. Pages 399–603 in *Hebrews—Revelation.* Vol. 12 of *The Expositor's Bible Commentary.* Grand Rapids: Zondervan.

Kelly, J. N. D.

1977. *A Commentary on the Epistles of Peter and of Jude.* Black's New Testament Commentaries. London: Adam & Charles Black.

Kennedy, H. A. A.

1979. The Epistle to the Philippians. Pages 397–473 in *Expositor's Greek Testament, vol. III.* Edited by W. R. Nicoll. Repr., Grand Rapids: Eerdmans.

Kenyon, Frederic G.

1933. *The Chester Beatty Biblical Papyri: Descriptions and Texts of Twelve Manuscripts on Papyrus of the Greek Bible.* Fasciculus II. London: Emery Walker Ltd.

1934. *The Chester Beatty Biblical Papyri.* Fasciculus III. London: Emery Walker Ltd.

1936. *The Chester Beatty Biblical Papyri.* Supplement. London: Emery Walker Ltd.

1940. Hesychius and the Text of the New Testament. Pages 245–250 in *Mémorial Lagrange.* Uppsala: Seminarium Neotestamentium Upsaliense.

1949. *The Text of the Greek Bible.* London: Duckworth.

Kilpatrick, George D.

1967. Übertreter des Gesetzes, Jak. 2,11. *Theologische Zeitschrift* 23:433.

Kim, Young-Kyu

1988. Paleographic Dating of $\mathfrak{P}^{46}$ to the Later First Century. *Biblica* 69:248–257.

Klijn, A. F. J.

1957. Stephen's Speech—Acts vii.2–53. *New Testament Studies* 4:25–31.

Kohlenberger, John, E. W. Goodrick, and James A. Swanson

1995. *Exhaustive Concordance to the Greek New Testament.* Grand Rapids: Zondervan.

Kubo, Sakae

1965. *$\mathfrak{P}^{72}$ and the Codex Vaticanus.* Studies and Documents 27. Salt Lake City: University of Utah Press.

1981. Jude 22–23: Two-division Form or Three? Pages 239–253 in *New Testament Textual Criticism: Its Significance for Exegesis.* Edited by Eldon J. Epp and Gordon Fee. Oxford: Clarendon.

Lane, William L.

1974. *The Gospel according to Mark.* Grand Rapids: Eerdmans.

1991. *Hebrews.* 2 vols. Word Biblical Commentary 47A–47B. Waco, Texas: Word.

Laurentin, R.

1957. *Structure et Théologie de Luc I–II.* Paris: Gabalda.

Liefeld, Walter L.

1984. Luke. Pages 797–1059 in *Matthew, Mark, Luke.* Vol. 8 of *The Expositor's Bible Commentary.* Grand Rapids: Zondervan.

Lightfoot, J. B.

1879. *St. Paul's Epistles to the Colossians and Philemon.* New York: Macmillan.

1893. *Biblical Essays.* London: Macmillan.

1903. *St. Paul's Epistle to the Philippians.* London: Macmillan.

1904. *Notes on the Epistles of St. Paul.* London: Macmillan.

Lincoln, Andrew
1990. *Ephesians.* Word Biblical Commentary 42. Waco, Texas: Word.

Lindars, Barnabas
1958. Matthew, Levi, Lebbaeus, and the Value of the Western Text. *New Testament Studies* 4:220–222.

Longenecker, Richard N.
1981. The Acts of the Apostles. Pages 207–573 in *John—Acts.* Vol. 9 of *The Expositor's Bible Commentary.* Grand Rapids: Zondervan.
1990. *Galatians.* Word Biblical Commentary 41. Waco, Texas: Word.

Lyon, Robert W.
1958. A Re-examination of Codex Ephraemi Rescriptus. *New Testament Studies* 5:260–272.

Mantey, J. R.
1939. The Mistranslation of the Perfect Tense in John 20:23; Mt 16:19 and Mt 18:18. *Journal of Biblical Literature* 58:243–249.

Marshall, I. Howard
1978. *The Gospel of Luke.* New International Greek Testament Commentary. Grand Rapids: Eerdmans.

Martin, Ralph
1986. *2 Corinthians.* Word Biblical Commentary 40. Waco, Texas: Word.
1988. *James.* Word Biblical Commentary 48. Waco, Texas: Word.

Martin, Victor
1956. *Papyrus Bodmer II: Évangile de Jean chap. 1–14.* Cologny/Génève: Bibliotheca Bodmeriana.
1958. *Papyrus Bodmer II Supplément: Évangile de Jean chap. 14–21.* Cologny/Génève: Bibliotheca Bodmeriana.

Martin, Victor, and Rudolf Kasser
1961. *Papyrus Bodmer XIV-XV, Évangile de Luc chap. 3–24, Évangile de Jean chap. 1–15.* Cologny/Génève: Bibliotheca Bodmeriana.

Mayor, Joseph B.
1907. *The Epistle of St. Jude and the Second Epistle of St. Peter.* Repr., Grand Rapids: Baker, 1965.

McArthur, H. K.
1973. Son of Mary. *Novum Testamentum* 15:38-58.

Merell, Jean
1938. Nouveaux fragments du papyrus IV. *Revue Biblique* 47:5–22.

Metzger, Bruce
1958. How Many Times Does "epiousios" Occur Outside the Lord's Prayer? *Expository Times* 69:52-54.
1977. *The Early Versions of the New Testament.* Oxford: Clarendon.
1981. *Manuscripts of the Greek Bible.* Oxford: Oxford University Press.
1992. *The Text of the New Testament:* Its Transmission, Corruption, and Restoration. 3rd ed. Oxford: Oxford University Press.

1994. *A Textual Commentary on the Greek New Testament.* 2nd ed. New York: United Bible Societies.

2003. The New Testament: Its Background, Growth, and Content. 3rd ed. Nashville: Abingdon.

Michaels, J. Ramsey

1988. *1 Peter.* Word Biblical Commentary 49. Dallas: Word.

Mill, John

1723. *Novum Testamentum Graece.* 2nd ed. Leipzig.

Miller, J. Edward

2003. Some Observations on the Text-critical Function of the Umlauts in Vaticanus, with Special Attention to 1 Corinthians 14.34–35. *Journal for the Study of the New Testament* 26:217–236.

Milne, H. J. M., and T. C. Skeat

1938. *The Scribes and Correctors of the Codex Sinaiticus.* Oxford: Oxford University Press.

Moo, Douglas J.

1985. *The Letter of James.* Tyndale New Testament Commentaries. Grand Rapids: Eerdmans.

Morris, Leon

1971. *The Gospel according to John.* Grand Rapids: Eerdmans.

1981. Hebrews. Pages 3–158 in *Hebrews—Revelation.* Vol. 12 of *The Expositor's Bible Commentary.* Edited by F. Gaebelein. Grand Rapids: Zondervan.

1984. *1 and 2 Thessalonians.* Rev. ed. Tyndale New Testament Commentaries. Grand Rapids: Eerdmans.

1992. *The Gospel according to Matthew.* Pillar New Testament Commentary. Grand Rapids: Eerdmans.

Moule, C. F. D.

1953. *An Idiom Book of New Testament Greek.* Cambridge: Cambridge University Press.

Moulton, James, and George Milligan

1972. *The Vocabulary of the Greek New Testament.* Grand Rapids: Eerdmans.

Nestle, Eberhard

1901. *Introduction to the Textual Criticism of the Greek New Testament.* Translated by William Edie. London: Williams & Norgate.

1911. The Honeycomb in Luke xxiv. *Expository Times* 22:567–568.

Newman, Barclay, and Eugene Nida

1980. *A Translator's Handbook on the Gospel of John.* New York: United Bible Societies.

Niccum, Curt

1997. The Voice of the Manuscripts on the Silence of Women: The External Evidence for 1 Cor 14:34–5. *New Testament Studies* 43:242–255.

Nolland, John

1989–1993. *Luke.* 3 vols. Word Biblical Commentary 35A–35C. Dallas: Word.

O'Brien, Peter T.

1982. *Colossians, Philemon.* Word Biblical Commentary 44. Waco, Texas: Word.

O'Callaghan, Jose

1981. La variante ειϲ/ελθων en Mt 9,18. *Biblica* 62:104–106.

Osborne, Grant

1992. Resurrection. Pages 673–688 in *Dictionary of Jesus and the Gospels.* Edited by Joel B. Green, Scot McKnight, and I. Howard Marshall. Downers Grove, Ill.: InterVarsity.

Osburn, Carroll D.

1976. The Christological Use of I Enoch i. 9 in Jude 14, 15. *New Testament Studies* 23:334–341.

1981. The Text of 1 Corinthians 10:9. Pages 201–212 in *New Testament Textual Criticism: Its Significance for Exegesis.* Edited by Eldon J. Epp and Gordon Fee. Oxford: Clarendon.

Parker, D. C.

1992. *Codex Bezae: An Early Christian Manuscript and Its Text.* Cambridge: Cambridge University Press.

1997. *The Living Text of the Gospels.* Cambridge: Cambridge University Press.

Payne, Philip

1995. Fuldensis, Sigla for Variants in Vaticanus, and 1 Cor 14:34–5. *New Testament Studies* 41:240–262.

1998. MS. 88 as Evidence for a Text without 1 Cor 14:34–5. *New Testament Studies* 44:152–158.

Payne, Philip, and Paul Canart

2000. The Originality of Text-critical Symbols in Codex Vaticanus. *Novum Testamentum* 42:105–113.

Petzer, Jacobus

1989. Contextual Evidence in Favour of ΚΑΥΧΗΣΩΜΑΙ in 1 Corinthians 13.3. *New Testament Studies* 35:229–253.

1994. The History of the New Testament Text—Its Reconstruction, Significance and Use in New Testament Textual Criticism. Pages 11–36 in *New Testament Textual Criticism, Exegesis, and Early Church History.* Edited by B. Aland and J. Delobel. Contributions to Biblical Exegesis and Theology 7. Kampen: Pharos.

Plooij, D.

1929. *The Ascension in the "Western" Textual Tradition.* Afdeeling letterkunde, Deel 67, Serie A, No. 2. Amsterdam.

Plummer, Alfred

1896. *A Critical and Exegetical Commentary on the Gospel according to St. Luke.* International Critical Commentary. Edinburgh: T&T Clark.

Porter, Calvin

1962. Papyrus Bodmer XV ($\mathfrak{P}^{75}$) and the Text of Codex Vaticanus. *Journal of Biblical Literature* 81:363–376.

1967. John ix. 38, 39a: A Liturgical Addition to the Text. *New Testament Studies* 13:387–394.

Ramaroson, L.

1977. Une lecture de Éphésians 1,15–2,10. *Biblica* 58:388–410.

Rhodes, Erroll

1968. The Corrections of Papyrus Bodmer II. *New Testament Studies* 14:271–281.

Richards, E. Randolph

1991. *The Secretary in the Letters of Paul.* Wissenschaftliche Untersuchungen zum Neuen Testament 2/42.Tübingen: J. C. B. Mohr.

Roberts, Colin H.

1935. *An Unpublished Fragment of the Fourth Gospel in the John Rylands Library.* Manchester: Manchester University Press.

1953. An Early Papyrus of the First Gospel. *Harvard Theological Review* 46:233–247.

Ropes, J. H.

1926. *The Acts of the Apostles.* Part I in *The Beginnings of Christianity.* Edited by F. J. Foakes Jackson and K. Lake. London: Macmillan.

Ross, J. M.

1987. Another Look at Mark 8:26. *Novum Testamentum* 29:97–99.

1992. The Extra Words in Acts 18:21. *Novum Testamentum* 34:247–249.

Royse, James Ronald

1981. Scribal Habits in Early Greek New Testament Papyri. Ph.D. diss. Graduate Theological Union.

1983. The Treatment of Scribal Leaps in Metzger's *Textual Commentary. New Testament Studies* 29:539–551.

2008. *Scribal Habits in Early Greek New Testament Papyri.* Leiden: Brill.

Sailors, Timothy B.

2000. Wedding Textual and Rhetorical Criticism to Understand the Text of 1 Thessalonians 2:7. *Journal of the Study of the New Testament* 80:81–98.

Sanders, Henry A.

1912. *The New Testament Manuscripts in the Freer Collection, Part I: The Washington Manuscript of the Four Gospels.* New York: Macmillan.

1927. A Papyrus Fragment of Acts in the Michigan Collection. *Harvard Theological Review* 20:1–19.

1935. *A Third-century Papyrus Codex of the Epistles of Paul.* Humanistic Series 38. Ann Arbor: University of Michigan Press.

Schmid, Joseph

1955–1956. *Studien zur Geschichte des griechischen Apokalypse-Textes.* 2 vols. Munich: Zink.

Schnackenburg, Rudolf

1982–1987. *The Gospel according to St. John.* 3 vols. New York: Crossroad.

Silva, M.

1992a. *Philippians.* Baker Exegetical Commentary on the New Testament. Grand Rapids: Baker.

1992b. The Text of Galatians: Evidence from the Earliest Greek Manuscripts. Pages 17–25 in *Scribes and Scripture: New Testament Essays in Honor of J. Harold Greenlee.* Edited by David A. Black. Winona Lake: Eisenbrauns.

2002. Response. Pages 141–150 in *Rethinking New Testament Textual Criticism.* Edited by David A. Black. Grand Rapids: Baker.

Skeat, T. C.

1938. The Lilies of the Field. *Zeitschrift für die neutestamentliche Wissenschaft* 37:211–214.

1988. The "Second-First" Sabbath (Luke 6:1): The Final Solution. *Novum Testamentum* 30.2:103–106.

1997. The Oldest Manuscript of the Four Gospels? *New Testament Studies* 43:1–34.

Smalley, Stephen S.

1984. *1, 2, 3 John.* Word Biblical Commentary 51. Waco, Texas: Word.

Smothers, Edgar
1958. Two Readings in Papyrus Bodmer II. *Harvard Theological Review* 51:111–122.

Stott, John R. W.
1988. *The Letters of John.* Tyndale New Testament Commentaries. Leicester, England: InterVarsity.

Swanson, Reuben
1995–2003. *New Testament Greek Manuscripts.* 8 vols. Pasadena: William Carey.

Swete, H. B.
1916. The Faithful Sayings. *Journal of Theological Studies* 18:1-7.

Tasker, R. V. G.
1949. The Chester Beatty Papyrus of the Apocalypse of John. *Journal of Theological Studies* 50:60–68.
1964. Notes on Variant Readings. Pages 411–445 in *The Greek New Testament: Being the Text Translated in the New English Bible.* London: Oxford University Press.

Testuz, Michael
1959. *Papyrus Bodmer VII–IX: L'Épître de Jude, les deux Épîtres de Pierre, les Psaumes 33 et 34.* Cologny/Génève: Bibliotheca Bodmeriana.

Thompson, Edward M.
1912. *An Introduction to Greek and Latin Palaeography.* Oxford: Clarendon.

Thrall, Margaret E.
1981. "Putting On" or "Stripping Off" in 2 Corinthians 5:3. Pages 221–237 in *New Testament Textual Criticism: Its Significance for Exegesis.* Edited by Eldon J. Epp and Gordon Fee. Oxford: Clarendon.

Tregelles, Samuel P.
1854. *An Account of the Printed Text of the Greek New Testament.* London: Samuel Bagster & Sons.
1857–1879. *The Greek New Testament.* 6 vols. London: Samuel Bagster & Sons.

Turner, Nigel
1965. *Grammatical Insights into the New Testament.* Edinburgh: T&T Clark.

Vine, W. E.
1970. *The Epistles of John.* Grand Rapids: Zondervan.

Vitelli, G., and G. Mercati
1932. *Papiri greci e latini della Società Italiana.* Vol. 10. Florence: Societá Italiana.

Wallace, Daniel
1993. Reconsidering "The Story of Jesus and the Adulteress Reconsidered." *New Testament Studies* 39:290–296.
2001. Innovations in Text and Translation of the NET Bible, New Testament. *The Bible Translator* 52.3:335–349.

Warren, William
1998. The Textual Relationship of 𝔓[4]. Paper presented at the annual meeting of the Society of Biblical Literature. Orlando, Fla.

Wessel, Walter

1984. Mark. Pages 601–796 in *Matthew, Mark, Luke.* Vol. 8 of *The Expositor's Bible Commentary.* Grand Rapids: Zondervan.

Westcott, Brooke F.

1881. *The Gospel according to St. John.* London: Macmillan.

1886. *The Epistles of St. John.* London: Macmillan.

Westcott, Brooke F., and Fenton J. A. Hort

1881. *The New Testament in the Original Greek.* Cambridge: Macmillan.

1882. *The New Testament in the Original Greek: Introduction and Appendix.* New York: Harper & Brothers.

Wikgren, Allen

1967. Some Problems in Jude 5. Pages 147–152 in *Studies in the History and Text of the New Testament in Honor of Kenneth Willis Clark.* Edited by B. L. Daniels and M. J. Suggs. Studies and Documents 29. Salt Lake City: University of Utah Press.

1981. The Problem in Acts 16:12. Pages 171–178 in *New Testament Textual Criticism: Its Significance for Exegesis.* Edited by Eldon J. Epp and Gordon Fee. Oxford: Clarendon.

Williams, C. S. C.

1951. *Alterations to the Text of the Synoptic Gospels and Acts.* Oxford: Basil Blackwell.

Williams, James

1974. Proposed Renderings from Some Johannine Passages. *The Bible Translator* 25:351–353.

Wilson, J. M.

1923. *The Acts of the Apostles, Translated from the Codex Bezae.* London: Macmillan.

Zuntz, Günther

1953. *The Text of the Epistles.* London: Oxford Press.